T0419164

The Cambridge Handbook of Cognitive Development

How does cognition develop in infants, children and adolescents? This handbook presents a cutting-edge overview of the field of cognitive development, spanning basic methodology, key domain-based findings and applications. Part I covers the neurobiological constraints and laws of brain development, while Part II covers the fundamentals of cognitive development from birth to adulthood: object, number, categorization, reasoning, decision-making and socioemotional cognition. Part III covers educational and school-learning domains, including numeracy, literacy, scientific reasoning skills, working memory and executive skills, metacognition, curiosity-driven active learning and more. Featuring chapters written by the world's leading scholars in experimental and developmental psychology, as well as in basic neurobiology, cognitive neuroscience, computational modelling and developmental robotics, this collection is the most comprehensive reference work to date on cognitive development of the twenty-first century. It will be a vital resource for scholars and graduate students in developmental psychology, neuroeducation and the cognitive sciences.

OLIVIER HOUDÉ is Professor of Psychology at the University of Paris, where he is the honorary director of the Laboratory of Psychology at the Sorbonne. He is an academician at the Institut de France. One of the world's leading specialists of cognitive development, he is Editor in Chief of the *Dictionary of Cognitive Science* (2004).

GRÉGOIRE BORST is Professor of Psychology at the University of Paris, where he is the director of the Laboratory of Psychology at the Sorbonne. A rising star in the areas of cognitive development and neuroeducation, he is also a member of the board of the *Journal of Experimental Child Psychology*.

The Cambridge Handbook of Cognitive Development

Edited by

Olivier Houdé
University of Paris

Grégoire Borst
University of Paris

CAMBRIDGE
UNIVERSITY PRESS

University Printing House, Cambridge CB2 8BS, United Kingdom

One Liberty Plaza, 20th Floor, New York, NY 10006, USA

477 Williamstown Road, Port Melbourne, VIC 3207, Australia

314–321, 3rd Floor, Plot 3, Splendor Forum, Jasola District Centre, New Delhi – 110025, India

103 Penang Road, #05–06/07, Visioncrest Commercial, Singapore 238467

Cambridge University Press is part of the University of Cambridge.

It furthers the University's mission by disseminating knowledge in the pursuit of
education, learning, and research at the highest international levels of excellence.

www.cambridge.org
Information on this title: www.cambridge.org/9781108423878
DOI: 10.1017/9781108399838

First published 2022

A catalogue record for this publication is available from the British Library.

Library of Congress Cataloging-in-Publication Data
Names: Houdé, Olivier, editor. | Borst, Grégoire, 1977- editor.
Title: The Cambridge handbook of cognitive development / edited by Olivier Houdé,
    Université de Paris V, Grégoire Borst, Université de Paris V.
Description: 1 Edition. | New York, NY : Cambridge University Press, 2022. | Series: Cambridge
    handbooks in psychology | Includes bibliographical references and index.
Identifiers: LCCN 2021033329 (print) | LCCN 2021033330 (ebook) | ISBN 9781108423878 (hardback) |
    ISBN 9781108436632 (paperback) | ISBN 9781108399838 (epub)
Subjects: LCSH: Cognition in children. | Developmental psychology. | Piaget, Jean, 1896-1980.
Classification: LCC BF723.C5 C36 2022 (print) | LCC BF723.C5 (ebook) | DDC 155.4/13–dc23
LC record available at https://lccn.loc.gov/2021033329
LC ebook record available at https://lccn.loc.gov/2021033330

ISBN 978-1-108-42387-8 Hardback
ISBN 978-1-108-43663-2 Paperback

Contents

Part III Education and School-Learning Domains

The plate section can be found between pp. 534 and 535.

Figures

Tables

Contributors

DANIEL ANSARI, University of Western Ontario, Canada

RENÉE BAILLARGEON, University of Illinois, USA

DEON T. BENTON, Carnegie Mellon University, USA

NEELTJE E. BLANKENSTEIN, Leiden University, the Netherlands

AGNÈS BLAYE, Aix-Marseille University, France

GRÉGOIRE BORST, University of Paris, France

ARNAUD CACHIA, University of Paris, France

LISA CHALIK, Yeshiva University, USA

JEAN-PIERRE CHANGEUX, Collège de France and Pasteur Institute, France

NICOLAS CHEVALIER, University of Edinburgh, UK

EVELINE A. CRONE, Leiden University, the Netherlands

ANTONIO DAMASIO, University of Southern California, USA

HANNA DAMASIO, University of Southern California, USA

WIM DE NEYS, University of Paris and CNRS, France

JESSICA DUBOIS, University of Paris and INSERM, France

YARROW DUNHAM, Yale University, USA

PETER A. EDELSBRUNNER, ETH Zürich, Switzerland

MONIQUE ERNST, NIMH, USA

ANDREAS FALCK, Institut Jean Nicod, ENS-Ulm, PSL, CNRS, Paris, France and Lund University, Sweden

DARREN FREY, University of Paris and CNRS, France

CLAUDIE GAILLARD, NIMH, USA

MARIE-LINE GARDES, University Lyon-1 and CNRS, France

SUSAN A. GELMAN, University of Michigan, USA

MARIEL K. GODDU, University of California, Berkeley, USA

ALISON GOPNIK, University of California, Berkeley, USA

JOSH GOWIN, University of Colorado School of Medicine, USA

KEITH HAPPANEY, City University of New York

OLIVIER HOUDÉ, University of Paris, France

PIERRE JACOB, Institut Jean Nicod, ENS-Ulm, PSL and CNRS, Paris, France

TORKEL KLINGBERG, Karolinska Institute, Sweden

EUGENIA KULAKOVA, University College London, UK

BART LARSEN, University of Pittsburgh, USA

NATHAN T. T. LAU, University of Western Ontario, Canada

YI LIN, University of Illinois, USA

BEATRIZ LUNA, University of Pittsburgh, USA

JEAN-FRANÇOIS MANGIN, University Paris-Saclay and INSERM, France

ANTONIA MISCH, Ludwig Maximilian University of Munich, Germany

PHUONG NGOC DINH, Carnegie Mellon University, USA

ARDAVAN S. NOBANDEGANI, McGill University, Canada

PIERRE-YVES OUDEYER, INRIA, France

ASHLEY PARR, University of Pittsburgh, USA

TOMÁŠ PAUS, University of Montreal, Canada

JISKA S. PEPER, Leiden University, the Netherlands

JOSEF PERNER, University of Salzburg, Austria

CONRAD PERRY, Swinburne University of Technology, Australia

KASKA PORAYSKA-POMSTA, Centre for Educational Neuroscience, UCL Institute of Education, UK

MICHAEL I. POSNER, University of Oregon, USA

JÉRÔME PRADO, University Lyon-1 and CNRS, France

EVA RAFETSEDER, University of Stirling, UK

DAVID H. RAKISON, Carnegie Mellon University, USA

ORMA RAVINDRANATH, University of Pittsburgh, USA

ERIN ROBY, NYU Grossman School of Medicine

MARGOT ROELL, University of Paris and CNRS, France

MARY K. ROTHBART, University of Oregon, USA

BRUNO SAUCE, Karolinska Institute, Sweden

RALPH SCHUMACHER, ETH Zürich, Switzerland

ROSE M. SCOTT, University of California, Merced, USA

THOMAS R. SHULTZ, McGill University, Canada

ROBERT S. SIEGLER, Carnegie Mellon University, USA

CLAIRE DE SMID, University College London, UK

MAAYAN STAVANS, University of Illinois, USA

NIKOLAUS STEINBEIS, University College London, UK

ELSBETH STERN, ETH Zürich, Switzerland

BRENT STRICKLAND, Institut Jean Nicod, ENS-Ulm, PSL, CNRS, Paris, France and ABS, SCI, UM6P, Rabat, Morocco

MICHAEL S. C. THOMAS, Birkbeck, University of London, UK,

KRISTY VANMARLE, University of Missouri – Columbia, USA

JACQUES VAUCLAIR, Aix-Marseille University, France

ARNAUD VIAROUGE, University of Paris and CNRS, France

PHILIP DAVID ZELAZO, University of Minnesota, USA

JOHANNES C. ZIEGLER, Aix-Marseille University and CNRS, France

MARCO ZORZI, University of Padova, Italy

Introduction

Cognitive Development Studies: From the History of Psychology to the Current Trends in Cognitive Sciences

Olivier Houdé and Grégoire Borst

The history of cognitive development studies began with the Greek philosopher Plato (Houdé, 2019)[1]. In the centre of Raphael's famous fresco, *The School of Athens* (1512) in the Vatican Museum in Rome, Italy, we see Plato (428–347 BC) and Aristotle (384–322 BC). Plato is pointing upwards to the 'Heaven of Ideas', while Aristotle, his pupil at the Academy, stretches his hand forward, symbolizing the earthly world. Indeed, for Aristotle (who does not believe in the Ideas as such), the general and the particular are transmitted here.

I.1 Step 1: The Ancient Roots of Innatism and/or Empiricism

For Plato, souls, thought of as 'immortal', have already contemplated the world of Ideas – i.e., the Good, the True, and the Beautiful – during their prenatal period. Birth disturbs this process. That is why 'the body is a tomb', according to the philosopher's expression. Nevertheless, thanks to a psychological phenomenon of *reminiscence*, triggered by the perception of concrete things in the sensible world (relations, numbers, and qualities), we can rediscover the innate Ideas. For example, Plato states that we grasp the idea of perfect equality with pieces of wood that are almost equal, but that the 'equal' itself does not reside in the pieces of wood. It is we ourselves who, from sensible objects, infer their essence. In the same way, when we look at six knucklebones, we cannot say that the number six is in any one

of them, or in all of them together, since it is we ourselves who have made the connection between the Idea and the objects. Even Meno's slave, who appears in the dialogue of the same name, is able to deduce, starting from a right-angled triangle, Pythagoras's theorem: *the square of the hypotenuse is equal to the sum of the squares of the other two sides.* A century before Plato, the geometer Pythagoras (580–495 BC) had indeed demonstrated this theorem – a 'discovery of the True'.

According to Plato, these immutable Ideas are latent knowledge: they are within us from birth, without our knowing it. In this already subtle psychology, it is not a question of *ignorance* but of *latency*: dormant truths for which man seeks. It is at the cost of a mental effort, often requiring a whole education, that the innate Ideas can (re)appear. They are recalled and reactivated. Hence the importance, from a Platonic perspective, of the *maieutics* of Socrates, the art of 'giving birth to minds' (Socrates' mother was apparently a midwife), causing doubt and astonishment in one's interlocutor. Plato thus underlines the educational role of the social environment. However, learning is not a matter of filling the mind, seen as an empty *tabula rasa* ('blank slate'),

---

[1] Even before Socrate and Plato, there were pre-Socratic thinkers whose conceptions already looked forward to cognitive development, such as Parmenides (sixth–fifth century BC), who thought that perception was an illusion, and indeed a fraud, compared to thought.

by means of mere sensation, as it is in Aristotle, and as the young Theaetetus, an empiricist, suggests in a Socratic dialogue narrated by Plato. On the contrary, the Ideas are already present from birth, as a pre-existing cognitive store, a capital sum of reason that can be reactivated. Here we identify the ancient root of the *rationalist and innatist* trend that stretched for two millennia, right up to the 'core knowledge' of the infant cognitive psychology, according to Elizabeth S. Spelke (2000), via Descartes, Kant, Noam Chomsky (1975) and Jerry Fodor (1983).

Plato also anticipated the cerebrocentric approach: he already located the rational part of the soul (mind, intellect, reason) in the brain, whereas his pupil Aristotle, at the School of Athens, still located it in the heart (cardiocentrism). Plato, however, placed desire and its impulses in the lower abdomen, and the will in the heart. We now know that everything is in the brain (Changeux, 1985, 2012), including the mapping of desires and emotions through feelings, even though the brain's relations with the whole body are always intimate and continuous (Damasio, 1994, 2018).

Let us return to Raphael's fresco, *The School of Athens*, and Aristotle's place in it. According to Aristotle, at birth we are a *tabula rasa*. Thus, it is only within things themselves that their essence is to be found, and not in a superior Idea that transcends them.

What interests Aristotle is the discovery of *what the earthly world is made of*, the 'genera of being': quality, quantity, relation, place, time, action, etc., and their subdivisions. That is why his approach is encyclopaedic and known as 'systematic': he classifies diversity. Aristotle has thus influenced separate branches of knowledge: psychology, logic and zoology, all of which include the *logos*, implying reason and language. Aristotle distinguishes between external objects, mental images and their communication by words; but in order to understand the world and to speak correctly of it, he wishes to establish a rigorous logical reasoning that connects objects to words: a science of sciences. Therefore, he is important to philosophy, certainly, but he also prefigures the psychology of reasoning. Indeed, we owe him the discovery of the 'syllogism'.

Aristotle used logic to detect and refute the errors of reasoning, the sophisms and paralogisms, of his contemporaries in Greece (sophisms corresponds to the fake news of today, Lazer et al., 2018). Here lies the ancient root of the study of the cognitive biases of reasoning (Evans, 1989; Kahneman, 2011) and the psychological forms of syllogisms – the rules of mental logic (Braine & O'Brien, 1998) and visual-spatial models (Johnson-Laird, 2001).

A fundamental problem nevertheless remained for Aristotle: if the science of syllogisms aims at the objective knowledge of the world, how do we obtain the first true propositions, which do not themselves result from a prior deduction? Indeed, we can produce an argument whose conclusion (c) is logical (valid) but has a premise (either a or b) that is false. For example, if (a) *all men are immortal* and (b) *Socrates is a man*, then (c) *Socrates is immortal*. However, Socrates, a Greek philosopher, and the master of Plato, was mortal! How can we ensure that the initial proposals are trustworthy? This is where induction and empiricism find their place in Aristotle's theory. Not believing in the Ideas of Plato (as starting principles that are inside us without our knowledge), he appeals to a *sure and certain* faculty of recognition and judgment, which results from perception: there is no Idea without such a prior impression. Psychological empiricism is therefore inevitable. The *tabula rasa* is a corollary of the science of syllogisms.

According to Aristotle, the senses and induction lie at the origin of everything. From sensation arises memory, from memory comes experience and from *reasoned* experience (syllogism) comes the conception of the universal. It is through this inductive empirical process alone – without needing first to attain the pre-existing Ideas – that we can grasp the indemonstrable elements or axioms that are seen as trustworthy, appropriate and self-evident. From these the necessary deductions will then follow.

At birth, the intellect is similar to a tablet on which nothing is currently written, argues Aristotle in his *Peri psychès* (*On the Soul*) – arguably the first comprehensive treatise on psychology in history (just as the *Organon* was for logic). He describes in fine detail how a sensible object causes a specialized activity of the cognitive function. The latter does not receive the sensible form 'from without', but re-creates it 'from within', from its own powers, when it is affected from without. This nuanced empiricism (internal re-creation) already foreshadows the cognitive process of assimilation-accommodation described by Jean Piaget (2015; Piaget & Inhelder, 1969). According to Plato's pupil, the powers of the cognitive function come from a general breath of life, 'the soul', shared by all animate beings: plants, endowed with faculties of nourishment and growth; animals, endowed with faculties of motion and perception in addition to the preceding ones; and humans, who also benefit from the cognitive faculties of thought, of reasoning. In this way, three souls intertwined by epigenesis form a hierarchy in man: vegetative, sensitive and intellective. Human intelligence is an extension of biological adaptation, once again prefiguring the work of Piaget. The living world of Aristotle, however, is fixed: it is a *scala naturae* ('scale of beings') created by God, in which man dominates an eternal universe (like that of Socrates and Plato), not a transformist world in evolution of the kind later discovered by Buffon, Lamarck and Darwin. Unable to imagine this revolution in

biology, Aristotle, as a good logician, wished to avoid an infinite regress: so, he formulated the hypothesis of a god being, the cause of all, and himself uncaused – in other words, the 'first cause'.

I.2 Step 2: The Renaissance of Innatism and/or Empiricism

According to the French philosopher René Descartes (1596–1650), men are composed of two natures: the body and the soul, the latter being specifically defined as a 'thinking substance'. He compares the body to a pipe organ, in which animal spirits act like the air between the ducts in some pipes. Body and soul may well be joined together and united by the pineal gland in the brain (the epiphysis), but only the body is a machine. This difference in nature (or substance) between the soul and the body constitutes what is called 'Cartesian dualism', which left a permanent mark on psychology: the body was the domain of physiologists and doctors, the soul was the domain of psychologists.

Descartes was an innatist, like Plato. Indeed, his thought drew on the *rationalism and innatism* of Ancient times. The Cartesian method and rules were designed to discover the Ideas and properly develop them. In Descartes, human doubt stems from an imperfection in method, whereas God is perfection. Thus, to the question 'From where do we get this precious treasure that is our intelligence?', Descartes, in his *Treatise on Man* (1664), answers with the self-evident and apparently inescapable truth: God has deposited in our minds, from birth, clear and distinct logical and mathematical ideas, the core of human intelligence. An infant is thus 'potentially intelligent' (a concept very common these days) but is intelligent thanks to God's gift. This divine explanation would be shattered by nineteenth-century biology and Darwin's description of a natural biological evolution of animal and human intelligence – excluding God from the explanation.

In the same way, the Cartesian dualism between the mind (or soul) and the body would be shattered by the neurosciences of the twentieth century – prefigured in Ancient times by the Greek physicians Herophilus and Galen – through the mechanistic study of the brain as an organ of thought, especially using brain imaging techniques. Moreover, Descartes' correlative theory of machine-animals was directly challenged by La Mettrie's *Man a Machine* (1748), which, though written in the eighteenth century, already foreshadowed contemporary artificial intelligence (the brain-machine), a branch of computer science. Finally, even though Descartes wrote a *Treatise on the Passions*, it was the dualism between the soul and the body that Damasio would denounce in *Descartes' Error* (1994). demonstrating, with the help of contemporary neuroscience and the 'somatic marker theory' that we think with our bodies and our emotions in a system of generalized equilibrium called homeostasis (Damasio & Carvalho, 2013). Damasio (2003) agreed more with Baruch Spinoza (1632–1677), who, somewhat later in the seventeenth century, came closer to modern neurobiology than had Descartes by bringing mind and body together, ascribing to the emotions a central role in human survival and culture.

After Descartes, at the Age of Enlightenment, a new and famous cognitive problem added new fuel to the debate between the advocates of innatism and empiricism: the 'Molyneux's problem', named after an Irish scholar who asked the English philosopher and physician John Locke (1632–1704) whether a man who was born blind, then grew old and was cured, would be able to distinguish by sight, without touching them, a sphere and a cube placed on a table in front

of him – assuming that he had previously learned to distinguish these two objects by touch alone. Molyneux (1688 [1978]) himself believed that he would not. Locke was of the same opinion, for, according to him, visual ideas and tactile ideas were acquired independently by sense experience; and in this case, *the necessary association between the two* had not been made. It is now known that intermodal touch-vision transfer is possible at a central level in the brain, even in an infant, so the answer to Molyneux's problem is therefore 'yes' from the point of view of the contemporary psychology of cognitive development. But the problem fascinated the eighteenth century, which debated opposite points of view.

Molyneux's problem, apparently technical and limited in scope, is historically important because it corresponded to a more general key question, which aroused lively debate in the eighteenth century: what is the role of the environment and experience in the construction of our knowledge? Locke, who inaugurated the Enlightenment in England, answered this question with his empirical philosophy: knowledge results directly from the experience of the reality of the senses. Our ideas are not of divine origin (as in Descartes) but come from perception. It is out in the world that they are found; they do not lie innate within us. Otherwise, how can we explain the diversity of men, the ignorance of children, savages, idiots, and so on? Locke was a paediatrician and tutor to the children of an important politician in England, Lord Ashley; what Locke was aiming for was the *upbringing of a young English gentleman* but he also understood how each culture and each epoch has its own infancy. Hence his psychology of the child and of education, a corollary of his empiricism. Locke, like Montaigne, was struck by the weight of custom and habit, and the role of circumstances. From his observations, from his travels, from the stories he heard, he deduced that human understanding was a matter of environment, of education, and a 'reflection of nature'.

Thus, in his *Essay Concerning Human Understanding* (1690), Locke refuted Descartes' innatist psychology (and all those that had preceded it ever since Plato). Inspired rather by Aristotle, he made the human mind a *tabula rasa* on which sensations are formed during childhood, shaping ideas that associate and combine, from the simple to the complex. He defined the idea as 'whatsoever is the Object of the Understanding when a Man thinks' (a representation). According to Locke, experience can be applied either to the external objects of the environment (association between *sensation* and idea) or to the internal operations of the mind (reflection through the association of ideas). He thought that ideas couldn't be separated from consciousness. Becoming aware of ideas is an awakening of consciousness. Education to ideas is an awakening of consciousness.

In the problem of Molyneux, the man born blind possesses the conscious experience of an association between the tactile sensation and the idea of a sphere, but not between the visual sensation and the same sphere. So, nothing in his previous experience allows him to associate the two in his mind (hence Locke's negative answer). The missing mechanism, very simply, was *association*. What Locke wanted to discover, in line with the Newtonian scientific spirit and in opposition to Descartes, was a simple psychological mechanism, a functioning law that regulated the mind, the mental realm. This was the association between sensations and ideas, and the association between ideas themselves. Thus, association governed the 'world of ideas', that is, the world of psychology, like the mechanism of gravitation theorized by Newton, whose physics governed the fall of bodies and the relations between celestial bodies. Locke's work acceded to a request

Newton had expressed in the *Principia* (1687): finding for the mind, as he had done for space, one, and only one, universal principle of operation.

However, this principle or mechanism of association of ideas necessarily implies a psychology of education. This is what Locke proposes in *Some Thoughts Concerning Education* (1693), in which he outlines a psychology of the child. With a clean slate as his starting point, Locke understands that the powers of the mind will demand social incentives and models if they are to develop. The *mechanism* needs to be educated, and he insists on the role of imitation and play. A properly understood education must use games that are both free and challenging, but it must reserve a place for spontaneous imitation. What fascinates Locke in children is their drive and enthusiasm, that childlike zest that bursts forth in action, play and even schoolwork. In action, as in play, this was, in his view, all an expression of *freedom*.

Locke had all it needed to be a child psychologist, but he did no more than touch on the essential problem: that of mental structures or frameworks. This was the main issue that Anglo-Saxon empiricism failed to address: beyond the mental content of knowledge (ideas), is there an active centre of the mind, a set of structures to which ideas cling? Locke came close to this when, in line with Aristotle, he described the child's powers of both feeling and reflecting. However, he said nothing about how these sentient and cognitive powers are structured (or structure themselves) in the mind. Returning to Descartes' innatism, Emmanuel Kant (1724–1804) will say that these powers were already in existence: for him, they were an *a priori* of understanding.

Following on from Locke, David Hume (1711–1776), a Scottish philosopher who was an acquaintance of Rousseau, completed the project of empiricism in the same scientific, mechanistic and Newtonian spirit. He insisted on our faculty of *imagination* that worked on the basis of sensations: we *imagine* ideas, which involves a certain margin of uncertainty. In order to understand how the very powerful human imagination associates ideas with each other on the basis of experience by bonding them together (by 'attraction' as Newton would have put it), Hume described more precisely than Locke three sub-processes: (a) the spatial or temporal *contiguity* of objects in reality, a contiguity which configures our memory and the mental evocation of ideas; (b) the *resemblance* of each copy to the general idea; (c) the *cause and effect relationship* that underpins our belief system and our practical knowledge.

According to Hume, these processes of 'assembly' can operate incredibly fast in the human mind. His empiricism was original, very cognitive in nature (memory, beliefs, etc.) and even prefigured Daniel Kahneman's *system 1* today (Kahneman, 2011).

In France, Étienne Bonnot de Condillac (1714–1780) formulated a so-called sensualist version of Anglo-Saxon empiricism in his *Essay on the Origin of Human Knowledge* (1746): all our understanding, from perception to judgment, is *and must be* derived wholly from sensations. This means that we need to reform and purify our language so that it will organize sensations in such a way as to impose a precise correlation between words and things. That is what Condillac, a member of the French Academy, advocated to the scholars and philosophers of his time: they needed to express their knowledge in a correct, pure, clear language so that everyone would be able to grasp that knowledge. This was also the aim of Diderot in the *Encyclopédie*. Condillac wrote his *Grammar*, *The Art of Writing*, *The Art of Thinking*, *The Art of Reasoning*, and so on with this aim. In his main work, *The Treatise on Sensations* (1754), he explained that

the understanding was like an inert 'statue' that resided within us before existing in the outside world; contact with the world through the senses gave this statue life in the following order: smell, hearing, taste, sight, touch. The ideas derived from these five senses were simply sensations designated by words that represented things. These sensations developed and combined, thereby shaping the understanding. However, this still leaves the problem of the mysterious inert statue from which it all began!

From Locke to Condillac, empiricism assumed various different forms in order to promote the same general psychology that marked a revolt against the Cartesian *cogito*: for the empiricists, the environment shaped reason. Nevertheless, the question of the powers of the understanding touched on by Locke in his psychology of the child, and the 'inert statue' within us in Condillac, reveals the difficulty empiricism encounters in giving an account of the frameworks of the mind, which can structure and perhaps even precede the experience of sensations. Without this, the associations of ideas by the empirical connections of contiguity, resemblance, or cause and effect, as in Hume, remain contingent, 'scattered around' by circumstances without any real active centre (self, or *cogito*, in Descartes' phrase). This is where Leibniz, Wolff and Kant contributed to the debate.

The German mathematician Gottfried Leibniz (1646–1716) refuted Locke's thesis on the non-innate nature of ideas point by point. His critique promoted the view that there are Ideas that exist *independently of us*. According to Leibniz, the understanding is innate and allows us to process the data from experience through 'necessary ideas': that is why he gives the answer 'yes' to Molyneux's problem. By definition, these ideas are not contingent; that is, they do not depend on environmental circumstances, contrary to what the empiricists believed. Moreover, Leibniz observes that when the understanding, endowed with its necessary ideas (the self, the *cogito*), meets the perceptual world, representations emerge, which are not always very clear, mixed with an infinity of 'little perceptions' that can confuse consciousness and reflection and sometimes even elude them altogether. This view was still quite different from that of Locke, who supposed that ideas derived from the senses could not be separated from consciousness. In the end, one has the impression that, for Leibniz, the role of the environment was not positive or, at least, not as able to structure mental life as the empiricists seemed to suggest.

A pupil of Leibniz, Christian Wolff (1678–1754), then published a two-part treatise on psychology *Psychologia empirica* (1732) and *Psychologia rationalis* (1734) that forged a remarkable methodological synthesis, paving the way for Kant. As these titles indicate, Wolff distinguishes between two types of psychology. One is *empirical*: it needs to be based on external or internal observation, through introspection, and to lay bare the laws of human conduct and the faculties of the soul by measurement and calculation, like in physics. Wolff called this very prophetically 'psychometry', heralding Fechner's psychophysics in the next century. The other psychology is *rational* and belongs to pure reason: it enables us to determine *a priori*, by reasoning, as in algebra or geometry, what the faculties of the soul must be. Wolff advocates combining these two psychologies; the second kind is also able to feed on data known *a posteriori*. Thus, almost all-future psychology found itself already defined.

After Leibniz and Wolff, their disciple Kant formulated propositions that are still current in today's psychology, in line with a tradition that went back to Plato via Descartes. He said that pure concepts exist in us innately, as mental frameworks or 'categories of the understanding'; these do not come from the sensible world (the environment of the empiricists). Kant, following Wolff, gives the name 'pure reason' to so-called transcendental, metaphysical knowledge, superior to and outside of the world. This exists *a priori*, independently of our sensations. These *necessary and universal* cognitive principles relating to space, time, number, etc., are in us from birth, but only sensible experience, from infancy to adulthood, can *reveal them*. Thus, according to Kant, reason neither alone (rationalism) nor sensations alone (empiricism) make it possible to know the world. The intermediary here is the 'schema', which links pure, innate concepts with *intuitions*, for example intuitions of space, time, number, etc. that are linked to sensible experience and its representations. Thus, the schemas, or frameworks, of the mind allow us to make judgments about reality. This notion of a schema (or scheme) would be made famous in the twentieth century by Piaget, who made it the basic unit in his constructivist (non-innatist) theory of intelligence in the child. Other current programmes in the non-Piagetian cognitive sciences are more innatist and follow Kant in considering the possibility of *a priori* mental frameworks which sensible experience reveals from infancy to adulthood. This is the case with Dehaene and Brannon's (2010) view: 'Space, Time, and Number: A Kantian Research Program'.

The path travelled since the Renaissance shows that the history of psychology has been punctuated by a cognitive reform. In the seventeenth century, cognitive reform began with Descartes, the discoverer of the *cogito*, and Pascal, the critic of reason, who promoted *finesse* against *geometry*; but he was still reckoning without a mechanistic science (that of Copernicus, Galileo and Newton) that had not yet affected psychology. We had to wait for empiricists like Locke and Hume *to move on from the laws of space to those of the mind*. Like nature, the mind itself could now be something to be observed, analysed and understood from an external scientific perspective. The new explanation, however, still lacked 'frameworks', and Kant restored them: pure concepts and innatism, *schemas for sensible experience*. Kant thus saw rationalism and empiricism as two sides of the same coin. While his approach was metaphysical, the repercussions of the *a priori* on psychology were still great, forming a kind of tradition leading from Plato to Descartes and then on to the innatism of the current cognitive sciences.

I.3 Step 3: From Innatism/Empiricism Duality to Jean Piaget's Constructivism

In the nineteenth century, the English naturalist Charles Darwin (1809–1882), in *The Origin of Species* (1859), formulated the hypothesis – now accepted – of a general mechanism of *natural selection* that applies to *populations* and is based on a two-fold principle. The first principle is the *variation* of characteristics, generation after generation (the genetic origin of this random variation would be understood only after Darwin, thanks to Mendel's laws). The second principle is the *selection* by survival and reproduction of those who have (by chance) the combination of characteristics best suited to their environment. The effect of the environment is therefore indirect, and there is no longer, as in Lamarck, a heredity of acquired characteristics (by daily habit). To this, Darwin adds a world-shattering new idea: *all* living things have a common ancestry, because life on earth has a unique origin, from bacteria and blue algae to man!

Thus Darwin introduced into science and psychology the idea of a *natural* evolution of animal and human intelligence or cognition through *phylogenesis* or the evolution of species, a process lasting millions of years, in which matter, life and thought are intertwined – thus excluding God from scientific explanation (and, by the same token, ruling out the divine-innate ideas of Descartes and Plato). In *The Expression of Emotions in Man and Animals* (1872), Darwin described in detail studies on the expressions on the face and the emergence of language in children. The baby he observed was his own son, Doddy Darwin. This was the century of the first monographs devoted to children: the French historian Hippolyte Taine (1828–1893) and the English physiologist William Preyer (1841–1897) both reported observations taken from their own children. The Americans Stanley Hall and Arnold Gesell would later develop methods that are more systematic.

In the twentieth century, this idea of an evolution of intelligence was taken up again in the study of *ontogeny* – the idea that, from infancy to adulthood, body and mind evolve. The Swiss Jean Piaget (1896–1980) developed this in the psychology of the child's cognitive development and the French Changeux in neurobiology (his 'neural-mental Darwinism'). According to the latter theory, Darwin's variation–selection mechanisms also operate in the brain itself, affecting cognitive representations within *neuronal populations* – a theory that Changeux (1983, 2012) shares with the American Nobel Laureate in Physiology or Medicine Gerald Edelman (1929–2014). In fact, all scientific psychology has to consider two timescales: *phylogenesis*, or the evolution of species (Darwin), and *ontogenesis*, that is, development from infant to adult (including embryogenesis). In addition, there is a cognitive 'microgenesis', which corresponds to the much shorter time taken up by learning or by the brain when solving a task: months, days, hours, minutes, fractions of seconds, i.e., milliseconds.

In the twentieth century, the most dominant figure in the study of cognitive development was Piaget. His very new approach was the basis of genetic (in the sense of *ontogenesis*, not genomic) psychology and epistemology. Piaget's contribution to the history of psychology and ideas in general was to produce a real synthesis between empiricism (from Aristotle to Locke and Hume) and innatism (from Plato to Descartes and Kant). He rejected both trends as too simplistic and proposed a third intermediate way: *constructivism*. In his experimental and clinical studies involving children, he demonstrated the construction of psychological structures, from the stage of sensorimotor *schemes* (as in Kant) in the infant to the stages of concrete operations in the child and then the formal (abstract) operations in the adolescent. This comprised the genesis of logico-mathematical intelligence, from intuitive and illogical levels in infants and preschool children to the logical levels in school children and adolescents, a view now revised by post-Piaget thinkers. Others supplemented it by focusing on the more emotional, social and cultural origins of human cognition: namely the Russian psychologist Lev Vygotski (1896–1934), opening the way to the American psychologists Jerome Bruner (1915–2016) and Michael Tomasello (b. 1950).

Challenging both the empiricism of Locke, Hume and Condillac, who believed everything derives from experience through association and practice, and innatism (the opposing theory), which explains everything through innate structures (see Plato and Descartes, but also Kant and his *a priori* forms of sensitivity), Piaget proposed an intermediate theory, called 'constructivism'. It holds that intellectual structures, i.e. our thoughts, our mental operations, have a genesis specific to them (cognitive ontogenesis). From birth to adulthood, they are gradually *constructed*, stage by stage (like going upstairs one-step at a time), in the context of the interaction between an individual and his or her

environment – or, in more biological terms, between a body and its environment. In this interaction, what is essential for Piaget, is the *action* of a child on objects that surround it (exploring, handling and 'experimentation'), a concept very different from the idea of 'passive' learning (association and practice) specific to empiricism.

I.4 Step 4: Neo- and Neuro-constructivism in Cognitive Sciences

The purpose of this *Cambridge Handbook of Cognitive Development* is to provide comprehensive and detailed work on cognitive and brain development, since the seminal work of Piaget. That is for 40 years (1980–2020).

During the last decades, detailed behavioural studies have shown that Piaget underestimated the cognitive and logical (even scientific) capabilities of infants, as shown by the American psychologists Renée Baillargeon, Alison Gopnik, Elisabeth Spelke and Karen Wynn for example (Gopnik, 1999, 2012). Conversely, Piaget overestimated the cognitive capabilities of adolescents and adults, which are often biased by illogical intuitions and overlearned strategies (or heuristics) they fail to inhibit, as shown by the Israeli-American psychologist Daniel Kahneman (2011), Nobel laureate in Economic sciences in 2002 – and other authors, namely the British Jonathan Evans (1989, 2003).

Therefore, cognitive developmental psychologists are now facing a big paradox: the early smart skills of infants and the late illogical ones of older children and even adults. The new challenge is therefore to account not only for an incremental stage-by-stage process like in Piaget's approach, but also for a non-linear dynamical system of growth (Siegler, 1996). Within such a system, competing strategies, i.e., intuitive ones (heuristics) and logical ones (exact algorithms), may occur in the developing brain with different weights at any point in time, depending on the context and individual differences. This dynamical modelling introduces less regular developmental curves containing perturbations, bursts and collapses. Often, in some contexts, children fail to inhibit misleading heuristics (Borst & Houdé, 2014; Houdé, 2019), which explains these developmental irregularities, formerly called horizontal and vertical 'décalages' by Piaget ('only to save face', because it was a very strong objection to his incremental and structuralist theory). In fact, 'décalages' are not the exception, as Piaget thought, but the rule!

The current non-linear and dynamical approach better matches with the complexity of cognitive development that all the parents and teachers watch every day. It also points to the brain attentional and cognitive-control mechanisms as the key factors of development.

The general aim of the handbook is to present, illustrate and summarise this new epistemology of cognitive and brain development that we call 'neo- and neuro-constructivism' (in line with Mareschal & Johnson, 2007). 'Neuro' because of, after Piaget's time, the development of brain imaging techniques and their use in experimental psychology conducted to study both brain construction and cognitive development. Within this co-construction, we must also now consider the multiple mechanisms by which genes may influence behaviour, having in mind, as Changeux states in this book (Chapter 2), that:

the human brain is, neither John Locke's blank slate (*tabula rasa*) deprived of any pre-existing innate structure – or, in a modern language, a random network of undifferentiated neurons fully instructed by experience – nor a fully genetically determined, irrevocably hard-wired neuronal architecture ... It is a unique compromise between an eminently variable, intrinsically rich, connectivity and a set of

species-specific, genetically determined, rules, which unambiguously make our brain that of *Homo sapiens*.

To achieve this general 'neo- and neuro-constructivism' aim, we have invited current leading scholars from neurobiology, developmental cognitive neuroscience, experimental child psychology and computational modelling.

I.5 Overview of the Handbook Contents

An opening section (Part I) covers the neurobiological constraints and laws of cognitive development: *how the brain constructs cognition*. Damasio and Damasio (Chapter 1) describe and explain how life regulation and feelings motivate the cultural mind, from the dawn of life to humans today, through *phylogenesis*. Then, in Chapter 2, Changeux explores the key principles of *epigenesis*, synapse selection, cultural imprints and human brain development, from molecules to cognition. Chapter 3, by Cachia, Mangin and Dubois, presents the current mapping of the human brain from the preterm period to infancy using 3D magnetic resonance imaging (MRI). Next, Chapter 4, by Paus, continues this description by the human brain development and maturation processes from infancy to adolescence. Then, Posner and Rothbart (Chapter 5) add an important focus on genetic and experiential factors in brain development using the examples of executive attention and self-regulation. Finally, Luna et al. ends this Part I developmental description by the brain basis, underlying the transition from adolescence to adulthood in Chapter 6.

The following section (Part II) covers the fundamentals of cognitive development, from infancy to adolescence and young adulthood. A first subsection covers the roots of thinking in infancy. It starts with Vauclair's description of the differences between humans (from infancy), great apes and monkeys in cognition (Chapter 7). Then, the following chapters explore infant physical reasoning about objects (Lin, Stavans, and Baillargeon, Chapter 8), categorization (Rakison, Benton, and Dinh, Chapter 9), numerical cognition (vanMarle, Chapter 10), theory of mind (Scott, Roby, and Baillargeon, Chapter 11), social-moral cognition (Falck, Strickland, and Jacob, Chapter 12), and scientific thinking and reasoning (Goddu and Gopnik, Chapter 13). A final chapter deals with computational approaches to cognitive development in infancy (Nobandegani and Shultz, Chapter 14).

A second subsection covers cognitive development during childhood and adolescence. It starts with language and categorization in young children (Gelman, Chapter 15). Then, the authors explore the question of numerical strategy choices in preschool and schoolchildren (Siegler, Chapter 16) and the role of inhibitory control in these choices (Roell, Houdé, Borst and Viarouge, Chapter 17). The following chapters present several other facets of cognitive development during childhood and adolescence. In Chapter 18, Perner, Kulakova and Rafetseder examine theory of mind and counterfactual reasoning together. In Chapters 19 and 20, Happaney and Zelazo, and Chevalier and Blaye describe the general role of executive functions and flexibility. In Chapter 21, Frey and De Neys explore the reasoning biases through dual processes (intuition versus logic). Then Chalik, Misch and Dunhan deal with social cognitive development in Chapter 22. Finally, Chapters 23 and 24 examine the functioning of cognitive control, decision-making and motivation in children and adolescents (Blankenstein, Peper and Crone; Ernst, Gowin and Gaillard).

The last section (Part III) covers the education and school-learning domains. Our aim here is to formulate a set of cognitive principles for evidence-based education (Lau and Ansari, Chapter 25). Ziegler, Perry and Zorzi start with the question of literacy and normal versus impaired reading, in Chapter 26. Chapter 27 explores numerical cognition and mathematical reasoning in the classroom (Prado and Gardes). Then, Edelsbrunner, Schumacher and Stern examine scientific reasoning skills in light of general cognitive development, in Chapter 28. Chapter 29, by Klingberg and Sauce, presents a focus on working memory training, from the laboratory to school. In addition, Steinbeis and de Smid draw a more general overview of working memory, cognitive flexibility and inhibition trainings or interventions at school, in Chapter 30. Chapter 31, by Oudeyer, deals with curiosity-driven learning and opens the field to developmental robotics. Finally, Thomas and Porayska-Pomsta show the power of neurocomputational methods in education, Chapter 32.

In each section, from Part I to Part III, beyond the specific cognitive or school domains, the authors analyse and discuss in depth the more general processes at the root of brain and cognitive development.

So, from Plato to neuroscientists today, beyond the outdated opposition between innatism and empiricism, we hold in hand for the twenty-first century a new and rich neuroconstructivist epistemology of cognitive development brilliantly illustrated by the contributions of the experts of this Handbook.

References

Borst, G., & Houdé, O. (2014). Inhibitory control as a core mechanism for cognitive development and learning at school. *Perspectives on Language and Literacy* (Special Issue on Executive functions, ed. A. Diamond), *17*, 41–44.

Braine, M., & O'Brien, D. (eds.) (1998). *Mental Logic*. Hove: Erlbaum.

Changeux, J. P. (1983). *L'Homme neuronal*. Paris: Fayard.

Changeux, J. P. (1985). *Neuronal Men: The Biology of Mind*. Princeton, NJ: Princeton University Press.

Changeux, J. P. (2012). *The Good, the True, and the Beautiful: A Neuronal Approach*. New Haven, CT: Yale University Press.

Chomsky, N. (1975). *Reflections on Language*. New York: Pantheon Books.

Condillac, E. B. (1746). *An Essay on the Origin of Human Knowledge*. Cambridge, UK: Cambridge University Press.

Condillac, E. B. (1754). *Traité des sentations*. Paris: Bure l'aîné.

Damasio, A. (1994). *Descartes's Error: Emotion, Reason and the Human Brain*. New York: Putnam.

Damasio, A. (2003). *Looking for Spinoza: Joy, Sorrow, and the Feeling Brain*. Orlando, FL: Harcourt.

Damasio, A. (2018). *The Strange Order of Things: Life, Feeling, and the Making of Cultures*. New York: Pantheon Books.

Damasio, A., & Carvalho, G. (2013). The nature of feelings: Evolutionary and neurobiological origins. *Nature Reviews Neuroscience, 14*, 143–152.

Darwin, C. (1859). *On the Origin of Species*. London: John Murray.

Darwin, C. (1872). *The Expression of Emotions in Man and Animals*. London: John Murray.

Dehaene, S., & Brannon, E. M. (2010). Space, time, and number: A Kantian research program. *Trends in Cognitive Sciences, 14*, 517–519.

Descartes, R. (1664). *L'Homme*. Paris: Charles Angot.

Evans, J. (1989). *Bias in Human Reasoning*. Hillsdale, NJ: Erlbaum.

Evans, J. (2003). In two minds: Dual-process accounts of reasoning. *Trends in Cognitive Sciences, 7*, 454–459.

Fodor, J. (1983). *The Modularity of Mind*. Cambridge, MA: MIT Press.

Gopnik, A. (1999). *The Scientist in the Crib*. New York: Harper Collins.

Gopnik, A. (2012). Scientific thinking in young children. Theoretical advances, empirical research and policy implications. *Science, 337*, 1623–1627.

Houdé, O. (2019). *3-System Theory of the Cognitive Brain: A Post-Piagetian Approach*. New York: Routledge.

Johnson-Laird, P. (2001). Mental models and deduction. *Trends in Cognitive Sciences, 5*, 434–442.

Kahneman, D. (2011). *Thinking, Fast and Slow*. New York: Farrar, Straus and Giroux.

La Mettrie, J. O. (1748). *L'Homme Machine*. Leyde.

Lazer, D. M. J., Baum, M., Benkler, Y., et al. (2018). The science of fake news. *Science, 359*, 1094–1096.

Locke, J. (1690). *Essay Concerning Human Understanding*. London.

Locke, J. (1693). *Some Thoughts Concerning Education*. London: A. and J. Churchill.

Mareschal, D., & Johnson, M. (2007). *Neuroconstructivism: How the Brain Constructs Cognition*. Oxford: Oxford University Press.

Molyneux, W. (1978). Letter to John Locke, 7 July 1688. In E. S. Beer (eds.), *The Correspondence of John Locke* (Vol. 3, Letter n. 1064). Oxford: Clarendon Press.

Newton, I. (1987). *Philosophiae naturalis principia mathematica*. London: W. Dawson and sons.

Piaget, J. (2015). *The Psychology of Intelligence*. London: Routledge.

Piaget, J., & Inhelder, B. (1969). *The Psychology of the Child*. New York: Basic Books.

Siegler, R. (1996). *Emerging Minds: The Process of Change in Children's Thinking*. New York: Oxford University Press.

Spelke, E. S. (2000). Core knowledge. *American Psychologist, 55*, 1233–1243.

Wolff, C. (1732). *Psychologia empirica*. Frankfurt.

Wolff, C. (1734). *Psychologia rationalis*. Frankfurt.

Part I
Neurobiological Constraints and Laws of Cognitive Development

1 How Life Regulation and Feelings Motivate the Cultural Mind

A Neurobiological Account

Antonio Damasio and Hanna Damasio

1.1 Sociocultural Phenomena Are Not Restricted to Humans

Few ideas are in greater need of correction than the common-sense notion that cultures are born exclusively of the human mind and constitute an entire novelty in the history of life. Somewhat distractedly and with the usual high regard that humans reserve for themselves, cultures are frequently thought of as purely human creations. For example, behaviors that result in moral regulation or in social and political organization, as well as activities tied to economical exchanges or the management of illness, are assumed to have been constructed by the grace of standard and explicit human intelligence. The human contemplation of facts, the process of reasoning over those facts, and the consequent knowledge writ large would have been the engines behind the production of cultures. Fine human cognition and sound human reasoning would explain the newness of such phenomena.

One understands why this scenario may be plausible, at first pass, and yet it is far removed from reality in numerous ways. Here are the facts. Simple organisms with only one cell and not even a nucleus, of the kind present at the dawn of life, around 4 billion years ago, already exhibited sociality. Groups of such organisms would band together to assist each other and improve their lot, but such groups could also fight other groups and compete with them for access to vital resources (Diggle et al., 2007;

Hughes & Sperandio, 2008; Jousset et al., 2013; Naviaux, 2014; Nealson & Hastings, 2006; Persat et al., 2015; Rainey & Rainey, 2003). The social behaviors already included traits that resemble, in their essence, critical features of what, today, we designate as human cultures. It is an established fact that complex social arrangements began to appear in evolution long before multicellular organisms did, in fact, long before there were nervous systems, even simple ones (Table 1.1). As for cultural phenomena unquestionably worthy of that name, they certainly began to occur before there were vertebrates on the planet, as can be demonstrated by the elaborate compendium of social insect behaviors. The organization and the variety of roles played by bees and ants in their hives and nests is, for all practical purposes, "cultural" (Wilson, 2012).

Lest our statements be dismissed as crude and naïve, it is important to acknowledge that the degree of complexity of the non-human social behaviors to which we are referring is no match for the current social behavior of humans. But the critical point we are trying to establish here is that, nonetheless, the contours of the fundamental kinds of such non-human social behaviors resemble those of human cultures and that the fundamental consequences of such human and non-human behaviors are also comparable (Damasio, 2018). They revolve around the issue of maintaining the life process within the bounds set by homeostatic regulation. It is critical for our

Table 1.1. *Stages of life*

Beginning of Earth	around 4.5 billion years
Chemistry and Protocells	4.0 to 3.8 billion years
First Cells	3.8 to 3.7 billion years
Eukaryotic Cells	2 billion years
Multicellular Organisms	700 to 600 million years
Nervous Systems	around 500 million years

argument that the non-human social behaviors be part of a manifestly intelligent struggle to maintain conditions of existence compatible with the optimization of the life process and conducive to survival. In other words, the later appearance and subsequent development of human cultures in the history of life has had a main consequence: assisting and promoting the life-regulation processes whose ensemble is known as *homeostasis*. But that process of assisting and promoting life regulation was already established, practiced, and ongoing long before humans made their debut in evolution. The main consequence of non-human complex social behaviors – those behaviors we like to designate as "pro-cultural" – has long been the assisting and promoting of homeostasis. In a curious way, terms such as "pro-cultural," "pre-cultural," and even "cultural" simply mean "pro-homeostatic."

It is also important to acknowledge that non-human social behaviors developed and have continued to operate and evolve in non-human species, in the absence of conscious mental processes and in the absence of overt, explicit, deliberate creativity. In the vast majority of non-human organisms, the "author" responsible for the "pre-cultural behaviors" is the life process itself. That "leading responsible author" is not – as is obvious in the case of humans and of a number of animal species – the singular mind of one individual, conscious of a specific need and capable of reasoning

creatively that the need can potentially be met by carrying out a specific action. Here is an illustration of our idea: when humans began to make use of warfare and also of pacts of cooperation, they were identifying problems and implementing solutions thanks to the fact that they were conscious and that their minds were capable of image-based reasoning. For all intents and purposes, they were guided by their creativity. But were humans really "inventing" solutions from scratch or were they, more plausibly, adjusting and perfecting pre-existing and quite competent solutions that their minds were now revealing and making explicit? After all, un-minded, non-conscious, and quite humble non-humans had responded comparably to such situations, long before, in the history of evolution. They had generated similar solutions in the absence of overt reasoning, in a manner that does not even qualify for "intuition," given how spontaneously and directly the actions appeared to spring fully formed from the living organism.

What was the essential mechanism, the "spring," as it were? It was, we believe, the *non-explicit, hidden sensing*, at any given moment, of the *degree of success or failure* of *internal life operations*, combined with the *concomitant and equally hidden sensing of the external conditions, at that moment*. We believe that using such terms as "mind" or "consciousness" for this process of non-explicit, non-imagetic sensing is not appropriate, although thinkers whose work we respect do so; that is the case with Arthur Reber (see Reber, 2019). We have begun to use the term "sentience" to describe such evaluative conditions, leaving out the vaguely conscious connotation associated with the word sentience. In brief, the "evaluation" of the life situation, no matter how covert, was responsible for adjusting life regulation, as needed, in keeping with the equally unstated, covert goal of maintaining the life of the organism. From a varied menu of many possibilities of response and after several of them were tried out, effective responses were selected and adopted for the future.

What was the overall mechanism behind the discovery of effective solutions? "Why," "how," and by "whom" were solutions found and implemented?

In our current perspective, in most living creatures and for most of the duration of life on earth, the process of creating complex social behaviors has not been conscious, has not been minded or reasoned, and has not depended on the presence of nervous systems. Matters proceeded as outlined above based on "sentience" and on a fundamental "competence" that adjusted life parameters accordingly. We also believe, however, that once nervous systems appeared in the biological scene a novel and multi-pronged development began to loom. We propose that there were several fundamental steps in that development.

The first step consisted of the development of *feeling*, which, as we will discover in Section 1.3, amounts to *a mental experience of the state of life in the respective organism*. This is the de facto initiation of the grand process of consciousness. In order to do their job – advise their owner of the conditions of the organism – *feelings have to be conscious*, they have to pertain, unequivocally, to *their* specific organism. If feelings had not been *necessarily* conscious, their practical consequences would have been negligible. For example, a situation of pain would not have constituted a protective defense, nor would pleasure have been an incentive. We know today that, by and large, feelings are achieved by interactions of non-neural and neural parts of the organism. We address the physiology of feeling in Section 1.3.

The second step was the emergence of *consciousness proper*, concerning not only the organism but plenty of other objects, actions, and processes. To imagine how this additional step could have come about, consider the following. The occurrence of feelings, no matter how modest, *coinciding with* or even *caused by* the presence of varied objects, actions, and processes, allows those constituents to be referred to their respective body and thus become "known" to their respective organism. In other words, *consciousness proper* begins with genuinely informative homeostatic feelings; such feelings – as well as others generated by standard emotive processes – are then naturally and spontaneously "applied" to and "associated" with other objects, actions, and processes. As a consequence, they too become connected to "their" organisms, which is another way of saying that they become "known" to the organism or that the organism is "conscious" of their presence.

The third step was the expansion of the *cognitive* machinery, an expansion responsible for refined imagetic perception of the world surrounding the organism as well as for the emergence of imagetic flow and of narrative making, both assisted by memory and reasoning. Intriguingly, this third step also amplified the organism's ability to experience the "world within," and expand the reaches of the feeling process itself.

In conclusion, we need to consider not one step but three, operating cooperatively but with distinct contributions. *Feeling* (the first step), which was primarily a motivator and guide of homeostatic behavior, enabled the second step – *consciousness proper* – by allowing the body reference that is integral to feelings to be applied to numerous other objects, actions, and processes. But *expanded cognition* (the third step) took advantage of the organism reference and promoted and perfected responses and permitted the invention of new solutions. These creative results accounted for the elaborate social behaviors which came to serve as the roots of cultural instruments and practices in the full sense of the term culture.

In summary, and in essence, the roots of cultural phenomena are to be found in the process of life regulation, that is, in *homeostasis*. Eventually, along with the development of *affective* processes and of their central feature – *feelings* – there arises a required expansion/complement: *consciousness proper*. The primary role of feelings and the indispensable presence of specific organism references are the critical features that allow homeostatic needs to motivate and guide the production of cultures. But the ultimate implementation of cultures also depends on the cognitive capabilities to which we allude above.

All of these stepwise processes – feelings, consciousness, and an expanded cognitive capacity – were in place before humanity first appeared. The entire range of cultural behaviors, the ones that emerged non-consciously along with the ones that were deliberately constructed by conscious, cognitively rich, creative minds, were the consequence of homeostatic needs. They still ARE. They follow the natural tendency of living organisms to respond to homeostatic needs efficiently and thus maintain life.

Eventually, when humans constructed collections of moral behaviors and religious beliefs, invented justice systems, practiced politics and economics, developed medicine, science, and technology, and engaged in the arts, they were still attempting to promote homeostasis by relying on (a) feelings, (b) the consciousness that they partly enable, and (c) a cognitive apparatus where imagination, memory, reasoning, and ultimately language had expanded spectacularly the possibilities of creative response.

1.2 From Life Regulation to Feeling

It is manifestly impossible to reconstitute the early evolutionary trajectory that begins with the processes of life regulation and ends with the emergence of feelings. Evolution cannot be described by a single line; there are several paths, parallel and intersecting, and different results, not to mention dead ends. It is reasonable, however, to point to probable stages and advance hypotheses about the capabilities of varied organisms along their evolutionary path, given the design of those organisms. When we consider unicellular organisms, with or without a nucleus, we simultaneously confront very simple and yet very complex creatures. There are rich processes of life contained within the perimeter defined by the cell membrane. Outside of that membrane there is the universe of other organisms and non-living objects; inside, there is an organized process of life, dependent on several organelles, each of which hails from even simpler life forms.

The machinery of life is through and through a world of chemistry, vulnerability, and transience. It is a world of atoms – those that are listed in the Periodic Table of Mendelev – combined and recombined in varied admissible arrangements so as to form molecules. The intelligence of this world has a specific but unstated aim – preserving the life process that consists of transforming energy, via metabolism, so that, for example, movements can be produced in response to chemical, mechanical, or thermal stimuli, arriving at the cell membrane. This intelligence is naturally embedded in the primary physical structure but modified by secondary chemical combinations, the resulting molecules, and their functional consequences. The life situation differs from the world of pure physics that undergirds the artificial intelligence of robots. It is vulnerable, even fragile, and it relies on continuous labors in order to stave off decline and extinction (Crick, 1981; Damasio & Damasio, 2021; De Duve, 1995, 2005; Dyson, 1999; Gantí, 2003; Man & Damasio, 2019; Schrodinger, 1944).

The term homeostasis refers to a collection of processes aimed at maintaining the operations of life within parameters compatible with its continuation (e.g., pH, temperature, presence, and amount of certain molecules). There is no single "optimal" or "best" life state. There are several states that are conducive to life marching on and several states that announce the opposite. At both ends of the range lies dysfunction, disease, and death. When decline or danger are *internally and non-consciously sensed*, a number of corrections are automatically instituted aimed at maintaining life. In the vast majority of creatures that ever have lived, this effective rescue operation does not require consciousness or reason. This qualification continues to apply to the present moment: for most creatures alive today the saving corrections of homeostasis are engaged unknowingly and only unknowingly. Matters are remarkably different when we transpose the micro-level situation to the level of humans: *when life operations become problematic humans feel malaise; if the problem persists, we feel sick; and if nothing is done to solve the problem we die. When sources of energy are lacking, we feel hunger, when hydration dips we are thirsty; cut our airflow and we feel "air hunger."* Intriguingly, at the other end of the behavioral range, exorbitant attempts at homeostatic correction can result in manic activity and also announce sickness and death. More often than not, in one way or another, humans try to respond to the felt warnings and take advantage of them. In other words, humans have dual homeostatic controls, the early automated version and the newer feeling variety further elaborated on by consciousness proper (Bernard, 1879; Berridge & Kringelbach, 2015; Cannon, 1929, 1932; Craig 2002, 2003, 2009; Damasio & Carvalho, 2013; Damasio & Damasio, 2021; Richter, 1943; Torday, 2015).

It is imperative and helpful, once we introduce an illustration that comes from the human level, to add that the likelihood of anything comparable to explicit feeling or explicit cognition in unicellular organisms is quite low. We know, today, a little bit about the physiological complexity required for mental phenomena such as ours – for example, the ability to make maps on the basis of which imagetic representations can arise. One can make a partial exception for primordial feelings, where the imagetic component would be minimal and where the action of chemical molecules would dominate. But robust and in all probability specific feelings also require neural structures. Mental phenomena with any degree of specificity are difficult to conceive when we consider that mental phenomena would have to be generated from chemical pathways within the cytoplasm of a single cell, even when we grant that cell a number of differentiated processes and devices – a nucleus and organelles such as mitochondria. What such processes and devices do is remarkable, no doubt, but they have their hands full running a risk-prone chemical factory. Thinking is not likely to result from that primary assignment.

What we are claiming here is that the level of complexity of unicellular organisms is not suggestive of the presence of mind processes. Why not? We venture (and wager) that there are no images to be found in single cells, alone or combined in a narrative flow; that there are no devices or processes capable of constructing representations of themselves and of their "parts," let alone representations of the world exterior to the cell. We believe that there are, instead, complex chemical states, maintained within certain bounds; that there is production of energy which can be channeled to movement and permits responses to stimuli or the spontaneous initiation of actions, provided the responses and actions are helpful, in some way, to the continuation of life in that organism. At any moment, continuously, the cell exhibits a particular chemical "state of life" that can be closer or further away from the most useful operational ranges for that particular organism. The part of the range toward which "states of life" tend to gravitate naturally defines the success or failure of the ongoing state of life. That degree of success or failure can express itself by certain overall actions of a cell – for example, relaxing its membrane, quietening its activities; or, on the contrary, by agitating its motions, constricting its perimeter and literally shrinking. Importantly, however, in simple organisms, those active expressions would NOT have a prominent mental counterpart. There would be no pronounced "mental state" to accompany the states conducive to life's continuation within a cell or to its demise. We suggest that, if single cells could have had *a mental expression of the state of life within their organism*, then that expression would have been a *feeling*, a natural translation of the goodness or badness of the state of life relative to its intrinsic goal: persist, maintain itself.

Our current position is that the entire sequence of processes – from basic life state to the mental expression of that state, a feeling – becomes possible only in organisms equipped with nervous systems of a certain degree of complexity. Still, we are open to the possibility that a number of species without nervous systems but with considerable multisystem differentiation might conceivably generate early stages of a feeling-like process and produce a basic sense of existence, a sense of being.

For the moment we need to face the reality that dating the beginning of feelings and connecting that beginning to specific species is not satisfactorily established. We need to accept that there is a gray zone, conceivably occupied by multicellular organisms with internal organ differentiation and with or without simple nervous systems, in which a general "sense of being" might be possible.

Beyond the gray zone, however, it is reasonable to imagine multicellular organisms with abundant internal organ differentiation and progressively more complex nervous systems with elaborate central components. And it is within such organisms that we expect feelings to have blossomed and have been capable of providing both a sense of being *and* an early manifestation of organism-based perspective on which consciousness can be based. In such organisms it is possible to conceive a broad range of homeostatic feelings thanks to the influence of circulating molecules on the operation of internal organs as well as on neural networks. Such molecules naturally help produce "valence," the one-word synonym for the *quality* of the life state relative to its fundamental goal: persisting.

1.3 The Physiology of Feelings

Given the significance of homeostasis and of feeling for the generation of social behaviors and, eventually, of cultures, it is important to address our current understanding of the physiology behind the emergence of feelings.

Nervous systems first appeared around 500 million years ago. As suggested in Section 1.2, although we are open to the possibility of primordial feelings emerging even earlier, we favor the hypothesis that full-fledged feelings require the presence of neural structures and fairly complex ones at that. The simpler variety of feelings would depend upon the action of chemical molecules. The configuration of the neural circuitry as determined by a particular chemical environment would signify and, in a way, "represent" a certain life state, a particular region or position along the homeostatic range. But the intriguing and often neglected issue as one attempts to describe this process is that, in this case, the "representation" does not constitute a conventional "perception" of a certain body state.

"Neural representation" and "actual body state" work in integrated fashion to be "felt" rather than simply perceived. They "interact." This distinction also points unceremoniously to the core of the feeling problem. We, the subjects of feeling, do not merely inspect "representations" or "perceptions" of our internal states telescoped by our senses to our brains. We, the subjects of feeling, are directly privy to such states and the term feeling designates that intimate process. The "perceiver/experiencer" *of a certain state of life within an organism turns out to be that same organism.* At first glance, the statement appears paradoxical and even absurd, but it turns out to be, upon reflection, the source of an explanation for the distinction between what is simply "perceived" and what is "felt" (Carvalho & Damasio, 2021).

In the typical situation of perceiving objects or events in the world external to an organism, there is a clear distinction and distance between the perceptual organ and the object of perception. This is not so in the world of feeling where there is no distance between perceiver and object of perception. There is, instead, an integration and fusion of the two participants, subject and object, such that they become difficult to tease apart. We believe that the difficulty in separating perceiver and perceived is part and parcel of the mechanisms behind the ability to feel.

When the retina (and, subsequently, the visual cortices) map a certain object in the surround of the organism, retina and object exist in separate realms, one inside the organism, the other outside. The perceived object cannot intervene in the process of perception directly, nor interfere with the chain of physiological changes that are occurring in different layers of the retina and in the varied cortical regions toward which the retina projects its signals. The same applies to the sounds processed in the cochlea relative to the auditory cortices or to the shape of objects touched by the skin of one's fingers. But when we are said to perceive the state of contraction of an internal organ such as the gut or perceive the consequences of opioid molecules circulating in our organism, the "perceiver" and what is being "perceived" *inhabit the same physiological space and can interact physically within the process. This is a fundamental distinction between the typical process of interoception (part of which is also known as visceroception) and the processes of exteroception.*

Exteroceptive processes such as seeing, hearing, and touching operate differently from interoception and even from proprioception (the perceptual system that refers to striated muscles and voluntary movement). Exteroception relies on perceptual maps which plot spatial patterns in one or more dimensions. Interoception begins to operate at the level of chemical molecules involved in altering the actual function and shape of viscera directly or via intermediate neural activity. At more complex structural levels, interoception also makes use of maps. For example, when we feel a contraction of the gut and call it a "colic," or the reduction of caliber of the trachea that hallmarks asthma. In such situations, feelings conform more closely to the notion of perception, but the process is still distinct from typical exteroception for obvious reasons. To a considerable extent, when it comes to feeling, the "subject" and the "object" merge, at least in part, and become less distinct. When we talk of "perception" under such circumstances we must add that the circumstances are unusual and, in a way, paradoxical. Helena De Preester has devoted particular effort to illuminating this problem (De Preester, 2019; Henry, 1963).

In conclusion, in a curious way, we might say that we generally do not need to "perceive" the physiological changes that underly our feelings because we *feel* them instead. Feelings offer themselves to our mental experience, *directly*. We believe that this is due to the fact that the relationship between the neural devices that probe our life state and those same life states is of *close intimacy and oneness*.

Recent results are helping us glean the physiological features and processes behind the intimacy that result in feeling. Some of them concern fundamental peculiarities of the neural hardware related to affect (Carvalho & Damasio, 2019, 2021; Carvalho et al., 2019). The most important among them has to do with the kind of neurons involved in the physiology of feeling. Those neurons turn out to be predominantly non-myelinated. This amounts to depriving their axons of the insulation material – the myelin – that separates the axon cable from its chemical surround. For practical purposes this feature opens the axons of the respective neurons to the influence of varied chemical molecules present in their environment. The nervous system and the surrounding non-nervous organism structures partake of intimate chemical interactions. As a result, in addition to the neuron signaling that depends on the activity or quiescence of synapses, nature adds to the mix another kind of signaling – known as Non-Synaptic-Signaling – along with an infinity of graded states beyond simply "on" and "off."

One dramatic consequence of such circumstances occurs in nerve structures whose axons are aligned in parallel, in a sort of palisade, as is the case with the vagus nerve, a nerve which is crucially involved in feeling processes. As a result of the lack of myelin in the vagus nerve, it is possible for electrical impulses to be conducted sideways, orthogonally to the direction of the nerve, such that conduction spreads *across* the bunched axons rather than along them. This phenomenon is known as *ephapsis*, and it enriches the menu of neural communication to include not just synaptic but also ephaptic conduction.

We must note yet another contributor to the intimacy of interoceptive processes: the fact that certain structures of the interoceptive system lack a blood-brain-barrier. This is manifestly the case in the neural ganglia that bring signals from everywhere in the organism's soma to the central nervous system, namely, the spinal ganglia distributed up and down the spinal cord, and the trigeminal ganglia in the brainstem. There is no blood-brain-barrier in part of the ganglia, and in its absence the neurons become open to the direct influence of molecules circulating in the blood capillaries and in cerebrospinal fluid. They are in the same chemical bath. This is perhaps the closest degree of intimacy between "body" and nervous system.

In brief, thanks to the expression of homeostatic states in the process of feeling, our cognitive processes can be informed and advised of the momentary life conditions of our organism, thus becoming conscious and acting accordingly in a large variety of situations, including our social human experiences. It should be apparent that both the functional "rationale" for consciousness and the "problem" of explaining its physiology, are approachable through the avenue of feeling.

1.4 The Role of Emotions

In our attempt to provide a neuro-biological account of the development of cultures we have so far evoked feelings, consciousness, and cognitive processes. Clearly, we give pride of place to affect but we have not yet mentioned the phenomena that are most frequently, and incorrectly, invoked as the virtual emblem of affect: *emotions*. Where do emotions fit in our account? What are emotions and where do they stand relative to feelings? These definitions and relationships have recently become more approachable. So here are the critical distinctions (Damasio, 2018, chapters 7 and 8, 2021).

First, as we have seen, feelings are through and through experiences of life states, although, as we have just shown, they form a distinct class of experiences.

Second, the fundamental variety of feelings is the one we have been highlighting: *homeostatic*. These feelings correspond to life states such as *well-being, malaise, pain, hunger, thirst,* and *desire*.

Third, emotions (and to a great extent drives and motivations) are *highly established, easily repeatable, largely involuntary action-programs*. Some of the actions in the program are only internal (contraction of smooth muscles of viscera, secretion of certain molecules), and some can be observed externally (relaxation or contraction of striated muscles, specific patterns of facial expression or gait). We can observe emotions in other creatures, of course, but we can also *feel* them in ourselves when we experience them as *emotional feelings*.

Fourth, *emotional feelings are transient modifications of the ongoing homeostatic state, large and small, caused by the deployment of emotional action-programs*. In brief, emotional feelings are transient variations (one might also call them "disturbances") of the ever-flowing homeostatic states. Consequently, emotional feelings *constitute variations on the theme of homeostatic feelings*.

Fifth, unlike homeostatic states and their respective feelings, which are part and parcel of the essential life process, emotions are *elaborate concerts of actions* that evolved to address and cope with specific problems faced by organisms, including problems posed by life in a social setting. That is why emotion programs prominently include fear, anger, joy, sadness, compassion, love, pride, humility, disgust, and contempt. To a greater or smaller degree, all of them constitute attempts to resolve, in a prompt, unreasoned manner, a problem posed by life, especially in *society*.

Emotions are "triggered" by the ongoing circumstances of life. The presence and perception of particular objects or events "engages" emotional responses which result in subsequent emotional feelings.

The flowing of events in the narratives of our lives is replete with emotive reactions and their attendant feelings, thus irrevocably intermixing cognition and affect.

We have discussed the role of affect in cultural life using the notion of "somatic marker" in domains as diverse as ethics, esthetics, economics, and politics. (See, for example, Damasio's *The Strange Order of Things* 2018; and Verweij & Damasio, 2019.)

1.5 Building Cultures

We have outlined three steps responsible for the building of complex social behaviors and, eventually, of cultures in the full sense. The three steps are: (1) *feelings*, the translation of homeostatic states into *hybrid somatic and mental experiences*; (2) *consciousness proper*, the largely feeling-derived functional arrangement that refers mental representations to an ongoing life process unfolding in a *specific organism*; and (3) the expansion of *cognitive* abilities responsible for translating in imagetic terms the presence of objects, actions, consequences, and qualities, actually occurring in the world external to the organism or imagined on the basis of reasoning over images, freshly minted or recalled from memories. The flow of images in a conscious mental process is well designated by the term *narrative*. Narratives are the fundamental currency of mental life, responsible simultaneously for telling the story of what things are and of how they interact in time but also capable of telling us what things can become or even ought to be (Kaplan et al., 2016).

Plain narratives operate on the basis of imagetic representations, spatial patterns more or less faithful to the originals that they stand for, often schematically simplified to the point of abstraction or translated in the form of symbols. The most commonly used set of symbols belongs to verbal languages. It is quite common for narratives to make use of both direct imagetic representations as well as linguistic translations.

One of the intriguing aspects of narratives is that they act upon organisms by using not only cognitive processes – reasoning, recall of previously memorized material, creation of new compositions – but also by prompting all manner of *affective reactions*, namely, *drives*, *motivations*, and *emotions*. As noted in Section 1.4, as these affective reactions are organized and deployed, organisms apprehend their significance and consequences via *emotive feelings*. The process sounds complicated at first but really is not. It is best conceived when one realizes that as life flows with all its attending vagaries, the introduction in its midst of an emotion or drive operates primarily by having the sets of actions that constitute, say, an emotion *disturb* the ongoing life process. The disturbance is such that, for example, certain visceral parameters are temporarily altered – the typical examples being cardiac and respiratory rhythms; gut activity; and myriad endocrine reactions. In other words, the ongoing cognitive narrative is responsible for prompting affective responses; such responses, for example, emotions, alter the flow of life so that the contents of the flowing narrative are not merely *accompanied* by affective phenomena – in a parallel track – but actually *modified and accompanied* by those phenomena. Moreover, in a wave of subsequent reciprocation, the new contents of the now enriched cognitive narrative can generate their own emotive responses.

The consequences of this arrangement are manifold. First, feelings introduce within the mental process information regarding the state of life in the organism and make that information count if it happens to be relevant. One can say that feelings plant, within the cognitive, creative process, the latest bulletins from the homeostasis front. Second, the idea that cognitive processes might operate independently from the world of feeling is pure fantasy and the same applies to the idea that the processes of life regulation and cognition would operate independently of each other.

The link between life regulation/homeostasis and the creation of cultures hinges on this curious physiological arrangement.

1.6 In Closing

In this essay we have tried to demonstrate the integral connection between biological phenomena and the development of cultures. We are following sound historical precedents. The moral philosophy of Adam Smith was grounded on understanding human affairs from a biological perspective. Intriguingly, Charles Darwin was influenced by Adam Smith as he applied selection mechanisms to cultural phenomena in *The Descent of Man*, as Marciano and Pelissier (2000) have demonstrated. But the close connection between Darwin and Smith reminds us that both were well aware of the precarity of life and of the extraordinary machinations behind its regulation at nonconscious as well as conscious levels.

References

Bernard, C. (1879). *Leçons sur les Phénomènes de la Vie Communs aux Animaux et aux Végétaux*. Paris: Librarie J. B. Baillière et Fils, Reprints from the Collection of the University of Michigan Library.

Berridge, K. C., & Kringelbach, M. L. (2015). Pleasure Systems in the Brain. *Neuron, 86*(3), 646–664.

Cannon, W. B. (1932). *The Wisdom of the Body*. New York: Norton.

Cannon, W. B. (1929). Organization for physiological homeostasis. *Physiological Review, 9*(3), 399–431.

Carvalho, G. B., & Damasio, A. (2019). Non-synaptic transmission and the foundations of affect. *Preprints*, doi: 10.20944/ preprints201901.0252.v1.

Carvalho, G. & Damasio, A. (2021). Interoception and the Origin of Feelings: A New Synthesis, *BioEssays*, https:// doi.org/10.1002/ bies.202000261.

Carvalho, G. B., Mulpuri, Y., Damasio, A., & Spigelman, I. (2019). A role for the P2Y1 receptor in nonsynaptic cross-depolarization in the rat dorsal root ganglia. *Neuroscience, 423*, 98–108.

Craig, A. D. (2002). How do you feel? Interoception: The sense of the physiological condition of the body. *Nature Reviews Neuroscience, 3*(8), 655–666.

Craig, A. D. (2003). Interoception: The sense of the physiological condition of the body. *Current Opinion in Neurobiology, 13*(4), 500–505.

Craig, A. D. (2009). How do you feel – now? The anterior insula and human awareness. *Nature Reviews Neuroscience, 10*(1), 59–70.

Crick, F. (1981). *Life Itself: Its Origins and Nature*. New York: Simon and Schuster.

Damasio, A. (2018). *The Strange Order of Things: Life, Feeling, and the Making of Cultures*. New York: Pantheon Books.

Damasio, A. (2021). *Feeling and Knowing*, New York: Pantheon Books.

Damasio, A. & Carvalho, G. B. (2013). The nature of feelings: Evolutionary and neurobiological origins. *Nature Reviews Neuroscience, 14*, 143–152.

Damasio, A. & Damasio, H. (2021). Are there two kinds of consciousness or will one kind suffice? *Journal of Consciousness Studies*.

De Duve, C. (1995). *Vital Dust: The Origin and Evolution of Life on Earth*. New York: Basic Books.

De Duve, C. (2005). *Singularities: Landmarks in the Pathways of Life*. New York: Cambridge University Press.

De Preester, H. (2019). Subjectivity as a sentient perspective and the role of interoception. In M. Tsakiris, & H. De Preester (eds.), *The Interoceptive Mind* (1st ed., pp. 293–306). Oxford: Oxford University Press.

Diggle, S. P., Griffin, A. S., Campbell, G. S., & West, S. A. (2007). Cooperation and conflict in quorum-sensing bacterial populations. *Nature, 450*, 411–414.

Dyson, F. (1999). *Origins of Life*. New York: Cambridge University Press.

Ganti, T. (2003). *The Principles of Life*. New York: Oxford University Press.

Henry, M. (1963). *L'Essence de la Manifestation* (1st ed.). Paris: Presses Universitaires de France.

Hughes, D. T., & Sperandio, V. (2008). Inter-kingdom signaling: Communication between bacteria and their hosts. *Nature Reviews Microbiology, 6*(2), 111–120.

Jousset, A., Eisenhauer, N., Materne, E., & Scheu, S. (2013). Evolutionary history predicts the stability of cooperation in microbial communities. *Nature Communications, 4*, 2573.

Kaplan, J., Gimbel, S. I., Dehghani, M., Immordino-Yang, M. H., Sagae, K., Wong, J. D., ... Damasio, A. (2016). Processing narratives concerning protected values: A cross-cultural investigation of neural correlates. *Cerebral Cortex, 27*(2), 1428–1438.

Man, K., & Damasio, A. (2019). Homeostasis and soft robotics in the design of feeling machines. *Nature Machine Intelligence, 1*, 446–452.

Marciano, A., & Pelissier, M. (2000). The influence of Scottish enlightenment on Darwin's theory of cultural evolution. *Journal of the History of Economic Thought, 22*(2), 239–249.

Naviaux, R. K. (2014). Metabolic features of the cell danger response. *Mitochondrion, 16*, 7–17.

Nealson, K. H., & Hastings, J. W. (2006). Quorum sensing on a global scale: Massive numbers of bioluminescent bacteria make milky seas. *Applied and Environmental Microbiology, 72*(4), 2295–2297.

Persat, A., Nadell, C. D., Kim, M. K., Ingremeau, F., Siryaporn, A., Drescher, K., . . . Stone, H. A. (2015). The mechanical world of bacteria. *Cell*, *161*(5), 988–997.

Rainey, P. B., & Rainey, K. (2003). Evolution of cooperation and conflict in experimental bacterial populations. *Nature, 425*, 72–74.

Reber, A. (2019). *The First Minds: Caterpillars, Karyotes, and Consciousness.* New York: Oxford University Press.

Richter, C. P. (1943). Total self-regulatory functions in animals and human beings. *Harvey Lecture Series, 38*(63), 1942.

Schrodinger, E. (1944). *What Is Life?* Dublin: Institute for Advanced Studies at Trinity College.

Torday, J. S. (2015). A central theory of biology. *Medical Hypotheses, 85*(1), 49–57.

Verweij, M., & Damasio, A. (2019). The somatic marker hypothesis and political life. *Oxford Research Encyclopedia of Politics.* https://doi.org/10.1093/acrefore/9780190228637.013.928.

Wilson, E. O. (2012). *The Social Conquest of the Earth.* New York: Liveright Publishing Corporation.

2 Epigenesis, Synapse Selection, Cultural Imprints, and Human Brain Development
From Molecules to Cognition

Jean-Pierre Changeux

2.1 Introduction: The Singularity of Brain Organization and Synaptic Epigenesis

The human brain is neither John Locke's "blank slate" deprived of any pre-existing innate structure – or, in a modern AI language, a random network of undifferentiated neurons fully instructed by experience – nor a fully genetically determined, irrevocably hard-wired neuronal architecture. Neither is it represented by the simplistic yet very popular deep-learning artificial networks. The 85–100 billion neurons of the human brain and their synaptic connections, that arose over million years of evolution and for each individual brain over almost 15 years of postnatal development, possess an original organization unmatched by any of our current computers. It is a unique compromise between an eminently variable, intrinsically rich connectivity and a set of species-specific, genetically determined, rules, which unambiguously make our brain that of *Homo sapiens*.

From a systemic point of view, the brain may be described as a dynamic assembly of multiple functional and reciprocally inter-regulated levels of structural organization, bottom-up, from molecule to consciousness and, conversely, top-down from cognitive functions to molecular processes, unified in a single global system. Actually, the brain may be viewed as the seat of multiple nested spontaneous evolutions operating concomitantly through variation–selection–amplification ("Darwinian") mechanisms (Barkow et al., 1992; Campbell, 2016; Changeux, 1983, 1985; Changeux & Danchin, 1976; Changeux et al., 1973; Edelman, 1987, 2006; Morange et al., 2016). These evolutions develop on strikingly different time scales: from the million years of the descent of man up to the 100 ms of psychological processes. They further operate from diverse variable units distributed in parallel at multiple nested levels of physical organization through variation–selection–amplification mechanisms creating profound intertwining between the developing (and adult) neuronal organization of the brain and the constantly evolving physical, social, and cultural environment. The brain's morphogenesis is progressive, with forms becoming intricated within forms, including possibly, at each step, sensitive phases of interactions with the environment. This dual relationship between the developing brain and its environment introduces an essential variability in the anatomy and functional architecture of the brain, which makes any individual human brain unique from both a

I would like to thank Professor Olivier Houdé for his valuable support and discussions. This project has received funding from the European Union's Horizon 2020 Framework Programme for Research and Innovation under Specific Grant Agreement No. 945539 (Human Brain Project SGA3).

connectional and a behavioral point of view (Changeux, 2017).

The aim of this chapter is to present and discuss a theory – initially expressed as a mathematical model (Changeux et al., 1973) – that gives access to such "epigenetic" inscription of environmental features within the developing connectivity of the brain. These views were consistent at the time with the behavioral observations of the newborn "learning by unlearning" (Mehler 1982) and with the then available knowledge of molecular biology. They did not need to refer to any sort of "instructive" or so-called Lamarckian mechanism (Piaget 1976; Quartz & Sejnowski, 1997). Furthermore, the term "epigenesis" (or "epigenetics") was used in a sense close to its original definition by Waddington (1942) and to his concept of the "epigenetic landscape" to illustrate how external events, some random, combine with inherited information coded in the genes to produce acquired variability between individuals from the same species. A well-established case is the acquisition of oral and written language, which, as discussed in Section 2.7, leaves important connectomic traces in the brain, which are re-learned, from one generation to the next.

This meaning differs from the concept of DNA "epigenetics" subsequently used in molecular biology to refer to unrelated mechanisms of DNA covalent modifications such as methylation and/or chromatin remodeling, which contribute to the regulation of genes expression without altering the DNA sequence (Lucchesi, 2019). The long-term heritability of such phenotypic changes has been suggested but heavily questioned. In addition, DNA "epigenetics" deals with gene expression at the level of the single nucleus of the nerve cell, while each individual neuron may establish up to 100,000 synapses available for synaptic epigenesis. Several levels of brain organization thus distinguish restricted DNA "epigenetics" from a broader synaptic epigenesis.

In the brain, the macromolecular level holds a decisive role by imposing inescapable bottom up physical constraints upon higher – up to the highest – functions (Changeux, 1983, 1985, 2017). First of all, the evolution of the species-specific features of the brain is grounded in the genes of the organism – in particular those which determine the "proto-organization" (Arcaro & Livingstone, 2017; Geschwind & Rakic, 2013; Rakic, 1976) or scaffolding of human brain connectivity – that we have referred to as the "genetic envelope" (Changeux et al., 1973). Yet, the issue of the evolution of the genetic envelope compared to the brain phenotype raises an interesting paradox. From mouse to humans, the size of the brain and, in parallel, its total number of neurons, increases from approximately 40–70 million to 85 billion (plus 50 billion glial cells), and the number of specialized cortical areas per hemisphere rises from about 10 in primitive mammals to as many as 180 in humans (Markov et al., 2013). In addition, the intrinsic connectivity, especially in the cerebral cortex, dramatically increases in diversity, leading to the ultimate development of oral language in less than 1 million years (Goulas et al., 2019).

By contrast, the full genome sequences now available for many species – mouse, monkey, chimpanzee, humans, and fossil human ancestors (Paabo, 2013) – are striking in their relative uniformity. The haploid genome comprises no more than about 20,000 gene coding sequences (only 1.2 percent of the human genome) and this number does not vary significantly from mouse to humans (Geschwind & Rakic, 2013; Paabo, 2013; Somel et al., 2013; Vallender et al., 2006). The coding genome itself appears highly conserved, especially for brain proteins, even at the most recent stages of hominization. The available comparative genomic data unambiguously reveal that the observed increase of brain anatomical and functional complexity does not reflect a parallel increase in the complexity of the genome (Dumas et al., 2019). This may be seen as an "astonishing evolutionary parsimony" (Changeux 1983, 1985, 2017). Still, at this stage, the actual few discrete genetic regulatory events that determined the fast increase in brain complexity during the past million years of hominization remain unidentified. These might include discrete changes in genomic organization, including gene duplications (Suzuki et al., 2018), DNA regulatory sequences (Petr et al., 2019; Weyer & Paabo, 2016), and others concerning the relationships between genes and phenotypes that have been under-evaluated within the classical "one gene–one protein–one phenotype" paradigm. The selective stabilization hypothesis is here presented as one mechanism, which might contribute to this evolutionary parsimony (Changeux 1983, 2017).

2.2 The Model of Changeux–Courrège–Danchin (CCD), 1973

During embryonic and postnatal development, the million billion synapses that form the adult human brain network do not assemble, like the parts of a computer, according to a plan that defines with great precision the disposition of all individual components. If this were the case, the slightest error in the instructions for carrying out this program could have catastrophic consequences. The mechanism proposed, on the contrary, relies upon the variability of developing interneuronal connections (within the mentioned genetic envelope) and the progressive setting of robust synapses through trial-and-error mechanisms that formally resemble an evolutionary process by variation–selection

(Arcaro & Livingstone, 2017; Blakemore et al., 1981; Changeux, 2017; Changeux & Danchin, 1976; Changeux et al., 1973; Edelman, 1978; Kasthuri & Lichtman, 2003; Purves & Lichtman, 1980; Rakic, 1976; Rakic et al., 1986; Shatz & Stryker, 1978; Sretavan et al., 1988). A most important and unique feature of human brain evolution is the extension of postnatal development for up to fifteen years. An approximately five-fold increase in brain weight accompanies this development, during which about half of all adult synaptic connections are formed at a very fast pace (approximately 0.5 million synapses per second) (Lagercrantz et al., 2010). The model was essentially designed to apply for the postnatal period of synaptogenesis of the human brain but may also account for some earlier steps of prenatal synaptogenesis and for the adult brain, yet to a lower extent (Petanjek et al., 2011).

On formal grounds, the original concept (CCD model, Changeux et al., 1973) has been extended with the "neural Darwinism" (Edelman, 1978), the group-selection theory of higher brain functions (Edelman, 1981), and more recently with the theory of symmetry breaking in space-time hierarchies (Pillai & Jirsa, 2017), among others.

The CCD model is based on the principle that interneuronal contacts, the synapses, mediate information transfers through the system (Figure 2.1). At nested critical periods during the development of the brain, the phenotypic variability of nerve cell distribution and position, as well as the exuberant spread and the multiple transient connectivity configurations resulting from the growth cone wanderings, produce a broad diversity of synaptic connections. This transient diversity is then reduced by the selective stabilization of some of the labile contacts and elimination (or retraction and/or pruning) of others. Excitatory as well as inhibitory synapses may

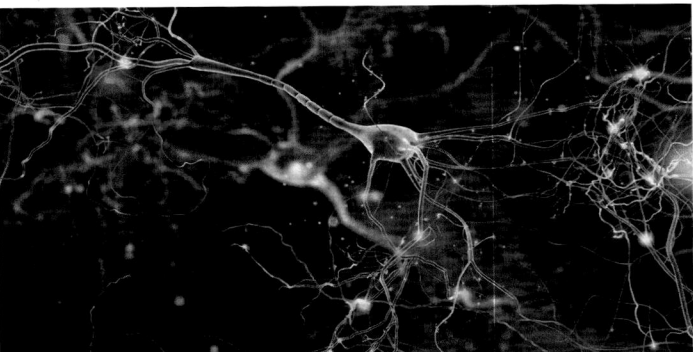

Figure 2.1 The neurone and the interneuronal connections through the synapse in the human brain
A black-and-white version of this figure will appear in some formats.
For the color version, please refer to the plate section.

exist under at least three connective states: Labile (L), Stable (S), and Degenerate (D); only states L and S transmit nerve impulses and the acceptable transitions between states are L→S, L→D, and S→L. A critical implication of the model is that evolution of the connective state of individual synaptic contacts is governed globally, and within a given time window, by the total activity afferent onto the postsynaptic soma during a prior time interval of determinate length (evolutive power of the soma). It includes, as a particular case, the standard Hebbian time-coincidence relationship and the popular statement "cells that fire together wire together." Activity of the postsynaptic cell in turn regulates, in a retrograde manner, the stabilization and/or elimination of afferent synapses.

The maximum wiring and the main stages of development of the network of synaptic connections, as well as the evolutive power and the integrative power (after the usual "firing" mechanism) of each soma are determinate expressions of the genetic endowment (the "genetic envelope" of the network). The emergence during growth of a large number of labile synapses is provided by this species-specific envelope. The associative property

that results from the "learning process" is structurally printed as a particular pattern of such organization. This pattern results often from the selection by functioning of particular pathways among a large number of labile synapses (especially during growth). Such trial-and-error mechanisms formally resemble the variation–selection process of an evolutionary Darwinian but epigenetic process (Campbell, 2016) (see Figure 2.2).

A nesting of many such elementary steps occurs in the course of development. The growth of axons toward their targets – the dendrites of target neurons in the central nervous system or muscle cells in the periphery – involves cell-surface recognition molecules, possibly ones unique to the specific category of connections. The axon terminals branch exuberantly at first. But, then, depending on the state of activity of the target neuron – either intrinsic spontaneous firing or evoked by external inputs – some synapses are eliminated (pruned), while others are strengthened and stabilized. In post-natal life, an important part of the activity in the network results from inputs from the environment and so the epigenetic selection of synapses represents learning in the network.

Growth

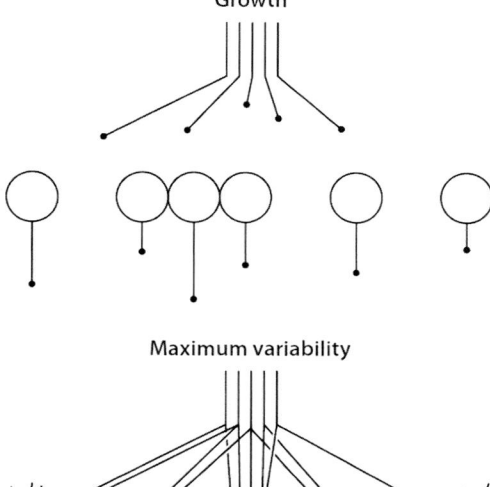

Maximum variability

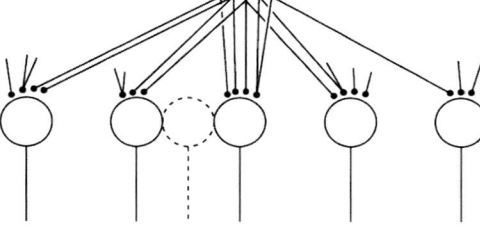

Selective stabilization

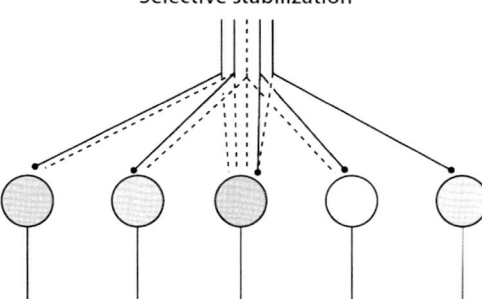

Figure 2.2 Schematic representation of the hypothesis of epigenesis by selective stabilization of synapses. From Changeux, 1983, 1985
A black-and-white version of this figure will appear in some formats. For the color version, please refer to the plate section.

2.3 The Variability Theorem and the "Multiple Realizability" of Brain Functions

The CCD model or theory accounts for the interactions that take place between the brain and its physical, social, and cultural environment in the course of cognitive development. But it accounts in addition for a property largely under-evaluated in brain research: the variability in the brain's connectivity and in behavior between individuals, which is associated with the variability of the environment and would be superimposed on that created by the variability of the genome.

As mentioned, in the course of the proposed epigenesis, diversification of neurons belonging to the same category occurs by the acquisition of the precise pattern of connections it establishes (and neurotransmitter/receptors it synthesizes) (Changeux, 1983, 1985). An unexpected but critical feature of the theory is that it may account for the constancy of some behaviors, despite such epigenetic variability of the connectivity. This idea was originally stated as the "variability theorem" (CCD model) that "different learning inputs may produce different connective organizations and neuronal functioning abilities, but the same behavioral abilities" (Changeux et al., 1973, p. 2976). Thus, the neuronal connectivity code exhibits "degeneracy" (see Edelman, 1978; Edelman & Gally, 2001; Tononi et al., 1999), that is, different code words (connection patterns) may carry the same meaning (function).

One prediction of the variability theorem is that the synaptic connectivity of genetically identical individuals (i.e., monozygotic twins) may display phenotypic variance. This was initially demonstrated using serial electron microscopy scans of genetically identical individuals (identical twins). In the small invertebrate Daphnia magna, the number of cells is fixed and the main categories of contacts (between optic sensory cells and optic ganglion neurons) are preserved from one isogenic individual to another. Yet, the exact number of synapses and the precise form of the axonal branches vary between pairs of identical twins

(Macagno, Lopresti, & Levinthal, 1973). Similar findings have been reported in the case of the Müller cells of a parthenogenetic fish (*Poecilia formosa*) (Levinthal, Macagno, & Levinthal, 1976), and thus they are not restricted to invertebrates. In a general manner, a phenotypic variance of the connectivity exists. This has been exquisitely demonstrated in the rat, where a detailed left–right comparison of interscutularis muscle innervation by the same motor neurons (Lu et al., 2009) revealed a profound variability of axon branching. This has been confirmed with the nervous system of isogenic Caenorhabditis, which was until recently viewed as precisely wired up to the individual synapse level (Oren-Suissa et al., 2016). Yet, the Daphnia, the worm, the fish, and individuals all swim similarly, and the left and right limbs of the rat also work the same!

In mammals, the variation also affects the number of neurons. For instance, in the case of the cerebellum of the mouse, the division and migration of Purkinje cells in consanguineous strains are not subject to as rigorous and precise a determinism as the laying down of neurons in invertebrates (Goldowitz & Mullen, 1982; Oster-Granite & Gearhart, 1981). The variability becomes microscopic and may even affect its chemistry, such as the type of neurotransmitter through activity dependent switches (Spitzer, 2017) or the pattern of transmitters and coexisting messengers synthesized (Hokfelt et al., 1986, 2018) of entire populations of neurons.

At a much higher level of complexity, humans with language areas located either in the left or right hemispheres, or in both, are indistinguishable by the way they speak or think! In monozygotic twins, differences in manual preferences have even been discovered, which by itself is a sign of variance at the behavioral level. In vivo measurements using magnetic resonance imaging of the planum temporale further reveal brain images that differ between left- and right-handed twins, which is more pronounced in the right-handed one (Sommer et al., 2002; Steinmetz et al., 1995).

In humans, most of the information available on anatomy derives from individuals taken from genetically heterogeneous populations. Nevertheless, even under such conditions, the substantial variability noticed, and, thus, the development of the fine details of the brain connectivity pattern, is expected to include a stochastic element. Chance plays a part in determining exactly which synapses survive. Nevertheless, the behavior may remain constant between individuals. These views are consistent with recent formal descriptions of brain behavior as a low-dimensional process emerging from a network's dynamics depending on the symmetry and invariance properties of the network connectivity (Pillai & Jirsa, 2017). These authors show that given behavioral patterns can be accomplished through the use of distinct architectures utilizing (at least partly) different functional modes (engaging the same or different neuro-muscular linkages) (Perdikis et al., 2011). They conclude that since the different control structures are likely to draw on distinct neural network components, this prediction speaks to the concept of degeneracy, which is precisely what we proposed as "variability" in the early formulation of the CCD theory (Changeux et al., 1973). There is no contradiction between epigenetic "Darwinian" selection and the occurrence of behavioral universals. The synapse selection model offers a neural example to "multiple realizability" – that is, the non-unique (degenerate) mapping of a given "invariant" function to the underlying neural organization (Changeux et al., 1973; Pillai & Jirsa, 2017). This let some cognitivist philosophers incorrectly "believe" that, in particular because of this degenerate mapping, the attempts to define a precise relationship between the connectional organization of the brain and its cognitive – in particular language – abilities is either irrelevant (Fodor, 1983) or even might remain a "mystery" forever (see Chomsky, in Hauser et al., 2014).

2.4 Cellular and Molecular Mechanisms of Synapse Selection

Both the spontaneous and the evoked activity may contribute to the synapse selection process. In this framework, the suggestion was made that reward signals received from the environment may control the developmental evolution of connectivity (Hull, 1943; Skinner, 1981; Thorndike, 1911; see also Gisiger & Kerszberg, 2006; Gisiger et al., 2005). Positive reward is signaled by neurons in the brain stem that release dopamine in the frontal cortex, whereas serotonin neurons signal negative reward, or punishment (Dehaene & Changeux, 1991, 2000; Kobayashi & Schultz, 2014; Stauffer et al., 2016). The evolution of connectivity through selection has been tested using a network simulation that can learn to do specific tasks when given simple positive and negative rewards (Gisiger et al., 2005). Before learning, the connectivity in the network is largely diffuse and unstructured and task completion is unsuccessful. After learning, the selected connections form a coherent and organized network that can complete tasks successfully. This is illustrated in the case of a visual delayed-matching-to-sample (Gisiger et al., 2005) or in a logical reasoning task (Houdé et al., 2000), both involving a prefrontal network. Further work should establish the actual contribution of reward to synapse selection in the course of development.

The cellular and molecular mechanisms involved in synapse selection are rather diverse. They include GABAergic inhibition,

which contributes to the "opening" of the critical period where synapse selection occurs (Hensch, 2005; Werker & Hensch, 2015). A shift in the excitatory–inhibitory balance is associated with the maturation of fast-spiking GABAergic inhibitory neurons that synthesize parvalbumin and are localized in layers III/IV of the cerebral cortex (Takesian & Hensch, 2013). Pharmacological agents that accelerate GABAergic circuit function (such as benzodiazepines acting as positive allosteric modulators of $GABA_A$ receptors) elicit precocious onset, whereas genetic manipulations (such as the deletion of genes involved in GABA synthesis) or environmental disruption (such as dark rearing or hearing loss) lead to a delay of the critical period.

During early postnatal development, microglia undergo morphological maturation that matches synaptic maturation and possess phagocytic properties, which led to the hypothesis that microglia may have a role in the elimination of exuberant synaptic connections during development. This hypothesis is supported by studies that reported the appearance of excess immature synapses in mice lacking either the fractalkine (Cx3cl1/Cx3cr1) or complement component (C1q/C3/CR3) microglia signaling pathways (Paolicelli et al., 2011; Weinhard et al., 2018).

Following gene expression in the course of synapse selection in the visual system, it was found that among the genes regulated by neural activity are the MHC (major histocompatibility) Class I family genes (Corriveau et al., 1998). This finding was rather unexpected because these genes – HLA genes in humans – are involved in cellular immunity and were previously not thought to be expressed by neurons. Other components of a signaling system for Class I MHC are also present in neurons, including their receptor, PirB (Kim et al., 2013). The study of mice deleted for theses diverse molecular components revealed that they are required for activity-dependent synapse selection (Huh et al., 2000). Homologs are present in the human brain and may have some relevance for understanding brain wiring developmental disorders including Alzheimer's disease (Kim et al., 2013).

Neurotrophic factors, including nerve growth factor (NGF), brain-derived neurotrophic factor (BDNF), neurotrophin-4 (NT-4), and neurotrophin-3 (NT-3) (Mandolesi et al., 2005), are important regulators of visual cortical plasticity (Huang et al., 1999). In transgenic mice in which the postnatal rise in BDNF in the forebrain was genetically accelerated, a precocious termination of the critical period of ocular dominance plasticity was found, which correlated with an accelerated maturation of GABAergic inhibitory circuitry. Neurotrophic factors are important modulators of synaptic epigenesis and brain development in general.

In addition, homeoproteins, such as Otx2, have been reported to have a role in synaptic evolution during critical periods of development (Prochiantz & Di Nardo, 2015). For instance, Otx2 accumulates in an activity-dependent manner inside the fast-spiking GABAergic neurons. Intriguingly, Otx2 is not expressed by these cells but instead is imported through diffusion from one or several external sources (Spatazza et al., 2013). Therefore, it was proposed that, in the mouse, Otx2 accumulation by fast spiking neurons cells is necessary and sufficient for a binocular critical period opening at twenty days after birth and closing at forty days (Prochiantz & Di Nardo, 2015).

Other work has revealed detailed mechanisms involved in synapse selection at the molecular level. Activity-dependent changes in the diffusion dynamics of postsynaptic receptors present under the nerve terminals have been recorded even if the density of receptors remains stable under the nerve

ending (Triller & Choquet, 2008). Also, allosteric transitions of the NMDA receptor traps the diffusible D1 dopamine receptor, resulting in an increase in dendritic spines bearing dopamine receptors (Scott et al., 2006). Such plasticity phenomena might possibly be altered in neuropsychiatric disorders.

Several molecular and cellular mechanisms are available for the active selection process to take place. They are themselves under stringent genetic control and belong to the genetic envelope of the species.

2.5 Anatomical and Physiological Evidence Supporting the Selective-Stabilization of Synapses Model

The classical Wiesel and Hubel experiments with the cat about the effects of monocular deprivation on binocular vision are consistent with the selective stabilization hypothesis (Hubel & Wiesel, 1965; LeVay et al., 1980; Shatz & Stryker, 1978; Sretavan & Stryker, 1988). If, during a critical period in early life, one eye is allowed to see normally, whereas the vision of the other eye is occluded, most of the cortical cells, even those in the deprived eye's columns, lose their ability to respond to the deprived eye (Hubel & Wiesel, 1970; Hubel et al., 1977; Shatz & Stryker, 1978; Wiesel & Hubel, 1963). This physiological loss of response is followed within one week by a dramatic retraction of the branches of deprived geniculocortical arbors and is later followed by a compensatory expansion of the arbors of the open eye (Antonini & Stryker, 1996; LeVay et al., 1980; Rakic, 1976). The effects of deprivation can be reversed to a limited extent during the critical period but they later become irreversible (Antonini & Stryker, 1998; Blakemore et al., 1981; Movshon, 1976; van Sluyters, 1978; Wiesel & Hubel, 1965). An example of such an irreversible effect of epigenetic experience in humans is amblyopia, an eye disorder characterized by impaired vision in one eye that otherwise appears normal. It may be viewed as a "cortical blindness" that occurs during early childhood, as a consequence of cataract or strabysmus.

Early demonstrations of the process of synapse stabilization accompanied by synapse elimination of supernumerary nerve endings include work on motor neurons innervating skeletal muscle cells (Benoit & Changeux, 1975, 1978; Gouzé et al., 1983; Henderson et al., 1986; O'Brien et al., 1977; Rakic et al., 1986; Turney & Lichtman, 2012). In the adult, there is only one motor nerve ending per muscle fiber, but at birth several active motor nerve endings converge to a common endplate (Redfern, 1970). All of them except one are subsequently eliminated and the state of activity of the neuromuscular junction plays a decisive role in this elimination (Benoit & Changeux, 1975, 1978). This epigenetic step results in the formation of the motor units, which work together to coordinate the contraction of the whole muscle (Buchtal & Schmalbruch, 1980).

In the cerebellar cortex, similarly, the interactions between parallel fiber and climbing fiber synapses on Purkinje cells reveal heterosynaptic competition during development. The mature monoinnervation of Purkinje cells) by their climbing fiber, afferents from the inferior olivary nucleus is preceded by a transient stage of multiple innervation (Mariani & Changeux, 1980). In the rat, synapse exuberance reaches a maximum of up to five climbing fibers per Purkinje cell (about 3.5 on average) on postnatal day 5 and then regresses until monoinnervation is established on postnatal day 14–15. Granule cell precursors suppression by postnatal X-irradiation indicates that granular cells are not involved in the early part of climbing fiber synapse elimination but only the final phase, after postnatal day 8, would

be driven by parallel fibers activity (Lohof et al., 1996). Genetic mutations have also been shown to alter synaptic epigenesis in the mouse (Changeux & Mikoshiba, 1978).

The innervation of the sympathetic submandibular ganglion cells undergoes profound reorganization during postnatal development, leaving individual ganglion cells in the adult innervated by many-fold fewer axons than they were at birth (Lichtman, 1977, 1980; Sheu et al., 2017).

These and many other studies (Bailly et al., 2018; Kano & Hashimoto, 2012; Ko et al., 2011; Li et al., 2017; Luo & O'Leary, 2005) have shown that, when neuronal activity is artificially modified, synaptic elimination is altered. At variance with the "Lamarckist-constructivist" scheme (Quartz & Sejnowski, 1997), blocking the activity maintains a high number of connections. Activity thus enhances synaptic elimination. As I have said in the past, "to learn is to eliminate" (Changeux, 1983, 1985). Many groups (Shatz, Lichtman, and others) have since abundantly documented this. Extending this idea to postnatal cognitive development itself (from object permanence in infants to logical reasoning in adolescents and adults), Olivier Houdé said, "to develop is to inhibit" (Houdé, 2000, 2019).

The classical information-processing scheme of the nervous system is based on the notion that its internal states of activity directly result from interactions with the outside world. In fact, from very early on, there is intense spontaneous electrical and chemical activity within the nervous system of the embryo and the fetus (Hamburger, 1970; Provine & Ripley, 1972). Chick embryos move within the egg as early as after two days of incubation. These spontaneous movements are blocked by curare (Levi Montalcini, 1936, see 2000) and coincide with electrical activity of the same frequency arising in spinal cord neurons. In the human, these movements start during the eighth week of embryonic development and diversify during the following months. Such spontaneous activity develops in a strictly endogenous manner and results from molecular oscillators consisting of slow and fast ionic channels (Berridge & Rapp, 1979). The cost of this activity in terms of structural genes is very small and bears no relation to its enormous potential for interaction and combination, which results from the activity's eventual contribution to the epigenesis of neuronal synaptic networks. In the retina, the spontaneous activity of the ganglion cells (Galli-Resta & Maffei, 1988) forms correlated patterns, or waves (Maffei & Galli-Resta, 1990, confirmed by Meister et al., 1991; Shatz, 1996).

The mechanism of wave initiation and propagation is not fully understood, yet it involves synaptic transmission mediated by nicotinic acetylcholine receptors (nAChRs) (Feller et al., 1996; Penn et al., 1998). These waves of endogenous retinal activity are shown to play an important role in the epigenesis of neural networks through selective synapse stabilization. In mice deprived of the high-affinity nAChR beta2 subunit (Picciotto et al., 1995, 1998; Zoli et al., 1998), the pattern of retinogeniculate and retinocollicular projections was found to be altered (Rossi et al., 2001). In contrast, although alpha 4 subunit is the predominant partner of the beta 2 subunit in the formation of brain high affinity nAChRs, its deletion did not cause defects in retinofugal segregation. The initial developmental phase of retinal projections looked normal in beta 2 mice until postnatal day 4. This result, together with previous observations showing that the anatomy and the spatial resolution of the retina were normal in beta 2 mice, indicate that the deficit observed at later ages is not due to defects in retinal ganglion cells, programmed cell death or path finding errors of optical nerve fibers, but to the aberrant segregation of ipsilateral and contralateral axons at the target level. Consistent with these data, the beta-2 deleted mice show an expansion of the binocular subfield of the primary visual cortex and a decrease in visual acuity at the cortical level but not in the retina. The nAChR beta 2 subunit is thus necessary for the developmental epigenesis of the visual system at both anatomical and physiological levels (Grubb et al., 2003; Rossi et al., 2001).

The example of the visual system may plausibly be extended to other sensory motor systems and to a broader framework of a formal architecture of thalamocortical areas, in which top-down activity generated in hierarchically higher cortical areas plays a key role. Multiple nested "waves" of synaptic epigenesis take place during the postnatal development of the adult brain. As a consequence, a net decline of the total envelope of synaptic connections, which themselves sum up this laminated development, is observed (Huttenlocher & Dabholkar, 1997). In the primary visual cortex, for example, after a burst of synapse formation between the ages of three and four months, synaptic density reaches its peak at 140–150 percent of adult levels between the ages of four and twelve months, after which the mean number of synapses per neuron declines (Huttenlocher, 1990). The decline observed during late childhood plausibly reflects the underlying rich nesting of selection steps in a cascade of critical periods that proceeds far beyond puberty. In rats, the maximum synaptic density is reached within a few weeks after birth, whereas in humans it takes over three years (Bourgeois, 1997). Moreover, rats show little loss of synapses after maximum density is reached. On the other hand, in humans there is a steady decline until the total number stabilizes about the time of puberty (Bourgeois, 1997; Huttenlocher & Dabholkar, 1997; Petanjek et al., 2011), reflecting the initial exuberance and later pruning of connections. In contemporary humans, the process of synaptic refinement goes far beyond puberty: learning is lifelong (Petanjek et al., 2011). When H. sapiens appeared in Africa about 100,000 years ago, half the average life span of around 30 years would have been taken up with building the brain. Cat and monkey show intermediate stages of this process as life span and infant dependency increases. This major distinction between lower mammals and humans has to be borne in mind to understand the evolutive process of brain humanization. This places severe limitations on using lower mammals as models for human psychiatric and neurological conditions.

2.6 Epigenesis of Higher Brain Functions and Global Integration

Among the cortical connections established in postnatal life are the long-range tracts between the frontal areas (Fuster, 2015) and other brain cortical areas (including sensory ones) (Collin & van den Heuvel, 2013; de Lange et al., 2019; Goldman-Rakic, 1988, 1999; Hagmann et al., 2008). Some years ago, the "global neuronal workspace" hypothesis was suggested, according to which these long-range connections, primarily between prefrontal, parietotemporal and cingulate cortices, yield subjective conscious experience (Dehaene & Changeux, 2011; Dehaene et al., 1998) by broadcasting signals to multiple brain areas, thus allowing sensory inputs – such as seeing, hearing – conscious access to a whole brain "global workspace" (Baars, 1989).

Long-range connections, mostly originating from the pyramidal neurons in cortical layers II and III, are particularly abundant in the prefrontal cortex (von Economo & Koskinas, 1925), and form white matter bundles, several of which originate from the prefrontal areas (Dejerine, 1895; Pugliese et al., 2009).

Particularly important are these connections involved in planning, decision making, thought, and socialization, which have evolved most dramatically between mice and humans (see Dehaene & Changeux 2011; Houdé, 2000, 2019).

The ontogeny and postnatal development of long-range connectivity expectedly reveal phases of exuberance and phases of selection and axonal pruning (Collin & van den Heuvel, 2013). Around birth, all major white matter tracts appear to be in place (Dubois et al., 2006; Hermoye et al., 2006), with at birth an over-representation of long-range connectivity followed rapidly by a decrease on the macroscopic scale. In nonhuman primates, a staggering 70 percent of callosal connections are eliminated (Innocenti & Price, 2005; LaMantia & Rakic, 1990). In human newborns, the evolution is slower. It has been suggested that the phase of exuberant axonal removal at the age of two years is completed accompanied by increasing information processing and cognitive – in particular language – development together with the "theory of mind" acquisition (Collin & van den Heuvel, 2013). The evolution continues during adolescence until adulthood with decreasing segregation and increasing integration mainly driven by modulation of connections stability and strength (Hagmann et al., 2010). It is expected to have major consequences on the laying down of cultural imprints, including the "epigenetic rules" associated with socialization.

One essential aspect of postnatal development in the human brain is the epigenesis of long-range connections establishment (Huttenlocher & Dabholkar, 1997) between different cortical areas, especially those of the GNW linking the parieto-temporal-cingulate cortices with the prefrontal lobes, which are the centers for decision-making, rational thinking, and social interaction. It is expected that these different areas develop rather independently (as for instance the visual areas for each eye) but need a strong synapse selection step to integrate them into a unique global workspace at the scale of the individual (as an integrated binocular vision in the visual system).

One question currently asked is whether these long-range connections are especially vulnerable to some pathologies (Wei et al., 2019). For instance, the onset of schizophrenia has been linked to susceptibility genes coding for several proteins involved in synaptic selection or pruning, such as ERBB4, SLC1A3, RAPGEF4, and CIT28; the last is also involved in bipolar disorder (Karlsgodt et al., 2008). Links with NEUREXIN 1, which is involved in synapse formation and stabilization, have been reported (Cook & Scherer, 2008). Also, various mutations linked to autism are in genes that are involved in synapse formation and stabilization such as NEUROLIGINS 3/4, NEUREXIN 1, and SHANK 3, which code for synaptic adhesion and stability proteins (Bourgeron, 2009; Huguet et al., 2016). Significantly, the long-range connections might be affected differentially by susceptibility mutations that are known to affect synaptogenesis in general (Scott-Van Zeeland et al., 2010). In addition, increased synapse elimination by microglia in schizophrenia patient-derived models of synaptic pruning has been observed (Sellgren et al., 2019). A particular vulnerability of long-range connections might result, for instance, from a very low nucleo-cytoplasmic ratio and/or changes in the long-distance transport of essential cellular components along the axons, which could explain the specificity of the schizophrenic or autistic phenotypes as distinct from the mental retardation expected from global deficits in synaptogenesis.

One way this vulnerability was tested was to compare the dendritic branching of pyramidal neurons in wild-type mice and mutant mice,

mentioned above, which lack the beta 2-subunit of the nAChR (Ballesteros-Yáñez et al., 2010). Loss of this subunit prevents the high-affinity binding of the neurotransmitter acetylcholine and, therefore, mice lacking the beta 2-subunit show a characteristic behavioral deficit: their exploratory drive, which is one of the most cognitive aspect of mouse behavior, is reduced, although their navigation abilities, a more automatic activity, are unaffected. Even though establishing a fair analogy between mouse behavior and human psychology may look far-fetched, it has been hypothesized that these mice might possibly be showing an alteration in elementary conscious access (Avale et al., 2011; Koukouli et al., 2017).

These studies on mice may be relevant to a possible effect of chronic nicotine use on long-range connectivity. In humans, diffusion tensor imaging (DTI), which allows the measurement of the location, orientation, and anisotropy of the white-matter tracts in the brain, has shown reduced integrity in the frontal white matter in people who are cocaine dependent or who abuse heroin. The same method has revealed that prenatal and adolescent exposure to tobacco smoke alters the development of the microstructure of the white matter, with increased fractional anisotropy in the right and left frontal regions, and in the genu of the corpus callosum (Changeux & Lou, 2011; Kangiser et al., 2019). These observations suggest that nicotine may also act directly on white matter and there is electrophysiological evidence that supports a direct action of nicotine on axon conduction, possibly at the level of the node of Ranvier (Changeux, 2010). Thus, there is support for an epigenetic control of the global neuronal workspace connectivity by nicotine at the white matter level. This work further implies that drugs of abuse like nicotine may interfere with the functioning of the long-range cortical connections, to the extent that addicts may lose some conscious self-control of their actions (Changeux & Lou, 2011; Joutsa et al., 2011; Rømer Thomsen et al., 2013). These observations strengthen the still hypothetical conclusion that the epigenesis of long-range connections plays a critical role in elementary conscious access.

2.7 Social and Cultural Imprints

The extension of the postnatal period of development in humans has been essential for the genesis and internalization of culture, as well as for the acquisition and transmission of individual experience. Among the many manifestations of cultural evolution, writing, and reading appear as recent inventions. Writing can be traced back to abstract cave drawings, dated around 30,000 BCE. Clay counting tokens are known from Mesopotamia (9,000 BCE) and the first pictograms from Ur are from around 4,000 BCE. Writing and reading is a recent cultural invention that evolved into distinct sub-systems and puts considerable demands to our cognitive system. The acquisition of reading and writing may be viewed as a typical example of epigenetically led down "cultural circuits."

Historically, the first evidence for specialized writing and reading circuits in the brain was the discovery by the French neurologist Dejerine (1914) of pure alexia, also known as alexia without agraphia. Individuals with pure alexia suffer from severe reading problems, while other language-related skills such as naming, oral repetition, auditory comprehension, or writing are typically intact. Alexia results from cerebral lesions in circumscribed brain regions including the supramarginal and angular gyri. New specialized sets of connections have been selected and consolidated as a consequence of written language learning. More recently, the circuits involved in literacy

have been examined using brain imaging. They confirm Dejerine's pioneering insight. These studies (Castro-Caldas et al., 1998) took advantage of behavioral evidence of different phonological processing in illiterate versus literate subjects. During repetition of real words, the literate and illiterate groups performed similarly and activated similar areas of the brain. In contrast, illiterate subjects had more difficulty correctly repeating pseudowords and did not activate the same neural structures as literates. Comparison of positron-emission tomography (PET) scans from illiterate and literate groups showed a considerable shift in activation. For instance, in a pseudowords–words contrast, activation in the literate group was stronger in the right frontal opercular–anterior insular region, left anterior cingulate, left lentiform nucleus and anterior thalamus/hypothalamus compared with the illiterate group (Carreiras et al., 2009; Castro-Caldas et al., 1998). These conclusions have been consolidated and further expanded with functional magnetic resonance imaging (fMRI) scans from illiterate and literate groups (Dehaene et al., 2010). Acquisition of reading and writing may be viewed as an example of epigenetically laid down "cultural circuits" following epigenetic appropriation of fast developing connections around five-to-six years of age. It operates at a time of still very rapid synaptogenesis and persists into adulthood (Dehaene et al., 2010).

Interestingly, occidental alphabetic writing systems recruit circuits which differ in part from those mobilized by the Chinese ideographic systems. In French readers reading French, activations were enhanced in left-hemisphere visual area V1, with the strongest differences between French words and their controls found at the central and horizontal meridian representations. In contrast, Chinese readers reading Chinese showed enhanced activations in intermediate visual areas

V3v/hV4, absent in French participants (Szwed et al., 2014).

Written language learning is one of many social and cultural imprints acquired during the human brain's development. Cognitive development per se, i.e. acquisition of *object* unit and permanence in infants, then *number*, *categorization* and *reasoning* operations in children and adolescents, depend both on brain inner regulation processes and socio-cultural imprints (Houdé, 2000, 2019). Thus, the adult human brain connectivity may be viewed as a complex intertwining of cognitive, social, and cultural circuits epigenetically laid down during development within the framework of a human-specific genetic envelope. Important bridges could then be established between the gene expression level and the highest level of the interaction of the brain with its social and cultural environment.

2.8 Conclusion: The Habitus of the Human Subject

Even if advocated by such a distinguished scholar as Piaget (1976), there is no compelling evidence whatsoever that the culturally acquired phenotypes may sooner or later become genetically transmitted. They have to be learned at each generation from adults to children and epigenetically transmitted from generation to generation, starting even in the womb of the mother, until the adult stage. Teaching reading and writing in five-to-six-year-old children requires elaborate pedagogic strategies, which in a general manner are absent in non-human primates (Premack, 2007).

As a major consequence, the acquisition of skills and practices associated with the symbolic experience and emotional labelling characteristic of rational thinking (science), rules of conduct (ethics), and shared feelings (art) become stably internalized epigenetically in

the connectivity of the brain and become exclusive of others. Their "forgetting" is considerably slower than their speed of acquisition through synapse stabilization processes. They contribute to what Bourdieu refers to as the "habitus" of the subject: internalized routine modes of perception, action, and evaluation, which often last a lifetime (Changeux, 2006). Possibly, since the domestication of fire, the grouping of human individuals into stable, autonomous, and geographically dispersed societies has led to the differentiation and divergence of cultures between human groups with separate languages, knowledge back-grounds, techniques and, most of all, systems of beliefs, thus raising cultural fences. These fences, as already noted by Levi Strauss (1952), are such that, because of its different culture, "the other" may no longer be regarded as a human being. A "dehumanization" process frequently accompanies the diversification of cultures (Changeux, 2018, 2019). Most often, a widespread "ethnocentrism" of the subject takes place, where he/she considers his/her own culture as "The only One Culture" existing on earth. Such cultural habitus acquired in the child and "printed" in its brain remains stable for years or even decades. It manifests itself, for instance, in the accent in spoken language. It can only be fully renewed with the re-learning step that takes place with the next generation (Changeux, 2018, 2019).

Finally, social and cultural evolution is associated with variable synaptic efficacy and the establishment of extracerebral memories in the form of spoken, written, and pictorial material, with a time range of 100 milliseconds to thousands of years. Spoken and written language and, perhaps even more significantly, artistic activity are seminal innovations that distinguish humans from other primates; they drove the development of modern civilization and have probably also been central to the expansion of human mental capacities. More important for my thesis, language, writing, and cognitive development in general (about objects, numbers, categorizations, and reasonings or decision-makings) rely on epigenetic cultural transmission framed within a robust human-specific genetic envelope. The huge postnatal increase in the size of the human brain – the adult brain weights five times that of the newborn infant and about 50 percent of the adult brain's connections develop after birth (Bourgeois, 1997; Huttenlocher & Dabholkar, 1997) – offers the developing brain the opportunity for intense self-regulations and social and cultural interactions.

From a neuroscientific perspective, ethical and social norms may therefore be conceived as spatiotemporal patterns of neuronal activity that can be mobilized within the "conscious neuronal workspace" and stored as long-term traces in brain memory (Changeux, 2018; Evers & Changeux, 2016; Farisco et al., 2018). In more general terms, the prefrontal region of the cerebral cortex acts as a "temporal buffer" between past events and future actions and contributes to decision-making within the context of the individual's history. In such a neuronal workspace, "neurally encoded rules" associate a context with a specific behavioral response in a top-down manner. This is referred to as cognitive control (Houdé, 2019) and coordinates thoughts or actions in relation to internal goals. Brain imaging fMRI revealed a hierarchical cascade of executive processes, which are implemented in distinct regions, from the posterior premotor to rostral lateral prefrontal cortex, typically Brodman's area 46 (Houdé & Tzourio-Mazoyer, 2003; Houdé et al., 2000, 2011; Koechlin, 2016). Behavioral rules are sorted at these nested levels of information processing, the highest-level ones controlling the underlying ones closer to the senses. This scheme may be extended assuming that ethical or social norms control rules and part of the

"concurrent behavioral strategies" in decision-making (Evers & Changeux, 2016). From birth on, and possibly even prenatally, the baby is exposed to a social and cultural environment. During its development, an epigenetic selection of neuronal networks accompanies the acquisition of the ethical rules of the social community to which the child and his/her family belong. These ethical rules are often linked with symbolic representations of the cultural community, and the acquisition of such ethical rules and symbolic systems has been compared to language acquisition. Yet, to justify such cultural differences, written language, holy books, moral rules, sexual practices, food, or clothing rituals among others are evoked as irreducible transcendentals even more fundamental than political or economical differences. The universe of cultural differences and thus of potential conflicts is immense. How to face this dramatic situation? How to overcome the cultural epigenetic fences that plague our planet?

One possibility to consider is to make an effort to gain some distance with respect to the emotions mobilized by what is believed to be a "transcendental" act of faith. This might be achieved, at the individual level, through the understanding that such belief is simply an acquired cultural trait invented and epigenetically perpetuated by the brains of humans in society to consolidate their social bond. Following Durkheim, such social facts would possess an objective reality that could be "studied like a physicist studies the physical world," taking into account the fact that they are produced and propagated in a steadily evolving socio-historic context. Within this context, the possibility of developing in the brain new ethical rules of "good life with and for the other" in just institutions (Changeux & Ricoeur, 2000) or "epigenetic proaction" has been proposed (Evers & Changeux, 2016). Another possibility, advocated by Levi-Strauss, is to look for a "coalition of cultures." Such a coalition would favor the evolution of cultures supporting progress and cooperation rather than exclusion, resulting in the breakdown of the cultural fences.

Last, a possibility – seemingly easier to achieve – is to be found in education. Cultural differences are infused into the child brain already at birth (possibly even before for language), in the family environment and consolidated by the schooling system. Secular education is a system of public education, where conspicuous symbolic (religious or philosophical) systems as well as the biased unilateral presentation of the diversity of symbolic systems have been banned. Still it has been recognized as one of the best systems in the world to learn and practice tolerance and respect for cultural differences (Changeux, 2018; Evers & Changeux 2016).

In conclusion, we are neurobiologically predisposed toward specific values, such as self-interest, empathy, sociality and so on, and our brain structures develop in response to ethical and social norms in our cultural and social context. Given the long-lasting plasticity of our brains and the underlying synaptic epigenesis mechanisms involved, we may influence, both biologically and culturally, how the brain responds to and constructs new norms with the aim to account for a harmonious future of humanity in our fast-evolving planet.

References

Antonini, A., & Stryker, M. (1996). Plasticity of geniculocortical afferents following brief or prolonged monocular occlusion in the cat. *Journal of Comparative Neurology, 369,* 64–82.

Antonini, A., & Stryker, M. (1998). Effect of sensory disuse on geniculate afferents to cat visual cortex. *Visual Neuroscience, 15,* 401–409.

Arcaro, M., & Livingstone, M. (2017). Retinotopic organization of scene areas in Macaque inferior temporal cortex. *Journal of Neuroscience, 37,* 7373–7389.

Avale, M. E., Chabout, J., Pons, S., et al. (2011). Prefrontal nicotinic receptors control novel social interaction between mice. *The FASEB Journal, 25,* 2145–2155.

Baars, J. (1989). *A Theory of Consciousness.* Cambridge: Cambridge University Press.

Bailly, Y., Rabacchi, S., Sherrard, R. M., et al. (2018). Elimination of all redundant climbing fiber synapses requires granule cells in the postnatal cerebellum. *Scientific Reports, 8,* Article number: 10017.

Ballesteros-Yáñez, I., Benavides-Piccione, R., Bourgeois, J.-P., Changeux, J.-P., & DeFelipe, J. (2010). Alterations of cortical pyramidal neurons in mice lacking high-affinity nicotinic receptors. *PNAS, 107,* 11567–11572.

Barkow, J., Cosmides, L., & Tooby, J. (1992). *The Adapted Mind: Evolutionary Psychology and the Generation of Culture.* Oxford: Oxford University Press.

Benoit, P., & Changeux, J. P. (1975). Consequences of tenotomy on the evolution of multiinnervation in developing rat soleus muscle. *Brain Research, 99,* 354–358.

Benoit, P., & Changeux, J. P. (1978). Consequences of blocking the nerve with a local anaesthetic on the evolution of multiinnervation at the regenerating neuromuscular junction of the rat. *Brain Research, 149,* 89–96.

Berridge, M., & Rapp, P. (1979). A comparative survey of the function, mechanism and control of cellular oscillators. *Journal of Exprerimental Biology, 81,* 217–279.

Blakemore, C., Garey, L., & Vital-Durand, F. (1981). Orientation preferences in the monkeys visual cortex. *Journal of Physiology, 319,* 78.

Bourgeois, J. P. (1997). Synaptogenesis, heterochrony, and epigenesis in the mammalian neocortex. *Acta Paediatrica, 422,* 27–33.

Bourgeron, T. (2009). A synaptic trek to autism. *Current Opinion in Neurobiology, 19,* 231–234.

Buchtal, F., & Schmalbruch, H. (1980). Motor unit of mammalian muscle. *Physiological Reviews, 60,* 90–142.

Campbell, J. O. (2016). Universal Darwinism as a process of Bayesian inference. *Frontiers in System Neuroscience*, doi:10.3389/fnsys.2016.00049

Carreiras, M., Seghier, M. L., Baquero, S., et al. (2009). An anatomical signature for literacy. *Nature*, *461*, 983–986.

Castro-Caldas, A., Petersson, K. M., Reis, A., Stone-Elander, S., & Ingvar, M. (1998). The illiterate brain. Learning to read and write during childhood influences the functional organization of the adult brain. *Brain*, *121*, 1053–1063.

Changeux, J. P. (1983). *L'Homme neuronal*. Paris: Fayard. English translation, Neuronal Man: The Biology of Mind. Princeton, NJ: Princeton University Press.

Changeux, J. P. (1985). *Neuronal Man: The Biology of Mind*. Princeton, NJ: Princeton University Press.

Changeux, J. P. (2006). Les bases neurales de l'habitus. In G. Fussman (ed.), *Croyance, raison et déraison* (pp. 143–158). Paris: Odile Jacob.

Changeux, J. P. (2010). Nicotine addiction and nicotinic receptors: Lessons from genetically modified mice. *Nature Reviews Neuroscience*, *11*, 389–401.

Changeux, J. P. (2017). Climbing brain levels of organization from genes to consciousness. *Trends in Cognitive Sciences*, *21*, 168–181.

Changeux, J. P. (2018). Mon rêve est qu'il puisse y avoir une éducation laïque universelle. In *Colloque Henri Caillavet les libertés en question?* (pp. 1–5).

Changeux, J. P. (2019). Two cultures and our encyclopaedic brain. *European Review*, *27*, 54–65.

Changeux, J. P., Courrège, P., & Danchin, A. (1973). A theory of the epigenesis of neuronal networks by selective stabilization of synapses. *PNAS*, *70*, 2974–2978.

Changeux, J. P., & Danchin, A. (1976). Selective stabilisation of developing synapses as a mechanism for the specification of neuronal networks. *Nature*, *264*, 705–712.

Changeux, J. P. & Lou, H. (2011). Emergent pharmacology of conscious experience: New perspectives in substance addiction. *The FASEB Journal*, *25*, 2098–2108.

Changeux, J. P., & Mikoshiba, K. (1978). Genetic and "epigenetic" factors regulating synapse formation in vertebrate cerebellum and neuromuscular junction. *Progress in Brain Research*, *48*, 43–66.

Changeux, J. P., & Ricoeur, P. (2000). *What Makes Us Think? A Neuroscientist and a Philosopher Argue about Ethics, Human Nature and the Brain*. Princeton, NJ: Princeton University Press.

Cook, E., & Scherer, S. (2008). Copy-number variations associated with neuropsychiatric conditions. *Nature*, *455*, 919–923.

Collin, G., & van den Heuvel, M. (2013). The ontogeny of the human connectome: Development and dynamic changes of brain connectivity across the life span. *Neuroscientist*, *19*, 616–628.

Corriveau, R., Huh, G., & Shatz, C. (1998). Regulation of class I MHC gene expression in the developing and mature CNS by neural activity. *Neuron*, *21*, 505–520.

de Lange, A. M., Kaufmann, T., van der Meer, D., et al. (2019). Population-based neuroimaging reveals traces of childbirth in the maternal brain. *PNAS*, *116*, 22341–22346.

Dehaene, S., & Changeux, J. P. (1991). The Wisconsin card-sorting test: Theoretical analysis and modeling in a neuronal network. *Cerebral Cortex*, *1*, 62–79.

Dehaene, S., & Changeux, J. P. (2000). Reward-dependent learning in neuronal networks for planning and decision making. *Progress in Brain Research*, *126*, 217–229.

Dehaene, S., & Changeux, J. P. (2011). Experimental and theoretical approaches to conscious processing. *Neuron*, *70*, 200–227.

Dehaene, S., Kerszberg, M., & Changeux, J. P. (1998). A neuronal model of a global workspace in effortful cognitive tasks. *PNAS*, *95*, 14529–14534.

Dehaene, S., Pegado, F., Braga, L. W., et al. (2010). How learning to read changes the cortical networks for vision and language. *Science*, *330*, 1359–1364.

Dejerine, J. (1895). *Anatomie des centres nerveux.* Paris: Rueff et Cie.

Dejerine, J. (1914). *Sémiologie des affections du système nerveux.* Paris: Masson.

Dubois, J., Poupon, C., Thirion, B., et al. (2006). Exploring the early organization and maturation of linguistic pathways in the human infant brain. *Cerebral Cortex, 26,* 2283–2298.

Dumas, G., Malesys, S., & Bourgeron, T. (2019). Systematic detection of divergent brain protein-coding genes in human evolution and their roles in cognition. *BioRxiv.* doi: https://doi.org/10.1101/658658

Edelman, G. (1978). Group selection and phasic reentrant signaling: A theory of higher brain function. In G. M. Edelman, & V. B. Mountcastle (eds.), *The Mindful Brain: Cortical Organization and the Group-Selective Theory of Higher Brain Function* (pp. 51–98). Boston, MA: MIT Press.

Edelman, G. (1981). Group selection as the basis for higher brain function. In F. O. Schmitt, F. G. Worden, G. Adelman, & S. G. Dennis (eds.), The *Organization of the Cerebral Cortex* (pp. 535–563). Boston, MA: MIT Press.

Edelman, G. (1987). *Neural Darwinism: The Theory of Neuronal Group Selection.* New York: Basic Books.

Edelman, G. (2006). *Second Nature: Brain Science and Human Knowledge.* New Haven, CT: Yale University Press.

Edelman, G., & Gally, J. (2001). Degeneracy and complexity in biological systems. *PNAS, 98,* 13763–13768.

Evers, K., & Changeux, J. P. (2016). Proactive epigenesis and ethical innovation: A neuronal hypothesis for the genesis of ethical rules. *EMBO Reports, 17,* 1361–1364.

Farisco, M., Salles, A., & Evers, K. (2018). Neuroethics: A conceptual approach. *Cambridge Quarterly of Healthcare Ethics, 27,* 717–727.

Feller, M. B., Wellis, D. P., Stellwagen, D., Werblin, F. S., & Shatz, C. J. (1996). Requirement for cholinergic synaptic transmission in the propagation of spontaneous retinal waves. *Science, 272,* 1182–1187.

Fodor, J. (1983). *The Modularity of Mind. An Essay on Faculty Psychology.* Boston, MA: MIT Press.

Fuster, J. (2015). *The Prefrontal Cortex.* Cambridge, MA: Academic Press.

Galli-Resta, L., & Maffei, L. (1988). Spontaneous impulse activity of rat retinal ganglion cells in prenatal life. *Science, 242,* 90–91.

Geschwind, D., & Rakic, P. (2013). Cortical evolution: Judge the brain by its cover. *Neuron, 80,* 633–647.

Gisiger, T., & Kerszberg, M. (2006). A model for integrating elementary neural functions into delayed-response behavior. *PLoS Computational Biology 2*(4): e25. https://doi.org/10.1371/journal.pcbi.0020025

Gisiger, T., Kerszberg, M., & Changeux, J.P. (2005). Acquisition and performance of delayed-response tasks: A neural network model. *Cerebral Cortex, 15,* 489–506.

Goldowitz, D., & Mullen, R. (1982). Nuclear morphology of ichthyosis mutant mice as a cell marker in chimeric brain. *Developmental Biology, 89,* 261–267.

Goldman-Rakic, P. (1988). Topography of cognition: Parallel distributed networks in primate association cortex. *Annual Review of Neuroscience, 11,* 137–156.

Goldman-Rakic, P. (1999). The physiological approach: Functional architecture of working memory and disordered cognition in schizophrenia. *Biological Psychiatry, 46,* 650–661.

Goulas, A., Betzel, R., & Hilgetag, C. (2019). Spatiotemporal ontogeny of brain wiring. *Science Advances, 5,* eaav9694.

Gouzé, J. L., Lasry, J. M., & Changeux, J. P. (1983). Selective stabilization of muscle innervation during development: A mathematical model. *Biological Cybernetics, 46,* 207–215.

Grubb, M. S., Rossi, F. M., Changeux, J. P., & Thompson, I. D. (2003). Abnormal functional organization in the dorsal lateral geniculate nucleus of mice lacking the β2 subunit of the nicotinic acetylcholine receptor. *Neuron, 40,* 1161–1172.

Hagmann, P., Cammoun, L., Gigandet, X., et al. (2008). Mapping the structural core of human cerebral cortex. *PLoS Biology, 6,* e159.

Hagmann, P., Sporns, O., Madan, N., et al. (2010). White matter maturation reshapes structural connectivity in the late developing human brain. *PNAS*, *107*, 19067–19072.

Hamburger, V. (1970). Embryonic motility in vertabrates. In F. Schmitt (ed.), *The Neurosciences: Second Study Program* (pp. 210–220). New York: Rockefeller University Press.

Hauser, M.D., Yang, C., Berwick, R. C., et al. (2014). The mystery of language evolution. *Frontiers in Psychology*, *5*, doi: 10.3389/fpsyg .2014.00401

Henderson, C. E., Benoit, P., Huchet, M., Guenet, J. L., & Changeux, J. P. (1986). Increase of neurite-promoting activity for spinal neurons in muscles of 'paralysé' mice and tenotomised rats. *Brain Research*, *390*, 65–70.

Hensch, T. (2005). Critical period plasticity in local cortical circuits. *Nature Reviews Nruroscience*, *6*, 877–888.

Hermoye, L., Saint-Martin, C., Cosnard, G., et al. (2006). Pediatric diffusion tensor imaging: Normal database and observation of the white matter maturation in early childhood. *NeuroImage*, *29*, 493–504.

Hokfelt, T., Fuxe, K., & Pernow, P. (eds.) (1986). Coexistence of neuronal messengers: A new principle in chemical transmission. *Progress in Brain Research*, *68*, 1–411.

Hokfelt, T., Barde, S., Xu, Z.-Q. D., et al. (2018). Neuropeptide and small transmitter coexistence: Fundamental studies and relevance to mental illness. *Frontiers in Neural Circuits*, *12*(106). doi: 10.3389/fncir.2018.00106

Houdé, O. (2000). Inhibition and cognitive development: Object, number, categorization, and reasoning. *Cognitive Development*, *15*, 63–73.

Houdé, O. (2019). *3-System Theory of the Cognitive Brain: A Post-Piagetian Approach.* New York: Routledge.

Houdé, O., Zago, L., Mellet, E., et al. (2000). Shifting from the perceptual brain to the logical brain: The neural impact of cognitive inhibition training. *Journal of Cognitive Neuroscience*, *12*, 721–728.

Houdé, O., Pineau, A., Leroux, G., et al. (2011). Functional MRI study of Piaget's conservation-of-number task in preschool and school-age children: A neo-Piagetian approach. *Journal of Experimental Child Psychology*, *110*, 332–346.

Houdé, O., & Tzourio-Mazoyer, N. (2003). Neural foundations of logical and mathematical cognition. *Nature Reviews Neuroscience*, *4*, 507–514.

Huang, Z. J., Kirkwood, A., Pizzorusso, T., et al. (1999). BDNF regulates the maturation of inhibition and the critical period of plasticity in mouse visual cortex. *Cell*, *98*, 739–755.

Hubel, D., & Wiesel, T. (1965). Receptive fields and functional architecture in two nonstriate visual areas (18 and 19) of the cat. *Journal of Neurophysiology*, *28*, 229–289.

Hubel, D., & Wiesel, T. (1970). The period of susceptibility to the physiological effects of unilateral eye closure in kittens. *Journal of Physiology*, *206*, 419–436.

Hubel, D., Wiesel, T., & LeVay, S. (1977). Plasticity of ocular dominance columns in monkey striate cortex. *Philosophical Transactions of the Royal Society of London B: Biological Sciences*, *278*, 377–409.

Huguet, G., Benabou, M., & Bourgeron, T. (2016). The genetics of autism spectrum disorders. In P. Sassone-Corsi, & Y. Christen (eds.), *A Time for Metabolism and Hormones* (pp. 101–129). Berlin: Springer Verlag.

Huh, G. S., Boulanger, L. M., Du, H., et al. (2000). Functional requirement for class I MHC in CNS development and plasticity. *Science*, *290*, 2155–2159.

Hull, C. (1943). *Principles of Behavior: An Introduction to Behavior Theory.* New York: Appleton-Century.

Huttenlocher, P. (1990). Morphometric study of human cerebral cortex development. *Neuropsychologia*, *28*, 517–527.

Huttenlocher, P., & Dabholkar, A. (1997). Regional differences in synaptogenesis in human cerebral cortex. *Journal of Comparative Neurology*, *387*, 167–178.

Innocenti, G., & Price, D. (2005). Exuberance in the development of cortical networks. *Nature Reviews Neuroscience*, *6*, 955–965.

Joutsa, J., Saunavaara, J., Parkkola, R., Niemelä, S., & Kaasinen, V. (2011). Extensive abnormality of brain white matter integrity in pathological gambling. *Psychiatry Research: Neuroimaging, 194,* 340–346.

Kangiser, M. M., Thomas, A. M., Kaiver, C. M., & Lisdahl, K. M. (2019). Nicotine effects on white matter microstructure in young adults. *Archives of Clinical Neuropsychology, 35,* 10–21.

Kano, M., & Hashimoto, L. (2012). Activity-dependent maturation of climbing fiber to Purkinje cell synapses during postnatal cerebellar development. *Cerebellum, 11,* 449–450.

Karlsgodt, K. H., van Erp, T. G. M., Poldrack, R. A., et al. (2008). Diffusion tensor imaging of the superior longitudinal fasciculus and working memory in recent-onset schizophrenia. *Biological Psychiatry, 63,* 512–518.

Kasthuri, N., & Lichtman, J. (2003). The role of neuronal identity in synaptic competition. *Nature, 424,* 426–430.

Kim, T., Vidal, G. S., Djurisic, M., et al. (2013). Human LilrB2 is a β-amyloid receptor and its murine homolog PirB regulates synaptic plasticity in an Alzheimer's model. *Science, 341,* 1399–1404.

Ko, H., Hofer, S. B., Pichler, B., et al. (2011). Functional specificity of local synaptic connections in neocortical networks. *Nature, 473,* 87–91.

Kobayashi, S., & Schultz, W. (2014). Reward contexts extend dopamine signals to unrewarded stimuli. *Current Biology, 24,* 56–62.

Koechlin, E. (2016). Prefrontal executive function and adaptive behavior in complex environments. *Current Opinion in Neurobiology, 37,* 1–6.

Koukouli, F., Rooy, M., Tziotis, D., et al. (2017). Nicotine reverses hypofrontality in animal models of addiction and schizophrenia. *Nature Medicine, 23,* 347–354.

Lagercrantz, H., Hanson, M. A., Ment, L. R., & Peebles, D. M. (eds.) (2010). *The Newborn Brain.* Cambridge: Cambridge University Press.

LaMantia, A., & Rakic, P. (1990). Axon overproduction and elimination in the corpus callosum of the developing rhesus monkey. *Journal of Neuroscience, 10,* 2156–2175.

LeVay, S., Wiesel, T., & Hubel, D. (1980). The development of ocular dominance columns in normal and visually deprived monkeys. *Journal of Comparative Neurology, 191,* 1–51.

Levi Montalcini, R. (2000). From Turin to Stockholm via St. Louis and Rio de Janeiro. *Science, 287*(5454), 809.

Levi Strauss, C. (1952). *Race et histoire.* Paris: UNESCO.

Levinthal, F., Macagno, E., & Levinthal, C. (1976). Anatomy and development of identified cells in isogenic organisms. *Cold Spring Harbor Symposia on Quantitative Biology, 40,* 321–331.

Li, W., Bellot-Saez, A., Phillips, M. L., et al. (2017). A small-molecule TrkB ligand restores hippocampal synaptic plasticity and object location memory in Rett syndrome mice. *Disease Models & Mechanisms, 10,* 837–845.

Lichtman, J. (1977). The reorganization of synaptic connexions in the rat submandibular ganglion during post-natal development. *The Journal of Physiology, 273,* 155–177.

Lichtman, J. (1980). On the predominantly single innervation of submandibular ganglion cells in the rat. *The Journal of Physiology, 302,* 121–130.

Lohof, A., Delhaye-Bouchaud, N., & Mariani, J. (1996). Synapse elimination in the central nervous system: Functional significance and cellular mechanisms. *Reviews in Neurosciences, 7,* 85–101.

Lu, J., Tapia, J. C., While, O. L., & Lichtman, J. W. (2009). The interscutularis muscle connectome. *PLoS Biology, 7,* e1000108.

Lucchesi, J. (2019). *Epigenetics, Nuclear Organization & Gene Function.* Oxford: Oxford University Press.

Luo, L., & O'Leary, D. (2005). Axon retraction and degeneration in development and disease. *The Annual Review of Neuroscience, 28,* 127–156.

Macagno, E., Lopresti, V., & Levinthal, C. (1973). Structure and development of neuronal connections in isogenic organisms: Variations and similarities in the optic system of Daphnia magna. *PNAS, 70,* 57–61.

Maffei, L., & Galli-Resta, L. (1990). Correlation in the discharges of neighboring rat retinal ganglion cells during prenatal life. *PNAS, 87,* 2661–2864.

Mandolesi, G., Menna, E., Harauzov, A., et al. (2005). A role for retinal brain-derived neurotrophic factor in ocular dominance plasticity. *Current Biology, 15,* 2119–2124.

Mariani, J., & Changeux, J. P. (1980). Intracellular recordings of the multiple innervation of Purkinje cells by climbing fibers in the cerebellum of the developing rat. *Comptes rendus des seances de l'Academie des sciences. Serie D, Sciences naturelles, 291,* 97–100.

Markov, N., Ercsey-Ravasz, M., Van Essen, D. C., et al. (2013). Cortical high-density counterstream architectures. *Science, 342,* 1238406.

Mehler, J. (1982). Dips and drops: A theory of cognitive development. In T. Bever (ed.), *Regressions in Development: Basic Phenomena and Theoretical Alternatives* (pp. 133–152). Hillsdale, NJ: Erlbaum.

Meister, M., Wong, R. O., Baylor, D. A., & Shatz, C. J. (1991). Synchronous bursts of action potentials in ganglion cells of the developing mammalian retina. *Science, 252,* 939–943.

Morange, M., Wolff, F., & Worms, F. (eds.) (2016). *L'Homme neuronal 30 ans après, Dialogue avec Jean-Pierre Changeux.* Paris: Rue d'Um.

Movshon, J. (1976). Reversal of the physiological effects of monocular deprivation in the kitten's visual cortex. *The Journal of Physiology, 261,* 125–174.

O'Brien, R., Purves, R., & Vabova, G. (1977). Effect of activity on the elimination of multiple innervation in soleus muscle of rats. *Journal of Physiology, 271,* 54–55.

Oren-Suissa, M., Bayer, E., & Hobert, O. (2016). Sex-specific pruning of neuronal synapses in Caenorhabditis elegans. *Nature, 533,* 206–211.

Oster-Granite, M., & Gearhart, J. (1981). Cell lineage analysis of cerebellar Purkinje cells in mouse chimeras. *Developmental Biology, 85,* 199–208.

Paabo, S. (2013). The human condition: A molecular approach? *Cell, 157,* 216–226.

Paolicelli, R. C., Bolasco, G., Pagani, F., et al. (2011). Synaptic pruning by microglia is necessary for normal brain development. *Science, 333,* 1456–1458.

Penn, A. A., Riquelme, P. A., Feller, M. B., & Shatz, C. J. (1998). Competition in retinogeniculate patterning driven by spontaneous activity. *Science, 279,* 2108–2112.

Perdikis, D., Huys, R., & Jirsa, V. (2011). Complex processes from dynamical architectures with time-scale hierarch. *PLoS ONE, 6.* doi: 10.1371/journal.pone.0016589

Petanjek, Z., Judaš, M., Šimic, G., et al. (2011). Extraordinary neoteny of synaptic spines in the human prefrontal cortex. *PNAS, 108,* 13281–13286.

Petr, M., Pääbo, S., Kelso, J., & Vernot, B. (2019). Limits of long-term selection against Neandertal introgression. *PNAS, 116,* 1639–1644.

Piaget, J. (1976). *Le comportement, moteur de l'évolution.* Paris: Gallimard.

Picciotto, M. R., Zoli, M., Léna, C., et al. (1995). Abnormal avoidance learning in mice lacking functional high-affinity nicotine receptor in the brain. *Nature, 374,* 65–67.

Picciotto, M. R., Zoli, M., Rimondini, R., et al. (1998). Acetylcholine receptors containing the beta2 subunit are involved in the reinforcing properties of nicotine. *Nature, 391,* 173–177.

Pillai, A., & Jirsa, V. (2017). Symmetry breaking in space-time hierarchies shapes brain dynamics and behavior. *Neuron, 94,* 1010–1026.

Premack, D. (2007). Human and animal cognition: Continuity and discontinuity. *PNAS, 104,* 13861–13867.

Prochiantz, A., & Di Nardo, A. (2015). Homeoprotein signaling in the developing and adult nervous system. *Neuron, 85,* 911–925.

Provine, R., & Ripley K. (1972). Neural correlates of embryonic motility in the chick. *Brain Research, 45,* 127–134.

Pugliese L., Catani, M., Ameis, S., et al. (2009). The anatomy of extended limbic pathways in Asperger syndrome: A preliminary diffusion tensor imaging tractography study. *NeuroImage, 47,* 427–434.

Purves, D., & Lichtman, J. (1980). Elimination of synapses in the developing nervous system. *Science, 210,* 153–157.

Quartz, S., & Sejnowski, T. (1997). The neural basis of cognitive development: A constructivist manifesto. *Behavioral and Brain Sciences, 20,* 537–556.

Rakic, P. (1976). Prenatal genesis of connections subserving ocular dominance in the rhesus monkey. *Nature, 261,* 467–471.

Rakic, P., Bourgeois, J. P., Eckenhoff, M. F., Zecevic, N., & Goldman-Rakic, P. S. (1986). Concurrent overproduction of synapses in diverse regions of the primate cerebral cortex. *Science, 4747,* 232–235.

Redfern, P. (1970). Neuromuscular transmission in new-born rats. *The Journal of Physiology, 209,* 701–709.

Rømer Thomsen, K., Joensson, M., Lou, H. C., et al. (2013). Altered paralimbic interaction in behavioral addiction. *PNAS, 110,* 4744–4749.

Rossi, F. M., Pizzorusso, T., Porciatti, V., et al. (2001). Requirement of the nicotinic acetylcholine receptor β2 subunit for the anatomical and functional development of the visual system. *PNAS, 98,* 6453–6458.

Scott, A., Zelenin, S., Malmersjö, S., et al. (2006). Allosteric changes of the NMDA receptor trap diffusible dopamine 1 receptors in spines. *PNAS, 103,* 762–767.

Scott-Van Zeeland, A. A., Abrahams, B. S., Alvarez-Retuerto, A. I., et al. (2010). Altered functional connectivity in frontal lobe circuits is associated with variation in the autism risk gene CNTNAP2. *Science Translational Medicine, 2,* 56–80.

Sellgren, C. M., Gracias, J., Watmuff, B., et al. (2019). Increased synapse elimination by microglia in schizophrenia patient-derived models of synaptic pruning. *Nature Neurosciences, 22,* 374–385.

Shatz, C. (1996). Emergence of order in visual system development. *PNAS, 93,* 602–608.

Shatz, C., & Stryker, M. (1978). Ocular dominance in layer IV of the cat's visual cortex and the effects of monocular deprivation. *Journal of Physiology, 281,* 267–283.

Sheu, S.-H., Tapia, J. C., Tsuriel, S., & Lichtman, J. W. (2017). Similar synapse elimination motifs at successive relays in the same efferent pathway during development in mice. *eLife, 6,* e23193. doi: 10.7554/eLife.23193

Skinner, B. (1981). Selection by consequences. *Science, 213,* 501–504.

Somel, M., Liu, X., & Khaitovich, P. (2013). Human brain evolution: Transcripts, metabolites and their regulators. *Nature Reviews Neuroscience, 14,* 112–127.

Sommer, M., Koch, M. A., Paulus, W., Weiller, C., & Büchel, C. (2002). Disconnection of speech-relevant brain areas in persistent developmental stuttering. *Lancet, 360,* 380–383.

Spatazza, J., Lee, H. H. C., Di Nardo, A. A., et al. (2013). Choroid plexus-derived Otx2 homeoprotein constrains adult cortical plasticity. *Cell Reports, 3,* 1815–1823.

Spitzer, N. (2017). Neurotransmitter switching in the developing and adult brain. *Annual Review of Neuroscience, 40,* 1–19.

Sretavan, D., Shatz, C., & Stryker, M. (1988). Modification of retinal ganglion cell axon morphology by prenatal infusion of tetrodotoxin. *Nature, 336,* 468–471.

Stauffer, W. R., Lak, A., Yang, A., et al. (2016). Dopamine neuron-specific optogenetic stimulation in Rhesus macaques. *Cell, 166,* 1564–1571.

Steinmetz, H., Herzog, A., Schlaug, G., Huang, Y., & Jäncke, L. (1995). Brain (A) symmetry in monozygotic twins. *Cerebral Cortex, 5,* 296–300.

Sretavan, W., & Stryker, M. (1988). Modification of retinal ganglion cell morphology by prenatal infusion of tetrodotoxin. *Nature, 336,* 468–471.

Suzuki, I. K., Gacquer, D., Van Heurck, R., et al. (2018). Human-specific *NOTCH2NL* genes expand cortical neurogenesis through Delta/Notch regulation. *Cell, 173,* 1370–1384.

Szwed, M., Qiao, E., Jobert, A., Dehaene, S., & Cohen, L. (2014). Effects of literacy in early visual and occipitotemporal areas of Chinese and French readers. *Journal of Cognitive Neurosciences, 26,* 459–475.

Takesian, A., & Hensch, T. (2013). Balancing plasticity/stability across brain development. *Progress in Brain Research, 207,* 3–34.

Thorndike, E. (1911). *Animal Intelligence.* New York: Macmillan.

Tononi, G., Sporns, O., & Edelman, G. (1999). Measures of degeneracy and redundancy in biological network. *PNAS*, *96*, 3257–3262.

Triller, A., & Choquet, D. (2008). New concepts in synaptic biology derived from single-molecule imaging. *Neuron*, *59*, 359–374.

Turney, S., & Lichtman, J. (2012). Reversing the outcome of synapse elimination at developing neuromuscular junctions in vivo: Evidence for synaptic competition and its mechanism. *PLoS Biology*, *10*, e1001352. doi: 10.1371/journal.pbio .1001352

Vallender, E., Mekel-Bobrov, N., & Lahn, B. T. (2006). Genetic basis of human evolution. *Trends in Neurosciences*, *31*, 637–644.

van Sluyters, R. (1978). Reversal of the physiological effects of brief periods of monocular deprivation in the kitten. *The Journal of Physiology*, *284*, 1–17.

von Economo, C., & Koskinas, G. (1925). *Atlas of Cytoarchitectonics of the Adult Human Cerebral Cortex*. Basel: Karger. Trans, rev, L. C. Triarhou, 2008.

Waddington, C. (1942). Canalization of development and the inheritance of acquired characters. *Nature*, *150*, 563–565.

Wei, Y., de Lange, S. C., Scholtens, L. H., et al. (2019). Genetic mapping and evolutionary analysis of human-expanded cognitive networks. *Nature Communications*, *10*, Article number: 4839.

Werker, J., & Hensch, T. (2015). Critical periods in speech perception: New directions. *Annual Review of Psychology*, *66*, 173–196.

Weyer, S., & Paabo, S. (2016). Functional analyses of transcription factor binding sites that differ between present-day and archaic humans. *Molecular Biology and Evolution*, *33*, 316–322.

Weinhard, L., di Bartolomei, G., Bolasco, G., et al. (2018). Microglia remodel synapses by presynaptic trogocytosis and spine head filopodia induction. *Nature Communications*, *9*, 1228.

Wiesel, T., & Hubel, D. (1963). Effects of visual deprivation on morphology and physiology of cells in the cats lateral geniculate body. *Journal of Neurophysiology*, *26*, 978–993.

Wiesel, T., & Hubel, D. (1965). Extend of recovery from the effects of visual deprivation in kittens. *Journal of Neurophysiology*, *28*, 1060–1072.

Zoli, M., Léna, C., Picciotta, M. R., & Changeux, J. P. (1998). Identification of four classes of brain nicotinic receptors using β2 mutant mice. *Journal of Neuroscience*, *18*, 4461–4472.

3 Mapping the Human Brain from the Prenatal Period to Infancy Using 3D Magnetic Resonance Imaging

Cortical Folding and Early Grey and White Maturation Processes

Arnaud Cachia, Jean-François Mangin, and Jessica Dubois

3.1 Introduction

Human brain development is a complex and dynamic process that begins during the first weeks of pregnancy and lasts until early adulthood. This chapter will focus on the developmental window from the prenatal period to infancy, probably the most dynamic period across the entire lifespan. The availability of non-invasive three-dimensional Magnetic Resonance Imaging (MRI) methodologies has changed the paradigm and allows investigations of the living human brain structure – for example, micro- and macrostructural features of cortical and subcortical regions and their connections, including cortical sulcation/gyrification, area, and thickness, as well as white matter microstructure and connectivity, see Boxes 1–3 (Sections 3.6.1–3.6.3) – beginning *in utero*. Because of its relative safety, MRI is well-adapted to

Arnaud Cachia was supported by the "Agence National pour la Recherche," "Institut Universitaire de France," and the "Fondation pour la Recherche Médicale." Jean-François Mangin was supported by the European Union's HBP-SGA2 (grant agreement n°785907), FRM (DIC20161236445), ANR (IFOPASUBA, PremaLocom, Folddico), and the Blaise Pascal Chair of Region Ile de France and Université Paris-Saclay to W. Hopkins. Jessica Dubois was supported by the "Fondation de France," the Fyssen Foundation, the Médisite Foundation, and the IdEx Université de Paris (ANR-18-IDEX-0001).

study individuals at multiple time points and to longitudinally follow the changes in brain structure and function that underlie the early stages of cognitive development.

Before the advent of brain imaging tools, structural brain changes were inferred from *post-mortem* data with major concerns about their generalizability due to the questionable good health of the studied individuals with very young death. On the other hand, despite the advantages of *in vivo* MRI, MRI cannot measure structural changes at the cellular or molecular levels, and the physiological interpretation of MRI signal is not straightforward nor univocal. A detailed description of early developmental mechanisms (e.g., formation of the neural tube, neuronal migration, and differentiation), as well as the early brain organization in transitory compartments such as the subplate can be found in complementary reviews (Kostovic & Judas, 2015; Stiles & Jernigan, 2010).

In addition, MRI data acquired on the early stage of brain development are very noisy due to the acquisition constraints (e.g., fetus movements, short acquisition duration), and difficult to analyze due to the low spatial resolution and the age-dependent tissue contrast and structure size. The comparison of anatomical brain measures derived from MRI across ages should therefore remain cautious. However, despite these limitations, the spatial and temporal patterns of developmental changes observed in recent MRI studies reflect patterns that were observed *post-mortem*, demonstrating the validity and compatibility of these methods (Dehaene-Lambertz & Spelke, 2015; Dubois et al., 2015)

We here review how the cortex grows and gets convoluted, the microstructural maturation of the gray and white matter, and their cognitive correlates in normal condition (see Anderson et al., 2011; Miller et al., 2016, in pathological conditions).

3.2 The Early Development of the Brain Cortex

3.2.1 Cortical Volume

The last weeks of pregnancy and the first postnatal months are marked by an intense increase in cortical volume (Dubois & Dehaene-Lambertz, 2015) which progressively slows down after two years of age until adolescence. Changes in cortical volume are driven by changes in cortical thickness (CT) and cortical surface area (CSA), two complementary macrostructural features of the cortex anatomy with distinct genetic (Panizzon et al., 2009; Raznahan et al., 2011) and developmental (Raznahan et al., 2011) mechanisms. The classical "radial unit hypothesis" (Rakic, 1988, 2000) assumes that the CSA of a given cortical area essentially reflects the number of cortical columns, while CT essentially reflects the number and size of cells within a column and packing density, as well as the number of connections and the extent of their myelination (Eickhoff et al., 2005).

During fetal life, the total cortical volume increases from 10 cm^3 at 18 weeks of gestational age (wGA), to 30 cm^3 at 27 wGA, and 150 cm^3 at 39 wGA (Andescavage et al., 2017; Makropoulos et al., 2016), reaching 200 cm^3 one month after birth and 600 cm^3 at two

years old (Knickmeyer et al., 2008) (Figure 3.1a). The total CSA of the fetus brain at 27 wGA is around 150 cm^2 (Makropoulos et al., 2016), reaching 600–800 cm^2 one month after birth, 1,300 cm^2 at five months, and 2,000 cm^2 at twenty-four months (Dubois et al., 2019; Lyall et al., 2015).

The cortical volume increase is more important during the first postnatal year (~100 percent) than during the second year (~20 percent) (Gilmore et al., 2012). Developmental rates differ among brain regions, with important cortical volume increases in parietal and occipital regions in utero (Rajagopalan et al., 2011) and in association cortices, particularly in the frontal and parietal lobes, after birth (Gilmore et al., 2012). During the first two years after birth, brain growth is mainly due to gray matter development (Gilmore et al., 2007; Knickmeyer et al., 2008), which is no more the case later (Matsuzawa et al., 2001).

3.2.2 Cortical Morphology

Parallel to volumetric changes, early brain development is characterized by dramatic changes in cortex morphology due to the cortical folding process that begins from ten weeks of fetal life (Feess-Higgins & Larroche, 1987; Welker, 1988) (Figure 3.1a and Box 2, Section 3.6.2). During the third trimester of pregnancy, the cerebral cortex changes from a relatively smooth, lissencephalic, surface to a complex folded structure that closely resembles the morphology of the adult cortex (Figure 3.1a). The precise mechanism underlying cortical folding is still unknown. However, several factors likely contribute to the prenatal processes that influence the shape of the folded cerebral cortex, including cortical growth, apoptosis (i.e., programmed cell death), differential expansion of superior and inferior cortical layers, differential growth of the cortical mantle relatively to the underlying white

a. Growth and folding of the brain

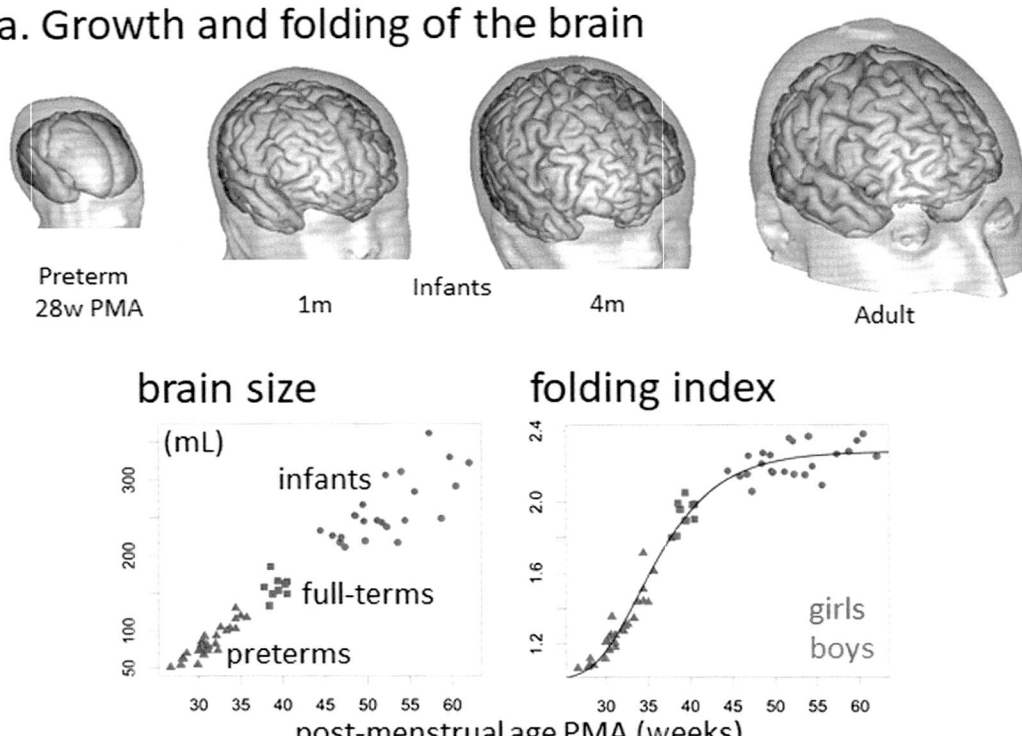

b. Maturation of cortical microstructure in infants

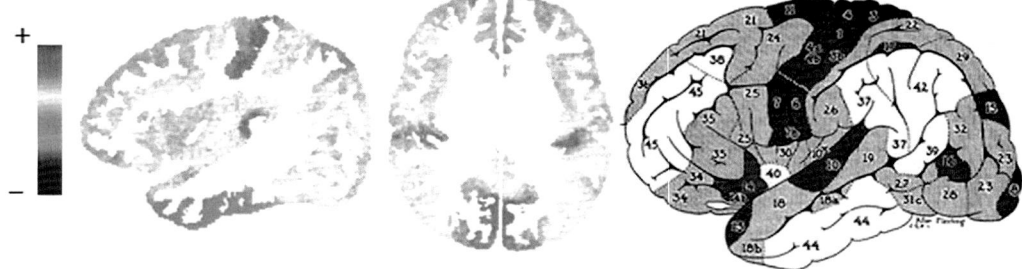

Figure 3.1 Structural changes of the brain during development. (a) The brain shows intense growth and folding during the last weeks of pregnancy and the first months of infancy, as demonstrated with anatomical MRI. Illustrations are provided for a preterm newborn at twenty-eight weeks of post-menstrual age (PMA), infants (at one and four months after birth), and an adult. Measures of brain size and folding index as a function of age provide a quantitative illustration of these intense changes (adapted from Dubois et al. (2019)). (b) The cortex also shows dramatic changes in microstructure complexity and maturation. A recent multi-parametric MRI approach highlighted strong differences between cortical regions in infants between one and five months of age. Colored maps adapted from Lebenberg et al. (2019), in agreement with post-mortem map of subcortical myelination by Flechsig (1920) adapted from Von Bonin (1950)

A black-and-white version of this figure will appear in some formats. For the color version, please refer to the plate section.

matter (Tallinen et al., 2016), transitory compartments such as the subplate (Rana et al., 2019), differential neuropil developments (Llinares-Benadero & Borrell, 2019; Mangin et al., 2019), differential tangential expansion induced by a genetics-based protomap, and/or structural connectivity through axonal tension forces (see Borrell, 2018; Foubet et al., 2019; Kroenke & Bayly, 2018; Zilles et al., 2013, for recent reviews on the phylogenetic, cellular, and mechanical factors of the cortical folding process). The folding process might enable an increase in the cortical surface area while maintaining the volume of the axons required for interconnecting the areas and thus relatively short distances and reasonable communication times between distant brain regions (Klyachko & Stevens, 2003). Macroscopic (morphological/volumetric) and microscopic (cellular) features of the cortex are therefore intrinsically interrelated. For instance, it has been shown that the cortical ribbon is thicker in the gyral areas and thinner in the sulcal areas and neurons located in the deep layers of gyri are squeezed from the sides and appear elongated while neurons that reside in the deep layers of sulci are stretched and look flattened (Hilgetag & Barbas, 2006, 2009).

Dedicated MRI tools and morphometric analyses have enabled us to map in detail the developing cortical surface and growth patterns in fetuses as young as 20 wGA (Habas et al., 2012). These in vivo studies confirm earlier post-mortem observations (Chi et al., 1977) and show a precise timing: stable primary folds appear around 20 wGA, secondary folds around 32 wGA, and highly variable tertiary folds around term (Chi et al., 1977). The gyrification (the apparition of the gyri, the "mountains" of the cortical relief) and the sulcation (the apparition of the sulci, the "valleys" of the cortical relief) become manifest after 24 wGA (Rajagopalan et al., 2011), and greatly heightens during the last weeks before birth (Dubois et al., 2008b, 2019). Although some

variability is observed among individuals, the regional pattern is consistent over the brain surface: sulcation starts in the central region and proceeds first toward the parietal, temporal, and occipital lobes, and second toward the frontal lobe (Dubois et al., 2008b; Ruoss et al., 2001). The heritability of the cortical folding is estimated between 0.2 and 0.5 (Le Guen et al., 2018), supporting a major role of early environmental factors like alcohol exposure (De Guio et al., 2014), intrauterine growth restriction, or twin pregnancy (Dubois et al., 2008a) in the cortical folding process. The morphology of the cortical folding at birth can then be considered a retrospective marker of fetal brain development. It can also be used as a prognostic marker of later functional development. Indeed, cortical sulcation at birth in preterms has been shown to predict infants' neurobehavioral development several weeks later (Dubois et al., 2008a; Kersbergen et al., 2016).

The development of the volumetric and morphological features of the brain, although governed by specific mechanisms, are not independent. The cortical folding index scales uniformly across species and individuals as a function of the product of CSA and the square root of CT (Mota & Herculano-Houzel, 2015). As early as 23 wGA, CSA and total brain volume were also found to be related by a scaling law whose exponent predicts later neurodevelopmental impairment in preterms (Kapellou et al., 2006).

At birth, the cortical surface area is three times smaller than in adults, but the cortex is roughly similarly folded, and the most variable regions among individuals are the same across newborns and adults (Hill et al., 2010). Unlike quantitative features of cortical anatomy such as CSA or CT which can take decades to attain the levels observed in adulthood (Giedd & Rapoport, 2010; Li et al., 2014; Raznahan et al., 2011), the qualitative features of the cortex anatomy, such as the sulcal patterns

(Cachia et al., 2016; Tissier et al., 2018) or the incomplete hippocampal inversion (Bajic et al., 2008; Cury et al., 2015) are determined in utero and are stable after birth. The analysis of such trait features of the brain can thus provide information on the prenatal constraints imposed by the structure of some specific brain regions on later cognitive development.

3.2.3 Study of the Fetal Foundation of Cognition Using the Sulcal Patterns

Several studies have reported that subtle variations of the in utero environment, as indexed by birth weight, are accompanied by differences in postnatal cognitive abilities (Raznahan et al., 2012; Shenkin et al., 2004; Walhovd et al., 2012). In addition to such a global proxy measure of "uterine optimality" (Raznahan et al., 2012), analysis of the sulcal patterns can provide information on the prenatal constraints imposed by the structure of some specific brain regions on later cognitive development.

Several studies in typically developed participants reported long-term influence of cortical sulcation at birth on cognition several years and decades later (for a review in impaired cognition, see Mangin et al., 2010). For instance, a critical region of the cognitive control is the dorsal anterior cingulate cortex (ACC) (Petersen & Posner, 2012) which presents two qualitatively distinct sulcal patterns: a "single" type when only the cingulate sulcus is present and a "double parallel" type when a paracingulate sulcus runs parallel to the cingulate sulcus. An asymmetrical sulcal pattern of the ACC (i.e., different sulcal pattern in left and right hemispheres) was found to be associated with

higher cognitive control in children at age five (Cachia et al., 2014), and four years later (Borst et al., 2014), as well as in adults (Fornito et al., 2004; Tissier et al., 2018) (Figure 3.2). A similar effect was found in children and adults for the inferior frontal cortex (IFC), another key region of cognitive control (Tissier et al., 2018). These early neurodevelopmental constraints on later cognitive efficacy are not fixed nor deterministic. Indeed, only a part (15–20 percent) of the cognitive variability is explained by the sulcal pattern variability (Borst et al., 2014; Cachia et al., 2014; Tissier et al., 2018). In addition, different environmental backgrounds, either after birth, such as bilingualism (Cachia et al., 2017; Del Maschio et al., 2018), or before birth, such as twin pregnancy (Amiez et al., 2018), can modulate the effect of the sulcal pattern on cognition. Sulcal studies also revealed that cognitive abilities requiring intensive learning and training, such as numeracy or literacy, can also be traced back to early stages of brain development. Indeed, the pattern (continuous or interrupted sulcus) of the posterior part of the left lateral occipito-temporal sulcus (OTS) hosting the visual word form area (VWFA) predicts reading skills in ten-years-old children (Borst et al., 2016) and in adults (Cachia et al., 2018) (Figure 3.2). The presence or absence of branches sectioning the horizontal branch of the intra-parietal sulcus (HIPS), a key region for processing numbers, is related to individual differences in symbolic number comparison and math fluency abilities in children and adults.[1]

3.2.4 Cortical Microstructure

These macro-structural changes, with increasing cortical folding and thickness with age, are probably the visible markers of the microstructural evolution occurring in the cortical plate over preterm and early post-term, marked by synaptic outburst and pruning, modifications

---

[1] Roell, M., Cachia, A., Matejko, A., Houdé, O., Ansari, D., & Borst, G. (Submitted). Sulcation of the intraparietal sulcus is related to childrens symbolic but not non-symbolic number skills.

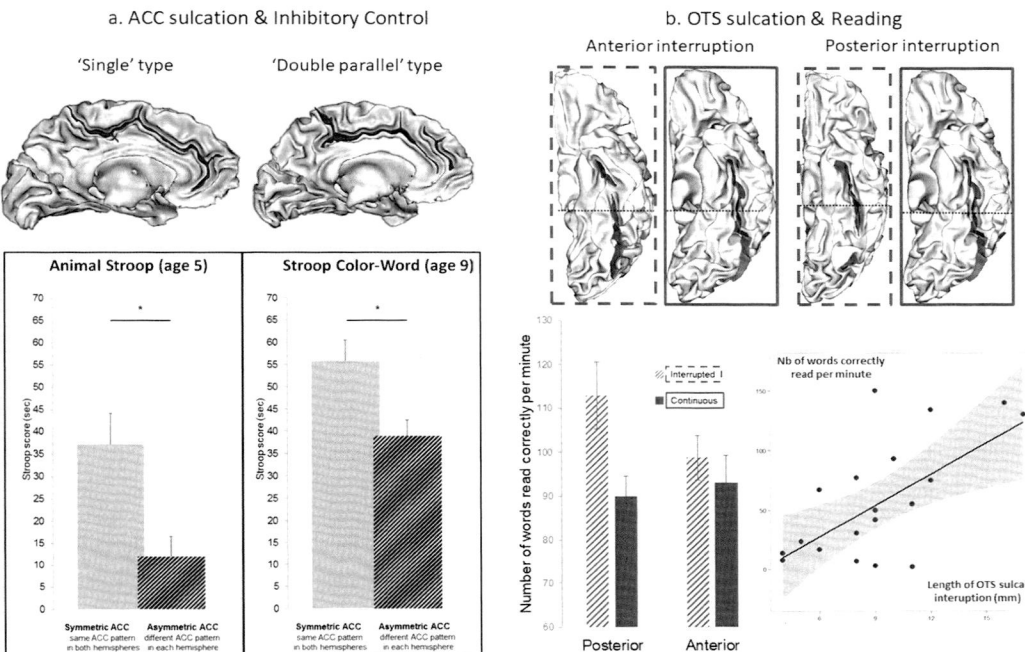

Figure 3.2 Cortical sulcation and cognitive efficiency. (a) Effects of the sulcation of the anterior cingulate cortex (ACC) on inhibitory control efficiency. Upper panel: the ACC can have two types of sulcal patterns: "single" type when only the cingulate sulcus was present and "double parallel" type when a paracingulate sulcus ran parallel to the cingulate sulcus (sulci are depicted in blue on the gray/white interface). Lower panel: Mean Stroop interference scores at age 5 (on the Animal Stroop task) and at age 9 (on the Color-Word Stroop task) in children with symmetrical (single or double parallel type in both hemispheres) and asymmetrical (single type in the right hemisphere and double type in the left hemisphere or vice versa) ACC sulcal patterns. Children with asymmetrical ACC sulcal patterns have better inhibitory control efficiency than children with symmetrical ACC sulcal patterns. Adapted from Borst et al. (2014) and Cachia et al. (2014). (b) Effect of Occipito-Temporal Sulcus (OTS) sulcation on reading ability. Upper panel: the left posterior OTS hosting the visual word form area (VWFA) can have two types of sulcal patterns: "continuous" type or "interrupted" type in case of a sulcal interruption located posteriorly, below the back dashed line. Lower panel: Number of words reads correctly in children or adult participants with continuous (in plain gray) or interrupted (in hatched gray) left OTS. Participants with interrupted OTS have better reading efficiency than participants with continuous OTS. The number of words read per minute is positively correlated with the length of the sulcal interruption. Adapted from Borst et al. (2016) and Cachia et al. (2018) A black-and-white version of this figure will appear in some formats. For the color version, please refer to the plate section.

in dendritic branching and fiber myelination. For instance, histological studies showed that cortical synaptogenesis starts from 16 wGA, and the peak in synapse density depends on

the brain region (Huttenlocher & Dabholkar, 1997; Kwan et al., 2012).

In recent years, several MRI methods have been used to provide quantitative information on these mechanisms in vivo (Box 3, Section 3.6.3). Diffusion MRI, notably diffusion tensor imaging, or DTI (Huppi & Dubois, 2006), has shown the different brain layers (cortical plate, subplate, inner layer) in post-mortem fetuses from 13 wGA (Huang et al., 2013, 2009) and in vivo preterm newborns from 25 wPMA (Maas et al., 2004). In the cortical plate, a complex age-related evolution is observed for the diffusion properties of water molecules (Dudink et al., 2010; McKinstry et al., 2002). This tissue first shows some anisotropy from 26 wGA/PMA with a radial orientation of the main tensor direction which might rely on the early radial deployment of glial fibers and apical dendrites of pyramidal neurons (Ball et al., 2013; Ouyang et al., 2019). This transient radial alignment was quantified by a radiality index that measures the directional coherence between the diffusion tensor and the cortical surface (Eaton-Rosen et al., 2017). Thereafter the cortical plate becomes isotropic from around 36 wGA/PMA with the elongation and complex branching of neuronal connections (basal dendrites for the pyramidal neurons and thalamo-cortical afferents), and the decrease in cortical anisotropy seems to stop at around 38 wPMA (Batalle et al., 2019). Besides, some reported an increase in DTI mean diffusivity between 26 and 32 wPMA (McKinstry et al., 2002), whereas most others have described a steady decrease with age (Batalle et al., 2019; Ouyang et al., 2019). This suggested competing mechanisms, such as a decrease in neuronal density associated with programmed cell death versus an increase in glial cells, addition of neuropils between the neuronal somas, decreasing water content, etc. To decipher between these complex microstructural changes, recent studies have used more elaborate diffusion models (e.g. Neurite Orientation Dispersion and Density Imaging, NODDI) (Batalle et al., 2019; Eaton-Rosen et al., 2015). Before 38wPMA, the neurite

density index (NDI) decreases and the orientation dispersion index (ODI) increases, consistently with a predominant increase in dendritic arborization and neurite growth. After this age, ODI plateaus and NDI increases in primary sensori-motor regions, suggesting that the 38–47 wPMA period might be dominated by increasing cellular and organelle density. Thus these microstructural changes are not linear, at least for some regions, and they are not uniform over the brain (Ball et al., 2013; Deipolyi et al., 2005). In particular, cortical sulci might show a more complex microstructure than gyri early on (Ball et al., 2013).

Diffusion parameters are also sensitive to the regional heterogeneity in cortical development. The occipital lobe shows the most rapid decrease in radiality index, and the frontal and temporal the least ones (Eaton-Rosen et al., 2017). Similarly, functionally distinct regions show different patterns of anistropy decrease from 20 to 35 wGA (Yu et al., 2017), which highlights the asynchronous rate of maturation across cortical areas. DTI parameters further revealed advanced cortical maturation of the primary auditory cortex by 28 wPMA, while rapid changes take place in the non-primary cortex of Heschl's gyrus between 26 and 42 wPMA (Monson et al., 2018). In a recent exploratory study, sharper changes in cortical microstructure were related to a more rapid increase in cerebral blood flow in preterms from 32 to 45 wPMA (Ouyang et al., 2017b).

During infancy, the evolution of cortical microstructure is complex. The growth of connections between neurons is first intense and exuberant through synaptogenesis and the extension of dendritic arborization. Then this phase is followed by an elimination of useless connections through a pruning mechanism, to select and maintain only functionally efficient connections. This occurs over different age periods for different cortical regions depending on the functions and the environmental stimulations. Accompanying this process, the dendritic and axonal fibers get myelinated, mostly during the early post-term period. Postmortem studies showed that brain regions have different maturational trajectories relatively to the myelination of sub-cortical white matter fibers (Flechsig, 1920). This mechanism can be explored *in vivo* with MRI by taking advantages of changes in T1 and T2 signals (two complementary standard macroscopic measures depending on different features of the brain anatomy at cellular level) induced by modifications in water and iron contents (Ouyang et al., 2019). Differences in myelination across cortical regions get stronger from 36 to 44 wPMA, as observed in premature infants with the T1w/T2w ratio (Bozek et al., 2018). The asynchrony of maturation across primary and associative regions was also recovered over the infant language network during the first postnatal months based on T2w images (Leroy et al., 2011), and during the second year based on T1w images (Travis et al., 2014). Multiparametric MRI approaches combining DTI, relaxometry (e.g., quantitative T1), or multi-compartment approaches (e.g., myelin water fraction) have also highlighted differences in the microstructural and maturational properties of cortical regions in preterms at term equivalent age (Friedrichs-Maeder et al., 2017), in infants (Lebenberg et al., 2019) (Figure 3.1b), and in toddlers (Deoni et al., 2015). All these changes observed with distinct MRI measurements probably reflect a complex interplay between several mechanisms, such as the development of dendritic arborization, the proliferation of glial cells, and/or the myelination of intra-cortical fibers.

3.2.5 Maturation of Central Grey Matter Nuclei

Marked microstructural changes are also observed in central gray nuclei throughout development, with an age-related decrease in DTI diffusivities and an increase in anisotropy over the preterm period and infancy (Mukherjee et al., 2001; Neil et al., 1998; Qiu et al., 2013), suggesting intense membrane proliferation and fiber myelination. In parallel and simultaneously with white matter regions, T1 decreases gradually over central gray nuclei (Schneider et al., 2016), as T2 does (Bultmann, Spineli, Hartmann, & Lanfermann, 2018). The developing microstructural properties are better characterized by comparing multiple parameters (e.g., DTI, NODDI, T1, magnetization transfer ratio, fraction of water related to myelin). This enables us to disentangle between maturational mechanisms (e.g., concentration of myelin-associated macromolecules, water content) (Melbourne et al., 2016; Nossin-Manor et al., 2013). Much like the cortical regions, the maturational patterns differ across nuclei, notably across thalamic substructures (Poh et al., 2015).

3.3 The Early Development of White Matter

In interaction with the development of cortical regions, intense and intermingled processes of growth and maturation are occurring within the brain white matter from the preterm period to infancy (Dubois et al., 2014, 2015, 2016a). All major long-distance fibers are observed by term birth (Figure 3.3a), while short-distance fibers (e.g. U-fibers) mainly develop during the first post-natal year. All these anatomical connections further refine through several complementary mechanisms. After an exuberant growth and proliferation, useless and redundant connections are pruned during childhood, whereas the ongoing myelination process stabilizes the functionally relevant ones and increases the efficiency of the information transfer between distant brain regions. Whereas the number of neurons and microglia

a. Tractography of white matter bundles

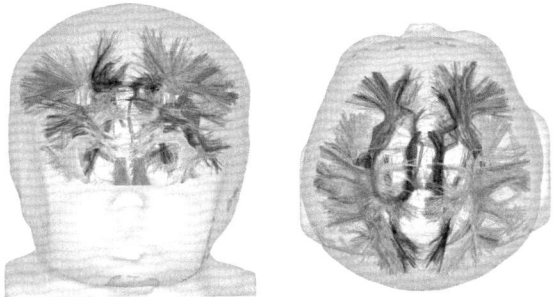

b. Maturation of white matter bundles in infants

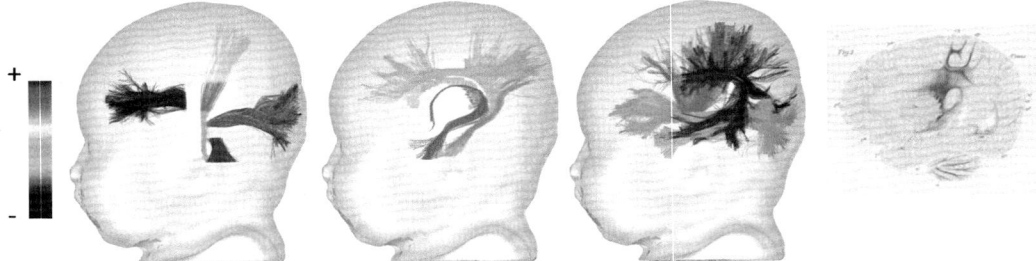

c. Maps of water fraction related to myelin

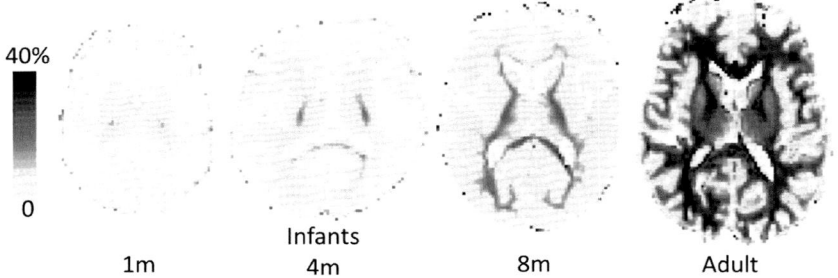

Figure 3.3 Structural changes of the white matter during development. (a) The brain shows an early organization in networks, with white matter bundles connecting distant and close regions, as illustrated here with diffusion MRI and tractography reconstructions in a one-month old infant. (b) The white matter also shows intense maturation after birth through the myelination process (Yakovlev & Lecours, 1967). A recent multi-parametric MRI approach confirmed strong differences between bundles in infants between one and five months of age (adapted from Dubois et al. (2015) and Kulikova et al. (2015) in agreement with a post-mortem map of subcortical myelination by Flechsig (1920) adapted from Von Bonin (1950)). (c) Different MRI techniques inform on myelination, such as the one computing the fraction of water related to myelin. These maps highlight the progression of myelination from central regions to the periphery. Adapted from Kulikova et al. (2016)

A black-and-white version of this figure will appear in some formats. For the color version, please refer to the plate section.

remains almost the same postnatally, the number of oligodendrocytes and astrocytes drastically increases in the white matter during the first 3 years, attaining two-thirds of the corresponding numbers in adults (Sigaard et al., 2016). The inhibitory role of oligodendrocytes and myelin on neuritic growth may partly explain the weak plasticity of the adult brain (Ng et al., 1996). In addition to the early brain organization in specific networks, a major developmental characteristic is the asynchronous progression of maturation across brain regions: for instance, sensory regions develop early on and quickly, whereas associative regions are slowly developing until the end of adolescence.

3.3.1 Developing Architecture of White Matter Bundles

Recent post-mortem and in vivo studies using diffusion MRI combined with physical models (e.g., diffusion tensor imaging DTI, high angular resolution diffusion imaging HARDI) and sophisticated tractography tools (cf. Box 3, Section 3.6.3) have confirmed and extended the knowledge on bundles growth and organization which previously relied on histological dissections. Nevertheless, several issues are related to these techniques in the developing brain (Dubois et al., 2016a). For instance, fetal and neonatal MRI is limited by motion-related constraints and spatial resolution issues (Dubois et al., 2014). Besides, the biological interpretation is not straightforward: not only do the axons participate in the depicted anisotropy of water diffusion, but also the radial glial fibers and the penetrating blood vessels, particularly during the preterm period (Xu et al., 2014).

The development of fiber systems proceeds in a sequential way (projection, callosal, and association) (Vasung et al., 2017), and transient fetal patterns of connectivity are observed

before the formation of stable connections (Dubois et al., 2015; Kostovic & Jovanov-Milosevic, 2006; Vasung et al., 2010). During the early fetal period (9–15 weeks post-conception wPC), major fiber pathways are growing and pathfinding within the intermediate zone. Some afferent (e.g., thalamo-cortical) and efferent (cortico-subcortical) fibers have already been observed, as well as several limbic bundles (e.g., fornix, cingulum) (Huang et al., 2006; Vasung et al., 2010). Before penetrating into the cortical plate, thalamo-cortical fibers make connections with neurons of the subplate zone (Kostovic & Rakic, 1990). During the midfetal period (15–23 wPC), major efferent fibers penetrate their targets in sub-cortical structures, and cortico-cortical callosal fibers and some associative connections (e.g., uncinate, inferior longitudinal, fronto-occipital fasciculi) begin to emerge (Huang et al., 2009; Judas et al., 2005; Vasung et al., 2017). In fetuses in utero, the pyramidal tract, the splenium, and genu of the corpus callosum are observed from 18 weeks of gestational age (wGA) (Bui et al., 2006; Kasprian et al., 2008; Pontabry et al., 2013), while the uncinate and inferior fronto-occipital fascicles are depicted from 20 wGA (Mitter et al., 2015).

During the early preterm period (24–28 wPC), afferent fibers that were waiting in the subplate start making connections within neurons of the cortical plate (of the future cortical layer IV), leading to the establishment of the permanent connectivity while the transient fetal circuitry still exists within the subplate (Kostovic & Judas, 2006; Vasung et al., 2016). Limbic cortico-cortical connections are well developed in the cingulate, entorhinal and hippocampal cortices (Kostovic et al., 1993). Some associative (e.g. inferior longitudinal fasciculus) and limbic bundles (cingulum, fornix) can be visualized in 3D in fetuses in utero (Mitter et al., 2015). During the late preterm period (29–34 wPC), long associative and commissural bundles are quickly developing, likely originating from pyramidal neurons of cortical layer III (Schwartz & Goldman-Rakic, 1991), and these bundles can be identified in preterm newborns (Dudink et al., 2007; Partridge et al., 2004). Short cortico-cortical fibers further grow and enter the cortex through the remnant subplate (Kostovic et al., 2014b; Takahashi et al., 2012).

At term birth, elaborate connectivity is established, allowing infants to acquire functional abilities. Notably, in infants born preterm, cognitive performances at two years are related with thalamocortical connectivity at term-equivalent age (Ball et al., 2015). U-fibers further develop (Kostovic et al., 2014a), and cortico-cortical connectivity is reorganized by several processes including the pruning of callosal fibers (LaMantia & Rakic, 1990) which probably extends until the end of the first post-natal year (Kostovic & Rakic, 1990; Kostovic et al., 2014a; Petanjek et al., 2011). During early infancy, all major white matter bundles and short-range connections are identified despite their weak maturation: commissural bundles of the corpus callosum (genu, body and splenium), projection bundles (cortico-spinal and spino-thalamic tracts, optic radiations, anterior limb of the internal capsule), limbic bundles (fornix and cingulum), and associative bundles (external capsule, uncinate, arcuate, superior, and inferior longitudinal fascicles) (Dubois et al., 2006; Kulikova et al., 2015). The trajectory and morphology of these bundles remain stable between birth and two years of age (Geng et al., 2012).

In recent years, the developing architecture of anatomical networks has also been detailed based on connectivity matrices (Keunen et al., 2017b), by measuring the degree of connections for all pairs of brain regions. Already at thirty weeks of post-menstrual age (wPMA), the structural connectome demonstrates a small-world modular organization like in the adult brain (van den Heuvel et al., 2015), and cortical hubs are highly connected to form a "rich club" (Ball et al., 2014). This topology further refines with age (van den Heuvel et al., 2015), becoming more clustered around term (Brown et al., 2014) and showing an increase in global efficiency and integration, and a decrease in segregation during the first two post-natal years (Yap et al., 2011).

3.3.2 White Matter Maturation

Concurrently and subsequently to the development of connections, the white matter bundles progressively mature and become functionally efficient through the myelination process. This includes several steps, and proceeds from the neuron body to the periphery (McCart & Henry, 1994). It occurs in the human brain from the second part of pregnancy to the end of adolescence, with a peak during the first post-natal year (Baumann & Pham-Dinh, 2001; Van der Knaap & Valk, 1995a, 1995b). It progresses at different ages and rates depending on the regions, bundles, and networks (Baumann & Pham-Dinh, 2001; Brody et al., 1987; Flechsig, 1920; Gilles et al., 1983; Kinney et al., 1988; Yakovlev, 1962; Yakovlev & Lecours, 1967), and follows a caudo-rostral gradient, from the center to the periphery, occurring earlier and faster in sensory pathways (somatosensory, vision, audition) than in motor ones, and in projection fibers than in associative ones (Figure 3.3b).

The myelination process can be quantified through several MRI parameters (Dubois et al., 2014, 2016a), which show intense changes after term birth and during the first post-natal months, and differences in maturation across white matter bundles (Dubois et al., 2008c, 2016b; Kulikova et al., 2015). With myelination, the water content decreases, thus the proton density decreases, while the macromolecule tissue volume (Mezer et al., 2013) increases (Yeatman et al., 2014). This mechanism, together with changes in water molecules compartmentalization (Matsumae et al., 2001) and increase of protein and lipid contents (Barkovich et al., 1988; Kucharczyk et al., 1994), lead to decreases in T1 and T2 relaxation times with age during the "pre-mye-linating" state and with the chemical maturation of the myelin sheath (Barkovich et al., 1988; Baumann & Pham-Dinh, 2001; Deoni et al., 2012; Engelbrecht et al., 1998; Haselgrove et al., 2000; Leppert et al., 2009; Poduslo & Jang, 1984).

DTI parameters also capture some aspects of this maturational pattern (Huppi & Dubois, 2006; Neil et al., 2002). During the preterm period, diffusivities decrease, while anisotropy increases in most white matter regions (Kersbergen et al., 2014) except at cross-roads locations (Nossin-Manor et al., 2015). During infancy and childhood, transverse diffusivity decreases more than longitudinal diffusivity (Dubois et al., 2008c; Geng et al., 2012; Krogsrud et al., 2015), leading to an anisotropy increase (Dubois et al., 2014). These parameters might be sensitive to the proliferation of glial cell bodies, the extension of oligodendroglial processes, and their ensheathment around axons (Dubois et al., 2008c; Nossin-Manor et al., 2013, 2015; Zanin et al., 2011). Several other MRI parameters can be measured to quantify the maturation as they vary with the density of myelin-associated macromolecules and axonal cytoskeleton components: magnetic susceptibility (Li et al., 2013), magnetization transfer imaging or ratio (Kucharczyk et al., 1994; McGowan, 1999; Xydis et al., 2006).

Recently, several modeling approaches have been proposed to characterize distinct pools of water molecules with different microstructural properties (Dubois et al., 2014, 2016a). Based on relaxometry data, some have allowed us to estimate the volume fraction of water related to myelin, which drastically increases with age in the white matter (Deoni et al., 2011, 2012; Kulikova et al., 2016) (Figure 3.3c). Based on diffusion data, some have characterized the intra-neurite volume fraction that relies on the fibers maturation, and the neurite orientation dispersion that depends on fiber crossings and fanning (Dean et al., 2017; Kunz et al., 2014). Other approaches have taken benefit of several MRI parameters that provide complementary information in the developing white matter (Dubois et al., 2014, 2016a). Larger axons and a thicker myelin sheath contribute to faster conduction, but there is a trade-off between axon size and myelin thickness due to spatial constraints imposed by the brain dimensions (Fields, 2008). The relationship between axon size and myelin thickness is captured in a parameter called the myelin g-ratio, defined as the ratio of the inner (axon) to the outer (axon plus myelin) diameter of the fiber. The g-ratio can be estimated using relaxometry and diffusion MRI data (Stikov et al., 2015). The g-ratio decreases with myelination (Dean et al., 2016; Melbourne et al., 2016) and its variations have been associated with cognition and disease (Fields, 2008). Finally, multi-parametric approaches have combined T1, T2, and DTI parameters with clustering (Lebenberg et al., 2015) or mathematical distance to the adult stage (Kulikova et al., 2015) to better highlight the patterns of maturation across regions and bundles.

3.3.3 White Matter Maturation and Functional Development

A few recent studies have related the developmental changes in white matter networks and the psychomotor acquisitions in infants and children. Based on the fraction of water related to myelin, cognitive scales for receptive and expressive language (O'Muircheartaigh et al.,

2014) and processing speeds (Chevalier et al., 2015) have been linked to the maturation of fronto-temporal regions and of occipital regions, respectively. A longitudinal study over the first 5 years showed that children with above-average ability might have differential trajectories of maturation compared to average and below average ability children (Deoni et al., 2016). This suggested that infants might benefit from an early period of prolonged maturation associated with protracted plasticity, and independently of socioeconomic status, gestational age, and weight at birth. The increasing accuracy and speed of processing complex sentences in children have been related to the DTI microstructural properties of the arcuate fasciculus which connects fronto-temporal regions of the language network (Skeide et al., 2016). This tract anisotropy measured at term equivalent age in preterm-born infants is also associated with individual differences in linguistic and cognitive abilities at two years of age, independently of the degree of prematurity (Salvan et al., 2017). Considering structural connections over the whole brain, the white matter anisotropy in neonates has even been related to behavioral functioning at five years of age (Keunen et al., 2017a).

Despite being informative, such behavioral measures correspond to complex processes that only reflect the white matter maturation in an indirect and composite way. In fact myelination is known to increase the conduction velocity of the nerve impulse along axonal fibers (Baumann & Pham-Dinh, 2001), which either leads to a decrease in the response latency at constant pathway length, or to a preserved latency compensating for a growing length (Salami et al., 2003). Recently some studies have tackled this issue by directly comparing structural and functional markers of the white matter maturation, combining MRI and electro- or magnetoencephalography (EEG/MEG) in the same subjects (Dubois et al., 2016a). These latter techniques enable us to measure the latency of evoked responses (i.e., the averaged responses over multiple trials following successive stimulations), and to identify its age-related decrease in infants. The following studies investigated whether this gradual acceleration in the peak latencies during infancy might be used as a proxy of the bundles myelination (see Dubois et al., 2016a for a more extensive review).

The visual modality develops mainly after birth, and infants' visual capacities drastically improve in a few months. Successive EEG/MEG visual evoked responses are recorded in occipital regions. At term birth, the small EEG positive component P1 (~P100 in adults) is detected at a latency that decreases strongly and quickly with age (Harding et al., 1989; McCulloch & Skarf, 1991; Taylor et al., 1987), from around 260 ms in neonates to around 110–120 ms at 12–14 weeks of age, depending on the pattern size (McCulloch et al., 1999). This suggests a progressive increase in conduction velocity in afferent visual pathways related to fiber myelination (Lee et al., 2012), together with other maturational processes (e.g., retina and cortical development).

These functional changes have been compared to the microstructural evolution of visual bundles throughout development, focusing on the latency of P1 and its transfer from contralateral to ipsilateral hemisphere in the case of lateral stimuli. While taking the infants' age into account, the variability in P1 conduction velocity across infants has been related to the DTI maturation of optic radiations (Adibpour et al., 2018a; Dubois et al., 2008d) (Figure 3.4a). This observation has been further extended to cortico-cortical connections. When stimuli are presented laterally (i.e., in a single hemifield), visual responses are first observed in the contralateral hemisphere, then in the ipsilateral hemisphere. In infants, the

a. Visual responses to central stimuli in relation with visual pathways

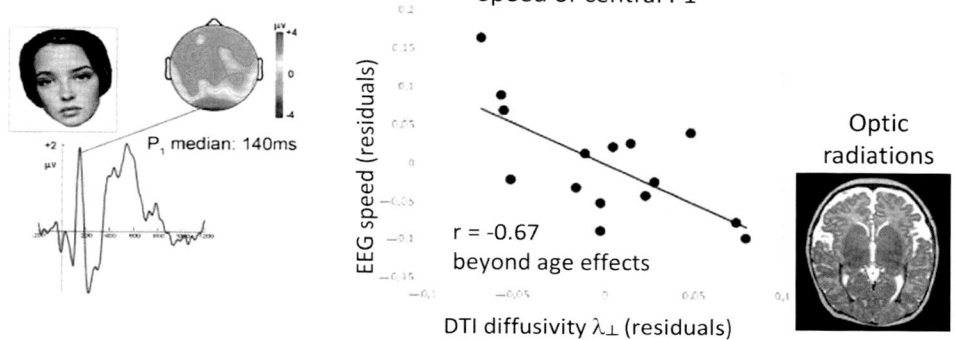

b. Visual responses to lateral stimuli in relation with callosal tracts

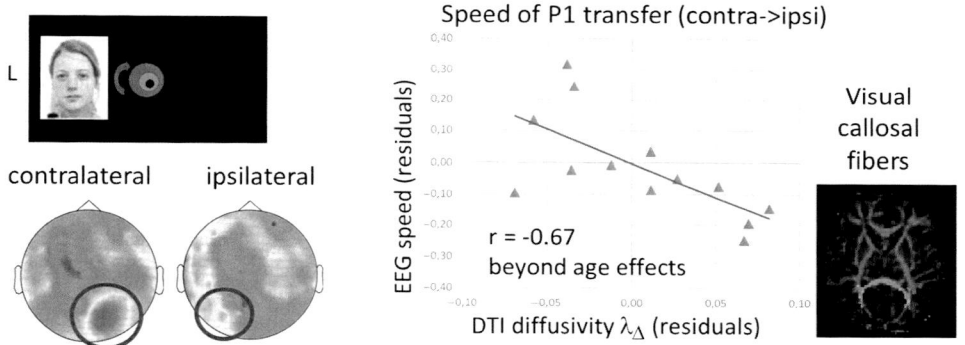

c. Auditory responses to lateral stimuli in relation with callosal tracts

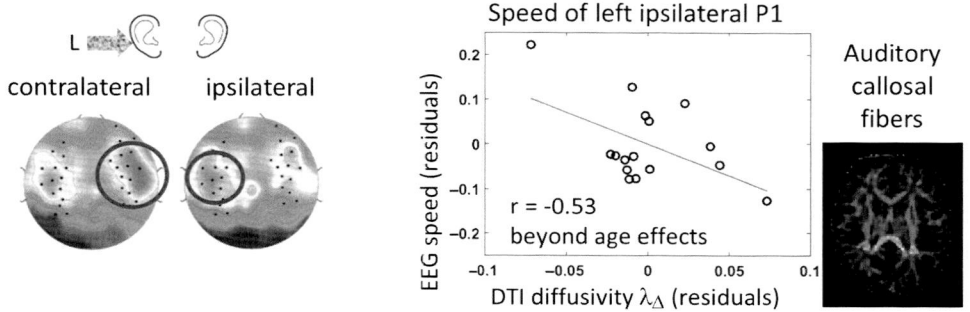

Figure 3.4 Relationships between functional and structural markers of development. (a) During infancy, the speed of P1 responses to visual stimuli increases with age, while the visual pathways become myelinated, resulting in changes of DTI indices (e.g., a decrease in transverse diffusivity $\lambda_\perp$ in the optic radiation). Recent studies have shown that these functional and structural markers of visual maturation are related beyond age dependencies (adapted from Dubois et al. (2008d)). (b) Similar relationships have been observed for responses to visual stimuli presented laterally (in one hemifield at a time). The speed of the responses transfer, from the contralateral to the ipsilateral hemisphere, is related to the maturation of callosal fibers connecting visual regions (adapted from Adibpour et al. (2018a)).

velocity of this inter-hemispheric transfer has been related to the maturation of the visual fibers of the corpus callosum (Adibpour et al., 2018a) (Figure 3.4b), in a similar way to P1 and optic radiations. In six-to-twelve-year-old children, the MEG P1 latency has been further related to the white matter properties of visual and motor association regions (Dockstader et al., 2012).

So far, no developmental study has related the anatomical and functional maturation in the somatosensory modality, despite intense development during the preterm period and major changes in electrophysiological responses throughout infancy (Dubois et al., 2016a). Only a controversial study in adults (Horowitz et al., 2015; Innocenti et al., 2015) has suggested that the N140 inter-hemispheric transfer time depends on the axon diameter of callosal fibers connecting primary somatosensory cortices.

As for the auditory modality, it is already functional *in utero*, but its development is more protracted throughout infancy and toddlerhood than the visual and somatosensory modalities. Thus, evoked responses show extended developmental changes throughout the first post-natal years (Dubois et al., 2016a), and this might make the comparison with white matter maturation difficult in infants (Adibpour et al., 2015).

Following auditory monaural stimulations (i.e., syllables presented in one ear at a time), early responses (P2) are observed in infants both on the contralateral and ipsilateral sides because, as in the adult brain, both types of pathways are already functional (Adibpour et al., 2018b, 2020). The latencies of these different responses decrease with age (Adibpour et al., 2020), and ipsilateral responses are significantly longer in the left than in the right hemisphere, which is not the case in infants with agenesis of the corpus callosum (Adibpour et al., 2018b). These results might suggest that contralateral responses are transmitted, via callosal fibers, more from the right to the left hemisphere than the opposite. Such functional asymmetries could influence the early lateralization of the language network and reinforce an initial bias during development. The comparison of DTI, structural, and EEG functional measures in infants further outlined that the speed of the left ipsilateral response (the same one that is slower in the right hemisphere) tends to vary with the microstructure of auditory callosal fibers (namely the more these fibers have an advanced maturation, the higher the speed (Adibpour et al., 2020)) (Figure 3.4c), suggesting the involvement of auditory callosal fibers in the emergence of this lateralized response. Afterwards, the decrease in the latency of MEG P2m during childhood has been related to the DTI maturation of acoustic radiations (Roberts et al., 2009).

Reliable correlations between the properties of evoked responses and the maturation of white matter pathways remain scarce so far. Further studies in the somatosensory and auditory modalities are required to confirm the results obtained in the visual modality. And

---

Figure 3.4 (*cont.*) (c) Such relationships are more difficult to demonstrate for the auditory system because of strong asymmetries in the latency of responses to lateral stimuli (presented in one ear at a time) (Adibpour et al., 2018b). It seems that the speed of the left ipsilateral responses is related to the maturation of callosal fibers connecting auditory regions (adapted from Adibpour et al. (2020)). This suggests that early structural biases might lead to the functional lateralization for speech processing in the left hemisphere

A black-and-white version of this figure will appear in some formats. For the color version, please refer to the plate section.

comparing the anatomo-functional changes across modalities within the same subjects would help to characterize the asynchronous development of brain networks and explore their sensitivity to distinct critical periods and to various environmental stimulations.

3.4 Perspectives: Toward an Integrative Approach

Besides further investigations of each piece of the complex puzzle of the early brain development, a critical challenge consists in combining all the pieces together so as to provide an integrative view of the neurocognitive development. This integrative approach raises methodological issues to characterize processes spanning different structures, scales, functions, and ages (Betzel & Bassett, 2017; van den Heuvel et al., 2019) and requires sound epistemological debate for interdisciplinary crosstalks. We provide, in Sections 3.4.1 and 3.4.2, recent integrative attempts regarding: (i) connectivity development at the structural and functional levels and (ii) white matter connectivity and grey matter maturation.

3.4.1 Relating the Development of The Structural and Functional Connectivity

Recent advances in neuroimaging techniques have enabled the simultaneous quantification of both anatomical and functional connectivity at the macroscale in pediatric populations (Ouyang et al., 2017a). These studies have reported hierarchical structural maturation from primary to higher-order cortices, with important individual variability, which is partially paralleled by functional development (Cao et al., 2017). For instance, the thalamocortical connectivity patterns in infants reveals good spatial agreement between structural and functional MRI modalities in general but with regional variations that are

system-specific (Ferradal et al., 2019): regions involving primary-sensory cortices exhibit greater structural/functional overlap, whereas higher-order association areas such as temporal and posterior parietal cortices show divergence in spatial patterns of each modality. In addition, analysis of the structural and functional brain networks from fetal life to 2 years of age suggest that the structural network remains ahead and paves the way for the development of the functional brain network (Zhao et al., 2018) and cognitive and behavior performance (Wee et al., 2017). The development of the functional connectome is reconfigured through the integration and segregation processes, contributed by increasing long-range functional connectivity and decreasing short-range functional connectivity, respectively (Cohen et al., 2008; Fair et al., 2007, 2009). Synaptic over-growth and the pruning that follows it as well as the myelination process, regulated by spatiotemporal transcriptomic profiles (Silbereis et al., 2016), are the major factors for reshaping the development and tuning of functional brain networks. The bridge between these microscale neuronal processes and macroscale connectome reconfiguration still need to be directly established because current in vivo noninvasive neuroimaging techniques have low spatial resolution (around 1 mm) that cannot approach cellular scales.

3.4.2 Relating the Patterns of Grey and White Matter Maturation

Spatial and functional gradients of development have been described for the dynamic interplay of cerebral gray and white matter using histological and multimodal neuroimaging approaches. Synchronous development between cortical gray matter (GM) and adjacent white matter (WM) were observed in primary motor, primary visual, visual association, and prefrontal regions, with maturation in primary motor and sensory regions preceding maturation of association areas (Smyser et al., 2016). Around term age, the development of thalamic substructures – connecting to the frontal, precentral, postcentral, temporal and parieto-occipital cortices – is synchronized with the maturation of their respective thalamo-cortical connectivity (Poh et al., 2015). More generally, the advancement of GM and WM maturation is inter-related and dependent on the underlying brain connectivity architecture (Friedrichs-Maeder et al., 2017). Particularly, corresponding maturation levels are found in GM regions and their incident WM connections, and also in GM regions connected through a WM tract. From one to six years of age, regional measures of cortical thickness were found to be partially driven by changes in adjacent white matter myelination, suggesting that cortical and white matter maturation reflect distinct, but complementary, neurodevelopmental processes (Croteau-Chonka et al., 2016).

3.5 Conclusion

Human brain development is a complex and dynamic process that begins during the first weeks of pregnancy and lasts until early adulthood. This chapter focuses on the developmental window from the prenatal period to infancy and showed how the cortex grows and gets convoluted, the microstructural maturation of the gray and white matter, and their cognitive correlates in normal condition. To summarize, the last weeks of pregnancy and the first postnatal months are marked by an intense increase in cortical volume which progressively slows down after 2 years of age until adolescence. These changes are driven by changes in cortical thickness and cortical surface area, two complementary macrostructural features of the cortex anatomy with distinct genetic

and developmental mechanisms. In parallel to volumetric changes, early brain development is characterized by dramatic change in cortex morphology due to the cortical folding process that begins from ten weeks of fetal life. During the third trimester of pregnancy, the cerebral cortex changes from a relatively smooth surface to a complex folded structure that closely resembles the morphology of the adult cortex. The morphology of the cortical folding is a marker of early neurodevelopment predisposition and its analysis has evidenced the long-term effect of fetal life on later cognitive development. These macro-structural changes of the cortex are associated with cellular changes. The growth of neuronal connections is first intense through synaptogenesis and the extension of dendritic arborization and then followed by an elimination of useless connections through a pruning mechanism, to select and maintain only functionally efficient connections. This occurs over different age periods for different cortical regions depending on the functions and the environmental stimulations. In interaction with the cortical development, intense and intermingled processes of growth and maturation are also occurring within the white matter. At birth, elaborate connectivity is established, allowing infants to acquire functional abilities. Concurrently and subsequently to the development of connections, the white matter bundles progressively mature and become functionally efficient through the myelination process, early and fast for the sensory regions while slow and long-lasting for the associative regions. All these cellular and macroscopic changes in white matter networks contribute to cognitive development in infants and children, but direct evidence of such relationships remains scarce so far. Finally, besides further investigations of these different age-, scale-, and function-specific processes, the ultimate challenge will be to combine all these complementary facets of the neurocognitive development into a comprehensive integrative model.

3.6 Boxes

3.6.1 Box 1: Measuring the Cerebral Volumes

The first approaches to quantifying the volume of a brain structure from an MRI image were simply hand-drawing them. Gradually, this tedious approach was replaced by algorithmic methods for automatically segmenting regions of interest (ROI). There is a wide variety of such methods, but the most common ones are based on software freely distributed throughout the community (Freesurfer, FSL, SPM, volbrain, etc.). Most of them fit a brain template to the brain to be segmented by deforming it. This brain template is associated with an atlas of predefined ROI, generally hand-drawn, which then automatically adjusts to the structures of the brain to be segmented. Some particularly complex structures such as the hippocampus and its subfields require dedicated development. The cortex itself, due to its surface geometry, often requires considering not only the volume of one of its subdivisions, but also its average thickness (Fischl, 2012). During the last decade, it has become important to use for segmentation not a single atlas but a set of atlases in order to benefit from a better modeling of the inter-individual anatomical variability (Manjón & Coupé, 2016). For each brain structure, the atlas that most closely resembles the brain to be segmented is used as the model. Usual automatic segmentation methods frequently require hours of computation to segment a brain, but deep-learning approaches are on the way to performing the analysis in a few seconds.

A notorious weakness of the ROI approach is that it imposes a parcellation of the brain which is not necessarily ideal for the question asked. If the anatomical structure of interest does not behave homogeneously, for instance relative to its maturation or its involvement in a physio-pathological process, estimating its overall volume does not provide much sensitivity. To overcome this difficulty, the neuroimaging community uses a strategy that comes from the world of neurosurgical planning, which has become an inescapable paradigm for functional mapping. It provides brains with a universal coordinate system that matches them without explicit concern for the details of their anatomy. This coordinate system is the result of an algorithmic operation very similar to the one used for automatic segmentation: the brain to be studied is deformed to make it look as much as possible like a template brain endowed with the coordinate system. This operation is called "spatial normalization." The coordinate system then plays the role of a Global Positioning System (GPS). It should be noted that this operation also aligns the structures of this brain with those of the template brain, but this is not really used for the coordinate-based analyses. It is then possible to quantify the brain volume locally, point by point, without any a priori hypothesis (Ashburner & Friston, 2000). The most frequent brain template is an average brain obtained from a large number of previously normalized brains. There is an iterative side to this construction of the average brain which is regularly refined by improving brain alignment techniques. The ancestral three-dimensional coordinate system coming from neurosurgery is called the Talairach space. It corresponds to a single brain used by neurosurgeons as an atlas. Today we more commonly use the MNI space, proposed by the Montreal Neurological Institute, derived from the Talairach space but based on an average of 152 brains. When the object of study is the cortex, one often prefers to opt for a system with only two coordinates very similar to the longitude and latitude used to locate oneself on the surface of the earth (Fischl, 2012).

What do you measure once a brain has been spatially normalized? The simplest possibility is to focus on a tissue, the grey or white matter, and quantify the amount of tissue aggregated in each voxel of the image (a 3D pixel) after spatial normalization. This quantity can be deduced from the deformation field allowing the studied brain to be adjusted to the brain template. Usually, we do not take into account the global scaling factors that allow at the beginning of the normalization process to correct global differences in length, width, or height with respect to the template. This strategy is called Voxel-Based Morphometry (VBM). An alternative is to compare the deformation fields themselves, which can shed light on the nature of the spatial transformations that result, for example, from brain development or an atrophy process. This is called Deformation-Based Morphometry (DBM). When focusing on the cortex using a two-dimensional coordinate system, the thickness of the cortex at each point on its surface is compared across subjects. It should be noted that the current consensus is to extract this thickness in the native space of the subject, and thus to discard any correction linked to the dimensions of the brain.

The different brain morphometric strategies are now relatively stabilized and applied systematically throughout the community. On the other hand, when it comes to studying brain development, many methodological questions remain relatively open. With regard to the ROI approach, automatic segmentation methods are less well developed, especially as one moves backwards in age, but the rise of deep learning seems to be solving the problem. However, it will still have to be taken into account that as a structure matures, MRI contrasts change and do not necessarily allow volumes to be quantified in an equivalent

manner from one age to another. For approaches based on spatial normalization, the issue is more complex, as it is difficult to free normalization from the effects of development. The first difficulty is the same as for ROI approaches, the evolution of MRI contrasts with maturation impacting alignment with the brain template. But the major difficulty lies in the choice of the brain template. Using an adult brain template has consequences that are difficult to understand on the final interpretation of the results. Using a family of templates dedicated to each age group is often preferred, but then it remains to align the templates of this family as well as possible. This question becomes particularly difficult when looking at the antenatal period where the patterns of cortical folding differ significantly from one age group to the next. An interesting strategy is to use alignment methods that explicitly impose the alignment of specific cortical sulci (Lebenberg et al., 2018).

3.6.2 Box 2: Measuring the Cortex Morphology

Despite the maturity of morphometric approaches based on spatial normalization, some questions tend to resist them with respect to cortex morphology. Indeed, the interindividual variability of cortical sulci is such (Figure 3.5) that its consequences on normalization are not really understood (Mangin et al., 2016). Consequently, detecting a difference between two groups of individuals with VBM does not necessarily imply a difference in volume but sometimes essentially a local difference in the folding pattern. The strategy based on the measurement of cortex thickness does not escape this difficulty, especially since there is a close correlation between cortical surface geometry and cortex thickness: the cortex is noticeably thicker at the top of the gyri than at the bottom of the folds (Wagstyl et al., 2018).

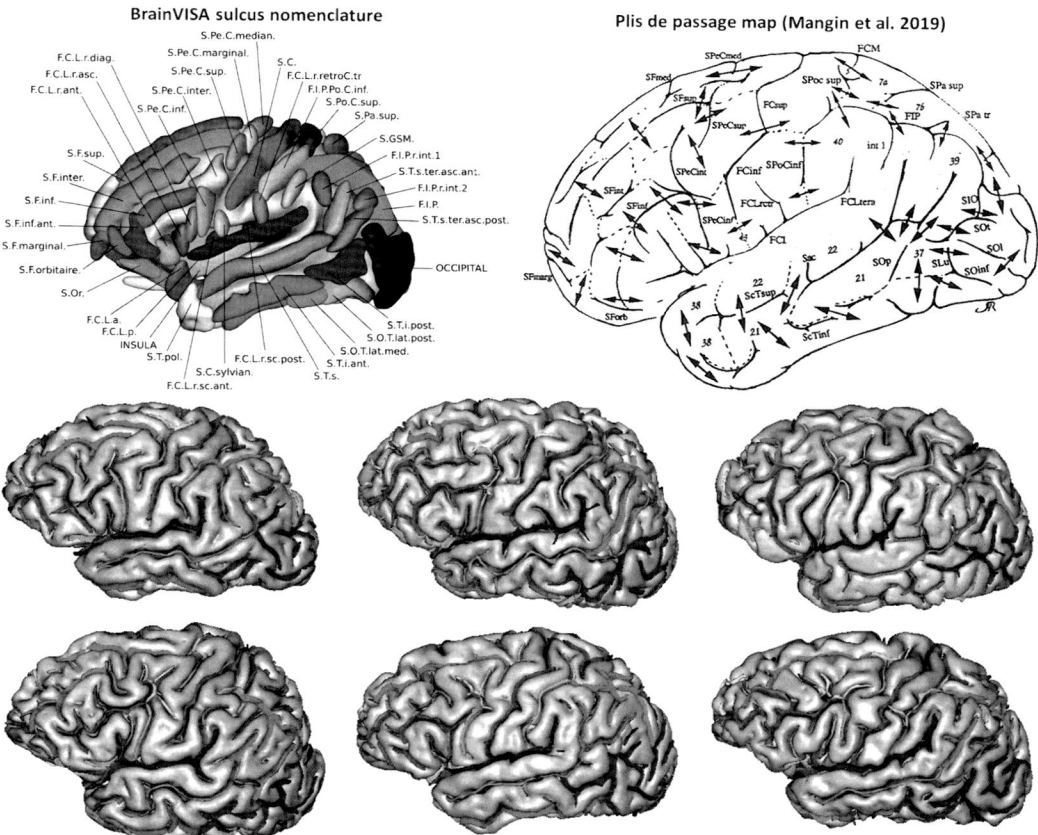

Figure 3.5 Top: Sulcus nomenclature and map of the standard sulcus interruptions. Bottom: The sulcus nomenclature projected on six different left hemispheres
A black-and-white version of this figure will appear in some formats. For the color version, please refer to the plate section.

The first studies of cortical morphology were based on the concept of the gyrification index (GI), a ratio that makes it possible to evaluate the amount of cortex buried in the folds. Historically, this ratio was based on contour lengths measured in 2D sections, which led to major biases. Today, thanks to the automatic segmentation of the cortical ribbon, it is possible to obtain a global 3D gyrification index based on the ratio between the surface area of the cortical surface and that of the convex envelope of the cortex. In addition, the 2D spatial normalization of the

cortex surface (Fischl, 2012) can be used to obtain a similar local gyrification index, calculated at each point, but which is not very easy to interpret. The global gyrification index can also be enriched by quantifying the amount of energy required by the folding of a cortex for different frequency bands (Germanaud et al., 2014), a bit like an EEG signal decomposition into alpha, beta, and theta waves. This approach is of particular interest for the study of development, as there is a correspondence between these bands and primary, secondary, and tertiary folding (Dubois et al., 2019).

To overcome the difficulties associated with spatial normalization when studying cortical morphology, it is sometimes preferable to return to the approach of ROI. One of the software distributed in the community, brainVISA, allows the segmentation of more than 100 sulci (Perrot et al., 2011). These virtual objects correspond to a negative 3D print of the folds of the cortex. They are automatically identified using an artificial intelligence approach, trained on a database where they have been identified by human experts. Then, for each of the sulci, it is possible to quantify simple morphometric parameters such as the length, depth, or distance between the two walls, a marker of local atrophy (Mangin et al., 2010). We can then follow the evolution of these parameters from the onset of the sulcus to adulthood. It is also possible to test whether pathologies of developmental origin have an impact on these parameters. To go further, more sophisticated sulcus shape characterization, such as qualitative features (e.g., sulcus interruptions, absence/presence of a fold) are of interest, but they still require visual observation to be reliable. Unsupervised machine learning approaches under development are in the process of developing a dictionary of the most frequent local folding patterns in the general population. This strategy will allow better modeling of the normal variability of cortical folding, which should lead to automated techniques for anomaly detection. Each type of abnormality is likely to indicate a specific developmental event impacting brain architecture. These abnormalities could assist in patient stratification.

One of the major difficulties of the ROI approach focusing on cortical sulci lies in the weaknesses of their definition in the anatomical literature. Large sulci are often interrupted, each sulcus piece being susceptible to connecting with the others in various ways. This recombination process often leads to ambiguous configurations for the usual anatomical nomenclature, which creates difficulties for the morphometric study of sulci. These difficulties have led to the proposal of an alternative nomenclature of cortical folding defined at a lower scale level (Mangin et al., 2019). This nomenclature is based on unbreakable entities called "sulcal roots," supposedly present in each brain. These sulcal roots can be separated by transverse gyri historically called "passage folds," often buried in the depths of the grooves (see Figure 3.5). At present, the best way to project this nomenclature into a brain is to rely on local maxima of depth of the cortical surface called sulcal pits (Lohmann et al., 2008). Several studies have shown good reproducibility of the pits map across individuals and ages. One of the current research programs is to understand the genesis of these pits in antenatal images and their possible links with early brain architecture. Several studies have shown differences in the organization of the pits map in the context of abnormal development.

3.6.3 Box 3: Measuring the White Matter Microstructure and Connectivity with Diffusion MRI

Conventional anatomical MRI can easily distinguish grey matter from white matter (WM), but provides little information about their microscopic structure. Diffusion MRI (dMRI), on the other hand, exploits the random motions of water in tissue to provide microstructure features that were previously only accessible by histology (Johansen-Berg & Behrens, 2013). Diffusion MRI reveals regularities in the microscopic geometry of cells through its impact on the diffusion of water molecules (the diffusion process is disturbed by the cell membranes). These perturbations lead to MR signal heterogeneities, for example in the extent of the diffusion process in each direction of space. Typically, in white matter, the amplitude of this process is greater in the

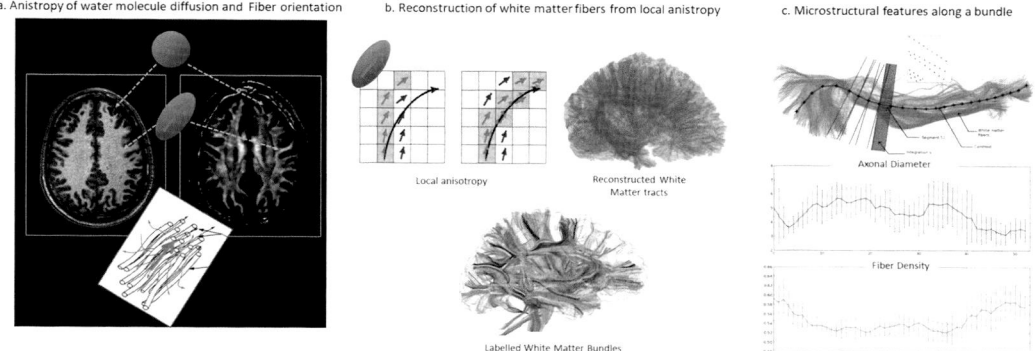

a. Anistropy of water molecule diffusion and Fiber orientation   b. Reconstruction of white matter fibers from local anistropy   c. Microstructural features along a bundle

Local anisotropy

Reconstructed White Matter tracts

Labelled White Matter Bundles

Axonal Diameter

Fiber Density

Figure 3.6 White matter microstructure and connectivity with diffusion MRI. (a) Water molecule diffusion is isotropic (sphere) in grey matter and anisotropic (ellipsoid) in grey matter. The main direction of water molecule diffusion (red arrow) indicates the main direction of the white matter fibers. (b) Whole white matter tracts can be mathematically reconstructed step-by-step using local tract direction derived from diffusion anisotropy. Main white matter bundles can be identified from all reconstructed tracts. (c) Microstructural features (e.g., axonal diameter, fiber density) can be estimated along each white matter bundle

A black-and-white version of this figure will appear in some formats. For the color version, please refer to the plate section.

direction of the fibers, whereas it is hindered and restricted in transverse directions of the fibers (Figure 3.6a).

This local anisotropy of the water diffusion process in WM has led to a flagship application of diffusion MRI: the mapping of structural connectivity. This application has a major impact since dissection only allows the observation of the largest WM pathways, whereas diffusion MRI can reveal, for the first time, the large pathways but also short connections such as U-shaped fibers in vivo (Guevara et al., 2017). Over the last twenty years, a wide variety of models have been proposed to decode the diffusion signal in each MRI voxel. The aim is to estimate the direction of the WM fibers locally in order to be able to reconstruct the trajectory of the fascicles step by step (Figure 3.6b). The major difficulty lies in the complexity of the geometry of the fiber crossings, which constitute most of the white matter. The most recent approaches, based on acquisition sequences that probe the diffusion of water in a large number of spatial directions, now make it possible to decipher a large part of these crossings, even though ambiguous situations still remain. It is nevertheless possible today to map more than a hundred bundles to study their integrity or their maturation. Dedicated measurements are derived from the diffusion of water for this purpose. They are averaged either throughout the bundle or along a central axis (Figure 3.6c). The Fractional Anisotropy (FA), which quantifies the amplitude of diffusion in the direction of the fibers versus in transverse directions, is generally maximal when a bundle is in good condition: the membranes and myelin sheaths that disrupt diffusion constitute barriers that are difficult to cross. On the other hand, when the bundle becomes disorganized, for example due to degeneration, FA decreases. The same type of considerations can be used to interpret diffusion variations induced by brain development and fiber myelination.

A range of recent microstructure imaging techniques have been proposed to tackle various histological features (Alexander et al., 2019): neurite (axon or dendrite) density, axon diameter distributions, cell shape, myelin density, myelin water fraction, etc. These techniques often combine diffusion imaging with quantitative relaxometry (the estimation of T1 and T2 relaxation times at the core of magnetic resonance). Most of these techniques fit a model relating the microscopic tissue features to MR signals in each voxel to produce microstructure maps. For instance, axon diameter stems from a simple model consisting of parallel impermeable cylinders, which is fitted in each voxel to a set of varying diffusion weighting in order to recover estimates of cylinder size and packing. Current models have several limitations, mainly related to the few model parameters that can be estimated with practical acquisition protocols. While these advanced technologies are still in progress, they have great appeal for studying brain development and maturation.

References

Adibpour, P., Dehaene-Lambertz, G., & Dubois, J. (2015). Relating the structural and functional maturation of visual and auditory white matter pathways with diffusion imaging and event-related potentials in infants. *Proceedings of ISMRM Meeting*, May 30–June 5, 2015, Toronto, p. 645.

Adibpour, P., Dubois, J., & Dehaene-Lambertz, G. (2018a). Right but not left hemispheric discrimination of faces in infancy. *Nature Human Behaviour*, 2, 67–79.

Adibpour, P., Dubois, J., Moutard, M. L., & Dehaene-Lambertz, G. (2018b). Early asymmetric inter-hemispheric transfer in the auditory network: Insights from infants with corpus callosum agenesis. *Brain Structure and Function*, 223, 2893–2905.

Adibpour, P., Lebenberg, J., Kabdebon, C., Dehaene-Lambertz, G., & Dubois, J. (2020). Anatomo-functional correlates of auditory development in infancy. *Developmental Cognitive Neuroscience*, 42, 100752.

Alexander, D. C., Dyrby, T. B., Nilsson, M., & Zhang, H. (2019). Imaging brain microstructure with diffusion MRI: Practicality and applications. *NMR in Biomedicine*, 32, e3841.

Amiez, C., Wilson, C. R. E., & Procyk, E. (2018). Variations of cingulate sulcal organization and link with cognitive performance. *Scientific Reports*, 8, 13988.

Anderson, V., Spencer-Smith, M., & Wood, A. (2011). Do children really recover better? Neurobehavioural plasticity after early brain insult. *Brain*, 134, 2197–2221.

Andescavage, N. N., du Plessis, A., McCarter, R., Serag, A., Evangelou, I., Vezina, G., Robertson, R., & Limperopoulos, C. (2017). Complex trajectories of brain development in the healthy human fetus. *Cerebral Cortex*, 27, 5274–5283.

Ashburner, J., & Friston, K. J. (2000). Voxel-based morphometry – The methods. *Neuroimage*, 11, 805–821.

Bajic, D., Wang, C., Kumlien, E., Mattsson, P., Lundberg, S., Eeg-Olofsson, O., & Raininko, R. (2008). Incomplete inversion of the hippocampus – A common developmental anomaly. *European Radiology*, 18, 138–142.

Ball, G., Aljabar, P., Zebari, S., Tusor, N., Arichi, T., Merchant, N., Robinson, E. C., Ogundipe, E., Rueckert, D., Edwards, A. D., & Counsell, S. J. (2014). Rich-club organization of the newborn human brain. *Proceedings of the National Academy of Sciences (USA)*, 111, 7456–7461.

Ball, G., Pazderova, L., Chew, A., Tusor, N., Merchant, N., Arichi, T., Allsop, J. M., Cowan, F. M., Edwards, A. D., & Counsell, S. J. (2015). Thalamocortical connectivity predicts cognition in children born preterm. *Cerebral Cortex*, 25, 4310–4318.

Ball, G., Srinivasan, L., Aljabar, P., Counsell, S. J., Durighel, G., Hajnal, J. V., Rutherford, M. A., & Edwards, A. D. (2013). Development of cortical microstructure in the preterm human brain. *Proceedings of the National Academy of Sciences (USA)*, *110*, 9541–9546.

Barkovich, A. J., Kjos, B. O., Jackson, D. E., Jr., & Norman, D. (1988). Normal maturation of the neonatal and infant brain: MR imaging at 1.5 T. *Radiology*, *166*, 173–180.

Batalle, D., O'Muircheartaigh, J., Makropoulos, A., Kelly, C. J., Dimitrova, R., Hughes, E. J., Hajnal, J. V., Zhang, H., Alexander, D. C., David Edwards, A., & Counsell, S. J. (2019). Different patterns of cortical maturation before and after 38 weeks gestational age demonstrated by diffusion MRI in vivo. *Neuroimage*, *185*, 764–775.

Baumann, N., & Pham-Dinh, D. (2001). Biology of oligodendrocyte and myelin in the mammalian central nervous system. *Physiological Reviews*, *81*, 871–927.

Betzel, R. F., & Bassett, D. S. (2017). Multi-scale brain networks. *Neuroimage*, *160*, 73–83.

Borrell, V. (2018). How cells fold the cerebral cortex. *Journal of Neuroscience*, *38*, 776–783.

Borst, G., Cachia, A., Tissier, C., Ahr, E., Simon, G., & Houdé, O. (2016). Early cerebral constraint on reading skills of 10-years-old children. *Mind, Brain and Education*, *10*, 47–54.

Borst, G., Cachia, A., Vidal, J., Simon, G., Fischer, C., Pineau, A., Poirel, N., Mangin, J. F., & Houde, O. (2014). Folding of the anterior cingulate cortex partially explains inhibitory control during childhood: A longitudinal study. *Developmental Cognitive Neuroscience*, *9*, 126–135.

Bozek, J., Makropoulos, A., Schuh, A., Fitzgibbon, S., Wright, R., Glasser, M. F., Coalson, T. S., O'Muircheartaigh, J., Hutter, J., Price, A. N., Cordero-Grande, L., Teixeira, R., Hughes, E., Tusor, N., Baruteau, K. P., Rutherford, M. A., Edwards, A. D., Hajnal, J. V., Smith, S. M., Rueckert, D., Jenkinson, M., & Robinson, E. C. (2018). Construction of a neonatal cortical surface atlas using multimodal surface matching in the developing human connectome project. *Neuroimage*, *179*, 11–29.

Brody, B. A., Kinney, H. C., Kloman, A. S., & Gilles, F. H. (1987). Sequence of central nervous

system myelination in human infancy. I. An autopsy study of myelination. *Journal of Neuropathology & Experimental Neurology*, *46*, 283–301.

Brown, C. J., Miller, S. P., Booth, B. G., Andrews, S., Chau, V., Poskitt, K. J., & Hamarneh, G. (2014). Structural network analysis of brain development in young preterm neonates. *Neuroimage*, *101*, 667–680.

Bui, T., Daire, J. L., Chalard, F., Zaccaria, I., Alberti, C., Elmaleh, M., Garel, C., Luton, D., Blanc, N., & Sebag, G. (2006). Microstructural development of human brain assessed in utero by diffusion tensor imaging. *Pediatric Radiology*, *36*, 1133–1140.

Bultmann, E., Spineli, L. M., Hartmann, H., & Lanfermann, H. (2018). Measuring in vivo cerebral maturation using age-related T2 relaxation times at 3T. *Brain and Development*, *40*, 85–93.

Cachia, A., Borst, G., Tissier, C., Fisher, C., Plaze, M., Gay, O., Riviere, D., Gogtay, N., Giedd, J., Mangin, J. F., Houde, O., & Raznahan, A. (2016). Longitudinal stability of the folding pattern of the anterior cingulate cortex during development. *Developmental Cognitive Neuroscience*, *19*, 122–127.

Cachia, A., Borst, G., Vidal, J., Fischer, C., Pineau, A., Mangin, J. F., & Houde, O. (2014). The shape of the ACC contributes to cognitive control efficiency in preschoolers. *Journal of Cognitive Neuroscience*, *26*, 96–106.

Cachia, A., Del Maschio, N., Borst, G., Della Rosa, P. A., Pallier, C., Costa, A., Houde, O., & Abutalebi, J. (2017). Anterior cingulate cortex sulcation and its differential effects on conflict monitoring in bilinguals and monolinguals. *Brain and Language*, *175*, 57–63.

Cachia, A., Roell, M., Mangin, J. F., Sun, Z. Y., Jobert, A., Braga, L., Houde, O., Dehaene, S., & Borst, G. (2018). How interindividual differences in brain anatomy shape reading accuracy. *Brain Structure and Function*, *223*, 701–712.

Cao, M., Huang, H., & He, Y. (2017). Developmental connectomics from infancy through early childhood. *Trends in Neurosciences*, *40*, 494–506.

Chevalier, N., Kurth, S., Doucette, M. R., Wiseheart, M., Deoni, S. C., Dean, D. C., 3rd, O'Muircheartaigh, J., Blackwell, K. A., Munakata, Y., & LeBourgeois, M. K. (2015). Myelination is associated with processing speed in early childhood: Preliminary insights. *PLoS ONE, 10*, e0139897.

Chi, J. G., Dooling, E. C., & Gilles, F. H. (1977). Gyral development of the human brain. *Annals of Neurology, 1*, 86–93.

Cohen, A. L., Fair, D. A., Dosenbach, N. U. F., Miezin, F. M., Dierker, D., Van Essen, D. C., Schlaggar, B. L., & Petersen, S. E. (2008). Defining functional areas in individual human brains using resting functional connectivity MRI. *Neuroimage, 41*, 45–57.

Croteau-Chonka, E. C., Dean, D. C., 3rd, Remer, J., Dirks, H., O'Muircheartaigh, J., & Deoni, S. C. (2016). Examining the relationships between cortical maturation and white matter myelination throughout early childhood. *Neuroimage, 125*, 413–421.

Cury, C., Toro, R., Cohen, F., Fischer, C., Mhaya, A., Samper-Gonzalez, J., Hasboun, D., Mangin, J. F., Banaschewski, T., Bokde, A. L., Bromberg, U., Buechel, C., Cattrell, A., Conrod, P., Flor, H., Gallinat, J., Garavan, H., Gowland, P., Heinz, A., Ittermann, B., Lemaitre, H., Martinot, J. L., Nees, F., Paillere Martinot, M. L., Orfanos, D. P., Paus, T., Poustka, L., Smolka, M. N., Walter, H., Whelan, R., Frouin, V., Schumann, G., Glaunes, J. A., Colliot, O., & Imagen Consortium. (2015). Incomplete hippocampal inversion: A comprehensive MRI study of over 2000 subjects. *Frontiers in Neuroanatomy, 9*, 160.

De Guio, F., Mangin, J. F., Riviere, D., Perrot, M., Molteno, C. D., Jacobson, S. W., Meintjes, E. M., & Jacobson, J. L. (2014). A study of cortical morphology in children with fetal alcohol spectrum disorders. *Human Brain Mapping, 35*, 2285–2296.

Dean, D. C., 3rd, O'Muircheartaigh, J., Dirks, H., Travers, B. G., Adluru, N., Alexander, A. L., & Deoni, S. C. (2016). Mapping an index of the myelin g-ratio in infants using magnetic resonance imaging. *Neuroimage, 132*, 225–237.

Dean, D. C., 3rd, Planalp, E. M., Wooten, W., Adluru, N., Kecskemeti, S. R., Frye, C., Schmidt, C. K., Schmidt, N. L., Styner, M. A., Goldsmith, H. H., Davidson, R. J., & Alexander, A. L. (2017). Mapping white matter microstructure in the one month human brain. *Scientific Reports, 7*, 9759.

Dehaene-Lambertz, G., & Spelke, E. S. (2015). The infancy of the human brain. *Neuron, 88*, 93–109.

Deipolyi, A. R., Mukherjee, P., Gill, K., Henry, R. G., Partridge, S. C., Veeraraghavan, S., Jin, H., Lu, Y., Miller, S. P., Ferriero, D. M., Vigneron, D. B., & Barkovich, A. J. (2005). Comparing microstructural and macrostructural development of the cerebral cortex in premature newborns: Diffusion tensor imaging versus cortical gyration. *Neuroimage, 27*, 579–586.

Del Maschio, N., Sulpizio, S., Fedeli, D., Ramanujan, K., Ding, G., Weekes, B. S., Cachia, A., & Abutalebi, J. (2019). ACC sulcal patterns and their modulation on cognitive control efficiency across lifespan: A neuroanatomical study on bilinguals and monolinguals. *Cerebral Cortex, 29*, 3091–3101.

Deoni, S. C., Dean, D. C., 3rd, O'Muircheartaigh, J., Dirks, H., & Jerskey, B. A. (2012). Investigating white matter development in infancy and early childhood using myelin water faction and relaxation time mapping. *Neuroimage, 63*, 1038–1053.

Deoni, S. C., Dean, D. C., 3rd, Remer, J., Dirks, H., & O'Muircheartaigh, J. (2015). Cortical maturation and myelination in healthy toddlers and young children. *Neuroimage, 115*, 147–161.

Deoni, S. C., Mercure, E., Blasi, A., Gasston, D., Thomson, A., Johnson, M., Williams, S. C., & Murphy, D. G. (2011). Mapping infant brain myelination with magnetic resonance imaging. *Journal of Neuroscience, 31*, 784–791.

Deoni, S. C., O'Muircheartaigh, J., Elison, J. T., Walker, L., Doernberg, E., Waskiewicz, N., Dirks, H., Piryatinsky, I., Dean, D. C., 3rd, & Jumbe, N. L. (2016). White matter maturation profiles through early childhood predict general cognitive ability. *Brain Structure and Function, 221*, 1189–1203.

Dockstader, C., Gaetz, W., Rockel, C., & Mabbott, D. J. (2012). White matter maturation in visual and motor areas predicts the latency of visual activation in children. *Human Brain Mapping*. *33*, 179–191.

Dubois, J., Adibpour, P., Poupon, C., Hertz-Pannier, L., & Dehaene-Lambertz, G. (2016a). MRI and M/EEG studies of the white matter development in human fetuses and infants: Review and opinion. *Brain Plasticity*, *2*, 49–69.

Dubois, J., Benders, M., Borradori-Tolsa, C., Cachia, A., Lazeyras, F., Ha-Vinh Leuchter, R., Sizonenko, S. V., Warfield, S. K., Mangin, J. F., & Huppi, P. S. (2008a). Primary cortical folding in the human newborn: An early marker of later functional development. *Brain*, *131*, 2028–2041.

Dubois, J., Benders, M., Cachia, A., Lazeyras, F., Leuchter, R. H. V., Sizonenko, S. V., Borradori-Tolsa, C., Mangin, J. F., & Huppi, P. S. (2008b). Mapping the early cortical folding process in the preterm newborn brain. *Cerebral Cortex*, *18*, 1444–1454.

Dubois, J., & Dehaene-Lambertz, G. (2015). Fetal and postnatal development of the cortex: Insights from MRI and genetics. In Arthur W. Toga (ed.), *Brain Mapping: An Encyclopedic Reference* (Vol. 2, pp. 11–19). Cambridge, MA: Academic Press.

Dubois, J., Dehaene-Lambertz, G., Kulikova, S., Poupon, C., Huppi, P. S., & Hertz-Pannier, L. (2014). The early development of brain white matter: A review of imaging studies in fetuses, newborns and infants. *Neuroscience*, *276*, 48–71.

Dubois, J., Dehaene-Lambertz, G., Perrin, M., Mangin, J. F., Cointepas, Y., Duchesnay, E., Le Bihan, D., & Hertz-Pannier, L. (2008c). Asynchrony of the early maturation of white matter bundles in healthy infants: Quantitative landmarks revealed noninvasively by diffusion tensor imaging. *Human Brain Mapping*, *29*, 14–27.

Dubois, J., Dehaene-Lambertz, G., Soares, C., Cointepas, Y., Le Bihan, D., & Hertz-Pannier, L. (2008d). Microstructural correlates of infant functional development: Example of the visual pathways. *Journal of Neuroscience*, *28*, 1943–1948.

Dubois, J., Hertz-Pannier, L., Dehaene-Lambertz, G., Cointepas, Y., & Le Bihan, D. (2006). Assessment of the early organization and maturation of infants' cerebral white matter fiber bundles: A feasibility study using quantitative diffusion tensor imaging and tractography. *Neuroimage*, *30*, 1121–1132.

Dubois, J., Kostovic, I., & Judas, M. (2015). Development of structural and functional connectivity. In A. W. Toga (ed.), *Brain Mapping: An Encyclopedic Reference* (Vol. 2, pp. 423–437). Cambridge, MA: Academic Press.

Dubois, J., Lefevre, J., Angleys, H., Leroy, F., Fischer, C., Lebenberg, J., Dehaene-Lambertz, G., Borradori-Tolsa, C., Lazeyras, F., Hertz-Pannier, L., Mangin, J. F., Huppi, P. S., & Germanaud, D. (2019). The dynamics of cortical folding waves and prematurity-related deviations revealed by spatial and spectral analysis of gyrification. *Neuroimage*, *185*, 934–946.

Dubois, J., Poupon, C., Thirion, B., Simonnet, H., Kulikova, S., Leroy, F., Hertz-Pannier, L., & Dehaene-Lambertz, G. (2016b). Exploring the early organization and maturation of linguistic pathways in the human infant brain. *Cerebral Cortex*, *26*, 2283–2298.

Dudink, J., Lequin, M., van Pul, C., Buijs, J., Conneman, N., van Goudoever, J., & Govaert, P. (2007). Fractional anisotropy in white matter tracts of very-low-birth-weight infants. *Pediatric Radiology*, *37*, 1216–1223.

Dudink, J., Buijs, J., Govaert, P., van Zwol, A. L., Conneman, N., van Goudoever, J. B., & Lequin, M. (2010). Diffusion tensor imaging of the cortical plate and subplate in very-low-birth-weight infants. *Pediatric Radiology*, *40*, 1397–1404.

Eaton-Rosen, Z., Melbourne, A., Orasanu, E., Cardoso, M. J., Modat, M., Bainbridge, A., Kendall, G. S., Robertson, N. J., Marlow, N., & Ourselin, S. (2015). Longitudinal measurement of the developing grey matter in preterm subjects using multi-modal MRI. *Neuroimage*, *111*, 580–589.

Eaton-Rosen, Z., Scherrer, B., Melbourne, A., Ourselin, S., Neil, J. J., & Warfield, S. K. (2017). Investigating the maturation of microstructure and radial orientation in the preterm human cortex with diffusion MRI. *Neuroimage, 162,* 65–72.

Eickhoff, S., Walters, N. B., Schleicher, A., Kril, J., Egan, G. F., Zilles, K., Watson, J. D., & Amunts, K. (2005). High-resolution MRI reflects myeloarchitecture and cytoarchitecture of human cerebral cortex. *Human Brain Mapping, 24,* 206–215.

Engelbrecht, V., Rassek, M., Preiss, S., Wald, C., & Modder, U. (1998). Age-dependent changes in magnetization transfer contrast of white matter in the pediatric brain. *AJNR American Journal of Neuroradiology, 19,* 1923–1929.

Fair, D. A., Cohen, A. L., Power, J. D., Dosenbach, N. U. F., Church, J. A., Miezin, F. M., Schlaggar, B. L., & Petersen, S. E. (2009). Functional brain networks develop from a "local to distributed" organization. *PLoS Computational Biology, 5,* e1000381.

Fair, D. A., Dosenbach, N. U. F., Church, J. A., Cohen, A. L., Brahmbhatt, S., Miezin, F. M., Barch, D. M., Raichle, M. E., Petersen, S. E., & Schlaggar, B. L. (2007). Development of distinct control networks through segregation and integration. *Proceedings of the National Academy of Sciences, 104,* 13507–13512.

Feess-Higgins, A., & Larroche, J. C. (1987). *Development of the Human Foetal Brain. An Anatomical Atlas.* Paris: INSERM CNRS.

Ferradal, S. L., Gagoski, B., Jaimes, C., Yi, F., Carruthers, C., Vu, C., Litt, J. S., Larsen, R., Sutton, B., Grant, P. E., & Zollei, L. (2019). System-specific patterns of thalamocortical connectivity in early brain development as revealed by structural and functional MRI. *Cerebral Cortex, 29,* 1281–1229.

Fields, R. D. (2008). White matter in learning, cognition and psychiatric disorders. *Trends in Neurosciences, 31,* 361–370.

Fischl, B. (2012). FreeSurfer. *Neuroimage, 62,* 774–781.

Flechsig, P. (1920). *Anatomie des Menschlichen Gehirn und Rückenmarks, auf myelogenetischer grundlage.* Stuttgart: G. Thieme.

Fornito, A., Yucel, M., Wood, S., Stuart, G. W., Buchanan, J. A., Proffitt, T., Anderson, V.,

Velakoulis, D., & Pantelis, C. (2004). Individual differences in anterior cingulate/paracingulate morphology are related to executive functions in healthy males. *Cerebral Cortex, 14,* 424–431.

Foubet, O., Trejo, M., & Toro, R. (2019). Mechanical morphogenesis and the development of neocortical organisation. *Cortex, 118,* 315–326.

Friedrichs-Maeder, C. L., Griffa, A., Schneider, J., Huppi, P. S., Truttmann, A., & Hagmann, P. (2017). Exploring the role of white matter connectivity in cortex maturation. *PLoS ONE, 12,* e0177466.

Geng, X., Gouttard, S., Sharma, A., Gu, H., Styner, M., Lin, W., Gerig, G., & Gilmore, J. H. (2012). Quantitative tract-based white matter development from birth to age 2 years. *Neuroimage, 61,* 542–557.

Germanaud, D., Lefevre, J., Fischer, C., Bintner, M., Curie, A., des Portes, V., Eliez, S., Elmaleh-Berges, M., Lamblin, D., Passemard, S., Operto, G., Schaer, M., Verloes, A., Toro, R., Mangin, J. F., & Hertz-Pannier, L. (2014). Simplified gyral pattern in severe developmental microcephalies? New insights from allometric modeling for spatial and spectral analysis of gyrification. *Neuroimage, 102,* 317–331.

Giedd, J. N., & Rapoport, J. L. (2010). Structural MRI of pediatric brain development: What have we learned and where are we going? *Neuron, 67,* 728–734.

Gilles, F., Shankle, W., & Dooling, E. (1983). Myelinated tracts: Growth patterns. In F. Gilles, A. Leviton, & E. Dooling (eds.), *The Developing Human Brain* (pp. 117–183). Boston, MA: Butterworth Heinemann.

Gilmore, J. H., Lin, W., Prastawa, M. W., Looney, C. B., Vetsa, Y. S., Knickmeyer, R. C., Evans, D. D., Smith, J. K., Hamer, R. M., Lieberman, J. A., & Gerig, G. (2007). Regional gray matter growth, sexual dimorphism, and cerebral asymmetry in the neonatal brain. *Journal of Neuroscience, 27,* 1255–1260.

Gilmore, J. H., Shi, F., Woolson, S. L., Knickmeyer, R. C., Short, S. J., Lin, W., Zhu, H., Hamer, R. M., Styner, M., & Shen, D. (2012). Longitudinal development of cortical and subcortical gray matter from birth to 2 years. *Cerebral Cortex, 22*, 2478–2485.

Guevara, M., Román, C., Houenou, J., Duclap, D., Poupon, C., Mangin, J. F., & Guevara, P. (2017). Reproducibility of superficial white matter tracts using diffusion-weighted imaging tractography. *Neuroimage, 147*, 703–725.

Habas, P. A., Scott, J. A., Roosta, A., Rajagopalan, V., Kim, K., Rousseau, F., Barkovich, A. J., Glenn, O. A., & Studholme, C. (2012). Early folding patterns and asymmetries of the normal human brain detected from in utero MRI. *Cerebral Cortex, 22*, 13–25.

Harding, G. F., Grose, J., Wilton, A., & Bissenden, J. G. (1989). The pattern reversal VEP in short-gestation infants. *Electroencephalography and Clinical Neurophysiology, 74*, 76–80.

Haselgrove, J., Moore, J., Wang, Z., Traipe, E., & Bilaniuk, L. (2000). A method for fast multislice T1 measurement: Feasibility studies on phantoms, young children, and children with Canavan's disease. *Journal of Magnetic Resonance Imaging, 11*, 360–367.

Hilgetag, C. C., & Barbas, H. (2006). Role of mechanical factors in the morphology of the primate cerebral cortex. *PLoS Computational Biology, 2*(3), e22.

Hilgetag, C. C., & Barbas, H. (2009). Sculpting the brain. *Scientific American, 300*, 66–71.

Hill, J., Dierker, D., Neil, J., Inder, T., Knutsen, A., Harwell, J., Coalson, T., & Van Essen, D. (2010). A surface-based analysis of hemispheric asymmetries and folding of cerebral cortex in term-born human infants. *Journal of Neuroscience, 30*, 2268–2276.

Horowitz, A., Barazany, D., Tavor, I., Bernstein, M., Yovel, G., & Assaf, Y. (2015). In vivo correlation between axon diameter and conduction velocity in the human brain. *Brain Structure and Function, 220*, 1777–1788.

Huang, H., Jeon, T., Sedmak, G., Pletikos, M., Vasung, L., Xu, X., Yarowsky, P., Richards, L. J., Kostovic, I., Sestan, N., & Mori, S. (2013). Coupling diffusion imaging with histological and gene expression analysis to examine the dynamics of cortical areas across the fetal period

of human brain development. *Cerebral Cortex, 23*, 2620–2631.

Huang, H., Xue, R., Zhang, J., Ren, T., Richards, L. J., Yarowsky, P., Miller, M. I., & Mori, S. (2009). Anatomical characterization of human fetal brain development with diffusion tensor magnetic resonance imaging. *Journal of Neuroscience, 29*, 4263–4273.

Huang, H., Zhang, J., Wakana, S., Zhang, W., Ren, T., Richards, L. J., Yarowsky, P., Donohue, P., Graham, E., van Zijl, P. C., & Mori, S. (2006). White and gray matter development in human fetal, newborn and pediatric brains. *Neuroimage, 33*, 27–38.

Huppi, P. S., & Dubois, J. (2006). Diffusion tensor imaging of brain development. *Seminars in Fetal and Neonatal Medicine, 11*, 489–497.

Huttenlocher, P. R., & Dabholkar, A. S. (1997). Regional differences in synaptogenesis in human cerebral cortex. *The Journal of Comparative Neurology, 387*, 167–178.

Innocenti, G. M., Caminiti, R., & Aboitiz, F. (2015). Comments on the paper by Horowitz et al. (2014). *Brain Structure and Function, 220*, 1789–1790.

Johansen-Berg, H., & Behrens, T. E. J. (2013). *Diffusion MRI: From Quantitative Measurement to In Vivo Neuroanatomy*. Cambridge, MA: Academic Press.

Judas, M., Rados, M., Jovanov-Milosevic, N., Hrabac, P., Stern-Padovan, R., & Kostovic, I. (2005). Structural, immunocytochemical, and MR imaging properties of periventricular crossroads of growing cortical pathways in preterm infants. *AJNR American Journal of Neuroradiology, 26*, 2671–2684.

Kapellou, O., Counsell, S. J., Kennea, N., Dyet, L., Saeed, N., Stark, J., Maalouf, E., Duggan, P., Ajayi-Obe, M., Hajnal, J., Allsop, J. M., Boardman, J., Rutherford, M. A., Cowan, F., & Edwards, A. D. (2006). Abnormal cortical development after premature birth shown by altered allometric scaling of brain growth. *PLoS Medicine, 3*, e265.

Kasprian, G., Brugger, P. C., Weber, M., Krssak, M., Krampl, E., Herold, C., & Prayer, D. (2008).

In utero tractography of fetal white matter development. *Neuroimage, 43*, 213–224.

Kersbergen, K. J., Leemans, A., Groenendaal, F., van der Aa, N. E., Viergever, M. A., de Vries, L. S., & Benders, M. J. (2014). Microstructural brain development between 30 and 40 week corrected age in a longitudinal cohort of extremely preterm infants. *Neuroimage, 103*, 214–224.

Kersbergen, K. J., Leroy, F., Isgum, I., Groenendaal, F., de Vries, L. S., Claessens, N. H. P., van Haastert, I. C., Moeskops, P., Fischer, C., Mangin, J. F., Viergever, M. A., Dubois, J., & Benders, M. (2016). Relation between clinical risk factors, early cortical changes, and neurodevelopmental outcome in preterm infants. *Neuroimage, 142*, 301–310.

Keunen, K., Benders, M. J., Leemans, A., Fieret-Van Stam, P. C., Scholtens, L. H., Viergever, M. A., Kahn, R. S., Groenendaal, F., de Vries, L. S., & van den Heuvel, M. P. (2017a). White matter maturation in the neonatal brain is predictive of school age cognitive capacities in children born very preterm. *Developmental Medicine & Child Neurology, 59*, 939–946.

Keunen, K., Counsell, S. J., & Benders, M. J. (2017b). The emergence of functional architecture during early brain development. *Neuroimage, 160*, 2–14.

Kinney, H. C., Brody, B. A., Kloman, A. S., & Gilles, F. H. (1988). Sequence of central nervous system myelination in human infancy. II. Patterns of myelination in autopsied infants. *Journal of Neuropathology & Experimental Neurology, 47*, 217–234.

Klyachko, V. A., & Stevens, C. F. (2003). Connectivity optimization and the positioning of cortical areas. *Proceedings of the National Academy of Sciences (USA), 100*, 7937–7941.

Knickmeyer, R. C., Gouttard, S., Kang, C., Evans, D., Wilber, K., Smith, J. K., Hamer, R. M., Lin, W., Gerig, G., & Gilmore, J. H. (2008). A structural MRI study of human brain development from birth to 2 years. *Journal of Neuroscience, 28*, 12176–12182.

Kostovic, I., & Jovanov-Milosevic, N. (2006). The development of cerebral connections during the first 20–45 weeks' gestation. *Seminars in Fetal and Neonatal Medicine, 11*, 415–422.

Kostovic, I., Jovanov-Milosevic, N., Rados, M., Sedmak, G., Benjak, V., Kostovic-Srzentic, M., Vasung, L., Culjat, M., Huppi, P., & Judas, M. (2014a). Perinatal and early postnatal reorganization of the subplate and related cellular compartments in the human cerebral wall as revealed by histological and MRI approaches. *Brain Structure and Function, 219*, 231–253.

Kostovic, I., & Judas, M. (2006). Prolonged coexistence of transient and permanent circuitry elements in the developing cerebral cortex of fetuses and preterm infants. *Developmental Medicine & Child Neurology, 48*, 388–393.

Kostovic, I., & Judas, M. (2015). Embryonic and fetal development of the human cerebral cortex. In A. W. Toga (ed.), *Brain Mapping: An Encyclopedic Reference* (Vol. 2, pp. 423–437). Cambridge, MA: Academic Press.

Kostovic, I., Kostovic-Srzentic, M., Benjak, V., Jovanov-Milosevic, N., & Rados, M. (2014b). Developmental dynamics of radial vulnerability in the cerebral compartments in preterm infants and neonates. *Frontiers in Neurology, 5*, 139.

Kostovic, I., Petanjek, Z., & Judas, M. (1993). Early areal differentiation of the human cerebral cortex: entorhinal area. *Hippocampus, 3*, 447–458.

Kostovic, I., & Rakic, P. (1990). Developmental history of the transient subplate zone in the visual and somatosensory cortex of the macaque monkey and human brain. *The Journal of Comparative Neurology, 297*, 441–470.

Kroenke, C. D., & Bayly, P. V. (2018). How forces fold the cerebral cortex. *Journal of Neuroscience, 38*, 767–775.

Krogsrud, S. K., Fjell, A. M., Tamnes, C. K., Grydeland, H., Mork, L., Due-Tonnessen, P., Bjornerud, A., Sampaio-Baptista, C., Andersson, J., Johansen-Berg, H., & Walhovd, K. B. (2015). Changes in white matter microstructure in the developing brain – A longitudinal diffusion tensor imaging study of children from 4 to 11 years of age. *Neuroimage, 124*, 473–486.

Kucharczyk, W., Macdonald, P. M., Stanisz, G. J., & Henkelman, R. M. (1994). Relaxivity and magnetization transfer of white matter lipids at MR imaging: Importance of cerebrosides and pH. *Radiology, 192*, 521–529.

Kulikova, S., Hertz-Pannier, L., Dehaene-Lambertz, G., Buzmakov, A., Poupon, C., & Dubois, J. (2015). Multi-parametric evaluation of the white matter maturation. *Brain Structure and Function, 220*, 3657–3672.

Kulikova, S., Hertz-Pannier, L., Dehaene-Lambertz, G., Poupon, C., & Dubois, J. (2016). A new strategy for fast MRI-based quantification of the myelin water fraction: Application to brain imaging in infants. *PLoS ONE, 11*, e0163143.

Kunz, N., Zhang, H., Vasung, L., O'Brien, K. R., Assaf, Y., Lazeyras, F., Alexander, D. C., & Huppi, P. S. (2014). Assessing white matter microstructure of the newborn with multi-shell diffusion MRI and biophysical compartment models. *Neuroimage, 96*, 288–299.

Kwan, K. Y., Sestan, N., & Anton, E. S. (2012). Transcriptional co-regulation of neuronal migration and laminar identity in the neocortex. *Development, 139*, 1535–1546.

LaMantia, A. S., & Rakic, P. (1990). Axon overproduction and elimination in the corpus callosum of the developing rhesus monkey. *Journal of Neuroscience, 10*, 2156–2175.

Le Guen, Y., Auzias, G., Leroy, F., Noulhiane, M., Dehaene-Lambertz, G., Duchesnay, E., Mangin, J. F., Coulon, O., & Frouin, V. (2018). Genetic influence on the sulcal pits: On the origin of the first cortical folds. *Cerebral Cortex, 28*, 1922–1933.

Lebenberg, J., Labit, M., Auzias, G., Mohlberg, H., Fischer, C., Rivière, D., Duchesnay, E., Kabdebon, C., Leroy, F., Labra, N., Poupon, F., Dickscheid, T., Hertz-Pannier, L., Poupon, C., Dehaene-Lambertz, G., Hüppi, P., Amunts, K., Dubois, J., & Mangin, J. F. (2018). A framework based on sulcal constraints to align preterm, infant and adult human brain images acquired in vivo and post mortem. *Brain Structure and Function, 223*, 4153–4168.

Lebenberg, J., Mangin, J. F., Thirion, B., Poupon, C., Hertz-Pannier, L., Leroy, F., Adibpour, P., Dehaene-Lambertz, G., & Dubois, J. (2019). Mapping the asynchrony of cortical maturation in the infant brain: A MRI multi-parametric clustering approach. *Neuroimage, 185*, 641–653.

Lebenberg, J., Poupon, C., Thirion, B., Leroy, F., Mangin, J.-F., Dehaene-Lambertz, G., & Dubois, J. (2015). Clustering the infant brain tissues based on microstructural properties and maturation assessment using multi-parametric MRI. *Paper presented at the 2015 IEEE 12th International Symposium on Biomedical Imaging (ISBI)*.

Lee, J., Birtles, D., Wattam-Bell, J., Atkinson, J., & Braddick, O. (2012). Latency measures of pattern-reversal VEP in adults and infants: Different information from transient P1 response and steady-state phase. *Investigative Ophthalmology & Visual Science, 53*, 1306–1314.

Leppert, I. R., Almli, C. R., McKinstry, R. C., Mulkern, R. V., Pierpaoli, C., Rivkin, M. J., & Pike, G. B. (2009). T(2) relaxometry of normal pediatric brain development. *Journal of Magnetic Resonance Imaging, 29*, 258–267.

Leroy, F., Glasel, H., Dubois, J., Hertz-Pannier, L., Thirion, B., Mangin, J. F., & Dehaene-Lambertz, G. (2011). Early maturation of the linguistic dorsal pathway in human infants. *Journal of Neuroscience, 31*, 1500–1506.

Li, G., Nie, J., Wang, L., Shi, F., Gilmore, J. H., Lin, W., & Shen, D. (2014). Measuring the dynamic longitudinal cortex development in infants by reconstruction of temporally consistent cortical surfaces. *Neuroimage, 90*, 266–279.

Li, G., Nie, J., Wang, L., Shi, F., Lin, W., Gilmore, J. H., & Shen, D. (2013). Mapping region-specific longitudinal cortical surface expansion from birth to 2 years of age. *Cerebral Cortex, 23*, 2724–2733.

Llinares-Benadero, C., & Borrell, V. (2019). Deconstructing cortical folding: genetic, cellular and mechanical determinants. *Nature Reviews Neuroscience, 20*, 161–176.

Lohmann, G., von Cramon, D. Y., & Colchester, A. C. (2008). Deep sulcal landmarks provide an organizing framework for human cortical folding. *Cerebral Cortex, 18*, 1415–1420.

Lyall, A. E., Shi, F., Geng, X., Woolson, S., Li, G., Wang, L., Hamer, R. M., Shen, D., & Gilmore, J. H. (2015). Dynamic development of regional cortical thickness and surface area in early childhood. *Cerebral Cortex, 25*, 2204–2212.

Maas, L. C., Mukherjee, P., Carballido-Gamio, J., Veeraraghavan, S., Miller, S. P., Partridge, S. C., Henry, R. G., Barkovich, A. J., & Vigneron, D. B. (2004). Early laminar organization of the human cerebrum demonstrated with diffusion tensor imaging in extremely premature infants. *Neuroimage, 22*, 1134–1140.

Makropoulos, A., Aljabar, P., Wright, R., Hüning, B., Merchant, N., Arichi, T., Tusor, N., Hajnal, J. V., Edwards, A. D., Counsell, S. J., & Rueckert, D. (2016). Regional growth and atlasing of the developing human brain. *Neuroimage, 125*, 456–478.

Mangin, J. F., Jouvent, E., & Cachia, A. (2010). In-vivo measurement of cortical morphology: Means and meanings. *Current Opinion in Neurology, 23*, 359–367.

Mangin, J. F., Le Guen, Y., Labra, N., Grigis, A., Frouin, V., Guevara, M., Fischer, C., Riviere, D., Hopkins, W. D., Regis, J., & Sun, Z. Y. (2019). "Plis de passage" deserve a role in models of the cortical folding process. *Brain Topography, 32*, 1035–1048.

Mangin, J. F., Lebenberg, J., Lefranc, S., Labra, N., Auzias, G., Labit, M., Guevara, M., Mohlberg, H., Roca, P., Guevara, P., Dubois, J., Leroy, F., Dehaene-Lambertz, G., Cachia, A., Dickscheid, T., Coulon, O., Poupon, C., Rivière, D., Amunts, K., & Sun, Z. Y. (2016). Spatial normalization of brain images and beyond. *Medical Image Analysis, 33*, 127–133.

Manjón, J. V., & Coupé, P. (2016). volBrain: An online MRI brain volumetry system. *Frontiers in Neuroinformatics, 10*, Article 30, 1–14.

Matsumae, M., Kurita, D., Atsumi, H., Haida, M., Sato, O., & Tsugane, R. (2001). Sequential changes in MR water proton relaxation time detect the process of rat brain myelination during maturation. *Mechanisms of Ageing and Development, 122*, 1281–1291.

Matsuzawa, J., Matsui, M., Konishi, T., Noguchi, K., Gur, R. C., Bilker, W., & Miyawaki, T. (2001). Age-related volumetric changes of brain gray and white matter in healthy infants and children. *Cerebral Cortex, 11*, 335–342.

McCart, R. J., & Henry, G. H. (1994). Visual corticogeniculate projections in the cat. *Brain Research, 653*, 351–356.

McCulloch, D. L., Orbach, H., & Skarf, B. (1999). Maturation of the pattern-reversal VEP in human infants: A theoretical framework. *Vision Research, 39*, 3673–3680.

McCulloch, D. L., & Skarf, B. (1991). Development of the human visual system: Monocular and binocular pattern VEP latency. *Investigative Ophthalmology & Visual Science, 32*, 2372–2381.

McGowan, J. C. (1999). The physical basis of magnetization transfer imaging. *Neurology, 53*, S3–S7.

McKinstry, R. C., Mathur, A., Miller, J. H., Ozcan, A., Snyder, A. Z., Schefft, G. L., Almli, C. R., Shiran, S. I., Conturo, T. E., & Neil, J. J. (2002). Radial organization of developing preterm human cerebral cortex revealed by non-invasive water diffusion anisotropy MRI. *Cerebral Cortex, 12*, 1237–1243.

Melbourne, A., Eaton-Rosen, Z., Orasanu, E., Price, D., Bainbridge, A., Cardoso, M. J., Kendall, G. S., Robertson, N. J., Marlow, N., & Ourselin, S. (2016). Longitudinal development in the preterm thalamus and posterior white matter: MRI correlations between diffusion weighted imaging and T2 relaxometry. *Human Brain Mapping, 37*, 2479–2492.

Mezer, A., Yeatman, J. D., Stikov, N., Kay, K. N., Cho, N. J., Dougherty, R. F., Perry, M. L., Parvizi, J., Hua, L. H., Butts-Pauly, K., & Wandell, B. A. (2013). Quantifying the local tissue volume and composition in individual brains with magnetic resonance imaging. *Nature Medicine, 19*, 1667–1672.

Miller, S. L., Huppi, P. S., & Mallard, C. (2016). The consequences of fetal growth restriction on brain structure and neurodevelopmental outcome. *Journal of Physiology, 594*, 807–823.

Mitter, C., Prayer, D., Brugger, P. C., Weber, M., & Kasprian, G. (2015). In vivo tractography of fetal association fibers. *PLoS ONE, 10*, e0119536.

Monson, B. B., Eaton-Rosen, Z., Kapur, K., Liebenthal, E., Brownell, A., Smyser, C. D., Rogers, C. E., Inder, T. E., Warfield, S. K., & Neil, J. J. (2018). Differential rates of perinatal maturation of human primary and nonprimary auditory cortex. *eNeuro, 5*. doi: 10.1523/ENEURO.0380-17.2017 eN-NWR-0380-17 [pii]

Mota, B., & Herculano-Houzel, S. (2015). Brain Structure. Cortical folding scales universally with surface area and thickness, not number of neurons. *Science, 349*, 74–77.

Mukherjee, P., Miller, J. H., Shimony, J. S., Conturo, T. E., Lee, B. C., Almli, C. R., & McKinstry, R. C. (2001). Normal brain maturation during childhood: Developmental trends characterized with diffusion-tensor MR imaging. *Radiology, 221*, 349–358.

Neil, J. J., Miller, J., Mukherjee, P., & Huppi, P. S. (2002). Diffusion tensor imaging of normal and injured developing human brain – A technical review. *NMR in Biomedicine, 15*, 543–552.

Neil, J. J., Shiran, S. I., McKinstry, R. C., Schefft, G. L., Snyder, A. Z., Almli, C. R., Akbudak, E., Aronovitz, J. A., Miller, J. P., Lee, B. C., & Conturo, T. E. (1998). Normal brain in human newborns: apparent diffusion coefficient and diffusion anisotropy measured by using diffusion tensor MR imaging. *Radiology, 209*, 57–66.

Ng, W. P., Cartel, N., Roder, J., Roach, A., & Lozano, A. (1996). Human central nervous system myelin inhibits neurite outgrowth. *Brain Research, 720*, 17–24.

Nossin-Manor, R., Card, D., Morris, D., Noormohamed, S., Shroff, M. M., Whyte, H. E., Taylor, M. J., & Sled, J. G. (2013). Quantitative MRI in the very preterm brain: Assessing tissue organization and myelination using magnetization transfer, diffusion tensor and T(1) imaging. *Neuroimage, 64*, 505–516.

Nossin-Manor, R., Card, D., Raybaud, C., Taylor, M. J., & Sled, J. G. (2015). Cerebral maturation in the early preterm period-A magnetization transfer and diffusion tensor imaging study using voxel-based analysis. *Neuroimage, 112*, 30–42.

O'Muircheartaigh, J., Dean, D. C., 3rd, Ginestet, C. E., Walker, L., Waskiewicz, N., Lehman, K., Dirks, H., Piryatinsky, I., & Deoni, S. C. (2014). White matter development and early cognition in babies and toddlers. *Human Brain Mapping, 35*, 4475–4487.

Ouyang, M., Dubois, J., Yu, Q., Mukherjee, P., & Huang, H. (2019). Delineation of early brain development from fetuses to infants with diffusion MRI and beyond. *Neuroimage, 185*, 836–850.

Ouyang, M., Kang, H., Detre, J. A., Roberts, T. P. L., & Huang, H. (2017a). Short-range connections in the developmental connectome during typical and atypical brain maturation. *Neuroscience & Biobehavioral Reviews, 83*, 109–122.

Ouyang, M., Liu, P., Jeon, T., Chalak, L., Heyne, R., Rollins, N. K., Licht, D. J., Detre, J. A., Roberts, T. P., Lu, H., & Huang, H. (2017b). Heterogeneous increases of regional cerebral blood flow during preterm brain development: Preliminary assessment with pseudo-continuous arterial spin labeled perfusion MRI. *Neuroimage, 147*, 233–242.

Panizzon, M. S., Fennema-Notestine, C., Eyler, L. T., Jernigan, T. L., Prom-Wormley, E., Neale, M., Jacobson, K., Lyons, M. J., Grant, M. D., Franz, C. E., Xian, H., Tsuang, M., Fischl, B., Seidman, L., Dale, A., & Kremen, W. S. (2009). Distinct genetic influences on cortical surface area and cortical thickness. *Cerebral Cortex, 19*, 2728–2735.

Partridge, S. C., Mukherjee, P., Henry, R. G., Miller, S. P., Berman, J. I., Jin, H., Lu, Y., Glenn, O. A., Ferriero, D. M., Barkovich, A. J., & Vigneron, D. B. (2004). Diffusion tensor imaging: Serial quantitation of white matter tract maturity in premature newborns. *Neuroimage, 22*, 1302–1314.

Perrot, M., Riviere, D., & Mangin, J. F. (2011). Cortical sulci recognition and spatial normalization. *Medical Image Analysis, 15*, 529–550.

Petanjek, Z., Judas, M., Simic, G., Rasin, M. R., Uylings, H. B., Rakic, P., & Kostovic, I. (2011). Extraordinary neoteny of synaptic spines in the human prefrontal cortex. *Proceedings of the National Academy of Sciences (USA)*, *108*, 13281–13286.

Petersen, S. E., & Posner, M. I. (2012). The attention system of the human brain: 20 years after. *Annual Review of Neuroscience*, *35*, 73–89.

Poduslo, S. E., & Jang, Y. (1984). Myelin development in infant brain. *Neurochemical Research*, *9*, 1615–1626.

Poh, J. S., Li, Y., Ratnarajah, N., Fortier, M. V., Chong, Y. S., Kwek, K., Saw, S. M., Gluckman, P. D., Meaney, M. J., & Qiu, A. (2015). Developmental synchrony of thalamocortical circuits in the neonatal brain. *Neuroimage*, *116*, 168–176.

Pontabry, J., Rousseau, F., Oubel, E., Studholme, C., Koob, M., & Dietemann, J. L. (2013). Probabilistic tractography using Q-ball imaging and particle filtering: Application to adult and in-utero fetal brain studies. *Medical Image Analysis*, *17*, 297–310.

Qiu, A., Fortier, M. V., Bai, J., Zhang, X., Chong, Y. S., Kwek, K., Saw, S. M., Godfrey, K., Gluckman, P. D., & Meaney, M. J. (2013). Morphology and microstructure of subcortical structures at birth: A large-scale Asian neonatal neuroimaging study. *Neuroimage*, *65*, 315–323.

Rajagopalan, V., Scott, J., Habas, P. A., Kim, K., Corbett-Detig, J., Rousseau, F., Barkovich, A. J., Glenn, O. A., & Studholme, C. (2011). Local tissue growth patterns underlying normal fetal human brain gyrification quantified in utero. *Journal of Neuroscience*, *31*, 2878–2887.

Rakic, P. (1988). Specification of cerebral cortical areas. *Science*, *241*, 170–176.

Rakic, P. (2000). Radial unit hypothesis of neocortical expansion. *Novartis Foundation Symposia*, *228*, 30–42; discussion 42–52.

Rana, S., Shishegar, R., Quezada, S., Johnston, L., Walker, D. W., & Tolcos, M. (2019). The subplate: A potential driver of cortical folding? *Cerebral Cortex*, *29*, 4697–4708.

Raznahan, A., Greenstein, D., Lee, N. R., Clasen, L. S., & Giedd, J. N. (2012). Prenatal growth in humans and postnatal brain maturation into late adolescence. *Proceedings of the National Academy of Sciences (USA)*, *109*, 11366–11371.

Raznahan, A., Shaw, P., Lalonde, F., Stockman, M., Wallace, G. L., Greenstein, D., Clasen, L., Gogtay, N., & Giedd, J. N. (2011). How does your cortex grow? *Journal of Neuroscience*, *31*, 7174–7177.

Roberts, T. P., Khan, S. Y., Blaskey, L., Dell, J., Levy, S. E., Zarnow, D. M., & Edgar, J. C. (2009). Developmental correlation of diffusion anisotropy with auditory-evoked response. *Neuroreport*, *20*, 1586–1591.

Ruoss, K., Lovblad, K., Schroth, G., Moessinger, A. C., & Fusch, C. (2001). Brain development (sulci and gyri) as assessed by early postnatal MR imaging in preterm and term newborn infants. *Neuropediatrics*, *32*, 69–74.

Salami, M., Itami, C., Tsumoto, T., & Kimura, F. (2003). Change of conduction velocity by regional myelination yields constant latency irrespective of distance between thalamus and cortex. *Proceedings of the National Academy of Sciences (USA)*, *100*, 6174–6179.

Salvan, P., Tournier, J. D., Batalle, D., Falconer, S., Chew, A., Kennea, N., Aljabar, P., Dehaene-Lambertz, G., Arichi, T., Edwards, A. D., & Counsell, S. J. (2017). Language ability in preterm children is associated with arcuate fasciculi microstructure at term. *Human Brain Mapping*, *38*, 3836–3847.

Schneider, J., Kober, T., Bickle Graz, M., Meuli, R., Huppi, P. S., Hagmann, P., & Truttmann, A. C. (2016). Evolution of T1 relaxation, ADC, and fractional anisotropy during early brain maturation: A serial imaging study on preterm infants. *AJNR American Journal of Neuroradiology*, *37*, 155–162.

Schwartz, M. L., & Goldman-Rakic, P. S. (1991). Prenatal specification of callosal connections in rhesus monkey. *The Journal of Comparative Neurology*, *307*, 144–162.

Shenkin, S. D., Starr, J. M., & Deary, I. J. (2004). Birth weight and cognitive ability in childhood: A systematic review. *Psychological Bulletin*, *130*, 989–1013.

Sigaard, R. K., Kjaer, M., & Pakkenberg, B. (2016). Development of the cell population in the brain white matter of young children. *Cerebral Cortex*, *26*, 89–95.

Silbereis, J. C., Pochareddy, S., Zhu, Y., Li, M., & Sestan, N. (2016). The cellular and molecular landscapes of the developing human central nervous system. *Neuron, 89,* 248–268.

Skeide, M. A., Brauer, J., & Friederici, A. D. (2016). Brain functional and structural predictors of language performance. *Cerebral Cortex, 26,* 2127–2139.

Smyser, T. A., Smyser, C. D., Rogers, C. E., Gillespie, S. K., Inder, T. E., & Neil, J. J. (2016). Cortical gray and adjacent white matter demonstrate synchronous maturation in very preterm infants. *Cerebral Cortex, 26,* 3370–3378.

Stikov, N., Campbell, J. S., Stroh, T., Lavelee, M., Frey, S., Novek, J., Nuara, S., Ho, M. K., Bedell, B. J., Dougherty, R. F., Leppert, I. R., Boudreau, M., Narayanan, S., Duval, T., Cohen-Adad, J., Picard, P. A., Gasecka, A., Cote, D., & Pike, G. B. (2015). In vivo histology of the myelin g-ratio with magnetic resonance imaging. *Neuroimage, 118,* 397–405.

Stiles, J., & Jernigan, T. L. (2010). The basics of brain development. *Neuropsychology Review, 20,* 327–348.

Takahashi, E., Folkerth, R. D., Galaburda, A. M., & Grant, P. E. (2012). Emerging cerebral connectivity in the human fetal brain: An MR tractography study. *Cerebral Cortex, 22,* 455–464.

Tallinen, T., Chung, J. Y., Rousseau, F., Girard, N., Lefèvre, J., & Mahadevan, L. (2016). On the growth and form of cortical convolutions. *Nature Physics, 12,* 588.

Taylor, M. J., Menzies, R., MacMillan, L. J., & Whyte, H. E. (1987). VEPs in normal full-term and premature neonates: Longitudinal versus cross-sectional data. *Electroencephalography and Clinical Neurophysiology, 68,* 20–27.

Tissier, C., Linzarini, A., Allaire-Duquette, G., Mevel, K., Poirel, N., Dollfus, S., Etard, O., Orliac, F., Peyrin, C., Charron, S., Raznahan, A., Houde, O., Borst, G., & Cachia, A. (2018). Sulcal polymorphisms of the IFC and ACC contribute to inhibitory control variability in children and adults. *eNeuro, 5.* doi: 10.1523/ENEURO.0197-17.2018

Travis, K. E., Curran, M. M., Torres, C., Leonard, M. K., Brown, T. T., Dale, A. M., Elman, J. L., & Halgren, E. (2014). Age-related changes in tissue signal properties within cortical areas important for word understanding in 12- to 19-month-old infants. *Cerebral Cortex, 24,* 1948–1955.

van den Heuvel, M. P., Kersbergen, K. J., de Reus, M. A., Keunen, K., Kahn, R. S., Groenendaal, F., de Vries, L. S., & Benders, M. J. (2015). The neonatal connectome during preterm brain development. *Cerebral Cortex, 25,* 3000–3013.

van den Heuvel, M. P., Scholtens, L. H., & Kahn, R. S. (2019). Multiscale neuroscience of psychiatric disorders. *Biological Psychiatry, 86,* 512–522.

Van der Knaap, M.S., & Valk, J. (1995a). Myelin and white matter. In M. S. Van der Knaap, & J. Valk (eds.), *Magnetic Resonance of Myelin, Myelination and Myelin Disorders* (pp. 1–17). Berlin: Springer-Verlag.

Van der Knaap, M. S., & Valk, J. (1995b). Myelination and retarded myelination. In M. S. Van der Knaap, & J. Valk (eds.), *Magnetic Resonance of Myelin, Myelination and Myelin Disorders* (pp. 37–65). Berlin: Springer-Verlag.

Vasung, L., Huang, H., Jovanov-Milosevic, N., Pletikos, M., Mori, S., & Kostovic, I. (2010). Development of axonal pathways in the human fetal fronto-limbic brain: Histochemical characterization and diffusion tensor imaging. *Journal of Anatomy, 217,* 400–417.

Vasung, L., Lepage, C., Rados, M., Pletikos, M., Goldman, J. S., Richiardi, J., Raguz, M., Fischi-Gomez, E., Karama, S., Huppi, P. S., Evans, A. C., & Kostovic, I. (2016). Quantitative and qualitative analysis of transient fetal compartments during prenatal human brain development. *Frontiers in Neuroanatomy, 10,* 11.

Vasung, L., Raguz, M., Kostovic, I., & Takahashi, E. (2017). Spatiotemporal relationship of brain pathways during human fetal development using high-angular resolution diffusion MR imaging and histology. *Frontiers in Neuroscience, 11,* 348.

Von Bonin, G. (1950). *Essay on the Cerebral Cortex.* Springfield, IL: Charles C. Thomas Publisher.

Wagstyl, K., Lepage, C., Bludau, S., Zilles, K., Fletcher, P. C., Amunts, K., & Evans, A. C. (2018). Mapping cortical laminar structure in the 3D BigBrain. *Cerebral Cortex*, *28*, 2551–2562.

Walhovd, K. B., Fjell, A. M., Brown, T. T., Kuperman, J. M., Chung, Y., Hagler, D. J., Jr., Roddey, J. C., Erhart, M., McCabe, C., Akshoomoff, N., Amaral, D. G., Bloss, C. S., Libiger, O., Schork, N. J., Darst, B. F., Casey, B. J., Chang, L., Ernst, T. M., Frazier, J., Gruen, J. R., Kaufmann, W. E., Murray, S. S., van Zijl, P., Mostofsky, S., & Dale, A. M. (2012). Long-term influence of normal variation in neonatal characteristics on human brain development. *Proceedings of the National Academy of Sciences (USA)*, *109*, 20089–20094.

Wee, C. Y., Tuan, T. A., Broekman, B. F., Ong, M. Y., Chong, Y. S., Kwek, K., Shek, L. P., Saw, S. M., Gluckman, P. D., Fortier, M. V., Meaney, M. J., & Qiu, A. (2017). Neonatal neural networks predict children behavioral profiles later in life. *Human Brain Mapping*, *38*, 1362–1373.

Welker, W. (1988). Why does cerebral cortex fissure and fold? *Cerebral Cortex*, *8B*, 3–135.

Xu, G., Takahashi, E., Folkerth, R. D., Haynes, R. L., Volpe, J. J., Grant, P. E., & Kinney, H. C. (2014). Radial coherence of diffusion tractography in the cerebral white matter of the human fetus: Neuroanatomic insights. *Cerebral Cortex*, *24*, 579–592.

Xydis, V., Astrakas, L., Zikou, A., Pantou, K., Andronikou, S., & Argyropoulou, M. I. (2006). Magnetization transfer ratio in the brain of preterm subjects: Age-related changes during the first 2 years of life. *European Radiology*, *16*, 215–220.

Yakovlev, P. I. (1962). Morphological criteria of growth and maturation of the nervous system in man. *Research Publications – Association for Research in Nervous and Mental Disease*, *39*, 3–46.

Yakovlev, P. I., & Lecours, A. R. (1967). The myelogenetic cycles of regional maturation in the brain. In A. Minowski (ed.), *Regional Development of the Brain in Early Life* (pp. 3–69). Oxford: Blackwell.

Yap, P. T., Fan, Y., Chen, Y., Gilmore, J. H., Lin, W., & Shen, D. (2011). Development trends of white matter connectivity in the first years of life. *PLoS ONE*, *6*, e24678.

Yeatman, J. D., Wandell, B. A., & Mezer, A. A. (2014). Lifespan maturation and degeneration of human brain white matter. *Nature Communications*, *5*, 4932.

Yu, Q., Ouyang, A., Chalak, L., Jeon, T., Chia, J., Mishra, V., Sivarajan, M., Jackson, G., Rollins, N., Liu, S., & Huang, H. (2017). Structural development of human fetal and preterm brain cortical plate based on population-averaged templates. *Cerebral Cortex*, *26*, 4381–4391.

Zanin, E., Ranjeva, J. P., Confort-Gouny, S., Guye, M., Denis, D., Cozzone, P. J., & Girard, N. (2011). White matter maturation of normal human fetal brain. An in vivo diffusion tensor tractography study. *Brain and Behavior*, *1*, 95–108.

Zhao, T., Xu, Y., & He, Y. (2019). Graph theoretical modeling of baby brain networks. *Neuroimage*, *185*, 711–727.

Zilles, K., Palomero-Gallagher, N., & Amunts, K. (2013). Development of cortical folding during evolution and ontogeny. *Trends in Neurosciences*, *36*, 275–284.

4 Development and Maturation of the Human Brain, from Infancy to Adolescence

Tomáš Paus

This chapter describes basic principles and key findings regarding the development and maturation of the human brain, the former referring to the pre-natal and early post-natal periods, and the latter concerning childhood and adolescence. In both cases, we focus on brain structure as revealed *in vivo* with multi-modal magnetic resonance imaging (MRI). We begin with a few numbers about the human brain and its cellular composition, and a brief overview of a number of MRI-based metrics used to characterize age-related variations in grey and white matter. We then proceed with synthesizing current knowledge about developmental and maturational changes in the cerebral cortex (its thickness, surface area and intracortical myelination), and the underlying white matter (volume and structural properties). To facilitate biological interpretations of MRI-derived metrics, we introduce the concept of virtual histology. We conclude the chapter with a few notes about future directions in the study of factors shaping the human brain from conception onwards.

4.1 General Introduction

4.1.1 Brain in Numbers

Our capacity to process information depends on the smooth functioning of neuronal networks, which consist of both neuronal and non-neuronal cells. In the cerebral cortex, the two main classes of neurons are pyramidal cells (~70 per cent of all neurons) and inter-neurons (~30 per cent) (Druga, 2009; Sloper et al., 1979). Non-neuronal cells are mostly glia, namely astrocytes (~19 per cent of all glial cells), microglia (~6 per cent) and oligodendrocytes (~75 per cent) (Pelvig et al., 2008), as well as endothelial and mural cells of the cerebral vasculature (Figure 4.1). The human brain of 1.5 kg (adult) has eighty-six billion neurons and eighty-five billion non-neuronal cells; sixteen billion neurons (sixty billion non-neuronal cells) are found in the cerebral cortex, while sixty-nine billion neurons (and sixteen billion non-neuronal cells) are in the cerebellum. Note the strikingly different ratio between the non-neuronal cells and neurons in the cerebral cortex (3.76 non-neuronal cells to one neuron) and the cerebellum (0.23 non-neuronal cells to one neuron) (Azevedo et al., 2009).

Axons – the cellular extensions of neurons carrying electrical impulses as well as various cargoes (e.g., vesicles, mitochondria) between the cell body and synapse (Paus et al., 2014) form a network that totals an astounding 176,000 km in length (adult) (Marner & Pakkenberg, 2003). The length of individual axons varies by four orders of magnitude, from micrometres (inter-neurons) to centimetres (corticospinal neurons). Schüz and Braitenberg (2002) classified axons into three different groups based on their length and location in the human brain: (1) short (<3 mm) axons within the cortex (intra-cortical

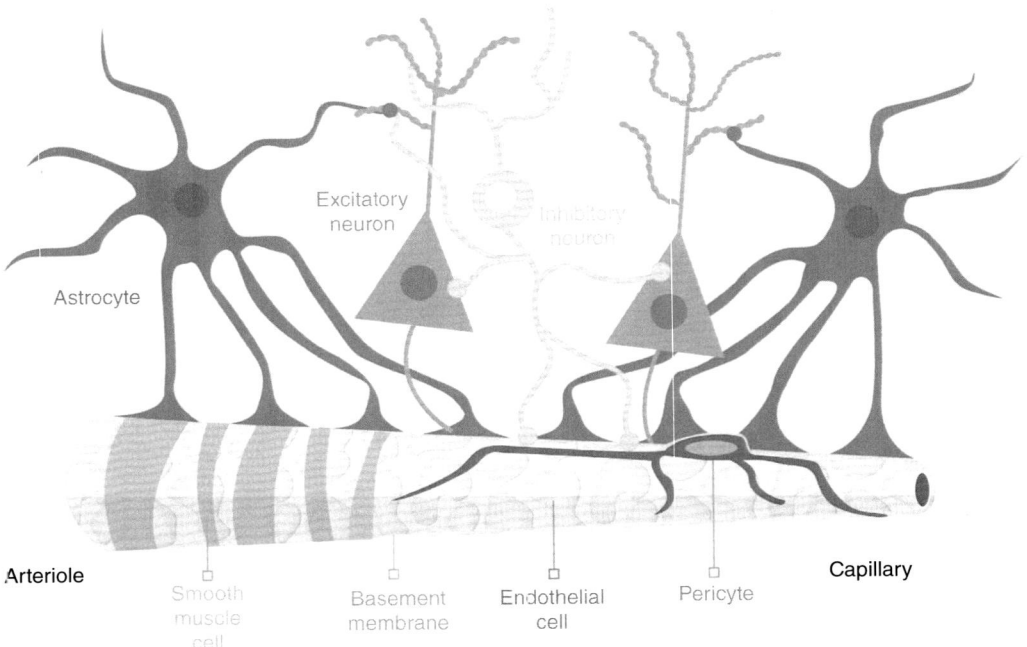

Figure 4.1 Neurovascular unit. From Hermann et al. (2015)
A black-and-white version of this figure will appear in some formats. For the colour version, please refer to the plate section.

horizontal axons); (2) longer (3–30 mm) axons in white matter adjacent to the cortex (U-fibres); and (3) very long (>30 mm) axons organized in bundles connecting different lobes within a hemisphere (e.g., longitudinal fascicles) and across hemispheres (corpus callosum). They estimated that the majority of axons are located within the short group (i.e., within the cerebral cortex), with only 4 per cent of all axons found in the very-long group containing the long-range fibre bundles (Schüz & Braitenberg, 2002). Axon diameter is related to its length, and the thickness of the myelin sheath varies with axon diameter (Paus & Toro, 2009).

Variations in the cellular composition of the cerebral cortex and those in the relative abundance of thick-or-thin and more-or-less myelinated axons affect MRI signals. We come back to the neurobiology underlying various MRI-based metrics in Section 4.3. But let us now review briefly what can be measured with MRI to capture development and maturations of the human brain.

4.1.2 Imaging the Brain

Over the past thirty+ years, MRI has become the method of choice for studying both structure and function of the human brain across the lifespan. This is due to its versatility (same scanner used for measuring a variety of brain phenotypes[1]), availability (e.g., ~ 11,000 MRI units in the United States) and the non-invasive nature of MRI technology, namely

---

[1] Phenotypes are organism's observable characteristics. Clearly, MRI allows us to observe – *in vivo* – many characteristics of the human brain that, in the past, could be observed only *post mortem*.

no exposure to ionizing radiation (not the case in Computerized Axial Tomography [CAT scan] and Positron Emission Tomography [PET scan]). The non-invasiveness makes MRI particularly suitable for research studies of brain development in the general (non-clinical) population. The majority of MRI scanners come equipped with basic hardware and software, allowing one to acquire a wide variety of brain 'images' using a particular temporal sequence of radiofrequency pulses, gradients and read-outs (a 'scan') (Moore & Chung, 2017) These scans allow one to capture different types of MR signal, which is based on electromagnetic energy emitted by precessing nuclei of hydrogen; Box 4.1 describes the basic principles of MRI and the main sources of contrast in some of the common types of images acquired in developmental studies, namely T1-weighted and T2-weighted images, Diffusion Tensor Images (DTI) and Magnetization Transfer (MT) images.

Using these images, one can derive a number of characteristics as informative with regards to normal and abnormal brain development. Thus, owing to the high contrast between grey and white matter, T1-weighted images are particularly useful for estimating – using automatic image-processing tools – the size of the cerebral cortex and its subdivisions (thickness, surface area) (Fischl & Dale, 2000) and volumes of various subcortical structures, such as the hippocampus (Pipitone et al., 2014). Quantitative estimates of T1 and T2 relaxation times provide valuable information about tissue properties of various grey-matter (e.g., cerebral cortex) and white-matter (e.g., corpus callosum) structures. Images of Myelin Water Fraction (MWF) and Magnetic Transfer Ratio (MTR) capture – in a complementary fashion – the *relative* amount of myelin in a given 3D voxel (relative to other types of tissue occupying the same voxel, such as the axon) (Bjornholm et al., 2017) . Finally,

DTI-derived estimates of mean diffusivity (MD) and fractional anisotropy (FA) reflect constraints imposed on water diffusion by the geometry (and biological properties) of cellular elements that make up a given voxel of imaged tissue. Taking advantage of this feature when modelling spatial patterns of water motion across voxels, the so-called tractography is used commonly to identify bundles of fibres (Jbabdi et al., 2015). Note that this approach works well for long-range fibres, which constitute, however, only ~4 per cent of all axons (Schüz & Braitenberg, 2002) These MRI-derived metrics provide a toolbox with which one can embark on mapping development and maturation of the human brain *in vivo*.

4.2 Development

The growth of the human cerebral cortex begins with the emergence of the ventricular (the fifth post-conception week) and subventricular (seventh post-conception week) zones (Zecevic et al., 2005). The radial unit hypothesis provides a framework for global (proliferation) and regional (distribution) expansion of the primate cerebral cortex emanating from the two zones (Figure 4.3) (Rakic, 1974)

The two most common MRI-derived metrics of the human cerebral cortex, namely the surface area and thickness, provide insights into different developmental processes, each with a different timeline. Thus, 'cortical surface area' reflects primarily the tangential growth of the cerebral cortex during prenatal development; the phase of *symmetric division of progenitor cells* in the proliferative zones during the first trimester is particularly important for the tangential growth through additions of ontogenetic columns (Rakic, 1988). The subsequent phase of *asymmetric division* continues to increase the number of ontogenetic columns (and thus surface area) but it also

Box 4.1   Principles of Magnetic Resonance Imaging (adapted from Paus (2013))

Nuclei that have an odd number of nucleons (protons and neutrons) possess both a magnetic moment and angular momentum (or spin). In the presence of an external magnetic field, such nuclei 'line up' with the main (external) magnetic field and precess (or spin) around their axis at a rate proportional to the strength of the magnetic field, emitting electromagnetic energy as they do. The hydrogen atom contains only a single proton and therefore precesses when exposed to a magnetic field.

In the majority of MR imaging studies, precessing nuclei of hydrogen associated with water and fat are the source of the signal. The signal is generated and measured in the following way. First, the person is exposed to a large static magnetic field (B_0) that aligns hydrogen nuclei along the direction of the applied field. In scanners most commonly used in research studies, the strength of B_0 is 1.5 or 3 Tesla; B_0 is oriented horizontally, pointing from head to toe along the long axis of the cylindrical magnet. Second, a pulse of electromagnetic energy is applied at a specific radiofrequency (RF), with an RF coil placed around the head. This radiofrequency is the same as the precession frequency of the imaged nuclei at a given strength of B_0. The RF pulse rotates the precessing nuclei away from their axes, thus allowing one to measure, with a receiver coil, the time it takes for the nuclei to 'relax' back to their original position pointing along B_0. The spatial origin of the signal is determined using subtle, position-related changes in B_0 induced by gradient coils (switching of the gradient coils generates the knocking noise heard during scanning).

The most common pulse sequences used to characterize brain structure are T1- and T2-weighted images, DTI and MTR. We will review these in turn (for a more detailed overview of pulse sequences, see Roberts and Mikulis (2007)).

Contrast in structural T1- and T2-weighted MR images is based on local differences in proton density (number of hydrogen nuclei per unit of tissue volume) and on the following two relaxation times: (1) longitudinal relaxation time (T1); and (2) transverse relaxation time (T2). Thus, longitudinal (T1) relaxation time represents an exponential recovery of the total magnetization over time. In a complex manner, it depends on the local structural pattern (lattice: an array of points repeating periodically in three dimensions) assumed by the hydrogen nuclei; in the brain, the more structured the tissue, the shorter T1. Transverse (T2) reflects the local 'dephasing' rate for precessing nuclei due to local magnetic-field non-homogeneities, with a concomitant decay of the total MR signal; in the brain, the more structured the tissues, the more rapid the de-phasing and hence the shorter the T2. Relaxation times, and therefore tissue 'brightness' on T1- and T2-weighted images, depend on a variety of biological and structural properties of the brain tissue. Water content is one of the most important influences on T1 in the brain: the more water there is in a given tissue compartment, the longer T1 – and the lower the signal on a T1-weighted image – will be in that compartment. In the adult brain, T1 is the longest in cerebrospinal fluid, intermediate in grey matter and the shortest in white matter. Lipid content in white matter may also influence T1, through magnetic interactions with hydrogen nuclei of the lipids, which are hydrophobic. Iron content is another important influence, primarily by changing local magnetic non-homogeneities: the higher the iron content, the shorter the T2. Finally, the anatomical arrangement of axons may influence the amount of interstitial water and, in turn, T1 values; more tightly bundled axons would have shorter T1 and therefore appear brighter on T1-weighted images.

The introduction of diffusion tensor imaging (DTI) in the mid-1990s opened up new avenues for *in vivo* studies of white-matter microstructure (Le Bihan, 1995). This imaging technique allows one to estimate several parameters of water diffusion, such as mean diffusivity (MD) and fractional anisotropy (FA). The latter parameter reflects the degree of water-diffusion directionality; voxels containing water that moves predominantly along a single direction have higher FA. In white matter, FA is believed to depend on structural properties of fibre tracts, including the relative alignment of individual axons, how tightly they are packed (which affects the amount of interstitial water), myelin content and axon diameter.

Finally, magnetization-transfer (MT) imaging is another MR technique employed in studies of the structural properties of white matter. Contrast in MT images reflects the interaction between free water and water bound to macromolecules (McGowan, 1999). The macromolecules of myelin are the dominant source of the MT signal in white matter (Kucharczyk et al., 1994). Post-mortem studies revealed a significant positive correlation between myelin content and MTR (Schmierer et al., 2004, 2008).

The fastest way to acquire magnetization-transfer data is to use a dual acquisition, with and without a MT saturation pulse. MTR images are calculated as the percentage signal-change between the two acquisitions (Pike, 1996). Mean MTR values, subsequently, can be summed across all white-matter voxels constituting, for example, the four lobes of the brain.

Multi-modal imaging of brain structure, that is a combination of multiple 'scans' of the person's brain during a single session, is particularly helpful for deriving multiple brain phenotypes and triangulating their neurobiological underpinnings. Figure 4.2 shows a particular example of such a multi-modal protocol, as employed in one of our population-based studies of the human brain (Bjornholm et al., 2017).

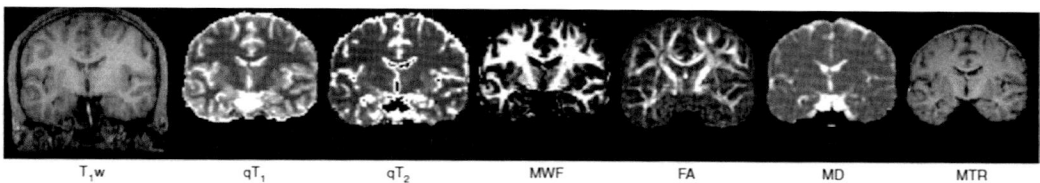

T₁w   qT₁   qT₂   MWF   FA   MD   MTR

Figure 4.2 Coronal slices of multimodal images of brain structure acquired in members of a birth cohort when they reached twenty years of age. T_1W, T1-weighted image; qT_1, T1 relaxation time; qT_2, T2 relaxation time; MWF, Myelin Water Fraction; FA, Fractional Anisotropy; MD, Mean Diffusivity; MTR, Magnetization Transfer Ratio. From Lerch et al. (2017)

begins to contribute to the 'thickness of the cerebral cortex' formed by post-mitotic neurons migrating from the proliferative zones to the cortical plate in the inside-out manner (Rakic, 1988). Ionizing radiation of the (monkey) foetus during early gestation reduces surface area (sparing cortical thickness) while the same radiation applied in midgestation affects both the surface area and cortical thickness (Selemon et al., 2013). As will be shown in the following paragraphs, the surface area remains stable after early childhood, while cortical thickness continues to change during adolescence (and beyond).

At birth, the human brain has reached ~420 cm³ in volume (~36 per cent of adult value) (Knickmeyer et al., 2008). Post-natal growth is particularly rapid during the first two years: the brain volume doubles by the end of the first year (855 cm³; 72 per cent of

adult value) and increases further to reach 83 per cent (983 cm³) of adult values by the end of the second year (Knickmeyer et al., 2008). In mammals, the cerebral cortex represents the majority of brain tissue; with its cortical grey and white matter combined, the mass of the cerebral cortex constitutes 82 per cent of the total brain mass in humans (Herculano-Houzel, 2009). Not surprisingly, there is a tight relationship between the brain volume and surface area of the cerebral cortex ($r^2 \sim 0.7$) (Toro et al., 2008). Gilmore and colleagues provided estimates of age-related changes in the volumes of grey and white matter during foetal development, as well as those in the surface area and thickness of the cerebral cortex after birth (Figure 4.4) (Gilmore et al., 2018).

The most dramatic tangential growth of the cerebral cortex (i.e., increase in surface area) takes place during the first two post-natal

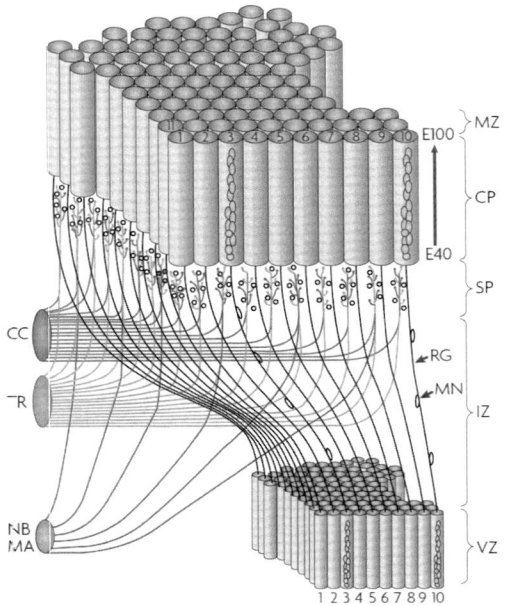

Figure 4.3 The radial unit hypothesis. 'The model of radial neuronal migration that underlies columnar organization based on Rakic (1974, 1995). The cohorts of neurons generated in the VZ traverse the intermediate zone (IZ) and subplate zone (SP) containing "waiting" afferents from several sources (cortico–cortical connections (CC), thalamic radiation (TR), nucleus basalis (NB), monoamine subcortical centres (MA)) and finally pass through the earlier generated deep layers before settling in at the interface between the cortical plate (CP) and marginal zone (MZ). The timing of neurogenesis (E40–E100) refers to the embryonic age in the macaque monkey (Bystron et al., 2006; Rakic, 1974, 1988). (The positional information of the neurons in the VZ and corresponding protomap within the SP and CP is preserved during cortical expansion by transient radial glial scaffolding. Further details can be viewed in the Rakic laboratory animated video of radial migration. RG, radial glia cell; MN, migrating neuron'. Legend to Figure 3 in Rakic (2009)

A black-and-white version of this figure will appear in some formats. For the colour version, please refer to the plate section.

years; cortical thickness appears to increase the most during the first year and continues to change (decrease) during adolescence (see Section 4.3). Note, however, that estimating thickness during the first year of life is quite challenging given the switch of relaxation time in grey and white matter at some point in this period (possibly due to decreases in water content in both tissue compartments) (Paus et al., 2001).

The robust growth of the cerebral cortex during the first two years of life is mirrored in age-related changes in white matter. As one would expect, the steep increases in white-matter volume during the first two years of life (Matsuzawa et al., 2001) are accompanied by changes in structural properties of white matter, as estimated using some of the MRI techniques shown in Figure 4.2. As reviewed recently by Lebel and Deoni (2018), most of these (and similar) metrics show a steep change during this period (Figure 4.5).

Zooming onto one of the metrics, namely Myelin Water Fraction (MWF), an index of myelin content, we can appreciate the steep increase in this parameter across various compartments of white matter in the infant brain (Figure 4.6). The rate of change in MWF appears to peak during the first two years of life across all regions examined in this study, with some subtle differences between the four cerebral lobes and virtually no differences across the corpus callosum (genu, body and splenium) (Dean et al., 2015). Although myelination is likely to be one of the main factors driving age-related changes in structural properties of white matter, illustrated in Figures 4.5 and 4.6, the complexity of the underlying neurobiology prevents one to draw such categorical conclusions based on observational data only.

To summarize, the human brain develops at a fast pace during the first three post-conception years. This is reflected in particular in the exponential increase of the surface area of the

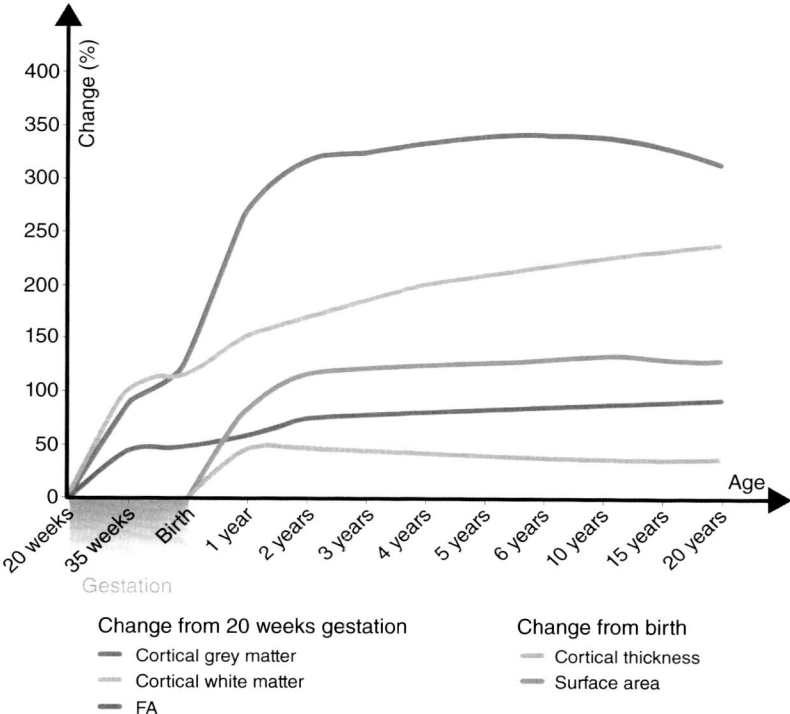

Figure 4.4 Estimated trajectories of cortical grey-matter and white-matter volumes during prenatal development, and cortical surface-area and thickness in post-natal development. From Gilmore et al. (2018)
A black-and-white version of this figure will appear in some formats. For the colour version, please refer to the plate section.

cerebral cortex and the volume of white matter, the latter tissue compartment including mostly axons either originating or terminating in the cerebral cortex. During the same (post-natal) period, there is also a dramatic change in the structural properties of white matter that, in part, reflect the initial wave of myelination. Thus, to put it simply, *development* of the human brain is completed by two-to-three years of age, but its *maturation* continues.

4.3 Maturation

After the phase of rapid growth described in Section 4.2, the brain continues to change throughout childhood and adolescence (and

beyond). As we will see, these age-related *maturational* changes are gradual and rather subtle. This picture changes somewhat during puberty and adolescence.[2]

4.3.1 Grey Matter

Figure 4.7 illustrates the gradual change in whole-brain (absolute) volumes of grey and

---

[2] As defined by Sisk and Foster, '... puberty refers to the activation of the hypothalamus–pituitary–gonadal axis that culminates in gonadal maturation. Adolescence refers to the maturation of adult social and cognitive behaviors' (Sisk & Foster, 2004, p. 1040).

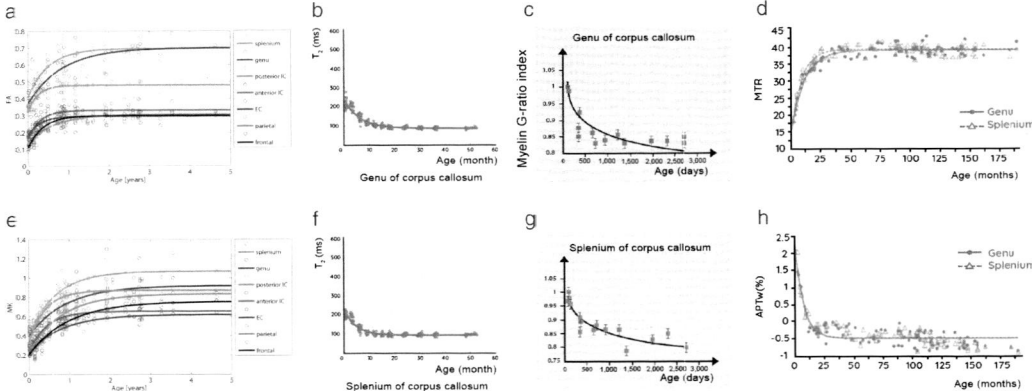

Figure 4.5 Developmental trajectories of structural properties of white matter during infancy and early childhood, as revealed with multi-modal MRI. Note different units (days, months, years) and ranges on the *x*-axis of the individual plots. DTI, Diffusion Tensor Imaging; DKI, Diffusion Kurtosis Imaging (a and e); T2 Relaxometry (b and f), g-ratio (c and g), MTR, Magnetization Transfer Ratio; APT, Amide Proton Transfer (d and h). From Lebel and Deoni (2018)
A black-and-white version of this figure will appear in some formats. For the colour version, please refer to the plate section.

white matter using cross-sectional data acquired in the NIH-PD project (Brain Development Cooperative Group, 2012). On average (based on table 4 in Brain Development Cooperative Group, 2012), volumes of grey matter in the brains of pre-pubertal children (four-to-ten years of age) were somewhat larger (by ~10 per cent), while volumes of white matter were slightly smaller (by ~10 per cent) as compared with the volumes obtained in seventeen-to-eighteen year old participants. Contrast this growth rate (~10 per cent over ten years) with that during early post-natal development (~100 per cent over two years; Figure 4.4).

When it comes to age-related changes in grey matter of the cerebral cortex, the initial report by Giedd and colleagues suggested a non-linear trajectory between four and eighteen years of age, with the cortical volumes increasing to about ten-to-twelve years of age (frontal and parietal lobes), and then gradually decreasing (Giedd et al., 1999). But no such non-linear age curves have been observed in subsequent reports of cortical volumes, including the first (cross-sectional) analysis of data acquired in the NIH-PD study discussed (Brain Development Cooperative Group, 2012). Global and regional volumes of grey matter of the cerebral cortex are the product of surface area and cortical thickness. Based on a combination of cross-sectional and longitudinal data from the NIHD-PD Study (753 scans, one-to-three per scans per participant), cortical thickness decreases between five and twenty years of age in a linear fashion (Figure 4.8) (Ducharme et al., 2016); this observation has been confirmed in other datasets and re-analyses (Walhovd et al., 2017). One possible explanation of discrepancies between the early and subsequent reports may be the influence of artefacts related to head movement during scanning (more common in younger subjects); non-linear trajectories were observed only if scans with such

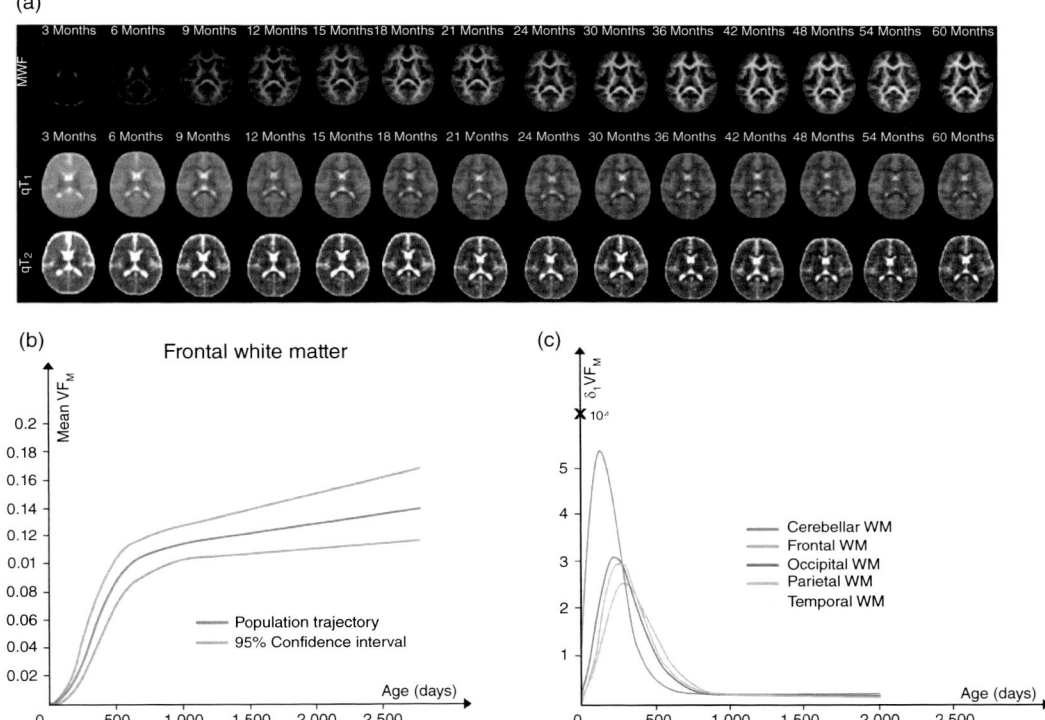

Figure 4.6 Myelin water fraction (MWF) and relaxation times in the developing brain. (a) Parametric images of MWF, T1 and T2 relaxation times during infancy and early childhood (from 3 to 60 months); (b) Mean values of MWF (denoted as VF_M on the y-axis) as a function of age in white matter of the frontal lobe; (c) Curves of the growth rate (denoted as $\delta_1 VF_M$ on the y-axis) in MWF in white matter of the four cerebral lobes and in the cerebellum. WM, White Matter. (a) from Lebel and Deoni (2018); (b) and (c) from Dean et al. (2015)
A black-and-white version of this figure will appear in some formats. For the colour version, please refer to the plate section.

artefacts were not excluded from the analysis (Ducharme et al., 2016).

Let us now review briefly maturational changes in the adolescent cerebral cortex. Using cross-sectional data from the Saguenay Youth Study (Pausova et al., 2007, 2017), we can see age-related decreases in cortical thickness, which appear to be more pronounced in male versus female adolescents (Figure 4.9, top); note that, in the same individuals, the surface area does not vary with age (Figure 4.9, bottom).

4.3.1.1 Virtual Histology of the Human Cerebral Cortex

Since the initial reports in the late 1990s (Giedd et al., 1999), neurobiological interpretations of age-related decreases in the cortical grey-matter have varied from stressing 'synaptic pruning' (Giedd et al., 1999) to emphasizing intra-cortical myelination· (Gogtay et al., 2004; Paus, 2005). To address the gap between *in vivo* (MRI) and *ex vivo* (histology) observations (Paus, 2018), we have recently developed a 'virtual histology' approach aimed at

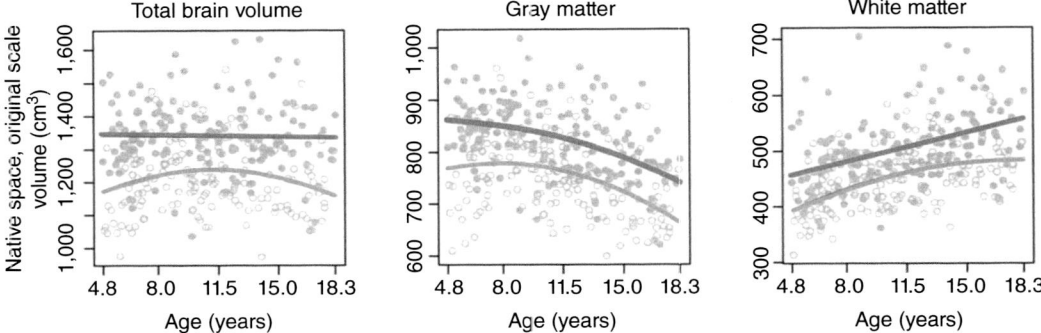

Figure 4.7 Total brain volume, as well as whole-brain (absolute) volumes of grey- and white-matter, derived from a combination of T1-weighted, T2-weighted and Proton Density-weighted images obtained in the NIH Paediatric Study. Cross-sectional age curves are indicated in blue (males) and red (females). In all three plots, the y-axis does not start at 0 cm^3; the differences between the youngest (five years of age) and oldest (eighteen years of age) do not exceed 10 per cent. From the Brain Development Cooperative Group (2012)

A black-and-white version of this figure will appear in scme formats. For the colour version, please refer to the plate section.

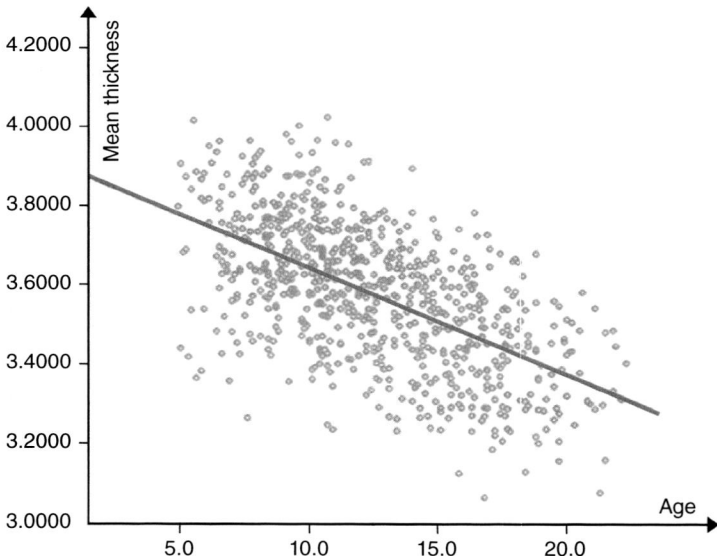

Figure 4.8 Decrease in cortical thickness between ten and twenty years of age. From Ducharme et al. (2016)

A black-and-white version of this figure will appear in some formats. For the colour version, please refer to the plate section.

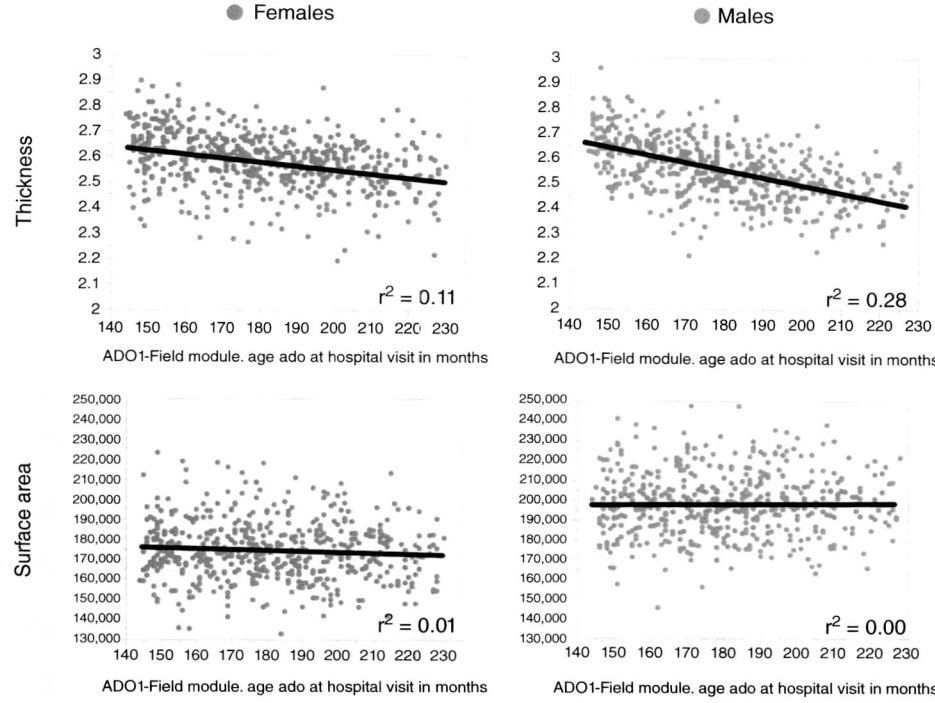

Figure 4.9 Cortical thickness and surface area in female (n = 509) and male (n = 479) adolescents. Data from the Saguenay Youth Study (Pausova et al., 2017)
A black-and-white version of this figure will appear in some formats. For the colour version, please refer to the plate section.

estimating cellular contributions to inter-regional variations in various MRI-derived metrics across the human cerebral cortex (Shin et al., 2018). Using this approach, we ask which of the cell types found in the cerebral cortex explains best inter-regional variations of a metric of interest, such as cortical thickness or age-related cortical thinning. We do so by comparing the profile of a given MRI-derived metric with profiles of cell-specific gene expression across the same cortical regions. To do so, we first extracted gene-expression data from the Allen Human Brain Atlas (Hawrylycz et al., 2012) and estimated the mean values of gene expression for each of thirty-four cortical regions segmented by FreeSurfer per hemisphere (French & Paus,

2015). Using a two-stage procedure, we identified genes with consistent inter-regional profiles of their expression (2,511 out of the total of 20,737 genes passed this filter). From these 'consistent' genes, we selected cell type-specific genes as markers of nine types of cells, namely pyramidal neurons, interneurons, astrocytes, microglia, oligodendrocytes, ependymal, endothelial and mural (pericytes and vascular smooth muscle cells) cells; these cell-specific marker-genes were identified (in the mouse brain) by others using single-cell transcriptomes (Zeisel et al., 2015). Finally, *across* the thirty-four 'FreeSurfer' regions of the left hemisphere (Desikan-Killiany atlas), we related expression profiles of these cell-specific markers to those in cortical thickness measured with

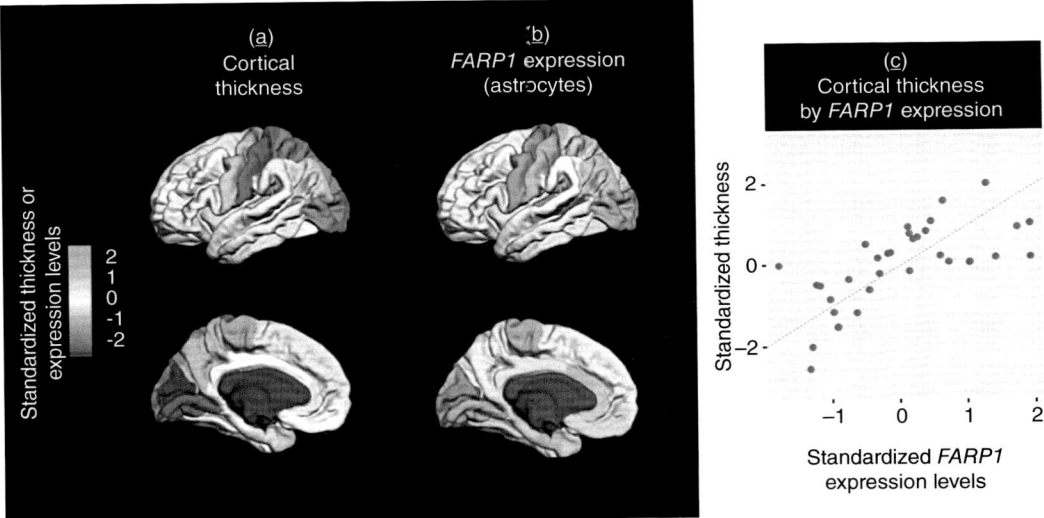

Figure 4.10 Virtual histology. Lateral (first row) and medial (second row) views of cortical thickness (Saguenay Youth Study) and gene expression levels (the Allen Human Brain Atlas). (a) Distribution of the standardized average cortical thickness measurements across the thirty-four cortical regions obtained from 981 SYS adolescents; (b) Distribution of the standardized median gene-expression level for *FARP1* (obtained from the Allen Human Brain Atlas); (c) Cortical thickness in the thirty-four cortical regions plotted as a function of *FARP1* expression in the same regions. The ranges of the standardized thickness values and expression levels are indicated by the colour-scale bar on the left. From Paus (2018)
A black-and-white version of this figure will appear in some formats. For the colour version, please refer to the plate section.

MRI in the same set of regions in 987 adolescents. Figure 4.10 illustrates this approach by showing inter-regional variations in cortical thickness (left) and expression of *FARP1*, one of fifty-four gene markers of astrocytes (middle), and their correlation across the thirty-four cortical regions (right).

In our first study using this approach, we determined that inter-regional profiles of cortical thickness (in the adolescent brain) are related to the expression profiles of three cell types, namely astrocytes, microglia and (CA1) pyramidal cells, but not to any other cell type; altogether, the three cell types explained about 70 per cent of variance in inter-regional differences in cortical thickness (Shin et al., 2018). Furthermore, we observed that the same three

cell types also contribute to inter-regional variations in cortical thinning during adolescence; in male adolescents only, we have also observed a contribution of oligodendrocytes to the inter-regional profile of cortical thinning (Shin et al., 2018). In a follow-up study, we used the same approach to identify the cellular substrate of cross-sectional and longitudinal profiles of magnetization transfer ratio (MTR), a scan sensitive to the relative density of macromolecules (including myelin) in the sampled tissue (Henkelman et al., 2001). We found that CA1 pyramidal cells and ependymal cells explain the cross-sectional profiles of MTR in the cerebral cortex, while oligodendrocytes matched closely the longitudinal profiles of the same MRI-derived metric (Patel et al., 2019). Taking these two studies together, we speculate that cortical thickness is dominated by dendritic arborization while cortical thinning during adolescence reflects intra-cortical myelination (which makes grey matter less 'grey'), the latter consistent with the results obtained in another study (Whitaker et al., 2016).

To summarize, during childhood and adolescence, the key age-related variations in the human cerebral cortex include those in its thickness and structural properties (rather than its surface area, as seen during infancy). Studies with virtual histology suggest that inter-regional variations and thickness and thinning during adolescence are best explained by parallel variations in pyramidal cells, astrocytes and microglia. It is likely, but not proven, that these cells drive the dynamics in dendritic arborization. Finally, it is now clear that intra-cortical myelination contributes to the pattern of cortical thinning during adolescence, as well as to the age-related changes in the structural properties captured with multimodal MRI of the cerebral cortex during this developmental period.

4.3.2 White Matter

As seen in Figure 4.7, the overall volume of white matter continues to increase during childhood and adolescence (by ~10 per cent). Structural properties of white-matter fibre tracts also continue to change during this period; for example, FA in fibre tracts increases by ~20 per cent between five and twenty-five years of age (Figure 4.11).

During adolescence, the volume of white matter increases more steeply in males as compared with females (Figure 4.12). In male adolescents, this change is at least in part driven by the increasing levels of testosterone; adolescents with a more (versus less) 'efficient' variant of the androgen-receptor gene show a stronger relationship between circulating levels of bioavailable testosterone and white-matter volume (Perrin et al., 2008).

Given the parallel *decrease* in MTR values in white matter during male adolescence, we interpreted these findings as reflecting the radial growth of the axon (i.e., an increase in axon diameter) rather than myelination (Perrin et al., 2008). This interpretation was confirmed in a follow-up study in rats where we revealed, with electron microscopy, sex differences in axon diameter (M>F); these sex differences were eliminated by castration (after weaning) (Pesaresi et al., 2015).

Axons of larger diameter contain a higher number of microtubules, a key component of the axonal cytoskeleton important for axonal transport (Paus et al., 2014). In an *in vitro* experiment, we showed that adding synthetic testosterone to a tissue culture of sympathetic neurons increases axon diameter and – most importantly – modulates anterograde transport of vesicles (Pesaresi et al., 2015).

Axon diameter appears to be an important contributor to MR signals in white matter. As compared with adjacent white matter, fibre tracts containing large-diameter (long) (Paus & Toro, 2009) axons, such as the cortico-spinal tract, have lower intensity on T1-weighted images (Herve et al., 2009; Pangelinan et al., 2016), as well as longer T1 and T2 relaxation times and lower MTR (Herve et al., 2011). Across the corpus callosum (anterior to posterior), variations in the relative density of large and small fibres (established by histology) are tracked almost perfectly by T1 and T2 relaxation times and the values of Myelin Water Fraction (MWF) but less so by FA and MD (Figure 4.13) (Bjornholm et al., 2017), thus emphasizing the importance of multi-modal imaging for the interpretations of MRI data.

To summarize, both the volume and structural properties of white matter continue to change during childhood and adolescence.

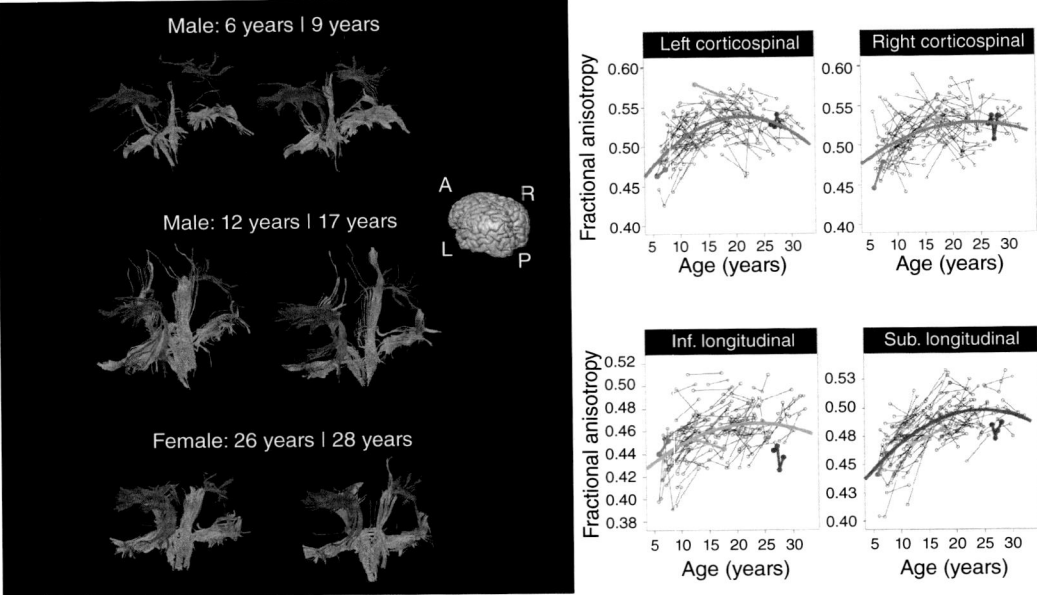

Figure 4.11 'Individual tractography results for the superior longitudinal fasciculus (orange), inferior longitudinal fasciculus (magenta), and corticospinal tracts (green) are shown in three representative healthy individuals at different ages. The whole dataset is shown in scatterplots at right, with data from the individuals shown at left identified in colour. The scatter plots show later maturation in the superior longitudinal fasciculus compared to the other regions. Ages of peak FA values were twenty-one and twenty-three years for the left and right corticospinal tracts, and twenty-four and twenty-five years for the inferior and superior longitudinal fasciculi, respectively.' Legend to Figure 5 in Lebel and Deoni (2018)

A black-and-white version of this figure will appear in some formats. For the colour version, please refer to the plate section.

Testosterone exerts a strong influence on the axon during male adolescence, influencing both its structure (radial growth) and function (axonal transport).

4.4 Future Directions

In 1989, the Child Psychiatry Branch of the National Institute of Mental Health (USA) initiated the first systematic MRI-based study of brain development during childhood and adolescence (Giedd et al., 2015). Over the last thirty years, other groups have established a number of population-based cohorts, with sample sizes exceeding 1,000 individuals, including the Saguenay Youth Study (Pausova et al., 2007), IMAGEN (Schumann et al., 2010), Generation R (White et al., 2013), the Philadelphia Neurodevelopmental Cohort (Satterthwaite et al., 2014) and the Paediatric Imaging, Neurocognition and Genetics (PING) Study (Jernigan et al., 2016). These efforts continue, with the latest addition being the Adolescent Brain Cognitive Development (ABCD) study that has recruited over 11,000 children (nine-to-ten years old) to participate in longitudinal assessments of their brains and behaviour throughout adolescence (Garavan et al., 2018). These observational datasets will continue generating new knowledge about

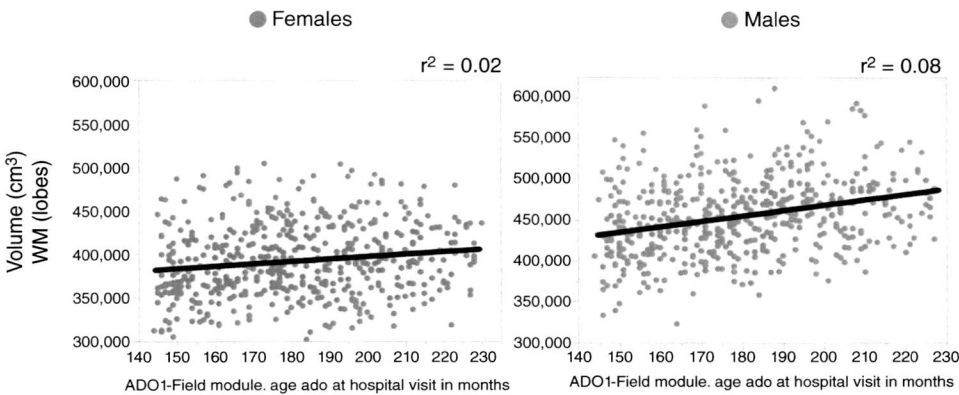

Figure 4.12 Volume of white matter (cerebral lobes) in female (n = 509) and male (n = 476) adolescents. Data from the Saguenay Youth Study (Pausova et al., 2017)

A black-and-white version of this figure will appear in some formats. For the colour version, please refer to the plate section.

forces shaping the brains of (mostly) typically developing children and adolescents. Where do we go from here?

First, I would argue for establishing large (n > 1,000) population-based cohorts over-sampled for children and adolescents who have been *exposed to a well-recognized risk* vis-à-vis early brain development. Longitudinal follow-up of these individuals would provide valuable information about factors modifying their developmental trajectories, both in negative (vulnerability) and positive (resilience) manners.

Second, we need to enhance assessment of the *environment* surrounding participants in our studies throughout their lives. The developing human being is under a myriad of influences related to his/her physical environment (e.g., air, trees), built environment (e.g., transportation) and, most importantly, social environment (family, peers, neighbours) (Ruiz Jdel et al., 2016). There are a growing number of examples whereby data science in general, and 'population informatics' in particular (Kum et al., 2014), show the power of extracting information about social and built

environment from various digital sources (e.g., satellite images, social media, patterns of mobile-phone use) and relating it to phenomena such as brain maturation (Parker et al., 2017), wellbeing (Kardan et al., 2015), obesity (Maharana & Okanyene Nsoesie, 2018), health (Abnousi et al., 2018) and social relationships (David-Barrett et al., 2016; Gruzd & Haythornthwaite, 2013). Twitter-based studies of social behaviour include, for example, a cyclic nature of coordinated social activity (Morales et al., 2017) or public attention and temporal patterns of tweets on specific social issues (Peng et al., 2017). To start, such information – mapped in space and time – can be considered at an aggregate level (e.g., neighbourhood, census tract) and related to the individual member of a cohort through a geospatial information system (Paus, 2016).

Third, there is a great desire to uncover *causal* influences shaping the developing brain. But observational studies do not allow for causal inferences to be made, although the use of Mendelian randomization (Davey-Smith & Hemani, 2014) has become a method of choice in this context. Some would argue that the

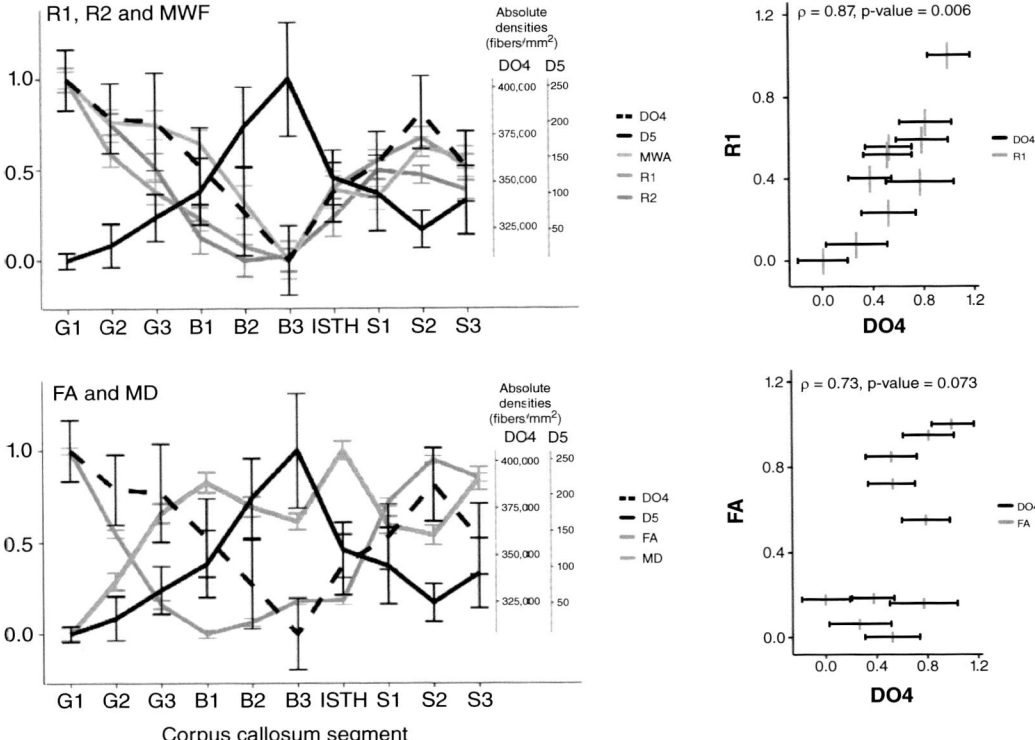

Figure 4.13 Multimodal imaging of the human corpus callosum: a comparison with histology. Left: Anterior–posterior profiles of callosal mid-sagittal histology (black; histological data are from Aboitiz et al. (1992)) and MRI measures (colour) with 95 per cent confidence intervals. All values were scaled to 0–1. Original absolute densities for 'small' (D04 for d > 0.4 μm) and 'large' (D5 for d > 5 μm) axons are shown on the right side of the plots. R1 and R2 (relaxation rate 1 and 2), MWF (myelin-water fraction), FA (fractional anisotropy) and MD (mean diffusivity). Right: Spearman correlations between R1 (top) and FA (bottom) and the density of 'small' axons. G1–G3, segments of the genu; B1–B3, segments of the body; ISTH, Isthmus; S1–S3, segments of the splenium. From Paus (2018) modified from Bjornholm et al. (2017).

A black-and-white version of this figure will appear in some formats. For the colour version, please refer to the plate section.

ultimate test of a hypothesis is an experiment. In studies of human development, interventions represent unique opportunities for examining causal effects of a variety of influences tested by randomizing individuals (or groups of individuals) into 'experimental' and 'control' arms and measuring outcomes before and after the intervention (see Houdé et al., 2000 for a seminal example using brain imaging in a reasoning task, before and after training). Randomized control trials and quasi-experimental designs have been used, for example, to evaluate the effects of breasfeeding on cognitive development (Kramer et al., 2008) or the effectiveness of various psycho-social interventions on mental health in children and adolescents (Sandler et al., 2014). Incorporating state-of-the-art assessment of brain and behaviour in future interventions has the potential to provide insights relevant for understanding brain development as well as mechanisms underlying the success (or failure) of a given intervention.

References

Abnousi, F., Krumholz, H. M., & Rumsfeld, J. S. (2018). Social determinants of health in the digital age: Determining the source code for nurture. *JAMA*, *321*, 247–248.

Aboitiz, F., Scheibel, A. B., Fisher, R. S., & Zaidel, E. (1992). Fiber composition of the human corpus callosum. *Brain Research*, *598*, 143–153.

Azevedo, F. A., Carvalho, L. R., Grinberg, L. T., et al. (2009). Equal numbers of neuronal and nonneuronal cells make the human brain an isometrically scaled-up primate brain. *The Journal of Comparative Neurology*, *513*, 532–541.

Bjornholm, L., Nikkinen, J., Kiviniemi, V., et al. (2017). Structural properties of the human corpus callosum: Multimodal assessment and sex differences. *Neuroimage*, *152*, 108–118.

Brain Development Cooperative Group (2012). Total and regional brain volumes in a population-based normative sample from 4 to 18 years: The NIH MRI Study of Normal Brain Development. *Cerebral Cortex*, *22*, 1–12.

Bystron, I., Blakemore, C., Rakic, P., & Molnar Z. (2006). The first neurons of the human cerebral cortex. *Nature Neuroscience*, *9*, 880–886.

Davey-Smith, G., & Hemani, G. (2014). Mendelian randomization: Genetic anchors for causal inference in epidemiological studies. *Human Molecular Genetics*, *23*, R89–R98.

David-Barrett, T., Kertesz, J., Rotkirch, A., et al. (2016). Communication with family and friends across the life course. *PLoS ONE*, *11*, e0165687.

Dean, D. C., 3rd, O'Muircheartaigh, J., Dirks, H., et al. (2015). Characterizing longitudinal white matter development during early childhood. *Brain Structure and Function*, *220*, 1921–1933.

Druga, R. (2009). Neocortical inhibitory system. *Folia Biologica*, *55*, 201–17.

Ducharme, S., Albaugh, M. D., Nguyen, T. V., et al. (2016). Trajectories of cortical thickness maturation in normal brain development – The importance of quality control procedures. *Neuroimage*, *125*, 267.

Fischl, B., & Dale, A. M. (2000). Measuring the thickness of the human cerebral cortex from magnetic resonance images. *Proceedings of the National Academy of Sciences (USA)*, *97*, 11050–11055.

French, L., & Paus, T. A. (2015). FreeSurfer view of the cortical transcriptome generated from the Allen Human Brain Atlas. *Frontiers in Neuroscience*, *9*, 323.

Garavan, H., Bartsch, H., Conway, K., et al. (2018). Recruiting the ABCD sample: Design considerations and procedures. *Developmental Cognitive Neuroscience*, *32*, 16–22.

Giedd, J. N., Blumenthal, J., Jeffries, N. O., et al. (1999). Brain development during childhood and adolescence: A longitudinal MRI study. *Nature Neuroscience*, *2*, 861–863.

Giedd, J. N., Raznahan, A., Alexander-Bloch, A., et al. (2015). Child psychiatry branch of the National Institute of Mental Health longitudinal structural magnetic resonance imaging study of human brain development. *Neuropsychopharmacology*, *40*, 43–49.

Gilmore, J. H., Knickmeyer, R. C., & Gao, W. (2018). Imaging structural and functional brain development in early childhood. *Nature Reviews Neuroscience*, *19*, 123–137.

Gogtay, N., Giedd, J. N., Lusk, L., et al. (2004). Dynamic mapping of human cortical development during childhood through early adulthood. *Proceedings of the National Academy of Sciences (USA)*, *101*, 8174–8179.

Gruzd, A., & Haythornthwaite, C. (2013). Enabling community through social media. *Journal of Medical Internet Research*, *15*, e248.

Hawrylycz, M. J., Lein, E. S., Guillozet-Bongaarts, A. L., et al. (2012). An anatomically comprehensive atlas of the adult human brain transcriptome. *Nature*, *489*, 391–399.

Henkelman, R. M., Stanisz, G. J., & Graham, S. J. (2001). Magnetization transfer in MRI: A review. *NMR in Biomedicine*, *14*, 57–64.

Herculano-Houzel, S. (2009). The human brain in numbers: A linearly scaled-up primate brain. *Frontiers in Human Neuroscience, 3,* 31.

Hermann, D. M., Buga, A. M., & Popa-Wagner, A. (2015). Neurovascular remodeling in the aged ischemic brain. *Journal of Neural Transmission (Vienna), 122*(Suppl 1), S25–S33.

Herve, P. Y., Cox, E. F., Lotfipour, A. K., et al. (2011). Structural properties of the corticospinal tract in the human brain: A magnetic resonance imaging study at 7 Tesla. *Brain Structure and Function, 216,* 255–262.

Herve, P. Y., Leonard, G., Perron, M., et al. (2009). Handedness, motor skills and maturation of the corticospinal tract in the adolescent brain. *Human Brain Mapping, 30,* 3151–3162.

Houdé, O., Zago, L., Mellet, E., et al. (2000). Shifting from the perceptual brain to the logical brain: The neural impact of cognitive inhibition training. *Journal of Cognitive Neuroscience, 12,* 721–728.

Jbabdi, S., Sotiropoulos, S. N., Haber, S. N., Van-Essen, D. C., & Behrens, T. E. (2015). Measuring macroscopic brain connections in vivo. *Nature Neuroscience, 18,* 1546–1555.

Jernigan, T. L., Brown, T. T., Hagler, D. J., Jr., et al. (2016). The Pediatric Imaging, Neurocognition, and Genetics (PING) data repository. *Neuroimage, 124,* 1149–1154.

Kardan, O., Gozdyra, P., Misic, B., et al. (2015). Neighborhood greenspace and health in a large urban center. *Scientific Reports, 5,* 11610.

Knickmeyer, R. C., Gouttard, S., Kang, C., et al. (2008). A structural MRI study of human brain development from birth to 2 years. *Journal of Neuroscience, 28,* 12176–12182.

Kramer, M. S., Aboud, F., Mironova, E., et al. (2008). Breastfeeding and child cognitive development: New evidence from a large randomized trial. *Archives of General Psychiatry, 65,* 578–584.

Kucharczyk, W., Macdonald, P. M., Stanisz, G. J., & Henkelman, R. M. (1994). Relaxivity and magnetization transfer of white matter lipids at MR imaging: Importance of cerebrosides and pH. *Radiology, 192,* 521–529.

Kum, H. C., Krishnamurthy, A., Machanavajjhala, A., & Ahalt, S. (2014). Social genome: Putting big data to work for population informatics. *Computer 47,* 56–63.

Le Bihan, D. (1995). Molecular diffusion, tissue microdynamics and microstructure. *NMR Biomedicine, 8,* 375–386.

Lebel, C., & Deoni, S. (2018). The development of brain white matter microstructure. *Neuroimage, 182,* 207–218.

Lerch, J. P., Van der Kouwe, A. J., Raznahan, A., et al. (2017). Studying neuroanatomy using MRI. *Nature Neuroscience, 20,* 314–326.

Maharana, A., & Okanyene Nsoesie, E. (2018). Use of deep learning to examine the association of the built environment with prevalence of neighborhood adult obesity. *JAMA Network Open, 1,* e181535.

Marner, L., & Pakkenberg, B. (2003). Total length of nerve fibers in prefrontal and global white matter of chronic schizophrenics. *Journal of Psychiatric Research, 37,* 539–547.

Matsuzawa, J., Matsui, M., Konishi, T., et al. (2001). Age-related volumetric changes of brain gray and white matter in healthy infants and children. *Cerebral Cortex, 11,* 335–342.

McGowan, J. C. (1999). The physical basis of magnetization transfer imaging. *Neurology, 53,* S3–S7.

Moore, M. M., & Chung, T. (2017). Review of key concepts in magnetic resonance physics. *Pediatric Radiology, 47,* 497–506.

Morales, A. J., Vavilala, V., Benito, R. M., & Bar-Yam, Y. (2017). Global patterns of synchronization in human communications. *Journal of the Royal Society, Interface, 14,* 20161048.

Pangelinan, M. M., Leonard, G., Perron, M., et al. (2016). Puberty and testosterone shape the corticospinal tract during male adolescence. *Brain Structure and Function, 221,* 1083–1094.

Parker, N., Wong, A. P., Leonard, G., et al. (2017). Income inequality, gene expression, and brain maturation during adolescence. *Scientific Reports, 7,* 7397.

Patel, Y., Shin, J., Gowland, P. A., et al. (2019). Maturation of the human cerebral cortex during adolescence: Myelin or dendritic arbor? *Cerebral Cortex*, *29*, 3351–3362.

Paus, T. (2005). Mapping brain maturation and cognitive development during adolescence. *Trends in Cognitive Science*, *9*, 60–68.

Paus, T. (2013). *Population Neuroscience.* Berlin: Springer-Verlag.

Paus, T. (2016). Population neuroscience. *Handbook of Clinical Neurology*, *138*, 17–37.

Paus, T. (2018). Imaging microstructure in the living human brain: A viewpoint. *Neuroimage*, *182*, 3–7.

Paus, T., Collins, D. L., Evans, A. C., et al. (2001). Maturation of white matter in the human brain: A review of magnetic resonance studies. *Brain Research Bulletin*, *54*, 255–266.

Paus, T., Pesaresi, M., & French, L. (2014). White matter as a transport system. *Neuroscience*, *276*, 117–125.

Paus, T., & Toro, R. (2009). Could sex differences in white matter be explained by g ratio? *Frontiers in Neuroanatomy*, *3*, 14.

Pausova, Z., Paus, T., Abrahamowicz, M., et al. (2007). Genes, maternal smoking, and the offspring brain and body during adolescence: Design of the Saguenay youth study. *Human Brain Mapping*, *28*, 502–518.

Pausova, Z., Paus, T., Abrahamowicz, M., et al. (2017). Cohort profile: *The Saguenay Youth Study* (SYS). *International Journal of Epidemiology*, *46*, e19.

Pelvig, D. P., Pakkenberg, H., Stark, A. K., & Pakkenberg, B. (2008). Neocortical glial cell numbers in human brains. *Neurobiology of Aging*, *29*, 1754–1762.

Peng, T. Q., Sun, G., & Wu, Y. (2017). Interplay between public attention and public emotion toward multiple social issues on Twitter. *PLoS ONE*, *12*, e0167896.

Perrin, J. S., Herve, P. Y., Leonard, G., et al. (2008). Growth of white matter in the adolescent brain: Role of testosterone and androgen receptor. *Journal of Neuroscience*, *28*, 9519–9524.

Pesaresi, M., Soon-Shiong, R., French, L., Kaplan, D. R., Miller, F. D., & Paus, T. (2015). Axon diameter and axonal transport: In vivo and in vitro effects of androgens. *Neuroimage*, *115*, 191–201.

Pike, G. B. (1996). Pulsed magnetization transfer contrast in gradient echo imaging: A two-pool analytic description of signal response. *Magnetic Resonance in Medicine*, *36*, 95–103.

Pipitone, J., Park, M. T., Winterburn, J., et al. (2014). Multi-atlas segmentation of the whole hippocampus and subfields using multiple automatically generated templates. *Neuroimage*, *101*, 494–12.

Rakic, P. (1974). Neurons in rhesus monkey visual cortex: Systematic relation between time of origin and eventual disposition. *Science*, *183*, 425–427.

Rakic, P. (1988). Specification of cerebral cortical areas. *Science*, *241*, 170–176.

Rakic, P. (1995). A small step for the cell, a giant leap for mankind: A hypothesis of neocortical expansion during evolution. *Trends in Neuroscience*, *18*, 383–388.

Rakic, P. (2009). Evolution of the neocortex: A perspective from developmental biology. *Nature Reviews Neuroscience*, *10*, 724–735.

Roberts, T. P., & Mikulis, D. (2007). Neuro MR: Principles. *Journal of Magnetic Resonance Imaging*, *26*, 823–837.

Ruiz Jdel, C., Quackenboss, J. J., & Tulve, N. S. (2016). Contributions of a child's built, natural, and social environments to their general cognitive ability: A systematic scoping review. *PLoS ONE*, *11*, e0147741.

Sandler, I., Wolchik, S. A., Cruden, G., et al. (2014). Overview of meta-analyses of the prevention of mental health, substance use, and conduct problems. *Annual Review of Clinical Psychology*, *10*, 243–273.

Satterthwaite, T. D., Elliott, M. A., Ruparel, K., et al. (2014). Neuroimaging of the Philadelphia neurodevelopmental cohort. *Neuroimage*, *86*, 544–553.

Schmierer, K., Scaravilli, F., Altmann, D. R., Barker, G. J., & Miller, D. H. (2004). Magnetization transfer ratio and myelin in postmortem multiple sclerosis brain. *Annals of Neurology*, *56*, 407–415.

Schmierer, K., Wheeler-Kingshott, C. A., Tozer, D. J., et al. (2008). Quantitative magnetic resonance of postmortem multiple sclerosis brain before and after fixation. *Magnetic Resonance in Medicine, 59*, 268–277.

Schumann, G., Loth, E., Banaschewski, T., et al. (2010). The IMAGEN study: Reinforcement-related behaviour in normal brain function and psychopathology. *Molecular Psychiatry, 15*, 1128–1139.

Schüz, A., & Braitenberg, V. (2002). *The Human Cortical White Matter: Quantitative Aspects of Cortico-Cortical Long-Range Connectivity.* London: Taylor & Francis.

Selemon, L. D., Ceritoglu, C., Ratnanather, J. T., et al. (2013). Distinct abnormalities of the primate prefrontal cortex caused by ionizing radiation in early or midgestation. *The Journal of Comparative Neurology, 521*, 1040–1053.

Shin, J., French, L., Xu, T., et al. (2018). Cell-specific gene-expression profiles and cortical thickness in the human brain. *Cerebral Cortex, 28*, 3267–3277.

Sisk, C. L., & Foster, D. L. (2004). The neural basis of puberty and adolescence. *Nature Neuroscience, 7*, 1040–1047.

Sloper, J. J. (1973). An electron microscopic study of the neurons of the primate motor and somatic sensory cortices. *Journal of Neurocytology, 2*, 351–359.

Sloper, J. J., Hiorns, R. W., & Powell, T. P. (1979). A qualitative and quantitative electron microscopic study of the neurons in the primate motor and somatic sensory cortices.

Philosophical Transactions of the Royal Society of London B: Biological Science, 285, 141–171.

Toro, R., Perron, M., Pike, B., et al. (2008). Brain size and folding of the human cerebral cortex. *Cerebral Cortex, 18*, 2352–2357.

Walhovd, K. B., Fjell, A. M., Giedd, J., Dale, A. M., & Brown, T. T. (2017). Through thick and thin: A need to reconcile contradictory results on trajectories in human cortical development. *Cerebral Cortex, 27*, 1472–1481.

Whitaker, K. J., Vertes, P. E., Romero-Garcia, R., et al. (2016). Adolescence is associated with genomically patterned consolidation of the hubs of the human brain connectome. *Proceedings of the National Academy of Sciences (USA), 113*, 9105–9110.

White, T., El Marroun, H., Nijs, I., et al. (2013). Pediatric population-based neuroimaging and the Generation R Study: The intersection of developmental neuroscience and epidemiology. *European Journal of Epidemiology, 28*, 99–111.

Zecevic, N., Chen, Y., & Filipovic, R. (2005). Contributions of cortical subventricular zone to the development of the human cerebral cortex. *The Journal of Comparative Neurology, 491*, 109–122.

Zeisel, A., Munoz-Manchado, A. B., Codeluppi, S., et al. (2015). Brain structure. Cell types in the mouse cortex and hippocampus revealed by single-cell RNA-seq. *Science, 347*, 1138–1142.

5 Genetic and Experiential Factors in Brain Development

The Examples of Executive Attention and Self-regulation

Michael I. Posner and Mary K. Rothbart

5.1 Goals and Organization of the Chapter

Executive attention is a brain network that includes the anterior cingulate cortex (ACC), the anterior insula and adjacent areas of the mid-prefrontal cortex and underlying striatum. In adult studies it is often activated by requiring a person to withhold a dominant response in order to perform a subdominant response (Posner & Rothbart, 2007a, 2007b). The ability to control our thoughts, feelings, and behavior develops over time and is called self-regulation. The self-regulatory view fits well with evidence of brain activation, functional and structural connectivity, and individual differences. Moreover, the self-regulatory view helps us understand how brain networks relate to important real-life functions and provides a perspective on how the shift takes place between infancy, where regulation is chiefly under the control of the caregiver, and later life, where self-control is increasingly important.

During infancy and childhood, the executive attention network is one of three attention networks that develop to carry out the functions of alerting, orienting, and executive control (Fan et al., 2002; Posner & Fan, 2008). Alerting refers to achieving and maintaining a state of optimal readiness to process and respond to input. Orienting refers to the selection of information from sensory input. Executive attention includes mechanisms for monitoring and resolving conflict among thoughts, feelings, and responses.

In this chapter we first examine the development of each of these networks. Of particular importance in this section is how control is exercised in infancy and early childhood. We then examine the genes related to each of the brain networks. We discuss candidate gene strategies as well as genetic nurturing and discuss how each method can be made more hypothesis driven. This section also considers the role of the environment, in particular parenting, in interaction with genes. In Section 5.5 we consider how training can influence the development of brain networks in adults. Both development and training induce changes in white matter through increasing myelination, thus improving connectivity. We consider how training effects might be used to illuminate the behavioral consequences of brain changes found in development.

5.2 Development of Attention Networks

5.2.1 Anatomy

It is now possible to define the anatomy of each of the attention networks in adults and then to use resting state magnetic resonance imaging (MRI) to follow their development (Fair et al., 2007). Although there is still much

The research for this chapter was supported by Office of Naval Research Grants N00014–15-1-2022 and N00014–15-2148 to the University of Oregon.

that we do not know about each of the networks, recent data allows us to attempt to trace attention networks into infancy (Gao et al., 2014, 2017) and perhaps even *in utero* (Thomason et al., 2014).

The *alerting network* involves the brain's norepinephrine system that arises in the locus coeruleus of the midbrain and synapses in frontal and parietal lobes of each cerebral hemisphere (Petersen & Posner, 2012). In the posterior part of each hemisphere, norepinephrine (NE) acts mainly upon more dorsal brain networks involving parietal areas. There is little change due to NE within ventral visual object recognition areas in comparison with great NE modulation of the more dorsal areas involved with orienting of attention (Morrison & Foote, 1986). This anatomy supports the behavioral finding that the rate of buildup of information about the identity of an object varies little with alertness, while the speed of response varies greatly (Posner, 1978).

Studies of phasic alerting often use warning signals that precede a target event. A warning signal induces two phases of brain activity: one that occurs before the target appears and the other following the target. Changes prior to the target are found in phasic alertness, and they reflect mainly a suppression of ongoing brain activity (Kahneman, 1973). In the central nervous system, there is a negative shift in scalp-recorded electrical activity (contingent negative variation, or CNV) that begins with the warning signal and may remain present until target presentation. This negative electrical change appears to arise at least in part in the anterior cingulate and adjacent structures. The ACC is a gateway to autonomic responses, so it should be of no surprise that the alert state is also indexed by widespread autonomic changes such as slowing of heart rate and a decrease in skin conductance. The generally inhibitory state includes a dominance of the parasympathetic autonomic system over the sympathetic system. State change following the occurrence of the target generally involves sympathetic dominance, including increased heart rate.

The warning signal triggers neural activity in the locus coeruleus, which is the source of the neuromodulator norepinephrine (NE, Pfaff & Kieffer, 2008; Posner, 2008). Warning signal effects can be blocked by drugs such as guanfacine and clonidine, which have the effect of reducing NE release. Drugs that increase NE release can also enhance the warning signal effect (Petersen & Posner, 2012). The effect of the warning signal on performance is generally to reduce reaction time, sometimes increasing error rate. However, specific effects may depend upon details of experimental design, such as the length and variability of the warning interval (Jaffard et al., 2007).

The *orienting network* (also called the Fronto-Parietal Network) has been studied extensively in humans and non-human primates (Corbetta & Shulman, 2002). The *orienting network* involves the frontal eye fields and areas of the superior (dorsal) and inferior (ventral) parietal lobe. Subcortical areas such as the superior colliculus and pulvinar are also involved. Primate research and fMRI studies of humans have suggested that the more dorsal areas are related to voluntary (endogenous) orienting, while the more ventral areas dominate in more automatic (exogenous) orienting (Corbetta & Shulman, 2002).

Covert orientation of attention can be studied when not enough time is allowed to move the eyes and/or head, or by instructing humans to attend to the cue without looking at it. The close connection of eye movements to covert shifts of attention has led to studies examining the relation of eye movements to attention shifts with no movement. In general the same brain areas are active before saccades and before covert shifts of attention (Corbetta & Shulman, 2002). However, cellular studies in alert monkeys have found that within the frontal eye fields there exist two different but overlapping populations of cells. One is active prior to saccades and the other before attention shifts not leading to saccades (Thompson et al., 2005). These findings suggest that eye, head, and covert attention movements rather than having the same mechanism become coordinated through learning in early development. In adults it becomes difficult, but still possible to separate them.

The *executive network* (also called the cingulo-opercular network in fMRI studies) includes dorsal and ventral areas of the anterior cingulate cortex (ACC) and adjacent medial prefrontal cortex, anterior insula, and areas of the subcortical striatum. The executive attention network is involved in the regulation of feelings (emotions), thoughts (cognitions), and actions (see Petersen & Posner, 2012, for more detail). The ACC, one of the main nodes of the executive attention network, has been linked to a variety of specific functions related to self-regulation. These include the monitoring of conflict (Botvinick et al., 2001), control of working memory (Duncan et al., 2000), regulation of emotion (Bush et al., 2000), and response to error (Holroyd & Coles, 2002). In emotion studies, the cingulate is often seen as part of a network involving the orbital frontal cortex and amygdala, regulating our emotional response to input. Activation of the anterior cingulate is observed when people are asked to control their natural reactions to strong positive (Beauregard et al., 2001) or negative emotions (Ochsner et al., 2002). Analysis of functional connectivity between brain areas has shown that when emotionally neutral sensory information is involved, there is strong connectivity between the dorsal ACC and the relevant sensory area (Crottaz-Herbette & Mennon, 2006). When control of emotion is involved, connectivity is mainly found between the ventral ACC and the amygdala (Etkin et al., 2006).

Specific brain networks have been identified while the person is at rest in correlations of activation between separate brain areas (functional connectivity) known to implement functions of attention in adults such as orienting (Frontal-Parietal network) and executive control (Cingulo-Opercular network) (Dosenbach et al., 2007). Graph theory has been used to trace the development of specific networks from infancy (Gao et al., 2013, 2014, 2017) to adulthood (Matthews & Fair, 2015). Most of the graphical depictions of changed connections have used functional imaging, examining correlations among activated sites, mainly from resting MRI, although some studies use diffusion tensor imaging (DTI) to measure the efficiency of specific pathways. Functional imaging stresses the overall connection between neural areas, while diffusion tensor imaging stresses the efficiency of particular pathways. The two can be related, particularly for longer range connections (Becker et al., 2016). However, there is some convergence of these methods on points that include (a) the existence of many networks at birth, (b) the abundance of short distance functional connectivity in early development, and (c) an increase of long-distance functional connections during later development. The increase in long connections is often reported in imaging studies using functional connectivity, while most DTI studies show chiefly increased axonal density and myelination in later development. Improved axonal efficiency, however, might differentially favor longer connections (Vértes & Bullmore, 2015).

Task-related MRI can be informative of the function of a brain network by relating the anatomy obtained from functional imaging studies to performance of a specific task. An fMRI study (Fjell et al., 2012) of 750 persons from four to twenty-one years old found that, early in childhood (up to seven years of age), the size of the anterior cingulate in the right hemisphere is the best predictor of the ability to resolve conflict, as measured by reaction time differences between congruent and incongruent flankers. Little improvement is found in the ability to resolve conflict in this task beyond age seven (Rueda et al., 2004). However, after age seven overall reaction time continues to improve, mainly through changes in the efficiency of connections through myelination.

Not only the size but also the shape of the ACC seems to be important in predicting the efficiency of executive attention. One recent study (Cachia et al., 2014) used anatomical MRI and three-dimensional reconstruction of cortical folds to investigate the effect of the ACC sulcal pattern on the ability to resolve conflict. Sulcal pattern proved to be a reliable feature of individual ACC anatomy from age seven to adulthood (Cachia et al., 2016). This pattern was also related to the resolution of conflict in the Stroop task, a classical behavioral index of ACC efficiency, in five-year-old preschoolers. Higher efficiency of executive attention, that is, lower Stroop interference, was found for both reaction time (RT) and error rates, in children with asymmetrical ACC sulcal patterns (i.e., a different pattern in each hemisphere) than for children with symmetrical patterns (i.e., similar patterns in both hemispheres). Critically, ACC sulcal pattern had no effect on performance in forward and backward digit span tasks, suggesting that ACC sulcal pattern contributes to the ability to resolve conflicts but not to the ability to maintain information in working memory. Overall evidence indicates that the size and pattern of ACC anatomy is an early constraint on the development of human executive ability, presumably because the more efficient form of ACC anatomy produces better ability to resolve conflict (Caccia et al., 2014, 2016; Fjell et al., 2012).

5.2.2 Connectivity

The presence of correlations in activations between distant brain areas even when no task is required has given rise to the use of resting state MRI to trace brain networks. Since resting connectivity analysis requires no task, it can be studied during infancy (Gao et al., 2017) and even *in utero* (Thomason et al., 2014, 2015). This has been a major achievement in development where there has always been great difficulty in finding tasks appropriate to widely varying ages.

Many resting state MRI studies trace development (Dosenbach et al., 2007; Fair et al., 2007) by the use of graph theory which has proven to be a convenient way of portraying the development of brain networks. These studies have suggested that adults have more separate orienting and executive attention networks; these are less differentiated in children. Children aged nine show many short connections. Adults show more segregation of the orienting and executive networks and more long connections between distant brain areas (Dosenbach et al., 2007; Fair et al., 2007, 2008). Even before birth, connectivity between nodes within networks increases and some areas, such as the posterior cingulate, appear to become particularly related to cortical areas prior to birth (Thomason et al., 2014, 2015).

During the first year of life the anterior cingulate shows little or no connectivity to other areas.

After the first year, infants begin the slow process of developing long-range connectivity typical of adults. In general, resting state studies have used functional connectivity measures, that is, correlations among remote brain areas to study connectivity.

As in any new method, many questions arise in the use of resting state to trace the development of brain networks. Studies have been questioned because of the likelihood that movement in the scanner is reduced with age, favoring short connections which are less influenced by movement (Van Dijk et al., 2012). While efforts have been made to compensate for movement, the best way to measure changes in connectivity with age while avoiding the motion artifact is currently a very active field of investigation (Parkes et al., 2018).

Studies using diffusion tensor imaging to study connectivity have been less supportive of the increase of long-range connections with age. While an increase of long connections over development is often reported in functional connectivity studies, most diffusion imaging studies show mainly increased axonal density and myelination in later development (Vértes & Bullmore, 2015). Improved axonal efficiency through myelination, however, might differentially favor longer connections providing some convergence between the functional and structural MRI approaches. Another, perhaps more traditional way to validate resting state studies is to examine the same networks while performing tasks, as we do in Section 5.2.3.

5.2.3 Behavior

It is important to be able to determine which changes in the brain are most related to the obvious differences in behavior between infants and adults. Individuals differ in the efficiency of each of the attentional networks. One way of exploring these differences is by using the Attention Network Test (ANT), designed to evaluate alerting, orienting, and executive attention (Fan et al., 2002). This test can be performed by children from age four, adults, and animals because it does not rely on language. The efficiency of the alerting network is examined by changes in RT resulting from a warning signal. The efficiency of orienting is examined by changes in RT that accompany cues indicating where the target

will occur. The efficiency of the executive network is the increased time to resolve conflict when the target arrow is surrounded by flankers that point in the opposite direction. The behavioral scores obtained from this test are largely independent (Fan et al., 2002), although slight variations have shown them to be correlated in some studies (Fan et al., 2009; Pozuelos et al., 2014), and they have to be integrated in many of the complex tasks of real life. Brain scans using the ANT reveal somewhat independent anatomies similar to those summarized for individual networks in Section 5.2.2. Both resting state and task methods indicate that orienting and alerting networks are somewhat functional from birth (Fan et al., 2005), even though they show improvement up until adulthood.

The ANT has been studied between ages six and adults by Rueda et al. (2004). Reaction time improves over this period. However, each of the individual networks show their own pattern of improvement. The alerting network tends to improve over the entire period, with phasic alerting improving from age six to adulthood. Orienting generally shows little improvement after the age of six. Perhaps this is because the method used in the ANT is extremely simple; other tests have shown improvements after age six when orienting requirements are more complex, for example, when they involve distracting objects or when the cue indicates only the probability that the target will occur at the cued location. The executive network as measured by the ANT does not show differences after about seven–eight years of age. This may be because of the simplicity of the flanker test, but note that this fits with the age for which the anatomical size of the ACC is related to differences in RT between congruent and incongruent flankers (Fjell et al., 2012) and also fits with the integration of the anterior cingulate and midprefrontal cortex, which resting state studies show takes place over this period.

When does the executive network begin to function? The resting state MRI data suggests this occurs within the first year or two of life, although changes in connectivity continue to occur after that period. A study of seven-month old infants viewing visual displays developed by Wynn (1992) showed longer orienting when a display was in error, and this behavior was associated with activating a set of scalp electrodes at the frontal midline that have been localized to the anterior cingulate, an important node of the executive network (Berger et al., 2006). However, the lack of connections of the ACC to remote areas was shown in infants' apparent inability to use errors to slow their behavior on the next trial. The most frequent adult response to a self-made error is to slow down during the next trial, and evidence for this kind of control was found to emerge around three years of age (Jones et al., 2003). The match between resting state MRI and the error detection findings suggests a common course of development between brain connectivity and behavior.

A longitudinal study starting at seven months of age found evidence of both behavioral and neural mechanisms of self-regulation (Posner et al., 2014a; Rothbart et al., 2011). The earliest form of regulation appears to come from the orienting rather than the executive network. This conclusion was based on several findings. First, parent reports of their child's orienting to the environment were correlated with reports of the child's (Posner et al., 2014a) higher positive and lower negative affect. A direct test was also done on the role of orienting to novel objects in soothing of infant distress. Distressed infants, while orienting to a novel object, showed reduced signs of overt distress, but the overt distress returned to the pre-distraction level when that orienting was broken (Harman et al., 1997).

This led us to suggest that the amygdala or other limbic areas maintain the distress, but that its overt expression is controlled by the orienting network.

Second, when confronted with novel objects, some seven-month old infants orient for a long period before reaching toward them. This tendency for a cautious reach was positively related to the number of anticipations infants made in orienting to a repeating sequence of visual events. These striking observations showed that infants faster in orienting to repeated visual sequences, often in anticipation of the object's appearance, exercised stronger control over reaching for an object by moving toward it more slowly, thus showing caution in the face of novelty.

Was rapid orienting to repeated locations controlled by the executive or the orienting network? Our longitudinal study (Posner et al., 2014a) found that anticipations at seven months were more closely related to the ANT measure of the orienting network at four years than to the executive network. Examination of the children at seven years also found that the time spent by infants examining a novel toy before starting to reach for it was related to the efficiency of the orienting network at age seven years.

Results of this longitudinal study suggest that, early in life, orienting serves to regulate both positive and negative affect (Posner et al., 2014a; Rothbart et al., 2011). In this view, both orienting and executive networks serve regulatory functions during infancy. Later in development, higher effortful control is consistently related to low negative emotion in questionnaire and laboratory studies, and effortful control has been consistently related to measures of executive attention (Rothbart, 2011). Executive attention appears to dominate in regulating emotions and thoughts, but orienting still serves as a control system, for example in the tendency to look away from frightening stimuli. The parallel use of the two networks fits with the findings of Dosenbach et al. (2007) that in adults the frontal-parietal (orienting) network controls behavior at short time intervals, while the cingulo-opercular (executive) network exercises strategic control over long intervals.

Some of the mechanisms reported for adult control of cognition and emotion are similar to those developing during this early period of childhood. Studies of connectivity of the ACC during selection of visual or auditory stimuli show that the ACC works to inhibit the non-selected modality (Crottaz-Herbette & Mennon, 2006). Control by the executive network also occurs within the visual modality when an unexpected visual stimulus summons activation of the executive network during visual orienting (Shulman et al., 2009) or when a misleading visuospatial heuristic had to be inhibited during a counting task (Houdé et al., 2011). The emotion of fear involves a ventral ACC/prefrontal cortex circuit which connects to the amygdala (Bush et al., 2000). There is evidence that amygdala activity can be suppressed by this circuit both when participants are instructed to ward off fear reactions (Etkin et al., 2006) and in natural fear situations (Bishop, 2007). While the brain mechanism may be common to all ages, specific cognitive strategies such as re-appraisal (Kanske et al., 2011) for inhibiting fear develop over the life span (Rothbart & Sheese, 2007).

Posner et al.'s (2014a) longitudinal study was also able to determine some of the possible origins of the attention networks by correlating the temperament dimensions measured from parent report data at seven-months with the later ANT performance at seven years. The dimensions significantly related to each network are shown in Table 5.1. One important result is that each network has a different set of predictors. The predictors are most often emotional, found in measures of infant temperament as rated by parent, which are correlated with later performance in the ANT. The orienting network at seven years is predicted best by parent report of the child's approach

Table 5.1. *Correlations between temperament measures at seven months and ANT scores at seven years*

Parent Rating Scale			
	Alerting[a]	Orienting[b]	Executive Attention[c]
Perceptual Sensitivity	0.56	0.18	−0.07
Duration of Orienting	0.55	0.01	0.03
Approach	0.29	0.76*	−0.28
Soothability	0.13	0.56	−0.24
Smiling and Laughter	0.17	0.06	−0.60*
Vocal Reactivity	0.24	0.20	−0.64*
Cuddliness	−0.04	0.08	−0.64*
Positive Affect (higher order)	0.43	0.38	−0.58*

• significant at p < 0.05.
Adapted from Posner et al. (2014a).
[a]For alerting, a positive correlation indicates stronger alerting.
[b]For orienting, a positive correlation indicates stronger orienting.
[c]For executive attention, a negative correlation means more efficient resolution of conflict, whereas a longer time to resolve conflict means less efficient resolution.

and soothability. Further evidence of the importance of early temperament is that in the current study, smiling and laughter as reported by the parents best predicted the efficiency of the executive network at seven years. A previous study found that the slope of heart rate deceleration predicted intensity of smiling at three months (Brock et al., 1986), consistent with the idea of the ACC relation to autonomic control.

In summary, we find that the orienting network provides the main control over behavior and emotion during infancy and early childhood. Orienting remains an important basis for control, but in later childhood the executive network provides the dominant control. This is supported by many findings (Rothbart & Rueda, 2005) showing the central role of effortful control during child development and its correlation with conflict resolution as measured by the ANT during this period. The best infant predictors of the efficiency of later attention networks involve parent observation of chiefly reactive temperamental dimensions, including emotion and vocal expression as well

as tendency to approach. A different set of predictors is involved with each of the attentional networks (see Table 5.1). While reaction time and alerting continue to improve up until adulthood, the executive network as measured by the ANT improves in efficiency up until about age seven years, and similarly the size of the ACC is a dominant predictor of the efficiency of resolving conflict up until about age seven years. While general improvements in various executive functions continue to develop, it may be that basic skills involving conflict remain fixed at an early age.

5.3 How Genes and Environment Interact in Development

5.3.1 Attention Genes

Each of the attention networks is associated with a dominant neuromodulator, as shown in Table 5.2. This suggests that genes associated with a specific modulator should be related to a particular attention network (Green et al., 2008). There have been many questions raised

Table 5.2. *Brain attention networks, anatomy, dominant modulators, and genetic alleles*

Network	Modulator	Genes
Alerting	Norepinephrine	ADRA2A
Locus Coeruleus		NET
Right Frontal Cortex		
Right Parietal Cortex		
Orienting	Acetycholine	APOE
Superior Parietal Lobe		
Temporal Parietal Junction		
Superior Colliculus		
Pulvinar		
Executive	Dopamine	DRD4, DAT1, COMT
Anterior cingulate		
Anterior Insula		MAOA, DBH
Mid Prefrontal Cortex		
Striatum	Serotonin	TPH2, 5HTT

Adapted from Green et al. (2008)

about replication of studies using the candidate gene approach (Zhu & Zhao, 2007), the method used by the studies in Table 5.2. However, unlike many candidate gene studies, the genes here are associated with particular networks, and studies use the ANT or other tasks to determine if a particular polymorphism is associated with the network that uses a specific neuromodulator. This provides a degree of theoretical basis for the polymorphism's function that is often missing from candidate gene studies. Findings have generally supported the association between genes and the network-related neuromodulators, as shown in Table 5.2. For example, the association of the executive attention system with dopamine supports the examination of several genes related to dopamine transmission in relation to early attention networks. Several of these genes are discussed in Section 5.3.2, where we concentrate on gene × environment interactions, particularly those linking parenting and genetics (also see Posner & Rothbart, 2018).

5.3.2 Genes and Gene-by-Environment Interactions

5.3.2.1 COMT

The Catechol-O-methyl transferase gene (COMT) plays an important role in dopamine metabolism by modulating extracellular levels of dopamine. Different alleles of the COMT gene have consistently been shown to be related to executive attention in adults and older children (Blasi et al., 2005; Diamond et al., 2004). COMT is also related to aspects of executive attention in toddlers (Sheese et al., 2007). Haplotypes of the COMT gene (Diatchenko et al., 2005) were related to both anticipatory looking and nesting cup skill at eighteen–twenty months, skills that predicted effortful control at three–four years. At seven

months, COMT was also related to positive affect, as reported by parents, and at seven years to executive attention, as measured by the ANT. The relation of COMT to parent-reported positive affect and laboratory cognitive skill supports the finding shown in Table 5.1 that the effectiveness of executive attention at age seven years is predicted by parental report of positive affect in infancy.

We also found that COMT showed an interaction between temperament and parenting quality. Those infants with the Val allele of COMT were faster to reach for novel toys during the motor approach task, and received higher scores on the temperament measure of approach to novelty. Two year old infants with the Met allele of COMT showed enhanced dishabituation to the novel stimulus during the habituation task, and received higher scores on the temperament measures of attention and effortful control (Voelker et al., 2009). The relation of the COMT gene to attention may help to explain how COMT contributes both to stability and to flexibility in the behavior of seven-month-old-infants depending upon how attention is directed (Markant et al., 2014).

5.3.2.2 DRD4

The seven-repeat allele of the DRD4 gene has been linked both to attention deficit hyperactivity disorder (ADHD) and to the temperamental dimension of risk taking (Swanson et al., 2000). There has also been considerable evidence that the environment can have a strong influence in the presence of the seven-repeat allele, but not when they are absent (Bakermans-Kranenburg & Van Ijzendoorn, 2006; van Ijzendoorn & Bakermans-Kranenburg, 2006). Bakermans-Kranenburg et al. (2008) have also performed a parent training intervention, finding that parent training decreased externalizing behavior, but only for those children with the DRD4 seven-repeat allele. This finding is important because assignment to the training group was random, ensuring that the result was not due to something about the parents other than the training.

A longitudinal study (Posner et al., 2014a) used raters to measure parenting quality in a caregiver/child interaction, and found a strong interaction between genes and parenting. For children without the seven-repeat polymorphism, variations in parenting were unrelated to the children's scores on impulsivity and risk taking. For children carrying the seven-repeat gene variant, however, variations in parenting quality were related to child behavior (Sheese et al., 2007), producing a Gene (seven repeat or not) × Environment interaction of the type found by the Netherlands group.

It seems paradoxical that the seven-repeat allele associated with developmental psychopathology (attention deficit hyperactivity disorder) is also under positive selective pressure in recent human evolution (Ding et al., 2002; Wang et al., 2006). Why should an allele related to ADHD be positively selected? One possibility is that positive selection of the seven-repeat allele arises from its association with increased effect of environmental influences on child behavior (Belsky & Pluess, 2009). Parenting provides training for children in the values favored by their culture, and the influence of the environment upon a particular child could be critical to this training.

In the Sheese et al. (2007) paper, attention did not appear to be the mechanism by which the genetic variation influenced the child's behavior at two years. However, a link between the DRD4 and attention as rated by parents did appear at age four years and older (Sheese et al., 2012). Thus, the mechanisms of influence of the DRD4 seem to depend on the connectivity of the network it influences. It is important to consider the multiple mechanisms by which genes may influence behavior.

Clearly one important mechanism lies in the executive attention network we have been discussing in this chapter, but there must be other pathways that influence behavior through other non-attentional mechanisms.

5.3.2.3 CHRNA4

Often a single gene may affect more than one neuromodulator and thus more than one attention system. In the case of CHRNA4 there is an effect on the orienting network via its influence on cholinergic modulation as well as its dopamine influence on executive attention. The nicotinic cholinergic polymorphisms in the CHRNA4 gene have been associated with nicotine dependence in humans and with cognitive performance in visuospatial attention (Parasuraman et al., 2005). However, the same polymorphism in the CHRNA4 gene has also been shown to have an influence on a visual oddball task thought to involve the cingulate (Winterer et al., 2007).

During infancy the T/T allele of CHRNA4 is related to better performance in anticipatory looking, but at eighteen months children with C/C homozygotes have higher scores on questionnaire measures of effortful control (Voelker et al., 2009). In a spatial attention task known to involve the orienting network, Parasuraman et al. (2005) report that adults with the C/C allele show higher benefits and lower costs than those with the T/T or T/C alleles. These genetic findings provide support for future research on development of control, investigating when children with higher levels of control by orienting in infancy may be slower to show the conversion to control by the executive network.

5.4 Genetic Nurture

Parental genes not passed on to the offspring may also have an influence on the nurturing of the child. Recent studies show a substantial effect of these non-transmitted parental genes on the educational attainment (EA) of the child (Kong et al., 2018).

To examine these non-direct genetic effects, the study focused on 21,637 Icelanders born between 1940 and 1983, where non-transmitted genes of each parent were determined. The EA was predicted both by the transmitted genes shared by parent and child and the non-transmitted parental genes not shared by the child. The influence of the transmitted genes on child EA was substantial, but an estimated 34 percent of the overall genetic effect was due to non-transmitted parental genes and, thus, the genetic nurture effect.

The genes of the parent that were not transmitted to the child produce a parental environment selected in part by the parental genes, and that environment in turn can influence the child nurture. In such a case it is not direct genetic transmission but genes of the parent working through the environment that influence the child. Genetic nurturing could also work on dimensions of attention and self-regulation. For example, genes influencing the self-regulation of the parent could obviously make the home environment more or less chaotic or predictive and thus have a strong influence on the development of the child self-regulatory phenotype.

5.5 Simulating Development through Training

In this chapter we have summarized some of the changes in brain mechanisms of attention from infancy to adulthood. These findings are based largely on behavioral and imaging studies. Although research over limited periods of infancy and early childhood is possible, it is obviously extremely difficult to collect a longitudinal study over the twenty-year period from birth to young adulthood. It would be useful to

have a method to examine the brain changes in a more accessible way.

Recently a possible method for doing this has arisen. The most prominent change in brain development between children and adults is in the white matter connections, particularly between remote cortical and subcortical areas. Among these are the connections of the anterior cingulate, which plays a central place in cognitive and emotional control. One of the many important behavioral changes between children and adults is the dramatic increase in speed of responding. Likely the white matter changes in part underlie this behavioral change. In recent years we have learned that many forms of training, including working memory, meditation, and motor skills also produce changes in white matter (Wang & Young, 2014). They appear to do so by increasing both the fibers within an axon and the amount of myelin surrounding the axon. The reaction time in a very simple task like the ANT improves by 400 milliseconds during development from seven to twenty-five years. The effects of practice on this task also improve reaction time, but by an amount of about 1/10 that of the developmental effect.

Meditation training research has used Diffusion Tensor Imaging (DTI) to trace increases in fractional anisotropy (FA) of white matter connections (Tang et al., 2010). FA increases signify improved white matter connections between brain areas. It was found that FA was increased following two–four weeks of IBMT in comparison with a relaxation training control. At two weeks, Axial Diffusivity (AD) was reduced (Tang et al., 2012). Reduced RD is thought to be related to increases in axonal density. After four weeks, connectivity as measured by both AD and RD (Radial Diffusivity, thought to be related to increased myelination) was improved (Tang et al., 2012). These changes occurred in pathways surrounding the Anterior Cingulate Cortex (ACC).

How might a purely mental practice like meditation produce a change in white matter? Evidence from multiple sclerosis has shown that dormant oligodendrocytes could become active and produce myelin (Beirowski, 2013). Other studies in mice and humans found increased myelination in adults following various forms of learning, including juggling, working memory, and meditation (Wang & Young, 2014). In the case of meditation, increased theta is frequently found in frontal areas following training (Xue et al., 2014). It was suggested that theta could serve to activate dormant oligodendrocytes, which could increase myelin and improve connectivity (Posner et al., 2014b).

A mouse model system was used to test this idea. Lasers were implanted in the ACC of mice who had been genetically bred to increase output of cells in the ACC with pulses of light (Piscopo et al., 2018; Weible et al., 2017). When the output of the ACC was increased by rhythmic stimulation in the range of 1–8 Hz there was an increase in active oligodendrocytes (the cells that myelinate axons).

Electron-micrographs, magnified 16,000 times, were used to compare g ratio (axonal diameter/axonal diameter + myelin) in stimulated versus non-stimulated mice. The ratio was similar to those usually reported from the central nervous system of mice for the non-stimulated controls and was significantly reduced in the stimulated mice. The reduced g ratio is associated with improved connectivity. A behavioral effect of stimulation was that time spent in the light when given a choice between light and dark areas of the cage was increased in those mice in the stimulation group compared to unstimulated controls (Weible et al., 2017). Choice of the light is usually taken as a sign of reduced anxiety and/or increased exploration. The size of these

behavioral effects is greater the smaller the g ratio (Piscopo et al., 2018).

Efforts at electrical modulation of neural activity in adult humans have usually involved DC stimulation of frontal areas. The results of these studies are complex and beyond what we can cover here (for a recent review see (Chrysikou et al., 2017). Fewer studies have used pulsed modulation as described in the mouse work cited in the previous paragraph, and these have been more successful (Luu et al., 2016). For example, pulsed stimulation designed to produce synchronous rhythms from the midline and lateral frontal areas improved executive function (Reinhart, 2017). This finding suggests that pulsed low frequency stimulation of the frontal lobes might produce similar changes to those found after meditation training. The exact mechanisms of these effects are still unclear, but the mouse data suggests that white matter changes might be involved.

Since, in development, axons occur first and later they are myelinated (Stiles & Jernigan, 2010), the time course of changes with meditation might mimic what is found in development to some degree (Tang et al., 2010, 2012). While it is not yet clear how improved connectivity occurs in adult human learning, if it reflects a similar set of brain changes that occur in development, it could provide an efficient way to relate measurable changes in the brain to changes in behavior. We might find that axonal density relates to one form of behavioral change, while myelination improves a different set of behaviors. Since both of these brain changes occur in development, the adult work might at the very least suggest what behavioral changes need to be explored in the developing brain.

In conclusion, this chapter summarizes changes in brain networks related to attention and self-regulation between infancy and adulthood. A frontal and parietal network related to orienting provides a basis for control of distress and behavior in infancy, while later regulation reflects an executive network including the anterior cingulate that provides control of emotion and resolution of conflict. Differences among people in network efficiency reflect the interaction of genetic and environmental influences. A strategy involving adult training is outlined to further our understanding on which brain changes influence different forms of emotional and cognitive control.

References

Bakermans-Kranenburg, M. J., & Van Ijzendoorn, M. H. (2006). Gene–environment interaction of the dopamine D4 receptor (DRD4) and observed maternal insensitivity predicting externalizing behavior in preschoolers. *Developmental Psychobiology, 48,* 406–409.

Bakermans-Kranenburg, M. J. Van Ijzendoorn, M. H., Pijlman, F. T. A., Mesman, J., & Juffer, F. (2008). Experimental evidence for differential susceptibility: Dopamine receptor polymorphism (DRD4 VNTR) moderates intervention effects on toddlers externalizing behavior in a randomized controlled trial. *Developmental Psychology, 44,* 293–300.

Beauregard, M., Levesque, J., & Bourgouin, P. (2001). Neural correlates of conscious self-regulation of emotion. *Journal of Neuroscience, 21,* RC165.

Becker, C. O., Pequite, S., Pappas, G. J., Miller, M. B., Grafton, S. T., Bassetti, D. S., & Preciado, V. M. (2016). Accurately predicting functional connectivity from diffusion imaging. arXiv.org > q-bio > arXiv:1512.02602v3.

Beirowski, B. (2013). Concepts for regulation of axon integrity by enwrapping glia. *Frontiers in Cellular Neuroscience, 7,* 256.

Belsky, J., & Pluess, M. (2009). Beyond diathesis stress: Differential susceptibility to environmental influences. *Psychological Bulletin, 135,* 624–652.

Berger, A., Tzur, G., & Posner, M. I. (2006). Infant babies detect arithmetic error. *Proceeding of the National Academy of Science USA, 103,* 12649–12553.

Bishop, S. J. (2007). Neurocognitive mechanisms of anxiety. *Trends in Cognitive Sciences, 11,* 307–316.

Blasi, G., Mattay, G. S., Bertolino, A., Elvevåg, B., Callicott, J. H., Das, S., et al. (2005). Effect of Catechol-O-Methyltransferase *val met* genotype on attentional control. *Journal of Neuroscience, 25,* 5038–5045.

Botvinick, M. M., Braver, T. S., Barch, D. M., Carter, C. S., & Cohen, J. D. (2001). Conflict monitoring and cognitive control. *Psychological Review, 108,* 624–652.

Brock, S. E., Rothbart, M. K., & Derryberry, D. (1986). Heart-rate deceleration and smiling in 3 month-old infants. *Infant Behavior and Development, 9,* 403–414.

Bush, G., Luu, P., & Posner, M. I. (2000). Cognitive and emotional influences in the anterior cingulate cortex. *Trends in Cognitive Science, 4,* 215–222.

Cachia, A., Borst, G., Tissier, C., Fisher, C., Plaze, M., et al. (2016). Longitudinal stability of the folding pattern of the anterior cingulate cortex during development. *Developmental Cognitive Neuroscience, 19,* 122–127.

Cachia, A., Borst, G., Vidal, J., Fischer, C., Pineau, A., Mangin, J. F., & Houdé, O. (2014). The shape of the ACC contributes to cognitive control efficiency in preschoolers. *Journal of Cognitive Neuroscience, 26,* 96–106.

Chrysikou, E. G., Berryhill, M. E., Bikson, M., & Coslett, H. B. (2017). Revisiting the effectiveness of transcranial direct current brain stimulation for cognition: Evidence, challenges, and open questions. *Frontiers in Human Neuroscience, 11,* 448.

Corbetta, M., & Shulman, G. L. (2002). Control of goal-directed and stimulus-driven attention in the brain. *Nature Reviews Neuroscience, 3,* 201–215.

Crottaz-Herbette, S., and Mennon, V. (2006). Where and when the anterior cingulate cortex modulates attentional response: Combined fMRI and ERP evidence. *Journal of Cognitive Neuroscience, 18,* 766–780.

Diamond, A., Briand, L., Fossella, J., & Gehlbach, L. (2004). Genetic and neurochemical modulation of prefrontal cognitive functions in children. *American Journal of Psychiatry, 161,* 125–132.

Diatchenko, L., Slade, G. D., Nackley, A. G., Bhalang, K., Sigurdsson, A., Belfer, I., et al. (2005). Genetic basis for individual variations in pain perception and the development of a chronic pain condition. *Human Molecular Genetics, 14,* 135–143.

Ding, Y. C., Chi, H. C., Grady, D. L., Morishima, A., Kidd, J. R., Kidd, K. K., et al. (2002). Evidence of positive selection acting at the human dopamine receptor D4 gene locus. *Proceedings of the National Academy of Sciences (USA), 99,* 309–314.

Dosenbach, N. U., Fair, D. A., Miezin, F. M., Cohen, A. L., Wenger, K. K. R., Dosenbach, A. T., et al. (2007). Distinct brain networks for adaptive and stable task control in humans. *Proceedings of the National Academy of Sciences (USA), 104,* 11073–11078.

Duncan, J., Seitz, R. J., Kolodny, J., Bor, D., Herzog, H. Ahmed, A., et al. (2000). A neural basis for general intelligence. *Science, 289,* 457–460.

Etkin, A., Egner, T., Peraza, D. M., Kandel, E. R., & Hirsch, J. (2006). Resolving emotional conflict: A role for the rostral anterior cingulate cortex in modulating activity in the amygdala. *Neuron, 51,* 871–882.

Fair, D. A., Cohen, A. L., Dosenbach, U. F., Church, J. A., Meizin, F. M., Barch, D. M., et al. (2008). The maturing architecture of the brain's default network. *Proceedings of the National Academy of Sciences (USA), 105,* 4028–4032.

Fair, D. A., Dosenbach, N. U. F., Church, J. A., Cohen, A. L., Brahmbhatt, S., Miezin, F. M., et al. (2007). Development of distinct control networks through segregation and integration. *Proceedings of the National Academy of Sciences (USA), 104,* 13507–13512.

Fan, J., Gu, X., Guise, K. G., Liu, X., Fossella, J., Wang, H., & Posner, M. I. (2009). Testing the behavioral interaction and integration of attentional networks. *Brain and Cognition, 70,* 209–220.

Fan, J., McCandliss, B. D., Fossella, J., Flombaum, J. I., & Posner, M. I. (2005). The activation of attentional networks. *Neuroimage, 26,* 471–479.

Fan, J., McCandliss, B. D., Sommer, T., Raz, M., & Posner, M. I. (2002). Testing the efficiency and independence of attentional networks. *Journal of Cognitive Neuroscience, 3,* 340–347.

Fjell, A. M., Walhovd, K., Brown, T., Kuperman, J., Chung, Y., Hagler, D., et al. (2012). Multimodal imaging of the self-regulating brain. *Proceedings of the National Academy of Sciences (USA), 109,* 19620–19625.

Gao, W., Alcauter, S., Elton, A., Hernandez-Castillo, C. R., Smith, J. K., Ramirez, J., & Lin, W. (2014). Functional network development during the first year: Relative sequence and socioeconomic correlations. *Cerebral Cortex, 25,* 2919–2928.

Gao, W., Gilmore, J. H., Shen, D., Smith, J. K., Zhu, H., & Lin, W. (2013). The synchronization within and interaction between the default and dorsal attention networks in early infancy. *Cerebral Cortex, 23,* 594–603.

Gao, W., Lin, W., Grewen, K., & Gilmore, J. H. (2017). Functional connectivity of the infant human brain: Plastic and modifiable. *Neuroscientist, 23,* 169–184.

Green, A. E., Munafo, M. R., DeYoung, C. G., Fossella, J. A., Fan, J., & Gray, J. R. (2008). Using genetic data in cognitive neuroscience: From growing pains to genuine insights, *Nature Neuroscience Review, 9,* 710–720.

Harman, C., Rothbart, M. K., & Posner, M. I. (1997). Distress and attention interactions in early infancy. *Motivation and Emotion, 21,* 27–43.

Holroyd, C. B., & Coles, M. G. H. (2002). The neural basis of human error processing: Reinforcement learning, dopamine and error-related negativity. *Psychological Review, 109,* 679–709.

Houdé O., Pineau, A., Leroux, G., Poirel, N., Perchey, G., Lanoë, C., et al. (2011). Functional MRI study of Piaget's conservation-of-number task in preschool and school-age children:

A neo-Piagetian approach. *Journal of Experimental Child Psychology, 110*, 332–346.

Jaffard, M., Benraiss, A., Longcamp, M., Velay, J.-L., & Boulinguez, P. (2007). Cueing method biases in visual detection studies. *Brain Research, 1179*, 106–118.

Jones, L. B., Rothbart, M. K., & Posner, M. I. (2003). Development of executive attention in preschool children. *Developmental Science, 6*, 498–504.

Kahneman, D. (1973). *Attention and Effort*. Englewood Cliffs, NJ: Prentice Hall.

Kanske, P., Heissler, J., & Schoenfelder, S. (2011). How to regulate emotion? Neural networks for reappraisal and distraction. *Cerebral Cortex, 21*, 1379–1388.

Kong, A., Thorleifsson, G., Frigge, M. I., Vilhjalmsson, B. J., & Stefansson, K. (2018). The nature of nurture: Effects of parental genotypes. *Science, 359*, 424–428.

Luu, P., Arumugam, E. M. E., Anderson, E., Gunn, A., Rech, D., Turovets, S., & Tucker, D. M. (2016). Slow-frequency pulsed transcranial electrical stimulation for modulation of cortical plasticity based on reciprocity targeting with precision electrical head modeling *Frontiers in Human Neuroscience, 10*, 377.

Markant, J., Cicchetti, D., Hetzel, S., & Thomas, K. M. (2014). Contributions of COMT Val[158] Met to cognitive stability and flexibility in infancy. *Development Science, 17*, 396–411.

Matthews, M., & Fair, D. A., (2015). Research review: Functional brain connectivity and child psychopathology – Overview and methodological consideration for investigators new to the field. *Journal of Child Psychology and Psychiatry, 56*, 400–414.

Morrison J. H., & Foote, S. L. (1986). Noradrenergic and serotoninergic innervation of cortical, thalamic and tectal visual structures in Old and New World monkeys. *The Journal of Comparative Neurology, 243*, 117–128.

Ochsner, K. N., Bunge, S. A., Gross, J. J., & Gabrieli, J. D. E. (2002). Rethinking feelings: An fMRI study of the cognitive regulation of emotion. *Journal of Cognitive Neuroscience, 14*, 1215–1229.

Parasuraman, R., Greenwood, P. M., Kumar, R., & Fossella, J. (2005). Beyond heritability: Neurotransmitter genes differentially modulate visuospatial attention and working memory. *Psychological Science, 16*, 200–207.

Parkes, L., Fulcher, B., Yücel, M., & Fornito, A. (2018). An evaluation of the efficacy, reliability, and sensitivity of motion correction strategies for resting-state functional MRI *Neuroimage, 171*, 415–436.

Petersen, S. E., & Posner, M. I. (2012). The attention system of the human brain: Twenty years after *Annual Review of Neuroscience, 35*, 71–89.

Pfaff, D. W., & Kieffer, B. L. (2008). Molecular and biophysical mechanisms of arousal, alertness, and attention. *Annals of the New York Academy of Sciences, 1129*, xi.

Piscopo, D. M., Weible, A. P., Rothbart, M. K., Posner, M. K. I., & Niell, C. M. (2018). Mechanisms of white matter change in mice given low frequency stimulation. *Proceedings of the National Academy of Sciences (USA), 115*, 6639–6646.

Posner, M. I. (1978). *Chronometric Explorations of Mind*. Hillsdale, NJ: Lawrence Erlbaum Associates.

Posner, M. I. (2008). Measuring alertness. *Annals of the New York Academy of Sciences, 1129*, 193–199.

Posner, M. I., & Fan, J. (2008). Attention as an organ system. In J. R. Pomerantz (ed.), *Topics in Integrative Neuroscience* (Ch. 2; pp. 31–61). New York: Cambridge University Press.

Posner, M. I., & Rothbart, M. K. (2007a). Research on attention networks as a model for integration of psychological science *Annual Review of Psychology, 58*, 1–23.

Posner, M. I., & Rothbart, M. K. (2007b). *Educating the Human Brain*. Washington, DC: APA Books.

Posner, M. I., & Rothbart, M. K. (2018). Parenting and human brain development. In M. R. Sanders, & A. Morawska (eds.), *Handbook of Parenting and Child Development Across the Lifespan* (pp. 173–200). New York: Springer.

Posner, M. I., Rothbart, M. K., Sheese, B. E., & Voelker, P. (2014a). Developing attention:

Behavioral and brain mechanisms. *Advances in Neuroscience, 2014*, 405094.

Posner, M. I., Tang, Y. Y., & Lynch, G. (2014b). Mechanisms of white matter change induced by meditation. *Frontiers in Psychology, 5*, 1220.

Pozuelos, J. P., Paz-Alonso, P. M., Castillo, A., Fuentes, L. J., & Rueda, M. R. (2014). Development of attention networks and their interactions in childhood. *Developmental Psychology, 50*, 102405–102415.

Reinhart, R. M. G. (2017). Disruption and rescue of interareal theta phase coupling and adaptive behavior. *Proceedings of the National Academy of Sciences (USA), 114*, 201710257.

Rothbart, M. K. (2011). *Becoming Who We Are*. New York: Guilford Press.

Rothbart, M. K., & Rueda, M. R. (2005). The development of effortful control. In U. Mayr, E. Awh, & S. W. Keele (eds.), *Developing Individuality in the Human Brain: A Tribute to Michael I. Posner* (pp. 167–188). Washington, DC: American Psychological Association.

Rothbart, M. K., & Sheese, B. E. (2007). Temperament and emotion regulation. In J. J. Gross (ed.), *Handbook of Emotion Regulation* (pp. 331–350). New York: Guilford Press.

Rothbart, M. K., Sheese, B. E., Rueda, M. R., & Posner, M. I. (2011). Developing mechanisms of self-regulation in early life. *Emotion Review, 3*, 207–213.

Rueda, M., Fan, J., McCandliss, B. D., Halparin, J. D., Gruber, D. B., Lercari, L. P., et al. (2004). Development of attentional networks in childhood. *Neuropsychologia, 42*, 1029–1040.

Sheese, B. E., Rothbart, M. K., Voelker, P., & Posner, M. I. (2012). The dopamine receptor D4 gene 7 repeat allele interacts with parenting quality to predict effortful control in four-year-old children. *Child Development Research, 2012*, 863242.

Sheese, B. E., Voelker, P. M., Rothbart, M. K., & Posner, M. I. (2007). Parenting quality interacts with genetic variation in dopamine receptor DRD4 to influence temperament in early childhood. *Development & Psychopathology, 19*, 1039–1046.

Shulman, G. L., Astafiev, S. V., Franke, D., Pope, D. L. W., Snyder, A. Z., McAvoy, M. P., & Corbett, M. (2009). Interaction of stimulus-driven reorienting and expectation in ventral and dorsal frontoparietal and basal ganglia-cortical networks. *Journal of Neuroscience, 29*, 4392–4407.

Stiles, J., & Jernigan, T. L. (2010). The basics of brain development. *Neuropsychological Review, 20*, 327–348.

Swanson, J., Oosterlaan, J., Murias, M., Schuck, S., Flodman, P., Spence, M. A., et al. (2000). Attention deficit/hyperactivity disorder children with a 7-repeat allele of the dopamine receptor D4 gene have extreme behavior but normal performance on critical neuropsychological tests attention. *Proceedings of the National Academy of Sciences (USA), 97*, 4754–4759.

Tang, Y.-Y., Lu, Q., Fan, M., Yang, Y., & Posner, M. I. (2012). Mechanisms of wWhite matter changes induced by meditation. *Proceedings of the National Academy of Sciences (USA), 109*, 10570–10574.

Tang, Y. Y., Lu, Q., Geng, X., Stein, E. A., Yang, Y., & Posner, M. I. (2010). Short term mental training induces white-matter changes in the anterior cingulate. *Proceedings of the National Academy of Sciences (USA), 107*, 16649–16652.

Thomason, M. E., Brown, J. A., Dassanayake, M. T., Shastri, R., Marusak, H. A., Hernandez-Anrade, E., et al. (2014). Intrinsic functional brain architecture derived from graph theoretical analysis in the human fetus. *PLoS ONE, 9*, e94423.

Thomason, M. E., Grove, L. E., Lozon, T. A., Vila, A. M., Ye, Y. Q., Nye, M. J., et al. (2015). Age-related increases in long-range connectivity in fetal functional neural connectivity networks in utero. *Developmental Cognitive Neuroscience, 11*, 96–104.

Thompson, K. G., Biscoe, K. L., & Sato, T. R. (2005). Neuronal basis of covert spatial attention in the frontal eye fields. *Journal of Neuroscience, 25*, 9479–9487.

Van Dijk, K. R., Sabuncu, M. R., & Buckner, R. L. (2012). The influence of head motion on intrinsic functional connectivity MRI. *NeuroImage, 59*, 431–438.

Van Ijzendoorn, M. H., & Bakermans-Kranenburg, M. J. (2006). DRD4 7-repeat polymorphism moderates the association between maternal unresolved loss or trauma and infant disorganization, *Attachment and Human Development, 8*, 291–307.

Vértes, P. E., & Bullmore, E. T. (2015). Annual research review: Growth connectomics – The organization and reorganization of brain networks during normal and abnormal development. *Journal of Child Psychology and Psychiatry, 56*, 299–320.

Voelker, P., Sheese, B. E., Rothbart, M. K., & Posner, M. I. (2009). Variations in COMT gene interact with parenting to influence attention in early development. *Neuroscience, 164*, 121–130.

Wang, E. T., Kodama, G., Baldi, P., & Moyzis, R. K. (2006). Global landscape of recent inferred Darwinian selection for *Homo sapiens. Proceedings of the National Academy of Science (USA), 103*, 135–140.

Wang, S., & Young, K. M. (2014). White matter plasticity in adulthood. *Neuroscience, 276*, 148–160.

Weible, A. P., Piscopo, D. M., Rothbart, M. K., Posner, M. I., & Niell, C. M. (2017). Rhythmic brain stimulation reduces anxiety-related behavior in a mouse model based on meditation training. *Proceedings of the National Academy of Sciences (USA), 114*, 2532–2537.

Winterer, G., Musso, F., Konrad, A., Vucurevic, G., Stoeter, P., Sander, T., & Gallinat, J. (2007). Association of attentional network function with exon 5 variations of the *CHRNA4* gene. *Human Molecular Genetics, 16*, 2165–2174.

Wynn, K. (1992). Addition and subtraction by human infants. *Nature, 358*, 749–750.

Xue, S., Tang, Y. Y., Tang, R., & Posner, M. I. (2014). Short-term meditation induces changes in brain resting EEG theta networks. *Brain and Cognition, 87*, 1–6.

Zhu, M., & Zhao, S. (2007). Candidate gene identification approach: Progress and challenges. *International Journal of Biological Studies, 3*, 420–427.

6 The Brain Basis Underlying the Transition from Adolescence to Adulthood

Beatriz Luna, Orma Ravindranath, Bart Larsen, and Ashley Parr

6.1 Introduction

Adolescence is primarily characterized by puberty (Vijayakumar et al., 2018) which demarcates sexual maturation that can start as young as 10–12 years of age (Parent et al., 2003) and proceeds until adult independence, which may continue until the mid-twenties (National Research Council, 2013). Adolescence is characterized as a time of a peak in sensation seeking (Chambers et al., 2003; Spear, 2000), the drive to explore novel experiences that generate increased sensations, despite possible long-term negative consequences (Zuckerman, 2008). While sensation seeking can be *adaptive*, including information seeking and exploration, to gain new experiences needed to optimally develop into an independent adult, it can also lead to risk-taking behavior, due to decision-making processes that weigh short-term rewards over long-term risks to survival. In fact, adolescents in the United States experience a four-fold increase in deaths over US adults due to risk-taking behaviors (e.g., crime, substance use, reckless driving) (Eaton et al., 2012). Thus, adolescents are often believed to lack forethought and behave in volatile and unpredictable ways. Adolescent peaks in sensation seeking, however, are present across species (Hodes & Shors, 2005; Stansfield & Kirstein, 2006) and across cultures (Steinberg et al., 2018), underscoring their adaptive nature. Adolescence is also a time for vulnerability to the emergence of psychopathology such as schizophrenia, mood disorders, anxiety, suicidality, and addiction (Paus et al., 2008). This adolescent vulnerability for emergence of psychopathology suggests that maturational processes unique to this period may impair development and/or reveal impairments that are present but unseen until puberty, becoming apparent as the brain transitions through adolescence and into adulthood. Thus, there is great interest in understanding the neurobiological mechanisms that underlie normative development to identify brain processes that may contribute to impaired development in adolescence.

As discussed in this chapter, adolescent brain maturation is widely understood as a unique time when *affective processes* – including reward sensitivity, motivation, and emotion – have heightened effects on behavior relative to *cognitive control processes*, including purposeful planned goal-directed behavior. Sensation seeking reflects this state as it is driven by the predominant influence of reward processing over deliberate cognitive control of behavior. Importantly, across mental illnesses there is a toll on both cognitive (Nigg, 2017) and reward (Blum et al., 2000) processing. Dual Systems Models of adolescence depict this unique weighing of affective over cognitive executive processes that lead to sensation seeking (Shulman et al., 2016). In particular, the engagement of the prefrontal cortex (PFC), which plays a primary role in executive cognitive function, is proposed to be undermined by affective processes engaging limbic regions including the ventral striatum (VS), which supports reward/motivation, and the amygdala, which supports emotion processing. The earliest model proposed that affective systems may mature earlier than executive prefrontal systems, resulting in a predominant influence of affect and reward over cognitive control (Casey et al., 2008; Somerville & Casey, 2010). More recent evidence indicates protracted maturation of limbic systems that may be more prolonged than prefrontal executive systems (Raznahan et al., 2014; Sowell et al., 1999) and evidence from animal models suggests that there may be a peak in the processing of the neurotransmitter dopamine that supports reward and motivation (detailed in Section 6.2.2). In light of these findings, newer models propose that the predominant influence of motivational systems may be due to a heightened sensitivity to rewards (Shulman et al., 2016). The "Maturation Imbalance Model" proposes that executive prefrontal systems have not yet matured to adult levels in adolescence and the peak in motivational systems can readily influence an immature cognitive control system (Steinberg et al., 2008). Finally, the model that we put forth, "The Driven Dual Systems Model," proposes that, in fact, adult level prefrontal executive systems are available by adolescence, but are unstable and driven by heightened sensitivity to rewards and motivation (Luna & Wright, 2016). Thus, adolescence can be viewed as a time when executive control processes are newly-gained, allowing complex goal directed plans, but these are influenced by the pursuit of rewards and sensation seeking. Thus, all models agree that adolescence is a time of increased influence of motivational/reward systems over cognitive control systems, whose level of maturity in adolescence is still under debate.

This chapter will present the current status of the literature indicating that cognitive and brain development through childhood can be seen as proceeding in an additive manner as abilities are gained and brain structure grows. By adolescence, there is evidence that adult levels of cognitive control are available, but the stability and reliability of their implementation improves as neural processes become more specialized. We will present evidence of maturational changes that proceed through adolescence, including brain function, structure, and connectivity that inform a model of adolescent specialization.

6.2 Functional Cognitive Development

As previously mentioned, Dual Systems models posit that the mechanism underlying increased sensation seeking and unreliable cognitive control in adolescence is the predominance of affective systems over cognitive control systems due to their differential maturational trajectories (Shulman et al., 2016). Therefore, it is important to understand the development of these two systems and their interactions to fully characterize functional development during adolescence and young adulthood. Here, we summarize current knowledge on the development of these functional systems and their effects on behavioral development.

6.2.1 Executive Control System

While the core aspects of executive function are available by adolescence (Amso & Johnson, 2005; Diamond & Goldman-Rakic, 1989), refinement of these abilities continues into adulthood (Luna et al., 2015). This protracted developmental trajectory is driven in part by the ability for the PFC to interact with other relevant brain regions. By mid-to-late adolescence, PFC function is accessible but can be highly unreliable and dependent on contextual factors. One of these still-developing abilities is inhibitory control, or the ability to suppress a prepotent response in favor of a goal-directed action (Bari & Robbins, 2013; Houdé, 2001, 2004; Luna, 2009). Although the ability to exert inhibitory control exists as early as infancy (Johnson, 1995), the rate of correct inhibitory responses significantly increases into adulthood (Dempster, 1992; Houdé, 2019; Houdé & Borst, 2015, Houdé et al., 2011; Luna et al., 2004). Inhibitory control is typically assessed with tasks that require suppression of distracting stimuli and impulsive responses in favor of a goal-driven response. These tasks include the antisaccade task, where participants must refrain from looking at a visual stimulus and look at its mirror location; the flanker task, where participants press a button in response to a cue flanked by distractors; the go no-go task, where participants must interrupt an established response pattern; and the stop-signal task, where participants must interrupt an ongoing behavior when prompted. Using these tasks, functional MRI (fMRI) studies have found both age-related increases and decreases in the recruitment of PFC regions (Luna et al., 2001; Marsh et al., 2006), likely due to either more optimal engagement of these regions with development, or greater effort exerted at younger ages to produce a correct cognitive response (Luna et al., 2010). In recent years, developmental decreases in prefrontal engagement through childhood have become the more predominant result (Alahyane et al., 2014; Ordaz et al., 2013), which are associated with age-related improvements in performance (Dwyer et al., 2014, Luna et al., 2004). However, these findings are based on cross-sectional data that can limit the ability to assess true developmental change due to cohort effects. Longitudinal studies provide a robust method to characterize within-participant developmental trajectories, providing a more direct view of individual rates of maturation. A longitudinal fMRI study

of inhibitory control using the antisaccade task showed that prefrontal activation decreased from childhood to adolescence, when it reached adult levels (Ordaz et al., 2013). However, activation within the dorsal anterior cingulate cortex (dACC) continued to increase into adulthood, as had been found in cross-sectional studies (Adleman, 2002; Velanova et al., 2008). Additionally, dACC activation was associated with superior performance, and mediated the relationship between age and inhibitory control performance. The dACC supports performance monitoring (Braver et al., 2001), and its connections to regions throughout the brain allow for efficient integration of several sources of information, making it an ideal hub for performance monitoring, by acting as an alert system to engage executive systems (Posner & Fan, 2008; Posner et al., 2014). Together, these results indicate that by adolescence, the PFC is functioning with adult-like maturity during cognitive control processes, but performance monitoring capabilities have not yet reached adult levels.

Another core component of executive function is working memory, the ability to maintain information over a brief period of time (seconds) for use in guiding goal-directed behavior (Baddeley, 1986). Working memory is typically measured using tasks that require a response that is determined by information that was processed and retained online. Such tasks include the memory-guided saccade task, where participants make an eye movement guided by the information in working memory of the cue location prior to a delay period; and the n-back task, where participants make a response based on a sequence of previously presented stimuli. The accuracy of working memory guided responses shows significant improvements through childhood and late adolescence (Conklin et al., 2007; Crone et al., 2006) and proceeding into young adulthood (Luna et al., 2004). fMRI studies show that developmental improvements in performance are associated with age-related changes in brain activity (O'Hare et al., 2008; Satterthwaite et al., 2013). Extant regions are recruited throughout development, but the degree and consistency of their engagement changes with development (Geier et al., 2009; Montez et al., 2017). Similar to inhibitory control, a longitudinal study found that activation of PFC decreased from childhood to adolescence, by which point it was successfully engaged at adult levels (Simmonds et al., 2017). In contrast, activation of the visual association cortex, where the information from working memory is stored in visual tasks (Postle et al., 2003), increased into adulthood (Simmonds et al., 2017), suggesting developmental improvements in ready engagement of optimal circuitry. Importantly, although mean performance improves with age, intrasubject variability across trials decreases (Montez et al., 2017). That is, while adolescents can execute adult-like responses on some trials, they still produce a high level of incorrect or imprecise responses, indicating that what improves with development is the ability to reliably generate correct responses. Additionally, intrasubject variability was associated with variability in the magnitude of the expression of whole brain patterns of cognitive function, both of which decreased through the adolescent period, illustrating specialization of key neural systems that stabilize in adulthood. A possible interpretation is that neural processes may be variably "testing" different magnitudes of activity in a Hebbian process to establish optimal brain function that results in optimal working memory. Together, these results suggest that, by adolescence, the PFC can operate at adult levels, but specialization within regions that support precision of responses continues into adulthood, which may be due to enhancements and specialization of PFC connectivity.

6.2.2 Affective Systems

Along with systems underlying cognitive control, affective systems also undergo significant development and specialization during adolescence. Past work has suggested that adolescents may be more sensitive to reward-related stimuli than children or adults (Casey et al., 2010; Geier & Luna, 2012), likely resulting from concurrent fluctuations within the DA system (Padmanabhan & Luna, 2014). Several studies suggest that adolescents may be hypersensitive to reward anticipation and/or reward receipt. For example, increased activation of the ventral striatum in adolescents compared to adults has been observed while anticipating whether a trial will be rewarded (Geier et al., 2010; Padmanabhan et al., 2011). However, some work has shown that ventral striatal activity may be decreased in adolescents when viewing an abstract reward cue (Bjork et al., 2004, 2010). Additionally, multiple studies of reward processing report decreased activation of the orbitofrontal cortex, which is involved in assessing reward value and linking reward to available actions, in adolescents compared to adults (Geier et al., 2010; Padmanabhan et al., 2011). These results suggest that the presence of a reward may lead to hyperactivity of the midbrain reward system in adolescence, coupled with decreased modulation from PFC structures (e.g., the orbitofrontal cortex). In social situations, adolescents also show striking differences compared to adults during reward processing tasks. One study showed that, in the presence of peers, adolescents had greater increases in ventral striatum activity in response to reward receipt compared to adults (Smith et al., 2015), and these increases have also been shown to predict subsequent risk-tasking in a laboratory setting (Chein et al., 2011).

Studies of emotion processing have largely consisted of tasks involving facial emotions, many of which reveal increased activation for emotional faces across brain regions in adolescents compared to adults. Specifically, the amygdala (Guyer et al., 2008; Killgore & Yurgelun-Todd, 2007), ventral striatum, ventromedial PFC (Pfeifer et al., 2011), and other areas of the PFC (Hare et al., 2008) all show increased activity during adolescence compared to both children and adults during emotional face stimuli tasks. The increased PFC activity observed in many of these studies may reflect increased cognitive control mechanisms recruited by adolescents in affective contexts, but few studies have attempted to test this directly.

How cognitive/prefrontal and affective/limbic systems interact may be particularly informative of unique maturation in adolescence. Research suggests that cognitive control abilities may be heavily influenced by motivational factors and affective context, particularly during adolescence. For example, studies have shown that, in the presence of impending rewards, adolescents show increased engagement of the ventral striatum in parallel to hyper-recruitment of regions that support the behaviors that lead to reward receipt (Padmanabhan et al., 2011; Paulsen et al., 2015). Furthermore, in the presence of an affective context such as emotionally arousing sounds, adolescents may exhibit poorer inhibitory control than adults, driven by lower state-based connectivity between the amygdala and executive control regions (Ravindranath et al., 2020). Overall, these findings suggest that, during adolescence, affective systems may have a greater influence on behavior, undermining cognitive systems.

6.3 Brain Structural Maturation

While the gross morphology of the brain is in place by mid-childhood as weight and size become established (Caviness et al., 1996), maturation continues through the adolescent period in parallel with developmental gains in cognitive control (Luna et al., 2015). Here we present the literature that delineates brain maturational changes in brain structure through the adolescent period.

6.3.1 Gray Matter

The gray matter is where neurons reside, enveloping the brain surface and nuclei within the brain. Adolescent maturation of the prefrontal cortex (PFC) is of special interest because of its primary role in executive functions through its whole brain systems-level connectivity and neural architecture that supports complex processing underlying planned goal-driven behavior (Fuster, 2008). Postmortem studies in human and non-human primates indicate that a primary brain maturational process involves the multiplication of synaptic connections (synaptogenesis) that is followed by the loss of less-used synaptic connections (synaptic pruning). Initial human postmortem studies found evidence for hierarchical brain maturation with synaptic pruning reaching adult levels in the visual cortex by childhood, followed by the auditory cortex by late childhood, and the PFC maturing throughout adolescence (Huttenlocher, 1990; Huttenlocher & Dabholkar, 1997). More recently, using a larger sample and more advanced techniques, evidence has been found for more prolonged synaptic maturation in PFC, with synaptogenesis proceeding into childhood followed by synaptic pruning extending into the third decade of life (Petanjek et al., 2011). The loss of unused synapses increases the signal-to-noise ratio in these areas, supporting more optimal processing that facilitates higher-level computations needed for cognitive control. Importantly, the prolonged duration of synaptic pruning in PFC suggests that this part of the brain, and thus cognition, experiences elevated plasticity believed to be necessary for the brain to adapt to the specific demands of the environment (Larsen & Luna, 2018). That said, other association areas, including regions that have high connectivity supporting complex processing (e.g., the parietal cortex), have not been studied extensively and may also undergo protracted maturation.

The advent of Magnetic Resonance Imaging (MRI) enabled the investigation of maturational changes in gray matter across the whole brain including cortical volume and thickness of not only PFC but other cortical and subcortical regions. The ability to characterize maturation of the PFC, which supports executive control, as well as subcortical regions such as the striatum and the amygdala, which support reward and emotion processing, respectively, is critical to the Dual Systems models of adolescent neurocognitive maturation. MRI studies have revealed that, similar to synaptic pruning, gray matter thickness increases through childhood, followed by a decrease in volume throughout adolescence, driven by cortical thinning and increases in white matter connectivity (Gogtay et al., 2004; Mills et al., 2016). In particular, PFC, but also other cortical regions including language areas in the temporal cortex and association areas of the visual cortex, are still maturing in adolescence. Similarly, subcortical regions, including the striatum and thalamus (Raznahan et al., 2014), and hippocampus (Daugherty et al., 2016), also show a protracted maturation through adolescence that may proceed later than cortical systems. Together, these studies provide compelling evidence that during adolescence, association areas supporting cognitive control and subcortical areas supporting affective processing and memory are still in an elevated state of plasticity and have not reached adult levels of stable processing.

6.3.2 White Matter

White matter is comprised of axons that transmit neuronal signals through long-range connections across the brain. During development, white matter tracts are enveloped with a fatty substance through "myelination," increasing speed and fidelity of neurotransmission supporting the ready engagement of top-down processing needed for executive function. Similar to synaptic pruning, early histological studies of postmortem brain tissue (Benes et al., 1994; Yakovlev et al., 1967) found hierarchical myelination with sensory areas reaching adult levels in early childhood, while association cortices, including frontal, parietal, and temporal cortices, matured into the second decade of life.

The findings of early histological studies have been corroborated by more recent work using in vivo neuroimaging techniques implemented with MRI, such as morphometry/volumetry, myelin mapping, and diffusion weighted imaging, which provides measures of the integrity of white matter. MRI morphometry studies, which parcellate white matter from gray matter and calculate the volume of white matter in the brain, show non-linear increases in white matter volume from childhood through young adulthood that plateau in mid-life (approximately the fourth and fifth decade of life), indicating a prolonged period of white matter maturation (Giedd et al., 1999; Rowley et al., 2017). Females consistently show earlier maturation of white matter volume compared to males, paralleling sex differences in pubertal timing (Lenroot & Giedd, 2006; Simmonds et al., 2014). Note that these MRI approaches cannot differentiate the contribution of myelination from other elements that make up white matter, including the number or size of the axons and water content (Paus, 2010). MRI myelin mapping techniques that use a specific MR contrast sensitive to myelin content – the T1w/T2w ratio (Glasser & Van Essen, 2011) – to carefully map myelin concentration within the cortex, also find evidence for increased myelination throughout adolescence, extending into later adulthood (Grydeland et al., 2013; Shafee et al., 2015). Notably, a unique quantitative myelin mapping technique known as magnetization transfer ratio (MTR) showed that while MTR slightly increased in females, it decreased in males during adolescence in a manner that corresponded with rising testosterone levels (Perrin et al., 2008, 2009).

Diffusion Weighted MRI (DWI) assesses white matter integrity by measuring the degree of diffusion of water molecules in tracts throughout the brain. Diffusion Tensor Imaging (DTI) is a DWI method that provides a measure of fractional anisotropy (FA), the ratio of diffusion along a primary fiber direction relative to perpendicular diffusion. Developmental studies of FA during adolescence have found that a number of major white matter pathways linking areas of the association cortex (involved in complex cognitive functions) show a significant increase in integrity through childhood into adolescence, where many have reached adult levels (Simmonds et al., 2014; Tamnes et al., 2011). The uncinate fasciculus and cingulum, which provide connectivity of prefrontal, limbic, and temporal regions, and support socioemotional processing, continue to mature into the twenties. These changes in white matter integrity have been found to depict periods of dynamic growth predominantly in childhood and early adolescence and into young adulthood in tracts supporting socioemotional processing (Simmonds et al., 2014). The protracted period of refinement of these pathways may reflect continued myelination and/or changes to axonal properties like axon width, directional coherence of axon bundles, or bundling density. A limitation of

FA measures is that it is undermined by crossing fibers limiting the ability to assess change in high cross-traffic regions (Pierpaoli et al., 2001). Recent approaches, such as those that measure quantitative anisotropy (QA), are more robust to the influence of crossing fibers (and other artifacts such as partial volume effects) than FA (Yeh et al., 2013). Studies using QA to investigate the development of cortico-subcortical connectivity relevant to affective processes have found that the QA *decreases* in specific connections during adolescence (Jalbrzikowski et al., 2017; Larsen et al., 2018). In particular, white matter fibers from cognitive networks that converge with fibers from limbic/affective regions in the basal ganglia, which determines action, show predominance of affective fibers in adolescence that changes to cognitive fibers predominating in adulthood (Larsen et al., 2018). This age-related change in the ratio of limbic/cognitive fibers was found to be driven by decreases in limbic fibers into adulthood while fibers from cognitive networks remained stable (Larsen et al., 2018). Similarly, QA shows a decrease in white matter integrity between the amygdala and PFC that parallels decreased functional connectivity (Jalbrzikowski et al., 2017). Together, DWI studies indicate that overall white matter tracts are strengthening predominantly during childhood but many including those supporting PFC systems are mature by mid-adolescence. In contrast, when focusing on cortico-subcortical connectivity, findings indicate decreases through adolescence providing a potential mechanism for decreases in the influence of affective systems into adulthood.

6.4 Brain Connectivity

6.4.1 Whole Brain Network Organization

The brain is continually in a state of activity as different brain regions integrate diverse sources of information. When focused on a task, specialized regions and their networks become increasingly engaged as reflected in task fMRI studies. When not engaged in a task, spontaneous neural activity between inherently functionally connected regions is evident (Newman, 2010). Resting state fMRI (rsfMRI) is obtained while participants are asked to do nothing and thus not be engaged in a task. This allows for the identification of regions that are communicating by recognizing correlations in the temporal structure of their spontaneous activity, known as *functional* connectivity. In this manner, groups of regions can be categorized as networks based on similar profiles of spontaneous activity. This approach has characterized approximately twenty networks (Menon, 2013) that correspond to different processes including: sensory systems (somatomotor and visual); cognitive processes (frontoparietal (FP) and cinguloopercular/salience (CO/Salience) networks); and, importantly, non-task related processing such as daydreaming or intro/retrospection (default mode (DM) network) (Power et al., 2011). These brain networks have a reliable organizational structure and together make up the brain connectome (Newman, 2010).

Developmental studies initially suggested that short-distance functional connections give way to long-distance connections with age, impacting the organization of larger networks (Fair et al., 2009; Fransson et al., 2011). However, since children move their heads more frequently during MRI scans, age-related differences in head motion artifacts were found to underlie initial age-related differences in network organization (Hallquist et al., 2013; Power et al., 2012). Advances in data processing methods (Hallquist et al., 2013; Power et al., 2014) and recent findings suggest that foundational aspects of functional network *organization*, or the formation of unique networks from individual brain

regions, are established early in development, while processes related to network *integration*, or the communication between different established groups of regions, continue to mature into adulthood (Hwang et al., 2013; Marek et al., 2015). This increase in network integration, particularly the integration of the cingulo-opercular/salience network, which is an important cognitive control network, was associated with age-related improvements in inhibitory control (Marek et al., 2015). Thus, the network structure of the brain is on-line through development, but the ability for networks to interact and exchange information continues to specialize through adolescence.

6.4.2 Prefrontal/Subcortical Connections

This section will discuss current knowledge on developmental changes in connectivity within the PFC-ventral striatum, PFC-amygdala, and PFC-hippocampus that underlie improvements in adolescents' ability to synthesize reward, affect, and memory information in order to support goal-oriented behavior.

6.4.2.1 Fronto-Striatal Connections

Developmental Dual Systems Models of adolescent development emphasize that the relative predominance of striatal signaling over prefrontal systems underlies increased sensation seeking and heightened exploration in adolescents (Shulman et al., 2016). Functional connectivity studies provide support for these models as they show developmental decreases in functional connectivity between the PFC and the VS through adolescence into adulthood (van Duijvenvoorde et al., 2016; Parr et al., 2021). A recent longitudinal study showed that these developmental decreases in PFC – VS functional connectivity were accompanied by developmental improvements in reward-guided decision-making, and decreases in real-world indices of risk-taking behavior into adulthood (Parr et al., 2021). Furthermore, these changes were supported by indices reflecting striatal dopamine-related neurophysiology (Parr et al., 2021). Providing further support for a dual-systems model of development, decreases in PFC – VS connectivity across adolescence may be driven by decreases in the predominance of striatal influence over PFC executive processing. As mentioned in Section 6.3.2, developmental changes in white matter connectivity show similar findings of decreases in white matter fiber integrity in limbic relative to cognitive inputs to the basal ganglia into adulthood (Larsen et al., 2018).

6.4.2.2 Fronto-Amygdala Connections

Through adolescence, enhancements in cognition support improvements in control over affective systems (Hare et al., 2008). Correspondingly, the amygdala (AMY) and the PFC, particularly the ventromedial PFC (vmPFC), and PFC/AMY connectivity have been implicated in emotional processing and the regulation of emotion (Blakemore, 2008; Steinberg, 2008). Initial task-based studies (primarily using emotional face paradigms) suggested a developmental decrease in mPFC-AMY task-related functional connectivity through childhood and adolescence, that was associated with age-related declines in AMY reactivity to emotional stimuli (Gee et al., 2013). Specifically, while processing negative emotion, youth showed stronger connectivity between the AMY and medial PFC which decreased into adulthood, suggesting maturation of systems required to regulate emotional processes (Silvers et al., 2017). Initial rsfMRI studies showed increases in PFC/AMY connectivity through adolescence (Gabard-Durnam et al., 2014).

However, a more recent study with a larger number of participants that included longitudinal data and replication using a large, publicly available fMRI dataset, found definitive decreases in connectivity between the medial PFC and AMY in parallel with decreases in structural white matter connectivity (Jalbrzikowski et al., 2017). This is in contrast to findings showing that the integrity of the uncinate fasciculus (UF), a major white matter tract that facilitates connectivity between PFC systems and subcortical regions such as the amygdala (also hippocampus – see Section 6.4.2.3), strengthen into adulthood. Together, these findings suggest that there may be dynamic decreases in the functional influence of emotional processing in the AMY on executive PFC processing as major white matter pathways strengthen, paralleling known developmental decreases in emotional reactivity.

6.4.2.3 Fronto-Hippocampal Connections

During adolescence, the ability to use prior experiences to support goal-directed behavior is facilitated, in part, by functional specialization among PFC-hippocampal (HPC) circuits (Murty et al., 2016). The HPC has been found to have a protracted development throughout adolescence into adulthood (Daugherty et al., 2016; Tamnes et al., 2014), potentially maturing on a longer timescale than the PFC (Murty et al., 2016). As described in Section 6.4.2.2, the UF provides connectivity between PFC and subcortical regions including HPC, which continues to strengthen through young adulthood (Lebel et al., 2012; Simmonds et al., 2014). Increases in white matter connectivity are believed to support developmental improvements in HPC associative memory processes, enhancing goal-directed behavior into adulthood (Ghetti & Bunge, 2012; Von

Der Heide et al., 2013). Functional studies have shown that greater reliance on the PFC accompanies improvements in associative memory processes in adolescence (Ofen et al., 2007), and that PFC-HPC connectivity may support associative memory processes as early as childhood/pre-adolescence (Riggins et al., 2016). However, the refinement of these circuits continues during adolescence, supporting developmental improvements in executive functions such as working memory (Finn et al., 2010), feedback learning (Voss et al., 2015), future planning (Calabro et al., 2020), and even arithmetic problem-solving (Qin et al., 2014). Rodent models have found that, during puberty, a rise in dopamine processing results in greater coupling between PFC and HPC, supporting the ability to integrate executive and associative processes (O'Donnell, 2010). This enhancement in the integration of PFC and HPC systems has led to the "experience-driven adaptive cognition" model (Murty et al., 2016), which proposes that adolescence may be a crucial period when experiences inform contextual learning, given that adolescents are gaining unique agency as individuals and are seeking new experiences outside the context of adult supervision. Thus, behaviors can be adapted across different contexts, defining a mode of operation that will define the individual and provide stability into adulthood. In the context of dual systems models which agree that sensation seeking is an adaptive means to gain new experiences, the integration of associative systems in the HPC provide a mechanism for integrating these formative experiences that will help determine adult trajectories.

Together, connectivity studies suggest a model where the influence of affect on prefrontal executive function is greater in adolescence, underlying sensation seeking that may be crucial for engaging memory systems to help establish behaviors that will predominate in adulthood.

6.5 Future Directions and Conclusions

This chapter presents the accumulated literature that inform a model of adolescent neurocognitive development characterized by specialization and refinement of core brain systems that will establish adult modes of operation. In particular, adolescence is a time when adult level executive function is available, but not in the controlled and flexible manner that it will be in adulthood. Influencing this new yet unstable decision-making resource is heightened affect and reward motivation that together support the elevated sensation seeking needed for brain specialization. These neurocognitive changes in the adolescent brain reflect a time when affect has the greatest influence over executive function, impacting decision-making. Neural specialization occurs through the strengthening and weakening of different connections, shifting the influence over behavior from reward and emotion toward executive systems. As such, adolescence is a time of critical period plasticity within higher-order association areas that specialize in the context of environmental demands interacting with a neurobiological genetic predisposition.

This time of specialization is also a period of increased risk for the emergence of psychopathology, including mood disorders, psychosis, and substance use. Thus, it is of great significance to understand the mechanisms at work during this period of transition to adulthood in order to inform preventive and intervention approaches. The next steps in the field include further investigation of the unique changes in different aspects of brain maturation, including neurotransmitter changes through adolescent development and how these interact with pubertal processes. Ultimately, the goal is to be able to precisely identify how unique brain processes affect specific aspects of development in order to enhance healthy development and limit the emergence of psychiatric disorders.

References

Adleman, N. E. (2002). A developmental fMRI study of the Stroop color-word task. *NeuroImage, 16,* 61–75.

Alahyane, N., Brien, D. C., Coe, B. C., Stroman, P. W., & Munoz, D. P. (2014). Developmental improvements in voluntary control of behavior: Effect of preparation in the fronto-parietal network? *NeuroImage, 98,* 103–117.

Amso, D., & Johnson, S. P. (2005). Selection and inhibition in infancy: Evidence from the spatial negative priming paradigm. *Cognition, 95,* B27–B36.

Baddeley, A. (1986). *Working Memory.* New York: Oxford University Press.

Bari, A., & Robbins, T. W. (2013). Inhibition and impulsivity: Behavioral and neural basis of response control. *Progress in Neurobiology, 108,* 44–79.

Benes, F. M., Turtle, M., Khan, Y., & Farol, P. (1994). Myelination of a key relay zone in the hippocampal formation occurs in the human brain during childhood, adolescence, and adulthood. *Archives of General Psychiatry, 51,* 477–484.

Bjork, J.M., Knutson, B., Fong, G. W., Caggiano, D. M., Bennett, S. M., & Hommer, D. W. (2004). Incentive-elicited brain activation in adolescents: Similarities and differences from young adults. *Journal of Neuroscience, 24,* 1793–1802.

Bjork, J. M., Smith, A. R., Chen, G., & Hommer, D. W. (2010). Adolescents, adults and rewards: Comparing motivational neurocircuitry recruitment using fMRI. *PLoS.ONE, 5,* e11440.

Blakemore, S.-J. (2008). The social brain in adolescence. *Nature Reviews Neuroscience, 9,* 267–277.

Blum, K., Braverman, E. R., Holder, J. M., Lubar, J. F., Monastra, V. J., Miller, D., . . . & Comings, D. E. (2000). The reward deficiency syndrome: a biogenetic model for the diagnosis and treatment of impulsive, addictive and compulsive behaviors. *Journal of psychoactive drugs, 32*(sup1), 1–112.

Braver, T. S., Barch, D. M., Gray, J. R., Molfese, D. L., & Snyder, A. (2001). Anterior cingulate cortex and response conflict: effects of frequency, inhibition and errors. *Cerebral Cortex, 11,* 825–836.

Casey, B. J., Jones, R. M., & Hare, T. A. (2008). The adolescent brain. *Annals of the New York Academy of Sciences, 1124,* 111–126.

Casey, B. J., Jones, R. M., Levita, L., Libby, V., Pattwell, S. S., Ruberry, E. J., . . . Somerville, L. H. (2010). The storm and stress of adolescence: Insights from human imaging and mouse genetics. *Developmental Psychobiology, 52,* 225–235.

Calabro, F. J., Murty, V. P., Jalbrzikowski, M., Tervo-Clemmens, B., & Luna, B. (2020). Development of hippocampal-prefrontal cortex interactions through adolescence. *Cerebral Cortex, 30*(3), 1548–1558.

Caviness, V. S., Kennedy, D. N., Bates, J. F., & Makris, N. (1996). The developing human brain: A morphometric profile. In R. W. Thatcher, G. R. Lyon, J. Rumsey, & N. Krasnegor (eds.), *Developmental Neuroimaging: Mapping the Development of Brain and Behavior* (pp. 3–14). New York: Academic Press.

Chambers, R. A., Taylor, J. R., & Potenza, M. N. (2003). Developmental neurocircuitry of motivation in adolescence: A critical period of addiction vulnerability. *The American Journal of Psychiatry, 160,* 1041–1052.

Chein, J., Albert, D., O'Brien, L., Uckert, K., & Steinberg, L. (2011). Peers increase adolescent risk taking by enhancing activity in the brain's reward circuitry. *Developmental Science, 14*(2), F1–10.

Conklin, H. M., Luciana, M., Hooper, C. J., & Yarger, R. S. (2007). Working memory performance in typically developing children and adolescents: Behavioral evidence of protracted frontal lobe development. *Developmental Neuropsychology*, *31*, 103–128.

Crone, E. A., Wendelken, C., Donohue, S., van Leijenhorst, L., & Bunge, S. A. (2006). Neurocognitive development of the ability to manipulate information in working memory. *Proceedings of the National Academy of Sciences*, *103*, 9315–9320.

Daugherty, A. M., Bender, A. R., Raz, N., & Ofen, N. (2016). Age differences in hippocampal subfield volumes from childhood to late adulthood. *Hippocampus*, *26*, 220–228.

Dempster, F. N. (1992). The rise and fall of the inhibitory mechanism: Toward a unified theory of cognitive development and aging. *Developmental Review*, *12*, 45–75.

Diamond, A., & Goldman-Rakic, P. S. (1989). Comparison of human infants and rhesus monkeys on Piaget's AB task: Evidence for dependence on dorsolateral prefrontal cortex. *Experimental Brain Research*, *74*, 24–40.

Dwyer, D. B., Harrison, B. J., Yücel, M., Whittle, S., Zalesky, A., Pantelis, C., ... Fornito, A. (2014). Large-scale brain network dynamics supporting adolescent cognitive control. *The Journal of Neuroscience*, *34*, 14096–14107.

Eaton, D. K., Kann, L., Kinchen, S., Shanklin, S., Flint, K. H., Hawkins, J., ... Wechsler, H. (2012). Youth risk behavior surveillance –United States, 2011. *Morbidity and Mortality Weekly Report Surveillance Summaries*, *61*, 1–162.

Fair, D. A., Cohen, A. L., Power, J. D., Dosenbach, N. U. F., Church, J. A., Miezin, F. M., ... Petersen, S. E. (2009). Functional brain networks develop from a "local to distributed" organization. *PLoS Computational Biology*, *5*, e1000381.

Finn, A. S., Sheridan, M. A., Kam, C. L. H., Hinshaw, S. & D'Esposito, M. (2010). Longitudinal evidence for functional specialization of the neural circuit supporting working memory in the human brain. *The Journal of Neuroscience*, *30*, 11062–11067.

Fransson, P., Aden, U., Blennow, M., & Lagercrantz, H. (2011). The functional architecture of the infant brain as revealed by resting-state fMRI. *Cerebral Cortex*, *21*, 145–154.

Fuster, J. M. (2008). *The Prefrontal Cortex*. London: Academic Press.

Gabard-Durnam, L. J., Flannery, J., Goff, B., Gee, D. G., Humphreys, K. L., Telzer, E., ... Tottenham, N. (2014). The development of human amygdala functional connectivity at rest from 4 to 23 years: A cross-sectional study. *NeuroImage*, *95*, 193–207.

Gee, D. G., Humphreys, K. L., Flannery, J., Goff, B., Telzer, E. H., Shapiro, M., ... Tottenham, N. (2013). A developmental shift from positive to negative connectivity in human amygdala-prefrontal circuitry. *The Journal of Neuroscience: The Official Journal of the Society for Neuroscience*, *33*, 4584–4593.

Geier, C. F., Garver, K., Terwilliger, R., & Luna, B. (2009). Development of working memory maintenance. *Journal of Neurophysiology*, *101*, 84–99.

Geier, C. F., & Luna, B. (2012). Developmental effects of incentives on response inhibition. *Child Development*, *83*, 1262–1274.

Geier, C. F., Terwilliger, R., Teslovich, T., Velanova, K., & Luna, B. (2010). Immaturities in reward processing and its influence on inhibitory control in adolescence. *Cerebral Cortex*, *20*, 1613–1629.

Ghetti, S., & Bunge, S. A. (2012). Neural changes underlying the development of episodic memory during middle childhood. *Developmental Cognitive Neuroscience*, *2*, 381–395.

Giedd, J. N., Blumenthal, J., Jeffries, N. O., Castellanos, F. X., Liu, H., Zijdenbos, A., ... Rapoport, J. L. (1999). Brain development during childhood and adolescence: A longitudinal MRI study. *Nature Neuroscience*, *2*, 861–863.

Glasser, M. F., & Van Essen, D. C. (2011). Mapping human cortical areas in vivo based on myelin content as revealed by T1- and T2-weighted MRI. *The Journal of Neuroscience: The Official Journal of the Society for Neuroscience*, *31*, 11597–11616.

Gogtay, N., Giedd, J. N., Lusk, L., Hayashi, K. M., Greenstein, D., Vaituzis, A. C., ... Thompson,

P. M. (2004). Dynamic mapping of human cortical development during childhood through early adulthood. *Proceedings of the National Academy of Sciences (USA)*, *101*, 8174–8179.

Grydeland, H., Walhovd, K. B., Tamnes, C. K., Westlye, L. T., & Fjell, A. M. (2013). Intracortical myelin links with performance variability across the human lifespan: Results from T1- and T2-weighted MRI myelin mapping and diffusion tensor imaging. *The Journal of Neuroscience*, *33*, 18618–18630.

Guyer, A. E., Monk, C. S., McClure-Tone, E. B., Nelson, E. E., Roberson-Nay, R., Adler, A. D., ... Ernst, M. (2008). A developmental examination of amygdala response to facial expressions. *Journal of Cognitive Neuroscience*, *20*, 1565–1582.

Hallquist, M. N., Hwang, K., & Luna, B. (2013). The nuisance of nuisance regression: Spectral misspecification in a common approach to resting-state fMRI preprocessing reintroduces noise and obscures functional connectivity. *NeuroImage*, *82*, 208–225.

Hare, T. A., Tottenham, N., Galvan, A., Voss, H. U., Glover, G. H., & Casey, B. J. (2008). Biological substrates of emotional reactivity and regulation in adolescence during an emotional go-no go task. *Biological Psychiatry*, *63*, 927–934.

Hodes, G. E., & Shors, T. J. (2005). Distinctive stress effects on learning during puberty. *Hormones and Behavior*, *48*, 163–171.

Houdé, O. (2001). Interference and inhibition (psychology of -). In N. J. Smelser and P. B. Baltes (eds.), *International Encyclopedia of the Social and Behavioral Sciences* (pp. 7718–7722). Oxford: Elsevier Science.

Houdé, O. (2004). Activation/inhibition. In O. Houdé (ed.), *Dictionary of Cognitive Science* (pp. 13–15). New York: Routledge.

Houdé, O. (2019). *3-System Theory of the Cognitive Brain: A Post-Piagetian Approach*. New York: Routledge.

Houdé, O., & Borst, G. (2015). Evidence for an inhibitory-control theory of the reasoning brain. *Frontiers in Human Neuroscience*, *9*, 148.

Houdé, O., Pineau, A., Leroux, G., Poirel, N., Perchey, G., Lanoë, C., ... Mazoyer, B. (2011). Functional MRI study of Piaget's conservation-of-number task in preschool and school-age children: A neo-Piagetian approach. *Journal of Experimental Child Psychology*, *110*, 332–346.

Huttenlocher, P. R. (1990). Morphometric study of human cerebral cortex development. *Neuropsychologia*, *28*, 517–527.

Huttenlocher, P. R., & Dabholkar, A. S. (1997). Regional differences in synaptogenesis in human cerebral cortex. *The Journal of Comparative Neurology*, *387*, 167–178.

Hwang, K., Hallquist, M. N., & Luna, B. (2013). The development of hub architecture in the human functional brain network. *Cerebral Cortex*, *23*, 2380–2393.

National Research Council (2013). *Improving the Health, Safety, and Well-Being of Young Adults – Workshop Summary*. Washington, DC: National Academies Press.

Jalbrzikowski, M., Larsen, B., Hallquist, M. N., Foran, W., Calabro, F., & Luna, B. (2017). Development of white matter microstructure and intrinsic functional connectivity between the amygdala and ventromedial prefrontal cortex: Associations with anxiety and depression. *Biological Psychiatry*, *82*, 511–521.

Johnson, M. H. (1995). The inhibition of automatic saccades in early infancy. *Developmental Psychobiology*, *28*, 281–291.

Killgore, W. D. S., & Yurgelun-Todd, D. A. (2007). Unconscious processing of facial affect in children and adolescents. *Social Neuroscience*, *2*, 28–47.

Larsen, B., & Luna, B. (2018). Adolescence as a neurobiological critical period for the development of higher-order cognition. *Neuroscience & Biobehavioral Reviews*, *94*, 179–195.

Larsen, B., Verstynen, T. D., Yeh, F.-C., & Luna, B. (2018). Developmental changes in the integration of affective and cognitive corticostriatal pathways are associated with reward-driven behavior. *Cerebral Cortex*, *28*, 2834–2845.

Lebel, C., Gee, M., Camicioli, R., Wieler, M., Martin, W., & Beaulieu, C. (2012). Diffusion tensor imaging of white matter tract evolution over the lifespan. *NeuroImage*, *60*, 340–352.

Lenroot, R. K., & Giedd, J. N. (2006). Brain development in children and adolescents: Insights from anatomical magnetic resonance imaging. *Neuroscience & Biobehavioral Reviews*, *30*, 718–729.

Luna, B. (2009). Developmental changes in cognitive control through adolescence. *Advances in Child Development and Behavior*, *37*, 233–278.

Luna, B., Garver, K. E., Urban, T. A., Lazar, N. A., & Sweeney, J. A. (2004). Maturation of cognitive processes from late childhood to adulthood. *Child Development*, *75*, 1357–1372.

Luna, B., Marek, S., Larsen, B., Tervo-Clemmens, B., & Chahal, R. (2015). An integrative model of the maturation of cognitive control. *Annual Review of Neuroscience*, *38*, 151–170.

Luna, B., Padmanabhan, A., & O'Hearn, K. (2010). What has fMRI told us about the development of cognitive control through adolescence? *Brain and Cognition*, *72*, 101–113.

Luna, B., Thulborn, K. R., Munoz, D. P., Merriam, E. P., Garver, K. E., Minshew, N. J., ... Sweeney, J. A. (2001). Maturation of widely distributed brain function subserves cognitive development. *NeuroImage*, *13*, 786–793.

Luna, B., & Wright, C. (2016). Adolescent brain development: Implications for the juvenile criminal justice system. In K. Heilbrun, D. DeMatteo, & N. E. S. Goldstein (eds.), *APA Handbook of Psychology and Juvenile Justice* (pp. 91–116). Washington, DC: American Psychological Association.

Marek, S., Hwang, K., Foran, W., Hallquist, M. N., & Luna, B. (2015). The contribution of network organization and integration to the development of cognitive control. *PLoS Biology*, *13*, e1002328.

Marsh, R., Zhu, H., Schultz, R. T., Quackenbush, G., Royal, J., Skudlarski, P., & Peterson, B. S. (2006). A developmental fMRI study of self-regulatory control. *Human Brain Mapping*, *27*, 848–863.

Menon, V. (2013). Developmental pathways to functional brain networks: Emerging principles. *Trends in Cognitive Sciences*, *17*, 627–640.

Mills, K. L., Goddings, A.-L., Herting, M. M., Meuwese, R., Blakemore, S.-J., Crone, E. A., ... Tamnes, C. K. (2016). Structural brain development between childhood and adulthood: Convergence across four longitudinal samples. *NeuroImage*, *141*, 273–281.

Montez, D. F., Calabro, F. J., & Luna, B. (2017). The expression of established cognitive brain states stabilizes with working memory development. *ELife*, *6*, e25606.

Murty, V. P., Calabro, F., & Luna, B. (2016). The role of experience in adolescent cognitive development: Integration of executive, memory, and mesolimbic systems. *Neuroscience and Biobehavioral Reviews*, *70*, 46–58.

Newman, M. E. J. (2010). *Networks: An Introduction*. Oxford: Oxford University Press.

Nigg, J. T. (2017). Annual research review: On the relations among self-regulation, self-control, executive functioning, effortful control, cognitive control, impulsivity, risk-taking, and inhibition for developmental psychopathology. *Journal of Child Psychology and Psychiatry, and Allied Disciplines*, *58*, 361–383.

O'Donnell, P. (2010). Adolescent maturation of cortical dopamine. *Neurotoxicity Research*, *18*, 306–312.

Ofen, N., Kao, Y.-C., Sokol-Hessner, P., Kim, H., Whitfield-Gabrieli, S., & Gabrieli, J. D. E. (2007). Development of the declarative memory system in the human brain. *Nature Neuroscience*, *10*, 1198–1205.

O'Hare, E. D., Lu, L. H., Houston, S. M., Bookheimer, S. Y., & Sowell, E. R. (2008). Neurodevelopmental changes in verbal working memory load-dependency: An fMRI investigation. *NeuroImage*, *42*, 1678–1685.

Ordaz, S. J., Foran, W., Velanova, K., & Luna, B. (2013). Longitudinal growth curves of brain function underlying inhibitory control through adolescence. *Journal of Neuroscience*, *33*, 18109–18124.

Padmanabhan, A., Geier, C. F., Ordaz, S. J., Teslovich, T., & Luna, B. (2011). Developmental changes in brain function underlying the influence of reward processing on inhibitory control. *Developmental Cognitive Neuroscience, 1,* 517–529.

Padmanabhan, A., & Luna, B. (2014). Developmental imaging genetics: Linking dopamine function to adolescent behavior. *Brain and Cognition, 89,* 27–38.

Parent, A.-S., Teilmann, G., Juul, A., Skakkebaek, N. E., Toppari, J., & Bourguignon, J.-P. (2003). The timing of normal puberty and the age limits of sexual precocity: Variations around the world, secular trends, and changes after migration. *Endocrine Reviews, 24,* 668–693.

Parr, A. C., Calabro, F., Larsen, B., Tervo-Clemmens, B., Elliot, S., Foran, W., Olafsson, V., & Luna, B. (2021). Dopamine-related striatal neurophysiology is associated with specialization of frontostraital reward circuitry through adolescence. Progress in Neurobiology, 201: 101997.

Paulsen, D. J., Hallquist, M. N., Geier, C. F., & Luna, B. (2015). Effects of incentives, age, and behavior on brain activation during inhibitory control: A longitudinal fMRI study. *Developmental Cognitive Neuroscience, 11,* 105–115.

Paus, T. (2010). Growth of white matter in the adolescent brain: Myelin or axon? *Brain and Cognition, 72,* 26–35.

Paus, T., Keshavan, M., & Giedd, J. N. (2008). Why do many psychiatric disorders emerge during adolescence? *Nature Reviews Neuroscience, 9,* 947–957.

Perrin, J. S., Hervé, P.-Y., Leonard, G., Perron, M., Pike, G. B., Pitiot, A., . . . Paus, T. (2008). Growth of white matter in the adolescent brain: Role of testosterone and androgen receptor. *The Journal of Neuroscience: The Official Journal of the Society for Neuroscience, 28,* 9519–9524.

Perrin, J. S., Leonard, G., Perron, M., Pike, G. B., Pitiot, A., Richer, L., . . . Paus, T. (2009). Sex differences in the growth of white matter during adolescence. *NeuroImage, 45,* 1055–1066.

Petanjek, Z., Judaš, M., Šimić, G., Rašin, M. R., Uylings, H. B. M., Rakic, P., & Kostović, I. (2011). Extraordinary neoteny of synaptic spines

in the human prefrontal cortex. *Proceedings of the National Academy of Sciences (USA), 108,* 13281–13286.

Pfeifer, J. H., Masten, C. L., Moore, W. E., Oswald, T. M., Mazziotta, J. C., Iacoboni, M., & Dapretto, M. (2011). Entering adolescence: resistance to peer influence, risky behavior, and neural changes in emotion reactivity. *Neuron, 69,* 1029–1036.

Pierpaoli, C., Barnett, A., Pajevic, S., Chen, R., Penix, L. R., Virta, A., & Basser, P. (2001). Water diffusion changes in Wallerian degeneration and their dependence on white matter architecture. *NeuroImage, 13,* 1174–1185.

Posner, M. I. & Fan, J. (2008). Attention as an organ system. In J. R. Pomerantz (ed.), *Topics in Integrative Neuroscience* (Ch. 2; pp. 31–61). New York: Cambridge University Press.

Posner, M. I., Rothbart, M. K., Sheese, B. E., & Voelker, P. (2014). Developing attention: Behavioral and brain mechanisms. *Advances in Neuroscience, 2014,* 405094.

Postle, B. R., Druzgal, T. J., & D'Esposito, M. (2003). Seeking the neural substrates of visual working memory storage. *Cortex, 39,* 927–946.

Power, J. D., Barnes, K. A., Snyder, A. Z., Schlaggar, B. L., & Petersen, S. E. (2012). Spurious but systematic correlations in functional connectivity MRI networks arise from subject motion. *NeuroImage, 59,* 2142–2154.

Power, J. D., Cohen, A. L., Nelson, S. M., Wig, G. S., Barnes, K. A., Church, J. A., . . . Petersen, S. E. (2011). Functional network organization of the human brain. *Neuron, 72,* 665–678.

Power, J. D., Mitra, A., Laumann, T. O., Snyder, A. Z., Schlaggar, B. L., & Petersen, S. E. (2014). Methods to detect, characterize, and remove motion artifact in resting state fMRI. *NeuroImage, 84,* 320–341.

Qin, S., Cho, S., Chen, T., Rosenberg-Lee, M., Geary, D. C., & Menon, V. (2014). Hippocampal-neocortical functional reorganization underlies children's cognitive development. *Nature Neuroscience, 17,* 1263–1269.

Ravindranath, O., Ordaz, S. J., Padmanabhan, A., Foran, W., Jalbrzikowski, M., Calabro, F. J., & Luna, B. (2020). Influences of affective context on amygdala functional connectivity during cognitive control from adolescence through adulthood. Developmental cognitive neuroscience, 45, 100836.

Raznahan, A., Shaw, P. W., Lerch, J. P., Clasen, L. S., Greenstein, D., Berman, R., ... Giedd, J. N. (2014). Longitudinal four-dimensional mapping of subcortical anatomy in human development. *Proceedings of the National Academy of Sciences (USA)*, *111*, 1592–1597.

Riggins, T., Geng, F., Blankenship, S. L., & Redcay, E. (2016). Hippocampal functional connectivity and episodic memory in early childhood. *Developmental Cognitive Neuroscience*, *19*, 58–69.

Rowley, C. D., Sehmbi, M., Bazin, P.-L., Tardif, C. L., Minuzzi, L., Frey, B. N., & Bock, N. A. (2017). Age-related mapping of intracortical myelin from late adolescence to middle adulthood using T1-weighted MRI. *Human Brain Mapping*, *38*, 3691–3703.

Satterthwaite, T. D., Wolf, D. H., Erus, G., Ruparel, K., Elliott, M. A., Gennatas, E. D., ... Gur, R. E. (2013). Functional maturation of the executive system during adolescence. *The Journal of Neuroscience*, *33*, 16249–16261.

Shafee, R., Buckner, R. L., & Fischl, B. (2015). Gray matter myelination of 1555 human brains using partial volume corrected MRI images. *NeuroImage*, *105*, 473–485.

Shulman, E. P., Smith, A. R., Silva, K., Icenogle, G., Duell, N., Chein, J., & Steinberg, L. (2016). The dual systems model: Review, reappraisal, and reaffirmation. *Developmental Cognitive Neuroscience*, *17*, 103–117.

Silvers, J. A., Insel, C., Powers, A., Franz, P., Helion, C., Martin, R., ... Ochsner, K. N. (2017). The transition from childhood to adolescence is marked by a general decrease in amygdala reactivity and an affect-specific ventral-to-dorsal shift in medial prefrontal recruitment. *Developmental Cognitive Neuroscience*, *25*, 128–137.

Simmonds, D. J., Hallquist, M. N., Asato, M., & Luna, B. (2014). Developmental stages and sex differences of white matter and behavioral development through adolescence: A longitudinal diffusion tensor imaging (DTI) study. *NeuroImage*, *92*, 356–368.

Simmonds, D. J., Hallquist, M. N., & Luna, B. (2017). Protracted development of executive and mnemonic brain systems underlying working memory in adolescence: A longitudinal fMRI study. *NeuroImage*, *157*, 695–704.

Smith, A. R., Steinberg, L., Strang, N., & Chein, J. (2015). Age differences in the impact of peers on adolescents' and adults' neural response to reward. *Developmental Cognitive Neuroscience*, *11*, 75–82.

Somerville, L. H., & Casey, B. J. (2010). Developmental neurobiology of cognitive control and motivational systems. *Current Opinion in Neurobiology*, *20*, 236–241.

Sowell, E. R., Thompson, P. M., Holmes, C. J., Jernigan, T. L., & Toga, A. W. (1999). In vivo evidence for post-adolescent brain maturation in frontal and striatal regions. *Nature Neuroscience*, *2*, 859–861.

Spear, L. P. (2000). Neurobehavioral changes in adolescence. *Current Directions in Psychological Science*, *9*, 111–114.

Stansfield, K. H., & Kirstein, C. L. (2006). Effects of novelty on behavior in the adolescent and adult rat. *Developmental Psychobiology*, *48*, 10–15.

Steinberg, L. (2008). A social neuroscience perspective on adolescent risk-taking. *Developmental Review*, *28*, 78–106.

Steinberg, L., Albert, D., Cauffman, E., Banich, M., Graham, S., & Woolard, J. (2008). Age differences in sensation seeking and impulsivity as indexed by behavior and self-report: Evidence for a dual systems model. *Developmental Psychology*, *44*, 1764–1778.

Steinberg, L., Icenogle, G., Shulman, E. P., Breiner, K., Chein, J., Bacchini, D., ... Takash, H. M. S. (2018). Around the world, adolescence is a time of heightened sensation seeking and immature self-regulation. *Developmental Science*, *21*, e12532.

Tamnes, C. K., Fjell, A. M., Østby, Y., Westlye, L. T., Due-Tønnessen, P., Bjørnerud, A., & Walhovd, K. B. (2011). The brain dynamics of intellectual development: Waxing and waning white and gray matter. *Neuropsychologia, 49,* 3605–3611.

Tamnes, C. K., Walhovd, K. B., Engvig, A., Grydeland, H., Krogsrud, S. K., Østby, Y., ... Fjell, A. M. (2014). Regional hippocampal volumes and development predict learning and memory. *Developmental Neuroscience, 36,* 161–174.

van Duijvenvoorde, A. C. K., Achterberg, M., Braams, B. R., Peters, S., & Crone, E. A. (2016). Testing a dual-systems model of adolescent brain development using resting-state connectivity analyses. *NeuroImage, 124,* 409–420.

Velanova, K., Wheeler, M. E., & Luna, B. (2008). Maturational changes in anterior cingulate and frontoparietal recruitment support the development of error processing and inhibitory control. *Cerebral Cortex, 18,* 2505–2522.

Vijayakumar, N., Op de Macks, Z., Shirtcliff, E. A., & Pfeifer, J. H. (2018). Puberty and the human brain: Insights into adolescent development. *Neuroscience & Biobehavioral Reviews, 92,* 417–436.

Von Der Heide, R. J., Skipper, L. M., Klobusicky, E., & Olson, I. R. (2013). Dissecting the uncinate fasciculus: disorders, controversies and a hypothesis. *Brain, 136,* 1692–1707.

Voss, J. L., O'Neil, J. T., Kharitonova, M., Briggs-Gowan, M. J., & Wakschlag, L. S. (2015). Adolescent development of context-dependent stimulus-reward association memory and its neural correlates. *Frontiers in Human Neuroscience, 9,* 581.

Yakovlev, P. I., Lecours, A. R., & Minkowski, A. (1967). The myelogenetic cycles of regional maturation of the brain. In A. Minkowski (ed.), *Regional Development of the Brain in Early Life* (pp. 3–70). Oxford: Blackwell Scientific.

Yeh, F.-C., Verstynen, T. D., Wang, Y., Fernández-Miranda, J. C., & Tseng, W.-Y. I. (2013). Deterministic diffusion fiber tracking improved by quantitative anisotropy. *PLoS ONE, 8,* e80713.

Zuckerman, M. (2008). Personality and sensation seeking. In G. J. Boyle, G. Matthews, & D. H. Saklofske (eds.), *The SAGE Handbook of Personality Theory and Assessment: Personality Theories and Models.* Thousand Oaks, CA: SAGE.

Part II

Fundamentals of Cognitive Development from Infancy to Adolescence and Young Adulthood

Introduction

Assembling the Building Blocks of Cognition in a Non-linear Dynamical System of Development

Grégoire Borst and Olivier Houdé

The scientific study of cognitive development in young children traces its roots back to Jean Piaget, a pioneer of this field in the twentieth century (Piaget, 1954, 1983). From infancy to adolescence, children progress through four psychological stages: (1) the sensorimotor stage, from birth to two years (when cognitive functioning is based primarily on biological reactions, motor skills, and perceptions); (2) the preoperational stage, from two to seven years (when symbolic thought and language become prevalent, but reasoning is illogical by adult standards); (3) the concrete operations stage, from seven to twelve years (when logical reasoning abilities emerge but are limited to concrete objects and events); and (4) the formal operations stage, at approximately twelve years (when thinking about abstract, hypothetical, and contrary-to-fact ideas becomes possible).

According to Piaget, the child, like the logician or mathematician, "models" objects, their properties, and their relations through a succession of cognitive frameworks, from primary biological reactions and motor skills to high-order formal thinking. After the age of twelve, children model a formal hypothetico-deductive logic that ultimately resembles the rational logic of scientists and mathematicians. Piaget was the first psychologist to take children's thinking seriously. His genius was based on the idea of building his child development theory on triple roots in epistemological, biological, and logico-mathematical foundations. Consequently, Piaget is now recognized as one of the precursors of cognitive science during the last century (Fischer & Kaplan, 2003).

II.1 Beyond Piaget

Piaget underestimated the cognitive capabilities of infants, preschoolers, and elementary schoolchildren, and he overestimated the capabilities of adolescents and adults, which are often biased by illogical intuitions and overlearned strategies (or heuristics) they fail to inhibit (Borst & Houdé, 2014; Houdé, 2000, 2019; Kahneman, 2011). During the last three decades, detailed behavioral studies of children's problem-solving led to a reconceptualization of cognitive development, from discrete Piagetian stages to one that is analogous to overlapping waves (Siegler, 1996, 1999). The latter is consistent with a neo-Piagetian approach of cognitive development, in which more and less sophisticated solutions compete for expression in the human brain. In this approach, inhibition of less sophisticated solutions by the prefrontal cortex is a critical component of children's conceptual insights associated with more advanced Piagetian stages (Houdé et al., 2000, 2011; Poirel et al., 2012).

At any point in time, children and adults potentially have available to them heuristics (i.e., intuitions) and logico-mathematical algorithms, or as Kahneman (2011) described, multiple levels of "thinking fast and slow." Heuristics are rapid, often global or holistic, useful strategies in many situations, *but sometimes they are misleading*, whereas algorithms are slow, demanding, and analytical strategies that *necessarily lead to a correct (i.e., logical) solution in every situation.* In general, children and adults prefer using fast heuristics spontaneously, but that choice does not indicate that they are illogical per se (Houdé, 2000) or that they are "happy fools" (De Neys et al., 2013). Psychologists had to be careful to avoid false negatives (Gelman, 1997), which is a strong tendency to say that those children or adults who fail a task are incompetent in the target domain of knowledge. A "presumption of rationality" is sometimes the best assessment.

Contrary to Piaget's theory, infants learn more about the outside world through information that is captured by their perceptual systems than through motor skills development (Baillargeon, 1995; Mandler, 1988; Spelke, 2000). Infant cognition studies evaluated both the capacity to interpret sensory data and the faculty for understanding and reasoning about complex physical and social events. In the last decades, theoretical ideas and empirical research in the field have demonstrated that very young children's learning and thinking mechanisms do remarkably resemble the basic processes of science, that is, probabilistic models and Bayesian learning methods (Gopnik, 2012). Infants can implicitly reason statistically (Téglás et al., 2011). From this point of view, the very young child is already seen as a "scientist in the crib" (Gopnik et al., 1999).

II.2 What Develops? Heuristics, Algorithms, Cognitive Control, and Inhibition of Misleading Strategies

The crucial question now is to understand why, despite these precocious abilities about physical and mathematical principles (even social and moral principles), older children, adolescents, and adults so often have poor

reasoning ability. How might we explain the systematic errors observed in humans at all stages of their cognitive development by Piaget (1954, 1983) in children and by post-Piagetian experimental psychologists of reasoning in adults (Evans, 1989, 2003; Kahneman, 2011; Kahneman & Tversky, 2000; Kahneman et al., 1982)?

For example, how might we explain the famous number-conservation error observed in children until the age of seven by Piaget and, after him, by all developmental psychologists around the world? It is an intriguing question because we know today that very young children are already capable of treating the number of items as invariable through irrelevant transformations (Antell & Keating, 1983; Gelman, 1972; Lipton & Spelke, 2003; Loosbroek & Smitsman, 1990; Mehler & Bever, 1967) and that they possess other protonumerical skills (Gelman & Meck, 1983; Gelman et al., 1986; Wynn, 1992, 1998). One of the main current explanations is that children learn heuristics, which are often useful in a large set of situations, but fail to inhibit them when, contrary to general practice, they are misleading (Borst & Houdé, 2014; Houdé, 2000, 2019). In the case of Piaget's number-conservation algorithm, the overlearned competing heuristic is "length-equals-number" (Houdé & Guichart, 2001).

This new theoretical approach is in line with Diamond's explanation of the A-not-B error in infants (Diamond, 1998) and assumes that cognitive development relies not only on the acquisition of knowledge of incremental complexity (Piaget, 1983), but also on the ability to inhibit previously acquired knowledge (Bjorklund & Harnishfeger, 1990; Dempster & Brainerd, 1995; Diamond, 1991, 1998; Harnishfeger, 1995; Houdé, 2000, 2019). Increasing evidence shows that the ability to inhibit previous knowledge is critical for developmental milestones, such as those defined by

Piaget's theory: object (permanence of-), number, categorization, and reasoning (Houdé, 2000, 2019). Inhibitory control of misleading strategies, an executive function performed by the prefrontal cortex (Aron et al., 2004, 2014), has been claimed necessary for acquisition and use of motor or cognitive algorithms in the fields of object permanence in infants (Bell & Fox, 1992; Diamond, 1991, 1998; Diamond & Goldman-Rakic, 1989), number conservation, and class inclusion in preschool and schoolchildren (Borst et al., 2012, 2013b; Houdé & Guichart, 2001; Perret et al., 2003), and logical reasoning in adolescents and adults (Houdé, 2007, 2019; Houdé & Tzourio-Mazoyer, 2003; Houdé et al., 2000).

One of the challenges of today's developmental research, in all domains of cognition, ranging from motor programming to high-order logical reasoning, is to account not only for a general and incremental process of coordination-activation capacities of structural units, schemes, or skills through ages and stages (Piaget, 1983, and all the 1980s neo-Piagetians: see the review book by Demetriou, 1988), but also for a general process of selection-inhibition of competing strategies, i.e., heuristics (or intuitions) and logico-mathematical algorithms, occurring with different weights at any point in time, depending on the context, in a non-linear dynamical system of growth (Borst & Houdé, 2014; Houdé, 2000, 2019; Siegler, 1996, 1999). Such cognitive models introduce less regular developmental curves containing perturbations, bursts, and collapses.

O'Reilly (1998) described six principles for biologically based computational models of cognition, one of which is inhibitory competition (see also Johnson, 2010). Resolving this "inhibition issue" is an important task for both developmental psychology and cognitive neuroscience. The most compelling magnetic resonance imaging (MRI) reports of structural changes with brain development during childhood and adolescence showed a sequence in which the higher-order association area, such as the prefrontal cortex sustaining inhibitory control, matures last (Casey et al., 2005). The sequence in which the cortex matures parallels the cognitive milestones in human development. First, the regions subserving primary functions, such as motor and sensory systems, mature the earliest; the temporal and parietal association cortices associated with basic language skills and spatial attention mature next; and the last to mature are the prefrontal cortex and its inhibitory-control ability.

Using fMRI (functional magnetic resonance imaging), from this theoretical perspective, we re-examined what occurs in the developing brain when school children are delayed in Piaget's number-conservation task (Houdé et al., 2011). Remember that when children are shown two rows of objects that contain an equal number of objects but that differ in length (because the objects in one of the rows had been spread apart), young children think that the longer one has more objects. Piaget's interpretation was that preschool children are still fundamentally intuitive (their reasoning being illogical by adult standards), or as he called them, "preoperational" (Stage 2), and hence limited to a perceptual way of processing information (here, based on length or, in certain cases, on density). When they are approximately six or seven years old, children understand the equivalency of quantities, regardless of apparent transformations. At this point, they are called "operational" or "conserving" (Stage 3), the criterion for logico-mathematical mastery of number. Our new hypothesis was that their main cognitive difficulty (beyond logico-mathematical cognition per se) was to efficiently inhibit through their prefrontal cortex the overlearned "length-equals-number" strategy, a heuristic that is often used both by children and adults in many school and everyday situations.

In a first fMRI study, we found that the cognitive change allowing children to access conservation (i.e., the shift from Stage 2 to Stage 3 in Piaget's theory) was related to the neural contribution of a bilateral parietofrontal network involved in numerical and executive functions (Houdé et al., 2011). These imaging results highlighted how the behavioral and cognitive stages that Piaget formulated during the twentieth century manifest in the brain with age. In a second fMRI study (Poirel et al., 2012), we demonstrated that the prefrontal activation (i.e., the blood-oxygen-level-dependent signal) observed when schoolchildren succeeded at the Piaget's number-conservation task was correlated to their behavioral performance on a Stroop-like measure of inhibitory function development (Wright et al., 2003). These new results in schoolchildren fit well with previous brain imaging data from our laboratory showing a key role of prefrontal inhibitory-control training when adolescents or adults (belonging to Stage 4 in Piaget's theory) spontaneously fail to block their perceptual intuitions (or bias, heuristics) to activate logico-mathematical algorithms (i.e., deductive rules) in reasoning tasks (Houdé, 2007, 2019; Houdé et al., 2000).

If we have "two minds in one brain," as stated by Evans (2003) or, in other words, two ways of thinking and reasoning, that is, "fast and slow" (Kahneman, 2011), currently called "System 1" (intuitive system) and "System 2" (analytic system), then the crucial challenge, for each child during cognitive development, is to learn to inhibit the misleading heuristics from System 1 when the more analytic and effortful System 2 (logico-mathematical algorithms) is the way to solve the problem (Borst & Houdé, 2014; Borst et al., 2013a; Houdé, 2000). It is what we called "System 3" (see Figure II.1), the executive-functions system, especially inhibitory control (Houdé, 2019). Within this post-Piagetian theoretical approach, we can now understand why, despite rich precocious knowledge about physical and mathematical principles observed in infants and young children (from object principle to pure reasoning), older children, adolescents, and adults so often have poor reasoning. The cost of blocking our intuitions is high and depends on the late maturation of the prefrontal cortex. Moreover, this executive ability remains delicate throughout our lifetime, and adults may sometimes need "prefrontal pedagogy" to learn inhibiting intuitive heuristics (or biases) in reasoning tasks (Houdé, 2007, 2019).

An innovative research question now is to better understand the cognitive roots of such powerful heuristics (intuitions and bias from System 1) that children and adults have so much difficulty inhibiting in some cases. New heuristics may appear and be overlearned at any time in the course of development because our brain is an irrepressible detector of regularities from its perceptual and cultural environment. For example, preschool children (more than infants) are often exposed, in "math books" in the classroom or in everyday scenes, to patterns of objects in which number and length covary (e.g., the 1-to-10 Arabic numbering series is frequently illustrated by increasing lines of drawn animals or fruits: one giraffe, two hippopotamus, three crocodiles, and so on), hence the overlearned and misleading "length-equals-number" heuristic, which is overactivated in Piaget's conservation of number task. A new avenue of research would be to assess the role of early sensitivity to statistical patterns (i.e., probability of hypotheses) and Bayesian inference (Gopnik, 2012) in the psychological construction of perceptual, motor, and cognitive heuristics (Houdé, 2015; Parpart et al., 2018). Moreover, the power of Bayesian learning might require, in some conflict situations, a strong antagonist process of inhibition for blocking heuristics when they are misleading.

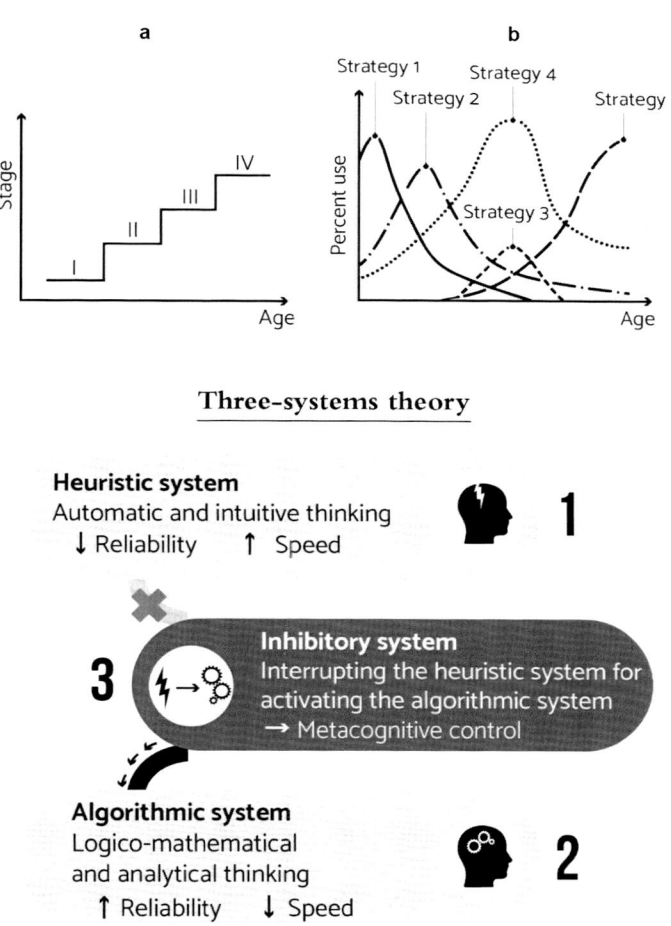

Figure II.1 Three-systems theory of the cognitive brain. (a) Piaget's theory or the "staircase model" of incremental progress stage by stage, from intuition to logic. (b) Non-linear development of cognitive strategies (R. Siegler) that come either from the fast and heuristic (intuitive) system or from the slow and algorithmic (logical) system at any age (D. Kahneman). When these two systems compete (System 1 versus System 2), our brain needs a third system, located in the prefrontal cortex, for inhibiting the too fast heuristic system and activating the logical one (Borst & Houdé, 2014; Houdé, 2019)
A black-and-white version of this figure will appear in some formats. For the color version, please refer to the plate section.

II.3 Other Paths for Assembling the Building Blocks of Cognition

The aforementioned theory of cognitive inhibition (including heuristics, algorithms, and inhibitory control) is only one of the possible paths for assembling the building blocks of cognition during development. The following chapters sometimes draw the same *executive-functions* path with different nuances, but also other paths. The chapters are divided into two subparts to address first the many early competencies of infants and their similarity and difference with other species, and then the development of these competencies from childhood to adolescence to young adulthood.

In the chapters dedicated to the origins of cognition, Vauclair (Chapter 7) starts by exploring the differences between humans, great apes, and monkeys in cognition, communication, language, and morality, to determine the phylogenetic process at play in each of these domains. The following chapters investigate in greater details the possible ontogenetic mechanisms that support the development of the building blocks within in each of these domains. Lin et al. (Chapter 8) describe how infants build a comprehension of the physical principles of the objects in their environment. Rakison et al. (Chapter 9) explain how categories emerge and develop in the infant brain. Then vanMarle (Chapter 10) addresses the early numerical abilities of infants and their development. Scott et al. (Chapter 11) examine the early ability to infer mental states of other individuals (theory of mind). Falck et al. (Chapter 12) describe the development of social-moral cognition during infancy. Goddu and Gopnik (Chapter 13) address the early scientific thinking and reasoning abilities of infants. Nobandegani and Shultz (Chapter 14) explain how to unravel the mechanisms of cognitive development during infancy by using computational approaches.

The remaining chapters cover cognitive development from childhood to adolescence and adulthood. Gelman (Chapter 15) describe the development of language and categorization in young children in relation to the early competencies observed in infants. Siegler (Chapter 16) then addresses the development of strategies used by pre-schoolers and school-aged children in numerical and arithmetic problems. Roell et al. (Chapter 17) explain how learning to inhibit interfering information and strategies is at the root of the development

of non-symbolic and symbolic numerical cognition. Perner et al. (Chapter 18) examine the development of theory of mind and counterfactual reasoning and the mechanisms that produce change in these domains with age. Happaney and Zelazo (Chapter 19) address the development of executive functions by the prism of their real life repercussion. Chevalier and Blaye (Chapter 20) describe how executive functions develop to allow children and adolescents to flexibility adapt to their environment. Frey and De Neys (Chapter 21) explore the development of reasoning with a dual process (intuition versus logic) account of reasoning abilities. Then Chalik et al. (Chapter 22) deal with social cognitive development. Blankenstein et al. (Chapter 23) address the role of cognitive control in the development of decision making from childhood and adulthood. Finally, Ernst et al. (Chapter 24) describe the most advanced tools to delineate how brain networks code motivated behaviors during the course of development.

References

Aron, A., Robbins, T., & Poldrack, R. (2004). Inhibition and the right inferior frontal cortex. *Trends in Cognitive Sciences*, 8, 170–177.

Aron, A., Robbins, T., & Poldrack, R. (2014). Inhibition and the right inferior frontal cortex: One decade on. *Trends in Cognitive Sciences*, 18, 177–185.

Antell, S., & Keating, D. (1983). Perception of numerical invariance in neonates. *Child Development*, 54, 695–701.

Baillargeon, R. (1995). Physical reasoning in infancy. In M. S. Gazzaniga (ed.), *The Cognitive Neurosciences* (pp. 181–204). Cambridge, MA: MIT Press.

Bell, M., & Fox, N. (1992). The relations between frontal brain electrical activity and cognitive development during infancy. *Child Development*, 63, 1142–1163.

Bjorklund, D., & Harnishfeger, K. (1990). The resources construct in cognitive development:

Diverse sources of evidence and a theory of inefficient inhibition. *Developmental Review, 10,* 48–71.

Borst, G., & Houdé, O. (2014). Inhibitory control as a core mechanism for cognitive development and learning at school. *Perspectives on Language and Literacy, 17,* 41–44.

Borst, G., Moutier, S., & Houdé, O. (2013a). Negative priming in logicomathematical reasoning: The cost of blocking your intuition. In W. De Neys, & M. Osman (eds.), *New Approaches in Reasoning Research – Current Issues in Thinking & Reasoning* (pp. 34–50). New York: Psychology Press.

Borst, G., Pineau, A., Poirel, N., Cassotti, M., & Houdé, O. (2013b). Inhibitory control efficiency in a Piaget-like class-inclusion task in school-age children and adults: A developmental negative priming study. *Developmental Psychology, 49,* 1366–1374.

Borst, G., Poirel, N., Pineau, A., Cassotti, M., & Houdé, O. (2012). Inhibitory control in number-conservation and class-inclusion tasks: A neo-Piagetian inter-tasks priming study. *Cognitive Development, 27,* 283–298.

Casey, B., Tottenham, N., Liston, C., & Durston, S. (2005). Imaging the developing brain: What have we learned about cognitive development? *Trends in Cognitive Sciences, 9,* 104–110.

De Neys, W., Rossi, S., & Houdé, O. (2013). Bats, balls, and substitution sensitivity: Cognitive misers are no happy fools. *Psychonomic Bulletin & Review, 20,* 269–273.

Demetriou, A. (ed.) (1988). *The Neo-Piagetian Theories of Cognitive Development.* Amsterdam: North-Holland.

Dempster, F., & Brainerd, C. (eds.) (1995). *Interference and Inhibition in Cognition.* New York: Academic Press.

Diamond, A. (1991). Neuropsychological insights into the meaning of object concept development. In S. Carey, & R. Gelman (eds.), *The Epigenesis of Mind: Essays on Biology and Cognition* (pp. 67–110). Hillsdale, NJ: Lawrence Erlbaum.

Diamond, A. (1998). Understanding the A-not-B error: Working memory vs. reinforced response, or active trace vs. latent trace. *Developmental Science, 1,* 185–189.

Diamond, A., & Goldman-Rakic, P. (1989). Comparison of human infants and rhesus monkeys on Piaget's AB task. *Experimental Brain Research, 74,* 24–40.

Evans, J. (1989). *Bias in Human Reasoning.* London: Erlbaum.

Evans, J. (2003). In two minds: dual-process accounts of reasoning. *Trends in Cognitive Sciences, 7,* 454–459.

Fischer, K., & Kaplan, U. (2003). Jean Piaget. In L. Nadel (ed.), *The Encyclopedia of Cognitive Science* (Vol. 1, pp. 679–682). London: Nature Publishing Group, Macmillan.

Gelman, R. (1972). Logical capacity of very young children. *Child Development, 43,* 75–90.

Gelman, R. (1997). Constructing and using conceptual competence. *Cognitive Development, 12,* 305–313.

Gelman, R., & Meck, E. (1983). Preschooler's counting. *Cognition, 13,* 343–359.

Gelman, R., Meck, E., & Merkin, S. (1986). Young children's numerical competence. *Cognitive Development, 1,* 1–29.

Gopnik, A. (2012). Scientific thinking in young children: Theoretical advances, empirical research, and policy education. *Science, 337,* 1623–1627.

Gopnik, A., Meltzoff, A., & Kuhl, P. (1999). *The Scientist in the Crib.* New York: William Morrow and Cie.

Harnishfeger, K. (1995). The development of cognitive inhibition: Theories, definition, and research evidence. In F. Dempster, & C. Brainerd (eds.), *Interference and Inhibition in Cognition* (pp. 176–204). New York: Academic Press.

Houdé, O. (2000). Inhibition and cognitive development: Object, number, categorization, and reasoning. *Cognitive Development, 15,* 63–73.

Houdé, O. (2007). First insights on neuropedagogy of reasoning. *Thinking & Reasoning, 13,* 81–89.

Houdé, O. (2015). Cognitive development during infancy and early childhood across cultures. In J. D. Wright (ed.), *International Encyclopedia of the Social and Behavioral Sciences* (pp. 43–50). Oxford: Elsevier Science.

Houdé, O. (2019). *3-System Theory of the Cognitive Brain: A Post-Piagetian Approach.* New York: Routledge.

Houdé, O., & Guichart, E. (2001). Negative priming effect after inhibition of number/length interference in a Piaget-like task. *Developmental Science, 4,* 71–74.

Houdé, O., Pineau, A., Leroux, G., Poirel, N., Perchey, G., Lanoë, C., Lubin, A., Turbelin, M.-R., Rossi, S., Simon, G., Delcroix, N., Lamberton, F., Vigneau, M., Wisniewski, G., Vicet, J.-R., & Mazoyer, B. (2011). Functional MRI study of Piaget's conservation-of-number task in preschool and school-age children: A neo-Piagetian approach. *Journal of Experimental Child Psychology, 110,* 332–346.

Houdé, O., & Tzourio-Mazoyer, N. (2003). Neural foundations of logical and mathematical cognition. *Nature Reviews Neuroscience, 4,* 507–514.

Houdé, O., Zago, L., Mellet, E., Moutier, S., Pineau, A., Mazoyer, B., & Tzourio-Mazoyer, N. (2000). Shifting from the perceptual brain to the logical brain: The neural impact of cognitive inhibition training. *Journal of Cognitive Neuroscience, 12,* 721–728.

Johnson, M. (2010). Interactive specialization: A domain-general framework for human functional brain development. *Developmental Cognitive Neuroscience, 1,* 7–21.

Kahneman, D. (2011). *Thinking, Fast and Slow.* New York: Farrar, Straus and Giroux.

Kahneman, D., Slovic, P., & Tversky, A. (1982). *Judgment under Uncertainty: Heuristics and Biases.* New York: Cambridge University Press.

Kahneman, D., & Tversky, A. (2000). *Choices, Values, and Frames.* New York: Cambridge University Press.

Lipton, J., & Spelke, E. (2003). Origins of number sense: Large number discrimination in human infants. *Psychological Science, 14,* 396–401.

Loosbroek, E., & Smitsman, A. (1990). Visual perception of numerosity in infancy. *Developmental Psychology, 26,* 916–922.

Mandler, J. (1988). How to build a baby: On the development of an accessible representational system. *Cognitive Development, 3,* 113–136.

Mehler, J., & Bever, T. (1967). Cognitive capacity of very young children. *Science, 158,* 141–142.

O'Reilly, R. (1998). Six principles for biologically based computational models of cortical cognition. *Trends in Cognitive Sciences, 11,* 455–462.

Parpart, P., Jones, M., & Love, B. (2018). Heuristics as Bayesian inference under extreme priors. *Cognitive Development, 102,* 127–144.

Perret, P., Blaye, A., & Paour, J.-L. (2003). Respective contributions of inhibition and knowledge levels in class inclusion development: A negative priming study. *Developmental Science, 6,* 283–286.

Piaget, J. (1954). *The Construction of Reality in the Child.* New York: Basic Books.

Piaget, J. (1983). Piaget's theory. In P. H. Mussen (ed.), *Handbook of Child Psychology* (Vol. 1, pp. 103–128). New York: Wiley.

Poirel, N., Borst, G., Simon, G., Rossi, S., Cassotti, M., Pineau, A., & Houdé, O. (2012). Number conservation is related to children's prefrontal inhibitory control: An fMRI study of a Piagetian task. *PLoS ONE, 7,* e40802.

Siegler, R. (1996). *Emerging Minds: The Process of Change in Children's Thinking.* New York: Oxford University Press.

Siegler, R. (1999). Strategic development. *Trends in Cognitive Sciences, 3,* 430–435.

Spelke, E. (2000). Core knowledge. *American Psychologist, 55,* 1233–1243.

Téglás E., Vul, E., Girotto, V., Gonzales, M., Tenenbaum, J.-B., & Bonatti, L. (2011). Pure reasoning in 12-month-old infants as probabilistic inference. *Science, 332,* 1054–1059.

Wright, I., Waterman, M., Prescott, H., & Murdoch-Eaton, D. (2003). A new Stroop-like measure of inhibitory function development: Typical developmental trends. *Journal of Child Psychology and Psychiatry, and Allied Disciplines, 44,* 561–575.

Wynn, K. (1992). Addition and subtraction by human infants. *Nature, 358,* 749–750.

Wynn, K. (1998). Psychological foundations of number: Numerical competence in human infants. *Trends in Cognitive Sciences, 2,* 296–303.

Subpart II.1
Infancy: The Roots of Human Thinking

7 Differences between Humans, Great Apes and Monkeys in Cognition, Communication, Language and Morality

Jacques Vauclair

The comparative psychology of human and nonhuman primates' cognition, communication, language and morality is a prime area of study for understanding not only the roots of these abilities in our cousins, but also their place in human evolution. The groundbreaking work in this area was undertaken by Yerkes (1916) and Koehler (1925). Both scientists studied the mental life of apes. Using ingenious apparatus and procedures, such as the multiple-choice experiment, Yerkes investigated what Piaget was later to call *object permanence*. He also invented the stacking experiment (a suspended banana can only be reached if two or more boxes are stacked one on top of another), which was subsequently popularized by Koehler's famous studies of problem-solving abilities in chimpanzees.

7.1 The Contemporary Study of Comparative Cognition

There is growing interest in combining different approaches in order to study primate cognition via one of two major programmes. The *generalist programme* is inspired by the concepts of human psychology (based notably on information processing theories). The *ecological programme*, influenced by ethologists, mainly concerns the ecology of behaviour. The former is generalist insofar as comparisons between species are designed to find out whether these species process structural information from the environment in comparable ways. These comparisons therefore serve to establish the identity of interspecific cognitive traits. The latter deals with the adaptation of animals, as well as their ability to solve problems in their natural environment. It favours the examination of spontaneous behaviours, more specifically, those that are ecologically valid for the species concerned. Thus, the main behaviours of interest are related to spatial abilities, individual recognition, and communication within the group or species. These two programmes raise different, but complementary, questions, and researchers in both camps have realized that it is much more in their interest to work together. Indeed, behavioural ecologists have already largely, if not totally, borrowed concepts of cognitive science and cognitive psychology to apply them to their discipline. Collaboration such as this allows comparative psychology to rediscover its links with evolutionary theory. For instance, research inspired by Piaget's theory of the development of intelligence in infants and children has offered a means of theorizing the cognitive skills of our closest relatives. Nonetheless, the ecology of behaviour remains more interested in the questions of ontogenesis and the cognitive processes responsible for complex behaviours (see Vauclair, 2012, for an overview).

7.2 Cognitive and Social Abilities of Non-human Primates

The investigation of cognitive abilities among non-human primates (NHPs) usually entails separating the cognitive processes concerned with knowledge about the physical domain from those involved in the social domain (see, for example, Parrish & Brosnan, 2012; Tomasello & Call, 1997; Vauclair, 1996). In the following sections, we summarize some of the findings in the field, based on this distinction.

7.2.1 Knowledge in the Physical Domain

7.2.1.1 Numerical Cognition

Evaluating quantities (including counting) represents one of the basic cognitive processes shared by primates. Several animal species, from insects to apes, can evaluate numbers and quantities (see Beran et al., 2015, for a review), but apparently only NHPs can perform some forms of counting.

A spectacular example of the mastery of cardinality was provided by Boysen and Berntson (1989), with Sheba the chimpanzee. Sheba was first trained on a one-to-one correspondence task involving round placards with black markers affixed to them (a blank placard corresponding to 0, one marker to the number 1, two markers to 2, and three markers to 3). In the first trial of the first phase, one food item was presented, and Sheba was encouraged to select the placard with one marker. In subsequent trials, two items, then three were presented, requiring the selection of the placard with the relevant number of markers. In the second phase, these markers were replaced with Arabic numbers, and Sheba was required to select the placard with the number that corresponded to the number of food items (1–3). A test of number comprehension was then

undertaken: an Arabic symbol was displayed on a video monitor and the chimpanzee was asked to select the placard bearing the corresponding number of markers. Finally, a functional counting task was introduced, by establishing three food sites in the laboratory that Sheba visited. Between one and three food items were placed in two of the three sites. Sheba was required to move from site to site and to attend to the arrays containing the food. She then returned to the starting position, where the number alternatives were available. Sheba reliably chose the correct number (0–5) corresponding to the sum of the items she had seen. Moreover, the chimpanzee's performances did not deteriorate when she was given a symbolic counting task (edible objects replaced by Arabic number placards). Sheba also spontaneously exhibited interesting behaviours similar to those demonstrated by human children during counting tasks (Boysen et al., 1995), namely tagging and partitioning. These behaviours included touching objects before selecting the number or moving each item in turn away from the others in the array before making the selection. These behaviours were equivalent to the pointing and verbalizing observed in children when they practise counting (e.g., Sarnecka & Carey, 2008).

This numerical ability to use tokens to represent quantities and then to make judgements and decisions about overall set values was also investigated by Beran (2004). Two chimpanzees were trained to collect sets of items on a computer screen by using a joystick to move a cursor into contact with those items. The task consisted of collecting the number of items that matched the value represented by an Arabic numeral. The chimpanzees performed above chance level for numbers up to seven. However, their performances decreased as the requested number of items increased.

This brief review suggests that quantification processes specific to numerical comprehension and elementary counting operations are at work in NHPs, even in the absence of a linguistic code. Moreover, after lengthy training on numerical material, apes (1) develop processes (e.g., approximate number system) that closely resemble those of humans, at least for processing small quantities and (2) like humans, engage the prefrontal cortex during numerical processing (Nieder, 2009).

7.2.1.2 Categorizing Abilities

A useful general framework for investigating categorizing abilities was provided by Herrnstein (1990), who identified five levels of increasing abstractness in categorization processes, including (1) discrimination, (2) categorization by rote, (3) open-ended categorization, (4) concepts, and (5) abstract relations. Level 5 is attained when an individual can use abstract relations not only between objects but also between concepts, such as in conceptual matching or conceptual identity. Although there is substantial evidence that several animal species are capable of performing the first three levels of categorization (see Thompson & Oden, 2000, for a review), the picture is far less clear with regard to Levels 4 and 5. Two criteria can be used to assess conceptual categorization: rapid response generalization from one exemplar to the whole set of exemplars of a given category; and categorization beyond the exemplars' perceptual similarity (e.g., based on their function instead). These abilities have been illustrated in a series of experiments. For example, Bovet and Vauclair (1998) trained monkeys (baboons) to divide objects into two different functional categories: foods and non-foods. Subsequent generalization tasks demonstrated a positive transfer to novel exemplars of the two categories – a Level 4 ability according to Herrnstein (1990). The same task (i.e., simple discrimination of items in a two-alternative

forced-choice procedure) was used in a follow-up study. In a test of perceptual identity (Experiment 1), the monkeys had to judge two physical objects as either the *same* (e.g., two apples) or *different* (e.g., an apple and a padlock). In a crucial test of conceptual identity (Experiment 2), they then had to combine their previously acquired skills to classify as the *same* two (different) objects that belonged to the same functional category (food or nonfood) and apply that learning to new exemplars. For example, they had to classify an apple and a banana, or a padlock and a cup as the *same*, and an apple and a padlock as *different* (Bovet & Vauclair, 2001). Similar abilities to judge the categorical abstract equivalence of same/different relationsbetween-relations were demonstrated by baboons in a computerized task (Flemming et al., 2013). These abilities correspond to Level 5 in Herrnstein's classification scheme.

7.2.1.3 Complex Tool Use

Given the power of humans to invent artefacts to make the best of the resources in their environment, the identification of tool use is a strong marker of intelligence. Many animal species, from insects to NHPs, manipulate objects to achieve goals, or even shape and transform them into tools. The complex termite *fishing* techniques invented by chimpanzees in the Republic of Congo were followed by cameras camouflaged in the vegetation (Sanz et al., 2004). The researchers first found that different tools are used, depending on whether the termite mounds are underground or above ground. In addition, some tools are simple probe-like rods used to recover any termites that become attached to them, while other, harder, tools are intended to perforate the nests. These two categories of tools can also be used sequentially: one to perforate the nest, the other to catch termites. Finally, chimpanzees practise a kind of recycling, as some re-use tools that have been discarded by others during previous visits to the termite mounds. The use of several kinds of tools by these populations of chimpanzees, associated with a hierarchical organization of the tools according to the goals to be reached, is undoubtedly one of the most complex examples of the use of functional objects in animal species (Sanz & Morgan, 2007).

7.2.2 Knowledge in the Social Domain

The main question addressed by researchers is whether social behaviours are governed by cognitive processes of variable complexity, as we saw for the physical domain. Several scientists (e.g., Humphrey, 1976; Kummer, 1982) have suggested that the emergence of cognitive abilities in NHPs needs to be conceived of as a function of the complexity of their social life. This assumption has been repeated over the years, and some authors (Seyfarth & Cheney, 2012) even consider that language evolved from the organization of social relations expressed in the vocal communication of monkeys. Another position is that cognition is unitary. As Bates (1979) imaginatively put it, the two realities (social and non-social) may refer to a common cognitive *software*. In other words, a set of common instruments (e.g., mastery of means-end relations) develops during human ontogeny and is applied to both realities, one sometimes earlier than the other. Accordingly, the use of tools (in the physical domain) corresponds to the solicitation of the Other, who is thus *instrumentalized* during social communication. Validating this hypothesis would require a research programme designed to highlight cognitive abilities in the non-social domain, and then to show that they also apply to the social field, in controlled experimental settings.

7.2.2.1 Understanding Social Relations

Without seeking to settle *a priori* the question of the supremacy of one type of cognition over the other, it is nonetheless relatively easy to show that abilities pertaining to the knowledge of physical objects (e.g., being able to distinguish between two or more objects, namely to classify them, count them, or establish relations of identity between them), have their equivalents in the social field. For example, recognizing a partner requires at the very least discrimination and categorization abilities. Similarly, associating with an ally within a social group involves the prior assessment of identity relationships, as well as numerical quantities, and so on.

The fact that NHPs, and indeed probably most vertebrates, recognize each other is unanimously acknowledged. In addition to having representations of their partners, primates can recognize relationships between familiar individuals and categorize these relationships on, say, a scale of social dominance. The best known illustration of these skills comes from a field experiment by Seyfarth et al. (1980), in which vervet monkeys heard the specific alarm calls produced by their conspecifics when predators were detected, played through a loudspeaker. There were three types of calls, corresponding to the three main predators (eagles, leopards and pythons). As in the wild, each type of call elicited an adapted response from the vervets (e.g., taking refuge in the trees when a python was signalled). The responses to the calls appeared to be independent of variations in the length and amplitude of the signal, as well as the age and state of arousal of the monkey that raised the alarm. As these calls refer to external objects and their production is controlled (e.g., an individual can increase the intensity of its calls in the presence of a related conspecific), they may possess a rudimentary form of semantization and, according to the authors, can be likened to *words*. Experiments using the same playback technique also suggest that a mother in a group of vervets can respond to the calls of her offspring, even if they are a long way apart. In addition, females can recognize the vocalizations of other mothers' offspring, and associate (by looking toward the loudspeaker) a mother with the calls of a specific juvenile.

The categorization of individuals within a group (offspring versus non-offspring) has also been investigated. Dasser (1988) showed that female macaques can identify mother–child pairs from slides featuring all the individuals making up their social group. Similarly, Bovet and Washburn (2003) found that macaques shown films representing various interactions between two unknown conspecifics could indicate which individual dominated the other. Monkeys are thus capable of conceptualizing the relationships between other monkeys and of using that knowledge to anticipate their reactions. This cognitive ability to control social relations relies on inference, which parallels the transitive reasoning demonstrated in the processing of physical objects (Thompson & Oden, 2000). For example, regarding dominance relations, let us imagine that C has been beaten by B, and sees B being beaten by A. In this situation, it is advantageous for C to be able to infer that A is probably stronger than he is, and that it is better to avoid conflict with him.

7.2.2.2 Self-Recognition

The importance of the face and, within it, the gaze, is paramount in all social situations. This part of our body serves to be recognized by others, but is paradoxically invisible to us. In humans, self-recognition in a mirror is a skill that is acquired relatively late, only emerging during the second year of childhood (Amsterdam, 1972). When they see themselves

in a mirror for the first time, most NHPs, along with other species, react as though they were in the presence of a conspecific or a stranger. By contrast, human children, chimpanzees, orangutans, and gorillas exhibit self-directed behaviours (e.g., exploring the inside of their mouth) instead of producing simple social responses. In short, these species pass the mark test first proposed by Gallup (1970) to test chimpanzees. A recent study (Chang et al., 2015) showed that if macaque monkeys are given lengthy training (touching a luminous mark on their face produced by a laser), they also pass the mark test.

7.2.2.3 Knowledge of Mental States: Do NHPs Have a *Theory of Mind*?

Under the dual impetus of cognitive ethology and attempts in analytic philosophy to naturalize the mind, the study of intentionality has become a major research theme in primatology. Thus, the levels of intentionality proposed by Dennett (1983) can be applied to the system of alarm calls in vervets described in Section 7.2.2.1. Level 1 intentionality would imply that X (the vervet producing an alarm call) wants Y (the receiving vervet) to make the appropriate response. Level 2 intentionality would imply that X wants Y to believe that there is a predator (e.g., a leopard) and that Y must seek refuge in a tree. Finally, Level 3 intentionality would mean that X wants Y to believe that X wants Y to take shelter in a tree. Analysis of the contexts of production and call responses points to Level 1, and perhaps Level 2, intentionality in the interpretation of the vervets' calls. If the assignment of intentions adequately describes the observed behaviours, then presumably the sender *knows* that its behaviour toward the recipient will influence its reaction. The sender may thus be able to manipulate the information sent to the recipient in order to deceive, if necessary.

Examples of this *Machiavellian intelligence* have been collected during observations of the spontaneous relations between NHPs (Byrne & Whiten, 1988). Several attempts have been made to experimentally study deception, but also, more generally, to understand the point of view that the Other may have of a situation. Premack and Woodruff (1978) proposed the expression *theory of the mind* to characterize the experimental study of mental states and the attribution of intentions to others. Starting from an operational definition of intentionality, which assumes that the sender of a message controls its content and understands its consequences for the addressee, these researchers examined situations of information manipulation between, for example, a chimpanzee and a human. They analysed the ability of a chimpanzee to mislead its partner or, as a corollary, to understand that it has itself been duped. The experimental context was a communication situation (pointing gesture) about the location of a box containing food. The chimpanzee was sometimes the informant, sometimes the recipient. The human partner was either friendly, sharing the food when the chimpanzee indicated the right box, or hostile, keeping the food, even if the chimpanzee had provided the right information. Results showed that chimpanzees can distinguish between these two types of partners, ceasing to follow the indications provided by a hostile partner or, in the production situation, deliberately giving that partner erroneous information about the location of the food box with the food.

7.2.2.4 Experimental Approach to Mental States

Children's gradual development and acquisition of the ability to attribute mental states to others (see, for example, Astington, 1993) can be used to investigate NHPs. Four different levels have been identified in theory of the mind.

Attribution of Perceptions

In humans, this ability is first exhibited between nine and twelve months, when infants begin to follow the gaze of adults and use gestures to direct other people's attention to objects or events of interest to themselves. When chimpanzees are given the choice between two treats, one visible to a dominant conspecific, the other hidden behind a screen, they head for the food that is invisible to their rival (Hare et al., 2001). By contrast, capuchin monkeys and macaques do not differentiate between the two treats (Hare et al., 2003). Chimpanzees therefore know that if their dominant conspecifics do not see the reward, they cannot stop them from taking it, whereas monkeys may be able to learn an effective strategy through trial-and-error, but cannot imagine it right away.

Attribution of Intentions

In an experiment with chimpanzees and children (aged six-to-eighteen months), two conditions were compared (Tomasello et al., 2005). In the first condition, an experimenter tried to give a toy to a child (or a candy to a chimpanzee), but failed, as the box containing it would not open. In the second condition, the experimenter deliberately kept the toy or candy. The six-month-olds did not distinguish between these two situations, but the chimpanzees and children aged nine months or older showed more signs of impatience in the second situation. In a more complex task, when the experimenter demonstrated his intention to perform an ultimately unsuccessful action (e.g., trying but failing to take a toy apart), the eighteen-month-olds and chimpanzees could go beyond simple imitation, performing in full the action that the adult had tried to perform, and showing that they were able to anticipate his intention. The twelve-month-olds could imitate the adult's actions if he reached his goal, but could not carry through an action that the demonstrator had tried unsuccessfully to perform.

Attribution of Knowledge

The test commonly used with children in this context is the *false belief* test. In the classic version of this test (Wimmer & Perner, 1983), children are shown a small scene played by two dolls, Sally and Anne. Sally puts a ball in a basket, then leaves. Anne then picks up the ball and hides it in a box. Sally comes back, and the experimenter asks the child, 'Where is Sally going to get her ball?'. Up to four or five years of age, the children answer 'In the box', as they cannot tell that Sally's knowledge is different from theirs. Call and Tomasello (1999) constructed a non-verbal version of this test to examine chimpanzees, orangutans, and children aged four or five years. In this version, the participant sees two identical boxes. An experimenter (the *hider*) places a reward in one of the boxes (the participant cannot see which one it is). Another experimenter (the *indicator*) looks and indicates where the reward is hidden by placing a mark on the correct box. Once the participant has learned to choose the box marked by the indicator, the test phase occurs. The indicator looks where the reward is hidden, then leaves. The hider then switches the boxes, and the indicator comes back and places the mark on the wrong box. To find the reward, participants must understand that, since the indicator does not know that the hider has switched the boxes, he or she marks the empty box and it is the other one that must be chosen. The five chimpanzees and two orangutans failed, as they continued to choose the marked box. As for the children, two of the fourteen four-year-olds, and eight of fourteen five-year-olds succeeded. Performances on this non-verbal version were strongly correlated with those on the classic (verbal) version of the test.

Reading Others' Thoughts

The latest research indicates that great apes can also *read the thoughts of others.* Earlier studies had shown that apes are remarkably competent at understanding what others want, and what others might know, based on what they themselves can see and hear. To demonstrate the reading of others' thoughts, a test initially developed for human children (Southgate et al., 2007) was used to show that great apes reliably look toward a place where an agent falsely believes an object to be located, even if they themselves know that the object is no longer there. Specifically, chimpanzees, bonobos and orangutans watched short videos while their gaze direction was recorded using an infrared eye-tracking device. The videos showed an experimenter hiding an object in a particular location. It then showed the object being moved to a second location by a human dressed up as King Kong (an unreal apelike character unfamiliar to the subjects and used to stimulate their engagement). Depending on the scenario, this change of location took place either in the presence or in the absence of the experimenter. In both conditions, the experimenter then came looking for the object. In the scenario where the experimenter did not see the object being moved, the eye-tracking data revealed that seventeen of the twenty-two apes correctly anticipated that the human would go to the wrong location to retrieve the object. This successful anticipation of where the human expected the object to be suggests that these primates understood his or her point of view (Krupenye et al., 2016). If other research confirmed these data, it would mean that the ability to conceive of a false belief is not specific to humans (this test is successfully performed by children from the age of two years), and has probably existed in primates for at least thirteen-to-eighteen million years, namely since the last common ancestors of chimpanzees, bonobos, orangutans and humans.

7.3 Communication and Language

Primates including humans use a set of communication signals to regulate their social exchanges. These signals are mainly conveyed through the oral and visual-gestural modalities. Examples of the former include the alarm calls of vervet monkeys (see Section 7.2.2.1) and the use of grunts by chimpanzees to announce that they have discovered food and are willing to share it (Slocombe & Zuberbühler, 2005). Chimpanzees also rely heavily on gestures and on a large repertoire of facial expressions for their spontaneous communication in the wild (see Hobaiter & Byrne, 2011, for a review). For example, extending an arm and touching the partner under the chin with the palm and fingers of the hand is used to beg for food from a dominant individual. Similarly, a young chimpanzee will invite a partner to play by raising one arm and simultaneously adopting a specific facial expression. These gestures are used flexibly, and if the initial invitation fails, the youth may well try another gesture from its repertoire, such as hitting the ground with its hands (Pollick & de Wall, 2007). These communicative signals of primates (vocalizations and gestures) not only regulate their social interactions but also trigger actions with partners. They are similarly involved in the ability of monkeys and apes to understand and respect the structure of certain social relationships (e.g., relations of dominance and kinship) and to establish coalitions and alliances. In this type of interaction, two or more individuals cooperate so that they are in a better position vis-à-vis their opponents. Two individuals may, for example, join forces to confront a conspecific who dominates each of

them individually. Kummer (1968) described a dominant behaviour called *threat under protection*, where one strategy is for X to choose Y as an ally, because Y occupies a dominant position in the hierarchy with respect to Z. Moreover, in the competition for grooming, X is often seen grooming the individual who occupies the highest position in the hierarchy. *Redirected aggression* also testifies to this knowledge of the social hierarchy. This is where X (or a relative of X) is attacked by Y, and X responds by attacking individuals related to Y.

To summarize, NHPs are able, like most mammals, to recognize other individuals in their group, form stable relationships with them, and predict their behaviour. Their communicative exchanges are also characterized – and this is probably specific to NHPs – by an understanding of the different social relations between individuals. This understanding allows the partners in these relationships to manipulate and, where appropriate, misuse them for their own benefit. Do these sophisticated means of reciprocal actions resemble those used by humans, and specifically those involved in language?

7.3.1 Human Language and NHP Communication

Whereas humans can use symbols and linguistic signs, it seems reasonable to hypothesize that NHPs only use signals in their intra- and interspecific communication. The difference between humans and NHPs obviously does not lie solely in the presence or absence of phonation, but rather in the cognitive skills that either emerge contemporaneously with or are derived from language. Ethologists and linguists have attempted to identify the most important features of language, so that their presence can be checked in other species. Hockett (1960)'s famous inventory contains thirteen such traits. A number of these traits are present in the communication systems of NHPs and of birds (e.g., transmission channel between the vocal and acoustic systems), but the most important attributes (double articulation, productivity, displacement in space and time) are lacking in animal communication systems, according to Hockett.

New discoveries (especially in primatology) have convinced researchers that key linguistic features (e.g., ability to *semantize* or certain arbitrariness of the signal in relation to its referent) can be found in the communication signals of animals. Given that other traits, such as metacognition and attribution of mental states to others (see above), are no longer deemed to be exclusively human, the frontier between animal communication and language has to be moved. The search for distinctive features in the structure and organization of language therefore has only a relative validity, insofar as the marking of the boundary can never be definitively fixed, depending on which features we choose to retain or reject.

7.3.1.1 Structural Differences between Signals, Symbols and Linguistic Signs

It is crucial to look for possible differences between signals (e.g., vocal ones), symbols (e.g., visual ones) and linguistic signs. Let us consider the case of arbitrariness, a hallmark of the language faculty. The relationship between two objects is said to be arbitrary if there is no resemblance between the two entities. As far as human speech is concerned, we have known since de Saussure (1966, originally published in 1916) that these entities are made up of material elements, namely the signifiers (sounds) and the signified (content). This relationship is described as *arbitrary*, for, in most cases, there is no physical or analogical resemblance between the sequence of sounds

and the content it represents. If we apply this definition to the chimpanzees Washoe (who communicates by gestures with a human) and Sarah (who arranges plastic symbols on a board), and the bonobo Kanzi (who manipulates visual symbols or lexigrams), we can conclude that these symbols have an arbitrary relationship with the various aspects of the reality they represent. Crucially, the arbitrariness of the substitution practised by the apes relates solely to the non-similarity between these substitutes and their referents. It does not imply what de Saussure referred to as *radical arbitrariness*, which is characteristic of the linguistic sign. The latter does not connect a substitute to an object, but a word to a concept or, in the vocabulary of linguistics, a signifier to a signified. Moreover, however varied and sophisticated the signalling systems (spontaneous or learned) used by NHPs may be, they do not exhibit the constitutive structure of language whereby each element or sign derives its meaning solely from its contrast with and opposition to all other signs (Vauclair, 2003).

One of the unique properties of language is therefore that words directly refer neither to entities nor to objects in the real world, but to other words or other signs organized in a system. As a sign refers to a concept, language manages a triangular relationship (object–sign–concept). It is precisely the triangularity of this systemic organization that seems to be lacking in the communication systems learned by apes, as signs can in no way be restricted to the simple accumulation of labels affixed to things. According to Hagège (1985), chimpanzees display a *representative intelligence*, 'that of the symbol as deferred notation of objects *in absentia*. But conceptual intelligence, which is linked to arbitrary signs and not to symbols, seems to be only human' (p. 102). Another characteristic of the organization of language is the presence of a syntax obeying strict rules, where word order plays a decisive role in meaning. Studies of *linguistically trained* chimpanzees suggest that this syntax is virtually non-existent. Chimpanzees can juxtapose two or three learned elements at best, and are unable to arrange them according to syntactic rules (for an example in bonobos, see Savage-Rumbaugh et al., 1986).

7.3.1.2 Functional Differences: Modalities of Communication

If we are to undertake a full comparison between language and animal communication, we need to consider not just structural differences, but also the function of the signals used in the two systems. This functional approach reveals a major difference between the use of symbols (e.g., by chimpanzees) and the use of words by children. In NHPs, this function is essentially imperative or injunctive. In other words, the signals are used in a context of requests (for an object, to go out, to play, etc.). In humans, in addition to this imperative modality, words are endowed with a declarative function whose purpose is to state information about the world. Through this declarative modality, language can be used to exchange information (Bates, 1976). Here, then, is a probable discontinuity between humans and apes regarding language. Consider the performance of the celebrated bonobo Kanzi, the most brilliant of the NHPs studied up to now (Savage-Rumbaugh, 1986). The developmental psychology literature tells us that at the age of one and a half years, the informative/declarative modality dominates a human child's language, and becomes systematic at around two and a half years, characterizing more than six out of ten productions (Bassano & Maillochon, 1994). The distribution of Kanzi's language productions (consisting of combinations of lexigrams and imperative gestures) is totally different

from that of children. At eight years, for example, 96 per cent of them were injunctive (Savage-Rumbaugh et al., 1986). The fact that his use of lexigrams is limited to a single modality can probably be explained in part by the constraints of the experimental environment, as the latter strongly encourages him to make requests for objects or activities. Nevertheless, studies indicate that although Kanzi (like the other apes taking part in these kinds of experiments) has learned the reference function of a substitute, he does not make spontaneous use of it beyond the restrictive framework in which these symbols have been acquired. If humans are so quick to use their first words to comment on the world and share their knowledge with others (because things have names), it is probably because these referential skills do not appear *de novo*. Rather, the ground is laid for these abilities well before language acquisition, through a set of early communicative activities between the infant and a competent adult. These interactions notably include joint attention (Bruner, 1983), which emerges at around four-to-six months of age, when the infant starts to follow his/her mother's gaze, in order to fixate the same object as her. This context of joint attention becomes more complex thereafter, with the addition of the pointing gesture making it possible to *designate* the location of the visually targeted object or third person with greater precision (see Vauclair & Cochet, 2013, for a review).

Returning to the comparison between apes and humans, the signals of the former fulfil a single objective, namely, to obtain a tangible result concerning an object or action. This function is observed both in exchanges between chimpanzees and between chimpanzees and their human teachers. Language, on the other hand, above and beyond this instrumental function, serves to draw other people's attention to objects or events, because these objects or events exist and because it is possible to name them. For example, children will say 'Air plane!' apparently to mean 'It's a plane!' or 'Look, I saw a plane!' In this context, they are simply communicating to share their interest in something with a listener, or to show that they know about this object. Communication can therefore be an end in itself, independently of any satisfaction related to the possession of a given object. Overall, the use of lexigrams or gestures by chimpanzees does not allow us to conclude that these symbols have the same function as linguistic signs, as control over the instrumental function of these lexigrams in the context of a test situation is sufficient to use them adaptively.

Interesting secondary properties emerge from the systemic organization of language. One of these peculiarities reported by Bickerton (1990) is that, whereas animals can only communicate about contexts that have biological significance for them (partners, food, predators), humans can communicate about anything and everything, including entities that do not exist (see fairy tales and science fiction). Finally, signs have the fundamental property of being bidirectional and intersubjective. In other words, people who use a word know that their partner knows the communicative meaning of that sign. This property means that the manipulation of language is based on the premise that representations are attributed between speakers. In animals' spontaneous communication, the signals are unidirectional. Thus, a young chimpanzee who touches the back of his mother to request her to bend down so that he can settle on her back would certainly not understand if a conspecific performed the same gesture on himself. This unidirectionality is also observed in some learned exchanges during pointing. For example, chimpanzees or baboons can understand and use pointing in a context of demand (pointing fingers at an experimenter to draw his

or her attention to a food item; see Meguerditchian & Vauclair, 2008, for examples), but they apparently cannot grasp the meaning of pointing in humans. This is probably because chimpanzees' actions typically serve as procedures for achieving goals, and do not constitute intersubjective communication conventions as they do in humans. This difference in use (signals serving to trigger actions versus signs used to share an experience) is based on another distinction: humans, and to lesser extent chimpanzees, consider their partners to be independent agents endowed with intentions. In a nutshell, although the ritualized spontaneous gestures of chimpanzees demonstrate their understanding of the effects these gestures have on their partners, it is as yet unclear whether these partners are perceived as intentional agents whose experience of the world can be, either temporally or permanently, influenced or shared.

7.3.2 Other Language-Related Psychological Discontinuities

Limitations in the modalities of communication, as well as in the attributive abilities of NHPs, lead us to envisage other aspects of discontinuity. For example, it is important to emphasize that the characteristics of linguistic structures are not confined to the register of verbal or intentional behaviours. They are also found in sign language, whether this language is spontaneously used, is used in association with speech, or constitutes a complete communication system, as is the case with the sign language of deaf people. These structures similarly underlie many human behaviours, particularly those related to tool use. Apes use and shape natural tools (see above), with chimpanzees cutting branches to *fish* for termites or cracking nuts with a *hammer* stone on a stump or a second stone that serves as an *anvil* (Boesch & Boesch, 1984). However, it is remarkable that these instruments are related to a single immediate function (obtaining food), and are not used to perform any other tasks, in contrast to the polysemy of linguistic signs. Thus, after fishing for termites, the chimpanzee does not use its tool to tickle some other non-edible animal, clean its teeth or scratch its ear. Likewise, the stone used to crack nuts is not used to manufacture another more advanced hammer, let alone make an ornament with a purely aesthetic value. Nor do chimpanzees enjoy throwing their hammer stones into a pond to make a splash.

Human tools and those of chimpanzees are thus partly distinct, as only the former are of lasting use. The ethnologist Leroi-Gourhan (1993) considered these tools to be closely related to words, in view of their permanence and universality. Another, related criterion that can help us distinguish animal tools from human tools is that manufactured human tools can be indefinitely improved. Unlike the use of linguistic signs, chimpanzees' use of tools is not synonymic. They do not use several different tools to perform the same task, and never undertake comparisons, keeping the *best* one and rejecting the others. In other words, apes do not seem to create toolkits that are structured like language, with elements arranged according to their differences and similarities within a system. According to Leroi-Gourhan (1993), the sequence of stages needed to make a tool such as a flint axe amounts to the use of a *syntax*. However, it must be emphasized that the systematic and continuous observation of wild chimpanzees in the Congo River Basin (Sanz et al., 2004) has highlighted considerable adaptability in these primates' use of tools. Thus, when they engage in termite fishing, they can visit two types of sites, namely underground termite nests and mound-shaped termite nests above ground. For the former, chimpanzees use sticks to pierce the nest, then smaller sticks to collect the termites. By contrast, for termite nests above ground, they make a hole with a short stick, then pick up the termites with a longer, more flexible branch.

Other cognitive and social skills are associated with language use. Thus, from a very early age, objects serve as the basis for activities that go beyond their immediate instrumental usage. For example, young children may engage in pretend play with a banana, using it as though it were a telephone or some other *transitional* object (in Winnicott, 1971's sense of the word), or with a teddy bear, using it as though it were a companion. By contrast, chimpanzees have no such symbolic repertoire, such that when they are given a banana, they will eat it if they are hungry, and ignore it if they are full. In other contexts, many species of NHP display aggressive, sexual or predatory *games*, but when they signal to their companions that they are playing, they do not engage in either pretend play or metaplay, which would allow them to negotiate agreements with their partners, as in the *Cat and mouse!* game. While it is true that chimpanzees can recognize themselves in a mirror, as demonstrated with Gallup (1970)'s mark test, they do not appear to use this skill to enhance their relationships with their partners, by paying attention to their appearance and to the way that others see them, as humans do. Certainly, no primatologist has ever thought of describing this self-recognition in terms of *narcissism* or modesty. Finally, although chimpanzees, among other animal species, seem to display preferences for certain objects of various shapes and colours, there is no evidence to suggest that they make even rudimentary aesthetic judgements, contrasting the *beautiful* with the *ugly*.

7.3.3 Reflection of Discontinuities in Cognition and Communication

The differences observed between humans and NHPs in the mastery of linguistic signs and the imputation of mental states are echoed in their respective cognitive and communicative abilities (Vidal & Vauclair, 1996). The attribution of knowledge and beliefs to others, and therefore the understanding of their role as agents endowed with intentions, can be observed in children's participation in tripartite activities including at least one partner and one object. These sociocognitive mechanisms allow them to engage in what Tomasello et al. (1993) called *cultural learning*, in which children discover the tools, artefacts and other symbols of their culture, by attempting to reproduce the relations of intentionality that adults have with these cultural objects. It is this involvement in cultural learning and the accumulation of knowledge over time that allow children to participate in the cognitive history of the species (Tomasello, 2019).

It must be emphasized that it is only because fellow humans are perceived of as intentional agents that cultural learning, and indeed any teaching, can begin. When the protagonists have representations of the knowledge and intentions of others, the *teacher* can attribute a state of either knowledge or ignorance to the *taught*. Moreover, in active teaching, the teacher can fine-tune this attribution according to the performance of the learner. Examples of the deliberate teaching of young individuals by competent adults are extremely rare in the NHP literature, as the young mostly acquire knowledge through either trial-and-error or observational learning (Halliday & Slater, 1983). With respect to teaching among apes, the only available data concern the active intervention of a mother chimpanzee during the long and laborious acquisition of a nut-cracking technique by a youth using a granite *hammer* (Boesch, 1991). The findings reported so far are thus in favour of a certain discontinuity between humans and NHPs, even though intermediate stages can be discerned in the evolutionary pathways and selection pressures that culminated in human social learning (Moore, 2013).

These considerations are not intended to diminish the interest or complexity of NHPs' spontaneous behaviours. They simply serve as a basis for comparing current primates and current humans on their interindividual communicative behaviours. Even if apes' performances share some characteristics with those of children, it would be naïve to expect their respective abilities to correspond completely. After all, chimpanzees, bonobos and humans are different species. Their specificities have led them to develop their own mechanisms for communicating and managing their relationships with their own environments. Those that have undergone particular development in humans include language and the systems that are partly derived from it, such as recursion in arithmetic. The presence both in humans and in NHPs of comparable brain hemispheric specialization for processing visual and acoustic cues (Hopkins & Vauclair, 2012), and the existence of rudimentary forms of symbolization in the use of such signals, nevertheless point to similarities between modern humans and current primates. These findings, associated with those obtained in *language* learning contexts among laboratory-trained apes, converge toward the idea that the components defining linguistic competencies may have appeared at different points in primate evolution. Nevertheless, only in modern humans (*Homo sapiens*) have all these components (cognitive and communicative) combined to form a single system that is both complex and very powerful (Vauclair, 1990).

The findings set out in this chapter are generally in favour of a discontinuity in cognition between humans and NHPs with respect to communication and language. Several avenues have been explored here to account for these differences in primate cognition, but there are others, not least those proposed by contemporary linguists such as Chomsky (1968), who postulated the existence of a universal grammar inscribed in a module of the brain, referring explicitly to Descartes' innate position (but see Hauser et al., 2002). Another thesis, advanced by the linguist Pinker (1994, 2013) and based on the Darwinian theory of evolution, is that language, like any other phenotypic characteristic, has evolved according to the laws of natural selection. This biological scenario contrasts with the cultural scenario whereby language appeared only recently (around 100,000 years ago), as a purely cultural artefact. The biological model has the advantage of acknowledging that the long evolutionary period that led to language in its current form was marked by a series of intermediate steps. This conception is therefore compatible with the idea that the language of our human ancestors shared properties with the communication systems of apes. Without fossil records, these intermediate steps are, of course, difficult to reconstruct. Nevertheless, the Darwinian evolutionary model is more plausible than other scenarios, as it allows the complexity of language as a system of representation and communication to be understood alongside that of other cognitive functions in humans (Vauclair, 1996).

7.4 The Question of Morality

The Darwinian perspective of continuity could easily apply to moral behaviours, broadly defined as any action or interaction that promotes group cohesion and the smooth functioning of the social group. As noted by Brosnan (2014), the moral behaviours of animals do not have to be understood as such by the individuals concerned. This means that these behaviours can exist even when the individuals themselves do not understand them to be *moral*, just as infants can exhibit moral behaviours before the onset of speech (Hamlin, 2013).

This field of inquiry was inaugurated in NHPs by de Waal (1996), who considered that several behaviours constitute the building blocks of moral systems, and kept sight of the fact that research needs to be limited to what animals (including humans) do, and not what they should do (Hall & Brosnan, 2016).

Several contexts have been examined to show evidence of the precursors of morality in NHPs, including (1) conflict resolution for promoting group harmony via reconciliation and consolation, (2) reciprocity via, for example, exchanges of food or grooming (e.g., for agonistic support), (3) responses to inequity (behaviour studied in collective tasks where cooperation is more effective if all the partners receive equal rewards), and (4) empathy, such as helping others or showing concern for them, indicating that individuals may understand the needs of others (the latter has only been the subject of a few experiments, but anecdotes are available). Thus, NHPs have a sense of reciprocity and fairness. For example, they can remember who did them favours and who did them wrong. Chimpanzees are also more likely to share food with those who have groomed them, and capuchin monkeys express displeasure if they are given a smaller reward than a partner for performing the same task (e.g., piece of cucumber instead of a grape; cited in Hall & Brosnan, 2016).

One specific bonus of this relatively novel comparative approach to morality in NHPs is that it allows the individuals' histories to be better controlled. For Tomasello (2016), human morality emanates from psychological processes of shared intentionality evolved to enable individuals to function effectively in ever more cooperative lifeways. A more general advantage is that it sheds light on the biological roots of moral behaviours in humans.

References

Amsterdam, B. (1972). Mirror self-image reactions before age two. *Psychobiology*, *5*, 297–305.

Astington, J. W. (1993). *The Child's Discovery of the Mind*. Cambridge, MA: Harvard University Press.

Bassano, D., & Maillochon, I. (1994). Early grammatical and prosodic marking of utterance modality in French. A longitudinal case study. *Journal of Child Language*, *21*, 649–675.

Bates, E. (1976). *Language and Context: The Acquisition of Pragmatics*. New York: Academic Press.

Bates, E. (1979). *The Emergence of Symbols. Cognition and Communication in Infancy*. New York: Academic Press.

Beran, M. J. (2004). Long-term retention of the differential values of Arabic numerals by chimpanzees (*Pan troglodytes*). *Animal Cognition*, *7*, 86–92.

Beran, M. J., Parrish, A. E., & Evans, T. A. (2015). Numerical cognition and quantitative abilities in nonhuman primates. In D. Geary, D. Berch, & K. Mann Koepke (eds.), *Evolutionary Origins and Early Development of Number Processing* (pp. 91–119). New York: Elsevier.

Bickerton, D. (1990). *Language and Species*. Chicago, IL: University of Chicago Press.

Boesch, C. (1991). Teaching among wild chimpanzees. *Animal Behaviour*, *41*, 530–532.

Boesch, C., & Boesch, H. (1984). Mental maps in wild chimpanzees: An analysis of hammer transports for nut cracking. *Primates*, *25*, 160–170.

Bovet, D., & Vauclair, J. (1998). Functional categorization of objects and of their pictures in baboons (Papio anubis). *Learning & Motivation*, *29*, 309–322.

Bovet, D., & Vauclair, J. (2001). Judgement of conceptual identity in monkeys. *Psychonomic Bulletin & Review*, *8*, 470–475.

Bovet, D., & Washburn, D. A. (2003). Rhesus macaques (*Macaca mulatta*) categorize unknown conspecifics according to their dominance relations. *Journal of Comparative Psychology*, *117*, 400–405.

Boysen, S. T., & Berntson, G. G. (1989). Numerical competence in a chimpanzee (*Pan troglodytes*). *Journal of Comparative Psychology*, *103*, 23–31.

Boysen, S. T., Berntson, G. G., Shreyer, T. A., & Hannan, M. B. (1995). Indicating acts during counting by a chimpanzee (*Pan troglodytes*). *Journal of Comparative Psychology*, *109*, 47–51.

Brosnan, S. F. (2014). Precursors of morality: Evidence for moral behaviors in non-human primates. In M. E. Christen, C. E. van Schaik, J. E. Fischer, M. E. Huppenbauer, & C. E. Tanner (eds.), *Empirically Informed Ethics: Morality between Facts and Norms* (pp. 85–98). Cham, Switzerland: Springer.

Bruner, J. S. (1983). *Child's Talk: Learning to Use Language*. New York: W. W. Norton & Company Inc.

Byrne, R., & Whiten, A. (1988). *Machiavellian Intelligence*. Oxford: Oxford University Press.

Call, J., & Tomasello, M. (1999). A nonverbal false belief task: The performance of children and great apes. *Child Development*, *70*, 381–395.

Chang, L., Fang, Q., Zhang, S., Poo, M., & Gong, N. (2015). Mirror-induced self-directed behaviors in rhesus monkeys after visual-somatosensory training. *Current Biology*, *25*, 1–6.

Chomsky, N. (1968). *Language and Mind*. New York: Harcourt, Brace & World.

Dasser, V. (1988). A social concept in Java monkeys. *Animal Behaviour*, *36*, 225–230.

de Saussure, F. (1966). *Course in General Linguistics*, ed. C. Bally, & A. Sechehaye. New York: McGraw-Hill.

de Waal, F. B. M. (1996). *Good Natured: The Origins of Right and Wrong in Primates and Other Animals*. Cambridge, MA: Harvard University Press.

Dennett, D. (1983). Intentional systems in cognitive ethology: The "Panglossian paradigm" defended. *The Behavioral and Brain Sciences*, *6*, 343–390.

Flemming, T. M., Thompson, R. K. R., & Fagot, J. (2013). Baboons, like humans, solve analogy by categorical abstraction of relations. *Animal Cognition*, *16*, 519–524.

Gallup, G. G. (1970). Chimpanzees: Self recognition. *Science*, *167*, 86–87.

Hagège, C. (1985). *L'homme de paroles*. Paris: Fayard.

Hall, K., & Brosnan, S. F. (2016). A comparative perspective on the evolution of moral behaviour. In T. K. Shackelford, & R. D. Hansen (eds.), *The Evolution of Morality* (pp. 157–176). Cham, Switzerland: Springer.

Halliday, T. R., & Slater, P. J. B. (eds.) (1983). *Animal Behaviour, Vol.3: Genes, Development and Learning*. Oxford: Blackwell Scientific Publications.

Hamlin, J. K. (2013). Moral judgment and action in preverbal infants and toddlers: Evidence for an innate moral core. *Current Directions in Psychological Science, 22*, 186–193.

Hare, B., Addessi, E., Call, J., Tomasello, M., & Visalberghi, E. (2003). Do capuchin monkeys, *Cebus apella*, know what conspecifics do and do not see? *Animal Behaviour, 65*, 131–142.

Hare, B., Call, J., & Tomasello, M. (2001). Do chimpanzees know what conspecifics know and do not know? *Animal Behaviour, 61*, 139–151.

Hauser, M. D., Chomsky, N., & Fitch, W. T. (2002). The faculty of language: What is it, who has it, and how did it evolve? *Science, 298*, 1569–1579.

Herrnstein, R. J. (1990). Levels of stimulus control: A functional approach. *Cognition, 37*, 133–166.

Hobaiter, C., & Byrne, R. W. (2011). The gestural repertoire of the wild chimpanzee. *Animal Cognition, 14*, 745–767.

Hockett, C. F. (1960). The origin of speech. *Scientific American, 203*, 88–96.

Hopkins, W. D., & Vauclair, J. (2012). Evolution of behavioral and brain asymmetries in primates. In M. Tallerman, & K. Gibson (eds.), *Handbook of Language Evolution* (pp. 184–197). Oxford: Oxford University Press.

Humphrey, N. (1976). The social function of intellect. In P. P. G. Bateson, & R. A. Hinde (eds.), *Growing Points in Ethology* (pp. 303–317). New York: Cambridge University Press.

Koehler, W. (1925). *The Mentality of Apes*. New York: Harcourt, Brace & Company Inc.

Krupenye, C., Kano, F., Hirata, S., Call, J., & Tomasello, M. (2016). Great apes anticipate that other individuals will act according to false beliefs. *Science, 354*, 110–114.

Kummer, H. (1968). *Social Organization of Hamadryas Baboons*. Chicago, IL: University of Chicago Press.

Kummer, H. (1982). Social knowledge in free-ranging primates. In D. R. Griffin (ed.), *Animal Mind–Human Mind* (pp. 113–130). Berlin: Springer Verlag.

Leroi-Gourhan, A. (1993). *Gesture and Speech*. Cambridge, MA: MIT Press.

Meguerditchian, A., & Vauclair, J. (2008). Vocal and gestural communication in nonhuman primates and the question of the origin of language. In L. S. Roska-Hardy, & E. M. Neumann-Held (eds.), *Learning from Animals?* (pp. 61–85). London: Psychology Press.

Moore, R. (2013). Social learning and teaching in chimpanzees. *Biology & Philosophy, 28*, 879–901.

Nieder, A. (2009). Prefrontal cortex and the evolution of symbolic reference. *Current Opinion in Neurobiology, 19*, 99–108.

Parrish, A. E., & Brosnan, S. F. (2012). Primate cognition. In V. S. Ramachandran (ed.), *The Encyclopedia of Human Behavior* (vol. 3, pp. 174–180). New York: Academic Press.

Pinker, S. (1994). *The Language Instinct: How the Mind Creates Language*. New York: W. Morrow and Co.

Pinker, S. (2013). *Language, Cognition and Human Nature*. New York: Oxford University Press.

Pollick, A. S., & de Waal, F. B. M. (2007). Ape gestures and language evolution. *Proceedings of the National Academy of Sciences (USA), 104*, 8184–8189.

Premack, D., & Woodruff, G. (1978). Does the chimpanzee have a theory of mind? *The Behavioral and Brain Sciences, 1*, 515–526.

Sanz, C., & Morgan, D. (2007). Chimpanzee tool technology in the Goualougo triangle, Republic of Congo. *Journal of Human Evolution, 52*, 420–433.

Sanz, C., Morgan, D., & Gulick, S. (2004). New insights into chimpanzees, tools, and termites from the Congo Basin. *American Naturalist, 164*, 567–581.

Sarnecka, B. W., & Carey, S. (2008). How counting represents number: What children must learn and when they learn it. *Cognition, 108*, 662–674.

Savage-Rumbaugh, E. S. (1986). *Ape Language. From Conditioned Response to Symbol.* New York: Columbia University Press.

Savage-Rumbaugh, E. S., McDonald, K., Sevcik, R. A., Hopkins, W. D., & Rubert, E. (1986). Spontaneous symbol acquisition and communicative use by pygmy chimpanzees (*Pan paniscus*). *Journal of Experimental Psychology: General, 115*, 211–235.

Seyfarth, R. M., & Cheney, D. L. (2012). Primate social cognition as a precursor to language. In K. Gibson, & M. Tallerman (eds.), *Oxford Handbook of Language Evolution* (pp. 59–70). Oxford: Oxford University Press.

Seyfarth, R. M., Cheney, D. L., & Marler, P. (1980). Monkey responses to three different alarm calls: Evidence of predator classification and semantic communication. *Science, 210*, 801–803.

Slocombe, K. E., & Zuberbühler, K. (2005). Functionally referential communication in a chimpanzee. *Current Biology, 15*, 1779–1784.

Southgate, V., Senju, A., & Csibra, G. (2007). Action anticipation through attribution of false belief in 2-year-olds. *Psychological Science, 18*, 587–592.

Thompson, R. K. R., & Oden, D. L. (2000). Categorical perception and conceptual judgments by nonhuman primates: The paleological monkey and the analogical ape. *Cognitive Science, 24*, 363–396.

Tomasello, M. (2016). *A Natural History of Human Morality.* Cambridge, MA: Harvard University Press.

Tomasello, M. (2019). *Becoming Human: A Theory of Ontogeny.* Cambridge, MA: The Belknap Press.

Tomasello, M., & Call, J. (1997). *Primate Cognition.* New York: Oxford University Press.

Tomasello, M., Carpenter, M., Call, J., Behne, T., & Moll, H. (2005). Understanding and sharing intentions: The ontogeny of cultural cognition. *The Behavioral and Brain Sciences, 28*, 675–735.

Tomasello, M., Kruger, A. C., & Ratner, H. H. (1993). Cultural learning. *The Behavioral and Brain Sciences, 16*, 495–552.

Vauclair, J. (1990). Primate cognition: From representation to language. In S. T. Parker, & K. Gibson (eds.), *Language and Intelligence in Monkeys and Apes: Comparative Developmental Perspectives* (pp. 312–329). Cambridge, UK: Cambridge University Press.

Vauclair, J. (1996). *Animal Cognition: Recent Developments in Comparative Psychology.* Cambridge, MA: Harvard University Press.

Vauclair, J. (2003). Would humans without language be apes? In J. Valsiner (Series ed.) & A. Toomela (Vol. ed.), *Cultural Guidance in the Development of the Human Mind: Vol. 7. Advances in Child Development within Culturally Structured Environments* (pp. 9–26). Greenwich, CT: Ablex Publishing Corporation.

Vauclair, J. (2012). Piaget and the comparative psychology of animal cognition. In E. Marti, & C. Rodríguez (eds.), *After Piaget* (pp. 59–72). New Brunswick, NJ: Transaction Publishers.

Vauclair, J., & Cochet, H. (2013). Ontogeny and phylogeny of communicative gestures, speech-gestures relationships and left hemisphere specialization for language. In R. Botha and M. Everaert (eds.), *Oxford Studies in the Evolution of Language: The Evolutionary Emergence of Human Language* (pp. 160–180). Oxford: Oxford University Press.

Vidal, J. M., & Vauclair, J. (1996). Un Animal politique autre qu'humain? *Epokhè, 6*, 35–55.

Wimmer, H., & Perner, J. (1983). Beliefs about beliefs: Representation and constraining function of wrong beliefs in young children's understanding of deception. *Cognition, 13*, 103–128.

Winnicott, D. W. (1971). *Playing and Reality.* London: Routledge.

Yerkes, R. M. (1916). *The Mental Life of Monkeys and Apes: A Study of Ideational Behavior.* New York: Holt & Co.

8 Infants' Physical Reasoning and the Cognitive Architecture that Supports It

Yi Lin, Maayan Stavans, and Renée Baillargeon

8.1 Introduction

Traditionally, research on early physical reasoning has focused on the simple types of physical events our distant human ancestors routinely observed and produced as they interacted with objects. These types include, for example, occlusion, containment, support, and collision events. Over the first two years of life, infants become increasingly sophisticated at reasoning about these events. How is this sophistication achieved? In this chapter, we describe three successive waves of infancy research that each brought to light critical components of the cognitive architecture that supports early physical reasoning and its development.

8.2 First Wave: Core Knowledge and Information-Processing Capabilities

The study of early physical reasoning began with Piaget (1952, 1954), who was the first researcher to systematically investigate the development of infants' physical knowledge. He examined their responses in various action tasks and concluded that infants initially possess little knowledge about the physical world. For example, after observing that infants under eight or nine months of age (henceforth young infants) do not search for objects they have observed being hidden, Piaget proposed that young infants lack a concept of *object permanence* and do not yet understand that objects are objective, permanent entities that continue to exist when out of sight. Piaget's conclusion that young infants understand very little about physical events was generally accepted until the 1980s, when researchers became concerned that his exclusive reliance on action tasks (the only ones available to him at the time) might have led him to underestimate infants' physical knowledge.

This concern led investigators to seek alternative methods for exploring young infants' physical reasoning. One method that proved particularly helpful in revealing hitherto unsuspected competencies was the *violation-of-expectation* (VOE) method (Baillargeon et al., 1985). This method takes advantage of infants' natural tendency to look longer at events that violate, as opposed to confirm, their expectations. In recent years, several variations of the VOE method have been developed. For example, researchers have found that infants spend more time exploring objects featured in unexpected as opposed to expected events (Stahl & Feigenson, 2015; Zhang & Wang, 2019) and select unexpected over expected events when allowed to choose what they see next (Jin et al., 2018). All of these VOE methods depend on infants' propensity to use their mental model of the world to predict how events will unfold; when an event does not unfold as expected, infants inspect it to glean information for revising their model, so as to better predict outcomes in the future.

8.2.1 Object Permanence Revisited

Over time, numerous VOE experiments on object permanence revealed that, contrary to what Piaget (1952, 1954) had claimed, even very young infants realize that objects continue to exist when out of sight (Baillargeon, 1993). For example, infants aged two and a half to five months detected a violation when an object was hidden behind a screen that then rotated through the space occupied by the object (Baillargeon, 1987; Baillargeon et al., 1985); when an object moved through an obstacle behind a screen (Baillargeon & DeVos, 1991; Spelke et al., 1992); when an object was hidden in one location and retrieved from a different location (Newcombe et al., 1999; Wilcox et al., 1996); when an object moved behind one screen and reappeared from behind a different screen without appearing in the gap between them (Aguiar & Baillargeon, 1999); when an object was hidden in a container that was then slid forward and to the side to reveal the object standing in the container's initial position (Hespos & Baillargeon, 2001b); and when an object disappeared from behind a screen (Wynn, 1992) or from under a cover (Wang et al., 2005).

These and other similar results provided converging evidence that from a very young age, infants can represent and reason about hidden objects. By the same token, these results also called into question the Piagetian view, prevalent during most of the twentieth century, that infants are limited sensorimotor processors incapable of representation or thought (Piaget, 1952, 1954). As might be expected, fierce controversies ensued as researchers steeped in the Piagetian tradition questioned these new VOE tasks and offered deflationary accounts for their findings. According to many of these accounts, infants looked longer at the unexpected than at the expected test event in each task because the familiarization events used to introduce the task inadvertently induced a transient and superficial preference for the unexpected event (Bogartz et al., 1997; Cashon & Cohen, 2000; Haith, 1998; Thelen & Smith, 1994). However, empirical tests of these alternative accounts provided little support for them: Even when given a VOE object-permanence task with no familiarization trials, only test trials, young infants still looked significantly longer at the unexpected than at the expected event, suggesting that they did possess a concept of object permanence (Wang et al., 2004).

Today, there is general agreement among developmental researchers that young infants can represent objects that go out of sight. Indeed, researchers often take advantage of this capacity to explore other facets of early cognition, such as infants' ability to track others' beliefs (Hyde et al., 2018; Kampis et al., 2015; Kovács et al., 2010; Southgate & Vernetti, 2014). For example, in a study using functional near-infrared spectroscopy (Hyde et al., 2018), seven-month-olds watched videotaped scenarios in which an agent saw a toy being hidden in one of two containers. Next, the agent either faced away while the toy was transferred to the other container (*false-belief* scenario) or witnessed this transfer (*true-belief* scenario). In each scenario, activation in the temporal-parietal junction (a brain region involved in the tracking of others' beliefs) was measured prior to the agent's search for the toy. Like adults (Hyde et al., 2015), infants showed more activation during the false- than the true-belief scenario, suggesting that they were tracking what information was available to the agent about the location of the hidden toy (see Chapters 12 and 13). This conclusion presumes, of course, that infants could represent the continued existence of the hidden toy.

8.2.2 Further Physical Expectations

The findings from VOE object-permanence tasks did not only demonstrate that young infants expect an object to continue to exist when out of sight: In many cases, due to the specific events shown, the findings provided evidence of additional physical expectations. In particular, they indicated that young infants already understand that an object cannot pass through space occupied by another object (Baillargeon et al., 1985; Spelke et al., 1992), cannot follow a discontinuous path through space (Aguiar & Baillargeon, 1999; Spelke et al., 1995a), and cannot exert a force on another object without contact (Kotovsky & Baillargeon, 2000; Spelke et al., 1995b).

Encouraged by these findings, investigators began exploring other aspects of infants' physical world, adapting the VOE method as needed for the purpose. It soon became clear that while young infants held the expectations listed above for both inert and self-propelled objects (including humans; Baillargeon et al., 1990; Saxe et al., 2006), the same was not true of other expectations, which differed for the two types of objects. For example, young infants detected a violation if an inert object suddenly began to move on its own, if it spontaneously reversed direction after being set into motion, if it failed to move when forcibly hit or pulled, and if it failed to fall when released in midair (Luo et al., 2009; Needham & Baillargeon, 1993; Saxe et al., 2007; Spelke et al., 1995b). Strikingly, all of these expectations differed for self-propelled objects: Young infants did not find it unexpected if a self-propelled object reversed direction on its own, if it failed to move when forcibly hit or pulled, and if it failed to fall when released in midair (Baillargeon et al., 2009b; Leslie & Keeble, 1987; Luo et al., 2009; Spelke et al., 1995b). These and related results suggested that when a novel object gives sufficient evidence of being self-propelled, young infants endow it with an internal source of energy and understand that it can use this energy to initiate or alter its own motion as well as to resist or exert external forces (Baillargeon et al., 2009b; Gelman, 1990; Leslie, 1994; Luo et al., 2009; Saxe et al., 2007).

8.2.3 Core Knowledge

The results summarized in Sections 8.2.1 and 8.2.2 hinted at remarkably sophisticated physical knowledge in young infants. As such, these results naturally gave rise to the following questions: Where did this knowledge come from? How could we explain its presence in young infants with limited motor skills and scant experience of the world?

An influential proposal, the *core-knowledge hypothesis*, suggested an answer to these questions. This hypothesis holds that infants are born with a skeletal framework of core principles and concepts that guides their reasoning about physical events (Baillargeon, 2008; Baillargeon & Carey, 2012; Carey, 2011; Gelman, 1990; Keil, 1995; Leslie, 1995; Spelke et al., 1992, 1995b; Ullman et al., 2017; Wellman & Gelman, 1992). Descriptions of these principles and concepts differ among researchers, and they have also changed substantially over time as new findings have come to light. Nevertheless, a common assumption is that young infants are capable of sophisticated reasoning about physical events because they are innately prepared by evolution to do so: Their skeletal framework places them in the right ball park, so to speak, to begin reasoning about events in ways that will make possible rapid learning about the physical world.

8.2.3.1 Core Principles

The core principles in the skeletal framework underlying infants' physical reasoning constrain their expectations about the displacements and interactions of objects and other physical entities. To the best of our knowledge, these principles include "persistence," "inertia," and "gravity" (these are introduced in quote marks to emphasize that they are only rudimentary versions of the principles used by physicists).

The persistence principle states that all other things being equal, objects persist, as they are, in time and space (Baillargeon, 2008; Baillargeon et al., 2009a). This principle has many corollaries, which dictate that an object cannot occupy the same space as another object (solidity) and cannot spontaneously disappear (continuity), break apart (cohesion), fuse with another object (boundedness), or change into a different object (unchangeableness) (Baillargeon, 2008; Baillargeon et al., 2009a; Spelke et al., 1992, 1995b). (Of course, objects can undergo such modifications through causal transformations, but our focus here is on spontaneous, unassisted, physically impossible modifications). The positive findings of the VOE object-permanence tasks reviewed earlier indicate that, from a young age, infants are sensitive to persistence violations (Aguiar & Baillargeon, 1999; Baillargeon, 1987; Hespos & Baillargeon, 2001b; Spelke et al., 1992; Wang et al., 2005; Wilcox et al., 1996; for related findings with non-solid substances, see Anderson et al., 2018; Hespos et al., 2016).

The *inertia* principle states that objects at rest will remain at rest and objects in motion will follow a smooth path without abrupt changes in direction or speed, unless they are acted upon by forces sufficient to alter their rest or motion states (Baillargeon et al., 2009b;

Luo et al., 2009). The evidence reviewed earlier that young infants find it unexpected if an inert object initiates its own motion, spontaneously reverses direction, or remains stationary when forcibly hit or pulled, indicates that, from an early age, infants are sensitive to inertia violations (Baillargeon et al., 2009b; Kosugi & Fujita, 2002; Kotovsky & Baillargeon, 2000; Luo et al., 2009; Saxe et al., 2007; Spelke et al., 1995b).

Finally, the *gravity* principle states that, all other things being equal, objects fall when unsupported (Baillargeon & DeJong, 2017). The evidence reviewed earlier that young infants find it unexpected if an inert object remains suspended in midair indicates that, from an early age, infants are sensitive to gravity violations (Baillargeon et al., 2009b; Luo et al., 2009; Needham & Baillargeon, 1993).

8.2.3.2 Core Concepts

The core concepts in the skeletal framework underlying infants' physical reasoning involve unobservable elements that help explain events' outcomes. Core concepts include "internal energy" and "force." As we saw in Section 8.2.3.1, when a novel object gives sufficient evidence of being self-propelled (e.g., begins to move on its own), young infants endow it with *internal energy* and recognize that it can use this energy to control its motion and to resist or exert forces (Baillargeon et al., 2009b; Gelman, 1990; Leslie, 1995; Luo et al., 2009; Saxe et al., 2007). When infants see an object hit another object, they represent a *force* – like a directional arrow – being exerted by the first object onto the second one (Kominsky et al., 2017; Kotovsky & Baillargeon, 1994, 2000; Leslie, 1995; Leslie & Keeble, 1987; Mascalzoni et al., 2013). There are no doubt other explanatory concepts that play an important role in infant's physical reasoning. Some of these, like the concept of *cause*, may be highly abstract and shared with other domains of core knowledge, such as psychological reasoning (Liu et al., 2019).

8.2.3.3 Kinds of Explanations

When watching physical events, infants bring to bear their core knowledge to build explanations for the events and predict how they will unfold. In these explanations, principles and concepts are woven together seamlessly. To illustrate, consider an experiment in which six-month-olds were first introduced to a novel self-propelled box (Luo et al., 2009). Next, the box rested behind a screen that lay flat on the apparatus floor, and infants saw one of two test events. In the *one-screen* event, the screen was lifted and lowered to reveal no box, and then it was lifted and lowered again to reveal the box once more. The *two-screen* event was identical except that a second screen stood upright to the right of the first; when raised, the first screen occluded the left edge of the second screen, making it possible for the box to surreptitiously move behind it.

Infants looked significantly longer if shown the one-screen as opposed to the two-screen event, suggesting that they (1) categorized the box as a self-propelled object, endowed with internal energy, (2) found it unexpected in the one-screen event when the box magically disappeared and reappeared, in violation of the persistence principle, and (3) inferred in the two-screen event that the box used its internal energy to slip behind the second screen when it "disappeared" and to return behind the first screen when it "reappeared." Control results with an inert box supported this interpretation, as infants then found both events unexpected. Together, these findings nicely illustrate how infants' core knowledge can support their physical reasoning and help them generate plausible explanations for novel or unfamiliar events.

Of course, the explanations infants build for physical events are typically shallow and lacking in mechanistic detail (Keil, 1995; Wilson & Keil, 2000) (e.g., how did the self-propelled box use its internal energy to move back and forth behind the screens?). As Keil (1995) noted, these are "kinds of explanations" (p. 261), rather than specific, detailed, mechanistic explanations. Nevertheless, infants' shallow causal understandings are sufficient to support many sophisticated inferences (Aguiar & Baillargeon, 2002; Saxe et al., 2005).

8.2.4 Information-Processing Capabilities

Although infants' core physical knowledge could explain their success at VOE object-permanence tasks, one important question remained: If infants could represent the continued existence of hidden objects from a very young age, why did they fail manual-search tasks for several months after they learned to reach for objects? The dissociation between the positive findings of VOE object-permanence tasks and the negative findings of manual-search tasks (see also Ahmed & Ruffman, 1998; Daum et al., 2009) remained the focus of heated debate for many years, until a new approach suggested a way of reconciling these divergent findings (Boudreau & Bushnell, 2000; Diamond, 2013; Keen & Berthier, 2004). Proponents of this *processing-load* approach suggested that (1) infants' information-processing resources are initially limited and improve gradually with age; (2) the processing demands of any action task depend on both the difficulty of the physical reasoning involved and the difficulty of the actions involved; and (3) infants may fail at an action task because the *combined demands* of the task overwhelm their limited resources. From this perspective, the reason why young infants who are able to reach for objects fail at manual-search tasks is not that they cannot represent a hidden object (they do so in VOE tasks; Baillargeon et al., 1985), and not that they cannot plan and execute means-end actions to retrieve an object (they do so in action tasks with partly visible objects; Shinskey, 2002). Rather, it is that doing *both* of these activities at once (i.e., representing a hidden object *and* planning and executing the actions necessary to retrieve it) overwhelms their limited information-processing capabilities.

The processing-load approach has led researchers to seek action tasks that minimize overall demands when investigating at what age infants first demonstrate specific physical knowledge in their actions. Several VOE findings have now been confirmed using low-demand action tasks, making clear that when task demands are kept at a minimum to avoid taxing infants' limited information-processing capacities, action tasks can reveal the same physical knowledge as VOE tasks (for a review, see Hauf et al., 2012).

8.3 Second Wave: Developments in the Physical-Reasoning System

As investigations continued, it soon became clear that one could not fully account for infants' physical reasoning by considering only their core knowledge and information-processing capabilities. A key difficulty was that when tested with subtle core violations that could not be discerned without attending to the specific properties of objects and their arrangements, infants often failed to detect these violations. When an object passed behind a large screen, for example, infants under three months did not detect a violation if the object failed to appear in a low opening in the screen (Aguiar & Baillargeon, 1999, 2002); infants under three and a half months did not detect a violation if the object failed to appear in a high opening in the screen (Baillargeon &

DeVos, 1991; Luo & Baillargeon, 2005); infants under seven and a half months did not detect a violation if the object surreptitiously changed pattern behind the screen (Wilcox, 1999; Wilcox et al., 2011); and infants under eleven and a half months did not detect a violation if the object surreptitiously changed color behind the screen (Káldy & Leslie, 2003; Wilcox & Chapa, 2004).

These and similar negative results with other events (Baillargeon, 1991; Baillargeon et al., 1992; Kotovsky & Baillargeon, 1998; Newcombe et al., 1999) led to two broad realizations. First, because infants apply their core knowledge not to events in the world but to *mental representations* of these events, they can detect subtle core violations involving specific properties of objects and their arrangements only if they include the relevant information in their event representations (e.g., when an object passes behind a screen, infants can detect a surreptitious change to the color of the object only if they include color information in their representation of the event). Second, the evidence that infants initially detect few violations and come to detect more and more with age indicates that their event representations are at first very sparse and become gradually richer and more detailed. Spurred by these realizations, researchers began to investigate how event representations develop over time (for detailed reviews, see Baillargeon et al., 2009a, 2011).

8.3.1 Event Representations

Research on early event representations has yielded a large body of evidence that we summarize in three sets of findings.

8.3.1.1 Event Categories and Vectors

As infants observe and produce physical events, they form distinct *event categories*, such as occlusion, containment, support, collision, covering, tube, and burying events (Casasola, 2008; Hespos & Baillargeon, 2001a, 2006; Kotovsky & Baillargeon, 2000; Mou & Luo, 2017; Newcombe et al., 1999; Wang & Baillargeon, 2006; Wang et al., 2005). Each event category represents a type of causal interaction between objects. To predict how events from a category will unfold over time, infants have to learn about multiple facets of the events; we refer to these facets as *vectors*. When an object is lowered into a container, for example, vectors for this containment event include: whether the object will fit into the opening of the container, whether it will protrude above the rim of the container, whether it will remain partly visible through the sidewalls of the container, and, when retrieved from a container large enough to contain multiple objects, whether it is the same individual object or a different object.

8.3.1.2 Rules and Causally Relevant Features

For each vector of an event category, infants acquire *rules* that identify *features* (i.e., properties of objects and their arrangements) that are causally relevant for predicting outcomes (Baillargeon et al., 1992; Hespos & Baillargeon, 2001a; Kotovsky & Baillargeon, 1998; Wang & Baillargeon, 2006; Wang et al., 2003, 2005, 2016; Wilcox, 1999). Once infants have identified a feature as relevant to an event category, from that point on they routinely include information about the feature when representing events from the category.

For some vectors, the rule needed to predict outcomes is fairly straightforward and is acquired without much difficulty. For example, infants as young as four and a half months of age realize that the width of an object relative to that of a container's opening determines whether the object can be lowered into the container (Goldman & Wang, 2019;

Wang et al., 2004). For other vectors, however, the rule needed to predict outcomes is more complex or multi-faceted, and infants acquire a series of rules that gradually approximate the correct rule, with each new rule revising or elaborating the one(s) before it. In the case of support events involving inert objects, for example, one key vector is whether an object will remain stable or fall when released in contact with another object (henceforth base). Initially, young infants have no particular expectation about the outcomes of these events; between about four and a half and thirteen and a half months of age, however, they identify a series of rules that help them predict these outcomes more and more accurately.

Thus, by about four and a half to five and a half months, infants acquire a *type-of-contact* rule: An object remains stable if released on top of a base, but not if released against or under it (Baillargeon, 1995; Hespos & Baillargeon, 2008; Merced-Nieves et al., 2020). By about six and a half months, they acquire a *proportion-of-contact* rule: An object on a base remains stable as long as 50 percent or more of its bottom surface is supported (Baillargeon et al., 1992; Hespos & Baillargeon, 2008; Luo et al., 2009). By about eight months, they acquire a *position-of-contact* rule: An object on a base can remain stable with less than 50 percent support as long as the middle of its bottom surface is supported (Dan et al., 2000; Huettel & Needham, 2000; Wang et al., 2016). Finally, by about thirteen months, infants acquire a *proportional-distribution* rule: When released with one end on a base, an object remains stable as long as the proportion of the entire object (not just its bottom surface) on the base is greater than that off the base (Baillargeon & DeJong, 2017). This last rule allows infants to correctly predict the outcomes of support events involving asymmetrical as well as symmetrical objects (e.g., an L-shaped box released with the rightmost 50 percent of its bottom surface on a base will fall, because the proportion of the entire box that is off the base is greater than that on the base).

8.3.1.3 Errors of Omission and Commission

By knowing what rules infants have acquired, researchers can predict the types of errors infants will produce in VOE tasks (Baillargeon & DeJong, 2017; Luo & Baillargeon, 2005; Wang et al., 2016; Zhang & Wang, 2019). *Errors of omission* occur when infants see a physically impossible event (e.g., in the laboratory) and view it as expected because it happens to be consistent with their faulty rule. An example of an error of omission is a five-month-old who fails to detect a violation when an object remains stable with only the leftmost 15 percent of its bottom surface supported, because this event is consistent with her type-of-contact rule (Baillargeon et al., 1992; Hespos & Baillargeon, 2008). In contrast, *errors of commission* occur when infants see a physically possible event (e.g., in the laboratory or in daily life) and find it unexpected because it happens to contradict their faulty rule. An example of an error of commission is a seven-month-old who detects a violation when an object remains stable with only the middle 33 percent of its bottom surface supported, because this event is inconsistent with her proportion-of-contact rule (Wang et al., 2016; Zhang & Wang, 2019).

8.3.2 Explanation-based Learning

How do infants acquire and revise their physical rules? There is growing evidence that *explanation-based learning* (EBL) is one of the key processes that enable them to do so (Baillargeon & DeJong, 2017; Wang, 2019; Wang & Baillargeon, 2008a; Wang & Kohne, 2007).

8.3.2.1 The EBL Process

EBL has three main steps (Baillargeon & DeJong, 2017), and the first is *triggering*. When infants encounter outcomes they cannot explain based on their current knowledge, the EBL process is triggered. In situations where no existing rule applies, infants may notice unexplained variation in events' outcomes (e.g., infants who have not yet acquired the first support rule, type-of-contact, may notice that objects released in contact with a base sometimes remain stable and sometimes fall). In situations where an existing rule does apply, infants may notice that, while some outcomes support the rule, others contradict it (e.g., infants who have acquired the type-of-contact rule may notice that objects released on top of a base sometimes remain stable, as predicted, but sometimes fall). Either way, exposure to the unexplained outcomes triggers EBL.

The second step in the EBL process is *explanation construction and generalization*. Infants first search for a potential feature whose values consistently map onto the different outcomes they have observed (e.g., when the feature has value x, one outcome is observed; when the feature has value y, a different outcome is observed). If they discover such a feature (infants' statistical-learning or regularity-detection processes must often play a key role in this discovery; Kirkham et al., 2002; Saffran & Kirkham, 2018; Saffran et al., 1996; Wang, 2019), they bring to bear their physical knowledge (i.e., core knowledge and acquired rules) to generate a plausible explanation for how the feature contributed to the observed outcomes. If they can construct such an explanation, they then generalize it, resulting in a candidate rule that incorporates only the relevant feature specified in the explanation.

The final step in the EBL process is *empirical confirmation*. Once a rule has been hypothesized, it must be evaluated against further empirical evidence, which will serve to either confirm or reject it. If the candidate rule proves accurate in predicting outcomes for a few additional exemplars, it is adopted, becomes part of infants' physical knowledge, and, from then on, helps guide prediction and action.

The EBL process makes clear why infants generally do not acquire rules based on spurious or accidental regularities in their environments: For a regularity to be adopted as a rule for an event category, it must be plausibly (even if shallowly) explained by infants' physical knowledge. Finally, the EBL process also makes clear why infants may require only a few exemplars to acquire a new rule. Because EBL combines both *analytic evidence* (i.e., the explanation that is constructed and generalized into a candidate rule) and *empirical evidence*, it makes possible highly efficient learning.

8.3.2.2 Teaching Experiments

The EBL process does not only make clear how infants acquire and revise their physical rules: It also suggests how infants might be "taught" a rule they have not yet acquired via exposure to EBL-designed observations (Baillargeon & DeJong, 2017; Wang, 2019; Wang & Baillargeon, 2008a; Wang & Kohne, 2007). One teaching experiment, for example, sought to teach eleven-month-olds the support rule of proportional distribution, which is typically not acquired until about thirteen months (Baillargeon & DeJong, 2017).

Infants first received three pairs of teaching trials. In each pair, an experimenter's gloved hand placed the right half of an asymmetrical box's bottom surface on a base and then released the box. Consistent with physical laws, the box fell when released with its smaller end on the base (*small-on* event), but it

remained stable when released in the reverse orientation, with its larger end on the base (*large-on* event). Each teaching pair involved a different asymmetrical box (e.g., a box shaped like a letter B on its back, a right-triangle box, and a staircase-shaped box). Following the teaching trials, infants saw two static test displays in which half of an L-shaped box's bottom surface lay on a base. In the *unexpected* display, the box's smaller end was supported; in the *expected* display, the box's larger end was supported.

Infants detected the violation in the unexpected test display, suggesting that they had acquired the proportional-distribution rule during the three pairs of teaching trials. How did these trials facilitate EBL? First, each small-on event contradicted infants' proportion-of-contact rule (i.e., the box fell even though half of its bottom surface rested on the base), and these unexplained outcomes triggered the EBL process. Second, because in each teaching pair the small-on and large-on events differed only in the box's orientation, infants could rapidly zero in on this information in their quest for an explanation. By bringing to bear their physical knowledge, infants could reason that (1) since an inert object falls when unsupported (in accordance with the gravity principle) but remains stable when released on a base because the base passively blocks its fall (in accordance with the solidity principle), then (2) it was plausible that in each teaching trial the base could block the fall of the asymmetrical box when half or more of the entire box was on the base, but not when half or more of the entire box was off the base – the larger unsupported portion of the box then caused it to tip off the base and topple to the apparatus floor. Armed with this explanation, infants could then hypothesize a proportional-distribution rule: An object released with one end resting on a base will remain stable as long as the proportion of the entire object that is on the base is greater than that off the base. Third, infants could confirm this hypothesized rule because across the teaching trials they saw three different asymmetrical boxes all behave in accordance with the rule (e.g., infants might have used the first two boxes to generate the rule, and the third box to confirm it).

Additional experiments indicated that infants no longer learned the proportional-distribution rule (i.e., failed to detect the violation in the unexpected test display) if the teaching trials were modified to disrupt one or more of the EBL steps. Thus, infants did not acquire the rule (1) when shown only teaching events consistent with their proportion-of-contact rule, so that the EBL process was not triggered (e.g., infants saw only large-on events); (2) when shown *reverse* teaching events for which they could construct no plausible explanation (e.g., in each teaching pair, the box now remained stable in the small-on event and fell in the large-on event); and (3) when shown too few distinct exemplars to generate and empirically confirm the rule (e.g., the three teaching pairs involved only two asymmetrical boxes, with one box appearing in both the first and third pairs). Finally, infants also failed to acquire the rule when shown teaching events that could in principle support EBL but made the search for an explanation harder (e.g., salient irrelevant differences were added to the teaching events, making it difficult for infants to rapidly zero in on the box's orientation as a critical feature).

8.3.3 Décalages

When introducing the second wave of research on early physical reasoning, we noted that when young infants are tested with subtle core violations that can be discerned only by attending to the specific properties of objects and their arrangements, they often fail to detect these violations. The research reviewed

in Section 8.3.2 helped explain these failures by showing that (1) infants typically succeed at reasoning about a feature in an event only if they have identified the feature as causally relevant for the event category involved; (2) after a feature is identified as relevant (with EBL playing an important role in this identification process), infants routinely encode information about the feature when representing events from the category; and (3) once information about a feature is included in an event's representation, it is interpreted by infants' physical knowledge, allowing them to detect subtle core violations involving the feature. These include *interaction* violations (i.e., objects interact in ways that are not physically possible given their properties) and *change* violations (i.e., objects spontaneously undergo changes that are not physically possible). To illustrate, consider the occlusion feature height, which is identified at about three and a half months. Infants who have acquired this feature detect an interaction violation if a tall object that is passing behind a screen of the same height fails to appear in a high opening in the screen (Baillargeon & DeVos, 1991; Baillargeon & Graber, 1987), or if a tall object becomes almost fully hidden when lowered behind a short occluder (Hespos & Baillargeon, 2001a; Mou & Luo, 2017). Infants also detect a change violation if an object is either much taller or much shorter after being briefly occluded (Goldman & Wang, 2019; Wang & Baillargeon, 2006). Thus, for any feature identified as causally relevant to an event category, there is *broad generalization within the category*: The feature is encoded for any event from the category (e.g., for any occlusion event), and it allows the detection of many types of violations involving the feature.

In contrast to infants' pervasive and flexible use of identified features *within* each event category, there is no evidence that infants transfer identified features *between* event categories: Features from one category are not passed on to other categories, even when equally relevant. This means that when infants happen to identify a feature at different ages in different event categories, striking *décalages* (to use a Piagetian term) or lags can be observed in their responses to similar events from the different categories. For example, five-to-six-month-olds detect a change violation if an object surreptitiously changes shape when behind an occluder (Káldy & Leslie, 2005; Wilcox, 1999) or when inside a container (Wang & Onishi, 2017), but not if it changes shape when buried in sand (Newcombe et al., 1999). Similarly, infants as young as three and a half months can detect interaction and change violations involving height in occlusion events, as we just saw, but such violations are not detected until much later in other event categories: at about seven and a half months in containment events, twelve months in covering events, and fourteen months in tube events (Hespos & Baillargeon, 2001a; Wang & Baillargeon, 2006; Wang et al., 2005).

Décalages between event categories have also been observed in action tasks. For example, six-month-olds correctly searched for a tall frog behind a tall as opposed to a short occluder – but they searched randomly when the occluders were replaced with a tall and a short container (the occluders were identical to the fronts of the containers) (Hespos & Baillargeon, 2006). Similarly, after being "taught" to attend to the feature height in covering events, nine-month-olds correctly searched for a tall toy under a tall as opposed to a short cover, thereby showing immediate generalization of the feature to novel events from the category – but they searched randomly when the covers were replaced with a tall and a short tube (the tubes were identical

to the covers without their tops; Wang & Kohne, 2007).

8.3.4 Object-File and Physical-Reasoning Systems

8.3.4.1 Multiple Representations

The growing evidence of marked décalages between event categories indicated that (1) identified features are not transferred across categories and (2) weeks or months can separate the identification of the same feature in different categories. Additional evidence indicated that when infants failed to include information about an unidentified feature in an event representation, it did not necessarily mean that they had not registered the feature at all (i.e., that their brains had not encoded it in any way). Strikingly, infants who failed to detect a violation involving a feature could sometimes be shown, using other tasks, to have registered the feature (Wang & Goldman, 2016; Wang & Mitroff, 2009).

In one experiment (Wang & Goldman, 2016), for example, twelve-month-olds saw an experimenter's hand lower a tall cover (cover condition) or a tall tube (tube condition) over a short block. Next, the hand lifted the cover or tube to reveal either the same block as before (no-change event) or a much taller block (change event). Consistent with prior findings that the feature height is identified at about twelve months in covering events but only at about fourteen months in tube events (Wang & Baillargeon, 2006; Wang et al., 2005), infants in the cover condition detected the change to the block's height, whereas those in the tube condition did not. However, infants did detect this change in a modified-tube condition in which they were briefly *turned away* from the apparatus while the tube was lowered over the block and lifted back again.

These results suggested that two distinct cognitive systems were involved in infants' responses. One system formed detailed representations of the test objects, including their heights. When infants witnessed no causal interaction in the test trial, as in the modified-tube condition, this first system guided infants' responses, leading to enhanced attention to the novel block in the change event (i.e., infants produced a novelty response). However, when infants did witness a causal interaction, as in the cover and tube conditions, a second system took over, built a specialized representation of the event, and used it to predict how the event would unfold. Because this second system had already identified height as a causally relevant feature for covering events, but not for tube events, it behaved differently in the two conditions. In the cover condition, the second system retrieved the height information from the first system and included it in the event's representation; when interpreted by infants' physical knowledge, this information allowed them to detect the persistence violation in the change event. In the tube condition, in contrast, the second system did not retrieve the height information from the first system, causing infants to fail to detect the persistence violation in the change event.

The notion that infants might form multiple representations of objects and hold information in one representation that they fail to use in another might be puzzling at first. However, this notion echoes extensive findings from the adult literature on change blindness. In particular, these findings show that (1) adults often fail to detect salient changes to attended objects that go briefly out of view, in both laboratory and real-world settings (Rensink et al., 1997; Simons & Levin, 1998; Simons et al., 2002) and (2) adults may overlook a featural change to an object, even though the information necessary to detect this change has been encoded, is maintained, and can be

accessed experimentally via photographic line-ups, probing questions, or more implicit measures (Angelone et al., 2003; Hollingworth et al., 2001; Mitroff et al., 2004).

8.3.4.2 The Two-System Model

In recent years, several multi-system models have been proposed (Baillargeon et al., 2011, 2012; Wang & Baillargeon, 2008b), building on prior research in the adult and infant literature (Huttenlocher et al., 1991, 2002; Kahneman et al., 1992; Leslie et al., 1998; Pylyshyn, 1989, 2007; Rips et al., 2006).

In the most recent of these models (Lin et al., 2021; Stavans et al., 2019), the two cognitive systems that contribute to early physical reasoning are the *object-file* (OF) system (Gordon & Irwin, 1996; Kahneman et al., 1992) and the *physical-reasoning* (PR) system (Baillargeon et al., 2011; Wang & Baillargeon, 2008b). The two systems serve different functions and have at least partly distinct neural substrates (Fischer et al., 2016; Grill-Spector et al., 2001). When infants see objects (e.g., in a picture book, a static scene, or an event), the OF system builds a temporary representation of the "where" and "what" information about each object, drawing on incoming perception as well as on stored knowledge, and it updates this information as needed. If the objects are involved in a causal interaction, the PR system also becomes engaged. It builds a specialized representation of the interaction that contains a subset of the information in the objects' files, and it uses this representation, together with its physical knowledge (i.e., core knowledge and acquired rules), to predict how the interaction will unfold.

To illustrate how the two systems operate, imagine that two objects, A and B, are resting on an apparatus floor. As infants view this static scene, the OF system builds a temporary representation of each object, which includes *spatiotemporal* ("where") information as well as *identity* ("what") information. Each type of information comprises broad categorical descriptors as well as more fine-grained featural descriptors. Now, imagine that A and B become involved in a causal interaction. This engages the PR system, which then builds a specialized representation of this event, in two steps. In the first, the PR system uses the OF system's spatiotemporal and identity categorical descriptors to categorize the event. For example, if B is identified as a container, the event is categorized as an *occlusion* event if A moves behind B, as a *collision* event if A hits B, and as a *containment* event if A is placed inside B. Once the PR system has categorized the event, it assigns event-specific roles to the objects (e.g., if A moves behind B, then A is assigned the role of occludee and B that of occluder). In the second step, the PR system accesses the list of features it has identified as causally relevant for predicting outcomes in the event category selected, and it then taps the OF system for information about these – and only these – features. The retrieved information (e.g., about the relative heights and widths of the occludee and occluder and about the shape and pattern of the occludee) is then added to the event's representation. Finally, the PR system brings to bear its physical knowledge to interpret the categorical and featural information in the event's representation and guide infants' responses.

The two-system model helps explain all of the findings summarized to this point in the chapter. First, it explains why very young infants can already detect some core violations (the spatiotemporal and identity categorical information included in the PR system's event representations is sufficient, when interpreted by the core knowledge, to allow the detection of these violations). Second, it explains why infants become able to detect more subtle core violations with development (once the PR system has identified a feature as causally relevant for an event category, it routinely taps the OF system for information about this feature when representing events from the category, making possible the detection of violations involving the feature). Finally, it explains why infants who detect a subtle core violation in an event from one category may fail to do so in a similar event from a different category, even though the featural information necessary to detect this violation is available in the OF system (the PR system only taps the OF system for information about identified features).

8.3.4.3 Carryover Effects

The two-system model also suggested new directions for research. In carryover experiments, researchers asked the following question: When infants see a sequence of two events that involve the same objects but belong to different event categories (e.g., a cover is placed first in front of and then over an object), does the PR system discard the featural information it requested from the OF system for the first event's representation, or does it *carry over* this information to the second event's representation, to save time and effort? If there is such a carryover, it should have positive consequences whenever (1) the second event depicts a subtle core violation that involves a particular feature and (2) this feature has been identified in the first event's category but not the second event's category. This is because information about the feature will be included in the first event's representation and, when carried over to the second event's representation, will allow infants to detect the violation in the event.

Several experiments have now demonstrated carryover effects in infants' detection of interaction violations (Baillargeon et al., 2009a; Wang, 2011; Wang & Baillargeon, 2005) and change violations (Wang & Onishi, 2017). For example, eight-month-olds detected an interaction violation when a short cover was first slid in front of a tall object, returned to its initial position, and then lifted and lowered over the object until it became fully hidden (Wang & Baillargeon, 2005). The height information that was carried over from the occlusion to the covering event enabled infants to detect a persistence violation that is typically not detected until about twelve months (Wang et al., 2005). Similarly, four-and-a-half-month-olds detected an interaction violation when a tall object was first slid in front of a short container, returned to its initial position, and then lifted and lowered into the container until it became almost fully hidden (Wang, 2011). Here again, the carryover of height information from the occlusion to the containment event enabled infants to detect a persistence violation that is typically not detected until about seven and a half months (Hespos & Baillargeon, 2001a). Additional results indicated that this effect was eliminated when a twenty-second delay was inserted between the two events (infants either were turned away from the apparatus or saw the tall object being moved back and forth next to the container) (Wang, 2011). There are thus temporal limits to carryover effects: As the interval between the two events increases, the PR system becomes more likely to discard the featural information from the first event and tap the OF system for the featural information it has identified as relevant to the second event.

8.3.4.4 Priming Effects

In carryover experiments, by definition, infants reason about a feature in a first event and then carry over the feature to a second, target event; in priming experiments, researchers asked whether infants would still succeed if instead of a first event they saw a *static array*

that highlighted the feature but gave them no opportunity to reason about its effect on an event's outcome (Baillargeon et al., 2009a; Lin et al., 2021; Wang, 2019). The rationale was that if (1) the static array rendered information about the feature more salient in the OF system and (2) this caused the OF system to spontaneously pass on this information when the PR system represented the target event, then (3) the PR system should be able to use the information to guide infants' responses to the event.

One priming experiment with twelve-month-olds, for example, focused on the feature color in containment events (Lin et al., 2021). Infants were assigned to a baseline or a priming condition. In the baseline condition, infants saw test events in which a brightly colored (e.g., orange) doll was lowered into a container too small to hold more than one doll. When lifted again, the doll was either the same as before (no-change event) or a different color (e.g., purple; change event). Infants failed to detect the change to the doll's color, indicating that their PR system had not yet identified color as a containment feature. The priming condition was identical to the baseline condition except that prior to the test events, infants saw a static array of four dolls differing only in color (orange, purple, yellow, pink). Infants now detected the change to the doll's color, suggesting that (1) the static array highlighted the information about the dolls' colors in the OF system; (2) this color information was spontaneously passed on to the PR system; and (3) when interpreted by the PR system's physical knowledge, this information allowed infants to detect the persistence violation in the change event. Additional priming experiments (Lin et al., 2021) indicated that following exposure to static arrays of objects differing only in height, eight-to-ten-month-olds succeeded at reasoning about height in tube events (recall that this feature is typically identified at about fourteen months; Wang et al., 2005): They detected a persistence violation if a tall object was much shorter after being briefly lowered into a tall tube, and they searched for a tall object in a tall as opposed to a short tube. Similarly, following exposure to static arrays of asymmetrical objects (Lin et al., 2021), seven-month-olds succeeded at reasoning about proportional distribution in support events (recall that this feature is typically identified at about thirteen months; Baillargeon & DeJong, 2017): They detected a gravity violation if an L-shaped box remained stable with its larger end unsupported.

Like the carryover experiments discussed in Section 8.3.4.3, these priming experiments demonstrate that when information about a feature is fortuitously included in an event representation, however it comes to be so, infants then bring to bear their physical knowledge to interpret this information, allowing them to succeed at VOE and action tasks involving the feature – even six months before they typically identify the feature!

8.3.5 Information-Processing Capabilities

In describing the two-system model, we focused mainly on simple situations involving a single event. What happens when two or more events occur side by side in quick succession, with each event involving different objects? As might be expected, infants' limited information-processing capacities begin to restrict how well they represent and reason about each event.

To illustrate, consider experiments in which six-month-olds saw occlusion events involving two identical screens, screen-1 and screen-2, and two objects that differed in shape, A and B (e.g., a red disk and a red triangle; Applin & Kibbe, 2019; Káldy & Leslie, 2005; Kibbe & Leslie, 2011, 2019). In the test events, A was

hidden behind screen-1, and then B was hidden behind screen-2. Infants detected a change violation if screen-2 was lifted to reveal A, but not if screen-1 was lifted to reveal B, suggesting that they had difficulty keeping track of the identity of the first-hidden object. Infants detected other violations involving this object, however, indicating that they did represent some information about it. For example, infants detected a violation if screen-1 was lifted to reveal no object at all (Kibbe & Leslie, 2011). Furthermore, when A and B differed in their ontological categories in that one was human-like and one was not (e.g., a doll's head and a ball), infants detected a violation if screen-1 was lifted to reveal B instead of A (Kibbe & Leslie, 2019).

Together, these results suggest that when A was hidden behind screen-1, the PR system began building an event representation, using the spatiotemporal and identity categorical descriptors provided by the OF system. However, the PR system was unable to adequately deal with the featural information for this event representation: When B was hidden behind screen-2, the PR system had to begin building an event representation for this second event, and it did not have sufficient information-processing resources to simultaneously (1) build this second event representation and (2) complete and/or maintain the first one. Thus, while the second event representation included both categorical and featural information about B, the first event representation included only categorical information about A (i.e., the PR system could not retrieve the featural information about A from the OF system and/or could not bind or maintain this information). As a result, infants detected a violation if screen-1 was lifted to reveal no object or an object from a different ontological category than A, but not an object that simply differed in shape from A.

These results support the two-system model, and also make clear how limitations in infants' information-processing capacities can hamper the operation of the PR system. Further results with older infants make the same point (Káldy & Leslie, 2003; Kibbe & Leslie, 2013): At nine months, infants detected a violation if either screen-1 or screen-2 was lifted to reveal the wrong object, but they failed with a more challenging situation involving three screens and three objects (for related findings with adults, see Strickland & Scholl, 2015).

8.4 Third Wave: Developments in the Object-File System

Although much of infants' physical reasoning could be explained by considering developments in their PR system and their information-processing capacities, as we saw in Sections 8.3.4 and 8.3.5, there remained a critical difficulty. Experiments with occlusion or containment events indicated that although infants detected interaction and change violations involving features they had identified for these categories, they nevertheless failed to detect *individuation* violations involving these same features. An individuation violation is a type of persistence violation in which fewer objects are revealed at the end of an event than were presented during the event, as though one or more objects had magically disappeared. Xu, Carey, and their colleagues were the first to report this baffling failure (Van de Walle et al., 2000; Xu & Carey, 1996; Xu et al., 2004), and similar results were subsequently obtained in a wide range of individuation tasks (for reviews, see Baillargeon et al., 2012; Stavans et al., 2019). In one task, for example, an experimenter's hand brought out two objects in alternation on either side of a large screen; for present purposes, let us assume that the objects belonged to the same basic-level category and differed only in their featural properties (e.g., a large red ball with blue dots and a small yellow ball with white stripes).

After several repetitions of this occlusion event, the screen was removed to reveal only one of the objects. Infants aged twelve months and younger failed to detect this violation, suggesting that they did not clearly expect to see two objects when the screen was removed, and hence that they were unable to individuate the objects in the occlusion event (i.e., to determine how many individual objects were present; Lin & Baillargeon, 2018; Lin et al., 2019; Stavans et al., 2019; Xu et al., 2004). To researchers familiar with the literature on early physical reasoning, these results were puzzling. By twelve months, most infants have identified size, pattern, and color as occlusion features, and the persistence principle dictates that these features cannot undergo spontaneous changes (e.g., a ball cannot spontaneously change size, pattern, or color). Why, then, did infants not infer that two objects were present behind the screen?

Controversy over the causes of infants' individuation failures persisted for many years, because most accounts could explain only a subset of available findings. However, it eventually became clear that by extending the two-system model described in the last section to consider not only developments in the PR system but also *developments in the OF system*, one could reconcile the findings of individuation tasks with those of other physical-reasoning tasks.

8.4.1 Individuation in the OF and PR Systems

Stavans et al. (2019) proposed that infants' individuation failures stem from catastrophic (as opposed to reconcilable) disagreements between the OF and PR systems. Here, we describe four key assumptions of their account.

8.4.1.1 Different Bases for Individuation

When a physical event comes to an end, infants successfully track the objects involved past the endpoint of the event as long as the OF and PR systems agree on how many objects are present. To individuate objects, each system uses somewhat different information: The OF system uses *categorical* information (i.e., the categorical descriptors in the objects' files), whereas the PR system uses *both categorical and featural* information (i.e., the categorical and featural information in the event's representation).

Why does the OF system not use the featural as well as the categorical information in its files to individuate objects in physical events? After all, in object-recognition tasks, the OF system does use the featural information at its disposal to detect changes (Oakes et al., 2006; Wang & Goldman, 2016; Wang & Mitroff, 2009). Why are things different in physical-reasoning tasks? According to the two-system model, the main reason has to do with infants' limited information-processing resources. During an event, the OF and PR systems are both engaged, but the PR system has priority: It must operate rapidly, online, to make sense of the unfolding event and predict its outcome. While this is happening (and taking up a sizeable portion of infants' information-processing resources), the OF system can do little more than track the objects in the event by checking their categorical descriptors. Thus, if two objects that come into view in alternation have different descriptors, the OF system infers that two objects are present; if they have the same descriptors, however, it infers that a single object is present and updates its featural properties.

In challenging situations that tax their information-processing resources, adults, too, tend to focus on objects' categorical descriptors; provided these are maintained across views, they fail to notice changes to objects' features (unless, of course, these changes are perceptually highly salient). For example, in an experiment inspired by the work of Xu

and Carey (1996), Simons and Levin (1998) embedded an occlusion event in a novel social interaction on a college campus. An actor who carried a map and was dressed as a construction worker (e.g., a young White man wearing a plain hard hat, black shirt, and white pants) approached individual students and asked for directions. In each case, the interaction between the actor and the student was interrupted by two confederates who passed between them, carrying a door. While occluded, the actor surreptitiously switched positions with one of the confederates, another young White man who also carried a map and was dressed as a construction worker, though in different clothing (e.g., a hard hat with a logo, a tool belt, a light blue shirt, and tan pants). Most students failed to notice the change to the actor, suggesting that they selectively compared the pre- and post-change actors' categorical descriptors (e.g., young, White, male construction worker requesting directions) and mistakenly inferred that a single actor was present because these descriptors remained constant across views.

8.4.1.2 Developments

In each system, significant developments occur with age in how objects are represented. In the OF system, more fine-grained spatiotemporal and identity categorical descriptors come to be used in objects' files. With respect to identity descriptors, for example, infants under twelve months typically do not spontaneously encode an isolated object's basic-level category, such as ball, toy duck, or cup (Pauen, 2002; Xu & Carey, 1996). However, they do encode more abstract or ontological descriptors, such as whether the object is human-like or non-human (Bonatti et al., 2002; Kibbe & Leslie, 2019), whether it is animate or inanimate (Setoh et al., 2013; Surian & Caldi, 2010), and whether it is a container (open at the top), a cover (open at the bottom), a tube (open at both ends), or a closed object (Mou & Luo, 2017; Wang et al., 2005). By their first birthday, infants begin to spontaneously encode objects' basic-level categories (Cacchione et al., 2013; Xu & Carey, 1996).

Turning to the PR system, two types of changes occur with development. First, because categorical descriptors are passed on to the PR system for its event representations, the OF system's more fine-grained categorical descriptors will also be available to the PR system. Second, as we saw in the last section of the chapter, the PR system includes more and more detailed information about objects' properties and arrangements as it learns, event category by event category, what features are causally relevant for predicting outcomes.

8.4.1.3 Catastrophic Disagreements

It follows from the preceding discussions that under some conditions, the OF and PR systems will disagree on how many objects are present. In particular, consider an occlusion event in which two objects (e.g., two different balls, as before) emerge in alternation on either side of a screen. Because the OF system can establish a continuous spatiotemporal trace between successive emergences, it assigns similar spatiotemporal categorical descriptors to each object. Disagreements between the two systems occur when (1) the OF system also assigns the same identity categorical descriptors to each object (e.g., nonhuman, inanimate, ball) and hence infers that a single object is present behind the screen, while (2) the PR system encodes distinct featural information about each object (e.g., large, red, blue dots; small, yellow, white stripes) and hence infers that two objects are present behind the screen. Stavans et al. (2019) refer to such disagreements as *catastrophic*. Before the screen is lowered, the OF signals

that a single object is present behind the screen, whereas the PR system signals that two objects are present. At this point, the OF realizes that its object file is corrupted: It does not cleanly refer to a single object in the world but instead contains a tangled mix of information that pertains to two separate objects. The OF system then discards its corrupted file, leading infants to have no expectation at all about how many objects will be revealed when the screen is lowered.

8.4.1.4 Reconcilable Disagreements

In catastrophic disagreements, the OF system represents a single object in a hiding location, whereas the PR system represents two objects in the same location. The systems cannot recover from such disagreements, leading to individuation failures. However, they *can* recover from other types of disagreements. In particular, consider an occlusion event in which two objects (e.g., two different balls) emerge in alternation on either side of a screen. Finally, one of the objects stops in plain view next to the screen, which is then lowered. The OF system will assign the same categorical descriptors to each object, will infer that a single object is present, and will conclude that this object is now resting in view, leaving no object behind the screen. In contrast, the PR system will encode distinct featural information about each object, will infer that two objects are present, and will conclude that while one is resting in view, the other remains hidden behind the screen. In this situation, the OF and PR systems have no disagreement about the object in view; their disagreement is only about whether objects remain behind the screen. The OF system assumes that there are none, whereas the PR system signals that one object still remains. Because the OF system currently has no object file linked to the area behind the screen, it can respond to the PR system's signal by adding one object file for that area. The OF and PR systems are then in agreement, leading infants to expect one object when the screen is lowered.

8.4.2 Predictions

The two-system model can explain a wide range of individuation findings, and here we focus on three predictions in particular (see Stavans et al., 2019, for additional predictions).

8.4.2.1 Prediction 1: Categorical Descriptors

According to the two-system model, young infants should succeed at an individuation task whenever the OF system assigns different identity categorical descriptors to the objects. In line with this analysis, twelve-month-olds (who use basic-level as well as ontological descriptors) succeed when tested with objects from different basic-level categories (e.g., a toy duck and a ball; Van de Walle et al., 2000; Xu & Carey, 1996), and nine-to-ten-month-olds (who use ontological but not basic-level descriptors) succeed when tested with objects from different ontological categories (e.g., a doll and a ball; Bonatti et al., 2002; Decarli et al., 2020; Surian & Caldi, 2010).

Although infants under twelve months typically fail to individuate objects that differ only in their basic-level categories, they succeed if induced to encode these categories via experimental manipulations (Futó et al., 2010; Stavans & Baillargeon, 2018; Xu, 2002). For example, in a *language-based* manipulation (Xu, 2002), nine-month-olds heard a distinct label (e.g., "Look, a duck!" or "Look, a ball!") as each object came into view during the occlusion event. Following this manipulation, infants detected a violation when the screen was lowered to reveal only one of the objects. Similarly, in a *function-based* manipulation

(Stavans & Baillargeon, 2018), four-month-olds first watched functional demonstrations for two different tools, one at a time (e.g., in one trial, a masher was used to compress sponges, and in another trial, tongs were used to pick them up). The two tools were then brought out in alternation from behind a screen, and infants detected a violation when the screen was lowered to reveal only one of the tools.

Finally, although twelve-month-olds typically fail to individuate objects they encode as merely featurally distinct, they succeed if they first see the objects play different roles in other events (recall that the OF system includes both incoming and stored information in objects' files). Thus, in a *role-based* manipulation (Lin et al., 2019), thirteen-month-olds first saw two blocks that differed only in pattern and color play different event roles in relation to a toy (e.g., in one trial, one block supported the toy, and in another trial, the other block was supported by the toy). The two blocks were then brought out in alternation from behind a screen, and infants detected a violation when the screen was lowered to reveal only one of the blocks.

8.4.2.2 Prediction 2: Catastrophic Disagreements

According to the two-system model, when the OF system signals that one object is present in a hiding location but the PR system signals that two objects are present, the OF system discards its corrupted object file, leading infants to hold no expectation at all about how many objects are present. Consistent with this analysis, after seeing two objects they encoded as merely featurally distinct emerge in alternation from behind a screen, eleven-month-olds detected no violation when the screen was lowered to reveal *no object at all* (Stavans et al., 2019). Similarly, after seeing two objects they encoded as merely featurally distinct being lifted, one at a time, from a large container, nine-month-olds detected no violation if the container *remained silent when shaken*, as though empty (Stavans et al., 2019).

8.4.2.3 Prediction 3: Reconcilable Disagreements

According to the two-system model, when the OF system signals that no object remains in a hiding location but the PR system signals that one object remains, the OF system then adds an object file for that location. In line with this analysis, positive findings have been obtained with five-to-eleven-month-olds in a variety of *remainder* tasks (Lin & Baillargeon, 2019; McCurry et al., 2009; Stavans et al., 2019; Wilcox & Baillargeon, 1998; Wilcox & Schweinle, 2002; Xu & Baker, 2005). In one experiment, for example, eleven-month-olds first saw two objects they encoded as merely featurally distinct emerge in alternation from behind a screen (Lin & Baillargeon, 2019). Next, one of the objects paused in plain view, and the screen was lowered to reveal an empty area – only the paused object was visible next to the screen. Infants detected the violation in this event, suggesting that the OF system successfully added an object file when the PR system signaled that an object remained behind the screen. Results were positive even if *three* featurally distinct objects emerged in alternation in the occlusion event. As long as the OF system assumed that no object remained behind the screen at the end of the event, (1) the PR system could signal that two objects still remained behind the screen and (2) the OF system could add two object files pointing to that area, leading infants to detect a violation when the screen was lowered to reveal only one object.

8.5 Conclusions

In this chapter, we sought to offer a historical overview that made clear how three successive waves of research on early physical reasoning over the past four decades not only led to a deeper understanding of the development of this ability but also helped shed light on the cognitive architecture needed to support it. In the first wave, demonstrations of early sensitivity to persistence, inertia, and gravity led to the suggestion that a *skeletal framework of core principles* guides infants' reasoning about physical events. In the second wave came the realization that infants often fail to adhere to these principles in their predictions and actions due to *limitations in their PR system*: Early in development, event representations in the PR system tend to be very sparse and often lack the featural information necessary for infants to respond appropriately. Over time, however, event representations become richer and more detailed as the PR system forms event categories and identifies causally relevant features for each category. Finally, the third wave made clear that even when featural information is included in an event representation, infants may still fail to adhere to the core principle of persistence in their predictions and actions due to *limitations in their OF system*: While the PR system uses both the categorical and featural information in its event representations to individuate objects in an event, the OF system uses only the categorical information in its object files for this purpose. When the two systems disagree as an event comes to an end (e.g., the PR system signals that two objects are present behind a screen, whereas the OF system signals that a single object is present), infants fail to track the objects past the endpoint of the event.

The two-system model provides a coherent, integrative framework for the findings from these three waves of research. As we saw, this model not only reconciles findings that initially appeared puzzling or even contradictory but also makes novel predictions that are being tested in different laboratories. Nevertheless, the two-system model still leaves many questions unanswered. For example, at what age does infants' OF system begin to use featural information to individuate objects in physical events, and what are the mechanisms responsible for this development? Could the OF system be induced to use featural information for this purpose at an earlier age, via experimental manipulations? The next wave of research should bring answers to these questions.

References

Aguiar, A., & Baillargeon, R. (1999). 2.5-month-old infants' reasoning about when objects should and should not be occluded. *Cognitive Psychology*, *39*, 116–157.

Aguiar, A., & Baillargeon, R. (2002). Developments in young infants' reasoning about occluded objects. *Cognitive Psychology*, *45*, 267–336.

Ahmed, A., & Ruffman, T. (1998). Why do infants make A not B errors in a search task, yet show memory for the location of hidden objects in a nonsearch task? *Developmental Psychology*, *34*, 441–453.

Anderson, E. M., Hespos, S. J., & Rips, L. J. (2018). Five-month-old infants have expectations for the accumulation of nonsolid substances. *Cognition*, *175*, 1–10.

Angelone, B. L., Levin, D. T., & Simons, D. J. (2003). The relationship between change detection and recognition of centrally attended objects in motion pictures. *Perception*, *32*, 947–962.

Applin, J. B., & Kibbe, M. M. (2019). Six-month-old infants predict agents' goal-directed actions on occluded objects. *Infancy*, *24*, 392–410.

Baillargeon, R. (1987). Object permanence in 3.5- and 4.5-month-old infants. *Developmental Psychology*, *23*, 655–664.

Baillargeon, R. (1991). Reasoning about the height and location of a hidden object in 4.5- and 6.5-month-old infants. *Cognition*, *38*, 13–42.

Baillargeon, R. (1993). The object concept revisited: New directions in the investigation of infants' physical knowledge. In C. E. Granrud (ed.), *Visual Perception and Cognition in Infancy* (pp. 265–315). Hillsdale, NJ: Erlbaum.

Baillargeon, R. (1995). A model of physical reasoning in infancy. In C. Rovee-Collier, & L. P. Lipsitt (eds.), *Advances in Infancy Research* (Vol. 9, pp. 305–371). Norwood, NJ: Ablex.

Baillargeon, R. (2008). Innate ideas revisited: For a principle of persistence in infants' physical reasoning. *Perspectives on Psychological Science*, *3*, 2–13.

Baillargeon, R., & Carey, S. (2012). Core cognition and beyond: The acquisition of physical and numerical knowledge. In S. Pauen (ed.), *Early Childhood Development and Later Outcome* (pp. 33–65). Cambridge: Cambridge University Press.

Baillargeon, R., & DeJong, G. F. (2017). Explanation-based learning in infancy. *Psychonomic Bulletin & Review*, *24*, 1511–1526.

Baillargeon, R., & DeVos, J. (1991). Object permanence in young infants: Further evidence. *Child Development*, *62*, 1227–1246.

Baillargeon, R., & Graber, M. (1987). Where's the rabbit? 5.5-month-old infants' representation of the height of a hidden object. *Cognitive Development*, *2*, 375–392.

Baillargeon, R., Graber, M., DeVos, J., & Black, J. (1990). Why do young infants fail to search for hidden objects? *Cognition*, *36*, 225–284.

Baillargeon, R., Li, J., Gertner, Y., & Wu, D. (2011). How do infants reason about physical events? In U. Goswami (ed.), *The Wiley-Blackwell Handbook of Childhood Cognitive Development*, *11* (2nd ed., pp. 11–48). Oxford: Blackwell.

Baillargeon, R., Li, J., Ng, W., & Yuan, S. (2009a). An account of infants' physical reasoning. In A. Woodward, & A. Needham (eds.), *Learning and the Infant Mind* (pp. 66–116). New York: Oxford University Press.

Baillargeon, R., Needham, A., & DeVos, J. (1992). The development of young infants' intuitions about support. *Early Development and Parenting*, *1*, 69–78.

Baillargeon, R., Spelke, E. S., & Wasserman, S. (1985). Object permanence in five-month-old infants. *Cognition*, *20*, 191–208.

Baillargeon, R., Stavans, M., Wu, D., Gertner, Y., Setoh, P., Kittredge, A. K., & Bernard, A. (2012). Object individuation and physical reasoning in infancy: An integrative account. *Language Learning and Development*, *8*, 4–46.

Baillargeon, R., Wu, D., Yuan, S., Li, J., & Luo, Y. (2009b). Young infants' expectations about self-propelled objects. In B. Hood, & L. Santos (eds.), *The Origins of Object Knowledge* (pp. 285–352). Oxford: Oxford University Press.

Bogartz, R. S., Shinskey, J. L., & Speaker, C. J. (1997). Interpreting infant looking: The event set × event set design. *Developmental Psychology*, *33*, 408–422.

Bonatti, L., Frot, E., Zangl, R., & Mehler, J. (2002). The human first hypothesis: Identification of conspecifics and individuation of objects in the young infant. *Cognitive Psychology*, *44*, 388–426.

Boudreau, J. P., & Bushnell, E. W. (2000). Spilling thoughts: Configuring attentional resources in infants' goal-directed actions. *Infant Behavior and Development*, *23*, 543–566.

Cacchione, T., Schaub, S., & Rakoczy, H. (2013). Fourteen-month-old infants infer the continuous identity of objects on the basis of nonvisible causal properties. *Developmental Psychology*, *49*, 1325–1329.

Carey, S. (2011). *The Origin of Concepts*. New York: Oxford University Press.

Casasola, M. (2008). The development of infants' spatial categories. *Current Directions in Psychological Science*, *17*, 21–25.

Cashon, C. H., & Cohen, L. B. (2000). Eight-month-old infants' perception of possible and impossible events. *Infancy*, *1*, 429–446.

Dan, N., Omori, T., & Tomiyasu, Y. (2000). Development of infants' intuitions about support relations: Sensitivity to stability. *Developmental Science*, *3*, 171–180.

Daum, M. M., Prinz, W., & Aschersleben, G. (2009). Means-end behavior in young infants: The interplay of action perception and action production. *Infancy*, *14*, 613–640.

Decarli, G., Franchin. L., Piazza, M., & Surian. L. (2020). Infants' use of motion cues in object individuation processes. *Journal of Experimental Child Psychology*, *197*, 104868.

Diamond, A. (2013). Executive functions. *Annual Review of Psychology*, *64*, 135–168.

Fischer, J., Mikhael, J. G., Tenenbaum, J. B., & Kanwisher, N. (2016). Functional neuroanatomy of intuitive physical inference. *Proceedings of the National Academy of Sciences (USA)*, *113*, E5072–E5081.

Futó, J., Téglás, E., Csibra, G., & Gergely, G. (2010). Communicative function demonstration induces kind-based artifact representation in preverbal infants. *Cognition*, *117*, 1–8.

Gelman, R. (1990). First principles organize attention to and learning about relevant data: Number and the animate-inanimate distinction as examples. *Cognitive Science*, *14*, 79–106.

Goldman, E. J., & Wang, S. H. (2019). Comparison facilitates the use of height information by 5-month-olds in containment events. *Developmental Psychology*, *55*, 2475–2482.

Gordon, R. D., & Irwin, D. E. (1996). What's in an object file? Evidence from priming studies. *Perception & Psychophysics*, *58*, 1260–1277.

Grill-Spector, K., Kourtzi, Z., & Kanwisher, N. (2001). The lateral occipital complex and its role in object recognition. *Vision Research*, *41*, 1409–1422.

Haith, M. M. (1998). Who put the cog in infant cognition? Is rich interpretation too costly? *Infant Behavior and Development*, *21*, 167–179.

Hauf, P., Paulus, M., & Baillargeon, R. (2012). Infants use compression information to infer objects' weights: Examining cognition, exploration, and prospective action in a preferential-reaching task. *Child Development*, *83*, 1978–1995.

Hespos, S. J., & Baillargeon, R. (2001a). Infants' knowledge about occlusion and containment events: A surprising discrepancy. *Psychological Science*, *12*, 141–147.

Hespos, S. J., & Baillargeon, R. (2001b). Reasoning about containment events in very young infants. *Cognition, 78,* 207–245.

Hespos, S. J., & Baillargeon, R. (2006). Décalage in infants' knowledge about occlusion and containment events: Converging evidence from action tasks. *Cognition, 99,* B31–B41.

Hespos, S. J., & Baillargeon, R. (2008). Young infants' actions reveal their developing knowledge of support variables: Converging evidence for violation-of-expectation findings. *Cognition, 107,* 304–316.

Hespos, S. J., Ferry, A. L., Anderson, E. M., Hollenbeck, E. N., & Rips, L. J. (2016). Five-month-old infants have general knowledge of how nonsolid substances behave and interact. *Psychological Science, 27,* 244–256.

Hollingworth, A., Williams, C. C., & Henderson, J. M. (2001). To see and remember: Visually specific information is retained in memory from previously attended objects in natural scenes. *Psychonomic Bulletin & Review, 8,* 761–768.

Huettel, S. A., & Needham, A. (2000). Effects of balance relations between objects on infant's object segregation. *Developmental Science, 3,* 415–427.

Huttenlocher, J., Duffy, S., & Levine, S. (2002). Infants and toddlers discriminate amount: Are they measuring? *Psychological Science, 13,* 244–249.

Huttenlocher, J., Hedges, L. V., & Duncan, S. (1991). Categories and particulars: Prototype effects in estimating spatial location. *Psychological Review, 98,* 352–376.

Hyde, D. C., Aparicio Betancourt, M., & Simon, C. E. (2015). Human temporal-parietal junction spontaneously tracks others' beliefs: A functional near-infrared spectroscopy study. *Human Brain Mapping, 36,* 4831–4846.

Hyde, D. C., Simon, C. E., Ting, F., & Nikolaeva, J. I. (2018). Functional organization of the temporal–parietal junction for theory of mind in preverbal infants: A near-infrared spectroscopy study. *Journal of Neuroscience, 38,* 4264–4274.

Jin, K. S., Houston, J. L., Baillargeon, R., Groh, A. M., & Roisman, G. I. (2018). Young infants expect an unfamiliar adult to comfort a crying baby: Evidence from a standard violation-of-expectation task and a novel infant-triggered-video task. *Cognitive Psychology, 102,* 1–20.

Kahneman, D., Treisman, A., & Gibbs, B. J. (1992). The reviewing of object files: Object-specific integration of information. *Cognitive Psychology, 24,* 175–219.

Káldy, Z., & Leslie, A. M. (2003). Identification of objects in 9-month-old infants: Integrating "what" and "where" information. *Developmental Science, 6,* 360–373.

Káldy, Z., & Leslie, A. M. (2005). A memory span of one? Object identification in 6.5-month-old infants. *Cognition, 97,* 153–177.

Kampis, D., Parise, E., Csibra, G., & Kovács, Á. M. (2015). Neural signatures for sustaining object representations attributed to others in preverbal human infants. *Proceedings of the Royal Society B: Biological Sciences, 282,* 20151683.

Keen, R. E., & Berthier, N. E. (2004). Continuities and discontinuities in infants' representation of objects and events. In R. V. Kail (ed.), *Advances in Child Development and Behavior* (Vol. 32, pp. 243–279). San Diego, CA: Elsevier Academic Press.

Keil, F. C. (1995). The growth of causal understandings of natural kinds. In D. Sperber, D. Premack, & A. J. Premack (eds.), *Causal Cognition: A Multidisciplinary Debate* (pp. 234–262). Oxford: Clarendon Press.

Kibbe, M. M., & Leslie, A. M. (2011). What do infants remember when they forget? Location and identity in 6-month-olds' memory for objects. *Psychological Science, 22,* 1500–1505.

Kibbe, M. M., & Leslie, A. M. (2013). What's the object of object working memory in infancy? Unraveling "what" and "how many." *Cognitive Psychology, 66,* 380–404.

Kibbe, M. M., & Leslie, A. M. (2019). Conceptually rich, perceptually sparse: Object representations in 6-month-old infants' working memory. *Psychological Science, 30,* 362–375.

Kirkham, N. Z., Slemmer, J. A., & Johnson, S. P. (2002). Visual statistical learning in infancy:

Evidence for a domain general learning mechanism. *Cognition, 83,* B35–B42.

Kominsky, J. F., Strickland, B., Wertz, A. E., Elsner, C., Wynn, K., & Keil, F. C. (2017). Categories and constraints in causal perception. *Psychological Science, 28,* 1649–1662.

Kosugi, D., & Fujita, K. (2002). How do 8-month-old infants recognize causality in object motion and that in human action? *Japanese Psychological Research, 44,* 66–78.

Kotovsky, L., & Baillargeon, R. (1994). Calibration-based reasoning about collision events in 11-month-old infants. *Cognition, 51,* 107–129.

Kotovsky, L., & Baillargeon, R. (1998). The development of calibration-based reasoning about collision events in young infants. *Cognition, 67,* 311–351.

Kotovsky, L., & Baillargeon, R. (2000). Reasoning about collision events involving inert objects in 7.5-month-old infants. *Developmental Science, 3,* 344–359.

Kovács, Á. M., Téglás, E., & Endress, A. D. (2010). The social sense: Susceptibility to others' beliefs in human infants and adults. *Science, 330,* 1830–1834.

Leslie, A. M. (1994). ToMM, ToBy, and Agency: Core architecture and domain specificity. In L. A. Hirschfeld, & S. A. Gelman (eds.), *Mapping the Mind: Domain Specificity in Cognition and Culture* (pp. 119–148). New York: Cambridge University Press.

Leslie, A. M. (1995). A theory of agency. In D. Sperber, D. Premack, & A. J. Premack (eds.), *Causal Cognition: A Multidisciplinary Debate* (pp. 121–149). Oxford: Clarendon Press.

Leslie, A. M., & Keeble, S. (1987). Do six-month-old infants perceive causality? *Cognition, 25,* 265–288.

Leslie, A. M., Xu, F., Tremoulet, P. D., & Scholl, B. J. (1998). Indexing and the object concept: developing "what" and "where" systems. *Trends in Cognitive Sciences, 2,* 10–18.

Lin, Y., & Baillargeon, R. (2018). Infants individuate objects with distinct prior event roles. *Paper presented at the Biennial International Congress of Infant Studies,* June 2018, Philadelphia, PA.

Lin, Y., & Baillargeon, R. (2019). Testing a new two-system model of early individuation. *Paper presented at the Biennial Meeting of the Cognitive Development Society,* September 2019, Louisville, KY.

Lin, Y., Li, J., Gertner, Y., Ng, W., Fisher, C. L., & Baillargeon, R. (2021). How do the object-file and physical-reasoning systems interact? Evidence from priming effects with object arrays or novel labels. *Cognitive Psychology, 125,* 101368.

Lin, Y., Stavans, M., & Baillargeon, R. (2019). Infants can use many types of categories to individuate objects. *Paper presented at the Biennial Meeting of the Society for Research in Child Development,* March 2019, Baltimore, MD.

Liu, S., Brooks, N. B., & Spelke, E. S. (2019). Origins of the concepts cause, cost, and goal in prereaching infants. *Proceedings of the National Academy of Sciences (USA), 116,* 17747–17752.

Luo, Y., & Baillargeon, R. (2005). When the ordinary seems unexpected: Evidence for incremental physical knowledge in young infants. *Cognition, 95,* 297–328.

Luo, Y., Kaufman, L., & Baillargeon, R. (2009). Young infants' reasoning about physical events involving inert and self-propelled objects. *Cognitive Psychology, 58,* 441–486.

Mascalzoni, E., Regolin, L., Vallortigara, G., & Simion, F. (2013). The cradle of causal reasoning: Newborns' preference for physical causality. *Developmental Science, 16,* 327–335.

McCurry, S., Wilcox, T., & Woods, R. (2009). Beyond the search barrier: A new task for assessing object individuation in young infants. *Infant Behavior and Development, 32,* 429–436.

Merced-Nieves, F. M., Aguiar, A., Dzwilewski, K. L. C., Musaad, S., Korrick, S. A., & Schantz, S. L. (2020). Association of prenatal maternal perceived stress with a sexually dimorphic measure of cognition in 4.5-month-old infants. *Neurotoxicology and Teratology, 77,* 106850.

Mitroff, S. R., Simons, D. J., & Levin, D. T. (2004). Nothing compares 2 views: Change blindness can occur despite preserved access to the changed information. *Perception & Psychophysics, 66,* 1268–1281.

Mou, Y., & Luo, Y. (2017). Is it a container? Young infants' understanding of containment events. *Infancy*, *22*, 256–270.

Needham, A., & Baillargeon, R. (1993). Intuitions about support in 4.5-month-old infants. *Cognition*, *47*, 121–148.

Newcombe, N., Huttenlocher, J., & Learmonth, A. (1999). Infants' coding of location in continuous space. *Infant Behavior and Development*, *22*, 483–510.

Oakes, L. M., Ross-Sheehy, S., & Luck, S. J. (2006). Rapid development of feature binding in visual short-term memory. *Psychological Science*, *17*, 781–787.

Pauen, S. (2002). The global-to-basic level shift in infants' categorical thinking: First evidence from a longitudinal study. *International Journal of Behavioral Development*, *26*, 492–499.

Piaget, J. (1952). *The Origins of Intelligence in Children*. New York: International Universities Press.

Piaget, J. (1954). *The Construction of Reality in the Child*. New York: Basic Books.

Pylyshyn, Z. (1989). The role of location indexes in spatial perception: A sketch of the FINST spatial-index model. *Cognition*, *32*, 65–97.

Pylyshyn, Z. W. (2007). *Things and Places: How the Mind Connects with the World*. Cambridge, MA: MIT Press.

Rensink, R. A., O'Regan, J. K., & Clark, J. J. (1997). To see or not to see: The need for attention to perceive changes in scenes. *Psychological Science*, *8*, 368–373.

Rips, L. J., Blok, S., & Newman, G. (2006). Tracing the identity of objects. *Psychological Review*, *113*, 1–30.

Saffran, J. R., Aslin, R. N., & Newport, E. L. (1996). Statistical learning by 8-month-old infants. *Science*, *274*, 1926–1928.

Saffran, J. R., & Kirkham, N. Z. (2018). Infant statistical learning. *Annual Review of Psychology*, *69*, 181–203.

Saxe, R., Tenenbaum, J., & Carey, S. (2005). Secret agents: 10- and 12-month-old infants' inferences about hidden causes. *Psychological Science*, *16*, 995–1001.

Saxe, R., Tzelnic, T., & Carey, S. (2006). Five-month-old infants know humans are solid, like inanimate objects. *Cognition*, *101*, B1–B8.

Saxe, R., Tzelnic, T., & Carey, S. (2007). Knowing who dunnit: Infants identify the causal agent in an unseen causal interaction. *Developmental Psychology*, *43*, 149–158.

Setoh, P., Wu, D., Baillargeon, R., & Gelman, R. (2013). Young infants have biological expectations about animals. *Proceedings of the National Academy of Sciences (USA)*, *110*, 15937–15942.

Shinskey, J. L. (2002). Infants' object search: Effects of variable object visibility under constant means-end demands. *Journal of Cognition and Development*, *3*, 119–142.

Simons, D. J., Chabris, C. F., Schnur, T., & Levin, D. T. (2002). Evidence for preserved representations in change blindness. *Consciousness and Cognition*, *11*, 78–97.

Simons, D. J., & Levin, D. T. (1998). Failure to detect changes to people during a real-world interaction. *Psychonomic Bulletin & Review*, *5*, 644–649.

Southgate, V., & Vernetti, A. (2014). Belief-based action prediction in preverbal infants. *Cognition*, *130*, 1–10.

Spelke, E. S., Breinlinger, K., Macomber, J., & Jacobson, K. (1992). Origins of knowledge. *Psychological Review*, *99*, 605–632.

Spelke, E. S., Kestenbaum, R., Simons, D. J., & Wein, D. (1995a). Spatiotemporal continuity, smoothness of motion and object identity in infancy. *British Journal of Developmental Psychology*, *13*, 113–142.

Spelke, E. S., Phillips, A., & Woodward, A. L. (1995b). Infants' knowledge of object motion and human action. In D. Sperber, D. Premack, & A. J. Premack (eds.), *Causal Cognition: A Multidisciplinary Debate* (pp. 44–78). Oxford: Clarendon Press.

Stahl, A. E., & Feigenson, L. (2015). Observing the unexpected enhances infants' learning and exploration. *Science*, *348*, 91–94.

Stavans, M., & Baillargeon, R. (2018). Four-month-old infants individuate and track simple tools following functional demonstrations. *Developmental Science, 21*, e12500.

Stavans, M., Lin, Y., Wu, D., & Baillargeon, R. (2019). Catastrophic individuation failures in infancy: A new model and predictions. *Psychological Review, 126*, 196–225.

Strickland, B., & Scholl, B. J. (2015). Visual perception involves event-type representations: The case of containment versus occlusion. *Journal of Experimental Psychology: General, 144*, 570–580.

Surian, L., & Caldi, S. (2010). Infants' individuation of agents and inert objects. *Developmental Science, 13*, 143–150.

Thelen, E., & Smith, L. B. (1994), *A Dynamic Systems Approach to the Development of Perception and Action.* Cambridge, MA: MIT Press.

Ullman, T. D., Spelke, E., Battaglia, P., & Tenenbaum, J. B. (2017). Mind games: Game engines as an architecture for intuitive physics. *Trends in Cognitive Sciences, 21*, 649–665.

Van de Walle, G. A., Carey, S., & Prevor, M. (2000). Bases for object individuation in infancy: Evidence from manual search. *Journal of Cognition and Development, 1*, 249–280.

Wang, S. (2011). Priming 4.5-month-old infants to use height information by enhancing retrieval. *Developmental Psychology, 47*, 26–38.

Wang, S. (2019). Regularity detection and explanation-based learning jointly support learning about physical events in early infancy. *Cognitive Psychology, 113*, 101219.

Wang, S., & Baillargeon, R. (2005). Inducing infants to detect a physical violation in a single trial. *Psychological Science, 16*, 542–549.

Wang, S., & Baillargeon, R. (2006). Infants' physical knowledge affects their change detection. *Developmental Science, 9*, 173–181.

Wang, S., & Baillargeon, R. (2008a). Can infants be "taught" to attend to a new physical variable in an event category? The case of height in covering events. *Cognitive Psychology, 56*, 284–326.

Wang, S., & Baillargeon, R. (2008b). Detecting impossible changes in infancy: A three-system account. *Trends in Cognitive Sciences, 12*, 17–23.

Wang, S., Baillargeon, R., & Brueckner, L. (2004). Young infants' reasoning about hidden objects: Evidence from violation-of-expectation tasks with test trials only. *Cognition, 93*, 167–198.

Wang, S., Baillargeon, R., & Paterson, S. (2005). Detecting continuity violations in infancy: A new account and new evidence from covering and tube events. *Cognition, 95*, 129–173.

Wang, S., & Goldman, E. J. (2016). Infants actively construct and update their representations of physical events: Evidence from change detection by 12-month-olds. *Child Development Research*, article 3102481.

Wang, S., Kaufman, L., & Baillargeon, R. (2003). Should all stationary objects move when hit? Developments in infants' causal and statistical expectations about collision events. *Infant Behavior and Development, 26*, 529–568.

Wang, S., & Kohne, L. (2007). Visual experience enhances infants' use of task-relevant information in an action task. *Developmental Psychology, 43*, 1513–1522.

Wang, S., & Mitroff, S. R. (2009). Preserved visual representations despite change blindness in infants. *Developmental Science, 12*, 681–687.

Wang, S., & Onishi, K. H. (2017). Enhancing young infants' representations of physical events through improved retrieval (not encoding) of information. *Journal of Cognition and Development, 18*, 289–308.

Wang, S., Zhang, Y., & Baillargeon, R. (2016). Young infants view physically possible support events as unexpected: New evidence for rule learning. *Cognition, 157*, 100–105.

Wellman, H. M., & Gelman, S. A. (1992). Cognitive development: Foundational theories of core domains. *Annual Review of Psychology, 43*, 337–375.

Wilcox, T. (1999). Object individuation: Infants' use of shape, size, pattern, and color. *Cognition, 72*, 125–166.

Wilcox, T., & Baillargeon, R. (1998). Object individuation in infancy: The use of featural information in reasoning about occlusion events. *Cognitive Psychology, 37*, 97–155.

Wilcox, T., & Chapa, C. (2004). Priming infants to attend to color and pattern information in an individuation task. *Cognition, 90*, 265–302.

Wilcox, T., Nadel, L., & Rosser, R. (1996). Location memory in healthy preterm and full-term infants. *Infant Behavior and Development, 19*, 309–323.

Wilcox, T., & Schweinle, A. (2002). Object individuation and event mapping: Developmental changes in infants' use of featural information. *Developmental Science, 5*, 132–150.

Wilcox, T., Smith, T., & Woods, R. (2011). Priming infants to use pattern information in an object individuation task: The role of comparison. *Developmental Psychology, 47*, 886.

Wilson, R. A., & Keil, F. C. (2000). The shadows and shallows of explanation. In F. C. Keil, & R. A. Wilson (eds.), *Explanation and Cognition* (pp. 87–114). Cambridge, MA: MIT Press.

Wynn, K. (1992). Addition and subtraction by human infants. *Nature, 358*, 749–750.

Xu, F. (2002). The role of language in acquiring object kind concepts in infancy. *Cognition, 85*, 223–250.

Xu, F., & Baker, A. (2005). Object individuation in 10-month-old infants using a simplified manual search method. *Journal of Cognition and Development, 6*, 307–323.

Xu, F., & Carey, S. (1996). Infants' metaphysics: The case of numerical identity. *Cognitive Psychology, 30*, 111–153.

Xu, F., Carey, S., & Quint, N. (2004). The emergence of kind-based object individuation in infancy. *Cognitive Psychology, 49*, 155–190.

Zhang, Y, & Wang, S. (2019). Violation to infant faulty knowledge induces object exploration by 7.5-month-olds in support events. *Paper presented at the Biennial Meeting of the Cognitive Development Society*, September 2019, Louisville, KY.

9 Infant Categorization

David H. Rakison, Deon T. Benton, and Phuong Ngoc Dinh

William James once famously wrote in his *Principles of Psychology* (1890 [2013]) that the infant "assailed by eyes, ears, nose, skin, and entrails at once, feels it all as one great blooming, buzzing confusion." According to James, infants are overwhelmed by the bombardment of information available to the senses, and consequently their ability to perceive and learn is limited in the first months of life. This perspective remained dominant in the early days of developmental psychology – perhaps reified by Piaget's (1952) claim that infants' rely on their senses and motor skills until two years of age – but the last forty years of research on this issue has revealed a startlingly different picture of infants' perceptual and cognitive abilities. For example, experimental work has demonstrated purportedly that infants in the first year of life can compute simple addition and subtraction (Wynn, 1992), have a basic grasp of certain physical principles (Baillargeon, 1987), perceive launching events as causal (Oakes & Cohen, 1990), have expectations about how animates – people and animals – engage in motion (Spelke et al., 1995), and interact with other animates (Hamlin et al., 2007), among other things.

Central to all of these early emerging capacities is the ability to categorize. Categorization is the ability to group together discriminable things based on some principle or rule and to respond to those items in terms of their class membership rather than as individuals (Bruner et al., 1956). Put another way, categorization is dealing with "a set of things as somehow equivalent: to put them in the same pile, or call them by the same name, or respond to them in the same way" (Neisser, 1987, p. 1). Categorization tends to refer to things – inanimate objects, animate entities, sounds, events – that exist in the world, but the ability to categorize relies on *concepts*, which are mental representations that incorporate the various features, properties, and structures that connect the things to be categorized in the mind. The structure of category knowledge – as represented by *representations* or *concepts* – is thought to vary considerably. There is evidence that some concepts are mentally stored as individual exemplars (e.g., faces) (Medin & Schaffer, 1978), while others are a list of necessary or defining features (e.g., birds have feathers) (Bruner et al., 1966), *prototypes* or averages of a category (e.g., a Golden Retriever dog) (Bomba & Siqueland, 1983), or a cluster of probabilistic and correlated features (e.g., things with beaks and feathers have claws) (Rosch, 1975; Rosch & Mervis, 1975).

The importance of categorization in human cognition cannot be understated. Categorization provides a framework by which humans and most – if not all – non-human animals encode and organize their experiences in a systematic fashion, which reduces the burden on memory. For example, instead of encoding that every individual dog that an infant has encountered can bark, this knowledge is extended – via categorization (and concepts) – to all dogs. The ability to categorize also supports inductive inferences about newly encountered instances of a class; for instance, once an individual categorizes an Australian Shepherd as a dog or as an animal, inferences can be made about what it likes to eat, what its progeny might be, and whether it likes to chew on bones. Categorization is also intimately connected to language such that words often refer to categories of objects (e.g., dogs) and events (e.g., walking the dog), or properties of those things (e.g., dogs have fur). Although the ability to categorize begins before infants can produce or comprehend words (e.g., Quinn et al., 1993), an unresolved and much debated issue concerns the causal direction between language and thought (Sapir, 1921; Whorf, 1956): is it the emergence of thoughts that drives language acquisition or are children's thoughts shaped or constrained by language? More broadly, the study of categorization is at the heart of key epistemic questions: Where does knowledge come from? How does knowledge change over developmental time?

Given the centrality of categorization to cognition early in and throughout the lifespan, there is now a considerable body of research on its developmental trajectory, its breadth (e.g., whether infants categorize different inputs similarly), and its application (e.g., whether cat and dog categorization is affected by, for example, pets in the home). There are also a number of theories to explain how infants categorize, and these theories differ in whether they regard this ability as underpinned by domain-general mechanisms that process a wide range of inputs (e.g., conditioning, associative learning, habituation, statistical learning, and imitation) or by domain-specific mechanisms that are specialized for categorization alone. In this chapter, we will first outline some of the prominent theories of early concept and category development and then describe some of the key findings in this area.

Although infants must learn to categorize diverse inputs – for example, sounds, labels, haptic information, objects, and events – we focus here primarily on early categorization of inanimate objects and animate entities, spatial categorization, and the effect of language on categorization. We made this choice for three reasons: first, these are our areas of expertise; second, there is a rich literature on these aspects of early categorization; and third, in our view these areas of research answer fundamental questions about the nature of infants' categorization abilities. We conclude by discussing a number of ongoing issues such as the nature of infants' representations, if and how infants' categorization in the laboratory mirrors that found in the wild, and the potential role of computational modeling in understanding infant categorization.

9.1 Theories of Infant Category and Concept Formation

As with many other fields in infant cognition, there exist two main perspectives on the mechanisms that underpin early category and concept formation. According to one perspective, infants form categories and concepts through domain-specific mechanisms (e.g., Mandler, 1992), skeletal systems (e.g., Gelman, 1990), core systems (e.g., Spelke & Kinzler, 2007, 2009), and modules (Gelman, 1990; Leslie, 1995; Mandler, 1992; Premack, 1990). The term *domain-specific mechanism* refers to processes that are dedicated or specialized for a single cognitive function and that facilitate learning for one type of input (e.g., animacy, math, physics). The rationale for this view is (at least) twofold. First, specialized mechanisms evolved for specific functions because the input has largely remained constant throughout evolution and thus such mechanisms are "prepared" for that input (Gelman & Coley, 1990). Second, the features and properties of categories are complex and multifaceted – especially those that are rarely, if ever, observable (e.g., that dogs have dog DNA or that they are self-propelled) – and it is assumed that more general mechanisms such as associative learning would be unable to extract these features from the input without constraints that specify what information is category-relevant and what information is not (Keil, 1981).

Domain-specific theories of categorization nonetheless vary considerably in their formulation. Rochel Gelman (1990; Gelman et al., 1995), for example, proposed that at birth there exist *skeletal causal principles* that include initial knowledge that directs learning of category-relevant cues. These principles allow infants to form conceptual schemes for inanimate objects and animate entities by guiding attention to motion and composition cues such as the energy sources and materials of entities and objects (e.g., animals have a renewable energy sources and inanimate objects do not). Thus, the reason seven-month-old infants are unsurprised when people, but not objects, engage in self-propelled motion (e.g., Spelke et al., 1995) is because the former category but not the latter one possesses those causally-relevant features that cause motion (e.g., legs) and internal, renewable sources of energy. In a similar vein, Leslie (1994, 1995) proposed that infants are born with three distinct modules that facilitate rapid category and concept formation. These modules allow infants to develop knowledge of the physical, causal, and psychology properties of objects. Specifically, the theory of body (TOBY) module processes the physical or mechanical properties of things, one subsystem of the theory of mind (TOMM) module processes the goal-directed and intentional properties of things, and the other subsystem of the TOMM processes objects' cognitive properties (e.g., attitudes, beliefs). On this account,

animate entities are perceived as causal agents because they possess an internal, renewable source of energy that can be transferred to other entities and objects (TOBY) and because they possess beliefs and are goal-directed (TOMM).

A final theory developed by Jean Mandler (1992, 2000, 2003) is at its core domain-specific: it has been applied almost exclusively to concept learning for animates and inanimates despite its presentation as a domain-general approach. According to this view, infants possess two mechanisms for category learning. The first mechanism processes the surface appearance of things (e.g., dogs have tails), which facilitates *perceptual* categorization whereby objects are categorized on the basis of their static surface features. The second is a process called *perceptual analysis* that recodes the perceptual input into an abstract and accessible format and supports *conceptual* categorization. Note that perceptual analysis is thought to differ from simple perception in that the former but not the latter is an active or purposeful process that involves attentively analyzing information in the perceptual array. The output of perceptual analysis is an *image-schema* – or *conceptual primitive* – that encapsulates how things move (e.g., dogs are self-propelled agents). These conceptual primitives allow infants to categorize things on the basis of their meaning such as category membership (e.g., these things are "dogs") or motion properties (e.g., dogs are self-propelled agents), rather than surface appearance. In this sense, "what holds a class such as animals together so that membership can be assigned to it is neither overall perceptual similarity nor a common perceptual features, but instead a notion of common kind" (Mandler & McDonough, 1996, p. 314).

In contrast to the domain-specific perspective, a number of theorists have argued that domain-general mechanisms – such as habituation, associative learning, conditioning, and imitation – are adequate to explain early category and concept formation. According to this view, domain-general mechanisms are sufficiently powerful to extract the statistical regularities that specify category membership (e.g., Jones & Smith, 1993; Oakes & Madole, 2003; Rakison & Lupyan, 2008), are parsimonious (Quinn & Eimas, 2000; Quinn et al., 2000), and are fundamentally developmental because they explain how infants' ability to form concepts and categories improves over time. Domain-general perspectives vary in their specifics, but they have in common the idea that concept acquisition – and therefore categorization – is a gradual process whereby new information is added to existing concepts in a minute-to-minute and day-to-day fashion.

Linda Smith and colleagues (Jones & Smith, 1993; Smith & Heise, 1992; Smith et al., 2003) formulated one of the first domain-general theories of early category and concept formation in infancy. According to Smith and collaborators, infants' ability to learn correlations in the world – essentially clusters of features and properties that co-occur – changes their conceptual similarity space and leads to increased attention to the features that make up those correlations (Smith & Heise, 1992). A similarity space here refers to the proximity of features in conceptual space: attention to shape over color in categorization leads the representational space for shape to become closer and the representational space for color to become more distanced. In this way, as infants' experience increases with the statistical regularities that define categories, their attention – guided by non-strategic *dumb attention mechanisms* (Smith et al., 1996) – is drawn to more relevant, sophisticated, and detailed perceptual information to form categories. This account explains why children at three years of age and older expect objects in the same category – as determined by count nouns, for example – to possess similar surface properties, and objects in different categories to possess dissimilar surface properties (Smith et al., 1992).

In a related vein, Quinn and Eimas (1996, 1997) proposed that infants form concepts and categories through a process of *continuous representational enrichment*. This process relies on a sensitive perceptual system that extracts fine details of similarity relations – such as whether one group of objects has a specific feature such as eyes in common – and uses these features to categorize. Depending on which features are available and diagnostic of class membership, infants may categorize on the basis of shape (e.g., Jones & Smith, 1993), functional object parts (e.g., Rakison & Cohen, 1999), or facial features (e.g., Quinn & Eimas, 1996). Less accessible properties (e.g., that dogs are entities that have dog DNA), according to this perspective, are acquired later through a relatively undefined process called "abstraction" as well as language-based formal learning.

Finally, Rakison (2003; Rakison & Hahn, 2004; Rakison & Lupyan, 2008; Rakison & Poulin-Dubois, 2001) offered a domain-general framework for early category and concept development labeled *constrained attentional associative learning* (CAAL). According to this view, infants learn concepts for things in the world through improvements in information-processing abilities – and particularly, associative processes – with representational knowledge and subsequent categorization abilities accruing over developmental time. This view differs from those of Smith and colleagues and Quinn and Eimas in two ways. First, it incorporates the notion that infants are born with a number of perceptual attention biases that help to constrain early concept learning. Second, with development, the relations that infants learn become increasingly constrained by the statistical regularities in the real world. For example, infants are born with a perceptual bias to prefer moving things more than static things and large things more than small things: these simple inherent biases mean that infants will attend, for example, to the way that animate objects move and the parts of those animate objects as they move and may associate the presence of one feature with the other. Furthermore, as infants' experience increases with statistical regularities in the real world, constraints begin to emerge on the kinds of relations that infants attend to and encode. This means that the relations that infants will attend to and encode are only those consistent with relations found in the real world. For example, infants will learn to associate dynamic parts with agency and static parts with recipiency – but not agency with static parts and recipiency with dynamic parts – presumably because these are the relations that infants experience in the real world. In this way, infants start to learn about the properties of objects that are only intermittently present in the perceptual array.

9.1.1 Predictions of the Theories of Infant Category and Concept Development

Theorists from both camps concur that infants' first categories – and the concepts on which those categories are based – are grounded in the surface appearance of things. However, there is debate about when and how infants start to rely on less obvious, intermittently available cues to categorize objects. Those who support a domain-specific perspective assume that specialized mechanisms, modules, or core knowledge systems cause infants relatively early in life to form abstract concepts for the psychological and motion-related properties of objects and entities. Those who support a domain-general perspective assume,

in contrast, that such properties are learned through all-purpose mechanisms – for example, associative learning, habituation, and conditioning – that extract statistical regularities for surface features (e.g., legs) as well as less available properties (e.g., dogs move non-linearly).

Although both views imply that early categorization – until six-to-eight months of age or so – will be grounded in the surface appearance of things (e.g., whether they have eyes, legs, their shape, or their color), they make quite different predictions about the basis for categorization beyond this point in developmental time. The domain-specificity perspective predicts that around nine months of age infants categorize things on the basis of category relatedness (e.g., these things are dogs), motion cues (e.g., these things are agents), or psychological properties (e.g., these things are goal-directed). In contrast, the domain-general perspective predicts that surface cues continue to act as the basis for categorization until at least twenty-four months of age. Children at this age may also categorize on the basis of, for example, how things move, but this knowledge will be part of an association between specific surface features (e.g., legs) and a movement property (e.g., acting as an agent). This means that top-down knowledge at this age about category membership (e.g., whether an object is an "animal" or a "cat") may be superseded by the appearance of things.

9.2 Categorization in Infancy: Empirical Evidence

In the following sections, we outline the primary findings on categorization in infancy. We focus here on infants' categorization of natural kinds – namely, animals – as well as categorization of space. We also discuss the effect of language on early categorization.

9.2.1 Categorization of Natural Kinds

Based on a series of classic studies, Eleanor Rosch and Carolyn Mervis suggested that categories are mentally represented as three hierarchical classes (e.g., Rosch, 1975, 1976, 1978; Rosch & Mervis, 1975). They proposed that the *superordinate* level – which covers expansive categories such as animals, vehicles, and furniture – is at the top of this hierarchy. Below this category level in the hierarchy are two more specific classes: the *basic-level* (e.g., dogs, cars, screwdrivers) and the *subordinate-level* (e.g., Australian Shepherds, race cars, flat-head screwdrivers). Rosch and Mervis proposed that the basic-level is "psychologically privileged" such that infants and children form categories at this level first. Basic-level labels, for example, are the first used by infants and children and within-category similarity for basic-level items tends to be greater than that for items at the other levels. It is only later in development that infants form categories at the superordinate- (animals, vehicles) and subordinate-levels (Rottweilers, pickup truck).

It was not until twenty years after Rosch and Mervis' work that researchers began to investigate infants' ability to categorize at the superordinate, basic, and subordinate level. Based on this research, there is now considerable evidence that infants' earliest representations for basic-level stimuli such as cats and dogs may be grounded in perceptual – or surface – features. Research by Quinn and colleagues provides perhaps the strongest support for this claim (e.g., Eimas & Quinn, 1994; French et al., 2004; Mareschal et al., 2002; Quinn et al., 1993). For example, Quinn et al. (1993) showed that the ability to categorize static pictures of cats and dogs emerges between three and four months of age. This technique involves two parts. In the first part, infants are repeatedly shown various pictures from the same category for a fixed amount of time, typically side-by-side. In the second part, infants are tested with a novel picture from the familiar category paired next to a novel picture from a novel category. In Quinn et al.'s (1993) study, for example, three-to-four-month-old infants were familiarized repeatedly to different pictures of either cats or dogs that were presented side-by-side. Following familiarization, infants were shown a picture of a new member of the familiar category (e.g., a cat if familiarized with cats) paired next to a new member of the novel category (e.g., a dog if familiarized with cats).

Quinn et al. (1993) hypothesized that infants would look longer at a novel category member if they formed a category of the familiar stimuli during the familiarization period. This means that if infants who were familiarized to pictures of different pictures of dogs perceived a novel dog – but not a novel cat – to be a familiar category member then at test they should look longer at the novel cat than at the novel dog. This pattern of looking would also indicate that infants had formed an exclusive category for dogs that included the novel dog but excluded the novel cat. The results demonstrated that, although infants familiarized to pictures of cats at test looked longer at a novel dog than a novel cat, infants familiarized to pictures of dogs looked equally long at test at a novel dog than a novel cat. These findings indicated that infants had formed an exclusive category for cats that excluded a novel dog, whereas they had formed an inclusive category for dogs that included both a novel cat and a novel dog.

Quinn et al. (1993) argued that these findings resulted from important perceptual differences between cats and dogs. In particular, they argued that the reason for the asymmetry in infants' categories was because dogs possessed features (e.g., eye length, nose length, tail length, body size) that varied to a greater extent than those of cats; that is, in the real world dogs tend to possess perceptual features that vary more than those of cats and that subsumed those of cats. This means that infants familiarized to pictures of dogs may well have seen both the novel cat and dog as plausible dogs. This speculation was confirmed in follow-up computational and behavioral research with three-to-four-month-old infants. In addition to demonstrating that a computational model showed similar exclusivity asymmetries when presented with the same images presented to infants (e.g., Mareschal et al., 2000), French et al. (2004) found that the asymmetry is eliminated when there is no overlap between the perceptual features of the cats and dogs. In particular, they found that when the dog features were made not to overlap the cat features – by morphing the features of the animals – both a computational model and three-to-four-month-old infants looked longer at the picture of the animal to which they had not been familiarized. In other words, infants and a model familiarized to pictures of cats looked longer at a novel picture of a dog than at a novel picture of a cat, whereas infants and a model familiarized to dogs looked longer at a novel cat than a novel dog. French et al. (2004) extended this finding to also show that the asymmetry can be reversed when the features of the cat stimuli overlapped those of the dog stimuli. When perceptual features of the cat stimuli varied more than, and overlapped with those of, the perceptual features of the dog stimuli, infants and a model familiarized to the pictures of cats at test looked equally long at the novel dog and cat pictures. In contrast, infants and a model familiarized to pictures of dogs at test looked longer at the picture of a novel cat than at the novel dog.

The results from these experiments were interpreted to mean not only that infants initially rely on perceptual features to categorize dogs and cats and other basic-level stimuli (e.g., Behl-Chadha, 1996; Eimas & Quinn,

1994), but also that the amount of perceptual overlap between categories influences how likely infants are to form exclusive or inclusive categories. However, it was unclear from these experiments how detailed the information presented to infants need to be for them to form exclusive categories. It was unknown, for example, whether infants can form exclusive categories for the silhouettes of dogs and cats – whereby the internal features of the dogs and cats were removed – and whether infants rely on information from the head region, the body region, or both the head and body region of these stimuli to form exclusive categories. Quinn et al. (2001) examined this issue by familiarizing infants either to silhouettes of whole dogs, silhouettes of whole cats, silhouettes of the heads of cats (or dogs), or silhouettes of the bodies of cats (or dogs). Infants in these conditions were then tested with a picture of a novel cat paired next to a picture of a novel dog in a manner consistent with their respective condition. Thus, infants familiarized to silhouettes of the heads of cats were tested with the silhouette of the head of a novel cat paired next to the silhouette of the head of a novel dog, whereas infants familiarized to silhouettes of whole dogs were tested with the silhouette of a novel dog paired next to that of a novel cat.

Quinn et al. (2001) found that three- to four-month-olds not only formed exclusive categories for cats and dogs from their silhouettes but also used information from the head region rather than the body region of these stimuli as the basis for categorization. Specifically, infants familiarized to silhouettes of whole dogs at test looked longer at the silhouette of a novel cat than at that of a novel dog. In contrast, infants familiarized to silhouettes of whole cats at test looked longer at the silhouette of a novel dog than at that of a novel cat. Likewise, infants familiarized to silhouettes of the heads of cats at test looked longer at the silhouette of the head of a novel dog than at that of a novel cat, whereas infants familiarized to silhouettes of the heads of dogs at test looked longer at the silhouette of the head of a novel cat than at that of a novel dog. Perhaps unsurprisingly, infants familiarized to silhouettes of the bodies either of cats or dogs at test looked equally long at the silhouettes of the bodies of the novel cat and dog. This is presumably because dogs and cats have similar body contours, which in turn may make it difficult to distinguish between the two categories.

These results are important for two reasons. First, they indicate that infants' ability to form exclusive categories for cats and dogs is influenced by the amount of perceptual overlap between the two basic-level categories. Second, they indicate that infants can use contour information alone from the head region, but not the body region, to form basic-level categories for cats and dogs. More generally, these results illustrate that infants' category knowledge of basic-level stimuli may be grounded in low-level perceptual, or surface, features.

According to Mandler (1992) this changes toward the end of the first year of life as infants begin to form what she calls conceptual categories. Mandler also proposed – based on her research with the *sequential touching* paradigm – that infants categorize first at the superordinate-level and not at the basic-level, as Rosch and Mervis (1975) suggested. In the sequential touching procedure (e.g., Mandler & Bauer, 1988; Mandler et al., 1991; Nelson, 1973; Rakison & Butterworth, 1998a, 1998b; Rakison & Cohen, 1999), eight objects – typically 3D scale model toys with four from one category and four from another – are placed randomly in front of an infant and their spontaneous touching to the objects is measured. The measure of categorization is whether infants touch sequentially those objects that

belong to the same category. For example, if infants touch sequentially – that is, greater than chance would predict – a number of dogs and then touch sequentially a number of birds, this is taken as evidence that they grouped the members of each class on some basis.

In one series of studies, Mandler et al. (1991; see also Mandler & Bauer, 1988) tested eighteen- and twenty-four-month-olds with different contrasts of basic-level categories from the same superordinate category (e.g., animals). Thus, the low contrast condition for animals was dogs and horses, and the high contrast condition was dogs and fish. Infants were also tested with a superordinate-level contrast of animals and vehicles. Infants' pattern of touching revealed that eighteen- and twenty-four-month-olds categorized the superordinate-level contrast of animals and vehicles but the younger group did not categorize low and moderate contrast basic-level groups (dogs and horses, dogs and rabbits) and the older group only categorized the moderate contrast (dogs and rabbits) but not the low contrast (dogs and horses). Based on these findings, Mandler et al. (1991; Mandler, 1992) argued that infants' categorization in these tasks could only have been based on conceptual knowledge of less obvious properties such as animacy or category relatedness; that is, according to Mandler, because the animals and vehicles looked different from each other – in terms of their surface features – infants could only have categorized them as different based on less obvious properties. Mandler and colleagues also concluded that the first categories that infants form are at the superordinate level – which they called the *global level* – with the ability to categorize basic-level contrasts emerging later in developmental time. This proposal has been supported by research with significantly younger infants. Quinn and Johnson (2000), using a paired-preference procedure, found that infants as young as two months of age form a category of mammals that exclude furniture, but are unable to form a category of cats that exclude elephants, rabbits, or dogs. Quinn and Johnson (2000) also found that this finding confirmed the predictions of a computational model – implemented as an autoassociator – in which global category-level representations emerged before basic category-level representations.

A number of researchers have disputed Mandler's conclusion that infants at the end of the first year start to use conceptual properties to categorize. For example, Rakison and Butterworth (1998a, 1998b), questioned Mandler et al.'s (1991; Mandler & Bauer, 1988) rationale that infants could only categorize animals as different from vehicles on the basis of less obvious cues such as animacy and category relatedness. They noted that the animal and vehicles stimuli, respectively, shared a number of surface features, such as legs among the animals and wheels among the vehicles, and they posited that infants may have used these features to categorize; that is, things with the same parts are classified as belonging to the same category. Note that this hypothesis does not dispute that "global" categories emerge prior to basic-level categories; rather, it is the basis for these categories that is under debate. However, this perspective does address why infants can categorize at the global level but not at the basic level: basic-level categories – such as cats and dogs – share a number of surface features (e.g., legs, eyes, tails, overall shape). If infants attend to such features to categorize then they would classify dogs and cats as the same kind of thing rather than as different things.

To test their hypothesis, Rakison and Butterworth (1998a) presented fourteen-, eighteen-, and twenty-two-month-olds with a number of different contrasts using the sequential touching procedure. In one experiment,

infants were tested with various global-level contrasts that either shared or did not share key parts, such as legs and wheels, (i.e., animals with legs, furniture with legs, and vehicles with wheels). They found that infants categorized different-part contrasts (e.g., animals versus vehicles, furniture versus vehicles) approximately eight months before they categorized same-part contrasts (e.g., animals versus furniture). In a second experiment, Rakison and Butterworth (1998a) used the same procedure with fourteen-, eighteen-, and twenty-two-month-olds but changed the parts of animals and vehicles so that they either had no shared parts (e.g., animals without legs), shared parts (e.g., animals and vehicles with legs and wheels), or possessed the parts of the other category (e.g., two of the four animals with wheels but no legs). Infants' sequential touching behavior across these contrasts supported the idea that shared parts such as legs and wheels are sufficient and perhaps necessary for categorization at the global-level. Infants in all three age groups failed to categorize the animals as different from the vehicle when the stimuli all possessed legs and wheels as well as when the stimuli had no such parts. When some members of each category had the parts that are typical of the other category (e.g., animals with wheels but no legs), infants at fourteen and eighteen months grouped objects on the basis of shared parts; that is, into groups of "things with legs" and "things with wheels" and not on the basis of category membership. These experiments provided evidence that object features or parts – and not conceptual knowledge of animacy or category relatedness (Mandler, 1992) – act as the basis for early categorization. Moreover, that infants formed *ad hoc* categories during one condition – that is, animals with wheels and vehicles with wheels – implies that these groupings may have formed categories *online* and without prior knowledge of the features of animals and vehicles (see also Jones & Smith, 1993; Oakes et al., 1997; Quinn et al., 1993).

In sum, research on infants' categorization of animals and vehicles suggests that surface features such as shape or object parts act as the basis for categorization in the first two years of life. Although it has been suggested that categories are formed on the basis of conceptual information (e.g., animacy, category relatedness) by the end of the first year of life, the evidence to support this view has been disputed both empirically and theoretically and is inconsistent with the results just discussed.

9.2.2 Spatial Categorization

Spatial categorization – the ability to discern different spatial relations between objects and recognize these relations among other objects or in novel instances – is fundamental to infants' ability to function in the world. This ability enables infants to parse the world based on these spatial categories (Quinn, 1994) and subserves the development of locomotion as well as a number of cognitive skills such as navigation and reading (Newcombe & Huttenlocher, 2000). Unsurprisingly, spatial categorization has attracted significant attention from the research community.

Piaget (1952) posited that infants perceive the world as unconnected, transient images well until their second year of life. However, subsequent research suggests that infants begin forming primitive spatial categories as early as sixty-one hours after birth. In one study, for example, Antell and Caron (1985) familiarized two groups of neonatal infants to three cards that depicted a black square positioned either above or below a black cross. Each group saw the configuration assigned to their group at the top, center, and bottom of the card, and they were tested with the unfamiliar image

positioned at the center of the card. Infants looked significantly longer at the unfamiliar image than the average of their last two familiarization trials. These results showed that sixty-one-hour-old infants could distinguish between above and below relations between two simple visual images. Using the habituation procedure, Gava et al. (2009) extended these findings to show that three-day-old infants discriminated between spatial categories of left and right relative to a vertical bar, even when there is high within-category variability in the object's position.

The ability of neonatal infants to group visual stimuli into simple spatial categories continues to develop throughout early infancy. For example, Quinn (1994, Experiment 2) familiarized two groups of three-month-old infants to four dots either above (Dot Above Line group) or below (Dot Below Line group) a horizontal bar. Infants in the Dot Above Line group looked longer at the test image with a single dot appearing below the line than the image with a dot above the line; the opposite pattern was observed for infants in the Dot Below Line group. These data suggested that three-month-old infants successfully formed spatial categories of above and below spatial relations and responded to novel instances based on these categories. Interestingly, infants' ability to form above and below spatial relations depended crucially on low-level perceptual manipulations: when the dots varied during familiarization (Quinn, 1994, experiment 1) or when the bar was removed (Quinn, 1994, experiment 3) during familiarization, infants did not show a decline in looking time across trials. This suggests that, although three-month-olds can form above and below spatial relations, their ability to do so is affected by perceptual changes to the familiarization stimulus, even when those changes do not affect the global spatial relation between the dots. The ability to form category representations for above and below spatial relations that are robust to low-level perceptual changes does not emerge until infants are between six and seven months of age (Quinn & Eimas, 1996). This developmental trend presumably results from increased real-world experience with different instances of above and below relations for the six-to-seven-month-olds compared to the three-month-olds.

Spatial categories more complex than above and below relations have been explored in other studies with the familiarization paradigm. Six- and seven-month-old infants are capable of forming a spatial category for the between spatial relation such that longer looking was obtained for dots outside two vertical bars than for dots in a novel location between the bars following familiarization to dots between the bars (Quinn et al., 1999). In a similar vein, Freeman et al. (1980) found that infants can form category representations for containment spatial relations: fifteen-month-olds, and to a lesser extent twelve-month-olds, performed better in the A-not-B visual search task when a toy was contained in an upright cup than when it was hidden underneath an inverted cup. A control experiment suggested that the previous data provided evidence for a developing representation of containment as a function of cups rather than the mere presence of an upward-facing cavity (Freeman et al., 1980, Experiment 2). Relations other than containment were investigated with habituation studies (e.g., Casasola & Cohen, 2002; Casasola et al., 2003; Hespos & Spelke, 2004). For example, Casasola and Cohen (2002) habituated English-learning ten- and eighteen-month-old infants to four different pairs of realistic toys bearing one of the following three spatial relationships: containment, support, and tight-fit. Results showed that infants in both age groups who were habituated to events of containment formed a category of this

relationship and generalized this category to novel object pairs. Despite those results, there was no evidence to suggest that these two age groups formed abstract categories of support or tight-fit relations: ten-month-olds responded solely based on perceptual novelty, whereas eighteen-month-olds responded to novel relationships only when familiar objects were involved.

The complexity of a spatial relation – support versus tight-fit, for example – is not the only factor that influences when and how well infants form a category of that spatial relation. Casasola and Park (2013) randomly assigned ten- and fourteen-month-old infants to be habituated to either two or six realistic exemplars of a specific spatial relation (containment or support). Although fourteen-month-old infants generally succeeded in forming a spatial category, regardless of the number of habituation exemplars, ten-month-old infants only succeeded when habituated to six exemplars. To form complex spatial categories, infants – especially those in the first year of life – may need a larger number of exemplars such that the spatial relationship between objects becomes salient. Additionally, Park and Casasola (2015) showed that eight- and fourteen-month-old infants generalized their category of support relation to new instances during test if they were habituated to embellished objects in a support relationship, whereas habituating infants to plain objects yielded no such results. Thus, the degree of perceptual complexity of the objects may factor into spatial categorization, especially for younger infants.

The findings covered to this point suggest at least two developmental trends in spatial categorization. First, infants acquire simple spatial categories (e.g., above versus below, left versus right) before complex ones (e.g., between, containment, support, tight-fit). Second, infants' spatial categories become more abstract with age: as infants mature, their spatial categorization abilities become less susceptible to changes in other, irrelevant perceptual dimensions (e.g., shape of object, degree of embellishment). However, it is possible to facilitate young infants' learning of more complex spatial relations in a variable environment by manipulating other factors (e.g., the number of training exemplars, the perceptual complexity of the objects involved). According to both Quinn et al. (1996, 1999) and Casasola and colleagues (Casasola & Cohen, 2002; Casasola & Park, 2013), the mechanisms that underpin both of these developmental progressions are domain-general; that is, infants' spatial categories develop as a result of the experience and ever improving information-processing abilities.

9.3 Categorization and Language

Infants' ability to categorize does not develop in a vacuum. A long-standing question in the developmental literature concerns the connection between categorization and language, especially given the lag between their developmental timelines. As mentioned in Section 9.2.2, infants form categories from as early as sixty-one hours after birth (Antell & Caron, 1985), yet they do not produce their first word until ten-to-twelve months of age (Waxman & Hall, 1993; see de Boysson-Bardies & Vihman, 1991 for language-specific differences in the production of first words). From this point, lexical acquisition continues at a slow and steady rate, resulting in a productive vocabulary size of 20 and 100 words by seventeen months (Dromi, 1987). By roughly seventeen months of age, infants enter the "naming explosion," during which they can learn as many as ten words a week (Dromi, 1987; see Goldfield & Reznick, 1990, for findings that suggest a gradual development of lexical acquisition in later infancy). Despite the developmental time lag, there exists a robust

positive correlation between categorization performance and productive vocabulary size. Gopnik and Meltzoff (1987), through a longitudinal study with fifteen- to twenty-month-old infants, showed that infants' complex categorization behavior in an object-sorting task accompanied the start of their "naming explosion," with an average 33.17-day gap between the two developmental milestones. Similarly, Nazzi and Gopnik (2001) found a strong positive correlation between categorization by object names in an object manipulation task and productive vocabulary size in twenty-month-old infants but not in sixteen-month-old infants. Given these observations, one may suspect a unidirectional relationship between categorization and language development such that categorization supports later lexical acquisition.

Though infants' ability to categorize develops earlier than their linguistic production, there is ample evidence suggesting that language could also impinge on categorization behavior. Studies by Waxman and colleagues (e.g., Waxman & Markow, 1995) provided some early experimental evidence for this link. Using a novelty preference paradigm, Waxman and Markow (1995, Experiment 1) familiarized infants of nine to twenty months of age with four trials of a category of toys. The toys were categorized by two sets of levels: basic (cars versus airplanes, cows versus dinosaurs) and superordinate (animals versus vehicles, animals versus tools). Infants in the basic level condition were familiarized with four exemplars of one of the contrastive categories (e.g., infants in the cars versus airplanes condition were familiarized with either four toy cars or four airplanes of different colors). Similarly, infants in the superordinate level condition were familiarized with four exemplars of different basic categories (e.g., infants in the animals versus vehicles condition were familiarized with either a brown horse, an orange tiger, a brown bear, and a panda, or a white roadster, a black sports car, a green truck, and a red airplane). Infants in the Word condition heard the instruction "Look, a(n) X" (where X stands for the type of object at the level of category that they were familiarized) during familiarization, whereas infants in the No Word condition heard the instruction "Look what's here." At test, all infants were presented with one object from the familiar category of toys and one from a novel category for forty-five seconds. Infants in the Word condition attended longer to the novel object than the familiar object compared to infants in the No Word condition. Although no age-based analysis was reported, the results at least suggested that object nouns were useful in tuning infants' attention toward the category of an object, especially at the superordinate level. The effect was not limited to nouns: adjective labels also guided eleven-month-olds' attention to novel objects at test (Waxman & Booth, 2003). These findings were consistent with the hypothesis that the onset of lexical acquisition encouraged infants to generalize the label of an object to other objects of the same category. Put another way, according to Waxman and colleagues, words serve as invitations to form categories.

Even more compelling evidence for the connection between language and categorization comes from studies of linguistic relativity (for an early discussion, see Whorf, 1940). One could return briefly to the domain of spatial categorization for some of this evidence. Choi and Bowerman (1991), in an observational study, investigated the spatial semantic organization of the English and Korean languages and toddlers' ability to learn specific spatial and motion categories (for more on this hypothesis, see a discussion by Cromer, 1974). Twenty-month-old English learners discerned events involving containment (*in*) and vertical support (*on*), regardless of the type of

contact or fit between objects. Korean infants at the same age made a distinction between tight-fit, various loose-fit, and loose contact events, but not between *in* and *on*. This early difference in spatial categorization mapped onto the divergence between the ways that space is conceptualized in English versus in Korean; that is, the relations that infants encode in the lab are constrained by how different languages conceptualize spatial relations. Thus, English-speaking infants will form spatial categories for containment and vertical-support spatial relations because these relations are used in English to describe how objects are positioned in relation to each other. In contrast, Korean-speaking infants will form spatial categories for fit relations because how objects fit together is emphasized more readily in Korean than how objects are positioned in relation to other objects. These findings were corroborated in later studies that used familiarization coupled with preferential looking (e.g., Choi et al., 1999; McDonough et al., 2003), and habituation (Casasola, 2005). Casasola and Bhagwat (2007) showed that eighteen-month-old English-learning infants use novel spatial particles (e.g., *in*, *on*) to facilitate their learning of spatial categories: the better the infant's productive capacity for spatial language, the stronger the effect. While English-learning infants distinguished between tight-fit and loose-fit containment relationships at eighteen months of age, their sensitivity to the difference faded by twenty-nine months compared to their twenty-nine-month-old Korean-learning peers (Choi, 2006). The connection between the acquisition of spatial categories and language is especially evident when considering what happens if the latter is absent: the lack of spatial language among five-year-old deaf homesigners in Istanbul, Turkey accompanies lower performance on the Spatial Mapping Task (Gentner et al., 2013). One needs not take the extreme theoretical position that language completely determines cognition to acknowledge that features of infants' linguistic environment bears on their categorization behavior.

Although many of these studies suffer from a small sample size, their combined findings are at least suggestive that language acquisition intertwines with categorization from early infancy. A potential mediating factor is attention: as children learn about words of the same class, they attend more and more to properties and dimensions relevant to those words (e.g., Yoshida & Smith, 2003), perhaps at the cost of decreasing sensitivity to other properties or dimensions (Best et al., 2013). The effects of language and context on categorization seem to extend beyond infancy and well into adulthood (e.g., Ji et al., 2004). In the case of spatial categories, linguistic spatial categories could tune a child's visual attention to particular spatial relationships and not others (for how such a pathway might be computationally instantiated in adults, see Regier & Carlson, 2001).

9.4 Other Issues

9.4.1 Do Infant Categorization Tasks Tap Real-World Knowledge?

An ongoing question relates to whether empirical work on infants' ability to categorize taps – or relies on – existing knowledge that they already possessed when they arrived at the laboratory or whether they create categories online based on the stimuli with which they are presented and the constraints of the experiment. This is a significant issue to address for empirical work that uses real-world stimuli and that seeks to draw inferences about infants' real-world categorization abilities. For example, it is possible that the babies in Quinn et al. (1993) possessed *a priori* concepts for cats and dogs prior to testing – presumably

as a result of their experience in the world – or that their representations for cats and dogs were generated during testing. There may also be important individual differences between infants such that some infants form online categories whereas others respond on the basis of existing category knowledge. To this end, there is evidence that four-months-old infants with and without pets show different scanning patterns when viewing images of cats and dogs (Hurley & Oakes, 2015; Kovack-Lesh et al., 2014). As Oakes (2010) pointed out, this issue may be intractable because the procedures that are suitable for very young infants – namely, familiarization and habituation – require that they be shown a sample of the exemplars prior to testing (e.g., French et al., 2004).

Some researchers have also argued that the type of task has an effect on this issue. For instance, Mandler (2000) proposed that visual familiarization and habituation can only generate – and access – perceptual categories that incorporate the surface features of objects because infants are shown two-dimensional images in such studies. According to this view, methods that use three-dimensional objects – such as the sequential touching and generalized imitation paradigms – can generate and access conceptual categories that go beyond perceptual, or surface, features. Yet others (e.g., Madole & Cohen, 1995; Rakison, 2005) have demonstrated that infants in the habituation paradigm can learn information and form categories that go beyond perceptual information such as the causal role and object function of objects and entities, which suggests that the presentation of 2-D images can lead to rich concepts and categories.

9.4.2 What Is the Nature of Infants' Representations?

A related question concerns the nature of the mental representations – or concepts – that infants generate and then use to categorize. There is now considerable evidence that these concepts take on a number of forms, although it remains an open question whether infants form a single representation of things in the world or multiple representation of the same things.

For example, infants within the first months of life are capable of forming categories by extracting correlations among surface features of things (Rakison & Poulin-Dubois, 2002; Younger & Cohen, 1986). These correlations are clusters of features that tend to co-occur – such as beaks and wings – and once represented they allow infants to predict or expect that if one feature is present then so will the other one. Infants also form representations that are prototypes – or averages –of the stimuli to which they are exposed and can do so for a wide range of stimuli including faces, animals, and geometric shapes (Bomba & Siqueland, 1983; Langlois et al., 1987). For instance, by three to four months of age infants can form prototypes of basic shapes such as triangles and squares such that, following familiarization with shapes that deviated from the prototype to different degrees (e.g. poor examples of a triangle), infants looked longer at a previously seen shape than at a previously unseen prototype. This implies that during familiarization infants generated a mental representation of the prototype and found it more familiar than a shape they had viewed earlier.

It has also been suggested that categories may be represented by their individual exemplars with new objects assigned to categories by comparing how similar they are to exemplars that have already been processed and stored (Brooks, 1978; Medin & Schaffer, 1978). In support of this view, there is evidence that under some conditions in categorization tasks adults remember individual instances and use them in subsequent category membership decisions (Brooks, 1978). However, this evidence is limited and the exemplar view has been criticized because it fails to explain how exemplar representations can support induction. Furthermore, there is no real difference between exemplar-based models and those which rely on prototypes because if the prototype encodes the full set of correlated features of a category then it can represent a number of exemplars (Medin et al., 1987; Murphy & Medin, 1985). One potentially fruitful avenue to pursue in this regard is to examine categorization abilities in individuals with developmental delays or disabilities (e.g., Johnson & Rakison, 2006).

9.5 Summary: The Way Forward

The goal of this chapter was to discuss the competing theories of infant concept and category formation and the research that has been taken as support for these theories. To this end, we outlined research that demonstrates that early in categorization young infants rely heavily on the perceptual, or surface, features to form categories for objects and spatial relations. We also showed that as infants develop, the categories and concepts they possess become increasingly more complex such that they begin to include features that rarely, if ever, occur together (e.g., Rakison & Benton, 2019). We argued that this developmental trend in concept and category acquisition presumably results from advancements in infants' cognitive abilities (e.g., improving information processing abilities, memory, and executive function), and increased exposure with real-world categories.

Despite the extensive body of research on infant category and concept formation, several open questions remain. For instance, it is unknown whether and to what extent infants' performance in categorization tasks reflect their real world category knowledge, their ability to form categories "on the fly" during testing, or a combination of both factors. In addition, it remains unclear whether infants' mental representation(s) of categories are supported by a single, prototypical representation or whether is it instantiated in, and aggregated across, multiple exemplars.

Computational models – in particular connectionist models – provide developmentalists with a tool for addressing many of the unresolved issues aforementioned. Although a number of computational techniques have been used to explain infant category and concept acquisition (e.g., Gopnik et al., 2004; Smith & Samuelson, 2003), we single out the connectionist approach for two reasons. First, many, if not the majority of, developmental models have been connectionist in design and have simulated a wide range of developmental findings (for reviews, see Benton & Rakison, 2018; Rakison & Yermolayeva, 2010; Yermolayeva & Rakison, 2014). Connectionist principles thus act as an organizing framework with which findings from seemingly disparate areas of developmental research cohere. Second, these models provide a concrete, mathematical, and mechanistic account of how infants acquire categories and concepts for things in the world. More specifically, these models enable researchers to test different assumptions about what is needed prior to a task to categorize objects and entities (e.g., real world experience) and to compare different accounts of how object categories are represented (e.g., prototype versus exemplar accounts of categorization) in light of the empirical data.

Despite the value of connectionist models in accounting for category and concept acquisition, it is worth noting that the flexibility of computational models in general – be they connectionist or Bayesian – can be their own drawback. One may be able to build a model that fits any subset of empirical data without yielding insight into, or gaining substantive support for, the proposed processes and mechanisms that underlie the phenomenon of interest. This issue can be addressed by designing experiments that test the assumptions of the model: if infants respond in a manner that is consistent with the model's predictions, this suggests that the model was informative because it was able to account for data on which it was not explicitly trained. This issue notwithstanding, computational modeling is a promising avenue that is worthy of further exploration because it can elucidate the processes underpinning concept and category acquisition. Given the value of computational modeling, it is critical that ongoing and future empirical work on this topic is to ground the assumptions behind a computational model.

Decades of developmental research on concept and category acquisition in infants have provided preliminary answers to the age-old question concerning the origin of knowledge. Further research with systematic and careful use of complementary methods, including computational modeling, is required to turn these preliminary answers into a richer and more complete picture of how humans acquire and represent categories and concepts of objects, events, and agents. Particular attention should be paid to the complex interplay between infants' developing categorization abilities and their real world experiences with objects and entities.

References

Antell, S. E., & Caron, A. J. (1985). Neonatal perception of spatial relationships. *Infant Behavior and Development, 8*, 15–23.

Baillargeon, R. (1987). Object permanence in 3 1/2- and 4 1/2-month-old infants. *Developmental Psychology, 23*, 655–664.

Behl-Chadha, G. (1996). Basic-level and superordinate-like categorical representations in early infancy. *Cognition, 60*, 105–141.

Benton, D. T., & Rakison, D. H. (2018). *Computational Modeling and What It Can Tell You about Behavior*. Thousand Oaks, CA: SAGE Research Methods Cases.

Best, C. A., Yim, H., & Sloutsky, V. M. (2013). The cost of selective attention in category learning: Developmental differences between adults and infants. *Journal of Experimental Child Psychology*, *116*, 105–119.

Bomba, P. C., & Siqueland, E. R. (1983). The nature and structure of infant form categories. *Journal of Experimental Child Psychology*, *35*, 294–328.

Brooks, L. (1978). Nonanalytic concept formation and memory for instances. In E. H. Rosch, and B. B. Lloyd (eds.), *Cognition and Categorisation* (pp. 169–211). Hillsdale, NJ: Lawrence Erlbaum Associates.

Bruner, J. S., Olver, R. R., & Greenfield, P. M. (1966). *Studies in Cognitive Growth*. New York: Wiley.

Bruner, R., Goodnow, J. J., and Austin, G. A. (eds.) (1956). *A Study of Thinking* (pp. 3–170). New York: Wiley.

Casasola, M. (2005). Can language do the driving? The effect of linguistic input on infants' categorization of support spatial relations. *Developmental Psychology*, *41*, 183–192.

Casasola, M., & Bhagwat, J. (2007). Do novel words facilitate 18-month-olds' spatial categorization? *Child Development*, *78*, 1818–1829.

Casasola, M., & Cohen, L. B. (2002). Infant categorization of containment, support and tight-fit spatial relationships. *Developmental Science*, *5*, 247–264.

Casasola, M., Cohen, L. B., & Chiarello, E. (2003). Six-month-old infants' categorization of containment spatial relations. *Child Development*, *74*, 679–693.

Casasola, M., & Park, Y. (2013). Developmental changes in infant spatial categorization: When more is best and when less is enough. *Child Development*, *84*, 1004–1019.

Choi, S. (2006). Influence of language-specific input on spatial cognition: Categories of containment. *First Language*, *26*, 207–232.

Choi, S., & Bowerman, M. (1991). Learning to express motion events in English and Korean: The influence of language-specific lexicalization patterns. *Cognition*, *41*, 83–121.

Choi, S., McDonough, L., Bowerman, M., & Mandler, J. M. (1999). Early sensitivity to language-specific spatial categories in English and Korean. *Cognitive Development*, *14*(2), 241–268.

Cromer, R. F. (1974). The development of language and cognition: The cognition hypothesis. In B. M. Foss (ed.), *New Perspectives in Child Development* (pp. 184–252). London: Penguin.

de Boysson-Bardies, B., & Vihman, M. M. (1991). Adaptation to language: Evidence from babbling and first words in four languages. *Language*, *67*, 297–319.

Dromi, E. (1987). *Early Lexical Development*. New York. Cambridge University Press.

Eimas, P. D., & Quinn, P. C. (1994). Studies on the formation of perceptually based basic-level categories in young infants. *Child Development*, *65*, 903–917.

Freeman, N. H., Lloyd, S., & Sinha, C. G. (1980). Infant search tasks reveal early concepts of containment and canonical usage of objects. *Cognition*, *8*, 243–262.

French, R. M., Mareschal, D., Mermillod, M., & Quinn, P. C. (2004). The role of bottom-up processing in perceptual categorization by 3- to 4-month old infants: Simulations and data. *Journal of Experimental Psychology: General*, *133*, 382–397.

Gava, L., Valenza, E., & Turati, C. (2009). Newborns' perception of left–right spatial relations. *Child Development*, *80*, 1797–1810.

Gelman, R. (1990). First principles organize attention to and learning about relevant data: Number and the animate-inanimate distinction as examples. *Cognitive Science*, *14*, 79–106.

Gelman, R., Durgin, F., & Kaufman, L. (1995). Distinguishing between animate and inanimates: Not by motion alone. In D. Sperber, D. Premack, & A. J. Premack (eds.), *Causal Cognition* (pp. 150–184). Oxford: Clarendon.

Gelman, S. A., & Coley, J. D. (1990). The importance of knowing a dodo is a bird: Categories and inferences in 2-year-old children. *Developmental Psychology*, *26*, 796.

Gentner, D., Özyürek, A., Gürcanli, Ö., & Goldin-Meadow, S. (2013). Spatial language facilitates spatial cognition: Evidence from children who lack language input. *Cognition, 127*, 318–330.

Goldfield, B. A., & Reznick, J. S. (1990). Early lexical acquisition: Rate, content, and the vocabulary spurt. *Journal of Child Language, 17*, 171–183.

Gopnik, A., Glymour, C., Sobel, D. M., Schulz, L. E., Kushnir, T., & Danks, D. (2004). A theory of causal learning in children: Causal maps and Bayes nets. *Psychological Review, 111*, 3.

Gopnik, A., & Meltzoff, A. (1987). The development of categorization in the second year and its relation to other cognitive and linguistic developments. *Child Development, 58*, 1523–1531.

Hamlin, J. K., Wynn, K., & Bloom, P. (2007). Social evaluation by preverbal infants. *Nature, 450*, 557.

Hespos, S. J., & Spelke, E. S. (2004). Conceptual precursors to language. *Nature, 430*, 453.

Hurley, K. B., & Oakes, L. M. (2015). Experience and distribution of attention: Pet exposure and infants' scanning of animal images. *Journal of Cognition and Development, 16*, 11–30.

James, W. (2013). *The Principles of Psychology.* Redditch, Worcestershire: Read Books Ltd.

Ji, L. J., Zhang, Z., & Nisbett, R. E. (2004). Is it culture or is it language? Examination of language effects in cross-cultural research on categorization. *Journal of Personality and Social Psychology, 87*, 57.

Johnson, C., & Rakison, D. H. (2006). Early categorization of animate/inanimate concepts in young children with autism. *Journal of Developmental and Physical Disabilities, 18*, 73–89.

Jones, S. S., & Smith, L. B. (1993). The place of perception in children's concepts. *Cognitive Development, 8*, 113–139.

Keil, F. C. (1981). Constraints on knowledge and cognitive development. *Psychological Review, 88*, 197–227.

Kovack-Lesh, K. A., McMurray, B., & Oakes, L. M. (2014). Four-month-old infants' visual investigation of cats and dogs: Relations with pet

experience and attentional strategy. *Developmental Psychology, 50*, 402.

Langlois, J. H., Roggman, L. A., Casey, R. J., Ritter, J. M., Rieser-Danner, L. A., & Jenkins, V. Y. (1987). Infant preferences for attractive faces: Rudiments of a stereotype? *Developmental Psychology, 23*, 363.

Leslie, A. (1994). ToMM, ToBy, and Agency: Core architecture and domain specificity. In L. Hirschfeld, & S. Gelman (eds.), *Mapping the Mind: Domain Specificity in Cognition and Culture* (pp. 119–148). New York: Cambridge University Press.

Leslie, A. (1995). A theory of agency. In D. Sperber, D. Premack, & A. J. Premack (eds.), *Causal Cognition* (pp. 121–141). Oxford: Clarendon.

Madole, K. L., & Cohen, L. B. (1995). The role of object parts in infants' attention to form-function correlations. *Developmental Psychology, 31*, 637.

Mandler, J. M. (1992). How to build a baby: II. Conceptual primitives. *Psychological Review, 99*, 587–604.

Mandler, J. M. (2000). Perceptual and conceptual processes in infancy. *Journal of Cognition and Development, 1*, 3–36.

Mandler, J. M. (2003). Conceptual categorization. In D. H. Rakison, & L. M. Oakes (eds.), *Early Category and Concept Development: Making Sense of the Blooming, Buzzing Confusion* (pp. 103–131). New York: Oxford University Press.

Mandler, J. M., & Bauer, P. J. (1988). The cradle of categorization: Is the basic level basic? *Cognitive Development, 3*, 247–264.

Mandler, J. M., Bauer, P. J., & McDonough, L. (1991). Separating the sheep from the goats: Differentiating global categories. *Cognitive Psychology, 23*, 263–298.

Mandler, J. M., & McDonough, L. (1996). Drinking and driving don't mix: Inductive generalization in infancy. *Cognition, 59*, 307–335.

Mareschal, D., French, R. M., & Quinn, P. C. (2000). A connectionist account of asymmetric category learning in early infancy. *Developmental Psychology, 36*, 635.

Mareschal, D., Quinn, P. C., & French, R. M. (2002). Asymmetric interference in 3- to 4-month olds' sequential category learning. *Cognitive Science, 26*, 377–389.

McDonough, L., Choi, S., & Mandler, J. M. (2003). Understanding spatial relations: Flexible infants, lexical adults. *Cognitive Psychology, 46*, 229–259.

Medin, D. L., & Schaffer, M. M. (1978). Context theory of classification learning. *Psychological Review, 85*, 207–238.

Medin, D. L., Wattenmaker, W. D., & Hampson, S. E. (1987). Family resemblance, conceptual cohesiveness, and category construction. *Cognitive Psychology, 19*, 242–279.

Murphy, G. L., & Medin, D. L. (1985). The role of theories in conceptual coherence. *Psychological Review, 92*, 289–316.

Nazzi, T., & Gopnik, A. (2001). Linguistic and cognitive abilities in infancy: When does language become a tool for categorization? *Cognition, 80*, B11–B20.

Neisser, U. (1987). From direct perception to conceptual structure. In U. Neisser (ed.), *Concepts and Conceptual Development* (pp. 11–24). London: Cambridge University Press.

Nelson, K. (1973). Some evidence for the cognitive primacy of categorisation and its functional basis. *Merrill-Palmer Quarterly, 19*, 21–39.

Newcombe, N., & Huttenlocher, J. (2000). *Making Space*. Cambridge, MA: MIT Press.

Oakes, L. M. (2010). Using habituation of looking time to assess mental processes in infancy. *Journal of Cognition and Development, 11*, 255–268.

Oakes, L. M., & Cohen, L. B. (1990). Infant perception of a causal event. *Cognitive Development, 5*, 193–207.

Oakes, L. M., Coppage, D. J., & Dingel, A. (1997). By land or by sea: The role of perceptual similarity in infants' categorization of animals. *Developmental Psychology, 33*, 396.

Oakes, L. M. & Madole, K. L. (2003). Principles of developmental change in infants' category formation. In D. H. Rakison, & L. M. Oakes (eds.), *Early Category and Concept Development: Making Sense of the Blooming, Buzzing Confusion* (pp. 159–192). New York: Oxford University Press.

Park, Y., & Casasola, M. (2015). Plain or decorated? Object visual features matter in infant spatial categorization. *Journal of Experimental Child Psychology, 140*, 105–119.

Piaget, J. (1952). *The Origins of Intelligence in Children*. New York: W. W. Norton & Co.

Premack, D. (1990). The infants' theory of self-propelled objects. *Cognition, 36*, 1–16.

Quinn, P. C. (1994). The categorization of above and below spatial relations by young infants. *Child Development, 65*, 58-69.

Quinn, P. C., Cummins, M., Kase, J., Martin, E., & Weissman, S. (1996). Development of categorical representations for above and below spatial relations in 3-to 7-month-old infants. *Developmental Psychology, 32*, 942–950.

Quinn, P. C., & Eimas, P. D. (1996). Perceptual organization and categorization. In C. Rovee-Collier, & L. Lipsitt (eds.), *Advances in Infancy Research* (Vol. 10, pp. 1–36). Norwood, NJ: Ablex Publishing.

Quinn, P. C., & Eimas, P. D. (1997). A reexamination of the perceptual-to-conceptual shift in mental representations. *Review of General Psychology, 1*, 171–187.

Quinn, P. C., & Eimas, P. D. (2000). The emergence of category representations during infancy: Are separate perceptual and conceptual processes required? *Journal of Cognition and Development, 1*, 55–61.

Quinn, P. C., Eimas, P. D., & Rosenkrantz, S. L. (1993). Evidence for representations of perceptually similar natural categories by 3-month-old and 4-month-old infants. *Perception, 22*, 463–475.

Quinn, P. C., Eimas, P. D., & Tarr, M. J. (2001). Perceptual categorization of cat and dog silhouettes by 3-to 4-month-old infants. *Journal of Experimental Child Psychology, 79*, 78–94.

Quinn, P. C., & Johnson, M. H. (2000). Global-before-basic object categorization in connectionist networks and 2-month-old infants. *Infancy, 1*, 31–46.

Quinn, P. C., Johnson, M. H., Mareschal, D., Rakison, D. H., & Younger, B. A. (2000).

Understanding early categorization: One process or two? *Infancy, 1,* 111–122.

Quinn, P. C., Norris, C. M., Pasko, R. N., Schmader, T. M., & Mash, C. (1999). Formation of a categorical representation for the spatial relation between by 6-to 7-month-old infants. *Visual Cognition, 6,* 569–585.

Rakison, D. H. (2003). Parts, categorization, and the animate-inanimate distinction in infancy. In D. H. Rakison, & L. M. Oakes (eds.), *Early Category and Concept Development: Making Sense of the Blooming Buzzing Confusion* (pp. 159–192). New York: Oxford University Press.

Rakison, D. H. (2005). A secret agent? How infants learn about the identity of objects in a causal scene. *Journal of Experimental Child Psychology, 91,* 271–296.

Rakison, D. H., & Benton, D. T. (2019). Second-order correlation learning of dynamic stimuli: Evidence from infants and computational modeling. *Infancy, 24,* 57–78.

Rakison, D. H., & Butterworth, G. E. (1998a). Infants' attention to object structure in early categorization. *Developmental Psychology, 34,* 1310–1325.

Rakison, D. H., & Butterworth, G. E. (1998b). Infants' use of object parts in early categorization. *Developmental Psychology, 34,* 49–62.

Rakison, D. H., & Cohen, L. B. (1999). Infants' use of functional parts in basic-like categorization. *Developmental Science, 2,* 423–432.

Rakison, D. H., & Hahn, E. (2004). The mechanisms of early categorization and induction: Smart or dumb infants? In R. Kail (ed.), *Advances in Child Development and Behavior* (Vol. 32, pp. 281–322). New York: Academic Press.

Rakison, D. H., & Lupyan, G. (2008). Developing object concepts in infancy: An associative learning perspective. *Monographs of the Society for Research in Child Development, 73,* 1–110.

Rakison, D. H., & Poulin-Dubois, D. (2001). Developmental origin of the animate-inanimate distinction. *Psychological Bulletin, 127,* 209–228.

Rakison, D. H., & Poulin-Dubois, D. (2002). You go this way and I'll go that way: Developmental changes in infants' attention to correlations among dynamic parts in motion events. *Child Development, 73,* 682–699.

Rakison, D. H., & Yermolayeva, Y. (2010). Infant categorization. *Wiley Interdisciplinary Reviews: Cognitive Science, 1,* 894–905.

Regier, T., & Carlson, L. A. (2001). Grounding spatial language in perception: An empirical and computational investigation. *Journal of Experimental Psychology: General, 130,* 273.

Rosch, E. (1975). Cognitive representations of semantic categories. *Journal of Experimental Psychology General, 104,* 192–233.

Rosch, E. (1976). Basic objects in natural categories. *Cognitive Psychology, 8,* 382–439.

Rosch, E. (1978). Principles of categorisation. In E. Rosch, & B. Lloyd (eds.), *Cognition and Categorisation* (pp. 27–48). Lawrence Erlbaum, NJ, Hillsdale.

Rosch, E., & Mervis, C. B. (1975). Family resemblances: Studies in the internal structure of categories. *Cognitive Psychology, 7,* 573–605.

Sapir, E. (1921). *An Introduction to the Study of Speech.* New York: Harcourt, Brace.

Smith, L. B., Colunga, E., & Yoshida, H. (2003). Making an ontology: Cross-linguistic evidence. In D. H. Rakison, & L. M. Oakes (eds.), *Early Category and Concept Development: Making Sense of the Blooming Buzzing Confusion* (pp. 275–302). New York: Oxford University Press.

Smith, L. B., & Heise, D. (1992). Perceptual similarity and conceptual structure. In B. Burns (ed.), *Percepts, Concepts, and Categories* (Vol. 93, pp. 233–272). Amsterdam: Elsevier.

Smith, L. B., Jones, S. S., & Landau, B. (1992). Count nouns, adjectives, and perceptual properties in children's novel word interpretations. *Developmental Psychology, 28,* 273–286.

Smith, L. B., Jones, S. S., & Landau, B. (1996). Naming in young children: A dumb attentional mechanism? *Cognition, 60,* 143–171.

Smith, L. B., & Samuelson, L. K. (2003). Different is good: Connectionism and dynamic systems theory are complementary emergentist approaches to development. *Developmental Science, 6,* 434–439.

Spelke, E. S., & Kinzler, K. D. (2007). Core knowledge. *Developmental Science, 10*, 89–96.

Spelke, E. S., & Kinzler, K. D. (2009). Innateness, learning, and rationality. *Child Development Perspectives, 3*, 96–98.

Spelke, E. S., Phillips, A., & Woodward, A. L. (1995). Infants' knowledge of object motion and human action. In D. Sperber, D. Premack, & A. J. Premack (eds.), *Causal Cognition* (pp. 150–184). Oxford: Clarendon.

Waxman, S., & Booth, A. (2003). The origins and evolution of links between word learning and conceptual organization: New evidence from 11-month-olds. *Developmental Science, 6*, 128–135.

Waxman, S. R., & Hall, D. G. (1993). The development of a linkage between count nouns and object categories: Evidence from fifteen-to twenty-one-month-old infants. *Child Development, 64*, 1224–1241.

Waxman, S. R., & Markow, D. B. (1995). Words as invitations to form categories: Evidence from 12-to 13-month-old infants. *Cognitive Psychology, 29*, 257–302.

Whorf, B. L. (1940). *Science and Linguistics* (pp. 207–219). Indianapolis, IN: Bobbs-Merrill.

Whorf, B. L. (1956). *Language, Thought, and Reality: Selected Writings of Benjamin Lee Whorf.* J. B. Carroll (Ed.). Cambridge, MA: Technology Press of MIT.

Wynn, K. (1992). Addition and subtraction by human infants. *Nature, 358*, 749–750.

Yermolayeva, Y., & Rakison, D. H. (2014). Connectionist modeling of developmental changes in infancy: Approaches, challenges, and contributions. *Psychological Bulletin, 140*, 224.

Yoshida, H., & Smith, L. B. (2003). Known and novel noun extensions: Attention at two levels of abstraction. *Child Development, 74*, 564–577.

Younger, B. A., & Cohen, L. B. (1986). Developmental change in infants' perception of correlations among attributes. *Child Development, 57*, 803–815.

10 Foundational Considerations

Does Primitive Number Sense Provide a Foothold for Learning Formal Mathematics?

Kristy vanMarle

Children with below average school entry mathematics knowledge are likely to remain behind their peers throughout schooling, and go on to face poor employment prospects and low wage-earning potential as adults. Previous research has identified key skills (number system knowledge) in the first-grade that predict math achievement ten years later. Recent studies have tried to identify early-emerging skills in infancy and during the preschool years that may provide a foundation upon which the formal skills they learn in school can be built. One candidate skill is the non-verbal ability to estimate and reason about numerosities that depends on an evolutionary ancient, and phylogenetically common, mechanism for representing quantities – the approximate number system (ANS). While there is evidence that ANS acuity (precision) predicts math achievement concurrently and prospectively, several studies have failed to find a link, or identified other quantitative skills (e.g., ordinal knowledge) or domain-general skills (e.g., intelligence, executive function, working memory) that are better predictors. Evidence for and against the claim that the ANS is a foundational skill that is critical for the development of formal mathematical knowledge is reviewed, followed by a synthesis of work by Geary and colleagues in which they examined the growth of many different domain-specific (quantitative) and domain-general skills longitudinally over four years. The findings suggest that the link between ANS acuity and math achievement is mediated by other skills,

especially cardinal knowledge. The ANS still remains a significant factor, however, because our findings also suggest that it plays an important role in the acquisition of cardinal knowledge, and the conceptual insight children appear to have when they first come to understand counting and the natural numbers.

In a world increasingly dependent upon technology and computing, having a strong knowledge of mathematics is more important than ever for social and economic success. Studies suggest that children's school entry (kindergarten) math skills are predictive of math achievement years later in adolescence (Duncan et al., 2007; Geary et al., 2013), which in turn affects future employability and wage-earning potential (Bynner, 1997; Parsons & Bynner, 1997; Ritchie & Bates, 2013; Rivera-Batiz, 1992). In a twelve-year longitudinal study by Rose and Betts (2004), both the number and the complexity of math courses taken during high school predicted wage earnings ten years after completing high school. Importantly, this study also showed that taking more, and more advanced, math courses helped diminish the gap in earnings between low-income and middle-income students (Rose & Betts, 2004).

But what if we can close the achievement gap earlier, for all students who struggle? Children who start school behind their peers in math tend to stay behind (Geary et al., 2013). Thus, a critical goal for developmental researchers is to determine whether there are earlier emerging number abilities that contribute to a child being ready (or not) to begin formal math learning in kindergarten. If we can determine which informal skills are most critical, we can then develop targeted interventions for at-risk children so that all children can start kindergarten with the informal number abilities they need to build upon as they begin to construct a formal number concept.

10.1 Informal "Number Sense"

Nearly four decades of research suggests that humans share with other animals a means for representing quantitative information (number, amount, duration, and so on) about behaviorally relevant objects and events in their environment. This "number sense" appears to be innately available (e.g., de Hevia et al., 2014; Izard et al., 2009) and does not depend on language. Instead, humans' early number sense derives primarily from two non-verbal mechanisms – an Approximate Number System (ANS) and the Object Tracking System (OTS) – that allow infants to represent and compute over quantities. These *non-verbal* number abilities may provide a foundation upon which young children begin to build their first *verbal* (symbolic) number representations.

Initially learning the verbal count list (i.e., "one," "two," "three," "four," ... "ten") around two years of age (at least for children from middle-class families), it can take children up to two more years before children fully understand the counting routine and how it can be used to determine the exact number of items (cardinality) in any set (Wynn, 1990, 1992). Initially, children move slowly and sequentially through the levels of "subset knower," mastering the exact meaning of each of the first few numbers in turn. Their understanding of the meaning of the number words is inferred from their performance on the GiveN task (Wynn, 1990, 1992), in which children are asked to give a puppet N toys from a pile. In the typical procedure, the puppet asks the child to give one-to-six items, starting with "one." If they give the correct number, the puppet then asks for N+1 on the next trial. If they make an error, they move down a set size (N−1) on the next trial. This "titration" continues until the child either gives the wrong number twice for a given set size (out of a maximum of three attempts), or when they correctly give six items on two trials. The highest set size they give correctly before they make two errors is considered their "knower-level." Wynn's (1990, 1992) original observations, as well as subsequent studies (Le Corre & Carey, 2007; Lee & Sarnecka, 2011), seem to suggest that development of cardinal understanding is truly stage-like. At first, around two and a half years of age, "one-knowers" can give exactly "one," but give a handful (or all the toys in the pile) for every larger number. About six months later, they become "two-knowers" and can give exactly "one" and "two" when asked, but no larger numbers. After about six more months, they become "three-knowers," and can give up to three items when asked. The next step, however, is different; when children can give exactly "four," they seem to suddenly appreciate the *cardinal principle* (CP), which states that the last number word in a count stands for the total number of items in the set (its cardinal value). At this point, the child is considered a "CP-knower." They seem to understand the counting procedure, and can use it to determine the cardinal value of any number in their count list. They also induce the *successor function*, realizing that moving one step forward in the count list means increasing the cardinality by adding one item to the set (Carey, 2009; Cheung et al., 2017; Le Corre & Carey, 2007). This last insight seems to emerge relatively late compared to cardinality, not occurring until children are about six years of age. Making this transition not only sets the stage for the acquisition of more complex formal math skills, but according to some researchers it also stands as a case of genuine conceptual change (e.g., Carey, 2011).

Despite empirical evidence suggesting that these early emerging abilities (especially number sense) are importantly linked to the acquisition of formal number knowledge, other findings suggest that domain-general abilities (e.g., intelligence, working memory, EF) likely also play a role (e.g., Blair & Razza, 2007; Bull et al., 2008; Bull & Scerif, 2001; Clark et al., 2010, and perhaps even a role more central than number sense (e.g., Gilmore et al., 2013; Huttenlocher et al., 1992). Importantly, early studies exploring the relationship between non-verbal abilities and math achievement often included measures for just one or two domain-general abilities, if any, raising the possibility that observed relationships between the ANS and math achievement could be mediated by one or more domain-general abilities.

Recent efforts have tried to disentangle just which abilities (domain-specific or domain-general) might be most important to the development of the number concept, but these studies are difficult to conduct. First, to properly study change (in number knowledge) over time, one really needs longitudinal data which is expensive and time consuming to collect. Second, "number knowledge" is a multi-faceted construct that encompasses a wide range of skills. Before a child acquires language, their number knowledge depends largely on their ANS, which supports estimation, ordinal comparisons (more and less relations), and non-verbal arithmetic. When children first begin to acquire numerical language (i.e., the count list) they gain a powerful new symbolic system that uses abstract symbols to represent quantities, but there is still a

great deal they must learn. Children must master the verbal count list, learn to recognize numerals and their relation to the verbal forms (i.e., that "2" and "two" are both pronounced /tōo/), and eventually come to understand the meaning of those symbols (cardinality). They must also learn procedural knowledge about the counting routine (i.e., the principles of counting, Gelman & Gallistel, 1978) and how counting can be used to determine the precise number of items in any set (cf. Gallistel & Gelman, 2000; Leslie et al., 2007, 2008). Thus, determining which early skills predict later math achievement means looking at a large number of candidate skills, which is challenging both practically and empirically.

An additional challenge is that on top of the host of domain-specific "quantitative" skills one needs to include to gain a comprehensive picture of which competencies matter most, one must also include measures of candidate domain-general abilities, including, for example, working memory, attention/executive function (EF), and intelligence (IQ). In other words, comprehensively assessing both domain-specific and domain-general skills in the same study can be difficult because there are so many tasks for subjects to complete. Moreover, collecting these data longitudinally means obtaining multiple assessments for each of these many tasks.

10.2 ANS Acuity and Math Achievement

Before their first birthday, infants depend on their analog number system (ANS) to estimate and compare the numerosity of large sets (>3; Lipton & Spelke, 2003; vanMarle, 2013; Xu & Spelke, 2000). A key property of the ANS is that it is limited by the precision of the underlying representations, which increases rapidly over the first year. Studies reveal that, at birth, two sets must differ at least three-fold (e.g., ten versus thirty) before an infant can reliably discriminate them (Coubart et al., 2014; Izard et al., 2009). By six months, infants can distinguish sets that differ two-fold (e.g., ten versus twenty) (Xu & Spelke, 2000). By nine months, precision has increased further, and infants can discriminate 1.5-fold differences (e.g., ten vs. fifteen) (Lipton & Spelke, 2003; Wood & Spelke, 2005). Precision continues to increase into adulthood, by which time most individuals can discriminate sets at roughly a nine-to-ten ratio (e.g., nine versus ten) (Halberda & Feigenson, 2008). By adulthood, the ANS is integrated with the verbal number system such that seeing the numeral "7" activates not only the visual representation of that numeral, but also the auditory representation of the word "seven," and the non-verbal ANS representation of seven as a magnitude (Dehaene et al., 2003; Gallistel & Gelman, 2000, 2005). Such integration across representations appears to begin once children understand cardinality (Geary et al., 2018).

Importantly, measurable and stable individual differences in the precision (acuity) of ANS representations are already evident in infancy. The first demonstration of this used a preferential looking change detection task to show that acuity at six months of age was correlated with acuity at nine months of age (Libertus & Brannon, 2010). Moreover, some studies reveal a correlation between early differences in ANS acuity and later math achievement both over the short-term and over relatively long periods of time. For example, in a landmark study in 2008, Halberda et al. (2008) demonstrated that ANS acuity at age fourteen was correlated retrospectively to math achievement scores as far back as kindergarten. For third grade math achievement, the correlation held even after accounting for individual differences in two domain-general skills (i.e., IQ and lexical access). Subsequent studies showed that in a sample of preschoolers, individual

differences in acuity were related to math achievement concurrently (Libertus et al., 2011), and also predicted math achievement six months later (Feigenson et al., 2013), controlling for age, expressive vocabulary, and time 1 math achievement. Even more impressive is the finding that ANS acuity at six months of age is correlated with math achievement at age three years (Starr et al., 2013). In older children, Gilmore et al. (2010) reported that an index of ANS acuity (non-verbal arithmetic) in kindergarten correlated with math achievement two months later, controlling for verbal IQ.

The importance of ANS acuity for math achievement is also evident when considering what factors contribute to non-normative development, as is the case with math learning disability (MLD or developmental dyscalculia). Children classified as MLD (e.g., by performing <10th percentile in math achievement for two consecutive academic years, see Geary, 2011; Shalev et al., 2005) struggle to learn numbers and arithmetic despite normal intelligence and learning in other domains (e.g., reading, writing; for reviews see Butterworth, 2010; Geary, 2011). Estimates suggest MLD affects about 7 percent of children and adolescents, with another 10 percent of children showing persistently low achievement specific to math learning. Processing of magnitudes is a core deficit in MLD (Geary, 2011), leading some researchers to suggest that MLD stems primarily from a poorly functioning ANS (e.g., Butterworth, 2005; De Smedt & Gilmore, 2011; Mazzocco et al., 2011; Piazza et al., 2010). Indeed, one study provides neuroimaging evidence that relative to typically achieving (TA) children, those with MLD showed poorer modulation of the right IPS (interparietal sulcus, believed to be the primary locus of the ANS, Dehaene et al., 2003; Edwards et al., 2016; Hyde, 2011) in response to numerical processing demands (Price et al.,

2007). For example, in a numerical discrimination task, harder discriminations (when the comparison sets are closer together, e.g., fifteen versus twenty) generally activate the IPS moreso than easier discriminations (when the sets are farther apart, e.g., ten versus twenty), while IPS activation generally increases with increasing difficulty. However, activation does not vary in accordance with the distance between comparison values for individuals with MLD.

But there is also evidence that other factors may contribute. For example, Rousselle and Noël (2007) suggest that MLD reflects a deficit in the ability to access the meaning of numerical symbols (retrieval), rather than a deficit in representing numerical magnitudes (encoding). Indeed, some studies suggest a role for working memory (Bull & Lee, 2014; Friso-van den Bos et al., 2013) and visuo-spatial skills (Cowan & Powell, 2014; Peng & Fuchs, 2016), as well as executive functioning, attention, and IQ (Espy et al., 2004; Shalev et al., 2005). Regardless, there is substantial evidence that above and beyond domain-general abilities, ANS acuity nonetheless remains correlated with MLD, at least in some studies.

Such findings as these suggest a potentially important link between early number sense (formalized as ANS acuity) and later emerging, formal number knowledge. However, several studies have also failed to find a relationship between ANS acuity and math achievement (Iuculano et al., 2008). For example, Lyons et al. (2014) examined seven different number skills, including mental arithmetic (their measure of math achievement), counting, dot estimation, numeral comparison, number line estimation, ordinal judgments for numerals, and numerosity match-to-sample, and found that none of them correlated with ANS acuity (dot comparison). Another study by Nosworthy et al. (2013) also failed to find evidence that ANS acuity is related to math

achievement. In a sample of children in grades one-to-three, while performance on both a symbolic comparison task (numeral comparison) and a non-symbolic comparison task (ANS acuity) was initially related to arithmetic competence, only symbolic comparison remained significant when reading ability and working memory were included in the analyses. A similar result was reported in kindergartners whose performance on a non-symbolic (ANS acuity) comparison task was unrelated to their performance on a symbolic numeral comparison task six months later (Sasanguie et al., 2014). Such findings have called into question just how robust the link is between ANS acuity and later math achievement, if it exists at all (cf. Libertus, 2019).

As can be seen in the above review, some studies include measures for domain-general abilities (e.g., IQ, verbal abilities), while others do not. Those that do often include measures for just one or two abilities, and the particular abilities chosen, can vary widely from study to study, even when the same underlying competency is being assessed. Further complicating matters, outcome measures, and predictor variables, including central constructs like math achievement and ANS acuity, are often assessed differently across different studies. For example, one study might operationalize "math achievement" as a score on a standardized, nationally-normed measure like the Test of Early Mathematics Achievement-3 (TEMA-3, Ginsburg & Baroody, 2003), while another uses one or more laboratory tasks, sometimes common (e.g., Give-a-number, Wynn, 1990; number line estimation, Siegler & Booth, 2004) and sometimes novel (e.g., verbal problem-solving, halving, and estimation, Soltész et al., 2010). This lack of consistency in measures and constructs raises concerns about how to interpret differing (or similar) findings across studies. Nonetheless, there are now many studies that explicitly test for domain-general abilities and their potential relationship with math achievement. Many of them find that abilities like working memory, attention, and IQ do predict math achievement, and moreover, that domain-general abilities may actually account for (i.e., statistically mediate) the often-assumed direct link between ANS acuity and math achievement.

10.3 Domain-General Abilities and Math Achievement

Although the ANS has been front and center for almost a decade as a leading candidate skill that may be the most critical for math learning, it is not the only focus of attention. Lyons and Beilock (2011), for example, examined whether an understanding of the *ordinal relations* between numerical symbols (i.e., accurately reporting whether a triad of Arabic numerals is in ascending order) predicts math achievement, irrespective of other abilities such as numeral recognition, numeral comparison, letter ordering, and working memory. While they did find that ANS acuity was related to math achievement, the relationship did not hold when symbolic ordinal relations were taken into account. However, the relationship between symbolic ordinal knowledge and math achievement remained significant, even when statistically accounting for all other covariates, including ANS acuity. The authors concluded that the ability to order numerical symbols, which may be distinct from ordering non-symbolic magnitudes (dot arrays) in the ANS, is ultimately what predicts math achievement (Lyons & Beilock, 2013). While this study did include several covariates, it had just one measure for domain-general abilities, that is, working memory. Importantly though, they did not focus on working memory as a predictor variable, just a covariate. The frequent use of domain-general measures as covariates, rather than predictor variables, is

(understandably) common among studies focusing on the relation between ANS and math achievement, but it leaves one wondering just what role they may play in the acquisition of formal math skills.

Several recent studies have been more systematic and comprehensive in their assessment of domain-general abilities (see Vanbinst & De Smedt, 2016 for review), and the data suggest that various abilities do contribute, above and beyond any influence of ANS acuity. Intelligence, for example, has long been known to predict academic performance (Walberg, 1984) and math ability, specifically (Deary et al., 2007; Geary, 2011), where it aids in the learning of novel symbolic information, which is critical for the learning of formal math. For instance, while the ability to discriminate non-symbolic quantities (e.g., number of dots, numbers of sounds) depends on dedicated, domain-specific systems, explicit processing of symbolic quantities (e.g., $4 + 7 = 11$) depends on domain-general neural systems that underlie abilities such as working memory and attentional networks (Geary, 2005; Geary & Moore, 2016). Likewise, because working memory underlies the ability to encode, maintain, and manipulate information, its integrity may be critical for the acquisition of a range of academic competencies, including numerical knowledge. Moreover, assuming Baddeley and Hitch's (1974, also Baddeley, 1996, 2002) model of working memory, the various subcomponents (phonological loop, visuospatial sketchpad, and the central executive) might influence the learning of formal math knowledge individually, or together. According to this model, the phonological loop allows auditory information to be maintained for a brief time with active rehearsal, and the visuospatial sketchpad maintains visual and/or spatial information in memory for a short time. These components are considered subordinate systems to the central executive, which is essentially working memory (i.e., updating) and regulates the two subcomponents, controlling the flow of information between what is currently in attentional focus and information represented in long-term memory (Baddeley & Hitch, 1974).

Several empirical findings link the integrity of these components to math achievement and the relationship is complicated. Geary et al. (2012b), for example, examined the role of the central executive, intelligence, and attention for math skill development and strategy choice when solving addition problems. Following children from first to fourth grade, they show that the contributions of these different domain-general abilities vary over time. At the beginning of first grade, central executive capacity predicted better fact retrieval and more sophisticated counting, above and beyond the role of working memory, intelligence, and attention. However, over time from first to fourth grade, the benefits of higher central executive capacity diminished (counting) or disappeared (fact retrieval), and central executive capacity instead predicted the early adoption of decomposition as an addition problem-solving strategy. Indeed, Geary et al.'s data suggest that intelligence, working memory, and attention also each independently contributed to the use of various addition strategies.

In another study, the phonological loop and the central executive have been implicated in arithmetic problem-solving (e.g., counting, mental arithmetic; Geary et al., 1991; Siegel & Ryan, 1989; Swanson & Sachse-Lee, 2001), and different domain-general abilities contribute to the development of different problem-solving strategies (Geary et al., 2012b). In addition, children with low academic achievement show particular deficits in central executive and visuo-spatial skills (Gathercole & Pickering, 2000). In a recent longitudinal study, working memory in grades one and two predicted math

achievement four months later, and one year later. However, the central executive uniquely predicted later performance at both time points, while the visuo-spatial sketchpad predicted performance after a few months, but not up to a year in advance (De Smedt et al., 2009).

Apart from working memory, researchers have explored other domain-general abilities. For instance, inhibitory control appears to be a factor that might be important for math learning. It has been implicated in the arithmetic fact retrieval deficits of children with MLD (De Visscher & Noël, 2014; Geary, 1993; Geary et al., 2012b). Consistent with that finding, when compared to ANS acuity, inhibitory control was not only related to math ability, but in at least one study, fully mediated the observed relationship between ANS acuity and math ability (Fuhs & McNeil, 2013). Looking over longer periods of development, Geary et al. (2017) recently showed that the relative importance of domain-general influence and domain-specific knowledge on math achievement varies depending on age. Over an eight-year span (first- to eighth-grade), domain-general skills were linked to math achievement throughout schooling, with working memory becoming more important with age. In contrast, although math-specific abilities were less important than domain-general abilities in the early grades, their importance increased over time until they were equally predictive of math achievement in the later grades.

Gilmore et al. (2013) have approached the issue of domain-specific versus domain-general skills by asking *why* the ANS measure is related to math ability. While the going assumption is that it is the fidelity (i.e., acuity) of the ANS representations that contributes to math achievement, there are other aspects of the typical ANS measure that might be driving the relationship and need to be examined.

Specifically, following Halberda and Feigenson (2008), many studies utilize a 2AFC dot discrimination task to measure ANS acuity. In this task, subjects view two dot arrays, side-by-side, and quickly judge (without counting) which array "has more dots." To control for non-numerical properties of the displays (e.g., surface area, density, item size), controls are often implemented within the procedure to ensure that behavior is based on number, per se. For example, in a common version of the procedure, half of the trials will be "congruent," while the other half are "incongruent." Congruent trials contain dots whose size is correlated with number – thus, the more numerous array also has greater dot density, surface area, and so on. Incongruent trials reverse that relationship so that the more numerous arrays have relatively less area, are less dense, etc., making it so that number and continuous extent are in conflict (i.e., anti-correlated).

Gilmore et al. (2013) exploited this procedural distinction to test the notion that inhibitory control plays a significant role in math achievement. Although overall, they found performance on the ANS measure was related to math achievement, when separated by trial type, it appeared the relationship was being driven primarily by performance on incongruent trials, when subjects had to inhibit the information about continuous extent in order to choose on the basis of number. In a follow-up experiment, an independent measure of inhibition was found to be related to math achievement and, when included as a covariate, it fully accounted for the link between ANS acuity and achievement (Gilmore et al., 2013). Together these findings suggest that inhibitory control may contribute to individual differences in math achievement, and may even explain variance previously thought attributable to ANS acuity.

Fuchs et al. (2010) also examined closely whether domain-specific and domain-general

skills and abilities might both be related to math achievement, but through distinct pathways. Two types of basic numerical information were tested: (1) speed and accuracy at manipulating small, exact numerosities (assessed by the number sets test; Geary et al., 2009) and (2) accuracy at placing numerals on a number line (assessed by the number line estimation task; Siegler & Booth, 2004). In addition, Fuchs et al. (2010) included eight different domain-general abilities/skills, to determine which individual skills, or constellations of skills, best predicted performance on their two outcome measures – procedural calculations (PC) and word problems (WP). With all eight domain-general abilities controlled, both basic number abilities (number sets and number line estimation) remained uniquely related to PC and WP. However, for PC virtually none of the eight domain-general skills contributed to performance, although some were uniquely related to WP (i.e., attention, language, central executive, and non-verbal problem-solving).

To summarize, although early investigations exploring what factors best predict math achievement in the classroom tended to focus primarily on one or two candidate skills, later investigations have been more comprehensive not just by including more candidate quantitative skills, but also by including domain-general skills (e.g., working memory, IQ, inhibitory control). This rather large body of data, only a sampling of which is discussed here, seems to suggest an important role for both domain-specific and domain-general abilities in the developmental of informal and formal mathematics skills.

In Section 10.4, I will describe a series of studies conducted by David Geary, Felicia Chu, and myself using a large ($n = \sim 200$) longitudinal dataset to determine the preschool quantitative skills that may be most central for predicting math achievement at school entry (first grade). In designing the study, we aimed to be as comprehensive as possible with regards to the domain-specific and domain-general skills under consideration. In all, we assessed performance on twelve different quantitative skills, including measures of both informal non-symbolic skills (e.g., ANS acuity, non-verbal arithmetic), as well as formal, symbolic skills (e.g., cardinality, numeral recognition). In addition, the longitudinal nature of our dataset allowed us to address questions of development and to glimpse potentially causal relationships between various preschool skills and later math achievement. Although the findings discussed here have been previously published, here the goal is to summarize and synthesize them in order to gain a broader perspective that can shed light on the development of quantitative knowledge and how it relates to the subsequent achievement in the domain of mathematics.

10.4 The Preschool Math Study: Predicting School Entry Math Achievement

As is clear from the discussion so far, an important goal for developmental psychologists is to determine what cognitive factors contribute to the acquisition and/or expression of early emerging number knowledge, and how this early informal knowledge may provide a critical foundation that essentially determines whether or not a child is ready to begin formal math education upon school entry. Understanding the developmental pathway from the use of primitive, intuitive ways of representing and operating over number (e.g., the ANS) to the use of the verbal counting system (e.g., the exact number system, or ENS, Libertus, 2015) and the development of more formalized number knowledge is interesting both theoretically and practically. From a philosophical standpoint, the transition from

primitive to formal knowledge of number can potentially inform our theories of conceptual change (e.g., Carey, 2004). From a practical standpoint, describing this developmental process can help us design assessments to identify at-risk children well before they enter school. Likewise, determining which early skills are especially critical for the acquisition of later, more complex concepts provides insights that can help us develop targeted interventions that aim to close the gap between at-risk and typically developing children before they start school.

10.4.1 General Methodology and Sample Characteristics

To that end, we followed a sample of almost 200 Title 1-program preschoolers through two years of preschool, kindergarten, and first grade. One limitation of previous research is that many studies were relatively narrow in their approach, often focusing on just one or two predictor variables (usually as a contrast), and similarly including, at most, one or two covariates. As previous research suggests, domain-general abilities appear to contribute in multiple ways to the development of math knowledge. However, even when they are included as part of the design, it is often as a control variable, rather than a potential explanatory variable. Of course, many studies have examined domain general abilities and their relationship to academic achievement overall (e.g., reading ability, Peng & Fuchs, 2016), as well as to math achievement in particular (e.g., Deary et al., 2007; Vanbinst & De Smedt, 2016), but they often have the same basic limitation. When domain-general abilities are the focus of the study, few other predictor variables, if any, are included (see Fuhs & McNeil, 2013). In our study we tried to be as broad as possible by including twelve different measures of quantitative knowledge, covering both informal and formal skills, as well as measures of IQ (Wechsler, 2001, 2002), preliteracy, EF, and math achievement (using a standardized assessment tool, TEMA-3). Through parental report, we also obtained demographic data on our sample that we included in our analyses (i.e., age, gender, race/ethnicity, and parental education). Thus, we were able to investigate the predictive power of a host of different factors for a variety of different outcome variables.

Previous studies were also often limited in power due to small sample size, and in terms of the representativeness of their sample. Thus, we attempted to obtain a large sample and worked hard to minimize attrition over the four years by offering incentives and using a mobile testing van to conduct testing sessions when a participant had moved. In addition, we drew our sample from the Title 1 preschool program managed through the local public school system. Title 1 is a federally-funded program for children at risk of academic failure and includes free preschool for two years prior to school entry. Besides offering free preschool to qualified children, many of whom are economically disadvantaged, the program is designed to assess, identify, and remediate potential developmental delays in cognitive abilities (e.g., reading/preliteracy, numbers/prenumeracy, problem-solving), social skills (e.g., communication, decision-making), and motor development (e.g., gross/fine motor aptitude, personal hygiene). Given that low-income children are at higher risk for poor achievement in multiple domains, utilizing a Title 1 sample increases the generalizability of our results since our sample is likely to be demographically similar to our population of interest (children at risk for poor math achievement).

All entering Title 1 preschoolers in the local public-school system were invited to participate in our study. Consent was obtained for 232 children. After excluding fourteen children for low IQ (IQ < 70), and twenty-one children for failing to complete the majority of the measures (e.g., from moving out of state), we had a final sample of 198 children (94 males). The final sample was of average intelligence ($M = 97$, SD = 15) and scored average on a standardized math achievement test ($M = 95$, SD = 14) at the end of preschool. Demographically, self-reported ethnic composition was 85 percent non-Hispanic, 10 percent Hispanic/Latino, with 5 percent unknown. Self-reported racial composition was 55 percent White, 24 percent Black, 8 percent Asian, and 13 percent one or more races. Fifty-eight percent of the sample earned less than $50k annually, with 38 percent earning less than $25k. Forty-two percent of participants reported receiving food assistance (e.g., food stamps), while 9 percent reported receiving housing assistance. Finally, 45 percent of the children had at least one parent with a high-school diploma and 35 percent had at least one parent with a college degree.

Understanding how children's number knowledge changes over time requires longitudinal data. Many of the previous studies demonstrating a link between ANS acuity and math achievement have done so using concurrent data (e.g., Halberda & Feigenson, 2008) and those using longitudinal designs have often covered a relatively short span of time (e.g., Gilmore et al., 2010). Our study spanned four years, through two years of preschool, kindergarten, and first grade. In Years one (Y1) and two (Y2), children completed our preschool quantitative battery (twelve tasks) twice each year. In addition, they completed our preschool cognitive battery (domain-general) in early spring of Y1 (IQ, EF, preliteracy) and Y2 (EF), and a standardized math achievement test late in the spring of each year of preschool. In kindergarten, children completed a primary quantitative battery (a subset

Table 10.1. *Sequence of tasks and approximate mean ages and ranges over four years*

Sequence of Tasks	Age of Children (years; months)
Year 1 Preschool	
Quantitative Session 1 (Fall)	Mean: 3; 10 Range: 3; 2–4; 4
Enumeration	
GiveN	
Point-to-x	
Magic box (OTS)	
Discrete quantity discrimination (ANS)	
Ordinal choice	
Quantitative Session 2 (Fall)	Mean: 3; 11 Range: 3; 2–4; 4
Verbal counting	
Non-verbal calculation	
Numeral recognition	
Numeral comparison	
Counting knowledge	
Continuous quantity discrimination	
Cognitive battery	Mean: 4; 1 Range: 3; 5–4; 8
Executive functions (Conflict EF scale)	
WPPSI-III (Receptive Vocabulary, Block Design, and Information)	
Letter recognition (PALS)	
Quantitative Session 1 (Spring)	Mean: 4; 2 Range: 3; 6–4; 9
Quantitative Session 2 (Spring)	Mean: 4; 3 Range: 3; 7–4; 10
Math achievement (Spring)	Mean: 4; 4 Range: 3; 8–4; 9
Test of Early Math Achievement (TEMA-3)	
Year 2 Preschool	
Quantitative Session 1 (Fall)	Mean: 4; 9 Range: 4; 1–5; 4
Cognitive battery	Mean: 5; 0 Range: 4; 4–5; 6
Executive functions	
Quantitative Session 2 (Fall)	Mean: 5; 2 Range: 4; 6–5; 8
Math achievement (Spring)	Mean: 5; 4 Range: 4; 10–5; 11
TEMA-3	
Kindergarten (Fall)	
Quantitative tasks	Mean: 5; 9 Range: 5; 1–6; 4

Table 10.1. (*cont.*)

Sequence of Tasks	Age of Children (years; months)
Verbal counting	Mean: 3; 10
	Range: 3; 2–4; 4
Discrete quantity discrimination (ANS)	
Number line estimation (NLE)	
Number sets (fluency)	
Continuous quantity discrimination	
Intelligence and academic achievement	Mean: 6; 2
	Range: 5; 6–6; 9
WIAT-II: Numerical Operatoins and Word Reading subtests	
Progressive Matricies	
First Grade (fall)	
Quantitative tasks	Mean: 6; 9
	Range: 6; 2–7; 2
Addition strategy	

of tasks from the preschool battery, plus two new, age appropriate, tasks (number line estimation and number sets). In first grade, children completed the primary quantitative battery, plus a new addition-strategy task. Table 10.1 shows a timeline of all the tasks administered, and mean ages at time of assessment (Chu et al., 2018; Geary et al., 2018).

We attempted to explore a wide range of candidate skills in preschool to determine empirically which were related to later math achievement and which were not. Obtaining multiple assessments (four time points during preschool, plus kindergarten and first grade assessments), allowed us to examine developmental change over time in foundational skills, as well as their changing relationships with math achievement over time. We included measures for domain-general skills (IQ, EF, preliteracy) that previous findings suggest may be important for learning math (and learning in general). Finally, we also collected demographic data, including parental education and correlates of socioeconomic status (SES), given that these factors can reasonably

be expected to influence school readiness and academic achievement. It should be noted that, in the following paragraphs, the various studies to be described will vary in their temporal scope (the number of years they cover) and in their sample size. We recruited children into our study in three cohorts (once each fall for three years). Thus, at the end of Y1, we had collected data from only about a third of our final sample. At the end of Y2, we had collected first year data from about two-thirds of our sample, but had two years' data for only the first cohort, and so on. Published research findings always encompassed the maximum number of subjects with complete data available up to that time point.

10.4.2 The ANS and Math Achievement

With the first published findings from our dataset we sought to establish, as previous studies have done, a link between ANS acuity and math ability (Chu et al., 2013). Using Y1 data from the first cohort ($n = 68$), we initially identified children in the sample who, based on their end of Y1 math achievement score, may be considered at high risk for poor math achievement and MLD. Using a natural break in the distribution of math achievement scores (between the twenty-second and twenty-seventh percentile), we labeled children ($n = 34$) below the twenty-second percentile to be "at-risk" for MLD. Compared to their TA peers ($n = 34$), the MLD at-risk group scored significantly lower on measures of intelligence, executive functions (EF), and preliteracy scores. However, even with those measures included as covariates, the MLD group still performed significantly lower than TA children in math achievement (Chu et al., 2013).

Critically, ANS acuity at the start of preschool was related to math achievement at the end of Y1, above and beyond the contribution of domain-general skills, thus replicating previous findings (e.g., Feigenson et al., 2013; Libertus et al., 2011). However, other quantitative skills proved important as well. Compared to the TA group, the MLD group showed smaller gains from the beginning to the end of Y1 for recognition of Arabic numerals, knowledge of number words, and cardinality, and showed deficits in understanding ordinal relations. Importantly, while being one standard deviation below the mean on the ANS task was associated with a 2.4-fold increase in being in the MLD group, the same deficit on the numeral, number words, cardinal, and ordinal tasks was associated with a 3.6–4.5-fold increase in the odds of MLD status (Chu et al., 2013). We concluded that these data offer some limited support for there being a genuine relationship between ANS and math ability, but that other quantitative skills also play an important role. Interestingly, domain-general factors showed little predictive power, with preliteracy being the only factor to reach significance; neither intelligence nor executive functions influenced the odds of MLD status.

10.4.3 Explaining the Link between ANS Acuity and Math Achievement

To follow up those initial findings, vanMarle et al. (2014) examined ANS acuity and its relationship to math achievement with a larger sample size ($n = 138$). As in Chu et al. (2013), here we again demonstrated that ANS acuity was related to math achievement at the beginning and end of Y1 of preschool, above and beyond the influence of age, sex, parental education, intelligence, executive functions, and preliteracy. We then conducted mediation analyses to further examine this link, as well as to explore any potential relationships between ANS acuity and the development of symbolic number skills (numeral recognition, numeral comparison, cardinality, and verbal counting) found by Chu et al. (2013) to be associated with math achievement. ANS accuracy was significantly associated with all four symbolic number skills. In turn, of those four skills, three (verbal counting, cardinality, and numeral recognition) were significant predictors of math achievement, and the only significant covariate was intelligence.

Importantly, mediation analyses revealed that the direct relation between ANS acuity and math achievement was no longer significant. The indirect effect between ANS and math achievement remained significant overall, as well as through verbal counting, cardinality, and numeral recognition. Cardinality accounted for 40 percent of the indirect effect, with the remainder accounted for by the other mediators. Thus, the apparent link between ANS acuity and math achievement is more complex than expected, and it may be mediated by other quantitative skills, especially cardinality.

Having empirically established that cardinality may be an important mediator, Chu et al. (2015) pitted ANS accuracy and cardinality against each other as predictors of math achievement. Now with Y1 data for all three cohorts, we had a larger sample size ($n = 191$) and more power to detect any differences. In independent regression analyses, both ANS accuracy and cardinality at the start of pre-school were significant predictors of math achievement at the end of Y1, with and without the inclusion of covariates (intelligence, preliteracy, executive function). However, when ANS and cardinality were entered simultaneously with the covariates, cardinality remained significant, but ANS acuity did not. Two mediation analyses confirmed these findings. In the first, the relationship between cardinality and math achievement remained significant, even when ANS acuity was included. In the second, however, the relationship between ANS acuity and math achievement was no longer significant once cardinality was included. Together, these findings not only provide evidence against a direct relation between ANS acuity and math achievement, but they also suggest a potentially critical role for cardinal knowledge.

10.4.4 What Drives Acquisition of Cardinal Knowledge?

It may not surprise some readers that cardinality emerged as an important predictor of math achievement in our sample. After all, acquiring cardinal knowledge is the first step children take as they begin to create a symbolic understanding of number (Carey, 2004; LeCorre & Carey, 2007). So, what drives the acquisition of cardinal knowledge? Because our data included assessments of many different quantitative skills, at multiple time points, we were able to address empirically a question that has been intensely debated for over four decades – how children come to understand numbers and counting?

As early as the 1970's, developmental psychologists like Rochel Gelman were challenging Piaget's (1952) constructivist view that children build a number concept slowly over several years, passing through a series of sequential stages in which their number knowledge undergoes qualitative change as they achieve key insights (e.g., conservation, abstraction, seriation, and classification), and eventually transition into a more advanced stage of number knowledge. In their seminal book *The Child's Understanding of Number*, Gelman and Gallistel (1978) lay out their alternative, nativist theory about how children come to reckon the number system. According to Gelman and colleagues (e.g., Gallistel & Gelman, 1992, 2000; Gelman, 1972, 1993; Gelman & Gallistel, 1978; Gelman & Greeno, 1989; Gelman & Meck, 1983; Leslie et al., 2007, 2008), the principles that determine the counting procedure (i.e., the "counting principles," Gelman & Gallistel, 1978) are embodied within representational mechanisms that are innately available, and that help not only to guide the child's attention to number and counting in their environment, but also to guide the child's own attempts to count as they learn to implement the procedure (Gelman & Meck, 1983).

Others have debated whether another specialized mechanism might be the source of the cardinal meanings of the number words (Briars & Siegler, 1984). As argued by Susan Carey (2004), the protracted and stage-like developmental progression of cardinal knowledge is inconsistent with the notion that children map number words directly onto underlying ANS representations. If they did, why does it take so long (two or more years) for children to achieve CP-knower status? After all, if the counting principles are built into the mechanism, the child might be able to grasp and realize them instead of having to construct them from the bottom up. Another troubling inconsistency for the ANS story is the performance break between small and large numbers. The first three numbers are learned slowly, one by one, and then suddenly when children learn "four," they seem to understand counting more deeply, and can use it to determine cardinality of any set (within the limits of their verbal count list).

But why is the break at "four"? The ANS does not predict any discontinuities. On the ANS, all values from the smallest to the largest are represented in the same way (Gallistel & Gelman, 2000, 2005). Carey (2004) suggests that, instead of the ANS, the object tracking system (OTS) provides the representations that become linked with the first few number words. Well-studied in adults (Kahneman et al., 1992; Pylyshyn & Storm, 1988; Scholl, 2001), the OTS is a capacity-limited, mid-level mechanism of visual attention comprised of a set of indexes, or pointers. The pointers can be assigned to visual objects and each pointer sticks to its object as it moves around the world, allowing the object to be tracked over time. Importantly, the system is capacity limited; it can track only as many objects as it has indexes, which in adults is about four (Pylyshyn & Storm, 1988; Scholl, 2001). The same mechanism has been studied in infants, and, like adults, they can track multiple objects simultaneously, but only up to a limit of three items (Feigenson & Carey, 2003; Feigenson et al., 2002; vanMarle, 2013). For Carey (2004), this system is a plausible mechanism because it creates episodic set representations that can be stored in long-term memory, and associated to the corresponding number words. The associations might form relatively slowly as word-set pairings may not be frequent in the linguistic input (Eason & Levine, 2017; Klibanoff et al., 2006; Ramani et al., 2015), explaining the protracted time course for learning the first few words. Likewise, the discontinuity at "four" is explained because the OTS can only index up to "three" items at a time.

Despite the fact that the OTS can account for certain aspects of the observed developmental progression in ways that the ANS cannot, there is nonetheless relatively little direct empirical evidence to suggest the OTS plays much of a role in the development of formal math skills more generally. It does not seem to be impaired in children with MLD, and there are no published findings (that I am aware of) that demonstrate discontinuities between small and large numbers in tasks involving symbolic number comparison, naming, or arithmetic (Piazza et al., 2010). Indirect evidence is reported by Le Corre and Carey (2007), who show that, when quickly estimating the number of dots in an array, only CP-knowers, and not subset-knowers, exhibited approximate knowledge for sets above four (i.e., their estimates scaled with number of dots and were more variable for larger than smaller numbers). This suggests that children begin to map the large number words onto ANS representations only after they transition to CP-knower status. On this account, the OTS is critical for learning the first three or four number words and also plays some role as children come to appreciate the cardinal principle and successor function when they become CP-knowers. However, its role diminishes once children understand counting and can begin to fix the meanings of the larger number words.

Despite this suggestive evidence, Gunderson et al. (2015) report contradictory results, showing that before having grasped the cardinal principle, subset-knowers can approximate sets for number words beyond their knower-level. Given the inconsistent findings and the relative dearth of direct investigation comparing what roles the ANS and OTS play in the acquisition of cardinal knowledge, and because our quantitative battery included a task measuring the OTS (non-verbal arithmetic, tracking additions and subtractions from small hidden sets), we were able to examine longitudinally (n = 198) whether there are links between ANS and cardinal knowledge, or OTS and cardinal knowledge, at the beginning (T1) and end (T2) of their first year of preschool (vanMarle et al., 2018).

We found that both the ANS and OTS were significant predictors of cardinal knowledge at T1, above and beyond the influence of sex, race/ethnicity, age, parental education, executive function, IQ, and preliteracy. However, by T2, only the ANS remained significant, suggesting the OTS may play some role in cardinal number acquisition, but only at the initial stages of the process. In contrast, ANS acuity was related to cardinal knowledge throughout the first year of preschool, suggesting perhaps a more central role in the process. Consistent with this interpretation, vanMarle et al. (2018) also showed that the critical transition from subset-knower at T1 to CP-knower at T2 was predicted by T1 ANS acuity, and not T1 OTS accuracy. Thus, this important milestone may depend more on the integrity of the ANS than the OTS, contrary to what some have suggested (Carey, 2004; Le Corre & Carey, 2007). It is of interest to note that some of the domain-general skills included in the analyses were related to cardinal knowledge. Specifically, at T1, in addition to ANS and OTS, we also found significant effects for age, IQ, and preliteracy. At T2, age and preliteracy both remained significant. Thus, although specialized mechanisms (ANS and OTS) are critical for the initial and subsequent (ANS) development of cardinal knowledge, domain-general processes also appear to play a role.

10.4.5 Beyond Preschool: How Early Quantitative Skills Promote School Readiness

Thus far, our data suggest that while both domain-general and domain-specific processes influence math achievement, the role for cardinal knowledge may be particularly important. Early-emerging, non-verbal abilities that depend on the ANS and the OTS (at least to some extent), appear to influence the acquisition of cardinal knowledge and, critically, the ANS specifically seems to predict the transition to CP-knower over one year of preschool. But how do these early abilities (cardinal knowledge, and CP-knower status) relate to math achievement at school entry?

Building on our earlier findings, Geary and vanMarle (2016) examined what beginning of preschool skills (Mean age = forty-six months) predict math achievement at the end of two years preschool (Mean age = sixty-four months). With a sample of 197 children, we used Bayesian and traditional frequentist regression methods to determine statistically which core non-symbolic and symbolic competencies best predicted math achievement just prior to entering kindergarten. Despite being correlated with math achievement, T1 ANS acuity was no longer significant once other non-symbolic skills and/or domain-general factors, were included. Likewise for all the other non-symbolic skills measured, including continuous quantity (i.e., area) discrimination, ordinal choice (relative quantity, judging which of two cups had more toys hidden in it), and non-verbal calculation, which were the strongest of the non-symbolic predictors (though not significant). For symbolic number skills, the most predictive measures were T1 cardinal knowledge, verbal counting, and numeral recognition.

Domain-general skills also proved important, with T1 non-verbal IQ and preliteracy being significant predictors of later math achievement, while executive function and verbal IQ were not significant. In the best Bayesian model, we found that non-verbal IQ, preliteracy, cardinality, verbal counting, and numeral recognition were most important for predicting later math achievement (Geary

& vanMarle, 2016). Importantly, this study also demonstrated that, contrary to previous claims (Carey, 2004; Le Corre & Carey, 2007; Wynn, 1992), children did perform well on math achievement tests at age five years, even if they were not CP-knowers at ages three or four, so long as they had begun to fix the meaning of at least the first few number words. Compared to children who were CP-knowers at T1, one-knowers and two-knowers (20 percent and 27 percent of our sample, respectively) scored about 0.5 SDs lower on their math achievement assessment just a few short months before entering kindergarten.

Taking a longer view, Chu et al. (2016) examined the beginning of preschool abilities ($n = 100$) and identified four core quantitative competencies that best predicted math achievement at the end of kindergarten. Next, we explored whether and how the domain-general abilities of IQ, executive functions, and preliteracy were related to growth in these core quantitative skills over two years of preschool. We finally compared our identified domain-specific competencies and domain-general abilities to determine how they each contribute to preschool math achievement (two years later) and kindergarten math and reading competency (three years later).

For domain-general abilities, both intelligence and executive functions predicted growth in the four quantitative skills, especially in the first year of preschool. End of preschool math achievement was best predicted by a combination of domain-general and domain-specific skills, with the domain-specific skills seemingly more related to achievement at the beginning of preschool, than at the end. Math achievement at the end of kindergarten was best predicted by preliteracy skills, cardinal knowledge, and ordinal choice. Such findings suggest that school entry math achievement, an important predictor of later math achievement (Cowan et al., 2011;

Geary, 2011; Geary et al., 2009, 2013), as well as earning potential and employability (e.g., Parsons & Bynner, 1997), depends on a few core number abilities (especially cardinal knowledge) and on domain-general abilities including intelligence and executive function. These findings also suggest a potential reason why domain-general abilities may matter. In our dataset, they seem to help children acquire critical quantitative skills, particularly those that are evolutionarily novel, which includes most of symbolic mathematics (Geary, 2005; Geary & Moore, 2016), and begins with children learning the meanings of the number words (i.e., cardinality).

Previous research suggests that the fluency with which children process symbolic magnitudes (Arabic numerals, collections of objects, and combinations of objects and numerals) predicts their current and future math achievement years later (Geary, 2011; Geary et al., 2009, 2013). Fluency is measured by the number sets task, illustrated in Figure 10.1, where children must quickly circle all the domino-style pairs (or triples) of non-symbolic (i.e., dot arrays) and symbolic (i.e., Arabic numerals) magnitudes that sum to match a target numeral (Geary et al., 2007, 2009). Geary et al. (2009) used first-grade performance on this test to accurately categorize two of three children diagnosed with MLD several years later, and nine of ten children who did not present MLD over that same period.

Because we assessed fluency using the number sets test in kindergarten, we were able to use the beginning of preschool performance on quantitative tasks, as well as domain-general tasks, to explore what early abilities predict fluency on the number sets test at school entry. In doing so, we were making a theoretical link between kindergarten/first-grade predictors of math achievement in adolescence, and preschool predictors of math achievement in kindergarten. Using a sample

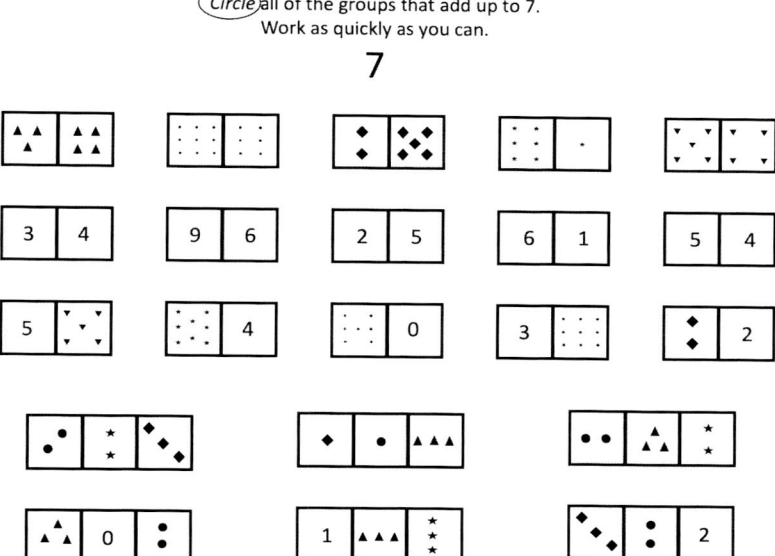

Figure 10.1 Example items from the number sets task. The number sets task (Geary et al., 2009) assesses the fluency with which children can access and manipulate symbolic and non-symbolic magnitudes. Children are given a sheet with multiple domino-style pairs (or triples) depicting non-symbolic (dot arrays) and symbolic (Arabic numerals) magnitudes, and asked to quickly circle every pair (triple) that sums to a target number (e.g., "5"). First-grade performance on this task predicts math learning disability (or its absence) several years later, and does so better than a standard math achievement test. Reprinted from Moore et al. (2016)

of 112 children, Moore et al. (2016) examined the beginning of preschool quantitative predictors (numeral recognition and comparison, ANS acuity, counting knowledge, cardinality, implicit arithmetic) of number sets (fluency) performance two years later in kindergarten. Controlling for the usual domain-general and demographic factors, two skills rose to the top – cardinal knowledge and non-verbal arithmetic – providing further evidence that fixing the meanings of the number words is a critical step that in turn allows the child to build fluent mappings between magnitudes and their corresponding auditory (i.e., number words) and visual (i.e., Arabic numerals) representations.

Extending these findings to first grade, we next asked whether another important outcome variable, i.e., the sophistication of problem-solving strategies, was predicted by any beginning of preschool quantitative skills. Previous findings suggest a link between strategy sophistication and later academic achievement (Siegler, 1988), particularly in the domain of mathematics (Geary et al., 2017). In our study, Chu et al. (2018) showed that, controlling for other factors, cardinal knowledge at the beginning of preschool again emerged as the strongest predictor variable from among a host of other symbolic and non-symbolic quantitative predictors. Thus, an early understanding of the meanings of the number words predicted the sophistication of children's addition strategies three years later above and beyond domain-general factors. The relationship between early cardinal knowledge and later sophistication of strategy choice was mediated by kindergarten symbolic (e.g., numeral comparison) and non-symbolic (e.g., ANS acuity) quantitative knowledge (Chu et al., 2018). This is consistent with the notion that individual differences in the ability to form memories for relational information (e.g., the associative relations among numbers, arithmetic problems, and their answers) may be key to later success in math, and also suggests that an early understanding of cardinal knowledge may be an integral step in the development of relational knowledge among the numerals (Geary & vanMarle, 2018).

10.5 Why Cardinal Knowledge Is the Most Important Early Emerging Number Skill

Thus far, I have discussed a series of findings from a relatively large longitudinal dataset which collectively point to cardinal knowledge being the most critical preschool skill for forecasting math competency at school entry and into first grade. Efforts to enhance this skill, or intervene with children who are delayed in developing cardinal knowledge, would benefit greatly from an understanding of *why* cardinal knowledge is so foundational. Because children typically acquire cardinal knowledge before entering school, and do so without explicit instruction beyond the natural instances of counting they witness or enact, it is important to identify the mechanisms through which this critical knowledge is acquired (vanMarle et al., 2014) and how it relates to the acquisition and growth of other skills (e.g., ordinality and relational knowledge, numeral recognition and comparison,

fluency in processing symbolic and non-symbolic magnitudes).

As described in Sections 10.4.2–10.4.4, having a solid grasp on the numerical relations (number system knowledge) in kindergarten mediated the link between beginning of preschool cardinal knowledge and strategy sophistication in first grade (Chu et al., 2018). To get at what might predict kindergarten (school entry) number system knowledge, Geary et al. (2018) focused on the transition from subset-knower to CP-knower. With a sample of 197 children, we found that, more than any other factor included in the model (quantitative, domain-general, demographic), the timing of becoming a CP-knower was the strongest predictor of first grade number system knowledge. And, importantly, the earlier a child transitioned to CP-status the better – rather than the shift itself being the critical element, the age of acquisition is what was central to later math achievement and school readiness.

This may not be surprising; it stands to reason that, if becoming a CP-knower helps children begin making associations between number words and their magnitudes, which in turn forms the basis for their number system knowledge, then a head start will give the child an advantage by school entry. This suspected advantage is not merely speculative. As reported in Geary and vanMarle (2018), children's symbolic knowledge grew faster after they transitioned to CP-knower. Prior to that, non-symbolic ordinal comparisons were more accurate than symbolic ordinal comparisons, but, after the transition, the reverse was true. Importantly, this pattern (greater growth of symbolic number knowledge after achieving CP-status) was independent of age, suggesting that simply understanding the cardinal values is not the key achievement. Rather, having time to build upon that new foundational understanding of the numbers and counting is what allows children to develop number system knowledge before they enter kindergarten.

10.6 Cardinal Knowledge As the Keystone

Throughout this chapter we have discussed a large body of research exploring what role early-emerging number abilities might play in the development of formal symbolic math once children begin school. We know that children who start school behind their peers tend to stay behind, which may compromise their potential for economic and social success later in adulthood (Parsons & Bynner, 1997). It is therefore in our best interest as a nation, and a global community, to better understand the development of the earliest, and possibly foundational, number skills. Despite a great deal of excitement and effort spent trying to find evidence that the ANS is the foundation linking our informal abilities to our achievement in formal mathematics, our data suggest that this link is indirect, and influences math achievement through its relationship with cardinal knowledge acquisition (vanMarle et al., 2014).

Cardinal knowledge, in contrast, was a robust predictor of math achievement directly, and through its influence on the development of number system knowledge. Importantly, the effects for cardinal knowledge were significant above and beyond the influence of the eleven other quantitative skills we assessed, as well as domain-general abilities and demographic factors. Because we ultimately hope that this work will inform the development of assessment tools (for the early identification of children at-risk for poor math achievement) and targeted interventions (for remediating deficits to bring children up to the performance level of their peers prior to school entry), we wanted to be as comprehensive as possible in what skills and abilities we

included in our measures. In addition, in many of the preschool math studies just described, we used Bayesian statistics to identify which constellation of factors was best, given the data, allowing us to objectively quantify how much adding or deleting a factor from a model affected its likelihood under the data.

Although other quantitative skills, like ordinal relations and numeral recognition, as well as domain-general abilities like intelligence and executive function, were also significant predictors of math achievement in some circumstances, cardinality remained our single strongest predictor, even after controlling for all of these other variables. Based on this set of findings, we would argue that cardinality, and, in particular, the age at which a child comes to understand cardinality, is a critical indicator of later math achievement. Finding meaning in the first mathematical symbols they encounter allows children to move forward in their learning, incrementally building on cardinal knowledge to develop relational number knowledge, much of which comprises their number system knowledge in kindergarten, which in turn constrains their addition strategy sophistication in first grade.

We hope that these findings will lead to further research that may (or may not) support our findings and the developmental progression our data suggests. For example, other candidate skills, such as knowledge of the successor function, may be related to the transition to CP-knower (Cheung et al., 2017). However, few studies have examined it as a simultaneous predictor of other quantitative competencies, or of math achievement. They are relatively understudied (but see the excellent work of David Barner and colleagues, e.g., Cheung et al., 2017; Davidson et al., 2012), leaving it an open question whether they are as important as cardinal knowledge appears to be. Moving forward, it will be the task of researchers and educators to develop interventions that target cardinal knowledge. For example, at this point in time, we still understand little about what causes children to transition to CP-knower. Future studies can elucidate these details and others as we work toward improving the long-term developmental outcomes for all individuals.

References

Baddeley, A. D. (1996). Exploring the central executive. *The Quarterly Journal of Experimental Psychology Section A, 49,* 5–28.

Baddeley, A. D. (2002). Is working memory still working? *European Psychologist, 7,* 85–97.

Baddeley, A. D., & Hitch, G. (1974). Working memory. In G. H. Bower (ed.), *The Psychology of Learning and Motivation: Advances in Research and Theory* (Vol. 8, pp. 47–89). New York: Academic Press.

Blair, C., & Razza, R. P. (2007). Relating effortful control, executive function, and false belief understanding to emerging math and literacy ability in kindergarten. *Child Development, 78,* 647–663.

Briars, D., & Siegler, R. S. (1984). A featural analysis of preschoolers' counting knowledge. *Developmental Psychology, 20,* 607–618.

Bull, R., Espy, K. A., & Wiebe, S. A. (2008). Short-term memory, working memory, and executive functioning in preschoolers: Longitudinal predictors of mathematical achievement at age 7 years. *Developmental Neuropsychology, 33,* 205–228.

Bull, R., & Lee, K. (2014). Executive functioning and mathematics achievement. *Child Development Perspectives, 8,* 36–41.

Bull, R., & Scerif, G. (2001). Executive functioning as a predictor of children's mathematics ability: inhibition, switching, and working memory. *Developmental Neuropsychology, 19,* 273–293.

Butterworth, B. (2005). The development of arithmetical abilities. *Journal of Child Psychology and Psychiatry, 46,* 3–18.

Butterworth, B. (2010). Foundational numerical capacities and the origins of dyscalculia. *Trends in Cognitive Sciences, 14,* 534–541.

Bynner, J. (1997). Basic skills in adolescents' occupational preparation. *The Career Development Quarterly, 45,* 305–321.

Carey, S. (2004). Bootstrapping and the origins of concepts. *Daedalus, 133,* 59–68.

Carey, S. (2009). *The Origin of Concepts.* New York: Oxford University Press.

Carey, S. (2011). Précis of the origin of concepts. *Behavioral and Brain Sciences, 34,* 113–124.

Cheung, P., Rubenson, M., & Barner, D. (2017). To infinity and beyond: Children generalize the successor function to all possible numbers years after learning to count. *Cognitive Psychology, 92,* 22–36.

Chu, F. W., vanMarle, K., & Geary, D. C. (2013). Quantitative deficits of preschool children at risk for mathematical learning disability. *Frontiers in Psychology, 4,* 195.

Chu, F. W., vanMarle, K., & Geary, D. C. (2015). Early numerical foundations of young children's mathematical development. *Journal of Experimental Child Psychology, 132,* 205–212.

Chu, F. W., vanMarle, K., & Geary, D. C. (2016). Predicting children's reading and mathematics achievement from early quantitative knowledge and domain-general cognitive abilities. *Frontiers in Psychology, 7,* 1–14.

Chu, F. W., vanMarle, K., Rouder, J., & Geary, D. C. (2018). Children's early understanding of number predicts their later problem-solving sophistication in addition. *Journal of Experimental Child Psychology, 169,* 73–92.

Clark, C. A. C., Pritchard, V. E., & Woodward, L. J. (2010). Preschool executive functioning abilities predict early mathematics achievement. *Developmental Psychology, 46,* 1176–1191.

Coubart, A., Izard, V., Spelke, E. S., Marie, J., & Streri, A. (2014). Dissociation between small and large numerosities in newborn infants. *Developmental Science, 17,* 11–22.

Cowan, R., Donlan, C., Shepherd, D. L., Cole-Fletcher, R., Saxton, M., & Hurry, J. (2011). Basic calculation proficiency and mathematics achievement in elementary school children. *Journal of Educational Psychology*, *103*, 786–803.

Cowan, R., & Powell, D. (2014). The contributions of domain-general and numerical factors to third-grade arithmetic skills and mathematical learning disability. *Journal of Educational Psychology*, *106*, 214–229.

Davidson, K., Eng, K., & Barner, D. (2012). Does learning to count involve a semantic induction? *Cognition*, *123*, 162–173.

de Hevia, M. D., Izard, V., Coubart, A., Spelke, E. S., & Streri, A. (2014). Representations of space, time, and number in neonates. *Proceedings of the National Academy of Sciences*, *111*, 4809–4813.

De Smedt, B., & Gilmore, C. K. (2011). Defective number module or impaired access? Numerical magnitude processing in first graders with mathematical difficulties. *Journal of Experimental Child Psychology*, *108*, 278–292.

De Smedt, B., Janssen, R., Bouwens, K., Verschaffel, L., Boets, B., & Ghesquière, P. (2009). Working memory and individual differences in mathematics achievement: A longitudinal study from first grade to second grade. *Journal of Experimental Child Psychology*, *103*, 186–201.

De Visscher, A., & Noël, M.-P. (2014). Arithmetic facts storage deficit: The hypersensitivity-to-interference in memory hypothesis. *Developmental Science*, *17*, 434–442.

Deary, I. J., Strand, S., Smith, P., & Fernandes, C. (2007). Intelligence and educational achievement. *Intelligence*, *35*, 13–21.

Dehaene, S., Piazza, M., Pinel, P., & Cohen, L. (2003). Three parietal circuits for number processing. *Cognitive Neuropsychology*, *20*, 487–506.

Duncan, G. J., Dowsett, C. J., Claessens, A., Magnuson, K., Huston, A. C., Klebanov, P., . . . Sexton, H. (2007). School readiness and later achievement. *Developmental Psychology*, *43*, 1428–1446.

Eason, S. H., & Levine, S. C. (2017). Math learning begins at home. *Zero to Three*, *37*, 35–44.

Edwards, L. A., Wagner, J. B., Simon, C. E., & Hyde, D. C. (2016). Functional brain organization for number processing in pre-verbal infants. *Developmental Science*, *19*, 757–769.

Espy, K. A., McDiarmid, M. M., Cwik, M. F., Stalets, M. M., Hamby, A., & Senn, T. E. (2004). The contribution of executive functions to emergent mathematic skills in preschool children. *Developmental Neuropsychology*, *26*, 465–486.

Feigenson, L., & Carey, S. (2003). Tracking individuals via object-files: Evidence from infants' manual search. *Developmental Science*, *6*, 568–584.

Feigenson, L., Carey, S., & Hauser, M. (2002). The representations underlying infants' choice of more: Object-files versus analog magnitudes. *Psychological Science*, *13*, 150–156.

Feigenson, L., Libertus, M. E., & Halberda, J. (2013). Links between the intuitive sense of number and formal mathematics ability. *Child Development Perspectives*, *7*, 74–79.

Friso-van den Bos, I., Van Der Ven, S. H., Kroesbergen, E. H., & Van Luit, J. E. (2013). Working memory and mathematics in primary school children: A meta-analysis. *Educational Research Review*, *10*, 29–44.

Fuchs, L. S., Geary, D. C., Compton, D. L., Fuchs, D., Hamlett, C. L., Seethaler, P. M., . . . Schatschneider, C. (2010). Do different types of school mathematics development depend on different constellations of numerical versus general cognitive abilities? *Developmental Psychology*, *46*, 1731–1746.

Fuhs, M. W., & McNeil, N. M. (2013). ANS acuity and mathematics ability in preschoolers from low-income homes: Contributions of inhibitory control. *Developmental Science*, *16*, 136–148.

Gallistel, C. R., & Gelman, R. (1992). Preverbal and verbal counting and computation. *Cognition*, *44*, 43–74.

Gallistel, C. R., & Gelman, R. (2000). Non-verbal numerical cognition: From reals to integers. *Trends in Cognitive Sciences*, *4*, 59–65.

Gallistel, C. R., & Gelman, R. (2005). Mathematical cognition. In K. Holyoak, & R. Morrison (eds.), *The Cambridge Handbook of*

Thinking and Reasoning (pp. 559–588). New York: Cambridge University Press.

Gathercole, S. E., & Pickering, S. J. (2000). Working memory deficits in children with low achievements in the national curriculum at 7 years of age. *British Journal of Educational Psychology, 70,* 177–194.

Geary, D. C. (1993). Mathematical disabilities: Cognitive, neuropsychological, and genetic components. *Psychological Bulletin, 114,* 345–362.

Geary, D. C. (2005). *The Origin of Mind: Evolution of Brain, Cognition, and General Intelligence.* Washington, DC: American Psychological Association.

Geary, D. C. (2011). Cognitive predictors of achievement growth in mathematics: A 5-year longitudinal study. *Developmental Psychology, 47,* 1539.

Geary, D. C., Bailey, D. H., & Hoard, M. K. (2009). Predicting mathematical achievement and mathematical learning disability with a simple screening tool: The number sets test. *Journal of Psychoeducational Assessment, 27,* 265–279.

Geary, D. C., Brown, S. C., & Samaranayake, V. A. (1991). Cognitive addition: A short longitudinal study of strategy choice and speed-of-processing differences in normal and mathematically disabled children. *Developmental Psychology, 27,* 787–797.

Geary, D. C., Hoard, M. K., Byrd-Craven, J., Nugent, L., & Numtee, C. (2007). Cognitive mechanisms underlying achievement deficits in children with mathematical learning disability. *Child Development, 78,* 1343–1359.

Geary, D. C., Hoard, M. K., & Nugent, L. (2012b). Independent contributions of the central executive, intelligence, and in-class attentive behavior to developmental change in the strategies used to solve addition problems. *Journal of Experimental Child Psychology, 113,* 49–65.

Geary, D. C., Hoard, M. K., Nugent, L., & Bailey, D. H. (2013). Adolescents' functional numeracy is predicted by their school entry number system knowledge. *PLoS ONE, 8,* e54651.

Geary, D. C., & Moore, A. M. (2016). Cognitive and brain systems underlying early mathematical development. *Progress in Brain Research, 227,* 75–103.

Geary, D. C., Nicholas, A., Li, Y., & Sun, J. (2017). Developmental change in the influence of domain-general abilities and domain-specific knowledge on mathematics achievement: An eight-year longitudinal study. *Journal of educational Psychology, 109,* 680–693.

Geary, D. C., & vanMarle, K. (2016). Young children's core symbolic and nonsymbolic quantitative knowledge in the prediction of later mathematics achievement. *Developmental Psychology, 52,* 2130–2144.

Geary, D. C., & vanMarle, K. (2018). Growth of symbolic number knowledge accelerates after children understand cardinality. *Cognition, 177,* 69–78.

Geary, D. C., vanMarle, K., Chu, F. W., Rouder, J., Hoard, M. K., & Nugent, L. (2018). Early conceptual understanding of cardinality predicts superior school-entry number-system knowledge. *Psychological Science, 29,* 191–205.

Gelman, R. (1972). Logical capacity of very young children: Number invariance rules. *Child Development, 43,* 75–90.

Gelman, R. (1993). A rational-constructivist account of early learning about numbers and objects. *Learning and Motivation, 30,* 61–96.

Gelman, R., & Gallistel, C. R. (1978). *The Child's Understanding of Number.* Cambridge, MA: Harvard University Press.

Gelman, R., & Greeno, J. G. (1989). On the nature of competence: Principles for understanding in a domain. In L. B. Resnick (ed.), *Knowing and Learning: Issues for a Cognitive Science of Instruction* (pp. 125–186). Hillsdale, NJ: Erlbaum.

Gelman, R., & Meck, E. (1983). Preschoolers' counting: Principles before skill. *Cognition, 13,* 343–359.

Gilmore, C. K., Attridge, N., Clayton, S., Cragg, L., Johnson, S., Marlow, N., & Inglis, M. (2013). Individual differences in inhibitory control, not non-verbal number acuity, correlate with mathematics achievement. *PLoS ONE, 8,* e67374.

Gilmore, C. K., McCarthy, S. E., & Spelke, E. S. (2010). Non-symbolic arithmetic abilities and mathematics achievement in the first year of formal schooling. *Cognition, 115,* 394–406.

Ginsburg, H. P., & Baroody, A. J. (2003). *Test of Early Mathematical Ability* (3rd ed.). Austin, TX: Pro-Ed.

Gunderson, E. A., Spaepen, E., & Levine, S. C. (2015). Approximate number word knowledge before the cardinal principle. *Journal of Experimental Child Psychology, 130,* 35–55.

Halberda, J., & Feigenson, L. (2008). Developmental change in the acuity of the "Number Sense": The approximate number system in 3-, 4-, 5-, and 6-year-olds and adults. *Developmental Psychology, 44,* 1457.

Halberda, J., Mazzocco, M. M., & Feigenson, L. (2008). Individual differences in non-verbal number acuity correlate with maths achievement. *Nature, 455,* 665.

Huttenlocher, J., Jordan, N. C., & Levine, S. C. (1992). A mental model for early arithmetic. *Journal of Experimental Psychology: General, 123,* 284–296.

Hyde, D. C. (2011). Two systems of non-symbolic numerical cognition. *Frontiers in Human Neuroscience, 5,* 1–8.

Iuculano, T., Tang, J., Hall, C. W., & Butterworth, B. (2008). Core information processing deficits in developmental dyscalculia and low numeracy. *Developmental Science, 11,* 669–680.

Izard, V., Sann, C., Spelke, E. S., & Streri, A. (2009). Newborn infants perceive abstract numbers. *Proceedings of the National Academy Sciences (USA), 106,* 10382–10385.

Kahneman, D., Treisman, A., & Gibbs, B. J. (1992). The reviewing of object files: Object specific integration of information. *Cognitive Psychology, 24,* 174–219.

Klibanoff, R. S., Levine, S. C., Huttenlocher, J., Vasilyeva, M., & Hedges, L. V. (2006). Preschool children's mathematical knowledge: The effect of teacher "math talk." *Developmental Psychology, 42,* 59–69.

Le Corre, M., & Carey, S. (2007). One, two, three, four, nothing more: An investigation of the conceptual sources of the verbal counting principles. *Cognition, 105,* 395–438.

Lee, M. D., & Sarnecka, B. W. (2011). Number-knower levels in young children: Insights from Bayesian modeling. *Cognition, 120,* 391–402.

Leslie, A. M., Gallistel, C. R., & Gelman, R. (2007). Where integers come from. In P. Carruthers, S. Laurence, & S. Stich (eds.), *The Innate Mind, Vol. 3: Foundations and the Future* (pp. 109–138). New York: Oxford University Press.

Leslie, A. M., Gelman, R., & Gallistel, C. R. (2008). The generative basis of natural number concepts. *Trends in Cognitive Sciences, 12,* 213–218.

Libertus, M. E. (2015). The role of intuitive approximation skills for school math abilities. *Mind, Brain, and Education, 9,* 112–120.

Libertus, M. E. (2019). Understanding the link between the approximate number system and math abilities. In D. C. Geary, D. B. Berch, & K. Mann-Koepke (eds.), *Mathematical Cognition and Learning: Cognitive Foundations for Improving Mathematical Learning,* (Vol. 5, pp. 91–106). New York: Elsevier.

Libertus, M. E., & Brannon, E. M. (2010). Stable individual differences in number discrimination in infancy. *Developmental Science, 13,* 900–906.

Libertus, M. E., Feigenson, L., & Halberda, J. (2011). Preschool acuity of the approximate number system correlates with school math ability. *Developmental Science, 14,* 1292–1300.

Lipton, J. S., & Spelke, E. S. (2003). Origins of number sense: Large number discrimination in human infants. *Psychological Science, 14,* 396–401.

Lyons, I. M., & Beilock, S. L. (2011). Numerical ordering ability mediates the relation between number-sense and arithmetic competence. *Cognition, 121,* 256–261.

Lyons, I. M., & Beilock, S. L. (2013). Ordinality and the nature of symbolic numbers. *Journal of Neuroscience, 33,* 17052–17061.

Lyons, I. M., Price, G. R., Vaessen, A., Blomert, L., & Ansari, D. (2014). Numerical predictors of arithmetic success in grades 1–6. *Developmental Science, 17,* 714–726.

Mazzocco, M. M., Feigenson, L., & Halberda, J. (2011). Impaired acuity of the approximate number system underlies mathematical learning disability (dyscalculia). *Child Development, 82*, 1224–1237.

Moore, A. M., vanMarle, K., & Geary, D. C. (2016). Kindergartners' fluent processing of symbolic numerical magnitude is predicted by their cardinal knowledge and implicit understanding of arithmetic 2 years earlier. *Journal of Experimental Child Psychology, 150*, 31–47.

Nosworthy, N., Bugden, S., Archibald, L., Evans, B., & Ansari, D. (2013). A two-minute paper-and-pencil test of symbolic and nonsymbolic numerical magnitude processing explains variability in primary school children's arithmetic competence. *PLoS ONE, 8*, e67918.

Parsons, S., & Bynner, J. (1997). Numeracy and employment. *Education and Training, 39*, 43–51.

Peng, P., & Fuchs, D. (2016). A meta-analysis of working memory deficits in children with learning difficulties: Is there a difference between verbal domain and numerical domain? *Journal of Learning Disabilities, 49*, 3–20.

Piaget, J. (1952). *The Child's Concept of Number*. London: Routledge & Kegan Paul.

Piazza, M., Facoetti, A., Trussardi, A. N., Berteletti, I., Conte, S., Lucangeli, D., ... Zorzi, M. (2010). Developmental trajectory of number acuity reveals a severe impairment in developmental dyscalculia. *Cognition, 116*, 33–41.

Price, G. R., Holloway, I., Räsänen, P., Vesterinen, M., & Ansari, D. (2007). Impaired parietal magnitude processing in developmental dyscalculia. *Current Biology, 17*, R1042–R1043.

Pylyshyn, Z. W., & Storm, R. W. (1988). Tracking multiple independent targets: Evidence for a parallel tracking mechanism. *Spatial Vision, 3*, 179–197.

Ramani, G. B., Rowe, M. L., Eason, S. H., & Leech, K. A. (2015). Math talk during informal learning activities in Head Start families. *Cognitive Development, 35*, 15–33.

Ritchie, S. J., & Bates, T. C. (2013). Enduring links from childhood mathematics and reading achievement to adult socioeconomic status. *Psychological Science, 24*, 1301–1308.

Rivera-Batiz, F. (1992). Quantitative literacy and the likelihood of employment among young adults in the United States. *Journal of Human Resources, 27*, 313–328.

Rose, H., & Betts, J. R. (2004). The effect of high school courses on earnings. *Review of Economics and Statistics, 86*, 497–513.

Rousselle, L., & Noël, M.-P. (2007). Basic numerical skills in children with mathematical learning disabilities: A comparison of symbolic vs. non-symbolic number magnitude processing. *Cognition, 102*, 361–395.

Sasanguie, D., Defever, E., Maertens, B., & Reynvoet, B. (2014). The approximate number system is not predictive for symbolic number processing in kindergarteners. *The Quarterly Journal of Experimental Psychology, 67*, 271–280.

Scholl, B. J. (2001). Objects and attention: The state of the art. *Cognition, 80*, 1–46.

Shalev, R. S., Manor, O., & Gross-Tsur, V. (2005). Developmental dyscalculia: A prospective six-year follow-up. *Developmental Medicine and Child Neurology, 47*, 121–125.

Siegel, L. S., & Ryan, E. B. (1989). The development of working memory in normally achieving and subtypes of learning disabled children. *Child Development, 60*, 973–980.

Siegler, R. S. (1988). Individual differences in strategy choices: Good students, not-so-good students, and perfectionists. *Child Development, 59*, 833–851.

Siegler, R. S., & Booth, J. L. (2004). Development of numerical estimation in young children. *Child Development, 75*, 428–444.

Soltész, F., Szűcs, D., & Szűcs, L. (2010). Relationships between magnitude representation, counting and memory in 4-to 7-year-old children: A developmental study. *Behavioral and Brain Functions, 6*, 13.

Starr, A., Libertus, M. E., & Brannon, E. M. (2013). Number sense in infancy predicts mathematical abilities in childhood. *Proceedings of the National Academy of Sciences, 110*, 18116–18120.

Swanson, H. L., & Sachse-Lee, C. (2001). Mathematical problem solving and working memory in children with learning disabilities: Both executive and phonological processes are important. *Journal of Experimental Child Psychology*, *79*, 294–321.

Vanbinst, K., & De Smedt, B. (2016). Individual differences in children's mathematics achievement: The roles of symbolic numerical magnitude processing and domain-general cognitive functions. *Progress in Brain Research*, *227*, 105–130.

vanMarle, K. (2013). Infants use different mechanisms to make small and large number ordinal judgments. *Journal of Experimental Child Psychology*, *114*, 102–110.

vanMarle, K., Chu, F. W., Li, Y., & Geary, D. C. (2014). Acuity of the approximate number system and preschoolers' quantitative development. *Developmental Science*, *17*, 492–505.

vanMarle, K., Chu, F. W., Mou, Y., Seok, J. H., Rouder, J., & Geary, D. C. (2018). Attaching meaning to the number words: Contributions of the object tracking and approximate number systems. *Developmental Science*, *21*, e12495.

Walberg, H. J. (1984). Improving the productivity of America's schools. *Educational Leadership*, *41*, 19–27.

Wechsler, D. (2001). *Wechsler Individual Achievement Test – Abbreviated II*. San Antonio, TX: Psychological Corp.

Wechsler, D. (2002). *Wechsler Preschool and Primary Scale of Intelligence* (3rd ed.). San Antonio, TX: Psychological Corp.

Wood, J. N., & Spelke, E. S. (2005). Infants' enumeration of actions: Numerical discrimination and its signature limits. *Developmental Science*, *8*, 173–181.

Wynn, K. (1990). Children's understanding of counting. *Cognition*, *36*, 155–193.

Wynn, K. (1992). Children's acquisition of the number words and the counting system. *Cognitive Psychology*, *24*, 220–251.

Xu, F., & Spelke, E. S. (2000). Large number discrimination in 6-month-old infants. *Cognition*, *74*, B1–B11.

11 How Sophisticated Is Infants' Theory of Mind?

Rose M. Scott, Erin Roby, and Renée Baillargeon

11.1 Introduction

Imagine the following scenario (inspired by true events): We are grocery shopping with our friend Anita, who notices a woman down the aisle and waves and smiles at her. The woman looks confused and walks away. Perplexed, Anita tells us that she spent the previous day training the woman, a new employee at their firm, and is surprised by her behavior because she thought they had established a friendly rapport. We suggest a possible explanation: Perhaps the woman did not recognize Anita outside of work. Later at the checkout line, we notice the woman standing with someone who is obviously her identical twin. In light of this new information, we revise our initial explanation: Anita must have waved at her trainee's twin, falsely believing her to be her trainee, and the twin responded with confusion because she had never met Anita before. Anita then joins us at the checkout, one of the twins waves happily to her, and the mystery is resolved with smiles all around.

As this everyday example illustrates, adults routinely attempt to infer others' mental states to make sense of their actions and interactions. Variously known as psychological reasoning, mental-state reasoning, mentalizing, mindreading, or theory of mind, this ability plays a vital role in everyday social life and is associated with a wide range of positive developmental outcomes, from improved cooperation to better academic performance (Butler, 2013; Cowell et al., 2017; Imuta et al., 2016; Takagishi et al., 2010). Considerable research has thus focused on when and how this important ability develops.

Over the past twenty-five years, our understanding of early psychological reasoning has undergone several substantial shifts, each prompted by new findings that revealed previously unsuspected competencies (for reviews, see Baillargeon et al., 2015, 2016; Scott, 2017b; Scott & Baillargeon, 2017). In this chapter, we outline the successive accounts of early psychological reasoning corresponding to these shifts. Section 11.2 describes earlier accounts, including constructivist, teleological, and conceptual-change accounts. Section 11.3 introduces the current debate between two-system and one-system accounts. Section 11.4 first reviews challenges to "signature limits" of early psychological reasoning proposed by two-system accounts, and Section 11.5 considers in detail one limit that has until now received scant attention, cognitive encapsulation. Finally, Section 11.6 outlines future research directions.

11.2 Earlier Accounts

11.2.1 Constructivist and Teleological Accounts

In the early 1990s, many researchers believed, following the Piagetian tradition, that infants

The redaction of this chapter was supported by an NSF grant to Rose M. Scott (1844416).

in the first year of life had no capacity for psychological reasoning and lacked any understanding of others as agents (Butterworth & Jarrett, 1991; Tomasello, 1999). However, new findings suggested that young infants could make sense of familiar actions by human agents (e.g., reaching for and grasping an object), though not by non-human agents (Kamewari et al., 2005; Meltzoff, 1995; Woodward, 1998, 1999). These findings led to *constructivist* or experience-driven accounts of early psychological reasoning (Woodward, 2005; Woodward et al., 2001). According to these accounts, as infants learned to act on objects, they became able to understand similar actions by similar agents. Over time, through the application of comparison and abstraction processes to the representations of their own actions and those of other agents, infants gradually constructed a more abstract understanding of intentional action, which could then be applied, broadly and flexibly, to novel actions and novel agents.

In time, constructivist accounts were called into question by new evidence that young infants could make sense of intentional actions by novel non-human agents, provided they received sufficient evidence to identify them as agents – specifically, evidence that these novel entities had internal control over their actions (Csibra, 2008; Csibra et al., 1999; Johnson et al., 2007; Luo & Baillargeon, 2005). These findings supported *teleological* accounts, which suggested that infants possessed a primitive cognitive system that enabled them to reason about the actions of any agents, whether human or non-human; this system was thought to be non-mentalistic in nature and, as such, to be qualitatively different from the mentalistic psychological-reasoning system of older children and adults (Csibra et al., 2003; Gergely & Csibra, 2003). According to such accounts, infants reasoned not about agents' mental states *per se*, but

rather about physical variables related to these mental states. When watching an agent act in a scene, infants generated a teleological explanation that specified the physical layout of the scene, the agent's actions, and the end-state the agent achieved. This teleological explanation, together with a core principle of *rationality* (all other things being equal, agents act rationally; Dennett, 1987; Gergely et al., 1995), was sufficient to allow infants to predict what the agent would do when the layout changed. For example, if agent-1 repeatedly jumped over an obstacle and then approached agent-2 on the far side of the obstacle, infants would expect agent-1 to travel to agent-2 in a straight line once the obstacle was removed (i.e., rational agents expend as little effort as possible to achieve end-states; Csibra et al., 1999; Gergely et al., 1995). Proponents of the teleological view argued that, with development, physical variables gradually became incorporated into a mentalistic system that made sense of agents' actions in terms of intentions and other mental states (Gergely & Csibra, 2003).

Implicit in teleological accounts was the assumption that infants were fundamentally egocentric: Because they attended only to physical variables, they could not distinguish between their own representation of a layout and that of an agent. Thus, if infants could see two objects but an agent could see only one of them, infants would be unable to distinguish between their representation of the scene (two objects) and that of the agent (one object). In time, however, new evidence indicated that infants did recognize that an agent could be ignorant about information that was available to them, but not to the agent. For example, they understood that an agent would be ignorant about an object that was hidden from her by a barrier (Choi et al., in press; Kim & Song, 2015; Luo & Baillargeon, 2007) or about an event she had not witnessed (Liszkowski et al., 2008; Luo & Johnson, 2009; Tomasello & Haberl, 2003).

In such cases, infants not only kept track of what the agent could see or had seen, but also non-egocentrically adopted the agent's representation of the scene to predict and interpret her actions.

Together, these findings suggested that infants might have something akin to a mentalistic system for reasoning about agents' actions. Further evidence for this conclusion came from investigations focusing on another facet of early social cognition, sociomoral reasoning. These investigations provided new evidence that infants (a) could identify novel non-human agents (Hamlin et al., 2007; Meristo & Surian, 2013), (b) could keep track, non-egocentrically, of what knowledge agents possessed or lacked about a scene (Meristo & Surian, 2013; Sloane et al., 2012), (c) could attribute to agents a wide range of positive (e.g., helping, comforting, giving) and negative (hindering, hitting, stealing) intentions (Hamlin et al., 2007; Hamlin & Wynn, 2011; Jin et al., 2018; Margoni et al., 2018), and (d) could distinguish between positive and negative intentions even if agents failed in their attempts to carry out these intentions (Dunfield & Kuhlmeier, 2010; Hamlin, 2013).

11.2.2 Conceptual-Change Accounts

Despite the wealth of evidence that infants could reason about agents' mental states, it remained unclear how similar infants' mentalistic system was to that of older children and adults. Infants were clearly able to understand simple mental states such as motivational states (e.g., intentions) and epistemic states (e.g., ignorance), but could they also understand more complex mental states such as false beliefs? According to *conceptual-change* accounts, the answer to this question had to be "No," because there was ample evidence suggesting that children younger than four years of age could not represent false beliefs.

This evidence came primarily from traditional or elicited-prediction tasks, which require children to answer a direct question about the likely behavior of a mistaken agent (Baron-Cohen et al., 1985; Gopnik & Astington, 1988; Perner et al., 1987; Wimmer & Perner, 1983). In one well-known transfer-of-location task (Baron-Cohen et al., 1985), children see Sally place a marble in a box; in her absence, the marble is moved to a nearby basket. Children are then asked where Sally will look for the marble when she returns. Beginning at around four years of age, children correctly indicate that Sally will look in the box, where she falsely believes the marble is located. In contrast, younger children incorrectly indicate that Sally will look in the basket, the marble's true location, suggesting an inability to appreciate Sally's false belief. This developmental pattern was widely replicated (Liu et al., 2008; Wellman et al., 2001), leading conceptual-change theorists to conclude that a fundamental leap took place in psychological reasoning at about age four, when children began to grasp the representational nature of the mind. False-belief understanding thus came to be viewed as a major developmental milestone that was not achieved until the preschool years and heralded a more sophisticated form of psychological reasoning (Carlson & Moses, 2001; de Villiers & de Villiers, 2003; Gopnik & Wellman, 1994; Perner, 1991).

Conceptual-change accounts were eventually challenged, however, by new evidence suggesting that children under age four can demonstrate false-belief understanding when tested with tasks other than traditional tasks. Non-traditional tasks do not require answering a direct question about the likely behavior of a mistaken agent (e.g., "Where will Sally look for her marble?"), but instead use alternative ways of assessing children's understanding of the agent's false belief. The first non-traditional task administered to infants (Onishi & Baillargeon, 2005) used the violation-of-expectation method, which takes advantage of infants' natural tendency to look longer at events that violate, as opposed to confirm, their expectations. In the task, fifteen-month-olds first saw an agent hide a toy in box-A as opposed to box-B. Next, infants received one of several belief-induction trials in which the agent came to hold either a true or false belief about the toy's location. In the subsequent test trial, the agent reached into either box-A or box-B and then paused. Infants expected the agent to reach into whichever box she believed contained the toy, regardless of whether her belief was true or false, and they detected a violation if she reached into the other box instead.

Since the publication of these results, over thirty reports have produced positive evidence of early false-belied understanding in six-to-thirty-six-month-olds (for a partial review, see Scott & Baillargeon, 2017).[1] These reports have used eleven different non-traditional methods, including (a) behavioral spontaneous-response tasks (violation-of-expectation, anticipatory-looking, preferential-looking, anticipatory-pointing, and affective-response tasks; Knudsen & Liszkowski, 2012; Moll et al., 2017; Onishi & Baillargeon, 2005; Scott et al., 2012; Southgate et al., 2007), (b) behavioral elicited-intervention or interactive tasks (helping and referential-communication tasks; Buttelmann et al., 2009; Southgate et al., 2010), and (c) neural spontaneous-response tasks (action-prediction, sustained-representation, belief-processing, and semantic-incongruity tasks; Forgács et al., 2019; Hyde et al., 2018; Kampis et al., 2015; Southgate & Vernetti, 2014). Non-traditional methods have yielded positive findings not only in Western cultures but also in non-Western cultures (Barrett et al., 2013).

11.3 More Recent Accounts

The converging findings from non-traditional tasks suggest that some capacity for reasoning about false beliefs is already present early in life. However, there is currently a heated debate about the exact nature of infants' false-belief understanding and psychological reasoning more generally. This debate primarily involves *two-system* accounts, which assume that traditional and non-traditional tasks are carried out by different psychological-reasoning systems (Apperly & Butterfill, 2009; Butterfill & Apperly, 2013; Low & Watts, 2013; Low et al., 2016), and *one-system* accounts, which assume that both types of tasks are carried out by the same psychological-reasoning system (Baillargeon et al., 2016; Carruthers, 2016; Scott & Baillargeon, 2017; Sodian et al., 2020). Deflationary accounts, which assume that infants' psychological reasoning can be explained in non-mentalistic terms using low-level stimulus factors, associations, or behavioral rules (Heyes, 2014; Perner, 2010; Ruffman, 2014), are not reviewed here. As Carruthers (2018) stated, "the consensus among most researchers in the field is that there are now too many infant studies, using too many variations in materials and methods, for [such accounts] to be plausible" (p. 11351).

---

[1] Positive findings have also been obtained with children between three and four years of age in a wide range of modified traditional and non-traditional tasks with reduced processing difficulties (Hansen, 2010; Rhodes & Brandone, 2014; Rubio-Fernandez & Geurts, 2013; Yazdi et al., 2006). However, proponents of conceptual-change accounts have argued that such results could simply be due to transitional children beginning to show the more mature form of psychological reasoning that typically emerges around age four (Gopnik & Wellman, 1994; Wellman et al., 2001). For this reason, we focus here on children aged thirty-six months and younger.

11.3.1 Two-System Accounts

According to *two-system* accounts, two distinct cognitive systems underlie human psychological reasoning (Apperly & Butterfill, 2009; Butterfill, & Apperly, 2013; Low & Watts, 2013; Low et al., 2016). The late-developing system, which emerges around four years of age, is non-automatic, slow, and flexible; it is capable of representing a wide range of false beliefs and enables correct responses in traditional tasks. The early-developing system, which emerges in infancy, is automatic, fast, and inflexible; it tracks belief-like states or "registrations" that are sufficient for success at most non-traditional tasks. For example, if an agent hides an object in one location and, in her absence, the object is moved to another location, the early-developing system can predict, by considering where the agent last encountered and registered the object, that upon her return she will search for it in its original (as opposed to its current) location. Thus, by tracking what information is available to agents about objects' locations and properties, even if it becomes outdated as events unfold, the early-developing system makes possible a minimal form of false-belief understanding.

Due to its primitive nature, the early-developing system has several "signature limits," beyond its failure in traditional tasks. One such limit is that although infants can represent false beliefs about the locations and properties of objects, as we just saw, they cannot represent false beliefs about objects' identities: Because registrations are minimal representations, they do not "allow for a distinction between what is represented and how it is represented" (Apperly & Butterfill, 2009, p. 963). Thus, if an infant and an agent view the same object but hold different beliefs about what it *is* (e.g., the infant knows it is a tree branch, but the agent mistakenly believes it is a snake), the early-developing system cannot

correctly predict the agent's actions. Another signature limit is that, because the early-developing system is "largely automatic and independent of central cognitive resources" (Low et al., 2016, p. 185), it has limited information-processing resources and cannot handle demanding situations in which predicting an agent's actions requires reasoning about multiple interlocking mental states that interact causally (Low et al., 2014). According to two-system theorists, such a complex causal structure "places demands on working memory, attention, and executive function that are incompatible with automaticity" (Butterfill & Apperly, 2013, p. 629). Yet another signature limit, related to the last, is that the early-developing system is largely encapsulated from the rest of cognition. This makes it fast and efficient, but also inflexible and sharply limited in its ability to integrate information from other cognitive processes when reasoning about agents' actions (Butterfill & Apperly, 2013).

11.3.2 One-System Accounts

According to *one-system* accounts, a single system underlies human psychological reasoning (Baillargeon et al., 2016; Carruthers, 2016; Scott & Baillargeon, 2017; Sodian et al., 2020; for earlier nativist accounts, see Leslie, 1987, 1994). This system emerges early in infancy, is mentalistic in nature, and is constrained by a principle of rationality, with corollaries of *consistency* (agents act in a manner consistent with their mental states) and *efficiency* (agents expend as little effort as possible when pursuing their goals) (Baillargeon et al., 2016). This principle is both descriptive and normative in nature: Infants use the principle, together with their representations of agents' mental states, not only to predict but also to *evaluate* agents' actions. Thus, infants are less likely to trust, learn from, or direct inquiries to agents who behave irrationally (Begus & Southgate, 2012; Koenig & Woodward, 2010; Poulin-Dubois et al., 2011; Zmyj et al., 2010).

Because one-system theorists assume that infants' psychological reasoning is qualitatively similar to that of older children and adults, they dispute all of the signature limits proposed by two-system accounts. Furthermore, they assume that young children fail at traditional tasks mainly because these tasks pose greater processing difficulties. Various descriptions of these difficulties have been offered, focusing on limitations in young children's executive functioning (Kloo et al., 2020; Leslie et al., 2004), pragmatic understanding (Hansen, 2010; Rubio-Fernandez & Geurts, 2016), or both (Helming et al., 2016; Westra & Carruthers, 2017). Building on these efforts, recent descriptions of early difficulties in traditional tasks have tended to include a wider range of factors (Antilici & Baillargeon, 2020; Roby & Scott, 2016; Scott & Baillargeon, 2017; Scott et al., 2020; Setoh et al., 2016).

According to the *expanded-processing-demands* view, for example, success at the Sally-Anne task depends on several different processes (Setoh et al., 2016). As children hear the story, they must comprehend it, and build and maintain a representation of Sally's false belief. When asked the test question ("Where will Sally look for her marble?"), they must interpret it as intended and decide how to respond. Because children typically begin this response-generation process by considering where the marble currently is, they must then inhibit that incorrect prepotent response to tap their representation of Sally's false belief. Finally, children must generate the correct response by naming or pointing to the marble's original location (e.g., the basket). According to the expanded-processing-demands view, young children may fail at the Sally-Anne task either because they lack sufficient skill at one or more

of the processes involved (e.g., they lack sufficient inhibitory control to inhibit the incorrect prepotent response triggered by the test question) or because they lack sufficient information-processing resources to handle the total processing demands of the task. This view is consistent with findings that improvements in various cognitive capacities – including inhibitory control, working memory, and verbal ability – contribute to success at traditional tasks (Carlson & Moses, 2001; Devine & Hughes, 2014; Duh et al., 2016; Milligan et al., 2007), as does practice at conversing about mental states (Hofmann et al., 2016; McAlister & Peterson, 2006; Ruffman et al., 2002; Wang & Su, 2009). Both cognitive advances and exposure to mental-state talk can help reduce the processing demands associated with answering direct questions about agents' false beliefs, thus enabling success at traditional tasks.

11.4 Evidence against Two-System Accounts

Do two-system or one-system accounts better describe early psychological reasoning? Over the past ten years, evidence has begun to accumulate that casts doubt on two-system accounts. In this section and Section 11.5, we review four such sets of findings.

11.4.1 Two Neurological Systems

Recent neuroscientific evidence provides no support for the claim that two systems with distinct neurological substrates and computational capacities underlie success in traditional and non-traditional tasks. First, investigations with adults, using either functional magnetic-resonance imaging (fMRI; Bardi et al., 2017) or functional near-infrared spectroscopy (fNIRS; Hyde et al., 2015), indicate that traditional and non-traditional tasks engage anatomically similar regions within the temporal-parietal junction (TPJ). Second, in a cross-sectional study (Richardson et al., 2018), children aged three-to-twelve years watched a silent animated movie, Pixar's "Partly Cloudy," while undergoing fMRI; in adults, this movie elicits the attribution of false beliefs and other mental states and thus activates the theory-of-mind brain network. Following the fMRI scan, children received a battery of behavioral tasks, including traditional false-belief tasks. Analyses of children's developing theory-of-mind network provided no support for "the prediction of a robust discontinuity in response, associated with the transition from failure to success on explicit false-belief tasks"; in the profiles of neural responses, the authors "saw no major discontinuity when children begin to systematically pass false-belief tasks" (Richardson et al., 2018, p. 8). Finally, in an fNIRS study, seven-month-old infants watched videos of three different transfer-of-location scenarios (Hyde et al., 2018): The agent faced away during the object's transfer from one container to another (false-belief scenario), she witnessed this transfer (true-belief scenario), or she faced away during the transfer but could infer it when she turned back because the containers were transparent (direct-perception scenario). In each scenario, activation in the TPJ was measured prior to the agent's search for the object. Like adults (Hyde et al., 2015), infants showed more TPJ activation during the false-belief scenario than during the true-belief and direct-perception scenarios, providing no support for claims of marked discontinuities in the development of false-belief understanding.

11.4.2 False Beliefs about Identity

Positive findings from various non-traditional tasks call into question the claim that infants are unable to represent false beliefs about identity (Buttelmann et al., 2015; Forgács et al., 2019, 2020; Scott & Baillargeon, 2009; Scott et al., 2015; Song & Baillargeon, 2008). For example, in one violation-of-expectation task (Scott & Baillargeon, 2009), eighteen-month-olds first received familiarization trials in which an agent sat behind a one-piece toy penguin that did not come apart and a disassembled two-piece penguin (Figure 11.1). Across trials, an experimenter placed the one-piece penguin and the disassembled two-piece penguin on platforms or in shallow containers; the side of each penguin (left or right) varied across trials. In each trial, the agent hid a small key in the bottom piece of the two-piece penguin and then assembled it; once assembled, the two-piece penguin looked identical to the one-piece penguin. In the test trials, the agent was initially absent; the experimenter assembled the two-piece penguin, placed it under a transparent cover, and then placed the one-piece penguin under an opaque cover. The agent returned with her key, reached for one of the covers, and then paused. Infants looked significantly longer when the agent reached for the opaque as opposed to the transparent cover (this effect reversed when the agent witnessed the experimenter's actions). These results indicated that infants expected the agent (a) to mistake the penguin visible under the transparent cover for the one-piece penguin (because the two-piece penguin was always disassembled at the start of the familiarization trials) and hence (b) to falsely conclude that the disassembled two-piece penguin was hidden under the opaque cover (because both penguins were always present in the familiarization trials). These results thus demonstrate that infants can reason about the actions of an agent who mistakes one object (the assembled two-piece penguin) for a different object (the one-piece penguin).

Familiarization Trials
Trials 1 and 2

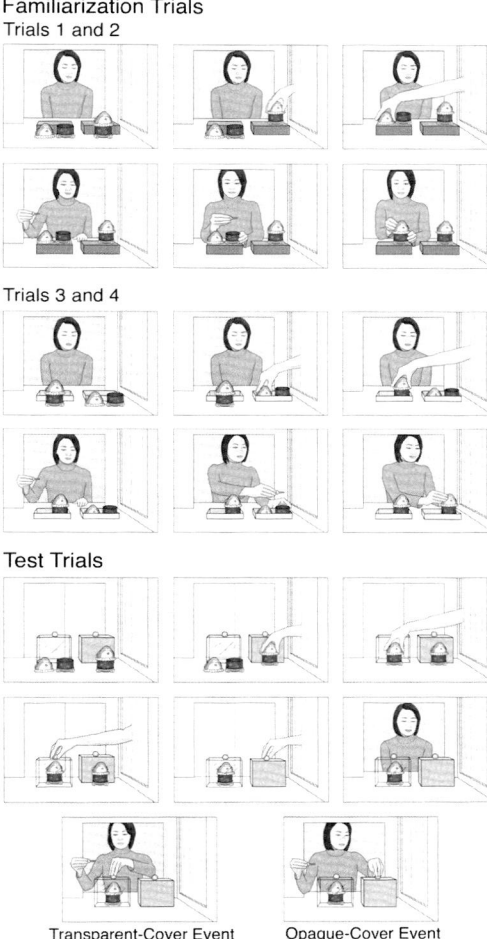

Trials 3 and 4

Test Trials

Transparent-Cover Event   Opaque-Cover Event

Figure 11.1 Familiarization and test trials shown in the false-belief condition of Scott and Baillargeon (2009). The order of the two test events was counterbalanced across infants

A black-and-white version of this figure will appear in some formats. For the color version, please refer to the plate section.

11.4.3 Interlocking Mental States

Positive findings from non-traditional tasks also cast doubt on the claim that infants are unable to represent multiple interlocking mental states that interact causally. For instance, to succeed in the task just described,

infants had to represent the agent's intention of hiding her key in the two-piece penguin, her mistaken belief that the penguin under the transparent cover was the one-piece penguin, and her ensuing mistaken inference that the disassembled two-piece penguin must be hidden under the opaque cover. Additional evidence comes from a study that explored seventeen-month-old infants' understanding of how an agent might go about implanting a false belief about the identity of an object in another agent (Scott et al., 2015). Infants were tested in a violation-of-expectation task in which a thief attempted to secretly steal a desirable rattling toy during its owner's absence by substituting a less desirable silent toy. Infants first watched a series of rattling-toy and silent-toy familiarization trials (Figure 11.2). In each rattling-toy trial, the owner entered with a different toy on a tray; she shook the toy, which rattled, placed it back on the tray and then left. In her absence, the thief picked up the toy, shook it, and then replaced it on the tray. When the owner returned, she stored the rattling toy in a treasure box. The silent-toy trials were similar except that the toy was silent, the thief did not play with it, and the owner discarded it in a trashcan. In the test trial, for the first time, the owner brought in a rattling test toy that was visually identical to a silent toy she had previously discarded in the trashcan. As before, she shook the toy and then left. In her absence, the thief picked up the rattling toy, peered into the trashcan, and selected either the matching silent toy (matching trial) or a non-matching silent toy (non-matching trial). The thief placed the silent toy on the owner's tray, hid the rattling test toy in a pocket, and then paused. Infants looked significantly longer if shown the non-matching as opposed to the matching trial, suggesting that they realized that (a) the thief sought to steal the rattling test toy without the owner's knowledge

Rattling-Toy Trials

Silent-Toy Trials

Test Trials

Each event began as shown above then continued as shown below.
Non-Matching Event

Matching Event

Figure 11.2 Familiarization and test trials shown in the deception condition of Scott et al. (2015) A black-and-white version of this figure will appear in some formats. For the color version, please refer to the plate section.

by substituting a discarded silent toy for the rattling test toy and (b) the thief could achieve this deceptive goal only by substituting the matching silent toy. Further results indicated that infants expected the returning owner to be deceived by this substitution and to store the matching silent toy in her treasure box. These results provide evidence that infants can reason about multiple interlocking mental states: To succeed at the task, infants had to represent the thief's deceptive goal of secretly stealing the rattling test toy by implanting in the owner a false belief about the identity of

the toy on the tray, and they had to reason that the thief could achieve this goal only by substituting a silent toy that was visually identical to the rattling toy – otherwise the owner would detect the substitution as soon as she returned and saw the silent toy.

11.4.4 Failure at Traditional Tasks

The central tenet of two-system accounts is that the early-developing system cannot support success at traditional, elicited-prediction tasks – only the late-developing system can do so. According to one-system accounts, however, young children who have sufficient verbal ability to comprehend the test question (e.g., "Where will Sally look for her marble?") should be able to determine the correct answer to this question as long as processing difficulties are sufficiently reduced, and there is growing evidence for this prediction. First, toddlers demonstrate false-belief understanding when the test question is addressed to a third party (Barrett et al., 2013; Garnham & Ruffman, 2001; He et al., 2012; Scott et al., 2012). In a non-traditional violation-of-expectation task, for example, two-and-a-half-year-olds found it unexpected when an adult who was asked where Sally would look for her toy answered incorrectly by pointing to the toy's current location, as opposed to the location corresponding to Sally's false belief (Scott et al., 2012). In line with the expanded-processing-demands view, because the test question was not directed at the toddlers, no response-generation process was initiated and no prepotent incorrect response had to be inhibited, enabling toddlers to correctly determine how the adult should answer the question.

Second, there is also evidence that when processing demands are appropriately reduced, toddlers can even correctly answer the test question themselves (Antilici & Baillargeon, 2020; Grosso et al., 2019; Scott et al., 2020; Setoh et al., 2016). In a modified traditional task, for example, toddlers heard a transfer-of-location story accompanied by a picture book: Emma found an apple in one of two containers, moved it to the other container, and then went outside to play with her ball; in her absence, her brother Ethan found the apple and took it away (Setoh et al., 2016). Emma then returned to look for her apple. In the test trial, children were shown pictures of the two containers and were asked the test question, "Where will Emma look for her apple?" The task included two modifications designed to reduce processing demands. One modification was that Emma's brother took the apple away to an undisclosed location instead of moving it to the other container. This modification built on findings that children aged three and a half years and older typically perform better at traditional tasks if the test object is absent from the scene (Bartsch, 1996; Wimmer & Perner, 1983), presumably because children then require less inhibitory control to suppress their knowledge of the object's current location when asked the test question. The other modification was that during the story, toddlers were asked two practice questions designed to reduce the response-generation demands of the test question. In one practice question, toddlers saw an apple and a banana and were asked, "Where is Emma's apple?"; in the other question, they saw a ball and a frisbee and were asked, "Where is Emma's ball?" These questions thus gave children practice interpreting a "where" question and producing a response by pointing to one of two pictures. With these two modifications, toddlers performed above chance in the test trial, pointing to the container Emma falsely believed held her apple. Additional experiments indicated that toddlers performed at chance if they received one or fewer practice trials, or if they received two practice trials that differed in form from the test trial, rendering them less effective at reducing

response-generation demands (for an extension of these findings to traditional moral-judgment tasks, see Margoni & Surian, 2020).

11.5 Cognitive Encapsulation

The results reviewed in Section 11.4 call into question the claims by two-system theorists that early psychological reasoning has a distinct neurological substrate and cannot support the attribution of false beliefs about identity, the representation of interlocking mental states, or success at traditional false-belief tasks. However, there remains one signature limit that is not addressed by these results: cognitive encapsulation. Thus, two-system theorists could argue that a critical distinction might still exist between early and more mature forms of psychological reasoning: It could be that this reasoning is at first largely encapsulated from the rest of cognition and, as such, tends to be inflexible, with sharp limits on children's ability to integrate information from other cognitive processes when reasoning about agents' actions.

Is early psychological reasoning cognitively encapsulated, as two-system accounts suggest? To our knowledge, this question has received little discussion so far. In this section, we address this issue by examining two well-studied examples from the developmental literature: early reasoning about preferences and about false beliefs. As will become clear, these examples paint a picture of early psychological reasoning that is more consistent with one-system accounts, in which cognitive processes and world knowledge are readily integrated, in a flexible and context-sensitive manner, into children's psychological reasoning.

11.5.1 Attributing Preferences to Others

In Woodward's (1998) seminal two-object task, five-, six-, and nine-month-olds first received familiarization trials in which an agent faced two different objects, object-A and object-B; in each trial, she grasped object-A and paused. In the test trials, the objects' locations were swapped, and the agent reached either for object-A in its new position (old-object event) or for object-B (new-object event). At all ages, infants looked longer at the new-object than at the old-object event. This result, which was widely replicated and extended to infants as young as three months of age (Cesana-Arlotti et al., 2020; Johnson et al., 2007; Luo, 2011; Scott & Baillargeon, 2013), suggests that (a) infants interpreted the agent's unvarying choice of object-A over object-B during the familiarization trials as signaling a preference for object-A; (b) they expected her to continue acting on this preference during the test trials, in accordance with the rationality principle; and (c) they therefore looked longer when she violated this expectation by reaching for object-B instead. Support for this interpretation came in part from one-object tasks that were identical to Woodward's two-object task except that only object-A was present during the familiarization trials (Bíró et al., 2011; Choi et al., 2018; Luo & Baillargeon, 2005; Song et al., 2014). Infants now looked equally at the old- and new-object events, suggesting that when no choice information was available in the familiarization trials, infants had no basis for attributing a preference to the agent and therefore held no expectations about which object she would select in the test trials.

The preceding interpretation of the two-object and one-object tasks is broadly consistent with the capabilities of the early-developing psychological-reasoning system, as described by two-system theorists. The same is true of several variants of these tasks. For example, the early-developing system could explain why infants fail to attribute to an agent a preference for object-A over object-B when the agent cannot see object-B in the familiarization trials (Kim & Song, 2015; Luo & Baillargeon, 2007), or when the agent is replaced by a different agent in the test trials (Buresh & Woodward, 2007; Henderson & Woodward, 2012). To the extent that the early-developing system can track simple epistemic states (e.g., what objects the agent can see) and motivational states (e.g., what objects the agent prefers) and views these as agent-specific, it is sufficient to explain these findings. However, this is not true of other findings from two-object tasks that require the integration of information from other cognitive processes and are thus inconsistent with a cognitively encapsulated system. We highlight five such findings here.

11.5.1.1 Engaging in Physical Reasoning

In a modified two-object task, researchers examined whether five-month-old infants would bring to bear their physical knowledge that wide objects cannot fit into narrow containers (Wang et al., 2004; see Chapter 8) when reasoning about an agent searching for a preferred wide toy (Ting et al., 2021). In each familiarization trial, the agent first saw an experimenter shake a wide toy that rattled and a narrow toy that did not (the side of each toy varied across trials); after the experimenter left, the agent consistently reached for and shook the wide toy, suggesting that she preferred it. In the test trial, the agent was initially absent, and the experimenter hid the wide toy in a wide box and the narrow toy in a narrow box; both toys had identical handles that protruded from the boxes. Next, the agent returned and reached for either the wide or the narrow box. Infants looked significantly longer if they saw the agent reach for the narrow as opposed to the wide box (this effect was eliminated when both boxes were wide, giving the agent no cue to the wide toy's location). These results suggest that infants were able to integrate their physical knowledge into their reasoning about the agent's actions: They expected her to share their knowledge that wide objects can fit only into wide containers and to search for her preferred toy accordingly.

11.5.1.2 Interpreting a Novel Label

By six months of age, infants understand the communicative function of speech and perceive words as linguistic conventions that are shared by members of the same speech community (Martin et al., 2012; Vouloumanos et al., 2014). This means that if agent-1 requests her preferred object from agent-2 using a novel label, infants expect agent-2 to understand this label and hence to know which object is being referred to. In one experiment, six-month-olds first received familiarization trials in which agent-1 repeatedly selected object-A over object-B (Vouloumanos et al., 2014). In the test trial, agent-1 could no longer reach the objects (she peered at them through a small window) and was joined by agent-2, who could reach both objects. Agent-1 looked at agent-2 and said, "Koba, koba!" Agent-2 then picked up either object-A (old-object event) or object-B (new-object event) and offered it to agent-1. Infants looked significantly longer if shown the new-object as opposed to the old-object event (this effect was eliminated if agent-1 coughed instead). These results suggest that infants interpreted agent-1's novel word as referring to her preferred object, and they expected agent-2 to share this linguistic knowledge and hence to know which object agent-1 was requesting.

11.5.1.3 Interpreting a Change in Label

Infants understand from a young age that words can serve as labels for objects (Bergelson & Swingley, 2012), and this has consequences for two-object tasks in which the agent utters a novel word in each trial prior to reaching for an object (Jin & Song, 2017; Song et al., 2014). In one experiment conducted in Korean (Jin & Song, 2017), twelve- and fourteen-month-olds first received familiarization trials in which the agent said a novel word (e.g., "Modi!") prior to selecting object-A as opposed to object-B. In the test trials, the agent said a different novel word (e.g., "Papu!") and then grasped either object-A (old-object event) or object-B (new-object event). At both ages, infants looked significantly longer at the old-object than at the new-object event, the opposite pattern from that usually found. These results suggest that infants did not interpret the agent's actions in the familiarization trials as demonstrating a preference for object-A; rather, they assumed that the label the agent produced signaled which object she would reach for, and they therefore interpreted the change in what she said in the test trials as signaling a change in which object she would grasp next.

11.5.1.4 Categorizing Objects

Beginning around their first birthday (perhaps due to advances in language acquisition), infants begin to spontaneously encode objects' basic-level categories (e.g., duck, ball, truck, or doll; see Chapters 8 and 10), and this has consequences for two-object tasks (Liu & Sun, 2018; Spaepen & Spelke, 2007). After watching familiarization trials in which an agent consistently chose object-A over object-B (Spaepen & Spelke, 2007), twelve-month-olds expected the agent to reach for object-A again in the test trials if the two objects were from different basic-level categories (e.g., a truck and a doll), but not if both objects were from the same category (e.g., two trucks that were perceptually distinct). These results suggest that infants interpreted the agent's repeated selection of object-A as signaling a preference for an object category (e.g., trucks), rather than a preference for a particular object (e.g., this truck). Thus, when the two objects were from the same category (e.g., trucks), infants had no expectation about which object the agent would select. Conversely, when the objects belonged to two different object categories and were replaced in the test trials with novel exemplars of these categories (e.g., a novel truck and a novel doll), infants still expected the agent to reach for the exemplar from the preferred category (i.e., the novel truck). Together, these results suggest that, at least by twelve months of age, infants integrate information about object categories when reasoning about agents' preferences.

11.5.1.5 Interpreting Ostensive Cues

According to natural-pedagogy theory, infants interpret ostensive cues as signaling "teaching" episodes intended to communicate general information about objects or events (Csibra & Gergely, 2009). Ostensive cues have been shown to affect responses in two-object tasks in which agents direct different emotional displays at object-A and object-B. In one experiment (Egyed et al., 2013), eighteen-month-olds first saw agent-1 express positive affect toward object-A and negative affect toward object-B. When no ostensive cues were used, infants assumed that agent-1 preferred object-A, and they were significantly more likely to select it in the test trial when she requested one of the objects ("Give me one of them!"). Moreover, consistent with prior findings, infants chose randomly between the two objects if agent-1 was replaced by agent-2 in the test trial. However, when agent-1's emotional displays were accompanied by ostensive cues (i.e., agent-1 called the infant's name, said, "Look!," and alternated her gaze between the

infant and the object), infants now gave object-A to agent-2 in the test trial. This last result suggests that infants (a) assumed that agent-1's ostensive displays were intended to teach them that object-A was pleasing but object-B was not and (b) expected agent-2 to share this knowledge and hence to also prefer object-A.

11.5.2 Attributing False Beliefs to Others

As was discussed in Section 11.2.2, over thirty reports have provided positive evidence of false-belief understanding in the first three years of life. These reports have used many different methods and have involved many different scenarios, with mistaken agents holding different false beliefs and producing different responses ranging from physical actions and emotional reactions to verbal responses (Forgács et al., 2009; Onishi & Baillargeon, 2005; Scott, 2017a; for a review, see Scott & Baillargeon, 2017). In this section, we focus on a subset of these reports to illustrate that, far from being encapsulated, early false-belief understanding is flexible, context-sensitive, and well integrated with other cognitive processes.

11.5.2.1 Engaging in Physical Reasoning

In a violation-of-expectation task (Bian et al., 2017), researchers examined whether ten-month-olds would bring to bear their physical knowledge that tall objects cannot be hidden in short containers (Hespos & Baillargeon, 2001; see Chapter 8) when reasoning about an agent who was playing a hide-and-seek game and searching for an object she mistakenly believed to be tall. In each familiarization trial, an agent sat at a window in the back wall of a puppet-stage apparatus behind a tall toy dog and two short containers. While an experimenter watched from a side window, the agent played with the dog briefly, put it down, and then hid herself by lifting a large cloth that filled her window ("I'm ready!"). Next, the experimenter placed the dog in one of the containers and then signaled the agent to return ("Ok!"). At that point, the agent lowered her cloth, grasped the dog's head, and paused. Across trials, different containers were used, and the side of the dog (left or right) was varied. The test trial was identical, with two exceptions: The containers were a tall and a short box, each closed with a lid, and the experimenter shortened the dog (its body could be collapsed by pressing firmly on its head) and hid it in the short box. When the agent returned, she grasped the lid of either the tall or the short box and then paused. Infants looked significantly longer if they saw the agent reach for the short as opposed to the tall box. These results suggest that infants expected the agent (a) to falsely believe that the dog was still tall and hence (b) to falsely conclude that it must be hidden in the tall box (this effect was eliminated if the agent saw the dog being shortened before hiding herself, as the short dog could then be hidden in either box). Infants were thus able to integrate their physical knowledge into their reasoning about the agent's actions: They expected her to share their knowledge that tall objects can be hidden only in tall containers and to search for the dog accordingly.

11.5.2.2 Detecting Semantic Incongruity

By the second year of life, infants' burgeoning word knowledge enables them to detect a violation when a spoken label is incongruent with an agent's false belief about an object's identity (Forgács et al., 2019, 2020). In a semantic-incongruity task measuring event-related potentials (ERPs; Forgács et al., 2019), fourteen-month-olds faced an agent who sat behind an occluder. A familiar object (e.g.,

an apple) was placed in front of the occluder, where it was visible to the infants but not the agent. The occluder was then lowered and the agent inspected the object. Next, the occluder was raised, the agent turned away, and the original object was replaced with a different familiar object (e.g., a car). The agent then turned back, and the occluder either remained raised (false-belief trials) or was lowered to reveal the new object (true-belief trials). Infants then heard a label that matched the current object ("car"). Analyses focused on the N400, an ERP component that indexes semantic processing: Adult listeners typically produce larger N400s to semantically incongruous statements (Kutas & Federmeier, 2011). In line with these results, infants exhibited significantly larger N400s to the label during the false-belief trials than during the true-belief trials, suggesting that they detected a violation when the label (though accurate from their perspective) was incongruous with the agent's false belief about the object's identity.

11.5.2.3 Engaging in Sociomoral Reasoning

From a young age, infants expect agents to approach someone with a good moral character, but to avoid someone with a bad moral character (Hamlin et al., 2007). This sociomoral knowledge has been shown to be integrated with infants' false-belief reasoning. In a violation-of-expectation task (Choi & Luo, 2015), fifteen-month-olds first saw agent-1 and agent-2 interact positively. In the next trial, while agent-1 was absent, agent-2 deliberately knocked down another agent, agent-3. In the test trials, agent-1 either ignored agent-2 (alone event) or continued to interact positively with her as before (together event). Infants looked significantly longer at the alone than at the together event (this effect reversed if agent-1 witnessed agent-2's harmful actions toward agent-3). Infants thus integrated their sociomoral knowledge into their reasoning about agent-1's actions: They expected her to continue interacting with agent-2 as long as she falsely believed in agent-2's good moral character.

11.5.2.4 Drawing Inferences Based on General Knowledge

In the false-belief tasks described thus far, the agent's false belief was based on information that was acquired during the experimental situation and became invalid (e.g., the toy was moved from box-A to box-B in the agent's absence). Other tasks have revealed that infants can also attribute false beliefs based on general knowledge about the world that happens not to hold true in the experimental situation (He et al., 2011; Scott et al., 2010). One violation-of-expectation task (Scott et al., 2010) built on prior findings that the greater the visual similarity between two objects, the greater the likelihood that eighteen-month-olds will generalize a non-obvious property from one object to the other (Welder & Graham, 2001). In the task, eighteen-month-olds first received a familiarization trial. An experimenter sat at a side window in a puppet-stage apparatus and faced a red toy with silver stars. Two additional toys stood at the rear of the apparatus: One was visually identical to the experimenter's toy (red test toy) and the other was green with yellow stripes (green test toy). The experimenter shook each toy in turn, thereby revealing that her toy and the green test toy rattled when shaken but the red test toy did not. In the test trial, an agent now sat behind the two test toys. The experimenter shook her toy and said, "Can you do it?" The agent then grasped either the red or green test toy and paused. Infants looked significantly longer if they saw the agent select the green as opposed to the red

test toy (this effect reversed if she witnessed the initial shaking of the toys). These results suggest that infants expected the agent (a) to share their knowledge that visually identical objects are more likely to share non-obvious properties than are non-identical objects and hence (b) to falsely expect the red test toy to rattle like the experimenter's toy.

11.5.2.5 Updating an Agent's False Belief

Because infants realize that language conveys information between communicative partners, they understand that a mistaken agent's false belief can be updated or corrected by an informed agent's appropriate utterance (Jin et al., 2019; Schulze & Buttelmann, 2021; Song et al., 2008). In a violation-of-expectation task (Song et al., 2008), eighteen-month-olds first saw an agent place a ball in a box. Next, while the agent was absent, an experimenter moved the ball to a nearby cup. The agent then returned, and the experimenter produced an utterance about the ball's location that was either informative ("The ball is in the cup!") or uninformative ("I like the cup!"). In the test trial, the agent was alone and reached for either the cup or the box and then paused. Infants who heard the informative utterance expected the agent to reach for the cup, suggesting that they considered this utterance sufficient to update the agent about where to find the ball. In contrast, infants who heard the uninformative utterance expected the agent to reach for the box, suggesting that they deemed the utterance insufficient to update the agent and hence expected her to continue believing that the ball was in the box.

11.5.2.6 Interpreting a Novel Label

By seventeen months of age, infants consider an agent's beliefs about a scene when determining the likely referent of the agent's verbal utterances (Southgate et al., 2010). In a referential-communication task, seventeen-month-olds first saw an agent place one novel object in box-A and a second novel object in box-B; the agent then left the room, and an experimenter swapped the locations of the objects. When the agent returned, she pointed to box-A, said it contained a "sefo," and asked the child, "Can you get the sefo for me?" Infants were significantly more likely to approach box-B, the box the agent had not pointed to (this effect reversed when the agent witnessed the swap of the objects' locations). These results suggest that infants recognized that the agent held a false belief about the objects' locations and intended to refer to the object in box-B when labeling the sefo.

11.5.2.7 Revising a Belief that was Incorrectly Computed

The ability to retrieve and reason about past events appears to improve markedly around age three years (Hayne, 2004), and this enables children to retrieve and revise a belief they incorrectly attributed to an agent. In a modified referential-communication task (Király et al., 2018), thirty-six-month-olds first saw an agent place two novel objects into two boxes; she then put on a pair of sunglasses and faced the boxes while the experimenter silently swapped the objects' locations. Next, the agent took off the sunglasses, put them in front of the child, and left the room with the experimenter. In their absence, the parent helped the child inspect the sunglasses and discover that they were completely opaque. The agent then returned, pointed to box-A, indicated that it contained a sefo, and asked the child to give it to her. Children were significantly more likely to approach box-B as opposed to box-A (this effect reversed when the sunglasses were transparent). These results suggest that children (a) retrieved the memory

that the agent had been wearing the sunglasses during the swap, (b) inferred that she did not see the swap and must falsely believe the objects were still in their original locations, and (c) concluded that she intended to refer to the object in box-B when labeling the sefo. Unlike thirty-six-month-olds, eighteen-month-olds expected the agent to know the objects' current locations whether the sunglasses were transparent or opaque. Thus, consistent with prior evidence on the development of episodic memory, only the thirty-six-month-olds were able to retrospectively revise the belief they had attributed to the agent after learning about the sunglasses' properties. This ability is, incidentally, the same one that was illustrated at the start of this chapter: We first attributed to Anita the true belief that the woman down the aisle was her trainee, but later inferred that Anita had in fact mistaken her trainee's identical twin for her trainee.

11.5.3 Cognitive Integration

Together, the twelve sets of findings described in the preceding sections on preference and false-belief tasks suggest that far from being cognitively encapsulated, early psychological reasoning is flexible, context-sensitive, and closely entwined with the rest of cognition. When reasoning about an agent's actions, infants and toddlers are able to integrate information from many different cognitive processes, including physical reasoning, socio-moral reasoning, categorization, language comprehension, general knowledge, and episodic memory. Moreover, as new knowledge is acquired and as new cognitive abilities emerge, children appear to immediately start integrating them into their psychological reasoning (Carruthers, 2018). These findings, together with those reviewed in Section 11.4 that call into question other signature limits proposed by two-system accounts, are all deeply problematic for these accounts. Instead, these various findings provide strong support for one-system accounts.

11.6 Future Directions

The evidence reviewed in this chapter is most consistent with the notion that a single mentalistic system guides human psychological reasoning, emerging early in infancy and gradually developing in sophistication over time. However, much remains to be understood about this development.

One important research direction will be to focus on more subtle facets of psychological reasoning. For example, there is extensive evidence that children become better over time at understanding that an agent's verbal statements or emotional displays do not always reflect what the agent truly thinks or feels, as in irony and sarcasm, white lies and other forms of benevolent social acting, and face-saving situations where one chooses to hide discomfiture from others (Baillargeon et al., 2013; Ma et al., 2011; Peterson et al., 2012; Wellman et al., 2011). Research efforts are getting under way to study at what age children first begin to understand such counterfactual displays.

Another important research direction, which is currently receiving a great deal of attention, is to better understand what factors drive performance in various psychological-reasoning tasks. We discuss two sets of relevant findings here.

11.6.1 Non-Replications and Component Abilities

Over the past few years, there have been several reports of failed attempts at replicating positive findings with infants and toddlers in non-traditional false-belief tasks (Crivello & Poulin-Dubois, 2018; Dörrenberg et al., 2018;

Kulke et al., 2018a; Poulin-Dubois et al., 2013; Powell et al., 2018; Priewasser et al., 2018; Yott & Poulin-Dubois, 2016). A few researchers have taken these non-replications to call into question the very existence of an early capacity for false-belief understanding (Kulke et al., 2018a; Poulin-Dubois et al., 2018; Powell et al., 2018). Such a conclusion is unlikely, however: As we saw earlier, over thirty reports, using eleven different behavioral and neural methods, have yielded positive evidence of early false-belief understanding in non-traditional tasks. To paraphrase Carruthers (2018), this represents too many studies, using too many variations in methods and stimuli, for such a conclusion to be plausible. A more constructive approach to these non-replications, we believe, is to examine what they reveal about the component abilities that contribute to success or failure at these tasks.

To draw an analogy, we saw earlier that two-and-a-half-year-old toddlers succeed at a traditional task using a transfer-of-location scenario when (a) inhibitory-control demands are reduced by removing the test object from the scene and (b) response-generation demands are also reduced by providing two practice questions similar in structure to the test question (Setoh et al., 2016). In contrast, toddlers fail when either of these modifications is altered. Together, this mix of positive and negative findings helps bring to light some of the component abilities that allow toddlers to correctly answer questions about others' false beliefs. In the same vein, we believe that negative findings in non-traditional tasks help shed light on some of the component abilities that contribute to success at these tasks.

In some non-replications, critical components were revealed by procedural changes that led to negative results (Crivello & Poulin-Dubois, 2018; Poulin-Dubois et al., 2013; Powell et al., 2018; Priewasser, et al., 2018).

To illustrate, consider two attempts at replicating the violation-of-expectation task of Onishi and Baillargeon (2005). In this task, all infants received a belief-induction trial that was separate from the test trial. For instance, infants in one condition received a belief-induction trial in which the toy moved in the agent's absence from box-A to box-B; this event was followed by a paused scene that ended when infants looked away and the trial ended. Because the toy moved for the first time in a self-propelled manner, this paused scene allowed infants time to process this new information and to work out its implications for the agent's actions. In their close replication of Onishi and Baillargeon (2005), Yott and Poulin-Dubois (2012) also used a belief-induction trial and replicated the original positive results. In contrast, Powell et al. (2018) did not use a separate belief-induction trial and obtained negative results. In the test trial, while the agent was briefly out of sight, the toy either moved from one box to the other on its own or was moved by a bystander; in either task, the agent reached for a box immediately after she returned. Together, these results suggest that in order to succeed at a violation-of-expectation false-belief task, infants must have sufficient time to process the relevant information and to form an expectation about what the agent will do before she initiates her actions (see also Schulze & Buttelmann, 2021).

In other non-replications, negative findings are less easily traced to procedural changes but seem to arise from more diffuse factors affecting participants' motivation. This is particularly true for the non-replications of the anticipatory-looking task Southgate et al. (2007) originally used with twenty-five-month-old toddlers and later extended to infants, older children, and adults (Senju et al., 2009, 2010, 2011). In this task, participants must anticipate where an agent who

holds a false belief about an object's location will search for it. Failed replications have been reported with toddlers, older children, and adults (Dörrenberg et al., 2018; Grosse Wiesmann et al., 2018; Kulke et al., 2018a, 2018b; Schuwerk et al., 2018). When commenting on these findings, Baillargeon et al. (2018) made two observations. First, the non-replications showed less correct anticipation in the true-belief familiarization trials than did the original studies, raising questions about participants' motivation to predict the agent's action. Second, test results across the non-replications showed no consistent pattern, with some studies reporting above-chance performance in one false-belief condition and below-chance performance in another, and other studies reporting at-chance performance across conditions. Together, these observations suggest that an anticipatory-looking false-belief task may yield positive findings only when everything about the task conspires to make participants highly engaged by the agent's actions so that they are focused on predicting what she will do next. At present, there is a multi-lab project under way (the "ManyBabies-2" project; e.g., Kampis & Hamlin, 2019) that is attempting to determine under what conditions infants are likely to robustly anticipate agents' actions.

11.6.2 Individual Differences

As the previous discussion illustrates, the capacity to represent mental states does not necessarily guarantee successful performance in a psychological-reasoning task. Rather, success can be influenced by properties of the task, as we just saw, as well as by differences across individuals. Decades of research with older children and adults have identified a number of factors that contribute to individual differences in performance on psychological-reasoning tasks. These include cognitive abilities (Carlson & Moses, 2001; Devine & Hughes, 2014; Duh et al., 2016; Milligan et al., 2007) as well as social factors such as exposure to conversations about mental states (Adrián et al., 2007; Ensor & Hughes, 2008; Ruffman et al., 2002; Slaughter et al., 2007), socioeconomic status (Cutting & Dunn, 1999; Devine & Hughes, 2018; Holmes et al., 1996; Hughes et al., 2000), and cultural background (Lecce & Hughes, 2010; Liu et al., 2008; Mayer & Träuble, 2013; Naito & Koyoma, 2006). To date, few studies have examined individual variation in infants' and toddlers' performance on the types of psychological-reasoning tasks that we have reviewed here. Thus, relatively little is known about individual differences in early psychological reasoning and the factors that might be responsible for such differences.

Researchers have recently begun to address these questions by examining whether the factors that predict psychological reasoning in preschool children also predict individual differences in toddlers' performance on non-traditional false-belief tasks (Glenwright et al., 2021; Kloo et al., 2020; Roby & Scott, 2018; Scott & Roby, 2015). In one study, individual differences in verbal ability predicted three-year-olds' performance on a preferential-looking task involving high verbal demands (Scott & Roby, 2015). Another study demonstrated that two-and-a-half-year-olds' exposure to mental-state terms (e.g., *think*, *know*) in conversations with their parents predicted their performance on an anticipatory-looking task (Roby & Scott, 2018). Together, these findings suggest continuity in the factors that influence psychological reasoning across early childhood. These findings also raise the possibility that at least some of the non-replications of non-traditional tasks stem from individual variability: If some individuals are highly motivated to anticipate an agent's behavior whereas others are less so, this could produce

chance performance at the group level. Exploring the factors that predict individual differences in early psychological reasoning, as well as the mechanisms underlying these relationships, thus presents a promising avenue for future research.

11.7 Conclusion

How sophisticated is infants' theory of mind? The evidence reviewed in this chapter suggests two broad conclusions. First, infants' psychological reasoning is driven by a single mentalistic system that is qualitatively similar to that of older children and adults. From a young age, this system enables infants (a) to infer agents' motivational, epistemic, and counterfactual mental states; (b) to attribute false beliefs with a wide range of propositional content, including false beliefs about identity; (c) to represent, under some conditions at least, complex arrays of interlocking mental states that interact causally; (d) to integrate world knowledge and information from other cognitive processes into their reasoning about agents' likely mental states; and finally (e) to use agents' mental states, together with a principle of rationality, to predict, interpret, and evaluate agents' actions and to guide their own actions toward agents.

Second, although infants' psychological reasoning system appears to be broadly similar to that of older children and adults, it is nevertheless considerably less sophisticated. The evidence we have reviewed points to at least three important differences between early and more mature psychological reasoning. One difference is that, with age, children become better able to cope with traditional and non-traditional false-belief tasks with high processing demands. Gradual improvements in cognitive capacities such as inhibitory control, working memory, and verbal ability help children better handle these demands, as does everyday practice at conversing about mental states with parents, siblings, and peers. Another difference is that when attempting to infer an agent's mental states, infants and toddlers cannot take into account world knowledge they have not yet acquired or information from cognitive processes (such as episodic memory) they are still developing. Finally, children become more skilled over time at understanding subtle facets of psychological reasoning, such as when agents offer verbal and emotional communications that do not convey what they truly think or feel.

References

Adrián, J. E., Clemente, R. A., & Villanueva, L. (2007). Mothers' use of cognitive state verbs in picture-book reading and the development of children's understanding of mind: A longitudinal study. *Child Development, 78*, 1052–1067.

Antilici, F., & Baillargeon, R. (2020). 2.5-year-olds pass an explicit unexpected-transfer false-belief task when processing demands are reduced. *Paper presented at the Biennial Meeting of the International Congress of Infant Studies*, July 2020, Glasgow, Scotland.

Apperly, I. A., & Butterfill, S. A. (2009). Do humans have two systems to track beliefs and belief-like states? *Psychological Review, 116*, 953–970.

Baillargeon, R., Buttelmann, D., & Southgate, V. (2018). Invited Commentary: Interpreting failed replications of early false-belief findings: Methodological and theoretical considerations. *Cognitive Development, 46*, 112–124.

Baillargeon, R., He, Z., Setoh, P., Scott, R. M., Sloane, S., & Yang, D. Y. J. (2013). False-belief understanding and why it matters. In R. Mahzarin, & S. A. Gelman (eds.), *Navigating the Social World: What Infants, Children, and Other Species Can Teach Us* (pp. 88–95). Oxford: Oxford University Press.

Baillargeon, R., Scott, R. M., & Bian, L. (2016). Psychological reasoning in infancy. *Annual Review of Psychology, 67*, 159–186.

Baillargeon, R., Scott, R. M., He, Z., Sloane, S., Setoh, P., Jin, K., ... Bian, L. (2015). Psychological and sociomoral reasoning in infancy. In M. Mikulincer, P. R. Shaver (eds.), E. Borgida, & J. A. Bargh (assoc. eds.), *APA Handbook of Personality and Social Psychology: Vol.1. Attitudes and Social Cognition* (pp. 79–150). Washington, DC: American Psychological Association.

Bardi, L., Desmet, C., Nijhof, A., Wiersema, J. R., & Brass, M. (2017). Brain activation for spontaneous and explicit false belief tasks overlaps: New fMRI evidence on belief processing and violation of expectation. *Social Cognitive and Affective Neuroscience, 12*, 391–400.

Baron-Cohen, S., Leslie, A. M., & Frith, U. (1985). Does the autistic child have a "theory of mind"? *Cognition, 21*, 37–46.

Barrett, H. C., Broesch, T., Scott, R. M., He, Z., Baillargeon, R., Wu, D., ... Laurence, S. (2013). Early false-belief understanding in traditional non-Western societies. *Proceedings of the Royal Society of London B: Biological Sciences, 280*, 20122654.

Bartsch, K. (1996). Between desires and beliefs: Young children's action predictions. *Child Development, 67*, 1671–1685.

Begus, K., & Southgate, V. (2012). Infant pointing serves an interrogative function. *Developmental Science, 15*, 611–617.

Bergelson, E., & Swingley, D. (2012). At 6–9 months, human infants know the meanings of many common nouns. *Proceedings of the National Academy of Sciences, USA, 109*, 3253–3258.

Bian, L., He, Z., & Baillargeon, R. (2017). False-belief understanding in young infants: Evidence from anticipatory-looking and violation-of-expectation measures. *Paper presented at the Biennial Meeting of the Society for Research in Child Development*, April 2017, Austin, TX.

Bíro, S., Verschoor, S., & Coenen, L. (2011). Evidence for a unitary goal concept in 12-month-old infants. *Developmental Science, 14*, 1255–1260.

Buresh, J. S., & Woodward, A. L. (2007). Infants track action goals within and across agents. *Cognition, 104*, 287–314.

Butler, A. G. (2013). Exploring the role of social reasoning and self-efficacy in the mathematics problem-solving performance of lower-and higher-income children. *Journal of Educational Research and Practice, 3*, 93–119.

Buttelmann, D., Carpenter, M., & Tomasello, M. (2009). Eighteen-month-old infants show false belief understanding in an active helping paradigm. *Cognition, 112*, 337–342.

Buttelmann, F., Suhrke, J., & Buttelmann, D. (2015). What you get is what you believe: Eighteen-month-olds demonstrate belief understanding in an unexpected-identity task. *Journal of Experimental Child Psychology, 131*, 94–103.

Butterfill, S., & Apperly, I. A. (2013). How to construct a minimal theory of mind. *Mind and Language, 28*, 606–637.

Butterworth, G., & Jarrett, N. (1991). What minds have in common is space: Spatial mechanisms serving joint visual attention in infancy. *British Journal of Developmental Psychology, 9*, 55–72.

Carlson, S. M., & Moses, L. J. (2001). Individual differences in inhibitory control and children's theory of mind. *Child Development, 72*, 1032–1053.

Carruthers, P. (2016). Two systems for mindreading? *Review of Philosophy and Psychology, 7*, 141–162.

Carruthers, P. (2018). Young children flexibly attribute mental states to others. *Proceedings of the National Academy of Sciences, USA, 115*, 11351–11353.

Cesana-Arlotti, N., Kovács, Á. M., & Téglás, E. (2020). Infants recruit logic to learn about the social world. Nature Communications, 11, 5999.

Choi, Y. J., & Luo, Y. (2015). 13-month-olds' understanding of social interactions. *Psychological Science, 26*, 274–283.

Choi, Y., Luo. Y., & Baillargeon, R. (in press). Can 5-month-old infants consider the perspective of a novel eyeless agent? New evidence for early mentalistic reasoning. Child Development.

Choi, Y. J., Mou, Y., & Luo, Y. (2018). How do 3-month-old infants attribute preferences to a human agent? *Journal of Experimental Child Psychology, 172*, 96–106.

Cowell, J. M., Lee, K., Malcolm-Smith, S., Selcuk, B., Zhou, X., & Decety, J. (2017). The development of generosity and moral cognition across five cultures. *Developmental Science, 20*, e12403.

Crivello, C., & Poulin-Dubois, D. (2018). Infants' false belief understanding: A non-replication of the helping task. *Cognitive Development, 46*, 51–57.

Csibra, G. (2008). Goal attribution to inanimate agents by 6.5-month-old infants. *Cognition, 107*, 705–717.

Csibra, G., Bíró, S., Koós, O., & Gergely, G. (2003). One-year-old infants use teleological representations of actions productively. *Cognitive Science, 27*, 111–133.

Csibra, G., & Gergely, G. (2009). Natural pedagogy. *Trends in Cognitive Sciences, 13*, 148–153.

Csibra, G., Gergely, G., Bíró, S., Koos, O., & Brockbank, M. (1999). Goal attribution without agency cues: The perception of 'pure reason' in infancy. *Cognition, 72*, 237–267.

Cutting, A. L., & Dunn, J. (1999). Theory of mind, emotion understanding, language, and family background: Individual differences and interrelations. *Child Development, 70*, 853–865.

de Villiers, J. & de Villiers, P. (2003). Language for thought: Coming to understand false beliefs. In D. Gentner, & S. Goldin-Meadow (eds.), *Language in Mind: Advances in the Study of Language and Thought* (pp. 335–384). Harvard, MA: MIT Press.

Dennett, D. C. (1987). *The Intentional Stance.* Cambridge, MA: MIT Press.

Devine, R. T., & Hughes, C. (2014). Relations between false belief understanding and executive function in early childhood: A meta-analysis. *Child Development, 85*, 1777–1794.

Devine, R. T., & Hughes, C. (2018). Family correlates of false belief understanding in early childhood: A meta-analysis. *Child Development, 89*, 971–987.

Dörrenberg, S., Rakoczy, H., & Liszkowski, U. (2018). How (not) to measure infant Theory of Mind: Testing the replicability and validity of four non-verbal measures. *Cognitive Development, 46*, 12–30.

Duh, S., Paik, J. H., Miller, P. H., Gluck, S. C., Li, H., & Himelfarb, I. (2016). Theory of mind and executive function in Chinese preschool children. *Developmental Psychology*, *52*, 582–591.

Dunfield, K. A., & Kuhlmeier, V. A. (2010). Intention-mediated selective helping in infancy. *Psychological Science*, *21*, 523–527.

Egyed, K., Király, I., & Gergely, G. (2013). Communicating shared knowledge in infancy. *Psychological Science*, *24*, 1348–1353.

Ensor, R., & Hughes, C. (2008). Content or connectedness? Mother–child talk and early social understanding. *Child Development*, *79*, 201–216.

Forgács, B., Gervain, J., Parise, E., Csibra, G., Gergely, G., Baross, J., & Király, I. (2020). Electrophysiological investigation of infants' understanding of understanding. Developmental Cognitive Neuroscience, 43, 100783.

Forgács, B., Parise, E., Csibra, G., Gergely, G., Jacquey, L., & Gervain, J. (2019). Fourteen-month-old infants track the language comprehension of communicative partners. *Developmental Science*, *22*, e12751.

Garnham, W. A., & Ruffman, T. (2001). Doesn't see, doesn't know: Is anticipatory looking really related to understanding or belief? *Developmental Science*, *4*, 94–100.

Gergely, G., & Csibra, G. (2003). Teleological reasoning in infancy: The naive theory of rational action. *Trends in Cognitive Sciences*, *7*, 287–292.

Gergely, G., Nádasdy, Z., Csibra G., & Bíró, S. (1995). Taking the intentional stance at 12 months of age. *Cognition*, *56*, 165–193.

Glenwright, M., Scott, R. M., Bilevicius, E., Pronovost, M., & Hanlon-Dearman, A. (2021). Children with autism spectrum disorder can attribute false beliefs in a spontaneous-response preferential-looking task. *Frontiers in Communication*, *6*, 146.

Gopnik, A., & Astington, J. W. (1988). Children's understanding of representational change and its relation to the understanding of false belief and the appearance-reality distinction. *Child Development*, *59*, 26–37.

Gopnik, A., & Wellman, H. M. (1994). The theory theory. In L. A. Hirschfeld, & S. A. Gelman (eds.), *Mapping the Mind: Domain Specificity in Cognition and Culture* (pp. 257–293). New York: Cambridge University Press.

Grosse Wiesmann, C. G., Friederici, A. D., Disla, D., Steinbeis, N., & Singer, T. (2018). Longitudinal evidence for 4-year-olds' but not 2-and 3-year-olds' false belief-related action anticipation. *Cognitive Development*, *46*, 58–68.

Grosso, S. S., Schuwerk, T., Kaltefleiter, L. J., & Sodian, B. (2019). 33-month-old children succeed in a false-belief task with reduced processing demands: A replication of Setoh et al. (2016). *Infant Behavior and Development*, *54*, 151–155.

Hamlin, J. K. (2013). Failed attempts to help and harm: Intention versus outcome in preverbal infants' social evaluations. *Cognition*, *18*, 451–474.

Hamlin, J. K., & Wynn, K. (2011). Young infants prefer prosocial to antisocial others. *Cognitive Development*, *26*, 30–39.

Hamlin, J. K., Wynn, K., & Bloom, P. (2007). Social evaluation by preverbal infants. *Nature*, *450*, 557–559.

Hansen, M. B. (2010). If you know something, say something: Young children's problem with false beliefs. *Frontiers in Psychology*, *1*, 23.

Hayne, H. (2004). Infant memory development: Implications for childhood amnesia. *Developmental Review*, *24*, 33–73.

He, Z., Bolz, M., & Baillargeon, R. (2011). False-belief understanding in 2.5-year-olds: Evidence from violation-of-expectation change-of-location, and unexpected-contents tasks. *Developmental Science*, *14*, 292–305.

He, Z., Bolz, M., & Baillargeon, R. (2012). 2.5-year-olds succeed at a verbal anticipatory-looking false-belief task. *British Journal of Developmental Psychology*, *30*, 14–29.

Helming, K. A., Strickland, B., & Jacob, P. (2016). Solving the puzzle about early belief-ascription. *Mind & Language*, *31*, 438–469.

Henderson, A. M., & Woodward, A. L. (2012). Nine-month-old infants generalize object labels, but not object preferences across individuals. *Developmental Science*, *15*, 641–652.

Hespos, S. J., & Baillargeon, R. (2001). Infants' knowledge about occlusion and containment events: A surprising discrepancy. *Psychological Science, 12*, 141–147.

Heyes, C. (2014). False belief in infancy: A fresh look. *Developmental Science, 17*, 647–659.

Hofmann, S. G., Doan, S. N., Sprungc, M., Wilson, A., Ebesutanie, C., Andrews, L. A. . . . Harris, P. L. (2016). Training children's theory-of-mind: A meta-analysis of controlled studies. *Cognition, 150*, 200–212.

Holmes, H. A., Black, C., & Miller, S. A. (1996). A cross-task comparison of false belief understanding in a Head Start population. *Journal of Experimental Child Psychology, 63*, 263–285.

Hughes, C., Adlam, A., Happé, F., Jackson, J., Taylor, A., & Caspi, A. (2000). Good test–retest reliability for standard and advanced false-belief tasks across a wide range of abilities. *Journal of Child Psychology and Psychiatry, 41*, 483–490.

Hyde, D. C., Aparicio Betancourt, M., & Simon, C. E. (2015). Human temporal-parietal junction spontaneously tracks others' beliefs: A functional near-infrared spectroscopy study. *Human Brain Mapping, 36*, 4831–4846.

Hyde, D. C., Simon, C. E., Ting, F., & Nikolaeva, J. I. (2018). Functional organization of the temporal–parietal junction for theory of mind in preverbal infants: A near-infrared spectroscopy study. *Journal of Neuroscience, 38*, 4264–4274.

Imuta, K., Henry, J. D., Slaughter, V., Selcuk, B. & Ruffman, T. (2016). Theory of mind and prosocial behavior in childhood: A meta-analytic review. *Developmental Psychology, 52*, 1192–1205.

Jin, K. S., Houston, J. L., Baillargeon, R., Groh, A. M., & Roisman, G. I. (2018). Young infants expect an unfamiliar adult to comfort a crying baby: Evidence from a standard violation-of-expectation task and a novel infant-triggered-video task. *Cognitive Psychology, 102*, 1–20.

Jin, K. S., Kim, Y., Song, M., Kim, Y. J., Lee, H., Lee, Y., . . . Song, H. J. (2019). Fourteen-to eighteen-month-old infants use explicit linguistic information to update an agent's false belief. *Frontiers in Psychology, 10*, 2508.

Jin, K. S., & Song, H. J. (2017). You changed your mind! Infants interpret a change in word as signaling a change in an agent's goals. *Journal of Experimental Child Psychology, 162*, 149–162.

Johnson, S. C., Shimizu, Y. A., & Ok, S. J. (2007). Actors and actions: The role of agent behavior in infants' attribution of goals. *Cognitive Development, 22*, 310–322.

Kamewari, K., Kato, M., Kanda, T., Ishiguro, H., & Hiraki, K. (2005). Six-and-a-half-month-old children positively attribute goals to human action and to humanoid-robot motion. *Cognitive Development, 20*, 303–320.

Kampis, D., & Hamlin, K. (2019). ManyBabies 2: Theory of mind in infancy. *Paper presented at the Biennial Meeting of the Society for Research in Child Development*, March 2019, Baltimore, MD.

Kampis, D., Parise, E., Csibra, G., & Kovács, Á. M. (2015). Neural signatures for sustaining object representations attributed to others in preverbal human infants. *Proceedings of the Royal Society B: Biological Sciences, 282*, 20151683.

Kim, E. Y., & Song, H. J. (2015). Six-month-olds actively predict others' goal-directed actions. *Cognitive Development, 33*, 1–13.

Király, I., Oláh, K., Csibra, G., & Kovács, Á. M. (2018). Retrospective attribution of false beliefs in 3-year-old children. *Proceedings of the National Academy of Sciences, USA, 115*, 11477–11482.

Kloo, D., Kristen-Antonow, S., & Sodian, B. (2020). Progressing from an implicit to an explicit false belief understanding: A matter of executive control? *International Journal of Behavioral Development, 44*, 107–115.

Knudsen, B., & Liszkowski, U. (2012). 18-month-olds predict specific action mistakes through attribution of false belief, not ignorance, and intervene accordingly. *Infancy, 17*, 672–691.

Koenig, M. A., & Woodward, A. L. (2010). Sensitivity of 24-month-olds to the prior inaccuracy of the source: Possible mechanisms. *Developmental Psychology, 46*, 815–826.

Kulke, L., ReiÔ, M., Krist, H., & Rakoczy, H. (2018a). How robust are anticipatory looking measures of Theory of Mind? Replication attempts across the life span. *Cognitive Development, 46*, 97–111.

Kulke, L., von Duhn, B., Schneider, D., & Rakoczy, H. (2018b). Is implicit theory of mind a real and robust phenomenon? Results from a systematic replication study. *Psychological Science, 29*, 888–900.

Kutas, M., & Federmeier, K. D. (2011). Thirty years and counting: Finding meaning in the N400 component of the event-related brain potential (ERP). *Annual Review of Psychology, 62*, 621–647.

Lecce, S., & Hughes, C. (2010). The Italian job?: Comparing theory of mind performance in British and Italian children. *British Journal of Developmental Psychology, 28*, 747–766.

Leslie, A. M. (1987). Pretense and representation: The origins of "theory of mind." *Psychological Review, 94*, 412–426.

Leslie, A. M. (1994). ToMM, ToBy, and agency: Core architecture and domain specificity. In L. A. Hirschfeld, & S. A. Gelman (eds.), *Mapping the Mind: Domain Specificity in Cognition and Culture* (pp. 119–148). New York: Cambridge University Press.

Leslie, A. M., Friedman, O., & German, T. P. (2004). Core mechanisms in 'theory of mind'. *Trends in Cognitive Sciences, 8*, 528–533.

Liszkowski, U., Carpenter, M., & Tomasello, M. (2008). Twelve-month-olds communicate helpfully and appropriately for knowledgeable and ignorant partners. *Cognition, 108*, 732–739.

Liu, D., Wellman, H. M., Tardif, T., & Sabbagh, M. A. (2008). Theory of mind development in Chinese children: A meta-analysis of false-belief understanding across cultures and languages. *Developmental Psychology, 44*, 523–531.

Liu, S., & Sun, R. (2018). Do great minds prefer alike? Thirteen-month-old infants generalize personal preferences across objects of like kind but not across people. *Frontiers in Psychology, 9*, 2636.

Low, J., Apperly, I. A., Butterfill, S. A., & Rakoczy, H. (2016). Cognitive architecture of belief reasoning in children and adults: A primer on the two-systems account. *Child Development Perspectives, 10*, 184–189.

Low, J., Drummond, W., Walmsley, A., & Wang, B. (2014). Representing how rabbits quack and competitors act: Limits on preschoolers' efficient ability to track perspective. *Child Development, 85*, 1519–1534.

Low, J., & Watts, J. (2013). Attributing false beliefs about object identity reveals a signature blind spot in humans' efficient mind-reading system. *Psychological Science, 24*, 305–311.

Luo, Y. (2011). Three-month-old infants attribute goals to a non-human agent. *Developmental Science, 14*, 453–460.

Luo, Y., & Baillargeon, R. (2005). Can a self-propelled box have a goal? Psychological reasoning in 5-month-old infants. *Psychological Science, 16*, 601–608.

Luo, Y., & Baillargeon, R. (2007). Do 12.5-month-old infants consider what objects others can see when interpreting their actions? *Cognition, 105*, 489–512.

Luo, Y., & Johnson, S. C. (2009). Recognizing the role of perception in action at 6 months. *Developmental Science, 12*, 142–149.

Ma, F., Xu, F., Heyman, G. D., & Lee, K. (2011). Chinese children's evaluations of white lies: Weighing the consequences for recipients. *Journal of Experimental Child Psychology, 108*, 308–321.

Margoni, F., Baillargeon, R., & Surian, L. (2018). Infants distinguish between leaders and bullies. *Proceedings of the National Academy of Sciences, USA, 115*, E8835–E8843.

Margoni, F., & Surian, L. (2020). Conceptual continuity in the development of moral judgment. *Journal of Experimental Child Psychology, 194*, 104812.

Martin, A., Onishi, K. H., & Vouloumanos, A. (2012). Understanding the abstract role of speech in communication at 12 months. *Cognition, 123*, 50–60.

Mayer, A., & Träuble, B. E. (2013). Synchrony in the onset of mental state understanding across cultures? A study among children in Samoa. *International Journal of Behavioral Development, 37*, 21–28.

McAlister, A., & Peterson, C. C. (2006). Mental playmates: Siblings, executive functioning, and theory of mind. *British Journal of Developmental Psychology, 24*, 733–751.

Meltzoff, A. N. (1995). Understanding the intentions of others: Re-enactment of intended acts by 18-month-old children. *Developmental Psychology, 31*, 838–850.

Meristo, M., & Surian, L. (2013). Do infants detect indirect reciprocity? *Cognition, 129*, 102–113.

Milligan, K., Astington, J. W., & Dack, L. A. (2007). Language and theory of mind: Meta-analysis of the relation between language ability and false-belief understanding. *Child Development, 78*, 622–646.

Moll, H., Khalulyan, A., & Moffett, L. (2017). 2.5-year-olds express suspense when others approach reality with false expectations. *Child Development, 88*, 114–122.

Naito, M., & Koyama, K. (2006). The development of false-belief understanding in Japanese children: Delay and difference? *International Journal of Behavioral Development, 30*, 290–304.

Onishi, K. H., & Baillargeon, R. (2005). Do 15-month-old infants understand false beliefs? *Science, 308*, 255–258.

Perner, J. (1991). *Understanding the Representational Mind*. Cambridge, MA: MIT Press.

Perner, J. (2010). Who took the cog out of cognitive science? Mentalism in an era of anti-cognitivism. In P. A. Frensch, & R. Schwarzer (eds.), *Cognition and Neuropsychology: International Perspectives on Psychological Science* (Vol. 1, pp. 241–261). Hove: Psychology Press.

Perner, J., Leekam, S. R., & Wimmer, H. (1987). Three-year-olds' difficulty with false belief: The case for a conceptual deficit. *British Journal of Developmental Psychology, 5*, 125–137.

Peterson, C. C., Wellman, H. M., & Slaughter, V. (2012). The mind behind the message: Advancing theory-of-mind scales for typically developing children, and those with deafness, autism, or Asperger syndrome. *Child Development, 83*, 469–485.

Poulin-Dubois, D., Brooker, I., & Polonia, A. (2011). Infants prefer to imitate a reliable person. *Infant Behavior and Development, 34*, 303–309.

Poulin-Dubois, D., Polonia, A., & Yott, J. (2013). Is false belief skin-deep? The agent's eye status influences infants' reasoning in belief-inducing situations. *Journal of Cognition and Development, 14*, 87–99.

Poulin-Dubois, D., Rakoczy, H., Burnside, K., Crivello, C., Dörrenberg, S., Edwards, K., . . .

Perner, J. (2018). Do infants understand false beliefs? We don't know yet – A commentary on Baillargeon, Buttelmann, and Southgate's commentary. *Cognitive Development, 48*, 302–315.

Powell, L. J., Hobbs, K., Bardis, A., Carey, S., & Saxe, R. (2018). Replications of implicit theory of mind tasks with varying representational demands. *Cognitive Development, 46*, 40–50.

Priewasser, B., Rafetseder, E., Gargitter, C., & Perner, J. (2018). Helping as an early indicator of a theory of mind: Mentalism or teleology? *Cognitive Development, 46*, 69–78.

Rhodes, M., & Brandone, A. C. (2014). Three-year-olds' theories of mind in actions and words. *Frontiers in Psychology, 5*, 263.

Richardson, H., Lisandrelli, G., Riobueno-Naylor, A., & Saxe, R. (2018). Development of the social brain from age three to twelve years. *Nature Communications, 9*, 1027.

Roby, E., & Scott, R. M. (2016). Rethinking the relationship between social experience and false-belief understanding: A mentalistic account. *Frontiers in Psychology, 7*, 1721.

Roby, E., & Scott, R. M. (2018). The relationship between parental mental-state language and 2.5-year-olds' performance on a nontraditional false-belief task. *Cognition, 180*, 10–23.

Rubio-Fernández, P., & Geurts, B. (2013). How to pass the false-belief task before your fourth birthday. *Psychological Science, 24*, 27–33.

Rubio-Fernández, P., & Geurts, B. (2016). Don't mention the marble! The role of attentional processes in false-belief tasks. *Review of Philosophy and Psychology, 7*, 835–850.

Ruffman, T. (2014). To belief or not belief: Children's theory of mind. *Developmental Review, 34*, 265–293.

Ruffman, T., Slade, L., & Crowe, E. (2002). The relation between children's and mothers' mental state language and theory-of-mind understanding. *Child Development, 73*, 734–751.

Schulze, C., & Buttelmann, D. (2021). Small procedural differences matter: Conceptual and direct replication attempts of the communication-intervention effect on infants' false-belief ascriptions. Cognitive Development, 59, 101054

Schuwerk, T., Priewasser, B., Sodian, B., & Perner, J. (2018). The robustness and generalizability of findings on spontaneous false belief sensitivity: A replication attempt. *Royal Society Open Science*, *5*, 172273.

Scott, R. M. (2017a). Surprise! 20-month-old infants understand the emotional consequences of false beliefs. *Cognition*, *159*, 33–47.

Scott, R. M. (2017b). The developmental origins of false-belief understanding. *Current Directions in Psychological Science*, *26*, 68–74.

Scott, R. M., & Baillargeon, R. (2009). Which penguin is this? Attributing false beliefs about object identity at 18 months. *Child Development*, *80*, 1172–1196.

Scott, R. M., & Baillargeon, R. (2017). Early false-belief understanding. *Trends in Cognitive Sciences*, *21*, 237–249.

Scott, R. M., & Baillargeon, R. (2013). Do infants really expect others to act efficiently? A critical test of the rationality principle. *Psychological Science*, *24*, 466–474.

Scott, R. M., Baillargeon, R., Song, H. J., & Leslie, A. M. (2010). Attributing false beliefs about non-obvious properties at 18 months. *Cognitive Psychology*, *61*, 366–395.

Scott, R. M., He, Z., Baillargeon, R., & Cummins, D. (2012). False-belief understanding in 2.5-year-olds: Evidence from two novel verbal spontaneous-response tasks. *Developmental Science*, *15*, 181–193.

Scott, R. M., Richman, J. C., & Baillargeon, R. (2015). Infants understand deceptive intentions to implant false beliefs about identity: New evidence for early mentalistic reasoning. *Cognitive Psychology*, *82*, 32–56.

Scott, R. M., & Roby, E. (2015). Processing demands impact 3-year-olds' performance in a spontaneous-response task: New evidence for the processing-load account of early false-belief understanding. *PLoS ONE*, *10*, e0142405.

Scott, R. M., Roby, E., & Setoh, P. (2020). 2.5-year-olds succeed in identity and location elicited-response false-belief tasks with adequate response practice. *Journal of Experimental Child Psychology*, *198*, 104890.

Senju, A., Southgate, V., Miura, Y., Matsui, T., Hasegawa, T., Tojo, Y., . . . Csibra, G. (2010).

Absence of spontaneous action anticipation by false belief attribution in children with autism spectrum disorder. *Development and Psychopathology*, *22*, 353–360.

Senju, A., Southgate, V., Snape, C., Leonard, M., & Csibra, G. (2011). Do 18-month-olds really attribute mental states to others? A critical test. *Psychological Science*, *22*, 878–880.

Senju, A., Southgate, V., White, S., & Frith, U. (2009). Mindblind eyes: An absence of spontaneous theory of mind in Asperger syndrome. *Science*, *325*, 883–885.

Setoh, P., Scott, R. M., & Baillargeon, R. (2016). Two-and-a-half-year-olds succeed at a traditional false-belief task with reduced processing demands. *Proceedings of the National Academy of Sciences, USA*, *113*, 13360–13365.

Slaughter, V., Peterson, C. C., & Mackintosh, E. (2007). Mind what mother says: Narrative input and theory of mind in typical children and those on the autism spectrum. *Child Development*, *78*, 839–858.

Sloane, S., Baillargeon, R., & Premack, D. (2012). Do infants have a sense of fairness? *Psychological Science*, *23*, 196–204.

Song, H. J., & Baillargeon, R. (2008). Infants' reasoning about others' false perceptions. *Developmental Psychology*, *44*, 1789–1795.

Song, H. J., Baillargeon, R., & Fisher, C. (2014). The development of infants' use of novel verbal information when reasoning about others' actions. *PLoS ONE*, *9*, e92387.

Song, H. J., Onishi, K. H., Baillargeon, R., & Fisher, C. (2008). Can an agent's false belief be corrected by an appropriate communication? Psychological reasoning in 18-month-old infants. *Cognition*, *109*, 295–315.

Southgate, V., Chevallier, C., & Csibra, G. (2010). Seventeen-month-olds appeal to false beliefs to interpret others' referential communication. *Developmental Science*, *13*, 907–912.

Southgate, V., Senju, A., & Csibra, G. (2007). Action anticipation through attribution of false belief by 2-year-olds. *Psychological Science*, *18*, 587–592.

Southgate, V., & Vernetti, A. (2014). Belief-based action prediction in preverbal infants. *Cognition*, *130*, 1–10.

Spaepen, E., & Spelke, E. (2007). Will any doll do? 12-month-olds' reasoning about goal objects. *Cognitive Psychology, 54*, 133–154.

Takagishi, H., Kameshima, S., Schug, J., Koizumi, M., & Yamagishi, T. (2010). Theory of mind enhances preference for fairness. *Journal of Experimental Child Psychology, 105*, 130–137.

Ting, F., He, Z., & Baillargeon, R. (2021). Five-month-old infants attribute inferences based on general knowledge to agents. *Journal of Experimental Child Psychology, 208*, 105126.

Tomasello, M. (1999). Having intentions, understanding intentions, and understanding communicative intentions. In P. D. Zelazo, J. W. Astington, & D. R. Olson (eds.), *Developing Theories of Intention: Social Understanding and Self-Control* (pp. 63–75). Mahwah, NJ: Erlbaum.

Tomasello, M., & Haberl, K. (2003). Understanding attention: 12-and 18-month-olds know what is new for other persons. *Developmental Psychology, 39*, 906–912.

Vouloumanos, A., Martin, A., & Onishi, K. H. (2014). Do 6-month-olds understand that speech can communicate? *Developmental Science, 17*, 872–879.

Wang, S., Baillargeon, R., & Brueckner, L. (2004). Young infants' reasoning about hidden objects: Evidence from violation-of-expectation tasks with test trials only. *Cognition, 93*, 167–198.

Wang, Y., & Su, Y. (2009). False belief understanding: Children catch it from classmates of different ages. *International Journal of Behavioral Development, 33*, 331–336.

Welder, A. N., & Graham, S. A. (2001). The influence of shape similarity and shared labels on infants' inductive inferences about nonobvious object properties. *Child Development, 72*, 1653–1673.

Wellman, H. M., Cross, D., & Watson, J. (2001). Meta-analysis of theory of mind development: The truth about false belief. *Child Development, 72*, 655–684.

Wellman, H. M., Fang, F., & Peterson, C. C. (2011). Sequential progressions in a theory-of-

mind scale: Longitudinal perspectives. *Child Development, 82*, 780–792.

Westra, E., & Carruthers, P. (2017). Pragmatic development explains the Theory-of-Mind scale. *Cognition, 158*, 165–176.

Wimmer, H., & Perner, J. (1983). Beliefs about beliefs: Representation and constraining function of wrong beliefs in young children's understanding of deception. *Cognition, 13*, 103–128.

Woodward, A. L. (1998). Infants selectively encode the goal object of an actor's reach. *Cognition, 69*, 1–34.

Woodward, A. L. (1999). Infants' ability to distinguish between purposeful and non-purposeful behaviors. *Infant Behavior and Development, 22*, 145–160.

Woodward, A. L. (2005). The infant origins of intentional understanding. *Advances in Child Development and Behavior, 33*, 229–262.

Woodward, A. L., Sommerville, J. A., & Guajardo, J. J. (2001). How infants make sense of intentional action. In B. F. Malle, L. J. Moses, & D. A. Baldwin (eds.), *Intentions and Intentionality: Foundations of Social Cognition* (pp. 149–169). Cambridge, MA: MIT Press.

Yazdi, A. A., German, T. P., Defeyter, M. A., & Siegal, M. (2006). Competence and performance in belief-desire reasoning across two cultures: The truth, the whole truth, and nothing but the truth about false belief? *Cognition, 100*, 343–368.

Yott, J., & Poulin-Dubois, D. (2012). Breaking the rules: Do infants have a true understanding of false belief? *British Journal of Developmental Psychology, 30*, 156–171.

Yott, J., & Poulin-Dubois, D. (2016). Are infants' theory-of-mind abilities well integrated? Implicit understanding of intentions, desires, and beliefs. *Journal of Cognition and Development, 17*, 683–698.

Zmyj, N., Buttelmann, D., Carpenter, M., & Daum, M. M. (2010). The reliability of a model influences 14-month-olds' imitation. *Journal of Experimental Child Psychology, 106*, 208–220.

12 Social Cognition and Moral Evaluation in Early Human Childhood

Andreas Falck, Brent Strickland, and Pierre Jacob

12.1 Intro: Human Social Cognition and Developmental Psychology

Human social cognition is the human capacity to process social stimuli, to intentionally convey socially relevant information to others, and to make use of socially transmitted information. Several human social cognitive capacities are special and set humans apart from non-human animals. Thanks to these capacities, humans are unique in their ability to create, maintain, and alter large social groups within which they coordinate, cooperate, and also compete. Moreover, there are few (if any) other biological species in which groups or crowds of individuals spend as much collective effort in attacking other groups or in defending their own group from the attacks of others (Boyer, 2018; Tooby & Cosmides, 2010). Humans also appear to be unique in their capacity for stable cultural transmission over many generations and for the pervasiveness of their moral cognitive concerns.

Human social cognition is a relatively recent and highly interdisciplinary topic of investigation in the cognitive sciences, ranging from evolutionary psychology to social cognitive neuroscience to developmental psychology. For example, evolutionary psychologists who advocate the "social brain hypothesis" have highlighted the correlation between the fact that humans have an unusually large brain in relation to their body size and the fact that they live in unusually large social groups, compared to all other biological species

(cf. Dunbar, 1992, 2003). Advocates of the so-called "Macchiavellian intelligence" hypothesis have suggested that the evolutionary arms race between the strategic demands for cooperation and competition among members of complex social groups must have placed strong selective pressures on human cognition, including the capacity to read others' minds or attribute mental states to others (cf. Byrne & Whiten, 1988; Humphrey, 1976).

This chapter focuses on a complementary body of work in developmental psychology, from the past forty years or so, devoted to the investigation of early social cognitive competencies in young human children and even in preverbal human infants. Now is a timely moment to write this chapter given that the field has undergone a recent transition in methods, that has radically changed how we understand the developmental origins of social cognition. Much early work relied on either action-based or verbal tasks, thus limiting researchers' ability to test for precocious

Département d'Etudes Cognitives receives support from Agence Nationale de la Recherche (grants ANR-10-IDEX-0001-02 PSL and ANR-17-EURE-0017 FrontCog). Andreas Falck gratefully acknowledges support from the Swedish Research Council, grant 2016-06783. Brent Strickland gratefully acknowledges support from PSL University (Aux Frontieres des Labex), grant IPFBW 2016-151. Pierre Jacob would like to acknowledge support from the European Research Council (ERC) under the European Union's Seventh Framework Program (FP7/2007-2013)/ERC Grant 609819.

abilities in pre-verbal infants. However, a shift occurred in developmental psychology in the 1980s with the advent of behavioral methods based on looking behavior. The violation-of-expectation method exploits the reliable tendency to look longer at unexpected rather than at expected events for the purpose of probing infant cognition. The anticipatory gaze method makes use of an eye-tracker to monitor infants' first gaze in anticipation of where an agent is likely to act. Though these methods were originally mainly applied to understand infants' representations of their non-social environment (e.g. their naive sense of physics and number), they have recently been applied to help reveal preverbal infants' expectations regarding their social environments.

Surprisingly, much developmental evidence suggests that early on young human children can represent both enduring (or stable) and episodic (or transient) social features of their conspecifics. For example, they can represent other people as agents, as speaking their mothers' tongue, as male or female, all of which are enduring social features likely to persist throughout an individual's lifespan. They can also attribute transient mental states to others, ranging from emotions to beliefs, most of which can change from moment to moment. In what follows, we first review developmental research into early sensitivity to, and understanding of, agency. Secondly, we review research into early theory of mind capacities to attribute mental states to others. Thirdly, we review research into early capacities to respond to cues of non-verbal communicative interactions, which are likely to play a crucial role in the process of cultural transmission. In the penultimate section, we review research into early sensitivity to in-group/out-group distinctions, including research about social essentialism in young children. Finally, we turn to the study of early moral cognition.

12.2 Early Perceptual Sensitivity to and Understanding of Agency in Human Infancy

Human infants and non-human animals display a remarkable ability to perceptually discriminate agents (i.e., living things which move about their environment autonomously) from non-agents in the earliest moments of life. For example, Vallortigara et al. (2005) showed that newly hatched chicks that had been reared in complete darkness prefer "point light displays" (i.e. displays with only minimal motion cues) which depict biological motion over those that depict closely matched but non-biological motion. Similarly, Simion et al. (2008) showed that two-day-old human infants have an ability to discriminate between equally unfamiliar biological and non-biological motion patterns, and that they have a preference to attend to displays containing biological motion.

It is important to appreciate that in these experiments the preferences for biological motion over non-biological motion are unlikely to be explained through familiarity to biological motion given both (a) the age of the participants (newborn humans or chicks) and (b) the fact that the displays in at least some conditions depicted motion patterns which are unlikely to be found in the participants' local environment (e.g., human infants being exposed to a display of a walking hen). Thus, these results strongly suggest an innate basis for "animacy detectors" within perception.

Consistent with the view that mechanisms dedicated to the tracking of animacy are deeply embedded in perception, we also see evidence for such "sophisticated" perceptual mechanisms in adults. For example, Gao et al. (2009) studied the perception of chasing, a form of biological motion, in displays that involved one geometric shape pursuing another geometric shape. Participants were asked to find the chasing figure amongst a set of otherwise identical geometric shapes. The authors demonstrated that observers' performance was systematically influenced by *chasing subtlety* (i.e., the degree to which the chaser deviated from perfectly "heat-seeking" pursuit) and *directionality* (how the shapes "face" each other), suggestive of a set of detection mechanisms with fairly specific "parameter settings," that in turn lead to predictable influences on behavior.

A separate demonstration of possible automatic mechanisms involved in the detection of animacy comes from New et al. (2007), in which adults saw repeating alternations between complex scenes and their duplicates with a single change, and were asked to spot the change. Participants were substantially better, in terms of both response time and accuracy, at detecting changes in animals relative to changes in all other categories of inanimate object. Along similar lines, Troje and Westhoff (2006) showed adults static point light displays in which the configural information (i.e., the relative positioning of the limbs) has been entirely disrupted. They found that participants were able to nevertheless accurately judge the motion direction of the figure (i.e. moving left or right). However, participants were impaired in detecting movement direction when the display was vertically inverted, suggesting that the adult visual system, like that of young infants, contains specific mechanisms for detecting animate motion and that these mechanisms are disrupted by inversion (but not by disrupting configural information).

Sensitivity to biological motion as well as socially relevant static displays is thus evident in adults' as well as infants' looking behavior. These overlapping sensitivities suggest a shared set of basic mechanisms that are present early in infancy and continue to exert an influence throughout the lifespan.

That an infant (or an adult) preferentially attends to a given type of display rather than another indicates discriminatory ability and relative interest, but says nothing regarding how they may represent different, but equally interesting displays. Some evidence for such differentiation comes from studies of infant imitation, to which we turn next.

Meltzoff and Moore (1983) offered preliminary evidence that neonates are able to imitate facial postures. Infants between one and seventy hours of age were shown an adult repeating two types of facial gestures in random order – either protruding their tongue or opening their mouth. The infants were more likely to respond to the protruding tongue with protruding their own tongue, and to the open mouth by opening their own mouth, than they were to respond with another gesture or not at all. In an earlier study (Meltzoff & Moore, 1977), slightly older infants (between twelve and seventeen days) were reported to also imitate lip protrusions and simple finger movements, in addition to tongue protrusions and mouth openings. Later in life infants could learn to imitate from reinforcement learning, for example by parents imitating the baby and then encouraging the baby when they continued doing what they just did. However, at this early age, the window for learning directly from social partners is still quite small. These results were interpreted as evidence for an early matching mechanism, whereby changes in the infants' visual inputs would be matched onto proprioceptive information from previous (in utero) experience of their own similar movements (Meltzoff & Moore, 1997).

Subsequent studies, however, have called into question some of these findings, and instead suggested that neonate imitation might be limited to tongue protrusions (Anisfeld, 1996; Oostenbroek et al., 2016) and have also challenged the hypothesis that infants imitate based on some matching between their own previously executed actions and others' seen actions. It might well be the case that the neonates stick out their tongue as an innate reflex triggered by some aspect of an observed pattern, or perhaps as a consequence of arousal due to interacting with another person (Oostenbroek et al., 2013). In a large study by Oostenbroek et al. (2016), infants were tested longitudinally at one, three, six, and nine weeks of age, and they were presented with a range of actions, including tongue protrusions. While Oostenbroek and colleagues found no clear-cut evidence for imitation of mouth opening, they found evidence for imitation of tongue protrusion, and they also found that infants are prone to stick their tongue out in response to other stimuli.

Another question that has been asked is: how well do infants distinguish goal-directed actions from other types of biological motion? A framework for studying the perception of goal-directed actions comes from an important discovery in the 1990s showing that macaque brains contain neurons that are active both when executing a specific manual action, and when observing someone (in the original study, a human) performing the same action (Gallese et al., 1996). Whereas the recording of activity of single cells is not viable in healthy humans, specific neural circuits that respond to both own and perceived actions have been identified in human brains using non-invasive neuroimaging techniques (Rizzolatti & Craighero, 2004). In infants, this "mirror neuron system" (MNS) has been primarily investigated with EEG, an electrophysiological technique that measures neural activity using electrodes mounted on the infant's head. These studies typically investigate mu- and alpha frequency band activation, previously shown in adults to correspond to MNS activity. Six-to-eight months infants' brains react differently to actions aimed at a target object, compared to actions without a clear goal

(Nyström, 2008; Nyström et al., 2010). Southgate et al. (2009) identified EEG activation in the alpha band that was elicited both when nine-month-old infants performed a grasping action themselves, and when they observed someone else grasp for an object. In addition to providing direct support for "mirror"-type activity in infancy, they also found that this activity started as soon as the goal of the action could be anticipated, corroborating the specificity for goal-directed (as opposed to other) action.

Using an anticipatory gaze task, Falck-Ytter et al. (2006) investigated infants' ability to anticipate the target of a manual action. They showed that adults and twelve-month-olds, but not six-month-olds, anticipated the goal of a human agent's action by looking in advance to the place where the agent was about to place an object. In contrast, if a mechanical robot arm moved the object only adults anticipated the goal in advance, suggesting again a preference for biological motion in early perception. Moreover, action anticipation by gaze in ten-month-olds is correlated with the infants' ability to look in advance at the target of their own actions (Rosander & von Hofsten, 2011). Twelve-month-olds playing with a caregiver keep visual focus on the object being played with, regardless of whether they themselves or the adult caregiver handles the object (Yu & Smith, 2013), suggesting a close coupling between MNS activity and visual attention at this age.

A final branch of research has focused on the ways in which the neonate (and adult) visual system is attuned to human faces. Two-day-old newborns preferentially orient toward faces or face-like stimuli over similarly complex but non-face stimuli (Johnson et al., 1991; Valenza et al., 1996). Newborn infants prefer to look at an upright face than at an inverted face. But they prefer an upright face only if the eye region exhibits a polarity contrast similar to the contrast between the dark iris and the white sclera characteristic of the human eye, not if it is reversed. This pattern has been hypothesized to reflect a bias toward potential communicative partners (Farroni et al., 2005). This selective processing of face-like stimuli has recently been suggested to be present even before birth (Reid et al., 2017). Human fetuses (eight months gestational age) turned their head more often toward a face-like configuration of dots projected onto the uterus wall than to an inverted version of the same projection. At four-to-five months infants follow an adult's gaze-shift, but only if the adult has antecedently made eye contact with them (Farroni et al., 2003).

12.3 Early Theory of Mind

What is known as *mindreading* is the cognitive capacity to attribute mental states (e.g., beliefs, desires, intentions, emotions and affective states) to self and others. In their seminal paper entitled "Does the chimpanzee have a theory of mind?," Premack and Woodruff (1978) called this capacity "theory of mind," on two grounds: first, the attributed mental states themselves are not observable. Secondly, by attributing mental states to an agent, one may understand and predict her likely observable behavior. Thus, theory of mind enables an observer to make sense of an agent's action by attributing to her a relevant desire to achieve her goal in the light of her relevant epistemic states (beliefs) about her immediate surroundings.

12.3.1 Rational Action, Goals, and Intentions

In the 1990s, the developmental investigation of infants' understanding of others' goals and motivations gave rise to three influential sets of findings, the first of which is that early on infants apply a "teleological stance" to others' goal-directed instrumental actions. In the familiarization trials of a series of studies, twelve-month-olds saw on a computer screen a goal-directed event whereby a small circle approached a larger circle by jumping over a rectangular obstacle. During the test phase, the rectangle that stood in between the two circles was removed and the infants either saw the small circle exhibit the same jumping behavior as before or approach the larger circle by moving in a straight line. The infants looked reliably longer at the same jumping action that they had already seen rather than at the novel straight-line approach that they had not seen before (Csibra et al., 1999; Gergely et al., 1995). These findings are consistent with the hypothesis that infants apply what Csibra and Gergely call the "teleological stance," namely that they attribute a goal to the agent and expect the agent to select the most efficient action as a means to fulfill his goal in the presence of local environmental constraints. Further research has shown that twelve-month-old infants are able to compute any one of the three components of the teleological stance from the other pair: the agent's goal, the agent's action-means, and the local environmental constraints (Csibra et al., 2003).

A second influential line of research was launched by Amanda Woodward's (1998, 1999) demonstration of the so-called Woodward effect. Six-month-olds were first habituated to seeing a human hand in a grasping posture repeatedly reach for and rest on the top of one of a pair of toys, e.g. the teddy bear, not the ball. In the test conditions, the toys' spatial positions were switched and the infants saw the hand either reach for the same toy (e.g. the teddy bear) at a new location or a new toy (e.g. the ball) at the previous location where the hand acted in the familiarization trials. Infants looked reliably longer when the hand reached for the new toy at the old location than for the old toy at the new location. Early studies showed that the Woodward effect disappeared if the human hand was either replaced by a mechanical device (e.g. an inanimate rod topped with a sponge or a mechanical claw) or if, instead of seeing a human hand in a grasping posture, infants saw the back of a human hand repeatedly drop on the same toy (Woodward, 1998, 1999).

The fact that the Woodward effect disappeared in both cases has been interpreted by Woodward herself and some of her colleagues as evidence that action understanding in human infancy is achieved by mirroring or mirror neuron activity (Hamlin et al., 2008; Sommerville et al., 2005; Woodward et al., 2009). Recall from Section 12.2 that mirror neuron activity in an observer's brain is taken to rest on motor familiarity with the agent's action and to enable an observer to understand the agent's action by covertly replicating her bodily movements. On this approach, the fact that mirror neurons failed to fire when a monkey observed an experimenter grasp a peanut with pliers seems like an anticipation of the disappearance of the Woodward effect when infants see an act performed by a mechanical claw (Rizzolatti et al., 1996, 2001; Umilta et al., 2001).

Further support for the mirroring interpretation of the Woodward effect comes from studies showing that active motor experience may enhance infants' understanding of others' goal-directed actions. For example, ten-month-olds, who initially failed to exhibit the Woodward effect when they saw an agent use a tool to fetch one of two toys, exhibited the Woodward effect after being actively trained to use the tool. Three-month-olds, who are notoriously unable to reach and grasp objects accurately, have also been shown not to exhibit the classical Woodward effect.

However, three-month-olds have been shown to exhibit the Woodward effect after being trained to grasp objects accurately with the use of sticky mittens, thus allowing the infants to grasp reached-for objects despite their lack of motor skill in this respect (Hamlin et al., 2008; Sommerville et al., 2005; Woodward et al., 2009).

This finding suggests that infants need some first-hand experience for the Woodward-effect to appear, thus lending support to mirror neuron accounts of the effect (Woodward et al., 2009). However, Skerry et al. (2013) have also trained a group of three-month-olds to accurately grasp a target by using sticky mittens. All infants saw an agent either efficiently reach an object by arching her arm over a barrier or inefficiently perform the same arching movements in the absence of a barrier. Only infants who had experienced sticky mittens looked longer when they saw an agent perform an inefficient action. Infants who had first-personal motor experience with mittens did not have first-personal motor experience with efficiently reaching for an object by arching their arm over a barrier. Skerry and colleagues conclude that, while motor experience with mittens might help three-month-old infants to attend to or identify the targets of others' goal-directed actions, the ability to compute the efficiency of actions must already be in place at this age. Similarly, motor experience with mittens might help three-month-old infants to better attend to the target of the agent's preference in the Woodward effect.

Consistent with this interpretation, many subsequent studies have also provided evidence for the presence of the Woodward effect when infants lack motor familiarity with the agent's action. For example, the Woodward effect is vindicated when infants see the back of a human hand not only contact a target but also displace it (Jovanovic et al., 2007; Kiràly et al., 2003). It also emerges when the agent is a box which provides robust cues of self-propelledness (Luo and Baillargeon, 2005) and when the agent is a rod topped with a sponge that provides robust cues of equifinal variations of behavior, whereby the rod uses different means to achieve a single goal (Biro & Leslie, 2007). Infants have even been shown to attribute a goal to an agent who performed a biologically impossible action, e.g., a human arm snaking around obstacles (Southgate et al., 2008). Thus, the agent need not exhibit any obvious perceptual similarity with a human (or even an animal) body. Nor need the agent's action be part of the infants' motor repertoire. Two conditions, however, seem necessary for the presence of the Woodward effect. First, the agent must exhibit self-propelled movements and provide evidence that they are able to produce equifinal variations of behavior. Secondly, the agent must face a choice between two competing targets. As Luo and Baillargeon (2005) have shown with five-month-olds and Luo (2011a) with three-month-olds, infants look longer when the agent approaches a new target at the old location rather than the same target at a new location, only if they first saw the agent repeatedly approach one of a pair of targets, not if there was only one target in the familiarization trials (cf. Jacob, 2012, for further discussion).

A third influential set of recent findings by Tomasello and his group has highlighted the central role of processes of so-called shared intentionality in early human children's social cognitive development. The shared-intentionality framework rests on the three following pillars. Making eye contact with an agent has been shown to trigger gaze-following in early human infancy (Farroni et al., 2003). Next, gaze-following is the basis for the early emergence of joint attention whereby two individuals are aware of attending to the same target. Finally, infants are taken to be uniquely motivated not only for joint attention, but also for forming joint goals and performing joint actions, with others (Tomasello, 2014; Tomasello et al., 2005). While Tomasello and colleagues have stressed the role of competitive interactions (especially in relation to food) among non-human apes, many of their studies have shown that, early on, young children are altruistically inclined to help an agent achieve her goal. Young children have been shown to help someone else by fetching an out-of-reach object, by sharing commodities and information with others. While Warnecken and Tomasello (2006, 2007, 2009) have shown that young children are inclined to help an agent whom they see trying and failing to achieve a goal, Liszkowski et al. (2006) offer evidence that eighteen- and even twelve-month-olds are motivated to point to objects which they believe an adult is looking for. More recently, Knudsen and Liszkowski (2012) have shown that twenty-four- and eighteen-month-olds spontaneously point to an object's location for the benefit of an agent, but only if the agent's goal is to retrieve the object and the agent has a false belief about its location, not if the agent either knows the object's location or her goal is not to retrieve it.

12.3.2 False-Belief Understanding

Following the publication and discussion of Premack and Woodruff's (1978) paper, much psychological research into the mindreading capacities of young human children, human adults, and non-human animals has focused on the capacity to attribute false beliefs to others. To be able to predict the likely action of a mistaken agent has been widely taken to show that one expects that another's action depends not merely on non-mental features of her environment, but on *her mental representation* of her environment. This research has given rise to importantly discrepant findings.

One strand of research based on verbal tasks initiated by Wimmer and Perner's (1983) paper has reliably shown that when directly asked to predict where a mistaken agent is likely to look for her toy (after the toy's location was changed in the agent's absence), most preschoolers (who know where the toy really is) incorrectly point to the toy's actual location. Most children correctly point to the empty location where the agent falsely believes her toy to be only when they are four and a half years old (Wellman et al., 2001).

Another strand of research based on non-verbal tests (including looking behavior, helping behaviour, and brain responses) has produced increasing evidence that preverbal infants expect an agent to act on the basis of the content of her true or false belief. For example, in their ground-breaking study, Onishi and Baillargeon (2005) found that fif-teen-month-olds look longer when an agent looks for her toy at its actual location rather than at the now empty location, when she did not see the toy's change of location. They also look longer when the agent looks for her toy at the now empty location rather than at the toy's actual location, when she saw the toy change location. Southgate and Vernetti (2014) found that the motor system of six-month-olds does not respond in the same way according to whether they are presented with an agent who falsely believes that a toy is in the box in front of her or whether she falsely believes the box to be empty. The same brain areas, the temporal-parietal junction in the right hemisphere (rTPJ), which are active when adults attribute false beliefs have been shown to be active in seven-month-old infants when they watch videos depicting a mistaken agent's action (Hyde et al., 2018).

Luo (2011b) investigated a combination of belief and preference attribution in ten-month-olds and showed that the Woodward effect appears even in the absence of a second non-preferred object, as long as the agent believes there to be a second object available to reach for. This suggests that infants can use information about others' beliefs in order to attribute preferences. Drawing on this result, Kampis et al. (2013) used a similar design, but replaced the agent from the familiarization trials by another agent in the test event. Interestingly, they found that the infants looked longer even when this new agent reached for the non-preferred object instead of the preferred object, suggesting that the infants generalized one agent's preference to another. Kampis and colleagues suggest that ten-month-old infants might not yet attribute mental states to specific agents, but are still able to represent the contents of others' beliefs and preferences in order to learn about the world.

There is presently no consensus on how to reconcile the discrepant developmental findings about false-belief understanding in early human childhood (see Chapter 11). Some researchers take it that only findings based on verbal false-belief tasks can reliably be taken as evidence for theory of mind. Their main burden is to offer a non-mentalistic account of the infant data. Other researchers take the infant data at face value as evidence for false-belief understanding in human infancy. Their main burden is to explain why verbal false-belief tasks are so challenging for preschoolers.

12.4 Natural Pedagogy in Infancy

According to evolutionary biologists, not all interactions between pairs of animals are com-municative (Maynard-Smith & Harper, 2003; Scott-Phillips, 2014). Only if both an agent's signal and his recipient's response have been shaped by evolution by natural selection do two animals communicate in the biological sense. For example, a vervet monkey's leopard alarm call and his recipient's escape response count as a communicative interaction. To the leopard itself, however, the vervet's call does not count as a communicative signal: instead, it is a *cue* of the monkey's presence. If a bird is scared by the vervet's call, the call does not count as a communicative signal either: instead, it *coerces* the bird's response.

Furthermore, not every communicative interaction involves so-called *ostensive* signals. What makes an agent's behavior ostensive is that its purpose is to provide the agent's recipient (or audience) with evidence that the agent has some communicative intention to convey information relevant to her recipient. Speech is a typical ostensive signal that conveys the speaker's communicative intention. Among non-verbal ostensive signals are making eye contact and smiling. Thus, in ostensive communicative interactions, an agent (e.g., Sally) has two related intentions: first, Sally has the informative intention to cause her recipient (e.g., Bob) to acquire a new mental state (e.g., a new belief). For example, Sally, who knows both that Bob is looking for his keys and where Bob's keys are, wants to make the location of his keys manifest to Bob. Secondly, she also has the communicative intention to make her informative intention manifest to Bob. Sally could tell Bob where his keys are either using linguistic stimuli (which are intrinsically ostensive) or ostensively pointing to their location.

There is evidence that very early on infants are attuned to both visual and auditory ostensive signals. Recall from Section 12.2 that infants are preferentially sensitive to being looked at. Infants' preference for a canonical orientation of another's frontal face has been interpreted as evidence for their early preparedness to be the recipients of communicative demonstrations (Csibra, 2010). Ostensive signals also exist in the auditory modality: for example, the special intonation pattern of infant-directed speech (so-called motherese)

can make it manifest that an infant is the intended recipient of speech. We know that newborns prefer speech over non-speech (Vouloumanos & Werker, 2007) and that they prefer their mother's voice over any other voice (Cooper & Aslin, 1990). By the age of four months, infants have been shown to prefer hearing their mother speak in infant-directed speech to a range of other acoustic stimulus (Csibra, 2010).

Since young infants follow gaze only after being looked at first (cf. Section 12.2), most if not all of their early learning from others' gaze takes place in communicative contexts. Six-month-olds have been shown to follow an adult's gaze to an object only if the adult first made eye contact with them or greeted them in motherese, not otherwise (Senju & Csibra, 2008). In a study by Csibra and Volein (2008), eight-month-olds first saw on a computer screen an adult ostensively greet them and make eye contact with them. Then the infants saw the adult shift her gaze toward one of two opaque barriers. Finally, an object was revealed behind the targeted or the non-targeted barrier. Infants' looking time indicated that they expected to find an object behind the barrier toward which the agent had shifted her gaze. Furthermore, in a detection study by Yoon et al. (2008), nine-month-olds were introduced to an object that an agent was either reaching for or ostensively pointing to. After the object was occluded for five seconds, the infants detected a change of its location, but not its visual properties, in the reaching context. The infants detected a change of the object's visual properties, but not its location, in the ostensive communicative context. This last finding has been interpreted as evidence that when infants perceive a novel object as the referent of an ostensive communicative act, they encode and remember better its enduring properties (e.g., its shape and color) than its transient properties, such as its location. In contrast, when infants' attention is drawn to the same object as the target of an agent's instrumental goal-directed action, they focus on its episodic location at the expense of its enduring visual features.

In a seminal study by Gergely et al. (2002), inspired by an earlier imitation study by Meltzoff (1988), fourteen-month-olds saw a model perform an odd action whereby she used her head rather than one of her hands in order to turn on a light box in front of her in two different conditions. In the so-called hands-occupied condition, the model used her hands to wrap herself within a shawl and hold the shawl around her shoulders. In the "hands-free" condition, she ostensibly placed her free hands on the table. Before performing her odd action, the model ostensively greeted the children. Like in Meltzoff's original study, Gergely and colleagues found that, while 69 percent of the children re-enacted the model's head action in the hands-free condition, only 21 percent did in the hands-occupied condition. Arguably, in the hands-occupied condition, the agent's choice of the head action looked to the children like an efficient means to achieve her goal of turning the light on. So most of the children selected their own hands, which were not occupied, as a means to turning the light on. But in the hands-free condition, the agent's choice of the head action must have looked opaque, as she might have used her hands, but she did not. So in the teleologically more opaque condition, most children decided to replicate the model's head-action. As reported in a later study, when the agent did not ostensively greet the children, the asymmetrical replication of the model's head-action in the hands-occupied and the hands-free condition disappeared (Király et al., 2003). These findings suggest that when the application of the teleological stance to an agent's instrumental action fails to make the action intelligible to young children, they turn

to what Csibra and Gergely (2009) call "natural pedagogy," whereby they assume that the agent's action is a non-verbal teaching demonstration from which they can expect to acquire some novel generic information.

Several studies further suggest that in the context of a non-verbal ostensive communicative interaction with an adult, toddlers, and even infants can encode not just episodic (or transient) but generic (or enduring) information. For example, eighteen-month-olds saw an agent display a positive emotional expression toward one object and a negative emotional expression toward another object, either in the context of ostensive signals or not. In both contexts, upon request by the same agent, the infants reliably gave her the object that had been the target of her earlier positive emotional display. But when a new agent requested an object, the infants also gave her the object that had been the target of the first agent's earlier positive emotional display in the ostensive context, but they were at chance in the non-ostensive context (Egyed et al., 2013).

A third study by Futó et al. (2010) shows how ostensive signals are likely to contribute to young children's acquisition of general (or generic) knowledge. In the familiarization trials of the first of three experiments by Futo et al. (2010), based on Xu and Carey's (1996) paradigm for investigating the capacity for object-individuation in infants, ten-month-olds were exposed to a non-verbal demonstration of the functions of a pair of toys. After the infants had been ostensively greeted in motherese, they first saw a human hand demonstrate the function of one toy on one side of a screen and the distinct function of a different toy on the other side of the screen, while the infants never saw the two toys together. After the screen was removed, the infants saw either both objects or only one of them. They looked reliably longer when they saw only one object rather than two. Further evidence showed that the effect of function demonstration on object-individuation depends on both the presence of ostensive signals and on an agent's manipulation of the toys. Finally, the infants saw exactly the same sequence of events as before except that they saw two functions being demonstrated with a single more complex toy (rather than two). Infants looked longer after the screen was removed and they discovered the single toy that they had actually seen, rather than the two distinct toys used in the first experiment. In other words, these infants experienced an illusion of being presented with two objects when in fact they saw only one.

Butler and Markman (2012) have further explored the cognitive mechanisms enabling young children to acquire generic information from the ostensive communicative demonstration of teachers. Four-year-olds were presented with eleven wooden blocks and taught that their name was "blicket." Only one out of eleven blickets had a (non-visible) magnetic tape on one end. The children were shown the unexpected property of the magnetic blicket: by applying the blicket with magnetic tape to paper clips, the experimenter picked up the paper clips, in three distinct conditions. In the pedagogical condition, the children were informed that they would be taught something novel and interesting before the magnetic property of the blicket was demonstrated. In the accidental condition, the experimenter accidentally dropped the magnetic blicket onto the paper clips. In the intentional condition, the experimenter deliberately placed the magnetic blicket onto the paper clips without ostensively addressing the infants. In all three conditions, after her demonstration, the experimenter placed all eleven blickets on the table and encouraged the children to play with them. Butler and Markman (2012) found that children's persistence in exploring the magnetic property of blickets in the face of mounting negative evidence was remarkably

stronger in the pedagogical than in either the accidental or the intentional condition. Butler and Markman argue that children assumed that they had been ostensively taught something about the *kind* of things called "blicket," not to be dismissed easily on the basis of counter-examples.

What the last findings strongly suggest is that in the presence of verbal or non-verbal ostensive communicative demonstrations young human children seem prone to a kind of cheap generalization which is reflected by generic sentences in natural languages, such as "ducks lay eggs," "tigers are striped," or "ticks carry Lyme disease" (which have long been studied by linguists and philosophers, Brandone et al., 2012; Leslie, 2007, 2008). What matters primarily to such generalizations is that they fit with psychological essentialism in that they provide general information about *kinds*, not just particulars. The propositional contents of such generic sentences, which are widely taken to be true by human adults, are clearly different from the contents of universally quantified sentences such as "all ducks lay eggs," "all tigers are striped," or "all ticks carry Lyme disease," which would be widely taken to be false. A single counterexample is sufficient to refute a universal generalization, but not the proposition expressed by a sentence with generic content. Despite the obvious fact that a majority of ducks, including males and infertile females, do not lay eggs, most adults would accept as true an utterance of the generic sentence "ducks lay eggs." Despite the known fact that a minute percentage of ticks actually carry Lyme disease, most adults would also accept as true an utterance of the generic sentence "ticks carry Lyme disease." Even for human adults who have acquired a natural language that makes them able to form other generalizations (e.g., universal ones) generics may be the default kind of human generalization. It may be the signature of preverbal infants' way of generalizing in response to non-verbal ostensive communicative demonstrations.

12.5 Early Understanding of Groups

Human social cognition also faces demands arising from the size and role of social groups in human social life. Humans benefit from in-group support, affiliation, and solidarity because they are unique among other biological species in depending on others not only for relevant information about their environment, but also for performing joint and collective actions that require coordination, cooperation, and communication. Coordination, cooperation, and communication among humans apply to kin and non-kin as well. Human adults have long been shown to display a preference for members of their own in-group at the expense of out-group members, even if the grouping is based on the flimsiest and most arbitrary criteria, such as the color of a scarf (Brewer, 1979; Tajfel et al., 1971). Similar phenomena have been demonstrated in three-year-old human children (Plötner et al., 2015). Like many other social animals, humans must attend to the costs and benefits of dominance hierarchies in their own social groups. More than any other social animals, they are also likely to suffer from racial prejudice, in-group bias, xenophobia, nationalism, and group conflicts ranging from civil wars to genocides (Boyer, 2018).

Contemporary humans in different parts of the world are known to speak approximately 6,500 different natural languages. One of the strongest cues of group membership in humans is therefore spoken native language. Moreover, which language an individual can speak is likely to be an enduring or stable social feature of the individual, thus increasing the possible value of keeping track of this information.

Given that infants are embedded in speech communities and speech patterns bear meaningful information about social relationships, it is perhaps no surprise that their preferences about who to attend to and who to interact with are informed by speech. Newborn human infants have been shown to have an early preference for listening to speech over non-speech that has been compared to birds' predisposition to attend to the vocalizations of conspecifics. In particular, they have been shown to exhibit a preference for the sound of their mother's voice and for their native language (Gervain & Mehler, 2010). Infants are the recipients of many of their caretakers' utterances. But they also process many verbal exchanges from a third-person perspective and there is evidence that they understand very early on the role of speech in communicative interactions, of which they are not the recipient (Martin et al., 2012).

Not only do they discriminate speech from non-speech, but they also understand that speech serves a communicative function. Infants' social preferences are also highly informed by speech patterns, consistent with their using speech type as a cue to group membership. Six-month-olds display a preference for a speaker of their native language by looking reliably longer at a person whose speech was a regular sequence of words from their native tongue rather than at a person whose speech was a sequence of words from their native tongue played backwards. Same age infants have been shown to prefer to receive a toy from a speaker of their native tongue rather than from a speaker of a foreign language (Kinzler et al., 2007) or to reach for a toy held and manipulated by a speaker of their native tongue rather than a foreign speaker (Kinzler et al., 2012). Twelve-month-olds have been shown to prefer a piece of food toward which a speaker of their native language had displayed positive affect over food toward which a speaker of a foreign language speaker has displayed either a negative of a positive affect (Shutts et al., 2009).

Accent is also likely to be a cue of group membership. Five-year-old children have been shown to choose to be friends with native speakers of their native language rather than with foreign-language or foreign-accented speakers, when presented with photographs and voice recordings of novel children (Kinzler et al., 2009). Five-to-six-year-olds have also been shown to prefer foreign-accented and pro-social (or nice) agents over native-accented and anti-social (or mean) agents (Kinzler & DeJesus, 2013). Accent has also been shown to trump race in five-year-olds: in a similar paradigm, children robustly used native accent, rather than race, to guide their social preferences (Kinzler et al., 2009).

Incipient group cognition is likely to interact with natural pedagogy in human infancy along the following lines. Recall from Section 12.2 that the role of the polarity contrast in infants' preference for an upright face has been interpreted as a bias toward potential communicative partners (Farroni et al., 2005). In a recent study, Begus et al. (2016) used electroencephalography (EEG) techniques in eleven-month-olds to record so-called *theta* activity, a neural rhythm in the brain shown to index active and selective preparation for encoding information in adults. In the first experiment, infants were familiarized with a pair of agents and a set of objects: the infants saw one agent (the informant) label the objects, while the other (non-informant) agent pointed to the objects without labeling them. In the second experiment, the infants saw the informant agent demonstrate the objects' functions, while the non-informant agent reached for the objects. In the third experiment, the infants saw one agent label objects in the infants' native tongue and the other agent label the same objects in a foreign language. At test, in the so-called

anticipation phase, just before either agent interacted with objects, the experimenters recorded theta activity and found that it was reliably stronger when infants faced the informant agent from whom they were most likely to receive useful information rather than the non-informant agent. This finding suggests that very early on infants are cognitively attuned to selecting the right opportunities to learn from informative others.

Human adults and older children uniquely derive much of their knowledge of the world from the verbal testimony of others, which can be either truthful or not. While infants do not have much of a choice about whether or not to trust their caretakers, older children must learn to selectively allocate their trust to others. On the one hand, confronted with a pair of informants, one of whom systematically mislabeled familiar objects, most three-to-four-year-olds have been shown to reliably discard the testimony of even a reliable source if it conflicts with their own perceptual experience (Clément et al., 2004). In the same situation, four-year-olds have also been shown to prefer the reliable, over the unreliable, source's label in relation to unfamiliar objects (Clément et al., 2004). On the other hand, although young children understand the contrast between a benevolent and a malevolent agent, they find it quite hard to detect a straight lie that is addressed to them. For example, when their task was to infer the falsity of a speaker's utterance from their understanding of the speaker's deceptive intent, most four-year-olds have been shown to fail (Mascaro and Sperber, 2009).

In the studies reviewed so far showing how language is a cue to group membership, young children and infants were the recipients of linguistic communicative signals. Nine-month-olds, however, have also been shown to be able to infer social affiliation on the basis of third-party linguistic exchanges, according to whether the partners spoke the same language or not (Liberman et al., 2017). Moreover, unlike other primates, humans seem to have uniquely multimodal imitative capacities, including especially the capacity for vocal imitation, without which human infants would be unlikely to learn a shared and arbitrary lexicon (Hauser et al., 2002). Thus, infants' understanding of imitation (or replicative behavior) has turned out to be a fruitful way to investigate their early understanding of third-party social affiliation.

In a first set of studies by Powell and Spelke (2013), seven- and eight-month-olds were shown to expect members of a group to act alike. The infants were shown videos depicting two groups of identical geometrical objects with a pair of eyes, one comprised of three orange stars and the other comprised of three purple trapezoids. Infants were first familiarized to seeing members of each group perform a typical sequence of dancing motions and sounds. Before the test trials, two members of each group displayed a type of action distinctive of their group (either jump or slide) accompanied by a sound also distinctive of their group. In the test trials, each member of each group performed the same action: half the infants saw both agents perform the action distinctive of one group. Half saw both agents perform the action distinctive of the other group. Every member of the pair of agents seen by all the infants performed an action (jump or slide) either congruent with that of its group (consistent trial) or incongruent with that of its group (inconsistent trial). Infants looked reliably longer at inconsistent than at consistent trials. In a second set of studies by Powell and Spelke (2018), also involving geometrical objects, infants saw one agent replicate the behavior of members of one group of two individuals, but not the behavior of members of a second group of two individuals. Four-month-olds were more surprised and

looked longer when the imitators approached and thereby affiliated with the group of agents that they had not imitated rather than those they had imitated. Infants did not have the converse expectation that the models would exhibit affiliative behavior toward the imitators. Powell and Spelke (2018) found that when presented with an imitator and a non-imitator, twelve-month-olds were significantly more likely to reach for the former than the latter.

To the extent that dominance is a fairly stable relation, members of a group must be able to keep track of dominance relations. In the familiarization trials of a study by Mascaro and Csibra (2012), twelve-month-olds saw a dominant agent prevail over a subordinate agent in a competitive situation. At test, infants were more surprised and looked longer when the expected subordinate agent was shown to prevail over the expected dominant agent. When they were familiarized to one sample of behavior displayed by one dominant agent over a subordinate, fifteen-month-olds (but not twelve-month-olds) were found to expect this pattern to generalize to other behavioral patterns involving the same agents. Infants were not shown to expect an agent who had already prevailed over one subordinate to prevail over a novel agent. Finally, fifteen-month-olds were familiarized to a transitive dominance relation involving three agents, such that B dominated A and C dominated B. The findings show that fifteen-month-olds did not extend their expectations of dominance to unobserved relationships (e.g., between C and A), even when they could have been established by transitive inference.

It has been recently argued that adult human psychology must include evolved cognitive mechanisms designed to garner support from other individuals, organize and maintain alliances, measure potential support from group members, and manage intergroup relations and conflicts (Boyer, 2018; Tooby & Cosmides, 2010). Kurzban and colleagues have further argued that in adults the encoding of others' racial or ethnic features might be a by-product of the cognitive machinery that evolved to detect coalitional alliances (Cosmides et al.,; Kurzban et al., 2001). There is some evidence for early sensitivity to ethnic differences in young children and even in infants. For example, three-month-old infants, but not one-month-olds, have been shown to discriminate their own, more commonly encountered, race, from other, less encountered, races (Kelly et al., 2005). Much work has shown the importance of psychological essentialism in young human children, that is, the belief that members of a category share a deep underlying nature or essence in virtue of which they are, and are likely to remain, fundamentally similar to one another. Psychological essentialism in young human children has been well documented in the biological, mentalistic, and social cognitive domains. For example, young children have been shown to assume that all exemplars of a biological species share hidden features (cf. Atran, 1995; Carey, 1995; Hirschfeld, 1995b for discussion), all humans have minds and mental states (cf. Section 12.3), and all members of social groups exemplify some common social categories (e.g., profession or race) (Gelman & Hirschfeld, 1999). Some evidence shows that pre-schoolers reason about race even if they do not readily exploit visually encoded information about it (Hirschfeld, 1995a).

Much coalitional psychology comprises inferences about in- and out-group membership. In a set of studies by Jin and Baillargeon (2017), seventeen-month-olds gave evidence that they entertained an abstract expectation of in-group support. When they saw live events in which a woman needed instrumental assistance to achieve her goal, they expected another woman to provide the necessary assistance (and were surprised if the latter did not help the former), only if they were aware that the two women were members of the same minimal group (see Section 12.6 for further discussion). In a study by Pietraszewski and German (2013), four-to-five-year-olds have been shown to understand the significance of "indirect social consequences," whereby the consequences of an observed interaction between a pair of human agents may extend far beyond the two interacting individuals. For instance, only the victim of a physical aggression is likely to feel pain. Friends of the victim uninvolved in the interaction are not likely to feel the victim's physical pain. But both the victim and his uninvolved friends are likely to feel anger at the aggressor. Pietraszewski and German (2013) found that preschoolers expected an uninvolved individual to feel anger if their friend had been the victim of an aggression, but not dizziness if their friend had endured a dizziness-inducing event. But Pietraszewski and German (2013) also found an interesting difference between adults and preschoolers: preschoolers expected, but adults did not expect, uninvolved friends of the aggressor and uninvolved friends of the victim to be angry to the same degree.

12.6 Early Moral Cognition

Historically speaking, moral philosophy has preceded the psychological investigation of human moral cognition in human adults and human children. Moral philosophy was mostly devoted to semantic, ontological, and epistemological issues: Do moral thoughts and utterances have truth-conditions? Do moral values fit in a naturalistic (causal) picture of the world? Can there be knowledge of moral values?

Research into moral psychology (including developmental psychology) of the past fifty or so years can be broken down along four dimensions: the contrast between a nativist and a non-nativist approach to the moral sense; the contrast between a rationalist and an emotivist approach to moral cognitive processes; the contrast between the capacity respectively for intuitive moral judgments and for moral justifications; and the role of cross-cultural studies of moral values for the study of human moral cognition.

Nativist views (e.g., Darwin, 1871) hold that humans' sense of morality is innately defined, be it innately good or innately evil. On the other hand, non-nativist views hold that our grasp of moral rules is a product of our experience with the world. For example, one popular non-nativist view was John Locke's empiricism (Locke, 1793) that claimed that children were essentially blank slates and only acquired their grasp of moral rules through experience provided by elders in their communities and households.

The second dimension along which we can categorize moral theories is the rational versus emotional divide. According to rationalist views (e.g., Kant, 1785), coming to understand and accept moral norms is the result of a rational or reason-based process. On the other hand, emotional views of morality (e.g., Hume, 1738) have claimed that our sense of right and wrong emerges primarily from our emotions and affective experiences (Buon et al., 2016).

The earliest work in cognitive psychology focusing on the development of morality (Kohlberg, 1976; Piaget, 1932) took a rationalist and non-nativist view of cognitive development. These theories asserted that moral understanding was "self-constructed." In other words, an understanding of moral norms is not given at birth, nor is it a product of mere learning from one's community. Instead children figure moral norms out for themselves, but only when they are capable of the appropriate forms of reasoning. The forms of reasoning that children are capable of are defined by various cognitive "stages."

The most influential "constructivist" view of moral development has been Kohlberg's (1976). Kohlberg's method was to present children with a narrated complex moral dilemma, for example, a husband steals a drug (which is wrong) in order to save his wife from cancer (which is right). Children are then asked to explain or justify their moral evaluation of the action. In the so-called pre-conventional stages of moral development, children were taken to reason only about consequences in deciding whether an action was right or wrong. So, for example, children might reason that stealing is wrong because they would get punished for it. Then around elementary school ages, children were taken to enter the so-called conventional stages in which they would reason from authority and normal behavior. So, for example, a child might reason that stealing is wrong because their teacher said it was wrong or because it is against the rules. One aspect of Kohlberg's view is that the child is expected to treat merely conventional rules (e.g., rules about what to wear to school) as moral rules: both are supposed to be processed as conventions using the same set of processes. Finally, in so-called post-conventional stages (which arrive after puberty), Kohlberg found that adolescents began to think for themselves about the underlying principles behind conventional rules, and he postulated that children were like ethicists capable of working out coherent ethical systems for themselves (Haidt, 2012). In these stages, children are taken to be capable of justifying a local dishonest act (e.g., stealing medicine) in pursuit of a higher good (e.g., saving a life).

This stage level view has been criticized on multiple grounds. First, children are often inconsistent in the types of responses they provide, and sometimes giving responses that span four or more stages (Krebs & Denton, 2005). Moreover, even very young children sometimes showed responses that were compatible with those one would only expect to find in the most advanced stages. Thus, Kohlberg's stages turned out not to be as clear-cut as they were meant to be (Keil, 2014). Secondly, Kohlberg's theory has been criticized on cross-cultural grounds. His theory was meant to be a universal theory regarding the stages of development for moral thought. However, if one were to use Kohlberg's methods to assess non-Western populations, one would conclude that some never make it past the pre-conventional stages (Keil, 2014; Kurtines & Greif, 1974). Instead, Kohlberg's system appears to be systematically biased in favor of Western moral systems that place a high priority on fairness, preventing harm, and the ability to question authority at the expense of loyalty, respect for authority, and purity, which have been shown to be important values in some cultures.

Thirdly, Kohlberg's system can be criticized on methodological grounds. Essentially Kohlberg's method assesses children's developing capacity to verbally justify and explain their own moral evaluations prompted by reflection on complex moral dilemmas, not their intuitive moral judgments. The main scientific question is the extent to which young human children's capacity for moral evaluation of human social interactions are correctly appraised by tasks that require them to verbally justify and explain their moral judgments. Recent developmental work in both social and non-social cognitive domains strongly suggests that the moral cognitive capacities of young human children (including preverbal infants) might be under-estimated by focusing on verbal tasks of justification.

A new fundamental step was taken by Turiel (1983; Turiel et al., 1987), who developed a verbal technique that bypassed some of these methodological problems by describing a scenario and asking young children simple "yes/no" questions (instead of asking them to generate complex explanations and justifications). Using this technique, Turiel et al. observed that, contrary to what Piaget and Kohlberg claimed, young children (as young as five years old) reason differently about moral norms and mere conventions. For example, children were told a story about another child going to school wearing pajamas whereas the school requires children to wear a uniform. Children were first asked: "Was it ok for the boy to do what he did?" Most children responded "No." Secondly, children were probed with a follow-up question: "What if the teacher said it was OK for the boy to wear pajamas? Would it be ok then?" Most answered "Yes." Finally, they were asked: "What if the boy were to wear pajamas in another school where this was allowed? Would it be ok then?" Most children also answered "Yes." Thus, children who respond in this way recognize that rules regarding clothing are mere social conventions. If, however, the questions were about harming others (as opposed to wearing clothes) and even if an adult says it is ok or if harming others is tolerated in a specific school, children judge that the harming is wrong. Thus, contrarily to what Kohlberg and Piaget postulated, children actually do treat conventional norms in a categorically different way from truly moral norms (where "moral" for Turiel et al. was operationally defined as "relating to harm").

So Turiel et al.'s methods illustrated major shortcomings in the more traditional psychological method based on assessing children's moral development by requesting them to offer verbal explanations and justifications of their moral evaluations. Nevertheless, this approach can still be criticized on two grounds (Haidt, 2012). First, like Kohlberg, the theory of human morality that emerged from this work appears to be biased toward secular

Western moral systems that place a high priority on preventing harm at the expense of other moral norms. Empirical psychological work on human moral cognition should take into account a wide range of moral values spread across different cultural and religious systems. These include things like respect for authority, patriotism, loyalty to family, honor, and purity. Consider for example the Hua of New Guinea who have a system of elaborate taboos pertaining to what men and women can eat (Haidt, 2012), These taboos stem from notions of bodily purity, which the Hua take to be moral (not conventional) rules that form the basis of judgments about others, duties, and relationships. Turiel et al., however, would classify these as mere social norms because food taboos do not relate to harm.

Secondly, despite the fact that Turiel et al.'s methods seem to be an improvement on Kohlberg's, they still fall short in the sense that they are meant to measure explicit, reason-based forms of morality. While explicit moral systems and deep reflection certainly plays a role in full mature moral thinking, more recent work has shown that the capacity for simple moral judgments might be dissociated from the capacity for higher-order moral justifications. In particular, "moral dumbfounding" scenarios (Haidt, 2001;[1] though see Royzman et al., 2015 for a critique) illustrate cases where people have an intuitive moral sense that some action is right or wrong, but in which they lack (and often come to recognize that they lack) good reasons to justify these moral judgments.

Consider the scenario from Figure 12.1, which is an example of an act that violates a conventional and harmless taboo, that is, taboo by a conventional norm but involves

no harm to either actor in the event. Participants would read a passage like this, and were then required to judge whether the action was acceptable. In the story in Figure 12.1, most (though not all) participants indicated that it was not acceptable for the brother and sister to make love. Participants would then be asked to justify why they thought it was wrong. People might then, for example, respond that if a pregnancy results from an incest, then the kid will likely be handicapped or deformed. At this point, the experimenter would push back and remind the participant that the couple took extra precautions to avoid a pregnancy, making it nearly impossible for the sister to become pregnant. In a similar fashion, the experimenter was able to "defeat" many other reasons provided by the participant until, ultimately, they were left with no good explanation as to why the act was not acceptable. But even in such circumstances, most participants still clung to the judgment that the act was wrong. These results thus show that moral intuitions (at least in some cases) fall short of, and precede, moral justifications and rationalizations. Haidt et al. (unpublished, see fn. 1) famously called "moral dumbfounding" the phenomenon whereby human adults are shown to have strong moral intuitions for which they cannot offer adequate justifications. According to Haidt and colleagues, these intuitions stem from certain categories of acts relating to the basic moral foundations of harm, fairness, loyalty, authority, and purity eliciting specific types of emotion (such as disgust), which serve to create moral intuitions.

On the basis of moral dumbfounding, Haidt (2001) put forward an influential "social intuitionist" model of moral reasoning in human adults, according to which intuitive moral judgments are mostly driven by emotional responses to a situation and the basic purpose of moral reasoning is to justify intuitive moral

---

[1] See also, Haidt, J., Björklund, F., & Murphy, S. (2000). Moral Dumbfounding: When Intuition Finds no Reason. Unpublished Manuscript.

Moral Dilemma (Incest)

Julie and Mark are brother and sister. They are travelling together in France on summer vacation from college. One night, they are staying alone in a cabin near the beach. They decide it would be interesting and fun if they tried making love. At the very least it would be a new experience for each of them. Julie is already taking birth control pills, but Mark uses a condom too just to be safe. They both enjoy making love, but they decide not to do it again. They keep that night as a special secret, which makes them feel even closer to each other. What do you think about that? Was it ok for them to make love?

Haidt, 2001

Figure 12.1 Example of a moral dilemma used by Haidt and colleagues in their "moral dumbfounding" experiments. Participants insist in upholding the taboo without being able to produce clear rational arguments for doing so, suggesting that intuitions play a larger role in our moral faculty than Kohlberg and others have argued.

judgments. Haidt's work was very influential in that it helped spur a paradigm shift in developmental psychology, as more and more attention turned to the origins of moral intuitions in development. One clear example is the work of Hamlin et al., (2007). In this study the experimenters presented six- and ten-month-old infants with a social scenario involving an agent (in the form of a simple geometric object with eyes) trying to get up a hill. The agent could be either helped up the hill by a "helper" or, in other conditions, prevented from going up the hill by a "hinderer." The authors found that, after habituation to such scenes, infants preferred to grab a helper over a neutral character but preferred the neutral character to hinderers, and they also directly preferred to play with a helper over a hinderer. Subsequent studies have replicated and extended these findings using different types of displays and agent goals (e.g., trying to open a box instead of trying to get up a hill; Hamlin & Wynn, 2012; though see Salvadori et al., 2015 for a non-replication in a similar experimental paradigm), and on a younger age group, with infants preferring helpers at three-months in a looking preference paradigm.

These results could be interpreted as showing that pre-verbal infants possess moral intuitions that guide the evaluation of certain social scenarios. Crucially in many of Hamlin's experiments (e.g. Hamlin et al., 2007), the results cannot be explained merely in terms of infant preferences for certain types of causal outcomes or interactions, as Piaget or Kohlberg might have predicted. This is due to the fact that the experimenters were careful to compare infants' looking time patterns in virtually identical "non-social" situations in which the helpers or hinderers moved and looked like simple inanimate objects. In these conditions, infant failed to prefer the inanimate objects that facilitated or prevented the main character from making their way up the hill. This detail is important because it suggests that the best explanation of the primary results is that infants evaluate the relationship between the agent's goals (i.e., to go up the hill) and the actions of the helpers or hinderers instead of merely focusing on purely causal (i.e. non-social) outcomes. In short, findings by Hamlin and colleagues about early infants' preferences for helpers over hinderers provides evidence that infants have an early sensitivity to harmful agents on the assumption that to prevent an agent to achieve her goal is to harm the agent.

Much further work on adults' responses to harmful actions has focused on the so-called trolley dilemmas, in which participants are asked whether it is licit to flip a switch to divert a trolley so as to sacrifice one individual for the sake of saving five. Findings in this paradigm have been interpreted as evidence for a two-systems approach to human moral cognition: while one so-called deontological system is taken to deliver emotional responses, the other system is taken to deliver utilitarian responses (Cushman et al., 2006; Greene et al., 2004; Mikhail, 2007). One robust finding in the developmental investigation of children's evaluation of harmful actions (between the ages of three and eight) has also been taken as evidence for the presence of a two-systems approach to children's moral cognition. Young children have been consistently shown to primarily attend to the causal role of harmful agents and to condemn agents that cause harm on the basis of the negative outcome of the agent's action. It takes time before children can take into account the agent's intention for the purpose of drawing relevant distinctions between intended harm, accidental harm, and attempted harm, and become able to both exculpate accidental harmful agents and to blame agents of merely attempted harmful actions. These findings have been taken as evidence for the dissociability between an early-emerging system for evaluating harm, on the basis of the agent's causal role, and a later-emerging system for evaluating harm based on the agent's intent (cf. Buon et al., 2013; Cushman et al., 2013).

Other, more recent work, has focused on other foundations. Buyukozer Dawkins et al. (2019) found that, in very simple contexts, nine-month-old infants expected an equal distribution of desirable resources (e.g., cookies) amongst similar characters, suggestion a precursor to the Haidtian foundation of fairness and equality. Bian et al. (2018) found, however, that these expectations were mitigated in one and a half-to-two and a half-year-olds by "in-group"/"out-group" affiliation. Thus, when an unequal amount of resources were present, toddlers expected that a character would give out a greater number to a member of their own group (as indicated by the puppets being the same or different kind of animal) than to a member of a different group (see also Jin & Baillargeon, 2017 for related findings). A number of papers also suggest that, just as infants expect others to show an in-group preference, they themselves prefer members of their own social group (Kelly et al., 2005; Kinzler et al., 2007).

12.7 Concluding Remarks

In the following concluding remarks, we briefly reflect on three outstanding issues raised by the recent experimental investigation of early human social cognition. First, it is controversial to what extent early social cognition is shaped by imitation and the activity of mirror neurons. Second, we shall reflect on the puzzle of the discrepant developmental findings about false-belief understanding and theory of mind in human childhood. Finally, we shall consider the puzzling developmental discrepancy between infants' moral intuitions and the immoral behavior of older children.

12.7.1 Imitation

In several influential papers, Meltzoff (2002, 2005, 2007) has proposed that imitation is a central mechanism for the development of early social cognition, including empathy and theory of mind. Broadly speaking, imitation involves the topographic resemblance between a model's observed behavior and the imitator's. But this topographic resemblance may be unobservable to the imitator who can rarely see her own relevant bodily parts (Heyes, 2018). On behalf of his "Like-me" framework, Meltzoff (2005, 2007) has suggested that infants are innately prepared to imitate others' actions, that mirror neuron activity underlies infants' imitative capacities, which in turn promote children's understanding of other minds. However, "imitation" does not refer to a single psychological mechanism. As a result, Meltzoff's influential framework raises at least three kinds of intriguing problems.

First of all, newborns' imitation is arguably best construed as a case of automatic motor mimicry (or contagion), not as the intentional replication of adults' facial expressions. But as discussed in detail in Section 12.1, the recent huge longitudinal study by Oostenbroek et al. (2016) has cast doubts on Meltzoff's hypothesis that human infants might be innately wired for imitation. Of the eleven movements demonstrated by adults to be replicated by infants, only tongue protrusion stood out as a possible candidate for infant imitation. It is presently an open question whether infants stick out their tongue as a specific imitative response or else in response to a wide range of arousing stimuli (for a response to Oostenbroek et al., 2016, see Meltzoff et al., 2018).

Secondly, Meltzoff's and Moore's (1977, 1983) reports of neonatal imitation of facial gestures have been taken as evidence for mirror neuron activity in newborns. However, the major problem for this hypothesis is that mirror neurons were first discovered in the brains of non-human primates and overt imitative behavior is far less common among non-human primates than among humans.

Nonhuman primates are widely taken to understand and emulate others' goals but rarely to faithfully replicate the exact action-means by which the agent achieved her goal (Tomasello, 2008).

Finally, while this is consistent with the view that mirror neurons in monkeys code an agent's goal (Rizzolatti & Sinigaglia, 2010), it undermines the hypothesis that mirror neuron activity is the neural basis of human imitative learning, that is, learning a new behavior from seeing another perform it. After being ostensively greeted by an adult model, human toddlers have been shown to emulate the model's goal when the efficiency of the model's action was manifest and to faithfully reproduce an agent's inefficient motor sequence when the teleological structure of the model's action was opaque (cf. Section 12.5). Thus, the capacity for ostensive communicative interactions, not mirror neuron activity, seems to underlie the faithful replication of a model's motor sequence, which in turn is central to human imitative learning (e.g., the cultural transmission of artistic skills). In short, whatever the strength of the evidence for automatic mimicry of facial expressions in newborns, there is a gap between it and the kind of imitative learning in toddlers, children, and adults that matters primarily for human cultural transmission.

12.7.2 Theory of Mind

We turn to the outstanding puzzle of the discrepant developmental findings about false-belief understanding, that is, the capacity to attribute true and false beliefs to others, in human childhood. In a nutshell, most preschoolers have been shown to fail verbal false-belief tests and point to the toy's actual location when asked to predict a mistaken agent's action. But findings based on non-verbal tests have been taken to show that pre-verbal infants expect an agent to act in accordance with the content of her true or false belief about an object's location.[2]

How to reconcile these discrepant developmental findings? The following crucial dilemma arises: do findings based on non-verbal false-belief tests provide sufficient evidence for genuine false-belief attribution, and hence for theory-of-mind, in human infancy? Or else, is success on verbal false-belief tasks necessary? Furthermore, if findings based on non-verbal tests do not reflect genuine false-belief attribution, then how should infants' responses to these tests be interpreted?

Whereas most psychologists agree that success on verbal false-belief tasks counts as evidence for genuine false-belief attribution, many find it ludicrous that preverbal infants might be able to attribute mental states (including false beliefs) to others. Their main burden is to explain the infant data by appealing to non-mentalistic processes. They have appealed to three-way associations, behavioral rules (e.g., Perner & Ruffman, 2005), and perceptual novelty (Heyes, 2014). According to another alternative, the "two-systems" approach, a minimal, efficient, but inflexible mindreading system enables infants to attribute registrations, which are not genuine beliefs, but belief-like states. Minimal mindreading is taken to be sufficient to account for the infant data. The more flexible full-blown mindreading system, which develops later, is taken to be necessary for success on verbal false-belief tests (Apperly & Butterfill, 2009). According to a recent so-called altercentric proposal, if an agent is present, infants in their first year spontaneously encode events, not from their own perspective, but from this agent's perspective (Southgate, 2020). This is in line with the suggestion by Kampis et al. (2013), based on their findings, that ten-month-olds may represent an agent's belief without attributing it to anyone. This suggests that the capacity to represent the content of an agent's belief may precede the full mindreading capacity to attribute beliefs to others.

Given that understanding the question asked by the experimenter is necessary for success on verbal false-belief tasks, false-belief-attribution cannot in and of itself be sufficient for success on verbal false-belief tasks. If so, then success on verbal false-belief tasks cannot be necessary for false-belief attribution. Following this line of thought, several psychologists have proposed to try and reconcile the discrepant developmental findings on the assumption that findings based on non-verbal tests provide evidence that infants can attribute genuine false-beliefs to others. Their main burden is to explain why verbal false-belief tasks are so challenging for preschoolers (see Chapter 11).

One possible explanation is the pragmatic account: in verbal false-belief tasks, not only are the children directly asked to predict the mistaken agent's likely action, but they are also provided with information that is ostensively communicated to them by the experimenter. To the extent that this information is ostensively communicated to them, children are likely to take it as relevant to answering the prediction question. But not all of this information is actually relevant to this task: in particular, the fact that Anne moves Sally's marble from the basket (where Sally placed it) to the box is irrelevant to predicting where Sally will look for her marble when she returns. The only relevant information is where Sally last placed her marble: this is

---

[2] Some recent studies have cast doubt on the replicability of some of the earlier results based on non-verbal false-belief tests (e.g., Dörrenberg et al., 2018). Further investigation is needed to explore the possible sources of the failure to replicate some of the non-verbal false-belief tests.

where she will look for it when she returns, whatever happened to the marble after she left the room. One possible way children may try to make the irrelevant information about the marble's actual location relevant is by turning the prediction question into the normative question "where should Sally look for her marble?" The correct answer to this normative question is the marble's actual location, which is where most preschoolers point to in response to the experimenter's question.

Further progress into the developmental investigation of mindreading is likely to emerge from the combination of three complementary sources: the investigation of phylogenetic precursors of the full human mindreading capacity in non-human primates; the potential role of social, linguistic, and cultural inputs to the ontogenetic development of mindreading in human children; and the application of non-intrusive brain imaging methods to human infants' brains.

12.7.3 Moral Competence and Immoral Behavior

Some fifty years ago the developmental investigation of moral cognition in the hands of Piaget and Kohlberg focused mostly on children's capacity to justify moral judgments at the expense of early moral intuitions. Until recently, most developmental psychologists took it for granted that moral competence is laboriously taught to naïve children by knowledgeable adults via a process of enculturation supported by language acquisition.

New experimental methods (based in particular on infants' looking time) have shown not only that preverbal infants and toddlers have robust moral intuitions about third-party harmful interactions and unfair allocation of resources, but also that they strongly prefer an agent who helped another achieve her goal rather than one who interfered with another's

goal (Hamlin, 2013; Hamlin et al., 2013; Kuhlmeier et al., 2003; Premack & Premack, 1997; Sloane et al., 2012).

However, it takes several years before children exhibit a moral behavior that is congruent with the moral competence displayed by infants' evaluation of others' social interactions. Young children have been shown to dislike receiving less than others, but not to mind others' receiving less than themselves. They have been shown to be willing to undertake costly actions in order to avoid such relative disadvantages for themselves. Furthermore, while three-year-olds have been shown not to be willing to share resources equally with other children, most five-year-olds have been shown to select a spiteful distribution over a fair distribution and only most nine-year-olds have been shown to share equally with others and to select a fair distribution (Sheshkin et al., 2014).

Sheskin et al. (2014) have recently argued that so-called life-history theory (an evolutionary approach to the costs and benefits of social cognition and behavior) sheds light on the discrepancy between infants' moral competence and children's immoral behavior. The basic assumption of life-history theory is that moral competence and moral behavior have different cost-benefit trade-offs. Arguably, the capacity for the moral evaluation of others' behavior is free from motivational costs. If so, then natural selection may have favored individuals who had early capacity for socially evaluating others. However, engaging in moral behavior is motivationally costly in the sense that any behavior requires some motivation. Furthermore, as argued by Baumard et al. (2013), moral behavior can be beneficial to an individual when the short-term costs of performing moral (e.g., altruistic) acts are outweighed by the long-term benefits derivable from mutualistic cooperation with others. In particular, in a relatively free market of cooperating partners, people are likely to select partners on the basis of their moral reputation, which in turn reflects their past moral behavior. Human life-history is characterized by an extended period of juvenile dependence restricted to resource transfers from kin. Only late in development do humans cooperate with non-kin. Only then does moral reputation become a relevant factor in partner selection for mutualistic interactions.

References

Anisfeld, M. (1996). Neonatal imitation. *Developmental Review, 11*, 60–97.

Apperly, I. A., & Butterfill, S. A. (2009). Do humans have two systems to track beliefs and belief-like states? *Psychological Review, 116*, 953–970.

Atran, S. (1995). Causal constraints on categories and categorical constraints on biological reasoning across cultures. In D. Sperber, D. Premack, & A. Premack (eds.), *Causal Cognition, a Multidisciplinary Debate* (pp. 205–233). Oxford: Clarendon Press.

Baumard, N., André, J.-B., & Sperber, D. (2013). A mutualistic approach to morality: The evolution of fairness by partner choice. *Behavioral and Brain Sciences, 36*, 59–122.

Begus, K., Gliga, T., & Southgate, V. (2016). Infants' preferences for native speakers are associated with an expectation of information. *Proceedings of the National Academy of Sciences, 113*, 12397–12402.

Bian, L., Sloane, S., & Baillargeon, R. (2018). Infants expect ingroup support to override fairness when resources are limited. *Proceedings of the National Academy of Sciences, 115*, 2705–2710.

Biro, S., & Leslie, A. (2007). Infants' perception of goal-directed action: Development through cue-based bootstrapping. *Developmental Science, 10*, 379–398.

Boyer, P. (2018). *Minds Make Societies, How Cognition Explains the World Humans Create.* New Haven, CT: Yale University Press.

Brandone, A. C., Leslie, S. J., Cimpian, A., & Gelman, S. A. (2012). Do lions have manes? For children, generics are about kinds rather than quantities. *Child Development, 83*, 423–433.

Brewer, M. B. (1979). In-group bias in the minimal intergroup situation: Cognitive–motivational analysis. *Psychological Bulletin, 86*, 307–324.

Buon, M., Habib, M., & Frey, D. (2016). Moral development: Conflicts and compromises. In J. A. Somerville, & J. Decety (eds.), *Social Cognition: Development Across the Life Span* (pp. 129–150). New York: Psychology Press.

Buon, M, Jacob, P., Loissel, E., & Dupoux, E. (2013). A non-mentalistic cause-based heuristic in human social evaluations. *Cognition, 126*, 149–155.

Butler, L. P., & Markman, E. M. (2012). Preschoolers use intentional and pedagogical cues to guide inductive inferences and exploration. *Child Development, 83*, 1416–1428.

Buyukozer Dawkins, M., Sloane, S., & Baillargeon, R. (2019). Do Infants in the first year of life expect equal resource allocations? *Frontiers in Psychology, 10*, 116.

Byrne, R. W., & Whiten, A. (eds.) (1988). *Machiavellian Intelligence: Social Expertise and the Evolution of Intellect in Monkeys, Apes and Humans.* Oxford: Blackwell.

Carey, S. (1995) On the origin of causal understanding. In D. Sperber, D. Premack, & A. Premack (eds.), (1995). *Causal Cognition, a Multidisciplinary Debate* (pp. 205–233). Oxford: Clarendon Press.

Clément, F., Koenig, M. A., & Harris, P. L. (2004). The ontogenesis of trust. *Mind and Language, 19*, 360–379.

Cooper, R. P., & Aslin, R. N. (1990). Preference for infant-directed speech in the first month after birth. *Child Development, 61*, 1584–1595.

Cosmides, L., Tooby, J., & Kurzban, R. (2003). Perceptions of race. *Trends in Cognitive Sciences, 7*, 173–179.

Csibra, G. (2010). Recognizing communicative intentions in infancy. *Mind and Language, 25*, 141–168.

Csibra, G., Bíró, S., Koós, O., & Gergely, G. (2003). One-year-old infants use teleological representations of actions productively. *Cognitive Science*, *27*, 111–133.

Csibra, G., & Gergely, G. (2009). Natural pedagogy. *Trends in Cognitive Sciences*, *13*, 148–153.

Csibra, G., Gergely, G., Bíró, S., Koós, O., & Brockbank, M. (1999). Goal attribution without agency cues: The perception of "pure reason" in infancy. *Cognition*, *72*, 237–267.

Csibra, G., & Volein, Á. (2008). Infants can infer the presence of hidden objects from referential gaze information. *British Journal of Developmental Psychology*, *26*, 1–11.

Cushman, F. A., Sheketoff, R., Wharton, S., & Carey, S. (2013). The development of intent-based moral judgment. *Cognition*, *127*, 6–21.

Cushman, F. A., Young, L., & Hauser, M. D. (2006). The role of conscious reasoning and intuition in moral judgment: Testing three principles of harm. *Psychological Science*, *17*, 1082–1089.

Darwin, C. (1871). *The Descent of Man, and Selection in Relation to Sex* (1st ed.). London: John Murray.

Dörrenberg, S., Rakoczy, H., & Liszkowski, U. (2018). How (not) to measure infant Theory of Mind: Testing the replicability and validity of four non-verbal measures. *Cognitive Development*, *46*, 12–30.

Dunbar, R. I. M. (1992). Neocortex size as a constraint on group size in primates. *Journal of Human Evolution*, *22*, 469–493.

Dunbar, R. I. M. (2003). The social brain: Mind, language, and society in evolutionary perspective. *Annual Review of Anthropology*, *32*, 163–181.

Egyed, K., Király, I., & Gergely, G. (2013). Communicating shared knowledge in infancy. *Psychological Science*, *24*, 1348–1353.

Falck-Ytter, T., Gredebäck, G., & von Hofsten, C. (2006). Infants predict other people's action goals. *Nature Neuroscience*, *9*, 878–879.

Farroni, T., Johnson, M. H., Menon, E., Zulian, L., Faraguna, D., & Csibra, G. (2005). Newborns' preference for face-relevant stimuli: Effects of contrast polarity. *Proceedings of the National Academy of Sciences*, *102*, 17245–17250.

Farroni, T., Mansfield, E. M., Lai, C., & Johnson, M. H. (2003). Infants perceiving and acting on the eyes: Tests of an evolutionary hypothesis. *Journal of Experimental Child Psychology*, *85*, 199–212.

Futó, J., Téglás, E., Csibra, G., & Gergely, G. (2010). Communicative function demonstration induces kind-based artifact representation in preverbal infants. *Cognition*, *117*, 1–8.

Gallese, V., Fadiga, L., Fogassi, L., & Rizzolatti, G. (1996). Action recognition in the premotor cortex. *Brain*, *119*, 593–609.

Gao, T., Newman, G. E., & Scholl, B. J. (2009). The psychophysics of chasing: A case study in the perception of animacy. *Cognitive Psychology*, *59*, 154–179.

Gelman, S., & Hirschfeld, L. (1999). How biological is essentialism? In S. Atran, & D. Medin (eds.), *Folk Biology* (pp. 403–446). Cambridge, MA: MIT Press.

Gergely, G., Bekkering, H., & Kiraly, I. (2002). Rational imitation in preverbal infants. *Nature*, *415*, 755.

Gergely, G., Nádasdy, Z., Csibra, G., & Bíró, S. (1995) Taking the intentional stance at 12 months of age. *Cognition*, *56*, 165–193.

Gervain, J., & Mehler, J. (2010). Speech perception and language acquisition in the first year of life. *Annual Review of Psychology*, *61*, 191–218.

Greene, J. D., Nystrom, L. E., Engell, A. D., Darley, J. M., & Cohen, J. D. (2004). The neural bases of cognitive conflict and control in moral judgment. *Neuron*, *44*, 389–400.

Haidt, J. (2001). The emotional dog and its rational tail: A social intuitionist approach to moral judgment. *Psychological Review*, *108*, 814–834.

Haidt, J. (2012). *The Righteous Mind: Why Good People Are Divided by Politics and Religion*. New York: Pantheon.

Hamlin, J. K. (2013). Moral judgment and action in preverbal infants and toddlers: Evidence for an innate moral core. *Current Directions in Psychological Science*, *22*, 186–193.

Hamlin, J. K., Hallinan, E. V., & Woodward, A. L. (2008). Do as I do: 7-month-old infants selectively reproduce others' goals. *Developmental Science*, *11*, 487–494.

Hamlin, J. K., Ullman, T., Tenenbaum, J., Goodman, N., & Baker, C. (2013). The mentalistic basis of core social cognition: Experiments in preverbal infants and a computational model. *Developmental Science, 16*, 209–226.

Hamlin, J. K., & Wynn, K. (2012). Who knows what's good to eat? Infants fail to match the food preferences of antisocial others. *Cognitive Development, 27*, 227–239.

Hamlin, J. K., Wynn, K., & Bloom, P. (2007). Social evaluation by preverbal infants. *Nature, 450*, 557–559.

Hauser, M. D., Chomsky, N., & Fitch, W. T. (2002). The faculty of language: What is it, who has it, and how did it evolve? *Science, 298*, 1569–1579.

Heyes, C. (2014). False belief in infancy: A fresh look. *Developmental Science, 17*, 647–659.

Heyes, C. (2018). *Cognitive Gadgets, the Cultural Evolution of Thinking.* Cambridge, MA: Harvard University Press.

Hirschfeld, L. (1995a). Do children have a theory of race? *Cognition, 54*, 209–252.

Hirschfeld, L. (1995b). Anthropology, psychology, and the meanings of social causality. In D. Sperber, D. Premack, & A. Premack (eds.) (1995). *Causal Cognition, a Multidisciplinary Debate* (pp. 205–233). Oxford: Clarendon Press.

Hume, D. (1738). *A Treatise of Human Nature: Being an Attempt to Introduce the Experimental Method of Reasoning into Moral Subjects.* New York: Oxford University Press.

Humphrey, N. (1976). The social function of the intellect. In P. P. G. Bateson, & R. A. Hinde (eds.), *Growing Points on Ethology* (pp. 303–317). Cambridge: Cambridge University Press.

Hyde, D. C., Simon, C. E., Ting, F., & Nikolaeva, J. I. (2018). Functional organization of the temporal–parietal junction for theory of mind in preverbal infants: A near-infrared spectroscopy study. *Journal of Neuroscience, 38*, 4264–4274.

Jacob, P. (2012). Sharing and ascribing goals. *Mind and Language, 27*, 202–229.

Jin, K., & Baillargeon, R. (2017). Infants possess an abstract expectation of ingroup support.

Proceedings of the National Academy of Sciences (USA), 114, 8199–8204.

Johnson, M. H., Dziurawiec, S., Ellis, H., & Morton, J. (1991). Newborns' preferential tracking of face-like stimuli and its subsequent decline. *Cognition, 40*, 1–19.

Jovanovic, B., Király, I., Elsner, B., Gergely, G., Prinz, W., & Aschersleben, G. (2007). The role of effects for infants' perception of action goals. *Psychologia, 50*, 273–290.

Kampis, D., Somogyi, E., Itakura, S., & Király, I. (2013). Do infants bind mental states to agents? *Cognition, 129*, 232–240.

Kant, I. (1785). *Groundwork of the Metaphysics of Morals,* various printings.

Keil, F. C. (2014). *Developmental Psychology: The Growth of Mind and Behavior.* New York: W. W. Norton.

Kelly, D. J., Quinn, P. C., Slater, A. M., Lee, K., Gibson, A., Smith, M, Ge, L., & Pascalis, O. (2005). Three-month-olds, but not newborns, prefer own-race faces. *Developmental Science, 8*, F31–F36.

Kinzler, K. D., & DeJesus, J. M. (2013). Children's sociolinguistic evaluations of nice foreigners and mean Americans. *Developmental Psychology, 49*, 655–664.

Kinzler, K. D., Dupoux, E., & Spelke, E. S. (2007). The native language of social cognition. *Proceedings of the National Academy of Sciences (USA), 104*, 12577–12580.

Kinzler, K. D., Dupoux, E., & Spelke, E. S. (2012). "Native" objects and collaborators: Infants' object choices and acts of giving reflect favor for native over foreign speakers. *Journal of Cognitive Development, 13*, 67–81.

Kinzler, K. D., Shutts, K., DeJesus, J., & Spelke, E. S. (2009). Accent trumps race in guiding children's social preferences. *Social Cognition, 27*, 623–634.

Kiràly, I., Jovanovic, B., Prinz, W., Aschersleben, G., & Gergely, G. (2003). The early origins of goal attribution in infancy. *Consciousness and Cognition, 12*, 752–769.

Knudsen, B., & Liszkowski, U. (2012). 18-month-olds predict specific action mistakes through attribution of false belief, not ignorance, and intervene accordingly. *Infancy, 17,* 672–691.

Kohlberg, L. (1976). Moral stages and moralization: The cognitive-developmental. In T. Lickona (ed.), *Moral Development and Behavior: Theory, Research and Social Issues* (pp. 31–53). New York: Holt, Rinehart and Winston.

Krebs, D. L., & Denton, K. (2005). Toward a more pragmatic approach to morality: A critical evaluation of Kohlberg's model. *Psychological Review, 112,* 629–649.

Kuhlmeier, V., Wynn, K., & Bloom, P. (2003). Attribution of dispositional states by 12-month-olds. *Psychological Science, 14,* 402–408.

Kurtines, W., & Greif, E. B. (1974). The development of moral thought: Review and evaluation of Kohlberg's approach. *Psychological Bulletin, 81,* 453–470.

Kurzban, R., Tooby, J., & Cosmides, L. (2001). Can race be erased? Coalitional computation and social categorization. *Proceedings of the National Academy of Sciences (USA), 98,* 15387–15392.

Leslie, S. J. (2007). Generics and the structure of the mind. *Philosophical Perspectives, 21,* 375–405.

Leslie, S. J. (2008). Generics: Cognition and acquisition. *Philosophical Review, 117,* 1–49.

Liberman, Z., Woodward, A. L., & Kinzler, K. D. (2017). Preverbal infants infer third-party social relationships based on language. *Cognitive Science, 41,* 622–634.

Liszkowski, U., Carpenter, M., Striano, T., & Tomasello, M. (2006). 12- and 18-month-olds point to provide information for others. *Journal of Cognition and Development, 7,* 173–187.

Locke, J. (1698). *An Essay Concerning Human Understanding.* London.

Luo, Y. (2011a). Three-month-old infants attribute goals to a non-human agent. *Developmental Science, 14,* 453–460.

Luo, Y. (2011b). Do 10-month-old infants understand others' false beliefs? *Cognition, 121,* 289–298.

Luo, Y., & Baillargeon, R. (2005). Can a self-propelled box have a goal?: Psychological reasoning in 5-month-old infants. *Psychological Science, 16,* 601–608.

Martin, A., Onishi, K. H., & Vouloumanos, A. (2012). Understanding the abstract role of speech in communication at 12 months. *Cognition, 123,* 50–60.

Mascaro, O., & Csibra, G. (2012). Representation of stable social dominance relations by human infants. *Proceedings of the National Academy of Sciences (USA), 109,* 6862–6867.

Mascaro, O., & Sperber, D. (2009). The moral, epistemic, and mindreading components of children's vigilance towards deception. *Cognition, 112,* 367–380.

Maynard-Smith, J., & Harper, D. (2003). *Animal Signals.* New York: Oxford University Press.

Meltzoff, A. N. (1988). Infant imitation after a 1-week delay: Long-term memory for novel acts and multiple stimuli. *Developmental Psychology, 24,* 470–476.

Meltzoff, A. N. (2002). Imitation as a mechanism of social cognition: Origins of empathy, theory of mind, and the representation of action. In U. Goswami (ed.), *Blackwell Handbook of Childhood Cognitive Development* (pp. 6–25). Oxford: Blackwell.

Meltzoff, A. N. (2005). Imitation and other minds: The "Like me" hypothesis. In S. Hurley, & N. Chater (eds.), *Perspectives on Imitation: From Neuroscience to Social Science* (Vol. 2, pp. 55–77). Cambridge, MA: MIT Press.

Meltzoff, A. N. (2007). "Like me": A foundation for social cognition. *Developmental Science, 10,* 126–134.

Meltzoff, A. N., & Moore, M. K. (1977). Imitation of facial and manual gestures by human neonates. *Science, 198,* 5.

Meltzoff, A. N., & Moore, M. K. (1983). Newborn infants imitate adult facial gestures. *Child Development, 54,* 702–709.

Meltzoff, A. N., & Moore, M. K. (1997). Explaining facial imitation: A theoretical model. *Early Development and Parenting, 6,* 179–192.

Meltzoff, A. N., Murray, L., Simpson, E., Heimann, M., Nagy, E., Nadel, J., Pedersen, E. J., Brooks, R., Messinger, D. S., Pascalis, L. D., Subiaul, F., Paukner, A., & Ferrari, P. F.

(2018). Re-examination of Oostenbroek et al. (2016): Evidence for neonatal imitation of tongue protrusion. *Developmental Science, 21*, e12609.

Mikhail, J. (2007). Universal moral grammar: Theory, evidence and the future. *Trends in Cognitive Sciences, 11*, 143–152.

New, J., Cosmides, L., & Tooby, J. (2007). Category-specific attention for animals reflects ancestral priorities, not expertise. *Proceedings of the National Academy of Sciences (USA), 104*, 16598–16603.

Nyström, P. (2008). The infant mirror neuron system studied with high density EEG. *Social Neuroscience, 3*, 334–347.

Nyström, P., Ljunghammar, T., Rosander, K., & von Hofsten, C. (2010). Using mu rhythm perturbations to measure mirror neuron activity in infants. *Developmental Science, 14*, 327–335.

Onishi, K. H., & Baillargeon, R. (2005). Do 15-month-old infants understand false beliefs? *Science, 308*, 255–258.

Oostenbroek, J., Slaughter, V., Nielsen, M., & Suddendorf, T. (2013). Why the confusion around neonatal imitation? A review. *Journal of Reproductive and Infant Psychology, 31*, 328–341.

Oostenbroek, J., Suddendorf, T., Nielsen, M., Redshaw, J., Kennedy-Costantini, S., Davis, J., & Slaughter, V. (2016). Comprehensive longitudinal study challenges the existence of neonatal imitation in humans. *Current Biology, 26*, 1334–1338.

Perner, J., & Ruffman, T. (2005). Infants' insight into the mind: How deep? *Science, New Series, 308*, 214–216.

Piaget, J. (1932). *The Moral Judgment of the Child.* London: Kegan, Paul, Trench, Trubner & Co.

Pietraszewski, D., & German, T. C. (2013). Coalitional psychology on the playground: Reasoning about indirect social consequences in preschoolers and adults. *Cognition, 126*, 352–363.

Plötner, M., Over, H., Carpenter, M., & Tomasello, M. (2015). The effects of collaboration and minimal-group membership on children's prosocial behavior, liking, affiliation, and trust.

Journal of Experimental Child Psychology, 139, 161–173.

Powell, L. J., & Spelke, E. S. (2013). Preverbal infants expect members of social groups to act alike. *Proceedings of the National Academy of Sciences (USA), 23*, E3965–E3972.

Powell, L. J., & Spelke, E. S. (2018). Human infants' understanding of social imitation: Inferences of affiliation from third party observations. *Cognition, 170*, 31–48.

Premack, D., & Premack, A. (1997). Infants attribute value ± to the goal-directed actions of self-propelled objects. *Journal of Cognitive Neuroscience, 9*, 848–856.

Premack, D., & Woodruff, G. (1978). Does the chimpanzee have a theory of mind? *Behavioral and Brain Sciences, 1*, 515–526.

Reid, V. M., Dunn, K., Young, R. J., Amu, J., Donovan, T., & Reissland, N. (2017). The human fetus preferentially engages with face-like visual stimuli. *Current Biology, 27*, 1825–1828.

Rizzolatti, G., & Craighero, L. (2004). The mirror-neuron system. *Annual Review of Neuroscience, 27*, 169–192.

Rizzolatti, G., Fadiga, L., Gallese, V., & Fogassi, L. (1996). Premotor cortex and the recognition of motor actions. *Cognitive Brain Research, 3*, 131–141.

Rizzolatti, G., Fogassi, L., & Gallese, V. (2001). Neurophysiological mechanisms underlying the understanding and imitation of action. *Nature Reviews Neuroscience, 2*, 661–670.

Rizzolatti, G., & Sinigaglia, C. (2010). The functional role of the parieto-frontal mirror circuit: interpretations and misinterpretations. *Nature Reviews Neuroscience, 11*, 264–274.

Rosander, K., & von Hofsten, C. (2011). Predictive gaze shifts elicited during observed and performed actions in 10-month-old infants and adults. *Neuropsychologia, 49*, 2911–2917.

Royzman, E., Kim, K., & Leeman, R. (2015). The curious tale of Julie and Mark: Unraveling the moral dumfounding effect. *Judgment and Decision Making, 10*, 296–313.

Salvadori, E., Blazsekova, T., Volein, A., Karap, Z., Tatone, D., Mascaro, O., & Csibra, G.

(2015). Probing the strength of infants' preference for helpers over hinderers: Two replication attempts of Hamlin and Wynn (2011). *PLoS ONE, 10,* e0140570.

Scott-Phillips, T. C. (2014). *Speaking Our Minds.* London: Palgrave MacMillan.

Senju, A., & Csibra, G. (2008). Gaze following in human infants depends on communicative signals. *Current Biology, 18,* 668–671.

Sheshkin, M., Bloom, P., & Wynn, K. (2014). Anti-equality: Social comparison in young children. *Cognition, 130,* 152–156.

Sheshkin, M., Chevallier, C., Lambert, S., & Baumard, N. (2014). Life-history theory explains childhood moral development. *Trends in Cognitive Sciences, 18,* 613–615.

Shutts, K., Kinzler, K. D., McKee, C. B., & Spelke, E. S. (2009). Social information guides infants' selection of foods. *Journal of Cognition and Development, 10,* 1–17.

Simion, F., Regolin, L., & Bulf, H. (2008). A predisposition for biological motion in the newborn baby. *Proceedings of the National Academy of Sciences (USA), 105,* 809–813.

Skerry, A. E., Carey, S. E., & Spelke, E. S. (2013). First-person action experience reveals sensitivity to action efficiency in prereaching infants. *Proceedings of the National Academy of Sciences (USA), 110,* 18728–18733.

Sloane, S., Baillargeon, R., & Premack, D. (2012). Do infants have a sense of fairness? *Psychological Science, 23,* 196–204.

Sommerville, J. A., Woodward, A. L., & Needham, A. (2005). Action experience alters 3-month-old infants' perception of others' actions. *Cognition, 96,* B1–B11.

Southgate, V. (2020). Are infants altercentric? The other and the self in early social cognition. *Psychological Review, 127,* 505–523.

Southgate, V., Johnson, M. H., & Csibra, G. (2008). Infants attribute goals even to biomechanically impossible actions. *Cognition, 107,* 1059–1069.

Southgate, V., Johnson, M. H., Osborne, T., & Csibra, G. (2009). Predictive motor activation during action observation in human infants. *Biology Letters, 5,* 769–772.

Southgate, V., & Vernetti, A. (2014). Belief-based action prediction in preverbal infants. *Cognition, 130,* 1–10.

Tajfel, H., Billig, M. G., Bundy, R. P., & Flament, C. (1971). Social categorization and intergroup behavior. *European Journal of Social Psychology, 1,* 149–177.

Tomasello, M. (2008). *Origins of Human Communication.* Cambridge, MA: MIT Press.

Tomasello, M. (2014). *A Natural History of Human Thinking,* Cambridge MA: Harvard University Press.

Tomasello, M., Carpenter, M., Call, J., Behne, T., & Moll, H. (2005). Understanding and sharing intentions: The origins of cultural cognition. *Behavioral and Brain Sciences, 28,* 675–691.

Tooby, J., & Cosmides, L. (2010). Groups in mind: The coalitional roots of war and morality. In H. Høgh-Olesen (ed.), *Human Morality & Sociality: Evolutionary & Comparative Perspectives* (pp. 191–234). New York: Palgrave MacMillan.

Troje, N. F., & Westhoff, C. (2006). The inversion effect in biological motion perception: Evidence for a "life detector"? *Current Biology, 16,* 821–824.

Turiel, E. (1983). *The Development of Social Knowledge: Morality and Convention.* Cambridge: Cambridge University Press.

Turiel, E., Killen. M., & Helwig, C. C. (1987). Morality: Its structure, function, and vagaries. In J. Kagan, & S. Lamb (eds.), *The Emergence of Morality in Young Children* (pp. 155–243). Chicago, IL: University of Chicago Press.

Umiltà, M. A., Kohler, E., Gallese, V., Fogassi, L., Fadiga, L., Keysers, C., & Rizzolatti, G. (2001). "I know what you are doing": A neurophysiological study. *Neuron, 32,* 91–101.

Valenza, E., Simion, F., Cassia, V. M., & Umiltà, C. (1996). Face preference at birth. *Journal of Experimental Psychology: Human Perception and Performance, 22,* 892.

Vallortigara, G., Regolin, L., & Marconato, F. (2005). Visually inexperienced chicks exhibit spontaneous preference for biological motion. *PLoS Biology, 3,* e208.

Vouloumanos, A., & Werker, J. F. (2007). Listening to language at birth: Evidence for a bias for speech in neonates. *Developmental Science, 10*, 159–164.

Warnecken, F., & Tomasello, M. (2006). Altruistic helping in human infants and young chimpanzees. *Science, 311*, 1301–1302.

Warnecken, F., & Tomasello, M. (2007). Helping and cooperation at 14 months of age. *Infancy, 11*, 271–294.

Warnecken, F., & Tomasello, M. (2009). Varieties of altruism in children and chimpanzees. *Trends in Cognitive Sciences, 13*, 397–402.

Wellman, H. M., Cross, D., & Watson, J. (2001). Meta-analysis of theory-of-mind development: The truth about false belief. *Child Development, 72*, 655–684.

Wimmer, H., & Perner, J. (1983). Beliefs about beliefs: Representation and constraining function of wrong beliefs in young children's understanding of deception. *Cognition, 13*, 103–128.

Woodward, A. L. (1998). Infants selectively encode the goal object of an actor's reach. *Cognition, 69*, 1–34.

Woodward, A. L. (1999). Infants' ability to distinguish between purposeful and non-purposeful behaviors. *Infant Behavior and Development, 22*, 145–160.

Woodward, A. L., Sommerville, J. A., Gerson, S., Henderson, A. M. E., & Buresh, J. (2009). The emergence of intention attribution in infancy. In B. Ross (ed.), *Psychology of Learning and Motivation* (Vol. 51, pp. 187–222). New York: Academic Press.

Xu, F., & Carey, S. (1996). Infants' metaphysics: The case of numerical identity. *Cognitive Psychology, 30*, 111–153.

Yoon, J. M. D., Johnson, M. H., & Csibra, G. (2008). Communication-induced memory biases in preverbal infants. *Proceedings of the National Academy of Sciences (USA), 105*, 13690–13695.

Yu, C., & Smith, L. B. (2013). Joint attention without gaze following: Human infants and their parents coordinate visual attention to objects through eye–hand coordination. *PLoS ONE, 8*, e79659.

13 Scientific Thinking and Reasoning in Infants and Young Children

Mariel K. Goddu and Alison Gopnik

13.1 Introduction

For more than three decades, researchers have characterized the dramatic changes in early cognitive development and the learning mechanisms that underlie those changes by analogy to the thinking of professional scientists. This "child-as-scientist" view has emphasized the parallels between: (1) the *evidence-based, theoretical nature* of both children's and scientists' knowledge, (2) the *rational process* by which that knowledge is updated and revised, and (3) *conceptual change*, the often radical alterations to epistemic content that can result from those revisions. In this chapter, we begin by laying out the fundamentals of scientific thinking and reasoning, situating it in an "interventionist" framework of causal reasoning. Next, we review the history of the "child-as-scientist" approach in this context. Then, we outline recent work, open questions, and future directions in research on the development of scientific thinking in infancy, early childhood, and beyond.

A nine-month-old infant, a nineteen-year-old backpacker, and a twenty-nine-year-old bioengineer are all reasoning about keys.

The nine-month-old has just made an exciting discovery: she has learned that grabbing and waving her parent's car keys can sometimes make a very exciting jingling sound. However, she is puzzled: sometimes this happens, but sometimes it does not – sometimes, she grabs them and waves them, but nothing jingles at all! Now, she is looking contemplatively at the keys on the table in front of her, wondering how she can make this desirable effect happen again.

The nineteen-year-old has just made an unfortunate discovery: she has learned that the key on the ring that so easily opened the door to her Barcelona hostel eight hours ago in broad daylight is posing some difficulty at 2AM in the dark after dancing. Now, she is frowning and looking back and forth between the doorknob and the keys in her hand, wondering why the door will not open up.

The twenty-nine year old has not made any discovery – yet. She is standing, lab coat- and goggles-clad, in a biomedical engineering lab, where she has spent the past three weeks engaged in a series of experiments to investigate which substrate will "unlock" a particular enzyme secreted by the pancreas of a mouse. She is wondering whether the solution she has just pipetted into her new cell culture will yield the biochemical indicator that is a telltale sign of the desired reaction.

The infant, the backpacker, and the researcher are each engaged in a process of *scientific reasoning*. In all cases, the reasoners face a problem or a question. And in all cases, the reasoners are attempting to resolve that question by making informative interventions that will help them deduce a solution or answer. In the course of their experimentation, they identify and manipulate potentially relevant causal variables that will produce a desired effect.

The process is dynamic and dramatic. The nine-month-old swipes and grasps at the keys; suddenly, she has them all clutched in her fist! She waves them around energetically ... but, there is no jingling. Meanwhile, the nineteen-year-old is growing increasingly frantic. She cycles through possible explanations why the door will not open: "Am I using the wrong key?"; "Am I turning it the wrong way?"; "Is there something wrong with the doorknob?" She curses softly, wishing she had not had that last *queimada*. The twenty-nine-year-old sighs, sets a timer for her reaction, and leaves the laboratory for her desk, where she consults the journal articles she has been reading. If this reaction does not work, then her hypothesis is wrong, and she will need to start trying a new set of reagents that operate by a different mechanism than the one that she and her collaborators have been banking on.

The cases are, of course, importantly different. The infant's reasoning takes place in the context of a still-developing understanding of the physical and social world in which she lives, without the help of mature logical and linguistic thought. The backpacker, by contrast, is equipped with explicit hypotheses, concepts, and prior knowledge about keys and doorknobs that she has learned from nineteen years of living and navigating the socially constructed, twenty-first century landscape of the human world. And the researcher is equipped with still further abstract conceptual knowledge, gleaned only through years of study and highly specific sociocultural indoctrination and apprenticeship with highly specialized equipment and tools. Those tools themselves were derived from literally millennia of scholars and thinkers pooling their knowledge, ideas, and practices.

The resolution of the cases, though, is once again similar. By chance, the infant manages to poke two fingers through the keyring without clutching all of the keys, and as she waves

them around this time – *aha!* – she hears the musical sound she has been waiting for. She grins. The backpacker, near tears, eventually looks up at the door in desperation and realizes, in a moment perhaps more "*Thank god!*" than "*Eureka!*" that she is, in fact ... on the wrong floor. The researcher's discovery, two hours later, is less obviously successful, but nonetheless informative: rather than what she had expected, her reaction yields instead an interesting compound that she will discuss with her lab mates and, in due time, analyze through three more weeks of experimentation into a replicable result that eventually makes sense in light of findings on a poster she sees at a conference.

In this chapter, we explore the claim that cognitive development in infants and young children is analogous to scientific theorizing, thinking, and reasoning. First, we outline the general characteristics of scientific thinking, emphasizing the search for causally relevant, or "difference-making," variables and relations. Then, we examine the history and role of the "child-as-scientist" analogy in the field of cognitive development. We describe a "first wave" of so-called theory theorists who used the analogy as a way of pointing to processes of conceptual change in early cognitive development and a "second wave" that has emphasized the rational process by which belief revision and updating takes place. Finally, we return to the scientific process, and discuss the many open questions and future directions that remain.

13.2 What Is Scientific Thinking?

There are many ways in which philosophers of science, science historians, science educators, and scientists themselves characterize scientific thinking and reasoning. Broadly, from the earliest philosophers to the most modern and specialized laboratory researchers, the aim of science has been to provide explanations for natural phenomena (Salmon, 1984). At the most basic level, science involves answering "why?" questions about events that are puzzling and mysterious. By undertaking steps to explore, investigate, and otherwise gather information about things we do not understand, we start on the road to scientific discovery (Ruchlis, 1963).

Once a research question and some hypotheses have been established, the scientific enterprise proceeds by empirical observation and experimentation. Scientists posit, test, and ultimately adopt those hypotheses, laws, or theories that prove to be the most broadly and powerfully predictive and explanatory, while discarding or revising those that do not. The practices and procedures for evaluating knowledge are just as important, if not more so, than the knowledge itself.

In science, the answers to the questions we pose are often, indeed primarily, *causal explanations*: scientists seek to discover the mechanisms that can account for what we observe. While there are a number of theoretical accounts of causal explanation, "interventionist" or "difference-making" accounts seem to most closely mirror and approximate the procedures used by scientists. These accounts emphasize the importance of identifying and manipulating causal variables in order to discern and determine the precise relations between those variables and the effects that they produce in some other variable of interest (e.g., Pearl, 2000, 2009; Pearl & Mackenzie, 2018; Spirtes et al., 1993; Woodward, 2003). In the vignettes described, each of the reasoners was engaged in an iterative process of identifying candidate causal variables that would explain, and ultimately make a difference to, the situation in which she found herself. By manipulating these candidate causal explanations, hypotheses, and variables, each was able to discover the reason for the effect she observed or experienced.

Framed in this way, at least one important aspect of the scientific discovery process might be broadly outlined as follows: First, a scientific reasoner must identify a *problem* or *question*. Then, they must imagine or propose *candidate solutions* or *answers* to the question. This second step involves identifying the candidate causal variables that will make a difference to the outcome or effect of interest that is specified by the research question: "Will swiping my hand harder make the keys do their jingle?"; "Will jiggling the knob help me open the door?"; "Will this more concentrated reagent make a difference to the concentration of the enzymes in my culture?" Third, a scientist must devise an *intervention*, a way of actually testing these candidate hypotheses or explanations: they must actually swipe the keys, jiggle the knob, or perform the reaction. Fourth, they must *interpret* their data, the results of their intervention. Sometimes, the results are straightforward (e.g., the door does not budge). But often, they are not: swiping the keys produces the *hint* of a jingle, but not the full-fledged phenomenon; adding the reagent produces a change to the enzyme concentration, but not the one that was anticipated. Finally, the reasoner must arrive at a *conclusion*: either they have attained a satisfactory answer, or they have discovered new questions for investigation.

Later, we return to this outline of the scientific method in our discussion of current work and future directions in the development of scientific thinking and reasoning in infants and young children. In Section 13.3, we turn to the history of the "child-as-scientist" analogy.

13.3 "Child-As-Scientist" in Historical Perspective

The "child-as-scientist" analogy as a view on children's cognitive development originated in the 1920s. Jean Piaget theorized that knowledge is neither innate nor completely learned: young children "construct" their knowledge through interactions with the environment. As they navigate their world, children's experiences change the way they think. According to Piaget's constructivist view, cognitive development is an iterative process between "assimilation" and "accommodation." In assimilation, the child integrates new information into existing conceptual structures. Conversely, in accommodation the child's representations must change in order to fit the new information (Flavell, 1963; Piaget, 1929). This view of cognitive development maps onto the distinctive relation between theory and evidence in scientific thinking. "Assimilation" corresponds to a situation in which one encounters new evidence that accords with one's existing theory, and "accommodation" corresponds to an instance that demands theory change.

In 1985, Susan Carey published *Conceptual Change in Childhood*, which detailed the conceptual changes in children's biological knowledge over time. For example: What does it look like for a child to shift from thinking of a whale as a fish to thinking of a whale as a mammal? This work emphasizes the changes in explanatory structure – theory change – that must occur when a child undergoes such a reconceptualization (Carey, 1985). Following the philosopher Quine who (1960) famously subscribes to a kind of semantic holism in which knowledge is a giant, interrelated "web of belief"), Carey holds that concepts can only be understood relative to the larger explanatory structures in which they are embedded. On Carey's view of conceptual change in childhood, Piaget's "accommodation" process ranges from instances of "belief revision" (mild tweaking) to dramatic "conceptual change" (total overhaul) (Carey, 1985). In the mid-1980s other researchers also formulated similar "theory theory" perspectives on

children's world knowledge and its changes throughout development (Gopnik, 1984; Karmiloff-Smith & Inhelder, 1974; Wellman, 1992).

Although their particular emphases have varied considerably, further investigations of the child as scientist idea have been united by two common ideas that link children's cognitive development to scientific thinking: (1) *Children's world knowledge resembles scientific theories* and (2) *Theory change in childhood resembles theory change in science.*

Theory theorists noted that children seem to privilege causal-explanatory knowledge: they seek answers to "why" questions, and they hold beliefs about invisible, underlying causes that give rise to observable features of objects, people, and aspects of the natural world (Carey, 1985; Gelman, 2003; Gopnik, 1998; Gopnik & Meltzoff, 1997; Keil, 1989). Children hold a variety of "naive theories" that they use to explain everyday phenomena. For example, they believe that people's behavior is caused by their mental states (e.g., Wellman & Woolley, 1990) and that biological phenomena are the result of unseen, internal attributes (e.g., Gelman et al., 1994).

The first wave of theory theory, the "intuitive theories" approach, was defined by its efforts to catalog the sweeping changes that occur in young children's world knowledge. If children's knowledge was structured like scientific theories, then the concepts embedded within those theories – the terms in which they were defined – could only change if the theories themselves did (Carey, 1985; Quine, 1960). This theory theory view of cognitive development was influenced by philosopher of science Thomas Kuhn, who coined the term "paradigm shift" to describe historical moments when scientific fields shift their views on a large scale. Kuhn argues that, in ordinary conditions, scientists do not actually innovate or make dramatic advances in exploring unknown worlds; on the contrary, they concentrate strictly on problems that can be explored within existing frameworks. It is only in times of crisis – often when the frameworks break down in light of new evidence that cannot be accounted for – that major changes in the structure of scientific knowledge occur. Kuhn (1962) referred to such events as "scientific revolutions."

As first wave theory theory evolved from the mid-1980s to the end of the twentieth century, the "intuitive theories" research program investigated the radical changes that occurred in infants' and young children's "intuitive" knowledge of major world domains: biology, physics, and psychology (Wellman & Gelman, 1998). Early theory-theorists emphasized three distinctive aspects of intuitive theories: their structure, their causal-explanatory function, and the dynamics by which they changed in light of new evidence. They also posited that children's intuitive theories were domain-specific: that is, they held different expectations about biological, physical, and psychological phenomena (Gopnik & Wellman, 2012).

13.3.1 Intuitive Theories of Biology

Infants and young children have clear and elaborate intuitions about biological entities. Their intuitions appear to be driven by a so-called essentialist bias that enables the assumption that externally observable features and behaviors are due to deeper, invisible underlying causes (Carey, 1985; Gelman, 2003). For example, fourteen-month-old infants already appear to use insides as a cue to expectations about biological behavior: when two characters share an external, but not an internal feature, infants will look longer when the characters' behavior is synchronous. In the absence of characters' movement, however, the infants do not show a preference, suggesting that they directly link internal properties to external behavior (Newman et al., 2008).

By preschool, children exhibit a reliable bias toward categorizing biological kinds by underlying causal "essences" over their perceptual features. When experimenters show children illustrations of two different animals with similar externalities (e.g., a bat and a sparrow with wings outstretched), yet provide information about causally relevant, internal similarities between the sparrow and a perceptually dissimilar other animal (e.g., a flamingo, who likes to eat the same kind of food), children willingly override perceptual similarity and categorize the birds together (Gelman & Markman, 1986, see Chapter 10). Across development, children's ability to "inductively project" or extend properties about biological organisms to increasingly distant category members grows increasingly sophisticated (Carey, 1985, 2009; Keil, 1989).

These changes seem to occur when children are exposed to increasing amounts of evidence that their intuitive theories must accommodate. For example, children who had experience taking care of a goldfish were better than non-caretakers at answering questions about observable and non-observable goldfish properties and reasoning about a similar but new animal (e.g., a frog) in a similar situation (Inagaki, 1990). Similarly, children raised in rural environments with firsthand access to animals showed a much less anthropocentric conception of animals and were more willing than urban children to inductively project internal features from humans to animals (Ross et al., 2003).

13.3.2 Intuitive Theories of the Physical World

First wave theory theory made a variety of surprising discoveries about very young children's knowledge of the physical world. Prior to this period, one important prevailing view was that babies did not have an understanding of "object permanence" – the fact that physical objects continue to exist out of sight – until late in the first year (Flavell, 1963). However, new experimental methods that used infant's propensity to look longer at surprising events allowed developmentalists to test that theory by setting up situations where object permanence was violated. Three- and four-month-olds who saw a rotating drawbridge appear to pass through a solid object looked longer at the stimulus than infants who saw the same display but without the apparent violation of solidity (Baillargeon, 1987). In research that followed, principles of object solidity and continuity were discovered in infants as young as two months (Carey, 2009). While the *innateness* of infants' object knowledge has not been demonstrated (i.e., in neonates), we know that even very young infants' object knowledge is theoretical. That is, they are surprised when these properties are violated in novel ways, with stimuli they have never seen. This suggests that the knowledge is abstract, general, and allows them to make causal predictions.

Interestingly, infants are *not* born with some other kinds of object concepts. For example, three-month-olds are unsurprised when experimenters show them objects that appear to float unsupported in the air (Baillargeon, 1998). Infants can, however, learn about new variables from data: for example, nine-month-olds who observe evidence from a series of covering events will learn to attend to the dimension of *height* (Wang & Baillargeon, 2008, see Chapter 12). Early knowledge and learning about the physical world are thus both scientific in their theoretical structure as well as in their responsiveness to new evidence.

13.3.3 Intuitive Theories of the Psychological World

The last domain in which first wave theory theory made critical observations of children's

conceptual change was the domain of psychology. Children have separate sets of expectations about activities that agents do versus the behavior of inanimate objects. Impressively, children as young as nine-to-eleven months old can make predictions about agents' goals and desires (e.g., Saxe et al., 2005; Woodward, 1999, see Chapter 12). One of the most striking conceptual changes in early intuitive theories of psychology occurs around eighteen months of age, when children begin to appreciate that other people may have preferences that differ from their own. While fourteen-month-olds will present an experimenter with a snack they themselves enjoy over a snack for which the experimenter has expressed a preference, eighteen-month-olds will abide by the other person's desires (Repacholi & Gopnik, 1997). This kind of appreciation seems to be the beginning of the young child's "theory of mind" (Astington et al., 1988). In one notable experiment, the false belief task (Wimmer & Perner, 1983), preschoolers open a candy box had been surprisingly filled with pencils prior to their encounter with it. Only four-year-olds – but not three-year-olds – were able to predict that an ignorant character who had just encountered the box without seeing inside would believe it was filled with candy, just as they had (Wimmer & Perner, 1983).

13.3.4 Summary

The first wave of theory theorists focused on investigating the typical progression of children's knowledge over development. Importantly, they noted that much of the knowledge that infants and young children accumulate is scientific in both its *responsiveness to evidence* and its focus on *causal explanatory mechanisms* such as unseen, internal forces. However, researchers still did not have a theory about the learning mechanisms that underwrote the changes they observed. In the second wave of theory theory, in the early 2000s, the focus shifted to investigating learning mechanisms.

Instead of querying children's knowledge of domain-specific causal structure in biology, physics, and psychology, the rational constructivist approach (also causal Bayes nets, or probabilistic models) seeks to investigate the underlying learning mechanisms that give rise to the complex mental landscapes they create. Researchers in this tradition take an approach that focuses on causal *learning*: How do children reason when they are given novel evidence about a causal system that they have never seen? Infants' and young children's causal inferences in such situations can shed light on the implicit strategies they use to construct and revise the causal knowledge that we know that they ultimately acquire.

In this section, we first review the history of the probabilistic model approach, and in particular the approach using causal Bayes nets, to understanding early causal reasoning. After explaining the computational formalism, we then explain how it works to solve the kinds of causal reasoning problems that young children and scientists have to solve: learning about conditional probabilities from causal structure, predicting the results of interventions, and learning causal structure from data. After reviewing the theory, we then explore the body of empirical evidence from causal learning studies with infants and children that support the second wave theory theorists' idea that children do in fact behave, in at least some situations, like ideal Bayesian learners.

13.3.5 Causal Interventionism

As early as two-to-three months of age, infants both notice their effects on the environment and are actively motivated to enact them. When experimenters tie a ribbon to a baby's foot and connect it to a mobile above their crib, the baby can learn to kick to make the mobile move. By six months of age, the baby can remember this contingency and generalize it to new situations – e.g., to new mobiles, to new crib environments, and across limbs. Causal intervention on the world is very compelling, even at this age: the reward consists in nothing more than the contingency of one's actions upon outcomes in the world (Greco et al., 1990).

Much of our everyday knowledge is constructed around pragmatic interventions such as this one – that is, those that produce a desired effect, or "make a difference" in the causal interventionist sense (Woodward, 2003). Although children are interested in causal explanation, they certainly cannot explain *all* of their knowledge, and in fact often acquire larger "framework" theories of a domain before the particulars (Keil et al., 2010). Even adults are notoriously bad at estimating their own causal-explanatory knowledge about how things work; most cannot explain how a flush toilet works, what a radio does, or why there are phases of the moon (Keil, 2006, 2012).

13.3.6 Causal Bayes Nets

The theoretical framework that rational constructivists have adopted to explain the way that young children learn so efficiently and scientifically about the world combines the ideas of causal interventionism with a Bayesian probabilistic approach to inference and learning (Gopnik, 2012; Gopnik & Wellman, 2012; Xu & Kushnir, 2013; Xu et al., 2009). This Bayesian framework – named after the eighteenth-century statistician and philosopher Reverend Thomas Bayes who invented it – was itself originally developed as a normative guide to describe how scientists *should*, ideally, interpret new data. Equation (13.1) is based on a relatively straightforward logic. Formally, the equation states that the likelihood of a particular hypothesis "given" (or "in light of") some data (the "posterior," on the left – P(H|E)) is proportional to both the *prior likelihood* of that hypothesis (P(H)) as well as to the *likelihood of the data* given that particular hypothesis (P(E|H)).

Bayes rule: P(H|E) ∝(P(E|H))(P(H)))

(13.1)

Say I am a child, and I see a gift on the table in the front hall. Here is the hypothesis I would like to evaluate: *Is that present for me?* I want to determine the posterior probability of this hypothesis. I have three possible hypotheses about what caused the appearance of the present. First, it could be my birthday. Second, it could be some other holiday – perhaps Christmas or my brother's birthday, which sometimes brings a consolation prize. Thirdly, it could be that I am being taken to a birthday party later today, and the present is, in fact, for someone else.

The likelihood of the evidence in light of the first two hypotheses – the likelihood of a present on my birthday, and the likelihood of a present on other special holidays – is extremely high. By contrast, I hardly ever receive presents when I'm going to someone else's birthday party. Should I jump for joy?

Not yet. The prior probability of birthdays and gift-giving holidays are both quite low. By contrast, there are a whole lot of kids in my preschool class. Most likely, that present is *not* for me … and I will be taken to a birthday party later.

Causal Bayes nets, represented in *directed graphs*, come from theoretical computer science, and they are an instantiation of precisely this logic. The graphs consist of networks of variables and causal "arrows" that show how different causes (represented by "nodes") in the graphs are related to effects probabilistically (Pearl, 2000; Spirtes et al., 1993). Bayes nets are a way to represent causal structure. If

you know something about the way in which some variables are causally connected by causality in the graph, then you can (1) make predictions about the *conditional probabilities* that certain events will occur, and you can also (2) make predictions about what might happen if you perform an *intervention* – if you altered the graph in some way (e.g., took away a variable, or cut off one of the causal connections).

As we have seen, causal Bayes nets and the predictions they enable us to make – that is, (1) and (2) – are exactly the sorts of causal reasoning problems we need to solve in the real world. But Bayes nets also provide a framework for solving an even more relevant and challenging problem, the one that infants and young children face. It allows us to solve backwards, evaluating the likelihood of a given hypothesized causal structure in light of the data that they see. Just like figuring out whether or not the birthday present is for them, Bayesian reasoning can allow children to figure out whether a certain domain or system in the world works the way they think it does.

13.3.7 Does the Theory Fit the Evidence?

One reason to be skeptical of such a formalized, idealized model of causal reasoning is that it comes from computer science and philosophy of science, not from empirical research in psychology. Over the past two decades, however, in the "second wave" of theory theory, rational constructivists have tested the fit between the theoretical ideas and the empirical evidence. Their empirical discoveries have largely corroborated the predictions of the probabilistic models formalism, and may be summarized in four categories:

1. children can exploit statistical regularities in the environment to make inferences about causal structure;

2. children can make inferences from interventions that they make or that they watch others make;

3. children can update their prior theories with new evidence; and

4. children can observe data to posit unobserved variables.

We will briefly review the empirical evidence for each of these in turn.

13.3.7.1 Children Can Infer Causal Structure

In the initial experiments, toddlers and young children observed covariation information about the effects (e.g., pleasing music) of certain blocks on a machine, a "blicket detector." With only minimal information about statistical contingencies, children were able to figure out which blocks were blickets. They could also generalize properties of the blickets to figure out which new ones might work (Gopnik & Sobel, 2000; Gopnik et al., 2001, 2004). These findings have been replicated many times, including in naturalistic settings: for example, children can use patterns of statistical covariation to determine whether the failure of a toy was due to their own incompetence or to the toy itself (Gweon & Schulz, 2011).

13.3.7.2 Children Can Learn from Interventions

Empirical evidence shows that children can both learn by observing evidence generated by others' interventions and design interventions of their own. In one compelling experiment, children were given pairs of large, plastic "pop" beads that could snap together and apart. They were either told that "some" of the beads would make a blicket detector activate, or "all" of the beads would. Children in the "some" beads condition did exactly what scientific thinking would predict: they unsnapped the pairs and tried each bead one

at a time. In another condition, children were again given the "all" or "some" instruction, but this time, the beads were glued together. Children in the "some" condition made a novel intervention: they tipped the pairs back and forth, testing one side at a time (Cook et al., 2011).

13.3.7.3 Children Can Update Their Prior Theories

In several compelling demonstrations of rational belief updating, experimenters present children with evidence that supports a belief that the children do not initially think is likely. In one case, children observed probabilistic evidence that favored a "no-contact" causal rule: a blicket machine was more likely to activate when the blicket was held *over* the machine. Children initially favored contact causality, but changed their behavior when they saw enough evidence (Kushnir & Gopnik, 2007). Another experiment demonstrated a change in naturalistic, domain-specific beliefs: initially, children did not believe that a psychological cause could result in a physical effect (e.g., nervousness leading to tummy ache). However, given enough evidence, young children were able to rationally update this belief (Schulz et al., 2007a).

13.3.7.4 Children Can Posit Unobserved Variables

Preschoolers can infer the existence of unobserved variables. In one study, children saw that the motion of two puppets covaried; they also saw that pulling on Puppet A did not move Puppet B, and that pulling Puppet B did not move Puppet A. From this evidence, children inferred the existence of a third variable that was responsible for moving both (Schulz & Gopnik, 2004). In another study, children who observed a machine that activate every time (i.e., behaved indeterministically) inferred that a hidden variable was causing the failures (Schulz & Somerville, 2006).

13.3.7.5 Summary

The emphasis of the rational constructivist agenda is not that children *are* ideal Bayesian learners; obviously, they are not. But the consistency with which children's actual causal learning fits the formalism has led to an optimism that these mechanisms might in fact be just the sort of cognitive mechanisms that would allow us to learn so much so quickly. The details of how and when these might apply are a topic of ongoing research and computational theorizing.

13.4 Future Directions

Over the past three decades, developmentalists have used the "child-as-scientist" metaphor to motivate fruitful investigations of children's cognitive development. The first wave theory theorists, the intuitive theories approach, emphasized that, like scientists, young children have structured, domain-specific theories of biology, physics, and psychology that undergo radical conceptual change over development. The rational constructivist approach emphasizes that, like scientists, young children use sophisticated causal reasoning skills to form abstract, theoretical representations of causal relations and update their theories in light of new data.

However, many open questions about the development of scientific thinking and reasoning remain unanswered. In the second section of this chapter, we outlined the scientific process as consisting of five parts:

1. *identifying a problem* or *question*;
2. *imagining or proposing a candidate solution or answer* to the question – that is,

identifying a candidate explanation, hypothesis, or causal variable that will make a difference to the outcome or effect of interest specified by the research question;

3. *devising an intervention*, a way of testing the candidate hypothesis or explanation;
4. *interpreting the data* produced by their intervention; and
5. *arriving at a* conclusion – i.e., determining whether they have attained a satisfactory answer, or whether continued investigation is necessary.

Here, we specify topics in ongoing research and investigation that pertain to each of these points of the scientific thinking and reasoning process.

13.4.1 Identifying a Problem or Question

Science starts with questions. What triggers investigation? A recent, now-famous study published in 2015 demonstrated that infants were more likely to selectively explore objects that violated their expectations (Stahl & Feigenson, 2015). Building on the first wave theory theorist assumption that children rapidly acquire domain-specific knowledge and strong expectations about the physical world, researchers showed eleven-month-old infants objects such as toy cars and balls that appeared to violate solidity (e.g., pass through a solid wall) or support (e.g., appear to float in the air). The infants who saw objects that violated these principles were more likely to explore them than they were to explore novel objects, and they explored them in ways that were consistent with the violation that they had witnessed (e.g., infants who saw objects violate solidity were more likely to bang the objects, where as those who saw objects violate support were more likely to drop them). This study is the first to demonstrate the violation of expectations in infants may lead to science-like intervention, in apparent search for explanation. Future research will be necessary to explore the ways in which early attention to violations of expectancy in infancy may develop into the motivation to explain or resolve more subtle inconsistencies and anomalies in their observations that we see during the preschool years (e.g., Legare et al., 2010; Schulz et al., 2008).

The relation between emotion, motivation, and investigation is also a promising avenue for future research: without wondering "Why?," scientific investigation cannot get off the ground. Although scientists, educators, and communicators often pay lip service to phenomena like "curiosity" and "wonder," there is limited empirical research investigating the developmental trajectory of these emotions and the role that they play in triggering scientific thinking and reasoning (Gopnik, 1988; Loewenstein, 1994; Silvia, 2008). Moreover, these emotional responses seemed to be linked to still other factors that may be relevant in explaining the development of scientific reasoning, such as attention, memory, the relation between attachment style and exploration behaviors, ego-resiliency, and the need for "cognitive closure" (Arend et al., 1979; Gottlieb et al., 2013; Kidd & Hayden, 2015; Mikulincer, 1997). Several initial studies suggest a role for "epistemic emotions," such as awe, in triggering adults' and children's curiosity for scientific phenomena (Gottlieb et al., 2018; Valdesolo et al., 2017). This research should be expanded and connected to extant research.

A complementary line of research to the triggers or antecedents of scientific inquiry and reasoning in early childhood should focus on the factors that may *prevent* initial inquiry. There is evidence to suggest that preschoolers do possess an early-developing ability to ask informative questions (Mills et al., 2010;

Ruggeri & Lombrozo, 2015; Ruggeri et al., 2017; see Ronfard et al., 2018 for a review). However, children may have difficulty mustering curiosity when it conflicts with social motivations such as challenging convention or authority (Butler, 2020; Kalish, 1998; Ruchlis, 1963). Children may also fail to be curious because they are satisfied with existing explanations, even when these explanations are not the standard adult or scientific explanations: for example, children are notoriously "promiscuous" teleological reasoners who accept purpose-based accounts of natural phenomena (Kelemen, 1999a, 1999b; Kelemen & DiYanni, 2005), and they also are more willing than adults to accept explanations that appeal to "inherence" (Cimpian & Steinberg, 2014).

Children may also fail to wonder, inquire, develop curiosity, or raise questions because they do not sense the gaps in their own knowledge or are unaware of their epistemic gaps. Kindergarteners vastly overestimate their own knowledge, and young children are notoriously bad at source-monitoring, often assuming that they have always known something that they just recently learned (Giles et al., 2002; Lockhart et al., 2017; Mills & Keil, 2004; O'Neill & Gopnik, 1991; Taylor et al., 1994). School-aged children do eventually develop an intuitive understanding of what people might be able or unable to learn on their own; however, further research is necessary to discover how children acquire this understanding, and the circumstances in which they may apply it to their own beliefs (Lockhart et al., 2016).

13.4.2 Identifying Causally Relevant Variables and Candidate Hypotheses

In studies with pre-specified causal variables and simple causal systems (e.g., blocks of different colors that cause or do not cause a toy to play music), even toddlers are able to identify causally relevant properties of objects such as shape or color. However, in everyday experience, it is far more difficult to pick out the types of variables that may be causally relevant, and to generate candidate causal hypotheses and explanations. How does this ability develop?

In addition to the domain-specific intuitive theories that they possess, a growing body of research suggests that children's hypothesis search may be constrained by higher order, abstract rules – "overhypotheses" – that operate in a "top-down" manner to guide and constrain a hypothesis search. This notion comes from computational accounts of Hierarchical Bayesian Models, but has seen some empirical support from several studies investigating early causal reasoning (Kemp et al., 2007; Tenenbaum et al., 2011). For instance, four-year-olds are able to infer that the abstract *form* of a causal relation – for instance, learning that two blocks must be present conjunctively in order for a machine to play music, or that two of the "same" (rather than two not same) blocks are required (Lucas et al., 2014; Walker & Gopnik, 2014; Walker et al., 2016). Four-year-olds are also able to make causal attributions based on evidence to indicate whether a character's trait (e.g., shyness) or a situational factor (e.g., the riskiness of a toy) is responsible for some causal outcome (e.g., the character's willingness to play on that toy or a new one (Seiver, Goodman, & Gopnik, 2013)).

Novel hypotheses may also be generated by processes of analogical reasoning. Researchers and theorists in the cognitive history and philosophy of science have long noted the role that analogical transfer seems to play in generating new ideas and sparking conceptual change (e.g., Gentner et al., 1997; Nersessian, 1999). While young children have often been assumed to be deficient in early reasoning about and transfer of abstract relations (e.g., Christie &

Gentner, 2010), one recent finding suggests that preschoolers are able to learn the abstract relations between the beginning and ending states of causal transformations and transfer them to predict novel causal outcomes (Goddu et al., 2020). This study builds on a previous finding that four-year-olds are able to match the abstract form of an effect to its cause (Magid et al., 2015). More research is needed to explore the other types of abstract causal knowledge that children may acquire to help them generate new hypotheses, and the role that analogy plays in this process.

Notably, even if children *are* able to generate novel hypotheses or identify novel causal variables, they may have difficulty reasoning about hypotheses that conflict with one another. Research in early reasoning about mutually exclusive, future possible outcomes suggests that this ability may not be in place until the school age years (Beck & Riggs, 2013; Beck et al., 2006; Leahy & Carey, 2020; Redshaw & Suddendorf, 2020). They may also have difficulty generating or entertaining hypotheses that are unlikely, or that violate social or moral conventions (Shtulman & Carey, 2007; Shtulman & Phillips, 2018). However, these findings themselves appear to conflict somewhat with the existing research that demonstrates that at least an *implicit* ability to reason about multiple hypotheses is present in the context of causal reasoning as early as sixteen months. Future research is necessary to explore the relation between these early successes in generating and reasoning about multiple possible hypotheses or causal explanations and the findings that older children struggle to consider them. One possibility is that causal explanations are in fact easier for very young children to consider; indeed, one recent study suggests that toddlers are able to identify, track, and apply multiple causal hypotheses in a causal learning task (Goddu,

Sullivan, & Walker, 2021). Another possibility is that children use rational sampling strategies to generate and test out new hypotheses serially (Bonawitz et al., 2014a, 2014b; Denison et al., 2013).

13.4.3 Devising Interventions

While there is research (reviewed in Section 13.3.7.2) to suggest that preschool aged children spontaneously design their own causal interventions in the course of free play, other research suggests that designing and tracking multiple interventions may place demands on attention and decision-making (Cook et al., 2011; Lapidow & Walker, 2020; Sobel & Kushnir, 2006). Additionally, while toddlers are able to successfully predict causal events, they may have difficulty generalizing from prediction to intervention, especially in multi-step causal sequences (Bonawitz et al., 2010). Further research is required to understand the development of successful intervention behaviors from successful causal prediction behaviors.

Interventions are also difficult due to the fact that early learners often face novel situations with causal variables that they have never seen. The ability to generalize from one causal system to another (e.g., that turning the hose spigot, like turning the bathtub knob, will release water) is critical for solving the so-called problem of variable choice – that is, where to intervene on a novel causal system in order to produce a novel effect. There is one recent study that suggests that three-, four-, and five-year-olds are able to learn and transfer their knowledge about difference-making variables to similar systems that contain new values of the same variables (Goddu & Gopnik, 2020). Future research is necessary to discover how this ability develops from infancy and toddlerhood.

13.4.4 Interpreting the Data

Once a reasoner has designed an intervention and enacted it, they are faced with the task of interpreting the results or outcomes of their actions. Are the results due to their successful manipulation of the variable they had in mind – the candidate variable or explanation specified by their research question – or are the observed effects due to the manipulation of some other, correlated variable that was not controlled for? The development of the ability to control variables and to reason about multiple candidate causal explanations are critical to interpreting data (Kuhn, 2002).

As noted in point (2), there is some research to suggest that children may have difficulty reasoning about multiple, conflicting possibilities (Beck et al., 2006; Leahy & Carey, 2020; Redshaw & Suddendorf, 2016, 2020). This is especially true when such reasoning involves thinking about counterfactuals – that is, reasoning about what could or would have been different, if particular variables or conditions had been different (e.g., Beck & Riggs, 2013; Rafetseder et al., 2010). These findings directly conflict with the second wave theory (i.e., probabilistic models and interventionist theories of causation) approaches, which are grounded on the (at least implicit) ability of learners to reason counterfactually (see Walker & Gopnik, 2013, for a review; see also Weisberg & Gopnik, 2013 for a review of counterfactual reasoning in young children's pretense). Additionally, despite some evidence of one-year-olds' implicit competence with "prelogical" disjunctive reasoning, children as old as five seem to have difficulty with deduction – for example, eliminating or ruling out candidate possibilities based on logic (Cesana-Arlotti et al., 2018; Mody & Carey, 2016). Further research is necessary to understand the link between infants' early reasoning about possibilities, counterfactuals, and evidence, and the explicit abilities that seem later developing, and more difficult.

13.4.5 Arriving at a Conclusion

The last step in the scientific process is the ability to evaluate the conclusion one has drawn from the evidence. Is the question answered, or the problem solved? Is the explanation satisfactory? While there are at present only a few studies examining children's early explanatory practices and preferences, findings suggest that children's ability to explain observations or the results of interventions is related to the extent to which they learn a given causal rule, and the extent to which they will continue to explore (or not explore) further evidence (Legare, 2012, 2014; Walker et al., 2014). Young children also seem to display at least some adult-like biases for explanatory scope and simplicity (Bonawitz & Lombrozo, 2012; Johnston et al., 2017; Walker et al., 2017). Further research is necessary to discover the developmental trajectory of these preferences, and the ways that they interact with others to develop early skills in scientific thinking and reasoning.

13.5 Conclusion

This chapter opened with three vignettes about individuals at very different life stages faced with very different situations: a nine-month-old trying to reproduce the jingling of her parents' car keys, a nineteen-year-old backpacker trying to unlock the door to her hostel, and a twenty-nine-year-old bioengineer studying a pancreatic enzyme. Each individual, we argued, was engaged in the process of scientific reasoning: she was searching for the resolution to a specific problem or question, and she was attempting to resolve that question by making informative interventions to deduce a solution or answer. We argued that the scientific

process fundamentally involves identifying and manipulating causally relevant variables, and observing the changes that result (or do not) in a surmised effect variable.

In addition to their structural similarity, these cases are striking for the additional reason that each of the individuals – the baby, the traveler, and the adult professional scientist – may all plausibly be instances from the same individual's lifetime. The nine-month-old may grow up and become a star STEM high school student, who becomes a chemical engineering major and Spanish minor and travels to Barcelona for spring break. After college, encouraged by her mentors, inspired by her colleagues – but most of all, inspired by the thrill of scientific discovery – she enters graduate school for chemical engineering. There, she falls in love with the particular intellectual challenges and peculiarities of the pancreas from a brief mention of its mysteries in a section of her textbook in a required organic chemistry course. Piqued, she turns to Google Scholar, explores some papers that further intrigue her, and discovers that a leading pancreatic enzyme researcher is actually at her university. She writes an email, meets the P.I., and before long is working in their lab.

There is continuity between the infant, the practical, rational reasoning of the adult college student in a tricky situation, and the carefully planned and controlled reasoning of the expert academic. Although the professional scientist explores for "purely epistemic" reasons, her drive to determine or deduce the general principle by which her enzyme operates has been in place since the very beginning of her life. (And, finding out the answer, of course, may lead to a set of pragmatic outcomes, too: finding a small piece of the cure to human pancreatic cancer, or securing funding for her next postdoctoral fellowship.) The early quest for certainty and control became, through social learning and experience, a finely tuned capacity for commonsense reasoning – which in turn became true scientific thinking and reasoning in the light of millennia of sociocultural practices and knowledge sharing. With continued hard work, curiosity, collaborations with inspiring colleagues, and a bit of luck, the young researcher will pass on her discoveries and findings to the next generation of children and young scientists.

References

Arend, R., Gove, F. L., & Sroufe, L. A. (1979). Continuity of individual adaptation from infancy to kindergarten: A predictive study of ego-resiliency and curiosity in preschoolers. *Child Development, 50*, 950–959.

Astington, J. W., Harris, P. L., & Olson, D. R. (eds.) (1988). *Developing Theories of Mind.* Cambridge: Cambridge University Press.

Baillargeon, R. (1987). Object permanence in 3½- and 4½-month-old infants. *Developmental Psychology, 23*, 655–664.

Baillargeon, R. (1998). Infants' understanding of the physical world. In M. Sabourin, F. Craik, & M. Robert (eds.), *Advances in Psychological Science, Vol. 2. Biological and Cognitive Aspects* (pp. 503–529). Hove: Psychology Press.

Beck, S. R., & Riggs, K. J. (2013). Counterfactuals and reality. In M. Taylor (ed.), *The Oxford Handbook of the Development of Imagination* (pp. 325–341). New York: Oxford University Press.

Beck, S. R., Robinson, E. J., Carroll, D. J., & Apperly, I. A. (2006). Children's thinking about counterfactuals and future hypotheticals as possibilities. *Child Development, 77*, 413–426.

Bonawitz, E., Denison, S., Gopnik, A., & Griffiths, T. L. (2014a). Win-stay, lose-sample: A simple sequential algorithm for approximating Bayesian inference. *Cognitive Psychology, 74*, 35–65.

Bonawitz, E., Denison, S., Griffiths, T. L., & Gopnik, A. (2014b). Probabilistic models, learning algorithms, and response variability: Sampling in cognitive development. *Trends in Cognitive Sciences, 18*, 497–500.

Bonawitz, E. B., Ferranti, D., Saxe, R., Gopnik, A., Meltzoff, A. N., Woodward, J., & Schulz, L. E. (2010). Just do it? Investigating the gap between prediction and action in toddlers' causal inferences. *Cognition, 115*, 104–117.

Bonawitz, E. B., & Lombrozo, T. (2012). Occam's rattle: Children's use of simplicity and probability to constrain inference. *Developmental Psychology, 48*, 1156.

Butler, L. P. (2020). The empirical child? A framework for investigating the development of scientific habits of mind. *Child Development Perspectives, 14*, 34–40.

Carey, S. (1985). *Conceptual Change in Childhood.* Cambridge, MA: MIT Press.

Carey, S. (2009) *The Origin of Concepts.* New York: Oxford University Press.

Cesana-Arlotti, N., Martín, A., Téglás, E., Vorobyova, L., Cetnarski, R., & Bonatti, L. L. (2018). Precursors of logical reasoning in preverbal human infants. *Science, 359*, 1263–1266.

Cimpian, A., & Steinberg, O. D. (2014). The inherence heuristic across development: Systematic differences between children's and adults' explanations for everyday facts. *Cognitive Psychology, 75*, 130–154.

Christie, S., & Gentner, D. (2010). Where hypotheses come from: Learning new relations by structural alignment. *Journal of Cognition and Development, 11*, 356–373.

Christie, S. & Gentner, D. (2014). Language helps children succeed on a classic analogy task. *Cognitive Science, 38*, 383–397.

Cook, C., Goodman, N. D., & Schulz, L. E. (2011). Where science starts: Spontaneous experiments in preschoolers' exploratory play. *Cognition, 120*, 341–349.

Denison, S., Bonawitz, E., Gopnik, A., & Griffiths, T. L. (2013). Rational variability in children's causal inferences: The sampling hypothesis. *Cognition, 126*, 285–300.

Flavell, J. H. (1963). *The Developmental Psychology of Jean Piaget.* New York: Van Nostrand Reinhold Company.

Gelman, S. A. (2003). *The Essential Child*. New York: Oxford University Press

Gelman, S. A., Coley, J. D., & Gottfried, G. M. (1994). Essentialist beliefs in children: The acquisition of concepts and theories. In L. A. Hirschfeld, & S. A. Gelman (eds.), *Mapping the Mind: Domain Specificity in Cognition and Culture* (pp. 341–365). Cambridge: Cambridge University Press.

Gelman, S. A., & Markman, E. M. (1986). Categories and induction in young children. *Cognition, 23*, 183–209.

Gentner, D., Brem, S., Ferguson, R. W., Markman, A. B., Levidow, B. B., Wolff, P., & Forbus, K. D. (1997). Analogical reasoning and conceptual change: A case study of Johannes Kepler. *The Journal of the Learning Sciences, 6*, 3–40.

Giles, J. W., Gopnik, A., & Heyman, G. D. (2002). Source monitoring reduces the suggestibility of preschool children. *Psychological Science, 13*, 288–291.

Goddu, M. K., & Gopnik, A. (2020). Learning what to change: Young children use "difference-making" to identify causally relevant variables. *Developmental Psychology, 56*, 275.

Goddu, M. K., Lombrozo, T., & Gopnik, A. (2020). Transformations and transfer: Preschool children understand abstract relations and reason analogically in a causal task. *Child Development, 91*, 1898–1915.

Goddu, M., K. & Walker, C. M. (2018). Toddlers and adults simultaneously track multiple hypotheses in a causal learning task. *Cognitive Science*. Available from https://cogsci.mindmodeling.org/2018/papers/0330/index.html. Last accessed July 30, 2021.

Gopnik, A. (1984). Conceptual and semantic change in scientists and children: Why there are no semantic universals. *Lingusitics, 21*.

Gopnik, A. (1998). Explanation as orgasm. *Minds and Machines, 8*, 101–118.

Gopnik, A. (2012). Scientific thinking in young children: Theoretical advances, empirical research, and policy implications. *Science, 337*, 1623–1627.

Gopnik, A., Glymour, C., Sobel, D. M., Schulz, L. E., Kushnir, T., & Danks, D. (2004). A theory of causal learning in children: Causal maps and Bayes nets. *Psychological Review, 111*, 3.

Gopnik, A., & Meltzoff, A. N. (1997). *Words, Thoughts, & Theories*. Cambridge, MA: MIT Press.

Gopnik, A., & Sobel, D.M. (2000). Detecting Blickets: How young children use information about novel causal powers in categorization and induction. *Child Development, 71*, 1205–1222.

Gopnik, A., Sobel, D. M., Schulz, L. E., & Glymour, C. (2001). Causal learning mechanisms in very young children: Two-, three-, and four-year-olds infer causal relations from patterns of variation and covariation. *Developmental Psychology, 37*, 620.

Gopnik, A., & Wellman, H. M. (2012). Reconstructing constructivism: Causal models, Bayesian learning mechanisms, and the theory theory. *Psychological Bulletin, 138*, 1085.

Gottlieb, J., Oudeyer, P. Y., Lopes, M., & Baranes, A. (2013). Information-seeking, curiosity, and attention: Computational and neural mechanisms. *Trends in Cognitive Sciences, 17*, 585–593.

Gottlieb, S., Keltner, D., & Lombrozo, T. (2018). Awe as a scientific emotion. *Cognitive Science, 42*, 2081–2094.

Greco, C., Hayne, H., & Rovee-Collier, C. (1990). Roles of function, reminding, and variability in categorization by 3-month-old infants. *Journal of Experimental Psychology: Learning, Memory, and Cognition, 16*, 617.

Gweon, H., & Schulz, L. (2011). 16-month-olds rationally infer causes of failed actions. *Science, 332*, 1524.

Inagaki, K. (1990). The effects of raising animals on children's biological knowledge. *British Journal of Developmental Psychology, 8*, 119–129.

Johnston, A. M., Johnson, S. G., Koven, M. L., & Keil, F. C. (2017). Little Bayesians or little Einsteins? Probability and explanatory virtue in children's inferences. *Developmental Science, 20*, e12483.

Kalish, C. (1998). Reasons and causes: Children's understanding of conformity to social rules and physical laws. *Child Development, 69*, 706–720.

Karmiloff-Smith, A., & Inhelder, B. (1974). If you want to get ahead, get a theory. *Cognition, 3*, 195–212.

Keil, F. C. (1989). *Concepts, Kinds, and Cognitive Development.* Cambridge, MA: MIT Press.

Keil, F. C. (2006). Explanation and understanding. *Annual Review of Psychology, 57*, 227–254.

Keil, F. C. (2012). Running on empty? How folk science gets by with less. *Current Directions in Psychological Science, 21*, 329–334.

Keil, F. C., Lockhart, K. L., & Schlegel, E. (2010). A bump on a bump? Emerging intuitions concerning the relative difficulty of the sciences. *Journal of Experimental Psychology: General, 139*, 1.

Kelemen, D. (1999a). The scope of teleological thinking in preschool children. *Cognition, 70*, 241–272.

Kelemen, D. (1999b). Why are rocks pointy? Children's preference for teleological explanations of the natural world. *Developmental Psychology, 35*, 1440.

Kelemen, D., & DiYanni, C. (2005). Intuitions about origins: Purpose and intelligent design in children's reasoning about nature. *Journal of Cognition and Development, 6*, 3–31.

Kemp, C., Perfors, A., & Tenenbaum, J. B. (2007). Learning overhypotheses with hierarchical Bayesian models. *Developmental Science, 10*, 307–321.

Kidd, C., & Hayden, B. Y. (2015). The psychology and neuroscience of curiosity. *Neuron, 88*, 449–460.

Kuhn, T. (1962) *The Structure of Scientific Revolutions.* Chicago, IL: The University of Chicago Press.

Kuhn, D. (2002). What is scientific thinking and how does it develop? In U. Goswami (ed.), *Blackwell Handbook of Childhood Cognitive Development* (pp. 371–393). Oxford: Blackwell Publishing.

Kushnir, T., & Gopnik, A. (2007). Conditional probability versus spatial contiguity in causal learning: Preschoolers use new contingency evidence to overcome prior spatial assumptions. *Developmental Psychology, 43*, 186.

Lapidow, E., & Walker, C. M. (2020). Informative experimentation in intuitive science: Children select and learn from their own causal interventions. *Cognition, 201*, 104315.

Leahy, B. P., & Carey, S. E. (2020). The acquisition of modal concepts. *Trends in Cognitive Science, 24*, 65–78.

Legare, C. H. (2012). Exploring explanation: Explaining inconsistent evidence informs exploratory, hypothesis-testing behavior in young children. *Child Development, 83*, 173–185.

Legare, C. H. (2014). The contributions of explanation and exploration to children's scientific reasoning. *Child Development Perspectives, 8*, 101–106.

Legare, C. H., Gelman, S. A., & Wellman, H. M. (2010). Inconsistency with prior knowledge triggers children's causal explanatory reasoning. *Child Development, 81*, 929–944.

Lockhart, K. L., Goddu, M. K., & Keil, F. C. (2017). Overoptimism about future knowledge: Early arrogance? *The Journal of Positive Psychology, 12*, 36–46.

Lockhart, K. L., Goddu, M. K., Smith, E. D., & Keil, F. C. (2016). What could you really learn on your own?: Understanding the epistemic limitations of knowledge acquisition. *Child Development, 87*, 477–493.

Loewenstein, G. (1994). The psychology of curiosity: A review and reinterpretation. *Psychological Bulletin, 116*, 75–98.

Lucas, C. G., Bridgers, S., Griffiths, T. L., & Gopnik, A. (2014). When children are better (or at least more open-minded) learners than adults: Developmental differences in learning the forms of causal relationships. *Cognition, 131*, 284–299.

Magid, R. W., Sheskin, M., & Schulz, L. E. (2015). Imagination and the generation of new ideas. *Cognitive Development, 34*, 99–110.

Mikulincer, M. (1997). Adult attachment style and information processing: Individual differences in curiosity and cognitive closure. *Journal of Personality and Social Psychology, 72*, 1217.

Mills, C. M., & Keil, F. C. (2004). Knowing the limits of one's understanding: The development of an awareness of an illusion of explanatory depth. *Journal of Experimental Child Psychology, 87*, 1–32.

Mills, C. M., Legare, C. H., Bills, M., & Mejias, C. (2010). Preschoolers use questions as a tool to acquire knowledge from different sources. *Journal of Cognition and Development, 11*, 533–560.

Mody, S., & Carey, S. (2016). The emergence of reasoning by the disjunctive syllogism in early childhood. *Cognition, 154*, 40–48.

Nersessian, N. J. (1999). Model-based reasoning in conceptual change. In L. Magnani, N. J. Nersessian, & P. Thagard (eds.), *Model-Based Reasoning in Scientific Discovery* (pp. 5–22). Boston, MA: Springer.

Newman, G. E., Herrmann, P., Wynn, K., & Keil, F. C. (2008). Biases towards internal features in infants' reasoning about objects. *Cognition, 107*, 420–432.

O'Neill, D. K., & Gopnik, A. (1991). Young children's ability to identify the sources of their beliefs. *Developmental Psychology, 27*, 390.

Pearl, J. (2000). *Causality: Models, Reasoning, and Inference.* New York: Cambridge University Press.

Pearl, J. (2009). *Causality.* New York: Cambridge University Press.

Pearl, J., & Mackenzie, D. (2018). *The Book of Why: The New Science of Cause and Effect.* New York: Basic Books.

Piaget, J. (1929). *The Child's Conception of the World.* London: Kegan Paul.

Quine, W. V. O. (1960). *Word and Object (Studies in Communication).* New York: Technology Press of MIT.

Rafetseder, E., Cristi-Vargas, R., & Perner, J. (2010). Counterfactual reasoning: Developing a sense of "nearest possible world." *Child Development, 81*, 376–389.

Redshaw, J., & Suddendorf, T. (2016). Children's and apes' preparatory responses to two mutually exclusive possibilities. *Current Biology, 26*, 1758–1762.

Redshaw, J., & Suddendorf, T. (2020). Temporal junctures in the mind. *Trends in Cognitive Sciences, 24*, 52–64.

Repacholi, B. M., & Gopnik, A. (1997). Early reasoning about desires: Evidence from 14-and 18-month-olds. *Developmental Psychology, 33*, 12.

Ronfard, S., Zambrana, I. M., Hermansen, T. K., & Kelemen, D. (2018). Question-asking in childhood: A review of the literature and a framework for understanding its development. *Developmental Review, 49*, 101–120.

Ross, N., Medin, D., Coley, J. D., & Atran, S. (2003). Cultural and experiential differences in the development of folk biological induction. *Cognitive Development, 18*, 25–47.

Ruchlis, H. (1963). *Discovering Scientific Method.* New York: Harper & Row.

Ruggeri, A., & Lombrozo, T. (2015). Children adapt their questions to achieve efficient search. *Cognition, 143*, 203–216.

Ruggeri, A., Sim, Z. L., & Xu, F. (2017). "Why is Toma late to school again?" Preschoolers identify the most informative questions. *Developmental Psychology, 53*, 1620–1632.

Salmon, W. C. (1984). *Scientific Explanation and the Causal Structure of the World.* Princeton, NJ: Princeton University Press.

Saxe, R., Tenenbaum, J. B., & Carey, S. (2005). Secret agents: Inferences about hidden causes by 10-and 12-month-old infants. *Psychological Science, 16*, 995–1001.

Schulz, L. E., Bonawitz, E. B., & Griffiths, T. L. (2007a). Can being scared give you a tummy ache? Naive theories, ambiguous evidence and preschoolers' causal inferences. *Developmental Psychology, 43*, 1124–1139.

Schulz, L. E., Goodman, N. D., Tenenbaum, J. B., & Jenkins, A. C. (2008). Going beyond the evidence: Abstract laws and preschoolers' responses to anomalous data. *Cognition, 109*, 211–223.

Schulz, L. E., & Gopnik, A. (2004). Causal learning across domains. *Developmental Psychology, 40*, 162.

Schulz, L. E., & Somerville, J. (2006). God does not play dice: Causal determinism and preschoolers' causal inferences. *Child Development, 77*, 427–442.

Shtulman, A., & Carey, S. (2007). Improbable or impossible? How children reason about the possibility of extraordinary events. *Child Development, 78*, 1015–1032.

Shtulman, A., & Phillips, J. (2018). Differentiating "could" from "should": Developmental changes in modal cognition. *Journal of Experimental Child Psychology, 165*, 161–182.

Silvia, P. J. (2008). Interest – The curious emotion. *Current Directions in Psychological Science, 17*, 57–60.

Simons, D. J., & Keil, F. C. (1995). An abstract to concrete shift in the development of biological thought: The insides story. *Cognition, 56*, 129–163.

Sobel, D. M., & Kushnir, T. (2006). The importance of decision making in causal learning from interventions. *Memory & Cognition, 34*, 411–419.

Spirtes, P., Glymour, C. N., Scheines, R., & Heckerman, D. (1993). *Causation, Prediction, and Search*. Cambridge, MA: MIT press.

Stahl, A. E., & Feigenson, L. (2015). Observing the unexpected enhances infants' learning and exploration. *Science, 348*, 91–94.

Taylor, M., Esbensen, B. M., & Bennett, R. T. (1994). Children's understanding of knowledge acquisition: The tendency for children to report that they have always known what they have just learned. *Child Development, 65*, 1581–1604.

Tenenbaum, J. B., Kemp, C., Griffiths, T. L., & Goodman, N. D. (2011). How to grow a mind: Statistics, structure, and abstraction. *Science, 331*, 1279–1285.

Valdesolo, P., Shtulman, A., & Baron, A. S. (2017). Science is awe-some: The emotional antecedents of science learning. *Emotion Review, 9*, 215–221.

Walker, C. M., Bonawitz, E., & Lombrozo, T. (2017). Effects of explaining on children's preference for simpler hypotheses. *Psychonomic Bulletin & Review, 24*, 1538–1547.

Walker, C. M., Bridgers, S., & Gopnik, A. (2016). The early emergence and puzzling decline of relational reasoning: Effects of knowledge and search on inferring abstract concepts. *Cognition, 156*, 30–40.

Walker, C. M., & Gopnik, A. (2013). Causality and imagination. In M. Taylor (ed.), *The Oxford Handbook of the Development of Imagination* (pp. 342–358). Oxford: Oxford University Press.

Walker, C. M., & Gopnik, A. (2014). Toddlers infer higher-order relational principles in causal learning. *Psychological Science, 25*, 161–169.

Walker, C. M., Lombrozo, T., Legare, C. H., & Gopnik, A. (2014). Explaining prompts children to privilege inductively rich properties. *Cognition, 133*, 343–357.

Wang, S. H., & Baillargeon, R. (2008). Can infants be "taught" to attend to a new physical variable in an event category? The case of height in covering events. *Cognitive Psychology, 56*, 284–326.

Weisberg, D. S., & Gopnik, A. (2013). Pretense, counterfactuals, and Bayesian causal models: Why what is not real really matters. *Cognitive Science, 37*, 1368–1381.

Wellman, H. M. (1992). *The Child's Theory of Mind*. Cambridge, MA: The MIT Press.

Wellman, H. M., & Gelman, S. A. (1998). Knowledge acquisition in foundational domains. In W. Damon (ed.), *Handbook of Child Psychology: Vol. 2. Cognition, Perception, and Language* (pp. 523–573). Hoboken, NJ: John Wiley & Sons Inc.

Wellman, H. M., & Woolley, J. D. (1990). From simple desires to ordinary beliefs: The early development of everyday psychology. *Cognition, 35*, 245–275.

Wimmer, H., & Perner, J. (1983). Beliefs about beliefs: Representation and constraining function of wrong beliefs in young children's understanding of deception. *Cognition, 13*, 103–128.

Woodward, A. L. (1999). Infants' ability to distinguish between purposeful and non-purposeful behaviors. *Infant Behavior and Development, 22*, 145–160.

Woodward, J. (2003). *Making Things Happen: A Theory of Causal Explanation*. New York: Oxford University Press.

Xu, F., Dewar, K., & Perfors, A. (2009). Induction, overhypotheses, and the shape bias: Some arguments and evidence for rational constructivism. In B. M. Hood, & L. Santos (eds.), *The Origins of Object Knowledge* (pp. 263–284). New York: Oxford University Press.

Xu, F., & Kushnir, T. (2013). Infants are rational constructivist learners. *Current Directions in Psychological Science, 22*, 28–32.

14 Computational Approaches to Cognitive Development

Bayesian and Artificial-Neural-Network Models

Ardavan S. Nobandegani and Thomas R. Shultz

14.1 Introduction

As in other sciences, formal modeling and simulation have assumed an important role in organizing and explaining cognitive development and providing a more unified account of its computational underpinnings. This chapter reviews research using two of the most influential approaches to such modeling: Bayesian and artificial neural networks. The techniques are explained for a general audience and concrete examples are described, providing both an in-depth and broad coverage of the literature.

In contrast to the common view that these two approaches are in competition, they may operate at distinctly different levels of analysis and thus potentially complement, enrich, and inspire each other (Shultz, 2007). Following a brief overview of the history of modeling of cognitive development, there is a more detailed review of how these two approaches have advanced understanding of cognitive development. There is also a discussion of some preliminary research suggesting how they might be integrated into a more general, cohesive approach that acknowledges their complementary roles.

14.2 History of Computational Modeling of Cognitive Development

The history of computational modeling of cognitive development resembles that of cognitive science more generally. Initial computational models of cognitive development employed symbolic rules (Klahr & Wallace, 1976; Klahr et al., 1987). These rules have an if–then conditional structure and explicitly reference objects and events. The next stage used artificial neural networks, sub-symbolic brain-like structures mimicking the functions of neurons and synapses (Elman, 1996; Shultz, 2003). The third stage addressed cognition under uncertainty using the formalisms of probability theory and Bayes rule to simulate selection of the best hypothesis to explain incoming data (Kemp et al., 2007; Tenenbaum et al., 2011). All three of these simulation approaches are still used, but each successive methodological stage substantially replaced the previous wave in terms of popularity and influence. As in science more generally, computational modeling of cognitive development consistently proved to be important in helping to explain and integrate empirical phenomena and generating predictions to guide new empirical research.

The focus here is on the Bayesian and neural-network approaches, and whether and how they can be integrated into a more general computational theory of cognitive development. Although they are often viewed as competitors and could generate different predictions, researchers are beginning to recognize that these two approaches can complement and enrich each other, in part because they operate at different levels of analysis

(Marr, 2010). Roughly, the Bayesian approach concentrates on a computational level of analysis (what the goal of the system is, and its optimal solution), while the neural-network approach emphasizes an implementational level (how the computation is implemented in neural systems). Both approaches can partake of the intermediate, algorithmic level of analysis (the algorithms employed in computation).

For each of these two methods, one computer simulation is presented in some detail, followed by several others that are described in less detail. This allows for both breadth and depth of coverage, although there are now many published studies that cannot be covered in the available space.

14.3 Neural Network Approaches

The range of cognitive developmental phenomena simulated by artificial neural networks is extensive, including classic Piagetian tasks and stages (e.g., conservation, seriation, transitivity, object permanence), many aspects of language acquisition (phonology, morphology, semantics, simple syntax), reading, concept learning, habituation of attention, early understanding of false belief, shift learning, disordered development, and a variety of other phenomena. There are several notable reviews of this literature on neural network simulation of cognitive development (Elman, 1996, 2005; Munakata & McClelland, 2003; Shultz, 2003, 2013, 2017; Shultz & Sirois, 2008; Thomas & Karmiloff-Smith, 2003; Westermann et al., 2006). None of them suggest or attempt an integration with Bayesian approaches.

An artificial neural network is comprised of neuronal units (representing neurons, either singly or in groups) connected by weights (representing synapses) (Figure 14.1). Each unit can be variously active, depending on the excitatory and inhibitory input it is receiving. Input units receive input signals from the environment, encoding the stimulus that the network has encountered. Those signals are transmitted by connection weights to hidden units, and then eventually on to output units, that encode some conclusion or action. Hidden units are effectively hiding from the environment, but they perform important computational transformations of their input at each successive network layer.

Many of the artificial neural networks simulating cognitive development use some kind of learning mechanism to reduce network error, the discrepancy between output-unit activations and a target signal, indicating what activation patterns the output units should produce in response to that particular input pattern. Network weights (representing synapses) are adjusted in order to reduce network error, eventually enabling correct performance on the problem the network is learning. As will be seen, some learning algorithms also recruit new hidden units as needed to increase expressive power (Shultz & Fahlman, 2010). This affords a distinction between learning (adjustment of connection weights) and development (a qualitative increase in computational power and expressivity due to hidden-unit recruitment). Still other neural-network models avoid error-reduction and supervised learning in

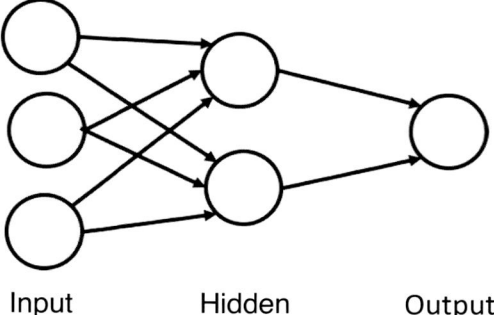

Input   Hidden   Output

Figure 14.1 A simple neural network with three layers. Units are represented as circles, connection weights as arrows

favor of unsupervised learning, often based instead on a correlational mapping of features from one network layer to another.

In comparison simulations, neural network models typically outperform symbolic rule-based models (Shultz, 2003, 2013). Constructive networks, in turn, often outperform static neural networks that do not improve their computational power. Static networks adjust connection weights to reduce error but often fail to capture the qualitative stages that characterize cognitive development in children, either by not being expressive enough to accurately learn the target function or so expressive that they mostly bypass intermediate developmental stages, failing to simulate the mistakes (non-normative solutions) that children make (Shultz et al., 2012).

14.3.1 Constructive Networks

Because three of the examples of neural network simulations utilize constructive networks, there is first a discussion of how these networks function. Among prominent constructive network algorithms are those in the cascade-correlation family. Cascade-correlation (CC) networks start with just input and output units, typically fully connected (Fahlman & Lebiere, 1990). They are feedforward networks trained in a supervised fashion with examples of particular input and target-output values. Hidden units required to deal with nonlinearity in the training patterns are recruited one at time, as needed. The algorithm alternates between output and input phases to reduce error and recruit helpful hidden units, respectively (Figure 14.2). The objective function to minimize during the output phase is:

$$E = \sum_o \sum_p (A_{op} - T_{op})^2$$

where E is error at the output units, A is actual output activation, and T is target output activation for unit o and pattern p. Error minimization is accomplished with the *Quickprop* algorithm, a fast variant of the generalized delta rule that uses curvature as well as slope of the error surface to compute weight changes (Fahlman, 1988). When error can no longer be reduced by adjusting weights entering the output units, the CC algorithm switches to input phase to recruit a hidden unit to supply additional computational power.

In the input phase, a pool of eight candidate hidden units is established, typically with sigmoid activation functions, and with initially random but trainable weights from the input units and any existing hidden units. These weights are trained by attempting to maximize a covariance C between candidate-hidden-unit activation and network error:

$$C = \frac{\sum_o |\sum_p (h_p - \langle h \rangle)(e_{op} - \langle e_o \rangle)|}{\sum_o \sum_p (e_{op} - \langle e_o \rangle)^2}$$

where h_p is activation of the candidate hidden unit for pattern p, $<h>$ is the mean activation of the candidate hidden unit for all patterns, e_{op} is residual error at output o for pattern p, and $<e_o>$ is the mean residual error at output o for all patterns. C is the absolute covariance between hidden-unit activation and network error summed across training patterns and output units and standardized by the sum of squared error deviations. The same Quickprop algorithm used for output-phase training is employed, but now with the goal of maximizing these covariances rather than reducing error (Fahlman, 1988). When these covariances stop increasing, the candidate with the highest absolute covariance is installed into the network, with its just-trained input weights frozen, and a random set of output weights, all with the negative of the sign of the covariance to give them a slight advantage in

a) Start of training.

b) First input phase.

c) Second output phase.

d) Second input phase.

e) Third output phase.

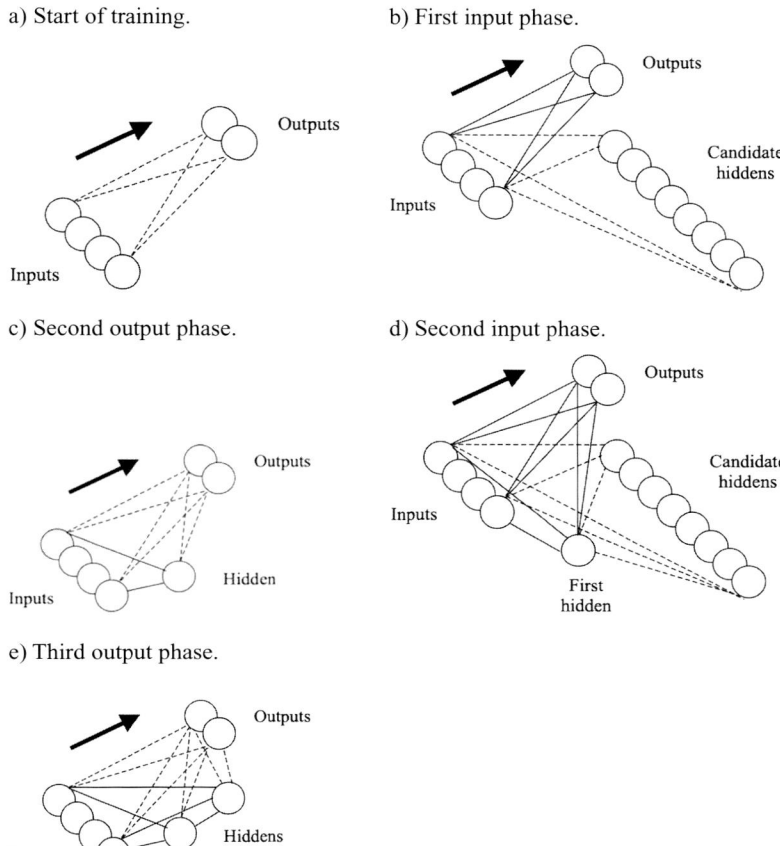

Figure 14.2 The first five phases of a CC network with four input units and two output units. Frozen input weights are represented by solid lines, trainable weights by dashed lines. Adapted from Shultz (2003)

reducing error on return to output phase. The other candidates are discarded, implementing a realistic proliferate-and-prune cycle.

The basic idea of the input phase is to select a candidate hidden unit whose activations track the network error observed in the last output phase. Once a new recruit is installed, CC returns to output phase to resume training of weights entering the output units in order to determine how to best use the new recruit in error reduction. CC networks have a uniformly deep topology with each hidden unit occupying its own layer.

A variant of CC called sibling-descendant cascade-correlation (SDCC) dynamically decides whether to install each new recruit on the current highest layer of hidden units (as a sibling) or on its own new layer (as a descendant) (Baluja & Fahlman, 1994). One-half of the candidate units exhibit sibling connectivity and the other half exhibit descendant connectivity. SDCC thus creates a wider variety of network topologies, normally with less depth and fewer cascaded connection weights, but otherwise performs much the same as CC on simulations of human experiments on learning

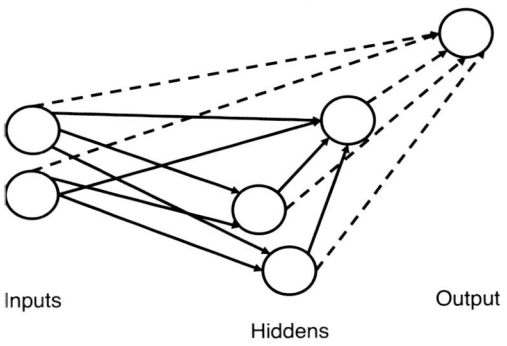

Inputs   Output

Hiddens

Figure 14.3 An SDCC network with two inputs, two layers of hidden units, and one output unit. The first layer of hidden units has two sibling units; the second layer of hidden units is a descendant of the first hidden layer, thus receiving input from that first layer. Frozen input weights are represented by solid lines, trainable weights by dashed lines

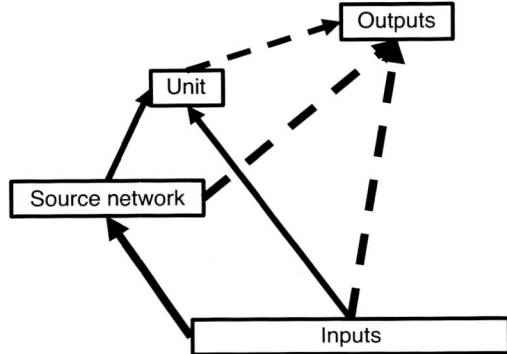

Figure 14.4 Example of a KBCC network that first recruited a previously-learnt source network and then a single hidden unit. Frozen input weights are represented by solid lines, trainable weights by dashed lines. The thicker arrows represent multiple input weights into multiple receptors. The thinner arrows entering the single hidden unit represent multiple inputs to one receptor. The thinner arrow exiting the single hidden unit represents a single sender connecting to multiple receptors

(Shultz & Bale, 2006). An example SDCC network is shown in Figure 14.3.

Another variant of CC is called knowledge-based cascade-correlation (KBCC). Rather than starting each new learning challenge from scratch, as if it knew nothing relevant, KBCC can recruit previously-learned networks, or indeed any differentiable function, in competition with single hidden units (Shultz & Rivest, 2001; Shultz et al., 2007). The new recruit is the candidate whose output correlates best with residual network error, just as in CC and SDCC. The candidate pool typically has a number of randomly initialized sigmoid units and a number of candidate source networks, i.e., networks previously trained on other tasks. The input weights to each of the source networks are randomly initialized to improve optimization. See Figure 14.4 for an example KBCC network that has recruited a previously-learned source network with relevant knowledge and then a single hidden unit. KBCC typically recruits the most relevant existing knowledge if any, and it is capable of

tweaking the recruited knowledge to suit the new learning task by adjusting output weights and recruiting single hidden units as needed. KBCC often speeds learning and sometimes even makes learning possible, for example, when it learned to detect prime integers by recruiting and using its previously acquired skill of divisibility testing (Shultz et al., 2007). Knowledge-based learning is effective, fast, and particularly realistic, as humans often leverage their existing relevant knowledge when learning new tasks.

In terms of developmental theory, constructive networks provide a clear separation between learning (weight adjustment) and development (via hidden-unit recruitment). They also afford a large advantage in autonomy over static, hand-designed networks. Finally, constructive networks from the CC family typically learn much faster than static networks, despite having to create the network interior (Fahlman & Lebiere, 1990). The speed advantage of constructive networks stems from greater hidden unit specialization and the use of both first and second derivatives of the error function in weight adjustments. Greater specialization of constructive networks is due to one-at-a-time recruitment and the freezing of input weights. Relatively greater specialization avoids the herd effect characteristic of hidden units in static networks that keep getting in each other's way. Use of the first two derivatives (slope and curvature) allows for more precision in adjusting the connection weights than just using the first derivative (slope), as in static backpropagation networks. Moreover, because these constructive networks adjust connection weights only one layer at a time, they do not require backpropagation of error across layers, which is widely considered to be implausible in biological neural networks.

14.3.2 The Balance-Scale Task

The balance-scale task has attracted several computational modeling efforts. On this task, a child is shown a rigid beam balanced on a fulcrum. The beam has pegs at regular intervals to the left and right of the fulcrum, and identical weights are placed on a peg on each side of the fulcrum (Figure 14.5). While the beam is horizontally stable, the child predicts which side of the beam will drop, or whether it will balance. Children progress through four regular stages (Boom & ter Laak, 2007; Boom et al., 2001; Siegler, 1976, 1996): (1) use weight information, (2) also use distance information when the weights are equal on each side, (3) compare the sums of weight and distance information across sides, and (4) compare the torques (products of weight and distance) across sides. Another important empirical regularity is that problems with large torque differences (left versus right) are easier for

children to solve than problems with small torque differences, torque difference being the absolute difference between the torques on each side (Ferretti & Butterfield, 1986).

Archimedes' principle of the lever specifies a rule that yields a correct answer to all such problems: compare the products of weight and distance across sides and predict that the side with the larger product (aka torque) will drop. A neural-network simulation using the cascade-correlation (CC) algorithm (Shultz et al., 1994) captured the four stages seen in children.

If performance at Stage 4 is diagnosed as being correct on 80 percent of balance-scale problems, some of which are difficult problems in which weight and distance cues conflict with each other, then even some older computational models, both symbolic (Schmidt & Ling, 1996) and connectionist cascade-correlation networks (Shultz et al., 1994), reach Stage 4. But if Stage 4 is defined by possession of a genuine multiplicative torque rule, as opposed to a mere addition rule, the modeling is more challenging. Because many conflict problems can be solved by just adding weight and distance, documentation of a torque rule must be supported by success on problems that cannot alternately be solved by an addition rule (Boom et al., 2001; Quinlan et al., 2007).

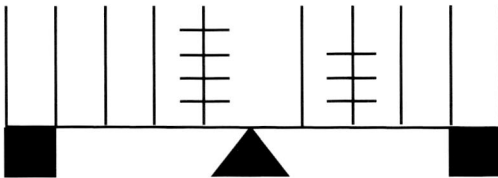

Figure 14.5 Example balance-scale problem, with four weights placed one peg from the fulcrum on the left side and three weights placed two pegs from the fulcrum on the right side. When the box supports are removed, this scale will tip to the right

With five pegs and five weights, an often used problem size in balance-scale simulations (Shultz et al., 1994), there are 625 total problems, of which only 200 are relatively difficult conflict problems in which weight and distance information, used alone, predict different outcomes. Only fifty-two of these conflict problems are torque problems that cannot be solved by mere addition; the other 148 are addition problems that can be solved by adding distance and weight on each side and comparing these sums.

An example of a problem that can be solved by addition (or torque) has left-side values of 2 and 4 versus right-side values of 3 and 2. In this case, both sums (6 > 5) and products (8 > 6) favor the left side to drop. A contrasting example that can only be solved using torque, but not by addition, has left-side values of 4 and 1 versus right-side values of 3 and 2. Although products favor the right side to drop (4 < 6), use of sums predict that the scale should balance (5 = 5). Note that these calculations are indifferent as to which measure is distance and which is weight.

An addition rule was routinely ignored in early computational models of balance-scale development, whether symbolic (Schmidt & Ling, 1996) or connectionist (Schapiro & McClelland, 2009; Shultz et al., 1994), just as it had been ignored in many older psychology experiments on the balance scale. But with evidence that at least some people use or follow a genuine torque rule, solving balance-scale problems that addition cannot solve (Boom et al., 2001; Quinlan et al., 2007), it became important to test computational models for their ability to acquire and use a genuine torque rule.

A recent constructive-network model simulated all of these effects, including in stage four a genuine torque rule capable of solving problems requiring comparison of torques (Dandurand & Shultz, 2014). As in previous models, balance-scale problems were presented as inputs and the networks learned to predict direction of tipping as outputs. There were three modules, each implemented as a constructive network. One employed an intuitive constructive SDCC network that learned to predict balance-scale results from examples alone. A second module had a neurally-implemented torque rule inserted in the recruitment pool of a KBCC network, mimicking the explicit teaching of torque in high-school science classes. To simulate the explicit teaching of a torque rule, the pool of candidates included torque-rule units, which executed the torque-rule function on their four inputs of weight and distance on the right and left sides of the balance scale:

$$TR = \frac{1}{1 + e^{-4TD}} \quad \text{where} \quad TD = (w_r d_r) - (w_l d_l)$$

Here, TR is torque rule, and TD is torque difference, computed as the difference between the torque on the right side and the left side of the fulcrum. TD was then passed through a steep sigmoid squashing function to obtain TR, an estimate of which side will tip down.

The third module, implemented as an SDCC network, learned to predict the accuracy of the intuitive network and then decided, for each balance-scale problem, whether to use the intuitive response or invoke the torque-rule module. This was similar to other tri-process models that use confidence in intuitive solutions to control access to more deliberative procedures (Thompson et al., 2011). All three networks had the usual balance-scale input of the weight and distance from fulcrum values on the left and right sides. The selection network had three additional inputs coding the torque-difference, the symmetry of weights, and the symmetry of distances (1 if symmetrical, 0 otherwise).

This model went through all four stages seen in children, whether measured by classic rule assessment (Siegler, 1976), Automatic Maxima Detection (Dandurand & Shultz, 2010), or Latent Class Analysis (LCA) (Boom & ter Laak, 2007; Quinlan et al., 2007). Automatic Maxima Detection is a statistical tool for measuring growth spurts in developmental data, among other phenomena. Spurts are characterized by a local increase in the rate of change, that is, a maximal value of velocity (first derivative) of the measure of interest, with respect to time. In between the documented growth spurts are stages, periods of little or no change.

Latent Class Analysis is a standard statistical technique that relates a set of observed (usually discrete) multivariate variables to a set of latent variables, in this case, stages. A class is characterized by a pattern of conditional probabilities that indicate the probability that variables take on particular values. It was noted that LCA typically found, in addition to the four stages seen in children, several small unreliable rule classes that do not replicate in either children's or simulation data (Dandurand & Shultz, 2010). The standard deviations of conditional probabilities were sixty-five to seventy times greater for these small, random classes than for the large, systematic rule classes. With such extraordinary variation, it is not surprising to also find that these small, random classes failed to replicate, either in children or in simulations. This suggests that Latent Class Analysis should be used with more care in diagnosing stages than is often the case. Just as non-replicable findings should be ignored in science more generally, so should non-replicable classes be ignored in applications of Latent Class Analysis. In particular, computational models should not be discredited for failing to generate results that Latent Class Analysis does not replicate. The ability to replicate is one of the strongest principles in science, and it should be consistently applied.

In short, this tri-partite model captured all and only the four stages that are replicated in children's data. The model also simulated the torque-difference effect and the documented pattern of human response times: faster on simple problems than on conflict problems (where pure weight and pure distance information yield different answers). The torque rule was invoked more on conflict problems than on simple problems. Overlapping waves of rule-based stages (Siegler, 1996) were also simulated (Figure 14.6). The weight rule peaked in the first stage and then diminished as other rules emerged. The weight-and-distance rule emerged next and peaked in the second stage. Then the addition rule emerged and peaked at the third stage. The final stage level was dominated by the torque rule. No other computational model has so far captured all of these balance-scale phenomena.

14.3.3 The Features-to-Correlations Shift in Category Learning

Infant research on category learning in the habituation/familiarization paradigm has discovered an interesting developmental shift from knowledge of independent features to relations between the features (Younger & Cohen, 1986). After repeated presentation of visual stimuli with correlated feature values, young infants (four-month-olds) showed more attention to stimuli with novel feature values than to stimuli with either correlated or uncorrelated familiar feature values. Older infants (ten-month-olds) recovered attention both to stimuli with novel feature values, and familiar but uncorrelated values, more than to stimuli with familiar correlated values. These results indicated that the younger infants had learned about individual feature values of the stimuli, but had not learned the correlations among the values. In contrast, the older infants had

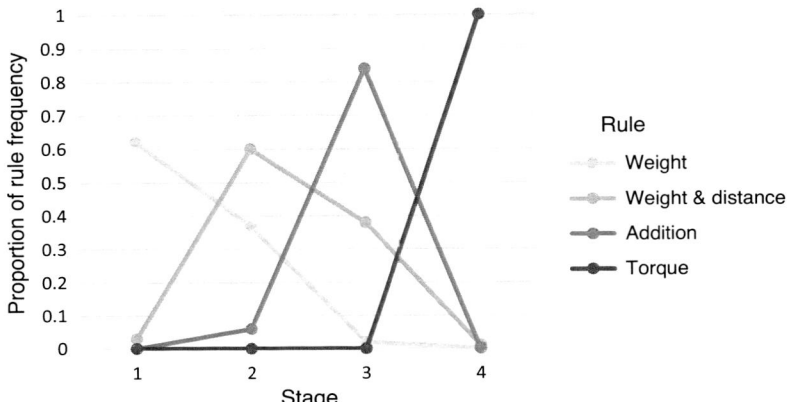

Figure 14.6 Proportion of LCA rule frequencies across stages, revealing overlapping waves in development

learned not only about stimulus feature values, but also about the pattern of correlations.

Emergence of this ability to understand correlations among feature values helps to resolve a longstanding controversy about whether perceptual development involves integration or differentiation of stimulus information. Psychological and simulation results here both favor the integration hypothesis by showing gradual understanding of relations among already discovered features. Infants of both ages learned about individual stimulus features, but older infants also learned how the features correlate with each other.

This developmental shift was simulated with constructive encoder networks (Shultz, 2010). Encoder networks learn to reproduce their inputs on their outputs, thus implementing recognition memory. Deeper learning by networks representing the older infants allowed them to understand the correlations as well as the features. In a kind of computational bakeoff, three other neural-network models did not cover these phenomena quite as well for various reasons: having weak effects, requiring extra parameters fitted by a programmer, taking far longer to learn, or not being able

to cover the shift from features to relations within testing sessions (Shultz & Cohen, 2004).

14.3.4 Taxonomic Word Learning

A neural-network model using two self-organizing maps (one for vision and another for audition, see Figure 14.7) and simple Hebbian learning explained the emergence of hierarchical taxonomies, fast mapping in early word learning, and the rapid increase in acquisition rate seen in late infancy (Mayor & Plunkett, 2010). Accuracy of word–object associations was directly related to the quality of prelexical, categorical representations in the networks. The model showed that adjustment of connection weights supported generalization of word–object associations, while pruning of weights minimized computational costs without diminishing accuracy. Simulated joint-attention between images and words accelerated and refined vocabulary acquisition. The model also explained a qualitative shift from associative to referential use, over-extension errors in both production and comprehension, typicality effects, a shift from prototype to exemplar-based effects, early

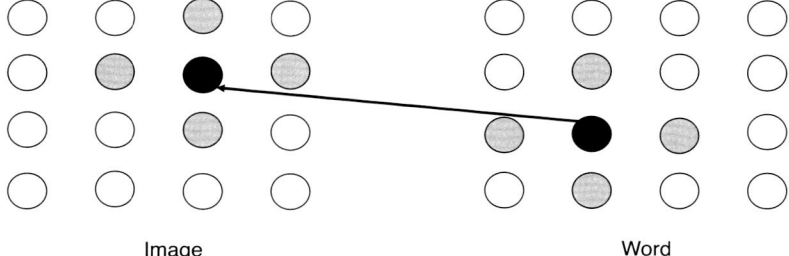

Image   Word

Figure 14.7 An example joint-attention event in word learning. When a word is presented to the auditory map, a coherent activity pattern emerges. Similarly, when an image is presented to the visual map, a selection of neurons is activated. Synapses connecting the two maps are adjusted using the Hebb rule: basically, neurons that fire together wire together. Adjusting synaptic strength to neurons neighboring (gray) a maximally active neuron (black) supports generalization and thus taxonomic responses. Adapted from Mayor and Plunkett (2010)

mispronunciations, and language deficiencies in Williams syndrome. More generally, the model showed how constraints on word learning, which are often regarded as domain-specific, can emerge from domain-general principles of learning.

14.3.5 Learning about False Beliefs in Others

Children eventually come to understand that other people have mental representations, a phenomenon that has frequently been studied with false-belief tasks (see Chapters 12 and 13). Two successive transitions have been noted in false-belief tasks. One is a shift from omniscient to representational (Wellman et al., 2001). An early, omniscient view is that other people always know the true state of the world. A later, representational view is that other people rely on representations that may or may not be accurate. The other documented developmental shift is from approach to avoidance. This is a change from initially succeeding only at tasks involving a desire to approach to eventually succeeding at tasks that involve

desires to either approach or avoid an object (Cassidy, 1998; Friedman & Leslie, 2005).

A comprehensive model of these transitions (Berthiaume et al., 2013) employed SDCC networks to simulate a non-verbal version of false-belief tasks in fifteen-month-olds (Onishi & Baillargeon, 2005). In that experiment, infants watched an agent hide an object in one of two boxes (either green or yellow). They next saw one of four belief-induction trials, leading the agent to form a true or false belief that the object was in the green or yellow box. Some infants saw the agent watch the object move from the green box to the yellow box, yielding a true belief that the object is in the yellow box. Other infants instead saw that the agent was absent as the object moved from the green box to the yellow box. In this case, the infant might think that the agent has a false belief that object is in the green box. The other two belief-induction trials induced a true belief that the object was in the yellow box and a false belief that it was in the green box. Finally, the infant saw one of two test trials in which the agent searched in either the green or the yellow box. They looked reliably longer at the apparatus when the agent did not search according to her supposed belief, whether true or false, indicating surprise due to a disconfirmed expectation.

Because it is unlikely that infants learn about search behavior during false-belief tasks, network training simulated presumed everyday experience with search behavior, while network testing simulated performance on the false-belief tasks used in the infant experiment. Input units coded the start and end locations of an object and whether the agent saw the object move from one box to another. Output units coded four different locations where the agent could search for the object. Before recruiting any hidden units, networks used location information to categorize training patterns by task, producing outcomes consistent with omniscient predictions for both approach and avoidance tasks. After recruiting a hidden unit, networks could distinguish false from true beliefs. With six hidden units, networks additionally used information on actor's attention to make representational predictions for both approach and avoidance.

These simulation results suggested that: (a) false-belief tasks cannot be solved by mere linear associations, (b) the omniscient-to-representational transition arises from overcoming a default true-belief attribution, and (c) the approach-to-avoidance transition is due to an avoidance search being less consistent than an approach search, as there are more possible locations where an object is not located than the one where it is actually located. Analysis of the internal structure of the networks showed categorization of the training patterns first by task (approach versus avoidance) and then by belief (true versus. false). This was the first model to autonomously construct and transition between belief structures and to simulate the two principal false-belief task transitions.

Given the same training and computational power, static backpropagation networks did not experience either transition as their error reductions stagnated within the first 100 training epochs.

The SDCC model and the infant data that it simulated also showed that a variety of proposed verbal hypotheses about false-belief transitions are not required to explain the two transitions (e.g., distinguishing beliefs from desires, development of executive function, language acquisition, or improvement in working memory).

Some previous computational models of false-belief tasks simulated the first transition, but not the second. In these models, the researchers inserted specific false-belief task information and transitions were accomplished via direct manipulation of some parameter value (O'Loughlin & Thagard, 2000; Triona et al., 2019), or selection from a limited set of pre-determined options (Goodman et al., 2006). The first of these models was a constraint-satisfaction neural-network, the second an ACT-R production system, and the third a Bayesian network.

14.3.6 Learning Transition Probabilities

Young infants are able to extract statistical structure from a stream of either auditory or visual information (Aslin et al., 1998; Bulf et al., 2011; French et al., 2004; Kirkham et al., 2002; Saffran et al., 1996; Tummeltshammer et al., 2017). Such abilities are important for the debate about *poverty-of-the-stimulus* in language acquisition, the issue of whether infants receive sufficient data to acquire language from learning alone.

Such learning of transition probabilities was simulated by a partially-recurrent autoencoder network that learned graded chunks of information on its connection weights and

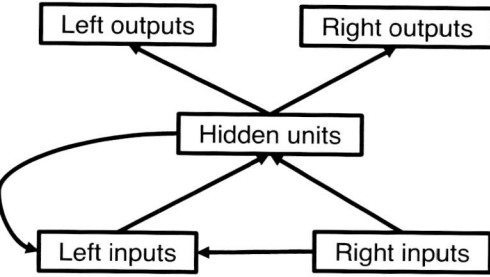

Figure 14.8 Architecture and information flow in the TRACX2 neural-network model. Adapted from Mareschal and French (2017)

recognized their recurrence, while drawing on co-occurrence statistics, as sketched in Figure 14.8 (Mareschal & French, 2017). An autoencoder network strives to learn to reproduce its input values on its output units, using a relatively compact layer of hidden units. Input values are encoded into a more abstract representation on the hidden units, which is in turn decoded to reproduce the input values on the output units.

The encoder network accurately simulated two infant experiments in audition and five in vision, including both forward and backward transitional probabilities and illusory conjunctions. In each time cycle, an item was presented to the right-side inputs. The left-side inputs were a blend of right-side input and hidden-unit activations from the previous cycle. A parameter called *delta* was the absolute difference between input and output activations. When delta was large (as was true with novel items), most of the contribution to the left-side inputs came from the right-side inputs. But when delta was small (as it was for more familiar items), most of the contribution to left-side inputs came from the hidden units. On each cycle, connection weights were updated to minimize the value of delta. Improvement with age was implemented by increasing a learning rate parameter.

14.4 Bayesian Approaches

Bayesian modeling is the other prominent approach to computational developmental psychology. Unlike neural-network approaches, Bayesian efforts target a computational level of analysis, striving to precisely characterize the computational task faced by children along with what they strive to achieve (their objective function).

Over the past fifteen years, Bayesian modeling has been successfully applied to a wide range of developmental topics, for example, numerical development (Piantadosi et al., 2012), intuitive theories and theory discovery (Goodman et al., 2011; Ullman et al., 2012), causal-structure learning (Gopnik et al., 2004), cross-domain causal reasoning (Schulz et al., 2007), social reasoning (Hamlin et al., 2013), grammar learning (Perfors et al., 2011b), and word learning and taxonomic generalizations (Xu & Tenenbaum, 2007). As with the neural-network literature, there is insufficient space to review all of the Bayesian work on cognitive development. But there are other competent and more complete reviews of Bayesian approaches to cognitive development (Gopnik & Bonawitz, 2015; Perfors et al., 2011a). They do not suggest or recommend integration with neural-network research.

What lies at the heart of a Bayesian model is the assertion of a probabilistic generative model responsible for producing the behavioral data of interest. This probabilistic generative model, which often takes the form of a causal Bayesian network, parameterized by prior probabilities and conditional probability distributions (Gopnik et al., 2004; Pearl, 2000), characterizes the abstract, structured knowledge representation that the Bayesian model assumes for explaining children's cognition.

Because Bayesian models serve as a computational-level explanation of behavioral effects, they make few or no assumptions about how their presumed knowledge representation would be implemented in neural circuits, and how inference algorithms would operate on those neural-level representations. Recent work in theoretical neuroscience has shed light on these fundamental questions (Gershman & Beck, 2017; Lochmann & Deneve, 2011).

14.4.1 Win-Stay, Lose-Sample: An Algorithm for Approximate Bayesian Reasoning

Bayes' rule provides a high-level computational model of how new evidence and current beliefs are combined to produce updated beliefs. However, the denominator in Bayes' rule is acknowledged to be computationally intractable because there are an indeterminately large number of hypotheses to consider. There is a lot of evidence that children approximate Bayes' rule as they accumulate more evidence, but the psychological processes underpinning this cognitive feat have remained largely unknown (see Chapter 13).

One idea that researchers are starting to explore is that children's algorithms only do a small amount of sampling from probability distributions in their Bayesian approximations (Bonawitz et al., 2014). To investigate how causal learning improves as new evidence is accumulated over time, Bonawitz et al. (2014) did experiments allowing analysis of changes in a learner's knowledge as more evidence was gradually presented.

They assumed that learners choose a hypothesis from a set, called the hypothesis set, given by $\mathcal{H} = \{h_1, h_2, \ldots, h_n\}$, where h_i denotes the ith hypothesis. They also assumed that $P(h_i)$ denotes the prior probability of hypothesis h_i, reflecting the learner's belief about h_i being the correct hypothesis, before having any evidence. Given hypothesis space

$\mathcal{H}$ and a prior distribution $P(h)$, a Bayesian learner should update their beliefs in light of new evidence. Receiving evidence d, the learner updates the belief in hypothesis h_i, using Bayes' rule:

$$P(h_i|d) = \frac{P(d|h_i)P(h_i)}{\sum_{i=1}^{n} P(d|h_i)P(h_i)} \qquad (14.1)$$

where $P(h_i|d)$ denotes the learner's updated belief in hypothesis h_i given evidence d, also known as the posterior probability of h_i given data d. $P(d|h_i)$ expresses the probability with which hypothesis h_i generates evidence d, also known as the likelihood. In general, the likelihood $P(d|h_i)$ could be any probability distribution. However, in the case of a deterministic likelihood, which simplifies this exposition, the likelihood is just 0 or 1 depending on whether or not the data d could be generated by h_i:

$$P(d|h_i) = \begin{cases} 1 \text{ if } d \text{ is consistent with } h_i \\ 0 \text{ otherwise} \end{cases}$$

$$\qquad (14.2)$$

This can be extended to cases where n datapoints $d_1, d_2, \ldots, d_n$ are observed by the learner. Assuming that $d_1, d_2, \ldots, d_{n-1}$ denote observations after $n-1$ trials, and upon observing d_n on the nth trial, the learner's updated belief about hypothesis h_i is given by

$$P(h_i|d_1, d_2, \ldots, d_{n-1}, d_n)$$
$$= \frac{P(d_n|h_i)P(h_i|d_1, d_2, \ldots, d_{n-1})}{\sum_{i=1}^{n} P(d_n|h_i)P(h_i|d_1, d_2, \ldots, d_{n-1})}$$
$$\qquad (14.3)$$

The intuition behind Eq. (14.3) is that a learner's updated belief about h_i upon receiving the evidence d_n on the nth trial, amounts to (1) evaluating the learner's belief about h_i prior to receiving the final evidence d_n, and solely based on past evidence $d_1, d_2, \ldots, d_{n-1}$ (captured by $P(h_i, d_1, d_2, \ldots, d_{n-1})$ in the numerator of Eq. 14.3), (2) verifying if the final evidence d_n is consistent with the hypothesis h_i [captured by $P(d_n, h_i)$ in the numerator of Eq. (14.3)], and, finally, (3) ensuring that the posterior distribution over h_i's sums to one, by performing normalization [the denominator of Eq. (14.3) serves this purpose].

In simple terms, upon receiving the first piece of evidence, d_1, the likelihood assigns a posterior probability of zero to hypotheses that are inconsistent with the data. Those hypotheses consistent with the data remain, with their updated probability being proportional to their prior probability, and the summation in the denominator operates over only those hypotheses. The same process recurs with each subsequent piece of evidence, with the posterior probability at each moment being the prior renormalized over the hypotheses consistent with all the evidence so far encountered.

Bonawitz et al. (2014) tested adults and preschoolers on two causal learning tasks, and showed that adults and preschoolers' behavior can be accounted for by a sequential algorithm, called the *win-stay, lose-sample* (WSLS). WSLS was inspired by the win-stay, lose-shift principle (Restle, 1962) which holds that learners maintain a hypothesis until they receive contradictory evidence. As opposed to exact Bayesian inference that requires evaluating the posterior probability of every hypothesis in light of the evidence acquired thus far, WSLS frugally requires hypothesis revision only if the latest piece of evidence contradicts the current hypothesis. They proposed WSLS as a rational algorithm for approximating computationally intractable Bayesian inference. For a deterministic likelihood, WSLS can be iteratively computed in three steps: (1) Sampling: Sample a hypothesis $h^{(0)}$ from the prior distribution $P(h)$; (2) Belief Updating: Upon observing the first piece of evidence d_1, evaluate $h^{(0)}$ by verifying if d_1 is consistent with $h^{(0)}$ [see Eq. (14.2)], and (3) Re-Sampling:

If d_1 is inconsistent with $h^{(0)}$ (i.e., $P(d|h^{(0)}) = 0$), sample a new hypothesis $h^{(1)}$ from the posterior distribution $P(h|d^{(0)})$ [see Eq. (14.3)]. Otherwise, set $h^{(1)} := h^{(0)}$.

This process can be iterated, replacing $h^{(0)}$ with $h^{(n)}$ and $d^{(1)}$ with $d^{(n+1)}$ in Steps 2 and 3, and $h^{(1)}$ with $h^{(n+1)}$ in Step 3. With slight modifications, WSLS can be extended to the case of having a stochastic likelihood. Using proof by induction, the authors show that WSLS always produces samples from the correct posterior distribution given in Eq. (14.3). WSLS has a strong dependency between consecutive hypotheses contemplated by the learner. As Step 3 indicates, if the stream of data remains consistent with a hypothesis h, WSLS maintains that hypothesis until contradictory evidence arrives.

The WSLS strategy made the best fit to three-to-five-year-olds' changing hypotheses (Bonawitz et al., 2014). Children were presented with initial evidence that was compatible with several different hypotheses and asked to guess again which hypothesis was correct as new evidence arrived. Each new piece of evidence tended to either confirm or disconfirm the child's current hypothesis, and each new hypothesis shaped the next one. Despite high variation in the sequence of hypotheses, on average children's responses approximated the ideal Bayesian solution. The WSLS algorithm predicted this approximate Bayesian response on aggregate and best matched hypothesis progressions. This was true for both children and adults, but the pattern held for children only when a new experimenter was used in each testing cycle. Perhaps young children think that their answers are wrong if the same adult keeps questioning them. The role of repeated questioning needs further study more generally, as it is unclear whether people would change their hypothesis every time it was disconfirmed by new evidence.

14.4.2 A Bayesian Account of Social Influences in Learning

Bayesian approaches not only explain individual learning, but are also starting to explore social learning (Bonawitz & Shafto, 2016). Children make inferences about the knowledge and goals of an informant who is selecting the data to be presented, thus enhancing their own learning. Such social information can lead to even stronger inferences and more rapid learning. Recent Bayesian models relate the knowledge and goals of a demonstrator to the teaching actions they choose to employ, and formalize how these purposeful actions influence learning.

Children represent and reason about others' beliefs and actions, and how informants sample from probability distributions. In weak (aka random) sampling, an informant provides only the basic information. Sampling is considered strong when samples are chosen by a knowledgeable person to aid learning, allowing stronger inferences about the data (Shafto et al., 2012). For example, four- and five-year-old children used the knowledge and intent of the informant to draw stronger inferences than would be afforded by the data alone (Bonawitz et al., 2011; Buchsbaum et al., 2011).

14.4.3 Bayesian Insights into Development

The rapid growth of Bayesian models has already provided several fresh insights into psychological development (Perfors et al., 2011a), some of which are summarized here:

1. Children rationally integrate a variety of information to update their posterior probabilities, taking account of what they know (prior probabilities) and new evidence (likelihoods). This is at a high, computational level, such that neither the processing algorithms nor brain implementation are typically specified.
2. There is a rational resolution of a natural trade-off between parsimony (priors) and goodness of fit (likelihoods).
3. The gap between innate and learning approaches can be bridged by Bayesian updating that selects the best hypothesis to explain the known data.
4. A lot can be learned quickly from very little data by taking account of current knowledge and information about how learning examples are selected (strong or weak, random or intentional).
5. High-level learning constraints need not be innate. Instead, they can be learned in hierarchical models, and are often learned quickly because they provide fewer options, thus requiring less evidence.
6. As Bayesian models often ignore cognitive limitations when deriving an optimal solution for a task, it is possible to identify deviations from rationality resulting from those cognitive limitations (e.g., constraints on time, memory, attention, and other resource limitations).

14.5 Prospects for Integrating Bayesian and Neural-Network Approaches to Development

It is only recently that developmental researchers have started exploring how the computations assumed by Bayesian models could be carried out by cognitive processes (Bonawitz et al., 2014). However, building bridges between the computational, algorithmic, and implementational levels of analysis has remained largely unexplored. Some Bayesian modelers have acknowledged that computational- and algorithmic-level models could turn out to be significantly different, without a clear one-to-one correspondence with the computational-level (Griffiths et al., 2012).

Given that Bayesian modeling of development has reached a reasonable level of maturity, it may be timely for researchers to begin to systematically integrate across Marr's (2010) levels, with the aim of answering the three key questions of what is computed, how it's computed, and how that computational algorithm is neurally implemented. It could be fruitful for developmental modelers to investigate this integrative approach in exploring basic developmental findings, with the goal of gaining insight about the computational underpinnings of both these and more complex cognitive tasks.

However, artificial neural-networks have had some limitations preventing them from performing probabilistically. They typically continue indefinitely trying to reduce error, which prevents them from efficiently learning probability distributions. As well, although they can deterministically learn categories from examples, they cannot probabilistically generate examples from the categories they have learned.

The first limitation can be overcome by allowing networks to track their own learning performance, enabling them to stop learning when they are no longer reducing error (Shultz & Doty, 2014). The second limitation can be overcome by inducing a normatively-justified probability distribution on the input–output mapping learned by deterministic neural networks; this provides a probabilistic interpretation of those neural networks, enabling them to use a Markov-chain Monte-Carlo (MCMC) algorithm to probabilistically generate samples (Nobandegani & Shultz, 2018). This allows for coherent bridging between neural-network and Bayesian cognition, and permits an integrative approach to computational developmental psychology.

As a single example, recent empirical work investigated the developmental origins of probabilistic reasoning in infancy, finding that six-month-old infants could generalize from a sample to a population, while four and a half-month-olds could not, suggesting a developmental shift in probabilistic abilities (Denison et al., 2013). A recent neural-network simulation showed that this developmental shift can be quantitatively accounted for (Nobandegani & Shultz, 2018).

In the infant experiment, four and a half- and six-month-olds were first shown four familiarization trials with two boxes, one containing a ratio of one pink to four yellow balls, and the other containing the opposite ratio. On each of six test trials, an experimenter drew a sample of, e.g., one pink and four yellow balls from one box and placed it in a small transparent container. Then the experimenter revealed that the source box had a four-to-one ratio of yellow to pink balls, while the other box had the opposite ratio. The six test trials alternated between a four pink and one yellow sample (relatively improbable, given the source) and a four yellow and one pink sample (more probable, given the source).

Results indicated that the older infants looked longer at an unexpected, improbable sample than at an expected, probable sample, while the younger infants looked about equally at both samples. Length of looking time in such experiments is conventionally interpreted as an indication of how surprised the infant is. It was concluded that the ability to generalize from samples to populations emerges at around six months of age, but underlying causal or computational mechanisms were not explored.

Because depth of learning, manipulated by the score-threshold (ST) parameter in SDCC, has been shown to capture numerous developmental phenomena (Shultz, 2010, 2012), ST was set to either 0.5 to represent the apparent deeper learning of the six-month-olds or the higher value of 0.63 to represent the apparent shallower learning of the four and a half-month-olds. In both conditions, SDCC ran in learning-cessation mode, ensuring that the networks would stop when they no longer made sufficient progress in reducing network error. The networks were trained on two samples illustrating the four-to-one and one-to-four color ratios of the samples drawn in the infant experiments. They were tested on nine replications of a four-to-one or one-to-four sample pattern, an approximation of what the infants saw in the boxes.

Results showed that these probability distributions were accurately learned only in the deeper-learning condition, in which two-to-three hidden units were recruited. In the shallow-learning condition, typically no hidden units were recruited. Error on test patterns represented surprise at seeing an unexpected event, here an improbable sample of five balls. This surprise was evident only with deeper learning. Also, only networks with deeper learning were able to accurately generate probable and improbable samples.

There are several other infant experiments of this sort showing that infants of six-to-twelve months can learn and use simple, discrete probability distributions. They learn these distributions very quickly, within a few minutes, and are more surprised when they see unexpected outcomes than expected outcomes. They can also use their just learned probability knowledge to search in containers that are more favorable for obtaining their preferred objects (Denison & Xu, 2014). This raises a deep puzzle because infants of these ages can neither count nor divide their counts by the sum of the counts in the standard way of computing probabilities. Results show that a model combining SDCC and MCMC can simulate both surprise and search behaviors in this range of infant experiments (Shultz & Nobandegani, 2020). The model suggests a novel, neurally plausible, and computationally sufficient explanation of how infants learn

probabilities and why infant behavior accords well with probability matching in these experiments. Alternative explanations based on known magnitude estimation techniques are unable to account for the infant data.

Starting with small and simple probability problems like these seems like a good way to begin exploring whether integration of neural-network learning with Bayesian ideas could be useful. Infants would seem to require a quick and accurate mechanism for learning and using probabilities. Whether neural-network methods could scale up to more complex Bayesian phenomena seen in older children and adults would likely be even more challenging.

References

Aslin, R. N., Saffran, J. R., & Newport, E. L. (1998). Computation of conditional probability statistics by 8 month old infants. *Psychological Science*, *9*, 321–324.

Baluja, S., & Fahlman, S. E. (1994). Reducing network depth in the cascade-correlation learning architecture. *Technical Report CMU-CS-94-209*, Carnegie Mellon University.

Berthiaume, V. G., Shultz, T. R., & Onishi, K. H. (2013). A constructivist connectionist model of transitions on false-belief tasks. *Cognition*, *126*, 441–458.

Bonawitz, E., Denison, S., Gopnik, A., & Griffiths, T. L. (2014). Win-Stay, Lose-Sample: A simple sequential algorithm for approximating Bayesian inference. *Cognitive Psychology*, *74*, 35–65.

Bonawitz, E., & Shafto, P. (2016). Computational models of development, social influences. *Current Opinion in Behavioral Sciences*, *7*, 95–100.

Bonawitz, E., Shafto, P., Gweon, H., Goodman, N. D., Spelke, E., & Schulz, L. (2011). The double-edged sword of pedagogy: Instruction limits spontaneous exploration and discovery. *Cognition*, *120*, 322–330.

Boom, J., Hoijtink, H., & Kunnen, S. (2001). Rules in the balance: Classes, strategies, or rules for the

Balance Scale Task? *Cognitive Development, 16,* 717–735.

Boom, J., & ter Laak, J. (2007). Classes in the balance: Latent class analysis and the balance scale task. *Developmental Review, 27,* 127–149.

Buchsbaum, D., Gopnik, A., Griffiths, T. L., & Shafto, P. (2011). Children's imitation of causal action sequences is influenced by statistical and pedagogical evidence. *Cognition, 120,* 331–340.

Bulf, H., Johnson, S. P., & Valenza, E. (2011). Visual statistical learning in the newborn infant. *Cognition, 121,* 127–132.

Cassidy, K. W. (1998). Three- and four-year-old children's ability to use desire- and belief- based reasoning. *Cognition, 66,* B1.

Dandurand, F., & Shultz, T. R. (2010). Automatic detection and quantification of growth spurts. *Behavior Research Methods, 42,* 809–823.

Dandurand, F., & Shultz, T. R. (2014). A comprehensive model of development on the balance-scale task. *Cognitive Systems Research, 31–32,* 1–25.

Denison, S., Reed, C., & Xu, F. (2013). The emergence of probabilistic reasoning in very young infants: Evidence from 4.5- and 6-month-olds. *Developmental Psychology, 49,* 243–249.

Denison, S., & Xu, F. (2014). The origins of probabilistic inference in human infants. *Cognition, 130,* 335–347.

Elman, J. L. (1996). *Rethinking Innateness: A Connectionist Perspective on Development.* Cambridge, MA: MIT Press.

Elman, J. L. (2005). Connectionist models of cognitive development: Where next? *Trends in Cognitive Sciences, 9,* 111–117.

Fahlman, S. E. (1988). An empirical study of learning speed in back-propagation networks. *Neural Networks, 6,* 1–19.

Fahlman, S. E., & Lebiere, C. (1990). The cascade-correlation learning architecture. In D. S. Touretzky (ed.), *Advances in Neural Information Processing Systems* (pp. 524–532). Los Altos, CA: Morgan Kaufmann.

Ferretti, R. P., & Butterfield, E. C. (1986). Are children's rule-assessment classifications invariant across instances of problem types? *Child Development, 57,* 1419–1428.

French, R. M., Mermillod, M., Mareschal, D., & Quinn, P. C. (2004). The role of bottom-up processing in perceptual categorization by 3- to 4-month-old infants: Simulations and data. *Journal of Experimental Psychology: General, 133,* 382–397.

Friedman, O., & Leslie, A. M. (2005). Processing demands in belief-desire reasoning: Inhibition or general difficulty? *Developmental Science, 8,* 218–225.

Gershman, S., & Beck, J. (2017). Complex probabilistic inference: from cognition to neural computation. In A. Moustafa (ed.), *Computational Models of Brain and Behavior* (p. 453). Hoboken, NJ: Wiley-Blackwell.

Goodman, N. D., Baker, C. L., Bonawitz, E. B., Mansinghka, V. K., Gopnik, A., & Wellman, H. M. (2006). Intuitive theories of mind: A rational approach to false belief. In *Proceedings of the 28th Annual Conference of the Cognitive Science Society* (pp. 1382–1387). Mahwah, NJ: Lawrence Erlbaum Associates.

Goodman, N. D., Ullman, T. D., & Tenenbaum, J. B. (2011). Learning a theory of causality. *Psychological Review, 118,* 110.

Gopnik, A., & Bonawitz, E. (2015). Bayesian models of child development. *Wiley Interdisciplinary Reviews: Cognitive Science, 6,* 75–86.

Gopnik, A., Glymour, C., Sobel, D., Schulz, L., Kushnir, T., & Danks, D. (2004). A theory of causal learning in children: Causal maps and Bayes nets. *Psychological Review, 111,* 1–31.

Griffiths, T. L., Chater, N., Norris, D., & Pouget, A. (2012). How the Bayesians got their beliefs (and what those beliefs actually are): Comment on Bowers and Davis. *Psychological Bulletin, 138,* 415–422.

Hamlin, K., Ullman, T., Tenenbaum, J., Goodman, N., & Baker, C. (2013). The mentalistic basis of core social cognition: Experiments in preverbal infants and a computational model. *Developmental Science, 16,* 209–226.

Kemp, C., Perfors, A., & Tenenbaum, J. B. (2007). Learning overhypotheses with hierarchical Bayesian models. *Developmental Science, 10,* 307–321.

Kirkham, N. Z., Slemmer, J. A., & Johnson, S. P. (2002). Visual statistical learning in infancy: Evidence for a domain general learning mechanism. *Cognition, 83*, 4–5.

Klahr, D., Langley, P., & Neches, R. (1987). *Production System Models of Learning and Development.* Cambridge, MA: MIT Press.

Klahr, D., & Wallace, J. G. (1976). *Cognitive Development: An Information Processing View.* Hillsdale; NJ: Erlbaum.

Lochmann, T., & Deneve, S. (2011). Neural processing as causal inference. *Current Opinion in Neurobiology, 21*, 774–781.

Mareschal, D., & French, R. (2017). Tracx2: A connectionist autoencoder using graded chunks to model infant visual statistical learning. *Philosophical Transactions of the Royal Society B: Biological Sciences, 372*, 20160057.

Marr, D. (2010). *Vision: A Computational Investigation into the Human Representation and Processing of Visual Information.* Cambridge, MA: MIT Press.

Mayor, J., & Plunkett, K. (2010). A neurocomputational account of taxonomic responding and fast mapping in early word learning. *Psychological Review, 117*, 1–31.

Munakata, Y., & McClelland, J. L. (2003). Connectionist models of development. *Developmental Science, 6*, 413–429.

Nobandegani, A., & Shultz, T. (2018). Example generation under constraints using cascade correlation neural nets. *CogSci.* Available from https://cogsci.mindmodeling.org/2018/papers/0456/index.html. Last accessed August 23, 2021.

O'Loughlin, C., & Thagard, P. (2000). Autism and coherence: A computational model. *Mind and Language, 15*, 375–392.

Onishi, K., & Baillargeon, R. (2005). Do 15-month-old infants understand false beliefs? *Science, 308*, 255–258.

Pearl, J. (2000). *Causality: Models, Reasoning and Inference.* Cambridge, MA: MIT Press.

Perfors, A., Tenenbaum, J., Griffiths, T., & Xu, F. (2011a). A tutorial introduction to Bayesian models of cognitive development. *Cognition, 120*, 302–321.

Perfors, A., Tenenbaum, J., & Regier, T. (2011b). The learnability of abstract syntactic principles. *Cognition, 118*, 306–338.

Piantadosi, S. T., Tenenbaum, J. B., & Goodman, N. D. (2012). Bootstrapping in a language of thought: A formal model of numerical concept learning. *Cognition, 123*, 199–217.

Quinlan, P. T., van der Maas, H. L. J., Jansen, B. R. J., Booij, O., & Rendell, M. (2007). Rethinking stages of cognitive development: An appraisal of connectionist models of the balance scale task. *Cognition, 103*, 413–459.

Restle, F. (1962). The selection of strategies in cue learning. *Psychological Review, 69*, 329–343.

Saffran, J. R., Aslin, R. N., & Newport, E. L. (1996). Statistical learning by 8-month-old infants. *Science, 274*, 1926–1928.

Schapiro, A. C., & McClelland, J. L. (2009). A connectionist model of a continuous developmental transition in the balance scale task. *Cognition, 110*, 395–411.

Schmidt, W., & Ling, C. (1996). A decision-tree model of balance scale development. *Machine Learning, 24*, 203–229.

Schulz, L. E., Bonawitz, E., & Griffiths, T. L. (2007). Can being scared cause tummy aches? Naive theories, ambiguous evidence, and preschoolers' causal inferences. *Developmental Psychology, 43*, 1124–1139.

Shafto, P., Goodman, N. D., & Frank, M. C. (2012). Learning from others: The consequences of psychological reasoning for human learning. *Perspectives on Psychological Science, 7*, 341–351.

Shultz, T. R. (2003). *Computational Developmental Psychology.* Cambridge, MA: MIT Press.

Shultz, T. R. (2007). The Bayesian revolution approaches psychological development. *Developmental Science, 10*, 357–364.

Shultz, T. R. (2010). Computational modeling of infant concept learning: The developmental shift from features to correlations. In L. M. Oakes, C. H. Cashon, M. Casasola, & D. H. Rakison (eds.), *Infant Perception and Cognition: Recent Advances, Emerging Theories, and Future Directions* (pp. 125–152). New York: Oxford University Press.

Shultz, T. R. (2012). A constructive neural-network approach to modeling psychological development. *Cognitive Development, 27*, 383–400.

Shultz, T. R. (2013). Computational models in developmental psychology. In P. D. Zelazo (ed.), *Oxford Handbook of Developmental Psychology, Vol. 1: Body and Mind* (pp. 477–504). New York: Oxford University Press.

Shultz, T. R. (2017). Constructive artificial neural-network models for cognitive development. In N. Budwig, E. Turiel, & P. D. Zelazo (eds.), *New Perspectives on Human Development* (pp. 13–26). Cambridge: Cambridge University Press.

Shultz, T. R., & Bale, A. C. (2006). Neural networks discover a near-identity relation to distinguish simple syntactic forms. *Minds and Machines, 16*, 107–139.

Shultz, T. R., & Cohen, L. B. (2004). Modeling age differences in infant category learning. *Infancy, 5*, 153–171.

Shultz, T. R., & Doty, E. (2014). Knowing when to quit on unlearnable problems: Another step towards autonomous learning. In J. Mayor, & P. Gomez (ed.), *Computational Models of Cognitive Processes* (pp. 211–221). London: World Scientific.

Shultz, T. R., & Fahlman, S. E. (2010). Cascade-correlation. In C. Sammut, & G. Webb (eds.), *Encyclopedia of Machine Learning Part 4/C* (pp. 139–147). Heidelberg, Germany: Elsevier.

Shultz, T. R., Mareschal, D., & Schmidt, W. C. (1994). Modeling cognitive development on balance scale phenomena. *Machine Learning, 16*, 57–86.

Shultz, T. R., Mysore, S. P., & Quartz, S. R. (2012). Why let networks grow? In D. Mareschal, S. Sirois, G. Westermann, & M. H. Johnson (eds.), *Neuroconstructivism: Perspectives and Prospects* (Vol. 2, pp. 65–98). Oxford: Oxford University Press.

Shultz, T. R., & Nobandegani, A. S. (2020). Probability without counting and dividing: A fresh computational perspective. In S. Denison, M. Mack, Y. Xu, & B. Armstrong (eds.), *Proceedings of the 42nd Annual Conference of the Cognitive Science Society* (pp. 1–7). Toronto ON: Cognitive Science Society.

Shultz, T. R., & Rivest, F. (2001). Knowledge-based cascade-correlation: Using knowledge to speed learning. *Connection Science, 13*, 43–72.

Shultz, T. R., Rivest, F., Egri, L., Thivierge, J.-P., & Dandurand, F. (2007). Could knowledge-based neural learning be useful in developmental robotics? The case of KBCC. *International Journal of Humanoid Robotics, 4*, 245–279.

Shultz, T. R., & Sirois, S. (2008). Computational models of developmental psychology. In R. Sun (ed.), *The Cambridge Handbook of Computational Psychology* (pp. 451–476). New York: Cambridge University Press.

Siegler, R. S. (1976). Three aspects of cognitive development. *Cognitive Psychology, 8*, 481–520.

Siegler, R. S. (1996). *Emerging Minds: The Process of Change in Children's Thinking*. New York: Oxford University Press.

Tenenbaum, J. B., Kemp, C., Griffiths, T. L., & Goodman, N. D. (2011). How to grow a mind: Statistics, structure, and abstraction. *Science, 331*, 1279–1285.

Thomas, M. S. C., & Karmiloff-Smith, A. (2003). Connectionist models of development, developmental disorders and individual differences. In R. J. Sternberg, J. Lautrey, & T. Lubart (eds.), *Models of Intelligence: International Perspectives* (pp. 133–150). Washington, DC: American Psychological Association.

Thompson, V. A., Prowse Turner, J. A., & Pennycook, G. (2011). Intuition, reason, and metacognition. *Cognitive Psychology, 63*, 107–140.

Triona, L. M., Masnick, A. M., & Morris, B. J. (2019). What does it take to pass the false belief task? An ACT-R model. *CogSci*. Available from https://escholarship.org/uc/item/49c346x1. Last accessed August 23, 2021.

Tummeltshammer, K., Amso, D., French, R. M., & Kirkham, N. Z. (2017). Across space and time: Infants learn from backward and forward visual statistics. *Developmental Science, 20*, e12474.

Ullman, T. D., Goodman, N. D., & Tenenbaum, J. B. (2012). Theory learning as stochastic search in the language of thought. *Cognitive Development, 27,* 455–480.

Wellman, H. M., Cross, D., & Watson, J. (2001). Meta-analysis of theory-of-mind development: The truth about false belief. *Child Development, 72,* 655–684.

Westermann, G., Sirois, S., Shultz, T. R., & Mareschal, D. (2006). Modeling developmental cognitive neuroscience. *Trends in Cognitive Sciences, 10,* 227–232.

Xu, F., & Tenenbaum, J. B. (2007). Word learning as Bayesian inference. *Psychological Review, 114,* 245–272.

Younger, B. A., & Cohen, L. B. (1986). Developmental change in infants' perception of correlations among attributes. *Child Development, 57,* 803–815.

Subpart II.2
Childhood and Adolescence: The Development of Human Thinking

15 Development of Qualitative Thinking
Language and Categorization

Susan A. Gelman

15.1 Introduction

This chapter examines the role of language in children's categorization. Children categorize every time they treat discriminably different items as in some way the same. A nine-month-old tosses a foam ball, a round candle, and American football, treating them all as throwable objects. A toddler points to a cow and calls it a "dog," treating all four-legged mammals as somehow alike. A three-year-old wisely observes, "Butterflies have bones," making a general claim about the abstract set of butterflies. Categories organize human experience, provide the building blocks of thought, and operate on every sort of content: objects, persons, events, mental states, abstract ideas, and logical elements.

Basic survival requires every organism to be capable of categorizing items in their environment: food versus non-food, predator versus prey, mate versus non-mate. And indeed, all organisms – chimps, cats, pigeons, bees – form categories. Infants, too, form and use categories, as Chapter 9 on infant cognition richly demonstrates. Clearly, then, at the most fundamental level, language isn't a necessary prerequisite to categorization.

Nonetheless, for humans, categories are often expressed in language. Thus, the study of how children categorize as they develop provides an opportunity to examine anew the age-old question of how language intersects with thought. This question can be broken down into several sub-questions: What is the nature of thought prior to language? How do categories change as children acquire names for things? How does language input influence children's categories? Do children learning different languages show differences in their categories and, if so, at what point in development?

This chapter selectively reviews a range of recent research findings that have examined these questions. The chapter is organized into four primary sections, each focusing on one key function of categories: efficiency, induction, communication, and organizing norms and moral judgments (see Murphy, 2002, regarding the first three functions). To provide a brief summary of these functions, consider the category of clams, each unique, each varying slightly from one another in size, coloration, texture, and shape. Having access to this category is *efficient* in that we don't have to keep track of each of the numerous and distinct individual objects we encounter but rather can reduce this tremendous variety to a single concept. The category fosters *induction*, that is, generalizing beyond what we have already experienced to make predictions about the future. For example, once we have eaten one clam and survived, we can infer that other clams will be edible, too. The category fosters *communication*, by means of a label that allows us to share ideas about clams with others. Finally, categories organize our *normative and moral judgments*. Category boundaries tell us what is or is not acceptable (for example, kosher laws dictate that it's acceptable to eat trout and salmon, but not eels or clams). For each of these key functions of categories, developmental evidence provides new insights into classic questions regarding how knowledge is constructed, and the links between language and thought.

15.2 Efficiency

Categories are efficient, in that they impose order on everyday experience. As we move through time and space, we are confronted with a world that is highly complex, multi-dimensional, and dynamic. By placing items into categories, we are able to overlook variability, reduce the amount of detail and complexity we need to consider, and focus on some features over others. In this section, I focus on the ways in which children construct efficient categories, and how language modifies or modulates these constructs.

15.2.1 Words As Invitations

From early in infancy, words "invite" children to form a category (Waxman & Markow, 1995). Hearing a word for a set of distinct items encourages children to note how the items relate to one another, and to form a category that includes them all. In one task, infants of six-to-twelve months of age viewed a series of different animals (e.g., duck, bear, lion, ...), one at a time, during a familiarization phase, and then during a test phase were presented with two items that had not appeared during familiarization: another animal (cat) and a non-animal (apple) (Perszyk & Waxman, 2018). Importantly, the study design manipulated whether or not a word accompanied the presentation of each item during familiarization. When children heard the same word with each animal during familiarization ("This is a toma ... This is a toma ... This is a toma ...") then, at test, they

looked longer at the item that was outside the category (a novelty preference; in this case, the apple). In other words, they treated the duck, bear, lion, etc., as constituting a category (animals). In contrast, if they heard no word during familiarization, then they failed to integrate the instances and did not form a category. A similar lack of categorization was found if children heard only a non-word auditory signal (such as a beep), or variable labels ("This is a blicket ... This is a toma ... This is a fep ..."). As children gain experience with different types of words in their language, grammatical cues guide increasingly subtle and differentiated expectations. For example, by eighteen-to-twenty-one months of age, different kinds of words signal different kinds of concepts (e.g., nouns ["This is a blick ..."] invite categories, whereas adjectives ["This is a blickish one ..."] invite properties, such as color) (Perszyk & Waxman, 2018).

Another conceptual understanding that is boosted by supplying words is the acquisition of what philosophers call "sortals" (Macnamara, 1987) – concepts that provide principles of individuation (how many) and identity (the same). One cannot answer either "How many are there?" or "Are they the same?" without specifying how many *what*, or the same *what*. This "what" is the sortal concept. For example, when counting farm animals, the answer to "How many animals are there?" will differ from "How many horses are there?" Sortal concepts undergo important developmental changes in infancy (Xu & Carey, 1996). For example, consider a task in which an object moves behind a screen and comes out the other side. If we were to watch a toy duck go behind the screen and a toy truck come out the other side, we would infer that there are two items behind the screen: one duck and one truck. Twelve-month olds do the same: when the screen is dropped, they look longer if only one object is revealed rather than two. However, ten-month-olds treat this event as displaying just one object that has switched features behind the screen – that is, they seem to have access just to the sortal "object," and not to the sortals "truck" and "duck." Xu and Carey (1996) argued that language may be implicated in this shift, as this period from ten-to-twelve months is roughly when children first acquire noun labels (but see Bergelson & Swingley, 2012). Even younger children, nine-month-olds, can succeed when each toy is explicitly labeled with a count noun as it emerges from behind the screen (Dewar & Xu, 2007).

15.2.2 Language Variation

All languages have names for things, but languages vary tremendously in how they carve up the world. This variation is found in vocabulary items (e.g., Schadenfreude is available in German but not English), conceptual detail (e.g., number of words for number; Frank et al., 2008), semantic structure (e.g., verbs in English and Spanish tend to encode different elements of an event; Talmy, 1985), and grammatical elements (tense, aspect, clusivity, polarity, mirativity, . . .). Studying how children acquire different languages, and the corresponding concepts that are expressed, sheds light on when and why conceptual development sets limits on the learning process, and when and why language-specific patterns shape children's categories.

Take, for example, the acquisition of evidentials, which are grammatical devices that some languages employ to mark how the speaker came to know something. Turkish requires a speaker to choose between two past-tense morphemes, indicating either that a speaker knows something directly (e.g., by perceiving it; -DI) or indirectly (hearsay or inference; –mIş). Ozturk and Papafragou (2016) found that Turkish-speaking children do not acquire this

distinction until about six-to-seven years of age, and that the linguistic distinction rests in part on developmental changes in children's ability to identify and remember sources of knowledge (aka source monitoring), which younger children have difficulty with. This is a case of a linguistic development following prior conceptual developments.

In contrast, consider the words used to refer to spatial relations (e.g., the apple is in the bowl, the cap is on the bottle). The English pronouns "in" and "on" correspond to spatial terms in Korean that overlap and cross-cut this conceptual space, distinguishing between tight fit (e.g., a cork in a bottle; kkita) versus loose fit (e.g., an apple in a bowl; nohta) (Bowerman & Choi, 2001). Young children acquire the system of their language from their earliest production of language, suggesting that language input guides the conceptual system from early in development, rather than a purely non-linguistic universal conceptual starting-point that then shifts as a function of language input (see also Casasola & Ahn, 2018, for evidence that exposure to this linguistic input affects children's concepts by eighteen months of age).

One of the more intriguing – yet understudied – ways in which language variation can form categories is that of "covert categories." Bowerman (2005, p. 239) refers to "a shadow world of hidden object categories: ways of classifying objects that are woven subtly into the semantics of the verbs, classifiers, prepositions, and other relational words of the language we speak." For example, in Korean, one class of items (hand, book, fan, . . .) can be the object of the verb "phyelchita" (open) and another class of items (box, door, bag, . . .) can be the object of the verb "yelta" (open). In contrast to English, which lumps all these elements into a single category, Korean incorporates a conceptual distinction that must be learned: *phyelchita* refers to spreading out something flat, whereas *yelta* refers to removing a barrier to interior space.

Another example are classifiers, which are used when referring to countable units. English has a very limited set of classifiers, such as *ball* (ball of wax) or *sheet* (sheet of paper). In contrast, other languages, such as Japanese, have well over 100 distinct classifiers. Eventually these categories are learned, not by rote but as conceptually grounded, as demonstrated by their productivity – that adults can generalize classifiers systematically to new instances. Children begin to extract the semantics of classifiers as early as preschool age (Yamamoto & Keil, 2000) though full acquisition is a prolonged process (Salehuddin & Winskel, 2009; Schwab et al., 2018).

15.2.3 Beyond the Tangible

Words refer not only to tangible objects and events, but also to non-visible or abstract constructs, including mental states (wishes, hopes), time (minute, hour), logical operators (or, not), or dimensions (color, quantity). Children are working on all of these concepts from early in development, and examining their development gives us the opportunity to tease apart the role of conceptual understanding and linguistic form in word acquisition. For example, although "no" is one of children's earliest words and appears prior to two years of age, understanding negation as a broad logical operator (relevant not only when rejecting something on offer but also to deny the truth of a proposition) is not robustly understood until age two or three (Austin et al., 2014; Feiman et al., 2015; Reuter et al., 2018).

When working out the meanings of non-object words, children may identify the broad semantic field to which a word belongs, prior to working out their more detailed meaning. For example, they know that minute, hour,

day, and year refer to time prior to knowing anything about how they differ from one another (Shatz et al., 2010; Tillman et al., 2017). This result suggests that children can glean meaning from a word's context of use – what Shatz et al. (2010) refer to as "word–word mappings."

15.2.4 Categories in Larger Structures

As suggested by the word–word mappings mentioned in Section 15.2.3, categories are not just isolated atomic units; they are embedded in larger structures. One important structure that has received much attention are class-inclusion hierarchies, in which smaller categories are nested in larger categories (e.g., beagles are dogs, dogs are animals, animals are living things). This hierarchical structure, with roughly three-to-five levels of lexicalized items, appears to be a linguistic and cultural universal (Atran, 1998). Furthermore, the middle level of abstraction (dog, table, shoe, car; AKA the basic level) is the most rapidly accessed and earliest learned (Horton & Markman, 1980; Mervis & Crisafi, 1982; Rosch et al., 1976). Adults make use of these structures to guide their inferences; for example, upon learning that a dog and an elephant share a feature, they will generalize it further than upon learning that a dog and a fox share a feature, because the former pair is more diverse and therefore has broader "coverage" of the animal domain (Osherson et al., 1990).

Children's access to these larger structures undergoes important developmental changes (Inhelder & Piaget, 1964; Markman, 1989; Unger & Fisher, 2019; Unger et al., 2016). For example, although children as young as five years of age are capable of drawing broader inferences from a diverse sample (three very dissimilar items) as compared to a homogeneous sample (three very similar items), they do so only for novel categories, and not for familiar categories until nine-to-ten years of age (Rhodes & Liebenson, 2015). In this case, younger children's knowledge of the structure of more familiar categories paradoxically stands in the way of making use of the diversity of the sample. More generally, developmental changes in children's access to and use of these structures are influenced by an array of factors, including children's expertise (Gobbo & Chi, 1986), their experiences with animals (Inagaki, 1990; Unger & Fisher, 2019), and the cultural and ecological context in which children are raised (Coley, 2012; Medin et al., 2010). At the same time, linguistic scaffolding allows even preschoolers to begin making headway on components of a given hierarchy (e.g., Anggoro et al., 2008; Gelman et al., 1989; Waxman, 1990).

15.3 Induction

Categories not only allow efficient retrieval of, and connections among, prior experiences; they also permit one to generalize to new instances and expand one's knowledge, a process known as induction. Indeed, induction may be the most valuable function of categories, as it allows us to predict, anticipate the future, and plan accordingly. Whereas *inductive inferences* extend beyond what is known with certainty, *deductive inferences* logically on follow from a set of propositions. For example, if a child observes a single squirrel eating a nut and then infers that squirrels eat nuts, this is an inductive inference. In contrast, if a child learns that all squirrels are rodents, and then infers that a particular squirrel is a rodent, that is a deductive inference that necessarily follows based on predicate logic. Induction is one crucial means by which we can extend our knowledge beyond the limits of what we directly experience, and has great survival value (Hollander et al., 1986).

15.3.1 Category-based Induction

Children rely on categories to make inductive inferences about novel, non-obvious properties, starting in infancy. For example, when babies are presented with a small can that makes an interesting wailing sound when turned upside-down, they try to elicit the same property in another can that is similar in appearance by also turning it upside-down (Baldwin et al., 1993). In this case, appearance alone is sufficient to indicate shared category membership, and the inductive inference follows.

However, category membership cannot always be directly inferred based on appearance alone. For example, in the animal kingdom looks may be deceiving, due to biological mechanisms such as camouflage, convergent evolution, mimicry, or sexual dimorphism. In such cases, adults rely on the language of experts to identify items and guide inferences. Interestingly, children do as well. In a classic study, Gelman and Markman (1986) showed preschool children triads of items (biological or non-biological natural kinds) for which category labels and similarity were pitted against one another. For example, one set included two birds (a blackbird and a flamingo, each referred to as "a bird") and a bat (which looked very similar to the blackbird in shape, color, and orientation; referred to as "a bat"). Children then learned contrasting facts about a non-obvious behavior of two of the items (e.g., what the flamingo and the bat feed their babies), and were asked which of the two facts was true of the third (the blackbird). By four years of age (and, in follow-up studies using simpler methods, by two-to-three years of age), children tended to answer based on the category label (Gelman & Coley, 1990; Gelman & Markman, 1987). This wasn't due to a simple matching strategy, because children did not make use of labels when asked to generalize superficial properties such as size or visibility, and they did make use of non-matching labels when they were semantically equivalent (e.g., "puppy" and "dog") (Gelman & Markman, 1986). By thirteen months of age, children also make use of category labels to guide their inferences about simple artifacts (Graham et al., 2004; Keates & Graham, 2008).

My colleagues and I have argued that the use of labels on this task is due to an "essentialist" conceptual framework for reasoning about categories in the natural world. Essentialism is an assumption that categories "carve up nature at its joints," and thus are inductively rich, immutable, with clear boundaries, and an internal, inherent, biological basis (Gelman, 2003, 2004). For clarity, I note two important caveats. First, essentialism is a psychological claim about concepts, not a metaphysical claim about the structure of the world. And indeed, people's intuitive essentialist beliefs may distort the complexity and variety of the world (Gelman & Rhodes, 2012; Leslie, 2013). Second, psychological essentialism is a placeholder concept with relatively little content (Medin, 1989). People may believe *that* there is an internal causal essence, but not know *what* the essence is.

Essentialism has been well-documented in adults, who explicitly endorse a variety of essentialist claims (Haslam et al., 2000; Mandalaywala et al., 2018; Shtulman & Schulz, 2008). Evidence for this framework in childhood comes from a variety of tasks, including identity judgments, word-learning, decisions about category boundaries, predicting the role of nature versus nurture in development (see Gelman, 2003; Gelman & Roberts, 2017, for review). Essentialist beliefs have been documented in children across a broad variety of cultural contexts, suggesting that essentialism is a fundamental component of how humans reason about animals (e.g., Astuti et al., 2004; del Rio & Strasser, 2011; Moya et al., 2015; Waxman et al., 2007).

Children's essentialist reasoning does not mean that children don't also make use of other sorts of information, such as perceptual similarity, statistical learning, or attentional and associative mechanisms (e.g., Smith et al., 2010). Indeed, evidence indicates that a variety of processes are important components to children's inductive reasoning (Davidson & Gelman, 1990; Fisher et al., 2015; Gelman & Davidson, 2013; Waxman & Gelman, 2009).

15.3.2 Stereotyping and Social Essentialism

Viewing categories within an essentialist framework may seem "smart" when applied to natural kinds, such as animals, plants, or natural substances. It is impressive that children so readily accept adult labels (e.g., to learn that an eel is a fish, not a snake) and go beyond the obvious to make inferences about the hidden nature of things. These findings indicate that preschool children are not limited to considering only the most obvious and concrete features of their experience, as many have classically argued (e.g., Inhelder & Piaget, 1964). Moreover, in broad strokes essentialism seems consistent with the assumption of scientists, that the world has a deep and non-obvious structure that can be revealed by careful and intensive study.

And yet, this same view of categories may be flawed and pernicious when applied to social categories, such as gender, race, or other social groupings (e.g., nationality, caste). Relying on category membership rather than individuating information is indeed the hallmark of stereotyping. Among adults, those who endorse essentialist accounts of race and gender often display more stereotyping and prejudice, and at the level of academic disciplines these essentialist beliefs seem to contribute to systemic imbalances in who enters which field of endeavor (Bastian & Haslam, 2007;

Keller, 2005; Leslie et al., 2015; Williams & Eberhardt, 2008).

There is now extensive evidence that young children engage in stereotyping and essentialist reasoning about at least some social categories from preschool age (Banaji & Gelman, 2013; Rhodes & Mandalaywala, 2017). Here I briefly mention just a few key points, illustrating with gender, as perhaps the most well-studied example. Young children engage in gender stereotyping and prejudice (Arthur et al., 2008). They treat boys and girls as categorically distinct (Rhodes & Gelman, 2009a) and view gender-linked properties as inborn and relatively impervious to environmental influence (Taylor et al., 2009). By six years of age, they also judge girls as less likely to be "really, really smart" than boys (Bian et al., 2017).

At the same time, there is substantial and important variation in what and when children stereotype and essentialize, as a function of cultural context (Astuti et al., 2004; Diesendruck, 2013). Thus, for example, the developmental course for social essentialism may increase, decrease, or stay the same with age, depending on the category (gender, race) and community (liberal, more diverse university city versus conservative, less diverse small town) (Rhodes & Gelman, 2009a; Rhodes & Mandalaywala, 2017). Language may also play a role in fostering stereotypes and essentialism, a topic I turn to next.

15.3.3 Generic Language

To this point I have discussed children's tendency to generalize information to category members on the basis of facts learned about individual category instances. Yet languages have a more direct mechanism for fostering category-based inferences, by means of generalizing statements that refer to the category as a whole, also known as generics (e.g., "Birds fly"). Generics have been attested in all languages (Gelman & Roberts, 2017) and are particularly relevant in the context of acquisition: they are frequent in child-directed speech, they are early-acquired and readily stored in children's memory, and they convey conceptually central properties (see Gelman, 2010, for review).

Children start producing and comprehending generics at about two and a half years of age. This in itself is notable, given that a generic refers to an abstract category that is not concretely present to the child (e.g., "Ducks waddle" refers to ducks in general), and that its meaning does not reduce to any simple rule or frequency (e.g., children understand that "Lions have manes" is true, although only male lions do so, but that "Lions are male" is not true, even though at least as many lions are male as have manes; Brandone et al., 2012). Rather than frequency, generics express features that are "core" or causally powerful (Cimpian & Markman, 2009; Gelman & Bloom, 2007). They exaggerate the prevalence of a feature in a category: one can assert generics on the basis of minimal evidence (as with the examples above), but upon hearing a novel generic, people assume that the feature has high prevalence. This leads to an asymmetry in which both children and adults exaggerate the prevalence relative to the evidence (Brandone et al., 2015; Cimpian et al., 2010). For example, upon learning that 70 percent of crullets have spots, both children and adults report that "Crullets have spots" is true, but upon learning that "Crullets have spots," on average they estimate that 95 percent of crullets have spots.

Of particular significance for the inductive power of categories, children (and adults) who hear generics about a novel category are more likely to treat that category in essentialist ways, for example, as having inductive potential, as being stable over time, and as having innately determined properties (Gelman et al., 2010; Rhodes et al., 2012). Generics are certainly not the only means by which stereotypes are conveyed to children (see also Gelman et al., 2004), but they are especially widespread and difficult to counteract.

15.4 Communication

Categories foster communication despite our vastly different experiences. So, for example, the category "birds" is shared by toddlers, poets, hunters, bird owners, and ornithologists, notwithstanding their radically different experiences with, and knowledge about, birds. Language is not required for sharing categories. For example, categories can be conveyed to others by non-linguistic means, including spatial separation (dangerous cleaning fluids out of reach at the top of the closet, soap at sink-level), adding features (long hair and dresses on girls, short hair and suspenders on boys), or differential non-verbal behaviors (e.g., eating ice cream with gusto versus grimacing when eating spinach), including ones that are quite subtle (Skinner et al., 2017).

Nonetheless, language has unique expressive power to rapidly and with high fidelity transmit information and advance cultural evolution (Kirby et al., 2008; Maynard Smith & Szathmáry, 1997; Pagel, 2017). As we have seen in Section 15.3, language has a wealth of devices for communicating categories, including labels (e.g., dog), grammatical morphemes (e.g., tense markers, classifiers, evidentials), covert categories (e.g., which items can be the object of which verbs), and generic language. Some of these concepts would be difficult or impossible to convey non-linguistically, including non-obvious category membership (e.g., referring to a legless lizard as a lizard rather than a snake) or the scope of a proposition (e.g., a property of "all lizards," "most lizards," "some lizards," or [generically] "lizards"). Thus, the communicative function of categories is especially important to understanding children's cognition, as the expression of categories in language permits the social transmission of knowledge from one generation to the next.

15.4.1 Testimony

Much of what children learn is not picked up via direct experience but rather through the testimony of others (Gelman, 2009; Harris et al., 2018). Children do not just passively receive others' input; rather, they actively seek testimony about category knowledge, by means of gestures (Shatz, 1987), questions (Chouinard, 2007; Frazier et al., 2009, 2016; Kemler-Nelson et al., 2004), and trying out erroneous labels (Gelman et al., 1998).

By two years of age, children rely on the testimony provided by others. They treat labels as conventional and thus shared among members of their speech community (Clark, 1992). They learn new concepts, including those with a non-obvious basis (Gopnik & Sobel, 2000). They learn category boundaries, and shift their category boundaries in response to language input (e.g., deciding that something that looked like a cat is actually a dog; Gelman & Markman, 1986; Jaswal & Markman, 2007).

At the same time, children are selective in which testimony they put their trust in – an adaptive strategy, given that speakers may be ignorant, misinformed, or downright deceptive. By preschool age, children evaluate a speaker's accuracy and then use that information when deciding whether to trust the information they provide. Thus, for example, young children refrain from learning from a speaker who repeatedly mislabels things (calls a ball a hat, calls a dog a duck), expresses uncertainly (I think it's a duck?), or is otherwise less nice, smart, or honest (Koenig & Harris, 2005; Lane et al., 2013; Sabbagh & Baldwin, 2001).

Children's attentiveness to speaker cues to reliability is consistent with the idea that children engage in a process of rational inference when evaluating speakers' communications (Sobel & Kushnir, 2013). When a speaker demonstrates category knowledge, children rely on the specifics of their knowledge – for example, they trust what a dog-expert tells them about dogs, but not necessarily regarding another domain that is outside their expertise (Koenig & Jaswal, 2011; Sobel & Corriveau, 2010). At the same time, children's skill in discerning what constitutes relevant expertise changes with age – for example, younger children are more likely to rely on the topic of an expert's knowledge (e.g., marbles), rather than the causal principles that organize their domain of expertise (e.g., physics) (Danovitch & Keil, 2004; Keil et al., 2008).

15.4.2 Learning from Others

As we have just seen, even toddlers are sensitive to the testimony of others, and employ a variety of relevant cues to evaluate information sources as more or less trustworthy. It should thus not be surprising that the language children hear has consequences for their conceptual development. One fruitful way this has been examined is by seeing how variation in the language that children hear corresponds to variation in children's skills and concepts, across a range of content areas, for example: math skills (Susperreguy & Davis-Kean, 2016), spatial reasoning (Pruden et al., 2011), and motivational frameworks for reasoning about intelligence (Gunderson et al., 2013).

One very instructive case involves the role of input language in children's theory of mind. Because mental states and mental processes are not directly observable, this is a domain in which variation in the language children

hear could have particularly meaningful consequences for their understanding. And, indeed, despite broadly consistent patterns across multiple cultures in the sequencing of steps in the development of theory of mind (Wellman & Liu, 2004), children who have access to richer mental state language during development are relatively more advanced in their theory-of-mind reasoning. Thus, children whose parents engage in more mental state talk have a more advanced theory of mind (Adrián et al., 2007; Taumoepeau & Reese, 2013), as do children with older (but not younger) siblings (Perner et al., 1994).

There is something of a "natural experiment" that has allowed researchers to gain new insights into the role of language input on theory of mind development, with the study of deaf children. Deaf children of deaf parents have a fully expressive, linguistically complex language model from birth, by means of whichever sign language their community uses (e.g., in the United States this would typically be ASL, but in other communities this would be another sign language). In contrast, deaf children of hearing parents (which constitutes roughly 95 percent of deaf children) typically have a substantially more limited language model, especially in their first few years, as their parents are rarely fully proficient in sign language and often only one parent is the designated signer. As a result, a child in this latter group "... begins with little discourse about persons' inner states, thoughts, and ideas; is likely to have restricted play with others; and generally has less access to the free-flowing, turn-taking, perspective-negotiating dance of social interactions" (Wellman, 2013, p. 72). Correspondingly, the linguistic environments of these two groups of children – on the one hand, deaf children of deaf parents, on the other hand, deaf children of hearing parents – are quite substantially different. And whereas deaf children of deaf parents develop theory-of-mind milestones on the same time-table as hearing children from the same community, deaf children of hearing parents show a considerable delay, taking about twelve years or more to reach the level that is reached in only four-to-six years by hearing children, or by deaf children of deaf parents (de Villiers & de Villiers, 2014; Wellman et al., 2011).

15.4.3 Language As a Social Category

As discussed in Section 15.3, language provides testimonial evidence to children as they construct categories and theories about the world. In these cases, the messages are explicitly expressed in the language, by means of category labels or propositional content. Yet this is not the only way that language provides important category information to children. A person's manner of speaking is also a powerful cue, albeit an indirect cue. Specifically, children draw rapid and far-reaching inferences about others as a function of the language, accent, dialect, register, and style with which they speak.

I start with language (e.g., English and French) and accent (e.g., English spoken with a native American accent versus a "foreign" French accent). Kinzler et al. (2007) noted that the language someone speaks, and the accent they employ, are "honest signals" to a person's background. That is, for most people, how someone speaks is a true indication of how they were raised; it is difficult to fake native-like accent and fluency in a language learned later in life. For this reason, Kinzler et al. hypothesized that children would use this sort of language variation as a social cue when evaluating others and guiding social interactions. Consistent with this hypothesis, children show keen sensitivity to language and accent when making social judgments. By five-to-six months, infants prefer to look at someone who speaks the same language as they do, or

with the same native accent; by ten months of age, babies reach for a toy offered by someone who speaks the same language as they do; and by five years of age, children prefer to be friends with someone who speaks the same language as them (Kinzler et al., 2007).

These findings have been replicated and extended in interesting ways to examine other language variants (e.g., regional accents; Kinzler & DeJesus, 2013), other populations (e.g., bilingual children), and other consequences (e.g., trust in a speaker's message) (DeJesus et al., 2017; Kinzler, 2013). There are many interesting questions regarding how this sensitivity plays out in different contexts as a function of the child's own language experiences.

Furthermore, how a person is addressed can also signal information about the addressee. For example, if a person is addressed in "foreigner talk" (slower, louder, simplified speech that is sometimes used when speaking with a non-native speaker; Ferguson, 1975), children as young as six years of age judge the person to be not quite as nice or smart as someone who is addressed in casual peer talk (Labotka & Gelman, 2019).

15.5 Norms and Moral Judgments

Sections 15.3 and 15.4 focus on widely-recognized functions of categories: efficiency, induction, and communication (Murphy, 2002). In this last section, I propose that categories have a fourth function, namely, to organize our judgments regarding norms and morality. A variety of norms and strictures are organized around category boundaries, such as kosher/non-kosher, adult/child, or male/female. Here I sketch out when, how, and why children treat categories as having normative weight.

The moral aspects of categories can be considered one (especially important) aspect of inductive potential. Just as we learn that clams are alive, that they are bivalves, and that they dig in the sand, we also learn that clams violate the kosher laws (a normative feature). Additionally, however, categories by their very nature may invite normative and moral responses, beyond any specific normative facts with which they are associated. First, categories are normative in the sense that they are conventional and shared by members of the speech community. We expect the categories we use and encode in language to be the same as others with whom we interact. Second, categories are normative in the sense that we often take descriptive regularities as reflecting how the world should be – a conflation of "is" with "ought." And third, category boundaries may be the locus of moral evaluations. Entities that cross over a category boundary may be treated as inherently dirty, out of place, or even monstrous (see Douglas, 1966). This possibility is hinted at by the variety of social issues for which categories are the ground-zero for moral judgments or debates: including transgender rights, political polarization, and policies or strife based on religious or national boundaries.

In the remainder of this section, I review research examining when and how children treat categories as normative in these three respects outlined above, and how language plays a role in these evaluations (see also Gelman & Roberts, 2017).

15.5.1 Categories As Conventional

By the time children produce their first words (at about twelve-to-thirteen months of age), they treat words as normative – that is, as conventional and shared with others in their speech community (Clark, 2005; Sabbagh & Henderson, 2007). By this point in development, the words children produce are those that they hear from others. This is not a general assumption about all behaviors; whereas

object labels are treated as generalizable across individuals, object preferences are not (Henderson & Woodward, 2012).

Another way in which young children treat labels as normative is adhering to a division of labor, whereby knowledge of the lexicon is dispersed unevenly throughout the speech community (Jaswal & Markman, 2007). The full lexicon is not thought to be contained in the head of each member of the community, but rather different members are more expert and can be relied upon as sources to learn from. Children preferentially accept labels from adults over children, and labels from experts over novices (Koenig & Harris, 2005), an expectation that fosters conformity. Children accept others' re-labelings, even when they defy their perceptions (e.g., when an object that looks like a rock is labeled "soap"; Lane et al., 2014). Moreover, this is not just a blind deference to authority; when children learn a new label, they then pass it along when talking to someone new (Jaswal et al., 2009). Moreover, children are more accepting when they understood the distinction between appearance and reality, and when the experimenter explicitly acknowledged things looked different from what they really were (i.e., the naming was not a mistake) (Lane et al., 2014).

15.5.2 Categories Are Not Just Descriptive but also Prescriptive

Children as well as adults have a strong intuition that what is descriptively true of a category is also prescriptively right, good, or desirable (Cimpian & Salomon, 2014; Cimpian & Steinberg, 2014; Tworek & Cimpian, 2016). For example, preschoolers report that not only is it true that fire trucks are red (a descriptive fact), but also that fire trucks have to be red, that it works best if fire trucks are red, that fire trucks always were and always will be red, and that it would not be right to change the color of fire trucks, even if everyone agreed to do so (Cimpian & Steinberg, 2014). This assumption that category regularities are prescriptively correct leads people to favor inherent explanations for why these regularities exist (there's something about the color red that's inherently appropriate for fire engines) and downplay or ignore structural explanations involving historical or contextual factors, such as the relative cost of red paint back in the earliest days of fire departments (Cimpian & Salomon, 2014; Cimpian & Steinberg, 2014; Tworek & Cimpian, 2016; though see Vasilyeva et al., 2018, for evidence that young children are capable of considering structural explanations).

Categories evoke normative judgments even when reasoning about wholly novel social kinds. Steven Roberts has conducted a series of experiments in which children of four-to-thirteen years of age were shown two groups of people (Hibbles and Glerks) that wore different clothing and were described as differing in several respects, including the food they ate, the music they listened to, the games they played, or the language they spoke (Roberts et al., 2017a, 2017b, 2019). Children negatively judged individuals who didn't conform to the behavior of the group (e.g., they reported that it was "not OK" for a Hibble to behave in a manner that was characteristic of Glerks). Note that the behaviors themselves were innocuous in content; there is nothing morally questionable about listening to a certain kind of music or eating a certain kind of berry. Rather, the negative judgment followed from not conforming to the group. Roberts et al. refer to this as a "descriptive-to-prescriptive" tendency.

This tendency was enhanced by linguistic cues, in the form of labels and generic language. Consider scenarios regarding two different individuals (rather than two different groups). When no linguistic information was provided, children no longer made normative

judgments (Roberts et al., 2017a, 2017b). It was only when the individuals were labeled as a Hibble and a Glerk, and/or the information was presented generically (e.g., "Hibbles listen to this kind of music"), that children disapproved of an individual not conforming to the regularity that was presented (Roberts et al., 2017a). These results suggest that category labels and generic statements may foster prescriptive interpretations of novel, innocuous behaviors in the social domain.

Another intriguing source of evidence regarding how categories may in and of themselves promote normative reasoning is the usage of the word "you" in English. In English, as in a broad range of unrelated languages, "you" has two distinct meanings, one specific and one generic. The specific meaning is what we canonically think of as the meaning of 'you' – namely, the individual or individuals whom a speaker is addressing (e.g., "I see that you have a question"). This meaning is highly specific and context-sensitive. Indeed, the very context-sensitivity of "you" is why it is considered a deictic, as the meaning shifts as a function of who is speaking, and to whom. In contrast, the generic meaning can be glossed as roughly "people in general" (e.g., "You have to crawl before you can walk"). This generic usage is neither specific nor context-sensitive. It is impersonal and does not specifically refer to anyone in context. Recent research with both children and adults shows that when a speaker shifts from a canonical, deictic usage of "you" to a generic usage of "you," the meaning shifts to become more normative – as expressing the right way to do things (Orvell et al., 2017, 2018, 2019).

15.5.3 Moral Evaluations of Category Boundaries

There are hints in the literature that category boundaries may be a magnet for moral evaluations. In 1744, the naturalist Carl Linnaeus, in his famous taxonomy of biological categories, named a flower "peloria," which is the Latin word for "monster" – not because it was somehow ugly or unpleasant but simply because it seemed to combine features of two different species. Linnaeus was so startled by this seeming hybrid that he at first thought that flowers from two different species had been glued together as a trick, writing: "This is certainly no less remarkable than if a cow were to give birth to a calf with a wolf's head" (Gustafsson, 1979). The point here is that combining categories was not just unusual, but also monstrous. Similarly, in her book *Purity and Danger*, the anthropologist Mary Douglas (1966) suggested that category boundaries are bound up with judgments of purity and holiness: "Holiness requires that individuals shall conform to the class to which they belong. And holiness requires that different classes of things shall not be confused." Again, crossing category boundaries is deemed somehow unholy or wrong.

More recently, work with adults suggests that those who endorse essentialism are more likely to endorse boundary-enhancing policies as well (Roberts et al., 2017c). Those with higher levels of essentialism were more likely to support policies that disadvantage certain social groups as well as policies that advantage certain social groups. Examples of the former include requiring that people use bathrooms that correspond to the sex they were assigned at birth, rather than their current gender identity, and the policies of the Trump administration in the United States, such as a wall between the United States and Mexico, and a ban on Muslim immigration. Examples of the latter include same-sex classrooms, and services that benefit LGBTQ individuals. Across a series of experiments, essentialism correlated with evaluative judgments of boundaries, even when controlling for education level, conservatism, religiosity, and LGBTQ attitudes.

At present, we know very little about how children reason about the crossing of boundaries, and whether they view hybrids as suspect in some way. Even infants have a tendency to treat categories as dichotomous (White et al., 2018), and older children view boundaries between natural kinds as absolute (Rhodes & Gelman, 2009b) and objectively correct (Diesendruck et al., 2013; Roberts & Gelman, 2015; Rhodes & Gelman, 2009a; Rhodes et al., 2014). Furthermore, as reviewed in Section 15.5.2, children negatively evaluate individuals who don't conform to their group (Roberts et al., 2017b). In future research, it would be important to examine how children think about items that combine features of different categories, and whether this elicits moral discomfort. These findings suggest that children may be susceptible to this moralizing of categories.

At the same time, recent work suggests that children are also looking to cues from their environment to modulate these expectations. Shutts and colleagues have studied gender concepts in explicitly non-gendered preschools in Sweden, and found that children who attend such schools are less stereotyped about gender (Shutts et al., 2017). Similarly, Kristina Olson has been studying gender non-conforming children and finding that these children – and their siblings – are less stereotyped about gender (Olson & Enright, 2018). And Marjorie Rhodes and I found that children growing up in a more diverse community show very different trajectories with essentialism (Rhodes & Gelman, 2009a). Studies are also discovering the precise cues that make a difference. Studying this interplay between intuitive biases and cultural cues is a critical direction for future research.

15.6 Conclusions

Children are born into a cultural system, encoded in language, that tells them which categories are relevant, and transmits hard-won discoveries from one generation to the next. The language used to express categories embodies cultural wisdom, serves as a tool of thought, and serves as an "honest signal" to categorizing our social world. The interplay of language input and children's processing biases reveal a complex story by which language builds on, and exerts influences on, categorization throughout development.

References

Adrián, J., Clemente, R., & Villanueva, L. (2007). Mothers' use of cognitive state verbs in picturebook reading and the development of children's understanding of mind: A longitudinal study. *Child Development, 78*, 1052–1067.

Anggoro, F. K., Waxman, S. R., & Medin, D. L. (2008). Naming practices and the acquisition of key biological concepts: Evidence from English and Indonesian. *Psychological Science, 19*, 314–319.

Arthur, A. E., Bigler, R. S., Liben, L. S., Gelman, S. A., & Ruble, D. N. (2008). Gender stereotyping and prejudice in young children: A developmental intergroup perspective. In S. R. Levy, & M. Killen (eds.), *Intergroup Attitudes and Relations in Childhood through Adulthood* (pp. 66–86). Oxford: Oxford University Press.

Astuti, R., Solomon, G. A., & Carey, S. (2004). Constraints on conceptual development: A case study of the acquisition of folkbiological and folksociological knowledge in Madagascar. *Monographs of the Society for Research in Child Development, 69*, 1–13.

Atran, S. (1998). Folk biology and the anthropology of science: Cognitive universals and cultural particulars. *Behavioral and Brain Sciences, 21*, 547–569.

Austin, K., Theakston, A., Lieven, E., & Tomasello, M. (2014). Young children's understanding of denial. *Developmental Psychology, 50*, 2061–2070.

Baldwin, D. A., Markman, E. M., & Melartin, R. L. (1993). Infants' ability to draw inferences about nonobvious object properties: Evidence from exploratory play. *Child Development, 64*, 711–728.

Banaji, M. R., & Gelman, S. A. (eds.) (2013). *Navigating the Social World: What Infants, Children, and Other Species Can Teach Us.* New York: Oxford University Press.

Bastian, B., & Haslam, N. (2007). Psychological essentialism and attention allocation: Preferences for stereotype-consistent versus stereotype-inconsistent information. *The Journal of Social Psychology, 147*, 531–541.

Bergelson, E., & Swingley, D. (2012). At 6–9 months, human infants know the meanings of many common nouns. *Proceedings of the National Academy of Sciences (USA), 109*, 3253–3258.

Bian, L., Leslie, S. J., & Cimpian, A. (2017). Gender stereotypes about intellectual ability emerge early and influence children's interests. *Science, 355*, 389–391.

Bowerman, M. (2005). Why can't you "open" a nut or "break" a cooked noodle? Learning covert object categories in action word meanings. In L. Gershkoff-Stowe, & D. H. Rakison (eds.). *Building Object Categories in Developmental Time* (pp. 227–262). Hove: Psychology Press.

Bowerman, M., & Choi, S. (2001). Shaping meanings for language: Universal and language-specific in the acquisition of spatial semantic categories. In S. C. Levinson, & M. Bowerman (eds.), *Language Acquisition and Conceptual Development* (No. 3, pp. 475–511). Cambridge: Cambridge University Press.

Brandone, A. C., Cimpian, A., Leslie, S. J., & Gelman, S. A. (2012). Do lions have manes? For children, generics are about kinds rather than quantities. *Child Development, 83*, 423–433.

Brandone, A. C., Gelman, S. A., & Hedglen, J. (2015). Children's developing intuitions about the truth conditions and implications of novel generics versus quantified statements. *Cognitive Science, 39*, 711–738.

Casasola, M., & Ahn, Y. A. (2018). What develops in infants' spatial categorization? Korean infants' categorization of containment and tight-fit relations. *Child Development, 89*, e382–e396.

Chouinard, M. M. (2007). Children's questions: A mechanism for cognitive development. *Monographs of the Society for Research in Child Development, 72*, vii–ix, 1–112.

Cimpian, A., Brandone, A. C., & Gelman, S. A. (2010). Generic statements require little evidence for acceptance but have powerful implications. *Cognitive Science, 34*, 1452–1482.

Cimpian, A., & Markman, E. M. (2009). Information learned from generic language becomes central to children's biological concepts: Evidence from their open-ended explanations. *Cognition, 113*, 14–25.

Cimpian, A., & Salomon, E. (2014). The inherence heuristic: An intuitive means of making sense of the world, and a potential precursor to psychological essentialism. *Behavioral and Brain Sciences, 37*, 461–480.

Cimpian, A., & Steinberg, O. D. (2014). The inherence heuristic across development: Systematic differences between children's and adults' explanations for everyday facts. *Cognitive Psychology, 75*, 130–154.

Clark, E. V. (1992). Conventionality and contrast: Pragmatic principles with lexical consequences. In E. F. Kittay, & A. Lehrer (eds.), *Frames, Fields, and Contrasts: New Essays in Semantic and Lexical Organization* (pp. 171–188). Hillsdale, NJ: Erlbaum.

Clark, E. V. (2005). Meaning: Development. In K. Brown (gen. ed.), *Encyclopedia of Language and Linguistics* (2nd ed., article 0840, pp. 577–584). London: Elsevier.

Coley, J. D. (2012). Where the wild things are: Informal experience and ecological reasoning. *Child Development, 83*, 992–1006.

Danovitch, J. H., & Keil, F. C. (2004). Should you ask a fisherman or a biologist?: Developmental shifts in ways of clustering knowledge. *Child Development, 75*, 918–931.

Davidson, N. S., & Gelman, S. A. (1990). Inductions from novel categories: The role of language and conceptual structure. *Cognitive Development, 5*, 151–176.

de Villiers, J. G., & de Villiers, P. A. (2014). The role of language in theory of mind development. *Topics in Language Disorders, 34*, 313–328.

DeJesus, J. M., Hwang, H. G., Dautel, J. B., & Kinzler, K. D. (2017). Bilingual children's social preferences hinge on accent. *Journal of Experimental Child Psychology, 164*, 178–191.

del Río, M. F., & Strasser, K. (2011). Chilean children's essentialist reasoning about poverty. *British Journal of Developmental Psychology, 29*, 722–743.

Dewar, K., & Xu, F. (2007). Do 9-month-old infants expect distinct words to refer to kinds? *Developmental Psychology, 43*, 1227–1238.

Diesendruck, G. (2013). Essentialism: The development of a simple, but potentially dangerous, idea. In M. R. Banaji, & S. A. Gelman (eds.), *Navigating the Social World: What Infants, Children, and Other Species Can Teach Us* (pp. 263–268). New York: Oxford University Press.

Diesendruck, G., Goldfein-Elbaz, R., Rhodes, M., Gelman, S. A., & Neumark, N. (2013). Cross-cultural differences in children's beliefs about the objectivity of social categories. *Child Development, 84*, 1906–1917.

Douglas, M. (1966). *Purity and Danger: An Analysis of Concepts of Pollution and Taboo*. Oxfordshire: Routledge and Keegan Paul.

Feiman, R., Carey, S., & Cushman, F. (2015). Infants' representations of others' goals: Representing approach over avoidance. *Cognition, 136*, 204–214.

Ferguson, C. A. (1975). Toward a characterization of English foreigner talk. *Anthropological Linguistics, 17*, 1–14.

Fisher, A. V., Godwin, E. K., & Matlen, B. (2015). Development of inductive generalization with familiar categories. *Psychonomic Bulletin & Review, 22*, 1149–1173.

Frank, M. C., Everett, D. L., Fedorenko, E., & Gibson, E. (2008). Number as a cognitive technology: Evidence from Pirahã language and cognition. *Cognition, 108*, 819–824.

Frazier, B. N., Gelman, S. A., & Wellman, H. M. (2009). Preschoolers' search for explanatory information within adult–child conversation. *Child Development, 80,* 1592–1611.

Frazier, B. N., Gelman, S. A., & Wellman, H. M. (2016). Young children prefer and remember satisfying explanations. *Journal of Cognition and Development, 17,* 718–736.

Gelman, S. A. (2003). *The Essential Child: Origins of Essentialism in Everyday Thought.* New York: Oxford University Press.

Gelman, S. A. (2004). Psychological essentialism in children. *Trends in Cognitive Sciences, 8,* 404–409.

Gelman, S. A. (2009). Learning from others: Children's construction of concepts. *Annual Review of Psychology, 60,* 115–140.

Gelman, S. A. (2010). Generics as a window onto young children's concepts. In F. J. Pelletier (ed.), *Kinds, Things, and Stuff: The Cognitive Side of Generics and Mass Terms* (New Directions in Cognitive Science, v. 12, pp. 100–121). New York: Oxford University Press.

Gelman, S. A., & Bloom, P. (2007). Developmental changes in the understanding of generics. *Cognition, 105,* 166–183.

Gelman, S. A., & Coley, J. D. (1990). The importance of knowing a dodo is a bird: Categories and inferences in 2-year-old children. *Developmental Psychology, 26,* 796–804.

Gelman, S. A., Coley, J. D., Rosengren, K., Hartman, E., & Pappas, A. (1998). Beyond labeling: The role of maternal input in the acquisition of richly-structured categories. *Monographs of the Society for Research in Child Development,* Serial No. 253, *63,* 1–157.

Gelman, S. A., & Davidson, N. S. (2013). Conceptual influences on category-based induction. *Cognitive Psychology, 66,* 327–353.

Gelman, S. A., & Markman, E. M. (1986). Categories and induction in young children. *Cognition, 23,* 183–209.

Gelman, S. A., & Markman, E. M. (1987). Young children's inductions from natural kinds: The role of categories and appearances. *Child Development, 58,* 1532–1541.

Gelman, S. A., & Rhodes, M. (2012). "Two-thousand years of stasis": How psychological essentialism impedes evolutionary understanding. In K. S. Rosengren, S. Brem, E. M. Evans, & G. Sinatra (eds.), *Evolution Challenges: Integrating Research and Practice in Teaching and Learning about Evolution* (pp. 3–21). Cambridge: Oxford University Press.

Gelman, S. A., & Roberts, S. O. (2017). How language shapes the cultural inheritance of categories. *Proceedings of the National Academy of Sciences (USA), 114,* 7900–7907.

Gelman, S. A., Taylor, M G., Nguyen, S. P., Leaper, C., & Bigler, R. S. (2004). Mother–child conversations about gender: Understanding the acquisition of essentialist beliefs. *Monographs of the Society for Research in Child Development, 69,* i–142.

Gelman, S. A., Ware, E. A., & Kleinberg, F. (2010). Effects of generic language on category content and structure. *Cognitive Psychology, 61,* 273–301.

Gelman, S. A., Wilcox, S. A., & Clark, E. V. (1989). Conceptual and lexical hierarchies in young children. *Cognitive Development, 4,* 309–326.

Gobbo, C., & Chi, M. (1986). How knowledge is structured and used by expert and novice children. *Cognitive Development, 1,* 221–237.

Gopnik, A., & Sobel, D. M. (2000). Detecting blickets: How young children use information about novel causal powers in categorization and induction. *Child Development, 71,* 1205–1222.

Graham, S. A., Kilbreath, C. S., & Welder, A. N. (2004). Thirteen-month-olds rely on shared labels and shape similarity for inductive inferences. *Child Development, 75,* 409–427.

Gunderson, E. A., Gripshover, S. J., Romero, C., Dweck, C. S., Goldin-Meadow, S., & Levine, S. C. (2013). Parent praise to 1-to 3-year-olds predicts children's motivational frameworks 5 years later. *Child Development, 84,* 1526–1541.

Gustafsson, Å. (1979). Linnaeus' peloria: The history of a monster. *Theoretical and Applied Genetics, 54,* 241–248.

Harris, P. L., Koenig, M. A., Corriveau, K. H., & Jaswal, V. K. (2018). Cognitive foundations of learning from testimony. *Annual Review of Psychology, 69,* 251–273.

Haslam, N., Rothschild, L., & Ernst, D. (2000). Essentialist beliefs about social categories. *British Journal of Social Psychology*, 39, 113–127.

Henderson, A. M., & Woodward, A. L. (2012). Nine-month-old infants generalize object labels, but not object preferences across individuals. *Developmental Science*, 15, 641–652.

Hollander, J. H., Holyoak, K. J., Nisbett, R. E., & Thagard, P. R. (1986). *Induction: Processes of Inference*. Cambridge, MA: MIT Press.

Horton, M. S., & Markman, E. M. (1980). Developmental differences in the acquisition of basic and superordinate categories. *Child Development*, 51, 708–719.

Inagaki, K. (1990). The effects of raising animals on children's biological knowledge. *British Journal of Developmental Psychology*, 8, 119–129.

Inhelder, B., & Piaget, J. (1964). *The Early Growth of Logic in the Child*. New York: Norton.

Jaswal, V. K., Lima, O. K., & Small, J. E. (2009). Compliance, conversion, and category induction. *Journal of Experimental Child Psychology*, 102, 182–195.

Jaswal, V. K., & Markman, E. M. (2007). Looks aren't everything: 24-month-olds' willingness to accept unexpected labels. *Journal of Cognition and Development*, 8, 93–111.

Keates, J., & Graham, S. A. (2008). Category markers or attributes: Why do labels guide infants' inductive inferences? *Psychological Science*, 19, 1287–1293.

Keil, F. C., Stein, C., Webb, L., Billings, V. D., & Rozenblit, L. (2008). Discerning the division of cognitive labor: An emerging understanding of how knowledge is clustered in other minds. *Cognitive Science*, 32, 259–300.

Keller, J. (2005). In genes we trust: the biological component of psychological essentialism and its relationship to mechanisms of motivated social cognition. *Journal of Personality and Social Psychology*, 88, 686.

Kemler-Nelson, D. G., Egan, L. C., & Holt, M. B. (2004). When children ask, "What is it?" what do they want to know about artifacts? *Psychological Science*, 15(6), 384–389.

Kinzler, K. D. (2013). The development of language as a social category. In M. R. Banaji, & S. A. Gelman (eds.), *Oxford Series in Social Cognition and Social Neuroscience. Navigating the Social World: What Infants, Children, and Other Species Can Teach Us* (pp. 314–317). New York: Oxford University Press.

Kinzler, K. D., & DeJesus, J. M. (2013). Northern = smart and Southern = nice: The development of accent attitudes in the United States. *Quarterly Journal of Experimental Psychology*, 66, 1146–1158.

Kinzler, K. D., Dupoux, E., & Spelke, E. S. (2007). The native language of social cognition. *Proceedings of the National Academy of Sciences (USA)*, 104, 12577–12580.

Kirby, S., Cornish, H., & Smith, K. (2008) Cumulative cultural evolution in the laboratory: An experimental approach to the origins of structure in human language. *Proceedings of the National Academy of Sciences (USA)*, 105, 10681–10686.

Koenig, M. A., & Harris, P. L. (2005). Preschoolers mistrust ignorant and inaccurate speakers. *Child Development*, 76, 1261–1277.

Koenig, M. A., & Jaswal, V. K. (2011). Characterizing children's expectations about expertise and incompetence: Halo or pitchfork effects? *Child Development*, 82, 1634–1647.

Labotka, D. & Gelman, S. A. (2019). *The Effect of Register on Children's Social Inferences about Addressees*. Baltimore, MD: Society for Research in Child Development Biannual Meeting.

Lane, J. D., Harris, P. L., Gelman, S. A., & Wellman, H. M. (2014). More than meets the eye: Young children's trust in claims that defy their perceptions. *Developmental Psychology*, 50, 865–871.

Lane, J. D., Wellman, H. M., & Gelman, S. A. (2013). Informants' traits weigh heavily in young children's trust in testimony and in their epistemic inferences. *Child Development*, 84, 1253–1268.

Leslie, S. J. (2013). Essence and natural kinds: When science meets preschooler intuition. *Oxford Studies in Epistemology*, 4, 108–165.

Leslie, S. J., Cimpian, A., Meyer, M., & Freeland, E. (2015). Expectations of brilliance underlie gender distributions across academic disciplines. *Science, 347,* 262–265.

Macnamara, J. (1987). *A Border Dispute.* Cambridge, MA: MIT Press.

Mandalaywala, T. M., Amodio, D. M., & Rhodes, M. (2018). Essentialism promotes racial prejudice by increasing endorsement of social hierarchies. *Social Psychological and Personality Science, 9,* 461–469.

Markman, E. M. (1989). *Categorization and Naming in Children: Problems in Induction.* Cambridge: MIT Press.

Maynard Smith, J., & Szathmary, E. (1997). *The Major Transitions in Evolution.* New York: Oxford University Press.

Medin, D. (1989). Concepts and conceptual structure. *American Psychologist, 44,* 1469–1481.

Medin, D., Waxman, S., Woodring, J., & Washinawatok, K. (2010). Human-centeredness is not a universal feature of young children's reasoning: Culture and experience matter when reasoning about biological entities. *Cognitive Development, 25,* 197–207.

Mervis, C. B., & Crisafi, M. A. (1982). Order of acquisition of subordinate-, basic-, and superordinate-level categories. *Child Development, 53,* 258–266.

Moya, C., Boyd, R., & Henrich, J. (2015). Reasoning about cultural and genetic transmission: Developmental and cross-cultural evidence from Peru, Fiji, and the United States on how people make inferences about trait transmission. *Topics in Cognitive Science, 7,* 595–610.

Murphy, G. (2002). *The Big Book of Concepts.* Cambridge, MA: MIT Press.

Olson, K. R., & Enright, E. A. (2018). Do transgender children (gender) stereotype less than their peers and siblings? *Developmental Science, 21,* e12606.

Orvell, A., Kross, E., & Gelman, S. A. (2017). How "you" makes meaning. *Science, 355,* 1299–1302.

Orvell, A., Kross, E., & Gelman, S. A. (2018). That's how "you" do it: Generic you expresses norms in early childhood. *Journal of Experimental Child Psychology, 165,* 183–195.

Orvell, A., Kross, E., & Gelman, S. A. (2019). "You" and "I" in a foreign land: The persuasive force of generic-you. *Journal of Experimental Social Psychology, 85,* 103869.

Osherson, D. N., Smith, E. E., Wilkie, O., Lopez, A., & Shafir, E. (1990). Category-based induction. *Psychological Review, 97,* 185.

Ozturk, O., & Papafragou, A. (2016). The acquisition of evidentiality and source monitoring. *Language Learning and Development, 12,* 199–230.

Pagel, M. (2017). Darwinian perspectives on the evolution of human languages. *Psychonomic Bulletin and Review, 24,* 151–157.

Perner, J., Ruffman, T., & Leekam, S. R. (1994). Theory of mind is contagious: You catch it from your sibs. *Child Development, 65,* 1228–1238.

Perszyk, D. R., & Waxman, S. R. (2018). Linking language and cognition in infancy. *Annual Review of Psychology, 69,* 231–250.

Pruden, S. M., Levine, S. C., & Huttenlocher, J. (2011). Children's spatial thinking: Does talk about the spatial world matter? *Developmental Science, 14,* 1417–1430.

Reuter, T., Feiman, R., & Snedeker, J. (2018). Getting to no: Pragmatic and semantic factors in two- and three-year-olds' understanding of negation. *Child Development, 89,* e364–e381.

Rhodes, M., & Gelman, S. A. (2009a). A developmental examination of the conceptual structure of animal, artifact, and human social categories across two cultural contexts. *Cognitive Psychology, 59,* 244–274.

Rhodes, M., & Gelman, S. A. (2009b). Five-year-olds' beliefs about the discreteness of category boundaries for animals and artifacts. *Psychonomic Bulletin & Review, 16,* 920–924.

Rhodes, M., Gelman, S. A., & Karuza, J. C. (2014). Preschool ontology: The role of beliefs about category boundaries in early categorization. *Journal of Cognition and Development, 15,* 78–93.

Rhodes, M., Leslie, S. J., & Tworek, C. M. (2012). Cultural transmission of social essentialism. *Proceedings of the National Academy of Sciences (USA), 109,* 13526–13531.

Rhodes, M., & Liebenson, P. (2015). Continuity and change in the development of category-based induction: The test case of diversity-based reasoning. *Cognitive Psychology, 82*, 74–95.

Rhodes, M., & Mandalaywala, T. M. (2017). The development and developmental consequences of social essentialism. *Wiley Interdisciplinary Reviews: Cognitive Science, 8*, e1437.

Roberts, S. O., & Gelman, S. A. (2015). Do children see in black and white? Children's and adults' categorizations of multiracial individuals. *Child Development, 86*, 1830–1847.

Roberts, S. O., Gelman, S. A., & Ho, A. K. (2017a). So it is, so it shall be: Descriptive regularities license children's prescriptive judgments. *Cognitive Science, 41*, 576–600.

Roberts, S. O., Ho, A. K., & Gelman, S. A. (2017b). Group presence, category labels, and generic statements foster children's tendency to enforce group norms. *Journal of Experimental Child Psychology, 158*, 19–31.

Roberts, S. O., Ho, A. K., & Gelman, S. A. (2019). The role of group norms in evaluating uncommon and negative behaviors. *Journal of Experimental Psychology: General, 148*, 374–387.

Roberts, S. O., Ho, A. K., Rhodes, M., & Gelman, S. A. (2017c). Making boundaries great again: Essentialism and support for boundary-enhancing initiatives. *Personality and Social Psychology Bulletin, 43*, 1643–1658.

Rosch, E., Mervis, C. B., Gray, W. D., Johnson, D. M., & Boyes-Braem, P. (1976). Basic objects in natural categories. *Cognitive Psychology, 8*, 382–439.

Sabbagh, M. A., & Baldwin, D. A. (2001). Learning words from knowledgeable versus ignorant speakers: Links between preschoolers' theory of mind and semantic development. *Child Development, 72*, 1054–1070.

Sabbagh, M. A., & Henderson, A. M. (2007). How an appreciation of conventionality shapes early word learning. *New Directions in Child and Adolescent Development, 115*, 25–37.

Salehuddin, K., & Winskel, H. (2009). An investigation into Malay numeral classifier acquisition through an elicited production task. *First Language, 29*, 289–311.

Schwab, J. F., Lew-Williams, C., & Goldberg, A. E. (2018). When regularization gets it wrong: Children over-simplify language input only in production. *Journal of Child Language, 45*, 1054–1072.

Shatz, M. (1987). Bootstrapping operations in child language. In K. E. Nelson, & A. Van Kleeck (eds.), *Children's Language* (Vol. 6, pp. 1–22). Hillsdale, NJ: Erlbaum.

Shatz, M., Tare, M., Nguyen, S. P., & Young, T. (2010). Acquiring non-object terms: The case for time words. *Journal of Cognition and Development, 11*, 16–6.

Shtulman, A., & Schulz, L. (2008). The relation between essentialist beliefs and evolutionary reasoning. *Cognitive Science, 32*, 1049–1062.

Shutts, K., Kenward, B., Falk, H., Ivegran, A., & Fawcett, C. (2017). Early preschool environments and gender: Effects of gender pedagogy in Sweden. *Journal of Experimental Child Psychology, 162*, 1–17.

Skinner, A. L., Meltzoff, A. N., & Olson, K. R. (2017). "Catching" social bias: Exposure to biased nonverbal signals creates social biases in preschool children. *Psychological Science, 28*, 216–224.

Smith, L. B., Colunga, E., & Yoshida, H. (2010). Knowledge as process: Contextually cued attention and early word learning. *Cognitive Science, 34*, 1287–1314.

Sobel, D. M., & Corriveau, K. H. (2010). Children monitor individuals' expertise for word learning. *Child Development, 81*, 669–679.

Sobel, D. M., & Kushnir, T. (2013). Knowledge matters: How children evaluate the reliability of testimony as a process of rational inference. *Psychological Review, 120*, 779–797.

Susperreguy, M. I., & Davis-Kean, P. E. (2016). Maternal math talk in the home and math skills in preschool children. *Early Education and Development, 27*, 841–857.

Talmy, L. (1985). Lexicalization patterns: Semantic structure in lexical forms. *Language Typology and Syntactic Description, 3*, 36–149.

Taumoepeau, M., & Reese, E. (2013). Maternal reminiscing, elaborative talk, and children's theory of mind: An intervention study. *First Language, 33*, 388–410.

Taylor, M.G., Rhodes, M., & Gelman, S.A. (2009). Boys will be boys, cows will be cows: Children's essentialist reasoning about human gender and animal development. *Child Development*, *80*, 461–481.

Tillman, K. A., Marghetis, T., Barner, D., & Srinivasan, M. (2017). Today is tomorrow's yesterday: Children's acquisition of deictic time words. *Cognitive Psychology*, *92*, 87–100.

Tworek, C. M., & Cimpian, A. (2016). Why do people tend to infer "ought" from "is"? The role of biases in explanation. *Psychological Science*, *27*, 1109–1122.

Unger, L., & Fisher, A. V. (2019). Rapid, experience-related changes in the organization of children's semantic knowledge. *Journal of Experimental Child Psychology*, *179*, 1–22.

Unger, L., Fisher, A. V., Nugent, R., Ventura, S. L., & MacLellan, C. J. (2016). Developmental changes in semantic knowledge organization. *Journal of Experimental Child Psychology*, *146*, 202–222.

Vasilyeva, N., Gopnik, A., & Lombrozo, T. (2018). The development of structural thinking about social categories. *Developmental Psychology*, *54*, 1735–1744.

Waxman, S. R. (1990). Linguistic biases and the establishment of conceptual hierarchies: Evidence from preschool children. *Cognitive Development*, *5*, 123–150.

Waxman, S. R., & Gelman, S. A. (2009). Early word-learning entails reference, not merely associations. *Trends in Cognitive Sciences*, *13*, 258–263.

Waxman, S. R., & Markow, D. B. (1995). Words as invitations to form categories: Evidence from 12- to 13-month-old infants. *Cognitive Psychology*, *29*, 257–302.

Waxman, S., Medin, D., & Ross, N. (2007). Folkbiological reasoning from a cross-cultural developmental perspective: Early essentialist notions are shaped by cultural beliefs. *Developmental Psychology*, *43*, 294–308.

Wellman, H. M. (2013). Universal social cognition. In M. Banaji, & S. Gelman (eds.), *Navigating the Social World: What Infants, Children, and Other Species Can Teach Us* (pp. 69–74). New York: Oxford University Press.

Wellman, H. M., Fang, F., & Peterson, C. C. (2011). Sequential progressions in a theory-of-mind scale: Longitudinal perspectives. *Child Development*, *82*, 780–792.

Wellman, H. M., & Liu, D. (2004). Scaling of theory-of-mind tasks. *Child Development*, *75*, 523–541.

White, H., Jubran, R., Chroust, A., Heck, A., & Bhatt, R. S. (2018). Dichotomous perception of animal categories in infancy. *Visual Cognition*, *26*, 764–779.

Williams, M. J., & Eberhardt, J. L. (2008). Biological conceptions of race and the motivation to cross racial boundaries. *Journal of Personality and Social Psychology*, *94*, 1033–1047.

Xu, F., & Carey, S. (1996). Infants' metaphysics: The case of numerical identity. *Cognitive Psychology*, *30*, 111–153.

Yamamoto, K., & Keil, F. (2000). The acquisition of Japanese numeral classifiers: Linkage between grammatical forms and conceptual categories. *Journal of East Asian Linguistics*, *9*, 379–409.

16 Development of Numerical Knowledge

Robert S. Siegler

Numerical knowledge is of great and growing importance. While children are attending school, numerical knowledge is essential for learning more advanced mathematics and science, and eventually for learning computer science, psychology, sociology, economics, and a host of other subjects. After children leave school, numerical knowledge is essential not just in STEM areas but also in a wide range of other occupations. Illustratively, a survey of more than 2,000 employed people in the United States, chosen through random digit dials, indicated that 94 percent reported using math in their work, including majorities in occupations classified as upper white collar, lower white collar, upper blue collar, and lower blue collar (Handel, 2016). Moreover, numerical proficiency is related to occupational success: numerical knowledge at age seven years predicts SES at age forty-two years, even after statistically controlling for IQ, years of education, reading skill, working memory, race, and family SES (Ritchie & Bates, 2013).

Reducing differences in numerical knowledge is also crucial for the goal of reducing educational and economic inequality. When children from low-income backgrounds enter kindergarten, their numerical knowledge lags a full year behind that of peers from middle class backgrounds (Jordan et al., 2006). That gap seems to have long-term consequences: Even after statistically controlling for a variety of relevant variables, the numerical knowledge of individual preschoolers' and kindergartners'

predicts their math achievement test scores in elementary school (Duncan et al., 2007) and even in high school (Watts et al., 2014). Moreover, the percentile differences between mathematical knowledge of children from wealthier and poorer backgrounds expand considerably over the course of schooling (Reardon, 2011).

In addition to these SES differences, racial differences are also substantial. On the 2013 National Assessment of Educational Progress, a test given to a nationally representative sample of more than 20,000 US students, the average math score of black twelfth graders was in the nineteenth percentile of the distribution of white peers (Hanushek, 2016). Reducing these gaps in mathematical knowledge between economic and racial groups seems essential to reducing inequality.

Numerical knowledge is also important for theoretical understanding of cognitive development. Understanding of numbers has long been recognized as a fundamental part of intellect. Kant (1781) classified it as one of a small number of categorical imperatives, categories so basic to understanding the world that people must be born with some useful intuitions regarding them. From Binet and Simon's (1905) original formulation to the present, intelligence tests have also consistently included assessments of numerical knowledge. More recently, developmental theorists with widely varying approaches, including Piagetian (Piaget, 1952), neo-Piagetian (Case & Okamoto, 1996), information processing

(Klahr & MacWhinney, 1998), core knowledge (Spelke & Kinzler, 2007), sociocultural (Gauvain, 2001), and evolutionary (Geary, 2008), have all argued that numerical development is fundamental to cognitive growth.

From the present perspective, numerical development involves two main types of acquisition – knowledge of individual numbers and knowledge of arithmetic – for each of three types of numbers – non-symbolic numbers, symbolic whole numbers, and symbolic rational numbers.[1] The integrated theory of numerical development provides a unified approach to understanding acquisition of knowledge about individual numbers and arithmetic combinations of numbers for all three types of numbers.

16.1 The Integrated Theory of Numerical Development

A basic tenet of the integrated theory is that numerical development is a process of representing increasingly precisely the magnitudes of increasing ranges and types of numbers (Siegler & Braithwaite, 2017; Siegler et al., 2011). This process starts in infancy and continues through childhood, adolescence, and adulthood. The current version of the theory identifies six key processes within numerical development:

1. Representing the magnitudes of non-symbolic numbers increasingly precisely;
2. Connecting non-symbolic representations of small sets to corresponding symbolic whole numbers;
3. Increasing the range of symbolic whole numbers that are accurately represented;

4. Representing the magnitudes of rational numbers increasingly accurately;
5. Learning procedures for solving symbolic whole number and rational number arithmetic problems; and
6. Connecting conceptual knowledge of individual symbolic whole and rational numbers, and arithmetic operations on the numbers.

One distinctive feature of the integrated theory is that understandings of rational and whole numbers are viewed as co-equal parts of numerical development. This development requires learning which properties of whole numbers apply to rational numbers and which do not (see Chapter 23). Some major commonalities are that whole and rational numbers express magnitudes and can be located and ordered on number lines. Some major differences are that whole numbers have unique predecessors and successors, but rational numbers do not, and that whole numbers are represented by a unique symbol within a given symbol system (e.g., "4" or "four") but rational numbers can be represented in infinite equivalent ways (1/4, 2/8, 3/12, 0.25, 0.250, . . .) Numerical development requires understanding of both types of numbers.

The integrated theory is also unusual among theories of numerical development in viewing arithmetic as central to the developmental process. Historically, arithmetic has been viewed as part of educational psychology, because it is taught explicitly in school, whereas understanding of individual numbers has been viewed as part of development because it receives much less attention in school. However, this distinction has become increasingly untenable, as evidence has emerged that arithmetic is rooted in biological evolution (e.g., Brannon & Merritt, 2011) and that formal education influences understanding of individual numbers as well as arithmetic (e.g., Halberda et al., 2008, see also Chapter 11).

---

[1] Other types of numbers, such as irrational and imaginary numbers, are not part of most children's numerical development and therefore are not considered here.

A third distinctive feature of the integrated theory is its assumption that knowledge of individual number magnitudes influences understanding of arithmetic. Knowledge of numerical magnitude has been found to be correlated with, predictive of, and causally related to arithmetic proficiency (Siegler & Braithwaite, 2017). This is not to deny that people can learn arithmetic through rote memorization, in which their knowledge of numerical magnitudes is decoupled from their knowledge of arithmetic. For example, many children (and teachers) who flawlessly solve fraction division problems cannot estimate plausible answers to fraction division problems or explain why the standard fraction division procedure works (Ma, 1999; Siegler & Lortie-Forgues, 2015). However, both correlational and causal evidence suggest that, at least in Western countries, knowledge of numerical magnitudes and arithmetic proficiency are closely linked.

Two visual metaphors are useful for understanding the perspective of the integrated theory on numerical development. One metaphor, the mental number line, is often used to describe how individual numbers are represented. This structure is usually depicted as static, but the integrated theory posits that it is actually dynamic: With numerical experience, the mental number line is extended rightward to include larger whole numbers, leftward to include negatives, and interstitially to include rational numbers. This sequence, together with approximate ages at which the most dramatic advances in magnitude knowledge occur in economically advanced societies, is depicted in Figure 16.1.

The other visual metaphor, which is particularly useful for thinking about development of arithmetic procedures, is that of overlapping waves. As shown in Figure 16.2(a), the overlapping waves model depicts people as using multiple approaches for prolonged periods of time. Development proceeds toward greater use of more advanced strategies (indicated by higher numbers and rightward placement in Figure 16.2), with new strategies fairly often being added to the repertoire and other strategies waxing and waning. The applicability of the approach to children's arithmetic is illustrated in Figure 16.2(b); for evidence regarding the applicability of overlapping waves theory to a wide variety of tasks, both mathematical and non-mathematical, see Siegler (1996).

Consistent with the integrated theory of numerical development, this chapter first examines the growth of understanding of the magnitudes of individual numbers, both whole and rational, and then links this development to the development of arithmetic, with both whole and rational numbers. Because a recent review focusing entirely on development of magnitude knowledge of individual numbers is already available (Siegler, 2016), this chapter summarizes that development fairly briefly and places greater emphasis on development of understanding of arithmetic. The chapter first examines individual numbers – non-symbolic numbers, symbolic whole numbers, and symbolic rational numbers – and then arithmetic with each type of number.

16.2 Individual Numbers

16.2.1 Non-symbolic Numbers

Infants can discriminate between stimuli, both visual (e.g., two sets of dots) and auditory (e.g., two sets of tones) that differ in number but are similar in dimensions that ordinarily covary with number, such as surface area and duration. The larger the ratio of the set sizes being compared, the faster and more accurate the discrimination. The non-symbolic representations are approximate rather than exact, and they reflect ratios rather than absolute numbers; this leads to discrimination of sets

Types of Numbers, Range of Numbers, and Primary Acquisition Period

Small whole numbers (≈ 3 to 5 years)

Large whole numbers (≈ 5 to 7 years)

Even larger whole numbers (≈ 7 to 12 years)

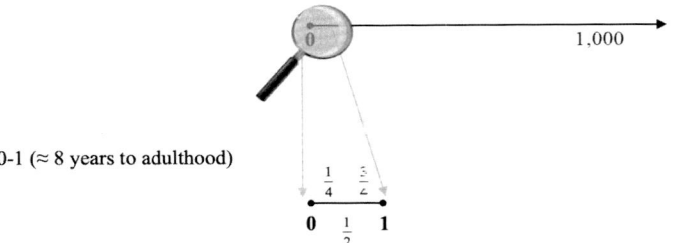

Fractions 0-1 (≈ 8 years to adulthood)

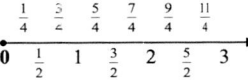

Fractions 0-N (≈ 11 years to adulthood)

Rational numbers— negative and positive (≈ 11 years to adulthood)

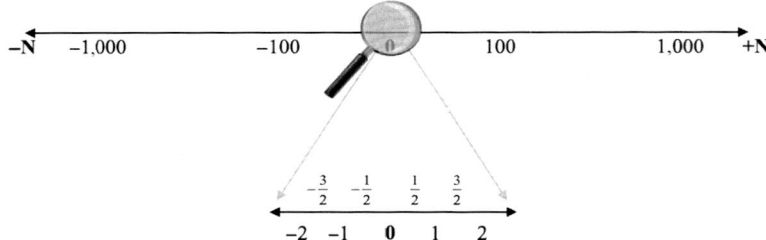

Figure 16.1 Development of understanding of different types of symbolic numbers, including the age range in which development is most dramatic

being more closely related to the ratio between the numbers of entities in the sets than to the absolute difference in number of entities in them.

With age and numerical experience, infants become able to discriminate between sets whose quantities differ by smaller ratios. For example, six-month-olds discriminate 2:1 but not 1.5:1 ratios, nine-month-olds discriminate 1.5:1 but not 1.3:1 ratios, and so on (Cordes & Brannon, 2008). The development continues long beyond infancy, with many educated adults consistently discriminating 1:14:1 ratios (Halberda & Feigenson, 2008). The brain areas that are most active in the discriminations are parts of the intraparietal sulcus

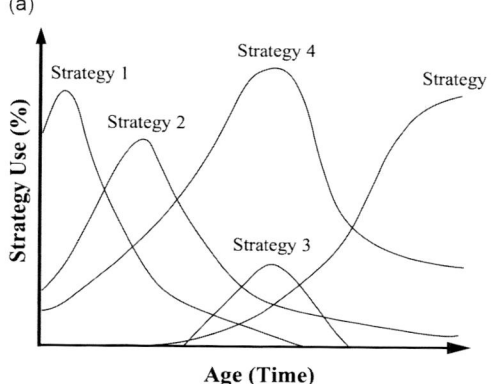

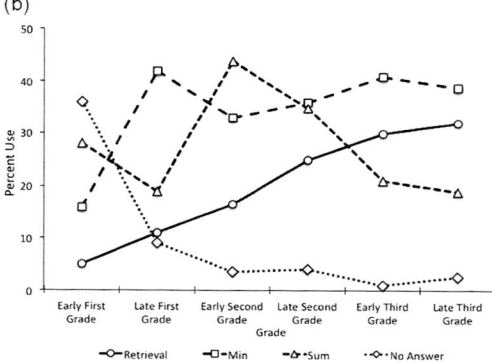

Figure 16.2 The overlapping waves model, (a) with idealized data and (b) with data from Svenson and Sjöberg's (1983) study of basic addition

(IPS) and the dorsolateral prefrontal cortex (DLPFC) (Dehaene, 2011).

The one known exception to this general ratio dependence is that discrimination of very small set sizes (one-to-four members) is faster, more accurate, and less variable than would be predicted from the ratios being discriminated (Piazza, 2011). The phenomenon is apparent not only among adults but also among infants, children, and even guppies (Agrillo et al., 2012). The superior processing of very small numbers appears to be due to subitizing, a

rapid pattern recognition mechanism applicable to a range of sensory modalities including vision, audition, and touch (Riggs et al., 2006).

16.2.2 Symbolic Numbers

16.2.2.1 From Non-symbolic Numbers to Small Symbolic Whole Numbers

Non-symbolic representations of small whole numbers provide a useful referent for learning the meaning of corresponding symbolic representations. For example, the spoken or written symbol for "3" can be mapped onto three dots, sounds, or touches.

Such mappings are useful for acquiring symbolic representations of small sets. Supporting this view, the same ratio dependence observed with comparisons of non-symbolic numbers is observed with comparisons of symbolic numbers; individual differences in the precision of young children's discriminations between non-symbolic numbers correlate both contemporaneously and longitudinally with symbolic numerical skills; and similar brain areas are used to process non-symbolic and symbolic numerical magnitudes (Nieder & Dehaene, 2009).

Other data, however, have called into question the nature of the relation. Ratio effects are present with many modalities other than number, such as odor discrimination (Parnas et al., 2013). Moreover, relations between individual differences in the precision of non-symbolic numerical magnitude discriminations and overall math achievement have turned out to be much weaker than originally claimed. Three meta-analyses of the relation (Chen & Li, 2014; Fazio et al., 2014; Schneider et al., 2018) found that the mean weighted correlation was $r = 0.20$ $r = 0.22$, and $r = 0.28$, respectively. Moreover, an internet study with more than 10,000 adult participants (Halberda et al., 2012) and an experimental study with

1,200 first through sixth graders (Lyons et al., 2014) both yielded correlations of $r = 0.21$. All of these remarkably similar relations are significant but weak.

One potential resolution of the controversy is that representations of non-symbolic magnitudes play an important role in early symbolic representations but a lesser role thereafter. A longitudinal study of the early development of understanding symbolic number words indicated that two- and three-year-olds learn the meanings of the symbolic numbers 1–4 by first attaching the word "one" to a single object; then doing the same for the word "two" and two objects; then for "three" and three objects. After attaching "four" to four objects, attachments of symbolic and non-symbolic numbers proceeds much faster (Le Corre & Carey, 2007).

Non-symbolic numbers likely play an important role in learning numbers somewhat beyond the subitizing range as well. Putting up fingers after being presented addition problems activates preschoolers' answers to problems with sums up to ten (Siegler & Shrager, 1984). Among both adults and children, fMRI data indicate a common neural substrate for finger representations and mental addition and subtraction of numbers one through ten (Andres et al., 2012; Berteletti & Booth, 2015). Moreover, Fazio et al.'s (2014) meta-analysis indicated that relations between the precision of non-symbolic numerical representations and overall math achievement are considerably stronger among children of five-years and younger, when the focus is on numbers one-to-ten, than it is with older children, where the focus is on larger numbers. Whether individual differences in the precision of non-symbolic representations of larger numbers also contribute to individual differences in later symbolic numerical knowledge remains an open question.

Acquisition of counting skills may also play a role in development of symbolic numerical

magnitude knowledge, but the relation is less direct than might be anticipated. Between ages three- and five-years, most children learn to count from one to ten. This might be interpreted as implying that they also know ordinal properties of the numbers they are counting (e.g., that seven is larger than six because seven comes after six when counting) and the distance between numbers (e.g., that the distance between seven and six is the same as that between one and two, because both pairs of numbers are counted consecutively). This is not the case, however. Many four- and five-year-olds who count flawlessly from one to ten are inaccurate in comparing the sizes of numbers in the same range (Ramani & Siegler, 2008, 2011).

Moreover, when preschoolers first learn about numerical magnitudes, they tend to represent their magnitudes as increasing logarithmically rather than linearly. For example, when presented a number line with zero at one end and ten at the other, three- and four-year-olds generally place consecutive small whole numbers, such as two and three, much farther apart on the number line than consecutive larger whole numbers, such as seven and eight. In contrast, five- and six-year-olds space the two pairs of numbers roughly equally (Berteletti et al., 2010). Thus, between ages three- and six-years, children's representations of symbolic single digit numbers progress from a roughly logarithmic to a roughly linear form.

16.2.2.2 From Small to Large Whole Numbers

This developmental sequence in magnitude representations recurs with larger ranges of numbers at older ages. Estimates of numbers between 0 and 100 progress from a roughly logarithmically increasing pattern at five- and six-years to a roughly linearly increasing pattern at seven- and eight-years (Geary et al., 2007). Estimates of numbers in the range

0–1,000 increase roughly logarithmically among seven- and eight-year-olds and roughly linearly at nine- and ten-years-old. Chinese children show the same developmental sequence at younger ages (Xu et al., 2013); children with math learning difficulties show it at older ages (Reeve et al., 2015). Even among adults, vestiges of logarithmic representations can be seen in transitory processes during a single number line estimation trial (Dotan & Dehaene, 2013). Encouragement to draw analogies between smaller and larger ranges of numbers (separated by powers of ten), and illustrations of how to do so, can extend the range of symbolic whole numbers on which children of a given age generate linear estimation patterns (Sullivan & Barner, 2014; Thompson & Opfer, 2010).

16.2.3 Individual Rational Numbers

16.2.3.1 Non-symbolic Rational Numbers

Development of non-symbolic rational numbers also begins in infancy. Six-month-old infants discriminate between sets in which one ratio is twice that of the other (e.g., after infants of this age are habituated to blue and yellow dots with a 2:1 ratio, they dishabituate when the ratio of blue to yellow dots switches to 4:1) (McCrink & Wynn, 2007). This ratio matches the ratios of non-symbolic whole numbers that infants discriminate at this age. Moreover, changes in non-symbolic ratio discrimination parallel those in discrimination of whole numbers. Six-month-olds discriminate speeds of moving objects (distance/ time) that differ by a 2:1 ratio but not ones that differ by a 3:2 ratio, whereas ten-month-olds discriminate both ratios (Möhring et al., 2017). Thus, age-related changes in ratio discrimination are not specific to whole numbers.

16.2.3.2 Symbolic Rational Numbers

Relative to symbolic whole numbers, learning the magnitudes of individual symbolic rational numbers begins considerably later and asymptotes at a much lower level. Both middle school children and community college adults err on 20–30 percent of fraction magnitude comparison problems with unequal-denominator fractions between zero and one (Bailey et al., 2014; Schneider & Siegler, 2010). Performance is even weaker when the set includes fractions between zero and five (Siegler & Pyke, 2013; Siegler et al., 2012). To convey the gap between knowledge of individual whole and rational numbers, second graders' number line estimates of whole numbers in the 0–100 range are more accurate than eighth graders' estimates of fractions on 0–5 number lines (Siegler & Booth, 2004; Siegler et al., 2012).

Difficulty in understanding magnitudes of individual rational numbers is in part due to difficulties interpreting fraction notation. However, the difficulty is not limited to fractions; fourth to eighth graders often predict that longer sequences of decimal digits imply larger magnitudes (e.g., that $0.123 > 0.45$) (Lortie-Forgues & Siegler, 2017; Resnick et al. 1989).

Along with these differences, knowledge of individual rational number magnitudes and whole number magnitudes also show several similarities. Distance effects are present on both rational and whole number magnitude comparison tasks among both children (Iuculano & Butterworth, 2011) and adults (Meert et al., 2010). Similarly, for both whole and rational numbers, relations are present between the precision of magnitude representations, as measured by number line estimation and magnitude comparison, and both arithmetic performance and overall math achievement (Schneider et al., 2017, 2018).

Longitudinal relations between young children's precision of whole number magnitude representations and older children's fraction magnitude representations have also been established (Jordan et al., 2013; Resnick et al., 2016). For example, precision of six-year-olds' whole number magnitude representations predicts precision of thirteen-year-olds' fraction magnitude representations, even after controlling for IQ, executive functioning, race, gender, and parental income and education (Bailey et al., 2014). Together, these findings indicate that although children progress further and faster in acquiring precise magnitude representations of individual whole numbers than individual rational numbers, important similarities also are present.

16.3 Arithmetic

Development of understanding of individual numbers and development of understanding of arithmetic are usually treated in isolation. Growth of understanding of individual numbers is often viewed as a phenomenon that reflects general developmental processes, occurring largely or completely independent of formal instruction (Dehaene, 2011). In contrast, growth of arithmetic is often viewed as driven largely or completely by instruction in formal educational settings. Seen from another perspective, one is viewed as part of developmental psychology, the other as part of educational psychology.

This distinction has broken down in recent years, however. Creatures that have not encountered any formal instruction, specifically non-human animals and human infants, show understanding of non-symbolic arithmetic as well as individual numbers (e.g., McCrink & Wynn, 2004; Piffer et al., 2013). Similarly, preschoolers discover symbolic arithmetic strategies, such as counting-on from the larger addend (e.g., solving 2 + 6 by counting "7, 8"), without any

relevant formal instruction (Siegler & Jenkins, 1989). These discoveries are not the product of trial and error; preschoolers show conceptual understanding of relatively advanced whole number arithmetic strategies even before they begin to use them (Siegler & Crowley, 1994).

Another reason for integrating development of understanding of individual numbers and arithmetic in the same theory is that once children begin school, development cannot be understood without considering experience in school. Children spend a high proportion of their waking hours in school and acquire many types of knowledge that influence their thinking in general as well as specific ways. Unsurprising from this perspective, knowledge of individual numbers and of arithmetic are correlated with, predictive of, and causally related to each other (e.g., Jordan et al., 2013; Libertus et al., 2011; Siegler & Ramani, 2009). Thus, integrating understanding of individual numbers and arithmetic within a single theory seems a worthwhile goal.

16.3.1 Non-symbolic Arithmetic

Infants can perform approximate arithmetic on their non-symbolic representations of individual whole numbers. In procedures used to study this ability, four- and five-month-olds are habituated to seeing correct outcomes of adding or subtracting sets of one-to-three objects, and then see implausible outcomes, produced by trickery (e.g., Wynn, 1992). In the face of such tricks, four- and five-month-olds show a longer looking time, presumably because they do not expect the implausible outcomes (Wynn, 1992). By age nine-months, infants react similarly to addition and subtraction with sets of five-to-ten objects (McCrink & Wynn, 2004). The brain areas activated in such non-symbolic arithmetic overlap considerably with those active in representing individual sets (Park et al., 2013).

16.3.2 Symbolic Whole Number Arithmetic

16.3.2.1 Basic Empirical Phenomena: Variability, Choice, and Change

Substantial consensus exists about the main features of the development of symbolic, whole number arithmetic (e.g., Geary & vanMarle, 2016; Verschaffel et al., 2007). The progression begins at three- or four-years of age, when preschoolers begin to solve symbolic whole number addition and subtraction problems with small single-digit addends (e.g., 2 + 2). Children use a variety of strategies to solve symbolic arithmetic problems from early in acquisition, a phenomenon that continues throughout childhood and adulthood, even on single-digit problems. Children learn all four arithmetic operations, with multi-digit as well as single-digit whole numbers, by the end of elementary school, typically age eleven-to-twelve years in the United States.

Many of the most striking phenomena of whole number symbolic arithmetic can be summarized under three headings: variability, choice, and change.

Variability of whole number arithmetic strategies is apparent from preschoolers' first efforts to solve simple arithmetic problems. Among the strategies emerging between three- and five-years are putting up fingers to represent each addend and counting the fingers starting with "one"; counting from one without any visible referent; putting up fingers and answering without any apparent counting; and retrieving answers from memory (Siegler & Shrager, 1984). Individual children typically use several of these strategies on different trials, so that the variability of strategy use is within children as well as between them. The strategies have distinctive profiles of speed and accuracy. For example, among the four- and five-year-olds in Siegler and Shrager (1984),

retrieval was faster than putting up fingers and answering without overt counting, and both were faster, though less accurate, than counting fingers.

Variability of whole number arithmetic strategies for solving single-digit problems is far from limited to preschoolers' addition. Such variability is present among both older children (e.g., Geary, 2006) and adults (e.g., LeFevre et al., 1996), for all four arithmetic operations (Siegler, 2006), and in all countries that have been studied (e.g., Verschaffel et al., 2007). Even adults at selective universities in the US use strategies other than retrieval to solve single-digit addition on 15–30 percent of problems. The most common alternatives to retrieval among school age children and adults are counting-on from the larger addend (e.g., solving 9 + 3 by counting "10, 11, 12") and decomposition (solving 9 + 3 by thinking ""10 + 3 = 13, 9 is 1 less than 10, so 9 + 3 = 12")(Campbell & Xue, 2001; LeFevre et al., 2003). The frequencies of strategies change with age and experience, but the variability of strategy use is constant.

Adaptive strategy choices. Choosing strategies in ways that produce desirable combinations of speed and accuracy is another pervasive phenomenon of whole number arithmetic (Siegler, 1996). When preschoolers, older children, or adults are presented a whole number arithmetic problem, they tend to rely on the fastest available strategy, retrieval, when they can execute it accurately. In contrast, when retrieval would be error prone, they usually rely on slower but surer "backup" strategies. This adaptive strategy choice was evident when the same individuals were presented three blocks of arithmetic problems and asked to solve one block via retrieval, one via calculator, and one via either retrieval or calculator (Siegler & Lemaire, 1997). The frequency with which university students and elderly adults chose to use the calculator in the condition where they were given a choice was strongly predicted by the differences in speed and accuracy between the two approaches in the conditions where they needed to use one approach on all trials. In the free choice condition, on problems where retrieval was faster and at least as accurate as calculator use, students usually used retrieval, but when calculator use was more accurate, students used that approach more often.

Change is a third omnipresent characteristic of whole number symbolic arithmetic. The types of changes that are most striking in the development of whole number arithmetic are acquisition of new strategies, increasing reliance on the more effective existing strategies, increasingly efficient execution of strategies, and increasingly adaptive choices among strategies (Lemaire & Siegler, 1995).

Generation of New Strategies

The prototypic change in children's mathematical thinking is discovery of a new strategy. This can involve either generation of a strategy where no appropriate strategy existed before or addition of a new strategy to a set of existing strategies. An example of the first is when preschoolers discover how to solve single digit addition problems through the sum strategy, which involves representing the first addend on the fingers of one hand, representing the second addend by the fingers of the other hand, and counting the combined fingers starting with "one." An example of the second type of discovery, again in the context of single digit addition, is when children, a year or two later, add the min strategy to their existing approaches. The min strategy involves counting up from the larger addend the number of times indicated by the smaller addend; thus, on 2 + 9, the child would start at 9 and say "10, 11."

Siegler and Jenkins (1989) examined discovery of the min strategy by presenting as many as 200 addition problems to preschoolers who did not use that strategy on a pretest, even on problems where its use would have saved considerable time. The results revealed several characteristics of the discovery process. Most of the preschoolers discovered the min strategy, with the number of trials before discovery varying among children from 8 to 200. Most children also discovered a previously undocumented approach, the shortcut sum strategy, shortly before discovering the min strategy. Similar to the sum strategy, the shortcut sum involved counting from one; unlike the sum strategy, it involved doing so only once. For example, on four plus two, the shortcut sum strategy involved counting "1, 2, 3, 4, 5, 6" rather than the "1, 2, 3, 4," "1, 2," "1, 2, 3, 4, 5, 6" involved in executing the sum strategy.

An interesting characteristic of strategy discovery is that it often occurs in domains where children already know accurate and reasonably efficient alternatives. This is evident in the addition example mentioned, in which children discovered the min strategy despite already knowing the sum strategy, which also generated consistently correct answers in the study. It is also evident in many other whole number arithmetic tasks. For example, in whole number division, children discover how to solve problems by adding the divisor repeatedly until reaching the dividend, by subtracting the divisor repeatedly from the dividend, and by retrieving answers from memory (Siegler, 1996). Often, the newly discovered strategies are faster or more accurate than existing strategies, at least on subsets of problems. Thus, in whole number subtraction, counting down from the minuend the number of times indicated by the subtrahend is faster on $11 - 2$ ("10 is 1, 9 is 2"), but counting from the subtrahend up to the minuend is faster on $11 - 9$ ("10 is 1, 11 is 2"). Children typically begin by counting down on all subtraction problems, but they soon learn to count up when that is faster and more accurate (Siegler, 1989).

Sometimes, newly discovered strategies are, at least initially, slower and less accurate, or at least no faster and no more accurate, when they are first discovered. To illustrate, although the min strategy becomes faster than the sum strategy for adding numbers, on the first trials on which the min strategy was used, it was neither faster nor more accurate than the sum strategy had been (Siegler & Jenkins, 1989). Why children persist in using new strategies despite such utilization deficiencies (Miller & Seier, 1994) in this and other domains is not well understood.

Increasing Use of More Efficient Strategies

Increasing use of more efficient strategies also plays a large a role in the development of whole number arithmetic. For example, kindergartners use the relatively inefficient sum strategy quite often, but arithmetic experience leads to decreasing use of it and increasing use of retrieval and the min strategy in first and second grade (Siegler, 1987). Both the min strategy and retrieval are faster and more accurate than the sum strategy, thus illustrating that the change in strategy use involved movement toward increased use of more efficient strategies.

Better Execution of All Strategies

Beyond discovering useful new strategies and relying increasingly on relatively effective existing strategies, children execute all of their whole number symbolic arithmetic strategies increasingly effectively as they gain experience using them. For example, in Siegler (1987), between kindergarten and second grade, error rates on retrieval trials decreased from 19 to 3 percent and mean solution times from 3.9 to 1.8 seconds. In the same study, min strategy errors decreased from 29 to 7 percent of trials and mean solution times from 6.0 to 3.9 seconds; and decomposition strategy errors decreased from 9 to 3 percent of trials and mean solution times from 6.9 to 3.2 seconds. Similar changes have been observed in subtraction and multiplication (Siegler, 1988, 1989).

More Adaptive Choices among Strategies

With arithmetic experience, children also choose which strategy to use increasingly adaptively. To illustrate, in Lemaire and Siegler (1995), multiplication strategy choices of French second graders were examined in the first ten days of their instruction on the topic, after two months of instruction, and after four months of instruction. During the first ten days of instruction, multiplication strategy choices were already fairly adaptive, in the sense that the more difficult the problem, the more often children used strategies other than retrieval. With multiplication experience, however, the correlation increased, with children increasingly focusing their use of backup strategies on problems where retrieval was less likely to yield correct answers.

Conceptual Understanding of Whole Number Arithmetic

Development of whole number arithmetic entails acquisition of conceptual understanding, as well as facts and procedures. Preschoolers and early elementary school children gain at least implicit, and often explicit, understanding of the commutative and associative properties (Baroody & Dowker, 2003). Children of the same ages discriminate between the "smartness" of strategies that are correct but that they do not yet use and strategies that are incorrect and that they do not use (Siegler & Crowley, 1994). Discovery of new strategies proceeds with little or no attempt to use flawed strategies (Siegler & Jenkins, 1989).

This smooth and rapid acquisition of conceptual understanding of whole number arithmetic seems partially due to whole number operations building on each other in transparent ways. Addition is grounded in counting (2 + 2 = 1, 2, 3, 4); subtraction builds on counting and addition (if 2 + 3 = 5, 5 − 3 = 2); multiplication is grounded in counting and addition (3 × 4 = 4 + 4 + 4); and division is the inverse of multiplication (if 3 × 4 = 12, 12 ÷ 4 = 3).

Magnitude knowledge provides further conceptual grounding for whole number arithmetic, in that it provides a means of checking the plausibility of answers. When presented verification tasks, both children and adults more quickly reject incorrect answers that are far from the correct one (e.g., 5 + 7 = 18) than incorrect answers that are closer to it (e.g., 5 + 7 = 14) (Ashcraft, 1982).

Other whole number arithmetic concepts take longer to develop. Not until fifth or sixth grade do most US students understand the equal sign, as measured by correct predictions on questions such as "3 + 4 + 5 = ___ + 5." Before then, most children solve such problems by stating the sum of the numbers to the left of the equal sign or the sum of all numbers in the problem, answering "12" or "17" to "3 + 4 + 5 = ___ + 5" (Alibali & Goldin-Meadow, 1993; McNeil, 2014).

Similarly, prior to fifth grade, most children do not spontaneously display understanding of the inversion principle with addition and subtraction, as measured by realizing that problems such as 18 + 43 − 43 can be answered without adding and subtracting. Even most high school students do not understand the principle as applied to multiplication and division (e.g., 18 × 43 ÷ 43) (Robinson, 2017). Moreover, conceptual understanding of multi-digit whole number arithmetic is less advanced than understanding of single-digit arithmetic, as seen in many second through fifth graders'

buggy subtraction errors, such as converting 208 − 135 into 238 − 105 before doing the subtraction (Brown & Van Lehn, 1982). Nonetheless, understanding of whole number symbolic arithmetic is far superior to understanding of rational number arithmetic, as described in Sections 16.3.3 and 16.3.4.

16.3.2.2 Modeling Development of Whole Number Arithmetic

Several computer simulations have been formulated that indicate how cognitive processes work together to produce development of whole number arithmetic. One model that produces a wide range of documented phenomena regarding the development of single-digit addition is that of Shrager and Siegler (1998). Their model, SCADS (Strategy Choice and Discovery Simulation), generates the variable strategy use, adaptive strategy choice, improving strategy execution, and strategy discovery characteristic of development of single digit addition.

SCADS begins with two strategies: retrieval and the sum strategy. As it is presented with addition problems, it continually adjusts the strength of alternative strategies, with their strengthening and weakening depending on the relative accuracies and speeds they generate on each problem. SCADS also strengthens associations between answers and the problem that led to the answers. Further, it forms a working memory trace of the execution of each strategy as it is executed, which is available during and immediately after the strategy is executed. Due to reinforcement of correct answers, connections between problems and their correct answer become increasingly dominant.

SCADS also includes an attentional spotlight and a goal sketch, both of which are crucial to strategy discovery. The attentional spotlight increases the cognitive resources devoted to execution of poorly learned strategies. The more often a strategy is used, the less cognitive resources its execution requires. As attentional resources are freed, SCADS allocates them to strategy change heuristics that operate on the working memory trace of the cognitive processes used on the immediately prior problem. The two strategy change heuristics in the model are: (1) If redundant sequences of behavior are detected, then delete one of the two sets of operators that generated the redundancy and (2) If a strategy's accuracy and speed are greater when the strategy is executed in a particular order, then create a variant of the strategy that always involves that order (e.g., a variant that always quantifies the larger addend first, rather than arbitrarily selecting which addend to quantify first).

These heuristics allow SCADS to consider a variety of strategies, both valid and flawed. A commonly generated flawed strategy was "count the first addend twice." However, another part of the metacognitive system, the goal sketch filter, prevented proposed strategies from being tried unless they met two criteria: that both addends be represented and that the quantified versions of both representations be included in the answer. Counting the first addend twice met neither filter, and thus was never tried.

SCADS' workings can be most easily understood by describing a specific run. On the run being described, solving about seventy addition problems freed enough attentional resources for SCADS to propose new strategies. The first three strategies that it proposed violated the goal sketch and therefore were not tried. On Problem 82, SCADS discovered a legal but inefficient strategy; the strategy passed the goal sketch filters, but it was rarely used, because it was less efficient than the sum strategy. A few problems later, SCADS generated the strategy of always representing the larger addend first. Some problems later, the simulation generated the shortcut sum strategy. Finally, a few trials later, on the problem 4 + 2, SCADS eliminated

the redundancy involved with counting from one and just counted "5, 6." That is, it used the min strategy.

Running SCADS thirty times indicated that it consistently generated a wide range of whole number addition phenomena. It used multiple strategies at all points in its run; it chose adaptively among strategies throughout its run but increasingly so as it gained experience; it became faster and more accurate with problem-solving experience; it always discovered the min strategy; it usually (though not always) discovered the shortcut sum before the min strategy; its discoveries followed correct as well as incorrect answers; and it never executed incorrect strategies (Shrager & Siegler, 1998). Also like the preschoolers in Siegler and Jenkins (1989), SCADS greatly increased its use of the min strategy after presentation of problems such as 2 + 21, which made its advantages over the sum strategy obvious.

16.3.3 Non-symbolic Rational Number Arithmetic

In principle, it would be possible to study non-symbolic rational number arithmetic. For example, people could be presented two sets of dots, each including blue dots and yellow dots, and be asked to estimate on a number line the sum of the two proportions of blue dots either by marking a number line or by stating a fraction or decimal that approximated the sum of the two proportions. However, no such studies of non-symbolic rational number arithmetic appear to have been conducted.

16.3.4 Symbolic Rational Number Arithmetic

Although rational number arithmetic has been studied far less than whole number arithmetic, it is also very important both in and out of school. For example, fraction arithmetic was part of more than half of the equations included on the reference sheets provided for recent Advanced Placement examinations in chemistry and physics (College Board, 2015). Rational number arithmetic is also used in many occupations. In a large study of the mathematics used by a wide range of white collar, blue collar, and service workers, Handel (2016) found that 68 percent of the 2,000 adults in his sample reported using rational number arithmetic in their jobs. This was less than the percentage reporting use of whole number arithmetic, but more than twice as large as the percentage reporting use of algebra, geometry, or any other more advanced mathematics.

Unfortunately, in the United States and many other Western countries, both children and adults often fail to master rational number arithmetic. In studies presenting all four fraction arithmetic operations, US university students erred on about 20 percent of problems using simple fractions (e.g., 2/3 + 4/5), and middle school students in both the United States and Belgium err on 20–40 percent of similar problems (Siegler & Braithwaite, 2017; Torbeyns et al., 2015). Results on the National Assessment of Educational Progress, a biennial study of many thousands of US fourth and eighth graders, students regularly show remarkable misunderstanding of fraction and decimal arithmetic. In one classic illustration, only 24 percent of US eighth graders correctly estimated the answer to 12/13 + 7/8 as being closer to 2 than to 1, 19, or 21 (Carpenter et al., 1981). When the same problem was presented to contemporary US eighth graders in 2014, accuracy had increased only to 27 percent correct (Siegler & Lortie-Forgues, 2015).

Learning of rational numbers seems to have a large impact on future mathematical development: In both Great Britain and the United States, fifth graders' knowledge of fractions predicts their math achievement test scores even after statistically controlling for whole number

arithmetic knowledge, working memory, reading comprehension, and socioeconomic status (Siegler et al., 2012). Teachers recognize this influence; in a survey of 1,000 US Algebra 1 teachers, difficulty with rational numbers was rated the second greatest source of difficulty in learning algebra, behind only the amorphous category "word problems."

16.3.4.1 Sources of Difficulty in Learning Rational Number Arithmetic

The many reasons why students have difficulty mastering rational number arithmetic can be divided into two broad classes: inherent reasons and culturally contingent reasons. *Inherent sources of difficulty* affect learning regardless of the society, the educational system, and the historical time period in which learning occurs. These sources include complex relations between whole number arithmetic and fraction arithmetic procedures; complex relations among different fraction arithmetic procedures; and the difficulty of estimating the magnitudes of individual fractions, which increases the difficulty of estimating, and thus of checking the plausibility of, answers to arithmetic problems.

Culturally contingent sources of difficulty vary with the sociocultural context in which learning occurs. They include teacher understanding of rational number arithmetic, characteristics of textbooks, and societal value on learning mathematics. Each of these is discussed in Section 16.3.4.3 (for a more in-depth discussion of these two types of difficulties, see Lortie-Forgues et al., 2015).

16.3.4.2 Inherent Sources of Difficulty

Complex Relations between Whole Number and Rational Number Arithmetic Procedures
Some aspects of whole number arithmetic hold true for rational number arithmetic, but others do not. For example, adding positive numbers

always yields an answer larger than either addend for both whole and rational numbers, and subtracting positive numbers always yields an answer smaller than the number being subtracted from, but multiplying rational numbers between 0 and 1 yields a produce smaller than either multiplicand, thus departing from the pattern with whole numbers. Avoiding overgeneralization from whole number arithmetic to rational number arithmetic is thus an inherent challenge for learners (Ni & Zhou, 2005; Siegler & Braithwaite, 2017).

Complex Relations among Rational Number Arithmetic Procedures

Standard procedures for the four rational number arithmetic operations are partially overlapping and partially distinct. For example, addition and subtraction of fractions require a common denominator, but neither multiplication nor division does. The procedure used in whole number arithmetic is applied independently to numerators and denominators in fraction multiplication, and sometimes can be with division, but never can be with fraction addition or subtraction. When adding and subtracting decimals with equal numbers of digits to the right of the decimal point, the placement of the decimal relative to the rightmost digit is maintained in the answer. In contrast, the number of decimal digits in the operands is added for multiplication, regardless of the equality or inequality of the number of decimal digits in the operands. Such complex relations are an inherent source of difficulty in learning rational number arithmetic.

Opaque Relations between Rational Number Procedures and Concepts

Why are equal denominators needed for adding and subtracting, but not multiplying or dividing? Why can the arithmetic operation be applied independently to the numerator and denominator when multiplying but not when adding or subtracting? Why do we add the number of decimal digits (digits to the right of the decimal point) when multiplying two decimals, but maintain the number of decimal digits when adding two decimals with the same number of decimal digits? Such questions are inherently difficult to explain to learners who lack knowledge of algebra, but it is unclear how algebra could be taught prior to rational numbers, which are pervasive in algebra.

16.3.4.3 Culturally Contingent Sources of Difficulty

Teachers' Understanding

Although teachers' possessing deep understanding of a topic does not guarantee strong learning, teachers' possessing only shallow understanding almost guarantees that learners' understanding will be weak. Unfortunately, many teachers in Western countries have limited understanding of rational number arithmetic. For example, when asked to explain the meaning of the problem $1\frac{3}{4} \div 1/2$, fewer than half of US and Belgian teachers were able to explain its meaning, other than citing the invert and multiply rule, whereas 90 percent of East Asian teachers provided coherent explanations of it (Depaepe et al., 2015; Luo et al., 2011; Ma, 1999). If teachers cannot explain a procedure, how can students be expected to understand it? Perhaps as a result of their shallow understanding of rational number arithmetic procedures, many US teachers emphasize rote memorization (National Mathematics Advisory Panel, 2008).

Textbook Problems

An analysis of the fraction arithmetic problems presented in three widely used US textbook series showed consistent biases in the types of problems that appeared (Braithwaite et al., 2017). Almost all problems that had equal denominators were addition and subtraction problems; multiplication and division were the operations in fewer than 10 percent of problems with equal denominators in all three textbook series but were roughly 50 percent of problems with unequal denominators in the textbooks. Such biased input seems to underlie children's highly frequent errors on multiplication and division problems with equal denominators, such as $3/5 \times 4/5 = 12/5$. Such errors appear to reflect overgeneralization of the addition/subtraction procedure of maintaining equal denominators in the answer. Such answers, which are consistent with the correct procedure for addition and subtraction, are in some data sets as frequent as correct answers among sixth and eighth graders (e.g., Siegler & Pyke, 2013).

Students' Limited Prerequisite Knowledge
Fraction arithmetic procedures require mastery of whole number arithmetic procedures, and a fairly sizable minority of students lack such mastery. For example, the sixth and eighth graders in Siegler and Pyke (2013) made whole number arithmetic errors on 21 percent of fraction arithmetic problems. Such errors make it difficult for students to know whether they used the correct rational number arithmetic procedure but made an execution error or whether they used an incorrect procedure.

16.3.4.4 Modeling Development of Fraction Arithmetic

Braithwaite et al. (2017) formulated a computer simulation of the development of fraction arithmetic, FARRA (Fraction Arithmetic Reflects Rules and Associations.) This production system model includes both correct and incorrect rules. Correct rules are those presented in the three textbook series that were examined; incorrect rules reflected procedures that would produce the most common errors

observed in prior studies. The incorrect rules reflected overgeneralization of the correct rules. For example, FARRA, like children, generated errors such as $3/5 * 4/5 = 12/5$ as frequently as it generated the correct answer (about 40 percent of trials for both answers). More generally, FARRA produced all major empirical phenomena identified in Braithwaite et al.'s review of the literature on fraction arithmetic:

- Low overall accuracy,
- Especially low accuracy on division problems,
- Variable responses within individual problems,
- Variable strategy use by individual children,
- Greater frequency of errors due to faulty strategies than incorrect execution of strategies,
- The most frequent strategy errors are independent whole number errors ($3/5 + 4/5 = 7/10$) and wrong fraction operation errors ($3/5 \times 4/5 = 12/5$), and
- Equal denominators increase addition and subtraction accuracy but decrease multiplication and division accuracy.

This simulation of fraction arithmetic resembles Shrager and Siegler's (1998) simulation of whole number arithmetic in its strategy choice mechanisms and its emphasis on the role of problem input. However, the two simulations differ in that the simulation of whole number arithmetic includes conceptual knowledge that prevents the simulation from discovering faulty strategies, whereas the simulation of fraction arithmetic includes no conceptual knowledge. This characteristic of the fraction arithmetic simulation is not due to any theoretical preference for purely procedural models – indeed, our preference was the opposite – but rather that a large body of data indicates that most US children do not use conceptual knowledge when solving fraction arithmetic problems. One example is the previously cited finding that more eighth graders choose 19 or 21 as the closest answers to 12/13 + 7/8 than choose 2. Another example is the high frequency of independent whole number errors, such as students answering that 1/2 + 2/3 = 3/5. Yet another example involved recent findings with sixth and seventh graders who were asked to estimate the location of two fractions on a 0–1 number line and later asked to locate the sum of the two addends on another 0–1 number line (Braithwaite et al., 2018). The children estimated that one of the two addends was larger than the sum on 52 percent of problems. Data such as these have led us to reluctantly conclude that most US middle school students do not apply conceptual understanding to fraction arithmetic, an assumption reflected in the Braithwaite et al. (2017) simulation model and one that likely contributed to the close fit of the model to children's performance.

16.4 Conclusions

The integrated theory of numerical development proposes that acquisition of knowledge about non-symbolic, whole, and rational numbers, as well as arithmetic combinations of such numbers, can be unified within a single framework. The present chapter illustrated how such a unification can illuminate both similarities and differences among different types of numerical knowledge. The most striking similarities were seen in the development of understanding of magnitudes of non-symbolic, whole, and rational numbers. With age and numerical experience, all types of magnitude knowledge become increasingly precise and are extended to an increasing range of numbers.

The most striking dissimilarities were seen in the role of conceptual knowledge in whole and rational number symbolic arithmetic.

Conceptual knowledge of whole number arithmetic was evident in adaptive choices among alternative arithmetic strategies and in useful constraints on discovery of new strategies. With rational number arithmetic, in contrast, conceptual knowledge seems to play little if any role; instead, association and generalization, both appropriate and inappropriate, appear to be the dominant processes for most students. The stereotype of students learning mathematical formulas by rote, rather than with conceptual understanding, does not seem to characterize most students' learning of whole number arithmetic, but it does seem to characterize their learning of rational number arithmetic.

The Common Core State Standards (2010) sought to address this problem by improving conceptual understanding of rational number arithmetic. This includes a variety of reasonable recommendations for doing so. However, many studies of rational number arithmetic cited in this chapter were published three-to-seven years after the CCSSI was published. The lack of conceptual knowledge evidenced by students in these very recent studies of rational number arithmetic might reflect the CCSSI not being implemented appropriately, or it might reflect the recommendations of the CCSSI being insufficient to meet the goal of students understanding rational number arithmetic. Whatever the reason, identifying means of improving conceptual understanding of rational number arithmetic is an important and pressing goal for teachers and researchers alike.

References

Agrillo, C., Piffer, L., Bisazza, A., & Butterworth, B. (2012). Evidence for two numerical systems that are similar in humans and guppies. *PLoS ONE, 7,* e31923.

Alibali, M. W., & Goldin-Meadow, S. (1993). Gesture-speech mismatch and mechanisms of learning: What the hands reveal about a child's state of mind. *Cognitive Psychology*, *25*, 468–523.

Andres, M., Michaux, N., & Pesenti, M. (2012). Common substrate for mental arithmetic and finger representation in the parietal cortex. *NeuroImage*, *62*, 1520–1528.

Ashcraft, M. H. (1982). The development of mental arithmetic: A chronometric approach. *Developmental Review*, *2*, 213–236.

Bailey, D. H., Siegler, R. S., & Geary, D. C. (2014). Early predictors of middle school fraction knowledge. *Developmental Science*, *17*, 775–785.

Baroody, A. J., & Dowker, A. (eds.) (2003). *The Development of Arithmetic Concepts and Skills: Constructing Adaptive Expertise*. Mahwah, NJ: Erlbaum.

Berteletti, I., & Booth, J. R. (2015). Perceiving fingers in single-digit arithmetic problems. *Frontiers in Psychology*, *6*, 226.

Berteletti, I., Lucangeli, D., Piazza, M., Dehaene, S., & Zorzi, M. (2010). Numerical estimation in preschoolers. *Developmental Psychology*, *41*, 545–551.

Binet, A., & Simon, T. (1905). New methods for the diagnosis of the intellectual level of subnormals. *L'Année Psychologique*, *11*, 191–244. Translated by Elizabeth S. Kite and reprinted in *The Development of Intelligence in Children* (1916). Baltimore: Williams & Wilkins.

Braithwaite, D. W., Pyke, A. A., & Siegler, R. S. (2017). A computational model of fraction arithmetic. *Psychological Review*, *124*, 603–625.

Braithwaite, D. W., Tian, J., & Siegler, R. S. (2018). Do children understand fraction addition? *Developmental Science*, *21*, e12601.

Brannon, E. M., & Merritt, D. J. (2011). Evolutionary foundations of the approximate number system. In S. Dehaene, & E. Brannon (eds.), *Space, Time and Number in the Brain: Searching for the Foundations of Mathematical Thought* (pp. 207–224). New York: Elsevier.

Brown, J. S., & Van Lehn, K. (1982). Toward a generative theory of "bugs." In T. P. Carpenter, J. M. Moser, & T. A. Romberg (eds.), *Addition and Subtraction: A Cognitive Perspective* (pp. 117–136). Hillsdale, N.J.: Erlbaum

Campbell, J. I., & Xue, Q. (2001). Cognitive arithmetic across cultures. *Journal of Experimental Psychology. General*, *130*, 299–315.

Carpenter, T. P., Corbitt, M. K., Kepner, H. S., Lindquist, M. M., & Reys, R. E. (1981). *Results and Implications from the Second Mathematics Assessment of the National Assessment of Educational Progress*. Reston, VA: National Council of Teachers of Mathematics.

Case, R., & Okamoto, Y. (1996). The role of central conceptual structures in the development of children's thought. *Monographs of the Society for Research in Child Development*, *61*, Nos. 1–2 (Serial No. 246).

Chen, Q., & Li, J. (2014). Association between individual differences in nonsymbolic number acuity and math performance: A meta-analysis. *Acta Psychologica*, *148*, 163–172.

College Board. (2015). *Advanced Placement Physics 1 Equations, Effective 2015* (pdf document). Available from https://secure-media .collegeboard.org/digitalServices/pdf/ap/ap-physics-1-equations-table.pdf. Last accessed August 2, 2021.

Cordes, S., & Brannon, E. M. (2008). Quantitative competencies in infancy. *Developmental Science*, *11*, 803–808.

Dehaene, S. (2011). *The Number Sense: How the Mind Creates Mathematics*. New York: Oxford University Press.

Depaepe, F., Torbeyns, J., Vermeersch, N., Janssens, D., Janssen, R., Kelchtermans, G., ... Van Dooren, W. (2015). Teachers' content and pedagogical content knowledge on rational numbers: A comparison of prospective elementary and lower secondary school teachers. *Teaching and Teacher Education*, *47*, 82–92.

Dotan, D., & Dehaene, S. (2013). How do we convert a number into a finger trajectory? *Cognition*, *129*, 512–529.

Duncan, G. J., Dowsett, C. J., Claessens, A., Magnuson, K., Huston, A. C., Klebanov, P., ... Japel, C. (2007). School readiness and later achievement. *Developmental Psychology, 43,* 1428–1446.

Fazio, L. K., Bailey, D. H., Thompson, C. A., & Siegler, R. S. (2014). Relations of different types of numerical magnitude representations to each other and to mathematics achievement. *Journal of Experimental Child Psychology, 123,* 53–72.

Gauvain, M. (2001). *The Social Context of Cognitive Development.* New York: The Guilford Press.

Geary, D. C. (2006). Development of mathematical understanding. In D. Kuhn, & R. S. Siegler (vol. eds.), *Cognition, Perception, and Language,* (pp. 777–810). W. Damon (gen. ed.), Handbook of child psychology (6th ed.). New York: John Wiley & Sons.

Geary, D. C. (2008). An evolutionarily informed education science. *Educational Psychologist, 43,* 179–195.

Geary, D. C., Hoard, M. K., Byrd-Craven, J., Nugent, L., & Numtee, C. (2007). Cognitive mechanisms underlying achievement deficits in children with mathematical learning disability. *Child Development, 78,* 1343–1359.

Geary, D. C., & vanMarle, K. (2016). Young children's core symbolic and non-symbolic quantitative knowledge in the prediction of later mathematics achievement. *Developmental Psychology, 52,* 2130–2144.

Halberda, J., & Feigenson, L. (2008). Developmental change in the acuity of the "Number sense": The approximate number system in 3-, 4-, 5-, and 6-year-olds and adults. *Developmental Psychology, 44,* 1457–1465.

Halberda, J., Ly, R., Wilmer, J. B., Naiman, D. Q., & Germine, L. (2012). Number sense across the lifespan as revealed by a massive Internet-based sample. *Proceedings of the National Academy of Sciences (USA), 109,* 11116–11120.

Halberda, J., Mazzocco, M. M. M., & Feigenson, L. (2008). Individual differences in non-verbal number acuity correlates with math achievement. *Nature, 455,* 665–668.

Handel, M. J. (2016). What do people do at work? A profile of U.S. jobs from the survey of workplace Skills, Technology, and Management Practices (STAMP). *Journal for Labour Market Research, 49,* 177–197.

Hanushek, E. A. (2016). What matters for student achievement: Updating Coleman on the influence of families and schools. *EducationNext, 16,* 23–30.

Iuculano, T., & Butterworth, B. (2011). Understanding the real value of fractions and decimals. *The Quarterly Journal of Experimental Psychology, 64,* 2088–2098.

Jordan, N. C., Hansen, N., Fuchs, L. S., Siegler, R. S., Gersten, R., & Micklos, D. (2013). Developmental predictors of fraction concepts and procedures. *Journal of Experimental Child Psychology, 116,* 45–58.

Jordan, N.C., Kaplan, D., Olah, L. N., & Locuniak, M. N. (2006). Number sense growth in kindergarten: A longitudinal investigation of children at risk for mathematics difficulties. *Child Development, 77,* 153–175.

Kant, I. (1781/2003). *Critique of Pure Reason,* trans. J. M. D. Meiklejohn. Mineola, NY: Dover.

Klahr, D., & MacWhinney, B. (1998). Information processing. In W. Damon (Series ed.) & D. Kuhn & R. S. Siegler (vol. eds.), *Handbook of Child Psychology: Vol. 2: Cognition, Perception & Language.* (5th ed., pp. 631–678). New York: Wiley.

Le Corre, M., & Carey, S. (2007). One, two, three, four, nothing more: An investigation of the conceptual sources of the verbal counting principles. *Cognition, 105,* 395–438.

LeFevre, J. A., Sadesky, G. S., & Bisanz, J. (1996). Selection of procedures in mental addition: Reassessing the problem-size effect in adults. *Journal of Experimental Psychology: Learning, Memory, and Cognition, 22,* 216–230.

LeFevre, J. A., Smith-Chant, B. L., Hiscock, K., Dale, K. E., & Morris, J. (2003). Young adults' strategic choices in simple arithmetic: Implications for the development of mathematical representations. In A. J. Baroody, & A. Dowker (eds.), *The Development of Arithmetic Concepts and Skills: Constructing Adaptive Expertise* (pp. 203–228). Mahwah, NJ: Erlbaum.

Lemaire, P., & Siegler, R. S. (1995). Four aspects of strategic change: Contributions to children's learning of multiplication. *Journal of Experimental Psychology: General, 124*, 83–97.

Libertus, M., Feigenson, L., & Halberda, J. (2011). Preschool acuity of the approximate number system correlates with school math ability. *Developmental Science, 14*, 1292–1300.

Lortie-Forgues, H., & Siegler, R. S. (2017). Conceptual knowledge of decimal arithmetic. *Journal of Educational Psychology, 109*, 374–386.

Lortie-Forgues, H., Tian, J., & Siegler, R. S. (2015). Why is learning fraction and decimal arithmetic so difficult? *Developmental Review, 38*, 201–221.

Luo, F., Lo, J., & Leu, Y. (2011). Fundamental fraction knowledge of pre-service elementary teachers: A cross-national study in the United States and Taiwan. *School Science and Mathematics, 111*, 164–177.

Lyons, I. M., Price, G. R., Vaessen, A., Blomert, L., & Ansari, D. (2014). Numerical predictors of arithmetic success in grades 1-6. *Developmental Science, 17*, 714–726.

Ma, L. (1999). *Knowing and Teaching Elementary Mathematics: Teachers Understanding of Fundamental Mathematics in China and the United States*. Mahwah, NJ: Erlbaum.

McCrink, K., & Wynn, K. (2004). Large-number addition and subtraction by 9-month-old infants. *Psychological Science, 15*, 776–781.

McCrink, K., & Wynn, K. (2007). Ratio abstraction by 6-month-old infants. *Psychological Science, 18*, 740–745.

McNeil, N. M. (2014). A change-resistance account of children's difficulties understanding mathematical equivalence. *Child Development Perspectives, 8*, 42–47.

Meert, G., Grégoire, J., & Noël, M.-P. (2010). Comparing the magnitude of two fractions with common components: Which representations are used by 10- and 12-year-olds? *Journal of Experimental Child Psychology, 107*, 244–259.

Miller, P. H., & Seier, W. L. (1994). Strategy utilization deficiencies in children: When, where, and why. In H. W. Reese (ed.), *Advances in Child Development and Behavior* (Vol. 25, pp. 108–156). New York: Academic Press.

Möhring, W., Liu, R., & Libertus, M. E. (2017). Infants' speed discrimination: Effects of different ratios and spatial orientations. *Infancy, 22*, 762–777.

National Mathematics Advisory Panel. (2008). *Foundations for Success: The Final Report of the National Mathematics Advisory Panel*. Washington, DC: US Department of Education.

Ni, Y., & Zhou, Y.-D. (2005). Teaching and learning fraction and rational numbers: The origins and implications of whole number bias. *Educational Psychologist, 40*, 27–52.

Nieder, A., & Dehaene, S. (2009). Representation of number in the brain. *Annual Review of Neuroscience, 32*, 185–208.

Park, J., Park, D. C., & Polk, T. A. (2013). Parietal functional connectivity in numerical cognition. *Cerebral Cortex, 23*, 2127–2135.

Parnas, M., Lin, A. C., Huetteroth, W., & Miesenböck, G. (2013). Odor discrimination in Drosophila: From neural population codes to behavior. *Neuron, 79*, 932–944.

Piaget, J. (1952). *The Child's Concept of Number*. New York: W. W. Norton.

Piazza, M. (2011). Neurocognitive start-up tools for symbolic number representations. In S. Dehaene, & E. Brannon (eds.), *Space, Time, and Number in the Brain: Searching for the Foundations of Mathematical Thought* (pp. 267–285). London: Elsevier.

Piffer, L., Petrazzini, M. E. M., & Agrillo, C. (2013). Large number discrimination in newborn fish. *PLoS ONE, 8*, e62466.

Ramani, G. B., & Siegler, R. S. (2008). Promoting broad and stable improvements in low-income children's numerical knowledge through playing number board games. *Child Development, 79*, 375–394.

Ramani, G. B., & Siegler, R. S. (2011). Reducing the gap in numerical knowledge between low- and middle-income preschoolers. *Journal of Applied Developmental Psychology, 32*, 146–159.

Reardon, S. F. (2011). The widening academic achievement gap between the rich and the poor: New evidence and possible explanations. In G. Duncan, & R. Murnane (eds.), *Whither Opportunity? Rising Inequality and the Uncertain Life Chances of Low-Income Children* (pp. 91–116). New York: Russell Sage Foundation Press.

Reeve, R. A., Paul, J. M., & Butterworth, B. (2015). Longitudinal changes in young children's 0–100 to 0–1000 number-line error signatures. *Frontiers in Psychology*, 6, Article 647.

Resnick, I., Jordan, N. C., Hansen, N., Rajan, V., Rodrigues, J., Siegler, R. S., & Fuchs, L. (2016). Developmental growth trajectories in understanding of fraction magnitude from fourth through sixth grade. *Developmental Psychology*, 52, 746–757.

Resnick, L. B., Nesher, P., Leonard, F., Magone, M., Omanson, S., & Peled, I. (1989). Conceptual bases of arithmetic errors: The case for decimal fractions. *Journal for Research in Mathematics Education*, 20, 8–27.

Riggs, K. J., Ferrand, L., Lancelin, D., Fryziel, L., Dumur, G., & Simpson, A. (2006). Subitizing in tactile perception. *Psychological Science*, 17, 271–272.

Ritchie, S. J., & Bates, T. C. (2013). Enduring links from childhood mathematics and reading achievement to adult socioeconomic status. *Psychological Science*, 24, 1301–1308.

Robinson, K. M. (2017). The understanding of additive and multiplicative arithmetic concepts. In D. C. Geary, D. B. Berch, R. Ochsendorf, & K. Mann Koepke (eds.). *Acquiring Complex Arithmetic Skills and Higher-Order Mathematical Concepts* (Vol. 3, Mathematical Cognition and Learning, pp. 21–46). San Diego, CA: Elsevier Academic Press.

Schneider, M., Beeres, K., Coban, L., Merz, S., Schmidt S., Stricker, J., & De Smedt, B. (2017). Associations of non-symbolic and symbolic numerical magnitude processing with mathematical competence: A meta-analysis. *Developmental Science*, 20, e12372.

Schneider, M., Merz, S., Stricker, J., De Smedt, B., Torbeyns, J., Verschaffel, L., & Luwel, K. (2018). Associations of number line estimation with mathematical competence: A meta-analysis. *Child Development*, 89, 1467–1484.

Schneider, M., & Siegler, R. S. (2010). Representations of the magnitudes of fractions. *Journal of Experimental Psychology: Human Perception and Performance*, 36, 1227–1238.

Shrager, J., & Siegler, R. S. (1998). SCADS: A model of children's strategy choices and strategy discoveries. *Psychological Science*, 9, 405–410.

Siegler, R. S. (1987). The perils of averaging data over strategies: An example from children's addition. *Journal of Experimental Psychology: General*, 116, 250–264.

Siegler, R. S. (1988). Strategy choice procedures and the development of multiplication skill. *Journal of Experimental Psychology: General*, 117, 258–275.

Siegler, R. S. (1989). Hazards of mental chronometry: An example from children's subtraction. *Journal of Educational Psychology*, 81, 497–506.

Siegler, R. S. (1996). Unidimensional thinking, multidimensional thinking, and characteristic tendencies of thought. In A. J. Sameroff, & M. M. Haith (eds.), *The Five to Seven Year Shift: The Age of Reason and Responsibility* (pp. 63–84). Chicago, IL: University of Chicago Press.

Siegler, R. S. (2006). Microgenetic analyses of learning. In W. Damon, & R. M. Lerner (Series eds.) & D. Kuhn & R. S. Siegler (vol. eds.), *Handbook of Child Psychology: Volume 2: Cognition, Perception, and Language* (6th ed., pp. 464–510). Hoboken, NJ: Wiley.

Siegler, R. S. (2016). Magnitude knowledge: The common core of numerical development. *Developmental Science*, 19, 341–361.

Siegler, R. S., & Booth, J. L. (2004). Development of numerical estimation in young children. *Child Development*, 75, 428–444.

Siegler, R. S., & Braithwaite, D. W. (2017). Numerical development. *Annual Review of Psychology*, 68, 187–213.

Siegler, R. S., & Crowley, K. (1994). Constraints on learning in non-privileged domains. *Cognitive Psychology*, 27, 194–227.

Siegler, R. S., Duncan, G. J., Davis-Kean, P. E., Duckworth, K., Claessens, A., Engel, M., . . .

Chen, M. (2012). Early predictors of high school mathematics achievement. *Psychological Science, 23*, 691–697.

Siegler, R. S., & Jenkins, E. A. (1989). *How Children Discover New Strategies*. Hillsdale, NJ: Erlbaum.

Siegler, R. S., & Lemaire, P. (1997). Older and younger adults' strategy choices in multiplication: Testing predictions of ASCM via the choice/no-choice method. *Journal of Experimental Psychology: General, 126*, 71–92.

Siegler, R. S., & Lortie-Forgues, H. (2015). Conceptual knowledge of fraction arithmetic. *Journal of Educational Psychology, 107*, 909–918.

Siegler, R. S., & Pyke, A. A. (2013). Developmental and individual differences in understanding fractions. *Developmental Psychology, 49*, 1994–2004.

Siegler, R. S., & Ramani, G. B. (2009). Playing linear number board games – but not circular ones – improves low-income preschoolers' numerical understanding. *Journal of Educational Psychology, 101*, 545–560.

Siegler, R. S., & Shrager, J. (1984). Strategy choices in addition and subtraction: How do children know what to do? In C. Sophian (ed.), *The Origins of Cognitive Skills* (pp. 229–293). Hillsdale, NJ: Erlbaum.

Siegler, R. S., Thompson, C. A., & Schneider, M. (2011). An integrated theory of whole number and fractions development. *Cognitive Psychology, 62*, 273–296.

Spelke, E. S., & Kinzler, K. D. (2007). Core knowledge. *Developmental Science, 10*, 89–96.

Sullivan, J., & Barner, D. (2014). The development of structural analogy in number-line estimation. *Journal of Experimental Child Psychology, 128*, 171–189.

Svenson, O., & Sjöberg, K. (1983). Evolution of cognitive processes for solving simple additions during the first three school years. *Scandinavian Journal of Psychology, 24*, 117–124.

Thompson, C. A., & Opfer, J. E. (2010). How 15 hundred is like 15 cherries: Effect of progressive alignment on representational changes in numerical cognition. *Child Development, 81*, 1768–1786.

Torbeyns, J., Schneider, M., Xin, Z. & Siegler, R. S. (2015). Bridging the gap: Fraction understanding is central to mathematics achievement in students from three different continents. *Learning and Instruction, 37*, 5–13.

Verschaffel, L., Greer, B., & De Corte, E. (2007). Whole number concepts and operations. In F. Lester (ed.), *Second Handbook of Research on Mathematics Teaching and Learning* (pp. 557–628). Charlotte, NC: Information Age.

Watts, T. W., Duncan, G. J., Siegler, R. S., & Davis-Kean, P. E. (2014). What's past is prologue: Relations between early mathematics knowledge and high school achievement. *Educational Researcher, 43*, 352–360.

Wynn, K. (1992). Addition and subtraction by human infants. *Nature, 358*, 749–750.

Xu, X., Chen, C., Pan, M., & Li, N. (2013). Development of numerical estimation in Chinese preschool children. *Journal of Experimental Child Psychology, 116*, 351–366.

17 Numerical Cognition and Executive Functions

Development As Progressive Inhibitory Control of Misleading Visuospatial Dimensions

Margot Roell, Olivier Houdé, Grégoire Borst, and Arnaud Viarouge

17.1 Introduction

Theories have ventured to explain how the human brain has gained the unique ability to develop mathematical concepts and theories. One theory states that mathematics has appeared as a by-product of the human language faculty (Chomsky, 2006). Alternatively, recent cognitive neuroscience research have postulated that mathematics arose from non-linguistic intuitions of numbers and space (Dehaene, 2011; Dillon et al., 2013). Indeed, studies have observed that infants (Starkey & Cooper, 1980; Starkey et al., 1983) and Amazonian indigenous adults with no education in Mathematics and who do not possess number words (Dehaene et al. 2008, Pica et al., 2004) display abstract proto-mathematical intuitions of arithmetic and geometry. These 'core knowledges' (Spelke & Kinzler, 2007) have been theorized to be the ontological building blocks that scaffold our ability for representing numbers symbolically and performing exact arithmetic (Starr et al., 2013). They have been found to be predictive of later, more complex mathematical abilities (Gilmore et al., 2010; Halberda et al., 2008; Starr et al., 2013), supporting the idea that complex mathematics would arise from core representations of number and space (Amalric & Dehaene, 2016). Extensive research has shown that numerical and spatial cognition were tightly connected (Hubbard et al., 2005). In some contexts, this relation between number and visuospatial dimensions, such as spatial extent or density, can lead to interferences which can hinder the development of math abilities.

Thus, we propose here that numerical cognition partly develops as a progressive ability to inhibit misleading visuospatial dimensions. Inhibitory control can be defined as an executive function that facilitates the suppression of prepotent responses in favour of efficient task processing (Dempster, 1992). Inhibition involves the ability to focus on task-relevant stimuli while resisting strong or automatic interference from task-irrelevant information (see Chapters 20 and 21). It is well documented within psychology and mathematics education literature that there is a relationship between inhibitory control and formal mathematic ability (Blair & Razza, 2007; Bull & Scerif, 2001; Cragg & Gilmore, 2014; Espy et al., 2004; St Clair-Thompson & Gathercole, 2006). Individuals with better inhibition skills also tend to perform better on tasks measuring mathematical ability.

Throughout this chapter, we shall investigate how numerical cognition develops as a progressive ability to inhibit misleading visuospatial dimensions, first examining intuitive pre-schooling non-symbolic numerical cognition and then post-schooling symbolic numerical cognition.

17.2 The Role of Inhibition in the Development of Non-symbolic Numerical Abilities

17.2.1 Number Conservation

Children under approximately seven years of age fail to solve Piaget's seminal number-conservation task (Piaget, 1952). This task consists of presenting two rows of tokens placed in one-to-one correspondence. Participants are then asked whether the two rows contain the same number of tokens or not. Once the equality is acknowledged by the participants, one of the two rows is transformed by spreading the tokens apart, so as to take up more space. Participants are then asked again whether the two rows contain the same or different number of tokens.

Children up to seven years of age are considered 'non-conservers' due to the fact that they make systematic errors in judging that there are more tokens in the longer row (the row that has been transformed). When children are able to correctly state that the two rows contain the same number of tokens after transformation, usually around seven-to-eight years of age, they are considered 'conservers', that is, they understand that the number represented by the set of tokens is invariant to the transformation.

According to Piaget (1968), success in the task is contingent on the understanding of the equivalence of numerical quantities and the reversibility of operations, that is, the ability to understand that the direct operation (i.e., spreading the dots) can be cancelled out by the reverse operations (i.e., bringing the dots back into their original position). For Piaget, non-conserver children have not yet reached the logico-mathematical reasoning stage and do not have a solid concept of numbers (Piaget, 1964).

Studies have since provided evidence that younger children have some intuitions on number conservation (see the seminal study by Mehler & Bever, 1967; but also Gelman, 1972). Specifically, studies recording oculomotor behaviour have shown that four-to-five-month-olds are capable of detecting the violation or conservation of number when presented with unexpected or expected numerical events (Wynn, 1992, 1995, 1998; Wynn et al., 2002). Note that the objection that neonate processing in this case may rely on non-numerical processes such as object identity and/or spatial location has been experimentally disproved (Dehaene et al., 1998; Koechlin et al., 1997; Simon et al., 1995).

A possible explanation for such discrepancy between the age at which children succeed at Piaget's number conservation task and the early numerical abilities reported in younger children is the strategy selected by children to solve a problem (Siegler, 1998, see Chapter 16). Indeed, it has been demonstrated that, at any given time, children possess several strategies for solving a problem (Siegler, 1995). According to this model, development should no longer be perceived as a linear and cumulative process relying on discrete stages as hypothesized by Piaget (1952) but as analogous to overlapping waves (Siegler, 1998). As one possesses several competing strategies, the selection of the appropriate strategy would rely on the ability to inhibit misleading strategies, particularly in interference tasks such as the number-conservation task (Houdé, 2000). According to neo-Piagetian theories, children make errors in the Piagetian task not because they lack the cognitive ability to understand the underlying concepts of the task but primarily because they fail to inhibit a misleading strategy (Houdé, 2000). Thus, children's failure in the number conservation task does not necessarily reflect an inability to grasp the number conservation principles per se but rather a failure to inhibit a misleading visuospatial bias, that is, the length-equals-number bias (Houdé & Guichart, 2001; Houdé et al., 2011).

Indeed, studies converge in showing that success in the number conservation task relies on the inhibition of misleading visuospatial dimensions rather than the activation of logico-mathematical reasoning capacities such as the reversibility of operations (Daurignac et al., 2006; Houdé & Guichart, 2001; Houdé et al., 2011; Joliot et al., 2009; Leroux et al., 2006, 2009).

Adapting the number-conservation task to a negative priming paradigm, researchers have systematically tested whether succeeding at the number-conservation task requires inhibiting the length-equals-number visuo-spatial bias (Daurignac et al., 2006; Houdé & Guichart, 2001; Houdé et al., 2011). The negative priming paradigm rests on the rationale that if a strategy (or distractor) is inhibited on a given item, then the activation of that strategy (or distractor) on the next item should be more difficult, as revealed by poorer performance (Tipper, 2001). Negative priming effects were originally reported in attentional tasks to reveal the inhibition of distractors (Tipper et al., 1991) and have been reported afterward in numerous tasks in various domains to reveal the inhibition of overlearned misleading strategies and biases (see Houdé & Borst, 2015). In their study using a number conservation task, Houdé and Guichart (2001) have demonstrated that nine-year-olds are slower to respond to items where the length of the rows and the number of tokens covariate (i.e., the longest row contains the highest number of tokens) after having responded to items where the length of the row and the number of tokens interfere (i.e., the longest row contains the same amount of tokens as the smallest row).

The negative priming effect suggests that children need to inhibit the length-equals-number bias to succeed at the number conservation task.

De Neys et al. (2014) have examined the critical question of whether children fail the number conservation task because they lack the executive resources to complete the inhibition process or whether they fail to detect that they need to inhibit in the first place.

It is important to note that inhibitory control accounts do not posit that one must always block the visuospatial dimensions (Brainerd & Reyna, 2001; De Neys & Vanderputte, 2011; De Neys et al., 2014; Jacobs & Klaczynski, 2002; Lubin et al., 2015). Visuospatial dimensions offer a valid and useful basis for our judgement as often in everyday situation length and quantity will covary. However, in number conservation the visuospatial dimension needs to be inhibited as it is misleading and violates the logical conservation principle. Efficient inhibition requires that one monitors for such conflicts and inhibits the visuospatial dimension when it is detected. Conflict detection may be implicit but is nonetheless a crucial building block for an efficient inhibition. Interestingly, De Neys et al. (2014) observed that non-conserving children did detect their number conservation errors. In their study, the majority of the preschoolers failed to give the correct answer (i.e., 60 percent incorrect response) in the standard conservation task, that is they were unable to state that the two rows were the numerically equal. However, they were all (i.e. 100 percent correct responses) able to state that the two rows were equal in the reverse number conservation condition. In this condition, they initially saw two rows containing the same amount of tokens but differing in length, then the longer row was contracted to give both rows equal length. Critically, they found that children who had failed the classic conservation task were far less confident in their response (mean confidence of 64 percent) in the classic number conservation task than in the reverse number conservation task (mean confidence of 98 percent). Although the non-conservers did not manage to give the correct response, they were not completely oblivious to their error, as indicated by their confidence rating, which suggests that they detected the conflict between the length-equals-number misleading strategy and the appropriate logical strategy to use in that context (i.e., reversibility).

These behavioural findings imply that success in the number conservation task relies on domain-general inhibitory ability, by which one inhibits the misleading visuospatial dimension. Moreover, inhibition failure should be conceived as a failure to complete the inhibition process rather than a failure to detect that inhibition is required (Lubin et al., 2015).

17.2.2 Approximate Number Sense

Since Piaget's work, research in the field of numerical cognition has shown that, well before becoming conservers, children and even infants have numerical competencies. In particular, many studies have demonstrated that infants possess an approximate number system (ANS), providing them with the ability to estimate and compare quantities. One characteristic of this ability is that it follows Weber's law, which means that the ability to perceive the difference between two quantities ultimately depends on their numerical ratio. For instance, in their ground-breaking study, Xu and Spelke (2000) showed that six-month-olds could discriminate between arrays of eight and sixteen dots (a 1:2 ratio), but not between eight and twelve dots (a 2:3 ratio). Subsequent studies have described the developmental trajectory of this numerical estimation ability, with a progressively increasing precision with age,

from a 1:3 discriminable ratio in newborns to a 9:10 ratio in adulthood (Halberda et al., 2008).

The question remains open of the factors of this development. Some studies point to the idea that the increase in precision of the ANS is not purely maturational, and that formal education in mathematics contributes to refining numerical representations (Nys et al., 2013; Piazza et al., 2013). Recently, several authors have posited that developing one's approximate number sense also implies learning to focus on the numerical aspect of the environment (Piazza et al., 2018), and to abstract the numerical dimension from other visuospatial dimensions of magnitude, echoing Piaget's work on number conservation. Inhibitory control seems to be a good candidate for such an abstraction process, and has been suggested by several authors as a central motor of numerical development (Clayton & Gilmore, 2015; Leibovich et al., 2017; Szücs et al., 2013a; Viarouge et al., 2019).

While looking time paradigms have been commonly used in infants, the task classically used in children and adults to assess the precision of numerical estimation, called the non-symbolic numerical comparison task, consists in asking the participants to judge which of two visually presented arrays contains the larger number of items (usually dots). The two arrays are rapidly flashed on a computer screen, so as to prevent counting of the dots. In all these paradigms, the arrays of dots carry not only numerical information, but also information regarding visuospatial dimensions, such as the size of the dots or the field area occupied by the dots. All these dimensions covary with numerosity, which makes it almost impossible to control for all of them simultaneously. For this reason, non-symbolic comparison tasks usually contain trials whereby some visuospatial dimensions are congruent with number (for instance the larger the number of dots in the array, the larger the total surface area occupied by the dots), and trials with an incongruence between number and non-numerical visuospatial dimensions (for instance, if the total surface area is maintained constant between both arrays, the average dot size will be smaller in the most numerous array).

Several authors have used these characteristics of the stimuli to generate congruent and incongruent trials in order to study the impact of specific visuospatial dimensions on numerical comparison. Using a variety of dimensions, congruency effects have been reported both in pre-schoolers and school-aged children (Defever et al., 2013; Fuhs & McNeil, 2013; Fuhs et al., 2016; Gilmore et al., 2016; Szücs et al., 2013a), as well as in adults (Anobile et al., 2014; Dakin et al., 2011; Gebuis & Gevers, 2011; Gebuis & Reynvoet, 2012, 2013; Hurewitz et al., 2006; Nys & Content, 2012; Sophian & Chu, 2008; Tibber et al., 2012). They generally show lower performance on incongruent than on congruent or neutral trials, and support the idea of the role of inhibitory control processes in the development of numerical representations (Fuhs & McNeil, 2013; Fuhs et al., 2016; Rousselle & Noël, 2008).

Also consistent with the idea of a development of numerical representation through a gradual focusing on number are training studies of the ANS (DeWind & Brannon, 2012; Fuhs et al., 2016). For instance, Fuhs et al. (2016) trained the ANS of pre-schoolers from low-income homes during eight ten-minute sessions over a period of four weeks on an adaptive non-symbolic numerical comparison task. They observed that children's improvements were mainly driven by their better performance on the number/total surface area incongruent trials, supporting the idea of an improvement of inhibitory control underlying the development of numerical acuity.

Moreover, the amplitude of the difference in performance between congruent and incongruent trials in non-symbolic numerical comparison tasks has been shown to be influenced by age (Defever et al., 2013; Gebuis et al., 2009; Soltész et al., 2010; Szücs et al., 2013b). For instance, Szücs et al. (2013b) used a non-symbolic comparison task including congruent and incongruent trials between number and visuospatial dimensions such as the average size of the dots and their total surface area. The authors found a larger congruency effect in seven-year-olds compared to adult participants, and suggested that their results could be due to the lower level of inhibitory control abilities in children (see also Defever et al., 2013). Congruency effects have not been consistently found in all the studies, with some studies reporting no difference in performance between incongruent and congruent trials in children or in adults (Odic et al., 2013, 2014) or higher performance in incongruent trials (Tokita & Ishiguchi, 2010). In order to provide converging evidence for the causal role of inhibition in the development of non-symbolic numerical comparison, Viarouge et al. (2019) adapted a non-symbolic comparison task to a negative priming paradigm in groups of seven-to-eight-year-olds and adults. They used pairs of dot arrays whereby number could be either congruent, incongruent, or neutral regarding aspects of the dots' size (using the *Size* dimension as defined in DeWind et al., 2015). Congruent pairs could be either preceded by neutral (in the control condition) or incongruent (in the test condition) pairs. The results showed significant negative priming effects in both age groups, reflecting the cognitive cost of blocking the non-numerical dimension on the subsequent numerical judgement. Interestingly, the amplitude of the negative priming effect was larger in children than in adults, which is consistent with the protracted development of inhibitory control until late adolescence (Luna et al., 2010). Previous studies comparing primary school children and adults have indeed shown that the amplitude of negative priming effects in various contexts could reveal the efficiency of the inhibitory control processes at play (e.g., Aïte et al., 2016; Borst et al., 2013a). The study by Viarouge et al. (2019) supports the idea that the development of numerical representations is rooted in the development of the ability to inhibit non-numerical visuospatial dimensions.

We have reviewed here evidence pointing toward the role of inhibitory control processes in the development of early numerical representations. Whether these early numerical abilities reflect an innate dedicated system for the processing of numerical information, or rather a general sense of magnitude from which the perception of numerosity is derived, has been the object of intense debate. However, both these alternative hypotheses are compatible with the idea that executive functions such as inhibitory control contribute to the development of numerical cognition. Consistent with the latter view, inhibitory control processes would allow us to extract number from a general representation of magnitude (Leibovich et al., 2017), while the former view would posit that, in order to develop their innate sense of number at all ages, one must learn to inhibit the interfering visuospatial dimensions (Clayton & Gilmore, 2015; see Cappelletti et al., 2014 for a study in ageing).

17.2.3 Neuroimaging Studies

Neuroimaging studies have further supported the role of inhibition in the development of non-symbolic numerical abilities. According to Houdé et al.'s (2011) fMRI study, the number conservation task may depend on a large-scale executive brain network that includes the activation of the parietal and prefrontal areas conjointly with the insula.

Regions such as the inferior frontal gyrus and the insula were found to be activated in children who succeeded in the number conservation task but not in children who failed (Houdé et al., 2011). Notably, these activations were observed in the inferior frontal gyrus usually linked to inhibitory control in working memory (Aron et al., 2004; Konishi et al., 1998; McNab et al., 2008) and known to be involved in both cognitive control (Miller, 2000) and number processing when conjointly activated with the IPS (Cappelletti et al., 2010; Dormal & Pesenti, 2009; Piazza et al., 2004). The Insula has also been found to be a core brain area specifically activated during executive function tasks, namely inhibition, response shifting, and working memory (Houdé et al., 2010). It is of note that although the IPS was conjointly activated during the task in participants that have succeeded and failed the task, this region was more activated in participants who had succeeded in the task. The activation of this network would allow one to surpass the misleading visuospatial bias and correctly focus on the comparison of numbers (Leroux et al., 2009).

In a follow up study, Poirel et al. (2012) demonstrated that the percentage of BOLD signal change in the inferior temporal gyrus and the insula was related to the change in inhibitory control efficiency, as reflected by children's performance on an Animal Stroop task. Additionally, no correlation was observed between the activation in these two regions of interest and the ability to manipulate numerical information in working memory, as reflected by children's performance in a Backward Digit Span task. Interestingly, the ability to manipulate numerical information in working memory was related to the activation of the IPS only in children that had succeeded in the number conservation task. Participants who failed the number conservation task did not present such a relation. As stated in Section 17.1, the reversibility of operation process is crucial to the success at the number conservation task. To determine that two rows of tokens of different lengths possess the same number of tokens, participants must maintain in working memory the two rows while mentally imagining what the two rows would look like when the tokens that are spread apart return to their original position. Moreover, as the IPS is recruited both for numerical processing and length processing as well as for the transformation of visuospatial mental images (Harris & Miniussi, 2003; Zacks, 2008), the authors suggest that the activation of IPS observed in the participants that succeeded in the number conservation task may reflect the ability to imagine the mirror visuospatial transformation of a perceptual transformation of objects (Poirel et al., 2012).

Regarding non-symbolic numerical comparison, the right inferior frontal gyrus was also found to be more activated for number/total surface area incongruent trials than for congruent trials, consistent with the idea of a higher inhibitory control demand in the incongruent condition (Wilkey et al., 2017). Another study looking at brain activations related to the congruency conditions of a non-symbolic numerical comparison task found different regions showing greater activations for incongruent trials: the left posterior cingulate gyrus and left precentral gyrus, both associated with cognitive control (Leibovich et al., 2015). Several methodological factors could explain the discrepancy between the results of these two studies. First, the age and school levels of the participants were not the same. While Wilkey et al. investigated late adolescents in twelfth grade, Leibovich et al.'s participants were young adult students. Second, the congruency conditions were not equivalent between the two studies. Leibovich et al. (2015) generated arrays of dots whereby number was either congruent or incongruent with five non-numerical dimensions of magnitude simultaneously (dot size, total circumference, total surface area, density and area extended). Combined with the different numerical ratios used in both studies, the levels of salience of the numerical and non-numerical dimensions, hence their levels of interference, are likely to be very different. Longitudinal studies are needed to systematically investigate the neural correlates of the inhibitory control processes involved in the development of non-symbolic numerical abilities.

EEG studies have revealed the modulation of centro-parietal N2 and fronto-central P3 components in an adaptation of the number conservation task (Borst et al., 2013b; Joliot et al., 2009; Leroux et al., 2006, 2009). The amplitude of the N2 and P3 component increased when the length and the number of tokens were in conflict (i.e., the two rows contains the same amount of tokens but one is longer than the other as it is spread apart) compared to when the length and the number of tokens covaried (i.e., the longer row contained more token that the shorter row). Both the N2 and the P3 components reflect conflict monitoring and inhibition of dominant responses (Anokhin et al., 2004; Kok, 1999; Nieuwenhuis et al., 2003). As stated in Section 17.1, one must detect the presence of a conflict between length and number and then inhibit the visuospatial bias to determine that the two rows have the same number of tokens when the length and numbers interfere. In their study, Borst et al. (2013b) demonstrated that the inhibitory control efficiency, as reflected by the difference in RTs between the condition in which the length and the number of tokens interfered and the condition in which the length and the number of tokens covaried, was related to the difference in amplitude of the P3 component in these two conditions. The authors argue that number conservation relies on two critical mechanisms: the inhibition of the misleading visuospatial dimension of length, and the activation of the reversibility of operation (Borst et al., 2013b). Few studies to date have investigated the inhibitory control processes at play in non-symbolic numerical comparison using EEG. Gebuis et al. (2010) used EEG to investigate the temporal course of the congruency effect between number and physical size in numerical comparison. They observed larger latency and smaller amplitude of the parietal P3 component during incongruent trials, suggesting a conflict processing at the stage of stimulus evaluation.

17.3 Inhibition in the Development of Symbolic Arithmetic

Interference of misleading visuospatial dimensions in numerical processing is not limited to non-symbolic numerical processing. Researchers have shown that visuospatial dimensions also interact with symbolic numerical processing. For instance, the mere perception of digits brings about an illusion of the perception of spatial extent (de Hevia et al., 2008, 2012). Participants overestimate significantly more the space delimited by large magnitude digits (e.g. 8 or 9) than the same space delimited by small magnitude digits (e.g. 1 or 2) (de Hevia et al., 2008). A follow-up study showed that this perceptive illusion was indeed evoked by the numerical magnitude carried by the digits, as it was not observed when using other ordered symbols such as letters (Viarouge & de Hevia, 2013). Moreover, the authors did not observe a similar illusion when the participants had to estimate levels of brightness, supporting the idea of a privileged link between the representations of number and spatial extent.

As for non-symbolic numerical processing, visuospatial dimensions have been found to interfere with numerical processing, and

inhibitory control processes are thought to be a key mechanism in order to overcome these interferences.

17.3.1 Symbolic Numerical Stroop

The numerical Stroop task first described by Besner and Coltheart (1979) provides a well-documented example of how inhibition of misleading visuospatial dimensions is crucial for accurate symbolic numerical processing. In a typical number Stroop experiment, both numerical magnitude and physical size of the numbers display vary and participants are to select the larger number in either the numerical or the physical dimension. Trials may be congruent, where the numerically larger number is physically larger (e.g., 3, 5); incongruent, where the numerically larger number is physically smaller (e.g. 3, 5) and neutral, where the numbers are displayed in the same size (e.g. 3, 5) for the numerical comparison task and where the same numbers are displayed in different sizes (e.g. 3, 3) for the physical comparison. The size congruity effect refers to slower reaction times yielded by incongruent trials compared to congruent trials (Besner & Coltheart, 1979; Henik & Tzelgov, 1982; Tzelgov et al., 1992). Importantly, the size congruity effect occurs in both numerical (Besner & Coltheart, 1979; Foltz et al., 1984; Henik & Tzelgov, 1982) and physical comparison (Schwarz & Ischebeck, 2003; Tzelgov et al., 1992). The size congruity effect in numerical comparison tasks has been interpreted as reflecting the interference from misleading visuospatial dimensions in numerical processing of magnitude (Dehaene et al., 1993; Duncan & McFarland, 1980).

The size congruity effect can already be observed in first graders when they are asked to compare the magnitude of two Arabic numerals of different sizes (Girelli et al., 2000; Rubinsten et al., 2002). That is, from the age of six years, in order to correctly compare the magnitude of two Arabic numbers of different sizes, children must inhibit the misleading visuospatial dimension, here physical size.

Interestingly, Girelli et al. (2000) found that the size congruity effect in the physical comparison task was absent in first graders, emerged only in third grade and was highly significant in fifth graders. The authors concluded that the autonomous processing of numerical information arises gradually over the course of learning as children's numerical skills and arithmetic knowledge progress (Girelli et al., 2000). Practicing one dimension should increase its automaticity, which in turn would increase its interference effect when the dimension is task-irrelevant. Physical size is automatically processed at a very early age and thus is less sensitive to developmental changes, whereas access to numerical magnitude from number symbols becomes automatic only through extensive learning experience, even though young children are able to compare numbers along the conceptual dimension.

Rubinsten et al. (2002) found similar patterns of results in their study, however they proceeded to investigate both the interference (incongruent – neutral) and facilitation (congruent – neutral) components of the size congruency effect and tested children at the beginning and the end of grade one, as well as third graders, fifth graders and adults. The authors found that size congruity effect in the physical task does not appear at the beginning of first grade. However, eight months later the first graders displayed a significant size congruency effect as well as an interference effect but no facilitation effect. Third, fifth graders and adults were found to display both a facilitation and an interference effect. Notably, facilitation has been suggested to be an indicator of automaticity as the task-irrelevant numerical magnitude facilitates the judgement

of physical size in the congruent conditions (Rubinsten et al., 2002). Interference would reflect attentional processing (Posner & Petersen, 1990) as the irrelevant numerical magnitude does not match the physical size of the number. Size congruity effect appears at the end of first grade and is interference based, becoming automatic at a more advanced age (Rubinsten et al., 2002). In a later study, Bugden and Ansari (2011) observed a size congruity effect in the physical comparison task in both first and second grade participants. Importantly, both first and second graders displayed similar interference and facilitation effects. The grade one and two children were tested near the end of the year, this time period is thought to have provided sufficient experience to the children for them to achieve some automaticity in numerical information to generate both facilitation and interference effects (Bugden & Ansari, 2011). Interestingly, Zhou et al. (2007) revealed a size congruity effect in both the numerical and physical comparison task in Chinese kindergartners. Such early onset of automatic numerical processing, according to the authors, is thought to be due to cross-cultural differences in early mathematical acquisition. Chinese children appear to have a greater daily exposure to number and early mathematical training during preschool and at home (Ho & Fuson, 1998). Interestingly, in their study, Borgmann et al. (2011) examined the effect of congruency proportions in the numerical Stroop task. Manipulation in congruency proportion in Stroop tasks usually entails a change in magnitude of the congruency effect. Borgmann et al. (2011) found that the proportion of congruent items had a significant effect on the numerical comparison task but not the physical comparison task. The authors argue that these findings point toward an asymmetrical processing of numerical and physical size information, with physical size information processed before information pertaining to numerical size (Borgmann et al., 2011).

These studies demonstrate that the automaticity of number processing develops with age and schooling. The inconsistent findings regarding the developmental changes of the size congruity effect and its automaticity could be the result of the difference in age of testing and differences in exposure to mathematics. These studies have nonetheless highlighted the difference between intentional and automatic processing of numbers. Regardless of the exact developmental time point when numerical processing becomes automatic, these studies have systematically highlighted the importance of inhibiting the misleading visuospatial dimension for processing numerical magnitude. Indeed, children display from early school years a size congruity effect in the numerical comparison task even when number processing is intentional.

17.3.2 Decimal Comparison and Inhibition of Misleading Visuospatial Dimensions

In a recent study, Roell et al. (2019a) investigated whether the interference between spatial and numerical processing extends to more complex arithmetic such as decimal number comparison. They focused on decimal number, as children and even educated adults have difficulty in comparing decimal numbers when the smallest decimal number has the greatest number of digits (3.453 versus 3.6) (Lortie-Forgues et al., 2015; Moskal & Magone, 2000; Resnick et al., 1989; Roche, 2005; Sackur-Grisvard & Léonard, 1985). So far, studies have mainly attributed this difficulty to a whole number bias, that is, an overgeneralization of whole number properties to rational numbers (Durkin & Rittle-Johnson, 2012; Resnick et al., 1989; Sackur-Grisvard &

Léonard, 1985; Vamvakoussi et al., 2012). The whole number bias consists of using a property of whole numbers, such as 'the greater the number of digits, the greater its magnitude', to compare decimal numbers in which the smallest one has the greatest number of digits after the decimal point (e.g., 3.453 versus 3.6) (Sackur-Grisvard & Léonard, 1985; Vamvakoussi et al., 2012; Van Dooren et al., 2015). However, a negative priming study in twelve-year-old adolescents recently demonstrated that the comparison of the magnitude of two decimal numbers in which the smallest decimal number has the greatest number of digits (3.453 versus 3.6) relies not only on the inhibition of the property of whole numbers such as the 'greater the number of digits, the greater its magnitude', but also on the inhibition of the physical lengths of the decimal numbers per se (Roell et al., 2017).

The authors examined (a) whether comparing the magnitude of two decimal numbers in which the smallest one has the greater number of digits after the decimal point and thus is the longest one (3.453 versus 3.6) requires one to inhibit non-numerical continuous dimensions, such as the lengths of the decimal numbers, not only in twelve-year-old adolescents but also in adults and (b) whether the inhibition of non-numerical continuous dimensions when comparing decimal numbers is specific to space, consistent with the functional overlap between the areas processing numbers and spatial extent in the IPS (see Cohen Kadosh et al., 2008 for a review), or extends to other non-numerical continuous dimensions such as luminance. To do so, they designed a negative priming task. In Roell et al.'s (2019a) study, adolescents and adults performed a negative priming task in which they were asked to compare the magnitude of two decimal numbers, the length of two lines or the luminance of two circles. Each trial consisted of a prime item followed by a probe item. Participants compared, on the prime item, the magnitude of two decimal numbers and later, on the probe item, the length of two lines (Line block) or the luminance of two circles (Luminance block). In the test condition, the probe items were preceded by a pair of decimal numbers in which the smallest number had the greatest number of digits after the decimal point and thus was the longest (e.g., 3.453 versus 3.6, a context in which the length of the decimal numbers interferes with their magnitude). In the control condition, the probe items were preceded by a pair of decimal numbers with the same number of decimal places and thus the same length (e.g., 3.389 versus 3.589, a context in which length is neither congruent nor incongruent with the magnitude of the decimal numbers to be compared).

Consistent with previous studies (Desmet et al., 2010; Resnick et al., 1989; Roell et al., 2017, 2019b; Sackur-Grisvard & Léonard, 1985; Stacey et al., 2001; Steinle & Stacey, 2003), the authors observed that participants required more time to compare the magnitude of two decimal numbers when the smallest one has the greatest number of digits after the decimal point (e.g., 3.453 versus 3.6) than when the two decimal numbers have the same number of decimal places (3.389 versus 3.589). Crucially, in the Line block, participants were less efficient at comparing the length of two lines after having compared the magnitude of two decimal numbers where the smallest one had the greatest number of digits after the decimal point (e.g., 3.453 versus 3.6, a context that requires one to inhibit the length of the numbers to compare their magnitude) than after having compared the magnitude of two decimal numbers with the same number of decimal places, (e.g., 3.389 versus 3.589, a context in which length neither interferes with nor facilitates the magnitude comparison). These findings suggest that the difficulty in comparing the magnitude of decimal numbers

is in part due to the difficulty of inhibiting the length of the numbers when it interferes with their magnitude, such as in a context in which the smallest decimal number has the largest number of digits (e.g., 3.453 versus 3.6).

These results show that, in addition to a whole number bias in decimal comparison (Sackur-Grisvard & Léonard, 1985; Vamvakoussi et al., 2012; Van Dooren et al., 2015), performances in this task are also impacted by a perceptual bias due to the interference between the magnitude of the numbers to be compared and their physical length.

The authors posit that such perceptual bias results from the progressive co-opting of neural circuits dedicated to the processing of non-numerical magnitudes, specifically spatial extent, for numerical cognition (Dehaene & Cohen, 2007). Interestingly, participants' responses to another continuous dimension of magnitude, luminosity, were not affected by the preceding decimal comparison. In the Luminance block, participants did not differ in their performance when comparing the luminance of two circles after having compared two decimal numbers where the smallest one had the greatest number of digits after the decimal point (e.g., 3.453 versus 3.6) or after comparing two decimal numbers with the same number of decimal places (e.g., 3.389 versus 3.589). These results are in line with previous studies questioning the existence of a shared system for the representation of different dimensions of magnitude. In particular, our results are consistent with the idea of shared but distinct representational systems with more overlap between some dimensions, such as number and spatial extent, and less overlap with others, such as luminance (de Hevia et al., 2012; Pinel et al., 2004; Viarouge & de Hevia, 2013).

One hypothesis is that neuronal recycling mechanisms are at the root of this overlap. Human mathematics would build from foundational concepts (space, time and number) by progressively co-opting cortical areas whose prior organization fits with cultural needs (Dehaene & Cohen, 2007). The Operational Momentum (OM) effect has been interpreted as a good example of neuronal recycling, as it is thought to be the result of the reuse of cortical circuits in the posterior superior parietal lobule (PSPL). OM describes a systematic bias, overestimating outcomes of simple addition and underestimating the outcome of subtraction problems (Knops et al., 2009a, 2009b, 2013; McCrink et al., 2007). Knops et al. (2009a, 2009b) were able to show that performing mental arithmetic, such as subtraction and addition, induces spatial biases (e.g., biases toward left-located responses when performing subtractions, and right-located responses when performing additions). Additionally, they demonstrated that these spatial biases recruit the same neural network in the PSPL involved in updating spatial information during saccadic eye movements (Knops et al., 2009a). In this study, the authors trained a multivariate classifier to distinguish between leftward and rightward saccades from brain activation measured in the PSPL. The classifier was subsequently able, without further training, using the left versus right saccade classification, to successfully differentiate between addition and subtraction trials whether performed with symbolic or non-symbolic material. These findings were interpreted by the authors as demonstrating that mental arithmetic superimposes on a parietal circuitry originally associated with spatial coding (Knops et al., 2009a). A similar mechanism could account for the cost of handling a length/numerical magnitude interference when comparing decimal numbers on the subsequent length-comparison task observed in our study. Indeed, the negative priming effect reported in Roell et al.'s (2019a) study, only when the probes required a length comparison

but not when they required a luminance comparison, suggests that neural circuits for processing non-numerical dimensions of magnitude such as space but not luminance might be co-opted, not only during the acquisition of simple mathematical skills but also during more complex ones such as symbolic decimal number processing. Mathematical learning could induce neuronal recycling in the IPS, that is, neurons originally dedicated to the processing of continuous non-numerical dimensions of magnitude could be co-opted to process numbers. As such, pre-existing properties of the neurons being recycled could induce such errors as those observed in decimal comparison, and inhibitory control might be a crucial mechanism in correcting errors induced by the neuronal recycling process. This hypothesis is in keeping with findings showing that overcoming systematic errors in reading, specifically mirror generalization errors (confusing 'b' for 'd' or 'p' for 'q'), relies on the capacity to inhibit the original function (here the mirror generalization process) of the recycled neurons in the left ventral occipito-temporal cortex (Ahr et al., 2016; Borst et al., 2015). Similarly, we suggest that decimal comparison errors may in part result from an interference between numerical and spatial magnitudes, which could itself originate in the functional overlap of the areas processing numbers and spatial extent in the IPS.

17.3.3 Neuroimaging Studies

It has been suggested that the size congruity effect in the numerical stroop task may be due to the fact that numerical and non-numerical comparison tasks share common cognitive mechanisms (Kaufmann et al., 2005; Marshuetz et al., 2000; Walsh, 2003). Kaufmann et al. (2005) examined the neural correlates of the size congruity effect in a symbolic numerical Stroop task. When comparing incongruent trials (e.g., 3 5) to congruent trials (e.g., 3 5), Kaufmann et al. (2005) observed a greater activation in fronto-parietal areas in incongruent trials. Activations related to both the numerical and physical comparison tasks were observed at the level of the anterior cingulate cortex (ACC), the dorsolateral prefrontal cortex (DLPFC) as well as the left and right precuneus and the middle and inferior frontal gyrus (Kaufmann et al., 2005). Studies investigating the classic word Stroop task have reliably found a stronger activation for incongruent trials in the ACC (Adleman et al., 2002; Pardo et al., 1990; Peterson et al., 2002) as well as the dorsolateral prefrontal cortex (DLPFC) (Bench et al., 1993; Pardo et al., 1990). Indeed, the ACC and the DLPC have been found to play a significant role in cognitive control (MacDonald, 2000). According to the conflict-monitoring theory (Botvinick, 2007; Botvinick et al., 2001) the role of the dorsal ACC is to signal conflict in information processing to the cognitive control system supported through the DLPFC. It has been conjectured that the cognitive control system will increase the activation of task-relevant information and inhibit task-irrelevant information, such as misleading visuospatial dimensions, to resolve the information processing conflict (Egner & Hirsch, 2005). The strong relationship between cognitive control efficiency and quantitative anatomical characteristics of the ACC, such as cortical thickness (Westlye et al., 2011), surface area (Fjell et al., 2012) and gray matter volume (Takeuchi et al., 2012) but also qualitative characteristics that are stable over time, such as sulcal morphometry (Borst et al., 2014; Cachia et al., 2016; Tissier et al., 2018) suggests that the ACC is one of the core structures responsible for inhibitory control. Ansari et al. (2006) found similar brain activation patterns in adults to Kaufmann et al. (2005). They also found that the DLPFC and the ACC were modulated by stimulus congruency in their numerical word Stroop task.

Kaufmann et al. (2006) aimed to extend their findings in adults (Kaufmann et al., 2005) to the developing brain by subjecting a group of eight-to-twelve-year-olds to the same stimuli and testing procedure.

Surprisingly, when comparing incongruent trials to congruent trials no activations became significant in the numerical condition. These results are highly surprising as the behavioural data did show a significant congruity effect for the numerical task. Moreover, physical size has been reliably shown to be a very salient stimulus feature (Henik & Tzelgov, 1982). In the physical comparison task, the congruity effect yielded left-sided activations in the inferior and middle frontal regions (extending to the DLPFC), in the inferior and medial occipital regions and in the posterior lobe of the cerebellum.

Building on Kaufmann et al.'s (2005, 2006) studies, Wood et al. (2009) wished to examine more precisely the impact of age on the neural correlates of inhibitory control in the numerical Stroop task. To do so, the authors used the same paradigm as Kaufmann et al.'s (2006) study with three different age groups (children of same age as Kaufman et al.'s study, young adults and elderly participants). Using a conjunction analysis, they were able to observe the brain areas commonly activated by all age groups: the left premotor cortex, the left IPS and the right lateral cerebellum. Activation in these regions was not modulated by age. The authors suggest that the cognitive functions subserved by these areas remain relatively constant throughout the life span. The DLPFC was not found to be activated in the conjunction analysis, suggesting its role when processing interference changes with age. Indeed, as for Kaufmann et al. (2005, 2006), Wood et al. found that children and adults recruit partially distinct fronto-parietal networks in response to inhibitory control. Children activated the DLPFC bilaterally and the anterior portions of the left parietal cortex whilst adults activated the left ACC, the right premotor cortex, left posterior parietal and right IPS. Maturation of the cortical circuits could offer a possible explanation for such a difference (Fair et al., 2009; Wood et al., 2009). According to Fair et al. (2009), the involvement and the functional connection of the fronto-parietal and cingulate structures is less proficient in children than in teenagers or adults.

Although children and elderly participants were significantly slower and less accurate than young adults, the behavioural effects of congruity were comparable across all groups in Wood et al.'s study. Relative to children, elderly participants needed to activate the DLPFC bilaterally, the left middle temporal gyrus, and the left middle cerebellum significantly more in order to reach the same efficiency in inhibitory control. Interestingly, children's poor performance in interference control was associated with weak DLPFC activation whereas comparable performance in elderly participants was accompanied by very strong DLPFC activation. Bub et al. (2006) have suggested that greater Stroop interference in children may not be due to a lack of ability to inhibit the relevant information but rather a failure to maintain the task set. This is in line with the lower levels of DLPFC activation observed in children, as the DLPFC has been found to be involved in maintenance of items in working-memory (Diamond & Goldman-Rakic, 1989; Dubois et al., 1994) as well as response selection (Hadland et al., 2001). Furthermore, it is well known that due to its late structural maturation the prefrontal cortex in children is still not fully operational (Diamond, 2000), whereas these regions are susceptible to ageing effects (Townsend et al., 2006). Wood et al.

(2009) suggest that poor interference/inhibitory control in children is most likely attributable to weak prefrontal recruitment, whereas in elderly participants, poor inhibitory control would be associated with compensatory mechanisms (e.g., higher DLPFC activation) necessary for keeping a certain level of cognitive function.

In their study, Pinel et al. (2004) explored the impact of other visuospatial dimensions on numerical comparison, examining not only the impact of physical size on number processing but also luminance. Participants were asked to perform three comparison tasks: a symbolic number comparison task in which participants compared the magnitude of two Arabic digits, a size comparison task in which they compared the size of two digits, and a luminance comparison task in which they compared the luminance of two digits. The same items were presented in all three comparison tasks, i.e., two digits were displayed on the screen that vary in numerical magnitude, physical size and luminance (e.g., 2 7), and participants were asked to focus on one of the three dimensions (i.e., number, size or luminance). Thus, in certain items, one (or two) of the continuous quantities could interfere with the comparison to perform on the third continuous quantity. For instance, in the number comparison task when presented with the following item (2 7), size is congruent with numerical magnitude (i.e., the greater digit is the taller one) but incongruent with luminance (i.e., the taller digit is the darker one, assuming that greater is associated with brighter; but see Smith & Sera, 1992 for evidence of a reversed association between brightness and magnitude). Thus, the interference between one dimension and the others could be estimated. Pinel et al. (2004) provided evidence of an interference (a) between size and number processing, (b) between size and luminance processing, but (c) not between luminance and number processing. In addition, the extent to which these three dimensions (i.e., number, size and luminance) interfered with each other was related to the degree of overlap of the brain activations elicited by these dimensions (Lammertyn et al., 2002). The activations elicited by number and size dimensions overlapped in the anterior horizontal segment of the IPS, while the activations elicited by size and luminance overlapped in the posterior part of the IPS and the ventral occipito-temporal cortex. Importantly, no overlap of activation was found for the luminance and number dimensions. Pinel and colleagues' findings point toward the existence of distinct but overlapping systems of representations of numerical and non-numerical dimensions of magnitude (see also Vogel et al., 2013) with more overlap between the number and space dimensions than between number and luminance (but see Cohen Kadosh et al., 2008). It is important to note that, in a similar study, Cohen Kadosh et al. (2008) did not find the same pattern of brain activation. They found that the right IPS exhibited activity modulation as a function of the interaction between luminance and numerical magnitude, independent of the comparison type. The difference in results might be due to the fact that Cohen Kadosh et al. (2008) only manipulated two dimensions in their task, numerical and luminance magnitude, whereas Pinel et al. (2004) manipulated three: physical size, numerical value and luminance level.

17.4 Conclusion

The representations of number and space are strongly related, as evidenced by multiple behavioural studies showing number/space interactions, and neuroimaging studies revealing overlap between brain regions involved in the processing of numerical and visuospatial information. We wish to claim here that, from early non-symbolic numerical abilities to formal, symbolic arithmetic, the development of numerical cognition relies in part on the ability to handle the possible interferences occurring between number and space. We further propose that inhibitory control is a key mechanism that allows children to overcome these interferences, both in order to develop their sense of the numerosity of a set of objects, and also later on during math education, in order to focus on the numerical dimension of an arithmetic problem when number conflicts with space-based heuristics.

This view of numerical development has important implications regarding math achievement and education, by suggesting a central role of executive functions and more specifically inhibitory control in the development of math abilities. Several authors have put forward the importance of executive functions for education in general. The studies reviewed here suggest that this could be particularly relevant for math education, and in particular for the development of numerical representations. Regarding early numerical abilities such as numerical estimation and comparison, some authors have posited that children's ability to handle the interference between number and visuospatial dimensions was a better predictor of math achievement than the precision of the numerical representation itself (Fuhs & McNeil, 2013; Gilmore et al., 2013, but see Keller & Libertus, 2015). Consistently, a study on a large group of children in their early school years covering a large range of achievement levels showed that dyscalculic children had specific difficulties in the incongruent trials of a non-symbolic numerical comparison task, and that performance in the incongruent trials was predictive of math achievement across all achievement levels (Wilkey et al., 2020). These studies suggest we should pay particular attention to the specific contexts in which number conflicts with visuospatial dimensions when teaching mathematics.

Several questions remain open regarding the inhibitory control processes at play in the development of arithmetic. First, we would like to stress here that this chapter focuses on specific contexts in which visuospatial dimensions conflict with number, but many other contexts are likely to require inhibitory control in arithmetic (see Blair et al., 2008 for a review). We previously mentioned the case of the whole number bias which can lead to errors when comparing decimal numbers, but which has also been shown to induce errors in the comparison of fractions, when children rely solely on a comparison of the numerators (DeWolf & Vosniadou, 2015; Gabriel et al., 2013; Resnick et al., 1989; Vamvakoussi et al., 2012; Van Hoof et al., 2013). We also know that inhibition can be required to block irrelevant strategies in counting in the context of verbal problems (e.g., when 'more' is used in the wording of a subtraction problem), or multi-digit subtractions including a zero. Studies have also demonstrated the automatic activation of incorrect number facts that need to be inhibited in order to find the correct solution of an arithmetic operation (Lubin et al., 2013, 2016).

Another question is that of the characterization of the inhibitory control processes involved in arithmetic. In particular, recent studies have started to investigate the question of the specificity of the inhibitory control processes. Is there a number-specific inhibitory control that allows children to ignore irrelevant dimensions of magnitude in order to focus on the numerical aspects of their environment? Some recent studies have started to argue for such a number-specific cognitive control (Wilkey et al., 2020). Characterizing the executive processes involved in mathematical cognition and their developmental trajectories, especially throughout school years,

appears fundamental in order to better adapt teaching methods to children's needs.

References

Adleman, N. E., Menon, V., Blasey, C. M., White, C. D., Warsofsky, I. S., Glover, G. H., & Reiss, A. L. (2002). A developmental fMRI study of the Stroop color-word task. *NeuroImage*, *16*, 61–75.

Ahr, E., Houdé, O., & Borst, G. (2016). Inhibition of the mirror generalization process in reading in school-aged children. *Journal of Experimental Child Psychology*, *145*, 157–165.

Aïte, A., Berthoz, A., Vidal, J., Roëll, M., Zaoui, M., Houdé, O., & Borst, G. (2016). Taking a third-person perspective requires inhibitory control: Evidence from a developmental negative priming study. *Child Development*, *87*, 1825–1840.

Amalric, M., & Dehaene, S. (2016). Origins of the brain networks for advanced mathematics in expert mathematicians. *Proceedings of the National Academy of Sciences (USA)*, *113*, 4909–4917.

Anobile, G., Cicchini, G. M., & Burr, D. C. (2014). Separate mechanisms for perception of numerosity and density. *Psychological Science*, *25*, 265–270.

Anokhin, A. P., Heath, A. C., & Myers, E. (2004). Genetics, prefrontal cortex, and cognitive control: A twin study of event-related brain potentials in a response inhibition task. *Neuroscience Letters*, *368*, 314–318.

Ansari, D., Fugelsang, J. A., Dhital, B., & Venkatraman, V. (2006). Dissociating response conflict from numerical magnitude processing in the brain: An event-related fMRI study. *NeuroImage*, *32*, 799–805.

Aron, A. R., Robbins, T. W., & Poldrack, R. A. (2004). Inhibition and the right inferior frontal cortex. *Trends in Cognitive Sciences*, *8*, 170–177.

Bench, C. J., Frith, C. D., Grasby, P. M., Friston, K. J., Paulesu, E., Frackowiak, R. S. J., & Dolan, R. J. (1993). Investigations of the functional anatomy of attention using the Stroop test. *Neuropsychologia*, *31*, 907–922.

Besner, D., & Coltheart, M. (1979). Ideographic and alphabetic processing in skilled reading of English. *Neuropsychologia*, *17*, 467–472.

Blair, C., Knipe, H., & Gamson, D. (2008). Is there a role for executive functions in the development of mathematics ability? *Mind, Brain, and Education*, *2*, 80–89.

Blair, C., & Razza, R. P. (2007). Relating effortful control, executive function, and false belief understanding to emerging math and literacy ability in kindergarten. *Child Development*, *78*, 647–663.

Borgmann, K., Fugelsang, J., Ansari, D., & Besner, D. (2011). Congruency proportion reveals asymmetric processing of irrelevant physical and numerical dimensions in the size congruity paradigm. *Canadian Journal of Experimental Psychology/Revue Canadienne de Psychologie Expérimentale*, *65*, 98–104.

Borst, G., Ahr, E., Roell, M., & Houdé, O. (2015). The cost of blocking the mirror-generalization process in reading: Evidence for the role of inhibitory control in discriminating letters with lateral mirror-image counterparts. *Psychonomic Bulletin & Review*, *22*, 228–234.

Borst, G., Cachia, A., Vidal, J., Simon, G., Fischer, C., Pineau, A., . . . Houdé, O. (2014). Folding of the anterior cingulate cortex partially explains inhibitory control during childhood: A longitudinal study. *Developmental Cognitive Neuroscience*, *9*, 126–135.

Borst, G., Poirel, N., Pineau, A., Cassotti, M., & Houdé, O. (2013a). Inhibitory control efficiency in a Piaget-like class-inclusion task in school-age children and adults: A developmental negative priming study. *Developmental Psychology*, *49*, 1366–1374.

Borst, G., Simon, G., Vidal, J., & Houdé, O. (2013b). Inhibitory control and visuo-spatial reversibility in Piaget's seminal number conservation task: A high-density ERP study. *Frontiers in Human Neuroscience*, *7*, 920.

Botvinick, M. M. (2007). Conflict monitoring and decision making: Reconciling two perspectives on anterior cingulate function. *Cognitive, Affective, & Behavioral Neuroscience*, *7*, 356–366.

Botvinick, M. M., Braver, T. S., Barch, D. M., Carter, C. S., & Cohen, J. D. (2001). Conflict monitoring and cognitive control. *Psychological Review*, *108*, 624–652.

Brainerd, C. J., & Reyna, V. F. (2001). Fuzzy-trace theory: Dual processes in memory, reasoning, and cognitive neuroscience. *Advances in Child Development and Behavior*, *28*, 41–100.

Bub, D. N., Masson, M. E. J., & Lalonde, C. E. (2006). Cognitive control in children: Stroop interference and suppression of word reading. *Psychological Science*, *17*, 351–357.

Bugden, S., & Ansari, D. (2011). Individual differences in children's mathematical competence are related to the intentional but not automatic processing of Arabic numerals. *Cognition*, *118*, 32–44.

Bull, R., & Scerif, G. (2001). Executive functioning as a predictor of children's mathematics ability: Inhibition, switching, and working memory. *Developmental Neuropsychology*, *19*, 273–293.

Cachia, A., Borst, G., Tissier, C., Fisher, C., Plaze, M., Gay, O., . . . Raznahan, A. (2016). Longitudinal stability of the folding pattern of the anterior cingulate cortex during development. *Developmental Cognitive Neuroscience*, *19*, 122–127.

Cappelletti, M., Didino, D., Stoianov, I., & Zorzi, M. (2014). Number skills are maintained in healthy ageing. *Cognitive Psychology*, *69*, 25–45.

Cappelletti, M., Lee, H. L., Freeman, E. D., & Price, C. J. (2010). The role of right and left parietal lobes in the conceptual processing of numbers. *Journal of Cognitive Neuroscience*, *22*, 331–346.

Chomsky, N. (2006). *Language and Mind* (3rd ed.). Cambridge: Cambridge University Press.

Clayton, S., & Gilmore, C. (2015). Inhibition in dot comparison tasks. *ZDM: The International Journal on Mathematics Education*, *47*, 759–770.

Cohen Kadosh, R., Cohen Kadosh, K., & Henik, A. (2008). When brightness counts: The neuronal correlate of numerical-luminance interference. *Cerebral Cortex*, *18*, 337–343.

Cragg, L., & Gilmore, C. (2014). Skills underlying mathematics: The role of executive function in the development of mathematics proficiency. *Trends in Neuroscience and Education, 3,* 63–68.

Dakin, S. C., Tibber, M. S., Greenwood, J. A., Kingdom, F. A. A., & Morgan, M. J. (2011). A common visual metric for approximate number and density. *Proceedings of the National Academy of Sciences (USA), 108,* 19552–19557.

Daurignac, E., Houdé, O., & Jouvent, R. (2006). Negative priming in a numerical Piaget-like task as evidenced by ERP. *Journal of Cognitive Neuroscience, 18,* 730–736.

de Hevia, M. D., Girelli, L., Bricolo, E., & Vallar, G. (2008). The representational space of numerical magnitude: Illusions of length. *The Quarterly Journal of Experimental Psychology, 61,* 1496–1514.

de Hevia, M. D., Vanderslice, M., & Spelke, E. S. (2012). Cross-dimensional mapping of number, length and brightness by preschool children. *PLoS ONE, 7,* e35530.

De Neys, W., Lubin, A., & Houdé, O. (2014). The smart nonconserver: Preschoolers detect their number conservation errors. *Child Development Research, 2014,* 1–7.

De Neys, W., & Vanderputte, K. (2011). When less is not always more: Stereotype knowledge and reasoning development. *Developmental Psychology, 47,* 432–441.

Defever, E., Reynvoet, B., & Gebuis, T. (2013). Task- and age-dependent effects of visual stimulus properties on children's explicit numerosity judgments. *Journal of Experimental Child Psychology, 116,* 216–233.

Dehaene, S. (2011). *The Number Sense: How the Mind Creates Mathematics* (Rev. and updated ed). New York: Oxford University Press.

Dehaene, S., Bossini, S., & Giraux, P. (1993). The mental representation of parity and number magnitude. *Journal of Experimental Psychology: General, 122,* 371.

Dehaene, S., & Cohen, L. (2007). Cultural recycling of cortical maps. *Neuron, 56,* 384–398.

Dehaene, S., Dehaene-Lambertz, G., & Cohen, L. (1998). Abstract representations of numbers in the animal and human brain. *Trends in Neurosciences, 21,* 355–361.

Dehaene, S., Izard, V., Spelke, E., & Pica, P. (2008). Log or linear? Distinct intuitions of the number scale in western and Amazonian indigene cultures. *Science, 320,* 1217–1220.

Dempster, F. N. (1992). The rise and fall of the inhibitory mechanism: Toward a unified theory of cognitive development and aging. *Developmental Review, 12,* 45–75.

Desmet, L., Grégoire, J., & Mussolin, C. (2010). Developmental changes in the comparison of decimal fractions. *Learning and Instruction, 20,* 521–532.

DeWind, N. K., Adams, G. K., Platt, M. L., & Brannon, E. M. (2015). Modeling the approximate number system to quantify the contribution of visual stimulus features. *Cognition, 142,* 247–265.

DeWind, N. K., & Brannon, E. M. (2012). Malleability of the approximate number system: Effects of feedback and training. *Frontiers in Human Neuroscience, 6,* 68.

DeWolf, M., & Vosniadou, S. (2015). The representation of fraction magnitudes and the whole number bias reconsidered. *Learning and Instruction, 37,* 39–49.

Diamond, A. (2000). Close interrelation of motor development and cognitive development and of the cerebellum and prefrontal cortex. *Child Development, 71,* 44–56.

Diamond, A., & Goldman-Rakic, P. S. (1989). Comparison of human infants and rhesus monkeys on Piaget's AB task: Evidence for dependence on dorsolateral prefrontal cortex. *Experimental Brain Research, 74,* 24–40.

Dillon, M. R., Huang, Y., & Spelke, E. S. (2013). Core foundations of abstract geometry. *Proceedings of the National Academy of Sciences (USA), 110,* 14191–14195.

Dormal, V., & Pesenti, M. (2009). Common and specific contributions of the intraparietal sulci to numerosity and length processing. *Human Brain Mapping, 30,* 2466–2476.

Dubois, B., Verin, M., Teixera-Ferreira, C., Thierry, A. M., Glowinski, J., Goldman-Rakic, P. S., & Christen, Y. (1994). *Motor and Cognitive Functions of the Prefrontal Cortex.* Berlin: Springer.

Duncan, E. M., & McFarland, C. E. (1980). Isolating the effects of symbolic distance, and semantic congruity in comparative judgments: An additive-factors analysis. *Memory & Cognition, 8*, 612–622.

Durkin, K., & Rittle-Johnson, B. (2012). The effectiveness of using incorrect examples to support learning about decimal magnitude. *Learning and Instruction, 22*, 206–214.

Egner, T., & Hirsch, J. (2005). Cognitive control mechanisms resolve conflict through cortical amplification of task-relevant information. *Nature Neuroscience, 8*, 1784–1790.

Espy, K. A., McDiarmid, M. M., Cwik, M. F., Stalets, M. M., Hamby, A., & Senn, T. E. (2004). The contribution of executive functions to emergent mathematic skills in preschool children. *Developmental Neuropsychology, 26*, 465–486.

Fair, D. A., Cohen, A. L., Power, J. D., Dosenbach, N. U. F., Church, J. A., Miezin, F. M., . . . Petersen, S. E. (2009). Functional brain networks develop from a 'local to distributed' organization. *PLoS Computational Biology, 5*, e1000381.

Fjell, A. M., Walhovd, K. B., Brown, T. T., Kuperman, J. M., Chung, Y., Hagler, D. J., . . . Gruen, J. (2012). Multimodal imaging of the self-regulating developing brain. *Proceedings of the National Academy of Sciences (USA), 109*, 19620–19625.

Foltz, G. S., Poltrock, S. E., & Plotts, G. R. (1984). Mental comparison of size and magnitude: Size congruity effects. *Journal of Experimental Psychology: Learning, Memory, and Cognition, 10*, 442–453.

Fuhs, M. W., & McNeil, N. M. (2013). ANS acuity and mathematics ability in preschoolers from low-income homes: Contributions of inhibitory control. *Developmental Science, 16*, 136–148.

Fuhs, M. W., McNeil, N. M., Kelley, K., O'Rear, C., & Villano, M. (2016). The role of non-numerical stimulus features in approximate number system training in preschoolers from low-income homes. *Journal of Cognition and Development, 17*, 737–764.

Gabriel, F. C., Szucs, D., & Content, A. (2013). The development of the mental representations of the magnitude of fractions. *PLoS ONE, 8*, e80016.

Gebuis, T., & Gevers, W. (2011). Numerosities and space; indeed a cognitive illusion! A reply to de Hevia and Spelke (2009). *Cognition, 121*, 248–252.

Gebuis, T., Herfs, I. K., Kenemans, J. L., De Haan, E. H. F., & Van der Smagt, M. J. (2009). The development of automated access to symbolic and non-symbolic number knowledge in children: An ERP study. *European Journal of Neuroscience, 30*, 1999–2008.

Gebuis, T., Kenemans, J. L., de Haan, E. H. F., & van der Smagt, M. J. (2010). Conflict processing of symbolic and non-symbolic numerosity. *Neuropsychologia, 48*, 394–401.

Gebuis, T., & Reynvoet, B. (2012). The interplay between nonsymbolic number and its continuous visual properties. *Journal of Experimental Psychology. General, 141*, 642–648.

Gebuis, T., & Reynvoet, B. (2013). The neural mechanisms underlying passive and active processing of numerosity. *Neuroimage, 70*, 301–307.

Gelman, R. (1972). Logical capacity of very young children: Number invariance rules. *Child Development, 43*, 75.

Gilmore, C., Attridge, N., Clayton, S., Cragg, L., Johnson, S., Marlow, N., . . . Inglis, M. (2013). Individual differences in inhibitory control, not non-verbal number acuity, correlate with mathematics achievement. *PLoS ONE, 8*, e67374.

Gilmore, C., Cragg, L., Hogan, G., & Inglis, M. (2016). Congruency effects in dot comparison tasks: Convex hull is more important than dot area. *Journal of Cognitive Psychology (Hove, England), 28*, 923–931.

Gilmore, C. K., McCarthy, S. E., & Spelke, E. S. (2010). Non-symbolic arithmetic abilities and mathematics achievement in the first year of formal schooling. *Cognition, 115*, 394–406.

Girelli, L., Lucangeli, D., & Butterworth, B. (2000). The development of automaticity in accessing number magnitude. *Journal of Experimental Child Psychology, 76*, 104–122.

Hadland, K. A., Rushworth, M. F. S., Passingham, R. E., Jahanshahi, M., & Rothwell, J. C. (2001). Interference with performance of a response selection task that has no working memory component: An rTMS comparison of the dorsolateral prefrontal and medial frontal cortex. *Journal of Cognitive Neuroscience, 13*, 1097–1108.

Halberda, J., Mazzocco, M. M. M., & Feigenson, L. (2008). Individual differences in non-verbal number acuity correlate with maths achievement. *Nature, 455*, 665–668.

Harris, I. M., & Miniussi, C. (2003). Parietal lobe contribution to mental rotation demonstrated with rTMS. *Journal of Cognitive Neuroscience, 15*, 315–323.

Henik, A., & Tzelgov, J. (1982). Is three greater than five: The relation between physical and semantic size in comparison tasks. *Memory & Cognition, 10*, 389–395.

Ho, C. S.-H., & Fuson, K. C. (1998). Children's knowledge of teen quantities as tens and ones: Comparisons of Chinese, British, and American kindergartners. *Journal of Educational Psychology, 90*, 536–544.

Houdé, O. (2000). Inhibition and cognitive development: Object, number, categorization, and reasoning. *Cognitive Development, 15*, 63–73.

Houdé, O., & Borst, G. (2015). Evidence for an inhibitory-control theory of the reasoning brain. *Frontiers in Human Neuroscience, 9*, 148.

Houdé, O., & Guichart, E. (2001). Negative priming effect after inhibition of number/length interference in a Piaget-like task. *Developmental Science, 4*, 119–123.

Houdé, O., Pineau, A., Leroux, G., Poirel, N., Perchey, G., Lanoë, C., . . . Mazoyer, B. (2011). Functional magnetic resonance imaging study of Piaget's conservation-of-number task in preschool and school-age children: A neo-Piagetian approach. *Journal of Experimental Child Psychology, 110*, 332–346.

Houdé, O., Rossi, S., Lubin, A., & Joliot, M. (2010). Mapping numerical processing, reading, and executive functions in the developing brain: An fMRI meta-analysis of 52 studies including

842 children: Meta-analysis of developmental fMRI data. *Developmental Science, 13*, 876–885.

Hubbard, E. M., Piazza, M., Pinel, P., & Dehaene, S. (2005). Interactions between number and space in parietal cortex. *Nature Reviews Neuroscience, 6*, 435–448.

Hurewitz, F., Gelman, R., & Schnitzer, B. (2006). Sometimes area counts more than number. *Proceedings of the National Academy of Sciences (USA), 103*, 19599–19604.

Jacobs, J. E., & Klaczynski, P. A. (2002). The development of judgment and decision making during childhood and adolescence. *Current Directions in Psychological Science, 11*, 145–149.

Joliot, M., Leroux, G., Dubal, S., Tzourio-Mazoyer, N., Houdé, O., Mazoyer, B., & Petit, L. (2009). Cognitive inhibition of number/length interference in a Piaget-like task: Evidence by combining ERP and MEG. *Clinical Neurophysiology, 120*, 1501–1513.

Kaufmann, L., Koppelstaetter, F., Delazer, M., Siedentopf, C., Rhomberg, P., Golaszewski, S., . . . Ischebeck, A. (2005). Neural correlates of distance and congruity effects in a numerical Stroop task: An event-related fMRI study. *NeuroImage, 25*, 888–898.

Kaufmann, L., Koppelstaetter, F., Siedentopf, C., Haala, I., Haberlandt, E., Zimmerhackl, L.-B., . . . Ischebeck, A. (2006). Neural correlates of the number-size interference task in children. *NeuroReport, 17*, 587–591.

Keller, L., & Libertus, M. (2015). Inhibitory control may not explain the link between approximation and math abilities in kindergarteners from middle class families. *Frontiers in Psychology, 6*, 685.

Knops, A., Thirion, B., Hubbard, E. M., Michel, V., & Dehaene, S. (2009a). Recruitment of an area involved in eye movements during mental arithmetic. *Science, 324*, 1583–1585.

Knops, A., Viarouge, A., & Dehaene, S. (2009b). Dynamic representations underlying symbolic and nonsymbolic calculation: Evidence from the operational momentum effect. *Attention, Perception, & Psychophysics, 71*, 803–821.

Knops, A., Zitzmann, S., & McCrink, K. (2013). Examining the presence and determinants of operational momentum in childhood. *Frontiers in Psychology, 4*, 325.

Koechlin, E., Dehaene, S., & Mehler, J. (1997). Numerical transformations in five-month-old human infants. *Mathematical Cognition, 3*, 89–104.

Kok, A. (1999). Varieties of inhibition: Manifestations in cognition, event-related potentials and aging. *Acta Psychologica, 101*, 129–158. https://doi.org/10.1016/S0001-6918(99)00003-7

Konishi, S., Nakajima, K., Uchida, I., Kameyama, M., Nakahara, K., Sekihara, K., & Miyashita, Y. (1998). Transient activation of inferior prefrontal cortex during cognitive set shifting. *Nature Neuroscience, 1*, 80–84.

Lammertyn, J., Fias, W., & Lauwereyns, J. (2002). Semantic influences on feature-based attention due to overlap of neural circuits. *Cortex, 38*, 878–882.

Leibovich, T., Henik, A., & Salti, M. (2015). Numerosity processing is context driven even in the subitizing range: An fMRI study. *Neuropsychologia, 77*, 137–147.

Leibovich, T., Katzin, N., Harel, M., & Henik, A. (2017). From 'sense of number' to 'sense of magnitude': The role of continuous magnitudes in numerical cognition. *The Behavioral and Brain Sciences, 40*, e164.

Leroux, G., Joliot, M., Dubal, S., Mazoyer, B., Tzourio-Mazoyer, N., & Houdé, O. (2006). Cognitive inhibition of number/length interference in a Piaget-like task in young adults: Evidence from ERPs and fMRI. *Human Brain Mapping, 27*, 498–509.

Leroux, G., Spiess, J., Zago, L., Rossi, S., Lubin, A., Turbelin, M.-R., . . . Joliot, M. (2009). Adult brains don't fully overcome biases that lead to incorrect performance during cognitive development: An fMRI study in young adults completing a Piaget-like task. *Developmental Science, 12*, 326–338.

Lortie-Forgues, H., Tian, J., & Siegler, R. S. (2015). Why is learning fraction and decimal arithmetic so difficult? *Developmental Review, 38*, 201–221.

Lubin, A., Rossi, S., Lanoë, C., Vidal, J., Houdé, O., & Borst, G. (2016). Expertise, inhibitory control and arithmetic word problems: A negative priming study in mathematics experts. *Learning and Instruction, 45*, 40–48.

Lubin, A., Simon, G., Houdé, O., & De Neys, W. (2015). Inhibition, conflict detection, and number conservation. *ZDM, 47*, 793–800.

Lubin, A., Vidal, J., Lanoë, C., Houdé, O., & Borst, G. (2013). Inhibitory control is needed for the resolution of arithmetic word problems: A developmental negative priming study. *Journal of Educational Psychology, 105*, 701–708.

Luna, B., Padmanabhan, A., & O'Hearn, K. (2010). What has fMRI told us about the development of cognitive control through adolescence? *Brain and Cognition, 72*, 101–113.

MacDonald, A. W. (2000). Dissociating the role of the dorsolateral prefrontal and anterior cingulate cortex in cognitive control. *Science, 288*, 1835–1838.

Marshuetz, C., Smith, E. E., Jonides, J., DeGutis, J., & Chenevert, T. L. (2000). Order information in working memory: FMRI evidence for parietal and prefrontal mechanisms. *Journal of Cognitive Neuroscience, 12*(suppl 2), 130–144.

McCrink, K., Dehaene, S., & Dehaene-Lambertz, G. (2007). Moving along the number line: Operational momentum in nonsymbolic arithmetic. *Attention, Perception, & Psychophysics, 69*, 1324–1333.

McNab, F., Leroux, G., Strand, F., Thorell, L., Bergman, S., & Klingberg, T. (2008). Common and unique components of inhibition and working memory: An fMRI, within-subjects investigation. *Neuropsychologia, 46*, 2668–2682.

Mehler, J., & Bever, T. G. (1967). Cognitive capacity of very young children. *Science, 158*, 141–142.

Miller, E. K. (2000). The prefrontal cortex and cognitive control. *Nature Reviews Neuroscience, 1*, 59–65.

Moskal, B. M., & Magone, M. E. (2000). Making sense of what students know: Examining the referents, relationships and modes students displayed in response to a decimal task. *Educational Studies in Mathematics, 43*, 313–335.

Nieuwenhuis, S., Yeung, N., van den Wildenberg, W., & Ridderinkhof, K. R. (2003). Electrophysiological correlates of anterior cingulate function in a go/no-go task: Effects of response conflict and trial type frequency. *Cognitive, Affective, & Behavioral Neuroscience, 3,* 17–26.

Nys, J., & Content, A. (2012). Judgement of discrete and continuous quantity in adults: Number counts! *Quarterly Journal of Experimental Psychology, 65,* 675–690.

Nys, J., Ventura, P., Fernandes, T., Querido, L., Leybaert, J., & Content, A. (2013). Does math education modify the approximate number system? A comparison of schooled and unschooled adults. *Trends in Neuroscience and Education, 2,* 13–22.

Odic, D., Hock, H., & Halberda, J. (2014). Hysteresis affects approximate number discrimination in young children. *Journal of Experimental Psychology. General, 143,* 255–265.

Odic, D., Libertus, M. E., Feigenson, L., & Halberda, J. (2013). Developmental change in the acuity of approximate number and area representations. *Developmental Psychology, 49,* 1103–1112.

Pardo, J. V., Pardo, P. J., Janer, K. W., & Raichle, M. E. (1990). The anterior cingulate cortex mediates processing selection in the Stroop attentional conflict paradigm. *Proceedings of the National Academy of Sciences (USA), 87,* 256–259.

Peterson, B. S., Kane, M. J., Alexander, G. M., Lacadie, C., Skudlarski, P., Leung, H.-C., . . . Gore, J. C. (2002). An event-related functional MRI study comparing interference effects in the Simon and Stroop tasks. *Cognitive Brain Research, 13,* 427–440.

Piaget, J. (1952). *The Child's Conception of Number.* London: Routledge and Kegan Paul (original in French, Piaget, J., & Szeminska, A., 1941).

Piaget, J. (1964). Part I: Cognitive development in children: Piaget development and learning. *Journal of Research in Science Teaching, 2,* 176–186.

Piaget, J. (1968). Quantification, conservation, and nativism. *Science, 162,* 976–979.

Piazza, M., De Feo, V., Panzeri, S., & Dehaene, S. (2018). Learning to focus on number. *Cognition, 181,* 35–45.

Piazza, M., Izard, V., Pinel, P., Le Bihan, D., & Dehaene, S. (2004). Tuning curves for approximate numerosity in the human intraparietal sulcus. *Neuron, 44,* 547–555.

Piazza, M., Pica, P., Izard, V., Spelke, E. S., & Dehaene, S. (2013). Education enhances the acuity of the nonverbal approximate number system. *Psychological Science, 24,* 1037–1043.

Pica, P., Lemer, C., Izard, V., & Dehaene, S. (2004). Exact and approximate arithmetic in an Amazonian indigene group. *Science, 306,* 499–503.

Pinel, P., Piazza, M., Le Bihan, D., & Dehaene, S. (2004). Distributed and overlapping cerebral representations of number, size, and luminance during comparative judgments. *Neuron, 41,* 983–993.

Poirel, N., Borst, G., Simon, G., Rossi, S., Cassotti, M., Pineau, A., & Houdé, O. (2012). Number conservation is related to children's prefrontal inhibitory control: An fMRI study of a Piagetian task. *PLoS ONE, 7,* e40802.

Posner, M., & Petersen, S. E. (1990). The attention system of the human brain. *Annual Review of Neuroscience, 13,* 25–42.

Resnick, L. B., Nesher, P., Leonard, F., Magone, M., Omanson, S., & Peled, I. (1989). Conceptual bases of arithmetic errors: The case of decimal fractions. *Journal for Research in Mathematics Education, 20,* 8.

Roche, A. (2005). Longer is larger – Or is it? *Australian Primary Mathematics Classroom, 10,* 11–16.

Roell, M., Viarouge, A., Hilscher, E., Houdé, O., & Borst, G. (2019a). Evidence for a visuospatial bias in decimal number comparison in adolescents and in adults. *Scientific Reports, 9,* 14770.

Roell, M., Viarouge, A., Houdé, O., & Borst, G. (2017). Inhibitory control and decimal number comparison in school-aged children. *PLoS ONE, 12,* e0188276.

Roell, M., Viarouge, A., Houdé, O., & Borst, G. (2019b). Inhibition of the whole number bias in decimal number comparison: A developmental negative priming study. *Journal of Experimental Child Psychology, 177*, 240–247.

Rousselle, L., & Noël, M.-P. (2008). The development of automatic numerosity processing in preschoolers: Evidence for numerosity-perceptual interference. *Developmental Psychology, 44*, 544–560.

Rubinsten, O., Henik, A., Berger, A., & Shahar-Shalev, S. (2002). The development of internal representations of magnitude and their association with Arabic numerals. *Journal of Experimental Child Psychology, 81*, 74–92.

Sackur-Grisvard, C., & Léonard, F. (1985). Intermediate cognitive organizations in the process of learning a mathematical concept: The order of positive decimal numbers. *Cognition and Instruction, 2*, 157–174.

Schwarz, W., & Ischebeck, A. (2003). On the relative speed account of number-size interference in comparative judgments of numerals. *Journal of Experimental Psychology: Human Perception and Performance, 29*, 507–522.

Siegler, R. S. (1995). How does change occur: A microgenetic study of number conservation. *Cognitive Psychology, 28*, 225–273.

Siegler, R. S. (1998). *Emerging Minds: The Process of Change in Children's Thinking*. New York: Oxford University Press.

Simon, T. J., Hespos, S. J., & Rochat, P. (1995). Do infants understand simple arithmetic? A replication of Wynn (1992). *Cognitive Development, 10*, 253–269.

Smith, L. B., & Sera, M. D. (1992). A developmental analysis of the polar structure of dimensions. *Cognitive Psychology, 24*, 99–142.

Soltesz, F., Szucs, D., & Szucs, L. (2010). Relationships between magnitude representation, counting and memory in 4- to 7-year-old children: A developmental study. *Behavioral and Brain Functions, 6*, 13.

Sophian, C., & Chu, Y. (2008). How do people apprehend large numerosities? *Cognition, 107*, 460–478.

Spelke, E. S., & Kinzler, K. D. (2007). Core knowledge. *Developmental Science, 10*, 89–96.

St Clair-Thompson, H. L., & Gathercole, S. E. (2006). Executive functions and achievements in school: Shifting, updating, inhibition, and working memory. *Quarterly Journal of Experimental Psychology, 59*, 745–759.

Stacey, K., Helme, S., & Steinle, V. (2001). Confusions between decimals, fractions and negative numbers: A consequence of the mirror as a conceptual metaphor in three different ways. *PME Conference, 4*, 4–217.

Starkey, P., & Cooper, R. (1980). Perception of numbers by human infants. *Science, New Series, 210*, 1033–1035.

Starkey, P., Spelke, E., & Gelman, R. (1983). Detection of intermodal numerical correspondences by human infants. *Science, 222*, 179–181.

Starr, A., Libertus, M. E., & Brannon, E. M. (2013). Infants show ratio-dependent number discrimination regardless of set size. *Infancy, 18*, 927–941.

Steinle, V., & Stacey, K. (2003). Grade-related trends in the prevalence and persistence of decimal misconceptions. *International Group for the Psychology of Mathematics Education, 4*, 259–266.

Szucs, D., Devine, A., Soltesz, F., Nobes, A., & Gabriel, F. (2013a). Developmental dyscalculia is related to visuo-spatial memory and inhibition impairment. *Cortex; a Journal Devoted to the Study of the Nervous System and Behavior, 49*, 2674–2688.

Szűcs, D., Nobes, A., Devine, A., Gabriel, F. C., & Gebuis, T. (2013b). Visual stimulus parameters seriously compromise the measurement of approximate number system acuity and comparative effects between adults and children. *Frontiers in Psychology, 4*, 444.

Takeuchi, H., Taki, Y., Sassa, Y., Hashizume, H., Sekiguchi, A., Nagase, T., ... Kawashima, R. (2012). Regional gray and white matter volume associated with Stroop interference: Evidence from voxel-based morphometry. *NeuroImage, 59*, 2899–2907.

Tibber, M. S., Greenwood, J. A., & Dakin, S. C. (2012). Number and density discrimination rely on a common metric: Similar psychophysical effects of size, contrast, and divided attention. *Journal of Vision*, *12*, 8.

Tipper, S. P. (2001). Does negative priming reflect inhibitory mechanisms? A review and integration of conflicting views. *The Quarterly Journal of Experimental Psychology Section A*, *54*, 321–343.

Tipper, S. P., Weaver, B., Cameron, S., Brehaut, J. C., & Bastedo, J. (1991). Inhibitory mechanisms of attention in identification and localization tasks: Time course and disruption. *Journal of Experimental Psychology: Learning, Memory, and Cognition*, *17*, 681–692.

Tissier, C., Linzarini, A., Allaire-Duquette, G., Mevel, K., Poirel, N., Dollfus, S., . . . Cachia, A. (2018). Sulcal polymorphisms of the IFC and ACC contribute to inhibitory control variability in children and adults. *eNeuro*, *5*.

Tokita, M., & Ishiguchi, A. (2010). How might the discrepancy in the effects of perceptual variables on numerosity judgment be reconciled? *Attention, Perception, & Psychophysics*, *72*, 1839–1853.

Townsend, J., Adamo, M., & Haist, F. (2006). Changing channels: An fMRI study of aging and cross-modal attention shifts. *NeuroImage*, *31*, 1682–1692.

Tzelgov, J., Meyer, J., & Henik, A. (1992). Automatic and intentional processing of numerical information. *Journal of Experimental Psychology: Learning, Memory, and Cognition*, *18*, 166–179.

Vamvakoussi, X., Van Dooren, W., & Verschaffel, L. (2012). Naturally biased? In search for reaction time evidence for a natural number bias in adults. *The Journal of Mathematical Behavior*, *31*, 344–355.

Van Dooren, W., Lehtinen, E., & Verschaffel, L. (2015). Unraveling the gap between natural and rational numbers. *Learning and Instruction*, *37*, 1–4.

Van Hoof, J., Lijnen, T., Verschaffel, L., & Van Dooren, W. (2013). Are secondary school students still hampered by the natural number bias? A reaction time study on fraction comparison tasks. *Research in Mathematics Education*, *15*, 154–164.

Viarouge, A., & de Hevia, M. D. (2013). The role of numerical magnitude and order in the illusory perception of size and brightness. *Frontiers in Psychology*, *4*, 484.

Viarouge, A., Houdé, O., & Borst, G. (2019). Evidence for the role of inhibition in numerical comparison: A negative priming study in 7- to 8-year-olds and adults. *Journal of Experimental Child Psychology*, *186*, 131–141.

Vogel, S. E., Grabner, R. H., Schneider, M., Siegler, R. S., & Ansari, D. (2013). Overlapping and distinct brain regions involved in estimating the spatial position of numerical and non-numerical magnitudes: An fMRI study. *Neuropsychologia*, *51*, 979–989.

Walsh, V. (2003). A theory of magnitude: Common cortical metrics of time, space and quantity. *Trends in Cognitive Sciences*, *7*, 483–488.

Westlye, L. T., Grydeland, H., Walhovd, K. B., & Fjell, A. M. (2011). Associations between regional cortical thickness and attentional networks as measured by the attention network test. *Cerebral Cortex*, *21*, 345–356.

Wilkey, E. D., Barone, J. C., Mazzocco, M. M. M., Vogel, S. E., & Price, G. R. (2017). The effect of visual parameters on neural activation during nonsymbolic number comparison and its relation to math competency. *NeuroImage*, *159*, 430–442.

Wilkey, E. D., Pollack, C., & Price, G. R. (2020). Dyscalculia and typical math achievement are associated with individual differences in number-specific executive function. *Child Development*, *91*, 596–619.

Wood, G., Ischebeck, A., Koppelstaetter, F., Gotwald, T., & Kaufmann, L. (2009). Developmental trajectories of magnitude processing and interference control: An fMRI study. *Cerebral Cortex*, *19*, 2755–2765.

Wynn, K. (1992). Addition and subtraction by human infants. *Nature*, *358*, 749–750.

Wynn, K. (1995). Infants possess a system of numerical knowledge. *Current Directions in Psychological Science*, *4*, 172–177.

Wynn, K. (1998). Psychological foundations of number: Numerical competence in human infants. *Trends in Cognitive Sciences, 2*, 296–303.

Wynn, K., Bloom, P., & Chiang, W.-C. (2002). Enumeration of collective entities by 5-month-old infants. *Cognition, 83*, B55–B62.

Xu, F., & Spelke, E. S. (2000). Large number discrimination in 6-month-old infants. *Cognition, 74*, B1–B11.

Zacks, J. M. (2008). Neuroimaging studies of mental rotation: A meta-analysis and review. *Journal of Cognitive Neuroscience, 20*, 31.

Zhou, X., Chen, Y., Chen, C., Jiang, T., Zhang, H., & Dong, Q. (2007). Chinese kindergartners' automatic processing of numerical magnitude in Stroop-like tasks. *Memory & Cognition, 35*, 464–470.

18 Developing Theory of Mind and Counterfactual Reasoning in Children

Josef Perner, Eugenia Kulakova, and Eva Rafetseder

The first part of this chapter focuses on the development of our theory of mind or folk psychology. The second part gives a brief overview of how counterfactual reasoning develops and how this development interacts with theory of mind development. In both parts our focus is on developmental research that speaks to basic issues: What is the nature of our folk psychology, its genetic or experiential basis, its kinship with executive control and pragmatics, and its cognitive mechanism? Is there an 'implicit' theory that even infants master? How does counterfactual reasoning differ from conditional reasoning and why should counterfactual reasoning be important for folk psychology? We examine what answers forty years of research have produced so far.

18.1 Theory of Mind

18.1.1 Forty Years of 'Theory of Mind': What Have We Learnt?

Our quick answer is 'no answers to the big questions, but interesting developmental detail'.

Our topic of investigation was christened in 1978 by Premack and Woodruff's provocative title, 'Does the chimpanzee have a theory of mind?' This gave rise to the theory that a theory is involved in mindreading. This original idea is enshrined in the term 'Theory of Mind'. But it need not be a theory and we thus sometimes use the less loaded term 'folk psychology'. Indeed, simulation theorists suggested that instead of using a theory we simulate other persons' mental states on our own mind. After forty years we still have no clear answer as to which process is used and when. We suggest paying attention again to these grand frameworks, especially since there are now more options on offer, like teleology and embodiment. The question of origin was dominated by nativism due to the increasing popularity of evolutionary psychology (Björklund, 2018) and fuelled by ever earlier evidence for theory of mind in infancy. Just how much infants understand is still hotly debated. In defence of nativism it was discovered that theory of mind and executive control are developmentally related. Another discovery was that earlier evidence can be mustered with indirect tests, suggesting that an 'implicit' theory precedes an explicit understanding. Unfortunately, the terms are just used descriptively when they should drive the theoretical analysis of the cognitive difference between implicit and explicit knowledge. Theory of mind also relates to language development, in particular, pragmatics, which provides an opportunity to investigate the common basis of these abilities. Finally, the question arises as to why counterfactual reasoning should have a central place in theory of mind development.

The work on this chapter was financially supported by the Austrian Science Fund Project 'FWF I 3518-G24' and by the Jacobs Foundation Fellowship 2017 1261 08.

18.1.2 The Grand Frameworks

'Theory of Mind' has become the label for our folk psychology: how we understand agents' intentional action and the workings of their mind. Its essentials can be demonstrated by the false belief story (Wimmer & Perner, 1983) about Mistaken Max:

Max puts his chocolate in the drawer, and leaves. He does not witness his mother moving it unexpectedly to the cupboard. On his return he is hungry and wants his chocolate. Where will he look for it?

According to the standard account, the child listening to this story has to engage in reasoning with reference to Max's mental states: 'Putting the chocolate into the drawer Max knows it's in there. But when it is unexpectedly transferred he'll keep thinking (false belief) it is still in the drawer. Now, (as I am being told) he wants to get his chocolate. So he will go to where he thinks it is: the drawer'.

The reason why such folk reasoning has been christened a 'theory' is the intuition that mental states are 'inner states' that cannot be observed but must be inferred,[1] and that they serve as theoretical terms in explaining and predicting behaviour. The theory that our folk psychology is a theory has been dubbed 'theory theory' (TT). TT is a body of knowledge of how given circumstances cause mental states, which in turn cause further mental states and/or behaviour. The knowledge consists of law-like generalizations of matters of fact, without consideration of people's justifying reasons for their actions. However, there are other views of how our folk psychology works.

'Simulation theory' (ST: Barlassina & Gordon, 2017; Gordon, 1986; Heal, 1986) claims that no theory is used but mental simulation. It is characterized by the absence of any existing knowledge about the mind. Instead, knowledge is gained by imagining oneself being in the other agent's situation, which triggers similar mental processes and action tendencies in one's own mind. This gained knowledge stems from one's own practical reasoning in the imagined situation and thus inherits the simulated agent's reasons for acting. Applied to Mistaken Max, simulation would proceed like this: 'I imagine being Max and imagine putting my chocolate into the drawer and then go out to play. On my return, where will I look for my chocolate? Naturally I should go to the drawer'. At that point the simulation stops and the child assigns the action tendency experienced while simulating Max to predict his actions.

Apart from the original work on simulation by Harris (1992), the few developmental studies that addressed the ST-TT distinction speak against simulation (Astington & Gopnik, 1988; Perner & Howes, 1992; Ruffman, 1996). However, data from early non-verbal action understanding suggest simulation use (Hauf & Prinz, 2005; Hauf et al., 2007), as infants' own action competence precedes their understanding of observed actions: Sommerville et al. (2005) enabled three-month-olds to manipulate Velcro surfaced objects by outfitting them with Velcro gloves, which made them interpret observed actions the way five-month-olds do (Woodward, 1998).

By and large, developmental research tacitly assumed TT. Some of its assumptions have come under scrutiny due to friction with action theory in the tradition of Anscombe (1957) and Davidson (1963). Anscombe defined intentional action as action with a

---

[1] This claim has been questioned by enactivist interaction theorists (Gallagher, 2007), who assume that infants understand others in terms of how they can interact with them. Mental states need not be inferred as they are deemed to be embodied in the interaction. It is unclear how exactly this is supposed to work for the false belief test.

good reason. TT has no place for such good reasons, as a central assumption is that the theory consists of law-like generalizations (Gopnik & Meltzoff, 1998). A simplified first-person version of the false belief scenario illustrates this point:

I put my sandwich in the drawer, and leave. On my return I am hungry and need something to eat. I go to the drawer.

When asked why I went to the drawer I will reply 'I haven't had anything to eat and have to get some food (objective goal) and I can get something from the drawer (objective fact)'. As good reasons for my action I offered objective facts that count in favour of my action (Scanlon, 1998), but no mental states, as TT would argue. There is the strong intuition that we see others act for the same kinds of reasons as we do ourselves. If we observe Max place his sandwich in the drawer, leave, and return hungry, we understand that he has good reasons to go to the drawer. And we therefore expect him to go there. After all, we treat Max as a rational being. If he wasn't rational we wouldn't know what to predict. Again, no mental states are part of this explanation based on reasons.

Explanation by reasons proceeds by means-ends reasoning: a worthwhile goal gives reason to act, and the facts that require a particular action to obtain the goal advocate that action. Because of its means–ends character, Perner and Roessler (2010) called it *teleology*. It differs from TT by assuming that people act like oneself for good objective reasons and not because their action is caused by their mental states. In this respect it is similar to ST (Gordon, 2001), where one presumably also uses reasons for deciding how to react when simulating. It differs from ST in that it doesn't require imagining oneself being in another agent's shoes and pretending to have this agent's beliefs and desires. Instead one reasons

from one's own perspective about what should happen (Max should not be hungry) and how to bring it about (Max should go to the drawer to get his sandwich and still his hunger).

Teleology captures our folk psychology better than TT if we agree that we treat others as rational agents who act for good reasons, and it works perfectly for cases where no misinformation or perspective differences are involved. This is the exact case in the false belief task, which puts a serious limitation on teleology. To close this explanatory gap, Perner and Roessler (2010) suggested using teleology counterfactually within other agents' perspectives (*teleology-in-perspective*): 'If his chocolate were still in the drawer, Mistaken Max would have good reason to go there to still his hunger. And we need to assume that Max will act as he should act if matters were as he thinks they are'. This makes counterfactual reasoning inherent in applying teleology in the false belief task. As we will see in Section 18.2, children's performance in different false belief tasks depends strictly on the level of counterfactual reasoning required, a finding that is difficult to accommodate for TT or ST.

18.1.3 Acquisition

Another pressing question concerns the origin of folk psychology. To what degree was it formed phylogenetically, and thus determined by our genes, and how much depends on ontogenetic experience in our lifetime?

18.1.3.1 Nativism

Through the rise of evolutionary psychology and the lack of a learning theory for concepts, it was argued that a theory of mind is so essential for humans, who are dependent on social interaction, that it must be innate. Leslie (1987, 1994) argued that mental concepts ('think', 'want', 'know') are innate and mature for active use around eighteen months of age with the emergence of pretend play. The ability to pretend is kin to counterfactual reasoning (Section 18.2) and understanding false beliefs. They all require distinguishing between what is true and what is assumed to be true. Leslie, therefore, had the problem to explain why children fail the false belief test until about four years old (Wellman et al., 2001), despite their earlier pretend play competence.

Several investigations tried to explain this developmental gap. To defend nativism, the core assumption is that the traditional false belief test poses unnecessary executive demands that prohibit younger children from expressing their knowledge about the mind. However, the evidence still leaves the original question unanswered, as the late mastery of the false belief task is not just a function of executive demands. Another line of argument bears on even earlier evidence of infants' sensitivity to false belief from 'implicit' tasks. The theoretically interesting question is whether these tasks show regular understanding earlier, or whether they tap into a different body of *implicit* knowledge. However, widespread problems replicating the early evidence are emerging (Section 18.1.6). A more recent argument focuses on the reliance on language and language-use (pragmatics) of the false belief test and whether it can explain the gap between early pretence and late mastery of the false belief test (Section 18.1.5).

18.1.3.2 Learning

The traditional alternative to innately specified knowledge is learning by experience. To acquire a theory of mind involves mastery of its constituent concepts like belief and desire. However, a general theory of concept learning is still lacking. A strong philosophical tradition is that concepts cannot be learnt on principle

and must be innately specified (Fodor, 1981). This issue is still far from resolved (Fodor, 2008; Margolis & Laurence, 2011), as shown by the discussion around Carey's (2009) claim that children acquire a genuinely new numerical insight with their understanding of the Cardinality principle around four years of age. Bayesian learning theorists have started to model theory of mind acquisition (Baker et al., 2017; Bello & Cassimatis, 2006; Stuhlmüller & Goodman, 2014) that also promises genuine concept acquisition through a rational learning process. Due to the complexity of this enterprise the modelling has to stay close to specific examples. One contribution empirical research could make is to provide more information about how theory of mind is represented in our minds, so that the modelling has a specification of what the learning is supposed to work on.

18.1.4 Executive Functions

Russell et al. (1991) found that passing the false belief task coincided with the ability to inhibit pointing to an object, when asked where that object was. This suggested that the false belief question was difficult because children could not inhibit answering with the chocolate's true location. Russell (1996) abandoned this view after finding that leaving children in the dark about the chocolate's new location did not bring any improvement. Only when the object is removed from the scene altogether ('disappear condition', Wimmer & Perner, 1983) do children produce more correct responses. The object's disappearance, however, might produce false positives: without a clear answer where Max should look for his chocolate children are more influenced by plausible cues, for example, where has Max seen his chocolate last, without actually inferring his belief. This is underlined by the fact that children who fail the traditional task still fail tasks that pose no evident inhibition problem. In Robinson and Mitchell's (1995) task children observe two identical looking twins put their ball into one of two locations. One twin leaves to get some milk while the other twin gets out the ball again, puts it into the other location, and leaves. They both return with their mother, who asks them to hand her their ball. Each twin goes to a different location. Which one had left earlier to get some milk? Children who failed the traditional belief task gave but a perfect guessing pattern on this question (Perner et al., 2002).

The link between theory of mind and executive function tasks consistently shows up in correlational studies, raising the question of whether they correlate because theory of mind tasks pose executive demands (expression account) or whether the relationship goes deeper. Powell and Carey (2017) went beyond correlation by depleting children's inhibitory power with a delay of gratification task which affected their responses on a subsequent belief task. This shows that inhibition plays a role in how well children can express their knowledge in the false belief task. It does not speak against a deeper relationship shown by the fact that performance on theory of mind tasks with high executive components correlate with executive measures as much as tasks with low or no executive component (Carlson et al., 2015). The consensus appears to be that the persistently found correlation goes beyond a mere problem of expression and reflects a deeper link (Devine & Hughes, 2014), with one playing a role in the emergence of the other (emergence or construction account). Russell (1996) held that executive control provides the foundations for developing a theory of mind. Alternatively, theory of mind might help understand and better control one's own mind (Perner & Lang, 1999; Wimmer, 1989). Longitudinal studies support the former theory.

This research emphasizes the need for a cognitive analysis of executive functioning that defines the features that are useful for theory of mind and common features that underlie the depletion phenomenon. The failure to inhibit wrong responses is not of the usual kind, where one is aware of having lost control and has given into temptation, e.g., peeking in the 'Marshmallow' test. On the contrary, children who fail the false belief task are convinced that their response is correct (Ruffman et al., 2001). The naïve question to ask is how the child's central executive knows which response or representation to inhibit. There must be some meta-intentional monitoring at work (Norman & Shallice, 1986; Perner, 1998). The observed correlations suggest that we can learn much by focusing our theoretical analysis on the cognitive commonalities between executive control and mental state attribution.

18.1.5 Language and Pragmatics

Just like the relationship with executive functions, the connection between general language skills and mindreading has been acknowledged for a long time. The false belief task is not only related to language in that the false belief question is necessarily verbal, but explicit false belief performance is also robustly correlated with general language skills (Milligan et al., 2007). In contrast, nonverbal tasks have generated some evidence for false belief understanding at younger ages (Scott & Baillargeon, 2017; but see Section 18.1.6 and Chapter 12). Semantically, the false belief question might not be particularly challenging. However, another aspect of language, pragmatic skills, has recently been emphasized as explanations of children's failure in explicit false belief tasks. The main idea is that children do not as much struggle with tracking and understanding Mistaken Max's belief, but rather fail because they misinterpret the experimenter's question.

Specifically, the pragmatic view stresses that in false belief tasks children are not only acting as spectators to the story but are also engaged in verbal communication with the experimenter. Communication can be considered a special form of interaction between agents. As the speaker's communicative goal is usually under-defined by the literal meaning of their utterance ('Have you seen my keys?'), children employ available non-literal information to infer the likely goal of the experimenter's question. For this they use – just as in the case of non-verbal actions – their assumption of rationality and relevance. Westra and Carruthers (2017) suggest that communication with adults usually focuses on cooperative and pedagogical goals. Children are thus more likely to assume that the experimenter is prompting them to help Mistaken Max, or that they are in a pedagogical situation and asked to display their knowledge about the true location of the displaced object. A question about a protagonist's mental state which the experimenter knows herself might be a less salient communicative goal for children to attribute to the experimenter.

Other accounts highlight the effort required to switch between observing the story from a detached perspective to engaging in a dialogue about it. Such a switch might distract children from the protagonists' mental states, instead guiding their attention to the knowledge shared with the experimenter, the object's true location (Helming et al., 2016). Modifications of the task which allow the child to remain in the observer's position and act out the protagonist's predicted behaviour seem to improve performance (Rubio-Fernández & Geurts, 2013; but see Garnham & Perner, 2001, and Priewasser et al., 2020). So do manipulations in which the experimenter addresses the false belief question to

themselves rather than to the child (He et al., 2011; Scott et al., 2012).

According to a classical Gricean account of communication, a fully-fledged theory of mind is required to understand the intention of the interlocutor (Grice, 1957). However, this view is at odds with the developmental reality, at least if theory of mind competence is equated with mastering the false belief task. Luckily, postulating early theory of mind competence is not the only way to embrace that young children can engage in communication and show pragmatic understanding. Minimalist requirement views overcome the problem by postulating an implicit notion of rationality, relevance, or teleology, which is sufficient to enable children to understand and engage in communicative acts (Breheny, 2006). Evidence that three-year-olds choose unfamiliar rather than known objects as the referent of a novel name has been interpreted as an early pragmatic effect of inferring speaker's intention – why introduce a novel word if an established name for the object already exists? (Diesendruck et al., 2003). However, only after four years are children flexible enough to overcome this pragmatic disambiguation to comply with other pragmatic task demands, such as selecting the familiar but edible object as the referent of the novel word, which the speaker intends to use as food (Haryu, 1991; Haryu & Imai, 1999). Notably, this ability correlates with false belief competence (Gollek & Doherty, 2016). Examples like these illustrate that the same communicative situation might pose different and even contradictory pragmatic demands, which seem to be mastered at different ages and might differ in their underlying cognitive mechanisms. Such observations resonate with interactionist accounts of language and mindreading (de Villiers, 2007), which suggest a bi-directional interrelation between language and mindreading and go beyond considering pragmatic constraints as mere obstacles of demonstrating false belief competence. As such, pragmatic accounts make valuable suggestions for potential methodological improvements by avoiding potential communicative ambiguity, yet they so far remain silent about the developmental trajectory of social cognition skills.

18.1.6 Early Sensitivity to False Belief: A Socioscientific Lesson

The nativist vision of an innate theory of mind was given great impetus by moving from direct test responses in the traditional false belief task to indirect indicators of understanding. In addition of asking children from which one of two doors a protagonist will emerge in search of an object, Clements and Perner (1994) observed children's eye gaze in anticipation of the protagonist's return. Most children as young as two years and eleven months looked at the door where the protagonist thought the object was, but answered the question with the door where the object was. Children of two and a half years showed no such dissociation. They looked at and answered with the door where the object was. When using a disappear condition (Section 18.1.4), anticipatory looking to the correct location was found in two-year-olds (Southgate et al., 2007). Using looking time in a violation of expectation study, the first signs of processing false beliefs was found at thirteen-to-fifteen months (Onishi & Baillargeon, 2005; Surian et al., 2007). Using interference of other's perspective on infants' looking time, even seven-month-olds were influenced by another agent's belief (Kovács et al., 2010), also shown at six months with neural activity measures (Kampis et al., 2015; Southgate & Vernetti, 2014). However, neural activation of the standard adult theory of mind network tends to emerge with passing the standard false belief task (Liu et al., 2009; Wiesmann et al., 2017).

At a 2017 ICPS-workshop in Vienna, Hannes Rakoczy and Louisa Kulke brought together researchers who had reported problems replicating such results. Table 18.1 summarizes a preliminary overview of successful and failed replications by Kulke and Rakoczy (2018), details of which can be found in a special edition of *Cognitive Development* (2018, Vol 46).

Table 18.1 shows that data from children younger than three years are difficult to replicate. A similar picture emerged from a recent meta-analysis (Barone et al., 2019). This is not to say that an early understanding does not exist, only that at present there is no reliable evidence for it (see also Chapter 12). The replication difficulties attest to the existence of effective but unknown experimental factors that happened to work favourably in the original studies but not when replication failed. The search for these factors has started (Baillargeon et al., 2018). Their effectiveness matters not only for replicability but also for the original interpretation, as illustrated here with three cases marked 'confound' in Table 18.1. In one case, Kulke et al. (2018) successfully replicated Low and Watts' (2013) version of Southgate et al.'s (2007) non-verbal anticipatory looking. Unfortunately, when the distracted agent turned her head back to the scene, it was always toward the box where she believed the object was. When this confound was resolved, children showed no looking preference. In another case, reaction time data from adults designed to validate the looking times of babies (Kovács et al., 2010) could be replicated by different research groups (Phillips et al., 2015). However, the effect was not due to adults' automatic representation of another agent's belief, but was driven by inconsistencies in the timing of an attention check. Thirdly, Buttelmann et al. (2009) reported that by eighteen months children's help with opening a box depended on their

Table 18.1. *Overview of replication success of early belief understanding studies from Kulke and Rakoczy (2018)*

Paradigm	Study	Age	Success/ Attempts	Commentary
Anticipatory Looking (verbal)	Clements and Perner (1994)	2 y 11 m	**7/7**	
Anticipatory Looking (non-verbal)	Southgate et al. (2007)	18 m	5/20	Confound
	Surian and Geraci (2012)	17 m	2/5	
	Low and Watts (2013)	3 y	**4/4**	
Violation of Expectation	Onishi and Baillargeon (2005)	14 m	4/9	Confound
	Träuble et al. (2010)	16 m	0/1	
	Schneider et al. (2012)	Adults	4/7	
	Kovács et al. (2010)	Adults	**4/4**	
		7 m	–	
Behavioural (helping)	Buttelmann et al. (2009)	18 m	1/7	Confound
	Southgate et al. (2010)	18 m	0/4	
Acting Out	Rubio-Fernandez and Guerts (2013)	2 y	0/4	
Brain Activity (EEG)	Southgate and Vernetti (2014)	6 m (μ)	–	
	Kampis et al. (2015)	7m	–	

understanding of the needy agent's beliefs. Several studies could not replicate this difference in helping behaviour. Only one study (Priewasser et al., 2018), designed with the help of the original authors, managed to just capture the effect. Yet, in a new condition the study showed that children's helping behaviour could also be explained by factors other than the agent's belief. This weakens the claim that the original difference is due to children's false belief understanding.

The replication crisis points at hidden factors that are necessary for replication but might simultaneously invalidate the original interpretation. More and careful investigation is needed to validate the findings of implicit false belief understanding.

18.1.7 Cognitive Analysis

Children's theory of mind competence develops. This can be due to changes in the theory of mind and/or changes in the ability to apply the theory. Both factors ask for a cognitive analysis. This chapter focuses on the *cognitive approach* which makes claims about subpersonal changes, that do not apply to the person but to cognitive processes or mechanisms (e.g., 'younger children's working memory is limited').

Leslie et al. (2004) proposed a mechanism of belief attribution consisting of a Theory of Mind Mechanism (ToMM) able to meta-represent beliefs and desires. It provides all possible beliefs that an agent might have in a given situation, for example, Max believes his chocolate is (1) in its original place or (2) in its current place. The different possibilities are then pruned by an inhibitory selection processor (SP), for example, it should inhibit belief (2). This theory has been used to test two models of how children solve avoidance–desire tasks where double inhibition is required. However intriguing this analysis is, it does not disclose the cognitive basis of the ToMM, of how it attributes and represents possible beliefs.

Apperly and Butterfill (2009; Butterfill & Apperly, 2013) proposed that children keep a memory of all facts and a separate memory of a subset of facts that were registered by another agent, for example, events that are encountered by the agent within his visual field. This subset is then used to predict what the agent will do. The registered facts function like beliefs but are not fully fledged beliefs. Adults and infants spontaneously show anticipatory looking (Section 18.1.6) when registered facts predict action as in the Clements and Perner (1994; Southgate et al., 2007) paradigm, but not when the agent's belief is based on confusion about identity, which involves understanding the intensionality or aspectuality[2] of belief (Low & Watts, 2013). This signature limit also applies to infants' early 'implicit' sensitivity to belief, but without an explanation of why we get earlier evidence from 'implicit' tasks than from the standard 'explicit' false belief task. Moreover, the theory does not provide an analysis of the fully fledged concept of belief that could accommodate the intensionality/aspectuality of belief.

A more encompassing mechanism has been proposed as mental files theory (Recanati, 2012). A mental file is a representation of an entity (object, person, etc.), its referent, which it tracks over time, recording all information about it. The notion of *coreferential files* is particularly important. If one hears of, for example, *Susi's teacher* and *Susi's aunt*, two files are deployed, one for each. When one finds out that they happen to be the same person, one can either *merge* the two files into one or *link* them. Linking leaves information collected when speaking about Susi's teacher separate from information collected when referring to her aunt, but the link makes information on one file (Susi's teacher is at school) available when one uses the other file to think about this person (Susi loves her aunt. Where is she? In school).

In an effort to explain persistent correlations between false belief tasks and alternative naming games (Doherty & Perner, 1998, 2020), Perner and Brandl (2005) suggested that we not only create different files[3] for an individual when it is named differently, but also in order to capture different perspectives of an object, for example, a *regular* file of Max's chocolate and its new location and a *vicarious*[4] file of his chocolate indexed to Max with the misinformation that the chocolate is still in its old location (see also Recanati (2012) on the resilient problems of the semantics of belief sentences).

Capturing different perspectives with co-referential files requires linking of the two files. The assumption that children cannot link co-referential files before four years provides an explanation of the developmental relation between alternative naming and false belief understanding. Younger children should therefore fail the false belief test and the alternative naming game (Perner & Leahy, 2016). A new prediction follows from this theory: before passing false belief tests children should have problems with identity statements ('Susi's teacher is her aunt'), which was confirmed in Perner et al., (2011).

Mental files theory can also explain why children have difficulties to account for the intensionality/aspectuality of belief (Apperly

---

[2] Intentionality or aspectuality of belief requires the understanding that an agent's belief about an object depends on the way in which the object is conceived. For instance, if I hear of Susi's teacher and her aunt I think of two people, even though they are the same person. I then see a person enter the school building and am told she is Susi's teacher. Then I know (and believe) that Susi's teacher is in the school building but I do not believe that her aunt is in there.

[3] They were talking of discourse referents (the linguists' versions of mental files: Karttunnen, 1976; Kamp, 1990)

[4] This is Recanati's (2012) term to indicate that these files are used vicariously for Max's files.

& Robinson, 1998; Russell, 1987) after they pass the false belief task. To show that passing the false belief task indexes children's acquisition of the concept of belief (including its intensionality), Rakoczy et al. (2015) attempted to show that the additional difficulty vanishes when unnecessary task features are eliminated. Perner et al. (2015; Huemer et al., 2018), however, showed that the additional difficulty with intensionality/aspectuality had not disappeared but re-emerged in a control condition. Mental files theory thus provides a subpersonal representational model from which testable predictions can be drawn. It also gives insight into how the concept of belief is implemented in representational procedures able to account for the 'belief like state' characterized by Butterfill and Apperly (2013) and the fuller concept of belief that incorporates the intensionality/aspectuality of belief.

Section 18.2 addresses the question of why counterfactual reasoning should be important for folk psychology. We begin with outlining how counterfactual reasoning differs from conditional reasoning and how children acquire this ability. We finish with evidence that teleology is used counterfactually within other agents' perspective in false belief tasks.

18.2 Counterfactual Reasoning

18.2.1 Counterfactual As a Special Case of Conditional Reasoning

Counterfactuals describe situations that could have possibly happened, but did not in actuality. Typically expressed as conditional statements of the form 'if p then q', counterfactuals are a particular kind of conditional where the information expressed in the antecedent p is 'either known or expected to be false' (Ginsberg, 1986, p. 35). Unlike other conditionals, counterfactuals elicit two representations, factual and counterfactual (Thompson

& Byrne, 2002), and handling such incompatibility requires enhanced cognitive resources (Ferguson & Cane, 2015; Kulakova et al., 2013). To reason counterfactually, one has to maintain representations of factual events, yet also manipulate them in line with the antecedent. In doing so, the reasoner stays as closely as possible to the actual world, only changing facts that depend on the counterfactual supposition (Edgington, 2011), and thereby adhering to the *nearest possible world constraint* (Lewis, 1973; Stalnaker, 1968). Some philosophers (e.g., Woodward, 2011) and developmental psychologists (e.g., Harris, 2000; Weisberg & Gopnik, 2013) are less restrictive in their definition of counterfactuals, also including pretence and future hypothetical reasoning (see Chapter 14). Irrespective of terminology, the fact that some, but not all, counterfactuals present challenges to young children (e.g., Rafetseder et al., 2010, 2013) and that future conditional questions are consistently easier than counterfactual questions (Beck et al., 2006; Riggs et al., 1998) asks for a refined approach.

To distinguish different types of reasoning applied by children who answer counterfactual questions, Rafetseder et al. (2013) used two conditions: in the one-track condition one puppet, Carol, dirtied the clean floor (see Harris et al., 1996); in the two-tracks condition Max and Carol dirtied the clean floor. In both conditions participants were asked the same counterfactual question 'If Carol had taken her dirty shoes off, would the floor be dirty or clean?' In the one-track condition almost all participants reasoned that the floor would be 'clean'. In the two-tracks condition, adults and older children reasoned that the floor would be 'dirty', while less than 20 per cent of the five-to-six-year-olds gave this answer.

There are two different theoretical positions about why children answer counterfactual tasks incorrectly. Some authors argue that counterfactual reasoning is brought about by improvements in executive functioning, specifically in inhibitory control (Beck et al., 2009), in cognitive flexibility (Burns et al., 2012), and in working memory (Drayton et al., 2011; Guajardo et al., 2009). In contrast, Rafetseder et al. (2010, 2013) argue that young children's problem with counterfactual tasks lies in their inability to follow the nearest possible world constraint. While *mature reasoning with counterfactuals* considers all features of the actual event that are causally and logically independent of the antecedent (e.g., Max still walked across the floor) and modifies everything causally and logically dependent on the antecedent (e.g., Carol's footprints have to be ignored), young children apply *basic reasoning with counterfactuals*, whereby they fail to follow this constraint. Like mature reasoners, they accept the antecedent to be true (Carol took her dirty shoes off), which suffices to compute the correct answer in the one-track condition. The two-tracks condition, however, additionally requires to hold fixed features that are independent of the antecedent, and children who fail to attend to causal dependencies (Nyhout et al., 2017) use basic strategies to construct the counterfactual world (for details see Leahy et al., 2014).

18.2.2 Acquisition

How is counterfactual reasoning acquired? An early indicator of counterfactual reasoning is pretend play (Buchsbaum et al., 2012; Leslie, 1987; Scott et al., 1999). Like for counterfactual reasoning, to engage in pretend play one has to represent the world as it is not. From around one and a half years children are able to pretend that a banana is a telephone. This raises the question of why children are able to engage in pretend play when they find it difficult to answer counterfactual questions until much later.

We can think of four possible answers: (1) Counterfactual questions are more demanding linguistically, phrased as if–then relations including a subjunctive. But from very early on children use words like 'would' to refer to hypothetical scenarios (Kuczaj & Daly, 1979) and are able to answer syntactically similar conditional questions (Beck et al., 2006). On the other hand, non-verbal alternatives that measure counterfactual emotions like regret or relief are not solved until five years (Weisberg & Beck, 2012), indicating that syntactic complexity may not cause the difference. (2) There is no need to integrate the identity of a banana into the pretend context of a telephone, despite representing both identities in parallel (Lillard, 1993). However, two and a half-year-olds are able to engage in complex pretend play, for example, Teddy pours pretend tea over a piece of chocolate. Although the chocolate is dry really, children claim that it is wet (Harris et al., 1993). The inference children draw in this case looks very much like the inference they draw when they reason counterfactually (i.e., 'If there had been tea in the pot, the chocolate would be wet', Perner, 2000, p. 386). They integrate the real world context (i.e., Teddy tilted the pot over the wooden block) into the pretend context (i.e., there is tea in the pot). (3) Pretend context supports children's mental imagination, which helps them reason with false propositions. Indeed, five-year-olds are more likely to reason from premises that run counter to what they believed to be true in the real world ('All cats bark') when it is presented in a pretend context (i.e., toy cats pretended to bark) rather than in a verbal context only (Dias & Harris, 1988). (4) A major difference is the time at which suppositions are introduced. In the pretend context, the pretend supposition is introduced at the beginning of the story, i.e., before an event unfolds, while counterfactual suppositions are introduced once the event has already happened. No study has yet investigated whether this factor explains the difference found between pretend play and counterfactual reasoning.

Other early indicators for children's understanding of counterfactuality are seen in their ability to imitate rationally and to understand 'almost'. When asked which horse almost fell off the table, two and a half-year-olds picked the horse at the edge of the table as opposed to the horse far away from the edge (Harris, 1997). However, children pass the task only at five years when they are given the choice between a horse at the edge and a horse that has already fallen to the floor (Beck & Guthrie, 2011). Rational imitation is also based on counterfactual reasoning by assessing what someone could have done differently (Paulus, 2012). Fourteen-months-olds use their head to turn on a lamp when they watch an adult do so with their hands free, but not with their hands occupied. In order for such imitation to be rational, children must realize that the adult could have acted differently in the hands free condition and thus must have had a good reason to use their head instead (Perner et al., 2004). Whether the head touch study shows rational imitation is, however, disputed (Paulus et al., 2011).

In sum, like for early false belief understanding, present evidence for early understanding of counterfactuality is not reliable and needs further investigation.

18.2.3 Counterfactuality in Theory of Mind

In the past two decades several studies suggested that counterfactuality is utilized in false belief reasoning (e.g., Riggs et al., 1998). Preschool-aged children's answers to false belief questions ('Where will Max look for his chocolate?') and counterfactual questions ('If mother had not baked a cake, where would the chocolate be?') are closely related, even when age, language skills, and executive functioning are controlled. False beliefs are counterfactual in that they contrast the known state of the world with something that is known to be false, yet is held true by somebody else (Section 18.1.3; although there are relevant differences, for example, counterfactuals are not believed to be true). Most evidence is correlational, and existing false belief tasks have not allowed for errors other than the reality bias. Recently, Rafetseder and Perner (2018) systematically varied the need to adhere to the nearest possible world constraint in counterfactual questions and build a false belief task that allowed for the same error types that are possible in counterfactual tasks. In the task, Ben makes blue footprints on the floor and either wipes them clean (one-track) or leaves the mess (two-tracks). Later, Sarah enters and adds red footprints. Mature reasoning with counterfactuals produces different answers to the counterfactual question (If Sarah had taken her dirty shoes off, what would the floor look like?) in the two conditions, 'clean' (one-track) and 'blue footprints' (two-tracks), while basic reasoning with counterfactuals produces the same answer 'clean' in both conditions. Answer types to counterfactual questions and false belief questions ('What does Ben think the floor looks like?') matched closely, and children gave much fewer correct answers to counterfactual and false belief questions of the two-tracks task, which requires adherence to the nearest possible world.

To explain the striking relation between false belief and counterfactual questions, domain general accounts focus on children's ability to inhibit what they know to be true (Beck et al., 2009) and their limited processing capacity (German & Nichols, 2003). Reducing such demands improves children's performance on false belief tasks (Robinson & Mitchell, 1995) and counterfactual tasks

(Beck et al., 2011). Yet, pre-school children are able to move away from what they know to be true and readily accept a different 'reality' in the context of pretence (Harris et al., 1993) and hypothetical reasoning (Beck et al., 2006). When inhibitory demands are kept constant, children still produce errors on some but not all counterfactual questions, and these errors do not always reflect a reality bias (Rafetseder et al., 2010). Pragmatic skills (Section 18.1.5) and information processing demands, that is, holding in mind and manipulating information, were also suggested to explain children's difficulties with false belief (Carlson et al., 2005) and counterfactual tasks (Drayton et al., 2011). Inferential complexity, however, only accounts for a small portion of performance differences on counterfactual tasks (Beck et al., 2010).

General frameworks of theory of mind, TT and ST (Section 18.1.2), face challenges to explain the relation between false belief and counterfactual tasks. TT does not predict that children, who make an error other than the reality bias on counterfactual questions, will make the same error on false belief questions. ST, in contrast, in its current form fails to address why a simulator should use counterfactual reasoning to arrive at another person's false belief, when in fact that person did not reason counterfactually herself to arrive at her mistaken belief.

Domain-specific accounts, adaptive modelling (for details see Peterson & Riggs, 1999) and teleology-in-perspective (Perner & Roessler, 2010) explicitly predict similar performance on both questions. Adaptive modelling assumes a common core process for counterfactual and false belief questions that explains the correlation, but fails to predict a difference in difficulty between the one- and two-tracks condition. Teleology-in-perspective, in contrast, assumes that reasoning with false belief is achieved by placing teleology into a counterfactual context. Perspective differences (e.g., what one knows but somebody else does not) function as the antecedent from which one either uses mature or basic reasoning with counterfactuals. Unlike adaptive modelling it leaves open which level of counterfactual reasoning, basic or mature, is used and can thus explain both, why children master only certain counterfactual and false belief questions at a particular age and why answers to counterfactual questions match answers to false belief questions.

18.3 Conclusion

We aimed at a forward-facing review. To steer future investigations, we focused on important questions about the cognitive basis of ToM that existing research has marginalized: Which grand framework is used, TT, ST, teleology? To what degree does children's evident increasing competence depend on factors extraneous to the theory like executive control and processing capacity or depend on genuine growth of their theory of mind? To answer these questions we need to know more about the cognitive basis of theory of mind and work on how basic conceptual structures can be learned. A useful insight is that theory of mind development concurs with other unfolding abilities, like executive function, language, pragmatics, and counterfactual reasoning. Instead of treating these as independent domains and asking which causes which, we advocate looking into shared cognitive structures in these domains.

References

Anscombe, G. E. M. (1957). *Intention*. Cambridge, MA: Harvard University Press.

Apperly, I. A., & Butterfill, S. A. (2009). Do humans have two systems to track beliefs and belief-like states? *Psychological Review, 116*, 953.

Apperly, I. A., & Robinson, E. (1998). Children's mental representation of referential relations. *Cognition, 67*, 287–309.

Astington, J. W., & Gopnik, A. (1988). Knowing you've changed your mind: Children's understanding of representational change. In J. W. Astington, P. L. Harris, & D. R. Olson (eds.), *Developing Theories of Mind* (pp. 193–206). Cambridge: Cambridge University Press.

Baillargeon, R., Buttelmann, D., & Southgate, V. (2018). Invited commentary: Interpreting failed replications of early false-belief findings: Methodological and theoretical considerations. *Cognitive Development, 46*, 112–124.

Baker, C. L., Jara-Ettinger, J., Saxe, R., & Tenenbaum, J. B. (2017). Rational quantitative attribution of beliefs, desires and percepts in human mentalizing. *Nature Human Behaviour, 1*, 0064.

Barlassina, L., & Gordon, R. M. (2017). Folk psychology as mental simulation. In E. N. Zalta (ed.), *The Stanford Encyclopedia of Philosophy* (Summer 2017 ed.). Available from https://plato.stanford.edu/entries/folkpsych-simulation/. Last accessed 4 August 2021.

Barone, P., Corradi, G., & Gomila, A. (2019). Infants' performance in spontaneous-response false belief tasks: A review and meta-analysis. *Infant Behavior and Development, 57*, 101350.

Beck, S. R., Carroll, D. J., Brunsdon, V. E., & Gryg, C. K. (2011). Supporting children's counterfactual thinking with alternative modes of responding. *Journal of Experimental Child Psychology, 108*, 190–202.

Beck, S. R., & Guthrie, C. (2011). Almost thinking counterfactually: Children's understanding of close counterfactuals. *Child Development, 82*, 1189–1198.

Beck, S. R., Riggs, K. J., & Gorniak, S. L. (2009). Relating developments in children's counterfactual thinking and executive functions. *Thinking & Reasoning, 15*, 337–354.

Beck, S. R., Riggs, K. J., & Gorniak, S. L. (2010). The effect of causal chain length on counterfactual conditional reasoning. *British Journal of Developmental Psychology, 28*, 505–521.

Beck, S. R., Robinson, E. J., Carroll, D. J., & Apperly, I. A. (2006). Children's thinking about counterfactuals and future hypotheticals as possibilities. *Child Development, 77*, 413–426.

Bello, P., & Cassimatis, N. (2006). Developmental Accounts of Theory-of-Mind Acquisition: Achieving Clarity via Computational Cognitive Modeling. *Paper presented at the Proceedings of the Annual Meeting of the Cognitive Science Society*, Vancouver, Canada.

Björklund, D. F. (2018). A metatheory for cognitive development (or 'Piaget is dead' revisited). *Child Development, 89*, 2288–2302.

Breheny, R. (2006). Communication and folk psychology. *Mind & Language, 21*, 74–107.

Buchsbaum, D., Bridgers, S., Weisberg, D. S., & Gopnik, A. (2012). The power of possibility: Causal learning, counterfactual reasoning, and pretend play. *Philosophical Transactions of the Royal Society of London B: Biological Sciences, 367*, 2202–2212.

Burns, P., Riggs, K. J., & Beck, S. R. (2012). Executive control and the experience of regret. *Journal of Experimental Child Psychology, 111*, 501–515.

Buttelmann, D., Carpenter, M., & Tomasello, M. (2009). Eighteen-month-old infants show false belief understanding in an active helping paradigm. *Cognition, 112*, 337–342.

Butterfill, S. A., & Apperly, I. A. (2013). How to construct a minimal theory of mind. *Mind & Language, 28*, 606–637.

Carey, S. (2009). Where our number concepts come from. *The Journal of Philosophy, 106*, 220.

Carlson, S. M., Claxton, L. J., & Moses, L. J. (2015). The relation between executive function and theory of mind is more than skin deep. *Journal of Cognition and Development, 16*, 186–197.

Carlson, S. M., Wong, A., Lemke, M., & Cosser, C. (2005). Gesture as a window on children's beginning understanding of false belief. *Child Development, 76*, 73–86.

Clements, W. A., & Perner, J. (1994). Implicit understanding of belief. *Cognitive Development, 9*, 377–395.

Davidson, D. (1963). Actions, reasons, and causes. *The Journal of Philosophy*, *60*, 685–700.

De Villiers, J. (2007). The interface of language and theory of mind. *Lingua*, *117*, 1858–1878.

Devine, R. T., & Hughes, C. (2014). Relations between false belief understanding and executive function in early childhood: A meta-analysis. *Child Development*, *85*, 1777–1794.

Dias, M. G., & Harris, P. L. (1988). The effect of make-believe play on deductive reasoning. *British Journal of Developmental Psychology*, *6*, 207–221.

Diesendruck, G., Markson, L., & Bloom, P. (2003). Children's reliance on creator's intent in extending names for artifacts. *Psychological Science*, *14*, 164–168.

Doherty, M. J., & Perner, J. (1998). Metalinguistic awareness and theory of mind: Just two words for the same thing? *Cognitive Development*, *13*, 279–305.

Doherty, M. J., & Perner, J. (2020). Mental files: Developmental integration of dual naming and theory of mind. *Developmental Review*, *56*, 100909.

Drayton, S., Turley-Ames, K. J., & Guajardo, N. R. (2011). Counterfactual thinking and false belief: The role of executive function. *Journal of Experimental Child Psychology*, *108*, 532–548.

Edgington, D. (2011). Causation first: Why causation is prior to counterfactuals. In C. Hoerl, T. McCormack, & S. R. Beck (eds.), *Understanding Counterfactuals, Understanding Causation: Issues in Philosophy and Psychology* (pp. 230–241). Oxford: Oxford University Press.

Ferguson, H. J., & Cane, J. E. (2015). Examining the cognitive costs of counterfactual language comprehension: Evidence from ERPs. *Brain Research*, *1622*, 252–269.

Fodor, J. A. (1981). The current state of the innateness controversy. In J. A. Fodor (ed.), *Representations* (pp. 257–316). Cambridge, MA: MIT Press.

Fodor, J. A. (2008). *LOT 2: The Language of Thought Revisited*. Oxford: Oxford University Press.

Gallagher, S. (2007). Simulation trouble. *Social Neuroscience*, *2*, 353–365.

Garnham, W. A., & Perner, J. (2001). Actions really do speak louder than words – but only implicitly: Young children's understanding of false belief in action. *British Journal of Developmental Psychology*, *19*, 413–432.

German, T. P., & Nichols, S. (2003). Children's counterfactual inferences about long and short causal chains. *Developmental Science*, *6*, 514–523.

Ginsberg, M. L. (1986). Counterfactuals. *Artificial Intelligence*, *30*, 35–79.

Gollek, C., & Doherty, M. J. (2016). Metacognitive developments in word learning: Mutual exclusivity and theory of mind. *Journal of Experimental Child Psychology*, *148*, 51–69.

Gopnik, A., & Meltzoff, A. N. (1998). *Words, Thoughts, and Theories (Learning, Development, and Conceptual Change)*. Cambridge, MA: MIT Press.

Gordon, R. M. (1986). Folk psychology as simulation. *Mind & Language*, *1*, 158–171.

Gordon, R. M. (2001). Simulation and reason explanation: the radical view. *Philosophical Topics*, *29*, 175–192.

Grice, H. P. (1957). Meaning. *The Philosophical Review*, *66*, 377–388.

Guajardo, N. R., Parker, J., & Turley-Ames, K. (2009). Associations among false belief understanding, counterfactual reasoning, and executive function. *British Journal of Developmental Psychology*, *27*, 681–702.

Harris, P. L. (1992). From simulation to folk psychology: The case for development. *Mind & Language*, *7*, 120–144.

Harris, P. L. (1997). On realizing what might have happened instead. *Polish Quarterly of Developmental Psychology*, *3*, 161–176.

Harris, P. L. (2000). *The Work of the Imagination: Understanding Children's Worlds*. Malden, MA: Wiley-Blackwell.

Harris, P. L., German, T., & Mills, P. (1996). Children's use of counterfactual thinking in causal reasoning. *Cognition*, *61*, 233–259.

Harris, P. L., Kavanaugh, R. D., Wellman, H. M., & Hickling, A. K. (1993). Young children's understanding of pretense. *Monographs of the*

Society for Research in Child Development, 58, i–107.

Haryu, E. (1991). A developmental study of children's use of 'mutual exclusivity' and context to interpret novel words. *The Japanese Journal of Educational Psychology, 39,* 11–20.

Haryu, E., & Imai, M. (1999). Controlling the application of the mutual exclusivity assumption in the acquisition of lexical hierarchies. *Japanese Psychological Research, 41,* 21–34.

Hauf, P., Aschersleben, G., & Prinz, W. (2007). Baby do–baby see!: How action production influences action perception in infants. *Cognitive Development, 22,* 16–32.

Hauf, P., & Prinz, W. (2005). The understanding of own and others' actions during infancy: 'You-like-Me' or 'Me-like-You'? *Interaction Studies, 6,* 429–445.

He, Z., Bolz, M., & Baillargeon, R. (2011). False-belief understanding in 2.5-year-olds: Evidence from violation-of-expectation change-of-location and unexpected-contents tasks. *Developmental Science, 14,* 292–305.

Heal, J. (1986). Replication and functionalism. In J. Butterfield (ed.), *Language, Mind, and Logic* (pp. 135–150). Cambridge: Cambridge University Press.

Helming, K. A., Strickland, B., & Jacob, P. (2016). Solving the puzzle about early belief-ascription. *Mind & Language, 31,* 438–469.

Huemer, M., Perner, J., & Leahy, B. (2018). Mental files theory of mind: When do children consider agents acquainted with different object identities? *Cognition, 171,* 122–129.

Kamp, H. (1990). Prolegomena to a structural account of belief and other attitudes. In C. A. Anderson (ed.), *Propositional Attitudes: The Role of Content in Logic, Language and Mind* (pp. 27–90). Stanford, CA: Center for study of language and information, Lecture Notes Series.

Kampis, D., Parise, E., Csibra, G., & Kovács, Á. M. (2015). Neural signatures for sustaining object representations attributed to others in preverbal human infants. *Proceedings of the Royal Society B, 282,* 20151683.

Karttunen, L. (1976). Discourse referents. In J. D. McCawley (ed.), *Notes from the Linguistic*

Underground (Syntax and Semantics, vol. 7, pp. 363–385). New York: Academic Press.

Kovács, Á. M., Téglás, E., & Endress, A. D. (2010). The social sense: Susceptibility to others' beliefs in human infants and adults. *Science, 330,* 1830–1834.

Kuczaj, S. A., & Daly, M. J. (1979). The development of hypothetical reference in the speech of young children. *Journal of Child Language, 6,* 563–579.

Kulakova, E., Aichhorn, M., Schurz, M., Kronbichler, M., & Perner, J. (2013). Processing counterfactual and hypothetical conditionals: An fMRI investigation. *NeuroImage, 72,* 265–271.

Kulke, L., & Rakoczy, H. (2018). Implicit theory of mind – An overview of current replications and non-replications. *Data in Brief, 16,* 101–104.

Kulke, L., von Duhn, B., Schneider, D., & Rakoczy, H. (2018). Is implicit theory of mind a real and robust phenomenon? Results from a systematic replication study. *Psychological Science, 29,* 888–900.

Leahy, B., Rafetseder, E., & Perner, J. (2014). Basic conditional reasoning: How children mimic counterfactual reasoning. *Studia Logica, 102,* 793–810.

Leslie, A. M. (1987). Pretense and representation: The origins of 'theory of mind'. *Psychological Review, 94,* 412.

Leslie, A. M. (1994). ToMM, ToBy, and Agency: Core architecture and domain specificity. In L. A. Hirschfeld, & S. A. Gelman (eds.). *Mapping the Mind: Domain Specificity in Cognition and Culture* (pp. 119–148). New York: Cambridge University Press.

Leslie, A. M., Friedman, O., & German, T. P. (2004). Core mechanisms in 'theory of mind'. *Trends in Cognitive Sciences, 8,* 528–533.

Lewis, D. (1973). *Counterfactuals.* Oxford: Basil Blackwell.

Lillard, A. S. (1993). Young children's conceptualization of pretense: Action or mental representational state? *Child Development, 64,* 372–386.

Liu, D., Sabbagh, M. A., Gehring, W. J., & Wellman, H. M. (2009). Neural correlates of children's theory of mind development. *Child Development, 80*, 318–326.

Low, J., & Watts, J. (2013). Attributing false beliefs about object identity reveals a signature blind spot in humans' efficient mind-reading system. *Psychological Science, 24*, 305–311.

Margolis, E., & Laurence, S. (2011). Learning matters: The role of learning in concept acquisition. *Mind & Language, 26*, 507–539.

Milligan, K., Astington, J. W., & Dack, L. A. (2007). Language and theory of mind: Meta-analysis of the relation between language ability and false-belief understanding. *Child Development, 78*, 622–646.

Norman, D., & Shallice, T. (1986). Attention to action: Willed and automatic control of behavior. In R. J. Davidson, G. E. Schwarts, & D. Shapiro (eds.), *Consciousness and Self-regulation: Advances in Research and Theory* (pp. 1–18). New York: Plenum Press.

Nyhout, A., Henke, L., & Ganea, P. A. (2017). Children's counterfactual reasoning about causally overdetermined events. *Child Development, 90*, 610–622.

Onishi, K. H., & Baillargeon, R. (2005). Do 15-month-old infants understand false beliefs? *Science, 308*, 255–258.

Paulus, M. (2012). Is it rational to assume that infants imitate rationally a theoretical analysis and critique. *Human Development, 55*, 107–121.

Paulus, M., Hunnius, S., Vissers, M., & Bekkering, H. (2011). Imitation in infancy: Rational or motor resonance? *Child Development, 82*, 1047–1057.

Perner, J. (1998). The meta-intentional nature of executive functions and theory of mind. In P. Carruthers, & J. Boucher (eds.), *Language and Thought: Interdisciplinary Themes* (pp. 270–283). Cambridge: Cambridge University Press.

Perner, J. (2000). About + belief + counterfactual. In P. Mitchell, & K. J. Riggs (eds.), *Children's Reasoning and the Mind* (pp. 367–401). Hove, East Sussex: Psychology Press.

Perner, J., & Brandl, J. L. (2005). File change semantics for preschoolers: Alternative naming and belief understanding. *Interaction Studies, 6*, 483–501.

Perner, J., & Howes, D. (1992). 'He thinks he knows': And more developmental evidence against the simulation (role taking) theory. *Mind & Language, 7*, 72–86.

Perner, J., Huemer, M., & Leahy, B. (2015). Mental files and belief: A cognitive theory of how children represent belief and its intensionality. *Cognition, 145*, 77–88.

Perner, J., & Lang, B. (1999). Development of theory of mind and executive control. *Trends in Cognitive Sciences, 3*, 337–344.

Perner, J., Lang, B., & Kloo, D. (2002). Theory of mind and self-control: More than a common problem of inhibition. *Child Development, 73*, 752–767.

Perner, J., & Leahy, B. (2016). Mental files in development: Dual naming, false belief, identity and intensionality. *Review of Philosophy and Psychology, 7*, 491–508.

Perner, J., Mauer, M. C., & Hildenbrand, M. (2011). Identity: Key to children's understanding of belief. *Science, 333*, 474–477.

Perner, J., & Roessler, J. (2010). Teleology and causal understanding in children's theory of mind. In J. H. Aguilar, & A. A. Buckareff (eds.), *Causing Human Actions: New Perspectives on the Causal Theory of Action*. Cambridge, MA: MIT Press.

Perner, J., Sprung, M., & Steinkogler, B. (2004). Counterfactual conditionals and false belief: A developmental dissociation. *Journal of Cognition and Development, 19*, 179–201.

Peterson, D. M., & Riggs, K. J. (1999). Adaptive modelling and mindreading. *Mind & Language, 14*, 80–112.

Phillips, J., Ong, D. C., Surtees, A. D., Xin, Y., Williams, S., Saxe, R., & Frank, M. C. (2015). A second look at automatic theory of mind: Reconsidering Kovács, Téglás, and Endress (2010). *Psychological Science, 26*, 1353–1367.

Powell, L. J., & Carey, S. (2017). Executive function depletion in children and its impact on theory of mind. *Cognition, 164*, 150–162.

Premack, D., & Woodruff, G. (1978). Does the chimpanzee have a theory of mind? *Behavioral and Brain Sciences, 1*, 515–526.

Priewasser, B., Fowles, F., Schweller, K., & Perner, J. (2020). Mistaken max befriends Duplo girl: No difference between a standard and an acted-out false belief task. *Journal of Experimental Child Psychology, 191*, 104756.

Priewasser, B., Rafetseder, E., Gargitter, C., & Perner, J. (2018). Helping as an early indicator of a theory of mind: Mentalism or teleology? *Cognitive Development, 46*, 69–78.

Rafetseder, E., Cristi-Vargas, R., & Perner, J. (2010). Counterfactual reasoning: Developing a sense of 'nearest possible world'. *Child Development, 81*, 376–389.

Rafetseder, E., & Perner, J. (2018). Belief and counterfactuality. *Zeitschrift für Psychologie, 226*, 110–121.

Rafetseder, E., Schwitalla, M., & Perner, J. (2013). Counterfactual reasoning: From childhood to adulthood. *Journal of Experimental Child Psychology, 114*, 389–404.

Rakoczy, H., Bergfeld, D., Schwarz, I., & Fizke, E. (2015). Explicit theory of mind is even more unified than previously assumed: Belief ascription and understanding aspectuality emerge together in development. *Child Development, 86*, 486–502.

Recanati, F. (2012). *Mental Files*. Oxford: Oxford University Press.

Riggs, K. J., Peterson, D. M., Robinson, E. J., & Mitchell, P. (1998). Are errors in false belief tasks symptomatic of a broader difficulty with counterfactuality? *Cognitive Development, 13*, 73–90.

Robinson, E. J., & Mitchell, P. (1995). Masking of children's early understanding of the representational mind: Backwards explanation versus prediction. *Child Development, 66*, 1022–1039.

Rubio-Fernández, P., & Geurts, B. (2013). How to pass the false-belief task before your fourth birthday. *Psychological Science, 24*, 27–33.

Ruffman, T. (1996). Do children understand the mind by means of simulation or a theory? Evidence from their understanding of inference. *Mind & Language, 11*, 388–414.

Ruffman, T., Garnham, W., Import, A., & Connolly, D. (2001). Does eye gaze indicate implicit knowledge of false belief? Charting transitions in knowledge. *Journal of Experimental Child Psychology, 80*, 201–224.

Russell, J. (1987). 'Can we say...?' Children's understanding of intensionality. *Cognition, 25*, 289–308.

Russell, J. (1996). *Agency. Its Role in Mental Development*. Hove: Erlbaum.

Russell, J., Mauthner, N., Sharpe, S., & Tidswell, T. (1991). The 'windows task' as a measure of strategic deception in preschoolers and autistic subjects. *British Journal of Developmental Psychology, 9*, 331–349.

Scanlon, T. (1998). *What We Owe to Each Other*. Cambridge, MA: Harvard University Press.

Schneider, D., Lam, R., Bayliss, A. P., & Dux, P. E. (2012). Cognitive load disrupts implicit theory-of-mind processing. *Psychological Science, 23*, 842–847.

Scott, F. J., Baron-Cohen, S., & Leslie, A. (1999). 'If pigs could fly': A test of counterfactual reasoning and pretence in children with autism. *British Journal of Developmental Psychology, 17*, 349–362.

Scott, R. M., & Baillargeon, R. (2017). Early false-belief understanding. *Trends in Cognitive Sciences, 21*, 237–249.

Scott, R. M., He, Z., Baillargeon, R., & Cummins, D. (2012). False-belief understanding in 2.5-year-olds: Evidence from two novel verbal spontaneous-response tasks. *Developmental Science, 15*, 181–193.

Sommerville, J. A., Woodward, A. L., & Needham, A. (2005). Action experience alters 3-month-old infants' perception of others' actions. *Cognition, 96*, 1–11.

Southgate, V., Chevallier, C., & Csibra, G. (2010). Seventeen-month-olds appeal to false beliefs to interpret others' referential communication. *Developmental Science, 13*, 907–912.

Southgate, V., Senju, A., & Csibra, G. (2007). Action anticipation through attribution of false belief by 2-year-olds. *Psychological Science, 18*, 587–592.

Southgate, V., & Vernetti, A. (2014). Belief-based action prediction in preverbal infants. *Cognition, 130*, 1–10.

Stalnaker, R. (1968). A theory of conditionals. In F. Jackson (ed.), *Conditionals* (pp. 98–112). Oxford: Oxford University Press.

Stuhlmüller, A., & Goodman, N. D. (2014). Reasoning about reasoning by nested conditioning: Modeling theory of mind with probabilistic programs. *Cognitive Systems Research, 28,* 80–99.

Surian, L., Caldi, S., & Sperber, D. (2007). Attribution of beliefs by 13-month-old infants. *Psychological Science, 18,* 580–586.

Surian, L., & Geraci, A. (2012). Where will the triangle look for it? Attributing false beliefs to a geometric shape at 17 months. *British Journal of Developmental Psychology, 30,* 30–44.

Thompson, V. A., & Byrne, R. M. (2002). Reasoning counterfactually: Making inferences about things that didn't happen. *Journal of Experimental Psychology: Learning, Memory, and Cognition, 28,* 1154.

Träuble, B., Marinović, V., & Pauen, S. (2010). Early theory of mind competencies: Do infants understand others' beliefs? *Infancy, 15,* 434–444.

Weisberg, D. P., & Beck, S. R. (2012). The development of children's regret and relief. *Cognition & Emotion, 26,* 820–835.

Weisberg, D. S., & Gopnik, A. (2013). Pretense, counterfactuals, and Bayesian causal models: Why what is not real really matters. *Cognitive Science, 37,* 1368–1381.

Wellman, H. M., Cross, D., & Watson, J. (2001). Meta-analysis of theory-of-mind development: The truth about false belief. *Child Development, 72,* 655–684.

Westra, E., & Carruthers, P. (2017). Pragmatic development explains the Theory-of-Mind Scale. *Cognition, 158,* 165–176.

Wiesmann, C. G., Schreiber, J., Singer, T., Steinbeis, N., & Friederici, A. D. (2017). White matter maturation is associated with the emergence of Theory of Mind in early childhood. *Nature Communications, 8,* 14692.

Wimmer, H. (1989). *Common-sense Mentalismus und Emotion: einige entwicklungspsychologische Implikationen Denken und Fühlen* (pp. 56–66). Berlin: Springer.

Wimmer, H., & Perner, J. (1983). Beliefs about beliefs: Representation and constraining function of wrong beliefs in young children's understanding of deception. *Cognition, 13,* 103–128.

Woodward, A. L. (1998). Infants selectively encode the goal object of an actor's reach. *Cognition, 69,* 1–34.

Woodward, J. (2011). Psychological studies of causal and counterfactual reasoning. In C. Hoerl, T. McCormack, & S. R. Beck (eds.), *Understanding Counterfactuals, Understanding Causation. Issues in Philosophy and Psychology* (pp. 16–53). Oxford: Oxford University Press.

19 Development of Executive Function Skills in Childhood

Relevance for Important Life Outcomes

Keith Happaney and Philip David Zelazo

Executive function (EF) skills are a set of neurocognitive skills required for the conscious, goal-directed control of thought, action, and emotion. These skills make it possible to sustain attention, keep goals and information in mind, refrain from responding immediately, resist distraction, tolerate frustration, consider the consequence of different behaviors, reflect on past experiences, and plan for the future (e.g., Diamond, 2013; Zelazo et al., 2016).

The construct of EF skills derives from observations of damage to the prefrontal cortex (PFC) and Luria's characterization of the PFC at the highest level in a hierarchy of brain regions, exerting top-down control over other brain regions, but also being influenced by them in a reciprocal, bi-directional fashion (e.g., Luria, 1966; Pribram, 1973; Stuss & Benson, 1986). Patients with damage to the PFC often show intact basic cognitive skills (e.g., memory, language) but considerable difficulty controlling or using those basic skills in an intentional, contextually appropriate way. For example, these patients have been found to respond to stimuli in an automatic, over-learned fashion – sometimes called utilization behavior (Lhermitte, 1983). These patients also display perseveration, continuing with strategies that are no longer adaptive (e.g., continuing to sort cards by shape in the Wisconsin Card Sorting Task despite corrective feedback from the examiner; e.g., Milner, 1963). In general, the behavior of these patients appears stimulus driven and inflexible, apparently reflecting a deficit in goal-directed problem-solving (e.g., Zelazo et al., 1997). Luria's research on the self-regulatory role of language in controlling behavior (e.g., Luria & Vinogradova, 1959) also provided a foundation for later work on the importance of rule use (self-directed speech) for EF skills (Bunge, 2004; Bunge & Wallis, 2008; Zelazo & Jacques, 1996; Zelazo et al., 2003).

Research on the development of EF skills in childhood and adolescence has often involved the use of neuropsychological tests designed to assess PFC function in adult patients (e.g., Becker et al., 1987; Levin et al., 1991; Passler et al., 1985; Welsh & Pennington, 1988; Welsh et al., 1991), as well as paradigms derived from the literature on nonhuman primates (e.g., delayed response; Diamond & Doar, 1989; Hunter, 1917; Jacobsen, 1936). These measures have typically been adapted for use with children (e.g., Archibald, & Kerns, 1999; Espy, 1997; Espy et al., 1999; Zelazo et al., 1996), and more recently there has been an effort to create standardized (reliable, validated, normed) measures of EF skill that can provide repeated assessments of EF skill across the lifespan (e.g., Carlson & Zelazo, 2014; Delis et al., 2004; Zelazo et al., 2013). Many of these paradigms, in turn, have also been used in a clinical context to examine the role of EF skills in various forms of developmental psychopathology, such as Attention Deficit/Hyperactivity Disorder (ADHD; e.g., Castellanos et al., 2006), conduct disorder (CD; e.g., Rubia,

2011), and autism spectrum disorder (ASD; e.g., O'Hearn et al., 2008). Thus, the study of EF has moved from a focus on neurologically impaired adults to the inclusion of typically and atypically developing children.

19.1 EF Skills

EF skills depend on increasingly well-understood neural circuits involving brain regions in PFC and other areas (e.g., Cole et al., 2013; Duncan, 2013), and they are typically measured behaviorally as three skills: inhibitory control, working memory, and cognitive flexibility (Miyake et al., 2000). *Inhibitory control* involves deliberately suppressing attention (or other resulting responses) to something (e.g., ignoring a distraction or stopping an impulsive utterance). *Working memory* involves not only holding things in the focus of attention but also manipulating this information, such as when keeping two numbers in mind and subtracting one from the other. *Cognitive flexibility* involves shifting attention and consequently thinking about a single stimulus in multiple ways – for example, when considering someone else's perspective on a situation. These skills can be thought of as *attention-regulation skills*, or ways of intentionally modulating attention (and hence, downstream responding) in the service of a goal – selectively (inhibitory control), over time (working memory), and flexibly (cognitive flexibility). Collectively, these skills allow for goal-directed problem-solving, flexible adaptation to changing circumstances, and intentional learning (Zelazo, 2015). Neuroimaging evidence from adults indicates that these three neurocognitive skills activate partially overlapping regions in the brain, and that there are common networks of activation across tasks, such as the frontoparietal control and dorsal attention networks (e.g., Cole et al., 2013; Duncan, 2013; Vincent et al., 2008).

In an initial study with undergraduate students, Miyake et al. (2000) used confirmatory factor analysis to show that performance on nine EF tasks loaded on the three correlated latent variables, shifting (flexibility), updating (of contents in working memory), and inhibition (inhibitory control). A subsequent study with children between the ages of eight and thirteen years revealed a similar factor structure extracted from eight EF measures (Lehto et al., 2003). More recently, research has supported a hierarchical, bifactor model involving a common EF latent variable together with updating and shifting variables (e.g., Miyake & Friedman, 2012).

These factors appear to emerge during development. Several studies with young children have found that EF measures load onto one factor (e.g., Brydges et al., 2012; Wiebe et al., 2008, 2011; Xu et al., 2013) or two factors (inhibitory control and working memory; Gandolfi et al., 2014; Lerner & Lonigan 2014; Miller et al., 2012; Schoemaker et al., 2012; Usai et al., 2014). Performance on these measures appears to become differentiated by middle childhood or adolescence as a bifactor structure emerges involving common EF and multiple specific factors (e.g., Cirino et al., 2018; Lee et al., 2013; Lehto et al., 2003; McAuley & White, 2011). Indeed, Shing et al. (2010) showed extremely high correlations between inhibitory control and working memory in children between four and seven years and between seven and nine and a half years ($r = 0.98$ and 0.82, respectively), but much more modest relations ($r = 0.32$) in children between nine and a half and fourteen and a half years of age. More recently, using data collected using the NIH Toolbox Cognitive Battery, Mungas et al. (2013) revealed a simpler factor structure in early childhood (three-to-six year-olds) than in children in middle childhood and adolescence (eight-to-fifteen year-olds), which in turn was simpler than in adults. These patterns of skill differentiation with age are consistent with the interactive specialization model of neurocognitive development, according to which experience results in the specialization (and long-range integration) of neural and cognitive functions (Johnson, 2011).

19.2 Hot versus Cool EF Skills

While EF skills in general concern the deliberate, effortful, top-down, self-regulatory processing dependent on PFC, considerable behavioral and neural evidence indicates that EF skills vary along a continuum from more "hot EF" to more "cool EF" (Zelazo & Müller, 2002; see Peterson & Welsh, 2014, for a review). Cool EF concerns top-down attentional control within relatively neutral and decontextualized contexts. By contrast, hot EF concerns the top-down attentional control of motivation and emotion, particularly with regard to the approach versus avoidance of motivationally relevant stimuli. Further, while dorsal and lateral regions of PFC are involved in cool EF, more ventral and medial regions of PFC have been implicated in performance on tasks of motivational and emotional significance. Lesion studies, neuroimaging studies, and research using transcranial direct stimulation (tCDS) point to the importance of the hot–cool continuum in EF (e.g., Bechara et al., 1994; Eslinger et al., 2004; Fonseca et al., 2012; Manes et al., 2002; Nejati et al., 2018).

19.2.1 Examples of Cool EF Skills in Early Childhood

Most of the laboratory-based tasks used to assess EF skills are of the cool variety. For example, the Dimensional Change Card Sort task (DCCS; Frye et al., 1995; Zelazo, 2006) is a cool measure of cognitive flexibility.

Participants are instructed to match a series of test cards to one of two target cards. For example, the two target cards might be a *blue boat* and a *red rabbit*, and participants are to sort cards by shape, boats versus rabbits. After several trials, participants are told to switch, and sort by color, red versus blue. While three-year-olds tend to perform well on pre-switch trials (before the sorting dimension changes), they continue to sort by the previously relevant dimension during post-switch trials, akin to the perseverative responding seen in frontal lobe patients on the WCST (Milner, 1963). Five-year-olds, by contrast, tend to switch their sorting strategy adaptively and perform well.

A common measure of cool *inhibitory control* in preschoolers is the Day/Night Stroop task (Gerstadt et al., 1994), in which children are shown either a light colored card containing a sun or a dark colored card containing a moon. In response to the sun cards, children are instructed to say, "Night," and in response to the moon cards, children are instructed to say, "Day," contrary to any automatic response tendency to describe the card shown. Unlike the standard Stroop (1935) task, the Day/Night Stroop does not depend on being literate.

To measure cool working memory in young children, researchers have sometimes used an adaptation of Petrides and Milner's (1982) self-ordered pointing task. For example, Hongwanishkul et al. (2005) found improvements in performance on a child version of the self-ordered pointing task between three and five years of age. On this task, children are shown three images (e.g., an image of a leaf, a rabbit, and a crayon), presented in different spatial arrangements on each trial, and told to point to a new item on each trial. If children respond correctly to the three-item array, a four-item array is shown, and so on, until children fail the task. As reviewed by

Gathercole (1998), performance on self-ordered pointing tasks improves across the preschool period. Luciana and Nelson (1998) assessed working memory in young children using the spatial working memory task of the Cambridge Neuropsychological Test Automated Battery (CANTAB; Robbins et al., 1994). On this task, performance improved between four and eight years of age, with eight-year-olds showing adult-level performance on some measures (although this may be due to ceiling effects on these measures).

Another measure of relatively cool working memory in young children is backward digit span (Pickering & Gathercole, 2001). The examiner tells children a series of numbers (digits) and children repeat them back in reverse order. If children are successful on four out of six trials, the number of digits increases. Backward digit span is also part of the Wechsler Intelligence Scale for Children (WISC; Wechsler, 1992).

19.2.2 Examples of Hot EF Skills in Early Childhood

What makes EF hot, and engages neural networks involving more ventral and medial regions of PFC, is the specific requirement of flexibly reappraising whether to approach or avoid a salient stimulus (e.g., Rolls, 2004). A wide range of measures that require the modification of the value of specific stimulus-reward associations have been found to depend on neural systems connecting ventral and medial PFC with mesolimbic regions including amygdala and striatum (see Happaney et al., 2004, for review). Examples include measures of reversal learning (in which a rewarded approach-avoidance discrimination must be reversed), delay of gratification and delay discounting (in which the value of an immediate reward must be reconsidered

relative to a larger delayed reward), and extinction (when a previously rewarded stimulus is no longer rewarded and must now be avoided).

Perhaps the most well-known measure of hot EF skills in early childhood is the delay of gratification task (e.g., Mischel et al., 1989). Children are given a choice between receiving one marshmallow now or waiting and receiving two marshmallows. The amount of time that four-year-olds waited predicted their SAT scores in high school (Shoda et al., 1990).

Another aspect of hot EF has sometimes been termed "affective decision making" (e.g., Prencipe & Zelazo, 2005). Interest in such decision-making began with the study of ventromedial prefrontal (VM-PFC) patients, characterized by Saver and Damasio (1991) as having "acquired sociopathy." These patients are not necessarily violent but tend to make disastrous decisions in their everyday lives. This maladaptive decision-making was captured by Bechara et al. (1994) using their Iowa Gambling Task (IGT). In this task, individuals must select cards from one of four decks in an attempt to win as much facsimile money as possible by the game's end (usually 100 trials). Two of these decks were advantageous in that choosing from them yielded small gains but, on average, even smaller losses. By contrast, the two disadvantageous decks, while yielding relatively large gains, led to even larger losses. When players begin the game, the larger wins on the disadvantageous decks make them appear to be a good choice. Across trials, however, what had previously appeared to be the good decks are gradually revealed to be bad ones. While healthy controls and patients without VM-PFC damage learned to switch from disadvantageous to advantageous decks over the course of the game, patients with VM-PFC damage continued to choose from the disadvantageous decks (Bechara et al., 1994). Interestingly, while controls showed anticipatory arousal (as indexed by changes in electrodermal activity) prior to choosing disadvantageously, VM-PFC patients showed no such arousal, suggesting that the ability to use emotions to inform decisions may be involved in the maladaptive decisions made by VM-PFC patients in everyday life (Bechara et al., 1996).

Kerr and Zelazo (2004) adapted the IGT to design the Children's Gambling Task (CGT). This task was simplified for use with preschool-age children and participants only had to choose from two decks (one advantageous and one disadvantageous), as opposed to four decks. Additionally, instead of monetary rewards, children were rewarded with small candies (mini-M&Ms). The number of M&Ms won or lost was indicated on the opposite side of the cards by small smiley or sad faces. Accumulated candies were collected in a narrow translucent graduated cylinder next to the child, providing a running tally of wins and losses. As in the Iowa Gambling Task, however, the options that at first appear advantageous (higher rewards) are revealed gradually to be disadvantageous (higher rewards but even higher losses), and vice versa. Kerr and Zelazo (2004) showed significant improvements in children's performance on the CGT between three and five years of age.

Cool EF skills (e.g., working memory) also appear to play a role in the IGT (Fellows & Farah, 2005; Hinson et al., 2003; Manes et al., 2002), and in other relatively complex "hot" EF tasks, such as the Less is More task (Carlson, 2005), perhaps because cool EF skills are often used to engage and modulate hot EF skills (e.g., Moriguchi & Shinahara, 2019). Finally, hot EF is also involved in deliberate emotion regulation, which involves intentionally modulating approach-avoidance reactions (Zelazo & Cunningham, 2007), including through reflection and cool EF skills, as occurs during reframing (e.g., Mischel et al., 1989), reappraising (Sheppes et al., 2015),

decentering (e.g., Bernstein et al., 2015), and psychological distancing (e.g., Kross et al., 2011; Travers-Hill et al., 2017).

19.2.3 Behavioral Support for the Utility of the Hot/Cool EF Distinction in Childhood

Behavioral evidence suggests that the hot/cool EF distinction can be observed in children as young as two years of age when hot EF skills are measured using tasks involving the need to delay approaching a tempting reward (e.g., Brock et al., 2009; Conway & Stifter, 2012; Smith-Donald et al., 2007; Sonuga-Barke, 2003; Willoughby et al., 2011; but see Allan & Lonigan, 2014). For example, studies with two-to-three-year-olds (Bernier et al., 2010, 2012) and three-to-four-year-olds (Carlson et al., 2014) found support for two factors in preschool children's performance on batteries of EF measures: cool EF ("conflict" tasks, such as the DCCS) and hot EF ("delay" tasks, such as delay of gratification). Willoughby et al. (2011) found support for hot and cool EF factors in a study with over 750 four-to-five-year-olds. A recent study with a diverse-SES sample of 1,900 two-to-five-year-olds also found support for hot and cool EF factors across multiple direct behavioral assessments of each construct (Montroy et al., 2019).

Evidence from young children indicates that whereas cool EF skills typically show stronger associations with academic outcomes, including math and reading, hot EF skills show stronger associations with problem behaviors in school (e.g., inattentive and overactive behavior; e.g., Bassett et al., 2012; Brock et al., 2009; Kim et al., 2013; Mann et al., 2017; Mulder et al., 2014; Thorell, 2007; Willoughby et al., 2011). For example, Brock et al. (2009) found that cool but not hot EF skills predicted school performance in preschoolers and kindergartners. The authors suggested that this lack of a connection between hot EF skills and school readiness might derive from the heavily supportive and individually tailored instructional practices in kindergarten, which make resistance to negative motivational influences less necessary. Willoughby et al. (2011) also administered various self-regulation tasks to a sample of children between three and five years of age and found that two latent factors (mapping onto cool and hot EF) best described the data. Importantly, while cool EF skills uniquely predicted academic performance (based on several subtests of the Woodcock-Johnson battery), hot EF skills uniquely predicted ratings of inattentive-overactive behavior. Another measure of cool EF skills in preschool shown to predict academic outcomes is the Head, Toes, Knees, and Shoulders (HTKS) task, in which children are required to follow increasingly complex sets of rules, such as following a pair of rules ("touch your head" and "touch your toes") and then being told to do the opposite of what is instructed (McClelland et al., 2014).

In general, there is now considerable research that has shown that EF skills are associated with both academic achievement (e.g., Allan et al., 2014; Best et al., 2011; Blair & Razza, 2007; McClelland et al., 2014) and socioemotional competence (e.g., Carlson & Moses, 2001; Frye et al., 1995; Rhoades et al., 2009; Riggs et al., 2006). While cool EF appears to be more strongly related than hot EF to academic outcomes (e.g., Willoughby et al., 2011), early hot EF skills nonetheless also predict later academic achievement (e.g., Mischel et al., 1989).

Groppe and Elsner (2014) examined 1,657 children aged six-to-eleven years and found that hot and cool EF skills related differently to other variables. Consistent with previous research (e.g., Hongwanishkul et al., 2005), cool but not hot EF was related to fluid intelligence, and whereas girls showed higher levels of cool EF than boys, boys showed higher levels of hot EF, consistent with evidence that ventromedial PFC function develops more rapidly in males (e.g., Clark & Goldman-Rakic, 1989; Kerr & Zelazo, 2004; Overman et al., 1996). In contrast, other research found hot but not cool EF skills to be related to emotional intelligence (Checa & Fernández-Berrocal, 2019).

19.2.4 Development of Hot and Cool EF Skills

A key dimension along which EF skills develop is revealed by age-related increases in the complexity of the rules that children can understand and use in order to regulate their behavior (Bunge & Zelazo, 2006; Crone & Steinbeis, 2017). On the DCCS and other measures of rule use, performance improves markedly in the preschool period. Relatively simple rules (e.g., stimulus-response associations and their reversal) appear relatively early in development and are associated more with the orbitofrontal cortex (OFC). Over the course of the preschool years, children are able to use increasingly complex rules. For example, research has found that even two and a half-year-olds successfully use a single arbitrary rule to sort pictures (e.g., Zelazo & Reznick, 1991), three-year-olds can use a pair of rules (e.g., shape rules in the DCCS), and five-year-olds can use a hierarchical set of rules, including a higher-order rule for switching between rule pairs (e.g., Zelazo et al., 2003, 2013).

The Minnesota Executive Function Scale (MEFS; Carlson & Zelazo, 2014) and the NIH Toolbox measures of EF (Zelazo et al., 2013) have helped characterize the development of cool EF skills across the lifespan.

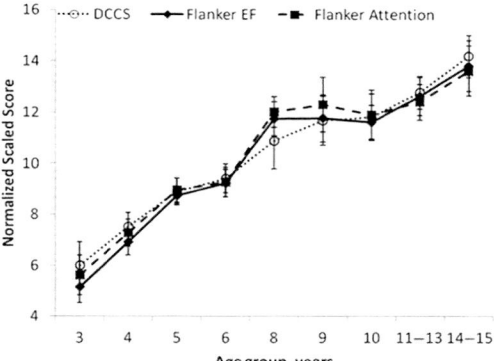

Figure 19.1 Performance on the NIH Toolbox DCCS test and the Toolbox Flanker Inhibitory Control ("Flanker EF") and Attention ("Flanker Attention") test across age groups. Pediatric data from a cross-sectional validation study of 476 participants aged three to eighty-five years. Error bars are ± 2 standard errors. Reproduced with permission from: Zelazo, P. D., Anderson, J. E., Richler, J., Wallner-Allen, K., Beaumont, J. L., & Weintraub, S. (2013). NIH Toolbox Cognition Battery (CB): Measuring executive function and attention. Monographs of the Society for Research in Child Development, *78*(4), 16–33

These measures are computer adaptive, have multiple levels of complexity, and yield scores that reflect both accuracy and reaction time, allowing for the use of the same measure from ages two to eighty-five years (e.g., Zelazo et al., 2013, 2014). On the NIH Toolbox measures (see Figure 19.1), cool EF skills develop rapidly during the preschool years, from about three to six years of age. These skills continue to improve at a slower rate until early adolescence, when there is another period of rapid improvement, and then they again improve more gradually until reaching a peak in the early twenties. Following this, in the general population, EF skills typically decline steadily with age, reaching a level of performance at age eighty-five that is comparable to that of six-year-olds.

Compared to cool EF skills, for which standardized measures are available, there is relatively little research on hot EF skills. Both hot and cool EF skills appear to show protracted development extending into adolescence, however. One study with children aged eight to fifteen years found that for cool EF, there was a transition toward more adult-like performance at around ten years of age, but for hot EF, this transition did not occur until around fourteen years (Prencipe et al., 2011). These findings may depend on the measures used, however, which may vary in developmental sensitivity.

19.3 Neurodevelopment of EF Skills

From the perspective of developmental neuroscience, brain development occurs largely as a function of experience: the activation of specific neural pathways, repeated over time, changes those pathways, rendering them more efficient. As children exercise their EF skills, they activate hierarchical networks involving the prefrontal cortex and other regions (e.g., other cortical regions, striatum, amygdala) as well as the long-range connections among them. These increasingly differentiated yet integrated networks allow for higher-order control over earlier developing and otherwise automatic functions, and they become more efficient with use (e.g., through synaptic pruning and myelination of axons; Kaller et al., 2017; Zatorre et al., 2013). PFC-dependent EF skills are among the last to mature, in part because they depend on the earlier development of more fundamental networks and skills. This protracted period during which both neural networks adapt to relevant environmental challenges is indicative of a relatively long window of neuroplasticity during which children acquire increasingly proficient EF skills mainly by using them, typically in the context of goal-directed problem-solving, and in early childhood, in the context of supportive mentoring.

19.3.1 Theoretical Approaches to EF Skills and their Development

Contemporary theoretical approaches to EF skills and their development generally seek to characterize EF skills at multiple levels of analysis, identify key dimensions along which development occurs, and articulate causal influences on this development. According to the Iterative Reprocessing (IR) model (Cunningham & Zelazo, 2007; Zelazo & Cunningham, 2007), for example, the development of EF skills is made possible by increases in the reflective reprocessing of information via neural circuits that coordinate hierarchically arranged regions of PFC (Bunge & Zelazo, 2006). This coordination permits increases in the hierarchical complexity of rules that can be formulated and maintained in working memory (Zelazo et al., 2003). More complex rule representations allow for more flexibility and control in a wider range of situations than previously possible.

A key trigger for reflection is the detection of uncertainty or conflict, which interrupts automatic processing and signals a need to proceed deliberately. The IR model proposes that conflict/uncertainty detection triggers reflection, or the active reprocessing of information, which in turn allows children to keep information actively in mind and to formulate more complex action-oriented rules that allow for greater cognitive flexibility and inhibitory control.

On the DCCS described earlier, for example, successful switching requires detecting the conflict between the two different games being played. Once children detect a problem, they can pause, interrupting the momentum of their behavior, and reflect on the task. When they do

so, they may recognize that they know two different ways of approaching the stimuli, and formulate a higher-order rule that allows them to switch between games (e.g., If it's the color game, then the red ones go here and the blue ones go there; but if it's the shape game, then the rabbits go here and the boats go there). Consistent with this account, research indicates that the N2 component of the event related potential (ERP), generated largely by neural activity in the anterior cingulate cortex (ACC) and taken as an index of conflict detection (Botvinick et al., 2004), differentiates children who pass and fail on the DCCS (Espinet et al., 2012), and that reflection training leads not only to improvements in children's EF skills, but also changes the amplitude of their N2 responses so that they resemble those of children who pass (Espinet et al., 2013). Importantly, the effects of reflection training were not limited to the DCCS but transferred to flexible perspective taking, an example of far transfer. Other studies have also found that reflection facilitates cognitive flexibility and the far transfer of trained skills (Hadley et al., 2019; Pozuelos et al., 2019). Reflection may help children appreciate the relevance of their newly acquired EF skills to problem-solving in new situations.

Reflection has been closely linked to EF skills in both developmental research (e.g., Lyons & Zelazo, 2011; Roebers, 2017) and neuropsychological studies (e.g., Ciurli et al., 2010), and evidence indicates it can be scaffolded using autonomy supportive techniques that encourage openness, exploration, curiosity, and agency (e.g., Marulis et al., 2020). A key feature of the IR model is that it captures the dynamic interaction between more bottom-up (e.g., limbic) and more top-down (cortical) influences on information processing and goal-directed behavior, and how this depends both on the strength of bottom-up influences and the degree of reflection.

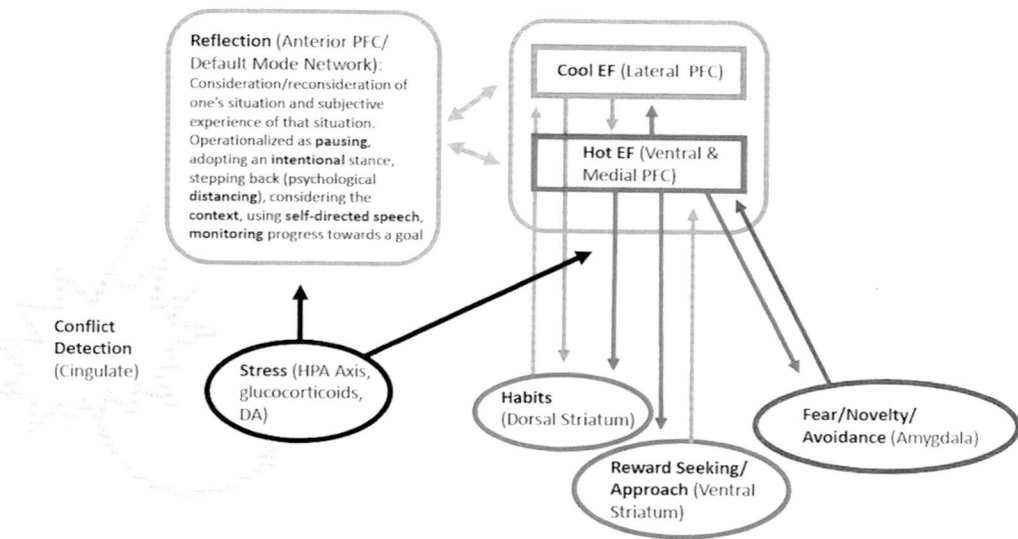

Figure 19.2 Neurocognitive processes (and structures) involved in deliberate fluid reasoning, intentional action, emotion regulation, and social function. Reprinted with permission from Zelazo, P. D. (2020). Executive function and psychopathology: A neurodevelopmental perspective. Annual Review of Clinical Psychology

Information may be processed with relatively little reflection (i.e., few iterations of reprocessing), relying more on limbic regions, or with more reflection, which allows for more aspects of a situation to be noticed and integrated into a construal (or interpretation), yielding a more complex characterization of the options at one's disposal.

Figure 19.2 highlights key interactions between more effortful, reflective processes and more automatic, bottom-up processes, primarily mediated by the striatum (habits, S-R associations) or amygdala (fear, emotional reactivity), among other regions (e.g., insula).

19.4 Positive and Negative Influences on Preschoolers' EF Skills

EF skills show considerable heritability in particular samples (e.g., Friedman et al., 2008). The development of EF skills depends crucially on experience, however, and there is

growing evidence that EF skills can be improved by practice and influenced by a wide range of circumstances and experiences, such as SES, stress, and the quality of early childhood care (e.g., Masten et al., 2012; Zelazo et al., 2018), that may affect children's opportunities and support for practicing EF skills. Children growing up in poverty typically perform worse on measures of EF than children from higher-SES families (e.g., Noble et al., 2015), and EF skills partially account for the relation between SES and school success (better than IQ or language; e.g., Fitzpatrick et al., 2014; Nesbitt et al., 2013). For example, in a socioeconomically and ethnically diverse sample of first graders, Noble et al. (2007) found that children from lower-SES families scored significantly worse on measures of working memory, cognitive control (go/no-go task and a Stroop-like task), and reward processing (a reversal learning task similar to the Children's Gambling Task as well as a delay of gratification task). Interestingly, while SES differences were found for the first two tasks (mapping onto cool EF) no such differences were found for reward processing (hot EF).

The pathway from poverty to poor EF skills is likely complex, but children from low-SES families are exposed to more chaos (e.g., Matheny et al., 1995; Micalizzi et al., 2019) and less environmental support for language acquisition (e.g., fewer words; Hart & Risley, 1995; Schmitt et al., 2011) and for EF skills (e.g., fewer opportunities to play games that require attention regulation; Korucu et al., 2019). These children are also more likely to be exposed to higher levels of noise, inconsistent caregiving, neglect or maltreatment, and malnutrition, all of which can lead to high levels of recurrent and uncontrollable stress (e.g., Blair & Raver, 2016; Evans, 2004; Farah et al., 2006; Lengua et al., 2007; Wass et al., 2019). There is evidence that negative effects of poverty on neurocognitive and social development are mediated in part by the toxic effects of stress on the development of PFC (e.g., Hanson et al., 2010; Sheridan et al., 2012) and on EF skills and school performance (e.g., Blair & Raver, 2015; Enlow et al., 2019; Kishiyama et al., 2009; Lupien et al., 2009; Sheridan et al., 2017; Shonkoff, 2011; Shonkoff et al., 2012). There is also evidence that good EF skills can serve as a protective factor against academic risks associated with poverty, however. In homeless and highly mobile children, having good EF skills increases their odds of success in school despite being homeless (Masten et al., 2012).

19.4.1 Stress

The human stress response is an evolutionary adaptation that functions to orchestrate behavioral and bodily responses to potentially threatening situations. Stress results in the release of glucocorticoids (cortisol) as well as catecholamines such as dopamine (DA) and norepinephrine (NE) that facilitate neural activity in PFC in an inverted U-shaped fashion; high levels overwhelm PFC function, resulting in more reactive and unregulated responding (e.g., Barnes et al., 2011; Joensson et al., 2015; Logue & Gould, 2014; Plessow et al., 2011; Robbins & Arnsten, 2009). Under moderately stressful conditions, such as when children are placed in a novel situation or face a demand slightly beyond their self-perceived ability, cortisol levels typically increase but return to baseline with increasing familiarization to the situation. Disruption of HPA axis function by exposure to high levels of stress undermines EF skills in the moment, because it hijacks attention (e.g., Liston et al., 2009; Shields et al., 2016). When high levels of stress are prolonged and uncontrollable, however, cortisol has toxic effects on neural structures important for EF (PFC and hippocampus; Kolb et al., 2017).

A study by Blair et al. (2005) illustrates the relation between cortisol activity and EF skills in preschoolers. Cortisol samples were collected from predominately white, lower-SES preschoolers at three time points: (1) prior to arriving at the lab, (2) after meeting the experimenter in this novel setting (a time when stress should be at its highest), and (3) after the child had become accustomed to the testing situation. The variable of interest was cortisol reactivity, operationally defined as changes in cortisol levels from time 1 to 2, and from time 2 to 3. Adaptive HPA responding would correspond to an increase in cortisol levels from time 1 to 2 and a decrease from time 2 to 3. This latter change represents an adaptive downregulation of the HPA axis after the perceived threat had abated. Results showed that greater cortisol reactivity was associated with better performance on EF measures of both cognitive flexibility and response inhibition. Further, EF performance mediated the relation between cortisol reactivity and teacher reports of children's self-regulation.

Research with children indicates that exposure to chronic stress is correlated over time with initially elevated stress hormone levels and subsequent blunted levels (and other disrupted stress physiology) along with diminished EF skills (e.g., Blair et al., 2011; Evans & Schamberg, 2009; Hostinar et al., 2014; Koss & Gunnar, 2018; Plamondon et al., 2015). Further, different Adverse Childhood Experiences (ACEs) may reveal different patterns of HPA dysregulation (Bruce et al., 2008; Cicchetti & Rogosch, 2001). Elevated cortisol levels in infancy have been found to be related to lower levels of short-term memory in four-year-olds (Bugental et al., 2010) as well as decreases in EF in three-year-olds (Blair et al., 2011). Given the role of PFC in the downregulation of the stress response, cortisol-induced damage to PFC may lead to the maintenance of chronically high levels of cortisol further undermining HPA regulation.

19.4.2 Parenting

Various parental characteristics may be expected to influence children's EF skills. For example, parental EF has been shown to make a unique contribution, over and above general intellectual functioning, in predicting children's EF (Jester et al., 2009). Further, evidence is mounting that parental EF may exert its influence on children's EF and behavioral regulation via specific parenting practices (e.g., DiStefano et al., 2018). One factor that has received considerable attention is the extent to which the parent supports the child's autonomy.

19.4.2.1 Autonomy Supportive Parenting

Autonomy supportive parenting includes the following factors (see DiStefano et al., 2018):

(1) providing help consistent with the child's skill level (i.e., scaffolding), (2) providing children with encouragement and praise, (3) taking children's perspectives, and (4) following children's lead in providing them with choices. In assessing autonomy support, a typical approach is to observe interactions within parent–child dyads, as children attempt to solve a problem (e.g., a puzzle) too difficult to solve on their own (e.g., DiStefano et al., 2018; Matte-Gagne & Bernier, 2011). Using this measure of autonomy support, Matte-Gagne and Bernier (2011) found parental autonomy support to predict children's EF skills. Parental SES was also positively related to the parents' autonomy support, consistent with previous research linking SES and parenting practices (e.g., Maccoby, 1980; McLoyd, 1998). Indeed, autonomy support requires the parent to flexibly adapt their parenting strategies to the needs of the child. Such sensitive parenting depends on reflection and EF skills and becomes more difficult under the stressful demands of economic insufficiency (see Conger et al., 2002).

Using Matte-Gagne and Bernier's measure of autonomy support, DiStefano et al. (2018) found parental autonomy support to predict children's performance on a version of the DCCS, the Minnesota Executive Function Scale (MEFS; Carlson & Zelazo, 2014), designed to assess cognitive flexibility across the lifespan. Importantly, autonomy support was found to mediate the relation between parental and child EF. In addition to flexibility, autonomy supportive parenting requires inhibitory control in order to fight the temptation to solve the task by oneself as opposed to allowing the child the freedom to do so. Thus, while genetic factors have been found to explain some of the variance in the relation between parent and child EF (e.g., Friedman et al., 2008; Jester et al., 2009), practices arguably deriving from parental EF may play a role in the intergenerational transmission of EF. It is important to note that while autonomy support predictably differed by maternal SES, the mediating effect of autonomy support on child EF held across levels of SES.

Specific aspects of autonomy supportive parenting such as scaffolding, and maintaining and redirecting children's attention during problem-solving, have also been found to predict children's EF, even after controlling for language ability and prior EF (Bernier et al., 2010; Hammond et al., 2012; Hughes & Ensor, 2009). Conway and Stifter (2012), for example, found that attentional redirection predicted children's EF at four and a half years of age. Experimental evidence also indicates that EF skills can be cultivated through autonomy supportive caregiver–child interactions (Meuwissen & Carlson, 2018).

19.4.2.2 The Home Environment

In addition to the potential effects of specific parenting practices on children's EF skills, the general home environment has been implicated in preschool children's developing EF. Children from low-SES families are exposed to more chaos (e.g., Matheny et al., 1995; Micalizzi et al., 2019) and less environmental support for EF skills (e.g., fewer opportunities to play games that require attention regulation; Korucu et al., 2019). Using the Home Observation for Measurement of the Environment (HOME; Bradley et al., 2011), the home environment predicted the trajectory of children's inhibitory control and cognitive flexibility between three and four years of age (Clark et al., 2014). Further, using the HOME, Mezzacappa et al. (2011) found that a stimulating home learning environment predicted children's attentional control. Such stimulation also served as a buffer against the negative effects of prenatal exposure to cigarettes on attentional control. Finally, scores on the

HOME were found to mediate the observed relation between maternal education and sustained attention, impulsivity, working memory, and planning in preschool and school-age children (Hackman et al., 2015).

Koruku et al. (2019) went beyond the more general HOME scale in focusing on EF-specific home activities in their "Home Executive Function Environment" (HEFE) scale. Scores on the HEFE were found to predict children's level of EF as assessed by the HTKS task (McClelland et al., 2014), over and above that of the general home learning environment.

19.4.3 Training and Other Experimental Influences on the Development of EF Skills

Experimental studies allow one to examine the causal impact of specific social interactions and/or cognitive strategies on children's EF skills. The literature on training effects on children's EF skills is reviewed in Chapter 32 (see also Diamond & Ling, 2016) and will not be repeated here. In short, however, the evidence suggests that individual EF skills and sometimes fluid intelligence can be improved through intensive training (e.g., Jaeggi et al., 2008; Mackey et al., 2011; Shinaver et al., 2014, for reviews). Preschool and kindergarten curricula (e.g., Tools of the Mind; Bodrova & Leong, 2001) and modular programs designed to complement these curricula (e.g. PATHS; Riggs et al., 2006) have been shown to lead to better EF skills and academic achievement. Although research to date has often failed to find evidence that trained EF skills generalize to different skills or contexts ("far transfer"; e.g., Melby-Lervåg et al., 2016), most interventions have not been well designed to promote far transfer. Research on learning shows clearly that to promote the far transfer of any skill, it is important to train that skill in a wide range of contexts (e.g., Smith, 1982). Newer evidence also indicates the importance not only of practicing EF skills in a variety of contexts but also of encouraging children to reflect upon them metacognitively so that they learn the purpose and utility of EF skills, as well as how and when to apply those skills in new situations (Espinet et al., 2013; Hadley et al., 2019; Pozuelos et al., 2019). Interventions focusing on reflection, decentering, metacognition, and psychological distancing have also been found effective for individuals with various forms of psychopathology (Moritz et al., 2014; Normann & Morina, 2018; Travers-Hill et al., 2017).

A well-known phenomenon is that teaching someone else something not only assists the learner but helps the teacher to gain a better grasp of the material. This may be because, in order to do so, the teacher must reflect on their own understanding of the material being taught in an attempt to explain it to another. Using this approach, Moriguchi et al. (2015) had three-to-five-year-old children teach a puppet to play the DCCS task. Children who received this training showed improvement on the DCCS as well as an associated increase in activity in the left lateral prefrontal cortex, as indexed by oxygenated hemoglobin.

Other research has explored influences on hot EF skills. For example, Kesek et al. (2011) examined the effect of implicit priming on four-year-olds' performance on a delay of gratification task. Manipulations were embedded within stories with accompanying illustrations. These stories, concerning a boy who had spent the day with his grandpa, were read to children. For one of two implicit priming conditions, children heard stories containing the words "larger" and "more," relating to the larger reward the children would receive if they were able to delay for an adequate amount of time. By contrast, in the immediate reward condition, children were primed to forgo the

opportunity for the larger reward. In this condition, the story contained words such as "quick" and "fast." In the control condition, children merely heard a story without any of these implicit primes embedded within it. The "delay" priming condition led to longer delay times than in the control condition, whereas the "immediate reward" condition led to decreases in delay time. In contrast, there was no effect of direct instructions to delay or to take the immediate reward. In essence, this study showed that, like adults (e.g., Bargh & Morsella, 2008), preschoolers are sensitive to implicit messages. This finding suggests that it is important not only to consider explicit messaging to children but also the influence of implicit suggestions, and it indicates that sometimes implicit suggestions are more effective.

19.5 Implications for Psychopathology

Difficulties with EF are a common feature of many clinical conditions with childhood or youth onset, including: Learning Disabilities (LD; e.g., Alloway et al., 2009; Toll et al., 2011), Attention Deficit/Hyperactivity Disorder (ADHD; e.g., Castellanos et al., 2006), conduct disorder (CD; e.g. Rubia, 2011), autism spectrum disorder (ASD; e.g., O'Hearn et al., 2008), obsessive-compulsive disorder (OCD; e.g., Pietrefesa & Evans, 2007), depression (e.g., Nelson et al., 2018), and anxiety (e.g., Carthy et al., 2010; Shi et al., 2017). From the perspective of developmental psychopathology (Cicchetti, 1984; Cicchetti & Tucker, 1994; Sroufe & Rutter, 1984), which takes a developmental systems view (e.g., Bronfenbrenner, 1979; Gottlieb, 1992; Sameroff, 1983) of the etiology and life course of atypical behavior, a wide range of variables and their interactions influence biological and psychological development and can result in psychopathology.

Zelazo (2020) suggested that the ubiquity of atypical EF development in psychopathology can be understood as a function of several considerations. For one, EF skills are particularly vulnerable to disruption due to their protracted development and the related protracted development of the PFC systems supporting them. Indeed, EF skills develop between infancy and early adulthood, leaving ample time for insult. Further, because EF is a higher-order function, perturbations in lower-order systems can feed forward and negatively influence the development of EF skills. As an illustration, disruption of the HPA axis feeds forward to adversely affect development of the PFC, hippocampus, and other regions. EF deficits, in turn, lead to further HPA axis dysfunction, creating a pernicious cycle. Finally, EF skills play a fundamental role in intentional action and flexible adaptation, necessary for intelligent behavior in general (e.g., Duncan, 2013). Disruption of these foundational EF skills, thus, has broad behavioral and developmental consequences across various domains, and across diagnostic categories of psychopathology (e.g., Moffitt et al., 2011).

Zelazo (2020) also proposed a simple neurodevelopmental model in which (1) Adverse Childhood Experiences (ACEs) and other sources of stress lead to (2) atypical development of PFC systems supporting EF, further leading to (3) an increased risk for general features of psychopathology, including impairments common to all categories as well as the severity of distress (e.g., Caspi et al., 2014; Castellanos-Ryan et al., 2016; Lahey et al., 2017; McLaughlin, 2016). EF difficulties common to various forms of psychopathology include reflection, task analysis and decomposition, sequencing, and monitoring. In a cross-sectional study of 2,395 six-to-twelve-year-olds, for example, performance on a battery of EF measures was associated with risk for a latent general psychopathology factor while not relating to other factors specific to given diagnoses (Martel et al., 2017). Difficulties with both hot and cool EF skills are transdiagnostic indicators of atypical development, therefore, in part because stress interferes with EF and its development, which in turn leads to impairments in the general, transdiagnostic features of atypical development

19.6 Conclusions

During the past decade, there has been considerable progress toward a more complete understanding of EF and its development during childhood. Evidence indicates that EF skills provide a foundation for goal-directed problem-solving, intentional learning, and flexible adaption to changing circumstances, and that early individual differences in EF skill predict long-term developmental outcomes. ACEs and other sources of stress appear to disrupt the development of neural systems supporting reflection and both hot and cool EF skills and may then lead to an increased risk for general, transdiagnostic features of a wide range of clinical conditions. Research is revealing the way in which experience shapes the neural circuitry underlying EF, and interventions targeting reflection have the potential to help reduce inequities in educational achievement and support children at risk for a wide range of difficulties. Intervention efficacy may be enhanced by mitigating disruptive bottom-up influences such as stress, and skills training that includes a reflective, metacognitive component helps promote the far transfer of trained skills.

References

Allan, N. P., Hume, L. E., Allan, D. M., Farrington, A. L., & Lonigan, C. J. (2014). Relations between inhibitory control and the development of academic skills in preschool and kindergarten: A meta-analysis. *Developmental Psychology, 50*, 2368–2379.

Allan, N. P., & Lonigan, C. J. (2014). Exploring dimensionality of effortful control using hot and cool tasks in a sample of preschool children. *Journal of Experimental Child Psychology, 122*, 33–47.

Alloway, T. P., Gathercole, S. E., Kirkwood, H., & Elliott, J. (2009). The Working Memory Rating Scale: A classroom-based behavioral assessment of working memory. *Learning and Individual Differences, 19*, 242–245.

Archibald, S. J., & Kerns, K. A. (1999). Identification and description of new tests of executive functioning in children. *Child Neuropsychology, 5*, 115–129.

Bargh, J. A., & Morsella, E. (2008). The unconscious mind. *Perspectives on Psychological Science, 3*, 73–79.

Barnes, J. J. M., Dean, A. J., Nandam, L. S., O'Connell, R. G., & Bellgrove, M. A. (2011). The molecular genetics of executive function: Role of monoamine system genes. *Biological Psychiatry, 69*, e127–e143.

Bassett, H. H., Denham, S., Wyatt, T. M., & Warren-Khot, H. K. (2012). Refining the Preschool Self-Regulation Assessment for use in preschool classrooms. *Infant and Child Development, 21*, 596–616.

Bechara, A., Damasio, A. R., Damasio, H., & Anderson S. W. (1994). Insensitivity to future consequences following damage to human prefrontal cortex. *Cognition, 50*, 7–15.

Bechara, A., Tranel, D., Damasio, H., & Damasio, A. R. (1996). Failure to respond autonomically to anticipated future outcomes following damage to prefrontal cortex. *Cerebral Cortex, 6*, 215–225.

Becker, M. G., Isaac, W., & Hynd, G. W. (1987). Neuropsychological development of nonverbal behaviors attributed to "frontal lobe" functioning. *Developmental Neuropsychology, 3*, 275–298.

Bernier, A., Carlson, S. M., Deschênes, M., & Matte-Gagné, C. (2012). Social factors in the development of early executive functioning: A closer look at the caregiving environment. *Developmental Science, 15*, 12–24.

Bernier, A., Carlson, S. M., & Whipple, N. (2010). From external regulation to self-regulation: Early parenting precursors of young children's executive functioning. *Child Development, 81*, 326–339.

Bernstein, A., Hadash, Y., Lichtash, Y., Tanay, G., Shepherd, K., & Fresco, D. M. (2015). Decentering and related constructs: A critical review and metacognitive processes model. *Perspectives on Psychological Science, 10*, 599–617.

Best, J. R. Miller, P. H., & Naglieri, J. A. (2011). Relations between executive function and academic achievement from ages 5 to 17 in a large, representative national sample. *Learning and Individual Differences, 21*, 327–336.

Blair, C., Granger, D., & Razza, R. P. (2005). Cortisol reactivity is positively related to executive function in preschool children attending head start. *Child Development, 76*, 554–567.

Blair, C., Granger, D., Willoughby, M., Mills-Koonce, R., Cox, M., Greenberg, M. T., et al. (2011). Salivary cortisol mediates effects of poverty and parenting on executive functions in early childhood. *Child Development, 82*, 1970–1984.

Blair, C., & Raver, C. C. (2015). School readiness and self-regulation: A developmental psychobiological approach. *Annual Review of Psychology, 66*, 711–731.

Blair, C., & Raver, C. C. (2016). Poverty, stress, and brain development: New directions for prevention and intervention. *Academic Pediatrics, 16*, S30–S36.

Blair, C., & Razza, R. P. (2007). Relating effortful control, executive function, and false belief understanding to emerging math and literacy ability in kindergarten. *Child Development, 78*, 647–680.

Bodrova, E., & Leong, D. J. (2001). Tools of the mind: A case study of implementing the Vygotskian approach in American early childhood and primary classrooms. *Innodata Monographs, 7*. Geneva: UNESCO International Bureau of Education.

Botvinick, M. M., Cohen, J. D., & Carter, C. S. (2004). Conflict monitoring and anterior cingulate cortex: An update. *Trends in Cognitive Sciences, 8,* 539–546.

Bradley, R. H., McKelvey, L. M., & Whiteside-Mansell, L. (2011). Does the quality of stimulation and support in the home environment moderate the effect of early education programs? *Child Development, 82,* 2110–2122.

Brock, L. L., Rimm-Kaufman, S. E., Nathanson, L., & Grimm, K. J. (2009). The contributions of "hot" and "cool" executive function to children's academic achievement, learning-related behaviors, and engagement in kindergarten. *Early Childhood Research Quarterly, 24,* 337–349.

Bronfenbrenner, U. (1979). *The Ecology of Human Development: Experiments by Nature and Design.* Cambridge, MA: Harvard University Press.

Bruce, J., Fisher, P. A., Pears, K. C., & Levine, S. (2008). Morning cortisol levels in preschool-aged foster children: Differential effects of maltreatment type. *Developmental Psychobiology, 51,* 14–23.

Brydges, C. R., Reid, C. L., Fox, A. M., & Anderson, M. (2012). A unitary executive function predicts intelligence in children. *Intelligence, 40,* 458–469.

Bugental, D. B., Schwartz, A. & Lynch, C. (2010). Effects of an early family intervention on children's memory: The mediating effects of cortisol levels. *Mind, Brain, and Education, 4,* 159–170.

Bunge, S. A. (2004). How we use rules to select actions: A review of evidence from cognitive neuroscience. *Cognitive, Affective, and Behavioral Neuroscience, 4,* 564–579.

Bunge, S. A., & Wallis, J. D. (2008). *Perspectives on Rule Guided Behavior.* New York: Oxford University Press.

Bunge, S. A., & Zelazo, P. D. (2006). A brain-based account of the development of rule use in childhood. *Current Directions in Psychological Science, 15,* 118–121.

Carlson, S. M. (2005). Developmentally sensitive measures of executive function in preschool children. *Developmental Neuropsychology, 28,* 595–616.

Carlson, S. M., & Moses, L. J. (2001). Individual differences in inhibitory control and children's theory of mind. *Child Development, 72,* 1032–1053.

Carlson, S. M., White, R. E., & Davis-Unger, A. C. (2014). Evidence for a relation between executive function and pretense representation in preschool children. *Cognitive Development, 29,* 1–16.

Carlson, S. M., & Zelazo, P. D. (2014). *Minnesota Executive Function Scale.* Saint Paul, MN: Reflection Sciences, LLC.

Carthy, T., Horesh, N., Apter, A., Edge, M. D., & Gross, J. J. (2010). Emotional reactivity and cognitive regulation in anxious children. *Behaviour Research and Therapy, 48,* 384–393.

Caspi, A., Houts, R. M., Belsky, D. W., Goldman-Mellor, S. J., Harrington, H. L., Israel, S., et al. (2014). The *p* factor: One general psychopathology factor in the structure of psychiatric disorders? *Clinical Psychological Science, 2,* 119–137.

Castellanos, F. X., Sonuga-Barke, E. J. S., Milham, M. P., & Tannock, R. (2006). Characterizing cognition in ADHD: Beyond executive dysfunction. *Trends in Cognitive Sciences, 10,* 117–123.

Castellanos-Ryan, N., Brière, F. N., O'Leary-Barrett, M., Banaschewski, T., Bokde, A., Bromberg, U., et al. (2016). The structure of psychopathology in adolescence and its common personality and cognitive correlates. *Journal of Abnormal Psychology, 125,* 1039–1052.

Checa, P., & Fernández-Berrocal, P. (2019). Cognitive control and emotional intelligence: Effect of the emotional content of the task: Brief Reports. *Frontiers in Psychology, 10,* 195.

Cicchetti, D. (1984). The emergence of developmental psychopathology. *Child Development, 55,* 1–7.

Cicchetti, D., & Rogosch, F. A. (2001). Diverse patterns of neuroendocrine activity in maltreated children. *Development and Psychopathology, 13,* 677–693.

Cicchetti, D., & Tucker, D. (1994). Development and self-regulatory structures of the mind. *Development and Psychopathology, 6,* 533–549.

Cirino, P. T., Ahmed, Y., Miciak, J., Taylor, W. P., Gerst, E. H., & Barnes, M. A. (2018). A framework for executive function in the late elementary years. *Neuropsychology, 32,* 176–189.

Ciurli, P., Bivona, U., Barba, C., Onder, G., Silvestro, D., Azicnuda, E., et al. (2010). Metacognitive unawareness correlates with executive function impairment after severe traumatic brain injury. *Journal of the International Neuropsychological Society, 16,* 360.

Clark, A. S., & Goldman-Rakic, P. S. (1989). Gonadal hormones influence the emergence of cortical function in nonhuman primates. *Behavioral Neuroscience, 103,* 1287–1295.

Clark, C. A., Martinez, M. M., Nelson, J. M., Wiebe, S. A., & Andrews Espy, K. (2014). Children's self-regulation and executive control: Critical for later years. *Wellbeing: A Complete Reference Guide* (pp. 1–30). Wiley Online Library.

Cole, M. W., Reynolds, J. R., Power, J. D., Repovs, G., Anticevic, A., & Braver, T. S. (2013). Multi-task connectivity reveals flexible hubs for adaptive task control. *Nature Neuroscience, 16,* 1348–1355.

Conger, R. D., Wallace, L. B., Sun, Y., Simons, R. L., McLoyd, V., & Brody, G. H. (2002). Economic pressure in African American families: A replication and extension of the family stress model. *Developmental Psychology, 38,* 179–193.

Conway, A., & Stifter, C. A. (2012). Longitudinal antecedents of executive function in preschoolers. *Child Development, 83,* 1022–1036.

Crone, E., & Steinbeis, N. (2017). Neural perspectives on cognitive control development during childhood and adolescence. *Trends in Cognitive Sciences, 21,* 205–215.

Cunningham, W. A., & Zelazo, P. D. (2007). Attitudes and evaluations: A social cognitive neuroscience perspective. *Trends in Cognitive Sciences, 11,* 97–104.

Delis, D., Kramer, J., Kaplan, E., & Holdnack, J. (2004). Reliability and validity of the Delis-Kaplan Executive Function System: An update. *Journal of the International Neuropsychological Society, 10,* 301–303.

Diamond, A. (2013). Executive functions. *Annual Review of Psychology, 64,* 135–168.

Diamond, A., & Doar, B. (1989). The performance of human infants on a measure of frontal cortex function, the delayed response task. *Developmental Psychobiology, 22,* 271–294.

Diamond, A., & Ling, D. S. (2016). Conclusions about interventions, programs and approaches for improving executive functions that appear justified and those that, despite much hype, do not. *Developmental Cognitive Neuroscience, 18,* 34–48.

DiStefano, R., Galinsky, E., McClelland, M. M., Zelazo, P. D., & Carlson, S. M. (2018). Autonomy-supportive parenting and associations with child and parent executive function. *Journal of Applied Developmental Psychology, 58,* 77–85.

Duncan, J. (2013). The structure of cognition: Attentional episodes in mind and brain. *Neuron, 80,* 35–50.

Enlow, M. B., Petty, C. R., Svelnys, C., Gusman, M., Huezo, M., Malin, A., et al. (2019). Differential effects of stress exposures, caregiving quality, and temperament in early life on working memory versus inhibitory control in preschool-aged children. *Developmental Neuropsychology, 44,* 339–356.

Eslinger, P. J., Flaherty-Craig, C. V., Benton, A. L. (2004). Developmental outcomes after early prefrontal cortex damage. *Brain and Cognition, 55,* 84–103.

Espinet, S. D., Anderson, J. E., & Zelazo, P. D. (2012). N2 amplitude as a neural marker of executive function in young children: An ERP study of children who switch versus perseverate on the Dimensional Change Card Sort. Developmental Cognitive Neuroscience, 2, S49–S58.

Espinet, S. D., Anderson, J. E., & Zelazo, P. D. (2013). Reflection training improves executive function in preschool children: Behavioral and neural effects. *Developmental Cognitive Neuroscience, 4,* 3–15.

Espy, K. A. (1997). The shape school: Assessing executive function in preschool children. *Developmental Neuropsychology*, *13*, 495–499.

Espy, K. A., Kaufmann, P. M., McDiarmid, M. D., & Glisky, M. L. (1999). Executive functioning in preschool children: Performance on A-not-B and other delayed response format tasks. *Brain and Cognition*, *41*, 178–199.

Evans, G. W. (2004). The environment of childhood poverty. *American Psychologist*, *59*, 77–92.

Evans, G. W., & Schamberg, M. A. (2009). Childhood poverty, chronic stress, and adult working memory. *Proceedings of the National Academy of Sciences (USA)*, *106*, 6545–6549.

Farah, M. J., Shera, D. M., Savage, J. H., Betancourt, L., Giannetta, J. M., Brodsky, N. L., et al. (2006). Childhood poverty: Specific associations with neurocognitive development. *Brain Research*, *1110*, 166–174.

Fellows, L. K., & Farah, M. J. (2005). Different underlying impairments in decision-making following ventromedial and dorsolateral frontal lobe damage in humans. *Cerebral Cortex*, *15*, 58–63.

Fitzpatrick, C., McKinnon, R. D., Blair, C. B., & Willoughby, M. T. (2014). Do preschool executive function skills explain the school readiness gap between advantaged and disadvantaged children? *Learning and Instruction*, *30*, 25–31.

Fonseca, R. P., Zimmermann, N., Cotrena, C., Cardoso, C., Kristensen, C. H., & Grassi-Oliveira, R. (2012). Neuropsychological assessment of executive functions in traumatic brain injury: Hot and cold components. *Psychology & Neuroscience*, *5*, 183–190.

Friedman, N. P., Miyake, A., Young, S. E., DeFries, J. C., Corley, R. P., & Hewitt, J. K. (2008). Individual differences in executive functions are almost entirely genetic in origin. *Journal of Experimental Psychology: General*, *137*, 201–225.

Frye, D., Zelazo, P. D., & Palfai, T. (1995). Theory of mind and rule-based reasoning. *Cognitive Development*, *10*, 483–527.

Gandolfi, E., Viterbori, P., Traverso, L., & Usai, M. C. (2014). Inhibitory processes in toddlers: A latent-variable approach. *Frontiers in Psychology*, *5*, 381.

Gathercole, S. E. (1998). The development of memory. *The Journal of Child Psychology and Psychiatry and Allied Disciplines*, *39*, 3–27.

Gerstadt, C., Hong, Y., & Diamond, A. (1994). The relationship between cognition and action: Performance of children 3 ½–7 years old on a Stroop-like day-night test. *Cognition*, *53*, 129–153.

Gottlieb, G. (1992). *Individual Development and Evolution: The Genesis of Novel Behavior*. New York: Oxford University Press.

Groppe K., & Elsner B. (2014). Executive function and food approach behavior in middle childhood. *Frontiers in Psychology*, *5*, 477.

Hackman, D. A., Gallop, R., Evans, G. W., & Farah, M. J. (2015). Socioeconomic status and executive function: Developmental trajectories and mediation. *Developmental Science*, *18*, 686–702.

Hadley, L. V., Acluche, F., & Chevalier, N. (2019). Encouraging performance monitoring promotes proactive control in children. *Developmental Science*, e12861.

Hammond, S. I., Müller, U., Carpendale, J. I. M., Bibok, M. B., & Liebermann-Finestone, D. P. (2012). The effects of parental scaffolding on preschoolers' executive function. *Developmental Psychology*, *48*, 271–281.

Hanson, J. L., Chung M. K., Avants, B. B., Shirtcliff, E. A., Gee, J. C., Davidson, R. J., et al. (2010). Early stress is associated with alterations in the orbitofrontal cortex: A tensor-based morphometry investigation of brain structure and behavioral risk. *Journal of Neuroscience*, *30*, 7466–7472.

Happaney, K., Zelazo, P. D., & Stuss, D. T. (2004). Development of orbitofrontal function: Current themes and future directions. *Brain and Cognition*, *55*, 1–10.

Hart, B., & Risley, T. (1995). *Meaningful Differences in the Everyday Experience of Young American Children*. Baltimore, MD: Brookes.

Hinson, J. M., Jameson, T. L., & Whitney, P. (2003). Impulsive decision making and working memory. *Journal of Experimental Psychology; Learning Memory and Cognition, 29*, 298–306.

Hongwanishkul, D., Happaney, K. R., Lee, W., & Zelazo, P. D. (2005). Hot and cool executive function: Age-related changes and individual differences. *Developmental Neuropsychology, 28*, 617–644.

Hostinar, C. E., Sullivan, R. M., & Gunnar, M. R. (2014). Psychobiological mechanisms underlying the social buffering of the hypothalamic-pituitary-adrenocortical axis: A review of animal models and human studies across development. *Psychological Bulletin, 140*, 256–282.

Hughes, C., & Ensor, R. (2009). How do families help or hinder the emergence of early executive function? *New Directions in Child and Adolescent Development, 123*, 35–50.

Hunter, W. S. (1917). The delayed reaction in a child. *Psychological Review, 24*, 74–87.

Jacobsen, C. F. (1936). Studies of cerebral function in primates. I. The functions of the frontal association areas in primates. *Comparative Psychology Monographs, 13*, 1–60.

Jaeggi, S. M., Buschkuehl, M., Jonides, J., & Perrig, W. J. (2008). Improving fluid intelligence with training on working memory. *Proceedings of the National Academy of Sciences (USA), 105*, 6829–6833.

Jester, J. M., Nigg, J. T., Puttler, L. I., Long, J. C., Fitzgerald, H. E., & Zucke, R. A. (2009). Intergenerational transmission of neuropsychological executive functioning. *Brain and Cognition, 70*, 145–153.

Joensson, M., Thomsen, K. R., Andersen, L. M., Gross, J., Mouridsen, K., Sandberg, K., et al. (2015). Making sense: Dopamine activates conscious self-monitoring through medial prefrontal cortex. *Human Brain Mapping, 36*, 1866–1877.

Johnson, M. H. (2011). Interactive specialization: A domain-general framework for human functional brain development? *Developmental Cognitive Neuroscience, 1*, 7–21.

Kaller, M. S., Lazari, A., Blanco-Duque, C., Sampaio-Baptista, C., & Johansen-Berg, H. (2017). Myelin plasticity and behaviour: Connecting the dots. *Current Opinion in Neurobiology, 47*, 86–92.

Kerr, A., & Zelazo, P. D. (2004). Development of "hot" executive function: The Children's Gambling Task. *Brain and Cognition, 55*, 148–157.

Kesek, A., Cunningham, W. A., Packer, D. J., & Zelazo, P. D. (2011). Indirect goal priming is more powerful than explicit instruction in children. *Developmental Science, 14*, 944–948.

Kim, S., Nordling, J. K., Yoon, J. E., Boldt, L. J., & Kochanska, G. (2013). Effortful control in "hot" and "cool" tasks differentially predicts children's behavior problems and academic performance. *Journal of Abnormal Child Psychology, 41*, 43–56.

Kishiyama, M. M., Boyce, W. T., Jimenez, A. M., Perry, L. M., & Knight, R. T. (2009). Socioeconomic disparities affect prefrontal function in children. *Journal of Cognitive Neuroscience, 21*, 1106-1115.

Kolb, B., Harker, L., de Melo, S., & Gibb, R. (2017). Stress and pre-frontal cortical plasticity in the developing brain. *Cognitive Development, 42*, 15–26.

Korucu, I., Rolan, E., Napoli, A. R., Purpura, D. J., & Schmitt, S. A. (2019). Development of the Home Executive Function Environment (HEFE) scale: Assessing its relation to preschoolers' executive function. *Early Childhood Research Quarterly, 47*, 9–19.

Koss, K. J., & Gunnar, M. R. (2018). Annual research review: Early adversity, the hypothalamic-pituitary-adrenocortical axis, and child psychopathology. *Journal of Child Psychology and Psychiatry, 59*, 327–346.

Kross, E., Duckworth, A., Ayduk, O., Tsukayama, E., & Mischel, W. (2011). The effect of self-distancing adaptive versus maladaptive self-reflection in children. *Emotion, 11*, 1032–1039.

Lahey, B. B., Krueger, R. F., Rathouz, P. J., Waldman, I. D., & Zald, D. H. (2017). A hierarchical causal taxonomy of psychopathology across the life span. *Psychological Bulletin, 143*, 142–186.

Lee, K., Bull, R., & Ho, R.M. (2013). Developmental changes in executive functioning. *Child Development, 84*, 1933–1953.

Lehto, J. E., Juujarvi, P., Kooistra, L., & Pulkkinen, L. (2003). Dimensions of executive functioning: Evidence from children. *British Journal of Developmental Psychology, 21*, 59–80.

Lengua L. J., Honorado, E., & Bush, N. R. (2007). Contextual risk and parenting as predictors of effortful control and social competence in preschool children. *Journal of Applied Developmental Psychology, 28*, 40–55.

Lerner, M. D., & Lonigan, C. J. (2014). Executive function among preschool children: Unitary versus distinct abilities. *Journal of Psychopathology and Behavioral Assessment, 36*, 626–639.

Levin, H. S., Culhane, K. A., Hartmann, J., Evankovich, K., Mattson, A. J., Harward, H., et al. (1991). Developmental-changes in performance on tests of purported frontal-lobe functioning. *Developmental Neuropsychology, 7*, 377–395.

Lhermitte, F. (1983). "Utilization behavior" and its relation to lesions to the frontal lobes. *Brain, 106*, 237–255.

Liston, C., McEwen, B. S., & Casey, B. J. (2009). Psychosocial stress reversibly disrupts prefrontal processing and attentional control. *Proceedings of the National Academy of Science (USA), 106*, 912–917.

Logue, S. F., & Gould, T. J. (2014). The neural and genetic basis of executive function: Attention, cognitive flexibility, and response inhibition. *Pharmacology Biochemistry and Behavior, 123*, 45–54.

Luciana, M., & Nelson, C. A. (1998). The functional emergence of prefrontally-guided working memory systems in four-to-eight-year-old children. *Neuropsychologia, 36*. 273–293.

Lupien, S. J., McEwen, B. S., Gunnar, M. R., & Heim, C. (2009). Effects of stress throughout the lifespan on the brain, behaviour and cognition. *Nature Reviews Neuroscience, 10*, 434–445.

Luria, A. R. (1966). *Higher Cortical Functions in Man* (2nd ed.). New York: Basic Books.

Luria, A. R., & Vinogradova, O. S. (1959). An objective investigation of the dynamics of semantic systems. *British Journal of Psychology, 50*, 89–105.

Lyons, K. E., & Zelazo, P. D. (2011). Monitoring, metacognition, and executive function: Elucidating the role of self-reflection in the development of self-regulation. *Advances in Child Development and Behavior, 40*, 379–412.

Maccoby, E. E. (1980). *Social Development*. San Diego, CA: Harcourt Brace Jovanovich.

Mackey, A. P., Hill, S. S., Stone, S. I., & Bunge, S. A. (2011). Differential effects of reasoning and speed training in children. *Developmental Science, 14*, 582–590.

Manes, F., Sahakian, B., Clark, L., Rogers, R., Antoun, N., Aitken, M., et al. (2002). Decision-making processes following damage to prefrontal cortex. *Brain, 125*, 624–639.

Mann, T. D., Hund, A. M., Hesson-McInnis, M. S., & Roman, Z. J. (2017). Pathways to school readiness: Executive functioning predicts academic and social-emotional aspects of school readiness. *Mind, Brain, and Education, 11*, 21–31.

Martel, M. M., Pan, P. M, Hoffmann, M. S., Gadelha, A., do Rosário, M. C., Jair, J., et al. (2017). A general psychopathology factor (*p* factor) in children: Structural model analysis and external validation through familial risk and child global executive function. *Journal of Abnormal Psychology, 126*, 137–148.

Marulis, L., Baker, S., & Whitebread, D. (2020). Integrating metacognition and executive function to enhance young children's perception of and agency in their learning. *Early Childhood Research Quarterly, 50*, 46–54.

Masten, A. S., Herbers, J. E., Desjardins, C. D., Cutuli, J. J., McCormick, C. M., Sapienza, J. K., et al. (2012). Executive function skills and school success in young children experiencing homelessness. *Educational Researcher, 41*, 373–384.

Matheny, A., Jr., Wachs, T. D., Ludwig, J., & Phillips, K. (1995). Bringing order out of chaos:

Psychometric characteristics of the Confusion, Hub-bub, and Order Scale. *Journal of Applied Developmental Psychology, 16*, 429–444.

Matte-Gagne, C., & Bernier, A. (2011). Prospective relations between maternal autonomy support and child executive functioning: Investigating the mediating role of child language ability. *Journal of Experimental Child Psychology, 110*, 611–625.

McAuley, T., & White, D. A. (2011). A latent variables examination of processing speed, response inhibition, and working memory during typical development. *Journal of Experimental Child Psychology, 108*, 453–468.

McClelland, M. M., Cameron, C. E., Duncan, R., Bowles, R. P., Acock, A. C., Miao, A., et al. (2014). Predictors of early growth in academic achievement: The Head-Toes-Knees-Shoulders task. *Frontiers in Psychology, 5*, 599.

McLaughlin, K. A. (2016). Future directions in childhood adversity and youth psychopathology. *Journal of Clinical Child & Adolescent Psychology, 45*, 361–382.

McLoyd, V. (1998). Socioeconomic disadvantage and child development. *American Psychologist, 53*, 185–204.

Melby-Lervåg, M., Redick, T. S., & Hulme, C. (2016). Working memory training does not improve performance on measures of intelligence or other measures of "far transfer": Evidence from a meta-analytic review. *Perspectives on Psychological Science, 11*, 512–534.

Meuwissen, A. S., & Carlson, S. M. (2018). An experimental study of the effects of autonomy support on preschoolers' self-regulation. *Journal of Applied Developmental Psychology, 60*, 11–23.

Mezzacappa, E., Buckner, J. C., & Earls, F. (2011). Prenatal cigarette exposure and infant learning stimulation as predictors of cognitive control in childhood. *Developmental Science, 14*, 881–891.

Micalizzi, L., Brick, L. A., Flom, M., Ganiban, J. M., & Saudino, K. J. (2019). Effects of socioeconomic status and executive function on school readiness across levels of household chaos. *Early Childhood Research Quarterly, 47*, 331–340.

Miller, M. R., Giesbrecht, G. F., Muller, U., McInerney, R. J., & Kerns, K. A. (2012). A latent variable approach to determining the structure of executive function in preschool children. *Journal of Cognition and Development, 13*, 395–423.

Milner, B. (1963). Effects of different brain lesions on card sorting. *Archives of Neurology, 9*, 90–100.

Mischel, W., Shoda, Y., & Rodriguez, M. L. (1989). Delay of gratification in children. *Science, 244*, 933–938.

Miyake, A., & Friedman, N. P. (2012). The nature and organization of individual differences in executive functions: Four general conclusions. *Current Directions in Psychology, 21*, 8–14.

Miyake, A., Friedman, N. P., Emerson, M. J., Witzki, A. H., Howerter, A., & Wager, T. D. (2000). the unity and diversity of executive functions and their contributions to complex "frontal lobe" tasks: A latent variable analysis. *Cognitive Psychology, 41*, 49–100.

Moffitt, T. E., Arseneault, L., Belsky, D., Dickson, N., Hancox, R. J., Harrington, H., et al. (2011). A gradient of childhood self-control predicts health, wealth, and public safety. *Proceedings of the National Academy of Sciences (USA), 108*, 2693–2698.

Montroy, J. J., Merz, C., Williams, J. M., Landry, S. H., Johnson, U. Y., Zucker, T. A., et al. (2019). Hot and cool dimensionality of executive function: Model invariance across age and maternal education in preschool children. *Early Childhood Research Quarterly, 49*, 188–201.

Moriguchi, Y., Sakata, Y., Ishibashi, M., & Ishikawa, Y. (2015) Teaching others rule-use improves executive function and prefrontal activations in young children. *Frontiers in Psychology, 6*, 894.

Moriguchi, Y., & Shinahara, I. (2019). Less Is More activation: The involvement of the lateral prefrontal regions in a "Less Is More" task. *Developmental Neuropsychology, 44*, 273–281.

Moritz, S., Andreou, C., Schneider, B. C., Wittekind, C. E., Menon, M., Balzan, R. P., et al. (2014). Sowing the seeds of doubt: A narrative review on metacognitive training in schizophrenia. *Clinical Psychology Review, 34*, 358–366.

Mulder, H., Hoofs, H., Verhagen, J., van der Veen, I., & Leseman, P. P. (2014). Psychometric properties and convergent and predictive validity of an executive function test battery for two-year-olds. *Frontiers in Psychology, 5*, 733.

Mungas, D., Widaman, K., Zelazo, P.D., Tulsky, D., Heaton, R. K., Slotkin, J., et al. (2013). VII. NIH toolbox Cognition Battery (CB): Factor structure for 3- to 15-year-olds. *Monographs of the Society for Research in Child Development, 78*, 103–118.

Nejati, V., Salehinejad, M. A., & Nitsche, M. A. (2018). Interaction of the left dorsolateral prefrontal cortex (L-dlPFC) and right orbitofrontal cortex (OFC) in hot and cold executive functions: Evidence from transcranial direct current stimulation (tDCS). *Neuroscience, 369*(Suppl C), 109–123.

Nelson, T. D., Kidwell, K. M., Nelson, J. M., Tomaso, C. C., Hankey, M., & Espy, K. A. (2018). Preschool executive control and internalizing symptoms in elementary school. *Journal of Abnormal Child Psychology, 46*, 1509–1520.

Nesbitt, K. T., Baker-Ward, L., & Willoughby, M. T. (2013). Executive function mediates socio-economic and racial differences in early academic achievement. *Early Childhood Research Quarterly, 28*, 774–783.

Noble, K. G., Houston, S. M, Brito, N. H., Bartsch, H., Kan., E., Kuperman, J. M., et al. (2015). Family income, parental education and brain structure in children and adolescents. *Nature Neuroscience, 18*, 773–778.

Noble, K. G., McCandliss, B. D., & Farah, M. J. (2007). Socioeconomic gradients predict individual differences in neurocognitive abilities. *Developmental Science, 10*, 464–480.

Normann, N., & Morina, N. (2018). The efficacy of metacognitive therapy: A systematic review and meta-analysis. *Frontiers in Psychology, 9*, 2211.

O'Hearn, K., Osato, M., Ordaz, S., & Luna, B. (2008). Neurodevelopment and executive function in autism. *Development and Psychopathology, 20*, 1103–1132.

Overman, W. H., Bachevalier, J., Schumann, E., & Ryan, P. (1996). Cognitive gender differences in very young children parallel biologically based cognitive gender differences in monkeys. *Behavioral Neuroscience, 110*, 673–684.

Passler, M. A., Isaac, W., & Hynd, G. W. (1985). Neuropsychological development of behavior attributed to frontal lobe functioning in children. *Developmental Neuropsychology, 1*, 349–370.

Peterson, E., & Welsh, M. C. (2014). The development of hot and cool executive functions in childhood and adolescence: Are we getting warmer? In S. Goldstein, & J. Naglieri (eds.), *Executive Functioning Handbook* (pp. 45–65). New York: Springer.

Petrides, M., & Milner, B. (1982). Deficits on subject-ordered tasks after frontal-and temporal-lobe lesions in man. *Neuropsychologia, 20*, 249–262.

Pickering, S. J., & Gathercole, S. E. (2001). *Working Memory Test Battery for Children*. London: Psychological Corp.

Pietrefesa, A. S., & Evans, D. W. (2007). Affective and neuropsychological correlates of children's rituals and compulsive-like behaviors: Continuities and discontinuities with Obsessive-Compulsive Disorder. *Brain and Cognition, 65*, 36–46.

Plamondon, A., Akbari, E., Atkinson, L., Steiner, M., Meaney, M. J., & Fleming, A. S. (2015). Spatial working memory and attention skills are predicted by maternal stress during pregnancy. *Early Human Development, 91*, 23–29.

Plessow, F., Fischer, R., Kirschbaum, C., & Goschke, T. (2011). Inflexibly focused under stress: Acute psychosocial stress increases shielding of action goals at the expense of reduced cognitive flexibility with increasing time lag to the stressor. *Journal of Cognitive Neuroscience, 23*, 3218–3227.

Pozuelos, J. P., Combita, L. M., Abundis, A., Paz-Alonso, P. M., Conejero, A., Guerra, S., et al. (2019). Metacognitive scaffolding boosts cognitive and neural benefits following executive attention training in children. *Developmental Science, 22*, e12756.

Prencipe, A., Kesek, A., Cohen, J., Lamm, C., & Zelazo, P. D. (2011). Development of hot and cool executive function during the transition to adolescence. *Journal of Experimental Child Psychology*, 108, 621–637.

Prencipe, A., & Zelazo, P. D. (2005). Development of affective decision-making for self and other: Evidence for the integration of first- and third-person perspectives. *Psychological Science, 16*, 501–505.

Pribram, K. H. (1973). The primate frontal cortex: Executive of the brain. In K. H. Pribram, & A. R. Luria (eds.), *Psychophysiology of the Frontal Kobes* (pp. 293–314). New York: Academic Press.

Rhoades, R. D., Greenberg, M. C., & Domitrovich, T. (2009). The contribution of inhibitory control to preschoolers' social–emotional competence. *Journal of Applied Developmental Psychology. 30*, 310–320.

Riggs, N. R., Greenberg, M. T., Kusché, C. A., & Pentz, M. A. (2006). The mediational role of neurocognition in the behavioral outcomes of a social-emotional prevention program in elementary school students: Effects of the PATHS curriculum. *Prevention Science, 7*, 91–102.

Robbins, T. W., & Arnsten, A. F. (2009). The neuropsychopharmacology of fronto-executive function: Monoaminergic modulation. *Annual Review of Neuroscience, 32*, 267–287.

Robbins, T. W., James, M., Owen, A. M., Sahakian, B. J., McInnes, L., & Rabbitt, P. (1994). Cambridge Neuropsychological Test Automated Battery (CANTAB): A factor analytic study of a large sample of normal elderly volunteer. *Dementia, 5*, 266–281.

Roebers, C. (2017). Executive function and metacognition: Towards a unifying framework of cognitive self-regulation. *Developmental Review, 45*, 31–51.

Rolls, E. T. (2004). The functions of the orbitofrontal cortex. *Brain and Cognition, 55*, 11–29.

Rubia, K. (2011). "Cool" inferior frontostriatal dysfunction in attention-deficit/hyperactivity disorder versus "hot" ventromedial orbitofrontal-limbic dysfunction in conduct disorder: A review. *Biological Psychiatry, 69*, e69–e87.

Sameroff, A. J. (1983). Developmental systems: Contexts and evolution. In W. Kessen (Series ed.) & P. H. Mussen (Vol ed.), *Handbook of Child Psychology: Vol. 1. History, Theories, and Methods* (pp. 238–294). New York: Wiley.

Saver, J. L., & Damasio, A. R. (1991). Preserved access and processing of social knowledge in a patient with acquired sociopathy due to ventromedial frontal damage. *Neuropsychologia, 29*, 1241–1249.

Schmitt, S. A., Simpson, A. M., & Friend, M. (2011). A longitudinal assessment of the home literacy environment and early language. *Infant and Child Development, 20*, 409–431.

Schoemaker, K., Bunte, T., Wiebe, S. A., Espy, K. A., Deković, M., & Matthys, W. (2012). Executive function deficits in preschool children with ADHD and DBD. *Journal of Child Psychology and Psychiatry, 53*, 111–119.

Sheppes, G., Suri, G., & Gross, J. J. (2015). Emotion regulation and psychopathology. *Annual Review of Clinical Psychology, 11*, 379–405.

Sheridan, M. A., Peverill, M., Finn, A. S., & McLaughlin, K. A. (2017). Dimensions of childhood adversity have distinct associations with neural systems underlying executive functioning. *Development and Psychopathology, 29*, 1777–1794.

Sheridan, M. A., Sarsour, K., Jutte, D., D'Esposito, M., & Boyce, W. T. (2012). The impact of social disparity on prefrontal function in childhood. *PLoS ONE, 7*, e35744.

Shi, R., Sharpe, L., & Abbott, M. (2017). A meta-analysis of the relationship between anxiety and attentional control. *Clinical Psychology Review, 72*, 101754.

Shields, G. S., Sazma, M. A., & Yonelinas, A. P. (2016). The effects of acute stress on core executive functions: A meta-analysis and comparison with cortisol. *Neuroscience & Biobehavioral Review, 68*, 651–668.

Shinaver, C. S., Entwistle, P. C., & Söderqvist, S. (2014). Cogmed WM training: Reviewing the reviews. *Applied Neuropsychology: Child, 3*, 163–172.

Shing, Y.L., Lindenberger, U., Diamond, A., Li, S.C., & Davidson, M. C. (2010). Memory maintenance and inhibitory control differentiate from early childhood to adolescence. *Developmental Neuropsychology, 35*, 679–697.

Shoda, Y., Mischel, W., & Peake, P. K. (1990). Predicting adolescent cognitive and self-regulatory competencies from preschool delay of gratification: Identifying diagnostic conditions. *Developmental Psychology, 26*, 978–986.

Shonkoff, J. P. (2011). Protecting brains, not simply stimulating minds. *Science, 333*, 982–983.

Shonkoff, J. P., Garner, A. S., Siegel, B. S., Dobbins, M. I., Earls, M. F., Garner, A. S., et al. (2012). The lifelong effects of early childhood adversity and toxic stress. *Pediatrics, 129*, e232–e246.

Smith, S. M. (1982). Enhancement of recall using multiple environmental contexts during learning. *Memory & Cognition, 10*, 405–412.

Smith-Donald, R., Raver, C. C., Hayes, T., & Richardson, B. (2007). Preliminary construct and concurrent validity of the preschool self-regulation assessment (PSRA) for field-based research. *Early Childhood Research Quarterly, 22*, 173–187.

Sonuga-Barke, E. J. S. (2003). The dual pathway model of AD/HD: An elaboration of neuro-developmental characteristics. *Neuroscience and Biobehavioral Reviews, 27*, 593–604.

Sroufe, L. A., & Rutter, M. (1984). The domain of developmental psychopathology. *Child Development. 55*, 17–29.

Stroop, J. R. (1935). Studies of interference in serial verbal reactions. *Journal of Experimental Psychology, 18*, 643–662.

Stuss, D. T., & Benson, D. F. (1986). *The Frontal Lobes*. New York: Raven Press.

Thorell, L. B. (2007). Do delay aversion and executive function deficits make distinct contributions to the functional impact of ADHD symptoms? A study of early academic skill deficits. *Journal of Child Psychology and Psychiatry, 48*, 1061–1070.

Toll, S. W., Van der Ven, S. H., Kroesbergen, E. H., & Van Luit, J. E. (2011). Executive functions as predictors of math learning disabilities. *Journal of Learning Disabilities, 44*, 521–532.

Travers-Hill, E., Dunn, B., Hoppitt, L., Hitchcock, C., & Dalgleish, T. (2017). Beneficial effects of training in self-distancing and perspective broadening for people with a history of recurrent depression. *Behaviour Research and Therapy, 95*, 19–28.

Usai, M. C., Viterbori, P., Traverso, L., & De Franchis, V. (2014). Latent structure of executive function in 5- and 6-year-old children: A longitudinal study. *European Journal of Developmental Psychology, 11*, 447–462.

Vincent, J. L., Kahn, I., Snyder, A. Z., Raichle, M. E., & Buckner, R. L. (2008). Evidence for a frontoparietal control system revealed by intrinsic functional connectivity. *Journal of Neurophysiology, 100*, 3328–3342.

Wass, S. V., Smith, C. G., Daubney, K. R., Suata, Z. M., Clackson, K., Begum, A., et al. (2019). Influences of environmental stressors on autonomic function in 12-month-old infants: Understanding early common pathways to atypical emotion regulation and cognitive performance. *Journal of Child Psychology and Psychiatry, 60*, 1323–1333.

Wechsler, D. (1992). *Wechsler Intelligence Scale for Children – Third Edition*. London: Psychological Corporation.

Welsh, M. C., & Pennington, B. F. (1988). Assessing frontal lobe functioning in children: Views from developmental psychology. *Developmental Neuropsychology, 4*, 199–230.

Welsh, M. C., Pennington, B. F., & Groisser, D. B. (1991). A normative-developmental study of executive function: A window on prefrontal function in children. *Developmental Neuropsychology, 7*, 131–149.

Wiebe, S. A., Espy, K. A., & Charak, D. (2008). Using confirmatory factor analysis to understand executive control in preschool children: I. Latent structure. *Developmental Psychology, 44*, 575–587.

Wiebe, S. A., Sheffield, T., Nelson, J. M., Clark, C. A. C., Chevalier, N., & Espy, K. A. (2011). The structure of executive function in 3-year-olds. *Journal of Experimental Child Psychology, 108*, 436–452.

Willoughby, M., Kupersmidt, J., Voegler-Lee, M., & Bryant, D. (2011). Contributions of hot and cool self-regulation to preschool disruptive behavior and academic achievement. *Developmental Neuropsychology, 36*, 162–180.

Xu, F., Han, Y., Sabbagh, M.A., Wang, T., Ren, X., & Li, C. (2013). Developmental differences in the structure of executive function in middle childhood and adolescence. *PLoS ONE, 8*, e77770.

Zatorre, R. J., Fields, R. D., & Johansen-Berg, H. (2013). Plasticity in gray and white: Neuroimaging changes in brain structure during learning. *Nature Neuroscience, 15*, 528–536.

Zelazo, P. D. (2006). The dimensional change card sort: A method of assessing executive function in children. *Nature Protocols, 1*, 297–301.

Zelazo, P. D. (2015). Executive function: Reflection, iterative reprocessing, complexity, and the developing brain. *Developmental Review, 38*, 55–68.

Zelazo, P. D. (2020). Executive function and psychopathology: A neurodevelopmental perspective. *Annual Review of Clinical Psychology, 16*, 14.1–14.24.

Zelazo, P. D., Anderson, J. E., Richler, J., Wallner-Allen, K., Beaumont, J. L., Conway, K. P., et al. (2014). NIH Toolbox Cognition Battery (CB): Validation of executive function measures in adults. *Journal of the International Neuropsychological Society, 20*, 620–629.

Zelazo, P. D., Anderson, J. E., Richler, J., Wallner-Allen, K., Beamont, J. L., & Weintraub, S. (2013). NIH Toolbox Cognition Battery (CB): Measuring executive function and attention. *Monographs of the Society for Research in Child Development, 78*, 16–33.

Zelazo, P. D., Blair, C. B., & Willoughby, M. T. (2016). Executive function: Implications for education. *US Department of Education*, 1–148. Available from https://ies.ed.gov/ncer/pubs/20172000/pdf/20172000.pdf. Last accessed August 4, 2021.

Zelazo, P. D., Carter, A., Reznick, J. S., & Frye, D. (1997). Early development of executive function: A problem-solving framework. *Review of General Psychology, 1*, 198–226.

Zelazo, P. D., & Cunningham, W. (2007). Executive function: Mechanisms underlying emotion regulation. In J. Gross (ed.), *Handbook of Emotion Regulation* (pp. 135–158). New York: Guilford.

Zelazo, P. D., Forston, J. L., Masten, A. S., & Carlson, S. M. (2018). Mindfulness plus reflection training: Effects on executive function in early childhood. *Frontiers in Psychology, 9*, 1–12.

Zelazo, P. D., Frye, D., & Rapus, T. (1996). An age-related dissociation between knowing rules and using them. *Cognitive Development, 11*, 37–63.

Zelazo, P. D., & Jacques, S. (1996). Children's rule use: Representation, reflection, and cognitive control. *Annals of Child Development, 12*, 119–176.

Zelazo, P. D., & Müller, U. (2002). Executive function in typical and atypical development. In U. Goswami (ed.), *Handbook of Childhood Cognitive Development* (pp. 445–469). Oxford: Blackwell.

Zelazo, P. D., Müller, U., Frye, D., & Marcovitch, S. (2003). The development of executive function in early childhood. *Monographs of the Society for Research on Child Development, 68*, vii–137.

Zelazo, P. D., & Reznick, J. S. (1991). Age related asynchrony of knowledge and action. *Child Development, 62*, 719–735.

20 Developing Cognitive Control and Flexible Adaptation during Childhood

Nicolas Chevalier and Agnès Blaye

20.1 What Is Cognitive Control?

Whereas performance on intelligence tests and their associated IQ indices are typically considered by parents and teachers as a visa for school success, research over the last couple of decades has revealed an even better predictor of life success than intelligence: cognitive control, that is, the goal-directed regulation of attention, thoughts and actions (Blair & Razza, 2007). Even young children, who tend to be 'all over the place', prone to tantrums and often engage in socially inappropriate behaviours, are not devoid of cognitive control skills. Emerging cognitive control during childhood supports increasingly complex thinking and reasoning, ensures steady gains in autonomy with age and allows children to respond increasingly adaptively to novel situations where no routine exists or multiple responses compete with one another. As such, cognitive control plays a key role in explicit learning, as it is initially required to guide actions (e.g., to decide on which keys to press while learning the piano), although it is progressively released as the newly learned skill becomes automated (Chein & Schneider, 2012). Furthermore, in the classroom, children need to engage cognitive control to raise their hands before talking, take turns, concentrate, follow instructions and stay on task. Indeed, cognitive control early in life predicts not only attention in the classroom and academic achievement but also other important outcomes such as health, income and relationship quality in adulthood (Daly et al., 2015; Moffitt et al., 2011). Children growing up in poverty generally show less efficient cognitive control than children from higher socioeconomic backgrounds (Noble et al., 2007) and poor cognitive control is often observed in children with developmental disorders (such as autism and ADHD; Christ et al., 2010; Geurts et al., 2004). In turn, poor cognitive control is a major risk factor for learning difficulties, academic failure, and cascading negative outcomes, including unsafe sex, drug abuse, and criminality in adolescence and adulthood (Moffitt et al., 2011).

The central role of cognitive control in child development has sparked exponential scientific interest in its neurocognitive processes and the mechanisms that drive changes with age. Cognitive control is achieved via prefrontally mediated goals guiding information processing in posterior brain regions. In other words, the goals that one is pursuing (i.e., intentions to achieve a specific action, perform a task or reach certain states of the world; Altmann & Trafton, 2002) are maintained in working memory and used to orient attention toward goal-relevant information in the environment and to select the most appropriate actions through top-down influences on sensory and motor systems. Such top-down influences may take the form of cross-frequency couplings between activity in frontal and posterior regions. Specifically, bursts of slow oscillations (in the alpha or theta bands) originating from the prefrontal cortex may result in synchronized rapid oscillations (gamma band) in posterior regions critical for goal attainment, and thus greater biasing of lower information processing pathways (Cavanagh & Frank, 2014; Helfrich & Knight, 2016; Verguts, 2017). Consistently, cognitive control training results in greater cross-frequency coupling in middle childhood (Barnes et al., 2016).

As cognitive control is supported by distributed neural networks, including prefrontal, anterior cingulate and parietal cortices, that is, association cortices that take among the longest to develop during childhood, and as its efficiency critically hinges on slow-building, long-range connections with distal, posterior regions (Raznahan et al., 2011; Shaw et al., 2008), it is no surprise that cognitive control follows a particularly protracted developmental trajectory (Diamond, 2013). Evidence of cognitive control is observed early in life, as infants successfully inhibit the impulse to search for objects where they previously retrieved them and instead search where they have seen them disappear last (Marcovitch & Zelazo, 1999). Although some important milestones are reached at preschool age, such as the ability to switch tasks once around four years of age and to switch back and forth from five years onwards (Doebel & Zelazo, 2015, see Chapter 19), cognitive control shows relatively steady progress throughout childhood, adolescence and until the mid-twenties (Zelazo & Carlson, 2012). At any specific age, what children can achieve is largely dependent on the amount of interference (conflict) that needs to be resolved in a particular situation, with tasks in which interference and thus cognitive demands are strongest being passed later in childhood. That being said, as will be addressed in detail later in this chapter, important changes in how children engage control are usually observed in middle childhood and adolescence (Crone, 2009; Munakata et al., 2012).

These changes progressively result in more efficient, flexible and adaptive behaviour with age, ranging from using the bathroom properly to organizing homework.

Both children and adults face the challenge of adjusting control engagement due to constant change in task demands, leading to inevitable moment-to-moment variations in the best way to engage control. For instance, as children cycle to school, they may ride through busy streets in which they must mobilize control to actively monitor for cars, traffic lights, pedestrians, etc., and then go through a quiet park where they can release control and perhaps engage attention in other activities (e.g., gathering their thoughts for the upcoming math exam) while still being able to quickly mobilize control if needed (e.g., if a dog unexpectedly runs across the bike path). Therefore, the developmental challenge may not necessarily consist of engaging more control with age, but instead of engaging it in a more flexible and differentiated fashion in order to respond adaptively to ever-changing task demands. In the rest of this chapter, we review evidence suggesting that control engagement becomes increasingly flexible with age and then address the mechanisms that may drive increasingly flexible adaptation during childhood.

20.2 Evidence for Increasingly Flexible Control Engagement with Age

As children grow older, they engage control in a more flexible way, hence more adaptively responding to changing task demands (e.g., Chevalier, 2015). Increasingly flexible engagement of cognitive control is evidenced by the progressive differentiation in the main components (or functions) of cognitive control alongside changes in the neural networks supporting cognitive control, the growing ability to up- or down-regulate how much control they exert, and better management of children's expanding repertoire of control strategies over the course of childhood.

20.2.1 Differentiation of Control Components and Neural Network Changes

A first line of evidence for increasing flexibility in control engagement comes from research on the latent structure (i.e., main components) of cognitive control, which uses confirmatory factor analysis to determine whether variance across multiple behavioural measures of cognitive control can be best summarized by one or several latent factors. Using this approach, a seminal study pointed out three correlated but partially separable components of mature cognitive control, suggesting that adults rely on different executive processes or at least engage them differently depending on whether task demands require (1) *inhibiting* irrelevant information or responses, (2) *updating* information in working memory, or (3) *shifting* between tasks, perspectives or mental operations (Miyake et al., 2000). Although separable, these components seem to partially overlap, perhaps because of the necessity to maintain goal-related information in working memory that is common to virtually all situations tapping cognitive control. More recently, the authors proposed a revised model including a common executive ability alongside shifting- and updating-specific abilities, but no inhibition-specific ability as all variance shared by inhibition measures was accounted for by the common executive ability (Miyake & Friedman, 2012).

In contrast, cognitive control seems much more unitary in preschool children, suggesting that preschool children mostly engage the same control processes regardless of specific task demands (Wiebe et al., 2008, 2011; Willoughby et al., 2012). It then progressively differentiates throughout childhood, with two components usually found in middle childhood (albeit not consistently the same two components across studies), and a three-component structure in adolescence similar to that observed in adults (Lee et al., 2013), suggesting that older children and adolescents progressively handle task demands in a finer-grained fashion with advancing age (see also Chapter 19). Although a recent review of the studies using confirmatory factor analysis pointed out the prevalence of these models in both childhood and adulthood, respectively, has been overestimated, it confirmed that available empirical evidence converges toward progressive differentiation of executive components during childhood and adolescence (Karr et al., 2018).

The differentiation of cognitive control components seems to be accompanied by differentiation in functional connectivity at the level of neural networks throughout childhood. In particular, the neural networks supporting cognitive control show both progressive segregation, that is, lower local functional connectivity within brain regions such as the prefrontal cortex and the anterior cingulate cortex, and integration, that is, greater distal functional connectivity across brain regions (e.g., between prefrontal and parietal cortices) (Barber et al., 2013; Ezekiel et al., 2013; Fair et al., 2007; Hwang et al., 2010; Kelly et al., 2009; Sherman et al., 2014; Uddin et al., 2011). Note, however, that greater motion-related noise in younger children, which was not properly accounted for in early work, may have resulted in overestimation of short-range connectivity at that age, and thus of the evidence for age-related segregation and integration during childhood (Fair et al., 2013; Grayson & Fair, 2017). Furthermore, later work showed that connectivity change is not as based on distance within the brain as initially thought, and connectivity change during childhood and adolescence also includes progressively greater cross-network connectivity, contributing to greater efficiency of cognitive control with age (Luna et al., 2015; Marek et al., 2015).

Changes in the functional connectivity between neural networks may reflect interactive specialization with age, the process by which cortical regions with originally broad and poorly defined functions become increasingly restricted to particular information processing through growing activity-dependent interactions with other regions (Johnson, 2011). In other words, different aspects of cognitive control, which may initially rely on largely overlapping brain regions and networks, may progressively be supported by more specialized regions and network with age and accumulated experiences. Consistently, greater frontoposterior connectivity is associated with better set-shifting performance in preschoolers (Buss & Spencer, 2018). As a result of specialization, prefrontal activation becomes increasingly focal with age (Durston et al., 2006; Marsh et al., 2006; Tamm et al., 2002; Tsujii et al., 2009). For instance, nine-year-old children show a diffuse pattern of prefrontal activation while completing the Go/No-Go task, which taps response inhibition, whereas most prefrontal activation is confined to the right ventrolateral PFC at eleven years of age (Durston et al., 2006), a region specialized in response inhibition in adults (Aron et al., 2003).

20.2.2 Cognitive Control Up- and Down-Adjustment

Not only is prefrontal activation in children diffuse, but it seems maximal even when demands on cognitive control are relatively low, suggesting poor modulation of control engagement in early childhood. Specifically, unlike adults who show increasing activation in ventral PFC with increasing interference on

the Go/No-Go task, school-age children show maximal activation even for lower interference levels (Durston et al., 2002; see also Davis et al., 2003). Similarly, on the task-switching paradigm, children recruit pre-SMA/SMA both when the task switches and when it repeats, whereas greater pre-SMA/SMA activation is observed in adults only in task switch trials (i.e., the most demanding trials; Crone et al., 2006). Although preschoolers engage just as much, if not more, prefrontal activation than elementary school-age children, they do not match prefrontal cortex recruitment to variations in task demands as effectively as older children, resulting in high prefrontal activation even when demands are relatively low and control could be released (Chevalier et al., 2019; see Chevalier et al., 2013, for consistent behavioural findings). Interestingly, a similar pattern is observed in a working memory updating task in teenagers from low socioeconomic status (SES) backgrounds. Relative to their high-SES counterparts, low-SES teenagers show greater prefrontal activation when task difficulty is low but lower activation when task difficulty is high, resulting in less prefrontal activation change as a function of task difficulty (Finn et al., 2017). Greater prefrontal activation release when demands are low may be achieved by relying more on posterior regions through automatized information processing (e.g., Durston et al., 2002), hence reducing the need for cognitive control engagement and promoting more economic cognitive functioning overall (Luna et al., 2010, 2015).

Although young children often show less variations in prefrontal cortex recruitment as a function of changing task demands than older children, they can under some circumstances show signs of adaptive control adjustments as revealed by the congruency sequence effect (CSE). This effect, also known as Gratton or conflict-adaptation effect, is well established in adults (Duthoo et al., 2014;

Egner, 2007; Gratton et al., 1992, for reviews) and generally considered a proxy for control modulation based on conflict that has just been encountered. Congruency effects have been evidenced in conflict tasks such as the colour–word Stroop (Stroop, 1935). Participants are presented with coloured colour words (e.g., the word "red" printed in blue) and asked to identify the print colour and resist the tendency to read the word. Two types of trials can be distinguished: conflictual incongruent trials where the word and print colour lead to different responses and congruent ones where both dimensions converge toward the same response. Congruency effects correspond to longer response times and potentially lower accuracy on incongruent trials, where a conflict has to be overcome, compared to congruent ones. The congruency sequence effect in turn corresponds to a smaller congruency effect after an incongruent trial than after a congruent one, hence suggesting better processing of conflicts when encountered in sequence. Although the congruency sequence effect was originally reported in the Stroop task, it is commonly observed in other paradigms involving conflict resolution (e.g., flanker task, Simon task). According to the most prominent conflict-monitoring account[1] (Botvinick et al., 2001), this effect reflects an adjustment of control in reaction to the conflict encountered on the previous incongruent trials. More specifically, when conflict is encountered, the dorsal anterior cingulate cortex (dACC) that monitors the occurrence of conflict would trigger up-regulation of control by sending a warning signal to the lateral PFC, which is responsible for biasing information processing toward task-relevant

information while ignoring task-irrelevant, interfering information. Such up-regulation of control would serve to reduce the impact of conflict on the upcoming trial.

Evidence in children is scarce but suggests that such modulation can already be observed in preschoolers (Ambrosi et al., 2016; Iani et al., 2014; Kray et al., 2012) and school-aged children (Blaye et al., 2018; Nieuwenhuis et al., 2006; Stins et al., 2007; Wilk & Morton, 2012). In a recent study, Erb, Moher, Sobel, and Song (2016) proposed to distinguish two distinct mechanisms underlying the congruency sequence effect. According to them, when a conflict is registered, conflict signal originating from dACC triggers (1) a threshold adjustment process that temporarily inhibits motor response and (2) a controlled selection process of the relevant response by the lateral PFC. Using a reach-tracking technique to measure responses in a flanker task with eight-to-ten-year-old children, ten-to-twelve-year-old pre-adolescents and young adults, Erb and Marcovitch (2019) observed congruency sequence effects in all age groups, but distinct developmental trajectories for the threshold adjustment process, which improved only until pre-adolescence, and the controlled selection of the correct response, which continued developing between pre-adolescence and adulthood. Interestingly however, most developmental studies failed to reveal significant changes with age in the magnitude of the congruency sequence effect (Blaye et al., 2018; Cragg, 2016; Larson et al., 2012; Smulders et al., 2018), which seems at odds with the above-mentioned inflexibility of control engagement in young children. Although the debate on whether the congruency sequence effect reflects conflict adaptation and hence proper control modulation is still ongoing, the conflict between the two lines of research may only be apparent. First, the conflict-monitoring account proposes that control

---

[1] For alternative associative- or temporal-learning-based accounts of congruency sequence effects, see for instance, Mayr et al. (2003), Hommel et al. (2004) and Schmidt (2013, 2019).

modulation results from a transient increase of control post-conflict encountered on trial N–1. The lower interference of conflict on trial N would then be a consequence of approaching the new trial with an up-regulated control. As will be described in Section 20.2.3, young children are more prone to engage control after conflict has already arisen, which then makes the present form of control modulation within their reach. Second, research in adults suggests that conflict adaptation can operate unconsciously (e.g., Atas et al., 2016; Linzarini et al., 2017; Van Gaal et al., 2010) and does not require awareness of conflict (Jiang et al., 2018). Although metacognition likely contributes to some aspects of flexible control engagement (see Section 2.3), explicitly representing how control is engaged may not be needed or even involved in congruency sequence effects, hence explaining why these effects can be observed from early on in development.

20.2.3 Variations in Cognitive Control Strategies

Greater flexibility in cognitive control engagement with age may also reflect a growing repertoire of control strategies, allowing children to adaptively use the strategy that best fits the current task demands. Despite the sparsity of studies, there is some evidence for variability across children in the way control is engaged, pointing out the potential coexistence of multiple control strategies (Dauvier et al., 2012). For instance, successful task switching at age five years is associated with different patterns of ventral prefrontal activation, and these patterns are predicted by earlier performance at age three years (Moriguchi & Hiraki, 2011). However, there is little evidence that young children can adaptively engage different control strategies as a function of changing task demands, and more active or advanced control strategies are not usually observed before

middle childhood, perhaps because the effort they require reduces their adaptiveness early in childhood. This is the case of strategies observed on working memory span tasks. Preschoolers seemingly engage no particular strategies, only passively maintaining the to-be-recalled items, whereas children from age seven years on show evidence of active attentional refreshing, which consists of quickly switching attention to the memoranda during processing episodes to prevent it from decaying (Camos & Barrouillet, 2011). Similarly, verbal rehearsal, like other verbal strategies, is generally observed only later in childhood (Fatzer & Roebers, 2012), even though language is a very powerful self-regulatory medium (Cragg & Nation, 2010), and gaze-based rehearsal of visuospatial information seems to shift from a reactive, cue-driven approach to a proactive, covert approach around that age (Morey et al., 2018).

The shift from reactive to proactive modes of engaging cognitive control is indeed a major transition during childhood observed across many tasks. Reactive and proactive control modes, which were introduced by the Dual Mechanisms of Control model (Braver & Burgess, 2007), differ in the temporal dynamics of control engagement. Reactive control is engaged as needed in the moment to resolve conflict after it has arisen (e.g., quickly gathering thoughts to answer an unexpected question during a class presentation), whereas proactive control consists of anticipating and actively preparing for upcoming conflict by configuring the cognitive system ahead of time in order to prevent conflict from arising (e.g., anticipating questions that are likely to be asked). Each control mode comes with its own advantages and disadvantages. Reactive control, which relies on fast goal-relevant information retrieval and only transient prefrontal activation, is the most viable option when upcoming tasks/conflict cannot be reliably predicted and it is thought to require less cognitive effort than proactive control. In contrast, proactive control is especially efficient, as it allows the cognitive system to arrive at the most appropriate response faster (as less conflict is experienced) than reactively solving conflict (in situations where both control modes are viable options). However, proactive control requires maintaining goal-relevant information in working memory over longer periods of time, resulting in sustained activation in the prefrontal cortex (Marklund & Persson, 2012), which makes this control mode particularly effortful. In addition, it is efficient only when upcoming events and potential conflict can be reliably predicted, as actively preparing for a task that never happens may be inefficient and even counterproductive. Indeed, engaging proactive control on a delayed-match-to-sample task when distraction during the retention delay increases the cost of this approach resulted in worse performance than reactive control engagement at age six years (Blackwell & Munakata, 2014).

Although young adults with high working-memory resources are more likely to engage control proactively than their lower working-memory resource counterparts, adults in general flexibly engage either control mode in order to best respond to changing task demands (Braver, 2012). In contrast, preschoolers do not yet flexibly engage these control modes. There is now a well-established progressive shift from reactive to proactive control during childhood. This shift has been observed in multiple tasks tapping response inhibition, task-switching, working memory, and prospective memory, and across multiple methods including behaviour, pupillometry, and EEG (Andrews-Hanna et al., 2011; Chatham et al., 2009; Chevalier et al., 2014, 2015; Doebel et al., 2017; Gonthier et al., 2019; Lucenet & Blaye, 2014; Munakata et al., 2012; Voigt et al., 2014). Specifically,

preschoolers tend to be biased toward reactive control, engaging this control mode even in situations where proactive control could have been more efficient (Munakata et al., 2012). Children start engaging proactive control around five-to-six years of age (Gonthier et al., 2019; Lucenet & Blaye, 2014), with proactive control strategies becoming increasingly efficient and elaborated throughout middle childhood and adolescence (e.g., Andrews-Hanna et al., 2011; Chatham et al., 2009; Polizzotto et al., 2018). This shift does not mean that from six years on proactive control replaces reactive control but instead that children more flexibly engage either form of control as a function of task demands with age. Indeed, the degree to which children engage proactive control at any age is influenced by contextual features such as the provision of reward, as shown by greater sustained prefrontal and parietal activation, in preadolescents, adolescents and adults on tasks with than without reward (Strang & Pollak, 2014).

Interestingly, although five-year-olds spontaneously engage reactive control even when proactive control would be more efficient, they can successfully engage control proactively if reactive control is made more difficult (Chevalier et al., 2015; Elke & Wiebe, 2017). Thus, proactive control is already part of children's repertoire before they engage it spontaneously, suggesting that young children's bias to reactive control may be due to a difficulty detecting situations in which proactive control would be especially efficient and/or a higher threshold for engaging this control mode, rather than a fundamental limitation of their cognitive system (e.g., not enough working memory resources). As proactive control engagement critically hinges on detection of cues that reliably signal upcoming tasks and young children especially struggle to detect and process environmental cues that signal relevant tasks (Blaye & Chevalier, 2011;

Chevalier & Blaye, 2009; Chevalier et al., 2011), greater attention to and processing of such cues with age may contribute to increasing use of proactive control in middle childhood (Chevalier et al., 2009).

20.3 Mechanisms Driving Increasingly Flexible Control Engagement

The question of the mechanisms underpinning flexible control engagement as a function of changing task demands is of paramount importance to fully understand developmental change in cognitive control during childhood. According to the Flexible Control Model (Muhle-Karbe et al., 2018), control adjustment is achieved through a reinforcement-learning mechanism that tracks task demands in order to minimize the prediction error or mismatch between the amount of control that was predicted (and thus exerted) and the amount of control that would have been needed for success. When there is little change in task demands (stable environments), the learning rate is low and predictions about the amount of control to be exerted are mostly based on the individual's large history of past experiences (i.e., knowledge base), whereas the learning rate rises when task demands change quickly (volatile environments) so that predictions are mostly based on very recent experiences. The anterior insula, dorsal striatum, and lateral prefrontal cortex may contribute to learning rate encoding, control demand predictions, and control adjustment based on these predictions, respectively. This model, however, does not emphasize the potential role of the dorsal anterior cingulate cortex (dACC), which is generally thought to be key to conflict detection and control adjustment (Botvinick et al., 2001; Gehring & Knight, 2000; Luna et al., 2015).

The dACC is central in the Expected Value of Control model (Shenhav et al., 2013).

According to this model, the cognitive system automatically computes the ratio between the expected benefit (i.e., reward) and cost (i.e., cognitive effort) of pursuing different tasks in order to select the most advantageous one and determine how much control to engage toward its attainment. The dACC may integrate the information about task demands and internal states (from high-order perception and the orbitofrontal cortex, respectively) and signals the need for control adjustment to the lateral prefrontal cortex (which actually exerts control by biasing activity in posterior regions). This model could be expanded by including computation of cost/benefit ratios of different control strategies and implementing the one with the most advantageous ratio (i.e., greatest expected reward for the lowest predicted cognitive effort).

The Integrative Component Model of Cognitive Control Development (Luna et al., 2015) also attributes a central role to dACC, as this model suggests that increasingly flexible control with age emerges from the progressive integration of the processes and neural networks supporting performance monitoring (in which dACC plays a prominent role) with those supporting information maintenance and inhibition. As experiences accumulate with age, patterns of within- and between-network connectivity supporting goal attainment (i.e., reward) in the face of specific task demands are strengthened while patterns associated with unsuccessful outcomes for the same task demands are weakened, leading to gains in control engagement flexibility and efficiency.

A central feature of flexible control engagement, based on these models, is building a large knowledge base of previous experiences to derive reliable predictions of (a) how much cognitive effort and thus control should be implemented and (b) which control strategy is most likely to succeed given particular task demands. Early in development, children may not have yet built such a knowledge base about the adequacy between different ways of engaging control and different task demands, hence leading to poor predictions. Over time and with increasing experiences, knowledge may progressively accumulate, leading to more accurate predictions from dACC. In addition, predictions about the need to adjust control engagement may be more clearly sent to lateral PFC as connectivity between dACC and lateral PFC increases due to greater links between the cingulo-opercular and the other networks with age (Kelly et al., 2009; Marek et al., 2015). Consistently, dACC volume is related to cognitive control performance during childhood (Fjell et al., 2012). Further, dorsolateral PFC activation was found to decrease while dACC activation increased on an antisaccade task between nine and twenty-two years of age, potentially because greater signal from dACC resulted in more refined control engagement in DLPFC (Ordaz et al., 2013).

Importantly, to compute accurate and reliable predictions about how to best engage control to meet task demands, the cognitive system needs at least three pieces of information: (1) information about available control resources (i.e., how much control and which control strategies could be engaged), (2) information about current task demands, and (3) information about progress toward goal attainment. An important question, thus, is to what extent children accurately represent how they engage control. Accurate representation of how control is engaged is essential to build a knowledge base of how well a particular approach or strategy was successful given specific task demands and, therefore, to predict whether the same approach is likely to succeed when similar task demands are met in the future. To our knowledge, only one study has investigated this question, by examining whether children accurately monitor how well they proactively prepare for the upcoming task in a cued task-switching paradigm in which they needed to switch back and forth between colour- and shape-matching tasks as a function of visual task cue presented ahead of the target, hence allowing children to proactively prepare for the upcoming task (by getting ready to process the relevant target dimension). Critically, proactive preparation was self-paced, meaning that children could take as long as they wanted to prepare for the upcoming task before triggering the next target themselves. At age six, children most often decided to trigger the target early, before they were fully prepared (as evidenced by gaze patterns), even though they did respond faster and more accurately on the minority of trials in which they waited until proactive preparation was complete. In contrast, ten-year-olds triggered the target when they were fully prepared in most trials, suggesting important progress in how accurately children monitor proactive control engagement with age (Chevalier & Blaye, 2016). Failure to accurately monitor proactive control engagement may lead younger children to misrepresent the situations in which this control mode would be especially efficient, hence potentially accounting at least partially for why they do not use proactive control in situations where it would benefit performance, unless reactive control is made more difficult (Chevalier et al., 2015). A pending question, though, is whether younger children do not accurately represent how and how well they engage control or whether they do not use this information to strategically optimize control engagement.

Regardless of the exact nature of this difficulty, these findings suggest that flexibility in control engagement may be intrinsically related to metacognitive abilities (see Roebers, 2017). Work on metacognitive development suggests that, as children grow older, they more accurately represent their own performance, when to engage more attention and which strategies to use to optimize learning. For instance, although five-year-olds can already tell easy- from hard-to-learn materials, only children aged six and older strategically devote more time to studying harder than easier materials (Destan et al., 2014). Similarly, children show increasing understanding of the role of deliberate practice for learning and more often engage in such practice before an expected assessment from four to seven years of age (Brinums et al., 2018). In addition, metacognition may influence control engagement through children's willingness to engage the cognitive effort that comes with cognitive control. For instance, seven-to-twelve-year-old children with a high subjective value of cognitive effort, that is, who perceive effort as valuable (perhaps because effortful situations often provide opportunities to learn), are more likely to engage proactive control, which requires earlier and more effort than reactive control, relative to children who perceive cognitive effort as costly (Chevalier, 2018). In addition, children with an intelligence growth mindset (i.e., children who think intelligence is malleable, seek effort, and perceive errors as sources of growth) perform better at school than children who hold a fixed intelligence mindset (i.e., children who perceive errors as threats and avoid effort; Claro et al., 2016; see also Haimovitz & Dweck, 2017). Despite the intrinsic links between cognitive control and metacognition developments, control adjustment is probably not entirely conscious and intentional, as some adjustments of control engagement largely operate outside of consciousness, as suggested by the above-mentioned research on congruency sequence effects.

Besides representation of control strategies, flexible control engagement likely relies on representation of task demands, as the best way to engage control is a function of the specific demands of each situation. Adults show clear sensitivity to variations in task demands and strategically use this information to optimize cognitive functioning by avoiding unnecessary cognitive effort. This is evidenced by their performance in the Demand Selection Task, in which participants select from which of two decks they want the next trial to be drawn. Unbeknown to them the two decks differ in cognitive demands as one deck requires frequent task switches (harder deck) while the other deck mostly requires task repetitions (easier deck). Across trials, adults develop a clear bias toward the easier deck, hence avoiding unnecessary cognitive effort and control (Gold et al., 2015; Kool et al., 2010). Importantly, participants with lower cognitive control, as evidenced by higher initial switch costs and greater need to engage prefrontal activity to succeed on the task, develop the most pronounced bias to the easier deck over time (Kool et al., 2010; McGuire & Botvinick, 2010), probably because extra (and unnecessary) cognitive effort is more taxing and thus more aversive for these individuals than their higher cognitive control counterparts.

As cognitive control is much less efficient in children than adults, one may argue that children should show an even greater bias to the easier deck in this task. Yet, children may not be as sensitive to variations in task demands and/or not use this information strategically to avoid unnecessary cognitive effort and control engagement, in which case they may not develop any bias toward the easier deck, even though it would be especially adaptive for them to do so. Indeed, unlike eleven-to-twelve-year-olds and young adults, six-to-seven-year-olds do not show a clear bias to either deck on the Demand Selection Task and fail to identify the easier deck when explicitly asked if one deck was easier than the other (Niebaum et al., 2019). Hence, young children do not appear sensitive to variations in task demands, which likely contributes to relatively rigid control engagement at that age. However, when five- and seven-year-old children are provided feedback on their performance on each deck and explicitly instructed to pick the easier deck, they now show a bias toward the easier deck (O'Leary & Sloutsky, 2017). Therefore, even younger children can use variations in task demands when guided to do so, which suggests that they need such scaffolding to either use this information or search for it spontaneously, and that this scaffolding may help them better monitor their performance across contexts.

Performance monitoring is indeed another essential element for flexible control engagement, as it provides information as to whether progress is made toward goal achievement and thus whether current cognitive control engagement should be maintained or adjusted. This information also contributes to building knowledge based on successful past experiences that can be used for later predictions about how to best engage control. Errors are especially important to monitor as they clearly signal the need to adjust up control to ensure success on the following trials. Error detection is accompanied in adults by an error-related negativity (ERN), that is, a marked frontocentral deflection in EEG data about 100 milliseconds following errors, relative to correct responses (e.g., Gehring et al., 1993). The error-related negativity may arise from the mismatch between the expected and actual responses (Falkenstein et al., 1991), it may constitute a negative learning reinforcement signal (Holroyd & Coles, 2002) or it may reflect conflict that lingers after the response has been made (Botvinick et al., 2001). In children, however, the error-related negativity is much less pronounced than in adults and it

progressively increases throughout childhood and adolescence (DuPuis et al., 2015; Ferdinand & Kray, 2014; Lo, 2018; Tamnes et al., 2013), suggesting that children get progressively better at monitoring performance errors and success with age. These findings are parallelled by increasingly greater dACC activation following errors than correct responses across groups of children, adolescents, and adults (Velanova et al., 2008). Indeed, as the error-related negativity originates in medial frontal regions, in particular dACC and the posterior cingulate cortex (PCC), greater connectivity between these regions and the lateral prefrontal cortex with age (Kelly et al., 2009; Marek et al., 2015) may account for improvement in performance monitoring throughout childhood.

At the behavioural level, post-error slowing (PES), which refers to slower response times in trials immediately following an error than a correct response, is typically considered a marker of performance monitoring, as it is thought to reflect control up-regulation to avoid subsequent error commission (e.g., Ridderinkhof et al., 2004). Children as young as three and a half have been found to slow down after errors (Jones et al., 2003), suggesting at first sight that children may monitor performance earlier than what has been reported based on error-related negativity findings. However, unlike error-related negativity findings which converge toward a clear progression during childhood, post-error slowing findings in children are particularly unclear. Some studies found that post-error slowing increased (Jones et al., 2003; Schachar et al., 2004), decreased (Gupta et al., 2009; Smulders et al., 2016; Torpey et al., 2012) or remained invariant (van de Laar et al., 2011; Wiersema et al., 2007) during childhood, while one study did not even find any evidence of post-error slowing in school-age children (Yordanova et al., 2011). Furthermore, post-error slowing does not correlate with the error-related negativity on a response inhibition task in five-to-seven-year-olds (Torpey et al., 2012). Thus, if post-error slowing does indeed reflect performance monitoring during childhood, which is far from established to date, it is a particularly unstable and unreliable marker that should be interpreted with caution. Rather than reflecting an online monitoring process and control up-regulation, post-error slowing may result from a continuation of the difficulty that led to the error in the first place (e.g., Carp & Compton, 2009) or reflect offline performance evaluation (Wiersema et al., 2007).

Although young children do not seem to monitor performance on their own (i.e., when no external information is provided), they already benefit from feedback, as shown by performance improvement when feedback is provided on multiple measures of cognitive control (e.g., O'Leary & Sloutsky, 2017). Indeed, even two- and three-year-olds show a greater frontal feedback-related negativity after negative than positive feedback, suggesting efficient feedback processing (Mai et al., 2011), although the feedback related negativity increases over childhood and, to a lesser degree, adolescence (Ferdinand & Kray, 2014). Further, encouraging reflection on children's own performance by making children select, between two feedback options, the feedback option that accurately reflects their performance on the prior trial promotes proactive control, as evidenced by greater P1 and N2 amplitudes on the flanker task in five-to-seven-year-old children, compared with conditions with no feedback or mere feedback provision (Hadley et al., 2020). Consistently, five-year-olds show more adult-like ERP markers on the flanker task after a short training involving metacognitive reflection on how to best engage control to meet task demands (Pozuelos et al., 2019). Yet, feedback processing and learning from feedback may continue to improve throughout childhood, through better discrimination between positive and negative feedback and extraction of increasingly rich information from feedback (Chevalier et al., 2009; Ferdinand & Kray, 2014; Meyer et al., 2013; Peters et al., 2014). Given that feedback processing is relatively efficient early in childhood, performance monitoring may initially rely primarily on external information and progressively shifts to more internal monitoring, as is observed in adults during learning (see Ferdinand & Kray, 2014). This possibility, however, will need to be investigated in future research.

20.4 Conclusion

Developing efficient cognitive control over thoughts and actions ensures increasingly adaptive and complex behaviours during childhood. As cognitive control is a multi-faceted, higher-order cognitive function, it is particularly challenging to chart out its developmental trajectory and disentangle the respective contribution of the multiple cognitive processes it involves. The research reviewed throughout this chapter shows that, unlike what had been assumed for years, the main challenge that children face probably is not to engage more control with age, but instead to engage control with increasing flexibility as a function of ever-changing task demands. In other words, cognitive control development may reflect increasingly flexible engagement of cognitive resources, rather than engagement of more cognitive resources with age. This includes up-regulation of control when cognitive demands increase as well as control release when demands decrease. Further, flexible engagement of control relies on an expanding repertoire of control strategies that allows optimal selection of the control strategies that are most likely to support goal attainment. Not only could these strategies reflect different dynamics of control across a series of trials within a task but also, as suggested by recent studies, they might also correspond to changes with age in the dynamics of control processes within each trial (Ambrosi et al., 2019, 2020).

The overall developmental trajectory of flexible control engagement might, however, conceal important individual and contextual differences. Recent research suggests that, among others, willingness to engage cognitive effort or implicit theories of intelligence might influence control adjustment. Considering the role of contexts, the nature of conflict may be key to understanding to what extent developmental changes in within-trial dynamics of control adjustment are observed or not (Ambrosi et al., 2020). In addition, whereas sensitivity to task demands seems to rely on explicit performance feedback, research on sequential conflict adaptation, at least in adults, suggests that control adjustment does not require consciousness. More generally, control adjustments following variable proportions of conflict, known as proportion congruency effects, may occur with no explicit representations of these variations (e.g., Crump et al., 2008). Indeed, proportion congruency effects can be observed even in preschoolers (Gonthier et al., 2021). Children may first experience 'automatic' control adjustment in contexts where it relies on some form of basic statistical learning. Such automatic control adjustment, through which children start experiencing the benefit of control adjustment, may lay the groundwork for later emergence of more complex forms of control adjustment that rely on explicit metacognition.

Considering that the development of control does not so much rely on more control than on more flexible control engagement has important implications in terms of the kind of interventions that might support control

development. Whereas encouraging more advanced control strategies might be counterproductive (Blackwell & Munakata, 2014), interventions should aim at promoting more flexibility in the selection of available control strategies. Although encouraging metacognitive reflection on performance and tasks demands may be critical in some contexts, letting children experience various proportions of task difficulties may be most effective in other contexts.

References

Altmann, E. M., & Trafton, J. G. (2002). Memory for goals: An activation-based model. *Cognitive Science, 26*, 39–83.

Ambrosi, S., Lemaire, P., & Blaye, A. (2016). Do young children modulate their cognitive control?: Sequential congruency effects across three conflict tasks in 5-to-6 year-olds. *Experimental Psychology, 63*, 117–126.

Ambrosi, S., Servant, M., Blaye, A., & Burle, B. (2019). Conflict processing in kindergarten children: New evidence from distribution analyses reveals the dynamics of incorrect response activation and suppression. *Journal of Experimental Child Psychology, 177*, 36–52.

Ambrosi, S., Śmigasiewicz, K., Burle, B., & Blaye, A. (2020). The dynamics of interference control across childhood and adolescence: Distribution analyses in three conflict tasks and ten age groups. *Developmental Psychology, 56*, 2262–2280.

Andrews-Hanna, J. R., Mackiewicz Seghete, K. L., Claus, E. D., Burgess, G. C., Ruzic, L., & Banich, M. T. (2011). Cognitive control in adolescence: Neural underpinnings and relation to self-report behaviors. *PLoS ONE, 6*, e21598.

Aron, A. R., Fletcher, P. C., Bullmore, E. T., Sahakian, B. J., & Robbins, T. W. (2003). Stop-signal inhibition disrupted by damage to right inferior frontal gyrus in humans. *Nature Neuroscience, 6*, 115–116.

Atas, A., Desender, K., Gevers, W., & Cleeremans, A. (2016). Dissociating perception from action during conscious and unconscious conflict adaptation. *Journal of Experimental Psychology: Learning, Memory, and Cognition, 42*, 866–881.

Barber, A. D., Caffo, B. S., Pekar, J. J., & Mostofsky, S. H. (2013). Developmental changes in within- and between-network connectivity between late childhood and adulthood. *Neuropsychologia, 51*, 156–167.

Barnes, J. J., Nobre, A. C., Woolrich, M. W., Baker, K., & Astle, D. E. (2016). Training working memory in childhood enhances coupling between frontoparietal control network and task-related regions. *Journal of Neuroscience, 36*, 9001–9011.

Blackwell, K. A., & Munakata, Y. (2014). Costs and benefits linked to developments in cognitive control. *Developmental Science, 17*, 203–211.

Blair, C., & Razza, R. P. (2007). Relating effortful control, executive function, and false belief understanding to emerging math and literacy ability in kindergarten. *Child Development, 78*, 647–663.

Blaye, A., Ambrosi, S., Lucenet, J., & Burle, B. (2018). The development of within and between-trials dynamics of inhibitory processes across childhood and adolescence. *Paper presented to the 48th Annual meeting of the Jean Piaget Society*, 31 May–2 June, Amsterdam, the Netherlands.

Blaye, A., & Chevalier, N. (2011). The role of goal representation in preschoolers' flexibility and inhibition. *Journal of Experimental Child Psychology, 108*, 469–483.

Botvinick, M. M., Braver, T. S., Barch, D. M., Carter, C. S., & Cohen, J. D. (2001). Conflict monitoring and cognitive control. *Psychological Review, 108*, 624–652.

Braver, T. S. (2012). The variable nature of cognitive control: A dual mechanisms framework. *Trends in Cognitive Sciences, 16*, 106–113.

Braver, T. S., & Burgess, G. C. (2007). Explaining the many varieties of working memory variation: Dual mechanisms of cognitive control. In A. Conway, C. Jarrold, M. Kane, A. Miyake, & J. Towse (eds.), *Variation in Working Memory* (pp. 76–106). Oxford: Oxford University Press.

Brinums, M., Imuta, K., & Suddendorf, T. (2018). Practicing for the future: Deliberate practice in early childhood. *Child Development, 86*, 2051–2058.

Buss, A. T., & Spencer, J. P. (2018). Changes in frontal and posterior cortical activity underlie the early emergence of executive function. *Developmental Science, 21*, e12602.

Camos, V., & Barrouillet, P. (2011). Developmental change in working memory strategies: From passive maintenance to active refreshing. *Developmental Psychology, 47*, 898–904.

Carp, J., & Compton, R. J. (2009). Alpha power is influenced by performance errors. *Psychophysiology, 46*, 336–343.

Cavanagh, J. F., & Frank, M. J. (2014). Frontal theta as a mechanism for cognitive control. *Trends in Cognitive Sciences, 18*, 414–421.

Chatham, C. H., Frank, M. J., & Munakata, Y. (2009). Pupillometric and behavioral markers of a developmental shift in the temporal dynamics of cognitive control. *Proceedings of the National Academy of Sciences (USA), 106*, 5529–5533.

Chein, J. M., & Schneider, W. (2012). The brain's learning and control architecture. *Current Directions in Psychological Science, 21*, 78–84.

Chevalier, N. (2015). The development of executive function: Toward more optimal coordination of control with age. *Child Development Perspectives, 9*, 239–244.

Chevalier, N. (2018). Willing to think hard? The subjective value of cognitive effort in children. *Child Development, 89*, 1283–1295.

Chevalier, N., & Blaye, A. (2009). Setting goals to switch between tasks: Effect of cue transparency on children's cognitive flexibility. *Developmental Psychology, 45*, 782–797.

Chevalier, N., & Blaye, A. (2016). Metacognitive monitoring of executive control engagement during childhood. *Child Development, 87*, 1264–1276.

Chevalier, N., Dauvier, B., & Blaye, A. (2009). Preschoolers' use of feedback for flexible behavior: Insights from a computational model. *Journal of Experimental Child Psychology, 103*, 251–267.

Chevalier, N., Huber, K. L., Wiebe, S. A., & Espy, K. A. (2013). Qualitative change in executive control during childhood and adulthood. *Cognition, 128,* 1–12.

Chevalier, N., Jackson, J., Revueltas Roux, A., Moriguchi, Y., & Auyeung, B. (2019). Differentiation in prefrontal cortex recruitment during childhood: Evidence from cognitive control demands and social contexts. *Developmental Cognitive Neuroscience, 36,* 100629.

Chevalier, N., James, T. D., Wiebe, S. A., Nelson, J. M., & Espy, K. A. (2014). Contribution of reactive and proactive control to children's working memory performance: Insight from item recall durations in response sequence planning. *Developmental Psychology, 50,* 1999–2008.

Chevalier, N., Martis, S. B., Curran, T., & Munakata, Y. (2015). Metacognitive processes in executive control development: The case of reactive and proactive control. *Journal of Cognitive Neuroscience, 27,* 1125–1136.

Chevalier, N., Wiebe, S. A., Huber, K. L., & Espy, K. A. (2011). Switch detection in preschoolers' cognitive flexibility. *Journal of Experimental Child Psychology, 109,* 353–370.

Christ, S. E., Kanne, S. M., & Reiersen, A. M. (2010). Executive function in individuals with subthreshold autism traits. *Neuropsychology, 24,* 590–598.

Claro, S., Paunesku, D., & Dweck, C. S. (2016). Growth mindset tempers the effects of poverty on academic achievement. *Proceedings of the National Academy of Sciences (USA), 113,* 8664–8668.

Cragg, L. (2016). The development of stimulus and response interference control in mid-childhood. *Developmental Psychology, 52,* 242–252.

Cragg, L., & Nation, K. (2010). Language and the development of cognitive control. *Topics in Cognitive Science, 2,* 631–642.

Crone, E. A. (2009). Executive functions in adolescence: Inferences from brain and behavior. *Developmental Science, 12,* 825–830.

Crone, E. A., Donohue, S. E., Honomichl, R., Wendelken, C., & Bunge, S. A. (2006). Brain regions mediating flexible rule use during development. *The Journal of Neuroscience, 26,* 11239–11247.

Crump, M. J. C., Vaquero, J. M. M., & Milliken, B. (2008). Context-specific learning and control: The roles of awareness, task relevance, and relative salience. *Consciousness and Cognition, 17,* 22–36.

Daly, M., Delaney, L., Egan, M., & Baumeister, R. F. (2015). Childhood self-control and unemployment throughout the life span: Evidence from two British cohort studies. *Psychological Science, 26,* 709–723.

Dauvier, B., Chevalier, N., & Blaye, A. (2012). Using finite mixture of GLMs to explore variability in children's flexibility in a task-switching paradigm. *Cognitive Development, 27,* 440–454.

Davis, E. P., Bruce, J., Snyder, K., & Nelson, C. A. (2003). The X-trials: Neural correlates of an inhibitory control task in children and adults. *Journal of Cognitive Neuroscience, 15,* 432–443.

Destan, N., Hembacher, E., Ghetti, S., & Roebers, C. M. (2014). Early metacognitive abilities: The interplay of monitoring and control processes in 5- to 7-year-old children. *Journal of Experimental Child Psychology, 126,* 213–228.

Diamond, A. (2013). Executive functions. *Annual Review of Psychology, 64,* 135–168.

Doebel, S., Barker, J. E., Chevalier, N., Michaelson, L. E., Fisher, V., & Munakata, Y. (2017). Getting ready to use control: Advances in the measurement of young children's use of proactive control. *PLoS ONE, 12,* e0175072.

Doebel, S., & Zelazo, P. D. (2015). A meta-analysis of the dimensional change card sort: Implications for developmental theories and the measurement of executive function in children. *Developmental Review, 38,* 241–268.

DuPuis, D., Ram, N., Willner, C. J., Karalunas, S., Segalowitz, S. J., & Gatzke-Kopp, L. M. (2015). Implications of ongoing neural development for the measurement of the error-related negativity in childhood. *Developmental Science, 18,* 452–468.

Durston, S., Davidson, M. C., Tottenham, N., Galvan, A., Spicer, J., Fossella, J. A., & Casey,

B. J. (2006). A shift from diffuse to focal cortical activity with development. *Developmental Science, 9*, 1–8.

Durston, S., Thomas, K. M., Yang, Y., Ulug, A. M., Zimmerman, R. D., & Casey, B. J. (2002). A neural basis for the development of inhibitory control. *Developmental Science, 5*, F9–F16.

Duthoo, W., Abrahamse, E. L., Braem, S., Boehler, C. N., & Notebaert, W. (2014). The heterogeneous world of congruency sequence effects: An update. *Frontiers in Psychology, 5*, 1–9.

Egner, T. (2007). Congruency sequence effects and cognitive control. *Cognitive, Affective, & Behavioral Neuroscience, 7*, 380–390.

Elke, S., & Wiebe, S. A. (2017). Proactive control in early and middle childhood: An ERP study. *Developmental Cognitive Neuroscience, 26*, 28–38.

Erb, C. D., & Marcovitch, S. (2019). Tracking the within-trial, cross-trial, and developmental dynamics of cognitive control: Evidence from the Simon task. *Child Development, 90*, e831–e848.

Erb, C. D., Moher, J., Sobel, D. M., & Song, J. H. (2016). Reach tracking reveals dissociable processes underlying cognitive control. *Cognition, 152*, 114–126.

Ezekiel, F., Bosma, R., & Morton, J. B. (2013). Dimensional change card sort performance associated with age-related differences in functional connectivity of lateral prefrontal cortex. *Developmental Cognitive Neuroscience, 5*, 40–50.

Fair, D. A., Dosenbach, N. U. F., Church, J. A., Cohen, A. L., Brahmbhatt, S., Miezin, F. M., ... Schlaggar, B. L. (2007). Development of distinct control networks through segregation and integration. *Proceedings of the National Academy of Sciences (USA), 104*, 13507–13512.

Fair, D. A., Nigg, J. T., Iyer, S., Bathula, D., Mills, K. L., Dosenbach, N. U. F., ... Milham, M. P. (2013). Distinct neural signatures detected for ADHD subtypes after controlling for micro-movements in resting state functional connectivity MRI data. *Frontiers in Systems Neuroscience, 6*, 1–31.

Falkenstein, M., Hohnsbein, J., Hoormann, J., & Blanke, L. (1991). Effects of crossmodal divided attention on late ERP components. II. Error processing in choice reaction tasks. *Electroencephalography and Clinical Neurophysiology, 78*, 447–455.

Fatzer, S. T., & Roebers, C. M. (2012). Language and executive functions: The effect of articulatory suppression on executive functioning in children. *Journal of Cognition and Development, 13*, 454–472.

Ferdinand, N. K., & Kray, J. (2014). Developmental changes in performance monitoring: How electrophysiological data can enhance our understanding of error and feedback processing in childhood and adolescence. *Behavioural Brain Research, 263*, 122–132.

Finn, A. S., Minas, J. E., Leonard, J. A., Mackey, A. P., Salvatore, J., Goetz, C., ... Gabrieli, J. D. E. (2017). Functional brain organization of working memory in adolescents varies in relation to family income and academic achievement. *Developmental Science, 20*, e12450.

Fjell, A. M., Walhovd, K. B., Brown, T. T., Kuperman, J. M., Chung, Y., Hagler, D. J., ... Dale, A. M. (2012). Multimodal imaging of the self-regulating developing brain. *Proceedings of the National Academy of Sciences (USA), 109*, 19620–19625.

Gehring, W. J., Goss, B., Coles, M. G. H., David, E., & Donchin, E. (1993). A neural system for error detection and compensation. *Psychological Science, 4*, 385–390.

Gehring, W. J., & Knight, R. T. (2000). Prefrontal–cingulate interactions in action monitoring. *Nature Neuroscience, 3*, 516–520.

Geurts, H. M., Verté, S., Oosterlaan, J., Roeyers, H., & Sergeant, J. A. (2004). How specific are executive functioning deficits in attention deficit hyperactivity disorder and autism? *Journal of Child Psychology and Psychiatry, and Allied Disciplines, 45*, 836–854.

Gold, J. M., Kool, W., Botvinick, M. M., Hubzin, L., August, S., & Waltz, J. A. (2015). Cognitive effort avoidance and detection in people with schizophrenia. *Cognitive, Affective & Behavioral Neuroscience, 15*, 145–154.

Gonthier, C., Ambrosi, S., & Blaye, A. (2021). Learning-based before intentional cognitive control: Developmental evidence for a dissociation between implicit and explicit control. *Journal of Experimental Psychology: Learning, Memory, and Cognition*. Advance online publication

Gonthier, C., Zira, M., Colé, P., & Blaye, A. (2019). Evidencing the developmental shift from reactive to proactive control in early childhood and its relationship to working memory. *Journal of Experimental Child Psychology, 177*, 1–16.

Gratton, G., Coles, M. G., & Donchin, E. (1992). Optimizing the use of information: Strategic control of activation of responses. *Journal of Experimental Psychology: General, 121*, 480–506.

Grayson, D. S., & Fair, D. A. (2017). Development of large-scale functional networks from birth to adulthood: A guide to the neuroimaging literature. *NeuroImage, 160*, 15–31.

Gupta, R., Kar, B. R., & Srinivasan, N. (2009). Development of task switching and post-error-slowing in children. *Behavioral and Brain Functions: BBF, 5*, 38.

Hadley, L. V., Acluche, F., & Chevalier, N. (2020). Encouraging performance monitoring promotes proactive control in children. *Developmental Science, 23*, e12861.

Haimovitz, K., & Dweck, C. S. (2017). The origins of children's growth and fixed mindsets: New research and a new proposal. *Child Development, 88*, 1849–1859.

Helfrich, R. F., & Knight, R. T. (2016). Oscillatory dynamics of prefrontal cognitive control. *Trends in Cognitive Sciences, 20*, 916–930.

Holroyd, C. B., & Coles, M. G. H. (2002). The neural basis of human error processing: Reinforcement learning, dopamine, and the error-related negativity. *Psychological Review, 109*, 679–709.

Hommel, B., Proctor, R. W., & Vu, K.-P. L. (2004). A feature-integration account of sequential effects in the Simon task. *Psychological Research, 68*, 1–17.

Hwang, K., Velanova, K., & Luna, B. (2010). Strengthening of top-down frontal cognitive

control networks underlying the development of inhibitory control: A functional magnetic resonance imaging effective connectivity study. *Journal of Neuroscience, 30*, 15535–15545.

Iani, C., Stella, G., & Rubichi, S. (2014). Response inhibition and adaptations to response conflict in 6- to 8-year-old children: Evidence from the Simon effect. *Attention, Perception & Psychophysics, 76*, 1234–1241.

Jiang, J., Correa, C. M., Geerts, J., & van Gaal, S. (2018). The relationship between conflict awareness and behavioral and oscillatory signatures of immediate and delayed cognitive control. *NeuroImage, 177*, 11–19.

Johnson, M. H. (2011). Interactive specialization: A domain-general framework for human functional brain development? *Developmental Cognitive Neuroscience, 1*, 7–21.

Jones, L. B., Rothbart, M. K., & Posner, M. I. (2003). Development of executive attention in preschool children. *Developmental Science, 6*, 498–504.

Karr, J. E., Areshenkoff, C. N., Rast, P., Hofer, S. M., Iverson, G. L., & Garcia-Barrera, M. A. (2018). The unity and diversity of executive functions: A systematic review and re-analysis of latent variable studies. *Psychological Bulletin, 144*(11), 1147–1185.

Kelly, A. M. C., Di Martino, A., Uddin, L. Q., Shehzad, Z., Gee, D. G., Reiss, P. T., . . . Milham, M. P. (2009). Development of anterior cingulate functional connectivity from late childhood to early adulthood. *Cerebral Cortex, 19*, 640–657.

Kool, W., McGuire, J. T., Rosen, Z. B., & Botvinick, M. M. (2010). Decision making and the avoidance of cognitive demand. *Journal of Experimental Psychology. General, 139*, 665–682.

Kray, J., Karbach, J., & Blaye, A. (2012). The influence of stimulus-set size on developmental changes in cognitive control and conflict adaptation. *Acta Psychologica, 140*, 119–128.

Larson, M. J., Clawson, A., Clayson, P. E., & South, M. (2012). Cognitive control and conflict adaptation similarities in children and adults. *Developmental Neuropsychology, 37*, 343–357.

Lee, K., Bull, R., & Ho, R. M. H. (2013). Developmental changes in executive functioning. *Child Development, 84*, 1933–1953.

Linzarini, A., Houdé, O., & Borst, G. (2017). Cognitive control outside of conscious awareness. *Consciousness and Cognition, 53*, 185–193.

Lo, S. L. (2018). A meta-analytic review of the event-related potentials (ERN and N2) in childhood and adolescence: Providing a developmental perspective on the conflict monitoring theory. *Developmental Review, 48*, 82–112.

Lucenet, J., & Blaye, A. (2014). Age-related changes in the temporal dynamics of executive control: A study in 5- and 6-year-old children. *Frontiers in Psychology, 5*, 1–11.

Luna, B., Marek, S., Larsen, B., Tervo-Clemmens, B., & Chahal, R. (2015). An integrative model of the maturation of cognitive control. *Annual Review of Neuroscience, 38*, 151–170.

Luna, B., Padmanabhan, A., & O'Hearn, K. (2010). What has fMRI told us about the development of cognitive control through adolescence? *Brain and Cognition, 72*, 101–113.

Mai, X., Tardif, T., Doan, S. N., Liu, C., Gehring, W. J., & Luo, Y.-J. (2011). Brain activity elicited by positive and negative feedback in preschool-aged children. *PLoS ONE, 6*, e18774.

Marcovitch, S., & Zelazo, P. D. (1999). The A-not-B error: Results from a logistic meta-analysis. *Child Development, 70*, 1297–1313.

Marek, S., Hwang, K., Foran, W., Hallquist, M. N., & Luna, B. (2015). The contribution of network organization and integration to the development of cognitive control. *PLoS Biology, 13*, 1–25.

Marklund, P., & Persson, J. (2012). Context-dependent switching between proactive and reactive working memory control mechanisms in the right inferior frontal gyrus. *NeuroImage, 63*, 1552–1560.

Marsh, R., Zhu, H., Schultz, R. T., Quackenbush, G., Royal, J., Skudlarski, P., & Peterson, B. S. (2006). A developmental fMRI study of self-regulatory control. *Human Brain Mapping, 27*, 848–863.

Mayr, U., Awh, E., & Laurey, P. (2003). Conflict adaptation effects in the absence of executive control. *Nature Neuroscience, 6*, 450–452.

McGuire, J. T., & Botvinick, M. M. (2010). Prefrontal cortex, cognitive control, and the registration of decision costs. *Proceedings of the National Academy of Sciences (USA), 107*, 7922–7926.

Meyer, A., Hajcak, G., Torpey, D. C., Kujawa, A., Kim, J., Bufferd, S., ... Klein, D. N. (2013). Increased error-related brain activity in six-year-old children with clinical anxiety. *Journal of Abnormal Child Psychology, 41*, 1257–1266.

Miyake, A., & Friedman, N. P. (2012). The nature and organization of individual differences in executive functions: Four general conclusions. *Current Directions in Psychological Science, 21*, 8–14.

Miyake, A., Friedman, N. P., Emerson, M. J., Witzki, A. H., Howerter, A., & Wager, T. D. (2000). The unity and diversity of executive functions and their contributions to complex 'Frontal Lobe' tasks: A latent variable analysis. *Cognitive Psychology, 41*, 49–100.

Moffitt, T. E., Arseneault, L., Belsky, D., Dickson, N., Hancox, R. J., Harrington, H., ... Caspi, A. (2011). A gradient of childhood self-control predicts health, wealth, and public safety. *Proceedings of the National Academy of Sciences (USA), 108*, 2693–2698.

Morey, C. C., Mareva, S., Lelonkiewicz, J. R., & Chevalier, N. (2018). Gaze-based rehearsal in children under 7: A developmental investigation of eye movements during a serial spatial memory task. *Developmental Science, 21*, e12559.

Moriguchi, Y., & Hiraki, K. (2011). Longitudinal development of prefrontal function during early childhood. *Developmental Cognitive Neuroscience, 1*, 153–162.

Muhle-Karbe, P. S., Jiang, J., & Egner, T. (2018). Causal evidence for learning-dependent frontal-lobe contributions to cognitive control. *The Journal of Neuroscience, 38*, 962–973.

Munakata, Y., Snyder, H. R., & Chatham, C. H. (2012). Developing cognitive control: Three key transitions. *Current Directions in Psychological Science, 21*, 71–77.

Niebaum, J. C., Chevalier, N., Guild, R. M., & Munakata, Y. (2019). Adaptive control and the avoidance of cognitive control demands across development. *Neurospychologia, 123*, 152–158.

Nieuwenhuis, S., Stins, J., Posthuma, D., Polderman, T. C., Boomsma, D., & Geus, E. (2006). Accounting for sequential trial effects in the flanker task: Conflict adaptation or associative priming? *Memory & Cognition, 34*, 1260–1272.

Noble, K. G., McCandliss, B. D., & Farah, M. J. (2007). Socioeconomic gradients predict individual differences in neurocognitive abilities. *Developmental Science, 10*, 464–480.

O'Leary, A. P., & Sloutsky, V. M. (2017). Carving metacognition at its joints: Protracted development of component processes. *Child Development, 88*, 1015–1032.

Ordaz, S. J., Foran, W., Velanova, K., & Luna, B. (2013). Longitudinal growth curves of brain function underlying inhibitory control through adolescence. *Journal of Neuroscience, 33*, 18109–18124.

Peters, S., Koolschijn, P. C. M. P., Crone, E. A., Van Duijvenvoorde, A. C. K., & Raijmakers, M. E. J. (2014). Strategies influence neural activity for feedback learning across child and adolescent development. *Neuropsychologia, 62*, 365–374.

Polizzotto, N. R., Hill-Jarrett, T., Walker, C., & Cho, Y. (2018). Normal development of context processing using the AXCPT paradigm. *PLoS ONE, 13*, e0197812.

Pozuelos, J. P., Combita, L. M., Abundis, A., Paz-Alonsa, P. M., Conejero, Á., Guerra, S., & Rueda, M. R. (2019). Metacognitive scaffolding boosts cognitive and neural benefits following executive attention training in children. *Developmental Science, 22*, e12756.

Raznahan, A., Shaw, P., Lalonde, F., Stockman, M., Wallace, G. L., Greenstein, D., . . . Giedd, J. N. (2011). How does your cortex grow? *The Journal of Neuroscience: The Official Journal of the Society for Neuroscience, 31*, 7174–7177.

Ridderinkhof, K. R., van den Wildenberg, W. P. M., Segalowitz, S. J., & Carter, C. S.

(2004). Neurocognitive mechanisms of cognitive control: The role of prefrontal cortex in action selection, response inhibition, performance monitoring, and reward-based learning. *Brain and Cognition, 56*, 129–140.

Roebers, C. M. (2017). Executive function and metacognition: Towards a unifying framework of cognitive self-regulation. *Developmental Review, 45*, 31–51.

Schachar, R. J., Chen, S., Logan, G. D., Ornstein, T. J., Crosbie, J., Ickowicz, A., & Pakulak, A. (2004). Evidence for an error monitoring deficit in attention deficit hyperactivity disorder. *Journal of Abnormal Child Psychology, 32*, 285–293.

Schmidt, J. R. (2013). Questioning conflict adaptation: Proportion congruent and Gratton effects reconsidered. *Psychonomic Bulletin & Review, 20*, 615–630.

Schmidt, J. R. (2019). Evidence against conflict monitoring and adaptation: An updated review. *Psychonomic Bulletin & Review, 26*, 753–771.

Shaw, P., Kabani, N. J., Lerch, J. P., Eckstrand, K., Lenroot, R., Gogtay, N., . . . Wise, S. P. (2008). Neurodevelopmental trajectories of the human cerebral cortex. *The Journal of Neuroscience: The Official Journal of the Society for Neuroscience, 28*, 3586–3594.

Shenhav, A., Botvinick, M. M., & Cohen, J. D. (2013). The expected value of control: An integrative theory of anterior cingulate cortex function. *Neuron, 79*, 217–240.

Sherman, L. E., Rudie, J. D., Pfeifer, J. H., Masten, C. L., McNealy, K., & Dapretto, M. (2014). Development of the default mode and central executive networks across early adolescence: A longitudinal study. *Developmental Cognitive Neuroscience, 10*, 148–159.

Smulders, S. F. A., Soetens, E., & van der Molen, M. W. (2016). What happens when children encounter an error? *Brain and Cognition, 104*, 34–47.

Smulders, S. F. A., Soetens, E. L. L., & van der Molen, M. W. (2018). How do children deal with conflict? A developmental study of sequential conflict modulation. *Frontiers in Psychology, 9*, 766.

Stins, J. F., Polderman, J. C. T., Boomsma, D. I., & de Geus, E. J. C. (2007). Conditional accuracy in response interference tasks: Evidence from the Eriksen flanker task and the spatial conflict task. *Advances in Cognitive Psychology*, *3*, 409–417.

Strang, N. M., & Pollak, S. D. (2014). Developmental continuity in reward-related enhancement of cognitive control. *Developmental Cognitive Neuroscience*, *10C*, 34–43.

Stroop, J. R. (1935). Studies of interference in serial verbal reactions. *Journal of Experimental Psychology*, *18*, 643.

Tamm, L., Menon, V., & Reiss, A. L. (2002). Maturation of brain function associated with response inhibition. *Journal of American Academy of Child and Adolescent Psychiatry*, *41*, 1231–1238.

Tamnes, C. K., Walhovd, K. B., Torstveit, M., Sells, V. T., & Fjell, A. M. (2013). Performance monitoring in children and adolescents: A review of developmental changes in the error-related negativity and brain maturation. *Developmental Cognitive Neuroscience*, *6*, 1–13.

Torpey, D. C., Hajcak, G., Kim, J., Kujawa, A., & Klein, D. N. (2012). Electrocortical and behavioral measures of response monitoring in young children during a Go/No-Go task. *Developmental Psychobiology*, *54*, 139–150.

Tsujii, T., Yamamoto, E., Masuda, S., & Watanabe, S. (2009). Longitudinal study of spatial working memory development in young children. *NeuroReport*, *20*, 759–763.

Uddin, L. Q., Supekar, K. S., Ryali, S., & Menon, V. (2011). Dynamic reconfiguration of structural and functional connectivity across core neurocognitive brain networks with development. *The Journal of Neuroscience: The Official Journal of the Society for Neuroscience*, *31*, 18578–18589.

van de Laar, M. C., van den Wildenberg, W. P. M., van Boxtel, G. J. M., & van der Molen, M. W. (2011). Lifespan changes in global and selective stopping and performance adjustments. *Frontiers in Psychology*, *2*, 357.

van Gaal, S., Lamme, V. A. F., & Ridderinkhof, K. R. (2010). Unconsciously triggered conflict adaptation. *PLoS ONE*, *5*, 6.

Velanova, K., Wheeler, M. E., & Luna, B. (2008). Maturational changes in anterior cingulate and frontoparietal recruitment support the development of error processing and inhibitory control. *Cerebral Cortex*, *18*, 2505–2522.

Verguts, T. (2017). Binding by random bursts: A computational model of cognitive control. *Journal of Cognitive Neuroscience*, *29*, 1103–1118.

Voigt, B., Mahy, C. E. V, Ellis, J., Schnitzspahn, K., Krause, I., Altgassen, M., & Kliegel, M. (2014). The development of time-based prospective memory in childhood: The role of working memory updating. *Developmental Psychology*, *50*, 2393.

Wiebe, S. A., Espy, K. A., & Charak, D. (2008). Using confirmatory factor analysis to understand executive control in preschool children: I. Latent structure. *Developmental Psychology*, *44*(2), 575–587.

Wiebe, S. A., Sheffield, T., Nelson, J. M., Clark, C. A. C., Chevalier, N., & Espy, K. A. (2011). The structure of executive function in 3-year-olds. *Journal of Experimental Child Psychology*, *108*, 436–452.

Wiersema, J. R., van der Meere, J. J., & Roeyers, H. (2007). Developmental changes in error monitoring: An event-related potential study. *Neuropsychologia*, *45*, 1649–1657.

Wilk, H. A., & Morton, J. B. (2012). Developmental changes in patterns of brain activity associated with moment-to-moment adjustments in control. *NeuroImage*, *63*, 475–484.

Willoughby, M. T., Blair, C. B., Wirth, R. J., & Greenberg, M. (2012). The measurement of executive function at age 5: Psychometric properties and relationship to academic achievement. *Psychological Assessment*, *24*, 226–239.

Yordanova, J., Kolev, V., Albrecht, B., Uebel, H., & Banaschewski, T. (2011). May posterior performance be a critical factor for behavioral deficits in attention-deficit/hyperactivity disorder? *Biological Psychiatry*, *70*, 246–254.

Zelazo, P. D., & Carlson, S. M. (2012). Hot and cool executive function in childhood and adolescence: Development and plasticity. *Child Development Perspectives*, *6*, 354–360.

21 Reasoning Bias and Dual Process Theory
Developmental Considerations and Current Directions

Darren Frey and Wim De Neys

21.1 Introduction: Reasoning Bias

If you are racing toward a cliff or a steep mountain drop-off, the sensible thing to do is to slow yourself down and stop – and as a matter of some urgency. Braking in this case is natural and intuitive. Yet, when you are hang gliding, not only should you not slow down as you approach a cliff, it is important that you accelerate, gaining velocity with every single stride as you approach the drop-off in order to have the necessary wind speed to fly. In the last moments before flight, you should be nearly sprinting toward the edge. For many aspiring hang gliders this can be quite challenging. A successful hang glide start requires you to override your intuitive tendency to stop when seeing a cliff. Although this natural "stopping" intuition is usually very useful, failing to control it when needed can have dramatic consequences.

In many reasoning and decision-making contexts people often face a similar need to control their intuitive responses (Evans & Over, 1996; Houdé, 1997, 2000; Kahneman, 2002; Tversky & Kahneman, 1974). Decades of research suggests that – just like aspiring hang gliders – even educated adults are not very good at it. In a wide range of classic reasoning tasks it has been shown that people readily violate the most elementary logical and probabilistic considerations because they

have a tendency to over-rely on intuitively cued, so-called "heuristic" problem solutions (Kahneman & Tversky, 1973). Consider the following illustration (an adaptation of the infamous base-rate neglect problem):

A psychologist wrote thumbnail descriptions of a sample of 1,000 participants consisting of five computer scientists and 995 attorneys. The description below was chosen at random from the 1,000 available descriptions.

Matt is a generally conservative, careful, and introverted person. He shows no interest in political and social issues and spends most of his free time on his many hobbies, which include collecting science fiction action figures, building model airplanes, and mathematical puzzles.

Which one of the following two statements is most likely?

a. Matt is a computer scientist.
b. Matt is an attorney.

Intuitively, when reading the personality description you'll readily infer that Matt is a computer scientist. The description fits with the stereotype of a nerdy and shy computer engineer. So if you had to base your conclusion solely on the provided description, that might be a reasonable answer: on average, there are presumably more shy and nerdy computer scientists than attorneys. However, in the problem you're also told that out of the 1,000 participants in the study only five were computer scientists. Logically speaking, this information about the proportion of computer

We would like to thank the Agence National de la Recherche (DIAGNOR, ANR-16-CE28–0010-01) for their support.

scientists and attorneys should support concluding the individual in question is likely to be an attorney. After all, it is not impossible for an attorney to be somewhat nerdy and introverted. Combined with the fact that there were many more attorneys than computer scientists to start with, it is safe to conclude that Matt is most likely an attorney. However, this is not what most people do. Even in studies with educated, adult university students, up to 80 percent of participants seem to neglect the base-rates and answer that Matt is most likely a computer scientist (e.g., De Neys & Glumicic, 2008). In general, the available evidence suggests that in cases in which an intuitive association cues a response that conflicts with more logical considerations (e.g., the role of base-rates), people seem to neglect the logical principle and opt for the intuitively cued conclusion (Evans & Over, 1996: Kahneman, 2011). Here, as in many other contexts, our intuitions are biasing our judgment and leading us astray.

21.2 Dual Process Theory

The dual process framework presents a simple and elegant explanation for the bias phenomenon (Evans, 2008; Kahneman, 2011). As Bago and De Neys (2020a) put it, at the most basic level, a dual process model posits that there are two different types of thinking, often referred to as System 1 and System 2 processing. System 1 (also referred to as intuitive, heuristic, or Type 1 processing) operates fast and effortlessly whereas System 2 (also referred to as deliberate, analytic, or Type 2 processing) is thought to be slower and effortful.

There are different types of dual process models but arguably the dominant framework has been the model put forward by prominent scholars such as Daniel Kahneman (Kahneman, 2011) or Jonathan Evans and

Keith Stanovich (Evans & Stanovich, 2013). At the heart of this model lays a serial view on the interaction between Systems 1 and 2. The key idea is that when people are faced with a reasoning problem, they will typically rely on the fast System 1 to generate an answer. This is the default system. If needed, people can activate System 2 in a later phase to intervene and correct System 1 output. But this System 2 engagement is not guaranteed. More generally, reasoners are conceived as cognitive misers who try to minimize cognitive effort (Kahneman, 2011; Kahneman & Frederick, 2005). Since System 2 thinking is hard, people will often refrain from recruiting it and stick to the default System 1 response.

So how exactly does this framework explain that reasoners are biased and violate basic logico-mathematical principles? Dual process theorists have highlighted that the key problem is that taking these logical principles into account typically requires demanding System 2 computations (e.g., Evans, 2003, 2008; Evans & Over, 1996; Kahneman, 2011; Stanovich & West, 2000). When the fast System 1 has provided us with a response, most reasoners will refrain from engaging the effortful System 2. Consequently, they will not detect that their intuitive answer conflicts with more logical considerations (Kahneman, 2011). Put differently, biased reasoners have a bias "blind spot" (De Neys, 2017); they are biased because they do not detect that their System 1 response is logically questionable. The few people who manage to give the correct response will be those who have sufficient motivation and resources to complete the deliberate System 2 computations, notice the conflict with their initial System 1 response, and override their intuition.

It is important to stress that although dual process theories of reasoning and decision-making point to System 1 as a primary source of reasoning bias, it is not disputed that in many instances responses generated by System 1 can be optimal (Evans, 2010; Kahneman, 2011; Stanovich, 2011). For example, recall the opening hang gliding case. One's reflex to slow down when approaching a cliff is vital, and in almost every context apart from hang gliding such a heuristic keeps us alive. Yet, in this particular case, knowing and applying a different rule is crucial. As in this case, there are many contexts in which there is no question that intuitive reasoning heuristics can be useful. Being able to make quick associations on the basis of stored knowledge will often be beneficial. However, the point is simply that sometimes intuitive reasoning heuristics can conflict with more logical considerations and will need to be corrected by the deliberate System 2. Conflicts of this sort – situations in which the heuristic and deliberative systems generate conclusions at odds with each other – seem to characterize many cognitive biases.

21.3 Developmental Misconceptions

The dual process framework can easily give rise to developmental misconceptions (Barrouillet, 2011). One of these is the so-called Illusion of Replacement. This misconception sees reasoning development as a replacement of one type of reasoning by another. More specifically, the idea is that over the course of development children would switch from System 1 to System 2 thinking. This view is akin to the classic Piagetian view in which a more intuitive type of processing would be gradually replaced by a more conceptual and logical type of thinking (Piaget, 1952). Various developmental scholars have long argued against the replacement view of reasoning development (e.g., Brainerd & Reyna, 2001; Brainerd et al., 2008; Houdé, 1997, 2000, 2007; Jacobs & Klaczynski, 2002; Klaczynski et al., 2001; Markovits & Barrouillet, 2004; Reyna & Farley, 2006;

Reyna et al., 2003). Likewise, dual process theory clearly conflicts with the replacement view; it is precisely the over-reliance on System 1 among adults that is conceived as the primary cause of bias within the dual process view. Hence, there is neither an empirical nor theoretical basis for the claim that System 1 thinking will disappear with age.

A related potential developmental dual process misconception is what one might label the illusion of a "developmental standstill." Markovits and Barrouillet (2004) have pointed out how the demonstration of the widespread bias in human reasoning initially led to a decreased interest in reasoning research among developmental scientists. The bias phenomenon seemed to point to a developmental standstill in human reasoning. That is, if the vast majority of educated adults fail to solve basic logical reasoning problems, one might easily get the impression that there doesn't seem to be a lot of development going on (De Neys, 2013). Consequently, as Markovits and Barrouillet put it, scholars might have been tempted to conclude that "there is no point in looking at the development of something that is not present."

However, the fact that even adults are often biased does not imply that reasoning does not develop. Both the capacity to engage in System 1 and System 2 thinking can increase with age, and reasoning at all ages can be conceived as an interplay between both systems (Barrouillet, 2011). When contrasting the performance of different age groups on a specific task, it is critical to fully consider this interplay. For example, when adults and children both face a conflict between a biasing heuristic and logical principle, there is evidence that adults are more likely to respond logically than children (e.g., Kokis et al., 2002). However, more generally one needs to bear in mind that System 1 also needs to develop with age. In many situations children might not have acquired the background knowledge that gives rise to biasing heuristic associations. For example, our introductory description of a nerdy and shy person will presumably not yet lead to the "it's a computer scientist!" hunch when presented to a six-year old. In cases when children lack the heuristic background knowledge, it has been found that children are more likely to respond correctly than adults (e.g., Davidson, 1995; De Neys & Vanderputte, 2011; Jacobs & Potenza, 1991; Klaczynski & Narashimham, 1998; Reyna & Brainerd, 1994; Stanovich et al., 2011). This does obviously not imply that children have a more developed System 2. Rather, they benefit from a less developed System 1 here (De Neys & Vanderputte, 2011).

21.4 Dual Process (R)evolution

The dual process model presents a very straightforward and appealing explanation for the reasoning bias phenomenon. Since its conception in the 1970s the model has become increasingly more influential. However, in recent years a number of findings have questioned core assumptions of the traditional dual process model (e.g., Bago & De Neys, 2017; Ball et al., 2017; Banks, 2017; De Neys, 2012; Houdé & Borst, 2014; Pennycook, 2017; Pennycook et al., 2015; Reyna, 2004; Thompson & Newman, 2017; Trippas & Handley, 2017). For example, many studies have now argued against the original bias "blind spot" assumption that entails that biased reasoners will not detect that their response conflicts with more logical considerations (De Neys, 2017). The available evidence seems to indicate that biased reasoners often do show bias or conflict sensitivity. In these studies, participants are presented with both classic reasoning problems – in which a cued heuristic response conflicts with a logical principle – and control, no-conflict problems. Small content transformations in the control

versions ensure that the intrinsic conflict in the classic version is removed. For example, a no-conflict problem of our introductory base-rate problem with the computer scientists and attorneys would simply switch the base-rate around (e.g., "There are 995 computer scientists and 5 attorneys in the sample"). Hence, in the control case both the description and base-rates cue the same response (i.e., "Matt is a computer scientist"). The rationale here is that people's bias or conflict sensitivity can be empirically tested by measuring how they process these different versions. If biased reasoners do not take logical principles (e.g., base-rates) into account, then whether or not they conflict with the cued heuristic response should not impact their reasoning.

The available evidence indicates that biased reasoners often do register conflict. For example, biased reasoners show increased response doubt (e.g., as reflected in lower response confidence and slightly longer decision latencies) when they give a biased answer on the conflict problems (e.g., De Neys & Glumicic, 2008; De Neys et al., 2013; Gangemi et al., 2015; Mevel et al., 2015; Pennycook et al., 2014b; Stupple et al., 2011; but see also Pennycook et al., 2012). They also show increased activation of brain areas that are supposed to mediate conflict and error detection (i.e., the Anterior Cingulate Cortex, e.g., De Neys et al., 2008; Simon et al., 2015; Vartanian et al., 2018).

Critically, the bias or conflict sensitivity is also observed under time-pressure and cognitive load (Bago & De Neys, 2017; Franssens & De Neys, 2009; Johnson et al., 2016; Pennycook et al., 2014a; Thompson & Johnson, 2014). These time-pressure and load manipulations are used to experimentally "knock-out" System 2 deliberation. Since System 2 processing is time and cognitive resource demanding we can minimize its impact by restricting participants' response time or burdening their cognitive resources with a demanding concurrent task. This allows us to determine whether a certain effect is driven by System 1 or System 2. In sum, in direct contrast with the bias blind spot hypothesis, available evidence indicates that biased reasoners not only show sensitivity to logic/heuristic conflict, they do so intuitively on the basis of mere System 1 processing.

In addition, the so-called corrective dual process assumption is also being questioned (Bago & De Neys, 2017, 2020b). Recall that in the traditional dual process framework, correct responses in case of conflict are assumed to result from a correction of the heuristic System 1 response after System 2 deliberation (e.g., Kahneman, 2011; Stanovich & West, 2000). However, evidence is amassing that correct responses in these cases are often also generated intuitively (e.g., Bago & De Neys, 2017, 2020b; Newman et al., 2017). Most direct evidence for this claim comes from studies that adopt a two-response paradigm (Thompson et al., 2011). In this paradigm, participants are asked to immediately respond with the first intuitive answer that comes to mind. Afterwards, they are allowed to take all the time they want to reflect on the problem and generate a final response. To make sure that the initial response is generated intuitively on the basis of System 1 processing, it has to be generated under stringent time-pressure and/or cognitive load (Bago & De Neys, 2017; Newman et al., 2017). This procedure allows us to examine the time-course of response generation and empirically determine which response is generated by System 1. Studies that adopted this approach clearly indicate that many reasoners who give a correct final response (i.e., after System 2 deliberation was allowed) already managed to give this response in the initial response stage in which they had to reason intuitively. Hence, *pace* the corrective assumption, correct responders do

not necessarily need to deliberate to correct a faulty intuition, their intuitive System 1 response is often already correct (Bago & De Neys, 2020a).

Based on these and related findings, various scholars have suggested it is time to revise the traditional dual process model and move to a "Dual Process Theory 2.0" (e.g., Bago & De Neys, 2017, 2020a; Ball et al., 2017; Banks, 2017; De Neys, 2012; Pennycook, 2017; Pennycook et al., 2015; Thompson & Newman, 2017; Trippas & Handley, 2017; see De Neys, 2017, for an overview). This new model upgrades our view of System 1. It entails that the response that is traditionally considered to be computed by System 2 can also be cued by System 1 (Bago & De Neys, 2020a; De Neys, 2012, 2017). Hence, System 1 is assumed to generate (at least) two different types of intuitive responses. For example, in the case of a classic reasoning task one of these is the traditional "heuristic" intuitive response that is based on semantic and other associations (e.g., the response cued by the stereotypical description in the base-rate problem). The critical second response is what we can refer to as a "logical" intuitive response which is based on elementary knowledge of basic logical and probabilistic principles (e.g., the role of base-rates). The underlying idea here is that even biased reasoners implicitly grasp elementary logical and probabilistic principles and activate this knowledge automatically when faced with a reasoning task. This intuitive logical knowledge allows one to detect that the heuristic intuition is questionable in cases of conflict without engaging in demanding System 2 computations.

The different intuitions within System 1 can have a different activation level or strength. For the modal reasoner, the heuristic intuition will typically be stronger than the logical intuition. Although the presence of a logical intuition allows people to detect conflict, selecting the logical response will still require deliberate System 2 intervention (which will often fail). However, for some individuals the logical intuition can actually be stronger than the heuristic intuition (Bago & De Neys, 2017; Pennycook et al., 2015). These are the reasoners likely to generate correct initial responses in the two-response paradigm (Bago & De Neys, 2020a). Interestingly, recent findings further suggest that they are also highest in cognitive capacity as measured by standard IQ tests (Raoelison et al., 2020; Thompson et al., 2018). This illustrates how the recent Dual Process Theory 2.0 advances are forcing us to re-conceptualize some cherished and widely held dual process beliefs. Where it was traditionally assumed that highly intelligent reasoners were more accurate because they managed to complete the demanding System 2 deliberation (De Neys, 2006; Stanovich & West, 2000), it seems that the IQ-logic correlation in classic reasoning tasks is primarily driven by System 1 (Raoelison et al., 2020; Thompson & Johnson, 2014). More intelligent reasoners simply have dominant logical intuitions (Raoelison et al., 2020; Thompson et al., 2018).

21.5 Developmental Dual Process Evolution

The theoretical dual process evolutions are also giving rise to new developmental explorations. For example, developmental studies on bias or conflict detection during reasoning have contrasted the detection efficiency in younger and older reasoners (e.g., De Neys & Feremans, 2013). Results of these studies suggest that, in contrast with adults, younger reasoners often struggle with bias detection. For example, the decreased response confidence for biased answers in adults is much less pronounced in younger reasoners (e.g., De Neys & Feremans, 2013; see De Neys, 2013 for a review). This presents further evidence against

the "developmental standstill" misconception. Although adults (just like younger children) will often be biased, a key developmental advancement seems to be that adults at least seem to be detecting that their heuristic judgment is logically questionable.

In addition, preliminary developmental studies that adopted the two-response paradigm indicate that the generation of initial correct responses is much less likely for young adolescents at the start of secondary education than for adults (e.g., Raoelison et al., 2021). This lends credence to the hypothesis that the occurrence of logical intuition among adults is the result of a learning process in which an initial deliberate System 2 computation becomes automatized and integrated into System 1 (e.g., De Neys, 2012; Evans, 2017; Stanovich, 2018). Repeated practice and exposure to logico-mathematical principles (e.g., through formal education in the school system) seem to be a critical factor for the development of our logical System 1 intuitions (De Neys, 2012). Although these findings will need to be further validated, they do suggest that the appearance of a developmental standstill – that the initial bias and dual process research might have unwillingly brought about – is more illusion than real.

21.6 Conclusion

In this chapter we have clarified how the reasoning bias phenomenon gave rise to the popular dual process framework. We pointed to common developmental dual process misconceptions and sketched recent evolutions in the dual process field and related emerging developmental work. Our hope is that this chapter might motivate at least some developmental scientists and students to join us in the future exploration of the interaction between intuitive and deliberate reasoning processes. Although important advances have been made, we are convinced that a deeper examination of the development of Systems 1 and 2 is critical for the further refinement of the dual process framework. A key challenge will be to further characterize the precise emergence and growth of "logical" and "heuristic" intuitions within System 1.

References

Bago, B., & De Neys, W. (2017). Fast logic?: Examining the time course assumption of dual process theory. *Cognition, 158*, 90–109.

Bago, B., & De Neys, W. (2020a). Advancing the specification of dual process models of higher cognition: A critical test of the hybrid model view. *Thinking & Reasoning, 26*, 1–30.

Bago, B., & De Neys, W. (2020b). The smart system 1: Evidence for the intuitive nature of correct responding on the bat-and-ball problem. *Thinking & Reasoning, 26*, 1–30.

Ball, L., Thompson, V., & Stupple, E. (2017). Conflict and dual process theory: The case of belief bias. In W. De Neys (ed.), *Dual Process Theory 2.0* (pp. 100–120). Oxford: Routledge.

Banks, A. (2017). Comparing dual process theories: Evidence from event-related potentials. In W. De Neys (ed.), *Dual Process Theory 2.0* (pp. 66–81). Oxford: Routledge.

Barrouillet, P. (2011). Dual process theories of reasoning: The test of development. *Developmental Review, 31*, 151–179.

Brainerd, C. J., & Reyna, V. F. (2001). Fuzzy-trace theory: Dual processes in memory, reasoning, and cognitive neuroscience. In H. W. Reese, & R. Kail (eds.), *Advances in Child Development and Behavior* (Vol. 28, pp. 41–100). San Diego, CA: Academic Press.

Brainerd, C. J., Reyna, V. F., & Ceci, S. J. (2008). Developmental reversals in false memory: A review of data and theory. *Psychological Bulletin, 134*, 343– 382.

Davidson, D. (1995). The representativeness heuristic and the conjunction fallacy effect in children's decision making. *Merrill-Palmer Quarterly, 41*, 328–346.

De Neys, W. (2006). Dual processing in reasoning: Two systems but one reasoner. *Psychological Science, 17*, 428–433.

De Neys, W. (2012). Bias and conflict a case for logical intuitions. *Perspectives on Psychological Science, 7*, 28–38.

De Neys, W. (2013). Heuristics, biases, and the development of conflict detection during reasoning. In H. Markovits (ed.), *The Developmental Psychology of Reasoning and Decision Making* (pp. 130–147). Hove: Psychology Press.

De Neys, W. (2017). Bias, conflict, and fast logic: Towards a hybrid dual process future? In W. De Neys (ed.), *Dual Process Theory 2.0* (pp. 47–65). Oxford: Routledge.

De Neys, W., & Feremans, V. (2013). Development of heuristic bias detection in elementary school. *Developmental Psychology, 49*, 258–269.

De Neys, W., & Glumicic, T. (2008). Conflict monitoring in dual process theories of thinking. *Cognition, 106*, 1248–1299.

De Neys, W., Rossi, S., & Houdé, O. (2013). Bats, balls, and substitution sensitivity: Cognitive misers are no happy fools. *Psychonomic Bulletin & Review, 20*, 269–273.

De Neys, W., & Vanderputte, K. (2011). When less is not always more: Stereotype knowledge and reasoning development. *Developmental Psychology, 47*, 432–441.

De Neys, W., Vartanian, O., & Goel, V. (2008). Smarter than we think when our brains detect that we are biased. *Psychological Science, 19*, 483–489.

Evans, J. St. B. T. (2003). In two minds: Dual-process accounts of reasoning. *Trends in Cognitive Sciences, 7*, 454–459.

Evans, J. St. B. T. (2008). Dual-processing accounts of reasoning, judgement and social cognition. *Annual Review of Psychology, 59*, 255–278.

Evans, J. St. B. T. (2010). Intuition and reasoning: A dual process perspective. *Psychological Inquiry, 21*, 313–326.

Evans, J. St. B. T. (2017). Dual process theories: Perspectives and problems. In W. De Neys (ed.), *Dual Process Theory 2.0* (pp. 137–155). Oxford: Routledge.

Evans, J. St. B. T., & Over, D. E. (1996). *Rationality and Reasoning*. Hove: Psychology Press.

Evans, J. St. B. T., & Stanovich, K. E. (2013). Dual-process theories of higher cognition advancing the debate. *Perspectives on Psychological Science*, *8*, 223–241.

Franssens, S., & De Neys, W. (2009). The effortless nature of conflict detection during thinking. *Thinking & Reasoning*, *15*, 105–128.

Gangemi, A., Bourgeois-Gironde, S., & Mancini, F. (2015). Feelings of error in reasoning – in search of a phenomenon. *Thinking & Reasoning*, *21*, 383–396.

Houdé, O. (1997). Rationality in reasoning: The problem of deductive competence and the inhibitory control of cognition. *Current Psychology of Cognition*, *16*, 108–113.

Houdé, O. (2000). Inhibition and cognitive development: Object, number, categorization, and reasoning. *Cognitive Development*, *15*, 63–73.

Houdé, O. (2007). First insights on neuropedagogy of reasoning. *Thinking & Reasoning*, *13*, 81–89.

Houdé, O., & Borst, G. (2014). Measuring inhibitory control in children and adults: Brain imaging and mental chronometry. *Frontiers in Psychology*, *5*, 616.

Jacobs, J. E., & Klaczynski, P. A. (2002). The development of decision making during childhood and adolescence. *Current Directions in Psychological Science*, *4*, 145–149.

Jacobs, J. E., & Potenza, M. (1991). The use of judgment heuristics to make social and object decisions: A developmental perspective. *Child Development*, *62*, 166–178.

Johnson, E. D., Tubau, E., & De Neys, W. (2016). The doubting system 1: Evidence for automatic substitution sensitivity. *Acta Psychologica*, *164*, 56–64.

Kahneman, D. (2002, December). Maps of bounded rationality: A perspective on intuitive judgement and choice. *Nobel Prize Lecture*. Available from http://nobelprize.org/nobel_prizes/economics/laureates/2002/kahnemann-lecture.pdf, Last accessed January 11, 2006.

Kahneman, D. (2011). *Thinking, Fast and Slow*. New York: Farrar, Straus and Giroux.

Kahneman, D. & Frederick, S. (2005). A model of heuristic judgement. In K. J. Holyoak, & R. G. Morrison (eds.), *The Cambridge Handbook of Thinking and Reasoning* (pp. 267–293). Cambridge, MA: Cambridge University Press.

Kahneman, D., & Tversky, A. (1973). On the psychology of prediction. *Psychological Review*, *80*, 237–251.

Klaczynski, P. A., Byrnes, J. B., & Jacobs, J. E. (2001). Introduction: Special issue on decision making. *Journal of Applied Developmental Psychology*, *22*, 225–236.

Klaczynski, P. A., & Narashimham, G. (1998). Representations as mediators of adolescent deductive reasoning. *Developmental Psychology*, *5*, 865–881.

Kokis, J. V., Macpherson, R., Toplak, M. E., West, R. F., & Stanovich, K. E. (2002). Heuristic and analytic processing: Age trends and associations with cognitive ability and cognitive styles. *Journal of Experimental Child Psychology*, *83*, 26–52.

Markovits, H., & Barrouillet, P. (2004). Why is understanding the development of reasoning important? *Thinking and Reasoning*, *10*, 113–121.

Mevel, K., Poirel, N., Rossi, S., Cassotti, M., Simon, G., Houdé, O., & Neys, W. D. (2015). Bias detection: Response confidence evidence for conflict sensitivity in the ratio bias task. *Journal of Cognitive Psychology*, *27*, 227–237.

Newman, I., Gibb, M., & Thompson, V. A. (2017). Rule-based reasoning is fast and belief-based reasoning can be slow: Challenging current explanations of belief -bias and base-rate neglect. *Journal of Experimental Psychology: Learning, Memory, and Cognition*, *43*, 1154–1170.

Pennycook, G. (2017). A perspective on the theoretical foundation of dual process models. In W. De Neys (ed.), *Dual Process Theory 2.0* (pp. 5–27). Oxford: Routledge.

Pennycook, G., Cheyne, J. A., Barr, N., Koehler, D. J., & Fugelsang, J. A. (2014a). Cognitive style and religiosity: The role of conflict detection. *Memory & Cognition*, *42*, 1–10.

Pennycook, G., Fugelsang, J. A., & Koehler, D. J. (2012). Are we good at detecting conflict during reasoning. *Cognition, 124,* 101–106.

Pennycook, G., Fugelsang, J. A., & Koehler, D. J. (2015). What makes us think? A three-stage dual-process model of analytic engagement. *Cognitive Psychology, 80,* 34–72.

Pennycook, G., Trippas, D., Handley, S. J., & Thompson, V. A. (2014b). Base rates: Both neglected and intuitive. *Journal of Experimental Psychology: Learning, Memory, and Cognition, 40,* 544–554.

Piaget, J. (1952/1941). *The Child's Conception of Number.* New York: Routledge & Kegan Paul.

Raoelison, M., Boissin, E., Borst, G., & De Neys, W. (2021). From slow to fast logic: The development of logical intuitions. *Thinking & Reasoning,* 1–25, online doi.org/10.1080/13546783.2021.1885488.

Raoelison, M., Thompson, V., & De Neys, W. (2020). The smart intuitor: Cognitive capacity predicts intuitive rather than deliberate thinking. Cognition, 204, 104381.

Reyna, V. F. (2004). How people make decisions that involve risk: A dual-processes approach. *Current Directions in Psychological Science, 13,* 60–66.

Reyna, V. F., & Brainerd, C. J. (1994). The origins of probability judgment: A review of data and theories. In G. Wright, & P. Ayton (eds.), *Subjective Probability* (pp. 239–272). New York: Wiley.

Reyna, V. F., & Farley, F. (2006). Risk and rationality in adolescent decision making: Implications for theory, practice, and public policy. *Psychological Science in the Public Interest, 7,* 1–44.

Reyna, V. F., Lloyd, F. J., & Brainerd, C. J. (2003). Memory, development, and rationality: An integrative theory of judgement and decision-making. In S. Schneider, & J. Shanteau (eds.), *Emerging Perspectives on Judgment and Decision Research* (pp. 201–245). New York: Cambridge University Press.

Simon, G., Lubin, A., Houdé, O., & De Neys, W. (2015). Anterior cingulate cortex and intuitive bias detection during number conservation. *Cognitive Neuroscience, 6,* 158–168.

Stanovich, K. E. (2011). *Rationality and the Reflective Mind.* Oxford: Oxford University Press.

Stanovich, K. E. (2018). Miserliness in human cognition: The interaction of detection, override and mindware. *Thinking & Reasoning, 24,* 423–444.

Stanovich, K. E., & West, R. F. (2000). Individual differences in reasoning: Implications for the rationality debate. *Behavioral and Brain Sciences, 23,* 645–665.

Stanovich, K. E., West, R. F., & Toplak, M. E. (2011). The complexity of developmental predictions from dual process models. *Developmental Review, 31,* 103–118.

Stupple, E. J., Ball, L. J., Evans, J. S. B., & Kamal-Smith, E. (2011). When logic and belief collide: Individual differences in reasoning times support a selective processing model. *Journal of Cognitive Psychology, 23,* 931–941.

Thompson, V. A., & Johnson, S. C. (2014). Conflict, metacognition, and analytic thinking. *Thinking & Reasoning, 20,* 215–244.

Thompson, V. A., & Newman, I. (2017). Logical intuitions and other conundra for dual process theories. In W. De Neys (ed.), *Dual Process Theory 2.0* (pp. 121–136). Oxford: Routledge.

Thompson, V. A., Pennycook, G., Trippas, D., & Evans, J. S. B. (2018). Do smart people have better intuitions? *Journal of Experimental Psychology: General, 147,* 945.

Thompson, V. A., Turner, J. A. P., & Pennycook, G. (2011). Intuition, reason, and metacognition. *Cognitive Psychology, 63,* 107–140.

Trippas, D., & Handley, S. (2017). The parallel processing model of belief bias: Review and extensions. In W. De Neys (ed.), *Dual Process Theory 2.0* (pp. 28–46). Oxford: Routledge.

Tversky, A., & Kahneman, D. (1974). Judgment under uncertainty: Heuristics and biases. *Science, 185,* 1124–1131.

Vartanian, O., Beatty, E. L., Smith, I., Blackler, K., Lam, Q., Forbes, S., & De Neys, W. (2018). The reflective mind: Examining individual differences in susceptibility to base rate neglect with FMRI. *Journal of Cognitive Neuroscience, 30,* 1011–1022.

22 Social Cognitive Development

The Intergroup Context

Lisa Chalik, Antonia Misch, and Yarrow Dunham

Throughout human history and across all human cultures, civilizations have organized themselves into social collectives, to the extent that it seems fair to say that social groups are the natural ecology of our species. In many ways, these groups play the same role as do categories in other domains; after all, the world is an incredibly complex place, and dividing it into categories is a powerful way to simplify this complexity and maximize efficiency in learning. In the social world, this way of working through complexity is especially important, given the extreme range of variability that exists across human individuals and communities. Children must navigate a world full of people with a range of properties that appear to have little in common with one another, posing a particularly difficult learnability problem. Social categorization allows children to work through this complexity by selecting features that denote meaningful differences between people (see Chapter 13). As a result, social categories become a fundamental lens through which we see the world.[1]

It should thus not be surprising that social categorization of some sort exists across all human societies, making it a human universal (Brown, 2004). However, there are important differences across human cultures in how groups are defined, which groups are viewed as important, and what the consequences of group membership are. Thus, it is important to consider how cognitive development unfolds in an intergroup context. In this chapter, we broadly explore how children across development understand social categories and use these categories to navigate the social world. In doing so, we aim to demonstrate where there is diversity across human cultures in how social categorization unfolds, and what aspects of this diversity are grounded in common psychological tendencies and mechanisms.

22.1 The Origins of Social Categorization in Infancy

Many social category-based tendencies can be documented early in infancy. Studies using visual preference paradigms have shown that infants are sensitive to social distinctions like race and gender by three months of age (Bar-Haim et al., 2006; Quinn et al., 2002), though the ways in which they understand these groups become refined throughout the first year of life. For example, by seven months, infants are aware of gender categories and recognize that these categories are broad enough to include individuals of multiple races

---

[1] For the purposes of this chapter, we will use the terms "social category" and "social group" interchangeably. Both of these terms are used ubiquitously throughout the literature on intergroup cognition, sometimes denoting the exact same concept, sometimes with slightly different connotations. Here, we use both terms to broadly refer to any collection of individuals that can be linked by some feature, be it a shared physical or psychological property, a common goal, a set of similar obligations, or otherwise.

(e.g., the category "female" can include both Black and White individuals), and by ten-to-eleven months, they make the corresponding inference for racial groups (e.g., the category "White" can include both women and men; Waxman & Grace, 2012). Also by ten-to-eleven months, infants distinguish people based on the languages they speak (Kinzler et al., 2007, 2012), their food preferences (Liberman et al., 2014; Mahajan & Wynn, 2012), and whether they are members of the majority or minority ethnicity in their cultural context (Singarajah et al., 2017). Thus, infants are capable of using social categories to classify individuals from quite early in life, potentially laying the groundwork for much of the social category-based processing that emerges across childhood.

Infants also use social group membership to make inferences about people's behavior (see Chapter 12). For example, seven-month-old infants expect members of a social group to perform similar actions (Powell & Spelke, 2013), and nine-month-olds expect people who speak the same language to affiliate with one another (Liberman et al., 2017). By seventeen months, infants use group membership to predict people's moral behavior, expecting people to preferentially help group members who are in need (Jin & Baillargeon, 2017), and by eighteen-to-twenty months, infants expect people to distribute limited resources in favor of ingroup members (Bian et al., 2018).

22.2 Social Categorization in Preschool and Beyond

22.2.1 What Inferences Do Young Children Make Based on Social Categories?

Throughout the preschool years, children further develop their understanding of social categories, using these categories as a base for a wide range of inferences about other people's properties and behaviors. However, doing so poses fundamental challenges: how do children know *which* inferences can be made on the basis of social categories? And how do they know *which* social category to use as the base of an inference, given that any individual belongs to multiple social categories? Research has now shown that children do not make the same types of inferences for all social groupings, suggesting an emerging understanding that different social collectives function in different ways. For example, some social category-based inferences, such as expectations about shared physical and psychological properties, are only evoked by a small subset of social distinctions. Gender is an example of a category that supports these inferences: Preschoolers believe that same-gender children will like the same kinds of toys and activities (Berndt & Heller, 1986; Biernat, 1991). However, children do not generally hold similar expectations about children who share membership in racial groups (Rhodes & Gelman, 2009).

By contrast, some social groupings evoke inferences about how people will act toward one another. For example, when thinking about novel social categories – groups defined by an arbitrary, previously meaningless characteristic, such as clothing color – children expect that people will act negatively toward outgroup rather than ingroup members (Chalik & Rhodes, 2018; Chalik et al., 2014; Rhodes, 2012). These findings – that different social categories serve different inferential purposes early in development – have lead researchers to conclude that children hold multiple *intuitive theories* – abstract, domain-specific, causal-explanatory frameworks (Gopnik & Wellman, 2012; Wellman & Gelman, 1992) – that guide their understandings of the social groups around them. Because developing in the intergroup context causes children to use social categories as a fundamental lens to view the world, these theories lay the groundwork for how children's social cognition will unfold for the rest of their lives.

One intuitive theory that appears to shape children's social category-based inferences as early as the preschool years is the belief that people who are members of the same social group are fundamentally similar to one another. For example, preschool-aged children use gender as a base for a wide range of inductive inferences (Taylor, 1996; Taylor et al., 2009), expecting same-gender individuals to share novel properties (Gelman et al., 1986) and predicting that girls and boys will behave in ways consistent with gender stereotypes, even in the presence of contrasting individuating information (e.g., a girl wanting to build airplanes instead of sew buttons will still behave in other stereotype-consistent ways; Berndt & Heller, 1986; Biernat, 1991). Additionally, by age five, children use a wide range of social distinctions (e.g., social status, ethnicity, religion, age group, profession) to predict that group members will share novel psychological and behavioral properties (e.g., liking to play a new type of game; Diesendruck & HaLevi, 2006; Waxman, 2010), and will be bound by similar rights and obligations (e.g., being required to help people; Kalish & Lawson, 2008).

Children also use social categories to make another set of inferences about people, using them to guide their predictions of how people will act toward one another. These inferences do not stem from an expectation of fundamental similarity among group members but might rather be the result of an early form of coalitional reasoning (Boyd & Richerson, 2009). Thus, they stem from an expectation that group members are obligated to interact cooperatively with one another. For example, as early as age three and across childhood,

children view harmful behaviors that occur among fellow social category members as serious, moral violations (i.e., these behaviors are wrong no matter what, regardless of the local context in which they occur), whereas they view harmful behaviors that occur between members of different social categories as wrong for more context-dependent reasons (i.e., these behaviors are less wrong if they are permitted in the local context; Rhodes & Chalik, 2013). Thus, children view social group members as morally obligated not to harm one another. This belief supports inferences about how people will behave in intergroup contexts; as early as age three, children predict that people are more likely to harm outgroup members than ingroup members (Chalik & Rhodes, 2014, 2018; Chalik et al., 2014; Rhodes, 2012) and are more likely to be friends with ingroup members than outgroup members (Chalik & Rhodes, 2018). Furthermore, by age four, children expect people to preferentially save ingroup members from harmful events (Chalik & Rhodes, 2018) and by age six, children expect people to direct a wide range of prosocial behaviors toward ingroup members rather than toward outgroup members (DeJesus et al., 2014; Rhodes, 2012). These predictions – distinct from the predictions of fundamental similarity that children make for categories like gender – may arise from children's belief that many social groups arise and are sustained via the collective intentions of their members *to be* members, a form of commitment which plausibly entails moral obligation (Noyes & Dunham, 2017).

22.2.2 Which Categories Do Children Use for these Inferences?

In addition to learning what types of inferences can be made on the basis of social categories, children also learn, quite early in life, *which* social categories are relevant for those inferences. Although category-based beliefs of some sort can be found in all cultural contexts, exactly *which* social categories evoke which kind of beliefs appears to depend on the cultural input children receive. This process has been described under the framework of Developmental Intergroup Theory (Bigler & Liben, 2006), which posits that children construct their own internal working model of how their social world is structured based on environmental messages they receive, such as perceptually salient attributes of the people around them, or explicit and implicit classification by means of labeling and societal structures. These messages form the basis from which children develop group-based preferences, beliefs, and stereotypes.

In fact, cultural input plays a role in the internalization of social categories as early as the first year of life. For example, Quinn et al. (2002) found that three-month-old infants' preferences for male and female faces depended on the gender of their primary caregiver – infants reared primarily by a female parent showed a looking preference for female faces, whereas the reverse was true for infants reared primarily by a male parent, suggesting that the way in which young infants view gender is shaped by the people that they are exposed to at the beginning of their lives. Similar findings have been documented with regard to race; infants show a looking preference for faces of their own race by three months, but this preference is not present in the first few days of life (Kelly et al., 2005). Furthermore, race-based preferences depend on the racial environment to which infants are exposed; infants who have not been raised in predominantly own-race environments (for example, Black children raised in White communities in Israel) do not show racial preferences in their looking behavior (Bar-Haim et al., 2006).

One psychological mechanism that fosters children's identification of social groups from which to make inferences is a pervasive cognitive bias known as psychological essentialism. Essentialism is the belief that certain categories have an underlying nature, an "essence," that gives them their identity and makes them fundamentally distinct from other kinds of things (Gelman, 2003; Medin & Ortony, 1989, see Chapter 15). In the social domain, then, essentialism functions such that individuals tend to represent certain social categories in the same way that they represent animal categories – as natural kinds that are homogeneous, unalterable, and inductively rich (Allport, 1954; Atran, 1990; Haslam et al., 2000; Rothbart & Taylor, 1992). For example, as early as age five, children see gender categories as objective, determined at birth, and predictive of gender-stereotypical properties, regardless of environmental input (e.g., a girl will collect dolls instead of tools, even if she was raised in a community of all boys; Rhodes & Gelman, 2009; Taylor et al., 2009). Four-year-old children even apply essentialist beliefs to novel social groups, if they have heard language suggesting that those groups are cohesive entities (Rhodes et al., 2012).

Social essentialism appears to be a universal phenomenon, occurring across cultures, having been documented in various communities around the United States (Hirschfeld, 1996; Rhodes & Gelman, 2009; Taylor et al., 2009), among Israeli children (Birnbaum et al., 2010; Diesendruck & HaLevi, 2006), and in communities in Chile (del Rio & Strasser, 2011), Madagascar (Astuti et al., 2004), India (Mahalingam, 2003), and Brazil (Sousa et al., 2002). However, there is a great deal of variation in how social essentialism plays out across cultures. For example, children from different religious communities in Israel differ in their essentialist beliefs about the stability of social category membership

(Diesendruck & Haber, 2009) and, in the United States, Black children view race as more stable than White children do (Kinzler & Dautel, 2012). Additionally, social essentialist beliefs change in culture-specific ways across development. Rhodes and Gelman (2009) documented that five-year-old American children in rural and urban communities showed similar tendencies to essentialize gender but not racial categories, but by age ten years, rural children began to show essentialist beliefs associated with race, whereas urban children of the same age did not share these beliefs, but instead began to see gender category boundaries as conventionalized. Furthermore, Chalik et al. (2017) studied American children from a variety of religious backgrounds and found that at age five, all of the children tested showed similar levels of essentialism when thinking about religious identity, but for ten-year-olds and adults, the degree to which participants held social essentialist beliefs depended on their own religion and level of religiosity. All of these studies, again, show that children use cultural input to identify the social categories that are relevant for the different types of group-based inferences they might make.

22.3 The Consequences of Viewing the World Through the Lens of Social Categorization

22.3.1 How Social Categorization Influences Children's View of Themselves

Seeing the world through the lens of social categorization deeply influences how we think about ourselves, in the form of what is commonly referred to as the *social identity* (Tajfel & Turner, 1979). The relation between social identity and the self-concept appears to develop during the elementary school years. For example, Bennett et al. (1998) found that

when shown instances of unfamiliar ingroup members acting negatively, seven-year-olds, but not five-year-olds, felt responsible for and embarrassed by these negative actions. Related research found that five-year-old children already display subtler signs of guilt and responsibility after they observed their ingroup members break someone else's possession (Over et al., 2016). Furthermore, by age five, children view themselves as particularly similar to children of the same gender if their gender identity has been made salient (Bennett & Sani, 2008a), and they recall words associated with their own groups (groups based on family, age, and gender) better than unrelated words, and to the same degree that they recall words associated with the self (Bennett & Sani, 2008b). Additionally, by age five and increasing across the elementary school years, children make memory errors in which they confuse themselves with ingroup members more than with outgroup members (Sani & Bennett, 2009). Thus, children identify deeply with their ingroups, and process information about the ingroup and the self similarly.

The connection between group identity and beliefs about the self undoubtedly has consequences for development. These consequences are often negative, as children often express and evaluate themselves in accordance with stereotyped beliefs about their own social categories (Witt, 1997). For example, elementary school girls begin to show lower self-confidence than boys in math abilities at the same age at which they begin to endorse the stereotype that boys are better than girls at math (Cvencek et al., 2011; Muzzatti & Agnoli, 2007). Furthermore, by age six, girls – but not boys – tend to avoid activities that are described as being for intelligent people, consistent with the common stereotype that women are less intelligent than men (Bian et al., 2017). In many cases, however, identifying as a member of a social group can have a positive influence on children's identity. For example, identifying as a member of a religious group may actually protect children from the internalization of prejudice: In a study by Dunham et al. (2014b), Muslim children preferred their own low-status group to higher-status Hindus, in contrast to children's caste-based preferences, where even children of low-status castes preferred the high-status group. These findings suggest that religious beliefs, which often focus on the spiritual goodness of the group, can prevent children from internalizing the negative stereotypes often associated with low-status groups. Furthermore, just being in a group at all, in the absence of stereotypes, can positively influence children's self-perceptions: In a study examining children's engagement in science, children who had been assigned to a novel group before completing a task reported higher self-efficacy in that task (Master et al., 2017), and children's enjoyment of and motivation to work on challenging tasks increases when they view those tasks as collaborative (Butler & Walton, 2013) or as related to group membership (Master & Walton, 2012).

22.3.2 How Social Categorization Influences Children's View of Others

The intergroup context also has powerful – if sometimes problematic – consequences for how we view others. As noted in Section 22.2.2, children use social categories as the basis of a range of inductive inferences; those inferences often include forms of intergroup bias (most notably prejudice and stereotyping) and can manifest in behavior (discrimination). By the preschool years, children express positive views of ingroup members and negative views of outgroup members across a variety of social distinctions, including race (Aboud, 1988; Rutland et al., 2005), gender (Halim et al., 2017; Hilliard & Liben, 2010), religion

(Heiphetz et al., 2013), and nationality (Barrett, 2007). Ingroup biases have even been documented with regard to groups that have no functional relevance; children who have been assigned to groups that are completely arbitrary and serve no functional purpose (so-called minimal groups; e.g., clothing color-based groups where assignment is done by a coin toss) report preferences for their ingroup members and make negative assumptions about outgroup members. Recent research has even found that children perceive of outgroup members as less human than their ingroup members (McLoughlin & Over, 2017; McLoughlin et al., 2018). These findings are sometimes interpreted as showing that ingroup favoritism is highly abstract, perhaps even the result of an evolved system for supporting within-group cooperation and between-group conflict (Dunham, 2018).

In addition to the explicit forms of bias documented above, some forms of ingroup bias are subtle, perhaps even occurring outside of awareness (Devine, 1989). To investigate this question, research on the development of intergroup attitudes has recently incorporated so-called implicit methods. The most commonly used measure to make this case, the Implicit Association Test (IAT; Greenwald et al., 1998), uses the structure of semantic memory to assess whether people have positive or negative associations with various social categories. Implicit measures have been commonly used to assess bias with regard to race; this work has shown that White children have a positive view of Whites and a negative view of Blacks as early as age six, and until at least age ten (Baron & Banaji, 2006; Dunham et al., 2006; reviewed in Olson & Dunham, 2010). Implicit ingroup biases have also been found in children with regard to religious groups (Heiphetz et al., 2013), gender categories (although boys show an increase in positivity toward females over time; Dunham et al., 2015), and even with respect to minimal groups (Dunham et al., 2011). Thus, most research suggests that children's implicit intergroup attitudes seem to develop early and remain stable across age groups (Dunham et al., 2008; but for an alternate perspective, see Degner & Wentura, 2010).

Interestingly, children's beliefs about their own social groups also appear to be influenced by social status (Griffiths & Nesdale, 2006). For example, no implicit race-based bias has been found in American children from low-status groups, such as Blacks (Newheiser & Olson, 2012) and Latinos (Dunham et al., 2007), and low-status children in racially-divided South Africa (Dunham et al., 2014a) and in the Hindu caste system (Dunham et al., 2014b) actually show implicit preferences in favor of higher status outgroups. Thus, ingroup favoritism is by no means a universal: It can be overridden by exposure to local views concerning the status of the groups involved.

22.3.3 Intergroup Bias in Children's Behavior and Learning

Children's preference for ingroup members over outgroup members often manifests in their behavior toward others. Children are more prosocial toward ingroup than outgroup members across a range of group distinctions; for example, they share resources preferentially with ingroup members (Dunham et al., 2011; Kinzler & Spelke, 2011; Kinzler et al., 2009, 2012; Renno & Shutts, 2015; Shutts, 2015), even when it is costly to them (i.e., when sharing requires them to give up some of their own resources; Benozio & Diesendruck, 2015; Fehr et al., 2008). Children also direct negative behavior (e.g., giving aversive objects) toward outgroup members, with this tendency beginning as early as the toddler years[2] and becoming more pronounced later in childhood (Buttelmann & Bohm, 2014).

Ingroup biases in childhood are also importantly *learning biases*, in that children prefer to learn new information from their ingroup members. For example, infants prefer objects and food that have been endorsed by speakers of their native language (Kinzler et al., 2012), and preferentially imitate actions that are modeled by their ingroup members (Buttelmann et al., 2013). Similarly, by the preschool years, children prefer to learn new information and actions from speakers of their own language (Corriveau et al., 2013; Howard et al., 2015) and prefer to play with objects that have been endorsed by their gender, age-based, or racial ingroup members (Shutts et al., 2010). Furthermore, the reverse patterns emerge when children are asked to learn from outgroup members; recent work has found that children tend to perform contrasting behaviors from ones that have been modeled by their outgroup members (Oostenbroek & Over, 2015).

The above research documents that children trust ingroup members far more than they trust many others. This selective trust in ingroup members is so strong that it overrides some other tendencies that children usually display; for example, children generally prefer to learn from groups of informants who are in consensus with one another, but they do so far less if the consensus group is made up of racial outgroup members (Chen et al., 2013). Also, children generally avoid antisocial individuals, but are sometimes willing to learn from ingroup members even after they have displayed antisocial behavior (Hetherington et al., 2014). Furthermore, children's selective trust in ingroup members is not limited to learning opportunities; children also trust their

---

[2] Chalik, L., & Wynn, K. Ingroup love and outgroup hate jointly motivate toddlers' social behavior. Under review.

ingroup members more to keep promises and secrets (Rotenberg & Cerda, 1994).

Social categorization also colors how children internalize new information about groups. For example, Over et al. (2017) gave five- to six-year-old children a choice between hearing a story that favored their ingroup and disfavored their outgroup, or one that favored their outgroup and disfavored their ingroup. Children consistently chose to hear the ingroup-favoring story, showing that they actively sought to learn information that was biased in favor of the ingroup. Children also preferred to teach biased information to others, thus promoting the social transmission of stereotypes and intergroup bias (Over et al., 2017). Additionally, children tend to recall more positive actions performed by ingroup than outgroup members (Bigler & Liben, 1993), interpret ambiguous events in ingroup-favoring ways (Dunham & Emory, 2014; Dunham et al., 2011), be more forgiving (and forgetful) of ingroup members' negative behavior (Corenblum, 2003; Dunham et al., 2011), and weigh positive and negative information in ways that favor their ingroup (Baron & Dunham, 2015; Schug et al., 2013). All of the processes documented here constitute mechanisms by which children generate support for their initial positive feelings about the ingroup, thus confirming and propagating the biases that they hold. Thus, even if some of the biases characterizing young children's views of groups are relatively modest in magnitude, when coupled with these learning biases their cumulative operation could be profound.

22.3.4 Intergroup Bias in Children's Adherence to and Enforcement of Norms

While many of the findings in Sections 22.3.1–22.3.3 could potentially be explained within the scope of an affective preference for ingroup members, other research shows that in some cases, the opposite is true: In certain circumstances, children are *less* lenient toward their ingroup members. More specifically, children hold harsher standards for ingroup members than for outgroup members when they are enforcing social norms. For example, Schmidt et al. (2012) found that three-year-old children protested more when conventional norms (e.g., the rules of playing a made-up game) were violated by ingroup members compared to outgroup members. These findings suggest two important points: First, from early on, children believe that social-conventional norms are specific to particular social groups and are not binding for outgroup members. Second, children see adherence to social-conventional norms as a crucial component of successful group functioning and thus take it upon themselves to actively enforce these norms, even when doing so entails directing protest at otherwise positively evaluated ingroup members.

Relatedly, one norm that children view as particularly important in the group context is loyalty. Children show a rudimentary appreciation of group loyalty at about age four, when they show a preference for *other* children who have played with racial ingroup members rather than children who have played with racial outgroup members (Castelli et al., 2007). Furthermore, from at least age five, children evaluate leaving a group to obtain individual benefits as morally wrong (Misch et al., 2014) and punish free riders who do not contribute to the common good (Yang et al., 2018). Loyalty in children's own behavior emerges around the same time; for example, by age five, children keep group secrets (Misch et al., 2016) and express commitment to their favorite sports teams, even in the face of defeat (James, 2001).

Children also display loyalty in their differential reactions to moral violations that have been performed by ingroup and outgroup members. For example, six-year-old children are more likely to punish people who allocate resources selfishly if those people are outgroup members, and are more likely to punish selfish allocators if the victims of those allocations are ingroup members (Jordan et al., 2014). They also tattle more on outgroup members' severe moral transgressions than ingroup members' similar transgressions (Misch et al., 2018). However, these overwhelming concerns for loyalty appear to change and interact with other moral concerns across development; by eight years of age, children punish unfair resource allocations that disadvantage both in- and out-group members equally (Jordan et al., 2014) and, with age, children increasingly allocate resources fairly to both ingroup and outgroup members (McAuliffe & Dunham, 2017).

Children's concern for loyalty is also apparent in their judgments of people who fail to support the ingroup: Research by Abrams et al. (2003, 2009) found that school-aged children judge ingroup members who do not preferentially support the ingroup more harshly than outgroup members who perform the same violation, suggesting an early onset of the so-called black sheep effect (where people evaluate deviant ingroup members more negatively than comparable outgroup members; Marques et al., 1988). These findings have been elucidated as part of a model of Developmental Subjective Group Dynamics (Abrams & Rutland, 2008), which suggests that, with age, children develop an increasingly sophisticated understanding of the complexities of group functioning, as well as an understanding of specific intergroup and intragroup norms and how they constrain behavior across

diverse contexts (e.g., Abrams et al., 2003, 2009; Rutland et al., 2010).

22.3.5 Theories of the Developmental Trajectory of Ingroup Bias

There are several theories explaining the developmental trajectories of children's ingroup bias and prejudice. For example, Developmental Intergroup Theory (Bigler & Liben, 2006), discussed in Section 22.2.2, focuses on how children use environmental messages to build an understanding of social structure (which includes stereotyping and ingroup bias) across development. Another account is Social-Cognitive Developmental Theory (Aboud, 1988), which states that children start to express negative views about outgroup members in the preschool years, but that these negative views decline after age seven, when children's increasing cognitive skills allow them to consider multiple dimensions of identity at the same time. Indeed, meta-analytic review suggests that children's explicit prejudice decreases with age (Raabe & Beelmann, 2011), though, as noted in Section 22.3.2, this may not be the case for implicit forms of bias, something this theoretical approach may have difficulty accounting for (Dunham et al., 2008). Other accounts focus more on children's own social identity and the idea that children, like adults, want to derive a positive self-identity from being a member of a social group that is comparatively superior to the outgroup (e.g., Nesdale & Flesser, 2001, Social Identity Development Theory). According to this account, once children have acquired an initial understanding of social groups, their desire to be positively distinct from others causes them to evaluate the outgroup negatively.

Another mechanism that might explain the trajectory of children's developing social biases is social essentialism, described in Section 22.2.2. It is clear that essentialism is associated with prejudice and stereotyping (Haslam et al., 2000; Keller, 2005; Prentice & Miller, 2007; Williams & Eberhardt, 2008); this might be because it leads people to attribute differences between groups to biological causes rather than to contextual factors (e.g., believing that there are more men in STEM fields because men are naturally better than women at science and math, rather than because boys are encouraged more than girls to develop an interest in those subjects; Salomon & Cimpian, 2014). The link between essentialism and prejudice has been documented in work with adults; for example, Keller (2005) demonstrated that people who held more social essentialist beliefs were more likely to stereotype, and that making essentialist information about social categories salient increased both levels of prejudice toward those categories and levels of ingroup bias. A version of this link has also been demonstrated in children; four-to-six-year-old children withhold resources from members of groups about which they hold essentialist beliefs (Rhodes et al., 2017). Thus, children's intergroup biases may develop alongside their developing essentialist beliefs. However, in the same study, children did not discriminate against essentialized group members in activities aside from resource distribution, so the link between essentialism and discrimination in early childhood may not be absolute, or may depend on other features of the categories in question.

22.3.6 The Internal Motivations that Underlie Children's Ingroup Biases

The most exhaustive examination of the findings reported above is incomplete without taking a closer look at the underlying motivation that drives much of this behavior. First of all, like adults, children have a strong desire

to belong (Baumeister & Leary, 1995), and being a member of a social group might guarantee protection, support, and cooperation when it comes to securing resources. Thus, the threat of being excluded from the group is so existential that it needs to be avoided at every cost; in turn, evidence suggests that affiliative tendencies can be activated even after minimal cues. For example, after being primed to think about the concept of ostracism by watching videos in which an animated shape was ostracized by others, five-year-old children drew more affiliative pictures (Song et al., 2015) and imitated an experimenter's action more closely (Over & Carpenter, 2009) than children who had watched control videos. In another study, children played Cyberball – a virtual ball-tossing game – with either ingroup or outgroup members who either included or excluded them from the game. Children who had been excluded by ingroup members later imitated the actions of another ingroup member more than children who had been included by ingroup members, illustrating their desire to re-establish inclusion in the group. Children who had been included or excluded by outgroup members, on the other hand, did not differ in their later imitative actions (Watson-Jones et al., 2016).

Children's need to belong also motivates them to present themselves in a favorable light toward their group members: Already by five years of age, children share more of their resources when they are being watched by ingroup members than when they are being watched by outgroup members, suggesting a desire to build up a good reputation in the eyes of their group (Engelmann et al., 2013). Four-year-old children also publicly conform to their peers' obviously wrong statements (e.g., identifying a picture of an animal), seemingly for affiliative reasons (Corriveau & Harris, 2010; Haun & Tomasello, 2011). Children's tendency to align their own behavior to that of their ingroup members is so robust that it sometimes even overrides their moral concerns: After children watched their ingroup members behave antisocially by withholding valuable resources from a third party, children's own tendency to behave prosocially was significantly reduced (Engelmann et al., 2016; Misch & Dunham, 2021).

22.4 Can We Avoid the Negative Consequences of Social Categorization?

Much of the research reviewed here suggests that intergroup bias is a natural result of the development of social cognition. Yet, this work also provides an opportunity to ask empirical questions about potential ways to improve outcomes for children developing in a world rife with intergroup conflict. How can we decrease ingroup bias and foster intergroup understanding? Because children are sensitive to moral transgressions from early on, some studies have investigated whether hearing about the antisocial behavior of ingroup members or the prosocial behavior of outgroup members can influence children's differential evaluations of them. Some of these studies have shown that being exposed to ingroup members who have performed antisocial behaviors can indeed attenuate children's ingroup bias (Hetherington et al., 2014; Wilks & Nielsen, 2018). Similar results have been found for children who are exposed to outgroup members performing prosocial behaviors, but to a somewhat lesser degree (Schug et al., 2013). Thus, exposing children to the full range of behaviors that people generally perform, rather than simply the positive behaviors that they naturally associate with ingroup members, could serve to reduce the ingroup bias that they would otherwise develop. Other research with adults suggests that inducing empathy for the outgroup might be an effective way to overcome ingroup bias (Batson et al., 1997; Finlay & Stephan, 2000). Similarly, in children, Sierksma et al. (2015) found that encouraging children to empathize with others who are not members of their peer ingroup diminishes their intentions to perform helpful actions preferentially toward the ingroup.

One particularly fruitful body of research into ways of reducing ingroup bias in children has focused on contact between children who are members of different social groups. Interacting with members of an outgroup, especially in the context of friendship, can improve attitudes toward those outgroup members (Allport, 1954; Pettigrew & Tropp, 2006). For example, a study in the United Kingdom found that three- to five-year-old White children in racially mixed classrooms did not show a pro-White bias, whereas children in racially homogenous classrooms did (Rutland et al., 2005a). Furthermore, children with more cross-race friendships show lower levels of racial bias (Binder et al., 2009; Rutland & Killen, 2015), and children in ethnically homogenous school settings tend to interpret ambiguous situations in biased ways and attribute negative stereotypes to outgroup members, but children in ethnically heterogeneous schools do not (McGlothlin & Killen, 2010; Rutland et al., 2005b). Thus, one way to reduce children's bias may be to put them in situations where they are more likely to directly interact with outgroup members.

However, a caveat to the above proposal is that it is not always possible or practical to simply place children in diverse environments. This concern has led researchers to examine the effectiveness of *extended contact* in reducing intergroup bias. In cases of extended contact, children may not themselves have had contact with outgroup members, but are aware of fellow group members who have (Cameron et al., 2006; Wright et al., 1997). Interventions to facilitate extended contact in school settings have successfully reduced prejudice in children. For example, reading illustrated stories about friendships between ingroup and outgroup children has led to more positive attitudes toward the outgroup across a number of studies (Cameron & Rutland, 2006; Cameron et al., 2006, 2007). Additionally, exposure to classroom materials that include images and symbols of diverse groups (e.g., in songs, books, and posters) can reduce the biases that children hold (Gaias et al., 2018).

Finally, another emergent body of work suggests that one reason children (and adults) rely on stereotypes and prejudices is because they have difficulty individuating outgroup members and so rely on category-level knowledge (the Perceptual-Social Linkage Hypothesis; Lee et al., 2017). Based on this hypothesis, researchers have experimented with cross-race individuation training as a way of reducing bias by reducing reliance on categories, with promising initial results (Qian et al., 2017). In brief, this work relies on the assumption that individual acts of categorization mediate between perception of individuals and the application of category-level beliefs to that individual (Dunham & Degner, 2013; Lee et al., 2017).

22.5 Conclusion

In this chapter, we have reviewed a great deal of research on the development of intergroup cognition, from the earliest origins of social categorization to the development and consequences of social category-based processing across childhood. In reviewing this work, we have aimed to highlight ways in which social categorization is deeply embedded in human psychology, shaping some of the most basic ways in which we view the world. The research reviewed here leaves open many interesting questions that will shape much of the work

done in developmental psychology over the years to come, but has also already brought us a long way in understanding just how influential social categorization is in shaping human development. Looking forward, we hope to see the field move toward an even more complete understanding of the development of social cognition that incorporates work across the lifespan, including adolescents and older adults, and that draws from the newest findings and methods across other areas of psychology, including comparative cognition and cognitive neuroscience. We trust that by continuing to ask questions about the roots of social cognition, researchers will uncover the basic psychological tendencies that will not only contribute to a fuller understanding of psychology, but that will allow us to facilitate positive outcomes for children developing in a dizzyingly complex social world.

References

Aboud, F. E. (1988). *Children and Prejudice*. New York: Blackwell.

Abrams, D., & Rutland, A. (2008). The development of subjective group dynamics. In S. R. Levy, & M. Killen (eds.), *Intergroup Attitudes and Relations in Childhood through Adulthood: Studies in Crime and Public Policy* (pp. 47–65). Oxford: Oxford University Press.

Abrams, D., Rutland, A., & Cameron, L. (2003). The development of subjective group dynamics: Children's judgments of normative and deviant in-group and out-group individuals. *Child Development*, *74*, 1840–1856.

Abrams, D., Rutland, A., Pelletier, J., & Ferrell, J. M. (2009). Children's group nous: Understanding and applying peer exclusion within and between groups. *Child Development*, *80*. 224–243.

Allport, G. (1954). *The Nature of Prejudice*. Cambridge: Addison Wesley.

Astuti, R., Solomon, G. E., & Carey, S. (2004). Constraints on conceptual development: A case study of the acquisition of folkbiological and folksociological knowledge in Madagascar. *Monographs of the Society for Research in Child Development, 69,* 1–135.

Atran, S. (1990). *Cognitive Foundations of Natural History.* New York: Cambridge University Press.

Bar-Haim, Y., Ziv, T., Lamy, D., & Hodes, R. M. (2006). Nature and nurture in own-race face processing. *Psychological Science, 17,* 159–163.

Baron, A. S., & Banaji, M. R. (2006). The development of implicit attitudes evidence of race evaluations from ages 6 and 10 and adulthood. *Psychological Science, 17,* 53–58.

Baron, A. S., & Dunham, Y. (2015). Representing "us" and "them": Building blocks of intergroup cognition. *Journal of Cognition and Development, 16,* 780–801.

Barrett, M. (2007). *Children's Knowledge, Beliefs and Feelings about Nations and National Groups.* Hove: Psychology Press.

Batson, C. D., Polycarpou, M. P., Harmon-Jones, E., Imhoff, H. J., Mitchener, E. C., Bednar, L. L., Klein, T. R., & Highberger, L. (1997). Empathy and attitudes: Can feeling for a member of a stigmatized group improve feelings toward the group? *Journal of Personality and Social Psychology, 72,* 105–118.

Baumeister, R. F., & Leary, M. F. (1995). The need to belong: Desire for interpersonal attachments as a fundamental human motivation. *Psychological Bulletin, 117,* 497–529.

Bennett, M., Lyons, E., Sani, F., & Barrett, M. (1998). Children's subjective identification with the group and in-group favoritism. *Developmental Psychology, 34,* 902–909.

Bennett, M., & Sani, F. (2008a). Children's subjective identification with social groups: A self-stereotyping approach. *Developmental Science, 11,* 69–75.

Bennett, M., & Sani, F. (2008b). The effect of comparative context upon stereotype content: Children's judgments of ingroup behavior. *Scandinavian Journal of Psychology, 49,* 141–146.

Benozio, A., & Diesendruck, G. (2015). From effort to value: Preschool children's alternative to

effort justification. *Psychological Science, 26,* 1423–1429.

Berndt, T. J., & Heller, K. A. (1986). Gender stereotypes and social inferences: A developmental study. *Journal of Personality and Social Psychology, 50,* 889–898.

Bian, L., Leslie, S. J., & Cimpian, A. (2017). Gender stereotypes about intellectual ability emerge early and influence children's interests. *Science, 355,* 389–391.

Bian, L., Sloane, S., & Baillargeon, R. (2018). Infants expect ingroup support to override fairness when resources are limited. *Proceedings of the National Academy of Sciences (USA), 115,* 2705–2710.

Biernat, M. (1991). Gender stereotypes and the relationship between masculinity and femininity: A developmental analysis. *Journal of Personality and Social Psychology, 61,* 351–365.

Bigler, R. S., & Liben, L. S. (1993). A cognitive-developmental approach to racial stereotyping and reconstructive memory in Euro-American children. *Child Development, 64,* 1507–1518.

Bigler, R. S., & Liben, L. S. (2006). A developmental intergroup theory of social stereotypes and prejudice. *Advances in Child Development and Behavior, 34,* 39–89.

Binder, J., Zagefka, H., Brown, R., Funke, F., Kessler, T., Mummendey, A., Maquil, A., Demoulin, S., & Leyens, J. P. (2009). Does contact reduce prejudice or does prejudice reduce contact? A longitudinal test of the contact hypothesis among majority and minority groups in three European countries. *Journal of Personality and Social Psychology, 96,* 843–856.

Birnbaum, D., Deeb, I., Segall, G., Ben-Eliyahu, A., & Diesendruck, G. (2010). The development of social essentialism: The case of Israeli children's inferences about Jews and Arabs. *Child Development, 81,* 757–777.

Boyd, R., & Richerson, P. J. (2009). Culture and the evolution of human cooperation. *Philosophical Transactions of the Royal Society B: Biological Sciences, 364,* 3281–3288.

Brown, D. E. (2004). Human universals, human nature & human culture. *Daedalus, 133,* 47–54.

Butler, L. P., & Walton, G. M. (2013). The opportunity to collaborate increases preschoolers' motivation for challenging tasks. *Journal of Experimental Child Psychology*, *116*, 953–961.

Buttelmann, D., & Bohm, R. (2014). The ontogeny of the motivation that underlies in-group bias. *Psychological Science*, *25*, 921–927.

Buttelmann, D., Zmyj, N., Daum, M., & Carpenter, M. (2013). Selective imitation of in-group over out-group members in 14-month-old infants. *Child Development*, *64*, 422–428.

Cameron, L., & Rutland, A. (2006). Extended contact through story reading in school: Reducing children's prejudice toward the disabled. *Journal of Social Issues*, *62*, 469–488.

Cameron, L., Rutland, A., & Brown, R. (2007). Promoting children's positive intergroup attitudes towards stigmatized groups: Extended contact and multiple classification skills training. *International Journal of Behavioral Development*, *31*, 454–466.

Cameron, L., Rutland, A., Brown, R., & Douch, R. (2006). Changing children's intergroup attitudes toward refugees: Testing different models of extended contact. *Child Development*, *77*, 1208–1219.

Castelli, L., De Amicis, L., & Sherman, S.J. (2007). The loyal member effect: On the preference for ingroup members who engage in exclusive relations with the ingroup. *Developmental Psychology*, *43*, 1347–1359.

Chalik, L., Leslie, S. J., & Rhodes, M. (2017). Cultural context shapes essentialist beliefs about religion. *Developmental Psychology*, *53*, 1178–1187.

Chalik, L., & Rhodes, M. (2014). Preschoolers use social allegiances to predict behavior. *Journal of Cognition and Development*, *15*, 136–160.

Chalik, L., & Rhodes, M. (2018). Learning about social category-based obligations. *Cognitive Development*, *48*, 117–124.

Chalik, L., Rivera, C., & Rhodes, M. (2014). Children's use of categories and mental states to predict social behavior. *Developmental Psychology*, *50*, 2360–2367.

Chen, E. E., Corriveau, K. H., & Harris, P. L. (2013). Children trust a consensus composed of outgroup members - but do not retain that trust. *Child Development*, *84*, 269–282.

Corenblum, B. (2003). What children remember about ingroup and outgroup peers: Effects of stereotypes on children's processing of information about group members. *Journal of Experimental Child Psychology*, *86*, 32–66.

Corriveau, K. H., & Harris, P. L. (2010). Preschoolers (sometimes) defer to the majority in making simple perceptual judgments. *Developmental Psychology*, *46*, 437–445.

Corriveau, K. H., Kinzler, K. D., & Harris, P. L. (2013). Accuracy trumps accent in children's endorsement of object labels. *Developmental Psychology*, *49*, 470–479.

Cvencek, D., Meltzoff, A. N., & Greenwald, A. G. (2011). Math-gender stereotypes in elementary school children. *Child Development*, *82*, 766–779.

Degner, J., & Wentura, D. (2010). Automatic prejudice in childhood and early adolescence. *Journal of Personality and Social Psychology*, *98*, 356.

DeJesus, J. M., Rhodes, M., & Kinzler, K. D. (2014). Evaluations versus expectations: Children's divergent beliefs about resource distribution. *Cognitive Science*, *38*, 178–193.

del Río, M. F., & Strasser, K. (2011). Chilean children's essentialist reasoning about poverty. *British Journal of Developmental Psychology*, *29*, 722–743.

Devine, P. G. (1989). Stereotypes and prejudice: Their automatic and controlled components. *Journal of Personality and Social Psychology*, *56*, 5–18.

Diesendruck, G., & Haber, L. (2009). God's categories: The effect of religiosity on children's teleological and essentialist beliefs about categories. *Cognition*, *110*, 100–114.

Diesendruck, G., & HaLevi, H. (2006). The role of language, appearance, and culture in children's social category-based induction. *Child Development*, *77*, 539–553.

Dunham, Y. (2018). Mere membership. *Trends in Cognitive Sciences*, *22*, 780–793.

Dunham, Y., Baron, A. S., & Banaji, M. R. (2006). From American city to Japanese village:

A cross-cultural investigation of implicit race attitudes. *Child Development*, *77*, 1268–1281

Dunham, Y., Baron, A. S., & Banaji, M. R. (2007). Children and social groups: A developmental analysis of implicit consistency in Hispanic Americans. *Self and Identity*, *6*, 238–255.

Dunham, Y., Baron, A. S., & Banaji, M. R. (2008). The development of implicit intergroup cognition. *Trends in Cognitive Sciences*, *12*, 248–253.

Dunham, Y., Baron, A. S., & Banaji, M. R. (2015). The development of implicit gender attitudes. *Developmental Science*, *18*, 469–483.

Dunham, Y., Baron, A. S., & Carey, S. (2011). Consequences of "minimal" group affiliations in children. *Child Development*, *82*, 793–811.

Dunham, Y., & Degner, J. (2013). From categories to exemplars (and back again). In M. R. Banaji, & S. A. Gelman (eds.), *Navigating the Social World: What Infants, Children, and Other Species Can Teach Us* (pp. 275–280). New York: Oxford University Press.

Dunham, Y., & Emory, J. (2014). Of affect and ambiguity: The emergence of preference for arbitrary ingroups. *Journal of Social Issues*, *70*, 81–98.

Dunham, Y., Newheiser, A. K., Hoosain, L., Merrill, A., & Olson, K. R. (2014a). From a different vantage: Intergroup attitudes among children from low- and intermediate-status racial groups. *Social Cognition*, *32*, 1–21.

Dunham, Y., Srinivasan, M., Dorsch, R., & Barner, D. (2014b). Religion insulates ingroup evaluations: The development of intergroup attitudes in India. *Developmental Science*, *17*, 311–319.

Engelmann, J. M., Herrmann, E., Rapp, D. J., & Tomasello, M. (2016). Young children (sometimes) do the right thing even when their peers do not. *Cognitive Development*, *39*, 86–92.

Engelmann, J. M., Over, H., Herrmann, E., & Tomasello, M. (2013). Young children care more about their reputation with ingroup members and potential reciprocators. *Developmental Science*, *16*, 952–958.

Fehr, E., Bernhard, H., & Rockenbach, B. (2008). Egalitarianism in young children. *Nature*, *454*, 1079–1083.

Finlay, K. A., & Stephan, W. G. (2000). Improving intergroup relations: The effects of empathy on racial attitudes. *Journal of Applied Social Psychology*, *30*, 1720–1737.

Gaias, L. M., Gal, D., Abry, T., Granger, K. L., & Taylor, M. (2018). Diversity exposure in preschool: Longitudinal implications for cross-race friendships and racial bias. *Journal of Applied Developmental Psychology*, *59*, 5–15.

Gelman, S. A. (2003). *The Essential Child: Origins of Essentialism in Everyday Thought.* Oxford: Oxford University Press.

Gelman, S., Collman, P., & Maccoby, E. (1986). Inferring properties from categories versus inferring categories from properties: The case of gender. *Child Development*, *57*, 396–404.

Gopnik, A., & Wellman, H. M. (2012). Reconstructing constructivism: Causal models, Bayesian learning mechanisms, and the theory theory. *Psychological Bulletin*, *138*, 1085–1108.

Greenwald, A. G., McGhee, D. E., & Schwartz, J. L. (1998). Measuring individual differences in implicit cognition: The implicit association test. *Journal of Personality and Social Psychology*, *74*, 1464.

Griffiths, J., & Nesdale, D. (2006). Ingroup and outgroup attitudes of ethnic majority and minority children. *International Journal of Intercultural Relations*, *30*, 735–749.

Halim, M. L. D., Ruble, D. N., Tamis-LeMonda, C. S., Shrout, P. E., & Amodio, D. M. (2017). Gender attitudes in early childhood: Behavioral Consequences and cognitive antecedents. *Child Development*, *88*, 882–899.

Haslam, N., Rothschild, L., & Ernst, D. (2000). Essentialist beliefs about social categories. *British Journal of Social Psychology*, *39*, 113–127.

Haun, D. B., & Tomasello, M. (2011). Conformity to peer pressure in preschool children. *Child Development*, *82*, 1759–1767.

Heiphetz, L., Spelke, E. S., & Banaji, M. R. (2013). Patterns of implicit and explicit attitudes in children and adults: Tests in the domain of religion. *Journal of Experimental Psychology: General*, *142*, 864–879.

Hetherington, C., Hendrickson, C., & Koenig, M. (2014). Reducing an in-group bias in preschool children: The impact of moral behavior. *Developmental Science, 17*, 1042–1049.

Hilliard, L. J., & Liben, L. S. (2010). Differing levels of gender salience in preschool classrooms: Effects on children's gender attitudes and intergroup bias. *Child Development, 81*, 1787–1798.

Hirschfeld, L. A. (1996). *Race in the Making.* Cambridge, MA: MIT Press.

Howard, L. H., Henderson, A. M., Carrazza, C., & Woodward, A. L. (2015). Infants' and young children's imitation of linguistic in-group and out-group informants. *Child Development, 86*, 259–275.

James, J. D. (2001). The role of cognitive development and socialization in the initial development of team loyalty. *Leisure Sciences, 23*, 233–261.

Jin, K., & Baillargeon, R. (2017). Infants possess an abstract expectation of ingroup support. *Proceedings of the National Academy of Sciences (USA), 114*, 8199–8204.

Jordan, J. J., McAuliffe, K., & Warneken, F. (2014). Development of ingroup favoritism in children's third-party punishment of selfishness. *Proceedings of the National Academy of Sciences (USA), 111*, 12710–12715.

Kalish, C. W., & Lawson, C. A. (2008). Development of social category representations: Early appreciation of roles and deontic relations. *Child Development, 79*, 577–593.

Keller, J. (2005). In genes we trust: The biological component of psychological essentialism and its relationship to mechanisms of motivated social cognition. *Journal of Personality and Social Psychology, 88*, 686–702.

Kelly, D. J., Quinn, P. C., Slater, A. M., Lee, K., Gibson, A., Smith, M., Ge, L., & Pascalis, O. (2005). Three-month-olds but not newborns prefer own-race faces. *Developmental Science, 8*, F31–F36.

Kinzler, K. D., & Dautel, J. (2012). Children's essentialist reasoning about language and race. *Developmental Science, 15*, 131–138.

Kinzler, K. D., Dupoux, E., & Spelke, E. S. (2007). The native language of social cognition. *Proceedings of the National Academy of Sciences (USA), 104*, 12577–12580.

Kinzler, K. D., Dupoux, E., & Spelke, E. S. (2012). "Native" objects and collaborators: Infants' object choices and acts of giving reflect favor for native over foreign speakers. *Journal of Cognition and Development, 13*, 67–81.

Kinzler, K. D., Shutts, K., DeJesus, J., & Spelke, E. S. (2009). Accent trumps race in guiding children's social preferences. *Social Cognition, 27*, 623–634.

Kinzler, K. D., & Spelke, E. S. (2011). Do infants show social preferences for people differing in race? *Cognition, 119*, 1–9.

Lee, K., Quinn, P. C., & Pascalis, O. (2017). Face race processing and racial bias in early development: A perceptual-social linkage. *Current Directions in Psychological Science, 26*, 256–262.

Liberman, Z., Kinzler, K. D., & Woodward, A. L. (2014). Friends or foes: Infants use shared evaluations to infer others' social relationships. *Journal of Experimental Psychology: General, 143*, 966–971.

Liberman, Z., Woodward, A. L., & Kinzler, K. D. (2017). Preverbal infants infer third-party social relationships based on language. *Cognitive Science, 41*, 622–634.

Mahajan, N., & Wynn, K. (2012). Origins of "us" versus "them": Prelinguistic infants prefer similar others. *Cognition, 124*, 227–233.

Mahalingam, R. (2003). Essentialism, culture, and power: Representations of social class. *Journal of Social Issues, 59*, 733–749.

Marques, J. M., Yzerbyt, V. Y., & Leyens, J. (1988). "The black sheep effect": Extremity of judgments toward ingroup members as a function of group identification. *European Journal of Social Psychology, 18*, 1–16.

Master, A., Cheryan, S., & Meltzoff, A. N. (2017). Social group membership increases STEM engagement among preschoolers. *Developmental Psychology, 53*, 201–209.

Master, A. & Walton, G. M. (2012). Minimal groups increase young children's motivation and learning on group-relevant tasks. *Child Development, 84*, 737–751.

McAuliffe, K., & Dunham, Y. (2017). Fairness overrides group bias in children's second-party punishment. *Journal of*

Experimental Psychology: General, 146, 485–494.

McGlothlin, H., & Killen, M. (2010). How social experience is related to children's intergroup attitudes. *European Journal of Social Psychology, 40,* 625–634.

McLoughlin, N., & Over, H. (2017). The developmental origins of dehumanization. *Advances in Child Development and Behavior, 54,* 153–178.

McLoughlin, N., Tipper, S. P., & Over, H. (2018). Young children perceive less humanness in outgroup faces. *Developmental Science, 21,* e12539.

Medin, D. L., & Ortony, A. (1989). Psychological essentialism. In S. Vosnaidou, & A. Ortony (eds.), *Similarity and Analogical Reasoning* (pp. 179–196). Cambridge, MA: Cambridge University Press.

Misch, A., & Dunham, Y. (2021). (Peer) group influence on children's prosocial and antisocial behavior. Journal of Experimental Child Psychology, 201, 104994.

Misch, A., Over, H., & Carpenter, M. (2014). Stick with your group: Young children's attitudes about group loyalty. *Journal of Experimental Child Psychology, 126,* 19–36.

Misch, A., Over, H., & Carpenter, M. (2016). I won't tell: Young children show loyalty to their group by keeping group secrets. *Journal of Experimental Child Psychology, 142,* 96–106.

Misch, A., Over, H., & Carpenter, M. (2018). The whistleblower's dilemma in young children: When loyalty trumps other moral concerns. *Frontiers in Psychology, 9,* 250.

Muzzatti, B., & Agnoli, F. (2007). Gender and mathematics: Attitudes and stereotype threat susceptibility in Italian children. *Developmental Psychology, 43,* 747–759.

Nesdale, D., & Flesser, D. (2001). Social identity and the development of children's group attitudes. *Child Development, 72,* 506–517

Newheiser, A. K., & Olson, K. R. (2012). White and black American children's implicit intergroup bias. *Journal of Experimental Social Psychology, 48,* 264–270.

Noyes, A., & Dunham, Y. (2017). Mutual intentions as a causal framework for social groups. *Cognition, 162,* 133–142.

Olson, K. R., & Dunham, Y. (2010). The development of implicit social cognition. In B. Gawronski, & B. K. Payne (eds.), *Handbook of Implicit Social Cognition: Measurement, Theory, and Applications* (pp. 241–254). New York: Guilford Press.

Oostenbroek, J., & Over, H. (2015). Young children contrast their behavior to that of out-group members. *Journal of Experimental Child Psychology, 139,* 234–241.

Over, H., & Carpenter, M. (2009). Eighteen-month-old infants show increased helping following priming with affiliation. *Psychological Science, 20,* 1189–1193.

Over, H., Eggleston, A., Bell, J., & Dunham, Y. (2017). Young children seek out biased information about social groups. *Developmental Science, 21,* 1–12.

Over, H., Vaish, A., & Tomasello, M. (2016). Do young children accept responsibility for the negative actions of ingroup members? *Cognitive Development, 40,* 24–32.

Pettigrew, T. F., & Tropp, L. R. (2006). A meta-analytic test of intergroup contact theory. *Journal of Personality and Social Psychology, 90,* 751–783.

Powell, L. J., & Spelke, E. S. (2013). Preverbal infants expect members of social groups to act alike. *Proceedings of the National Academy of Sciences (USA), 110,* E3965–E3972.

Prentice, D. A., & Miller, D. T. (2007). Psychological essentialism of human categories. *Current Directions in Psychological Science, 16,* 202–206.

Qian, M. K., Quinn, P. C., Heyman, G. D., Pascalis, O., Fu, G., & Lee, K. (2017). Perceptual individuation training (but not mere exposure) reduces implicit racial bias in preschool children. *Developmental Psychology, 53,* 845–859.

Quinn, P. C., Yahr, J., Kuhn, A., Slater, A. M., & Pascalis, O. (2002). Representation of the gender of human faces by infants: A preference for female. *Perception, 31,* 1109–1121.

Raabe, T., & Beelmann, A. (2011). Development of ethnic, racial, and national prejudice in childhood and adolescence: A multinational meta-analysis of age differences. *Child Development, 82*, 1715–1737.

Renno, M. P., & Shutts, K. (2015). Children's social category-based giving and its correlates: Expectations and preferences. *Developmental Psychology, 51*, 533–543.

Rhodes, M. (2012). Naïve theories of social groups. *Child Development, 83*, 1900–1916.

Rhodes, M., & Chalik, L. (2013). Social categories as markers of intrinsic interpersonal obligations. *Psychological Science, 24*, 999–1006.

Rhodes, M., & Gelman, S. A. (2009). A developmental examination of the conceptual structure of animal, artifact, and human social categories across two cultural contexts. *Cognitive Psychology, 59*, 244–274.

Rhodes, M., Leslie, S. J., Saunders, K., Dunham, Y., & Cimpian, A. (2017). How does social essentialism affect the development of inter-group relations? *Developmental Science, 21*, 1–15.

Rhodes, M., Leslie, S. J., & Tworek, C. M. (2012). Cultural transmission of social essentialism. *Proceedings of the National Academy of Sciences (USA), 109*, 13526–13531.

Rotenberg, K. J., & Cerda, C. (1994). Racially based trust expectancies of Native American and Caucasian children. *Journal of Social Psychology, 134*, 621–631.

Rothbart, M., & Taylor, M. (1992). Category labels and social reality: Do we view social categories as natural kinds? In G. R. Semin, & K. Fiedler (eds.), *Language, Interaction and Social Cognition* (pp. 11–36). Thousand Oaks, CA: Sage Publications, Inc.

Rutland, A., Cameron, L., Bennett, L., & Ferrell, J. (2005a). Interracial contact and racial constancy: A multi-site study of racial intergroup bias in 3–5 year old Anglo-British children. *Journal of Applied Developmental Psychology, 26*, 699–713.

Rutland, A., Cameron, L., Milne, A., & McGeorge, P. (2005b). Social norms and self-presentation: Children's implicit and explicit intergroup attitudes. *Child Development, 76*, 451–466.

Rutland, A., & Killen, M. (2015). A developmental science approach to reducing prejudice and social exclusion: Intergroup processes, social-cognitive development, and moral reasoning: A developmental science approach to reducing prejudice and social exclusion. *Social Issues and Policy Review, 9*, 121–154.

Rutland, A., Killen, M., & Abrams, D. (2010). A new social-cognitive developmental perspective on prejudice: The interplay between morality and group identity. *Perspectives on Psychological Science, 5*, 279–291.

Salomon, E., & Cimpian, A. (2014). The inherence heuristic as a source of essentialist thought. *Personality and Social Psychology Bulletin, 40*, 1297–1315.

Sani, F., & Bennett, M. (2009). Children's inclusion of the group in the self: Evidence from a self-ingroup confusion paradigm. *Developmental Psychology, 45*, 503–510.

Schmidt, M. F., Rakoczy, H., & Tomasello, M. (2012). Young children enforce social norms selectively depending on the violator's group affiliation. *Cognition, 124*, 325–333.

Schug, M. G., Shusterman, A., Barth, H., & Palatano, A. L. (2013). Minimal-group membership influences children's responses to novel experience with group members. *Developmental Science, 16*, 47–55.

Shutts, K. (2015). Young children's preferences: Gender, race, and social status. *Child Development Perspectives, 9*, 262–266.

Shutts, K., Banaji, M. R., & Spelke, E. S. (2010). Social categories guide young children's preferences for novel objects. *Developmental Science, 13*, 599–610.

Sierksma, J., Thijs, J. T., & Verkuyten, M. (2015). In-group bias in children's intention to help can be overpowered by inducing empathy. *British Journal of Developmental Psychology, 33*, 45–56.

Singarajah, A., Chanley, J., Gutierrez, Y., Cordon, Y., Nguyen, B., Burakowski, L., & Johnson, S. P. (2017). Infant attention to same- and other-race faces. *Cognition, 159*, 76–84.

Song, R., Over, H., & Carpenter, M. (2015). Children draw more affiliative pictures following priming with third-party ostracism. *Developmental Psychology, 51*, 831–840.

Sousa, P., Atran, S., & Medin, D. (2002). Essentialism and folkbiology: Evidence from Brazil. *Journal of Cognition and Culture, 2*, 195–223.

Tajfel, H., & Turner, J. (1979). An integrative theory of intergroup conflict. In W. G. Austin, & S. Worchel (eds.), *The Social Psychology of Inter-group Relations* (pp. 33–47). Monterey, CA: Brooks/Cole.

Taylor, M. G. (1996). The development of children's beliefs about social and biological aspects of gender differences, *Child Development, 67*, 1555–1571.

Taylor, M. G., Rhodes, M., & Gelman, S. (2009). Boys will be boys; cows will be cows: Children's essentialist reasoning about gender categories and animal species. *Child Development, 80*, 461–481.

Watson-Jones, R. E., Whitehouse, H., & Legare, C. H. (2016). In-group ostracism increases high-fidelity imitation in early childhood. *Psychological Science, 27*, 34–42.

Waxman, S. R. (2010). Names will never hurt me? Naming and the development of racial and gender categories in preschool-aged children. *European Journal of Social Psychology, 40*, 593–610.

Waxman, S. R., & Grace, A. D. (2012). Developing gender- and race-based categories in infants: Evidence from 7- and 11-month-olds. In G. Hayes, & M. Bryant (eds.), *Psychology of Culture* (pp. 159–175). Hauppauge, NY: Nova Science Publishers.

Wellman, H. M., & Gelman, S. A. (1992). Cognitive development: Foundational theories of core domains. *Annual Review of Psychology, 43*, 337–375.

Williams, M. J., & Eberhardt, J. L. (2008). Biological conceptions of race and the motivation to cross racial boundaries. *Journal of Personality and Social Psychology, 94*, 1033–1047.

Wilks, M., & Nielsen, M. (2018). Children disassociate from antisocial in-group members. *Journal of Experimental Child Psychology, 165*, 37–50.

Witt, S. D. (1997). Parental influence on children's socialization to gender roles. *Adolescence, 32*, 253–259.

Wright, S. C., Aron, A., McLaughlin-Volpe, T., & Ropp, S. A. (1997). The extended contact effect: Knowledge of cross-group friendships and prejudice. *Journal of Personality and Social Psychology, 73*, 73–90.

Yang, F., Choi, Y., Misch, A., Yang, X., & Dunham, Y. (2018). In defense of the commons: Young children negatively evaluate and sanction free-riders. *Psychological Science, 29*, 1598–1611.

23 Behavioral and Neural Development of Cognitive Control and Risky Decision-Making across Adolescence

Neeltje E. Blankenstein, Jiska S. Peper, and Eveline A. Crone

Adolescence, which is defined as the transition phase between childhood and adulthood, roughly between ten and twenty-two years of age, is marked by pronounced behavioral changes in cognitive control and decision-making (Crone & Dahl, 2012). For instance, adolescents show with advancing age an increased ability to control impulses and increases in goal-directed behavior (Hofmann et al., 2012). At the same time, adolescence is often characterized by an increase in exploratory and risk-taking behavior, possibly related to the need to develop independence from parents and develop their identity (Steinberg, 2008). In addition to these behavioral changes, adolescence is marked by profound neural changes both in functional brain activity and connectivity, and in terms of structural brain changes and connections (Mills & Tamnes, 2014). In this chapter, we will discuss current literature on two aspects that develop in tandem across adolescence, cognitive control (Section 23.1) and risky decision-making (Section 23.2; for an overview of paradigms to measure these two aspects, see Table 23.1), as well as their neural developmental patterns (for an overview of brain regions and connections, see Figure 23.1). Section 23.1 covers the development of cognitive control and how structural brain development and sex steroids contribute to this development. Section 23.2 discusses which underlying behavioral and functional neural factors contribute to the development of risky decision-making. Finally, Section 23.3 converges the two parts and considers avenues for future research.

23.1 Cognitive Control

Cognitive control has been described as the process by which goals or plans influence behavior. Hence, it is a form of goal-directed behavior and results from the selection of appropriate responses and ignoring or inhibiting inappropriate responses (see Chapters 20 and 21). Also referred to as executive control, cognitive control allows individuals to inhibit automatic or inappropriate responses and to keep information online in working memory. Cognitive control supports flexible, adaptive responses, and complex goal-directed thought (Crone & Steinbeis, 2017; Diamond, 2013; Luna et al., 2015; Miller & Cohen, 2001). Evidently, cognitive control is a multifaceted construct and relies on different functions, including working memory, behavioral inhibition, cognitive flexibility and monitoring of ongoing behavior (Diamond, 2013).

A large number of studies found that cognitive control skills rapidly improve from childhood into adolescence, reaching a plateau around late adolescence/early adulthood (for a review, see Diamond, 2013, see Chapter 20). Cognitive control is predictive for the development of academic achievement, for example, working memory and cognitive flexibility are

Table 23.1. *Overview of paradigms to measure cognitive control and risky decision-making across adolescence*

Name	Outcome measure	Example studies
Paradigms to measure cognitive control		
Marshmallow task	Delay of gratification	Shoda et al. (1990); Watts et al. (2018)
Delay Discounting study	Delay of gratification / area under curve	Peper et al. (2013b); Achterberg et al. (2016a)
Social Network Aggression Task	Self-control in response to social evaluations	Achterberg et al. (2017, 2018)
Paradigms to measure risky decision-making		
Heads-or-tails fMRI task	Neural sensitivity to rewards versus losses	Schreuders et al. (2018)
Hot Columbia Card fMRI Task	Risk and return sensitivity	van Duijvenvoorde et al. (2015)
Risk and Ambiguity task	Risk and ambiguity attitude	Tymula et al. (2012); Blankenstein et al. (2016)
Risk and Ambiguity fMRI task	Neural sensitivity to risk and ambiguity and outcome processing	Blankenstein et al. (2018)

related to better reading and mathematics achievements two years later (Peters et al., 2017). In the famous marshmallow study by Shoda et al. (1990) it was found that self-control (i.e., delay of gratification) in preschool was predictive for adolescent achievement, socio-emotional development, and brain structure development (Casey et al., 2011; Mischel et al., 2011; Shoda et al., 1990). These findings suggest that cognitive control is an important predictor for future development (see Chapter 20). It should be noted that a recent study could only partially replicate this effect (Watts et al., 2018), as controlling for factors such as family background, early cognitive ability, and the home environment reduced the explained variance considerably of self-control predicting adolescent outcomes (Watts et al., 2018). In addition, cohort effects in self-control have recently been reported as well: the average ability to delay gratification in children has improved from 1960 to 2000, such that children from the 2000s could – on average – wait two minutes longer for a delayed reward compared to children from the 1960s (Carlson et al., 2018). These findings show that environmental influences can impact the development of cognitive control. Indeed, age differences in decision-making and cognitive control can be modulated by differential kinds of incentives, such as monetary incentives (i.e., reward/loss) or social incentives (i.e., acceptance or rejection by the peer group; Achterberg et al., 2018; Kray et al., 2018; Tan et al., 2018).

Research has also reported a relation between *a lack* of cognitive control and detrimental developmental outcomes. For example, lack of (aberrant) cognitive control has been identified as a marker for susceptibility to develop impulse-related problems such as pathological gambling or addiction (van Timmeren, Daams, van Holst & Goudriaan, 2018). Furthermore, low levels of cognitive control have been associated with (neuro)psychiatric illnesses, such as schizophrenia

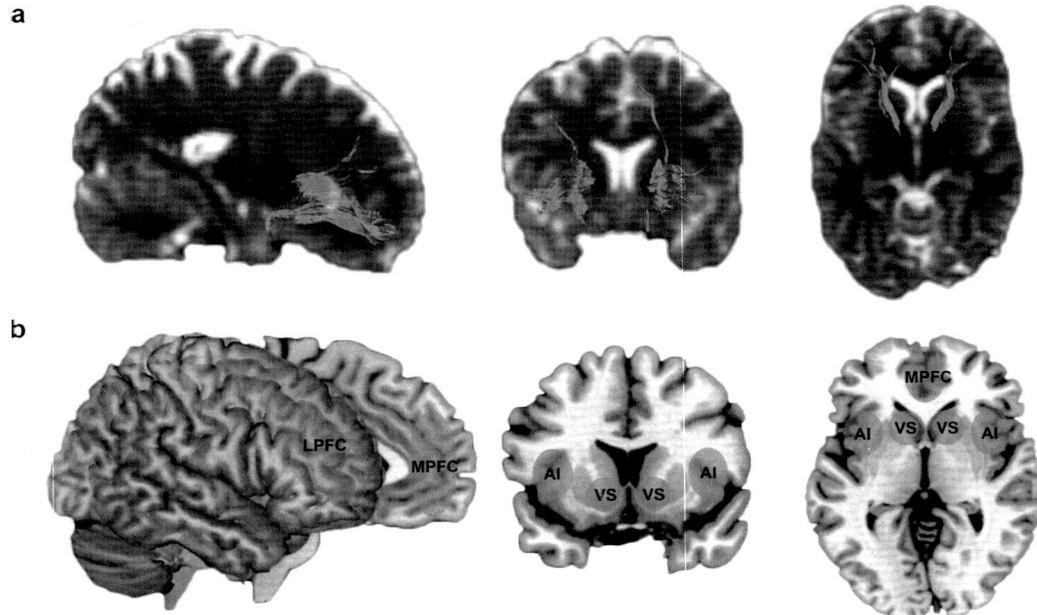

Figure 23.1 (a) Sagittal (left), coronal (middle), and axial (right) views of frontostriatal white matter bundles of one random participant (from Peper et al. (2013b) *Cerebral Cortex*, with permission). (b) Sagittal (left), coronal (middle), and axial (right) views of areas of activation involved in cognitive control and risky decision-making. LPFC = lateral prefrontal cortex; VS = ventral striatum; MPFC = medial prefrontal cortex; AI = anterior insula
A black-and-white version of this figure will appear in some formats. For the color version, please refer to the plate section.

(Matzke et al., 2017) and Attention Deficit Hyperactivity Disorder (ADHD) (Ma et al., 2016; Rubia, 2018). Recently, research has made significant progress in unraveling the neurocognitive processes that are associated with the development of cognitive control, leading to new insights in the mechanisms of cognitive control. In general, cognitive maturation closely follows the development of the prefrontal cortex (PFC) and its connections (Crone & Steinbeis, 2017), but different subparts of the PFC differentially relate to distinct aspects of cognitive control. Several examples of research linking behavioral development of self-control to brain development are described in Sections 23.1.1–23.1.3.

23.1.1 Cortico–Subcortical Connections and the Development of Self-Control

Longitudinal studies into the brain anatomy of typically developing children and adolescents reveal the largest gray matter volumes and cortical thickness during childhood followed by a steady decline during adolescence (Raznahan et al., 2011; Tamnes et al., 2017). In addition, the increases in functional and structural connectivity contribute to local and distal integrative processes and gradually shift the balance in the cortico–subcortical circuits toward the cognitive-control-dedicated brain regions (Genc et al., 2018; Koenis et al., 2018). The marked changes in connectivity are further evidenced by findings showing an initial wave of synaptic overproduction during childhood, which is followed by selective synaptic elimination during adolescence (Huttenlocher & Dabholkar, 1997). Together with the increase in axonal myelination, the elimination of (non-functional) synaptic connections is presumed to be part of the brain's "fine-tuning" mechanisms to maximize (metabolic) efficiency and functionality (Huttenlocher, 1979; Yakovlev et al., 1967).

The observation that the maturational processes on the brain level occur during the pubertal stage of adolescence, which is characterized by major physical changes including the development of secondary sexual characteristics, possibly suggests an interrelation between hormonal development and brain development (Herting & Sowell, 2017; Peper & Dahl, 2013). Puberty, the initial phase of adolescents which is characterized by large changes in physical appearance of adolescents, involves a surge in the sex steroid hormones testosterone and estradiol, and hallmarks the biological transition from a non-reproductive into a reproductive state (Nussey & Whitehead, 2001). There is now a fair amount of evidence from both animal and human studies, showing that the activational and organizational processes involved in brain maturation are partly mediated by pubertal (and adolescent) sex steroid hormones (Herting et al., 2015; Peper et al., 2013a; Wierenga et al., 2018). Research from our lab suggests that testosterone may play a substantial role in shaping white matter connectivity (Peper et al., 2015). Two-hundred and fifty-eight healthy volunteers aged between eight and twenty-five years underwent diffusion tensor imaging (DTI), a neuroimaging technique enabling the measurement of white matter connections in vivo. Tractographical analyses revealed associations between higher endogenous levels of testosterone, lower

quality of structural fronto-temporo–subcortical connectivity, and less behavioral inhibition in the form of aggressive personality (Peper et al., 2015). These findings possibly indicate that poorer cognitive control is related to less adequate inhibitory signal transfer from the cerebral cortex to the subcortical motivation circuits (Casey et al., 2016).

Support for this explanation comes from other DTI work that examined the relation between fronto-striatal fiber tracts and delayed discounting in forty healthy adults (Peper, et al., 2013b). Based on the previously mentioned Marshmallow task (Shoda et al., 1990), delay discounting evaluates cognitive control by examining the process of devaluation of a reward as a function of elapsed time. Volunteers who show a high rate of delay discounting typically discard an immediate small reward in favor of getting a significant larger reward after a prolonged period of time. Results revealed that lower integrity of the fronto-striatal tracts was correlated to lower rates of delayed discounting in both male and female participants. Furthermore, in the male participant group, endogenous testosterone levels were correlated to lower integrity of these fronto-striatal white-matter tracts (Peper et al., 2013b).

In our longitudinal study evidence was found that the integrity of the fronto-striatal white matter tracts predicted the development of cognitive control over time (Achterberg et al., 2016a). Separated by a two-year interval, 192 healthy volunteers between eight and twenty-six years underwent DTI and performed the delay-discounting task twice. Results showed that delay-discounting rates decreased with age (i.e., increased self-control to wait for a delayed reward), reaching the lowest discounting rates during late adolescence/early adulthood. Analyses of the neuro-anatomical data showed that the fronto-striatal tracts developed relatively fast during childhood and early adulthood, and showed little change during mid-adolescence. Particularly, the integrity of the frontal-striatal tracts during childhood and early adolescence predicted delay-discounting rates two years later. In sum, the presented results demonstrate the involvement of cortico–subcortical white matter tracts in cognitive control. Moreover, puberty-related sex steroids may be one of the underlying explanatory mechanisms for the relation between cortical–subcortical connectivity and delay discounting.

23.1.2 Social Self-Control

Another important form of behavioral control is social self-control. Social self-control includes for instance the inhibition of (unwanted) behavioral responses toward others, such as social aggression (Twenge et al., 2001). Negative social feedback (i.e., rejection) can trigger feelings of depression, frustration, or aggression (DeWall & Bushman, 2011). A relatively new field of research is concerned with studying the neural mechanisms underlying aggression after receiving negative social feedback (Achterberg et al., 2016b).

Accordingly, in our lab, the Social Network Aggression Task (SNAT) paradigm was used during which young adult participants were evaluated by peers according to a profile webpage they created at home (Achterberg et al., 2016b). First, neural activity was measured after (positive and) negative feedback of the peers on their profile page. Second, the participant was offered the possibility to retaliate by – after each feedback – sending out a loud noise blast to the peer. A longer duration of the noise blast was considered a measure of aggression (Achterberg et al., 2016b). It was found that noise blast duration was significantly longer after negative social feedback (disliking/rejection of

their profiles) than after positive or neutral feedback. Moreover, greater brain activation in the dorsal lateral PFC (dlPFC) and also the amygdala, hippocampus and parietal cortices) was associated with shorter noise blast duration after negative social feedback compared to neutral and positive feedback. This finding was interpreted as participants showing relatively high dlPFC activation after negative social feedback also displayed relatively higher aggression regulation (i.e., behavioral control) after experiencing negative social feedback (Achterberg et al., 2016b). In another study using the SNAT paradigm which was carried out in middle childhood (seven-to-ten years), similar brain–behavior interactions were found as in adults (Achterberg et al., 2017), rendering the SNAT a reliable tool to investigate social self-control in children and adults.

Taken together, social self-control is an important feature of studies into behavioral control, also from a developmental perspective, as the evaluation by others becomes especially salient during adolescence when teenagers are highly sensitive to acceptance and rejection by peers (Gunther Moor et al., 2010; Somerville et al., 2006).

23.1.3 Intermediate Conclusion

Improvements in cognitive and social self-control throughout adolescence are associated with development of (subregions within) the frontal lobe and with marked increases in white matter integrity of cortico–subcortical and fiber bundles in the frontal lobe. These connections are associated with stronger delay of gratification and less direct aggression (self-report) and social aggression (e.g., social rejection-evoked aggression). Owing to their organization and activational effects on brain tissue, sex steroid hormones are implicated in shaping the white-matter architecture underlying cognitive control. It is proposed that even though adolescents can exert cognitive control, the continuing refinement of the white matter structure makes the young individual increasingly robust to effectively deal with a variety of more complex and cognitively demanding tasks and life situations.

23.2 Risky Decision-Making

In parallel with the development of cognitive control, individuals undergo a vast array of changes in risky decision-making across adolescence. For instance, adolescence has often been associated with heightened risk-taking behavior such as heightened substance (ab) use, reckless driving, and unsafe sex, relative to childhood and adulthood (Dahl et al., 2018; Spear, 2018). Also in laboratory studies adolescents show elevated risky decision-making, especially under situations of immediate reward (Peper et al., 2013a), uncertainty (Figner et al., 2009), or social influence (Chein et al., 2011). Like cognitive control, risk taking is a multifaceted construct (Frey et al., 2017; Harden et al., 2016; Mamerow et al., 2016; van Duijvenvoorde et al., 2017) and different behavioral components of risk-taking mature along slightly different developmental non-linear curves (Peper et al., 2018). In addition, the pubertal hormones testosterone and estradiol contribute to the development of risk-taking, such that increases in testosterone and estradiol have been found to bolster risk-taking behavior and impulsive personality, and attenuated avoidance-like personality (Peper et al., 2018).

To better understand what drives this adolescent-specific maturation of risk-taking behavior, researchers made use of (economic) choice paradigms in which underlying sensitivities to different aspects of risk taking can be examined, such as sensitivity to rewards (e.g., winning versus losing) and risk (e.g., the probability of winning/losing). By investigating these separate sensitivities, it can be unraveled what aspects of risky choice behavior drive an individual's observed risk-taking behaviors across adolescent development. Moreover, including neuroimaging measures (such as fMRI) has proven valuable in understanding the underlying mechanisms of these sensitivities (Glimcher & Rustichini, 2004; van Duijvenvoorde & Crone, 2013). In Sections 23.2.1–23.2.3, an overview is given of recent behavioral and neuroimaging studies specifically focused on examining these different sensitivities to adolescent risk-taking. In particular, paradigms to measure these different aspects of risk-taking are discussed, as well as their developmental trajectories and neurobiological correlates.

23.2.1 Reward Sensitivity

It has been suggested that an important factor driving risk-taking behavior in adolescence is a heightened sensitivity to rewards (e.g., monetary gains). A way to examine this sensitivity to rewards is to study brain activation in response to rewards and losses during a simple gambling game. For example, our lab (Braams et al., 2014, 2015) studied changes in reward reactivity in the ventral striatum from childhood to young adulthood (eight-to-twenty-five years old; the "Braintime" sample), using a simple heads-or-tails tossing game in the MRI scanner. Here participants could either win or lose money depending on whether they correctly guessed heads or tails (i.e., if a participant matched the predetermined response of the computer they won money, and if they did not match this response they lost money). Using a two-wave longitudinal design, this study confirmed that ventral striatum activation in response to rewards versus losses is heightened in adolescence, as evidenced by a quadratic peak in ventral striatum reactivity in mid-adolescence (Braams et al., 2014, 2015). A number of studies have shown that adolescents' neural sensitivity to rewards is heightened relative to children and adults (Galvan et al., 2007; Schreuders et al., 2018; van Duijvenvoorde et al., 2016; Van Leijenhorst et al., 2010) and this adolescent peak in ventral striatum activity has been confirmed in a meta-analysis (Silverman et al., 2015).

An important question concerns the behavioral patterns that are associated with this rise and fall of ventral striatum activity in mid-adolescence. This question was addressed in a three-wave longitudinal study with the Braintime sample (eight-to-twenty-nine years; Schreuders et al., 2018). Similar to previous research, this study confirmed an adolescent-specific peak in ventral striatum activity which was estimated around the age of sixteen years. We further examined the contributions of individual differences in behavioral sensitivity to rewards. Specifically, we tested effects of state-like (the experienced enjoyment of winning versus losing money) and trait-like (the drive to obtain personal goals) behavioral reward sensitivity, on the increase in ventral striatum reactivity in early-to-mid adolescence (i.e., from eight to sixteen years old), followed by the decrease in mid-to-late adolescence and young adulthood (i.e., from sixteen to twenty-nine years old). It was found that the rise in this neural reactivity in early to mid-adolescence was related to the motivation to push boundaries to achieve goals that are personally relevant to the individual. In contrast, the subsequent decrease from mid-adolescence to early adulthood in ventral striatum activation was related to how those rewards are valued (Schreuders et al., 2018). Together, this study robustly documents that subcortical activation in response to rewards versus losses is heightened in mid-adolescence (see also Silverman et al., 2015, for a meta-analysis), and shows that the neural responses are related

to the behavioral experiences of rewards. Furthermore, other research showed that neural activity to rewards was related to a tendency to task risks in daily life (Galvan et al., 2007) and to alcohol consumption (Braams et al., 2016). Taken together, a heightened sensitivity to rewards is an important underlying factor driving risk-taking behavior in adolescence.

23.2.2 Risk Sensitivity

Although reward sensitivity in the ventral striatum has frequently been related to heightened risk-taking behavior in adolescence, risk-taking is often influenced by both rewards and the associated risk (i.e., the variability in outcomes). That is, when choosing to take a risk, individuals make a tradeoff between the potential risks and the potential rewards (Figner & Weber, 2011). As such, reward sensitivity is often convoluted with risk sensitivity. An example of a risky choice paradigm in which effects of reward and risk were disentangled is the study by van Duijvenvoorde et al. (2015), who administered the "hot" Columbia Card Task in the MRI scanner to a sample of children (eight-to-eleven years), adolescents (sixteen-to-nineteen years), and adults (twenty-five-to-thirty-four years). In this task, participants were presented with faced-down playing cards, and were asked to turn over cards one at a time, resulting in either a gain or a loss. Each gain card was added to participants' earnings, while a loss card terminated the trial. Participants could decide to stop turning cards at any time, cashing their earnings from the moment they decided to stop playing. Van Duijvenvoorde et al. (2015) disentangled risky choice behavior during this task into a return component (i.e., expected value, or the product of the probability of a reward and the amount of that reward) and a risk component (outcome variability).

Next, neural reactivity to changes in return (expected value) and risk (outcome variability) were compared across age groups. Neural reactivity in response to returns (expected value) increased linearly with age in a network of regions including the ventromedial PFC and the posterior cingulate cortex, also referred to as the "valuation network" of the brain. In contrast, neural reactivity in response to risk (outcome variability) peaked quadratically in adolescence, in the insula and dorsomedial PFC. Suggestively, adolescents may have a heightened emotional response to risks relative to children and adults, and in parallel engage more cognitive and regulatory processes when presented with risk (van Duijvenvoorde et al., 2015). Together, these findings show that mid-to-late-adolescence may not only be a phase of heightened reward sensitivity (in subcortical regions such as the nucleus accumbens: Schreuders et al., 2018), but also of heightened risk sensitivity (in conflict and uncertainty-related regions: van Duijvenvoorde et al., 2015).

23.2.2.1 Explicit Risk and Ambiguous Risk

In the studies described in Section 23.2, even though the outcomes of decisions were uncertain (i.e., guessing heads or tails correctly; winning or losing after turning over another card), participants did have explicit knowledge of the exact *probabilities* of these uncertain outcomes. For instance, the chance of guessing heads or tails correctly is 50 percent (Braams et al., 2015; Schreuders et al., 2018), and in the CCT, participants had knowledge of how many gain and loss cards were presented. However, risks in real life rarely present exact probabilities of different outcomes: they are often unknown or *ambiguous* (Tversky & Kahneman, 1992). Classic behavior economic work with adults has shown that even though individuals are generally averse to risk (known

probabilities), they are even more averse to ambiguity (unknown probabilities) than risk alone (Ellsberg, 1961; Von Gaudecker et al., 2011). How adolescents deal with these two types of risk has started to receive greater attention in recent years, as it has been suggested that these different types of risk differentially influence overt risk-taking behavior (Tversky & Kahneman, 1992).

The first to study how adolescents deal with risk and ambiguity was Tymula et al. (2012), who developed a binary risky choice task in which participants (thirty-three adolescents: twelve-to-seventeen years; thirty-one adults: thirty-to-fifty years) could choose between a sure option (i.e., a 100 percent chance of winning a small amount of money), or a gamble, which could yield more money but could also yield nothing. Specifically, the gambling option varied in amount, probability, and ambiguity level (i.e., the portion of the stimulus that was concealed to the participant, so that probabilities were (partially) unknown). Using a model-based method, the authors estimated individuals' behavioral preferences toward risk (known probabilities) and ambiguity (unknown probabilities). This study showed that adolescents were relatively more tolerant toward ambiguity (i.e., less ambiguity averse) than adults. Moreover, ambiguity tolerance, but not risk tolerance, was related to real life risk-taking behavior such as smoking and underage drinking, suggesting that adolescent risk-taking is driven by a tolerance to ambiguity. These findings were replicated in a more recent study from our lab (Blankenstein et al., 2016) using a similar paradigm (i.e., a wheel of fortune task) and the same model-based approach, in a continuous adolescent age range (ten-to-twenty-five years old, N = 157). Here, a linear decrease in ambiguity tolerance was observed across adolescence, and ambiguity tolerance was related to more real-life reckless behavior. Another recent behavioral study (van den Bos and Hertwig, 2017; eight-to-twenty-two years old, N = 105) also found pronounced age effects in ambiguity tolerance, i.e., an adolescent-specific peak in ambiguity tolerance, although in a loss domain, which also correlated with real-life risk-taking behavior. Together, these findings suggest that explicit risk (known probabilities) and ambiguous risk (unknown probabilities) differentially impact real-life risk-taking in adolescence.

To understand the neural mechanisms underlying risk and ambiguity processing in adolescence, we presented an fMRI adaptation of the wheel of fortune task to adolescents (Blankenstein et al., 2018; N = 198, twelve-to-twenty-five years old). Although there were no pronounced age differences in gambling behavior or neural processing (suggestively because no children (under twelve years old) were included), there were pronounced effects of individual differences in gambling behavior. That is, whereas individual differences in gambling under risk were related to activation in valuation regions of the brain (ventral striatum, parietal cortex), individual differences in gambling under ambiguity were related to regions associated with cognitive and affective processing (dMPFC, insula, DLPFC). These findings illustrate that different brain regions underlie risky and ambiguous gambling, which become particularly evident when including individual differences in task-based risk-taking. In addition, this paradigm also included decision outcomes. After choosing to gamble, participants were presented with gain or no gain outcomes. This allowed us to disentangle reward processing following risky gambles from reward processing following ambiguous gambles. Here it was shown that, although the ventral striatum coded reward processing irrespective of risk or ambiguity (indicative of a general signal of reward value), the MFPC particularly differentiated between gain and no gain outcomes following ambiguity. This suggests that this region may function as an informative saliency signal of ambiguous decision outcomes in particular, which may be applied to subsequent decisions (McCormick & Telzer, 2017; van Noordt & Segalowitz, 2012).

Furthermore, when including individual differences in indices of real-life risk-taking (such as self-reported rebellious behavior and the drive to obtain personal goals), activation in the LPFC was observed. Specifically, those individuals who reported to take more risks in daily life showed less activation in this region during reward outcome processing, independent of risk or ambiguity. This finding is in line with the idea that self-control (reflected in the LPFC) in response to general rewards is lowered for those who take more risks (Gianotti et al., 2009).

Taken together, these studies on risk and ambiguity processing and their neural correlates show that (1) risk and ambiguity are different aspects of risk-taking behavior in adolescence; (2) behavioral preferences under risk and ambiguity follow different developmental trajectories; and (3) risk and ambiguity are reflected in different brain systems. Finally, these studies highlight the importance of considering multiple aspects of risk-taking behavior (task-based and self-report measures) in the study of adolescent risk-taking.

22.2.3 Intermediate Conclusions

The rise in risk-taking behavior during adolescence is characterized by changes in brain function and structure, pubertal hormones, and behavioral sensitivities to underlying components of risk-taking, such as rewards, losses, and (explicit and ambiguous) risk. Moreover, different neural systems underlie these different components of risk-taking, further demonstrating that risk-taking is a multidimensional construct. By disentangling what underlying behavioral and neural components drive risk-taking, it can ultimately be studied who takes risks and why, and, in addition, how this contributes to our understanding of adolescents maturing into independent adults.

23.3 Conclusions and Future Directions

This chapter described the development of cognitive control and risky decision-making across adolescent development from a cognitive neuroscience perspective. Cognitive control development is often considered as the most important factor for resisting impulses and promoting future-oriented behavior, and it co-occurs in development with changes in how adolescents evaluate risks and rewards. The goal of this chapter was therefore to describe these changes in parallel and understand how these processes rely on partly similar and partly different neural structures.

We showed that cognitive control in terms of delay of gratification improves over the whole range of adolescence, peaking around late adolescence/early adulthood in both affective and social domains, and is partly mediated by stronger connectivity between the prefrontal cortex and limbic brain regions. These connections are associated with stronger delay of gratification and less direct aggression (self-report) and social aggression (e.g., social rejection-evoked aggression). Together these patterns suggest that adolescence is a period of significant cognitive advancements with improving control and goal flexibility (Crone & Dahl, 2012; Luna et al., 2015, see Chapter 21). Interestingly, risk-taking behavior shows a relative rise in adolescence, especially in the context of immediate rewards and social influences. These rises are associated with stronger activity in limbic brain regions when evaluating rewards. In search of mechanistic explanations for these changes, it was found that both these processes, that is, increased prefrontal cortex-limbic connectivity and stronger reward-related activity in limbic brain areas, are associated with the rise of the hormone testosterone, suggesting that these hormones may have multiple influences on neural circuits in the adolescent brain. Finally, components of risk-taking, such as risk and ambiguity processing, rely on partly overlapping and partly different circuits as cognitive control and reward sensitivity. This may explain why these processes are sometimes interpreted in parallel (i.e., poor cognitive control explains some parts of risk-taking behavior), but are not similar (i.e., additional brain circuits are involved in risk processing, such as the valuation network of the brain).

This multi-perspective view on adolescent development has received increased attention in recent years (e.g., dual-processing or circuit models, see Somerville & Casey, 2010 and Shulman et al., 2016) and shows the complexity of understanding the dynamic changes in behavioral and neural processes in adolescence. Inspection of data plots often shows that the elevated patterns of, for example, risk-taking in adolescence, are driven by subgroups of adolescents who engage in these behaviors (Willoughby et al., 2014) and have been examined in different phases of adolescents development (van Duijvenvoorde et al., 2016). Current research remains inconclusive with respect to the specific age or pubertal phases in which these relative changes in cognitive control and decision-making occur, although several longitudinal cohort studies which combine behavioral and neural assessment are currently ongoing (Casey et al., 2018).

Recent views also demonstrate the context-specificity of adolescent cognitive control and risky decision-making behaviors. An intriguing question concerns whether adolescents who show the largest increases in risk-taking in adolescence are more sensitive to contextual influences on behavior in general. These adolescents may show more risk-taking when risks result in higher incentives (Figner & Weber, 2011) or social acceptance (Chein et al., 2011), but may also show better cognitive control (Luna et al., 2015) and prosocial behavior (Do et al., 2017) when these behaviors are rewarded. An important question for future research is thus to examine which adolescents show the strongest contextual reward sensitivity. Subsequently, a crucial questions concerns which adolescents are characterized by a risk profile (suggesting a stronger tendency to engage in health-detrimental risk-taking behavior) and which adolescents are characterized by a "differential susceptibility" profile – that is, in some contextual circumstances they may engage in dangerous risk behaviors, but in other circumstances they may engage in risk behaviors to help others (i.e., "prosocial risk-takers," Do et al., 2017; Schriber & Guyer, 2016). For example, a higher tolerance to ambiguity has been associated with greater risk-taking behavior, but has also been associated with more trust and cooperation in adults (Vives & FeldmanHall, 2018).

Another important direction for future research is to understand the dynamics of change in terms of neural and hormonal influences. We showed several examples of how hormonal and neural development coincide, but it remains unclear whether these directly influence each other. Indeed, evidence based on animal and adult studies provide evidence for this hypothesis, although this has not yet been explicitly tested in adolescence. Also, the majority of studies suggest hormonal effects on reward valuation and connections with reward circuitry. However, it remains to be determined how and when hormonal development influences cognitive control and decision-making among multiple contexts, and whether there are sensitive periods for hormonal

influences on reward and cognitive control development. One approach to better understand these influences is by distinguishing between early and late pubertal adolescents and examining the developmental outcomes in terms of brain and behavior longitudinally (see Peper & Dahl, 2013).

Taken together, the current overview provided evidence for dynamic changes in multiple aspects of cognitive control and decision-making over the course of adolescent development, which are associated with dynamic neural changes in brain regions relevant for cognitive control and decision-making. There was consistent evidence for a role of prefrontal cortex-limbic activity and connectivity development in part explaining some of the behavioral improvements and changes observed during adolescence. New research approaches require better assessment of contextual influences and social–environmental influences on adolescent behavior and neural development. Such approaches will aid in understanding how these contextual influences predict long-term outcomes in terms of risk for adverse outcomes and opportunity for positive outcomes, such as (social) explorative behaviors.

References

Achterberg, M., Peper, J. S., Van Duijvenvoorde, A. C., Mandl, R. C., & Crone, E. A. (2016a). Fronto-striatal white matter integrity predicts development in delay of gratification: A longitudinal study. *Journal of Neuroscience, 36,* 1954–1961.

Achterberg, M., van Duijvenvoorde, A. C., Bakermans-Kranenburg, M. J., & Crone, E. A. (2016b). Control your anger! The neural basis of aggression regulation in response to negative social feedback. *Social Cognitive and Affective Neuroscience, 11,* 712–720.

Achterberg, M., van Duijvenvoorde, A. C. K., van der Meulen, M., Bakermans-Kranenburg,

M. J., & Crone, E. A. (2018). Heritability of aggression following social evaluation in middle childhood: An fMRI study. *Human Brain Mapping, 39,* 2828–2841.

Achterberg, M., van Duijvenvoorde, A. C. K., van der Meulen, M., Euser, S., Bakermans-Kranenburg, M. J., & Crone, E. A. (2017). The neural and behavioral correlates of social evaluation in childhood. *Developmental Cognitive Neuroscience, 24,* 107–117.

Blankenstein, N. E., Crone, E. A., van den Bos, W., & van Duijvenvoorde, A. C. K. (2016). Dealing with uncertainty: Testing risk- and ambiguity-attitude across adolescence. *Developmental Neuropsychology, 41,* 1–16.

Blankenstein, N. E., Schreuders, E., Peper, J. S., Crone, E. A., & van Duijvenvoorde, A. C. K. (2018). Individual differences in risk-taking tendencies modulate the neural processing of risky and ambiguous decision-making in adolescence. *NeuroImage, 172,* 663–673.

Braams, B. R., Peper, J. S., van der Heide, D., Peters, S., & Crone, E. A. (2016). Nucleus accumbens response to rewards and testosterone levels are related to alcohol use in adolescents and young adults. *Developmental Cognitive Neuroscience, 17,* 83–93.

Braams, B. R., Peters, S., Peper, J. S., Guroglu, B., & Crone, E. A. (2014). Gambling for self, friends, and antagonists: Differential contributions of affective and social brain regions on adolescent reward processing. *NeuroImage, 100,* 281–289.

Braams, B. R., van Duijvenvoorde, A. C. K., Peper, J. S., & Crone, E. A. (2015). Longitudinal changes in adolescent risk-taking: A comprehensive study of neural responses to rewards, pubertal development, and risk-taking behavior. *The Journal of Neuroscience, 35,* 7226–7238.

Carlson, S. M., Shoda, Y., Ayduk, O., Aber, L., Schaefer, C., Sethi, A., Wilson, N., Peake, P. K., & Mischel, W. (2018). Cohort effects in children's delay of gratification. *Developmental Psychology Journal, 54,* 1395–1407.

Casey, B., Cannonier, T., Conley, M. I., Cohen, A. O., Barch, D. M., Heitzeg, M. M., Soules, M. E., Teslovich, T., Dellarco, D. V., & Garavan, H. (2018). The adolescent brain cognitive development (ABCD) study: Imaging acquisition across 21 sites. *Developmental Cognitive Neuroscience, 32,* 43–54.

Casey, B. J., Galvan, A., & Somerville, L. H. (2016). Beyond simple models of adolescence to an integrated circuit-based account: A commentary. *Developmental Cognitive Neuroscience, 17,* 128–130.

Casey B. J., Somerville, L. H., Gotlib, I. H., Ayduk, O., Franklin, N. T., Askren, M. K., Jonides, J., Berman, M. G., Wilson, N. L., Teslovich, T., Glover, G., Zayas, V., Mischel, W., & Shoda, Y. (2011). Behavioral and neural correlates of delay of gratification 40 years later. *Proceedings of the National Academy of Sciences (USA), 108,* 14998–15003.

Chein, J., Albert, D., O'Brien, L., Uckert, K., & Steinberg, L. (2011). Peers increase adolescent risk taking by enhancing activity in the brain's reward circuitry. *Developmental Science, 14,* F1–10.

Crone, E. A., & Dahl, R. E. (2012). Understanding adolescence as a period of social-affective engagement and goal flexibility. *Nature Reviews Neuroscience, 13,* 636–650.

Crone, E. A., & Steinbeis, N. (2017). Neural perspectives on cognitive control development during childhood and adolescence. *Trends in Cognitive Science, 21,* 205–215.

Dahl, R. E., Allen, N. B., Wilbrecht, L., & Suleiman, A. B. (2018). Importance of investing in adolescence from a developmental science perspective. *Nature, 554,* 441.

DeWall, C. N., & Bushman, B. J. (2011). Social acceptance and rejection: The sweet and the bitter. *Current Directions in Psychological Science, 20,* 256–260.

Diamond, A. (2013). Executive functions. *Annual Review of Psychology, 64,* 135–168.

Do, K. T., Guassi Moreira, J. F., & Telzer, E. H. (2017). But is helping you worth the risk? Defining prosocial risk taking in adolescence. *Developmental Cognitive Neuroscience, 25,* 260–271.

Ellsberg, D. (1961). Risk, ambiguity, and the savage axioms. *The Quarterly Journal of Economics, 75,* 643–669.

Figner, B., Mackinlay, R. J., Wilkening, F., & Weber, E. U. (2009). Affective and deliberative processes in risky choice: Age differences in risk taking in the Columbia Card Task. *Journal of Experimental Psychology: Learning, Memory, and Cognition, 35,* 709.

Figner, B., & Weber, E. U. (2011). Who takes risks when and why? Determinants of risk taking. *Current Directions in Psychological Science, 20,* 211–216.

Frey, R., Pedroni, A., Mata, R., Rieskamp, J., & Hertwig, R. (2017). Risk preference shares the psychometric structure of major psychological traits. *Science Advances, 3,* e1701381.

Galvan, A., Hare, T., Voss, H., Glover, G., & Casey, B. (2007). Risk-taking and the adolescent brain: Who is at risk? *Developmental Science, 10,* F8–F14.

Genc, S., Smith, R. E., Malpas, C. B., Anderson, V., Nicholson, J. M., Efron, D., Sciberras, E., Seal, M. L., & Silk, T. J. (2018). Development of white matter fibre density and morphology over childhood: A longitudinal fixel-based analysis. *Neuroimage, 183,* 666–676.

Gianotti, L. R. R., Knoch, D., Faber, P. L., Lehmann, D., Pascual-Marqui, R. D., Diezi, C., Schoch, C., Eisenegger, C., & Fehr, E. (2009). Tonic activity level in the right prefrontal cortex predicts individuals' risk taking. *Psychological Science, 20,* 33–38.

Glimcher, P. W., & Rustichini, A. (2004). Neuroeconomics: The consilience of brain and decision. *Science, 306,* 447–452.

Gunther Moor, B., Van Leijenhorst, L., Rombouts, S. A., Crone, E. A., & Van der Molen, M. W. (2010). Do you like me? Neural correlates of social evaluation and developmental trajectories. *Social Neuroscience, 5,* 461–482.

Harden, K. P., Kretsch, N., Mann, F. D., Herzhoff, K., Tackett, J. L., Steinberg, L., & Tucker-Drob, E. M. (2016). Beyond dual systems: A genetically-informed, latent factor model of behavioral and self-report measures related to

adolescent risk-taking. *Developmental Cognitive Neuroscience, 25,* 221–234.

Herting, M. M., Gautam, P., Spielberg, J. M., Dahl, R. E., & Sowell, E. R. (2015). A longitudinal study: Changes in cortical thickness and surface area during pubertal maturation. *PLoS ONE, 10,* e0119774.

Herting, M. M., & Sowell, E. R. (2017). Puberty and structural brain development in humans. *Frontiers in Neuroendocrinology, 44,* 122–137.

Hofmann, W., Schmeichel, B. J., & Baddeley, A. D. (2012). Executive functions and self-regulation. *Trends in Cognitive Science, 16,* 174–180.

Huttenlocher, P. R. (1979). Synaptic density in human frontal cortex-developmental changes and effects of aging. *Brain Research, 163,* 195–205.

Huttenlocher, P. R., & Dabholkar, A. S. (1997). Regional differences in synaptogenesis in human cerebral cortex. *The Journal of Comparative Neurology, 387,* 167–178.

Koenis, M. M. G., Brouwer, R. M., Swagerman, S. C., van Soelen, I. L. C., Boomsma, D. I., & Hulshoff Pol, H. E. (2018). Association between structural brain network efficiency and intelligence increases during adolescence. *Human Brain Mapping, 39,* 822–836.

Kray, J., Schmitt, H., Lorenz, C., & Ferdinand, N. K. (2018). The influence of different kinds of incentives on decision-making and cognitive control in adolescent development: A review of behavioral and neuroscientific studies. *Frontiers in Psychology, 9,* 768.

Luna, B., Marek, S., Larsen, B., Tervo-Clemmens, B., & Chahal, R. (2015). An integrative model of the maturation of cognitive control. *Annual Review of Neuroscience, 38,* 151–170.

Ma, I., van Duijvenvoorde, A., & Scheres, A. (2016). The interaction between reinforcement and inhibitory control in ADHD: A review and research guidelines. *Clinical Psychology Review, 44,* 94–111.

Mamerow, L., Frey, R., & Mata, R. (2016). Risk taking across the life span: A comparison of self-report and behavioral measures of risk taking. *Psychology and Aging, 31,* 711–723.

Matzke, D., Hughes, M., Badcock, J. C., Michie, P., & Heathcote, A. (2017). Failures of cognitive control or attention? The case of stop-signal deficits in schizophrenia. *Attention, Perception, & Psychophysics, 79,* 1078–1086.

McCormick, E. M., & Telzer, E. H. (2017). Failure to retreat: Blunted sensitivity to negative feedback supports risky behavior in adolescents. *NeuroImage, 147,* 381–389.

Miller, E. K., & Cohen, J. D. (2001). An integrative theory of prefrontal cortex function. *Annual Review of Neuroscience, 24,* 167–202.

Mills, K. L., & Tamnes, C. K. (2014). Methods and considerations for longitudinal structural brain imaging analysis across development. *Developmental Cognitive Neuroscience, 9,* 172–190.

Mischel, W., Ayduk, O., Berman, M. G., Casey, B. J., Gotlib, I. H., Jonides, J., Kross, E., Teslovich, T., Wilson, N. L., Zayas, V., & Shoda, Y. (2011). 'Willpower' over the life span: Decomposing self-regulation. *Social Cognitive and Affective Neuroscience, 6,* 252–256.

Nussey, S., & Whitehead, S. (2001). *Endocrinology: An Integrated Approach.* Oxford: BIOS Scientific Publishers.

Peper, J. S., Braams, B. R., Blankenstein, N. E., Bos, M. G., & Crone, E. A. (2018). Development of multifaceted risk taking and the relations to sex steroid hormones: A longitudinal study. *Child Development, 89,* 1887–1907.

Peper, J. S., & Dahl, R. E. (2013). Surging hormones: Brain–behavior interactions during puberty. *Current Directions in Psychological Science, 22,* 134–139.

Peper, J. S., de Reus, M. A., van den Heuvel, M. P., & Schutter, D. J. (2015). Short fused? associations between white matter connections, sex steroids, and aggression across adolescence. *Human Brain Mapping, 36,* 1043–1052.

Peper, J. S., Koolschijn, P. C., & Crone, E. A. (2013a). Development of risk taking: Contributions from adolescent testosterone and the orbito-frontal cortex. *Journal of Cognitive Neuroscience, 25,* 2141–2150.

Peper, J. S., Mandl, R. C., Braams, B. R., de Water, E., Heijboer, A. C., Koolschijn, P. C., & Crone, E. A. (2013b). Delay discounting and frontostriatal fiber tracts: A combined DTI and MTR study on impulsive choices in healthy young adults. *Cerebral Cortex, 23,* 1695–1702.

Peters, S., Van der Meulen, M., Zanolie, K., & Crone, E. A. (2017). Predicting reading and mathematics from neural activity for feedback learning. *Developmental Psychology Journal, 53,* 149–159.

Raznahan, A., Shaw, P., Lalonde, F., Stockman, M., Wallace, G. L., Greenstein, D., Clasen, L., Gogtay, N., & Giedd, J. N. (2011). How does your cortex grow? *Journal of Neuroscience, 31,* 7174–7177.

Rubia, K. (2018). Cognitive neuroscience of attention deficit hyperactivity disorder (ADHD) and its clinical translation. *Frontiers in Human Neuroscience, 12,* 100.

Schreuders, E., Braams, B. R., Blankenstein, N. E., Peper, J. S., Güroğlu, B., & Crone, E. A. (2018). Contributions of reward sensitivity to ventral striatum activity across adolescence and early adulthood. *Child Development, 89,* 797–810.

Schriber, R. A., & Guyer, A. E. (2016). Adolescent neurobiological susceptibility to social context. *Developmental Cognitive Neuroscience, 19,* 1–18.

Shoda, Y., Mischel, W., & Peake, P. K. (1990). Predicting adolescent cognitive and self-regulatory competences from preschool delay of gratification – Identifying diagnostic conditions. *Developmental Psychology, 26,* 978–986.

Shulman, E. P., Smith, A. R., Silva, K., Icenogle, G., Duell, N., Chein, J., & Steinberg, L. (2016). The dual systems model: Review, reappraisal, and reaffirmation. *Developmental Cognitive Neuroscience, 17,* 103–117.

Silverman, M. H., Jedd, K., & Luciana, M. (2015). Neural networks involved in adolescent reward processing: An activation likelihood estimation meta-analysis of functional neuroimaging studies. *NeuroImage, 122,* 427–439.

Somerville, L. H., & Casey, B. J. (2010). Developmental neurobiology of cognitive control and motivational systems. *Current Opinion in Neurobiology, 20,* 236–241.

Somerville, L. H., Heatherton, T. F., & Kelley, W. M. (2006). Anterior cingulate cortex responds differentially to expectancy violation and social rejection. *Nature Neuroscience, 9,* 1007–1008.

Spear, L. P. (2018). Effects of adolescent alcohol consumption on the brain and behaviour. *Nature Reviews Neuroscience, 19,* 197.

Steinberg, L. (2008). A social neuroscience perspective on adolescent risk-taking. *Developmental Review, 28,* 78–106.

Tamnes, C. K., Herting, M. M., Goddings, A. L., Meuwes, R., Blakemore, S. J., Dahl, R. E., Guroglu, B., Raznahan, A., Sowell, E. R., Crone, E. A., & Mills, K. L. (2017). Development of the cerebral cortex across adolescence: A multisample study of inter-related longitudinal changes in cortical volume, surface area, and thickness. *Journal of Neuroscience, 37,* 3402–3412.

Tan, P. Z., Silk, J. S., Dahl, R. E., Kronhaus, D., & Ladouceur, C. D. (2018). Age-related developmental and individual differences in the influence of social and non-social distractors on cognitive performance. *Frontiers in Psychology, 9,* 863.

Tversky, A., & Kahneman, D. (1992). Advances in prospect theory: Cumulative representation of uncertainty. *Journal of Risk and Uncertainty, 5,* 297–323.

Twenge, J. M., Baumeister, R. F., Tice, D. M., & Stucke, T. S. (2001). If you can't join them, beat them: Effects of social exclusion on aggressive behavior. *Journal of Personality and Social Psychology, 81,* 1058–1069.

Tymula, A., Rosenberg Belmaker, L. A., Roy, A. K., Ruderman, L., Manson, K., Glimcher, P. W., & Levy, I. (2012). Adolescents' risk-taking behavior is driven by tolerance to ambiguity. *Proceedings of the National Academy of Sciences (USA), 109,* 17135–17140.

van den Bos, W., & Hertwig, R. (2017). Adolescents display distinctive tolerance to ambiguity and to uncertainty during risky decision making. *Scientific Reports, 7,* 40962.

van Duijvenvoorde, A. C. K., Blankenstein, N., Crone, E., & Figner, B. (2017). Towards a better understanding of adolescent risk taking: Contextual moderators and model-based

analysis. In M. E. Toplak, & J. A. Weller (eds.), *Individual Differences in Judgment and Decision-Making: A Developmental Perspective* (pp. 8–27). Hove: Psychology Press.

van Duijvenvoorde, A. C. K., & Crone, E. A. (2013). The teenage brain a neuroeconomic approach to adolescent decision making. *Current Directions in Psychological Science, 22,* 108–113.

van Duijvenvoorde, A. C. K., Huizenga, H. M., Somerville, L. H., Delgado, M. R., Powers, A., Weeda, W. D., Casey, B., Weber, E. U., & Figner, B. (2015). Neural correlates of expected risks and returns in risky choice across development. *The Journal of Neuroscience, 35,* 1549–1560.

van Duijvenvoorde, A. C. K., Peters, S., Braams, B. R., & Crone, E. A. (2016). What motivates adolescents? Neural responses to rewards and their influence on adolescents' risk taking, learning, and cognitive control. *Neuroscience & Biobehavioral Reviews, 70,* 135–147.

Van Leijenhorst, L., Moor, B. G., de Macks, Z. A. O., Rombouts, S. A., Westenberg, P. M., & Crone, E. A. (2010). Adolescent risky decision-making: Neurocognitive development of reward and control regions. *NeuroImage, 51,* 345–355.

van Noordt, S. J. R., & Segalowitz, S. J. (2012). Performance monitoring and the medial prefrontal cortex: A review of individual differences and context effects as a window on self-regulation. *Frontiers in Human Neuroscience, 6,* 197.

van Timmeren, T., Daams, J. G., van Holst, R. J., & Goudriaan, A. E. (2018). Compulsivity-related neurocognitive performance deficits in gambling disorder: A systematic review and meta-analysis. *Neuroscience & Biobehavioral Reviews, 84,* 204–217.

Vives, M.-L., & FeldmanHall, O. (2018). Tolerance to ambiguous uncertainty predicts prosocial behavior. *Nature Communications, 9,* 2156.

Von Gaudecker, H.-M., Van Soest, A., & Wengström, E. (2011). Heterogeneity in risky choice behavior in a broad population. *The American Economic Review, 101,* 664–694.

Watts, T. W., Duncan, G. J., & Quan, H. (2018). Revisiting the Marshmallow Test: A conceptual replication investigating links between early delay of gratification and later outcomes. *Psychological Science, 29*, 1159–1177.

Wierenga, L. M., Bos, M. G. N., Schreuders, E., Vd Kamp, F., Peper, J. S., Tamnes, C. K., & Crone, E. A. (2018). Unraveling age, puberty and testosterone effects on subcortical brain development across adolescence. *Psychoneuroendocrinology, 91*, 105–114.

Willoughby, T., Good, M., Adachi, P. J., Hamza, C., & Tavernier, R. (2014). Examining the link between adolescent brain development and risk taking from a social–developmental perspective (reprinted). *Brain and Cognition, 89*, 70–78.

Yakovlev, P., Lecours, A.-R., Minkowski, A., & Davis, F. (1967). *Regional Development of the Brain in Early Life*. Oxford: Blackwell Scientific.

24 The Triadic Neural Systems Model through a Machine-Learning Mill

Monique Ernst, Josh Gowin, and Claudie Gaillard

Fifteen years ago, the triadic neural systems model was proposed as a heuristic tool to study and clarify the neural mechanisms accounting for distinct typical adolescent behaviors. Whereas aspects of the models have been validated, the overall theory has not been comprehensively tested, mainly because of the lack of appropriate samples (i.e., large pediatric sample with follow-ups) and sufficiently powerful analytic tools. This situation can be remediated now, thanks to the availability of large longitudinal datasets and the emergence of machine learning (ML) tools in the neuroscience field. This chapter describes a "vision" of how the triadic neural systems model could be tested using ML methodology. In the name of clarity, fictitious concrete examples are presented, together with a concerted effort to keep this essay quite simple and accessible to the majority of clinical researchers. This comes at the expense of a critical review of assumptions and limitations that accompanies any analytical strategy. To mitigate this caveat, references to comprehensive publications are provided.

This work was supported by the Intramural Research Program of the National Institute of Mental Health, project number ZIAMH002798 (clinical protocol 02-*M*-0321, NCT00047853) to the Section on Neurobiology of Fear and Anxiety (SNFA). In addition, we wish to acknowledge Dr. Ryan Phillips for his assistance in the preparation of the manuscript.

24.1 Introduction

Adolescence is a period of rapid, formidable changes at all biological and behavioral levels. Particularly, adolescent behavior takes a distinct pattern, characterized by a peak in risk-taking and emotional intensity and lability, and accompanied by social transformation and a refinement in abstract thinking. These adolescent features have been described centuries ago (e.g., Aristotle (384–322 BC)) and are well-captured in the literature. Examples include the emotional intensity and social transformation in Romeo and Juliette (thirteen year-olds), and the Sturm and Drang (storm and stress) coined in the late 1700s to describe the passion and emotional turmoil of teenagers. Today's expressions of adolescent behaviors emphasize risk-taking, emotion intensity, and motivation for total engagement, which can take the form of substance abuse, radical behavior such as parachute flying, or, at the extreme, suicide attacker. The potentially disastrous consequences of these behaviors have prompted the search for underlying neural mechanisms. Accordingly, neural systems models have emerged, involving two (cognitive versus approach systems) or three systems (cognitive, approach, and avoidance) (e.g., Casey et al., 2008; Steinberg, 2008). The latter, the triadic neural systems model (Ernst et al., 2006), is the focus of this review.

The triadic model follows a very simple axiom governing motivated behaviors: when the organism encounters a stimulus, only two categories of responses are available. The organism can *approach* the stimulus or *avoid* the stimulus. The selection of the behavioral response naturally depends on the features of the stimulus and the state of the organism. These elements need to be integrated and evaluated to push the response toward one or the other option. This function can be supported by a *control* operator. This model is illustrated in Figure 24.1. Figure 24.1(a) features the behavior, and Figure 24.1(b) translates it at the neural systems level. Three neural systems supporting approach behavior, avoidance behavior, and a supervisory control function establish an equilibrium that determines appropriate behavior. If generically adult behavior is set as the optimal balance, the adolescent balance is represented as favoring

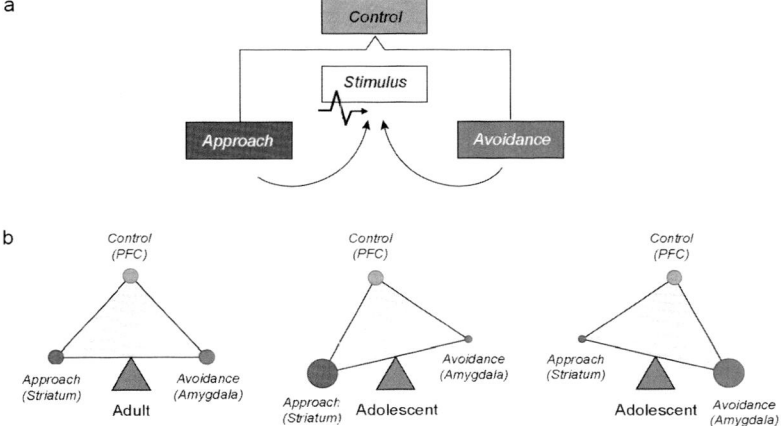

Figure 24.1 The triadic model. (a) This figure shows that, at the most elementary level, behavioral responses to a stimulus can take the two forms, approach or avoidance. The selection of the behavioral response is monitored or adjudicated by a supervisory controller (control system). In yellow is the stimulus (e.g., object, situation), purple is the approach response, red is the other possible avoidance response, and green is the controller. (b) This figure represents the neural translation (nodes of the triadic model) of the three behavioral entities described in (a). The term node refers to the brain regions that, together, form a neural system. The ventral striatum is the key node of the approach system, the amygdala of the avoidance system and the prefrontal cortex (PFC) of the control system. In addition, these three systems establish a balance that is represented as a triangle in equilibrium. The adult balance is used as the yardstick against which the adolescent balance is being compared. In an approach context, the adolescent balance is tilted toward the approach system, and away from the avoidance system, in a way that translates the proclivity of adolescent behavior toward approach, including risk-taking. In an avoidance context, the adolescent balance is tilted toward the avoidance system, and away from the approach system, in a way that translates the proclivity of adolescent behavior toward emotional intensity and lability, perhaps reflecting the peak onset of internalizing disorders in adolescence
A black-and-white version of this figure will appear in some formats. For the color version, please refer to the plate section.

the approach system. The triadic systems have been assigned to circuits that are recognized for their essential contribution to approach, avoidance, and control behavior. They are centered on the striatum for approach behavior, the amygdala for avoidance behavior, and the prefrontal cortex for the control system. At present, the maturation of these systems across adolescence has each been studied mostly independently and in a single context (e.g., positive stimuli for approach behavior). Until now, the testing of the whole model did not seem feasible for practical and analytic reasons. But now, the availability of large longitudinal datasets of pediatric samples (ABCD; Connectome; IMAGEN; Jernigan & Brown, 2018; NCANDA)[1] and the introduction of powerful ML tools to analyze complex data open new horizons. The goal of this chapter is to provide a window into these new possibilities.

This chapter consists of two parts. The first part reviews the triadic neural systems model (Ernst, 2014; Ernst et al., 2006). The second part proposes a strategy to test the full triadic model. For clarity we decided to follow concrete examples using fictitious studies. Fictitious datasets are used, and fictitious analyses and solutions are described. For the same reasons of parsimony and simplicity, no mathematical ML functions are presented, and the assumptions and limitations that come with any statistical analyses are not

---

[1] ABCD. Adolescent Brain Cognitive Development Home Page. Available from https://abcdstudy.org/; Connectome. The Human Connectome Project Home Page. Available from www .humanconnectomeproject.org/; IMAGEN. IMAGEN Consortium Home Page. Available from https://imagen-europe.com/; NCANDA. National Consortium on Alcohol and Neurodevelopment in Adolescence Home Page. Available from http:// ncanda.org/. All websites were last accessed August 16, 2021.

discussed. However, the readers are referred to publications that comprehensively cover these gaps. Ultimately, clinical researchers are introduced, in what we hope to be an easy and simple way, to a fairly new type of research, which may become critical in learning about brain mechanisms at the network level.

24.2 The Triadic Neural Systems Model

The triadic model consists of an approach, avoidance, and control module. It is a generic heuristic interpretation of how input information is processed at the brain neural-systems level to generate a motivated action output.

24.2.1 The Model

The fundamental assumption underlying this model is that approach and avoidance are mapped onto two separate, partly overlapping neural systems. The "approach system" classically supports positive-value encoding and underlies reward and motivation processing. The "avoidance system" supports negative-value encoding and captures punishment and negative emotion processing. Importantly, these two "approach" and "avoidance" systems are not just the mirror of one another (i.e., negative/positive). They hold distinct properties and respond to distinct rules. For example, "punishments weight more than rewards" (Tversky & Kahneman, 1992). The discipline of microeconomy demonstrates that the subjective value of a $5.00 loss equates the subjective value of a $10.00 gain (Tversky & Kahneman, 1992). Another example concerns the impact of uncertainty on behavior. Uncertainty carries a negative cost, and it increases avoidance but decreases approach. Naturally, this functional separation of the approach and avoidance systems is relative. Overlaps exist at both behavioral and neural levels.

Accordingly, motivation is common to both approach and avoidance systems. Indeed, motivation fuels approach and avoidance behaviors. For instance, "motivated avoidance" is another conceptualization of "active avoidance," a construct currently under investigation in the field of defensive responses (anxiety, fear) (Campese et al., 2016; Elliot & Covington, 2001; Tsutsui-Kimura et al., 2017). Similarly, emotion takes both negative and positive flavors. This behavioral overlap is reflected at the neural level, as addressed in Section 24.2.2.

The third module of the triadic model is the control system, which adjudicates courses of action between the approach and avoidance systems. In this chapter, "control" processes the formation of preference that is transferred to effector sites.

24.2.2 Neural Substrates

24.2.2.1 Approach System

The approach system is grounded in the striatum. The striatum is a relatively large multiplex structure, whose constituents include the caudate nucleus, nucleus accumbens, putamen, and pallidum. The striatum has been shown to be essential in the implementation of goals into actions. It plays this role through the processing of information along parallel striatal–thalamocortical–striatal loops (Balleine & O'Doherty, 2010). Although much of the research on the striatum has been on reward function and motivation (Berridge & Kringelbach, 2013; Berridge & Robinson, 2003), the past two decades have witnessed an additional focus on aversive processes (Campese et al., 2016; Delgado et al., 2011; Tsutsui-Kimura et al., 2017). While both

animal and human data indicate a role of the striatal circuitry in the processing of aversive stimuli (e.g., active avoidance), the exact mechanism remains unclear. Overall, the recruitment of the striatal circuitry predominates and is more consistent in the processing of appetitive than aversive information (Bromberg-Martin et al., 2010; Mirenowicz & Schultz, 1996).

24.2.2.2 Avoidance System

The avoidance system is grounded in the amygdala. The amygdala consists of multiple nuclei with distinct functions. These nuclei can be partitioned into three compartments: (1) an input compartment, receiving multimodal sensory information, (2) a processing compartment, that integrates and broadly interprets the sensory information coming from the cortex and hippocampus, and finally (3) an output compartment, that sends the processed signals to effector agents to code physiological and motor responses. The amygdala input receiver is assigned to the lateral nucleus and the output dispatcher to the extended amygdala (central nucleus of the amygdala and the bed nucleus of the stria terminalis). The information processing occurs in the basal/accessory basal nuclei. This information processing center has not typically been considered an "output region," but it does have an important one-way projection to the striatum to inform complex motor programs. The amygdala has raised considerable research on its function in the processing of aversive stimuli, including aversive learning (Goode & Maren, 2017; Sanford et al., 2017). Although its implication in reward learning is well-established (Balleine & Killcross, 2006; Maren, 2016; Wassum & Izquierdo, 2015), the amygdala responds prominently and more consistently to aversive than appetitive stimuli (Kragel & LaBar, 2016; Murphy et al., 2003).

24.2.2.3 Control System

The control system belongs to the prefrontal cortex (PFC). "Control" (or cognitive control) falls under the umbrella of executive function, which is essential to self-directed behavior (see Chapters 20 and 21). Multiple models have been proposed to describe the various aspects of executive function (e.g., working memory, inhibition, set shifting) and to map these onto specific brain regions (e.g., Banich, 2009). The common denominator of these is the PFC. The regional specialization of the PFC has been parsed out in several ways, depending on theoretical frameworks. For example, functional divisions can follow different directions, such as inferior-lateral versus mid-lateral PFC (Petrides, 2005), anterior versus posterior PFC (Christoff & Gabrieli, 2000), or medial versus left lateral versus right lateral PFC (Stuss & Alexander, 2007). The triadic model does not specify the putative PFC organization that adjudicates on courses of action. However, the framework most fit to accommodate the control of the direction of action (i.e., the decision proper) engages regions that integrate the value and salience tagged to the various options to decide on, and regions that modulate the weight of these value options (Figure 24.1). The former set of regions receives information (bottom-up process) and the latter applies the information to direct the course of action (top-down process). In other words, the first set of regions receives information from the approach (striatum) and avoidance (amygdala) systems, which is sent then to the second set. The second set of regions modulates the activity of the avoidance and/or approach systems, and provides the signal that is dispatched to effectors that implement the action. This framework has been used for neural mechanisms involved in the expression of defensive responses (Kouneiher et al., 2009; LeDoux & Daw, 2018), which we apply to motivated behaviors at large.

24.2.3 Triadic Model in Adolescence

The triadic model was initially formulated as a guide to study how brain maturational changes underlie the prototypical behavioral patterns of the adolescence period.

The behavioral shifts across adolescence, as described in Section 24.1, have been interpreted as an enhanced propensity for approach behaviors. Approach behaviors serve the evolutionary function of facilitating the search for novelties (exploratory) and the move toward independence. Indeed, adolescents do transition from childhood into adulthood, leaving the protective family nest and learning to independently navigate the world. The counterpart to these beneficial effects concerns a certain degree of blindness for potential negative consequences and an enhanced tolerance for possible failures.

Specifically, the triadic neural systems model posits that the proclivity for exploratory behavior is supported by both an increased reactivity of the approach neural system and a hypo-responsivity of the avoidance system. This balance may be dependent on the internal state of the individual and the context of the decision to make. Finally, the adjudication by the control neural system between approach and avoidance is becoming progressively more refined and efficient with age. This elementary description of the dynamics of the development of each unit of the triadic system accounts for the most commonly described changes in the adolescent motivated behavior, that is, risk-taking and improved cognition (Ernst, 2014; Ernst et al., 2011).

The triadic model also accounts for the intensification of emotional lability and the possibility of an exacerbation of negative emotions in adolescence. Indeed, the avoidance neural system, which also plays a critical role in emotional expression, has been shown to be hyperresponsive to aversive stimuli in adolescents compared to adults (e.g., Hare et al., 2008; Quevedo et al., 2009; Silvers et al., 2012). This finding suggests that, in a negative context, the adolescent may react more emotionally than the adult. Figure 24.1(b) schematizes this effect of context on the relative balance among the elements of the triadic model in adolescence.

This cursory description of how the triadic model is instantiated in adolescence, in a way that can explain typical adolescent behaviors, reveals obvious gaps. For example, it is unclear how the approach (appetitive) system is uniquely affected in aversive contexts in adolescence. The neural delineation of the circuits of each system is only partial. The amount and nature of overlaps among the systems is also unclear, and how these overlaps change with age and with context (appetitive versus aversive) has hardly been addressed. Section 24.3 explores how these limitations can be leveraged by the combined use of large datasets and ML tools.

24.3 Testing the Triadic Neural Systems Model

24.3.1 Introduction to Machine Learning Tools

The introduction of machine learning (ML) tools in neuroscience research has generated huge hope and excitement (e.g., Dwyer et al., 2018; Iniesta et al., 2016). These tools have gained enormous popularity among neuroscientists, particularly clinical neuroimagers. Together with the current move toward open science and data sharing, the time is ripe to attempt the validation or disproof of complex brain–behavior models.

The ML approach has been developed primarily by engineers for advancing the science of artificial intelligence. The application of these tools to neuroscience research, especially in the neuroimaging domain, is challenging because neuroscientists are not well-equipped to fully understand the properties and limitations of these complex mathematical tools and, conversely, engineers do not have a clear understanding of the fabric of clinical and neuroscience research. This implies that collaborative approaches are highly recommended when applying ML tools to neuroscientific questions. For example, ML applications require large datasets (several hundred to several thousand subjects). In addition, ML's initial solutions, computed in a first sample (training sample), must be tested in a new independent sample (test sample) (Varoquaux & Craddock, 2013; Varoquaux et al., 2017). This requirement can be a limitation for clinical applications, that is now leveraged by the emergence of large datasets made publicly available.

ML consists of algorithms that train computers to learn patterns from an array of variables (recognize a cat by using different measurements of a typical cat, such as the relative size of paws, tail, head, etc.). The computer learns patterns through automated, iterative, computations. These patterns can serve to classify data and to provide predictive models. It is important to realize that ML covers a variety of approaches that differ as a function of the goal of the study. For example, ML is divided into "supervised" and "unsupervised" algorithms (e.g., Tarca et al., 2007). Supervised ML assumes a ground truth (e.g., patient versus healthy groups; faces versus houses) and trains the computer to use data that will best predict the ground truth. Unsupervised ML is not predicated on a ground truth. It provides training to find reliable patterns in data that can inform the constituents of models. In other words, it attempts to classify objects (e.g., brain activation maps) according to their intrinsic properties, as opposed to similarity with some ground truth. As we present a strategy to test the triadic model, the use of supervised versus unsupervised approaches will become clear.

24.3.2 Overall Strategy for Testing the Triadic Neural Systems Model

The triadic neural systems model can be tested in three sequential stages to address three main aims (questions) needed to delineate (1) The functional architecture of each system: describe and validate the brain mapping of each system, the approach, avoidance and control system; (2) The dynamic interaction among the three systems: describe and validate how these systems work together to generate adaptive motivated actions; and (3) The maturation of the triadic model: how these three systems and their interactions develop with age. This approach is illustrated in Figure 24.2, which shows fictitious results. In other words, the number and location of the nodes (pattern of elements for each analysis) do not reflect actual data or real predictions (e.g., striatum not represented for the approach system). Figure 24.2 is meant to provide a concrete schematic representation to facilitate the description of the analytic paths.

To accomplish these aims, three types of data need to be collected concomitantly in healthy individuals: (1) behavioral and clinical characteristics (e.g., interviews, paper/pencil questionnaires), (2) task performance measures (e.g., reward task, avoidance task, and executive function task), and (3) neuroimaging data (resting state and task-based fMRI). These data need to be acquired in three different contexts (appetitive, aversive, and cognitive).

The first two questions do not require pediatric samples. Although it would be optimal for the samples of Questions 1 and 2 to be independent, it is not essential. The samples should be large enough to apply ML tools,

allowing for a larger subsample of >250 subjects to be used as a training sample to define the model, and a smaller subsample of >50 subjects to be used as the testing sample to validate the model. For Question 3, an optimal design would be that of a longitudinal study of a large community sample of children (e.g., n > 300). Research consortia, such as ABCD, NCANDA, IMAGEN, or Connectome, are currently collecting longitudinal behavioral and neuroimaging measures in large pediatric samples. Since these data are made available to the public, the present discussion is highly propitious.

24.3.3 Question 1: Functional Architecture of Each System

This question aims at defining the networks that are associated with the generation of three domains of behavior (approach, avoidance and cognitive control). Two types of data are used for this goal (behavioral and neural measures). The strategy to test Question 1 progresses in two steps for data organization (Figure 24.3) and the computation of the predictive model (Figure 24.4).

24.3.3.1 Data Organization/Reduction

The behavioral measures are expected to be numerous, including paper & pencil measures (self-report, interviews), task performance in both clinic and MRI (cognitive, motivation, emotion tasks), and physiological data (e.g., skin conductance, heart rate, EMG) (Figure 24.3). Therefore, a first step is to organize and reduce these measures to isolate latent factors most representative of the three domains of approach, avoidance, and control. In other words, rather than dictating which behaviors and questionnaires are associated with any one of the triadic systems, a data-driven approach can yield more objective and

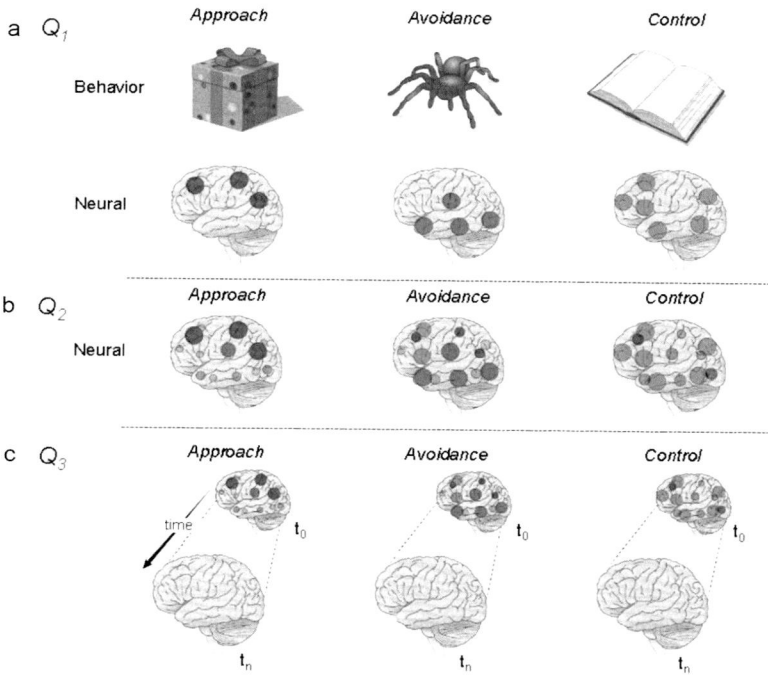

Figure 24.2 Overall strategy for testing the triadic neural systems model. The strategy involves three sequential stages of analyses, and fictitious data are used for clarity. (a) The upper panel addresses Question 1 and illustrates the two main analytic steps. First, the reduction and organization of behavioral variables into latent factors that map to the approach, avoidance, and cognitive domains. Second, the brain illustrations give the fictitious results of the predictive model (i.e., the core nodes that predict each of the three behavioral domain scores). In this fictitious example, three nodes map to the approach behavioral factor (A1–A3), four nodes to the avoidance factor (V1–V4), and six nodes to the control factor (C1–C6). (b) The middle panel addresses Question 2. It illustrates the fictitious neural predictors that are used to assess the functional overlaps and uniqueness of the three networks of the triadic model. Specifically, the thirteen neural nodes identified in Question 1 are all extracted in each task-related fMRI (approach, avoidance, and control), making up thirty-nine potential neural predictors. These extracted neural measures (n = 39) are submitted to ML algorithms. (c) The lower panel represents Question 3 showing the analyses being repeated at each follow-up time, based on a longitudinal study design A black-and-white version of this figure will appear in some formats. For the color version, please refer to the plate section.

valid categorization of behavioral data. Principal component analysis (PCA) (Gleason et al., 2015) is a reasonable approach to map existing behavioral data to distinct functional domains. This way, many metrics can be employed to reveal clusters of behavioral items that best describe the three behavioral domains of approach, avoidance, and control.

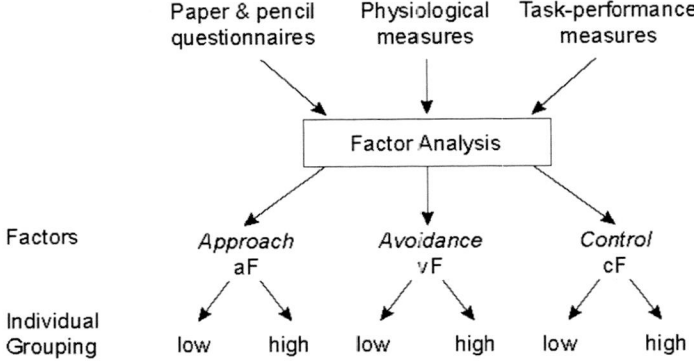

Figure 24.3 Strategy for addressing Question 1, Step-1: Behavioral data reduction and organization. This step pools together all behavioral variables, which are entered into a principal component analysis (PCA). The PCA is intended to provide the most representative factors depicting approach, avoidance, and cognitive control behavior by grouping those behavioral variables into components (factors) based on their intrinsic properties. The factors are labeled aF, vF, and cF, for the approach, avoidance, and cognitive control factor, respectively. Subjects can be classified as a function of their factor scores. Here, two groups for each factor, those with high and those with low scores, are represented. Of note, the number of groups is arbitrary. In addition, the factor scores could be used as continuous variables

Ultimately, this approach could provide one or two factor scores for each of the three behavioral domains. In addition, other factors, not related to the triadic domains, could emerge. Finally, the possibility for not being able to clearly identify an approach, avoidance, or cognitive factor is also possible, although the nature of the inputted items, all related to the behaviors of interest, make this possibility unlikely. For simplicity, only one behavioral factor for each domain will be used as illustration, and each factor score will define two groups, those with low scores and those with high scores. We will also not address the issue of additional unrelated factors. The next step is to identify which and how neural measures predict each behavioral domain, respectively.

24.3.3.2 The Predictive Model

This step identifies the activity patterns of the neural networks predicting each of the three behavioral domains, quantified by the data organization step as the three latent factors, approach factor (aF), avoidance factor (vF), and cognitive factor (cF). These domains are expected to be examined concurrently using the same procedure. This step uses ML tools for the supervised approach since the analysis provides solutions to a "ground truth" (e.g., low aF versus high aF). The ML algorithms (such as support vector machine model or random Forest model) implement iterative computations to train the computer to recognize the neural patterns that optimally predict the behavioral factor scores (aF, vF, and cF). In other words, the goal of these analyses is to

Supervised Machine Learning Algorithm

Behavioral Factors	Neural predictors		Solution
	Resting-state fMRI	Task-based fMRI	
		Approach Avoidance Control	

$Approach$ aF $= F(a^{(1)}\, a^{(2)}\, a^{(3)}\, a^{(4)}\, a^{(5)}\, a^{(6)} \ldots a^{(16)}\, a^{(17)}\, a^{(18)}\, a^{(19)}\, a^{(20)}\quad x^{(1)}\, x^{(2)}\, x^{(3)} \ldots x^{(i)}\quad y^{(1)}\, y^{(2)}\, y^{(3)} \ldots y^{(j)}\quad z^{(1)}\, z^{(2)}\, z^{(3)} \ldots z^{(k)});$

$Avoidance$ vF $= G(a^{(1)}\, a^{(2)}\, a^{(3)}\, a^{(4)}\, a^{(5)}\, a^{(6)} \ldots a^{(16)}\, a^{(17)}\, a^{(18)}\, a^{(19)}\, a^{(20)}\quad x^{(1)}\, x^{(2)}\, x^{(3)} \ldots x^{(i)}\quad y^{(1)}\, y^{(2)}\, y^{(3)} \ldots y^{(j)}\quad z^{(1)}\, z^{(2)}\, z^{(3)} \ldots z^{(k)});$

$Control$ cF $= H(a^{(1)}\, a^{(2)}\, a^{(3)}\, a^{(4)}\, a^{(5)}\, a^{(6)} \ldots a^{(16)}\, a^{(17)}\, a^{(18)}\, a^{(19)}\, a^{(20)}\quad x^{(1)}\, x^{(2)}\, x^{(3)} \ldots x^{(i)}\quad y^{(1)}\, y^{(2)}\, y^{(3)} \ldots y^{(j)}\quad z^{(1)}\, z^{(2)}\, z^{(3)} \ldots z^{(k)});$

Figure 24.4 Strategy for addressing Question 1, Step-2 & Step-3: Supervised ML step. Step-2 consists of the gathering of the neural predictors, and Step-3 of the use of a supervised ML algorithm. This ML algorithm computes the relative predictive value of the extracted neural measures. As such, it provides the components (nodes) of the neural networks that best predict the behavioral factors previously identified in Step-1 (Figure 24.3). The predictive model is represented as an equation, equation-F for aF, equation-G for vF, and equation-H for cF. The components aF, vF, and cF are the behavioral factors identified in Question 1 Step-1. More specifically, $a^{(1)}$ is the first extracted value of the resting state fMRI, up to $a^{(20)}$, which is the value of the last extracted value that passes the significant threshold set for the resting state study (the n = 20 is arbitrary). The variable $x^{(1)}$ is the extracted value of the most significant regional activation of the approach-task based fMRI, the last value being $x^{(i)}$ (n = i extracted values from the approach scan); $y^{(1)}$ corresponds to the avoidance domain $y^{(j)}$ (n = j extracted values from the avoidance scan); and $z^{(k)}$ to the control domain, the last value being $z^{(k)}$ (n = k extracted values from the control scan). The brain illustrations on the right of the equations represent the solution of the ML analysis, which identifies the nodes (neural predictors) that best predict aF, vF, and cF, respectively (i.e., have the highest weight). The number of these regional activations (or nodes) are arbitrarily set to three for the approach factor, four for the avoidance factor, and six for the control factor. These nodes define the neural networks that best predict reactivity to the behavioral domains of the triadic model
A black-and-white version of this figure will appear in some formats. For the color version, please refer to the plate section.

produce the most efficient (low-cost, low-noise) predictive model of a given behavior model using neural activity patterns as predictors.

The neural activity inputs (i.e., predictors) to the model consist of resting state connectivity measures, in the form of weights between hubs (e.g., ventral striatum to ventromedial prefrontal cortex), and regional BOLD activations during task-related fMRI (Figure 24.4).

One advantage of ML methods is that multiple neural variables can be examined as predictors of a given behavior in a single model, without violating the assumptions of the statistical model (e.g., t-tests are conducted with the assumption that the data is normally distributed). In Figure 24.4, we present three equations for each behavioral domain (F, G, H). Each equation is unique to its behavioral domain in terms of the parameters (computed by the ML algorithms) that weight the neural predictors. A higher weight signifies a more determinant role in predicting the behavior. The dominant predictors are those that also appear most determinant in decision trees, which maximize the output separation (subjects scoring high versus low on the behavioral domain). Furthermore, many ML models, by default, test interactions. For example, classification trees are a type of ML model where the sample is partitioned in a sequence of steps (e.g., Figure 24.5(a), two steps, tree sequentially split by gender and then by family history of substance use).

We present two simple fictitious examples of classification tree results in Figure 24.5. The first example (Figure 24.5(a)) uses demographic and clinical data to classify participants as high or low risk-takers. The model finds gender to be the strongest predictor of the propensity for risk-taking, with males more high risk-takers than females. The next in-line predictor is family history of substance use. A positive family history of substance use strongly increases the propensity for risk-taking in males, but less so in females. In other words, a positive family history confers risk that differs between males and females.

The second example (Figure 24.5(b)), also totally fictitious, is closer to the thematic of this paper, that is, neural predictors of a specific behavior. In this made-up example, the

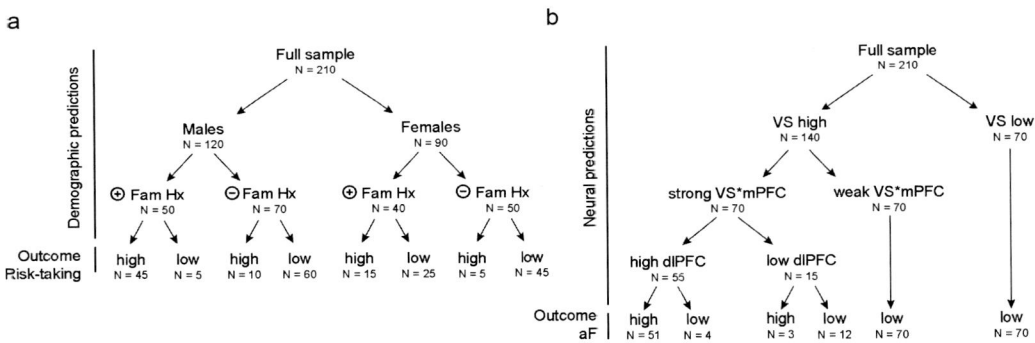

Figure 24.5 Two examples of solutions using classification tree algorithms. (a) Example 1 illustrates a ML classification of subjects into groups of high or low risk-takers (high versus low value of the outcome measure), as a function of sex and family history of substance use (fmhx-su). The sample is composed of 120 males and 90 females. The modulation of risk-taking by fmhx-su is different in males and females. Males with a positive fmhx-su are more prone to be high risk-takers (forty-five of fifty, 90 percent) compared to males without fmhx-su (ten of seventy, 14 percent). However, this factor does not seem to be as determinant in females, fifteen of forty females with a positive fmhx-su (38 percent) compared to five of fifty is 10% without fmhx-su. (b) Example 2 illustrates an ML classification of individuals as a function of high versus low propensity for approach behavior (high aF versus low aF) using neural predictors. This tree shows that the ventral striatum (VS) is the strongest predictor of high aF. All the individuals with low VS have low aF scores. In contrast, the association of high VS sensitivity with high aF is modulated by the connectivity of the VS*medial prefrontal cortex (mPFC) and by the activity of the dorsolateral prefrontal cortex (DLPFC). This tree clearly illustrates how such analyses can help clarify interactions among neural predictors of specific behaviors. VS = ventral striatum activation, VS*mPFC = intrinsic connectivity between VS and medial prefrontal cortex, DLPFC = dorsolateral prefrontal cortex

classification tree analysis reveals that approach behavior (e.g., aF) is most strongly (at the top of the tree) predicted by high ventral striatal (VS) response to reward, but only if the circuit's strength between VS and ventromedial PFC (VMPFC) is strong, and the dorsolateral PFC (DLPFC) response is high. ML would be able to identify this model, but linear models would not, unless the interaction term was specified (known a priori). With many potential interactions, it would be challenging for human researchers to consider all the possible interaction terms, but it is easy for a machine. Ultimately, a classification tree analysis would delineate the brain regions that matter in the modulation of approach behavior. In the theoretical example of Figure 24.5(b), the most powerful predictors are the VS, the VMPFC, and the DLPFC.

24.3.3.3 Output of the Predictive Model of the Characterization of the Three Neural Systems

Taken together, the expected output of Question 1 is the delineation of the main nodes engaged (via activation or connectivity) in each of the three functional domains. In addition to providing the identity of these nodes, Question 1 also reveals patterns of interactions that predict the degree of behavioral propensity toward either approach, avoidance or control. Here, these patterns of interactions are not used in the subsequent analyses and will not be addressed. Indeed, Question 2 will focus only on the nodes' identity, revealed in Question 1's solutions.

For illustration, we arbitrarily assign nodes to each neural system: approach system, A1, A2, A3, avoidance system, V1, V2, V3, V4, and control system, C1, C2, C3, C4, C5, C6. In actuality, some nodes are likely to be common to two or all three systems, but, for simplicity, this situation is not considered.

24.3.4 Question 2: Dynamic Interactions among the Three Systems

Question 2 examines how the neural predictors of all three behavioral domains (i.e., approach A1–A3, avoidance V1–V4, and control C1–C6) work together in each of the appetitive and aversive contexts. Indeed, the triadic model predicts that, in an appetitive context, the approach system will be specifically engaged and more tightly intra-connected, whereas the avoidance system will tend to be more silent (Ernst, 2014; Ernst & Spear, 2009). The opposite would characterize the neural pattern in an aversive context. The control network would manifest different couplings with the approach versus avoidance system as a function of the appetitive versus aversive context. We expect the reality to be more complex, particularly with expected interactions among nodes of the different neural systems. However, this is an acceptable starting hypothesis.

24.3.4.1 Question 2, Step-1

The neural predictors identified in Question 1 provide the variables for this analysis (Figure 24.6). Using the fictitious results of Question 1, these neural variables (nodes) are assigned to A1–A3 for approach, V1–V4 for avoidance, and C1–C6 for control. The strategy to query Question 2 consists of three steps, (1) the collection of all neural data in all three contexts (approach, avoidance, cognitive), (2) an ML "discovery" analysis, and (3) an ML "categorization" analysis.

The first data collection step (Figure 24.6(a)) is a re-examination of the task-based fMRI scans, in order to extract the values of the neural predictors (nodes) of all three contexts pooled together. In other words, the "approach" nodes (or regions of interest, ROIs) A1–A3 are also extracted from the control- and avoidance-related scans, the

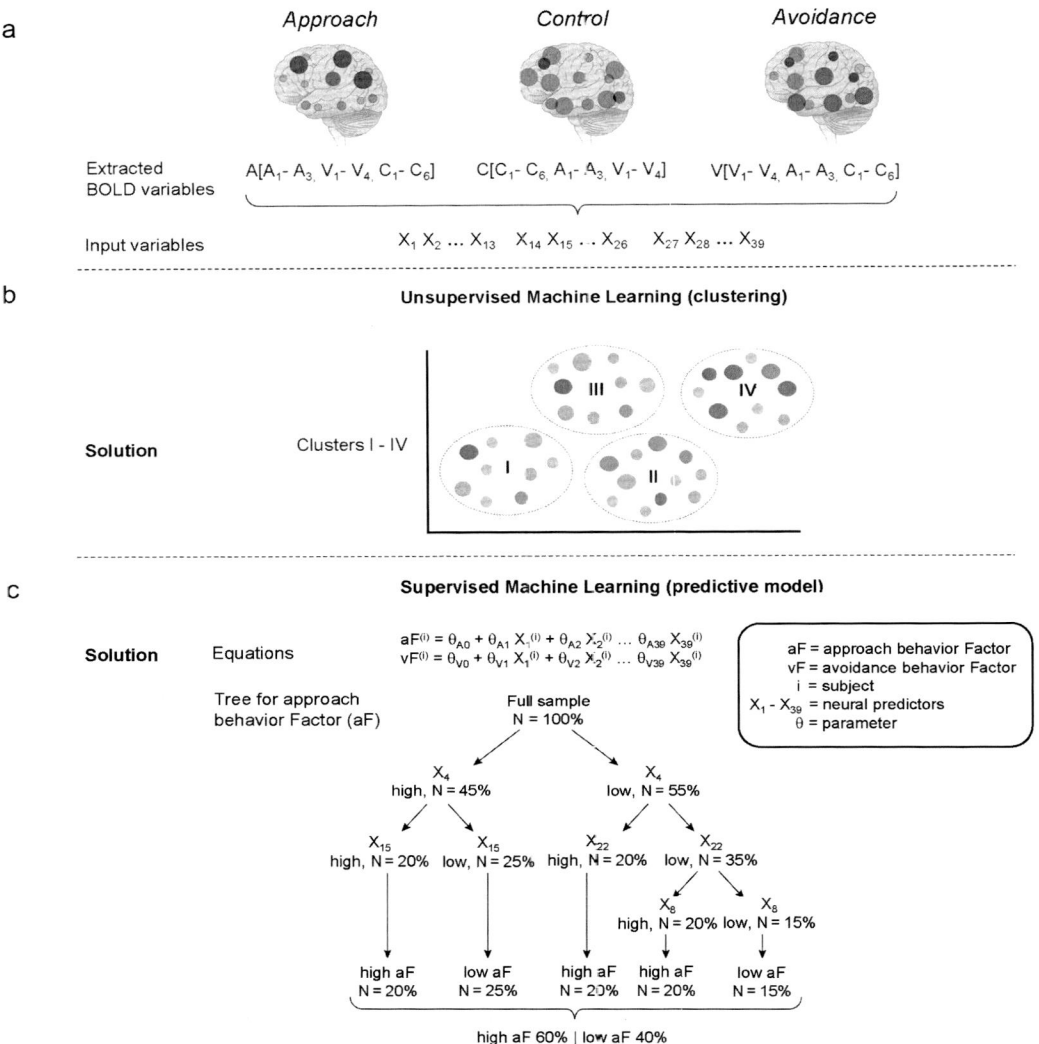

Figure 24.6 Strategy for Addressing Question 2, Step-1 to Step-3: Extraction of neural predictors, unsupervised ML clustering, and supervised ML to predict behavioral factors aF and vF. (a) Step-1: Extraction of neural predictors. This step consists of gathering all potential neural predictors of the behavioral factors identified in Question 1. These neural predictors (nodes) are now all extracted from every task-based fMRI scan (cognitive task fMRI, avoidance task fMRI, and approach task fMRI). The brain illustrations show the activation maps of all the nodes of interest, the approach nodes (purple), the avoidance nodes (red), and the control nodes (green), in each task-based fMRI scan. The extracted blood–oxygen-level-dependent (BOLD) variables are labeled A to refer to the approach domain (nodes A1–A3, associated with the approach domain in Question 1), V to refer to the avoidance domain (nodes V1–V4, associated with the avoidance domain in Question 1), and C to refer to the control domain (nodes C1–C6, associated with the control domain in Question 1). The schemes used for each domain are: A[A1–A3, V1–V4, C1–C6] (approach), V[V1–V4, A1–A3, C1–C6] (avoidance), and C[C1–C6, A1–A3, V1–V4] (control). The extracted thirty-nine regions of interest (ROIs)

"avoidance" ROIs V1–V4 from the control- and approach-related scans, and the "control" ROIs C1–C6 from the avoidance- and approach-related scans. Therefore, the number of potential neural predictors for Question 2 is tripled.

Theoretically, it would be possible to go from Step-1 to Step-3, but we believe that going directly to Step-3 would prevent the possibility of discovering new patterns of networks (clusters). These potentially new networks emerge in Step-2 as a function of the intrinsic characteristics of the neural variables, which may not be captured otherwise.

24.3.4.2 Question 2, Step-2

In the second step (Figure 24.6(b)), a "discovery analysis" organizes the neural data without a-priori guidance. Here, all the neural predictors (n = 39) are submitted to an unsupervised ML algorithm, a data clustering analysis (e.g.,

K-Means clustering, Mean-Shift Clustering). This step organizes the data into clusters. A cluster is defined by variables that have similar properties and which also differ from those of the other clusters. Furthermore, it is possible to assign (infer) a functional significance to each cluster based on their node composition. Of note, a clear separation of the clusters, as illustrated in Figure 24.6(b) is seldom the case, and intermediate steps may be necessary to clarify and interpret the clustering results. For illustration, Figure 24.6(b) displays a fictitious solution of four clusters, each containing a unique set of variables. In other words, the sum of the variables across the four clusters is thirty-nine, since it consists of all potential neural predictors extracted in Step-1.

24.3.4.3 Question 2, Step-3 and Solutions

In the third step (Figure 24.6(c)), the clusters are categorized based on their predictive value

Figure 24.6 (*cont.*) (thirteen per scan) are labelled X1 through X39. (b) Step-2: Unsupervised ML clustering. All the neural predictors (n = 39) are submitted to an unsupervised ML algorithm, which organizes the nodes into coherent clusters (nodes grouped into clusters as a function of their intrinsic characteristics). Here, the solution has been arbitrarily set to four clusters. The identity of the nodes within a given cluster can inform the likely underlying function of the cluster (i.e., striatal nodes can be inferred as mediating approach behavior). In other words, the clusters are composed of nodes which represent networks. This illustration shows a very clean separation of nodes into clusters. Such a clean picture is rarely the case, and more work is usually needed to conduct and interpret this type of analysis. Furthermore, it would have been possible to avoid this Step-2 and move directly from Step-1 to Step-3. However, such a short-cut would miss the opportunity to discover new networks (clusters) or to refine a priori hypotheses that are used in supervised ML. (c) Step-3: Supervised ML analysis. The clusters, predictors of the three behavioral domains, are used in two supervised ML algorithms, one for the approach domain and the other for the avoidance domain. The supervised ML algorithm leads to two types of solutions. The first type of solution uses a linear model to estimate the strength of each neural predictor. Each behavioral factor score is predicted by clusters associated with a constant unique parameter (theta) calculated by the ML algorithm. The second type of solution displays a decision tree to provide a hierarchical structure that represents the categorization of the sample as a function of the cluster values. In this example, the categorization leads to a sample divided into two groups, one group of individuals with low behavioral factor scores (in this example aF) and the other with high behavioral factor scores. This decision tree, which determines the propensity for approach behavior clearly shows how the different clusters (networks) work together to determine approach behavior

A black-and-white version of this figure will appear in some formats. For the color version, please refer to the plate section.

of the approach and avoidance behavioral domains (aF, vF). Because the triadic model does not predict how cognitive neural pattern changes in either an approach or avoidance context, this aspect is not considered here.

This analysis falls under the supervised ML approach, using learning algorithms of support vector machines or decision trees, as described in Question 1. To avoid confusion, in Question 1, the categorization analysis serves to identify each set of neural predictors that only relates to a given behavior, either approach (aF), avoidance (vF), or control (cF). Here, in Question 2, the categorization algorithm uses the clusters computed with all thirty-nine neural variables and classified them in function of their predictive value of the approach and avoidance behavioral factors (aF, vF) that were computed in Question 1.

In summary, two categorization algorithms are used, one for approach propensity and the other for avoidance propensity. Taken together, Step-3 provides data that test the theory underlying the triadic model, i.e., the relative independence of avoidance versus approach systems, and their interactions in approach and avoidance contexts. These results can be represented as equations and as trees (Figure 24.6(c)). The equations provide the parameters (thetas) that weigh the clusters values in predicting the behavior (aF, vF), which correspond to their relative power in predicting behavior. Trees have the advantage of depicting a hierarchical interactional organization of the neural predictors of behavior (see explanation of trees in Question 1).

24.3.5 Question 3: Maturation of the Triadic Neural Systems Dynamics

The strategy for Question 3 is the same as that employed to solve Question 2. The difference

is that this strategy is applied at each follow-up point (twelve, sixteen, and twenty years old). Accordingly, the neural predictors from our fictitious examples include thirteen node values × three contexts = thirty-nine neural datapoints for each follow-up data analysis. We summarize the steps below:

a. Step-1, Behavioral characterization. The predicted behavior outcome measures are computed as in Question 1, by conducting a factor analysis of all available behavioral data, at each follow-up.

b. Step-2, Data-driven organization of all thirty-nine ROIs at each follow-up. We expect slight differences in the clustering of the data across age-groups (fictitious example, Figure 24.7).

c. Step-3, Brain–behavior classification: This step gives rise to two types of results: trees that depict the hierarchical organization of predictors at each follow-up point, and equations that quantify the contribution of each cluster to a given behavioral domain, respectively. ML algorithms calculate the parameters of the equations that best characterize the value of the neural predictors of each of the three behavioral domains, at each follow-up point.

These results are expected to inform patterns of changes in the relative contribution of the key nodes of the neural systems of approach, avoidance, and control processes. These patterns can then be tested more specifically in hypothesis-driven studies.

24.4 Conclusion

In this chapter, we offer a preview of the potential contributions of the latest, so far most powerful, tools to help delineate how brain networks code motivated behaviors. Such potential windows into brain–behavior mechanisms can have invaluable implications

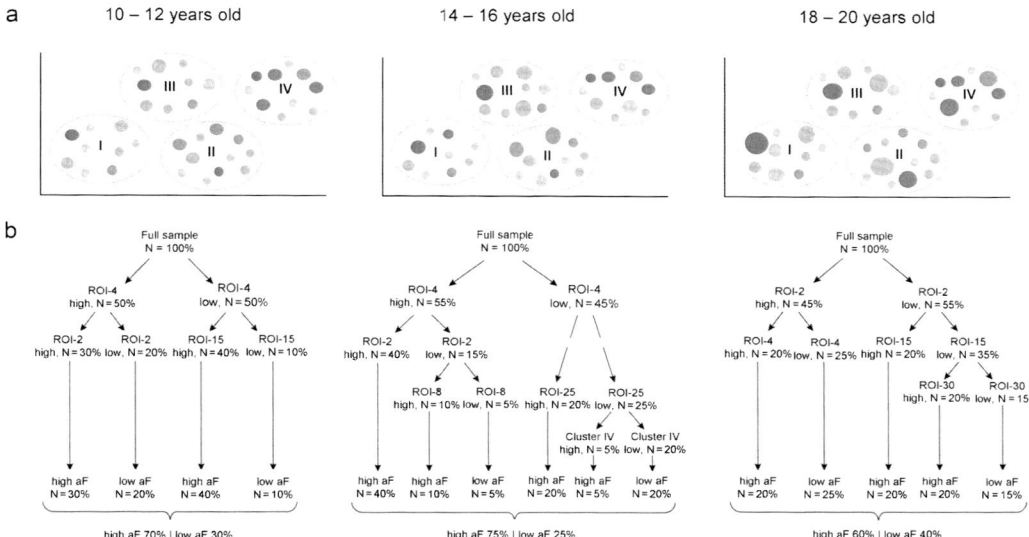

Figure 24.7 Fictitious results to Question 3: Decision trees across development. Fictitious examples of (a) composition of the clusters across ages and (b) changes in classification trees at different age groups. Differences among the composition of the clusters across ages can give clues as to how the nature of the networks evolve with maturation. Changes in classification trees at different age groups also informs the evolution of mechanisms underlying motivated behavior of approach in this example A black-and-white version of this figure will appear in some formats. For the color version, please refer to the plate section.

for understanding developmental changes in health and disease and can provide critical guides for refining and extending research in this field. Specifically, the present work illustrates how complex theoretical frameworks can be tested using large datasets that are becoming publicly available and sophisticated analytical tools like ML algorithms.

References

Balleine, B. W., & Killcross, S. (2006). Parallel incentive processing: An integrated view of amygdala function. *Trends in Neuroscience, 29,* 272–279.

Balleine, B. W., & O'Doherty, J. P. (2010). Human and rodent homologies in action control: Corticostriatal determinants of goal-directed and habitual action. *Neuropsychopharmacology, 35,* 48–69.

Banich, M. T. (2009). Executive function: The search for an integrated account. *Current Directions in Psychological Science, 18,* 89–94.

Berridge, K. C., & Kringelbach, M. L. (2013). Neuroscience of affect: Brain mechanisms of pleasure and displeasure. *Current Opinions in Neurobiology, 23,* 294–303.

Berridge, K. C., & Robinson, T. E. (2003). Parsing reward. *Trends in Neuroscience, 26,* 507–513.

Bromberg-Martin, E. S., Matsumoto, M., & Hikosaka, O. (2010). Dopamine in motivational control: Rewarding, aversive, and alerting. *Neuron, 68,* 815–834.

Campese, V. D., Sears, R. M., Moscarello, J. M., Diaz-Mataix, L., Cain, C. K., & LeDoux, J. E. (2016). The neural foundations of reaction and action in aversive motivation. In E. H. Simpson, & P. D. Balsam (eds.), *Behavioral Neuroscience of Motivation* (pp. 171–195). Cham: Springer International Publishing.

Casey, B. J., Jones, R. M., & Hare, T. A. (2008). The adolescent brain. *Annals of the New York Academy of Sciences, 1124*, 111–126.

Christoff, K., & Gabrieli, J. D. E. (2000). The frontopolar cortex and human cognition: Evidence for a rostrocaudal hierarchical organization within the human prefrontal cortex. *Psychobiology, 28*, 168–186.

Delgado, M. R., Jou, R. L., & Phelps, E. A. (2011). Neural systems underlying aversive conditioning in humans with primary and secondary reinforcers. *Frontiers in Neuroscience, 5*, 71.

Dwyer, D. B., Falkai, P., & Koutsouleris, N. (2018). Machine learning approaches for clinical psychology and psychiatry. *Annual Review of Clinical Psychology, 14*, 91–118.

Elliot, A. J., & Covington, M. V. (2001). Approach and avoidance motivation. *Educational Psychology Review, 13*, 73–92.

Ernst, M. (2014). The triadic model perspective for the study of adolescent motivated behavior. *Brain and Cognition, 89*, 104–111.

Ernst, M., Daniele, T., & Frantz, K. (2011). New perspectives on adolescent motivated behavior: Attention and conditioning. *Developmental Cognitive Neuroscience, 1*, 377–389.

Ernst, M., Pine, D. S., & Hardin, M. (2006). Triadic model of the neurobiology of motivated behavior in adolescence. *Psychological Medicine, 36*, 299–312.

Ernst, M., & Spear, L. P. (2009). Reward systems. In M. de Haan & M. R. Gunnar (eds.), *Handbook of Developmental Social Neuroscience* (pp. 324–341). New York: The Guilford Press.

Gleason, P. M., Boushey, C. J., Harris, J. E., & Zoellner, J. (2015). Publishing nutrition research: A review of multivariate techniques – Part 3: Data reduction methods. *Journal of the Academy of Nutrition & Dietetics, 115*, 1072–1082.

Goode, T. D., & Maren, S. (2017). Role of the bed nucleus of the stria terminalis in aversive learning and memory. *Learning & Memory, 24*, 480–491.

Hare, T. A., Tottenham, N., Galvan, A., Voss, H. U., Glover, G. H., & Casey, B. J. (2008). Biological substrates of emotional reactivity and regulation in adolescence during an emotional

go–nogo task. *Biological Psychiatry, 63*, 927–934.

Iniesta, R., Stahl, D., & McGuffin, P. (2016). Machine learning, statistical learning and the future of biological research in psychiatry. *Psychological Medicine, 46*, 2455–2465.

Jernigan, T. L., & Brown, S. A. (2018). Introduction. *Developmental Cognitive Neuroscience, 32*, 1–3.

Kouneiher, F., Charron, S., & Koechlin, E. (2009). Motivation and cognitive control in the human prefrontal cortex. *Nature Neuroscience, 12*, 939–945.

Kragel, P. A., & LaBar, K. S. (2016). Decoding the nature of emotion in the brain. *Trends in Cognitive Sciences, 20*, 444–455.

LeDoux, J., & Daw, N. D. (2018). Surviving threats: Neural circuit and computational implications of a new taxonomy of defensive behaviour. *Nature Reviews Neuroscience, 19*, 269–282.

Maren, S. (2016). Parsing reward and aversion in the amygdala. *Neuron, 90*, 209–211.

Mirenowicz, J., & Schultz, W. (1996). Preferential activation of midbrain dopamine neurons by appetitive rather than aversive stimuli. *Nature, 379*, 449–451.

Murphy, F. C., Nimmo-Smith, I., & Lawrence, A. D. (2003). Functional neuroanatomy of emotions: A meta-analysis. *Cognitive, Affective, & Behavioral Neuroscience, 3*, 207–233.

Petrides, M. (2005). Lateral prefrontal cortex: Architectonic and functional organization. *Philosophical Transactions of the Royal Society B: Biological Sciences, 360*, 781–795.

Quevedo, K. M., Benning, S. D., Gunnar, M. R., & Dahl, R. E. (2009). The onset of puberty: Effects on the psychophysiology of defensive and appetitive motivation. *Development and Psychopathology, 21*, 27–45.

Sanford, C. A., Soden, M. E., Baird, M. A., Miller, S. M., Schulkin, J., Palmiter, R. D., ... Zweifel, L. S. (2017). A central amygdala CRF circuit facilitates learning about weak threats. *Neuron, 93*, 164–178.

Silvers, J. A., McRae, K., Gabrieli, J. D. E., Gross, J. J., Remy, K. A., & Ochsner, K. N. (2012). Age-related differences in emotional reactivity, regulation, and rejection sensitivity in adolescence. *Emotion, 12*, 1235–1247.

Steinberg, L. (2008). A social neuroscience perspective on adolescent risk-taking. *Developmental Review, 28*, 78–106.

Stuss, D. T., & Alexander, M. P. (2007). Is there a dysexecutive syndrome? *Philosophical Transactions of the Royal Society of London B: Biological Science, 362*, 901–915.

Tarca, A. L., Carey, V. J., Chen, X. W., Romero, R., & Drăghici, S. (2007). Machine learning and its applications to biology. *PLoS Computational Biology, 3*, e116.

Tsutsui-Kimura, I., Bouchekioua, Y., Mimura, M., & Tanaka, K. F. (2017). A new paradigm for evaluating avoidance/escape motivation. *International Journal of Neuropsychopharmacology, 20*, 593–601.

Tversky, A., & Kahneman, D. (1992). Advances in prospect theory: Cumulative representation of uncertainty. *Journal of Risk and Uncertainty, 5*, 297–323.

Varoquaux, G., & Craddock, R. C. (2013). Learning and comparing functional connectomes across subjects. *Neuroimage, 80*, 405–415.

Varoquaux, G., Raamana, P. R., Engemann, D. A., Hoyos-Idrobo, A., Schwartz, Y., & Thirion, B. (2017). Assessing and tuning brain decoders: Cross-validation, caveats, and guidelines. *Neuroimage, 145*, 166–179.

Wassum, K. M., & Izquierdo, A. (2015). The basolateral amygdala in reward learning and addiction. *Neuroscience& Biobehavioral Reviews, 57*, 271–283.

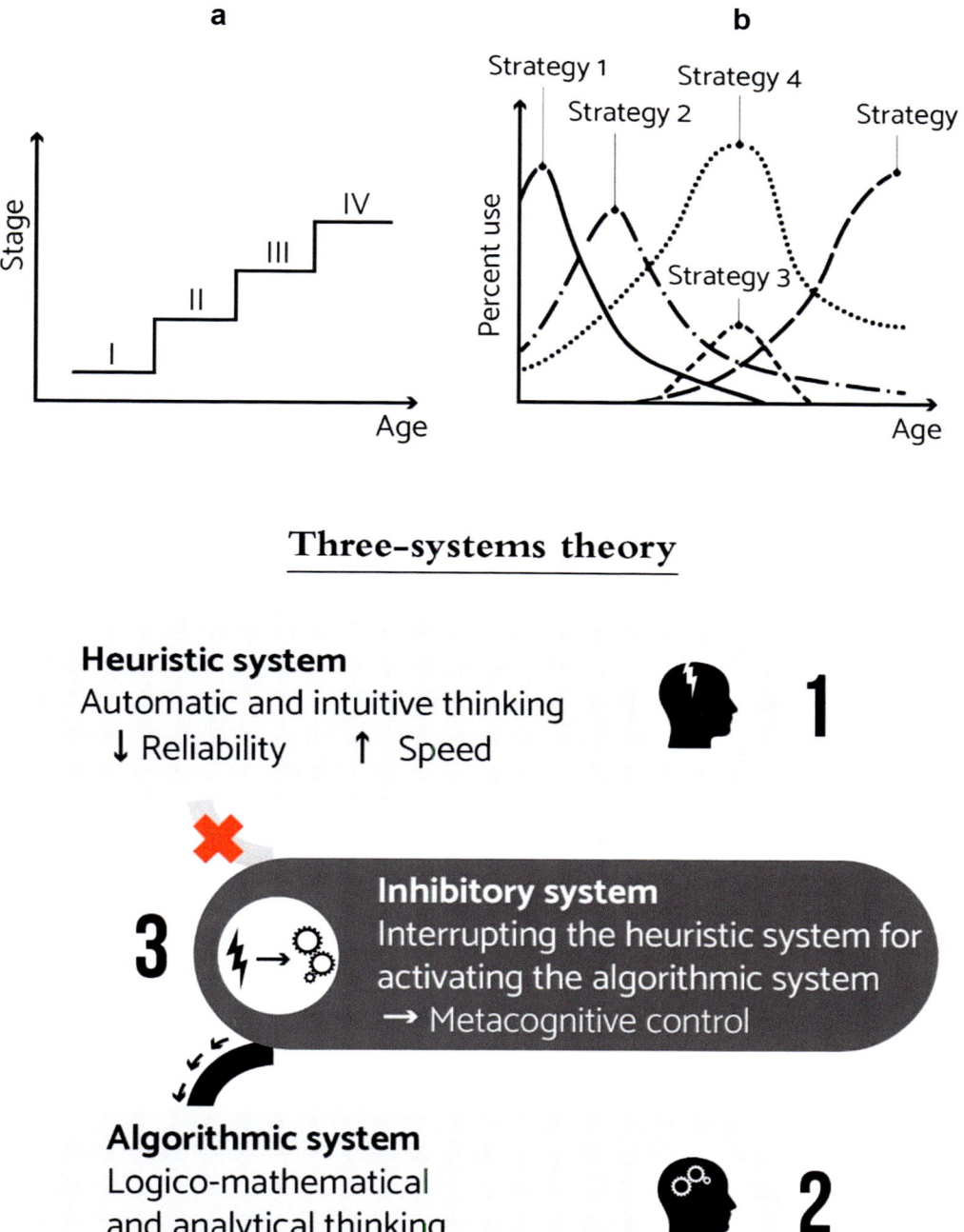

Figure II.1 Three-systems theory of the cognitive brain. (a) Piaget's theory or the "staircase model" of incremental progress stage by stage, from intuition to logic. (b) Non-linear development of cognitive strategies (R. Siegler) that come either from the fast and heuristic (intuitive) system or from the slow and algorithmic (logical) system at any age (D. Kahneman). When these two systems compete (System 1 versus System 2), our brain needs a third system, located in the prefrontal cortex, for inhibiting the too fast heuristic system and activating the logical one (Borst & Houdé, 2014; Houdé, 2019)

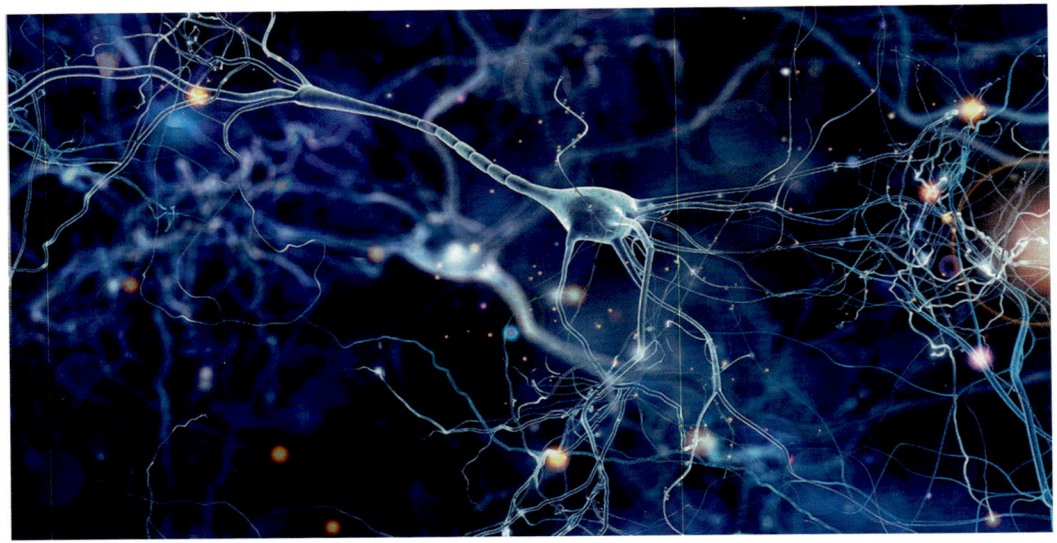

Figure 2.1 The neurone and the interneuronal connections through the synapse in the human brain

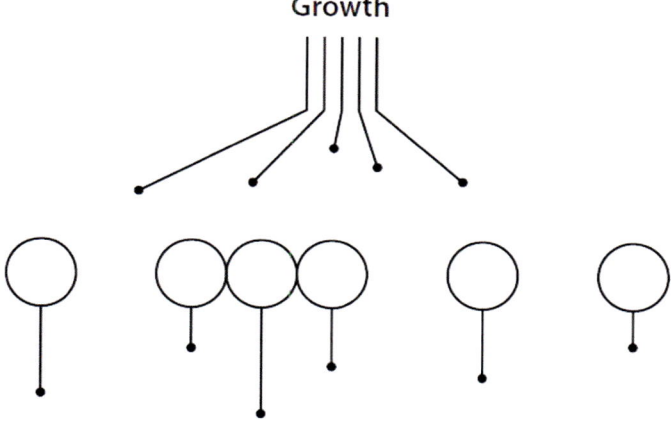

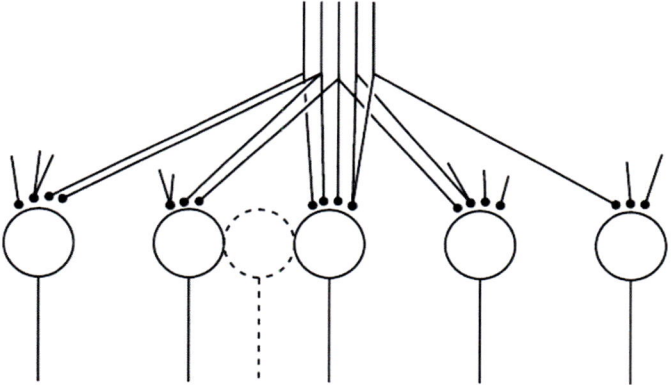

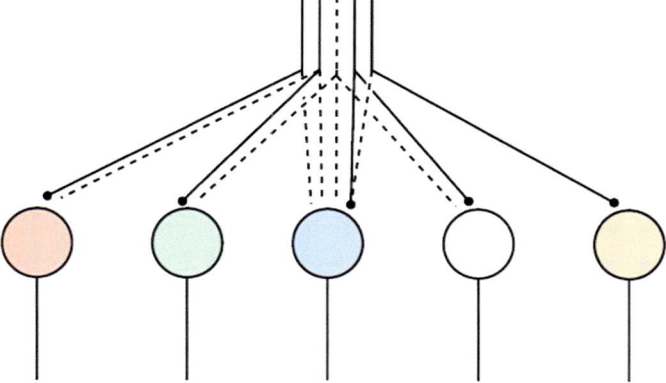

Figure 2.2 Schematic representation of the hypothesis of epigenesis by selective stabilization of synapses. From Changeux, 1983, 1985

a. Growth and folding of the brain

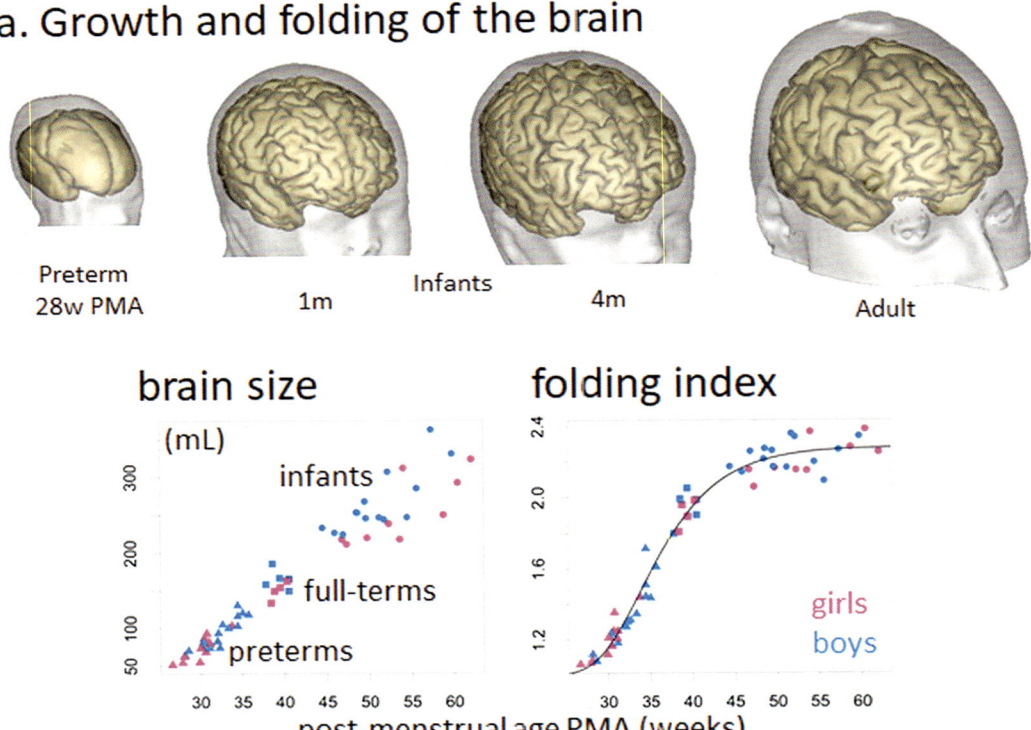

b. Maturation of cortical microstructure in infants

Figure 3.1 Structural changes of the brain during development. (a) The brain shows intense growth and folding during the last weeks of pregnancy and the first months of infancy, as demonstrated with anatomical MRI. Illustrations are provided for a preterm newborn at twenty-eight weeks of post-menstrual age (PMA), infants (at one and four months after birth), and an adult. Measures of brain size and folding index as a function of age provide a quantitative illustration of these intense changes (adapted from Dubois et al. (2019)). (b) The cortex also shows dramatic changes in microstructure complexity and maturation. A recent multi-parametric MRI approach highlighted strong differences between cortical regions in infants between one and five months of age. Colored maps adapted from Lebenberg et al. (2019), in agreement with post-mortem map of subcortical myelination by Flechsig (1920) adapted from Von Bonin (1950)

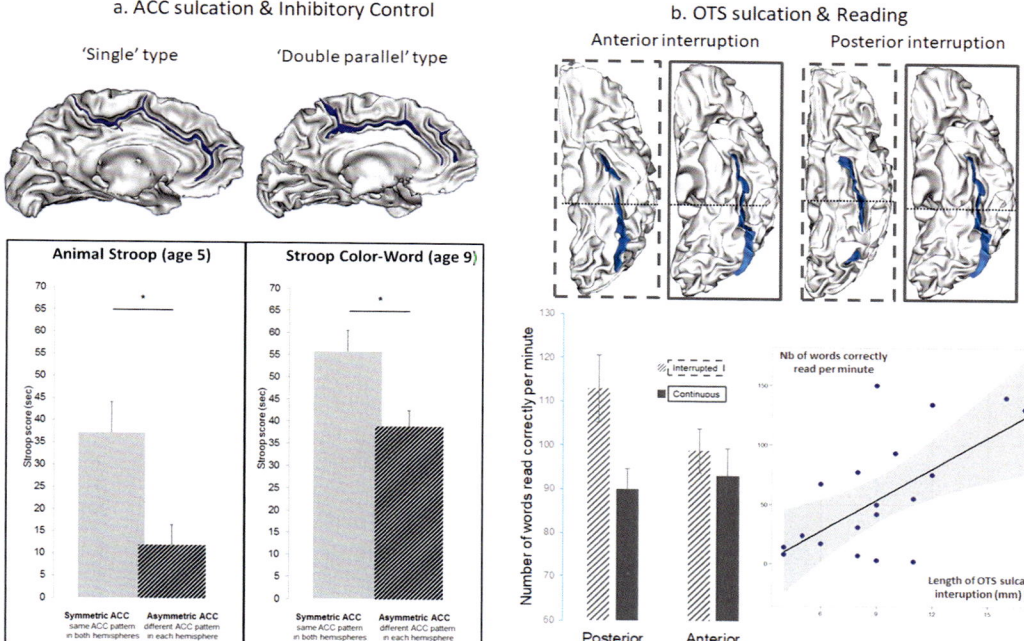

Figure 3.2 Cortical sulcation and cognitive efficiency. (a) Effects of the sulcation of the anterior cingulate cortex (ACC) on inhibitory control efficiency. Upper panel: the ACC can have two types of sulcal patterns: "single" type when only the cingulate sulcus was present and "double parallel" type when a paracingulate sulcus ran parallel to the cingulate sulcus (sulci are depicted in blue on the gray/white interface). Lower panel: Mean Stroop interference scores at age 5 (on the Animal Stroop task) and at age 9 (on the Color-Word Stroop task) in children with symmetrical (single or double parallel type in both hemispheres) and asymmetrical (single type in the right hemisphere and double type in the left hemisphere or vice versa) ACC sulcal patterns. Children with asymmetrical ACC sulcal patterns have better inhibitory control efficiency than children with symmetrical ACC sulcal patterns. Adapted from Borst et al. (2014) and Cachia et al. (2014). (b) Effect of Occipito-Temporal Sulcus (OTS) sulcation on reading ability. Upper panel: the left posterior OTS hosting the visual word form area (VWFA) can have two types of sulcal patterns: "continuous" type or "interrupted" type in case of a sulcal interruption located posteriorly, below the back dashed line. Lower panel: Number of words reads correctly in children or adult participants with continuous (in plain gray) or interrupted (in hatched gray) left OTS. Participants with interrupted OTS have better reading efficiency than participants with continuous OTS. The number of words read per minute is positively correlated with the length of the sulcal interruption. Adapted from Borst et al. (2016) and Cachia et al. (2018)

a. Tractography of white matter bundles

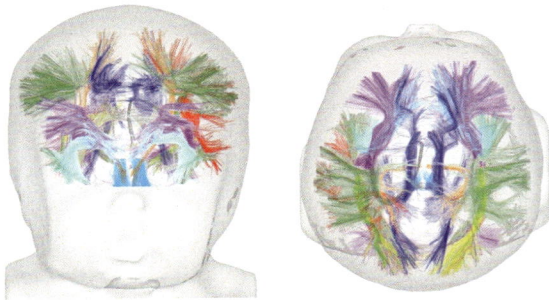

b. Maturation of white matter bundles in infants

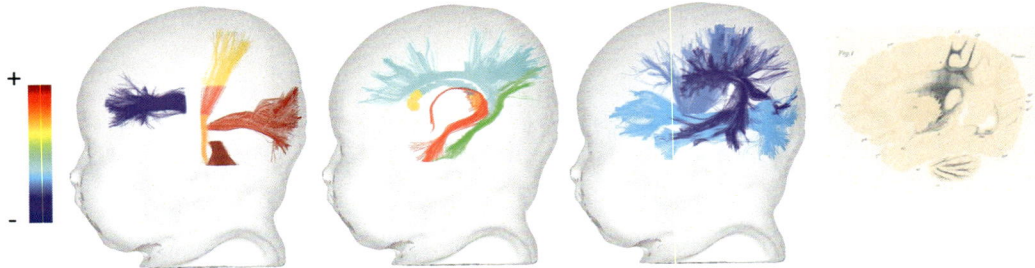

c. Maps of water fraction related to myelin

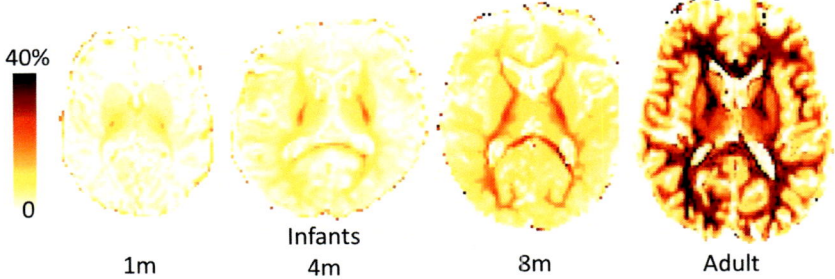

Figure 3.3 Structural changes of the white matter during development. (a) The brain shows an early organization in networks, with white matter bundles connecting distant and close regions, as illustrated here with diffusion MRI and tractography reconstructions in a one-month old infant. (b) The white matter also shows intense maturation after birth through the myelination process (Yakovlev & Lecours, 1967). A recent multi-parametric MRI approach confirmed strong differences between bundles in infants between one and five months of age (adapted from Dubois et al. (2015) and Kulikova et al. (2015) in agreement with a post-mortem map of subcortical myelination by Flechsig (1920) adapted from Von Bonin (1950)). (c) Different MRI techniques inform on myelination, such as the one computing the fraction of water related to myelin. These maps highlight the progression of myelination from central regions to the periphery. Adapted from Kulikova et al. (2016)

a. Visual responses to central stimuli in relation with visual pathways

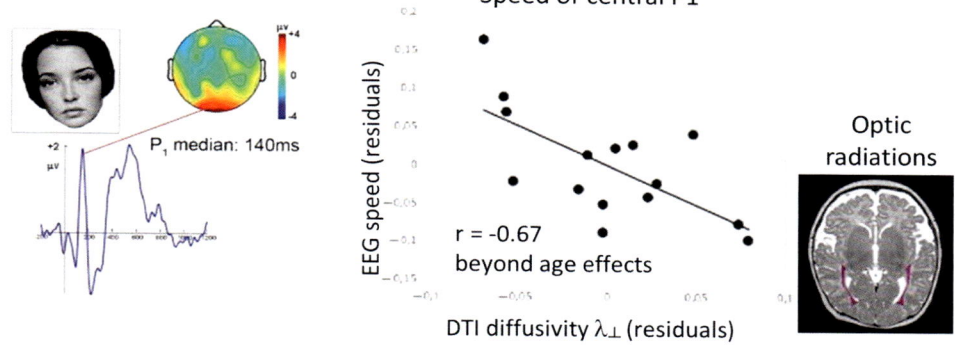

Speed of central P1

r = -0.67
beyond age effects

EEG speed (residuals)

DTI diffusivity $\lambda_\perp$ (residuals)

Optic radiations

P, median: 140ms

b. Visual responses to lateral stimuli in relation with callosal tracts

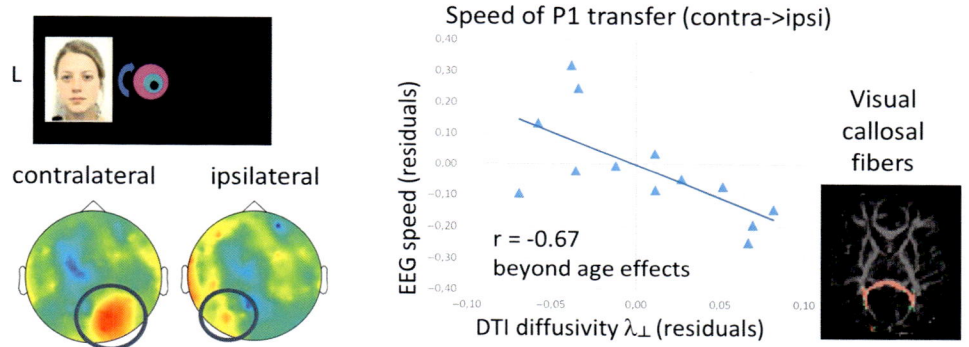

Speed of P1 transfer (contra->ipsi)

r = -0.67
beyond age effects

EEG speed (residuals)

DTI diffusivity $\lambda_\perp$ (residuals)

L

contralateral   ipsilateral

Visual callosal fibers

c. Auditory responses to lateral stimuli in relation with callosal tracts

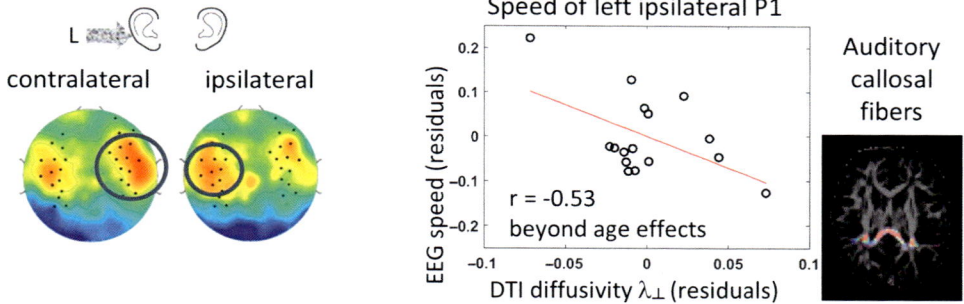

Speed of left ipsilateral P1

r = -0.53
beyond age effects

EEG speed (residuals)

DTI diffusivity $\lambda_\perp$ (residuals)

L

contralateral   ipsilateral

Auditory callosal fibers

Figure 3.4 Relationships between functional and structural markers of development. (a) During infancy, the speed of P1 responses to visual stimuli increases with age, while the visual pathways become myelinated, resulting in changes of DTI indices (e.g., a decrease in transverse diffusivity $\lambda_\perp$ in the optic radiation). Recent studies have shown that these functional and structural markers of visual maturation are related beyond age dependencies (adapted from Dubois et al. (2008d)). (b) Similar relationships have been observed for responses to visual stimuli presented laterally (in one hemifield at a time). The speed of the responses transfer, from the contralateral to the ipsilateral hemisphere, is related to the maturation of callosal fibers connecting visual regions (adapted from Adibpour et al. (2018a)). (c) Such relationships are more difficult to demonstrate for the auditory system because of strong asymmetries in the latency of responses to lateral stimuli (presented in one ear at a time) (Adibpour et al., 2018b). It seems that the speed of the left ipsilateral responses is related to the maturation of callosal fibers connecting auditory regions (adapted from Adibpour et al. (2020)). This suggests that early structural biases might lead to the functional lateralization for speech processing in the left hemisphere

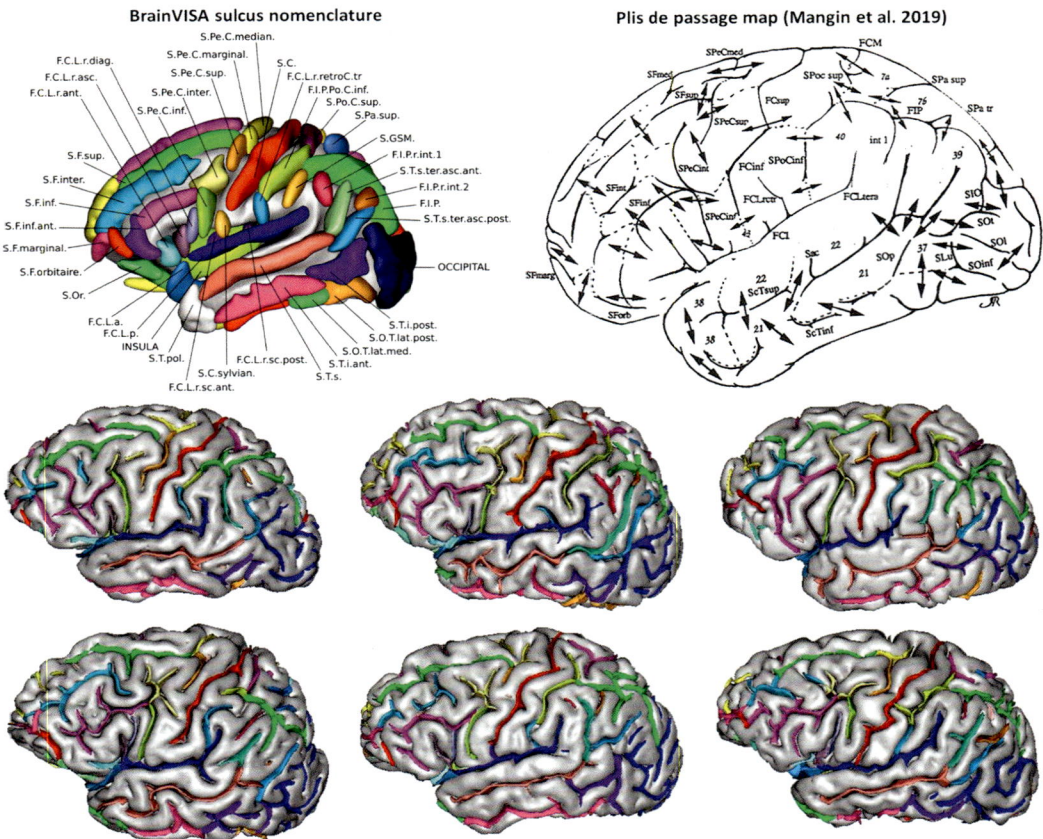

Figure 3.5 Top: Sulcus nomenclature and map of the standard sulcus interruptions. Bottom: The sulcus nomenclature projected on six different left hemispheres

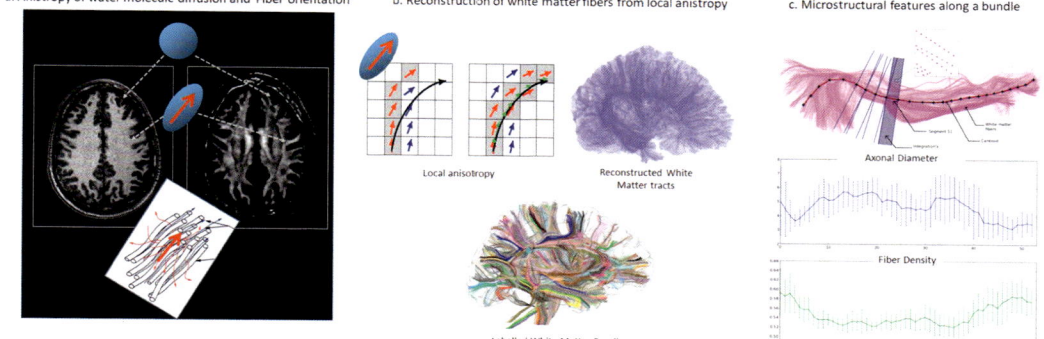

Figure 3.6 White matter microstructure and connectivity with diffusion MRI. (a) Water molecule diffusion is isotropic (sphere) in grey matter and anisotropic (ellipsoid) in grey matter. The main direction of water molecule diffusion (red arrow) indicates the main direction of the white matter fibers. (b) Whole white matter tracts can be mathematically reconstructed step-by-step using local tract direction derived from diffusion anisotropy. Main white matter bundles can be identified from all reconstructed tracts. (c) Microstructural features (e.g., axonal diameter, fiber density) can be estimated along each white matter bundle

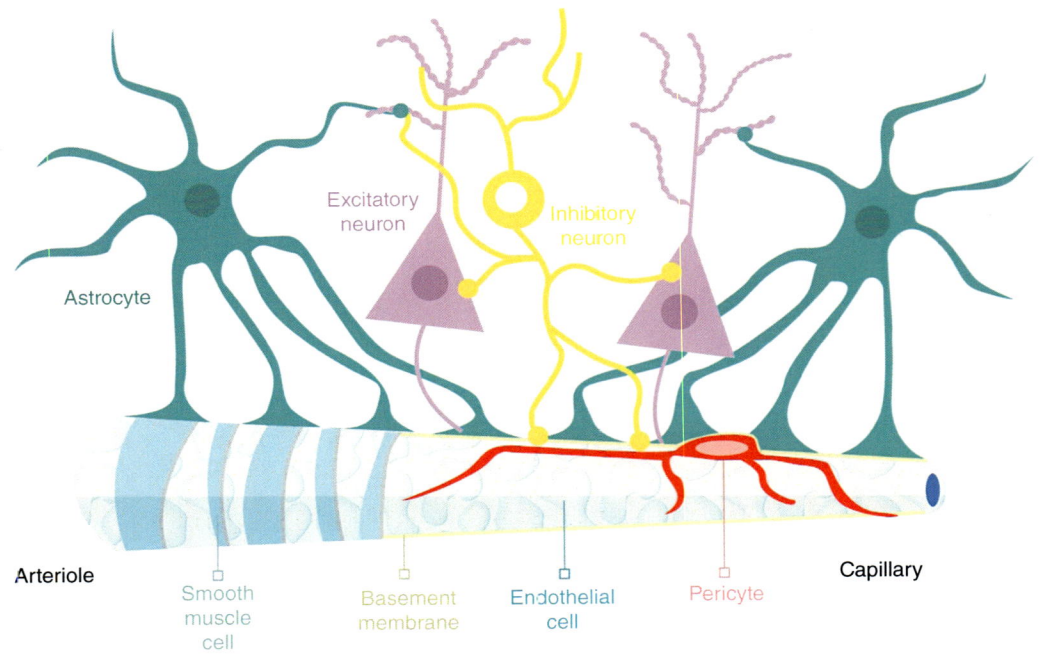

Figure 4.1 Neurovascular unit. From Hermann et al. (2015)

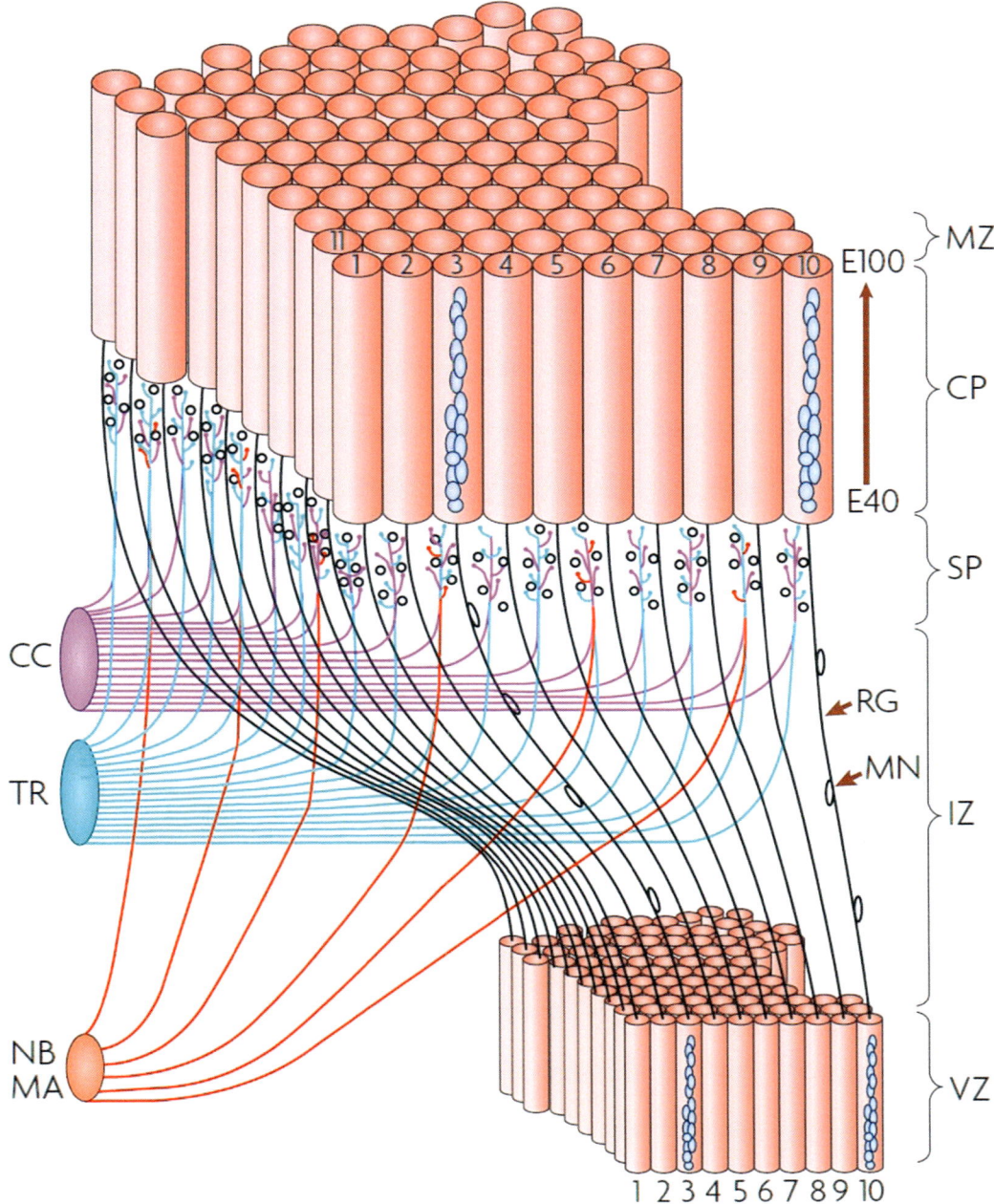

Figure 4.3 The radial unit hypothesis. 'The model of radial neuronal migration that underlies columnar organization based on Rakic (1974, 1995). The cohorts of neurons generated in the VZ traverse the intermediate zone (IZ) and subplate zone (SP) containing "waiting" afferents from several sources (cortico–cortical connections (CC), thalamic radiation (TR), nucleus basalis (NB), monoamine subcortical centres (MA)) and finally pass through the earlier generated deep layers before settling in at the interface between the cortical plate (CP) and marginal zone (MZ). The timing of neurogenesis (E40–E100) refers to the embryonic age in the macaque monkey (Bystron et al., 2006; Rakic, 1974, 1988). (The positional information of the neurons in the VZ and corresponding protomap within the SP and CP is preserved during cortical expansion by transient radial glial scaffolding. Further details can be viewed in the Rakic laboratory animated video of radial migration. RG, radial glia cell; MN, migrating neuron'. Legend to Figure 3 in Rakic (2009)

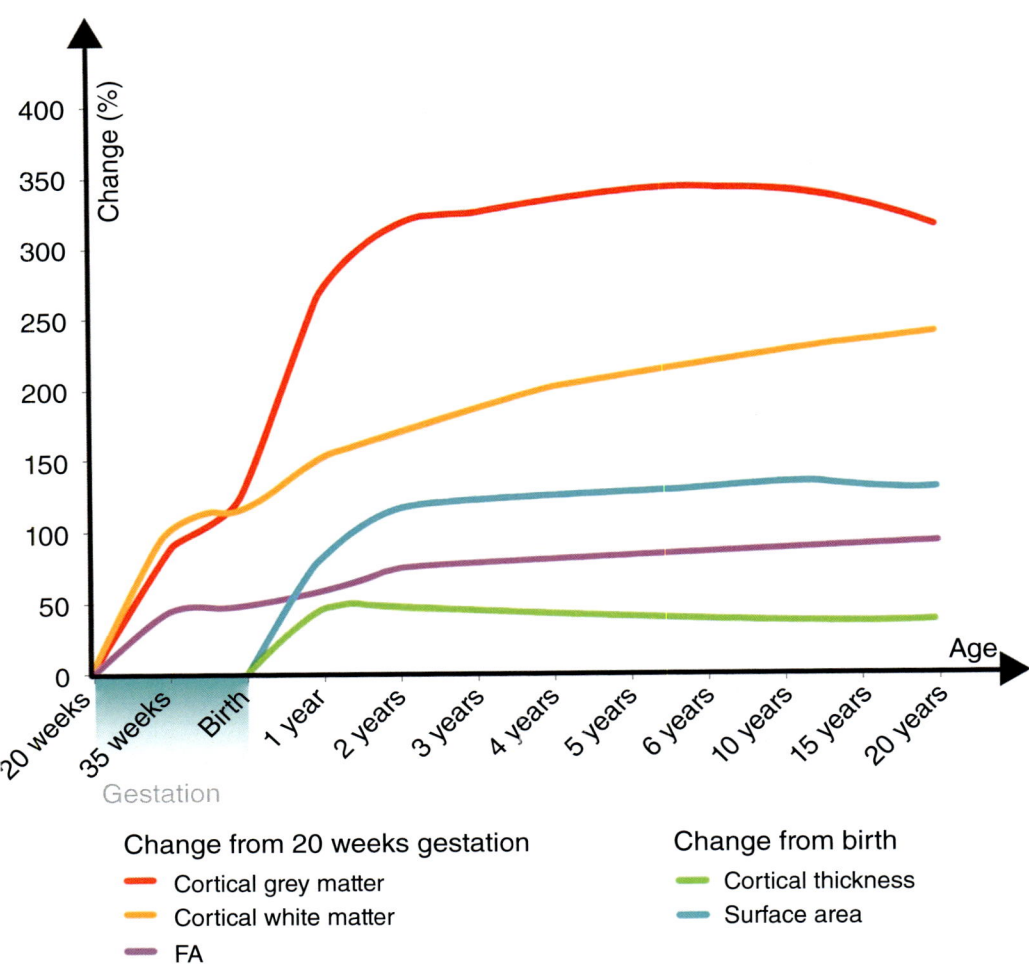

Figure 4.4 Estimated trajectories of cortical grey-matter and white-matter volumes during prenatal development, and cortical surface-area and thickness in post-natal development. From Gilmore et al. (2018)

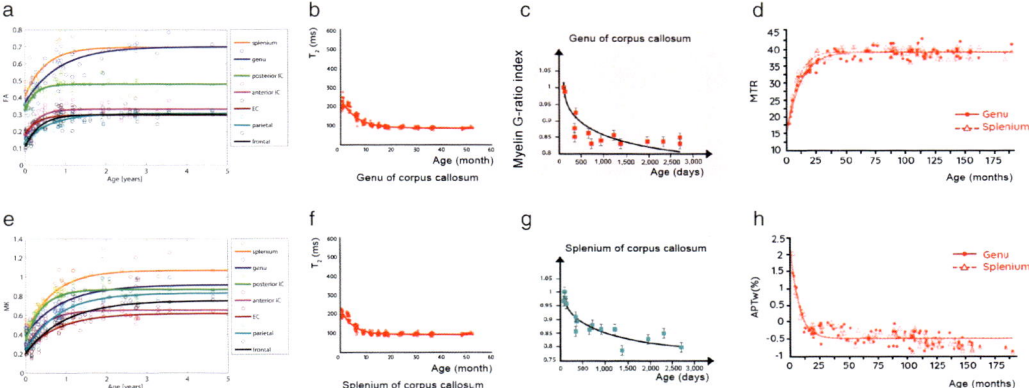

Figure 4.5 Developmental trajectories of structural properties of white matter during infancy and early childhood, as revealed with multi-modal MRI. Note different units (days, months, years) and ranges on the *x*-axis of the individual plots. DTI, Diffusion Tensor Imaging; DKI, Diffusion Kurtosis Imaging (a and e); T2 Relaxometry (b and f), g-ratio (c and g), MTR, Magnetization Transfer Ratio; APT, Amide Proton Transfer (d and h). From Lebel and Deoni (2018)

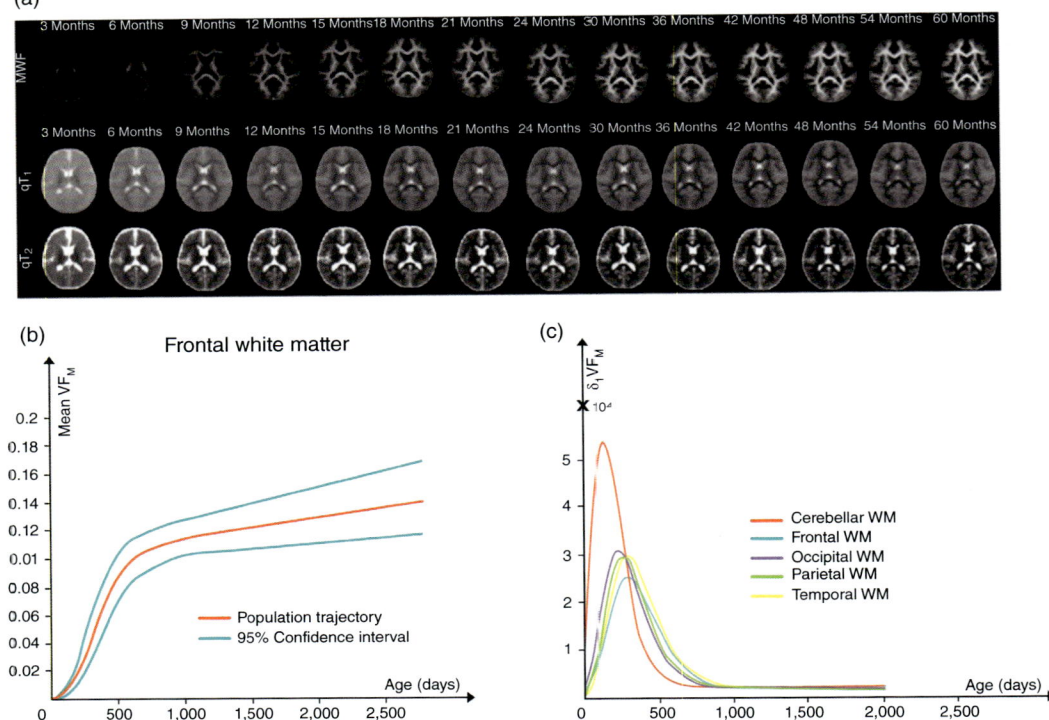

Figure 4.6 Myelin water fraction (MWF) and relaxation times in the developing brain. (a) Parametric images of MWF, T1 and T2 relaxation times during infancy and early childhood (from 3 to 60 months); (b) Mean values of MWF (denoted as VF_M on the y-axis) as a function of age in white matter of the frontal lobe; (c) Curves of the growth rate (denoted as $\delta_1 VF_M$ on the y-axis) in MWF in white matter of the four cerebral lobes and in the cerebellum. WM, White Matter. (a) from Lebel and Deoni (2018); (b) and (c) from Dean et al. (2015)

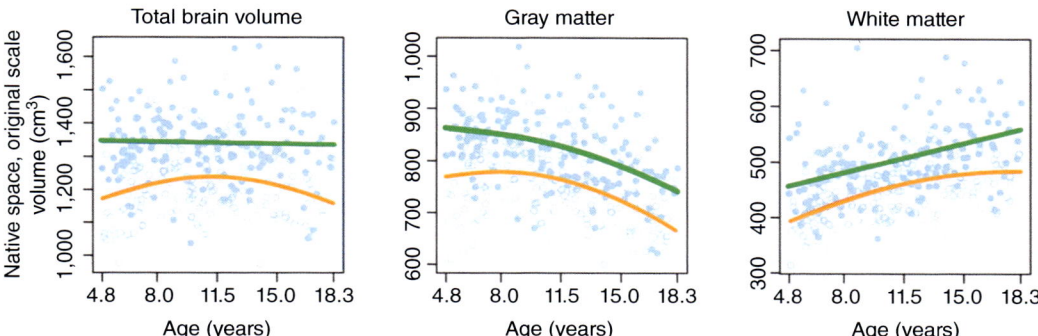

Figure 4.7 Total brain volume, as well as whole-brain (absolute) volumes of grey- and white-matter, derived from a combination of T1-weighted, T2-weighted and Proton Density-weighted images obtained in the NIH Paediatric Study. Cross-sectional age curves are indicated in blue (males) and red (females). In all three plots, the *y*-axis does not start at 0 cm³; the differences between the youngest (five years of age) and oldest (eighteen years of age) do not exceed 10 per cent. From the Brain Development Cooperative Group (2012)

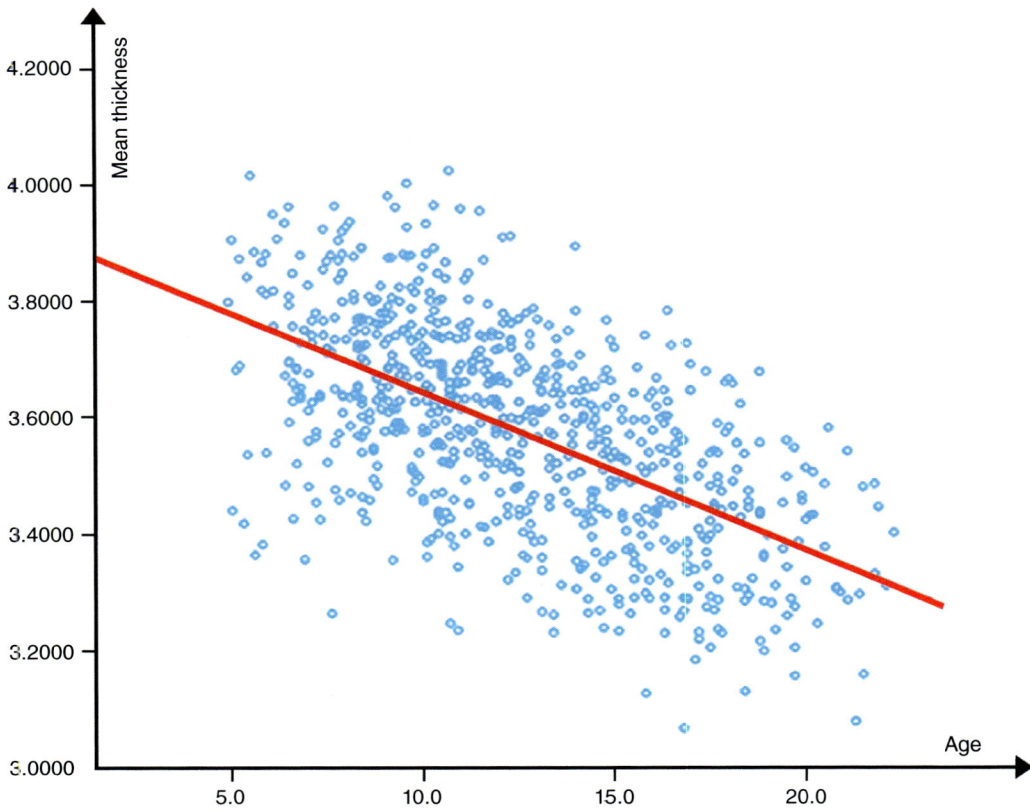

Figure 4.8 Decrease in cortical thickness between ten and twenty years of age. From Ducharme et al. (2016)

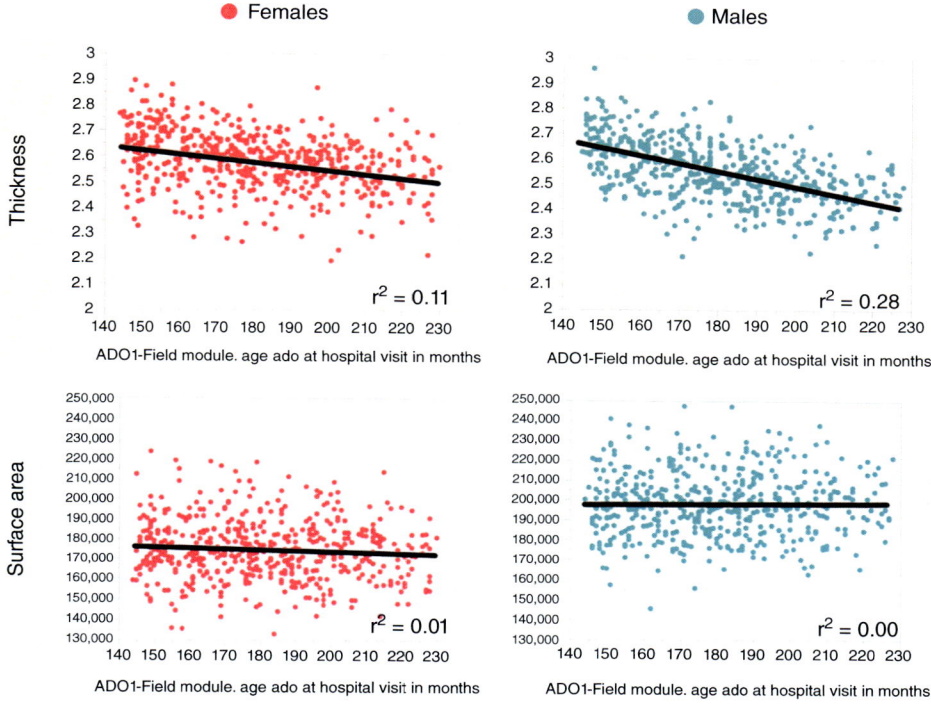

Figure 4.9 Cortical thickness and surface area in female (n = 509) and male (n = 479) adolescents. Data from the Saguenay Youth Study (Pausova et al., 2017)

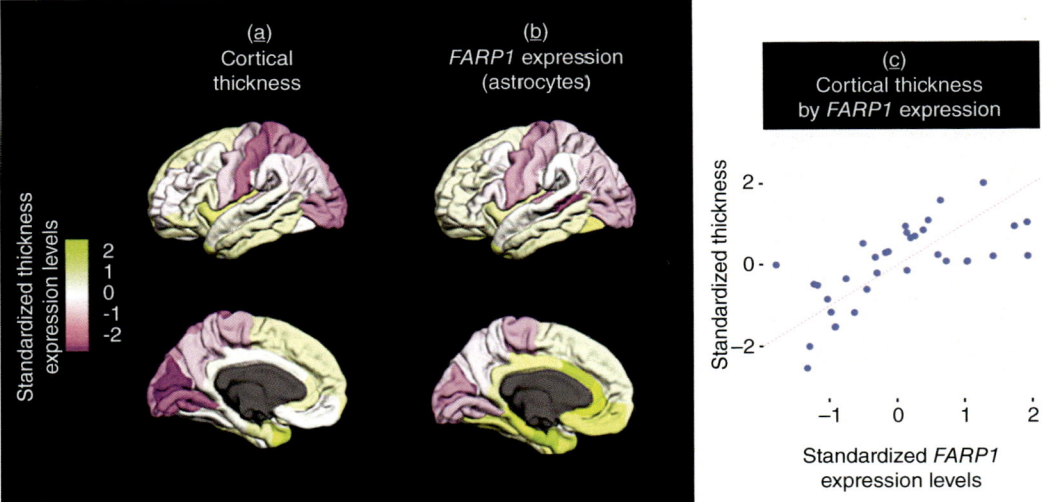

Figure 4.10 Virtual histology. Lateral (first row) and medial (second row) views of cortical thickness (Saguenay Youth Study) and gene expression levels (the Allen Human Brain Atlas). (a) Distribution of the standardized average cortical thickness measurements across the thirty-four cortical regions obtained from 981 SYS adolescents; (b) Distribution of the standardized median gene-expression level for *FARP1* (obtained from the Allen Human Brain Atlas). (c) Cortical thickness in the thirty-four cortical regions plotted as a function of *FARP1* expression in the same regions. The ranges of the standardized thickness values and expression levels are indicated by the colour-scale bar on the left. From Paus (2018)

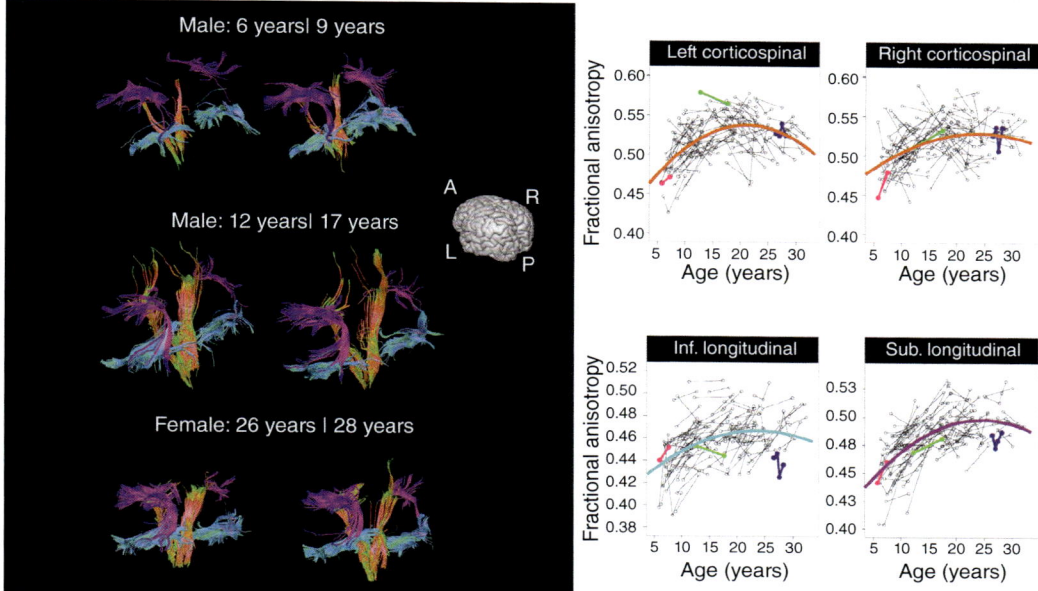

Figure 4.11 'Individual tractography results for the superior longitudinal fasciculus (orange), inferior longitudinal fasciculus (magenta), and corticospinal tracts (green) are shown in three representative healthy individuals at different ages. The whole dataset is shown in scatterplots at right, with data from the individuals shown at left identified in colour. The scatter plots show later maturation in the superior longitudinal fasciculus compared to the other regions. Ages of peak FA values were twenty-one and twenty-three years for the left and right corticospinal tracts, and twenty-four and twenty-five years for the inferior and superior longitudinal fasciculi, respectively.' Legend to Figure 5 in Lebel and Deoni (2018)

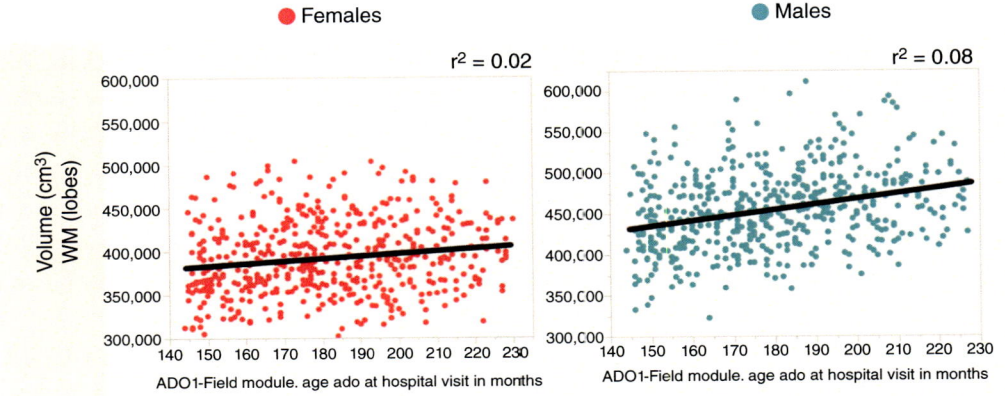

Figure 4.12 Volume of white matter (cerebral lobes) in female (n = 509) and male (n = 476) adolescents. Data from the Saguenay Youth Study (Pausova et al., 2017)

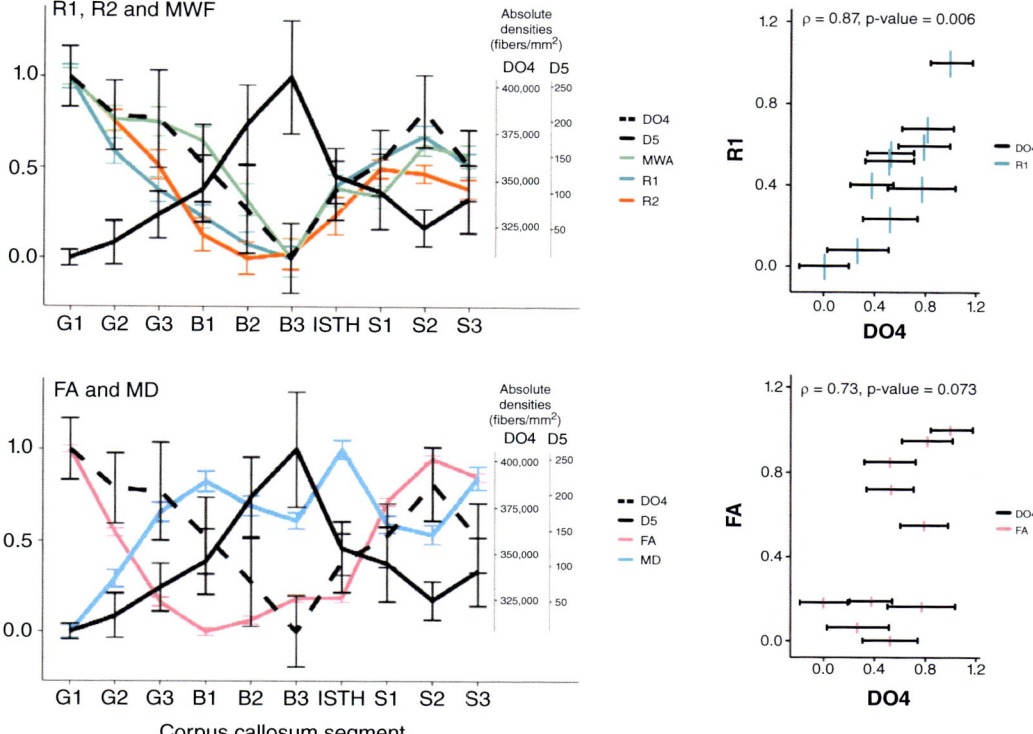

Figure 4.13 Multimodal imaging of the human corpus callosum: a comparison with histology. Left: Anterior–posterior profiles of callosal mid-sagittal histology (black; histological data are from Aboitiz et al. (1992)) and MRI measures (colour) with 95 per cent confidence intervals. All values were scaled to 0–1. Original absolute densities for 'small' (D04 for d > 0.4 µm) and 'large' (D5 for d > 5 µm) axons are shown on the right side of the plots. R1 and R2 (relaxation rate 1 and 2), MWF (myelin-water fraction), FA (fractional anisotropy) and MD (mean diffusivity). Right: Spearman correlations between R1 (top) and FA (bottom) and the density of 'small' axons. G1–G3, segments of the genu; B1–B3, segments of the body; ISTH, Isthmus; S1–S3, segments of the splenium. From Paus (2018) modified from Bjornholm et al. (2017).

Familiarization Trials
Trials 1 and 2

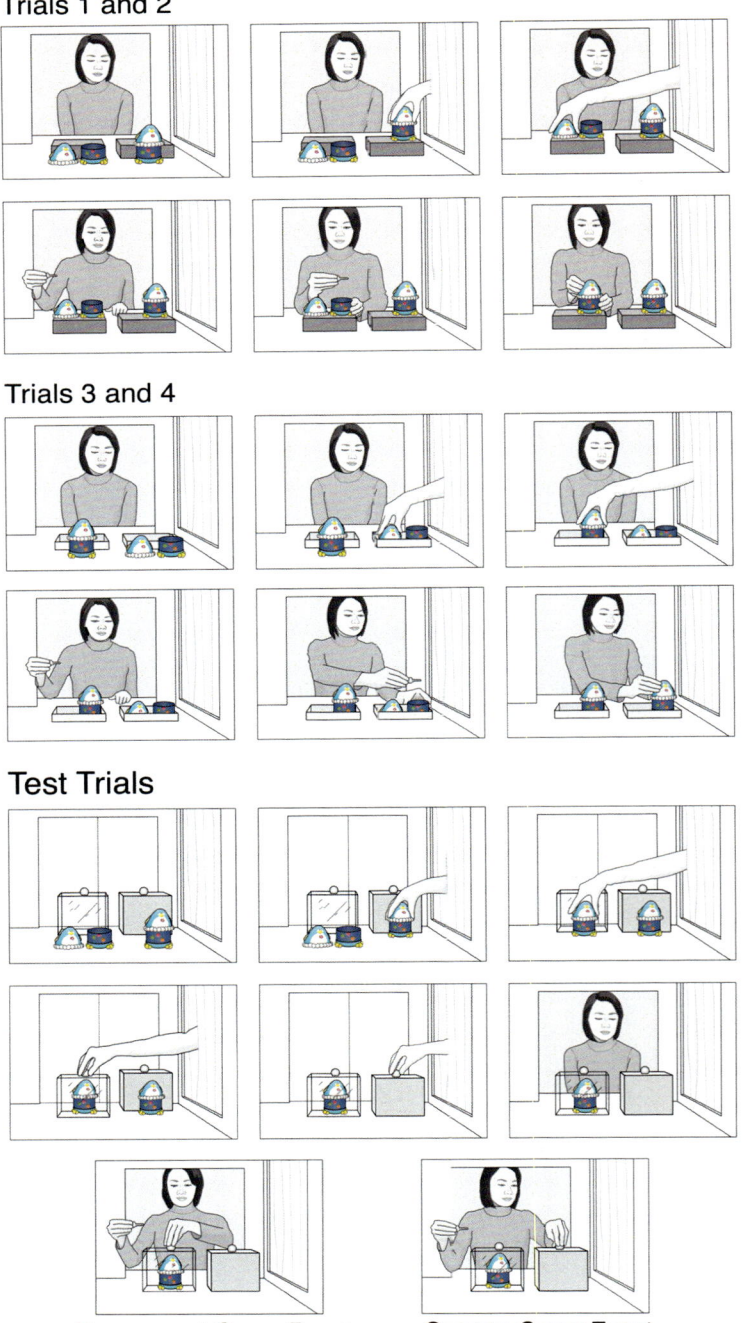

Trials 3 and 4

Test Trials

Transparent-Cover Event   Opaque-Cover Event

Figure 11.1 Familiarization and test trials shown in the false-belief condition of Scott and Baillargeon (2009). The order of the two test events was counterbalanced across infants

Rattling-Toy Trials

Silent-Toy Trials

Test Trials

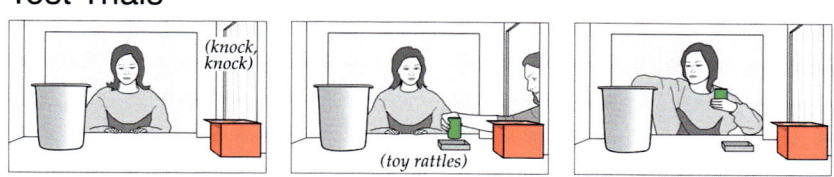

Each event began as shown above then continued as shown below.

Non-Matching Event

Matching Event

Figure 11.2 Familiarization and test trials shown in the deception condition of Scott et al. (2015)

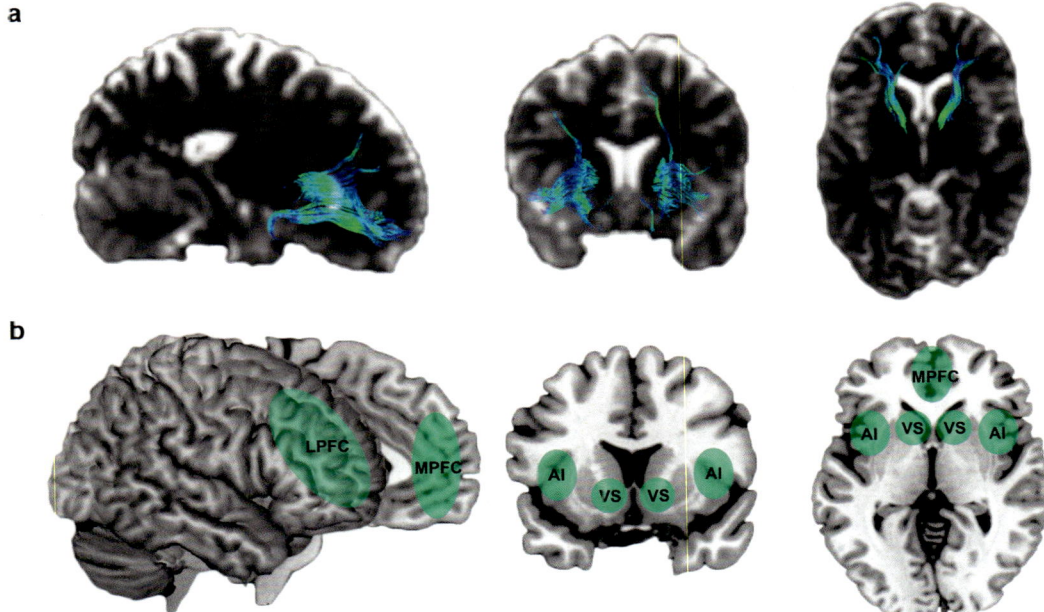

Figure 23.1 (a) Sagittal (left), coronal (middle), and axial (right) views of frontostriatal white matter bundles of one random participant (from Peper et al. (2013b) *Cerebral Cortex*, with permission). (b) Sagittal (left), coronal (middle), and axial (right) views of areas of activation involved in cognitive control and risky decision-making. LPFC = lateral prefrontal cortex; VS = ventral striatum; MPFC = medial prefrontal cortex; AI = anterior insula

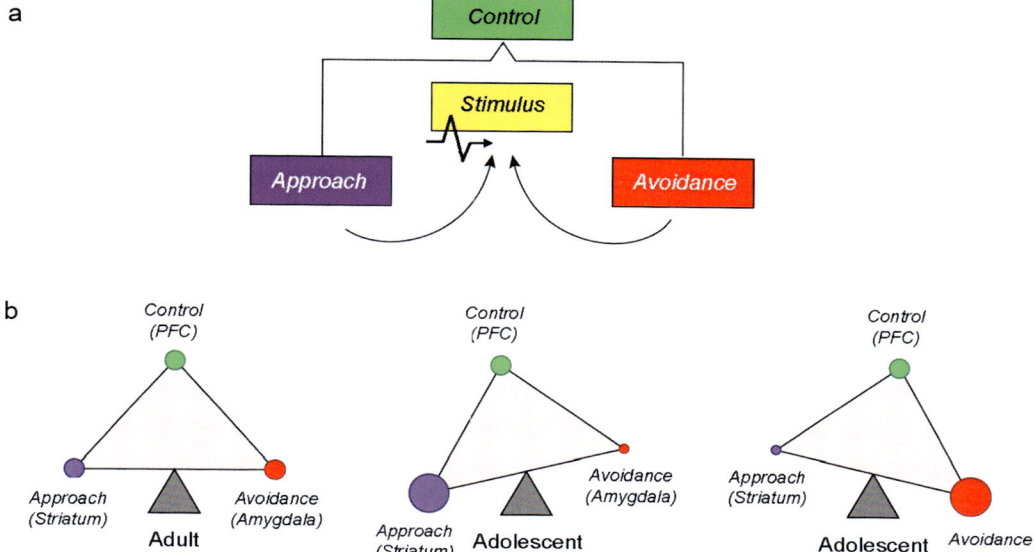

Figure 24.1 The triadic model. (a) This figure shows that, at the most elementary level, behavioral responses to a stimulus can take the two forms, approach or avoidance. The selection of the behavioral response is monitored or adjudicated by a supervisory controller (control system). In yellow is the stimulus (e.g., object, situation), purple is the approach response, red is the other possible avoidance response, and green is the controller. (b) This figure represents the neural translation (nodes of the triadic model) of the three behavioral entities described in (a). The term node refers to the brain regions that, together, form a neural system. The ventral striatum is the key node of the approach system, the amygdala of the avoidance system and the prefrontal cortex (PFC) of the control system. In addition, these three systems establish a balance that is represented as a triangle in equilibrium. The adult balance is used as the yardstick against which the adolescent balance is being compared. In an approach context, the adolescent balance is tilted toward the approach system, and away from the avoidance system, in a way that translates the proclivity of adolescent behavior toward approach, including risk-taking. In an avoidance context, the adolescent balance is tilted toward the avoidance system, and away from the approach system, in a way that translates the proclivity of adolescent behavior toward emotional intensity and lability, perhaps reflecting the peak onset of internalizing disorders in adolescence

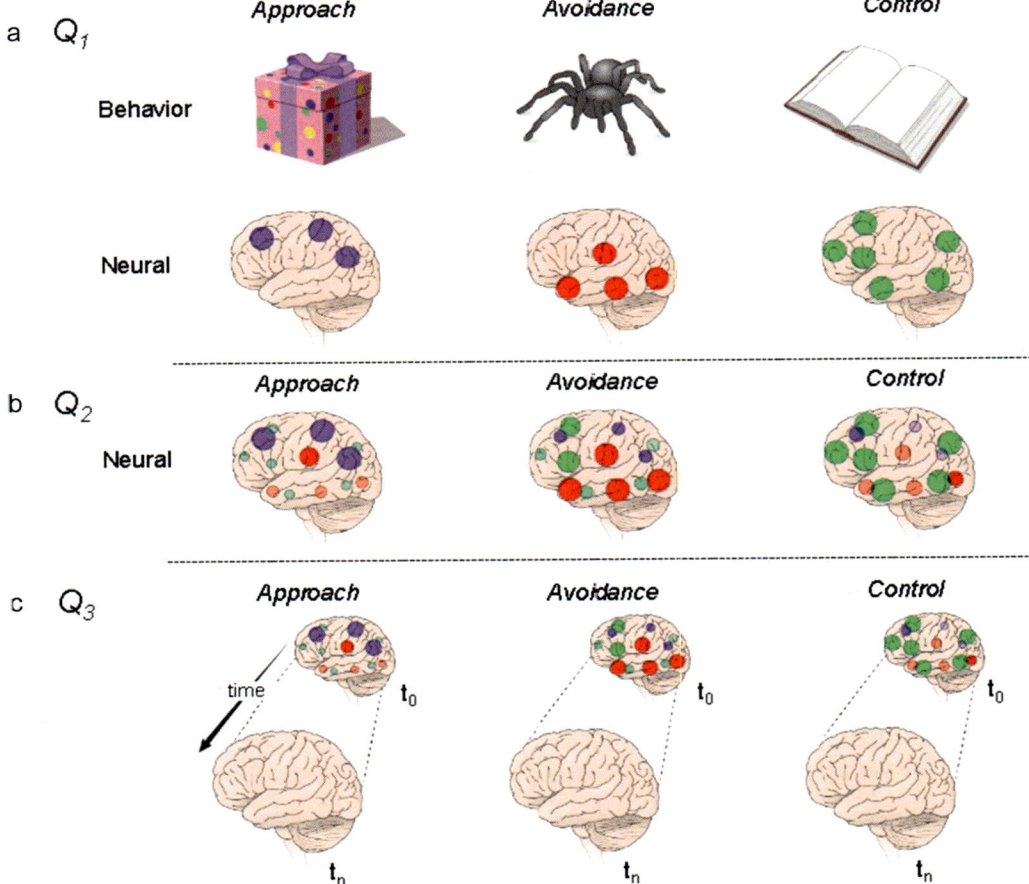

Figure 24.2 Overall strategy for testing the triadic neural systems model. The strategy involves three sequential stages of analyses, and fictitious data are used for clarity. (a) The upper panel addresses Question 1 and illustrates the two main analytic steps. First, the reduction and organization of behavioral variables into latent factors that map to the approach, avoidance, and cognitive domains. Second, the brain illustrations give the fictitious results of the predictive model (i.e., the core nodes that predict each of the three behavioral domain scores). In this fictitious example, three nodes map to the approach behavioral factor (A1–A3), four nodes to the avoidance factor (V1–V4), and six nodes to the control factor (C1–C6). (b) The middle panel addresses Question 2. It illustrates the fictitious neural predictors that are used to assess the functional overlaps and uniqueness of the three networks of the triadic model. Specifically, the thirteen neural nodes identified in Question 1 are all extracted in each task-related fMRI (approach, avoidance, and control), making up thirty-nine potential neural predictors. These extracted neural measures (n = 39) are submitted to ML algorithms. (c) The lower panel represents Question 3 showing the analyses being repeated at each follow-up time, based on a longitudinal study design

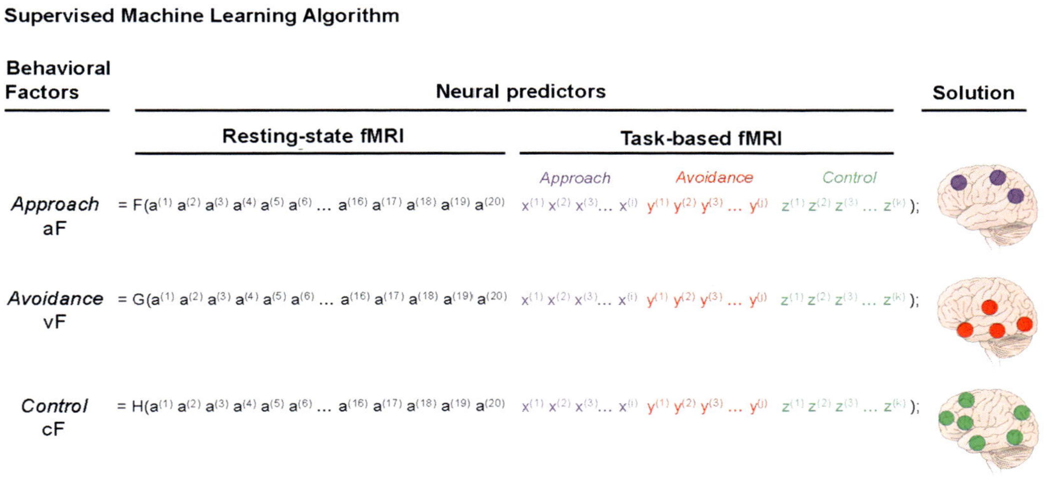

Supervised Machine Learning Algorithm

Behavioral Factors	Neural predictors		Solution
	Resting-state fMRI	Task-based fMRI	

Approach
aF
$= F(a^{(1)}\, a^{(2)}\, a^{(3)}\, a^{(4)}\, a^{(5)}\, a^{(6)} \ldots a^{(16)}\, a^{(17)}\, a^{(18)}\, a^{(19)}\, a^{(20)}\quad x^{(1)}\, x^{(2)}\, x^{(3)} \ldots x^{(i)}\quad y^{(1)}\, y^{(2)}\, y^{(3)} \ldots y^{(j)}\quad z^{(1)}\, z^{(2)}\, z^{(3)} \ldots z^{(k)}\,);$

Avoidance
vF
$= G(a^{(1)}\, a^{(2)}\, a^{(3)}\, a^{(4)}\, a^{(5)}\, a^{(6)} \ldots a^{(16)}\, a^{(17)}\, a^{(18)}\, a^{(19)}\, a^{(20)}\quad x^{(1)}\, x^{(2)}\, x^{(3)} \ldots x^{(i)}\quad y^{(1)}\, y^{(2)}\, y^{(3)} \ldots y^{(j)}\quad z^{(1)}\, z^{(2)}\, z^{(3)} \ldots z^{(k)}\,);$

Control
cF
$= H(a^{(1)}\, a^{(2)}\, a^{(3)}\, a^{(4)}\, a^{(5)}\, a^{(6)} \ldots a^{(16)}\, a^{(17)}\, a^{(18)}\, a^{(19)}\, a^{(20)}\quad x^{(1)}\, x^{(2)}\, x^{(3)} \ldots x^{(i)}\quad y^{(1)}\, y^{(2)}\, y^{(3)} \ldots y^{(j)}\quad z^{(1)}\, z^{(2)}\, z^{(3)} \ldots z^{(k)}\,);$

Task-based fMRI columns: *Approach*, *Avoidance*, *Control*

Figure 24.4 Strategy for addressing Question 1, Step-2 & Step-3: Supervised ML step. Step-2 consists of the gathering of the neural predictors, and Step-3 of the use of a supervised ML algorithm. This ML algorithm computes the relative predictive value of the extracted neural measures. As such, it provides the components (nodes) of the neural networks that best predict the behavioral factors previously identified in Step-1 (Figure 24.3). The predictive model is represented as an equation, equation-F for aF, equation-G for vF, and equation-H for cF. The components aF, vF, and cF are the behavioral factors identified in Question 1 Step-1. More specifically, $a^{(1)}$ is the first extracted value of the resting state fMRI, up to $a^{(20)}$, which is the value of the last extracted value that passes the significant threshold set for the resting state study (the n = 20 is arbitrary). The variable $x^{(1)}$ is the extracted value of the most significant regional activation of the approach-task based fMRI, the last value being $x^{(i)}$ (n = i extracted values from the approach scan); $y^{(1)}$ corresponds to the avoidance domain $y^{(j)}$ (n = j extracted values from the avoidance scan); and $z^{(k)}$ to the control domain, the last value being $z^{(k)}$ (n = k extracted values from the control scan). The brain illustrations on the right of the equations represent the solution of the ML analysis, which identifies the nodes (neural predictors) that best predict aF, vF, and cF, respectively (i.e., have the highest weight). The number of these regional activations (or nodes) are arbitrarily set to three for the approach factor, four for the avoidance factor, and six for the control factor. These nodes define the neural networks that best predict reactivity to the behavioral domains of the triadic model

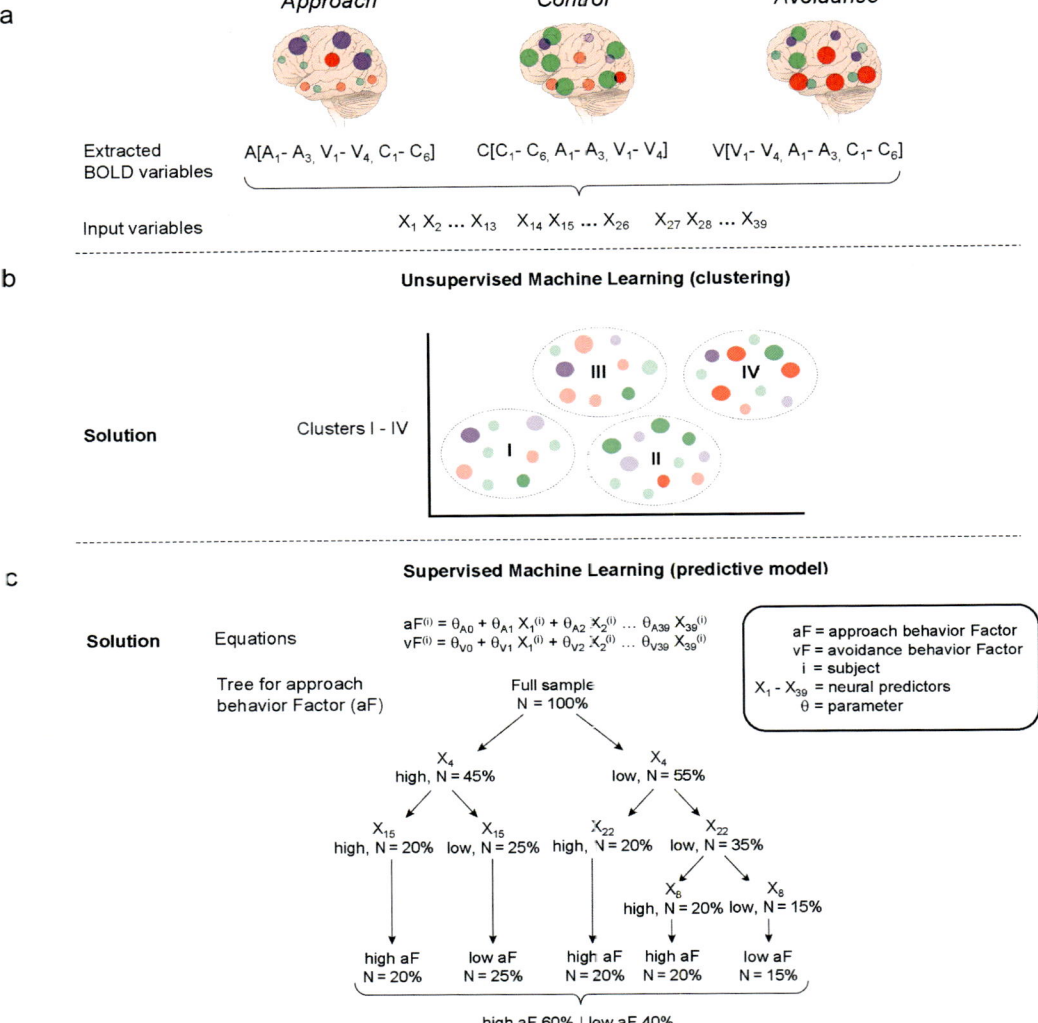

Figure 24.6 Strategy for Addressing Question 2, Step-1 to Step-3: Extraction of neural predictors, unsupervised ML clustering, and supervised ML to predict behavioral factors aF and vF. (a) Step-1: Extraction of neural predictors. This step consists of gathering all potential neural predictors of the behavioral factors identified in Question 1. These neural predictors (nodes) are now all extracted from every task-based fMRI scan (cognitive task fMRI, avoidance task fMRI, and approach task fMRI). The brain illustrations show the activation maps of all the nodes of interest, the approach nodes (purple), the avoidance nodes (red), and the control nodes (green), in each task-based fMRI scan. The extracted blood–oxygen-level-dependent (BOLD) variables are labeled A to refer to the approach domain (nodes A1–A3, associated with the approach domain in Question 1), V to refer to the avoidance domain (nodes V1–V4, associated with the avoidance domain in Question 1), and C to refer to the control domain (nodes C1–C6, associated with the control domain in Question 1). The schemes used for each domain are: A[A1–A3, V1–V4, C1–C6] (approach), V[V1–V4, A1–A3, C1–C6] (avoidance), and C[C1–C6, A1–A3, V1–V4] (control). The extracted thirty-nine regions of interest (ROIs)

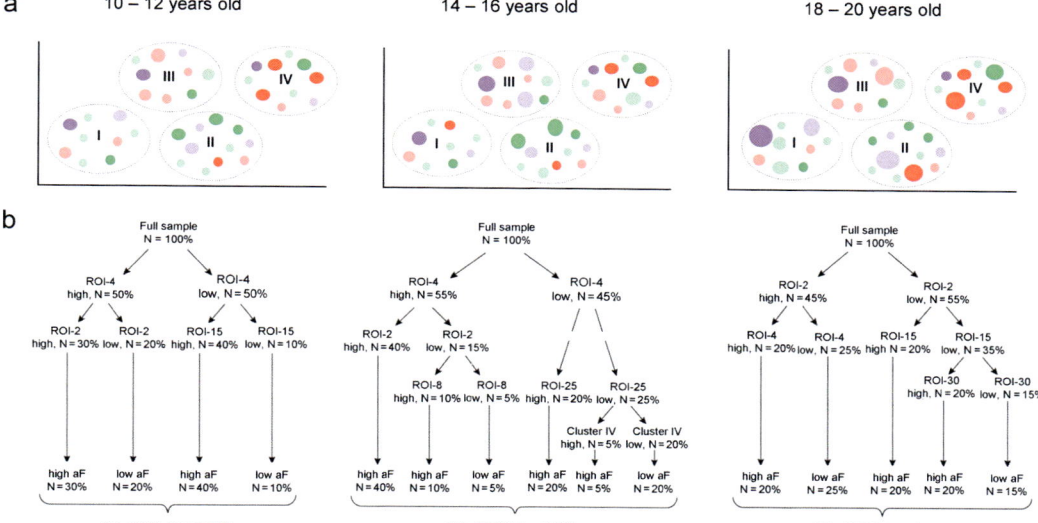

Figure 24.7 Fictitious results to Question 3: Decision trees across development. Fictitious examples of (a) composition of the clusters across ages and (b) changes in classification trees at different age groups. Differences among the composition of the clusters across ages can give clues as to how the nature of the networks evolve with maturation. Changes in classification trees at different age groups also informs the evolution of mechanisms underlying motivated behavior of approach in this example

---

Figure 24.6 (*cont.*) (thirteen per scan) are labelled X1 through X39. (b) Step-2: Unsupervised ML clustering. All the neural predictors (n = 39) are submitted to an unsupervised ML algorithm, which organizes the nodes into coherent clusters (nodes grouped into clusters as a function of their intrinsic characteristics). Here, the solution has been arbitrarily set to four clusters. The identity of the nodes within a given cluster can inform the likely underlying function of the cluster (i.e., striatal nodes can be inferred as mediating approach behavior). In other words, the clusters are composed of nodes which represent networks. This illustration shows a very clean separation of nodes into clusters. Such a clean picture is rarely the case, and more work is usually needed to conduct and interpret this type of analysis. Furthermore, it would have been possible to avoid this Step-2 and move directly from Step-1 to Step-3. However, such a short-cut would miss the opportunity to discover new networks (clusters) or to refine a priori hypotheses that are used in supervised ML. (c) Step-3: Supervised ML analysis. The clusters, predictors of the three behavioral domains, are used in two supervised ML algorithms, one for the approach domain and the other for the avoidance domain. The supervised ML algorithm leads to two types of solutions. The first type of solution uses a linear model to estimate the strength of each neural predictor. Each behavioral factor score is predicted by clusters associated with a constant unique parameter (theta) calculated by the ML algorithm. The second type of solution displays a decision tree to provide a hierarchical structure that represents the categorization of the sample as a function of the cluster values. In this example, the categorization leads to a sample divided into two groups, one group of individuals with low behavioral factor scores (in this example aF) and the other with high behavioral factor scores. This decision tree, which determines the propensity for approach behavior clearly shows how the different clusters (networks) work together to determine approach behavior

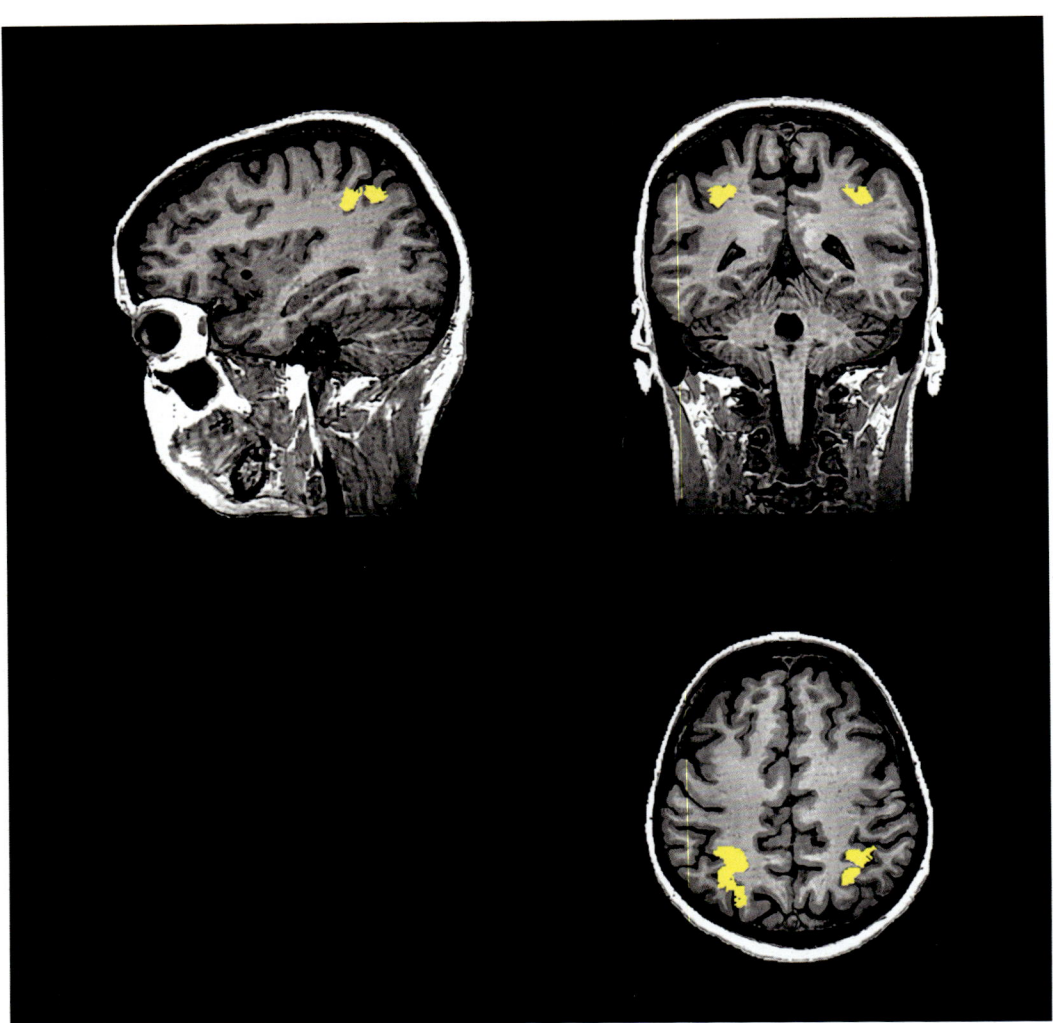

Figure 25.1 The intraparietal sulcus

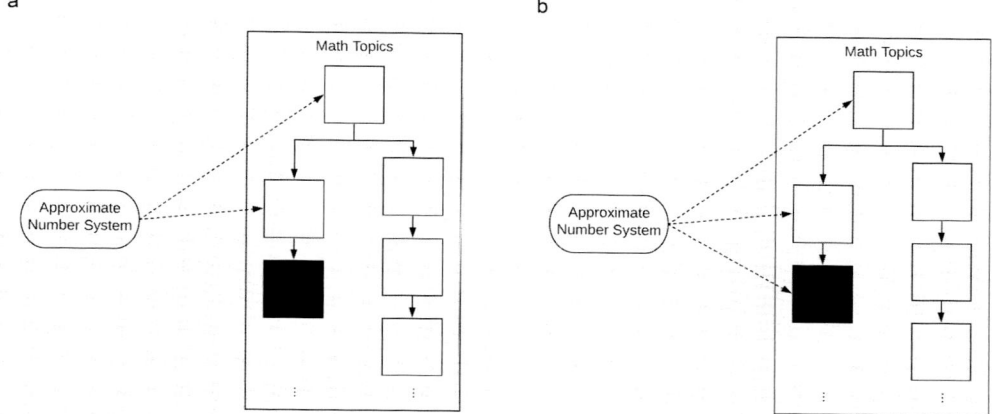

Figure 25.2 Two scenarios where ANS acuity will be related to the highlighted topic if prerequisite topics are not entered as a covariate to topic performance. In scenario A, there is a backdoor path through which ANS acuity would relate to the highlighted topic, and accounting for the ANS is not appropriate. In scenario B, even when the prerequisite topic is controlled for, the ANS is still related to the topic and, therefore, accounting for the ANS would be appropriate

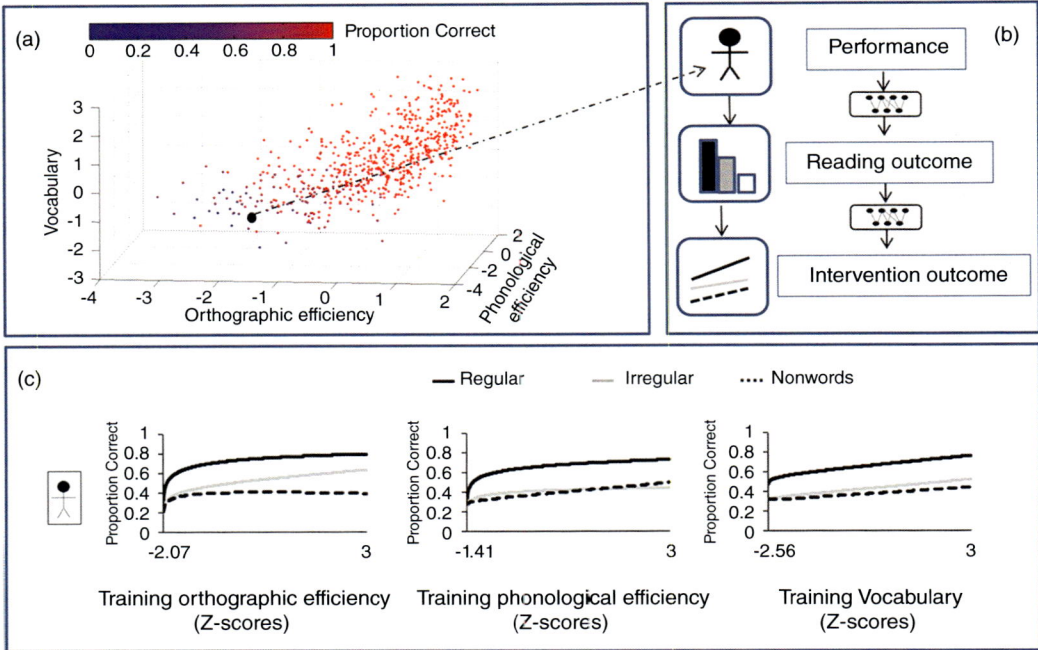

Figure 26.6 Predicting intervention outcomes through 'personalized' simulations. (a) Each child can be represented as a point in a three-dimensional deficit/performance space. (b) Depending on the performance of the child on the component tasks (her position in space), the model predicts the individual learning outcome. By systematically 'moving' the point along all possible dimensions (i.e., training the components), the model can predict intervention outcomes. (c) Simulated intervention outcomes for a child with a mixed profile on regular, irregular and non-words as a function of training orthographic efficiency, phonological efficiency and vocabulary. The x-axes are based on z-scores derived from the task scores of the 622 children, with the first number representing the measured performance of the child and the last number the maximum increase allowable after training.

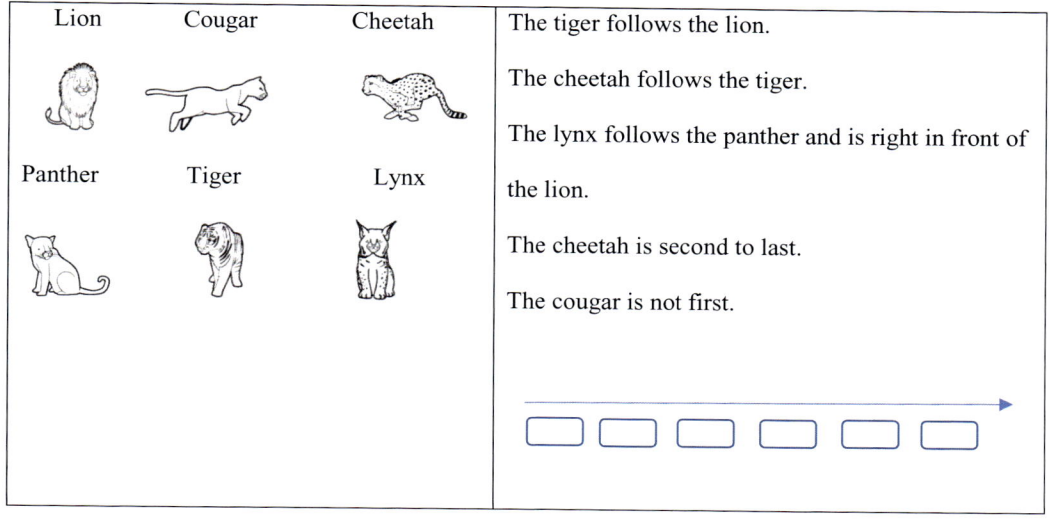

Figure 27.1 Example of materials used in the problem about transitive relations

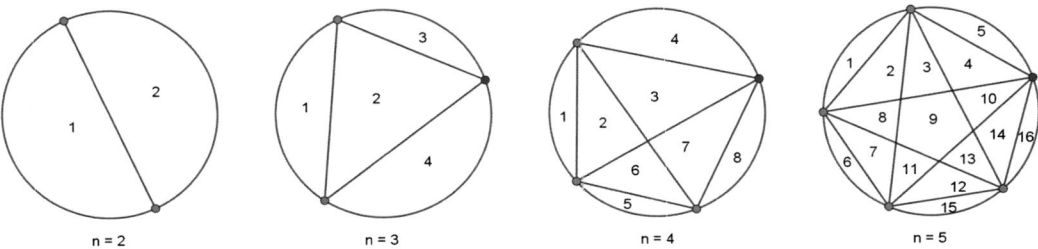

Figure 27.3 Examples of line configurations with different values of n in the geometry problem. For n = 2 there are two areas, for n = 3 there are four areas, for n = 4 there are eight areas, and for n = 5 there are sixteen areas. From these observations, students may use inductive reasoning to make the following conjecture: For n points on the circle, the number of areas is 2^{n-1}. However, perseverant students will realize that drawing lines with n = 6 leads to thirty-one areas (instead of thirty-two areas)! Thus, the formula must be incorrect

Recently, someone from Paul's school class started leaving letters on his table, without signing them. Paul wants to find out who it is! He leaves a cookie on his table.

And indeed, the next day the cookie is gone apart from some crumbs, and another letter has been left behind!

Good for Paul that he knows his classmates so well; he is quite sure that it is either Barbara or Sophie who leaves the letters, and he knows the following about them:

- Barbara likes eating Chocolate and Nuts, but no Cookies
- Sophie likes eating Cookies and Nuts a lot, but no Chocolate

Can you help Paul and tell him *Who is the mysterious letter-buddy?*

Figure 28.2 Can you help Paul to solve this riddle by providing your domain-general scientific reasoning skills?

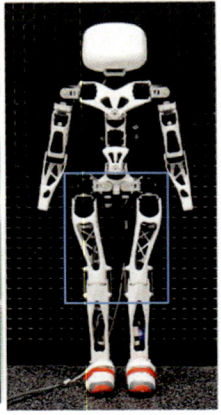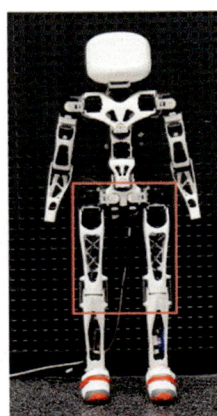

(a) bended thighs   (b) straight thighs

Figure 31.1 Open-source baby robots. Robots can help us model and study the complex interaction between the brain, the body, and the environment during cognitive development. Here we see two open-source robotic platforms used in laboratories. Being open-source allows open science through revealing all details in the experiments as well as replicability. Based on 3D printing, the Poppy platform allows fast and efficient exploration of various body morphologies (Lapeyre et al., 2014), such as leg shape (see alternatives on the right (a) and (b)), and how this can affect development of skills. Left: ICub; www.icub.org, right: Poppy www.poppy-project.org.

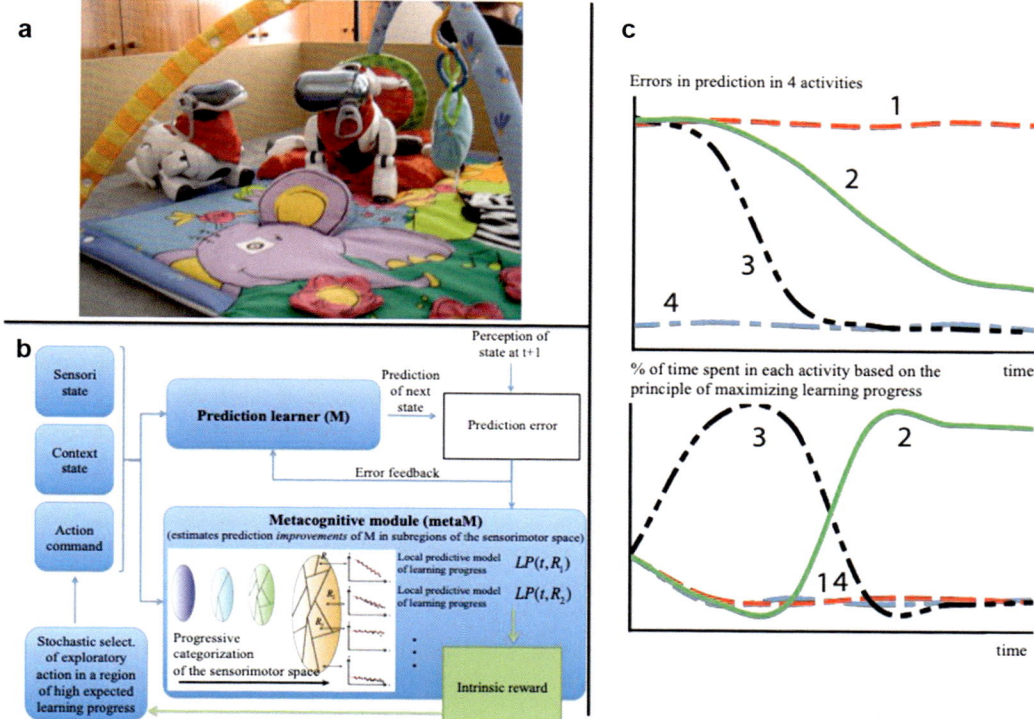

Figure 31.2 The playground experiment (Oudeyer & Kaplan, 2006; Oudeyer et al., 2007). (a) The learning context; (b) The computational architecture for curiosity-driven exploration in which the robot learner probabilistically selects experiences according to their potential for reducing uncertainty, that is, for learning progress; (c) Illustration of a self-organized developmental sequence where the robot automatically identifies, categorizes, and shifts from simple to more complex learning experiences. Figure adapted with permission from Gottlieb et al. (2013)

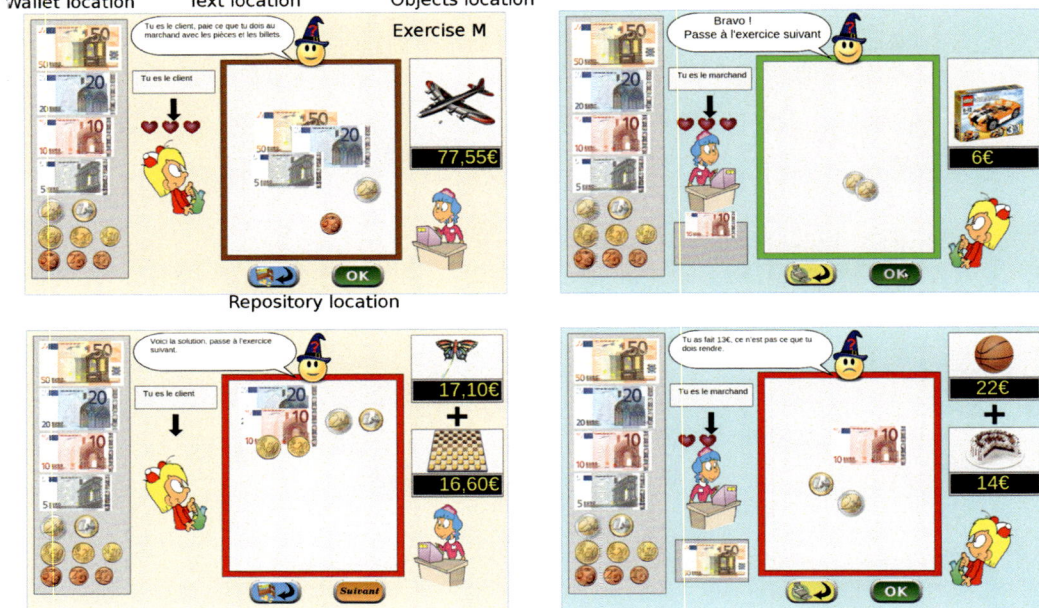

Figure 31.3 Educational game used in Clement et al. (2015): a scenario where elementary school children have to learn to manipulate money is used to teach them the decomposition of integer and decimal numbers. Four principal regions are defined in the graphical interface. The first is the wallet location where users can pick and drag the money items and drop them on the repository location to compose the correct price. The object and the price are present in the object location. Four different types of exercises exist: M (customer/one object), R (merchant/one object), MM (customer/two objects), RM (merchant/two objects). The intelligent tutoring system then dynamically proposes to students the exercises in which they are currently making maximal learning progress, targeting to maximize intrinsic motivation and learning efficiency

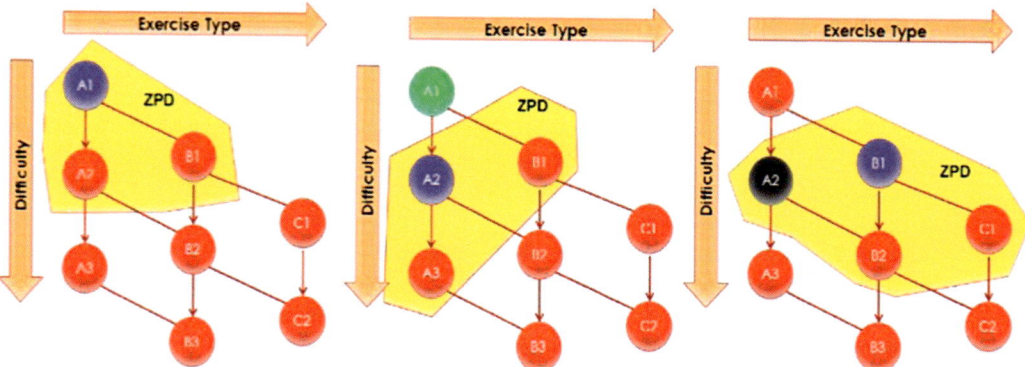

Figure 31.4 Example of the evolution of the zone-of-proximal development (ZPD) based on the empirical results of the student. The ZPD is the set of all activities that can be selected by the algorithm. The expert defines a set of preconditions between some of the activities (A1 → A2 → A3 ...), and activities that are qualitatively equal (A == B). Upon successfully solving A1 the ZPD is increased to include A3. When A2 does not achieve any progress, the ZPD is enlarged to include another exercise type C, not necessarily of higher or lower difficulty, for example, using a different modality, and A3 is temporarily removed from the ZPD. Adapted from Clement et al. (2015)

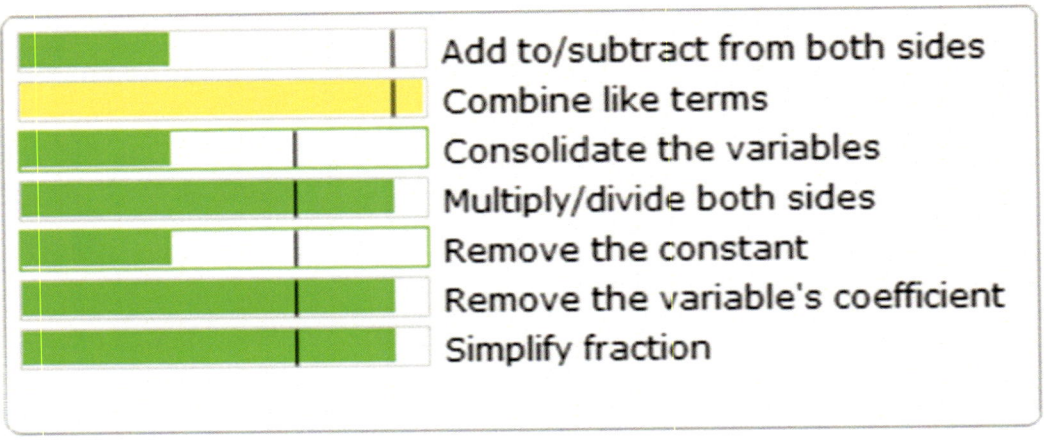

Figure 32.3 Long and Aleven's (2017) skills meter bars indicating the level of student skill mastery

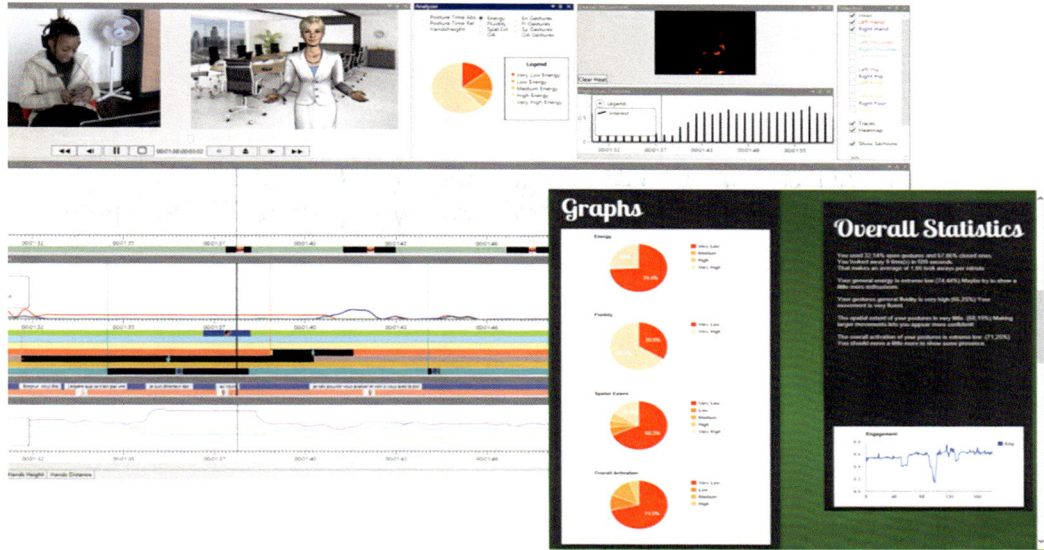

Figure 32.4 TARDIS scrutable OLM showing synchronized recordings of the learners interacting with the AI agents along with the interpretation of the learner's low-level social signals such as gaze patterns, gestures and voice activation in terms of higher-level judgements about the quality of those behaviours, e.g., energy in voice

Interaction Partner				
Condition	Computer Partner (CP)	Functional Robot (FR)	Anthropomorphic Robot (AR)	Human Partner (HP)
Humanlikeness	no human shape; no perceivable button pressing	no human shape; button pressing with artificial hands	humanlike shape; button pressing with humanlike hands	human shape; button pressing with human hands

Figure 32.5 Four conditions examined by Krach et al. (2008)

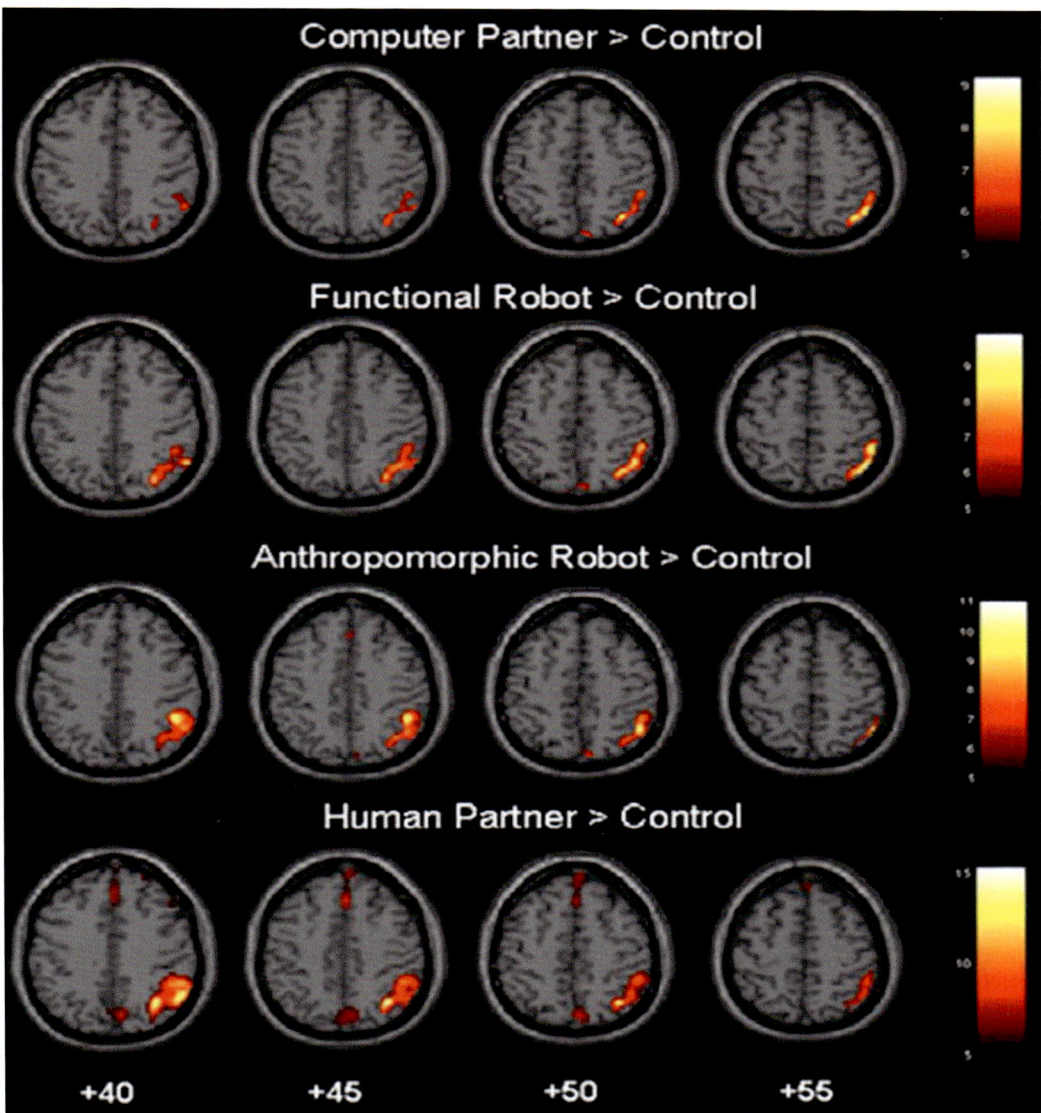

Figure 32.6 Regions associated with 'theory of mind' grow more active as the appearance of a technological opponent becomes more human-like, even when it is clearly not human (Krach et al. 2008)

Figure 32.7 A child playing with the ECHOES agent through the multi-touch screen interface (Left). The agent points to a flower that it wants a child to pick and put in the basket in a bid for attention and interaction with the child (Right)

Part III
Education and School-Learning Domains

25 Linking Cognitive Neuroscientific Research to Educational Practice in the Classroom

Nathan T. T. Lau and Daniel Ansari

In the past three decades, cognitive neuroscience has made substantial progress toward the understanding of how brain areas are associated with essential classroom skills – such as reading and arithmetic. This growing knowledge has inspired the possibility that these findings can be used to improve educational policy and practices. Indeed, ample enthusiasm can be seen in the field from the surge of reviews and discussion papers highlighting cognitive neuroscientific findings that may be relevant to educational practice (e.g., Blakemore & Frith, 2005; Goswami, 2004), and with the establishment of the peer-reviewed journal, *Mind, Brain, and Education*, and an international society of the same name to promote research linking cognitive neuroscience with education.

To date, one of the most successful and direct applications of cognitive neuroscience on education has been through increasing understanding of the causes of atypical development, such as dyscalculia (e.g., Butterworth, 2008), dyslexia (e.g., Eden et al., 2016), and autism (e.g., Anagnostou & Taylor, 2011). Within the field of mathematics education, studies on the origin of learning difficulties associated with dyscalculia have led to a greater understanding of the neural correlates (Bugden & Ansari, 2016) and behavioral profiles (Landerl et al., 2009) associated with the disorder. Application to education includes the deployment of diagnostic tools for early detection (e.g., Butterworth, 2003; Shalev et al.,

2005) as well as intervention programs that may help assuage the impact that dyscalculia has on learning (e.g., Kucian et al., 2011).

Furthermore, cognitive neuroscience has made progress in the identification and measurement of precursor skills that may predict success in later school-taught mathematical skills. For example, non-symbolic magnitude processing (Halberda & Feigenson, 2008), symbolic magnitude processing (De Smedt et al., 2009), spatial abilities (Hawes et al., 2015), and ordinal numerical abilities (e.g., Lyons & Beilock, 2011) have all been identified as potential basic predictors of children's future learning in the mathematics classroom. Individual variability of these skills has been demonstrated to be predictive of concurrent (e.g., Nosworthy et al., 2013) and future mathematics performance (e.g., Vanbinst et al., 2016). Interventions programs designed to train these component skills have been implemented with promising results (e.g., Dyson et al., 2013).

While cognitive neuroscience has made headway in influencing broader educational practice and policy, the influence that it has on day-to-day pedagogical practice is comparatively muted. By pedagogical practice, we are referring to the actions that educators take in designing and conducting classroom activities to aid students in learning of school-based mathematical topics. Indeed, the research community has expressed puzzlement concerning the fact that educators seem to disregard the inner workings of the brain in the classroom (e.g., Dehaene, 2008), which stand in contrast to their general enthusiasm toward the potential applications of cognitive neuroscientific findings (e.g., Pickering & Howard-Jones, 2007).

This situation is rather paradoxical: why is research in cognitive neuroscience struggling to influence practice in the classroom when it has made significant headway in other areas of education (such as atypical development)? In the following, we shall attempt to address this question specifically in the mathematics domain. For current purposes, we will not make a strong distinction between research findings from behavioral studies and neuroscientific studies. While the merits of behavioral versus neuroscientific research have been a topic of discussion (e.g., Bruer, 2016), the main concern of this chapter is addressing the reasons why the research is not used to inform classroom actions. As we will demonstrate in Sections 25.1–25.4, behavioral and neuroscientific research are often complementary in highlighting different aspects of development.

25.1 Knowledge Base for Teaching

Educators draw upon a large repertoire of knowledge in the classroom, and this knowledge influences the actions they take (Carpenter et al., 1996; Hoyle & John, 1995). However, different types of knowledge influence classroom actions in different manners. Before we can address why specifically cognitive neuroscientific research does not influence classroom actions, we first need to classify the types of knowledge that educators use, how this knowledge is then translated into action, and how research in cognitive neuroscience fits into this categorization.

At a glance, the teaching knowledge base can be broadly subdivided into two categories – *content knowledge* and *pedagogical knowledge*. Content knowledge refers to facts and concepts in a specific content domain, the structure of different facts in the domain, and the reasons why these facts and concepts are true (Schwab, 1982). For instance, in mathematics, the steps of long addition, why each step must be taken, and the knowledge of the prerequisites before long addition can be taught would constitute content knowledge. Pedagogical knowledge refers to a wide assortment of information that guides or constrains the actions that educators take in the classroom. This includes knowledge of learners, the learning process, curriculum, curricular goals, and educational contexts (Shulman, 1986, 1987). For example, knowledge on how students usually memorize material, their attention spans, and resources available in the classroom and the home would be considered part of pedagogical knowledge.

However, it has been argued that this dual categorization does not adequately describe the knowledge base that teachers rely upon to inform their actions in the classroom (Shulman, 1987). While content knowledge would describe the facts and concepts that educators need to transmit to students, it is deficient in describing the appropriate methods through which the transmission would best take place (i.e., knowing how to compute long addition versus knowing the best way to illustrate long addition to learners). Similarly, while pedagogical knowledge may lay out principles that guide or constrain educator actions in the classroom, it is lacking in providing the specific actions needed for the particular fact or concept being taught (i.e., knowing that students are biased toward looking at the numerator when comparing the sizes of two fractions versus knowing the best explanations to rectify and correct this bias).

Instead, it has been proposed that a third category of knowledge, dubbed *pedagogical content knowledge*, is the principal driver of teacher actions in the classroom (Grossman, 1990). As the name suggests, pedagogical content knowledge is a blending of content knowledge and pedagogical knowledge, and includes "how particular topics, problems, or issues are organized, represented, and adapted to the diverse interests and abilities of learners, and presented for instruction" (Shulman, 1987, p. 8). Put another way, pedagogical content knowledge is a specific instantiation of content knowledge, formatted in a way to be most conducive to student learning (Gess-Newsome, 1999). Pedagogical content knowledge would contain examples, representations, illustrations, and explanations of a topic, as well as ways to organize and structure these instigations to best cater to student characteristics and avoid student misunderstandings.

Importantly, it has been hypothesized that educators create pedagogical content knowledge through a process of transformation or translation of content knowledge while being informed by relevant pedagogical knowledge (Carter, 1990; Geddis, 1993). Even though pedagogical content knowledge is a blending of pedagogical and content knowledge, it is fundamentally examples and organizations of content knowledge. The role of pedagogical knowledge is to guide educators toward creating an appropriate set of pedagogical content knowledge, and the role of content knowledge is to be the medium that is transformed. For example, when planning lessons for single digit multiplication (content knowledge), an educator may be guided by the knowledge that the learning of multiplication relies heavily on memorization and that memorization is aided by sleep (pedagogical knowledge) and therefore design lessons to be staggered across multiple days (pedagogical content knowledge).

The three knowledge types, content knowledge, pedagogical knowledge, and pedagogical content knowledge, can be differentiated thusly. In any particular lesson, content knowledge can be construed as the facts and topics that educators are attempting to convey, and pedagogical knowledge would be the relevant surrounding knowledge that informs educators on how the lesson should be carried out. The ultimate actions that educators decide to take in the classroom are informed by pedagogical content knowledge, which refers to a specific set of examples, representations, illustrations, and explanations that the educator created for the purpose of teaching that specific topic.

25.2 The Generation of Pedagogical Content Knowledge

Two aspects of pedagogical content knowledge generation should be noted. First, the process itself and the corresponding output are topic-specific (Hashweh, 2005; Magnusson et al., 1999). The reason is that the generated examples, representations, illustrations, and explanations depend on the topic being taught. Even if two topics are informed by the same set of pedagogical knowledge, the generated pedagogical content knowledge would be specific to the topic being taught. For instance, educators will generate different examples (pedagogical content knowledge) depending on whether the topic being taught is addition or multiplication (content knowledge), even if the surrounding conditions (pedagogical knowledge) are the same. Consequently, this topic specificity would dictate what is considered relevant pedagogical knowledge to inform the process. Specifically, pedagogical knowledge can be general to all topics or specific to some or one topic in particular. For example, while the knowledge that younger children have shorter attention spans may apply to both addition and multiplication, the knowledge that multiplication may require more rote memorization is not relevant to generating examples for teaching addition.

Second, the generated pedagogical content knowledge can be idiosyncratic depending on the available pedagogical knowledge (Mason, 1999). Factors such as differences in student interest and abilities, available curricular material, and physical resource constraints may alter the pedagogical content knowledge that is generated at any instance. For example, the knowledge that a certain class of students tends to have shorter than normal attention spans may prompt the educator to generate examples and explanations that do not demand attention for too long of a period.

Importantly, one aspect of pedagogical knowledge that heavily alters the generated pedagogical content knowledge is the structure of the topics being taught and the students' progression through this structure. In the mathematics content domain, a topic is commonly viewed as the product that students are expected to produce and the operations and procedures used to generate the product, given a set of resources available to the students (e.g., the steps to produce the sum of two single digit numbers, given a horizontally presented question; Doyle, 1983; Stein et al., 1996). While different topics can be largely separated and the order of presentation may not be so important (e.g., addition and measurements), other topics are hierarchically organized (e.g., one-digit addition and two-digit addition). Students' current progress through this hierarchical structure (i.e., whether students have learned the topic on a lower rung of the hierarchy) influences the formation of pedagogical content knowledge. That is, generated instantiations for a more advanced topic in the hierarchy would differ depending on whether students possess some relevant prerequisite knowledge.

25.3 Cognitive Neuroscientific Research as Pedagogical Knowledge

Classifying educator knowledge under this three-way organization, research in cognitive neuroscience would squarely fall into the category of pedagogical knowledge – knowledge that is used to guide or constrict teacher actions in the classroom. The question that we queried at the beginning of this chapter can, therefore, be restated as such: why do educators seem to not view current cognitive neuroscientific research as relevant pedagogical knowledge when in the process of constructing pedagogical content knowledge from content knowledge?

In the following, we argue that this may be partly due to incompatibilities between, on the one hand, the current methods that cognitive neuroscientific research is attempting to link to education, and, on the other hand, the characteristics of the pedagogical content knowledge generation, specifically, that the generation process is topic-specific and that topics may be hierarchically organized. In the following, we shall illustrate this incompatibility using a case study, explore how current methods are attempting to link research to education, and discuss the incompatibilities that arise.

25.4 An Example of Cognitive Neuroscientific Research Potentially Relevant to Education

In the past few decades, the lion's share of research attention has been focused on the concept of an innate sense of numbers (see Chapter 11, on Infant numerical cognition). This so-called approximate number system (ANS) can be experienced when we estimate the number of people in a room or guess the number of gumballs in a machine. Converging evidence from developmental psychology (e.g., Xu & Spelke, 2000), animal psychology (e.g.,

Rugani et al., 2009), and comparative psychology (e.g., Cantlon & Brannon, 2006) suggest that humans are born with this ability and that humans and animals share this rudimentary system of quantity perception. In both humans and animals, quantity representations by means of the ANS are characterized by its imprecision. For most quantities,[1] the ANS follows the Weber-Fechner law whereby the ease of distinguishing between two quantities as represented by the ANS is related to the ratio of the two numbers rather than any absolute difference. Notably, when prohibited from counting, human adults showed similar performance characteristics to chimpanzees – suggesting that humans and animals rely on similar mechanisms to complete the task (Agrillo et al., 2012; Beran et al., 2011a, 2011b; Cantlon & Brannon, 2006).

The cross-species prevalence and seeming innateness suggest that the ANS is evolutionarily ancient. This has led researchers to examine whether this approximate sense of number may be related to learning and mastery of the uniquely human invention of symbolic numbers – the ability to represent numerical values using symbols, such as with written and spoken words. Interestingly, there is both behavioral and imaging evidence to suggest that these two systems are linked in humans. For instance, the behavioral characteristics of performances in a *non-symbolic* comparison task (i.e., deciding which of two arrays of dots have contained more dots) are very similar to the performances in a symbolic comparison task (i.e., deciding which of two symbolic numerals shown is larger). Indeed, both children's (e.g., Holloway & Ansari, 2008; Sasanguie et al., 2013) and adults' (e.g., Halberda et al., 2012; Nys et al., 2013) performance in the non-symbolic comparison task showed markers of the Weber-Fechner law – the distance and size effects. Notably, children's (e.g., Holloway & Ansari, 2008;

Sasanguie et al., 2012) and adults' (e.g., Sasanguie et al., 2017) task performance in symbolic number comparison mirrors these very same behavioral characteristics. These results suggest that the mechanisms that underlie symbolic and non-symbolic number comparison may be very similar or, indeed, may be underpinned by the same neural mechanisms.

Corroborating the results of these behavioral studies, several functional magnetic resonance imaging (fMRI) studies have shown that the parietal cortex – specifically the Intraparietal Sulcus (IPS) – is activated for both non-symbolic and symbolic comparison (Figure 25.1, see Nieder & Dehaene, 2009 for a review). Recently, imaging studies have employed an adaptation paradigm to examine the brain's response symbolic and non-symbolic numbers (e.g., Holloway et al., 2013; Piazza et al., 2007). Adaptation studies involve the repeated presentation of a specific quantity (either in symbolic or non-symbolic format), followed by a deviant number. During the repeated presentation, populations of neurons that are sensitive to the number are habituated to the repeated stimulus, and the presentation of the deviant number elicits a rebound effect that is sensitive to the distance between the adapter and deviant. Remarkably, it was observed that the IPS adaptation seem to occur irrespective of whether the adapter and deviant were cross-notation (e.g., adapting to a non-symbolic number and presenting with a symbolic number deviant or vice versa) or same notation (Piazza et al., 2007).

---

[1] This is true for quantities above four in humans. Humans have the ability to perceive quickly and accurately sets of items below four (Antell & Keating, 1983; Feigenson et al., 2002). There is some evidence to show that this ability may share the same mechanisms with the object tracking system (Chesney & Haladjian, 2011).

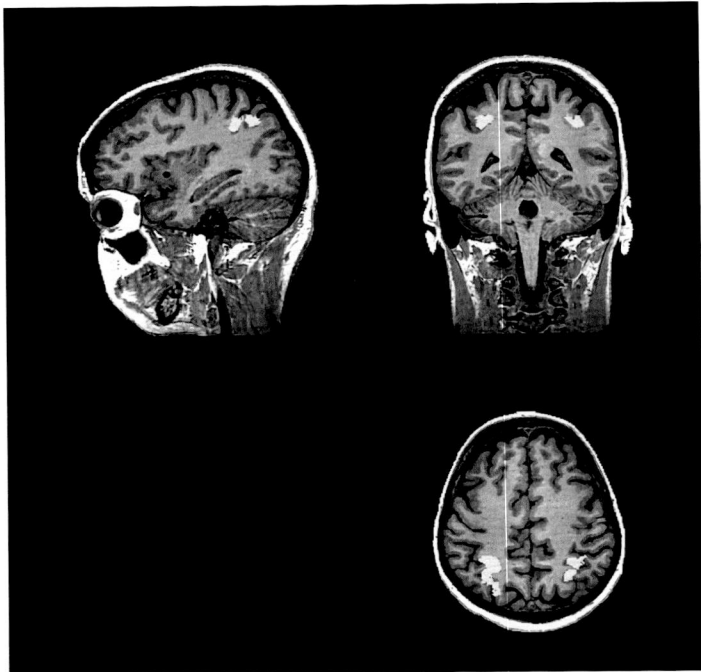

Figure 25.1 The intraparietal sulcus
A black-and-white version of this figure will appear in some formats. For
the color version, please refer to the plate section.

Additionally, Eger et al. (2009) recorded IPS activations to train a machine learning classifier to discriminate between different patterns of activation evoked by different symbolic and non-symbolic numerosities. The researchers found that the classifier was able to generalize between symbolic and non-symbolic number formats without accuracy loss (Eger et al., 2009). Taken together, these imaging results suggest that neurons in the IPS are agnostic toward whether the numbers presented were in symbolic or non-symbolic formats.

Given the preponderance of both behavioral and imaging evidence, some researchers have suggested that the neuro-circuitry for processing non-symbolic quantities has been co-opted to the task of processing symbolic quantities (Dehaene, 2005; Dehaene et al., 2003). As such, for adults, the semantic meaning that

we associate when viewing five objects, seeing the Arabic number "5," and listening to the spoken word "five" share the same underlying neural substrates (Dehaene, 2007; Feigenson et al., 2004). Developmentally, the shared neural substrates suggest that the learning of symbolic numbers may be scaffolded upon the ANS. Put succinctly, "when we learn number symbols, we simply learn to attach their arbitrary shapes to the relevant non-symbolic quantity representations" (Dehaene, 2007, p. 552). If the arbitrary shapes and sounds are indeed "mapped" to the ANS when children were first learning symbolic number, then those children with a stronger ANS acuity (i.e., those who can more accurately compare two non-symbolic numbers with a ratio closer to 1:1) would naturally be better positioned to attach these numerical symbols to the non-symbolic quantity of the ANS. Therefore, we can expect children with better ANS acuity to have an advantage in the acquisition of symbolic numerals (Gilmore et al., 2010; Libertus et al., 2011; Mazzocco et al., 2011).

25.5 Current Attempts at Applications to Education

The neuroscientific and behavioral evidence presented in Sections 25.1–25.4 suggests that symbolic number understanding may have its foundation built on an innate sense of approximate quantities. Given that the learning of symbolic numbers is often children's first step in learning mathematics and that virtually all mathematical topics require the understanding of symbolic numerals, it is not difficult to envision that ANS acuity may be related to performance in the mathematics classroom. Multiple lines of research have accordingly examined whether between-individual variability in ANS acuity are related to performance in mathematics. Statistically speaking, this involves operationalizing ANS acuity as a predictor variable and performance in mathematics as the outcome variable. A statistically significant relationship would suggest that all things being equal, a child with a stronger ANS acuity will perform better at the mathematical topic(s). Important to our discussion is how research studies operationalize mathematics performance, and how different ways of operationalization would affect the ease of integration into pedagogical practice. For current purposes, we categorize the extant research findings into two broad groups.

First, numerous studies have examined the relation between ANS acuity with general mathematics achievement in the context of other cognitive systems. For example, Halberda et al. (2008) have found that the ANS acuity of fourteen-year-olds can predict their past mathematics achievement above and beyond that of intelligence (Halberda et al., 2008), and numerous subsequent studies have since replicated and expanded on this relationship by showing that ANS acuity can predict both concurrent and future mathematics achievement (see Chen & Li, 2014 for a review). Further, this relationship has been expanded by other studies that have proposed other mathematics precursor skills that may mediate (e.g., symbolic number recognition; Peng et al., 2017) or moderate (e.g., inhibition; Gilmore et al., 2013) the relationship between ANS acuity and mathematics achievement.

Second, multiple studies have attempted to examine the link between ANS acuity and proficiency in specific mathematical topics, either early or late into formal education. For instance, some studies have found that preschooler's ANS acuity is predictive of their proficiency in early mathematical topics, such as familiarity with number words, cardinality, counting, and basic arithmetic (e.g., Libertus et al., 2011; Sella et al., 2016; van Marle et al., 2014). Finally, multiple studies have also hypothesized that ANS acuity is predictive of children's and adults' proficiency in more advanced mathematical topics. For example, studies have examined the link between ANS acuity and complex arithmetic (Jang & Cho, 2016) and fraction understanding (Siegler et al., 2013).

In Section 25.6, we shall take the role of the educator and examine the reasons why these two categories of research findings in cognitive neuroscientific are difficult to translate to educator actions.

25.6 Under-specificity of Research Findings Relating to Mathematics Achievement

We have argued in Section 25.1 that educator actions are most affected by pedagogical content knowledge, a blending of pedagogical knowledge and content knowledge. Pedagogical content knowledge is generated when an educator instantiates a specific topic in the content domain informed by pedagogical knowledge. Optimistically, one may conclude that given the finding that individual differences in ANS acuity is related to general mathematics achievement (e.g., Halberda et al., 2008), then accounting for the ANS when generating pedagogical content knowledge for any mathematical topics (e.g., illustrating basic numerical operations using examples of approximate quantities) should bring about beneficial results. However, given that the body of research findings relates the ANS to mathematics achievement (i.e., a set of mathematical topics) and that generating pedagogical content knowledge is topic-specific, two major assumptions would first need to be satisfied.

Mathematics achievement can be regarded as students' ability to learn a set of mathematical topics introduced in the classroom (grade 1 students may be expected to know simple addition, subtraction, measurement, etc.). The first assumption that needs to be satisfied is that ANS acuity is consistently predictive of each of the topics within the set. This is important because the process of generating pedagogical content knowledge is topic-specific, and educators need to generate pedagogical content knowledge for each topic one at a time. A consistent relationship (i.e., ANS acuity relating to performance in most or all topics) will give educators relatively high confidence in the beneficial results when integrating ANS knowledge in generating pedagogical content knowledge. While an inconsistent relationship (i.e., ANS acuity relating to performance in some topics but not others) would make uncertain whether integrating of ANS knowledge in generating pedagogical content knowledge is beneficial, and therefore more difficult to justify.

How do we know if this assumption holds in the case of ANS acuity? One way is to examine whether there are age-related differences in the strength of the relationship between ANS acuity and mathematics achievement. Since the criterion for mathematics achievement changes depending on grade level (i.e., the set of topics to measure achievement in grade 1 is different for that in grade 2), age-related changes in how ANS acuity relates to mathematics achievement would indicate that the relationship between ANS acuity and individual topics is inconsistent. Indeed, it was shown that the strength of the relationship between ANS acuity and mathematics achievement is the strongest early in development and attenuates as age increases (Xenidou-Dervou et al., 2017) and some studies have found that this relationship is altogether non-existent in adulthood (Inglis et al., 2011).

The second assumption that must be fulfilled is that the link between the ANS and mathematics achievement can be manipulated by pedagogical practice in a timely manner, either through action or inaction. Naturally, if the relationship between the ANS and mathematics achievement cannot be affected by educator actions, accounting for it when generating pedagogical content knowledge will not be beneficial. Prominently, this assumption can be violated if the path between ANS acuity and mathematics achievement is mediated by other cognitive factors. For instance, it has been proposed that symbolic number abilities (Price & Fuchs, 2016) and numerical ordering ability (Lyons & Beilock, 2011) fully mediate the relationship between the ANS and mathematics achievement. In such a case, both paths in the indirect relationship (i.e., the path between ANS and the mediator and the path between the mediator and mathematics achievement) would need to be manipulatable by pedagogical practice in a timely manner to justify integrating knowledge of the ANS and the mediators in generating pedagogical content knowledge. Further, even if both paths can be manipulated by pedagogical practice in a timely manner, the utility of integrating the ANS (i.e., accounting for the link between the ANS and the mediator) in the generation process is questionable.

In sum, solely knowing that ANS acuity is related to mathematics achievement is not enough to justify accounting for ANS acuity when generating pedagogical content knowledge. Two assumptions, a consistent relationship with individual topics and a direction, would first be fulfilled to provide enough justification that doing so would be beneficial. As such, solely knowing ANS acuity is related to mathematics achievement is not enough to justify integration, and additional research examining these assumptions would first need to take place. In the case of the ANS, there is extant research that suggests both assumptions are broken and, therefore, research relating ANS acuity with mathematics achievement cannot be used as justification for educators to integrate ANS knowledge into generating pedagogical content knowledge.

25.7 Accounting for the Hierarchical Structure of Mathematical Topics

In Section 25.6, we have argued that research studies that examine mathematics achievement are difficult to use due to the topic-specific nature of pedagogical content knowledge generation. Of course, there is an extant body of research that does examine the link between ANS acuity and specific mathematical topics. Most studies have mainly focused on topics early in education (e.g., Libertus et al., 2011; van Marle et al., 2014) but some research has also explored the relationship between ANS acuity with topics later in education (e.g., Siegler et al., 2013). While these studies are more conducive to be applied day-to-day

pedagogy, the interpretation of these results is often problematic due to, on the one hand, how researchers typically operationalize mathematical topics and, on the other hand, how educators view mathematical topics.

In both behavioral and imaging studies that examine complex behaviors, there is a need for researchers to determine the cognitive processes that can be considered primary (i.e., processes that are directly responsible for the computations underlying the behavior) or secondary (i.e., processes that support the primary processes). For instance, one way to disentangle primary from secondary cognitive processes in imaging research is through the subtraction paradigm, whereby participants are typically asked to complete the targeted behavior as well as a closely matched control task. Activations in areas of the brain are compared between the two conditions and regions of differences would reflect activation of the primary cognitive processes that underlie the complex task (Petersen et al., 1988). Similarly, in behavioral research, relationships between predictors (e.g., early basic mathematical skills) and predicted (e.g., basic arithmetic) variables are often tempered by co-varying away the influences of potential environmental (e.g., social-economic status and parental education level) and cognitive factors (e.g., general intelligence and executive functions). The utilization of these covariates allows researchers to verify whether a proposed cognitive system uniquely predicts the variance of the predicted variables over and above the predictive ability of the covariates.

These methods of controlling for secondary processes allow researchers to identify the likely cognitive systems that underlie specific mathematical topics. However, in the context of day-to-day pedagogy, these identification methods may not be entirely appropriate due to the sequential and hierarchal nature of classroom instruction. Recall that math topics tend to build on or modify learned mathematical topics (e.g., an educator may teach multi-digit arithmetic and use students' knowledge in simple one-digit arithmetic as a starting point), and that students' progression through this hierarchy would affect how pedagogical content knowledge is generated. In all likelihood, educators would tend to assume some previous knowledge when forming pedagogical content knowledge. As such, if research results do not make the distinction between cognitive processes that underlie already existing knowledge and cognitive processes that represent the modification of and building on existing knowledge, it would be difficult for educators to know whether the research results should be integrated into generating pedagogical content knowledge.

For example, using current research methods of separating primary from secondary processes, ANS acuity is related to simple arithmetic (e.g., Peng et al., 2017), complex arithmetic (e.g., Park & Brannon, 2014), and word problem solving (e.g., Träff, 2013). However, these skills are related hierarchically, whereby the simpler mathematical topics are nested inside the more complex mathematical topics (i.e., simple arithmetic is nested in complex arithmetic, and both are nested in word problem-solving), and they are taught in rough sequence over multiple school years. When teaching the more complex mathematical topic, educators would typically assume some existing knowledge in the simpler prerequisite topics and aim only to bridge the gap between existing knowledge and knowledge to be acquired. As such, research showing that the ANS is related to complex arithmetic may not be entirely useful to educators as the research findings do not distinguish between processes associated with complex arithmetic divorced from its prerequisite, simple arithmetic.

In sum, educators may not be entirely interested in what are considered primary processes

to researchers, as this classification does not commonly distinguish between cognitive systems relevant to existing knowledge and systems that are relevant to knowledge to be acquired (see Figure 25.2). Instead, the processes of interest to educators are the processes that contribute to or are modified when the more complex topics are being learned. In other words, educators are more interested in the cognitive processes that contribute uniquely after accounting for the mediating effects of knowledge in prerequisite topics. Of course, a cognitive system may be involved in the acquisition of both existing knowledge to to-be-acquired knowledge, in such a case, the removal of the mediating effects of prerequisite topics may effectively reduce the effect-size but would remain theoretically detectable.

This definition of cognitive processes of interest has two consequences. First, the often-used distinction between domain-general and domain-specific cognitive processes is not applicable in research attempting to bridge to education, as it is possible that after accounting for prerequisite topics only domain-general processes remain as statistically significant cognitive predictors. Second, the percentage of variance explained in the context of other cognitive processes is no guarantee of importance in teaching a specific mathematical topic as the accounted variance may be due to the relationship between these cognitive processes and the prerequisite topics.

To summarize with an example: successful execution of word problem-solving may require, among other things, complex arithmetic and the ability to determine and structure relevant information in the given problem. However, as students would be expected to have some proficiency in arithmetic when first learning word problem-solving, educators would right-fully desire to focus on helping students acquire the skills to select and to structure relevant information. In bridging research to education,

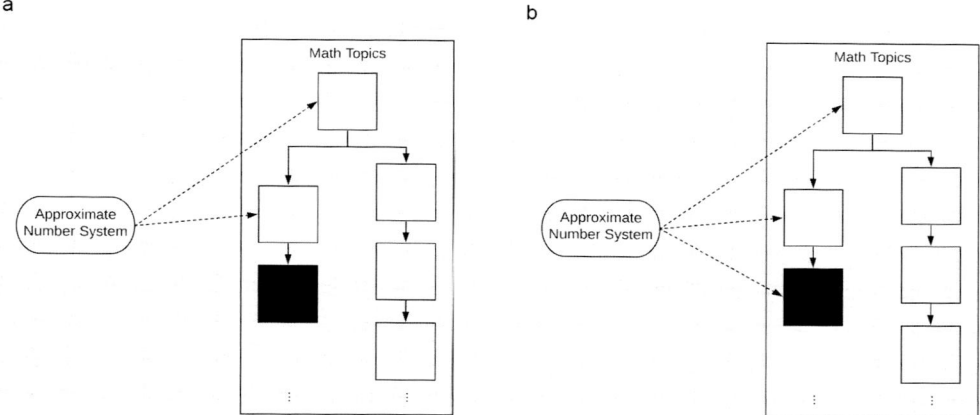

Figure 25.2 Two scenarios where ANS acuity will be related to the highlighted topic if prerequisite topics are not entered as a covariate to topic performance. In scenario A, there is a backdoor path through which ANS acuity would relate to the highlighted topic, and accounting for the ANS is not appropriate. In scenario B, even when the prerequisite topic is controlled for, the ANS is still related to the topic and, therefore, accounting for the ANS would be appropriate
A black-and-white version of this figure will appear in some formats. For the color version, please refer to the plate section.

researchers would need to provide information regarding the cognitive processes that underlie the ability to determine and to structure relevant information but not the processes that may underlie complex arithmetic. In this case, even if a cognitive process – for example, ANS acuity – accounts for a large amount of variance in problem-solving ability, it may still be an inappropriate target for pedagogy if it is only involved in arithmetic calculations and not the selecting and structuring of information. Using the prerequisite topic as a mediator will effectively reject cognitive processes that are not of interest for pedagogical purposes.

In conclusion, for research results to be more relevant to day-to-day pedagogy, potential mediating effects of prerequisites should be accounted for as an additional step. Utilized this way, researchers would be able to offer educators more in-depth and specific recommendations in ways to improve the teaching of specific mathematical topics.

25.8 Discussion

In Sections 25.1–25.7, we have described a framework of how pedagogical, content, and pedagogical content knowledge come together to influence pedagogical practice. We have argued that the reason why current research in cognitive neuroscience is not considered relevant to educators is due to incompatibilities between current research findings and the pedagogical content knowledge generation process. Specifically, we find that research that relates cognitive systems to general achievement tends to be too underspecified for the topic-specific generation process, and that the working definition of specific topics typically seen by educators and researchers tend to be different. These incompatibilities lead to a lack of integration of research in numerical cognition in education, as educators cannot easily utilize this knowledge when generating pedagogical content knowledge.

25.8.1 Pedagogical Knowledge Applicable to All Topics

We have advocated the need for topic specificity as a method to increase the relevance of cognitive neuroscientific research in Sections 25.1–25.7, however, we are not suggesting that the only method through which cognitive neuroscientific research may affect education is through this type of research. Indeed, pedagogical knowledge can be general to multiple topics or topic-specific, and similarly findings from cognitive neuroscience research can be general to multiple topics (e.g., memorization is aided by sleep) and topic specific (e.g., there is a tendency for students to focus on the numerator in fractions).

However, as we have seen in Section 25.6, research relating cognitive performance to general mathematics achievement does not necessarily translate to pedagogical knowledge applicable to all mathematical topics. We believe that research findings that apply to multiple topics are likely to be found when examining the learning process. Specifically, behaviors that enable or are required during the learning process (memorization, paying attention, pro-social behaviors, etc.) tend to be required for all topics that are presented in the classroom. As such, cognitive neuroscientific research that addresses these factors may be more relevant by virtue of being more applicable to a wide array of topics.

Indeed, studies that examine the neural correlates of student learning in mathematics have frequently found domain general areas in the brain, such as areas responsible for memory encoding and retrieval (Supekar et al., 2013), working memory, attention and planning (Soltanlou et al., 2017), linguistic functions (Gruber et al., 2001), and executive functions (Houde et al., 2012), to be related to the process of mastery of arithmetic. Consequently, research findings which illuminate the characteristics of these functions, ways to enhance these functions, or how these functions interact with one another would be of interest to educators.

25.8.2 Directionality and Topic Structure

In Sections 25.1–25.7, we have largely assumed that the directionality of influence goes from cognitive functions to task performance and we have largely disregarded the possibility that the acquisition of knowledge may refine cognitive ability. For instance, while the dominating hypothesis is that those with better ANS ability are better positioned to symbolic numbers (e.g., Feigenson et al., 2004), an alternative hypothesis could be that the acquisition of symbolic numbers refines the ANS (Mussolin et al., 2014). The direction of influence is important in ascertaining the benefit of integrating knowledge of cognitive functions in generating pedagogical content knowledge. In the case where the direction of influence goes from knowledge acquisition to improve cognitive function, integration would not bring about benefits. Therefore, longitudinal and training research designs should be used to supplement cross-sectional research.

Further, we have made the argument that research incorporating topic prerequisites as mediators would yield more relevant results for educators. We have made this argument under the assumption that topic boundary (i.e., what is considered a mathematical topic) and the hierarchical relationship between topic is known and rigid. This assumption is a simplification that deserves some elaboration. Both topic boundaries and topic prerequisites are, to some degree, subjective. The interchangeability of topic prerequisites (e.g., verbal and finger counting may interchangeably serve as prerequisites) and arbitrary nature of some topic boundaries (e.g., a topic defined as a student's ability to sum up to thirty; why not twenty-five, or forty?) would deny any chance for objective definitions of topic and their hierarchical structure. However, topic boundary and structure offered in most mathematics curriculums – created through generations of educator experience and trial-and-error – would be a practicable starting point for research. While this starting point would definitively be subjective, modifications to an existing structure (i.e., addressing whether there are more suitable ways to place topic boundaries and set prerequisites) are empirical questions that can be tested.

In conclusion, this chapter described the impediments of current cognitive neuroscientific research to day-to-day pedagogy. We believe that future research that is mindful of these difficulties will be able to design research that is more informative to educators.

References

Agrillo, C., Piffer, L., Bisazza, A., & Butterworth, B. (2012). Evidence for two numerical systems that are similar in humans and guppies. *PLoS ONE, 7*, e31923.

Anagnostou, E., & Taylor, M. J. (2011). Review of neuroimaging in autism spectrum disorders: What have we learned and where we go from here. *Molecular Autism, 2*, 4.

Antell, S. E., & Keating, D. P. (1983). Perception of numerical invariance in neonates. *Child Development, 54*, 695–701.

Beran, M. J., Decker, S., Schwartz, A., & Schultz, N. (2011a). Monkeys (*Macaca mulatta* and *Cebus apella*) and human adults and children (*Homo sapiens*) compare subsets of moving stimuli based on numerosity. *Frontiers in Psychology, 2*, 61.

Beran, M. J., Johnson-Pynn, J. S., & Ready, C. (2011b). Comparing children's *Homo sapiens* and chimpanzees' *Pan troglodytes* quantity judgments of sequentially presented sets of items. *Current Zoology, 57*, 419–428.

Blakemore, S.-J., & Frith, U. (2005). *The Learning Brain: Lessons for Education.* Hoboken, NJ: Blackwell Publishing.

Bruer, J. T. (2016). Where is educational neuroscience? *Educational Neuroscience, 1*, 1–12.

Bugden, S., & Ansari, D. (2016). Probing the nature of deficits in the 'approximate number system' in children with persistent developmental dyscalculia. *Developmental Science, 19*, 817–833.

Butterworth, B. (2003). *Dyscalculia Screener.* Glasgow: NFER Nelson Publishing Company Ltd.

Butterworth, B. (2008). Developmental dyscalculia. In J. Reed, & J. Warner-Rogers (eds.), *Child Neuropsychology: Concepts, Theory, and Practice* (pp. 357–374). Hoboken, NJ: John Wiley & Sons.

Cantlon, J. F., & Brannon, E. M. (2006). Shared system for ordering small and large numbers in monkeys and humans. *Psychological Science, 17*, 401–406.

Carpenter, T. P., Fennema, E., & Franke, M. L. (1996). Cognitively guided instruction: A knowledge base for reform in primary mathematics instruction. *The Elementary School Journal, 97*, 3–20.

Carter, K. (1990). Teachers' knowledge and learning to teach. *Handbook of Research on Teacher Education, 2*, 291–310.

Chen, Q., & Li, J. (2014). Association between individual differences in non-symbolic number acuity and math performance: A meta-analysis. *Acta Psychologica, 148*, 163–172.

Chesney, D. L., & Haladjian, H. H. (2011). Evidence for a shared mechanism used in multiple-object tracking and subitizing. *Attention, Perception, & Psychophysics, 73*, 2457–2480.

De Smedt, B., Verschaffel, L., & Ghesquière, P. (2009). The predictive value of numerical magnitude comparison for individual differences in mathematics achievement. *Journal of Experimental Child Psychology, 103*, 469–479.

Dehaene, S. (2005). Evolution of human cortical circuits for reading and arithmetic: The "neuronal recycling" hypothesis. In S. Dehaene, J. R. Duhamel, M. Hauser, & G. Rizzolatti (eds.), *From Monkey Brain to Human Brain* (pp. 133–157). Cambridge, MA: MIT Press.

Dehaene, S. (2007). Symbols and quantities in parietal cortex: Elements of a mathematical theory of number representation and manipulation. *Sensorimotor Foundations of Higher Cognition, 22*, 527–574.

Dehaene, S. (2008). Cerebral constraints in reading and arithmetic: Education as a "neuronal recycling" process. In A. Battro, K. Fischer, & P. Léna (eds.), *The Educated Brain: Essays in Neuroeducation* (pp. 232–247). Cambridge: Cambridge University Press.

Dehaene, S., Piazza, M., Pinel, P., & Cohen, L. (2003). Three parietal circuits for number processing. *Cognitive Neuropsychology, 20*, 487–506.

Doyle, W. (1983). Academic work. *Review of Educational Research, 53*, 159–199.

Dyson, N. I., Jordan, N. C., & Glutting, J. (2013). A number sense intervention for low-income kindergartners at risk for mathematics difficulties. *Journal of Learning Disabilities, 46*, 166–181.

Eden, G. F., Olulade, O. A., Evans, T. M., Krafnick, A. J., & Alkire, D. R. (2016). Developmental dyslexia. In G. Hickok, & S. L. Small (eds.), *Neurobiology of Language* (pp. 815–826). Cambridge, MA: Academic Press.

Eger, E., Michel, V., Thirion, B., Amadon, A., Dehaene, S., & Kleinschmidt, A. (2009). Deciphering cortical number coding from human brain activity patterns. *Current Biology, 19*, 1608–1615.

Feigenson, L., Carey, S., & Hauser, M. (2002). The representations underlying infants' choice of more: Object files versus analog magnitudes. *Psychological Science, 13*, 150–156.

Feigenson, L., Dehaene, S., & Spelke, E. (2004). Core systems of number. *Trends in Cognitive Sciences, 8*, 307–314.

Geddis, A. N. (1993). Transforming subject-matter knowledge: The role of pedagogical content knowledge in learning to reflect on teaching. *International Journal of Science Education, 15*, 673–683.

Gess-Newsome, J. (1999). Pedagogical content knowledge: An introduction and orientation. In J. Gess-Newsome, & N. G. Lederman (eds.), *Examining Pedagogical Content Knowledge* (pp. 3–17). Dordrecht: Springer.

Gilmore, C. K., Attridge, N., Clayton, S., Cragg, L., Johnson, S., Marlow, N., Simms, V., & Inglis, M. (2013). Individual differences in inhibitory control, not non-verbal number acuity, correlate with mathematics achievement. *PLoS ONE, 8*, e67374.

Gilmore, C. K., McCarthy, S. E., & Spelke, E. S. (2010). Non-symbolic arithmetic abilities and mathematics achievement in the first year of formal schooling. *Cognition, 115*, 394–406.

Goswami, U. (2004). Neuroscience and education. *British Journal of Educational Psychology, 74*, 1–14.

Grossman, P. L. (1990). *The Making of a Teacher: Teacher Knowledge and Teacher Education.* New York: Teachers College Press.

Gruber, O., Indefrey, P., Steinmetz, H., & Kleinschmidt, A. (2001). Dissociating neural correlates of cognitive components in mental calculation. *Cerebral Cortex, 11*, 350–359.

Halberda, J., & Feigenson, L. (2008). Developmental change in the acuity of the 'number sense': The approximate number system in 3-, 4-, 5-, 6-year-olds and adults. *Developmental Psychology, 44*, 1457–1465.

Halberda, J., Ly, R., Wilmer, J. B., Naiman, D. Q., & Germine, L. (2012). Number sense across the lifespan as revealed by a massive Internet-based sample. *Proceedings of the National Academy of Sciences (USA), 109*, 11116–11120.

Halberda, J., Mazzocco, M. M., & Feigenson, L. (2008). Individual differences in non-verbal number acuity correlate with maths achievement. *Nature, 455*, 665.

Hashweh, M. Z. (2005). Teacher pedagogical constructions: A reconfiguration of pedagogical content knowledge. *Teachers and Teaching, 11*, 273–292.

Hawes, Z., Moss, J., Caswell, B., & Poliszczuk, D. (2015). Effects of mental rotation training on children's spatial and mathematics performance:

A randomized controlled study. *Trends in Neuroscience and Education*, *4*, 60–68.

Holloway, I. D., & Ansari, D. (2008). Domain-specific and domain-general changes in children's development of number comparison. *Developmental Science*, *11*, 644–649.

Holloway, I. D., Battista, C., Vogel, S. E., & Ansari, D. (2013). Semantic and perceptual processing of number symbols: Evidence from a cross-linguistic fMRI adaptation study. *Journal of Cognitive Neuroscience*, *25*, 388–400.

Houde, O., Pineau, A., Leroux, G., Poirel, N., Perchey, G., Lanoë, C., Lubin, A., Turbelin, M. R., Rossi, S., Simon, G., Delcroix, N., Lamberton, F., Vigneau, M., Wisniewski, G., Vicet, J. R., & Mazoyer, B. (2012). Functional MRI study of Piaget's conservation-of-number task in preschool and school-age children: A neo-Piagetian approach. *International Journal of Psychology*, *47*, 332–346.

Hoyle, E., & John, P. D. (1995). *Professional Knowledge and Professional Practice*. London: Burns & Oates.

Inglis, M., Attridge, N., Batchelor, S., & Gilmore, C. K. (2011). Non-verbal number acuity correlates with symbolic mathematics achievement: But only in children. *Psychonomic Bulletin & Review*, *18*, 1222–1229.

Jang, S., & Cho, S. (2016). The acuity for numerosity (but not continuous magnitude) discrimination correlates with quantitative problem solving but not routinized arithmetic. *Current Psychology*, *35*, 44–56.

Kucian, K., Grond, U., Rotzer, S., Henzi, B., Schönmann, C., Plangger, F., Gälli, M., Martin, E., & von Aster, M. (2011). Mental number line training in children with developmental dyscalculia. *Neuroimage*, *57*, 782–795.

Landerl, K., Fussenegger, B., Moll, K., & Willburger, E. (2009). Dyslexia and dyscalculia: Two learning disorders with different cognitive profiles. *Journal of Experimental Child Psychology*, *103*, 309–324.

Libertus, M. E., Feigenson, L., & Halberda, J. (2011). Preschool acuity of the approximate number system correlates with school math ability. *Developmental Science*, *14*, 1292–1300.

Lyons, I. M., & Beilock, S. L. (2011). Numerical ordering ability mediates the relation between number-sense and arithmetic competence. *Cognition*, *121*, 256–261.

Magnusson, S., Krajcik, J., & Borko, H. (1999). Nature, sources, and development of pedagogical content knowledge for science teaching. In J. Gess-Newsome, & N. G. Lederman (eds.), *Examining Pedagogical Content Knowledge* (pp. 95–132). Dordrecht: Springer.

Mason, C. (1999). The TRIAD approach: A consensus for science teaching and learning. In In J. Gess-Newsome, & N. G. Lederman (eds.), *Examining Pedagogical Content Knowledge* (pp. 277–292). Dordrecht: Springer.

Mazzocco, M. M., Feigenson, L., & Halberda, J. (2011). Preschoolers' precision of the approximate number system predicts later school mathematics performance. *PLoS ONE*, *6*, e23749.

Mussolin, C., Nys, J., Content, A., & Leybaert, J. (2014). Symbolic number abilities predict later approximate number system acuity in preschool children. *PLoS ONE*, *9*, e91839.

Nieder, A., & Dehaene, S. (2009). Representation of number in the brain. *Annual Review of Neuroscience*, *32*, 185–208.

Nosworthy, N., Bugden, S., Archibald, L., Evans, B., & Ansari, D. (2013). A two-minute paper-and-pencil test of symbolic and nonsymbolic numerical magnitude processing explains variability in primary school children's arithmetic competence. *PLoS ONE*, *8*, e67918.

Nys, J., Ventura, P., Fernandes, T., Querido, L., Leybaert, J., & Content, A. (2013). Does math education modify the approximate number system? A comparison of schooled and unschooled adults. *Trends in Neuroscience and Education*, *2*, 13–22.

Park, J., & Brannon, E. M. (2014). Improving arithmetic performance with number sense training: An investigation of underlying mechanism. *Cognition*, *133*, 188–200.

Peng, P., Yang, X., & Meng, X. (2017). The relation between approximate number system and early arithmetic: The mediation role of numerical knowledge. *Journal of Experimental Child Psychology, 157*, 111–124.

Petersen, S. E., Fox, P. T., Posner, M. I., Mintun, M., & Raichle, M. E. (1988). Positron emission tomographic studies of the cortical anatomy of single-word processing. *Nature, 331*, 585.

Piazza, M., Pinel, P., Le Bihan, D., & Dehaene, S. (2007). A magnitude code common to numerosities and number symbols in human intraparietal cortex. *Neuron, 53*, 293–305.

Pickering, S. J., & Howard-Jones, P. (2007). Educators' views on the role of neuroscience in education: Findings from a study of UK and international perspectives. *Mind, Brain, and Education, 1*, 109–113.

Price, G. R., & Fuchs, L. S. (2016). The mediating relation between symbolic and nonsymbolic foundations of math competence. *PLoS ONE, 11*, e0148981.

Rugani, R., Fontanari, L., Simoni, E., Regolin, L., & Vallortigara, G. (2009). Arithmetic in newborn chicks. *Proceedings of the Royal Society B: Biological Sciences, 276*, 2451–2460.

Sasanguie, D., De Smedt, B., Defever, E., & Reynvoet, B. (2012). Association between basic numerical abilities and mathematics achievement. *British Journal of Developmental Psychology, 30*, 344–357.

Sasanguie, D., Göbel, S., Moll, K., Smets, K., & Reynvoet, B. (2013). Acuity of the approximate number sense, symbolic number comparison or mapping numbers onto space: What underlies mathematics achievement? *Journal of Experimental Child Psychology, 114*, 418–431.

Sasanguie, D., Lyons, I. M., De Smedt, B., & Reynvoet, B. (2017). Unpacking symbolic number comparison and its relation with arithmetic in adults. *Cognition, 165*, 26–38.

Schwab, J. J. (1982). *Science, Curriculum, and Liberal Education: Selected Essays.* Chicago, IL: University of Chicago Press.

Sella, F., Tressoldi, P., Lucangeli, D., & Zorzi, M. (2016). Training numerical skills with the adaptive videogame "The Number Race": A randomized controlled trial on preschoolers. *Trends in Neuroscience and Education, 5*, 20–29.

Shalev, R. S., Manor, O., & Gross-Tsur, V. (2005). Developmental dyscalculia: A prospective six-year follow-up. *Developmental Medicine and Child Neurology, 47*, 121–125.

Shulman, L. S. (1986). Those who understand: Knowledge growth in teaching. *Educational Researcher, 15*, 4–14.

Shulman, L. S. (1987). Knowledge and teaching: Foundations of the new reform. *Harvard Educational Review, 57*, 1–23.

Siegler, R. S., Fazio, L. K., Bailey, D. H., & Zhou, X. (2013). Fractions: The new frontier for theories of numerical development. *Trends in Cognitive Sciences, 17*, 13–19.

Soltanlou, M., Artemenko, C., Dresler, T., Haeussinger, F. B., Fallgatter, A. J., Ehlis, A.-C., & Nuerk, H.-C. (2017). Increased arithmetic complexity is associated with domain-general but not domain-specific magnitude processing in children: A simultaneous fNIRS-EEG study. *Cognitive, Affective, & Behavioral Neuroscience, 17*, 724–736.

Stein, M. K., Grover, B. W., & Henningsen, M. (1996). Building student capacity for mathematical thinking and reasoning: An analysis of mathematical tasks used in reform classrooms. *American Educational Research Journal, 33*, 455–488.

Supekar, K., Swigart, A. G., Tenison, C., Jolles, D. D., Rosenberg-Lee, M., Fuchs, L., & Menon, V. (2013). Neural predictors of individual differences in response to math tutoring in primary-grade school children. *Proceedings of the National Academy of Sciences (USA), 110*, 8230–8235.

Träff, U. (2013). The contribution of general cognitive abilities and number abilities to different aspects of mathematics in children. *Journal of Experimental Child Psychology, 116*, 139–156.

van Marle, K., Chu, F. W., Li, Y., & Geary, D. C. (2014). Acuity of the approximate number system and preschoolers' quantitative development. *Developmental Science, 17*, 492–505.

Vanbinst, K., Ansari, D., Ghesquière, P., & De Smedt, B. (2016). Symbolic numerical magnitude processing is as important to arithmetic as phonological awareness is to reading. *PLoS ONE, 11*, e0151045.

Xenidou-Dervou, I., Molenaar, D., Ansari, D., van der Schoot, M., & van Lieshout, E. C. (2017). Nonsymbolic and symbolic magnitude comparison skills as longitudinal predictors of mathematical achievement. *Learning and Instruction, 50*, 1–13.

Xu, F., & Spelke, E. S. (2000). Large number discrimination in 6-month-old infants. *Cognition, 74*, B1–B11.

26 Literacy

Understanding Normal and Impaired Reading Development through Personalized Large-Scale Neurocomputational Models

Johannes C. Ziegler, Conrad Perry, and Marco Zorzi

How do children learn to read? How do deficits in various components of the reading network affect learning outcomes? How does remediating one or several components change reading performance? In this chapter, we summarize what we know about learning-to-read and how previous computational models have tackled this issue. We then present our developmentally plausible computational model of reading acquisition and show how it helps to understand both normal and impaired reading development (dyslexia). In particular, we show that it is possible to simulate individual learning trajectories and intervention outcomes on the basis of three component skills: orthography, phonology and vocabulary. The work advocates a multi-factorial computational approach of

This research was supported by grants from the Australian Research Council (DP170101857), the European Research Council (210922-GENMOD), the Institute of Convergence ILCB (ANR-16-CONV-0002), the Excellence Initiative of Aix-Marseille University A*MIDEX (ANR-11-IDEX-0001-02), and the University of Padova (Strategic Grant NEURAT). These simulations were performed in part on the swinSTAR supercomputer at Swinburne University of Technology. We thank Robin Peterson, Bruce Pennington and Richard Olson for many insightful comments and discussions and for providing the behavioural data that were collected with support from the National Institutes of Health in the United States to the Colorado Learning Disabilities Research Center, grant number P50 HD027802.

understanding reading that has practical implications for dyslexia and intervention.

26.1 Literacy

Literacy is one of the greatest achievements of both human civilization and the human mind. Through reading and writing we are able to 'shape events in each other's brains ... bridging gaps of space, time and acquaintanceship' (Pinker, 1994, p. 15). One of the biggest challenges in cognitive and developmental sciences is to understand the complex machinery that is behind this extraordinary ability. As stated by Edmund Burke Huey, who was one of the pioneers of experimental psychology, 'to completely analyse what we do when we read, would almost be the acme of the psychologist's achievements, for it would be to describe many of the most intricate workings of the human mind' (Huey, 1908/1968, p. 6).

Ever since the first connectionist model of letter and word perception (McClelland & Rumelhart, 1981), computational models of reading have played an important role for our understanding of the 'intricate workings' that make it possible to read and comprehend written words (e.g., Coltheart et al., 2001; Perry et al., 2007, 2010; Plaut et al., 1996; Seidenberg & McClelland, 1989; Zorzi et al., 1998). Computational models of reading are computer programs that specify the 'ingredients' of the reading process and implement the units and computations that are necessary to transform visual information into linguistic information (phonemes, stress, words and meaning). Once a model is implemented, it can be used to simulate *real* reading performance in terms of reading latencies (how long it takes to compute the pronunciation of a word or pseudoword) and reading accuracy (whether the output of the model is correct or, with pseudowords, the same as people produce). Computational models further allow us to better understand reading impairments, such as developmental or acquired dyslexia (Coltheart et al., 2001). This is because model components can be 'impaired' in very specific and focal ways and the consequences of these impairments can be analysed through simulations (Harm and Seidenberg, 1999; Perry et al., 2019; Woollams, 2014; Ziegler et al., 2008, 2014). This allows one to understand the *causal* relation between deficits in components of the reading network and performance.

Interestingly, the first computational model of reading, the interactive activation model (McClelland & Rumelhart, 1981), did not have any phonological components (but see, Jacobs et al., 1998). Its goal was to simply describe how the system goes from letter features to whole words using the principles of activation, inhibition and feedback. The model was used to simulate the word superiority effect, that is, the finding that letter perception is facilitated when letters are embedded in real words compared to consonant strings (Grainger & Jacobs, 1994) and it made novel predictions, such as the existence of neighbourhood effects (Grainger, 1992). No learning occurred in the model and all connections were hard-wired. Subsequent models implemented phonological processes in order to tackle reading aloud. The models were tested with respect to their ability to simulate reading aloud latencies and the correct phonological output for words and non-words. Although some models used connectionist learning mechanisms to acquire the mapping between letter strings and their corresponding phonemes (Harm & Seidenberg, 1999; Plaut et al., 1996; Seidenberg & McClelland, 1989; Zorzi et al., 1998), it is probably fair to say that none of these models simulated reading development in a developmentally plausible way (for a discussion, see Ziegler et al., 2014). For example, the very influential reading model of Harm and Seidenberg (1999) used a three-layer network that learnt to map orthography onto a pre-trained phonological attractor network representing the child's initial knowledge about phonological structure. The model was trained by providing the orthography of about 3,000 words and then propagating the discrepancy (error) between the predicted and the actual phonology back to the weights between the orthographic, hidden and phonological layers. Although the model was able to learn 99 per cent of the training set after ten million trials, it is obvious that such a 'massive' and fully supervised learning process is very different from the way children learn to read (Castles et al., 2018; Share, 1995). An important challenge for the computational modelling of cognition is to shift toward more psychologically plausible learning regimens (e.g., unsupervised deep learning; Zorzi et al., 2013) and investigate the emergence of high-level representations, even in the absence of specific task demands (e.g., Di Bono & Zorzi, 2013; Hannagan et al., 2014; Testolin et al., 2017).

In the present chapter, we first summarize what we know about how children learn to read. We then present a developmentally plausible reading model that we have recently put forward (Ziegler et al., 2014). The model was tested against reading aloud data from a study of Peterson et al. (2012). We then present our recent attempt to 'personalize' these models to simulate normal and impaired individual learning trajectories (Perry et al., 2019). This approach has important implications for our understanding of dyslexia and allows us to predict intervention outcomes for any given child (Ziegler, Perry & Zorzi, 2020).

26.2 How Do Children Learn to Read?

Although the ultimate goal of learning-to-read is to comprehend what we read (Castles et al., 2018), the initial stages of learning-to-read are all about 'cracking' the orthographic code. That is, writing systems code spoken language (i.e., 'reading is speech written down') and children have to understand how this code works in their language. For example, in alphabetic writing systems, letters represent phonemes (the smallest units of speech) and, once children have understood the alphabetic principle and learnt the mappings between letters and sounds, they can decode words on their own and retrieve them from their phonological lexicon. Indeed, the great majority of children come to the task of learning to read with a fairly well-developed phonological lexicon (i.e., vocabulary), in which the phonological form of a word is associated with its meaning. This tight association between phonology and meaning results from language acquisition and 'there is almost no way to prevent it from happening, short of raising a child in a barrel' (Pinker, 2009, p. 29).

In alphabetic writing systems, children have to learn how letters or groups of letters map onto their corresponding phonemes. This is mainly done through the explicit teaching of letter–sound or grapheme–phoneme rules for the most basic correspondences. The child can then use these rules or associations to *decode* words, even if they have never seen them before. This process is referred to as *phonological decoding* (Share, 1995). Phonological decoding is at the heart of reading acquisition in all alphabetic writing systems because it provides an extremely parsimonious and straightforward way to retrieve the spoken

form and therefore the meaning of the thousands of words they have stored in their phonological lexicon (Ziegler & Goswami, 2005, 2006). In fact, as one would predict, the orthographic consistency of a writing system, which determines how easily basic grapheme–phoneme correspondences can be taught and learnt, very strongly predicts the rate of reading acquisition in different languages (Ziegler, 2018). The more inconsistent a writing system is, the longer it takes children to acquire basic reading skills. This can be seen as a proof-of-concept for the claim that phonological decoding is the *sine qua non* of reading acquisition in all alphabetic orthographies (Ziegler & Goswami, 2005). In non-alphabetic writing systems, children have to learn the correspondences between orthography and phonology at the levels of the syllable (Kana) or at the levels of morpho-syllables and whole words (Chinese), which is not a fundamentally different learning process but one that takes much longer because there are many more correspondences that need to be learned (Frost, 2012; Ziegler, 2006).

Once children have learnt basic decoding skills, explicit teaching is largely replaced by 'self-teaching' (Share, 1995). That is, children start to decode words autonomously. If they find a word in the phonological lexicon that fits the context, they create an orthographic representation for the decoded and retrieved word. Every successfully decoded word provides the child with a unique learning opportunity that allows the child to improve the decoding system and set up orthographic representations that directly link the written to the spoken word. Thus, phonological decoding provides a powerful self-teaching device because the explicit learning of a small set of spelling–sound correspondences allows the child to decode an increasingly large number of words, which bootstraps orthographic and lexical development (Share, 1995, 1999).

We refer to this learning loop as the phonological decoding self-teaching hypothesis (Ziegler et al., 2014).

26.3 A Developmental Computational Model of Reading

Given the fundamental role of phonological decoding and self-teaching for the initial stages of learning-to-read, we have tried to develop a computational model that implements the core principles of this theory (Ziegler et al., 2014). The model is depicted in Figure 26.1. In a nutshell, we first implemented a decoding network that was pre-trained on a small set of grapheme–phoneme correspondences (e.g., b→/b/, p→/p/). We chose to implement this process in a simple two-layer associative network which takes graphemes (letters or simple letter combinations such as TH, OO, AE) as input and phonemes as output. Such a network has no hidden layer, thus it cannot learn exceptions or irregular correspondences. During this stage, learning is supervised. We believe that this process mirrors most appropriately the explicit teaching of grapheme–phoneme

correspondences, as it occurs during early reading instruction (see, for example, the statutory requirements of the National curriculum in England (DfE, 2013; Hulme et al., 2012)).

From there on, the model enters the self-teaching phase. Thus, the model is presented with written words to be learnt, actually several thousands of written words, because we use models with real-size lexicons rather than toy models. The initially rudimentary decoding network generates a phoneme sequence that potentially activates entries in the phonological lexicon. If the correct word is in the phonological lexicon and passes a critical threshold, it is selected and a representation is set up in the orthographic lexicon (i.e., orthographic learning), which is connected to its phonological representation. Importantly, the internally generated phonological representation is then used as a teaching signal (i.e., self-teaching) to improve the decoding network.

In a first set of simulations (Ziegler et al., 2014), we assessed whether such a simple but developmentally plausible learning mechanism can work for a language like English, which is known for its rather difficult letter–sound

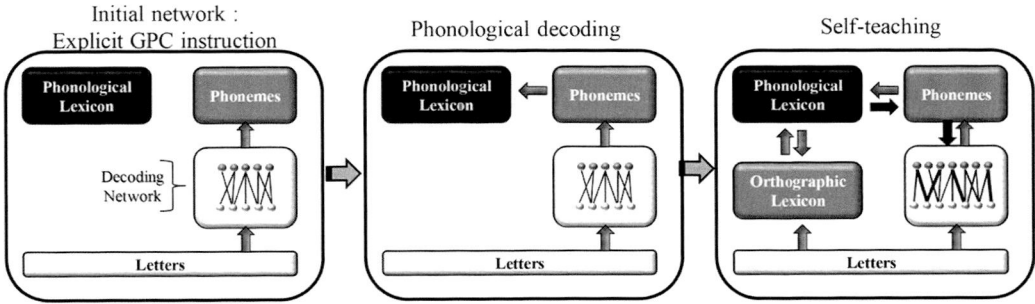

Figure 26.1 An implementation of the phonological decoding self-teaching hypothesis. After initial explicit teaching on a small set of grapheme–phoneme correspondences, the decoding network is able to decode words which have a pre-existing representation in the phonological lexicon but no orthographic representation. If the decoding mechanism activates a word in the phonological lexicon, an orthographic entry is created and the phonology is used as an internally generated teaching signal (black arrows) to refine and strengthen letter–sound connections, thereby improving the efficiency of the decoding network. Adapted from Ziegler et al. (2014)

mapping (e.g., Ziegler et al., 1997). We pre-trained the two-layer associative network with about sixty correspondences. After pre-training, the network was given more than 30,000 words and we checked whether the network was able to correctly learn these words. The results are presented in Figure 26.2.

The results showed that the model successfully learnt more than 80 per cent of the words. It was of interest to zoom into the phonological lexicon during learning to check how quickly the correct word had been activated. These results are presented in Figure 26.2(b). It can be seen that very rapidly in the course of learning, the most active item tended to be the correct word. This is a major reason why self-teaching works so well. In summary, this simulation provides a proof of concept for the claim that phonological decoding and self-teaching provide a powerful bootstrapping mechanism (Share, 1995, 1999) which allows the beginning reader to 'start small' (i.e., with a small set of explicitly taught letter–sound correspondences)

and to build upon this knowledge to 'self-learn' the majority of words (up to 80 per cent) through a simple decoding mechanism that gets more efficient with every successfully decoded word (for a similar approach, see Pritchard et al., 2018).

How do we learn irregular words, such as *yacht*, *aisle* or *choir*? To simulate irregular words learning/reading, we had to add a mechanism that gets irregular words into the orthographic lexicon (Perry et al., 2019). The basic idea was that children learn these words via direct instruction (e.g., flashcards). Direct instruction of irregular words is explicitly listed as one of the statutory requirements up to grade 4 (nine-to-ten years of age) in the National curriculum of England (DfE, 2013). We implemented this process in the following way: each time a phonological decoding attempt was unsuccessful, we allowed for the possibility that a word might enter the orthographic lexicon via direct instruction. We made this a probabilistic process where the

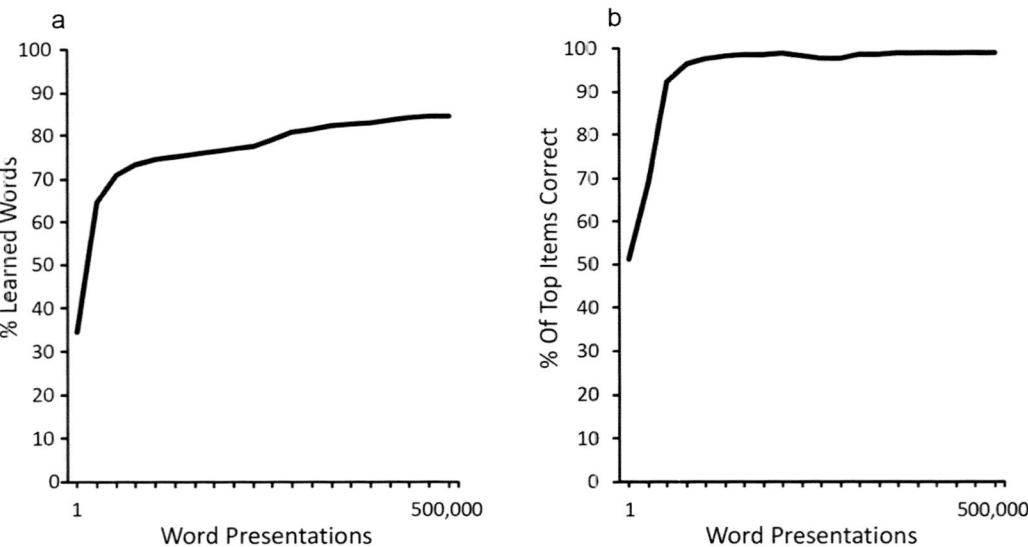

Figure 26.2 Simulations of learning to read through phonological decoding and self-teaching. (a) Percentage of correctly learnt words; (b) Percentage of items in each cohort where the correct item was also the most strongly activated item. Results taken from Ziegler et al. (2014)

chance that a word would enter the ortho-graphic lexicon varied as a function of a free parameter, which could be set as a function of the orthographic ability of each child or some assessment of his or her orthographic learning potential.

We then investigated the interplay between these two mechanisms in a large sample of 622 English-speaking children, which included good and poor readers (Peterson et al., 2012). Indeed, a large number of studies have suggested that good readers are initially efficient decoders and poor readers tend to be poor decoders (Gentaz et al., 2013). Poor readers are thus more reliant on direct instruction when learning to read than good readers. Figure 26.3(a) shows the proportion of words which entered the lexicon through decoding or direct instruction as a function of overall reading skill. Figure 26.3(b) complements the analysis by presenting the number of direct instruction attempts as a function of overall reading skill. As can be seen with the simulations of poor readers, only a small proportion of the words were learnt through decoding compared to direct instruction, and there were

far more attempts at direct instruction compared to the simulations of good readers. Alternatively, with the simulations of good readers, most of the words were learnt via decoding.

26.4 Modelling Dyslexia: The Multi-Deficit Component Approach

With a developmentally plausible and functioning learning model in place, we could ask how different deficits that are present at the outset of learning-to-read might affect the learning-to-read process (Perry et al., 2019). Our model has four critical components: letters, phonemes, phonological lexicon, and orthographic lexicon (see Figure 26.1). We have previously shown that one can impair these components and investigate the consequences of such low-level impairments for the learning-to-read process (Ziegler et al., 2014). For example, it is well known that many children with dyslexia have poor phoneme awareness skills (Landerl et al., 2013; Ziegler et al., 2010). We can assume that children with poor phoneme awareness would have problems of

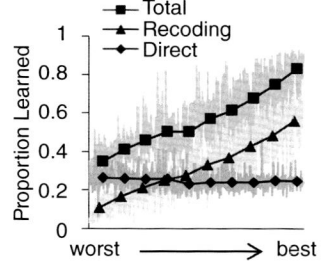
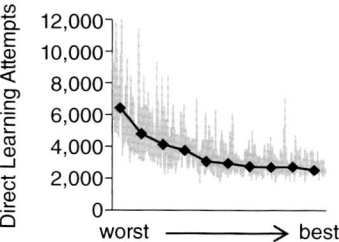

Figure 26.3 The use of decoding versus direct instruction as a function of reading skill. (a) Simulations show the proportion of words that were learned via self-generated decoding versus direct instruction as a function of the average reading performance of each child. (b) Number of direct instruction attempts. Note: the proportions of words in (a) do not add up to 1.0 because they refer to a full-size phonological lexicon, which includes words that were not learnt by either decoding or direct instruction for most of the simulated individuals. Results taken from Perry et al. (2019)

mapping letters onto phonemes, a process that is modelled by the two-layer associative decoding network. One can simulate such a deficit through the switching of phonetically similar phonemes during learning, which is a reasonable assumption because children with dyslexia tend to confuse phonetically similar phonemes (e.g., Ziegler et al., 2009). Thus, the core idea of the multi-deficit component approach was to estimate the efficiency of the component processes through component tasks and then create individual 'personalized' models for each subject to simulate their learning trajectory. This idea is illustrated in Figure 26.4.

In the simulations reported in Perry et al. (2019), we selected three component tasks from the above-mentioned study by Peterson et al. (2012), which contained reading aloud data (on regular, irregular and non-words) as well as performance measures in other non-reading tasks for 622 English-speaking children including 388 dyslexics. We specified how performance on these component tasks could map onto the component processes in the model. Orthographic choice was taken as a measure

for processing efficiency in the orthographic lexicon, phoneme deletion was taken as a measure for the efficiency of activating phonemes correctly and vocabulary score was taken as a measure of the size of a child's phonological lexicon. For each child, we used performance on these three tasks to create individual models, one for each child, in which the parameterization of the models' components and processes was changed using a simple linear function based on the child's performance on the three component tasks. In particular, performance in the orthographic choice task was used to parameterize the amount of noise in the orthographic lexicon and the probability that a word would be lexicalized if successfully decoded or found through direct instruction. Performance in the phoneme deletion task was used to parameterize the amount of noise in the decoding network during training, where noise was used probabilistically to swap correct phonemes to phonetically similar ones (Ziegler et al., 2014). Finally, the vocabulary score was used to set the size of the phonological lexicon, that is, how many words a child knows when they begin the task

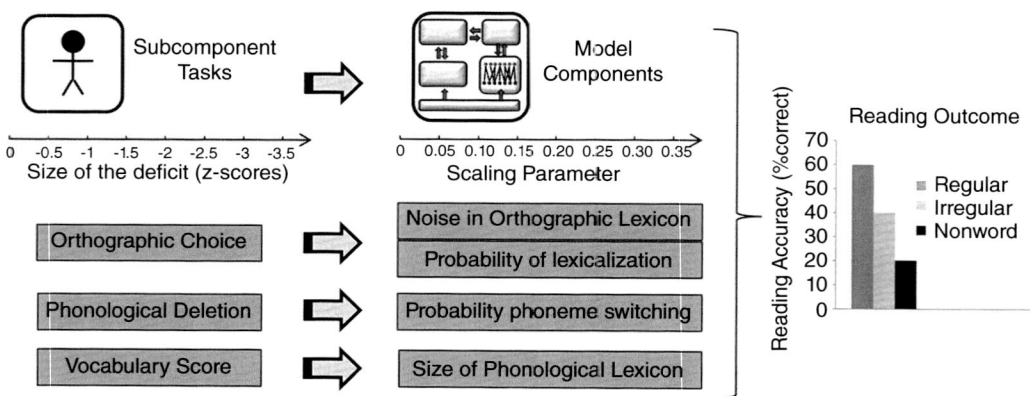

Figure 26.4 The individual-deficit simulation approach: the efficiency of various components of the reading network can be estimated individually for each child through performance on component tasks that map directly onto model components. The performance of each child in the three component tasks is used to individually set the parameters (scaling parameter) of the model in order to predict individual learning outcomes. Adapted from Perry et al. (2019)

of learning to read. Importantly, model parameters were not optimized to fit the individual reading scores, thereby preventing overfitting.

A full learning simulation was performed for each individual model and its performance after learning was assessed by presenting the same words and non-words used by Peterson et al. (2012). This allows a direct comparison between learning outcomes in the simulation and actual reading performance of the child that the simulation was meant to capture. Overall reading performance (percentage correct) averaged across the 622 simulations (Model) and 622 children (Human) is presented in Figure 26.5(a). These data are further broken down for dyslexic and normally developing readers. As can be seen from Figure 26.5(a), the overall means from the children and the predicted means of the model for the very same children are highly similar, both for the normally developing readers and

the dyslexics. That is, the model accurately simulated normal and impaired reading development on the basis of performance in three component tasks. To investigate how well the model captured inter-individual differences and reading outcomes, we plotted the actual versus predicted reading performance for the 622 children on the three reading outcome measures (Figure 26.5(b)). The fit was very good, as indexed by r-squares ranging between 0.63 and 0.72. That is, knowing a child's performance on only three component tasks of reading allows the model to predict their learning outcomes on regular, irregular and non-words with high accuracy.

26.5 Predicting Intervention Outcomes

The strong correlations between predicted and actual reading performance on different types

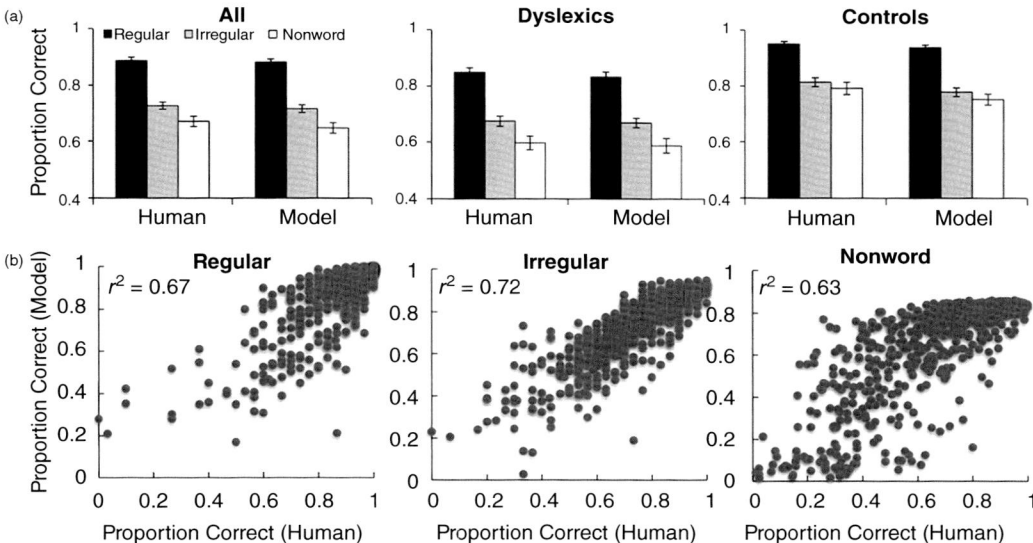

Figure 26.5 Predicted versus actual reading performance. (a) Proportion of correct responses on regular, irregular and non-words for the multi-deficit model (MDM) and humans on the whole data set (All, N = 622), children with dyslexia (Dyslexics, N = 388), and normally developing children (Controls, N = 234). (b) Predicted versus actual reading scores for regular, irregular and non-words for all children. Note: Error bars are 95 per cent confidence intervals. Results taken from Perry et al. (2019).

of words (see Figure 26.5(b)) make it possible to use the model as a tool to predict how remediating one component would change the reading performance on regular, irregular and non-words. That is, we set up a three-dimensional 'deficit'-space with each component task being one dimension such that each child could be represented as a point in this space (see Figure 26.6(a)). We then obtained simulations that sample the entire space, which makes it possible to predict how reading performance on words and non-words changes

as performance improves on a particular component task through intervention, for all possible combinations of deficits (see Figure 26.6(b)). This is illustrated for a given child with a mixed profile (Figure 26.6(c)). For this child, training orthographic skills helps word reading immediately but non-word reading remains poor. Training phonological skills, alternatively, does not initially help word reading much but longer-term increases occur due to better non-word reading allowing higher levels of self-teaching.

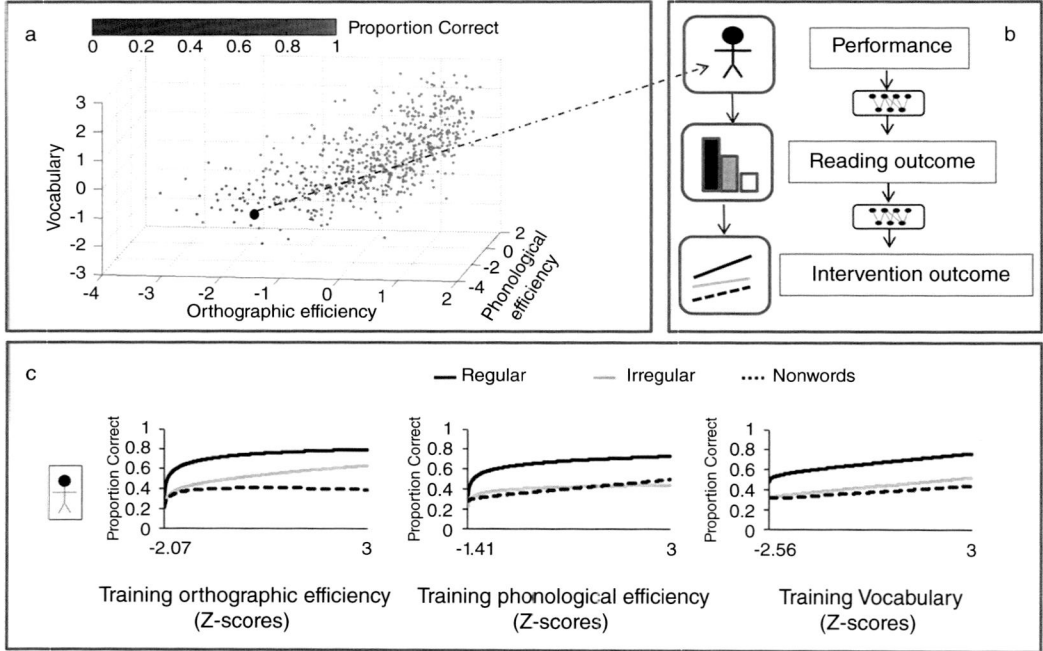

Figure 26.6 Predicting intervention outcomes through 'personalized' simulations. (a) Each child can be represented as a point in a three-dimensional deficit/performance space. (b) Depending on the performance of the child on the component tasks (her position in space), the model predicts the individual learning outcome. By systematically 'moving' the point along all possible dimensions (i.e., training the components), the model can predict intervention outcomes. (c) Simulated intervention outcomes for a child with a mixed profile on regular, irregular and non-words as a function of training orthographic efficiency, phonological efficiency and vocabulary. The x-axes are based on z-scores derived from the task scores of the 622 children, with the first number representing the measured performance of the child and the last number the maximum increase allowable after training.
A black-and-white version of this figure will appear in some formats. For the colour version, please refer to the plate section.

Although this was done for an individual child, the systematic computational exploration of the entire three-dimensional space allowed us to set up model-based applications that can predict 'personalized' intervention outcomes for any child. Such applications could help practitioners decide upon the most efficient intervention strategy for a given child as a function of their underlying deficits and actual reading scores. Being able to predict training outcomes is particularly useful when children show mixed patterns of deficits, which makes it difficult to decide on the extent to which different skills should be trained to improve reading most efficiently.

26.6 Conclusions

In the present chapter, we presented what we believe to be a developmentally plausible computational model of reading development. Even in a language with a complex spelling-to-sound system, such as English, such a model can indeed learn up to 80 per cent of words through decoding and self-teaching and almost all words if one adds direct instruction (Perry et al., 2019). The upshot of having a fully implemented developmental model is that such a model can be used to investigate how deficits that are present prior to reading or occur during reading development might cause the kind of reading impairments seen in children with dyslexia. For instance, we have shown how visual–attentional deficits in letter-position coding (Kohnen et al., 2012) can affect the entire learning-to-read process and how deficits in phoneme processing not only affect non-word reading but also the learning of regular or irregular words (Ziegler et al., 2014). Furthermore, our results showed that large-scale personalized computational modelling allowed us to predict reading outcomes for individual children and reading profiles of children with dyslexia, on the basis of performance on three component tasks (orthographic choice, phoneme deletion and vocabulary).

In the case of dyslexia, this novel computational approach not only allows us to establish causal relations between deficits and outcomes but also investigate how deficits that are present prior to reading affect the entire learning-to-read process. Importantly, the model can be used to predict how changing the efficiency of one component will change reading performance for an individual child. This is particularly important for deciding which remediation strategy is likely to be the most efficient for a given child. At a more conceptual level, the present work acknowledges the multi-factorial nature of dyslexia (Menghini et al., 2010; Paulesu et al., 2014; Pennington, 2006; Ziegler et al., 2008, 2019). That is, dyslexia might be caused by deficits at various levels and similar-looking reading impairments might have different underlying causes. Our simulations show that it is the combination of deficits and their relative size that determines a particular reading impairment. Importantly, reading performance alone is not sufficient to infer the underlying causes and decide upon appropriate remediation strategies.

References

Castles, A., Rastle, K., & Nation, K. (2018). Ending the reading wars: Reading acquisition from novice to expert. *Psychological Science in the Public Interest*, *19*, 5–51.

Coltheart, M., Rastle, K., Perry, C., Langdon, R., & Ziegler, J. (2001). DRC: A dual route cascaded model of visual word recognition and reading aloud. *Psychological Review*, *108*, 204–256.

DfE (2013). (Department for Education) Statutory guidance: National curriculum in England: Framework for key stages 1 to 4. Available from www.gov.uk/government/publications/national-curriculum-in-england-framework-for-key-stages-1-to-4. Last accessed 18 August 2021.

Di Bono, M., & Zorzi, M. (2013). Deep generative learning of location-invariant visual word recognition. *Frontiers in Psychology*, *4*, 635.

Frost, R. (2012). Towards a universal model of reading. *Behavioral and Brain Sciences*, *35*, 263–279.

Gentaz, E., Sprenger-Charolles, L., Theurel, A., & Colé, P. (2013). Reading comprehension in a large cohort of French first graders from low socio-economic status families: A 7-month longitudinal study. *PLoS ONE*, *8*, e78608.

Grainger, J. (1992). Orthographic neighborhoods and visual word recognition. In R. Frost, & L. Katz (eds.), *Orthography, Phonology, Morphology, and Meaning. Advances in Psychology* (Vol. 94, pp. 131–146). Oxford: North-Holland.

Grainger, J., & Jacobs, A. M. (1994). A dual read-out model of word context effects in letter perception: Further investigations of the word superiority effect. *Journal of Experimental Psychology: Human Perception & Performance*, *20*, 1158–1176.

Hannagan, T., Ziegler, J. C., Dufau, S., Fagot, J., & Grainger, J. (2014). Deep learning of orthographic representations in baboons. *PLoS ONE*, *9*, e84843.

Harm, M. W., & Seidenberg, M. S. (1999). Phonology, reading acquisition, and dyslexia: Insights from connectionist models. *Psychological Review*, *106*, 491–528.

Huey, E. B. (1908/1968). *The Psychology and Pedagogy of Reading*. New York: Macmillan.

Hulme, C., Bowyer-Crane, C., Carroll, J. M., Duff, F. J., & Snowling, M. J. (2012). The causal role of phoneme awareness and letter-sound knowledge in learning to read: Combining intervention studies with mediation analyses. *Psychological Science*, *23*(6), 572–577.

Jacobs, A. M., Rey, A., Ziegler, J. C., & Grainger, J. (1998). MROM-p: An interactive activation, multiple readout model of orthographic and phonological processes in visual word recognition. In J. Grainger, & A. M. Jacobs (eds.), *Localist Connectionist Approaches to Human Cognition* (Scientific Psychology Series, pp. 147–188). Mahwah, NJ: Lawrence Erlbaum Associates.

Kohnen, S., Nickels, L., Castles, A., Friedmann, N., & McArthur, G. (2012). When 'slime' becomes 'smile': Developmental letter position dyslexia in English. *Neuropsychologia*, *50*, 3681–3692.

Landerl, K., Ramus, F., Moll, K., Lyytinen, H., Leppanen, P. H., Lohvansuu, K., et al., (2013). Predictors of developmental dyslexia in European orthographies with varying complexity. *Journal of Child Psychology and Psychiatry*, *54*, 686–694.

McClelland, J. L., & Rumelhart, D. E. (1981). An interactive activation model of context effects in letter perception: 1. An account of basic findings. *Psychological Review 88*, 375–407.

Menghini, D., Finzi, A., Benassi, M., Bolzani, R., Facoetti, A., Giovagnoli, S., et al. (2010). Different underlying neurocognitive deficits in developmental dyslexia: A comparative study. *Neuropsychologia*, *48*, 863–872.

Paulesu, E., Danelli, L., & Berlingeri, M. (2014). Reading the dyslexic brain: Multiple dysfunctional routes revealed by a new meta-analysis of PET and fMRI activation studies. *Frontiers in Human Neuroscience*, *8*, 830.

Pennington, B. F. (2006). From single to multiple deficit models of developmental disorders. *Cognition*, *101*, 385–413.

Perry, C., Ziegler, J. C., & Zorzi, M. (2007). Nested incremental modeling in the development of computational theories: The CDP+ model of reading aloud. *Psychological Review*, *114*, 273–315.

Perry, C., Ziegler, J. C., & Zorzi, M. (2010). Beyond single syllables: Large-scale modeling of reading aloud with the Connectionist Dual Process (CDP++) model. *Cognitive Psychology*, *61*, 106–151.

Perry, C., Zorzi, M., & Ziegler, J. C. (2019). Understanding dyslexia through personalized large-scale computational models. *Psychological Science*, *30*, 386–395.

Peterson, R. L., Pennington, B. F., & Olson, R. K. (2012). Subtypes of developmental dyslexia: Testing the predictions of the dual-route and connectionist frameworks. *Cognition*, *126*, 20–38.

Pinker, S. (1994). *The Language Instinct*. New York: Harper Perennial Modern Classics.

Pinker, S. (2009). *Language Learnability and Language Development*. Cambridge, MA: Harvard University Press.

Plaut, D. C., McClelland, J. L., Seidenberg, M. S., & Patterson, K. (1996). Understanding normal and impaired word reading: Computational principles in quasi-regular domains. *Psychological Review*, *103*, 56–115.

Pritchard, S. C., Coltheart, M., Marinus, E., & Castles, A. (2018). A computational model of the self-teaching hypothesis based on the dual-route cascaded model of reading. *Cognitive Science*, *42*, 722–770.

Seidenberg, M. S., & McClelland, J. L. (1989). A distributed, developmental model of word recognition and naming. *Psychological Review*, *96*, 523–568.

Share, D. L. (1995). Phonological recoding and self-teaching: Sine qua non of reading acquisition. *Cognition*, *55*, 151–218.

Share, D. L. (1999). Phonological recoding and orthographic learning: A direct test of the self-teaching hypothesis. *Journal of Experimental Child Psychology*, *72*, 95–129.

Testolin, A., Stoianov, I., & Zorzi, M. (2017). Letter perception emerges from unsupervised deep learning and recycling of natural image features. *Nature Human Behaviour*, *1*, 657–664.

Woollams, A. M. (2014). Connectionist neuropsychology: Uncovering ultimate causes of acquired dyslexia. *Philosophical Transactions of the Royal Society B*, *369*, 20120398.

Ziegler, J. C. (2006). Do differences in brain activation challenge universal theories of dyslexia? *Brain & Language*, *98*, 341–343.

Ziegler, J. C. (2018). Différences inter-linguistiques dans l'apprentissage de la lecture. *Langue Francaise*, *119*, 35–49.

Ziegler, J. C., Bertrand, D., Tóth, D., Csépe, V., Reis, A., Faísca, L., et al. (2010). Orthographic depth and its impact on universal predictors of reading: A cross-language investigation. *Psychological Science*, *21*, 551–559.

Ziegler, J. C., Castel, C., Pech-Georgel, C., George, F., Alario, F. X., & Perry, C. (2008).

Developmental dyslexia and the dual route model of reading: Simulating individual differences and subtypes. *Cognition*, *107*, 151–178.

Ziegler, J. C., & Goswami, U. (2005). Reading acquisition, developmental dyslexia, and skilled reading across languages: A psycholinguistic grain size theory. *Psychological Bulletin*, *131*, 3–29.

Ziegler, J. C., & Goswami, U. (2006). Becoming literate in different languages: Similar problems, different solutions. *Developmental Science*, *9*, 429–436.

Ziegler, J. C., Pech-Georgel, C., George, F., & Lorenzi, C. (2009). Speech-perception-in-noise deficits in dyslexia. *Developmental Science*, *12*, 732–745.

Ziegler, J. C., Perry, C., & Zorzi, M. (2014). Modelling reading development through phonological decoding and self-teaching: Implications for dyslexia. *Philosophical Transactions of the Royal Society B*, *369*, 20120397.

Ziegler, J. C., Perry, C., & Zorzi, M. (2019). Modeling the variability of developmental dyslexia. In C. Perfetti, K. Pugh, & L. Verhoeven (eds.), *Developmental Dyslexia across Languages and Writing Systems* (pp. 350–371). Cambridge: Cambridge University Press.

Ziegler, J. C., Perry, C., & Zorzi, M. (2020). Learning to Read and Dyslexia: From Theory to Intervention Through Personalized Computational Models. *Current Directions in Psychological Science*, *29*(3), 293–300.

Ziegler, J. C., Stone, G. O., & Jacobs, A. M. (1997). What is the pronunciation for -ough and the spelling for u/? A database for computing feedforward and feedback consistency in English. *Behavior Research Methods, Instruments & Computers*, *29*, 600–618.

Zorzi, M., Houghton, G., & Butterworth, B. (1998). Two routes or one in reading aloud? A connectionist dual-process model. *Journal of Experimental Psychology: Human Perception & Performance*, *24*, 1131–1161.

Zorzi, M., Testolin, A., & Stoianov, I. P. (2013). Modeling language and cognition with deep unsupervised learning: A tutorial overview. *Frontiers in Psychology*, *4*, 515.

27 Reasoning in Mathematical Development

Neurocognitive Foundations and Their Implications for the Classroom

Jérôme Prado and Marie-Line Gardes

Relations are ubiquitous in mathematics, from the understanding of measurement and patterns to the acquisition of algebra and fractions. In line with this observation, a growing body of literature indicate that individual differences in mathematical skills are associated with individual differences in the ability to reason about relations. In the present chapter, we review these studies and discuss what is known about the neural and behavioral development of two major forms of relational reasoning (i.e., transitive reasoning and analogical reasoning). We argue that relational reasoning may not only relate to mathematical skills because both place demands on common general cognitive resources, but also because relational reasoning and numerical skills share some underlying neurocognitive representations. Finally, the educational implications of these studies are discussed. Notably, we suggest that teachers may help scaffold the development of relational reasoning skills in the classroom by promoting situations in which children are engaged in problem-solving.

In one of his many clever experiments, the pioneering developmental psychologist Jean Piaget asked several five- and six-year-olds to sell him some candies (Piaget, 1952). For each coin a child would get, Piaget would receive one candy. Children did not have much difficulty understanding this one for one exchange.

Given that the number of coins never exceeded children's counting ability, participants were also able to tell Piaget how many coins they had gained at the end of the trade. However, when children were asked to determine the number of candies that Piaget had received in exchange for the coins, they struggled to answer. In other words, children could not infer that if there was one coin for one candy, the number of coins and candies had to be identical.

This classic experiment illustrates the role inference making may play in the development of mathematical skills. Mathematical development is more than learning quantitative concepts. It is also learning to make inferences based on these concepts. In other words, mathematical development requires reasoning. It may thus appear surprising that relatively few developmental psychology studies have investigated how reasoning skills contribute to mathematical development. Part of the explanation may lie in the breakthrough discovery that, contrary to Piaget's assumptions, children do possess non-verbal mechanisms providing them with early intuitions about quantitative information (see Chapter 11). This has propelled investigations into young children's numerical knowledge, as well as into the extent to which early non-symbolic intuitions may underlie symbolic math skills (Feigenson et al., 2013). However, the finding that children may have domain-specific quantitative skills does not imply that a domain-general skill such as reasoning cannot

This research was supported by a grant from the Agence Nationale de la Recherche (ANR-14-CE30–0002).

contribute to mathematical development. In fact, there is increasing awareness in the cognitive literature that emerging mathematical skills in children are supported by various domain-general abilities, including working memory, executive control and attention (Fias et al., 2013; Houdé, 2019; Houdé et al., 2011). In keeping with this growing body of research, several studies suggest that reasoning skills also support several aspects of mathematical learning (Inglis & Attridge, 2017; Morsanyi & Szücs, 2014; Richland & Simms, 2015; Singley & Bunge, 2014). This may especially be the case of a particular type of reasoning that will be the focus of this chapter (i.e., reasoning about relations).

As stated in the previous paragraph, relations are ubiquitous in mathematics. For instance, early stages of mathematics education require children to use and combine words expressing relations (e.g., large/small, high/low, long/short) to compare sizes. Later on, understanding relations between numbers and operations (e.g., addition is inversely related to subtraction) is critical to master arithmetic. Relations are also central to algebra. That is, algebraic equations essentially indicate an equal relationship between two expressions in which numbers are related to variables. Finally, the importance of understanding relations between quantities is obvious when children learn fractions, which are defined by the relationship between the numerator and the denominator.

Relational reasoning, or the ability to attend to and manipulate relations, is fundamental to all of the activities described above. Sections 27.1 and 27.2 discuss two of the main types of relational reasoning involved in mathematical learning: transitive reasoning and analogical reasoning. We first describe what is meant by transitive reasoning, its relationship to mathematical learning, and subsequently turn to analogical reasoning. We end the chapter with a discussion of how to promote relational reasoning during mathematics learning.

27.1 Transitive Reasoning

Transitivity is a property that arises from a set of items that can be ordered along a single continuum. A relation is said to be "transitive" when it allows reasoners to infer a relationship between two items (e.g., A and C) from two other overlapping pairs (e.g., A and B; B and C). For example, the relation "older than" is transitive because it allows for the following type of inference:

(1)   Ann is older than Tom.
        Tom is older than Bill.
        Therefore, Ann is older than Bill

This inference is based on an ordering of items along a linear continuum. However, transitive relations are not necessarily linear. For instance, transitive inferences can also be made from sets that can be included in one another, such as in the inference in (2):

(2)   All tulips are flowers.
        All flowers are plants.
        Therefore, all tulips are plants.

As is clear from these examples, a transitive conclusion follows out of necessity from the premises. In other words, if the premises are true, the conclusion is necessarily true. This is the very definition of a "deduction," and this is why transitive reasoning is typically considered an instance of deductive reasoning.

The ability to recognize transitive relations and make associated inferences may contribute to the acquisition of many mathematical concepts. For example, transitive reasoning facilitates the extraction of ordinal information from sets of items and supports the understanding of hierarchical classification (Kallio, 1988; Newstead et al., 1985; Piaget & Inhelder, 1967; Rabinowitz & Howe, 1994). It is also an integral part of measurement skills in children (Bryant & Kopytynska, 1976; Piaget & Inhelder, 1967; Wright, 2001). These observations naturally suggest that transitive reasoning skills might be associated with mathematical performance. Several recent studies tested this hypothesis. For instance, Handley et al. (2004) asked children from nine to eleven years old to evaluate the validity of transitive inferences such as the one in (1). Importantly, the content of the arguments was arbitrary so that children did not have prior beliefs regarding the conclusion.[1] The authors found that reasoning accuracy on these neutral arguments was positively related to performance on a standardized mathematics test and a teacher-administered measure of numeracy. These relationships were specific to mathematical skills because no significant correlation was observed between reasoning accuracy and teacher-administered measures of reading or writing.

An issue with the study above is that transitive arguments were intermixed with conditional arguments (e.g., arguments of the form "If P then Q, there is a P, therefore there is a Q"). Because performance associated with transitive arguments was not separated from

performance associated with conditional arguments, it is unclear to what extent the relationships observed in Handley et al. (2004) are specific to transitive inferences. Two subsequent studies address this issue. Specifically, Morsanyi et al. (2017a, 2017b) found a specific relationship between transitive reasoning performance and mathematical abilities in adolescents and adults, respectively. It was also found that adult participants who were the most accurate at assessing the validity of a transitive inference were also the most accurate at positioning a given number on a bounded line with labeled endpoints (the so-called number-line task) (Morsanyi et al., 2017b). This latter finding raises the possibility that transitive reasoning and numerical processing may share some underlying mechanisms.

Some important evidence for the idea that common cognitive mechanisms underlie both transitive reasoning and numerical processing comes from neuroimaging studies. Indeed, processing transitive relations and processing numerical information appear to rely on the same region of the posterior parietal cortex, i.e., the intraparietal sulcus (IPS). On the one hand, the IPS is systematically activated in a wide range of numerical tasks, whether those involve quantity comparison (Ansari, 2008, see Chapter 28), mental arithmetic (Peters & De Smedt, 2017), ordinality judgments (Lyons et al., 2016), or fraction processing (Ischebeck et al., 2009; Jacob & Nieder, 2009). In numerical comparison tasks, for example, activity in the IPS typically increases as the distance between numbers decreases (Ansari, 2008; Hubbard et al., 2005). This "neural distance effect" mirrors the associated "behavioral distance effect" observed in those tasks (i.e., response times increase as the distance numbers decrease; Moyer & Bayer, 1976). It also suggests that quantities may be represented in the IPS along a spatial continuum or "mental

---

[1] A large body of literature has shown that inferences are influenced by the content of the premises when these are based on real-world content (for a review see Evans, 2003). For example, children and adults find it relatively difficult to infer a conclusion such as "Houses are bigger than skyscrapers" from the premises "Houses are bigger than trailers" and "Trailers are bigger than skyscrapers" because it is inconsistent with prior beliefs. They have to inhibit a belief bias (Houdé, 2019; Moutier et al., 2006). In contrast, it is relatively easy to infer a conclusion such as "Elephants are bigger than mice" from the premises "Elephants are bigger than dogs" and "Dogs are bigger than mice" because it is consistent with prior beliefs. In such cases, however, it is unknown whether participants attend to the logical structure of the arguments or whether their response is based on beliefs about the world.

number line" (Ansari, 2008; Hubbard et al., 2005): the smaller the distance between two quantities on the mental number line, the less distinguishable those quantities are and the longer it may take to compare them.

On the other hand, brain imaging studies indicate that transitive reasoning (typically measured by three-term arguments such as those exemplified in (1) and (2)) also relies on the IPS in adults (Prado et al., 2011). That is, over and above differences in experimental materials and procedures between studies, the neuroimaging literature consistently points to enhanced activity in the IPS during transitive reasoning tasks. Interestingly, when multiple premises are used in transitive reasoning tasks (e.g., A>B, B>C, C>D, D>E), a neural distance effect is found in the IPS (Hinton et al., 2010; Prado et al., 2010). That is, activity associated with evaluating pairs increases as the number of intervening items in a pair decreases (e.g., evaluating whether B>C is associated with more activity than evaluating whether B>D). As in numerical comparison tasks, this neural distance effect mirrors a behavioral distance effect that also characterizes transitive reasoning tasks with multiple premises (i.e., response time in evaluating pairs increases as the number of intervening items in a pair decreases) (Potts, 1972, 1974; Prado et al., 2008).

The presence of similar behavioral and neural signatures in number comparison and transitive reasoning tasks (i.e., the behavioral and neural distance effects) might indicate a common underlying mechanism. That is, both numbers and transitive orderings may be encoded along mental representations that may be spatial in nature and supported by mechanisms in the IPS. This hypothesis is supported by a study demonstrating that the exact same region of the IPS exhibits a neural distance effect in numerical comparison and transitive reasoning tasks in adults (Prado et al.,

2010). Therefore, the relationship between numerical and transitive reasoning skills may stem from a common reliance on IPS mechanisms supporting the ordering of items along a spatial dimension.

The idea that numerical processing and transitive reasoning would rely on a common mechanism in the IPS predicts that children with impairments in the IPS may exhibit impaired performance on both number processing and transitive reasoning tasks. Two studies confirm this prediction. First, Morsanyi et al. (2013) asked children with dyscalculia to solve linear transitive reasoning problems similar to that in (1). Dyscalculia is a disability affecting the acquisition of numerical and arithmetic skills that has been consistently linked to anatomical and functional impairments in the IPS (Ansari, 2008). The authors found that children with dyscalculia exhibited poor performance (as compared to typically developing children) in transitive reasoning problems with concrete content. In a recent study, Schwartz et al. (2018) further showed that children with dyscalculia struggle to integrate transitive relations such as in (1) and (2), even when the content is abstract and not affected by beliefs. In that study, brain activity was also measured while children were presented with transitive relations. The only region in which less activity was found in children with dyscalculia than in typically-developing children during transitive reasoning was the IPS. Thus, this study provides evidence that the poor transitive reasoning skills of children with dyscalculia may stem from functional impairments in the IPS (see also Schwartz et al., 2020).

How and when does transitive reasoning emerge in children? The first investigations into the development of transitive reasoning skills dates back to Piaget (Piaget, 1952; Piaget & Inhelder, 1967; Wright, 2001, 2012). The tasks used by Piaget to test transitive reasoning involved colored items that were shown to children. Specifically, children were typically presented with two overlapping pairs (e.g., A>B, B>C). They then had to establish the relationship between the two items that were never presented next to one another (e.g., A and C). Using this paradigm, Piaget found that transitive reasoning does not fully emerge until the age of seven or eight years. However, researchers have highlighted several issues with Piaget's methodology (Wright, 2001, 2012). First, when a transitive problem only involves three terms, one of the items in the conclusion is always at the top of the transitive hierarchy (i.e., A), whereas the other is always at the bottom (i.e., C). In other words, children can attach verbal labels to these items (e.g., "A is always the best" and "C is always the worst") and simply use these labels when presented with A and C, without having to engage in genuine reasoning. One simple way to address this caveat is to present participants with at least five premises (A>B, B>C, C>D, and D>E), such that a conclusion that does not involve endpoint items can be tested (i.e., B>D?) (Wright, 2012). Second, it has been argued that Piaget did not adequately ensure that children could remember the premises before evaluating the conclusion (Bryant & Trabasso, 1971). Using non-verbal problems with five premises and an extensive training protocol to ensure that premises were retained, Bryant and Trabasso (1971) demonstrated that children as young as four years could succeed in transitive reasoning tasks (see also Russell et al., 1996). Since that landmark study, transitive reasoning skills have been shown in many animal species, including non-human primates, rats, birds, and fish (Brannon & Terrace, 1998; Grosenick et al., 2007; Paz et al., 2004; Vasconcelos, 2008; see Chapter 7). Therefore, transitive reasoning appears to have a relatively ancient evolutionary history, perhaps because it has critical adaptive value in

facilitating the representation of hierarchies in socially organized species (Vasconcelos, 2008).

In sum, there is considerable evidence that, contrary to Piaget's assumptions, transitive reasoning emerges early in children. This does not mean, however, that transitive reasoning skills do not develop throughout elementary school. In fact, the transitive reasoning abilities observed in animals and young children (using paradigms that involve extensive training with non-verbal premises) may be supported by associative learning mechanisms that have little to do with the type of spatial representations thought to underlie transitive reasoning in adults (Frank, 2005; Frank et al., 2003; Vasconcelos, 2008). Indeed, even in paradigms that involve five transitive items (e.g., A>B, B>C, C>D, D>E), the endpoints (A and E) have asymmetric values in the sense that A is always the "best" item and E always the "worst." It is possible that, with extensive training and multiple repetitions of the premises, these asymmetric values transfer to the adjacent items (Delius & Siemann, 1998; Frank et al., 2003; von Fersen et al., 1991). In other words, B might develop a greater associative value than D because B is associated with the "best" item (i.e., A) and D is associated with the "worst" item (i.e., E). The past reinforcement history for each item might then underlie the transitive inference when B is chosen over D in animals and young children (von Fersen et al., 1991). Even though there is convincing evidence that transitive reasoning in adults relies on a representation of items along a spatial continuum, this strategy may not be readily available to young children (who might instead rely on associative learning mechanisms facilitated by a repeated exposition to premises). Thus, the development of transitive reasoning might be characterized by a transition from the use of associative learning mechanisms to a reliance on spatial ordering mechanisms in the IPS. Overall, both numerical processing and transitive reasoning may be characterized by an increase in specialization of the IPS for the representation of ordered information (Prado et al., 2010).

27.2 Analogical Reasoning

Broadly defined, analogical reasoning is the ability to reason with relational patterns (English, 2004). More specifically, analogical reasoning involves abstracting relational patterns and applying them to new entities. A conventional analogy typically takes the form "A is to B as C is to D" (this is formalized "A:B::C:D") and involves a mapping between some source items (i.e., A and B) and some target items (i.e., C and D). Consider for example the analogy in (3):

(3)   Automobile is to gas as sailboat is to?

Solving this analogy first requires reasoners to extract a relational pattern between two items, "automobile" and "gas" (i.e., A and B), before applying this pattern to a third item, "boat" (i.e., C). A probable conclusion can then be generated, i.e., "wind" (i.e., D). In (3), the relation between A and B ("powered by") is causal but relatively abstract. This makes the analogy more difficult than if it was based on a relation of physical similarity. Consider for example how the solution "melted snowman" comes naturally from the analogy in (4):

(4)   Chocolate bar is to melted chocolate as snowman is to?

Therefore, much like transitive reasoning, analogical reasoning requires relational processing. Unlike transitive reasoning, however, the solution of an analogy does not follow out of necessity from the available information. It can only be supported with varying degrees of strength (Bartha, 2013). In that sense, analogical reasoning belongs to the category of inductive reasoning.

Analogical reasoning plays a fundamental role in creativity (Holyoak & Thagard, 1995). As such, analogies have supported a number of important mathematical discoveries over the course of history (Polya, 1954). Consider for example how the famous mathematician Jean Bernoulli used an analogy with the path of the light to solve a classical problem in calculus of variation (the brachistochrone problem) (Polya, 1954; Sriraman, 2005). But analogical reasoning is not only relevant to expert mathematicians when solving complex problems. It is also a critical skill upon which young children and adolescents may rely on when learning mathematics and solving problems (for a neo-Piagetian theory on analogy through mapping structures in higher cognition, see Halford, 1992; Halford et al., 2010). For example, suppose that some students have used calculus to demonstrate that of all the rectangles with a given perimeter, the one with the greatest area is a square. These students may then infer that of all the boxes with a given surface area, the one with the greatest volume is a cube (Bartha, 2013). This is an example of an analogy in which students recognize a mapping (i.e., a similarity in relational structure) between a source problem (with rectangles and squares) and a target problem (with boxes and cubes). Younger children also rely on analogical reasoning when they are faced with pictorial representations (e.g., pizza slices, number lines) and manipulative materials (e.g., counters, blocks, rods). These have been termed "mathematical analogs" because they also essentially require children to recognize a structural relation between a source (i.e., the pictorial representation of manipulative) and a target (i.e., the mathematical concept to be acquired) (English, 2004). Finally, a relatively underappreciated fact is that teachers commonly use analogies in the classroom to illustrate concepts and procedures (Richland & Simms, 2015; Richland et al., 2004). In other words, analogies are at the heart of mathematics teachers' practices. There are many examples of such analogies. For instance, teachers may use the analogy of balancing a scale to illustrate how two sides of an equation should be equal. They may also use real world situations involving the manipulation of coins or candies to illustrate additive and subtractive concepts (Richland et al., 2004). Overall, there is no doubt that analogical reasoning plays a central role in mathematical learning, both from a learner's and a teacher's perspective.

Several cross-sectional and longitudinal studies indicate that analogical reasoning is related to mathematical development (Fuchs et al., 2005; Green et al., 2017; Primi et al., 2010; Taub et al., 2008). For instance, Fuchs et al. (2005) found that measures of geometric proportional analogies (i.e., sometimes called "matrix reasoning") at the beginning of first grade were related to math outcomes later during the year. Green et al. (2017) further found that a compound measure of relational reasoning (including matrix reasoning) predicted mathematical skills eighteen months later in children and adolescents. Primi et al. (2010) also demonstrated that verbal and spatial analogical reasoning skills were related to growth of mathematical skills from seventh to eighth grade.

Some important support for a foundational role of analogical reasoning in mathematical learning comes from the literature on "patterning," that is, the ability to extract a relational pattern within a given sequence in order to apply this pattern to another sequence (which could have different surface features) (Burgoyne et al., 2017; Rittle-Johnson et al., 2018). In a standard patterning task, children might be presented with alternating shapes of the same color, such as star–circle–star–circle. Children may then be given a set of red and blue squares and be asked to generate a similar pattern. If the pattern from the sequence of shapes is correctly extracted (i.e., A–B–A–B), children can infer the correct sequence of squares of different colors (i.e., red–blue–red–blue). Therefore, a patterning task requires children to recognize the similarity in relational structure (or mapping) between an initial (or source) sequence and a final (or target) sequence. As such, analogical reasoning skills are fundamental to patterning tasks. Cross-sectional and longitudinal studies have found a relationship between patterning performance and mathematical skills (Lee et al., 2011; Pasnak et al., 2016; Rittle-Johnson et al., 2016; Vanderheyden et al., 2011). For instance, Rittle-Johnson et al. (2016) demonstrated that patterning knowledge when children are in first grade predicts their mathematics achievement in fifth grade, independently of a number of cognitive abilities and mathematical skills.

Overall, there is considerable evidence supporting the role of analogical reasoning in mathematical development. As mentioned in the previous paragraphs of this section, however, analogies are not only used by learners but are also frequently employed by teachers to explain concepts and procedures. Interestingly, there is evidence that the quality of analogy-based instructions varies between teachers and that this has an influence of mathematical learning. This is suggested by a cross-cultural comparison of practices in the mathematics classroom (Richland et al., 2007). The authors analyzed videotapes of mathematics teachers in the United States as well as in two Asian regions in which students significantly outperform American students in international measures of mathematical attainment: Hong Kong and Japan. They did not find differences in terms of frequency of use of analogies by teachers across the three regions. However, there were differences in the extent to which these analogies adhered to principles that are known to facilitate and enhance the effectiveness of analogies. For example, teachers in Hong Kong and in Japan made greater use of strategies that enhanced the source of the analogy as compared to teachers in the United States, thereby reducing working-memory demands for students. These included the use of a familiar source analog and the use of visual aids. Analogies from teachers in Hong Kong and in Japan were also more likely to adhere to principles that draw attention to the relational comparison, such as using spatial cues highlighting the mapping between the source and target and using gestures and visualizations. Because students in Hong Kong and Japan typically achieve higher mathematical skills than children in the United States, the study suggests that an efficient use of analogies in the classroom may contribute to mathematical attainment (Richland et al., 2007).

What may be the neurocognitive foundation of the relationship between analogical reasoning and mathematical development? Of course, as is the case for other forms of reasoning, analogical reasoning may relate to mathematical skills because both place great demands on common general cognitive resources, such as working memory (Waltz et al., 2000). However, analogical reasoning is also (like transitive reasoning) a form of relational reasoning. Thus, it may support mathematical development because the ability to understand and manipulate relations is fundamental to mathematical knowledge. For instance, much like transitive reasoning, analogical reasoning has been found to activate regions in and around the IPS in tasks involving propositional analogies (Bunge et al., 2005; Wendelken et al., 2008) and matrix reasoning (Bunge et al., 2009; Crone et al., 2009; Dumontheil et al., 2010). A recent meta-analysis further found that activity associated with analogical reasoning (and relational reasoning more generally) in the posterior parietal lobe exhibit greater overlap with brain activity associated with numerical processing than with brain activity associated with working memory, attention, or linguistic processing (Wendelken, 2015). This is more consistent with the idea that parietal activity during analogical reasoning may reflect relational computations (a process that is involved in many mathematical tasks) than more general working memory or attentional demands.

The IPS, however, is not the only region involved in analogical reasoning. A large number of studies have also implicated a region located at the apex of the frontal cortex in analogical reasoning, that is, the rostrolateral prefrontal cortex (RLPFC) (Bunge et al., 2005; Wendelken et al., 2008; Wright et al., 2007). The RLPFC and the IPS may have different functional roles in analogical reasoning. For example, some authors have proposed that the IPS is specifically involved in the representation of relations (Singley & Bunge, 2014). In contrast, the RLPFC should support the integration of different mental relations (Bunge & Wendelken, 2009; Wendelken et al., 2008). Evidence for this idea comes from studies showing that the RLPFC is more active when participants compare the relations between two pairs of words (i.e., a classic analogy task) than when they process relations independently from one another (i.e., when they do not have to compare the relations) (Bunge et al., 2005; Wendelken et al., 2008). Interestingly, activity in the RLPFC does not vary with the associative strength of the relationship between words, suggesting that it is not involved in the retrieval of relations per se, but rather in their integration (Bunge et al., 2005; Wendelken et al., 2008). These findings on conventional analogies are consistent with studies on matrix reasoning, which also point to increased activity in the RLPFC when multiple geometric relations have to be considered jointly (as compared to the processing of one single relation) (Dumontheil et al., 2010). Therefore, neuroimaging studies suggest that a fronto-parietal network that includes the IPS (as well as neighboring parietal regions) and the RLPFC supports analogical reasoning.

It is interesting to note that the RLPFC develops more slowly than most other brain regions, only reaching maturity after adolescence (Dumontheil et al., 2008). In line with this observation, developmental studies have found increases of activity in the RLPFC (as well as in the IPS) from childhood to adolescence in analogical reasoning tasks (Crone et al., 2009; Dumontheil et al., 2010; Wright et al., 2007). More specifically, the RLPFC should become increasingly specialized for higher-order relational processing with age. For example, Wright et al. (2007) presented children from six to thirteen years and adults with visual analogy trials in which participants had to indicate which of four objects would complete the problem ("chalk is to chalkboard as pencil is to?). These trials (in which two relations have to be compared) were compared to semantic trials in which participants had to choose among several objects the one that was the most closely semantically related to a cued object. The results indicate age-related increases of activity in the RLPFC for both analogy and semantic trials in children. In contrast, adults showed increased activity in the RLPFC (as a function of accuracy) in analogy but not semantic trials. Using another visual analogy task, Wendelken et al., 2011) further found that activity in the RLPFC distinguishes between trials that require a comparison between two relations (i.e., an analogical judgment) and trials that only require the processing of a single relation in adolescents. However, no such difference was found before the age of fourteen years. Interestingly, that study showed that the RLPFC and the IPS are interconnected during the development of analogical reasoning. That

is, the degree of specialization of the RLPFC for relational integration was associated with the degree of cortical thinning in the parietal cortex. Therefore, as pointed out by Singley and Bunge (2014), structural development in the parietal lobe promotes RLPFC selectivity for higher-order problems, perhaps in that a more mature parietal cortex can complete lower-order tasks without taxing frontal regions.

Overall, the relatively delayed development of the brain system supporting analogical reasoning may explain some of the development of analogical reasoning skills in children. As for transitive reasoning, early findings on analogical reasoning skills of children come from Piaget. Piaget presented children with conventional analogical problems (such as the one in (3)) in a pictorial form. His main finding was that young children typically struggle to solve these problems, often relying on physical similarities between items rather than on relations between pairs of items (Inhelder & Piaget, 1958). This led Piaget to suggest that children might not be able to solve these types of problems before the age of eleven or so (Inhelder & Piaget, 1958). More recently, studies have found that the ability to solve classic analogical problems emerge much earlier, to the extent that children are familiar with the relations involved (Goswami & Brown, 1989; Richland et al., 2006; Singer-Freeman, & Goswami, 2001; Tunteler & Resing, 2002). For example, children as young as three years may be able to solve an analogy based on relations of physical causality, such as the one in (4) (Goswami & Brown, 1989). However, the fact remains that young children's analogical reasoning abilities are limited and only slowly improve through childhood and adolescence (such that only adolescents and adults may be able to solve the more abstract analogy in (3)). How can one explain this development? Clearly, one needs to have knowledge about the world to abstract relations and reason analogically. Therefore, with increasing knowledge, the relational similarity between different pairs of items should become increasingly salient (Rattermann & Gentner, 1998; Vendetti et al., 2015). Of course, because knowledge about the world increases with age, this may explain the increase in analogical reasoning performance with age.[2] Another ability that is likely to be important to improved analogical reasoning performance is the capacity to ignore information that is not relevant to the task, such as the physical similarities between items. Studies have shown that young children are very susceptible to distracting information in analogical reasoning tasks (Richland et al., 2006). Inhibiting such information is likely to require efficient executive control skills (including working memory and inhibition, Houdé, 2000, 2019), which also increase with age. Overall, the fact that increases in analogical reasoning performance with age is characterized by (i) a decrease in focus of similarities between items and (ii) an increase in focus on relational information between pairs of items is often characterized as a "relational shift" (Rattermann & Gentner, 1998). Before this relational shift, analogical reasoning remains difficult for young children. This is especially the case when relational patterns are more conceptual than perceptual, which is likely to be the case in many aspects of mathematical learning. Therefore, as stated by Vendetti et al. (2015, p. 102), "research suggests that elementary school children may need structured guidance when attempting to make relational comparisons between domains so that they draw the intended conclusion from the analogy."

27.3 Implications for the Classroom: The Role of Problem-Solving

As is made clear by the literature review in Section 27.2, there is little doubt that relational reasoning skills contribute to mathematical growth in children. Yet, we also reviewed evidence indicating that some of those skills only slowly develop from early childhood to late adolescence. Thus, education may play an important role in scaffolding children's relational reasoning abilities throughout the mathematics curriculum. An interesting way for teachers to promote reasoning in the classroom may be to have children engage in problem-solving, that is, "the cognitive process directed at achieving a goal when the problem solver does not initially know a solution method" (Mayer & Wittrock, 2006, p. 287). Indeed, following pioneering work by Lakatos (1976), Polya (1945), and Schoenfeld (1985), research in math education has often suggested that problem-solving may be an effective way of promoting mathematical reasoning (Törner et al., 2007). We point to five reasons for this. First, problem-solving allows students to apply mathematical knowledge and, in doing so, makes learning meaningful (Artigue & Houdement, 2007). For example, Gibel (2013) argues that solving problems is a situation in which students have to engage in reasoning processes, but also have to assess the validity of these processes. Second, problem-solving provides a context in which reasoning may serve different goals. For example, reasoning may support decision-making or the development of a general solving method (starting, for example, from specific instances). It may also promote arguments regarding the validity and relevance of the results. Third, problem-solving is an opportunity for students to encounter different modes of reasoning (Dias & Durand-Guerrier, 2005; Douek, 2010; Grenier, 2013). For

---

[2] Note, however, that this idea assumes that increases in performance stem from knowledge acquisition per se rather than from chronological age.

example, Gardes and Durand-Guerrier (2016) have shown that experimental approaches to mathematics learning may involve both deductive and inductive reasoning. An experimental approach to mathematics learning may also highlight what is a cornerstone of mathematical thinking, that is, the interplay between mathematical knowledge and heuristic processes (Polya, 1954). Fourth, problem-solving may encourage proof thinking in students (Balacheff, 1988). Finally, solving problems in the classroom is an ideal situation for students to engage in scientific debates, which may be beneficial to reasoning skills and critical thinking in general (Brousseau, 1997; Douek, 2010; Kuhn & Crowell, 2011).

Problems in the classroom may have different learning goals, and therefore may engage reasoning in different ways. It may be useful to break down mathematical problems into three different categories, depending on their learning goals: problems that focus on acquiring new concepts, problems that focus on strengthening already acquired concepts, and problems that focus on promoting investigative processes *in themselves*. Whereas the explicit goal of the first two types of problems may be to learn and practice some specific reasoning skills, the last type of problems may incidentally engage reasoning skills while students work out the solution of the problem. Consider for example the problems in (5) and (6):

(5)   A teacher gives children six strips of paper, each of a different length. The children have to order these strips from the smallest to the largest. After they are given the opportunity to work on the problem, the teacher points to the fact that one can start by putting down the smallest of the six strips, then (next to it) the smallest of the remaining five strips, and so on.

(6)   A teacher gives children several nesting cups (not nested) and a suitcase. Children have to store the cups in the suitcase. Because the suitcase is relatively small, the only way to store the cups is to nest them from the smallest to the largest.

The situation in (5) is an example of a problem whose explicit goal is to learn a new concept (i.e., serial order), using a particular technique. In contrast, the goal of the situation in (6) is merely to investigate and look for a solution. However, in doing so, children may apprehend serial order as a relevant reasoning strategy to solve the problem. Note that, in (5) as in (6), students can manipulate the materials to develop some reasoning and come up with a solution. They implement what can be described as an "experimental approach," in other words, a "back-and-forth between manipulation of objects and theoretical elaborations realized through the articulation of three processes: experimentation, formulation, and validation" (Gardes, 2018, p. 83). Such an experimental approach consists of making conjectures, testing them, modifying them and proving those that have withstood the test. This not only promotes inductive reasoning when student have to make conjectures, but also deductive reasoning when those conjectures have to be formally demonstrated (Polya, 1954).

Although having students to engage in problem-solving situations may be a prerequisite to promote reasoning skills in the classroom, it may not be sufficient. That is, for learning to occur, situations may need to adhere to some criteria. For example, students should work on problems by themselves, without the teacher's intervention (Brousseau, 1997). Problems should also (i) be challenging, (ii) concern a conceptual domain that is familiar to the students, and

(iii) induce neither the solution nor the solving method. Therefore, teachers should create an environment that encourages students to become involved in problem-solving.[3] It may also be beneficial for students to work in small groups, so that they can express ideas and explain their reasoning to others. Group work may also encourage students to take into account suggestions from others and encourage argumentation (Mercier et al., 2017). Finally, students may take part in debates. This would expose them to alternative perspectives and force them to engage in a process of formulation and validation of their solutions. Overall, a growing body of literature suggests that group discussions can be a very efficient way to increase reasoning performance in children and adults (Mercier & Sperber, 2011).

There area variety of scenarios in which students may engage in problem-solving, while taking into consideration all of the factors mentioned. However, just to give an example, suppose that (in a first session) students are split into small groups and given some time to solve a mathematical problem (without any intervention from the teacher). The teacher may then ask them to prepare a poster. A follow-up session may then be devoted to the presentation of these posters, as well as to collective discussions through a scientific debate (Arsac & Mante, 2007). Although this situation is just one among many possible scenarios, regular use of such problem-solving sessions in the classroom may help foster reasoning skills.

In Sections 27.3.1–27.3.3, we give some examples of problems that may teach transitive and analogical reasoning in young children. We then give an example of a problem in which both deductive and inductive reasoning are incidentally used when working out the solution.

27.3.1 Learning to Reason with Transitive Relations

Suppose that children are given the following instructions: "James is a tamer of big cats for a circus. James would like his cats to walk in line one behind the other. Can you help James keep his animals in line using the information provided?" (see Figure 27.1).

In order to successfully solve this problem, children must understand the transitive relations in the information provided. For example, from the first two sentences, children can infer the order lion, tiger, and cheetah. The cheetah can then be placed in the second to last position and a possible solution (or all possible solutions) can be proposed. It is easy to change the problem by changing some didactic variables (Brousseau, 1997): the number of animals, the number of constraints, the order of information, the number of correct solutions or the question asked. For example, explicitly asking who follows the lion would force children to use transitive reasoning. Overall, problems such as these may help show children how serial orders can be constructed from transitive relations. They can be solved by children individually or in groups, and even involve materials such as toy animals.

27.3.2 Learning to Reason by Analogy

In a typical patterning problem, children have to describe and reproduce a given alternating sequence (e.g., AABBAABB) using different sets of materials. For instance, children may be presented with a sequence made of alternating white and black diamonds. They are then

---

[3] By environment, we mean everything that may promote effective learning: material or non-material objects, state of current knowledge, documents, organization of interactions, etc. (Brousseau, 1997).

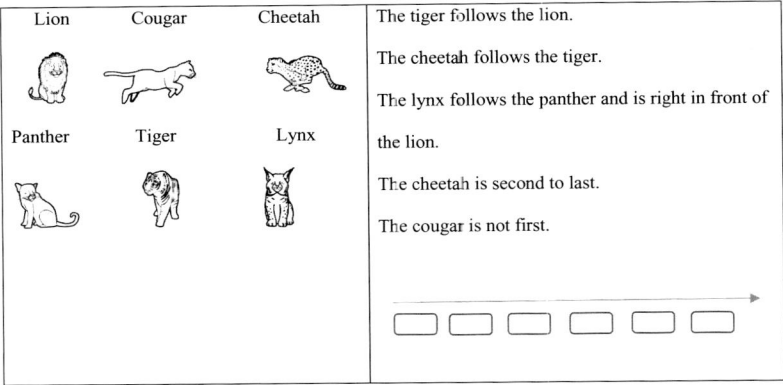

Figure 27.1 Example of materials used in the problem about transitive relations
A black-and-white version of this figure will appear in some formats. For the color
version, please refer to the plate section.

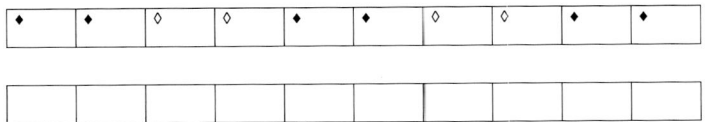

Figure 27.2 Example of materials used in the patterning problem

presented with an empty grid and given the following instructions: "Look carefully at the design I gave you. When you are done looking at it, hide it. Then, try to reproduce that design on the grid, with your tokens. When you think you are done, compare your design with the one I gave you" (see Figure 27.2). Children may work on such problems alone.

In order to successfully solve such a patterning problem, students need to notice what is unique about the design (i.e., the alternating sequence), so they can replicate it. Children who recognize the alternating pattern of two black diamonds and two white diamonds will succeed in reproducing the sequence with the same set of materials (black and white diamonds) but may also abstract the sequence if given a different set of materials (e.g., blue and yellow squares). In other words, several didactic variables can be manipulated, such as the pattern, the number of different tokens (shape and/or color), the initial design viewing time,

the presence of a grid, etc. The teacher may also encourage children to explicitly formulate the pattern by asking them to tell other children how to make the design.

The two problem-solving situations described here explicitly aim to teach relational reasoning. But even problems that may not necessarily be used to explicitly teach reasoning (e.g., problems that are used to promote investigative behavior) may encourage students to reason. For instance, these problems may highlight the difference between inductive reasoning (e.g., analogical reasoning) and deductive reasoning (e.g., transitive reasoning). An example of one such problem is given here.

27.3.3 Learning to Investigate: The Interplay between Inductive and Deductive Reasoning

Consider the following scenario (Aldon et al., 2017):

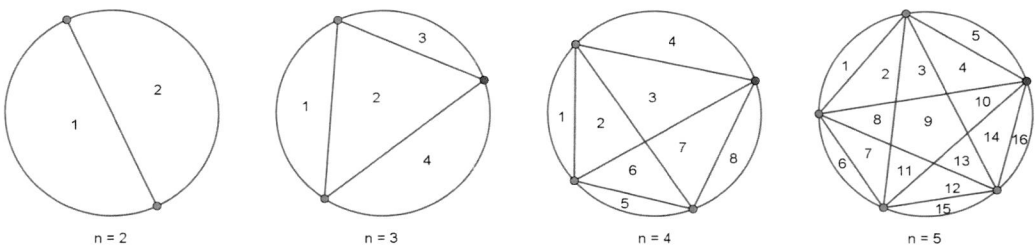

Figure 27.3 Examples of line configurations with different values of n in the geometry problem. For n = 2 there are two areas, for n = 3 there are four areas, for n = 4 there are eight areas, and for n = 5 there are sixteen areas. From these observations, students may use inductive reasoning to make the following conjecture: For n points on the circle, the number of areas is 2^{n-1}. However, perseverant students will realize that drawing lines with n = 6 leads to thirty-one areas (instead of thirty-two areas)! Thus, the formula must be incorrect

A black-and-white version of this figure will appear in some formats. For the color version, please refer to the plate section.

(7)   When two points are on a circle, the line joining them defines two areas within the disk. How about with three points? four points? and n points? What is the maximum number of areas possible within the disk?

A first step toward solving this problem often consists of drawing lines with the first few values of n. Figure 27.3 displays the number of areas corresponding to values of n from two to five.

One method that can be used to explain this surprising result is to come up with a formula after having systematically studied and enumerated several geometric configurations. For example, at the very beginning, there is only one point on the circle and only one area (i.e., the whole disk). Drawing another point (n = 2) adds a line, which itself adds an area (see Figure 27.3). Therefore, when n = 2, there is one line and two areas. With n = 3, there are three lines and each line adds one area. Thus, there are 1 + 3 = 4 areas. Students may then start to hypothesize that counting the areas is equivalent to counting the lines. In other words, it amounts to counting the combinations of two out of n points, i.e., $\binom{n}{2} = \frac{n(n-1)}{2}$. With n = 4, however it becomes

clear that this reasoning is insufficient. Indeed, there is one additional region every time two lines intersect. In fact, there are as many points of intersection as there are quadrilaterals whose corners are among the n points on the circle, that is, the number of combinations of four points among n: $\binom{n}{4} = \frac{n(n-1)(n-2)(n-3)}{4!}$. From this observation, students can derive the general formula of the maximum number of regions determined by n points on the circle:

$$1 + \binom{n}{2} + \binom{n}{4} = 1 + \frac{n(n-1)}{2} + \frac{n(n-1)(n-2)(n-3)}{4!}.$$

Overall, this situation illustrates the necessary interplay between inductive and deductive reasoning. Inductive reasoning is useful to make progress when looking for the solution of a problem. For example, it can be used to make conjectures. However, inductive reasoning does not always make it possible to validate the solution. Here, for instance, studying the geometric configuration with n = 6 makes it clear that the conjecture is wrong. But it does not explain why. Students need to use deductive reasoning when systematically studying how areas are added when points are drawn on the circle. This makes it possible to (i) find the correct solution given by a formula and (ii) demonstrate this formula.

27.4 Conclusion

Over the past decades, the literature on mathematical cognition has largely focused on the idea that primitive intuitions about quantities serve as a foundation for symbolic mathematics. This has notably led to the development of theories emphasizing how individual differences in the quality of magnitude representations affect math learning (Feigenson et al., 2013). Although this focus has allowed for significant progress to be made in the field, it is also clear that mathematical skills are wide ranging and go beyond basic representations of numerical magnitudes. In other words, mathematical skills are likely to involve multiple cognitive processes and representations. In the present chapter, we argue that the ability to understand and integrate relations is central to the development of mathematical skills. We have reviewed research indicating that such relational reasoning skills may be present early in development, but also considerably improve from childhood to adolescence. Thus, mathematics teachers may have an important role to play in nurturing relational reasoning skills in children. To reach this educational goal, they may use problem-solving situations in which students are confronted to different forms of relational reasoning as well as to the fundamental difference and complementarity between induction and deduction.

References

Aldon, G., Durand-Guerrier, V., & Ray, B. (2017). Problems promoting the devolution of the process of mathematisation: An example in number theory and a realistic fiction. In G. Aldon, F. Hitt, L. Bazzini, & U. Gellert (eds.), *Mathematics and Technology* (pp. 411–429). Cham, Switzerland: Springer.

Ansari, D. (2008). Effects of development and enculturation on number representation in the brain. *Nature Reviews Neuroscience, 9*, 278–291.

Arsac, G., & Mante, M. (2007). Les pratiques du problème ouvert. *SCEREN-CRDP de l'Académie de Lyon.*

Artigue, M., & Houdement, C. (2007). Problem solving in France: Research and curricular perspectives. *Zentral Blatt Für Didaktik Der Mathematik, 39*, 365–382.

Balacheff, N. (1988). Aspects of proof in pupils' practice of school mathematics. In D. Pimm (ed.), *Mathematics, Teachers and Children* (pp. 216–235). London: Hodder and Stoughton.

Bartha, P. (2013). Analogy and analogical reasoning. In E. N. Zalta (ed.), *The Stanford Encyclopedia of Philosophy.* Available from https://plato.stanford.edu/cite.html.

Brannon, E. M., & Terrace, H. S. (1998). Ordering of the numerosities 1 to 9 by monkeys. *Science, 282*, 746–749.

Brousseau, G. (1997). *Theory of Didactical Situations in Mathematics*, trans by N. Balacheff, M. Cooper, R. Sutherland, & V. Warfield. Dordrecht, NL: Kluwer.

Bryant, P. E., & Kopytynska, H. (1976). Spontaneous measurement by young children. *Nature, 260*, 773.

Bryant, P. E., & Trabasso, T. (1971). Transitive inferences and memory in young children. *Nature, 232*, 458–465.

Bunge, S., Helskog, E., & Wendelken, C. (2009). Left, but not right, rostrolateral prefrontal cortex meets a stringent test of the relational integration hypothesis. *Neuroimage, 46*, 338–342.

Bunge, S., & Wendelken, C. (2009). Comparing the bird in the hand with the ones in the bush. *Neuron, 62*, 609–611.

Bunge, S., Wendelken, C., Badre, D., & Wagner, A. (2005). Analogical reasoning and prefrontal cortex: Evidence for separable retrieval and integration mechanisms. *Cerebral Cortex, 15*, 239–249.

Burgoyne, K., Witteveen, K., Tolan, A., Malone, S., & Hulme, C. (2017). Pattern understanding: Relationships with arithmetic and reading development. *Child Development Perspectives, 11*, 239–244.

Crone, E., Wendelken, C., van Leijenhorst, L., Honomichl, R., Christoff, K., & Bunge, S. (2009). Neurocognitive development of relational reasoning. *Developmental Science, 12*, 55–66.

Delius, J. D., & Siemann, M. (1998). Transitive responding in animals and humans: exaption rather than adaption? *Behavioural Processes, 42*, 107–137.

Dias, T., & Durand-Guerrier, V. (2005). Expérimenter pour apprendre en mathématiques. *Repères IREM, 60*, 61–78.

Douek, N. (2010). Approaching proof in school: From guided conjecturing and proving to a story of proof construction. *Proceedings of the Sixth Congress of the European Society for Research in Mathematics Education*, January 28–February 1, 2009. Lyon, France.

Dumontheil, I., Burgess, P. W., & Blakemore, S. J. (2008). Development of rostral prefrontal cortex and cognitive and behavioural disorders. *Developmental Medicine & Child Neurology, 50*, 168–181.

Dumontheil, I., Houlton, R., Christoff, K., & Blakemore, S.-J. (2010). Development of relational reasoning during adolescence. *Developmental Science, 13*, 24.

English, L. D. (2004). *Mathematical and Analogical Reasoning of Young Learners*. Mahwah, NJ: Lawrence Erlbaum

Evans, J. S. (2003). In two minds: Dual-process accounts of reasoning. *Trends in Cognitive Science, 7*, 454–459.

Feigenson, L., Libertus, M. E., & Halberda, J. (2013). Links between the intuitive sense of number and formal mathematics ability. *Child Development Perspectives, 7*, 74–79.

Fias, W., Menon, V., & Szucs, D. (2013). Multiple components of developmental dyscalculia. *Trends in Neuroscience and Education, 2*, 43–47.

Frank, M. J. (2005). Dynamic dopamine modulation in the basal ganglia: A neurocomputational account of cognitive deficits in medicated and nonmedicated Parkinsonism. *Journal of Cognitive Neuroscience, 17*, 51–72.

Frank, M. J., Rudy, J. W., & O'Reilly, R. C. (2003). Transitivity, flexibility, conjunctive representations, and the hippocampus. II. A computational analysis. *Hippocampus, 13*, 341–354.

Fuchs, L. S., Compton, D. L., Fuchs, D., Paulsen, K., Bryant, J. D., & Hamlett, C. L. (2005). The prevention, identification, and cognitive determinants of math difficulty. *Journal of Educational Psychology, 97*, 493–513.

Gardes, M. L. (2018). Démarches d'investigation et recherche de problèmes. In G. Aldon (ed.), *Le Rallye mathématique, un jeu très sérieux!* (pp. 73–96). Poitiers: Canopée.

Gardes, M. L. & Durand-Guerrier, V. (2016). Designation at the core of the dialectic between experimentation and proving: A study in number theory. *Paper presented at the First Conference of International Network for Didactic Research in University Mathematics*. March 31–April 2, 2016, Montpellier, France.

Gibel, P. (2013). The presentation and setting up of a model of analysis of reasoning processes in mathematics lessons in primary schools. *Paper presented at the Proceedings of the Eighth Congress of the European Society for Research in Mathematics Education*. February 6–10, 2013, Manavgat-Side, Antalya, Turkey.

Goswami, U., & Brown, A. L. (1989). Melting chocolate and melting snowmen: Analogical reasoning and causal relations. *Cognition, 35*, 69–95.

Green, C. T., Bunge, S. A., Chiongbian, V. B., Barrow, M., & Ferrer, E. (2017). Fluid reasoning predicts future mathematical performance among children and adolescents. *Journal of Experimental Child Psychology, 157*, 125–143.

Grenier, D. (2013). Research situations to learn logic and various types of mathematical reasonings and proofs. *Paper presented at the Proceedings of the Eighth Congress of the European Society for Research in Mathematics Education*. February 6–10, 2013, Manavgat-Side, Antalya, Turkey.

Grosenick, L., Clement, T. S., & Fernald, R. D. (2007). Fish can infer social rank by observation alone. *Nature, 445*, 429–432.

Halford, G. (1992). Analogical reasoning and conceptual complexity in cognitive development. *Human Development, 35*, 193–217.

Halford, G., Wilson, W. H., & Phillips, S. (2010). Relational knowledge: The foundation of higher cognition. *Trends in Cognitive Sciences, 14,* 497–505.

Handley, S., Capon, A., Beveridge, M., Dennis, I., & Evans, J. S. B. T. (2004). Working memory, inhibitory control, and the development of children's reasoning. *Thinking & Reasoning, 10,* 175–195.

Hinton, E. C., Dymond, S., von Hecker, U., & Evans, C. J. (2010). Neural correlates of relational reasoning and the symbolic distance effect: Involvement of parietal cortex. *Neuroscience, 168,* 138–148.

Holyoak, K. J., & Thagard, P. (1995). *Mental Leaps: Analogy in Creative Thought.* Cambridge, MA: MIT Press.

Houdé, O. (2000). Inhibition and cognitive development: Object, number, categorization, and reasoning. *Cognitive Development, 15,* 63–73.

Houdé, O. (2019). *3-System Theory of the Cognitive Brain: A Post-Piagetian Approach.* New York: Routledge.

Houdé, O., Pineau, A., Leroux, G., Poirel, N., Perchey, G., Lanoë, C., ... Mazoyer, B. (2011). Functional MRI study of Piaget's conservation-of-number task in preschool and school-age children: A neo-Piagetian approach. *Journal of Experimental Child Psychology, 110,* 332–346.

Hubbard, E., Piazza, M., Pinel, P., & Dehaene, S. (2005). Interactions between number and space in parietal cortex. *Nature Reviews Neuroscience, 6,* 435–448.

Inglis, M., & Attridge, N. (2017). *Does Mathematical Study Develop Logical Thinking?: Testing the Theory of Formal Discipline.* Singapore: World Scientific.

Inhelder, B., & Piaget, J. (1958). *The Growth of Logical Thinking from Childhood to Adolescence: An Essay on the Construction of Formal Operational Structures.* New York: Basic Books.

Ischebeck, A., Schocke, M., & Delazer, M. (2009). The processing and representation of fractions within the brain: An fMRI investigation. *Neuroimage, 47,* 403–413.

Jacob, S. N., & Nieder, A. (2009). Notation-independent representation of fractions in the human parietal cortex. *Journal of Neuroscience, 29,* 4652–4657.

Kallio, K. D. (1988). Developmental difference in the comprehension of simple and compound comparative relations. *Child Development, 59,* 397–410.

Kuhn, D., & Crowell, A. (2011). Dialogic argumentation as a vehicle for developing young adolescents' thinking. *Psychological Science, 22,* 545–552.

Lakatos, I. (1976). *Proofs and Refutations.* Cambridge: Cambridge University Press.

Lee, K., Ng, S. F., Bull, R., Pe, M. L., & Ho, R. (2011). Are patterns important? An investigation of the relationships between proficiencies in patterns, computation, executive functioning and algebraic word problems. *Journal of Educational Psychology, 103,* 269–281.

Lyons, I. M., Vogel, S. E., & Ansari, D. (2016). On the ordinality of numbers: A review of neural and behavioral studies. *Progress in Brain Research, 227,* 187–221.

Mayer, R. E., & Wittrock, M. C. (2006). Problem solving. In P. A. Alexander, & P. H. Winne (eds.), *Handbook of Educational Psychology* (2nd ed., pp. 287–304). Mahwah, NJ: Erlbaum.

Mercier, H., Boudry, M., Paglieri, F., & Trouche, E. (2017). Natural-born arguers: Teaching how to make the best of our reasoning abilities. *Educational Psychologist, 52,* 1–16.

Mercier, H., & Sperber, D. (2011). Why do humans reason? Arguments for an argumentative theory. *Behavioral and Brain Sciences, 34,* 57–74.

Morsanyi, K., Devine, A., Nobes, A., & Szűcs, D. (2013). The link between logic, mathematics and imagination: Evidence from children with developmental dyscalculia and mathematically gifted children. *Developmental Science, 16,* 542–553.

Morsanyi, K., Kahl, T., & Rooney, R. (2017a). The link between math and logic in adolescence: The effect of argument form. In M. E. Toplak, & J. Weller (eds.), *Individual Differences in Judgment and Decision Making from a Developmental Context* (pp. 166–185). Hove: Psychology Press.

Morsanyi, K., McCormack, T., & O'Mahony, E. (2017b). The link between deductive reasoning and mathematics. *Thinking & Reasoning*, 24, 1–24.

Morsanyi, K., & Szücs, D. (2014). The link between mathematics and logical reasoning. In S. Chinn (ed.), *The Routledge International Handbook of Dyscalculia and Mathematical Learning Difficulties* (pp. 101–114). London: Routledge.

Moutier, S., Plagne, S., Melot, A.-M., & Houdé, O. (2006). Syllogistic reasoning and belief-bias inhibition in school children. *Developmental Science*, 9, 166–172.

Moyer, R. S., & Bayer, R. H. (1976). Mental comparison and the symbolic distance effect. *Cognitive Psychology*, 8, 228–246.

Newstead, S., Keeble, S., & Manktelow, K. (1985). Children's performance on set inclusion and linear ordering relationships. *Bulletin of the Psychonomic Society*, 23, 105–108.

Pasnak, R., Schmerold, K. L., Robinson, M. F., Gadzichowski, K. M., Bock, A. M., O'Brien. S. E., ... Gallington, D. A. (2016). Understanding number sequences leads to understanding mathematics concepts. *The Journal of Educational Research*, 109, 640–646.

Paz, Y. M. C. G., Bond, A. B., Kamil, A. C., & Balda, R. P. (2004). Pinyon jays use transitive inference to predict social dominance. *Nature*, 430, 778–781.

Peters, L., & De Smedt, B. (2017). Arithmetic in the developing brain: A review of brain imaging studies. *Developmental Cognitive Neuroscience*, 30, 265–279.

Piaget, J. (1952). *The Child's Conception of Number*. London: Routledge & Kegan Paul.

Piaget, J., & Inhelder, B. (1967). *The Child's Conception of Space*. London: Routledge & Kegan Paul.

Polya, G. (1945). *How to Solve It*. Princeton, NJ: Princeton University Press.

Polya, G. (1954). *Mathematics and Plausible Reasoning*. Princeton, NJ: Princeton University Press.

Potts, G. (1972). Information processing stragies used in the encoding of linear ordering. *Journal of Verbal Learning and Verbal Behavior*, 11, 727–740.

Potts, G. (1974). Storing and retrieving information about ordered relationship. *Journal of Experimental Psychology: General*, 103, 431–439.

Prado, J., Chadha, A., & Booth, J. (2011). The brain network for deductive reasoning: A quantitative meta-analysis of 28 neuroimaging studies. *Journal of Cognitive Neuroscience*, 23, 3483–3497.

Prado, J., Noveck, I. A., & Van Der Henst, J.-B. (2010). Overlapping and distinct neural representations of numbers and verbal transitive series. *Cerebral Cortex*, 20, 720–729.

Prado, J., Van der Henst, J.-B., & Noveck, I. A. (2008). Spatial associations in relational reasoning: evidence for a SNARC-like effect. *Quarterly Journal of Experimental Psychology (Colchester)*, 61, 1143–1150.

Primi, R., Ferrão, M. E., & Almeida, L. S. (2010). Fluid intelligence as a predictor of learning: A longitudinal multilevel approach applied to math. *Learning and Individual Differences*, 20, 446–451.

Rabinowitz, F. M., & Howe, M. L. (1994). Development of the middle concept. *Journal of Experimental Child Psychology*, 57, 418–449.

Rattermann, M. J., & Gentner, D. (1998). More evidence for a relational shift in the development of analogy: Children's performance on a causal-mapping task. *Cognitive Development*, 13, 453–478.

Richland, L. E., Holyoak, K. J., & Stigler, J. W. (2004). Analogy use in eighth-grade mathematics classrooms. *Cognition and Instruction*, 22, 37–60.

Richland, L. E., Morrison, R. G., & Holyoak, K. J. (2006). Children's development of analogical reasoning: insights from scene analogy problems. *Journal of Experimental Child Psychology*, 94, 249–273.

Richland, L. E., & Simms, N. (2015). Analogy, higher order thinking, and education. *Wiley Interdisciplinary Reviews: Cognitive Science*, 6, 177–192.

Richland, L. E., Zur, O., & Holyoak, K. J. (2007). Mathematics. Cognitive supports for analogies in the mathematics classroom. *Science*, 316, 1128–1129.

Rittle-Johnson, B., Fyfe, E. R., Hofer, K. G., & Farran, D. C. (2016). Early math trajectories:

Low-income children's mathematics knowledge from age 4 to 11. *Child Development, 88,* 1727–1742.

Rittle-Johnson, B., Zippert, E. L., & Boice, K. L. (2018). The roles of patterning and spatial skills in early mathematics development. *Early Childhood Research Quarterly, 46,* 166–178.

Russell, J., McCormack, T., Robinson, J., & Lillis, G. (1996). Logical (versus associative) performance on transitive inference tasks by children: Implications for the status of animals' performance. *The Quarterly Journal of Experimental Psychology, 49B,* 231–244.

Schoenfeld, A. (1985). *Mathematical Problem Solving.* Cambridge, MA: Academic press.

Schwartz, F., Epinat-Duclos, J., Léone, J., Poisson, A., & Prado, J. (2018). Impaired neural processing of transitive relations in children with math learning disability. *NeuroImage: Clinical, 20,* 1255–1265.

Schwartz, F., Epinat-Duclos, J., Léone, J., Poisson, A., & Prado, J. (2020). Neural representations of transitive relations predict current and future math calculation skills in children. *Neuropsychologia, 141,* 107410.

Singer-Freeman, K. E., & Goswami, U. (2001). Does half a pizza equal half a box of chocolates? Proportional matching in an analogy task. *Cognitive Development, 16,* 811–829.

Singley, A. T. M., & Bunge, S. A. (2014). Neurodevelopment of relational reasoning: Implications for mathematical pedagogy. *Trends in Neuroscience and Education, 3,* 33–37.

Sriraman, B. (2005). Mathematical and analogical reasoning of young learners. *ZDM – Mathematics Education, 37,* 506–509.

Taub, G. E., Floyd, R. G., Keith, T. Z., & McGrew, K. S. (2008). Effects of general and broad cognitive abilities on mathematics achievement. *School Psychology Quarterly, 23,* 187–198.

Törner, G., Schoenfeld, A. H., & Reiss, K. M. (2007). Problem solving around the world: Summing up the state of the art. *Zentral Blatt Für Didaktik Der Mathematik, 39,* 353.

Tunteler, E., & Resing, W. C. (2002). Spontaneous analogical transfer in 4-year-olds:

A microgenetic study. *Journal of Experimental Child Psychology, 83,* 149–166.

Vanderheyden, A. M., Broussard, C., Snyder, P., George, J., Meche Lafleur, S., & Williams, C. (2011). Measurement of kindergartners' understanding of early mathematical concepts. *School Psychology Review, 40,* 296–306.

Vasconcelos, M. (2008). Transitive inference in non-human animals: An empirical and theoretical analysis. *Behavioral Processes, 78,* 313–334.

Vendetti, M. S., Matlen, B. J., Richland, L. E., & Bunge, S. A. (2015). Analogical reasoning in the classroom: Insights from cognitive science. *Mind, Brain, and Education, 9,* 100–106.

von Fersen, L., Wynne, C. D., Delius, J. D., & Staddon, J. (1991). Transitive inference formation in pigeons. *Journal of Experimental Psychology Animal Behavior Processes, 17,* 334–341.

Waltz, J. A., Lau, A., Grewal, S. K., & Holyoak, K. J. (2000). The role of working memory in analogical mapping. *Memory & Cognition, 28,* 1205–1212.

Wendelken, C. (2015). Meta-analysis: How does posterior parietal cortex contribute to reasoning? *Frontiers in Human Neuroscience, 8,* 1042.

Wendelken, C., Nakhabenko, D., Donohue, S., Carter, C., & Bunge, S. (2008). "Brain is to thought as stomach is to??": Investigating the role of rostrolateral prefrontal cortex in relational reasoning. *Journal of Cognitive Neuroscience, 20,* 682–693.

Wendelken, C., O'Hare, E., Whitaker, K., Ferrer, E., & Bunge, S. (2011). Increased functional selectivity over development in rostrolateral prefrontal cortex. *Journal of Neuroscience, 31,* 17260–17268.

Wright, B. C. (2001). Reconceptualizing the transitive inference ability: A framework for existing and future research. *Developmental Review, 21,* 375–422.

Wright, B. C. (2012). The case for a dual-process theory of transitive reasoning. *Developmental Review, 32,* 89–124.

Wright, S., Matlen, B., Baym, C., Ferrer, E., & Bunge, S. (2007). Neural correlates of fluid reasoning in children and adults. *Frontiers in Human Neuroscience, 1,* 8.

28 Children's Scientific Reasoning Skills in Light of General Cognitive Development

Peter A. Edelsbrunner, Ralph Schumacher, and Elsbeth Stern

The desire to understand and explain patterns and regularities in terms of causal laws is part of human nature. This search for knowledge contributes to making the world predictable as well as controllable, and it enables the invention and production of technologies that help to improve quality-of-life. Although debates about criteria for good causal explanations and conclusive evidence are still a controversial topic of epistemology and theory of science, some widely accepted standards for scientific reasoning have emerged. The distinction between explanation and observation, and the control of variables strategy (CVS) for designing and evaluating experiments are two widely accepted concepts. Mastering the CVS means to vary only the levels of the focal variable in experimental designs while keeping all other potentially confounding variables constant across conditions.

28.1 The Emergence of Scientific Reasoning Skills during Childhood

As we will see in the present chapter, understanding and managing the distinction between theory and evidence and the CVS are two concepts that go hand in hand from the perspective of cognitive development. Only when we manage to coordinate theory and evidence as two distinct yet mutually interacting entities, we can make sure that our own beliefs and prior knowledge do adequately influence, but not negatively bias the design and interpretation of our experiments. The

coordination of theory and evidence in the application of the CVS and further scientific reasoning skills requires advanced cognitive processes. Therefore, the development of scientific reasoning skills depends significantly on our more general cognitive capabilities. At which age the general cognitive capabilities required for successful scientific reasoning develop, and how this development supports and constrains children's scientific reasoning, is in the focus of the present chapter.

Jean Piaget considered frequently observed violations of the CVS among children younger than twelve years as major evidence for his theory of cognitive development. Among other tasks, Inhelder and Piaget (1958) used the pendulum problem to demonstrate the transition from concrete to formal operational thought around the age of twelve. A schematic depiction of the pendulum task is provided in Figure 28.1.

In this task, participants are presented with a pendulum that allows varying the length of the string and the heaviness of the weight. The goal is to find out which of the following three factors is most important in determining the speed of swing of the pendulum: The length of the string, the heaviness of the weight, or the strength of the push. To find the correct answer, the participant has to grasp the idea of the experimental method – that is, to vary one variable at a time. For instance, trying different lengths with the same weight and the same strength of the push would adhere to this principle. A participant who neglects the CVS

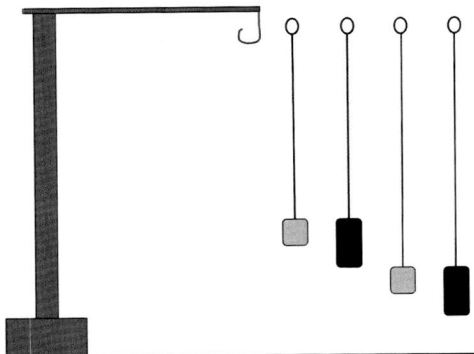

Figure 28.1 Setup of the pendulum task with the variables string length (two pendulums on the left: shorter; two pendulums on the right: longer) and heaviness of the weight (grey weights: lighter; black weights: heavier)

and simultaneously tries different lengths with different weights is likely to end up with the wrong answer. Somerville (1974), who was the first to present this task to a larger sample of 235 students between ten and fourteen years of age, found a strong increase of performance during this age period, while there was little variance within the age levels. These results confirmed a strong impact of a general mechanism of cognitive development on the CVS which, according to Piaget's theory, was the capability for abstract thinking.

This one-dimensional explanation of cognitive development was seriously challenged by numerous findings from the 1980s and 1990s on a variety of Piagetian tasks, among them the CVS (Stern, 2005). First, it turned out that task-specific characteristics like the context of the stories or the wording of the questions made some of the problems presented by Piaget and his team particularly difficult for younger children. By selecting a more familiar context and by some rewordings, much younger children were able to solve CVS tasks. Second, between-age variance in task performance has been found overlaid with strong within-age variation. This was particularly the

case when more heterogeneous samples were considered than had been the case in the earlier research in the 1970s. Personal traits as well as environmental factors seem to have a stronger impact on cognitive development than suggested by Piaget's theory. Both of these factors apply to the CVS and will be dealt with here.

We will first summarize central theories of scientific reasoning that connect the skills needed for systematic inquiry with more general cognitive development. These theories emphasize that scientific reasoning, which already starts developing in preschool age, stimulated by learning opportunities undergoes processes of refinement during later childhood. These theories also establish a substantial connection between children's scientific reasoning skills and their construction of domain-specific content knowledge, an assumption that is corroborated by recent evidence. In the second part, we will summarize findings on individual differences in scientific reasoning abilities, which occur at all age levels. These individual differences depend substantially on children's more general cognitive development. Differential relations with non-verbal and verbal cognitive abilities, as well as working memory and metacognitive factors will be summarized. Based on this overview, we will develop general conclusions about the aspects of cognitive development that are important for scientific reasoning during different periods of childhood.

28.2 Emergence and Refinement of Scientific Reasoning Abilities during Childhood

Studies based on the pendulum problem (e.g., Somerville, 1974) supported Piaget's classical theory according to which scientific reasoning emerges as a result of general brain maturation in early adolescence. However, the pendulum problem, as well as many other problems used in the Piagetian tradition, are out of touch with children's everyday life and therefore may have prevented the youngsters from focusing on the relevant information. In fact, Koerber et al. (2005) have documented the ability of children as young as four years of age to evaluate evidence in a context understandable for them. Children were asked about a single, dichotomous variable, namely which of two colors of chewing gum caused bad teeth. No instruction or feedback was provided. Cards depicted children with either bad or good teeth and either color of chewing gum. The number of cards depicting children with bad teeth varied per color, which led to conclusive, suggestive, and inconclusive conditions. Kindergartners correctly interpreted conclusive and suggestive evidence, but not inconclusive evidence. In other research, Klahr and Chen (2003) showed that kindergartners can even learn to interpret inconclusive evidence correctly when explicit feedback is given on their evaluation of evidence.

Such findings reveal similarities between children's activities in familiar inquiry settings and proceedings of scientists, who develop hypotheses, test their predictions, and revise them in light of evidence. In case of an unfamiliar context, the lack of domain-specific content knowledge prevents children from developing informative questions and engaging in systematic search processes to find out which inquiry activities work and which do not. Although mastery of CVS is central for appropriate scientific reasoning, it only works in a broader set of cognitive activities. These include asking appropriate questions, making sense of observations, revising prior beliefs, and restructuring existing knowledge in case of unexpected outcomes. Children's and even adolescents' difficulties in appropriately applying the CVS in unfamiliar contexts are partially due to their misconceptions about the goals of running experiments (Schauble et al.,

1991). Rather than viewing the goal of an experiment in finding out whether variables are causal or not (scientific goal orientation), many children and adolescents assume that experiments are run to produce desirable outcomes (engineering goal orientation). An engineering goal orientation is common among middle school children (Siler & Klahr, 2012). Such results suggest that CVS is not just a skill or procedure easy to teach and to learn, but rather requires conceptual restructuring of prior beliefs and knowledge, as has been demonstrated for many knowledge domains.

Research conducted throughout the 1980s showed that scientific reasoning skills can be trained in middle to late childhood with positive and lasting success (Ross, 1988). Chen and Klahr (1999) conducted a seminal study in which they showed that CVS training in elementary school can trigger substantial learning transfer across contexts and over time, both in more strongly and less strongly guided scenarios toward teaching CVS (Chen & Klahr, 1999). Lasting remote transfer over time particularly occurred in teacher-guided interventions (Strand-Cary & Klahr, 2008). During the past decades, elaborate educational interventions have boosted the development of CVS as well as other aspects of experimental design. Intervention studies now encompass the whole range of education from early elementary school to university, and low- and high achievers from diverse socioeconomic backgrounds (Lin & Lehman, 1999; Lorch et al., 2010, 2014; Zohar & Peled, 2008). In all of these populations, interventions have been designed that can successfully augment knowledge about experimental design in comparison to control groups (Chen & Klahr, 1999; Ross, 1988; Schwichow et al., 2015). A meta-analysis corroborates that the CVS can be trained very well across age groups and with rather little time investment (Schwichow et al., 2015).

In addition to CVS, another focus of past research was on the interpretation of covariation evidence (Ruffman et al., 1993) and belief revision based on counterevidence (e.g., Chinn & Brewer, 1998). Also in focus since the 1990s is the topic of epistemic beliefs, that is, beliefs about knowledge and its development (in educational contexts also called "nature of science"; see e.g., Hofer, 2004; Hofer & Pintrich, 1997; Kuhn et al., 2000; Schommer et al., 1997). A meta-analysis has shown that interventions on broader scientific reasoning beyond CVS skills reveal learning effects, although the number of studies is limited (Engelmann et al., 2016). Across different fields and for different aspects of scientific reasoning (experimentation, argumentation, epistemic beliefs/nature of science), the meta-analysis shows consistent moderate gains from interventions from primary school to higher education.

28.2.1 Scientific Reasoning Skills and Domain-Specific Content Knowledge

A discussion of cognitive factors influencing children's scientific reasoning first requires distinguishing between two central facets: First, *domain-general* scientific reasoning, which is based on principles that can be applied similarly across domains, and secondly *domain-specific* scientific reasoning, which is based on content knowledge that can be applied only to the respective domain. Domain-general scientific reasoning, for example, is required in the item presented in Figure 28.2.

In this item, understanding of the *determinacy* and *indeterminacy* of evidence is required: only one classmate likes cookies, and thus the evidence seems quite clear – it is a determinate situation. If, however, both classmates liked cookies, the evidence would be indeterminate, and Paul's cookie-test would be inconclusive. The situation described in this item is quite context-specific. The underlying domain-general principle of determinacy, however, is principally valid across any contexts and content domains. For example, in inquiry-based science education, the understanding of determinacy often plays a role, in that any scientific evidence can be determinate, or indeterminate, and has to be interpreted accordingly. Research on domain-general scientific reasoning was established in the

Recently, someone from Paul's school class started leaving letters on his table, without signing them. Paul wants to find out who it is! He leaves a cookie on his table.
And indeed, the next day the cookie is gone apart from some crumbs, and another letter has been left behind!
Good for Paul that he knows his classmates so well; he is quite sure that it is either Barbara or Sophie who leaves the letters, and he knows the following about them:
- Barbara likes eating Chocolate and Nuts, but no Cookies
- Sophie likes eating Cookies and Nuts a lot, but no Chocolate

Can you help Paul and tell him *Who is the mysterious letter-buddy?*

Lieber Paul,...
_____
_____
_____
...deine x.

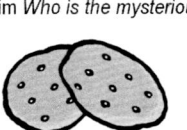

Figure 28.2 Can you help Paul to solve this riddle by providing your domain-general scientific reasoning skills?
A black-and-white version of this figure will appear in some formats. For the color version, please refer to the plate section.

A person is standing in a resting boat and tosses a big stone into the water behind the boat. Which of the following statements are true?

☐ The boat moves in the direction the stone was thrown.

☐ The stone displaces water and this is why the boat moves just slightly back and forth.

☐ If you let an inflated balloon whizz through the air, principally the same happens.

☐ The boat moves contrary to the direction the stone was thrown.

Figure 28.3 Item demanding domain-specific scientific thinking. From the basic Mechanics Concept Test (bMCT) in Hofer et al. (2017)

earlier-discussed work around Jean Piaget (e.g., Piaget & Inhelder, 1958).

Domain-specific scientific reasoning, on the other hand, is based on content knowledge that can only be meaningfully applied in its original domain, such as in the item presented in Figure 28.3.

In this item, in order to recognize that the third and fourth answer options are correct, applying conceptual understanding of Newton's third law of motion is demanded. Application of this conceptual knowledge is an instance of domain-specific scientific reasoning, because Newton's third law is bound to the domain of mechanics. The interrelation of these two types of scientific reasoning, based on domain-general skills and domain-specific content knowledge, has been emphasized as a general source of development of scientific reasoning skills.

The emergence of research on domain-specific scientific reasoning can be attributed to Bruner et al. (1956), who initiated a strand of research concerned with development and change in people's conceptions about scientific and natural phenomena. This is a domain-specific strand of research, because it is concerned with the concepts that people hold about

something, for example about a physical phenomenon. This research provided the basis for later research on *conceptual change* which, influenced by Thomas Kuhn's descriptions of paradigm changes (Kuhn, 1970), tries to elucidate how humans adapt and modify their concepts about scientific phenomena. For many academic fields, first and foremost in the STEM area (Science, Technology, Engineering, Mathematics), it has been demonstrated that experts and novices who use the same words may have entirely different representations of their meaning. This has been convincingly demonstrated for physics, and particularly in the area of mechanics, where it is a major source of mistakes and misunderstandings. Even high-school and university students who are easily able to apply the equations underlying Newton's axioms to solve quantitative word problems often still hold beliefs about force, inertia, and mass that are in line with many everyday experiences but incompatible with theories of physics (Hofer et al., 2018). Carey (1985) demonstrated discrepancies between young children's and adults' everyday concepts, such as "parents." For younger children, it mainly means "caring for kids," whereas adults focus on "having offspring."

Conceptual change takes place as a shift from characteristic to defining features. Vosniadou and Brewer (1992) provide a detailed analysis of children's concepts about the earth and humans living on it. Throughout childhood, children hold different concepts about the earth that might be influenced by the instruction and information from parents or peers they have received about basic astronomy. In late elementary school, most children understand that the earth is a sphere that orbits the sun even though it appears to be flat and stationary. However, children rarely seem to undergo a direct shift from the flat earth model to the spherical one. They rather construct several intermediate models with the attempt to integrate their intuitive knowledge and the instructed facts. They for instance draw a hollow sphere with humans living in it. Although most likely initiated by direct teaching, learning about complex and abstract concepts rarely ever shows itself in directly adopting the taught knowledge. Learners rather have to undergo integration of the incoming information into their prior knowledge, and this process is rarely ever characterized by a linear increase of performance. Much more likely is an erratic learning trajectory with performance in place under certain circumstances but not under others. This also seems to be the case for the emergence of scientific reasoning. Particularly in content areas dealing with demanding concepts, it is often difficult for children to apply principles of scientific reasoning that they already master successfully in other, more familiar content areas.

The domain-general approach initiated by Piaget and the domain-specific approach initiated by Bruner et al. (1956) and carried forward in conceptual change-research were unified within a major research framework in the late 1980s. Klahr and Dunbar (1988) modeled scientific reasoning by considering the

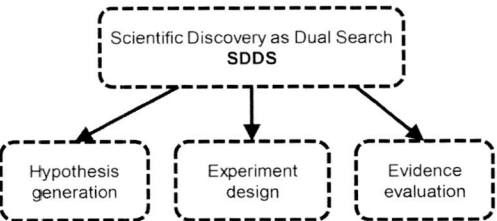

Figure 28.4 Main components of the SDDS model of scientific reasoning

impact of domain-specific knowledge change. Their *Scientific Discovery as Dual Search* (SDDS) model is conceptualized as a problem-solving process taking place in a hypothesis space and an experiment space with the aim to develop and revise hypotheses that can causally explain empirical evidence. To engage in this problem-solving process, three major cognitive processes are involved: Hypothesis generation, experimental design, and evidence evaluation (see Figure 28.4).

According to this model, the generation of hypotheses is influenced by prior knowledge about the investigated domain. Hypotheses lead to experiments that are conducted in order to produce evidence to test the hypotheses. The experimental design is also influenced by prior knowledge; for example, if children expect a causal relation between two factors, they are unlikely to design experiments that could potentially disprove such a relation (Schauble, 1996). An experiment is then conducted, and evidence is interpreted in order to evaluate whether it promotes a hypothesis, or whether the hypothesis has to be either rejected or revised in order to account for the accumulated evidence. This model of scientific reasoning explains why and how domain-specific knowledge and domain-general experimentation influence each other, unifying the two prior threads of research on scientific reasoning. The SDDS model has served as a fruitful framework for research on scientific reasoning across the last three decades, and it has also been used as a framework for synthesizing empirical evidence (Morris et al., 2012; Zimmerman, 2000, 2007).

Parallel to the SDDS model, Kuhn (1989) presented a theory of the development of scientific reasoning with a focus on the differentiation and coordination of theory and evidence. Understanding the difference between one's own beliefs and theories and the relevant empirical evidence is a key factor in developing scientific reasoning skills. The proposition of the relation between theory and evidence as the key to skilled scientific reasoning has been carried further by various researchers, including Köerber et al. (2014), Sodian et al. (1991) and Deanna Kuhn and her colleagues themselves (Kuhn et al., 2008, 2015). Within the overarching theory-evidence relation, Kuhn (2007) and Kuhn and Pease (2008) emphasize that beyond CVS, there are at least three central scientific reasoning skills. These encompass (a) the ability to coordinate effects of multiple causal influences on an outcome, (b) a mature understanding of the epistemological foundations of science, recognizing scientific knowledge as constructed by humans rather than simply discovered in the world, and (c) the ability to engage in skilled argumentation in the scientific domain, with an appreciation of argumentation as entailing the coordination of theory and evidence (Kuhn et al., 2008). Deanna Kuhn and her team delivered classroom-based interventions to students under the theme *multivariable causal reasoning*, which encompasses learning and applying CVS in designs with multiple variables, and also the schooling of epistemic beliefs and argumentation, in order to support understanding of the overarching theory-evidence relation (Kuhn et al., 2015). Starting in sixth grade, the continued intervention over three years showed a positive impact on students' ability to examine and coordinate multiple variables in finding out about causal relations.

As theorized in the SDDS model (Figure 28.1), domain-general scientific reasoning skills neither function nor develop independently of children's domain-specific content knowledge.

Seminal evidence on this inter-relation has been gathered by Schauble (1990, 1996). In a series of studies with fifth and sixth graders engaging in experimental inquiry of physics phenomena, Leona Schauble recorded and reported in detail how content knowledge about causal relations influences experimentation strategies, and how experimentation in turn influences the acquisition of content knowledge. In the inquiry settings, children had to engage in experimentation to find out causal relations between various variables. Children with more adequate prior knowledge about the variables of interest were more likely to apply valid experimentation strategies that were in accordance with the control of variables strategy (Schauble, 1996). Likewise, children with a better understanding of experimentation, thus applying more valid experimentation strategies, were able to draw more valid conclusions about causal relations between the variables of interest. This mutual relation was described as a bootstrapping process, connecting closely domain-specific content knowledge in science and domain-general scientific reasoning skills (Schauble, 1996). In addition, children who were able to draw causal inferences based on valid experimentation strategies reported more elaborate theoretical models of the underlying physics concepts, indicating that experimentation strategies do in turn not only support the acquisition of new beliefs, but also the development of adequate conceptual understanding.

This mutual relation is corroborated by further evidence from longitudinal and experimental designs. Van der Graaf et al. (2018) posed a CVS-task and an evidence evaluation-task twice on preschool children when they were four and five years old. They found that children's content knowledge on four topics in the domains of physics and biology could not only predict these two scientific reasoning skills at the first assessment, but also children's further development of both skills within one year. Furthermore, in the seminal study of Chen and Klahr (1999), training of the control-of-variables strategy in seven-to-ten year-olds promoted not just robust acquisition of this strategy and transfer to new situations, but also the ensuing acquisition of correct content knowledge by having acquired the new ability to conduct informative experiments. Thus, training in CVS led to gains in this ability, which allowed children to apply the strategy and use it to acquire new content knowledge about scientific concepts. In another study, first- to sixth-graders' knowledge of CVS was a substantial predictor of their domain-specific content knowledge. It could also predict students' content knowledge development controlling for their prior knowledge when they received experimentation-based education on floating and sinking (Edelsbrunner et al., 2019). Investigating the complementary perspective, Wagensveld et al. (2015) found that fourth and sixth graders' content knowledge showed predictive strength for their CVS skills before undergoing a training, and also for their ability to transfer newly acquired CVS skills after the training. In another longitudinal study, elementary school children's CVS skills increased after undergoing two years of teacher-guided inquiry education in basic physics (Schalk et al., 2019). The steady confrontation with the CVS in guided inquiry problems increased children's CVS skills although the underlying principles were never explicitly taught. The continued long-term application of the CVS across various content areas apparently triggered children's ability to transfer the underlying principles.

These results emphasize that children do generally not apply or develop scientific reasoning skills independently of the context of application. Therefore, the domain-specific content knowledge that children develop in formal and informal settings constitutes a significant factor in their development of scientific reasoning skills.

28.3 Individual Differences in Scientific Reasoning Abilities: The Impact of Broader Cognitive Competencies

In various areas of developmental psychology, the focus on between-age-group-differences has been accompanied by the within-age-group-perspective. Although it goes without question that age-related changes guided by brain maturation are steering cognitive development, significant variance within age groups occurs among cognitive competencies. These competencies are measured with intelligence tests, which attempt to highlight individual differences in humans' ability to "understand complex ideas, to adapt effectively to the environment, to learn from experience, to engage in various forms of reasoning, to overcome obstacles by taking thought" (Neisser, 1979, p. 217). Standardized intelligence tests are available for individuals from infancy on, but correlations between preschool measures and later intelligence are only moderate (Deary et al., 2000). Within-age group variance in intelligence measures during infancy and preschool age partly results from the different speeds of maturation. After entering school, intelligence quickly establishes itself as a stable trait. IQ measures stabilize and reach high long-term stability of $r > 0.80$, which is approached earlier in verbal than in non-verbal reasoning abilities (Schneider & Bullock, 2009). These patterns of intelligence development raise the question to what extent children's general cognitive abilities might act as a source of individual differences in scientific reasoning at different age levels. We will deal with this issue here.

For studies relating CVS or broader scientific reasoning skills to intelligence or general reasoning measures, it should be noted that correlations are sometimes estimated on the manifest level of observed sum scores, and sometimes on the latent level within a statistical model. In the latter case, measurement error (i.e., non-perfect reliability) is controlled for and correlation estimates therefore attenuated for measurement error bias. Thus, in the following overview it will be pointed out when correlations were estimated on the latent level, because these can be assumed to represent more appropriate estimates than deflated estimates on the manifest level.

Studies have shown that from preschool age onwards, substantial correlations exist between children's abilities in scientific reasoning and their general reasoning abilities. Van der Graaf et al. (2015) related four-to-six-year olds' achievement on an exclusion reasoning task, in which they had to identify which of four abstract figures differed from the others, to their achievement on dynamic hands-on tasks assessing CVS. Children's scores on the CVS task correlated slightly above $r = 0.40$ with their achievement on the exclusion task, indicating that non-verbal reasoning ability shows a substantial correlation with this central scientific reasoning skill already before children enter school. In another sample of four-to-five-year olds, van der Graaf et al. (2016) again found a correlation of about $r = 0.30$ between achievement on the exclusion task and on a similar yet non-dynamic hands-on CVS task. Additionally, a correlation of the same magnitude of $r = 0.29$ was found between the exclusion task and children's evidence evaluation skills. Piekny et al. (2013) used a task that required the recognition of the distinction between the goal to produce an outcome on the one hand, and to find something out on the other hand. Performance in this task and an intelligence measure revealed a non-significant correlation of $r = -0.07$ in a sample of four-year olds, and a significant yet weak correlation of $r = 0.19$ in the same sample one year later. These findings show that already before children undergo elementary schooling, their scientific reasoning skills are related to their more general non-verbal reasoning skills. Yet, these associations seem to be of limited strength. The low-to-moderate correlations might reflect different speeds of maturation in general reasoning ability. In addition, preschool measures do not cover the broad range of scientific reasoning skills used in tests for older children, which might also impact the estimates.

Studies run with elementary school children revealed significant but still moderate correlations between intelligence measures and CVS tasks as well as further tasks related to experimentation. Wagensveld et al. (2015) found a correlation of $r = 0.30$ between fourth- and sixth-graders CVS skills and Raven's progressive matrices reasoning test. In a subsequent training after initial assessment, this figural reasoning test could not predict children's acquisition of CVS skills beyond other cognitive factors. Thus, general reasoning ability showed a correlation with CVS but not with its acquisition during training. In second- to fourth-graders, Osterhaus et al. (2017) found a correlation of $r = 0.20$ between intelligence and experimentation skills. Further evidence from the Munich longitudinal study indicates that in late childhood and throughout adolescence, there are correlations varying between $r = 0.16$ and 0.42 between the skills to vary the focal dimension in an experimental design, to control confounding variables, and to recognize the necessity of a control group, with measures of intelligence (Bullock & Ziegler,

2009). Given that intelligence measures have reached a high stability at this age level, these still moderate correlations suggest that CVS is not merely a by-product of general reasoning abilities.

The picture changes when, in addition to CVS, broader scientific reasoning measures are applied that go beyond experimentation. Mayer et al. (2014) posed a pen-and-paper scientific reasoning test encompassing children's understanding of science and of theories, and their abilities to design experiments and to interpret data on fourth-graders. They found a correlation of $r = 0.62$ between a variable on the latent level representing these broad scientific reasoning skills, and another latent variable of children's intelligence, measured by a figural reasoning test. Notably, in psychometric analyses, the authors found that a model representing children's scientific reasoning skills and their reasoning ability as a single unitary trait exhibited a better model fit-complexity trade-off than modeling these two constructs as separate dimensions. Still, because of the strong yet limited correlation between the two constructs, the authors decided that from a psychometric view scientific reasoning and intelligence represent two distinct constructs. In another big sample of more than 1,000 second- to fourth-graders, Koerber et al. (2014) found a similar, strong correlation of $r = 0.63$ on the latent level between a broad scientific reasoning measure and children's achievement on a figural reasoning measure. This shows that on broader scientific reasoning measures, the correlation with general reasoning is substantially stronger.

The broader assessment of scientific reasoning skills used by Mayer et al. (2014), produced the substantial correlation of $r = 0.62$ with an intelligence measure. It is, however, not entirely clear what should be the common cognitive demands underlying the cognitive and metacognitive skills, beliefs, and knowledge subsumed under this scale. In addition to experimentation skills, data interpretation, as well as children's understanding of theories and hypothesis testing were considered. For such measures covering broader scientific reasoning skills, the common variance with general reasoning measures might stem from the ability to systematically handle complex information. The common variance across the tasks might reflect the kind of information processing that goes along with a greater learning potential. Activating the appropriate prior knowledge in the right order and relating it to the critical elements of the problem requires reasoning skills measured in intelligence tests. In the following, we will discuss further cognitive capacities assumed to guide differences in human intelligence, and how these relate to scientific reasoning skills.

28.3.1 Scientific Reasoning Skills and Verbal Abilities

The discussed studies relating intelligence to scientific reasoning have been based on nonverbal reasoning tests. These tests aim at assessing a broad reasoning or intelligence component that does not require mastering of a particular language. Such tests may only cover part of the abilities necessary for scientific reasoning. Given that scientific reasoning problems are genuinely language-based and require a very precise understanding and use of words, specific measures of verbal reasoning ability and comprehension can be expected to explain achievement differences beyond nonverbal intelligence.

The findings with kindergarten children are mixed. Piekny et al. (2013) found a nonsignificant correlation of $r = 0.10$ between four year-old preschool children's language skills assessed through a composite of grammar and vocabulary measures and their ability to differentiate between producing an outcome and conducting an experimental test. This correlation was similar and non-significant at $r = 0.08$ one year later when the same children were about five years old. In a study with 5.6 year old kindergarten children, van der Graaf et al. (2018) found significant correlations of $r = 0.31$, and $r = 0.32$, respectively, between children's grammar and vocabulary and their experimentation skills. Notably, controlling for prior experimentation skills one year earlier, these correlations remained stable. This result suggests that the development of grammar abilities and vocabulary boosts children's experimentation skills between age five and six years.

In elementary school age, Siler et al. (2010) reported a positive correlation of $r = 0.58$ between fifth-graders' ability to transfer the CVS after undergoing training and their verbal reasoning ability. Similarly, Wagensveld et al. (2015) found that verbal reasoning ability could predict fourth- and sixth-graders' acquisition of CVS skills in a training study. This predictive value of verbal reasoning remained stable when controlling for children's more general non-verbal reasoning ability. Osterhaus et al. (2017) also found a significant correlation of $r = 0.25$ between second- to fourth-graders language abilities and experimentation skills. On a broader measure of scientific reasoning, Koerber et al. (2014) found a strong correlation on the latent level of $r = 0.74$ with text comprehension in second- to fourth-graders. Also in fourth graders, Mayer et al. (2014) found a correlation between scientific reasoning and reading comprehension of $r = 0.44$.

Overall, these findings indicate that verbal skills are important for children's acquisition of CVS and broader experimentation skills. They also point out that verbal skills have an influence that goes beyond general non-verbal skills. In addition, similar to non-verbal skills,

the association between scientific reasoning skills and verbal skills is present already in kindergarten age but becomes stronger in elementary school age, and it is especially pronounced for broad measures of scientific reasoning that do not only encompass experimentation.

28.3.2 Scientific Reasoning and Working Memory

Regarding further factors of children's cognitive development, the concept of working memory is central in models of human cognition. To allow goal-directed behavior, conscious information processing and selective attention, only a fractional amount of incoming information passes into the working memory. Working memory is responsible for selecting, temporarily maintaining and manipulating this information during cognitive activity (for a summary, see Stern, 2017). It is the gatekeeper to long-term memory, where information acquired through experience and learning can be stored in different modalities as well as in symbol systems. Working memory regulates the interaction between incoming information from sensory memory and knowledge activated from long-term memory. It filters out (or inhibits, Houdé, 2000, 2019) irrelevant and distracting information to ensure that the necessary goals will be achieved undisturbed. Efficient information processing means that working memory is continuously selecting incoming information, aligning it with knowledge retrieved from long-term memory, and preparing responses for accomplishing requirements demanded by the environment or self-set goals. "Working memory functions" is the prominent answer given to the core question of developmental psychology, which is "What exactly changes during infancy, childhood, and adolescence?" Up to the age of three years, children fail in tasks that require goal switching (Zelazo et al., 2003), but from the age of four years onwards, working memory functions steadily increase and approach their full potential in adolescence. The explanatory power and the validity of working memory functions are substantiated by findings from brain science, which identified neural underpinnings of working memory functions in the frontal lobe. This brain area undergoes substantial changes in terms of synaptogenesis during childhood and adolescence (Arain et al., 2013). This extensive restructuring can account for a lack of cognitive control in this age period (Cohen et al., 2016).

Children's working memory is a general limitation, yet also a source of cognitive abilities during cognitive development. With respect to scientific reasoning skills, two aspects of working memory are considered central. The first is children's working memory capacity, which is not fully developed until adolescence. Barrouillet and Lecas (1999) posed conditional reasoning tasks and working memory span tasks on third-, sixth-, and ninth-graders. In the conditional reasoning tasks, students had to construct evidence patterns in accordance with hypotheses (e.g., "If you wear a white shirt, then you wear green trousers"). Their working memory span was found to be significantly related to students' achievement on this task similarly in all age groups. This supports the assumption that children's and adolescent's working memory span limits the number of mental models they can work concurrently, and thus their ability to coordinate a specific theory with covariation evidence.

A second aspect of working memory important for scientific reasoning skills is children's inhibition ability. Dual process theories of human reasoning distinguish between quick and intuitive cognitive procedures and consciously controlled ones. Causal reasoning problems in general and scientific reasoning in particular often provoke intuitive but wrong procedures (Verschueren et al., 2005; Vosniadou, 2014). In order to engage in successful scientific reasoning, children have to override their automatically activated intuitions by means of inhibition ability (Houdé, 2000, 2019).

Relations between children's inhibition ability and their scientific reasoning skills have been found in preschool age. Van der Graaf et al. (2016) found a correlation of $r = 0.27$ between children's experimentation skills and their inhibition ability, as well as a correlation of $r = 0.29$ with their evidence evaluation skills. For second- to fourth-graders inhibition ability and their experimentation skills a correlation of $r = 0.29$ was found (Osterhaus et al., 2017). In addition, taking into account children's prior achievement levels, inhibition can positively predict their development of evidence evaluation skills (van der Graaf et al., 2018). However, in a study by Mayer et al. (2014), inhibition was not related to a broad assessment of scientific reasoning skills. This finding might depend on the breadth of the scientific reasoning measure applied by the authors, because not all involved aspects, particularly those related to the nature of science, might be related to inhibition ability (Osterhaus et al., 2017). Applying a broader measure of scientific reasoning might increase the correlation with non-verbal and verbal intelligence measures, while it might decrease the association with inhibition and potentially also with other working memory functions. Therefore, in theorizing about the relation between scientific reasoning and working memory, it should be kept in mind that both of these constructs consist of various cognitive functions and processes, many of which might exhibit differential relations with each other. A study substantiated this assumption, showing in statistical simulations that differing correlations between scientific reasoning skills might add up to a misleading overall zero-correlation with external variables such as inhibition (Edelsbrunner & Dablander, 2019). A second explanation for inconsistent relations with inhibition might be low intercorrelations between different measures of inhibition, indicating the lack of a common underlying process and that findings might depend strongly on the nature of the inhibition measure (Rey-Mermet et al., 2018). The results by Mayer et al. (2014) nevertheless stand in contrast to the results reported on the relation between intelligence measures and scientific reasoning skills. While intelligence measures revealed significant correlations with CVS from elementary school on, and even more pronounced ones in later stages of schooling and on broader measures than just CVS, the pattern for the working memory function of inhibition was almost the other way around.

The two discussed working memory functions pose limitations on children's systematic inquiry behavior, as they constrain the use of scientific reasoning strategies. For capacity, Barrouillet and Lecas (1999) argue that due to children's limited working memory capacity, they can only work with a limited number of hypotheses, assumptions and pieces of evidence simultaneously. This also accounts for children's limited understanding of the relation between theory and evidence (Kuhn, 2006). The skilled coordination of theory and evidence is decisive for scientific reasoning. Therefore, the number of elements that can be handled simultaneously in working memory is important. Moreover, to prevent overload during problem-solving, the ability to inhibit as much as possible of the information not needed for problem-solving is crucial. The effect of inhibition according to Osterhaus et al. (2017) is assumed to stem from the fact that children initially understand scientific inquiry as a means for producing desirable

outcomes. In order to suppress the intuitive behavior of pursuing this aim and instead test for causal effects, children might have to use their inhibition ability. While there is some evidence corroborating relations between inhibition and scientific reasoning, more elaborate theories and experimental tests are required in order to establish the nature of this relation.

28.4 Scientific Reasoning, Theory of Mind, and Metacognition

Around age four years, children improve on tasks of theory of mind and are able to understand that someone may be acting based on a false belief about an object or event (see Chapters 12 and 19). Theory of mind is the ability to attribute different mental states to other people as to oneself (Premack & Woodruff, 1978). It is one of the earliest types of metacognition and an important step in children's cognitive development (Kuhn, 2000). In a commonly used false-belief task to assess children's theory of mind, an object is placed into a blue box while the experimenter, the child, and an additional person are present. After this third person has left the room, the experimenter takes the object out and puts it into another (e.g., red) box. The child is then asked into which box the third person will look for the object when she will come back to the room. If the child lacks a theory of mind and therefore does not understand that the third person has different knowledge about the object's location than the child himself, he will say that the person will look into the red box for the object, because this is the box which it is in. Scientific reasoning requires an understanding of uncertain and false knowledge. It is therefore thoroughly plausible that the development of scientific reasoning skills presupposes mastering the false-belief task.

Piekny et al. (2013) presented the false-belief task to children of around four years and assessed achievement on an experimentation task requiring the distinction between effect production and experimental tests one year later. They found a φ correlation coefficient of 0.34, while they could not find significant correlations between the two tasks at the first measurement points at four years of age, φ = −0.04, and also not at the second measurement point at five years of age, φ = 0.09. This result suggests that mastering the false belief task around the age of four can be a door opener for acquiring a basic understanding of scientific reasoning. Further research on how teachable moments for children from age four on can be recognized and used seems worthwhile.

In the course of elementary school, there is no evidence for a combined or even inter-weaved development of scientific reasoning and an advanced theory of mind, which is measured with the help of problems that include higher order beliefs and an appreciation of the recursive nature of mental states. Osterhaus et al. (2017) found a non-significant correlation of $r = 0.09$ between these variables. Within a model in which experimentation skills were represented as a latent variable and controlling for further cognitive and meta-cognitive variables, the relation remained just non-significant at $r = -0.17$.

Although closer relations between the theory of mind and scientific reasoning skills seem to be limited to the age of four-to-five years, mastering false belief tasks in its advanced version has been recognized as an important step in children's metacognitive development. Metacognition is defined as the awareness and the monitoring of one's own learning and thinking processes, and it therefore includes knowledge about one's own knowledge. Being aware of the certainty and uncertainty of one's own knowledge and beliefs bridges the gap between scientific reasoning and metacognition. There is evidence for the importance of metacognition in developing children's scientific reasoning skills. In a training study, Zohar and Dori (2012) found that emphasis on the metacognitive aspects of experimentation skills can trigger substantial learning gains and broad transfer effects in children's learning.

A further aspect of children's metacognitive development concerns children's beliefs about the nature of science, often referred to as epistemic beliefs (Kitchner, 1983). These encompass general beliefs about the structure and complexity of knowledge and insights, their emergence, certainty, and sources (Schommer et al., 1997). Nature of science assessments usually focus on an understanding of science as a subjective process of social interaction (Lederman, 1992). In developmental models, epistemic beliefs are conceptualized as stage-wise beliefs leading from children's beliefs that knowledge is absolute, objective, and certain, to multiplistic views that knowledge is more like opinion and that different subjects' opinions have equal value independent of their backing arguments (Kuhn et al., 2000). The final stage according to developmental models acknowledges that the logical value of different opinions is bound to the validity of arguments in favor and against the respective opinion.

A correlation between children's beliefs, knowledge, and views about the nature of science and the emergence of knowledge on the one hand and CVS on the other hand has been found (Mayer et al., 2014; Osterhaus et al., 2017). There is, however, an ongoing debate of whether epistemic beliefs and scientific reasoning should be conceptualized as a unitary construct, or whether they should be assessed separately. Empirical evidence usually shows cognitive facets of scientific reasoning, such as experimentation skills, and more metacognitive facets such as epistemic beliefs and nature of science should be separated.

Specifically, children's advanced theory of mind and inhibition ability share differential relations with these two aspects (Osterhaus et al., 2017), indicating that combining measures of experimentation and epistemic beliefs might lead to biased correlation patterns and inferences.

28.5 The Interaction between General Cognitive Abilities and Scientific Reasoning Skills: Insights from Multivariate Designs

Many of the studies summarized in this chapter related multiple variables associated with scientific reasoning and general cognitive abilities to each other within multivariate or longitudinal designs. Thanks to these study designs, we now have a better understanding of the learning trajectories of scientific reasoning, as well as of the more general cognitive precursors that guide the development of scientific reasoning skills. The integration of multiple variables and its combination with longitudinal or experimental data and elaborate theory is far more informative than studies focusing on bivariate relations. We summarize the findings of two studies that exemplify how a multivariate look at scientific reasoning can broaden our understanding. The schematic models behind two of these studies are depicted in Figure 28.5.

Figure 28.5 depicts the multivariate predictive relations that these studies found. While

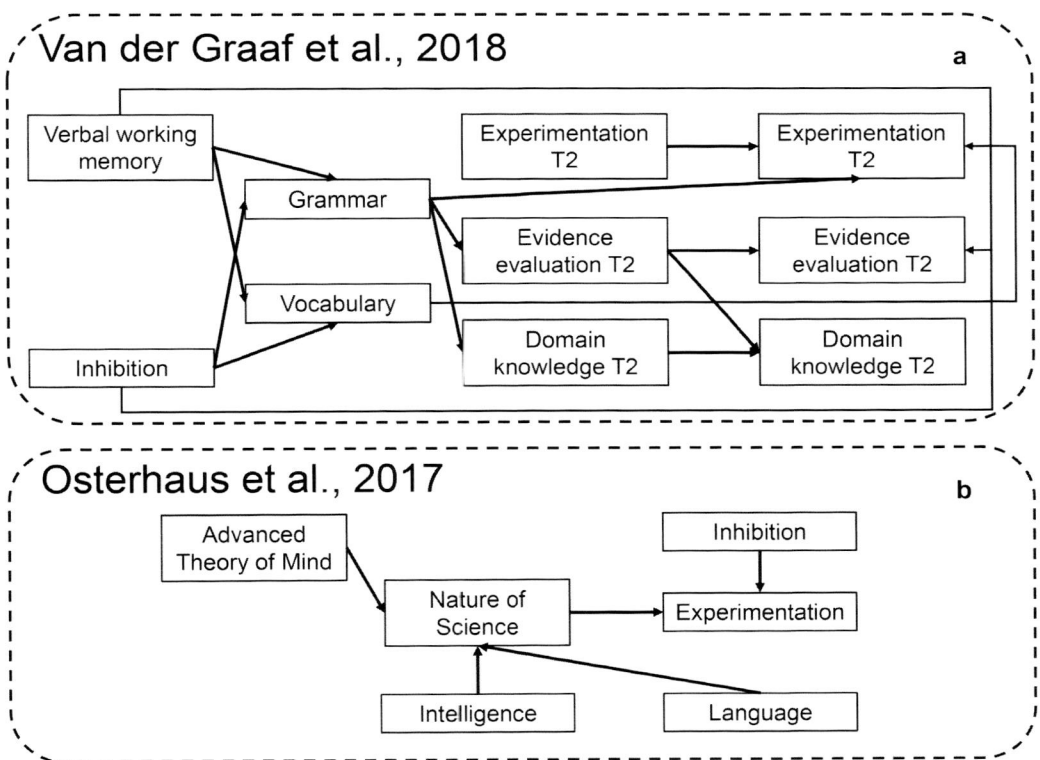

Figure 28.5 Schematic depiction of significant associations (all with positive regression weights) found in multivariate models of Osterhaus et al. (2017) (a) and van der Graaf et al. (2018) (b)

some of the bivariate associations from these studies have been discussed previously, a multivariate look reveals additional insights. Osterhaus et al. (2017; Figure 28.5(a)) assessed cognitive variables and scientific reasoning. Although this was a cross-sectional study, the combination of elaborate theory and a multivariate design allowed them to conclude that an advanced theory of mind predicts children's understanding of the nature of science, which in turn predicts their experimentation skills. Intelligence and inhibition could not predict experimentation skills beyond the predictive value of nature of science, indicating that the impact of these general cognitive variables on experimentation skills is potentially mediated through children's knowledge about the nature of science.

Van der Graaf et al. (2018; Figure 28.5(b)) did not just apply a multivariate design, but they also assessed preschool children repeatedly when they were four (first wave) and five (second wave) years old. They related children's scientific reasoning skills of experimentation and evidence evaluation to various cognitive abilities and domain-specific content knowledge. From their model, it is visible that evidence evaluation predicted the development of children's content knowledge, while the other direction of this connection was not found. In other words, the better children were able to interpret evidence, the bigger were their increases in content knowledge over one year. In addition, working memory variables (verbal WM and inhibition) impacted children's verbal development (grammar & vocabulary) and also their gains in evidence evaluation skills. Finally, the two verbal cognitive variables positively predicted children's development in experimentation skills. By including multiple variables related to scientific reasoning and general cognitive abilities within a longitudinal design, this model allowed for testing of these mutual predictions and

influences. These insights would not be possible based on the more common and less expensive design of relating two variables to each other.

28.6 Future Avenues

This overview shows that correlations exist between children's scientific reasoning skills and general verbal and non-verbal reasoning ability, moderately during kindergarten age and more substantially in elementary school age and on broader measures. Among preschool children, relations with working memory capacity exist, although inhibition ability and the development of an (advanced) theory of mind seem to be limited in their explanatory value for children's scientific reasoning, particularly on broader scientific reasoning measures. In addition, the relation between domain-general scientific reasoning skills and domain-specific content knowledge, which has been established by Leona Schauble's lab-based observational work in the 1990s, has been corroborated by recent correlational evidence and intervention studies relating students' scientific reasoning skills to their conceptual knowledge and learning.

Overall, these results encompass some moderate and some more substantial correlations between children's scientific reasoning skills and most variables related to children's general cognitive development. What can we learn from these inter-relations? A general point is that although children show tremendous development in some scientific reasoning skills, this development is significantly constrained by their more general cognitive development. This is particularly visible in the discussed constraints posed on children's scientific reasoning by their working memory development. What we can also learn from available evidence is that scientific reasoning skills should generally not be studied in isolation. These dependencies of scientific reasoning skills in childhood on more general cognitive development, and it's dynamics therewith, make it clear that scientific reasoning should not be examined in isolation. This can be understood in two ways. First, scientific reasoning skills constrain and can impact each other in their development. An example of this is the study by Osterhaus et al. (2017), who found that children's epistemic cognition impacts their experimentation skills. Since these two variables are related, leaving either out in a developmental or experimental design might bias parameters and resulting conclusions obtained from relating general cognitive variables to these variables, which are both often conceptualized as facets of scientific reasoning.

Second, multivariate studies have shown that including multiple cognitive predictor variables can better inform about which variable indeed impacts children's scientific reasoning. An example for this is the study by Wagensveld et al. (2015). Based on the bivariate associations found in this study, one might infer that children's non-verbal abilities impact their acquisition of CVS skills. A model taking into account multiple predictors showed that this relation is probably mostly caused by children's verbal skills, which turned out to be a more important predictor. The study by Osterhaus et al. (2017) also demonstrated the value of including multiple variables of scientific reasoning. Specifically, they found a predictive value of children's inhibition ability for their experimentation skills, however not for their understanding of the nature of science. As Osterhaus et al. (2017) discuss, this finding might explain why the study by Mayer et al. (2014) found a relation close to zero between inhibition ability and scientific reasoning. These authors scaled children's scientific reasoning skills based on a broad test that encompassed items related to experimentation as well as items related to the nature of science. Correlating this broad overall score with inhibition might have covered relations that were present in some scientific reasoning skills, but not in others. Thus, the study by Osterhaus et al. (2017), by including more than one scientific reasoning variable, could provide broad information on the differential relations of different facets of scientific reasoning and explain inconsistent prior findings.

Future studies might build on findings according to which children's scientific reasoning is influenced by their content knowledge and that scientific reasoning skills can be trained by making explicit use of existing knowledge. This might be valuable, particularly in educational settings. For example, by either first training children in CVS and then providing them with inquiry-based learning, or the other way around, it might be examined how both of these factors potentially interact in boosting children's future learning in regular science education in school (Edelsbrunner et al., 2019; Schalk et al., 2019).

By correlating scientific reasoning skills to other cognitive variables in future studies, researchers should be aware that variables stemming from typical experimental tasks developed in cognitive psychology do sometimes show limited reliability for individual differences. This has been argued recently, and corroborated by empirical data showing that stable within-person variance in typical working memory and further cognitive tasks is, on average, rather low (Hedge et al., 2018). This concerns also the Stroop task, which in different variations has also been used in the discussed studies to assess children's inhibition ability. In a retest-reliability study, Hedge et al. (2018) found limited short-term stability of $r = 0.60$. This lack of stability in the Stroop task as well as in other cognitive tasks might lead to biased correlations with individual differences in scientific reasoning, and it might limit the power to find significant correlations in such studies. This limitation provides another explanation why associations between inhibition ability and scientific reasoning are not always found (Mayer et al., 2014), and usually estimated to be rather moderate (Osterhaus et al., 2017).

Integrating and generalizing the findings discussed in this paper leads to the conclusion that in younger age, up to elementary school, limited working memory functions represent a major limiting factor of scientific reasoning. Later on, when most children's working memory capacity and functions are fully developed, more general reasoning abilities take over the key role in affecting children's scientific reasoning. Another conclusion from a more methodological view is that it is worth investing into studies that examine multiple scientific reasoning skills simultaneously. This is particularly informative in combination with multiple cognitive predictor variables, and in combination with a longitudinal or experimental design. While such studies draw on resources from researchers and participants, the discussed studies demonstrate that investment into elaborate study design allows insights into scientific reasoning that are not possible based on simpler designs. The continued combined investigation of scientific reasoning and general cognitive development promises to yield further insights into the key factors underlying children's cognitive development and how it can be supported.

References

Arain, M., Haque, M., Johal, L., Mathur, P., Nel, W., Rais, A., ... Sharma, S. (2013). Maturation of the adolescent brain. *Neuropsychiatric Disease and Treatment, 9*, 449.

Barrouillet, P., & Lecas, J.-F. (1999). Mental models in conditional reasoning and working memory. *Thinking & Reasoning, 5*, 289–302.

Bruner, J. S., Goodnow, J. J., & Austin, G. A. (1956). *A Study of Thinking*. New York: John Wiley.

Bullock, M., & Ziegler, A. (2009). Scientific reasoning: Developmental and individual differences. In F. E. Weinert, & W. Schneider (eds.), *Individual Development from 13 to 22: Findings from the Munich Longitudinal Study* (pp. 38–54). Cambridge: Cambridge University Press.

Carey, S. (1985). *Conceptual Change in Childhood*. Cambridge, MA: MIT press.

Chen, Z., & Klahr, D. (1999). All other things being equal: Acquisition and transfer of the control of variables strategy. *Child Development, 70*, 1098–1120.

Chinn, C. A., & Brewer, W. F. (1998). An empirical test of a taxonomy of responses to anomalous data in science. *Journal of Research in Science Teaching, 35*, 623–654.

Cohen, A. O., Breiner, K., Steinberg, L., Bonnie, R. J., Scott, E. S., Taylor-Thompson, K., ... Silverman, M. R. (2016). When is an adolescent an adult? Assessing cognitive control in emotional and nonemotional contexts. *Psychological Science, 27*, 549–562.

Deary, I. J., Whalley, L. J., Lemmon, H., Crawford, J. R., & Starr, J. M. (2000). The stability of individual differences in mental ability from childhood to old age: Follow-up of the 1932 Scottish Mental Survey. *Intelligence, 28*, 49–55.

Edelsbrunner, P. A., & Dablander, F. (2019). The psychometric modeling of scientific reasoning: A review and recommendations for future avenues. *Educational Psychology Review, 31*, 1–34.

Edelsbrunner, P. A., Schalk, L., Schumacher, R., & Stern, E. (2019). Variable control and conceptual change: A large-scale quantitative study in elementary school. *Learning and Individual Differences, 66*, 38–53.

Engelmann, K., Neuhaus, B. J., & Fischer, F. (2016). Fostering scientific reasoning in education – meta-analytic evidence from intervention studies. *Educational Research and Evaluation, 22*, 333–349.

Hedge, C., Powell, G., & Sumner, P. (2018). The reliability paradox: Why robust cognitive tasks do not produce reliable individual differences. *Behavior Research Methods*, *50*, 1166–1186.

Hofer, B. K. (2004). Epistemological understanding as a metacognitive process: Thinking aloud during online searching. *Educational Psychologist*, *39*, 43–55.

Hofer, B. K., & Pintrich, P. R. (1997). The development of epistemological theories: Beliefs about knowledge and knowing and their relation to learning. *Review of Educational Research*, *67*, 88–140.

Hofer, S. I., Schumacher, R., & Rubin, H. (2017). The test of basic mechanics conceptual understanding (bMCU): Using Rasch analysis to develop and evaluate an efficient multiple-choice test on Newton's mechanics. *International Journal of STEM Education*, *4*, 1–20.

Hofer, S. I., Schumacher, R., Rubin, H., & Stern, E. (2018). Enhancing physics learning with cognitively activating instruction: A quasi-experimental classroom intervention study. *Journal of Educational Psychology*, *110*, 1175–1191.

Houdé, O. (2000). Inhibition and cognitive development: Object, number, categorization, and reasoning. *Cognitive Development*, *15*, 63–73.

Houdé, O. (2019). *3-System Theory of the Cognitive Brain: A Post-Piagetian Approach*. New York: Routledge.

Inhelder, B., & Piaget, J. (1958). *The Growth of Logical Thinking: From Childhood to Adolescence*. Trans. A. Parsons, & S. Milgram. New York: Basic Books.

Kitchner, K. S. (1983). Cognition, metacognition, and epistemic cognition. *Human Development*, *26*, 222–232.

Klahr, D., & Chen, Z. (2003). Overcoming the positive-capture strategy in young children: Learning about indeterminacy. *Child Development*, *74*, 1275–1296.

Klahr, D. & Dunbar, K. (1988). Dual space search during scientific reasoning. *Cognitive Science*, *12*, 1–48.

Koerber, S., Mayer, D., Osterhaus, C., Schwippert, K., & Sodian, B. (2014). The development of scientific thinking in elementary school: A comprehensive inventory. *Child Development*, *86*, 327–336.

Koerber, S., Sodian, B., Thoermer, C., & Nett, U. (2005). Scientific reasoning in young children: Preschoolers' ability to evaluate covariation evidence. *Swiss Journal of Psychology*, *64*, 141–152.

Kuhn, T. S. (1970). The structure of scientific revolutions. In O. Neurath, R. Carnap, & C. Morris (eds.), *International Encyclopedia of Unified Science. Foundations of the Unity of Science* (vol. 2, no. 2, pp. 1–210). Chicago, IL: University of Chicago Press.

Kuhn, D. (1989). Children and adults as intuitive scientists. *Psychological Review*, *96*, 674–689.

Kuhn, D. (2000). Metacognitive development. *Current Directions in Psychological Science*, *9*, 178–181.

Kuhn, D. (2006). Do cognitive changes accompany developments in the adolescent brain? *Perspectives on Psychological Science*, *1*, 59–67.

Kuhn, D. (2007). Reasoning about multiple variables: Control of variables is not the only challenge. *Science Education*, *91*, 710–726.

Kuhn, D., Black, J., Keselman, A., & Kaplan, D. (2000). The development of cognitive skills to support inquiry learning. *Cognition and Instruction*, *18*, 495–523.

Kuhn, D., Iordanou, K., Pease, M., & Wirkala, C. (2008). Beyond control of variables: What needs to develop to achieve skilled scientific thinking? *Cognitive Development*, *23*, 435–451.

Kuhn, D. & Pease, M. (2008). What needs to develop in the development of inquiry skills? *Cognition and Instruction*, *26*, 512–559.

Kuhn, D., Ramsey, S., & Arvidsson, T. S. (2015). Developing multivariable thinkers. *Cognitive Development*, *35*, 92–110.

Lederman, N. G. (1992). Students' and teachers' conceptions of the nature of science: A review of the research. *Journal of Research in Science Teaching*, *29*, 331–359.

Lin, X., & Lehman, J. D. (1999). Supporting learning of variable control in a computer-based biology environment: Effects of prompting college students to reflect on their own thinking. *Journal of Research in Science Teaching, 36,* 837–858.

Lorch Jr, R. F., Lorch, E. P., Calderhead, W. J., Dunlap, E. E., Hodell, E. C., & Freer, B. D. (2010). Learning the control of variables strategy in higher and lower achieving classrooms: Contributions of explicit instruction and experimentation. *Journal of Educational Psychology, 102,* 90–101.

Lorch Jr, R. F., Lorch, E. P., Freer, B. D., Dunlap, E. E., Hodell, E. C., & Calderhead, W. J. (2014). Using valid and invalid experimental designs to teach the control of variables strategy in higher and lower achieving classrooms. *Journal of Educational Psychology, 106,* 18–35.

Mayer, D., Sodian, B., Körber, S., & Schwippert, K. (2014). Scientific reasoning in elementary school children: Assessment and relations with cognitive abilities. *Learning and Instruction, 29,* 43–55.

Morris, B. J., Croker, S., M., A., & Zimmerman, C. (2012). The emergence of scientific reasoning. In *Current Topics in Children's Learning and Cognition.* Rijeka, Croatia: InTech.

Neisser, U. (1979). The concept of intelligence. *Intelligence, 3,* 217–227.

Osterhaus, C., Koerber, S., & Sodian, B. (2017). Scientific thinking in elementary school: Children's social cognition and their epistemological understanding promote experimentation skills. *Developmental Psychology, 53,* 450–462

Piaget, J. & Inhelder, B. (1958). *The Growth of Logical Thinking from Childhood to Adolescence: An Essay on the Construction of Formal Operational Structures.* Abingdon, Oxon: Routledge.

Piekny, J., Grube, D., & Maehler, C. (2013). The relation between preschool children's false-belief understanding and domain-general experimentation skills. *Metacognition and Learning, 8,* 103–119.

Premack, D., & Woodruff, G. (1978). Does the chimpanzee have a theory of mind? *Behavioral and Brain Sciences, 1,* 515–526.

Rey-Mermet, A., Gade, M., & Oberauer, K. (2018). Should we stop thinking about inhibition? Searching for individual and age differences in inhibition ability. *Journal of Experimental Psychology: Learning, Memory, and Cognition, 44,* 501–526.

Ross, J. A. (1988). Controlling variables: A meta-analysis of training studies. *Review of Educational Research, 58,* 405–437.

Ruffman, T., Perner, J., Olson, D. R., & Doherty, M. (1993). Reflecting on scientific thinking: Children's understanding of the hypothesis-evidence relation. *Child Development, 64,* 1617–1636.

Schalk, L., Edelsbrunner, P. A., Deiglmayr, A., Schumacher, R., & Stern, E. (2019). Improved application of the control-of-variables strategy as a collateral benefit of inquiry-based physics education in elementary school. *Learning and Instruction, 59,* 34–45.

Schauble, L. (1990). Belief revision in children: The role of prior knowledge and strategies for generating evidence. *Journal of Experimental Child Psychology, 49,* 31–57.

Schauble, L. (1996). The development of scientific reasoning in knowledge-rich contexts. *Developmental Psychology, 32,* 102.

Schauble, L., Klopfer, L. E., & Raghavan, K. (1991). Students' transition from an engineering model to a science model of experimentation. *Journal of Research in Science Teaching, 28,* 859–882.

Schneider, W., & Bullock, M. (Hrsg.). (2009). *Human Development from Early Childhood to Early Adulthood: Findings from a 20 year Longitudinal Study.* New York: Psychology Press.

Schommer, M., Calvert, C., Gariglietti, G., & Bajaj, A. (1997). The development of epistemological beliefs among secondary students: A longitudinal study. *Journal of Educational Psychology, 89,* 37–40.

Schwichow, M., Croker, S., Zimmerman, C., Höffler, T., & Härtig, H. (2015). Teaching the control-of-variables strategy: A meta-analysis. *Developmental Review, 39,* 37–63.

Siler, S. A., & Klahr, D. (2012). Detecting, classifying, and remediating: Children's explicit and implicit misconceptions about experimental design. In R. W. Proctor, & E. J. Capaldi (eds.), *Psychology of Science: Implicit and Explicit Processes* (p. 137–180). Oxford: Oxford University Press.

Siler, S. A., Klahr, D., Magaro, C., Willows, K., & Mowery, D. (2010). Predictors of transfer of experimental design skills in elementary and middle school children. In *International Conference on Intelligent Tutoring Systems* (pp. 198–208). Berlin: Springer.

Sodian, B., Zaitchik, D., & Carey, S. (1991). Young children's differentiation of hypothetical beliefs from evidence. *Child Development, 62*, 753–766.

Somerville, S. C. (1974). The pendulum problem: Patterns of performance defining developmental stages. *British Journal of Educational Psychology, 44*, 266–281.

Stern, E. (2005). Knowledge restructuring as a powerful mechanism of cognitive development: How to lay an early foundation for conceptual understanding in formal domains. *BJEP Monograph Series II, Number 3-Pedagogy-Teaching for Learning, 155*, 155–170.

Stern, E. (2017). Individual differences in the learning potential of human beings. *NPJ Science of Learning, 2*, 2.

Strand-Cary, M., & Klahr, D. (2008). Developing elementary science skills: Instructional effectiveness and path independence. *Cognitive Development, 23*, 488–511.

van der Graaf, J., Segers, E., & Verhoeven, L. (2015). Scientific reasoning abilities in kindergarten: Dynamic assessment of the control of variables strategy. *Instructional Science, 43*, 381–400.

van der Graaf, J., Segers, E., & Verhoeven, L. (2016). Scientific reasoning in kindergarten: Cognitive factors in experimentation and evidence evaluation. *Learning and Individual Differences, 49*, 190–200.

van der Graaf, J., Segers, E., & Verhoeven, L. (2018). Individual differences in the development of scientific thinking in kindergarten. *Learning and Instruction, 56*, 1–9.

Verschueren, N., Schaeken, W., & d'Ydewalle, G. (2005). A dual-process specification of causal conditional reasoning. *Thinking & Reasoning, 11*, 239–278.

Vosniadou, S. (2014). Examining cognitive development from a conceptual change point of view: The framework theory approach. *European Journal of Developmental Psychology, 11*, 645–661.

Vosniadou, S. & Brewer, W. F. (1992). Mental models of the earth: A study of conceptual change in childhood. *Cognitive Psychology, 24*, 535–585.

Wagensveld, B., Segers, E., Kleemans, T., & Verhoeven, L. (2015). Child predictors of learning to control variables via instruction or self-discovery. *Instructional Science, 43*, 365–379.

Zelazo, P., Müller, U., Frye, D., Marcovitch, S., Argitis, G., Boseovski, J., . . . Carlson, S. (2003). The development of executive function in early childhood. *Monographs of the Society for Research in Child Development, 68*, I–151.

Zimmerman, C. (2000). The development of scientific reasoning skills. *Developmental Review, 20*, 99–149.

Zimmerman, C. (2007). The development of scientific thinking skills in elementary and middle school. *Developmental Review, 27*, 172–223.

Zohar, A. & Dori, Y. J. (eds.). (2012). *Metacognition in Science Education*. Dordrecht: Springer Netherlands.

Zohar, A., & Peled, B. (2008). The effects of explicit teaching of metastrategic knowledge on low- and high-achieving students. *Learning and Instruction, 18*, 337–353.

29 Working Memory Training

From the Laboratory to Schools

Torkel Klingberg and Bruno Sauce

29.1 Working Memory

29.1.1 The Many Concepts of Working Memory

As commonly defined in psychology, working memory (WM) is the ability to maintain and manipulate information in active attention. It includes narrow abilities such as auditory short-term storage, visual-spatial short-term storage, and attentional control. Despite a common definition, working memory is still quite a heterogeneous concept, and it can be measured in many distinct ways. WM was first proposed to be the memory for plans of future action (Miller et al., 1960). Later, the dual-store concept of WM by Alan Baddeley came to dominate cognitive psychology for a long time (Baddeley & Hitch, 1974). In that model, there are two separate domain-specific storage systems: the phonological loop (which stores verbal content) and the visuospatial sketchpad (which stores visuospatial content). And, as in many other models of WM since then, Baddeley's model proposes a central executive system (or attentional/processing component) that controls the flow of information from and to the two storage systems.

Based on empirical findings, there have been multiple revisions and new proposals for WM since Baddeley's model. In non-human animals, lesion studies and electrophysiological recordings from tasks described as "short term memory" or "delayed response" tasks revealed neural correlates of these types of memory to the prefrontal cortex (Fuster & Alexander, 1971; Kubota & Niki, 1971; Pribram et al., 1964). Afterwards, Patricia Goldman-Rakic made the link between this type of memory and WM (Goldman-Rakic, 1987). The sustained firing of prefrontal neurons found in electrophysiological recordings has been modeled with biologically realistic neural networks (Compte, 2000), and corresponding sustained activity has also been found using functional magnetic resonance imaging in humans (Postle et al., 2000). Together, these findings describe a standard model for visuospatial WM (Constantinidis & Klingberg, 2016). However, this model has been challenged by findings suggesting that memory during short intervals can occur without brain activity detected by fMRI (D'Esposito & Postle, 2015). More recently, hybrid models in which memory is retained both by sustained electrical activity and synaptic plasticity have also been suggested (Miller et al., 2018).

There are so many types of memories called WM that no definition fits perfectly. In its most wide concept, WM can be considered any type of on-line memory; not very distinct from other memories with a short delay such as short-term memory and sensory memory. The neural basis of WM might be multiple (Miller et al., 2018), and differ depending on stimulus modality, type of stimuli, and task requirements.

29.1.2 Working Memory Is Highly Relevant to Learning and Intelligence

Regardless of the specific concept used to define and measure it, WM is central to a wide range of cognitive tasks: from daily activities such as remembering instructions to sophisticated ones such as discussing politics. Research findings from the last two decades show that performance in working memory tasks is strongly correlated to learning and the general factor of intelligence – including fluid (abstract, reasoning-based) and crystallized (knowledge-based) measures (Conway et al., 2003). Individuals with higher scores on intelligence standardized tests also have a greater capacity for preserving reliable mental representations of relevant information in the short-term (Colom et al., 2016). Furthermore, statistical modeling of inter-individual differences has shown that updating/monitoring of WM is highly correlated with intelligence (Friedman et al., 2006). Surprisingly, other executive processes were not related to intelligence, such as shifting of mental sets and inhibition of prepotent responses (Friedman et al., 2006).

Why are WM and intelligence so tightly correlated? A possible cognitive explanation is that temporary storage is required for online processing in both reasoning and working memory. Reasoning and WM are clearly distinguishable mental operations, but limitations for short-term maintenance hinder the ability for problem-solving. WM might limit, for example, the number of relationships between elements that can be built and kept active during the reasoning process necessary for solving problems included in standard intelligence tests (Halford et al., 2007). Therefore, individual differences in intelligence can be accounted for by basic mental processes underlying memory span, namely, encoding, maintenance, updating, and retrieval (Jonides et al., 2008).

As reported by Martínez et al. (2011), online memory span factors such as WM are hardly distinguishable from fluid intelligence at the latent variable level. At that level of analysis, the difference between WM and intelligence as constructs might be very subtle. Engle (2018) has recently argued based on past research that the part of executive attention most relevant to WM tasks performance is the part that "maintains information in the maelstrom of divergent thought." And the part most relevant to intelligence tasks is the part that "disengages or unbind [relevant information] and functionally forgets it" (Engle, 2018). In other words, even though storage components might always play a critical role to both, the processing components important to WM might not be the ones important for intelligence.

As we present next, the heterogeneity in WM concepts/measures and the (subtle) differences between WM and learning/intelligence processes are likely relevant to the field of WM training – especially when related to educational outcomes.

29.2 Working Memory Training

29.2.1 Working Memory Development, Training, and Plasticity

WM has been traditionally regarded as a fixed trait, and one of the natural limitations on the information processing abilities of the human brain (Miller, 1956). Note, however, that throughout development, the WM of most children improves dramatically, and there are considerable inter-individual differences. At any given age, children differ in WM's capacity and rate of change, with some children developing their WM earlier and at a faster rate, while some others struggle far behind (Ullman et al., 2014). Why is that the case? The factors underlying the development of WM and the related inter-individual differences are still poorly understood. Even so, many researchers in the field default to a maturation/fixed interpretation – stating that the changes in WM over the years are under strict and inflexible genetic programing. Based on recent evidence, this maturation/fixed view of WM is likely to be incomplete.

In the first modern studies on WM training, one of the authors of this chapter, Klingberg gave children intensive and extensive training on visuospatial WM tasks for about forty-five minutes per day, five days per week for five weeks (Klingberg et al., 2002, 2005). These studies used mainly visuospatial tasks similar to the span-board task. The difficulty of the tasks was adapted close to the capacity limit of the children and the active control group received the same tasks, but the difficulty was not adapted. In those original studies, children did not only improve on the trained tasks but also in non-trained tasks (Klingberg et al., 2002, 2005). Since then, the method of WM training has been used as a tool to explore basic scientific questions: such as the question on the neural plasticity underlying WM (Constantinidis & Klingberg, 2016), and whether the neural basis of changes occurring during training corresponds to the changes underlying cognitive development during childhood.

Combined evidence from electrophysiology, neuroimaging, molecular genetics, and behavior genetics show some genes and associated brain activities in common between the WM gains during childhood development and the WM gains during WM training (for a review, see Klingberg, 2014). For example, our research group has previously found that WM development is predicted by both striatal volume and a polymorphism of the dopamine transporter gene – both factors are known to influence learning and brain plasticity (Nemmi et al., 2018). Furthermore, we found that a polymorphism in a dopamine receptor gene is associated with increased gains during WM training (Söderqvist et al., 2014). Recent studies with non-human animals reveal detailed evidence on the plasticity of WM. For example, particular factors underlying innately higher general cognitive abilities in mice can be recreated by WM training programs; including neuronal sensitivity in the prefrontal cortex and dopamine receptor turnover rates (Wass et al., 2013, 2018).

Together, these laboratory findings indicate that WM changes during childhood years and during weeks of training are both influenced by genetic factors on brain plasticity potential, which, in turn, modulate the effect of environmental factors. In contrast to the traditional view of a fixed WM, the new evidence suggest that WM is, to some extent, plastic, and show that WM training programs can have beneficial effects on an individual's WM.

29.2.2 Working Memory Training – Differences in Methods, Aims, and Populations

The rationale for the initial studies on WM training was not only to test if WM could be improved but also to test if this was beneficial for children with ADHD. That idea was based on the theory that deficits in WM are linked to inattention – a central aspect of the symptomatology of ADHD (Barkley, 1997). Neuroimaging shows that visuospatial WM and spatial attention are closely related concepts, both dependent on the prefrontal and intraparietal cortex (Jerde et al., 2012). Consistent with this, when children with attention deficits, either associated with ADHD or trauma, improved their WM, there was also a decrease in inattentive symptoms (Bigorra et al., 2016; Conklin et al., 2015; Green et al., 2012; Klingberg et al., 2005).

In 2008, Susanne Jaeggi and collaborators conducted the first WM training study using a different method: the dual n-back task (Jaeggi et al., 2008). The research also differed in two important aspects: the aim was not improving attention, but improving intelligence, and the participants were not children with ADHD, but healthy university students. The publication by Jaeggi et al. received major media attention and was a milestone in what came to be known as the brain training hype. The hype and the connection to commercial companies with claims that were not always based on solid research resulted in many academics reacting negatively, and a polarized discussion ensued.

There are now around 500 publications on WM training. However, the heterogeneity of WM's concepts is also reflected in the many different methods for improving WM. In addition to the Cogmed training and n-back training, other training approaches include using lists (Dahlin et al., 2008) or complex WM tasks (Chein & Morrison, 2010). Furthermore, WM training studies also differ in the schedules and support the training, the activities of control groups, the types of participants, and the outcome measures. Given the wide range of tasks to which WM capacity has been associated, studies testing the transfers of gains from WM to other abilities also differ: from "pure" measures, such as for intelligence and long-term memory, to more "ecological" measures directly relevant to education, such as reading and mathematics.

29.3 Overview of Working Memory Training in Education

Since the start of WM training programs twenty years ago, there has been an interest in testing whether a potentially increased WM after training can transfer (or generalize) to increased school performance. There have been attempts to summarize the literature from WM training, and there are mixed results. For example, a meta-analysis by Schwaighofer et al. (2015) concluded that WM training does not improve academic outcomes, while another study by Bergman Nutley and Söderqvist (2017) concluded that transfer occurs in some studies but with no significant effect in the majority of studies, though limited and dependent on other factors. Although qualitative and quantitative meta-analyses are certainly valuable to the field, their conclusions will reflect the specific designs of each study analyzed. As noted, WM training programs can be extremely heterogeneous, and this diversity and complexity are rarely taken into account by meta-analyses.

To give a glimpse of the field WM training in education, here we will overview a few studies that used the same WM training program, the Cogmed Working Memory Training, or "Cogmed Training" (Klingberg et al., 2005). Cogmed is the most widely used training program to date, and so represents a great platform for future refinements in going from the laboratory to schools. The Cogmed Training is a computerized training program with twelve different visuospatial and verbal WM span tasks that adapt to the capacity level of the trainee. Training is typically implemented during a period of five-to-seven weeks, thirty-to-forty minutes per day, five days a week, with weekly support from a certified coach that ensures compliance with the program.

Perhaps the most comprehensive study to date on Cogmed Training effects in education was recently performed by Berger et al. (2020). The study was a randomized control trial involving 572 children (six-to-seven-year-old first graders) that embedded Cogmed Training in regular teaching across thirty-one school classes. They found that training led to immediate and lasting gains in working memory capacity as well as relatively large gains in geometry skills, reading skills, and fluid IQ. Interestingly, the transfer effects emerged over time and only became fully visible after twelve months (at the end of this section, we discuss the relevance of this lagged, long-term effect in relation to the two main transfer routes for WM training). Finally, this study by Berger et al. (2020) also showed a direct effect on future school attainment: four years after the intervention, the children who received training had a 16 per cent higher probability of entering the academic track in secondary school.

Next, we discuss some Cogmed Training studies in more detail on the skills of reading and mathematics. The brief overview here is only supposed to illustrate a few examples and shed light on important points regarding transfer effects in schoolchildren. For a structured and extensive review of transfer from Cogmed Training, we recommend the study by Bergman-Nutley and Söderqvist (2017).

29.3.1 Transfer of Cogmed Training to Reading

Studies with Cogmed Training that assess reading gains by measuring passage comprehension frequently show positive results in both clinical and non-clinical samples (Dahlin, 2011; Egeland, Aarlien, & Saunes, 2013; Phillips et al., 2016). However, a study on reading after Cogmed Training in a sample of six- and seven-year-olds did not find reading gains (Roberts et al., 2016). The measures that the authors used to assess reading in a twelve-month follow-up were word reading, sentence comprehension, and spelling, and in a twenty-four-month follow-up, they used word reading and spelling. Note that these are all measures of simple word recognition and comprehension.

WM is only one of several processes that are necessary for reading. Previous research has shown WM to be predictive of certain aspects of reading at certain ages only. For example, WM does not predict simple word recognition

(Kibby et al., 2014) and reading comprehension when using simple sentences (compared to longer texts; Seigneuric & Ehrlich, 2005). This pattern might be behind the negative findings of the study by Roberts et al. (2016). Considering this point, it is not surprising that improvements were not observed in their measures. WM training studies should be careful at selecting appropriate outcome measures of transfer to school performance for each age bracket.

There is a clear difference in the processes supporting reading acquisition and reading comprehension (Chall, 1983). The role of the level of a child's WM gradually transitions from being just one of several processes underlying reading acquisition (learning to read) to later becoming a crucial process in reading comprehension of content (reading to learn). This matters because studies including students on both ends of reading proficiency are likely to see differential effects on the same outcome after WM training – such as in a study by Phillips et al. (2016) that included children ranging from age eight to sixteen years.

Even when WM is an important process for the educational outcome, if another process/ability is acting as a bottleneck for the outcome, then WM training alone is not likely to result in a noticeable transfer. Reading acquisition, for example, is more impacted by phonological awareness than by WM (Leather & Henry, 1994). However, if WM is impaired, then this is likely to disturb the decoding progress, which would make WM a bottleneck in those samples. In harmony with that idea, studies with Cogmed Training assessing reading proficiency in young children tend to show positive transfer on phonological awareness (Fälth et al., 2015; Foy, 2014), whereas studies assessing older children on this measure tend to find effects primarily in impaired samples (Dahlin, 2011; Egeland et al., 2013). Thus, WM training seems to transfer to reading only when it is a bottleneck for reading acquisition (i.e., the samples have lower WM than needed for the relevant learning process). The lesson here is that we should not expect WM training to have a homogeneous effect on reading proficiency. Instead, researchers in the field should explore the different levels of restriction that WM causes on the outcome and find in which situations WM training can make the most impact.

29.3.2 Transfer of Cogmed Training to Mathematics

Bergman-Nutley and Söderqvist (2017) summarized the thirteen studies using Cogmed WM training with mathematics as an outcome. Three of the studies showed significant improvement (Bergman-Nutley & Klingberg, 2014; Dahlin, 2013; Holmes & Gathercole, 2014). There were also positive effect sizes (Cohen's d > 0.25) in seven of the measures from the thirteen studies, but negative effect sizes in four measures.

At this point, it is unclear what explains the differences in results between studies, but it could include differences in outcome measures, population characteristics, sample sizes, and quality of training.

The importance of large sample sizes is discussed in Section 29.4.2. The question of population characteristics, such as diagnoses and baseline WM capacity, is discussed in Section 29.5.1. At this point, there is too little data to draw firm conclusions about the importance of baseline measures for Cogmed training. In particular, there is a lack of studies of typically-developing children.

For example, recent research examined the transfer to mathematics after increasing the amount of coaching during Cogmed training in nine-to-twelve year-olds (Nelwan et al., 2018). The authors found that the highly

coached group performed better in visual WM after training (though, surprisingly there were no differences for verbal WM) compared to a group who received a lesser amount of coaching and a non-trained group. More interestingly, the gains in mathematical ability were higher in the highly coached group right after the end of Cogmed training, and these children also retained their advantage in mathematics four months later compared to the other groups. This suggests that transfer effects from WM training might depend on the quality of the training and the engagement of the children.

The outcome measures used in training studies are important. Like with reading, WM is consistently found to relate to mathematical performance, and the specific patterns of this relation are complex. The relationship of mathematics and WM seems to change at different stages of development (De Smedt et al., 2009) and WM can be more or less important to different aspects of mathematics within the same age group (Wiklund-Hörnqvist et al., 2016). The attention/processing component of WM and visuospatial storage appear to be mostly recruited for learning and application of new mathematical skills

It's also worth noting the ways in which WM training can potentially impact education in general. Bergman-Nutley and Söderqvist (2017) defined two main routes for WM training to transfer to school performance: the learning route and the performance route. In the learning route, WM training will influence academic performance by improving learning capacity. This could be, for example, due to increased attention in class and from an increased capacity to process new information taught. In this route, effects from WM training would be more evident in the long-term, and outcome measures would match specific curricular content. In the performance route, WM will influence academic performance through

WM's direct involvement in academic tasks. So, effects from increased WM capacity from training would show on outcome measures of already learned skills that are tapping WM (and only if, before training, WM was a bottleneck for performing the learned skill, as opposed to other factors not affected by WM training such as speed of processing or knowledge of arithmetic).

29.4 Methodological Challenges

29.4.1 Methodological Aspects of Cognitive Interventions

A paper authored by forty-eight researchers (including one of the authors of this chapter, Klingberg) attempted to make headway in the often polarized discussion about cognitive training, in particular, to suggest guidelines for methodological practices (Shawn Green et al., 2019).

A first suggestion in the article was that "Behavioral interventions for cognitive enhancement can differ substantially in content and target(s) and thus a common moniker like 'brain training' can be misleading" (p. 3). We briefly discussed this problem in Section 29.3, and the situation becomes even worse in the broader literature where approaches used for enhancing cognitive ability by training include standard neuropsychological tasks, commercial computer games, and meditational practices. Some studies use a single task for the entire training while others use a wide range of tasks. Some studies use rigorous monitoring of subjects, while others just give access to a range of tasks to be "played" at home at leisure. Despite this, the term "brain training" is used as if it is a concept specific enough to answer the question of "does brain training work?" (Owen et al., 2010; Simons et al., 2016). Such a question is as scientifically meaningless as the question of whether "do

drugs work"! Instead, conclusions should be more specific, regarding method, subjects, and outcome.

Secondly, the paper by Shawn Green et al. (2019) suggests that it is important to make distinctions between different types of studies: (a) feasibility studies; (b) mechanistic studies; (c) efficacy studies; and (d) effectiveness studies, as described next.

Feasibility studies test the practical aspects of study design. In a drug trial, such a study might investigate possible side-effects of a drug. In an intervention study, a researcher might test whether the tasks are too difficult for the target population, but also evaluate economic, technical, and compliance problems. Feasibility studies can also give an indication of the expected effect size, and thus inform subsequent studies.

Mechanistic studies try to answer basic scientific questions about the neural or cognitive mechanisms by which an intervention works. They might involve neuroimaging, genetics, or try to use a wide range of cognitive tasks in order to pinpoint a cognitive effect.

Efficacy studies aim to test if an intervention causes cognitive or behavioral improvements above and beyond any placebo effects. The question can be framed as "Does the paradigm produce the anticipated outcome in the exact and carefully controlled population of interest when the paradigm is used precisely as intended by the researchers?" This type of study should ideally be done as a randomized, placebo-controlled, blinded trial, comparing the test–retest effect of the treatment group to the test–retest effect of a control group involved in some kind of meaningful alternative activity.

Finally, effectiveness studies try to answer the question of whether an efficient intervention is also effective in a real-world setting. This setting often includes non-compliant subjects who do not perform the training as intended or a wider range of included subjects who have not gone through a careful screening as in an efficiency study. This type of study might be especially relevant when an intervention is to be implemented in a school setting. The sample size of an effectiveness study should be based not only on effect sizes, as in an efficiency study, but also allow for drop-out and non-compliance, and could use an intent-to-treat analysis.

Another methodological problem that is especially relevant to WM training on school performance: studies typically have a wide age range of participants. As we discussed in the topics of reading and mathematics gains, a wide age range will induce large variance due to childhood development and how much WM is required by distinct processes. Furthermore, in the case of a study using standardized assessments (such the Wechsler Individual Achievement Test), the actual tasks performed by children within the same study will differ due to the assessment's wide inclusion of different mathematical domains (Raghubar et al., 2010), and the start and stop rules typically used within these assessments. All those problems make it difficult to interpret and generalize results. Therefore, the field of WM training needs more studies with a small range of age.

29.4.2 Statistical Power, Sample Size, and Latent Measures

Genetic research was for a long time troubled with a lack of replications and inconsistent findings. As technology made genotyping faster and less expensive, researchers realized that the effects of single nucleotide variability were very low, and that larger samples were required. The field of cognitive training is still young but will probably go in a similar direction. Effect size (ES) can be measured as Cohen's delta, which quantifies the change in the treatment group in terms of standard deviations, minus the effect of the change in the control group. Most interventions or drugs intended to improve cognitive function have a low-to-medium effect size. Antidepressants, such as SSRI, have an effect size of at best 0.3, but often around 0.2 (Kirsch, 2008). The effects of anticholinergic drugs on dementia is around 0.15. A meta-analysis of the effect of physical fitness on working memory showed a short-term effect of 0.15 and a long-term effect of 0.05 (Álvarez-Bueno et al., 2017). The effect of methylphenidate on WM is around 0.25 (Coghill et al., 2014). A meta-analysis on the effect of stimulating a "growth mindset" found an effect of less than 0.1 (Sisk et al., 2018). In the "What works clearinghouse," a cut-off of 0.25 is used to classify an intervention as effective.

We should not expect effects from WM training to be much higher than the typical effect size from other interventions in psychology. Any study aiming to evaluate the efficiency or effectiveness of WM training should thus have enough power to detect a 0.3 effect size. Power-calculations will depend on the data and statistical model, but, typically, in order to have a statistical power of 0.8, i.e., an 80 percent chance of finding a true effect is also statistically significant, we will require around 350 participants, 175 in each group. Most WM training studies to date have around fifty-to-sixty participants in total and are thus underpowered. This increases the risk of both false negative and false positive findings and contributes to the inconsistencies between studies.

When it comes to the effect of WM training on academic abilities, it is especially important to take long-term effects into account. A cognitive intervention might improve the ability of a child to pay attention, or keep information in WM, but does not install any new long-term memories or skills. It is not that you suddenly know Pythagoras theorem because you have a better working memory. A pre–post-test that mainly assesses knowledge would thus theoretically have no effect. As mentioned in Section 29.3.2, however, cognitive training might affect learning ability itself (via the learning route) rather than performance (via the performance route). If this is the case, studies need to allow for sufficient time between training and assessment for learning to take place. Therefore, long-term follow-ups are critical to the field, especially to test transfer from WM training via the learning route.

Although long-term follow-ups increase the risk of introducing confounding factors, this can be avoided with well-controlled designs. In these studies, a researcher should ensure that the education given to both groups is comparable for reliable conclusions. Some studies in the past (such as by Roberts et al., 2016) had selected children to take part in a WM training intervention, who are taken out of class to perform the intervention, thus missing out on some regular school lessons. In the long-term, having improved the WM of these students is unlikely to replace the education they have missed. If anything, that specific intervention design could even result in negative effects in school performance.

One last point on methods: Tests of WM transfer to school performance (such as for reading and mathematics) should, ideally, match the curriculum in each particular school. An outcome measure one or two years after WM training will be better if it reflects what the students have been learning in school. One method likely to be fruitful is the use of metrics that schools already use, such as exams and national achievement measures, since these are already designed to capture learning progress. Another possibility is to exploit the explosion of new forms of wearable technology. These could provide a host of reliable, valid, and scalable dependent variables of

improvements in education in scenarios outside of school, and that can also be tracked over long time periods (Shiffman et al., 2008). Of course, researchers need to keep in mind that the designs and protocols ought to respect the privacy and rights of participants, with special caution given the relative novelty of wearable technologies in research.

29.5 Visions for the Future of Working Memory Training in Education

29.5.1 Personalized Training

Most cognitive training interventions to date have used a one-size-fits-all approach, and not considered individual differences in either content or extent of training. The question of personal training, or personal learning, has some bad associations to a field of education promoted as "brain-based learning" – aimed to classify children according to their "learning style" as either auditory, visual, or tactile learners. This is one of the most prevalent brain myths among teachers but has no ground in science (Howard-Jones, 2014). The fact that the "astrological" explanation of inter-individual personality differences is nonsense does not mean that research about personality differences (nor astronomy) should be banned due to guilt-by-association. Serious research about inter-individual differences in learning might be very fruitful.

The clearest example of inter-individual differences might be that subjects differ in the rate of learning. One of the earliest examples of this is Thorndike's study from 1908: "The effect of practice in the case of a purely intellectual function" (Thorndike, 1908). When healthy volunteers were given practice in multiplying large numbers, all of them improved, but the difference in the amount of improvement was three-fold. Interestingly, he found that subjects with higher baseline abilities improved more, an effect later to be known as called the *Matthews effect*, or the *rich-get-richer* effect.

Similarly, the effect of WM training has been shown to be larger for subjects already at a relatively high level at baseline (Au et al., 2015; Jaeggi et al., 2008), and children with higher intelligence have larger transfer to non-trained WM tasks (Gathercole et al., 2019). Thus, the effect of WM training on academic abilities could be dependent on baseline characteristics. Evaluating differences in the impact of an intervention can ideally be done as showing an interaction between group (treatment or control) and baseline measures. For example, Nemmi et al. (2016) showed that the effect of WM training, when mathematical performance was the outcome measure, depended on baseline performance in a WM task. The interaction was positive, that is, in line with the *Matthews effect*. If this turns out to be a replicable finding, it is somewhat ironic that most studies of WM training to date have been including subjects with lower than average WM, which might have been preventing detection of any effect on WM gains.

Finally, the field of WM training in education may very well be one in which a big part of the impact from interventions reflects multiple interacting factors in addition to the intervention itself: such as diet, sleep, exercise, baseline levels of WM, baseline levels of skills, specific mindsets, specific motivational techniques, etc. Thus, WM training in the future ought to test these effects and take relevant individual differences into consideration.

29.5.2 Videogames and ESports

Videogames have been used for educational purposes since the early days of computers. Here, it's important to distinguish between educational videogames and cognitive training videogames.

Educational videogames are the oldest and most widespread in schools. They are software designed to help the teaching of curricular content (e.g., number division or multiplication tables) by gamifying typical exercises/homework and keeping students motivated and more in control of their learning. In an extensive meta-analysis, Clark et al. (2016) analyzed twelve years of research on educational videogames in postsecondary schools in areas such as Engineering, Natural Sciences, and Social Sciences. The meta-analysis found that digital games significantly enhanced student learning relative to non-game conditions, and that "augmented games," that is, games based on research and theories of learning, have a larger effect than plain educational games. Interestingly, he found that factors such as game mechanics characteristics, videogame genre, and narrative mattered to the effects (Clark et al., 2016). At least to some extent, it seems that educational games are becoming another useful pedagogical tool to educators – similar to video animations of a lesson (e.g., the mechanism of digesting food), field trips, and group activities.

In this chapter, however, we are primarily interested in the second, and newest type of videogames for educational purposes: cognitive training videogames. These games can be either designed based on cognitive tasks from research or originally designed for entertainment (such as popular commercial videogames) that happen to train cognition as a side-effect. Overall, these are all software that can potentially be used to motivate and automate the training of general abilities such as WM. Typical laboratory WM training tasks, such as the dual n-back, can be quite arduous and become tedious after a few weeks of daily training. Cognitive training videogames could solve that engagement problem and expand the audience for WM training.

The literature so far on the efficacy of cognitive training videogames is mixed. Many of these studies have focused on possible transfer effects on general abilities other than WM, such as visual tasks, reaction time, visuospatial rotation, and visual search (for a review, see Latham et al., 2013). Regarding WM, cross-sectional studies comparing expert video gamers with novices have commonly found superior performance of gamers on such tasks (e.g., Boot et al., 2008; Greenfield et al., 1994; West et al., 2008), and expert players have higher functional connectivity between attentional and sensorimotor networks (as expected from higher WM capacity) (Gong et al., 2015).

Of course, the results of these studies could merely mean that people with higher WM are more driven toward videogames (and are the people who keep playing them). As stronger evidence, two meta-analyses looked at the efficacy of cognitive training games in increasing WM and other related abilities (Powers et al., 2013). The first meta-analysis computed correlational and quasi-experimental studies comparing players with non-players and found that video game players were superior to non-players in measures of cognitive control/ executive functioning (also considered the processing component of WM). The second meta-analysis was on randomized, controlled interventions, and they also found positive, yet smaller, effects of video game training in cognitive control/executive functioning (among other measures less related to WM that also showed positive results). Furthermore, Palaus et al. (2017) concluded that distinct neural correlates of attention, cognitive control, and verbal and spatial working memory seem improved from different types of video games.

There are also negative results in the literature, however. Sala et al. (2017) conducted a meta-analysis and found small-to-null cognitive effects from playing video games, and null effects in cognitive abilities such as attention, spatial ability, cognitive control, and intelligence. And Gobet et al. (2014) found no effects of video game expertise on attention (flanker task and change detection). The mixed literature on cognitive training videogames somewhat mirrors the mess in the larger literature on cognitive training. Studies on videogames probably suffer from similar theoretical and methodological problems, as we discussed in the previous paragraphs. There are poorly designed studies, lack of agreement on parameters, small power, and meta-analyses ignoring differences between videogame genres (i.e., mixing apples and oranges, as a genre might not tap into WM at all, while another might require a lot of it).

Despite the mixed literature, the positive results so far and the increasing popularity of videogames represent a great potential for WM training in education. Videogames are a huge industry, and children of the current generation have videogames as an integral part of their day-to-day lives. A 2008 report in the US (Pew Research Center, 2008), for example, found that nearly all American teenagers aged twelve-to-seventeen play videogames (computer, web, console, or mobile games), totaling 99 percent of boys and 94 percent of girls. Regarding frequent gaming, there are significant gender differences, but the gap is not as large as people imagine – with 39 percent of boys and 22 percent of girls reporting daily gaming. And 34 percent of boys and 18 percent of girls in the US play video games for two hours or more daily. Furthermore, a 2017 report in the UK showed that children aged five-to-seven years spend an average of 7.3 hours per week playing videogames, while children aged twelve-to-fifteen spend a remarkable 12.2 hours per week playing them (Statista, 2017). These statistics, of course, mean that videogames for WM training are becoming easier to be adopted and implemented by schools, since both educators and students are now more familiar with the language of games, and can derive more motivation/pleasure from using them. If we can reliably increase WM via videogames, that would represent an immense help to WM training programs in education: in going from the laboratory to schools.

As a vision for the future of WM training videogames in schools, we see two potential and critical roles for researchers (these, of course, are not mutually exclusive).

Vision for role #1: Researches will directly help in the development of new cognitive training videogames. These laboratory-produced videogames would potentially borrow much from already existing WM training programs in psychology and combine them with principles in game design. Such as the way it was done, for example, with the app Vektor. There are a few guides and suggestions in the literature on how to build better memory training games. For example, Deveau et al. (2015) propose specific ways to augment the efficacy of WM training by borrowing from the fields of Perceptual Learning (research on reinforcement, multisensory facilitation and multi-stimulus training) and Computer Science (research on engaging environments from game design). This area, however, is still immature, and much work still needs to be done.

The advantage of laboratory-produced videogames is that they could be extremely effective at increasing WM per hour played compared to popular, standard videogames. Laboratory training programs are typically based on tests developed from decades of research in cognitive psychology and psychometrics, so there is high confidence that these tasks reliably and strongly tap the relevant construct (such as WM). The disadvantage of laboratory-produced videogames is that the vast majority of these games will not be as engaging and motivating as big-budget

videogames. It is unlikely that children will play these laboratory-produced games by themselves as pure entertainment. So, even though they are more effective at increasing WM per hour played, we cannot expect children to play for too many hours a week. In order to counter this problem, researchers and companies should be in closer contact with schools to implement these videogames as part of homework or during a set time in school. It is still unclear, however, if this approach could achieve voluntary playing in all children with the amount of playing needed to have cognitive effects.

Vision for role #2: Researches will help to provide evaluations and guides of already existing popular, commercial videogames. Some studies and laboratories will focus on testing which are the best videogames at improving cognitive abilities (e.g., WM, reasoning, intelligence) and school performance. As a proof of concept, a study by Baniqued et al. (2013) attempted to evaluate the cognitive abilities tapped by a variety of commercial videogames. They used twenty web-based commercial games and tested their relationship with a battery of cognitive tasks by using factor analyses. The authors found five interpretable cognitive groups with close correspondence to pre-defined game categorizations: working memory and reasoning games, spatial integration games, attention/ multiple object tracking games, and perceptual speed games. For example, games categorized to tap working memory and reasoning were robustly related to performance on working memory and fluid intelligence tasks. The methods used in Baniqued et al. (2013) could be used in the future to assess the best games to be used for WM training, and show that videogames can be heterogenous on the cognitive abilities they tap on. Furthermore, the diversity in cognitive requirements that Baniqued et al. (2013) found among games could also explain, in part, the mixed results in the video-game training literature.

In role #2, researchers would act the same way as nutritionists: suggesting which types of food are healthy, and how much of each should be consumed. Or, closer in analogy, the researcher's role would be of physical education experts in schools: suggesting the correct schedules of sports and exercising programs of already well-established activities, such as running, football, swimming, and basketball.

In fact, some videogames are gradually resembling traditional sports in many ways. ESports (electronic sports) is a form of organized, videogame competition between players or teams of players. ESports can be quite diverse (and, consequently, could be diverse in their requirements of distinct cognitive abilities), including the genre/modality of real-time strategy (e.g., StarCraft), fighting (e.g., Street Fighter), first-person shooter (e.g., Counter-Strike), multiplayer online battle arena (e.g., League of Legends), and digital card game (e.g., Hearthstone). Since the 2000s, eSports have become a significant factor in the entertainment industry, with audiences in numbers equal to leagues of traditional sports such as the NBA. Moreover, the competitive aspect of eSports is attracting the attention of the International Olympic Committee: some eSports are confirmed to be medal events in the 2022 Asian Games and are being considered for the 2024 Olympic Games. In this context, schools might in the future add eSports as part of recreational/break time and/or add eSports to the sports training curriculum. Further, it is likely that eSports will get amateur leagues within and between schools – similar to what already exists nowadays with football, swimming, volleyball, etc. (And similar to eSports college leagues that already exist in a few universities in the United States, for example.) If these visions

come true, the school environment will soon need studies on the effects of eSports on education and on cognitive training.

Extending the analogy of fitness/sports in our speculations of what could happen in the field's future: regarding role#1, small companies and gyms can create new and very effective exercising programs and group activities, and experts (such as personal trainers) can fine-tune these to smaller groups of individuals. This would be the role of researchers for WM training videogames. In role #2, well-established sports such as football, tennis, and swimming might not be the most effective at improving one's fitness, and cannot be changed, but their reach, engagement, and user numbers are much higher. The role of researchers would be choosing the best big-budget videogames and eSports at improving WM, as well as establishing the best schedules.

As far as we know, there is still no controlled research on the effect of eSports on WM. However, given some of the positives results with other popular videogames, the strategic and reasoning requirements of these games, and the number of hours played by children, it is likely that at least some of these games might be efficacious to WM. This, of course, is just informed speculation. However, the potential is there! Both roles of researchers in this vision could potentially bring enormous future gains to education using the method of WM training.

References

Álvarez-Bueno, C., Pesce, C., Cavero-Redondo, I., Sánchez-López, M., Martínez-Hortelano, J. A., & Martínez-Vizcaíno, V. (2017). The effect of physical activity interventions on children's cognition and metacognition: A systematic review and meta-analysis. *Journal of the American Academy of Child & Adolescent Psychiatry*, *56*, 729–738.

Au, J., Sheehan, E., Tsai, N., Duncan, G. J., Buschkuehl, M., & Jaeggi, S. M. (2015). Improving fluid intelligence with training on working memory: A meta-analysis. *Psychonomic Bulletin and Review*, *22*, 366–377.

Baddeley, A., & Hitch, G. (1974). Working memory. In K. W. Spence, & J. T. Spence (eds.), *The Psychology of Learning and Motivation* (pp. 47–87). New York: Academic Press.

Baniqued, P. L., Lee, H., Voss, M. W., Basak, C., Cosman, J. D., DeSouza, S., … Kramer, A. F. (2013). Selling points: What cognitive abilities are tapped by casual video games? *Acta Psychologica*, *142*, 74–86.

Barkley, R. A. (1997). Behavioral inhibition, sustained attention, and executive functions: Constructing a unifying theory of ADHD. *Psychological Bulletin*, *121*, 65–94.

Berger, E. M., Fehr, E., Hermes, H., Schunk, D., & Winkel, K. (2020). The impact of working memory training on children's cognitive and noncognitive skills. *Working Papers Gutenberg School of Management and Economics*. Available from https://ideas.repec.org/p/jgu/wpaper/2015.html. Last accessed August 18, 2021.

Bergman-Nutley, S., & Klingberg, T. (2014). Effect of working memory training on working memory, arithmetic and following instructions. *Psychological Research*, *78*, 869–877.

Bergman Nutley, S., & Söderqvist, S. (2017). How is working memory training likely to influence academic performance? Current evidence and methodological considerations. *Frontiers in Psychology*, *8*, 69.

Bigorra, A., Garolera, M., Guijarro, S., & Hervás, A. (2016). Long-term far-transfer effects of working memory training in children with ADHD: A randomized controlled trial. *European Child & Adolescent Psychiatry*, *25*, 853–867.

Boot, W. R., Kramer, A. F., Simons, D. J., Fabiani, M., & Gratton, G. (2008). The effects of video game playing on attention, memory, and executive control. *Acta Psychologica*, *129*, 387–398.

Chall, J. S. (1983). *Stages of Reading Development*. New York: McGraw-Hill.

Chein, J. M., & Morrison, A. B. (2010). Expanding the mind's workspace: Training and transfer effects with a complex working memory span task. *Psychonomic Bulletin & Review*, *17*, 193–199.

Clark, D. B., Tanner-Smith, E. E., & Killingsworth, S. S. (2016). Digital games, design, and learning: A systematic review and meta-analysis. *Review of Educational Research*, *86*, 79–122.

Coghill, D. R., Seth, S., Pedroso, S., Usala, T., Currie, J., & Gagliano, A. (2014). Effects of methylphenidate on cognitive functions in children and adolescents with attention-deficit/hyperactivity disorder: Evidence from a systematic review and a meta-analysis. *Biological Psychiatry*, *76*, 603–615.

Colom, R., Chuderski, A., & Santarnecchi, E. (2016). Bridge over troubled water: Commenting on Kovacs and Conway's process overlap theory. *Psychological Inquiry*, *27*, 181–189.

Compte, A. (2000). Synaptic mechanisms and network dynamics underlying spatial working memory in a cortical network model. *Cerebral Cortex*, *10*, 910–923.

Conklin, H. M., Ogg, R. J., Ashford, J. M., Scoggins, M. A., Zou, P., Clark, K. N., … Zhang, H. (2015). Computerized cognitive training for amelioration of cognitive late effects among childhood cancer survivors: A randomized controlled trial. *Journal of Clinical Oncology*, *33*, 3894–3902.

Constantinidis, C., & Klingberg, T. (2016). The neuroscience of working memory capacity and training. *Nature Reviews Neuroscience*, *17*, 438–449.

Conway, A. R., Kane, M. J., & Engle, R. W. (2003). Working memory capacity and its relation to general intelligence. *Trends in Cognitive Sciences*, *7*, 547–552.

D'Esposito, M., & Postle, B. R. (2015). The cognitive neuroscience of working memory. *Annual Review of Psychology*, *66*, 115–142.

Dahlin, E., Nyberg, L., Bäckman, L., & Neely, A. S. (2008). Plasticity of executive functioning in young and older adults: Immediate training gains, transfer, and long-term maintenance. *Psychology and Aging*, *23*, 720–730.

Dahlin, K. I. E. (2011). Effects of working memory training on reading in children with special needs. *Reading and Writing*, *24*, 479–491.

Dahlin, K. I. E. (2013). Working memory training and the effect on mathematical achievement in children with attention deficits and special needs. *Journal of Education and Learning, 2,* 118–133.

De Smedt, B., Janssen, R., Bouwens, K., Verschaffel, L., Boets, B., & Ghesquière, P. (2009). Working memory and individual differences in mathematics achievement: A longitudinal study from first grade to second grade. *Journal of Experimental Child Psychology, 103,* 186–201.

Deveau, J., Jaeggi, S. M., Zordan, V., Phung, C., & Seitz, A. R. (2015). How to build better memory training games. *Frontiers in Systems Neuroscience, 8,* 243.

Egeland, J., Aarlien, A. K., & Saunes, B. K. (2013). Few effects of far transfer of working memory training in ADHD: A randomized controlled trial. *PLoS ONE, 8,* e75660.

Engle, R. W. (2018). Working memory and executive attention: A revisit. *Perspectives on Psychological Science, 13,* 190–193.

Fälth, L., Jaensson, L., & Johansson, K. (2015). Working memory training – A Cogmed intervention. *International Journal of Learning, Teaching and Educational Research, 14,* 28–35.

Foy, J. G. (2014). Adaptive cognitive training enhances executive control and visuospatial and verbal working memory in beginning readers. *International Education Research, 2,* 19–43.

Friedman, N. P., Miyake, A., Corley, R. P., Young, S. E., DeFries, J. C., & Hewitt, J. K. (2006). Not all executive functions are related to intelligence. *Psychological Science, 17,* 172–179.

Fuster, J. M., & Alexander, G. E. (1971). Neuron activity related to short-term memory. *Science, 173,* 652–654.

Gathercole, S. E., Dunning, D. L., Holmes, J., & Norris, D. (2019). Working memory training involves learning new skills. *Journal of Memory and Language, 105,* 19–42.

Gobet, F., Johnston, S. J., Ferrufino, G., Johnston, M., Jones, M. B., Molyneux, A., . . . Weeden, L. (2014). "No level up!": No effects of video game specialization and expertise on cognitive performance. *Frontiers in Psychology, 5,* 1–9.

Goldman-Rakic, P. S. (1987). Circuitry of primate prefrontal cortex and regulation of behavior by representational memory. In F. Plum (ed.), *Handbook of Physiology* (pp. 373–417). New York: Oxford University Press.

Gong, D., He, H., Liu, D., Ma, W., Dong, L., Luo, C., & Yao, D. (2015). Enhanced functional connectivity and increased gray matter volume of insula related to action video game playing. *Scientific Reports, 5,* 9763.

Green, C. T., Long, D. L., Green, D., Iosif, A.-M., Dixon, J. F., Miller, M. R., . . . Schweitzer, J. B. (2012). Will working memory training generalize to improve off-task behavior in children with attention-deficit/hyperactivity disorder? *Neurotherapeutics, 9,* 639–648.

Greenfield, P. M., DeWinstanley, P., Kilpatrick, H., & Kaye, D. (1994). Action video games and informal education: Effects on strategies for dividing visual attention. *Journal of Applied Developmental Psychology, 15,* 105–123.

Halford, G. S., Cowan, N., & Andrews, G. (2007). Separating cognitive capacity from knowledge: A new hypothesis. *Trends in Cognitive Sciences, 11,* 236–242.

Holmes, J., & Gathercole, S. E. (2014). Taking working memory training from the laboratory into schools. *Educational Psychology, 34,* 440–450.

Howard-Jones, P. A. (2014). Neuroscience and education: Myths and messages. *Nature Reviews Neuroscience, 15,* 817–824.

Jaeggi, S. M., Buschkuehl, M., Jonides, J., & Perrig, W. J. (2008). Improving fluid intelligence with training on working memory. *Proceedings of the National Academy of Sciences (USA), 105,* 6829–6833.

Jerde, T. A., Merriam, E. P., Riggall, A. C., Hedges, J. H., & Curtis, C. E. (2012). Prioritized maps of space in human frontoparietal cortex. *Journal of Neuroscience, 32,* 17382–17390.

Jonides, J., Lewis, R. L., Nee, D. E., Lustig, C. A., Berman, M. G., & Moore, K. S. (2008). The mind and brain of short-term memory. *Annual Review of Psychology, 59,* 193–224.

Kibby, M. Y., Lee, S. E., & Dyer, S. M. (2014). Reading performance is predicted by more than phonological processing. *Frontiers in Psychology*, 5, 1–7.

Kirsch, I. (2008). Antidepressant drugs 'work', but they are not clinically effective. *British Journal of Hospital Medicine*, 69, 359.

Klingberg, T. (2014). Childhood cognitive development as a skill. *Trends in Cognitive Sciences*, 18, 573–579.

Klingberg, T., Fernell, E., Olesen, P. J., Johnson, M., Gustafsson, P., Dahlström, K., . . . Westerberg, H. (2005). Computerized training of working memory in children with ADHD – A randomized, controlled trial. *Journal of the American Academy of Child & Adolescent Psychiatry*, 44, 177–186.

Klingberg, T., Forssberg, H., & Westerberg, H. (2002). Training of working memory in children with ADHD. *Journal of Clinical and Experimental Neuropsychology*, 24, 781–791.

Kubota, K., & Niki, H. (1971). Prefrontal cortical unit activity and delayed alternation performance in monkeys. *Journal of Neurophysiology*, 34, 337–347.

Latham, A. J., Patston, L. L. M., & Tippett, L. J. (2013). The virtual brain: 30 years of video-game play and cognitive abilities. *Frontiers in Psychology*, 4, 1–10.

Leather, C. V., & Henry, L. A. (1994). Working memory span and phonological awareness tasks as predictors of early reading ability. *Journal of Experimental Child Psychology*, 58, 88–111.

Martínez, K., Burgaleta, M., Román, F. J., Escorial, S., Shih, P. C., Quiroga, M. Á., & Colom, R. (2011). Can fluid intelligence be reduced to 'simple' short-term storage? *Intelligence*, 39, 473–480.

Miller, E. K., Lundqvist, M., & Bastos, A. M. (2018). Working memory 2.0. *Neuron*, 100, 463–475.

Miller, G. A. (1956). The magical number seven, plus or minus two: Some limits on our capacity for processing information. *Psychological Review*, 63, 81–97.

Miller, G. A., Galanter, E., & Pribram, K. H. (1960). *Plans and the Structure of Behavior*. New York: Henry Holt & Co.

Nelwan, M., Vissers, C., & Kroesbergen, E. H. (2018). Coaching positively influences the effects of working memory training on visual working memory as well as mathematical ability. *Neuropsychologia*, 113, 140–149.

Nemmi, F., Helander, E., Helenius, O., Almeida, R., Hassler, M., Räsänen, P., & Klingberg, T. (2016). Behavior and neuroimaging at baseline predict individual response to combined mathematical and working memory training in children. *Developmental Cognitive Neuroscience*, 20, 43–51.

Nemmi, F., Nymberg, C., Darki, F., Banaschewski, T., Bokde, A. L. W., Büchel, C., . . . Klingberg, T. (2018). Interaction between striatal volume and DAT1 polymorphism predicts working memory development during adolescence. *Developmental Cognitive Neuroscience*, 30(February), 191–199.

Owen, A. M., Hampshire, A., Grahn, J. A., Stenton, R., Dajani, S., Burns, A. S., . . . Ballard, C. G. (2010). Putting brain training to the test. *Nature*, 465, 775–778.

Palaus, M., Marron, E. M., Viejo-Sobera, R., & Redolar-Ripoll, D. (2017). Neural basis of video gaming: A systematic review. *Frontiers in Human Neuroscience*, 11, 248.

Pew Research Center. (2008). Who Is Playing Games? Available from www.pewinternet.org/2008/09/16/part-1-1-who-is-playing-games/. Last accessed August 18, 2021.

Phillips, N. L., Mandalis, A., Benson, S., Parry, L., Epps, A., Morrow, A., & Lah, S. (2016). Computerized working memory training for children with moderate to severe traumatic brain injury: A double-blind, randomized, placebo-controlled trial. *Journal of Neurotrauma*, 33, 2097–2104.

Postle, B. R., Berger, J. S., Taich, A. M., & D'Esposito, M. (2000). Activity in human frontal cortex associated with spatial working memory and saccadic behavior. *Journal of Cognitive Neuroscience*, 12(suppl 2), 2–14.

Powers, K. L., Brooks, P. J., Aldrich, N. J., Palladino, M. A., & Alfieri, L. (2013). Effects of video-game play on information processing: A meta-analytic investigation. *Psychonomic Bulletin & Review*, 20, 1055–1079.

Pribram, K. H., Ahumada, A., Hartog, J., & Roos, L. (1964). A progress report on the neurological processes disturbed by frontal lesions in primates. In J. M. Warren, & K. Akert (eds.), *The Frontal Cortex and Behavior* (pp. 28–55). New York: McGraw-Hill.

Raghubar, K. P., Barnes, M. A., & Hecht, S. A. (2010). Working memory and mathematics: A review of developmental, individual difference, and cognitive approaches. *Learning and Individual Differences, 20*, 110–122.

Roberts, G., Quach, J., Spencer-Smith, M., Anderson, P. J., Gathercole, S., Gold, L., … Wake, M. (2016). Academic outcomes 2 years after working memory training for children with low working memory. *JAMA Pediatrics, 170*, e154568.

Sala, G., Tatlidil, K. S., & Gobet, F. (2017). Video game training does not enhance cognitive ability: A comprehensive meta-analytic investigation. *Psychological Bulletin, 144*, 111–139.

Schwaighofer, M., Fischer, F., & Bühner, M. (2015). Does working memory training transfer? A meta-analysis including training conditions as moderators. *Educational Psychologist, 50*, 138–166.

Seigneuric, A., & Ehrlich, M.-F. (2005). Contribution of working memory capacity to children's reading comprehension: A longitudinal investigation. *Reading and Writing, 18*, 617–656.

Shawn Green, C., Bavelier, D., Kramer, A. F., Vinogradov, S., Ansorge, U., Ball, K. K., … Witt, C. M. (2019). Improving methodological standards in behavioral interventions for cognitive enhancement. *Journal of Cognitive Enhancement, 3*, 2–29.

Shiffman, S., Stone, A. A., & Hufford, M. R. (2008). Ecological momentary assessment. *Annual Review of Clinical Psychology, 4*, 1–32.

Simons, D. J., Boot, W. R., Charness, N., Gathercole, S. E., Chabris, C. F., Hambrick, D. Z., & Stine-Morrow, E. A. L. (2016). Do "brain-training" programs work? *Psychological Science in the Public Interest, 17*, 103–186.

Sisk, V. F., Burgoyne, A. P., Sun, J., Butler, J. L., & Macnamara, B. N. (2018). To what extent and under which circumstances are growth mind-sets important to academic achievement? Two

meta-analyses. *Psychological Science, 29*, 549–571.

Söderqvist, S., Matsson, H., Peyrard-Janvid, M., Kere, J., & Klingberg, T. (2014). Polymorphisms in the dopamine receptor 2 gene region influence improvements during working memory training in children and adolescents. *Journal of Cognitive Neuroscience, 26*, 54–62.

Statista. (2017). Hours children spend gaming weekly in the United Kingdom (UK) from 2013 to 2017, by age group (in hours). Available from www.statista.com/statistics/274434/time-spent-gaming-weekly-among-children-in-the-uk-by-age/. Last accessed August 18, 2021.

Thorndike, E. L. (1908). The effect of practice in the case of a purely intellectual function. *The American Journal of Psychology, 19*, 374.

Ullman, H., Almeida, R., & Klingberg, T. (2014). Structural maturation and brain activity predict future working memory capacity during childhood development. *Journal of Neuroscience, 34*, 1592–1598.

Wass. C., Pizzo, A., Sauce, B., Kawasumi, Y., Sturzoiu, T., Ree, F., … Matzel, L. D. (2013). Dopamine D1 sensitivity in the prefrontal cortex predicts general cognitive abilities and is modulated by working memory training. *Learning & Memory, 20*, 617–627.

Wass, C., Sauce, B., Pizzo, A., & Matzel, L. D. (2018). Dopamine D1 receptor density in the mPFC responds to cognitive demands and receptor turnover contributes to general cognitive ability in mice. *Scientific Reports, 8*, 4533.

West, G. L., Stevens, S. A., Pun, C., & Pratt, J. (2008). Visuospatial experience modulates attentional capture: Evidence from action video game players. *Journal of Vision, 8*, 13.

Wiklund-Hörnqvist, C., Jonsson, B., Korhonen, J., Eklöf, H., & Nyroos, M. (2016). Untangling the contribution of the subcomponents of working memory to mathematical proficiency as measured by the national tests: A Study among Swedish third graders. *Frontiers in Psychology, 7*, 1–12.

30 Interventions for Improving Executive Functions during Development

Working Memory, Cognitive Flexibility, and Inhibition

Nikolaus Steinbeis and Claire Rosalie Smid

30.1 Introduction

Executive functions (EFs) comprise a set of cognitive skills harnessed for the regulation of behaviour and the pursuit of long-term goals. Sometimes referred to as cognitive control, this set of processes enables one to stay focused on a particular task and ignore distractions along the way (Diamond, 2013). There is some consensus that EFs can be decomposed into three core components, namely working memory, cognitive flexibility and inhibition (Miyake et al., 2000). *Working memory* (WM) allows the short-term retention and manipulation of information in mind (Baddeley, 1992); *inhibitory control* (IC) refers to the ability to suppress prepotent impulses and is also referred to as self-control or interference control (Logan et al., 1997); while *cognitive flexibility* (CF) is the ability to switch readily between different mental processes or task-demands (Eslinger & Grattan, 1993). These three EFs often operate jointly in a large variety of cognitive-development tasks. For the purposes of the present chapter, we also review the literature on attentional control (AC) (the ability to direct focus to the task at hand; Davidson et al., 2006).

Individually and in concert, EFs comprise a skill set that is critical for quality-of-life, impacting physical and mental health, as well as school readiness, and academic and job success (Diamond, 2013). Understandably, the interest in training and improving EFs

has as a result been considerable, both from a basic and an applied research perspective. Moreover, because of heightened brain plasticity during childhood and adolescence (Giedd & Rapoport, 2010; Gogtay et al., 2004; Mills et al., 2016), attention has turned increasingly to improving these functions during development (see Chapters 4 and 5). As a result, there has been a recent increase in the advocacy for early interventions (Heckman, 2006; Shonkoff & Levitt, 2010; Shonkoff et al., 2012). Understanding the mechanisms, effects and potential benefits of interventions in developmental populations is therefore crucial. Whereas this has been picked up at the level of policy, research has been slower to respond. Here, we will review evidence from EF training in both typical and atypical developmental populations, as well as in adults.

Our point of departure is that EF training can reliably improve performance on the training task. The more interesting (and obvious) question we focus on is whether such training leads to durable transfer onto other domains. We thus review and discuss transfer on tasks that are either structurally or conceptually closely related (i.e., near transfer; other EFs) as well as more distally related tasks tapping into different cognitive functions (i.e., intelligence, academic achievement). From this perspective, we also review the literature on EF training in clinical samples. While working memory training (WMT) is covered in greater detail in Chapter 29, to allow conclusions on EF training generally, we include some principal WMT studies. We review the available literature on training EF in children (and adolescents, where there is data available) and young adults separately. We include data on neural mechanisms if available and preface this by means of a section on neural circuitry of executive functions. Finally, in our discussion, we explore aspects that we consider critical when reviewing this literature, namely individual differences, motivation, the mechanism of training and factors likely to affect transfer, as well as meta-analyses (Smid et al., 2020).

30.2 Measuring Executive Functions

EF ability can be measured using a range of tasks that tap into its different components. It is helpful to illustrate the nature of these tasks, as interventions usually operate by manipulating the tasks' features. WM has been typically classified as the storage and manipulation of information (Baddeley & Hitch, 1974; D'esposito et al., 1995). Different tasks can tap into these WM functions, such as how simple memory tasks can test WM storage, either in verbal, numerical or visuospatial format, while tasks such as the backwards digit span (repetition of number sequence in backwards order with progressively longer sequences) measure the simultaneous ability of WM storage and manipulation (Baddeley & Hitch, 1974). Other WM tasks that are typically used to train WM include the n-back task, which entails monitoring the identity or location of a series of verbal or non-verbal stimuli and to indicate when the currently presented stimuli is identical to the one presented n-trials back (Owen et al., 2005).

To measure IC, the two main paradigms used are the Stop-Signal task and the Go/No-go task. In the Stop-Signal task, participants are asked to respond as fast as possible to a stimulus (Go-Signal), but to inhibit their response on trials when this Go-Signal is followed by a second stimulus (Stop-Signal). The interval between Go- and Stop-Signals (also known as Stop-Signal Delay; SSD) can vary; inhibition is easier on trials where the SSD is short (Verbruggen & Logan, 2008). In this task, subjects must balance speed with successful IC, which is thought to require proactive adjustments in response time, as measured by the Stop-Signal response time (SSRT) (Verbruggen & Logan, 2009). In the Go/No-go task, the Stop-Signal is presented without a prior Go-Signal (Rubia et al., 2001). Both, Stop-Signal and Go/No-go paradigms have a greater number of Go-Signals, which leads to a prepotent response to react to the stimulus that in turn needs to be inhibited. Interventions tend to focus on lowering the response window, the inter-trial intervals or varying the SSD in the Stop-Signal task.

For assessing CF, typically tasks are used that test the ability to adapt cognitive processing strategies to new and unexpected conditions, such as task-switching paradigms. In the task-switching paradigm, participants have to adapt their response to either react to the rule- or feature-domains, which change during the task. The measure of interest is performance (accuracy and speed) on trials where participants have to 'switch' from one strategy to the other, for example, selecting a response based on one of two varying stimulus dimensions compared to where the dimension remains constant (Davidson et al., 2006). An example of a task-switching paradigm is the Wisconsin Card Sorting Task (a card sorting task that switches random sorting rules a set number of turns), which measures the ability to change prior held beliefs (Monchi et al., 2001). This description of specific EF tasks serves as background to reviewing how task components are selectively varied to achieve training goals.

30.3 Executive Functions in the Brain

Both neuroimaging and lesion studies have been instrumental in identifying brain areas involved in EFs. The most consistently reported regions include the prefrontal cortex; especially the dorsolateral prefrontal cortex (DLPFC), the anterior cingulate cortex (ACC) and the right inferior frontal cortex (rIFC) (Berkman et al., 2009). These areas are also among the latest brain regions to mature (Giedd et al., 1999), making them particularly interesting from a developmental perspective. A recent meta-analysis of studies on the relationship between executive functioning and PFC volume found that larger PFC volume and cortical thickness was associated with better executive performance (Yuan & Raz, 2014). EFs have also been consistently linked to differential patterns of activations. Individual differences in both the intraparietal and prefrontal cortex are correlated to WM capacity differences among adults (Vogel & Machizawa, 2004), and between children and adults (Crone et al., 2006; Olesen et al., 2006). Neural network models suggest that stronger frontoparietal connectivity could be a potential mechanism underlying higher WM capacity (Buschkuehl et al., 2014; Klingberg, 2010; Langer et al., 2013; Schweizer et al., 2013).

IC has been consistently related to activity in the middle and inferior frontal gyrus (Garavan et al., 1999). A meta-analysis shows that the Go/No-go task reliably elicits activity in frontal regions (DLPFC, mPFC, inPFC) as well as the inferior parietal circuits (Simmonds et al., 2008), while the Stop-Signal task is reliably associated with activity in the right inferior frontal gyrus as well as the basal ganglia

(Chevrier et al., 2007). Another meta-analysis comparing the Go/No-go and Stop-Signal paradigms identified the bilateral anterior insular regions and the supplementary motor area as essential for accurate performance in both tasks, a so-called core system, with the middle frontal gyrus and inferior parietal lobule being more important for the Go/No-go than for the Stop-Signal task, while the Stop-Signal task saw more thalamic activity (Swick et al., 2011). Lastly, proactive inhibition was found to elicit more activity in the medial prefrontal cortex and the inferior parietal cortex, while reactive inhibition elicited more activity in the primary motor cortex, the supplementary cortex and the putamen (Jaffard et al., 2008).

For CF, a difference between reactive and spontaneous flexibility has been made, and the frontal lobe and basal ganglia have been identified as areas of interest (Eslinger & Grattan, 1993). In fMRI studies using task-switching paradigms, frontal regions such as the lateral and medial prefrontal cortex, DLPFC (Kim et al., 2011; Logue & Gould, 2014), as well as the posterior parietal cortex (PPC), the anterior cingulate cortex (ACC), anterior insula and subcortical structures such as the basal ganglia and superior colliculus have been identified (Leber et al., 2008).

30.4 The Benefits of Executive Function Training

30.4.1 Working Memory Training

30.4.1.1 Near Transfer Effects

WM is arguably the EF with the most training studies conducted. After a college student in the 1980s practiced number repetition until he could repeat seventy-nine digits (Ericcson et al., 1980), but then demonstrated a recall of merely six letters, it was thought that WMT might not generalize at all. Since then, however, a plethora of studies has shown that increases in WM capacity can in fact transfer to other measures of WM besides improvements on the training task. This is known as near transfer. Additionally, some studies have shown that WMT leads to structural (Metzler-Baddeley et al., 2016) as well as functional (McKendrick et al., 2014; Olesen et al., 2004; Takeuchi et al., 2010) brain changes in regions related to WM, such as the middle frontal gyrus and superior and inferior parietal cortices. These observed changes in brain structure and function suggest that the neural systems that underlie WM and potentially other EFs can be susceptible to training-induced plasticity. Several meta-analyses have shown that WMT can lead to improvements in other measures of WM (Schwaighofer et al., 2015), although some specified that these were only sustained short-term (Melby-Lervag & Hulme, 2013; Melby-Lervåg et al., 2016).

As with all programmes aiming to improve EFs, a crucial question is whether WMTs also transfer to other domains, such as educational outcomes or measures of intelligence (Holmes et al., 2009; Studer-Luethi et al., 2016). For typically-developing (TD) children, a recent meta-analysis of twenty-five WMT studies concluded that WMT leads to significant improvement on near transfer tasks, but that only little evidence was found for far transfer (Sala & Gobet, 2017). Many programmes have recently been criticized, since they were generally not found to lead to improvements to other domains (Melby-Lervag & Hulme, 2013; Melby-Lervåg et al., 2016; Minear et al., 2016; Thompson et al., 2013). This is an important issue when we consider that time spent in traditional education settings might be encroached by participating in an

EF training paradigm without any apparent benefit (Roberts et al., 2016). In Section 30.4.1.2 we review the literature on far transfer effects for TD and atypically-developing (AD) children, as well as young adults.

30.4.1.2 Far Transfer Effects

Typically-Developing (TD) Children
The most commonly studied transfer domains for WMT studies pertain to educational outcomes, as measured by testing mathematical skills and reading see Judd and Klingberg (2021). Nature Human Behavior. Several studies reported that using either *Cogmed*, a computerized adaptive WMT (Holmes et al., 2009), or a WMT in combination with a number line (Nemmi et al., 2016) or numeracy training (Kroesbergen et al., 2012; Passolunghi & Costa, 2016) led to improvements on measures of mathematical performance or numeracy ability. However, several other studies reported that they did not find differences in mathematical ability between their training and control groups, neither using adaptive *Cogmed* (Dunning et al., 2013) nor face-to-face training (Henry et al., 2014). Besides math. a relationship between WM and reading has long been hypothesized, whereby problems with reading might be partially due to WM difficulty (Lee Swanson et al., 2006). Thus, WMT might be beneficial to children's' reading comprehension. While the study using a face-to-face WMT saw no improvements in mathematics, it did lead to significantly higher reading comprehension scores compared to children in the active and passive control groups (Henry et al., 2014).

Lastly, a relationship between WMT and intelligence has been proposed, and fluid intelligence in particular. It has been suggested that since WM capacity requires the active maintenance of information and simultaneous processing, it therefore recruits an executive attention-control mechanism to combat interference and that this ability is mediated by portions of the prefrontal cortex (Conway et al., 2003). In addition, WM capacity has been found to be highly correlated to measures of IQ (Colom et al., 2008). Therefore, increasing WM capacity might also translate to improvements in measures of intelligence. Several studies using the adaptive n-back paradigm with TD children have reported improvements in fluid (Jaeggi et al., 2011; Peng et al., 2017; Studer-Luethi et al., 2016) or crystallized (Studer-Luethi et al., 2016) intelligence.

Atypically-Developing (AD) Children

WM interventions, in particular *Cogmed*, were originally marketed as an intervention for ADHD. Several studies showed that WMT led to improvements in ADHD symptoms (Beck et al., 2010; Bigorra et al., 2016; Green et al., 2012; Johnstone et al., 2010; Klingberg et al., 2005; Wong et al., 2014), as well as improvement on other measures of WM (Green et al., 2012; Wong et al., 2014) or complex reasoning (Klingberg et al., 2005).

Similar to the studies with TD children, several studies found that WMT led to improved academic performance in the form of reading in atypical populations. Studies have reported that adaptive *Cogmed* WMT led to improvements in EF ability (Bigorra et al., 2016), while the computerized *Jungle Memory* training was reported to lead to improvements in spelling and verbal and non-verbal ability (Alloway et al., 2013), and another adaptive WMT led to improvements on visual rhyming and reading fluency for children with dyslexia (Luo et al., 2013). Lastly, one meta-analysis on the effects of WMT in children and adolescents with learning disabilities found that WMT leads to reliable short-term improvements in near transfer tasks, as well as some reading improvement, when compared to control groups. These results could be sustained up until eight months after training, and that children over ten years seemed to benefit more from improvements in verbal WM than younger children (Peijnenborgh et al., 2016).

Typical Young Adults

The literature on WMT for young adults is substantial, with most studies focusing on whether WMT could lead to improvements in fluid intelligence. An influential study reported dosage-dependent improvement in fluid intelligence using an adaptive dual n-back task in a study with thirty-four young adults (Jaeggi et al., 2008). Since then, many studies have sought to replicate this, with either positive (Jaušovec & Jaušovec, 2012) or negative findings (Redick et al., 2013).

As a much debated topic, several meta-analyses have concluded that there is no convincing evidence that WMT transfers to fluid intelligence (Melby-Lervåg et al., 2016; Redick, 2015; Redick et al., 2013), academic performance (Redick et al., 2015) or any other type of far transfer (Clark et al., 2017; Melby-Lervag & Hulme, 2013). Other meta-analyses show that there are small effect sizes for WMT far transfer only (Au et al., 2015; Schwaighofer et al., 2015; Soveri et al., 2017).

However, there are still studies that reported far transfer, although not necessarily to fluid intelligence. A study with thirty-two participants found that an emotional dual n-back task led to increased performance in affective cognitive control, as compared to the placebo training, which consisted of a feature match task with shapes, which posed minimal demand on WM (Schweizer et al., 2013). This suggests that affectively contextualized WMT could indeed lead to benefits such as improved emotion regulation (Engen & Kanske, 2013). This could be of interest for clinical populations that suffer from affective dysregulation (Johnson, 2012)

30.4.2 Inhibitory Control Training

Interventions impacting IC have been much rarer (see Houdé et al., 2000, for a seminal brain imaging study on young adults). This is in large part due to failed early attempts of improving IC following training (Cohen & Poldrack, 2008; Logan & Burkell, 1986). It was concluded that IC was a largely automatic process, which could not be altered by means of targeted interventions, let alone lead to transfer effects. Since then, this picture has undergone some revision. We will begin tracing Inhibitory Control Training (ICT) studies in development and then discuss the literature on adults. Given the paucity of studies on ICT and Cognitive Flexibility Training (CFT), we will discuss the following studies in greater detail.

30.4.2.1 TD and AD Children

In one of the first ICT studies in children, Thorell et al. (2009) studied four-to-five year old children and divided them into a WMT or an ICT group, as well as an active and a passive control group. Children trained over a period of five weeks with fifteen-minutes of training each school day (6.25 hours of training in total). IC was trained by the means of five tasks based on the Stop-Signal task, the Go/No-go and the flanker task, which is a task aimed at training the stopping of ongoing and prepotent responses as well as interference control. The difficulty of the tasks was adaptive to performance levels, which was achieved through decreasing the response window. Children were given a battery of tests measuring IC, visuospatial and verbal WM, response speed, problem-solving, visual attention and sustained attention. Performance on the training tasks improved from the first to the last session for all tasks apart from the Stop-Signal task. In terms of transfer, WMT improved both types of WM, as well as

sustained attention, whereas ICT did not lead to improvements on any of the transfer tasks. The authors argued that inhibition is hard to train because of the relatively short-lived nature of the process required for stopping ongoing or prepotent responses. The authors also conceded that their manipulation of difficulty was suboptimal (i.e., response window) and this would necessarily make the inhibition process short-lived.

Using a similar type of adaptive training, Johnstone et al. (2010) employed a joint ICT and WMT with forty seven-to-twelve year old children diagnosed with ADHD. Children were divided into a performance sensitive, adaptive (high intensity) as well as a non-performance sensitive training group (low intensity). Training lasted five weeks and consisted of five weekly twenty-minute sessions at home (8.25 hours training in total). In the high intensity training group, difficulty was adapted by means of increasing the items to be remembered for the WMT and by decreasing the response window in the ICT. While children in the high intensity group were found to demonstrate less symptoms of inattention and hyperactivity compared to the low intensity group, no group differences could be found on any other measures including a Go/No-go task, resting state EEG or ERPs.

Another study capitalised on the properties of a pre-existing computer game known as *Fruit Ninja*, which mimics the structural properties of a Go/No-go task (i.e., 'slice the fruits; avoid the bombs') to train IC in four year olds (Liu et al., 2015). The training was adaptive in as far as children were encouraged to slice thirty more fruits than in the previous round. The control training was a colouring game. Training spanned three weeks with four weekly fifteen-minute sessions for the ICT (three hours training in total) and two weekly fifteen-minute sessions for the colouring game training (1.5 hours training in total). Whereas the group playing *Fruit Ninja* improved their performance on the training task compared to the control group, this did not transfer onto any other task (i.e., interference control, Go/No-go, digit span and Raven's progressive matrices). Using EEG, the authors did find an ERP effect during the Go/No-go task on the N200, which was larger in the ICT group but only for girls.

In a study by Zhao et al. (2018), a group of children aged ten-to-twelve years and a group of adults aged eighteen-to-twenty-four years completed either an ICT based on the Go/No-go task or sand painting training. Each group trained on twenty successive weekdays for approximately twenty minutes (about six hours of training in total). Task difficulty in the ICT was achieved by decreasing or increasing the inter-stimulus interval (ISI). If the mean percentage of correct responses was over 90 per cent, the ISI would be reduced by 200 milliseconds, whereas if the percentage of correct responses was between 60–90 per cent the ISI would remain the same and it would be increased by 200 milliseconds with correct responses below 60 per cent. The sand painting group was not adaptive, but the authors argued that this activity required focussed attention, perseverance and patience and being equally motivating. Transfer of training effects was assessed by looking at performance on tasks assessing response inhibition, interference control, WM updating, task-switching and non-verbal fluid intelligence at three- and six-month follow-up sessions and/or an immediate post-training sessions. Significant training improvements and positive transfer effects to a similar response inhibition task with other stimuli were observed for both children and adults. Reliable albeit short-lived transfer effects were only found for the children, specifically to WM updating and task switching.

Other types of ICT include interventions that capitalize on associating appetitive cues with inhibition of behaviour. Recent findings suggest that inhibition can be engaged automatically and is affected by both supra- and subliminally presented primes (Linzarini et al., 2017). Theoretical models of action control imply a close correspondence between approach and avoidant behavioural tendencies (i.e., respond and inhibit) on the one hand and reward and punishment on the other (Verbruggen et al., 2014). Thus, reward-related cues ought to be associated with activation of motor behaviour, whereas punishment-related cues should be associated with inhibition of behaviour. These patterns have been borne out empirically (Guitart-Masip et al., 2012), whereby models claim a bi-directional relationship between the two dimensions (i.e., valence and action). Thus, repeated approach responses to neutral cues increases positive evaluation of those cues (Woud et al., 2011, 2013). As a result, these associations lend themselves for interventions aiming to reduce appetite for unhealthy foods. Porter et al. (2018) tested this directly in four-to-eleven-year-old children who were presented with cards depicting either healthy or unhealthy food items, which in turn were paired with Go- and No-go-Signals, respectively (100 per cent pairing of Go-healthy food and No-go unhealthy food). A control training used a comparable procedure but changed the stimulus-action pairings to 50 per cent each. Each training session consisted of four blocks of thirty-two trials. The transfer task consisted of making a choice from a range of both trained and novel food cards. Children in the 100 per cent pairing chose significantly more healthy items than children in the control condition after the training compared to before. These findings indicate that stimulus-action pairings can lead to behavioural change in associated transfer domains in developmental samples.

30.4.2.2 Adults

In one of the first ICT studies, Cohen and Poldrack (2008) tested forty-seven adults with a mean age of 21.1 years using a serial reaction time (SRT) task in combination with a Stop-Signal task. The Stop-Signal task consisted of the SRT with 33 per cent auditory Stop-Signal trials. Importantly, the SSD varied after the onset of the SRT stimulus using two independent staircase functions. SSD increased by fifty milliseconds if participants inhibited their response correctly. Training occurred over three one-hour sessions over the course of one week (three hours training in total). The authors found no effect of training on inhibition and concluded that IC was untrainable.

More recently, Enge et al. (2014), assigned 122 healthy adults to either an adaptive or a non-adaptive ICT group (comprised of Go/No-go and Stop-signal tasks). Each group trained for three weeks, three times a week for half an hour (4.5 hours training in total). All subjects were tested on IC, interference control and fluid intelligence before, immediately after and four months after training. In the Go/No-go training, adaptation was implemented by shifting the response window to stimuli contingent on trial-by-trial performance, while in the Stop-signal task this was done by means of increasing or decreasing the SSD. These values did not change for the non-adaptive group. It was found that whereas adaptive training improved IC, this was true to an equal extent in the non-adaptive group. No transfer was found on interference control or fluid intelligence.

In arguably the best example of training IC, Berkman et al. (2014) only used a Stop-Signal task. Sixty adult participants were divided into two equal-sized groups, an inhibition and a so-called sham training group. Whereas the inhibition group had to inhibit responding to an adaptively changing Stop-Signal, the sham training also performed the stop task but without inhibiting in response to the Stop-Signal (i.e., a semi-active control group). The authors found that SSRTs improved in the inhibition

group pre–post training compared to the active sham group. Equally, the slope in SSRT across the ten training sessions decreased significantly and in a linear fashion, showing improvement on the task. The imaging analysis showed an increase in right IFG activity in the inhibition group post-training during the cue period compared to the sham group. This suggests that this training enhanced activity of IFG in a proactive way, as opposed to a reactive one. Beauchamp et al. (2016) tested whether this training would have an effect on an untrained task known to elicit activity in similar brain regions, namely emotion-regulation. Whereas no effects of training were found on reappraisal ratings of images with negative valence, participants in the training group showed a significant reduction in activity in left IFG and supramarginal gyrus during emotion regulation compared to the sham group. This suggests some transfer at the neural level from training IC.

Verbruggen et al. (2012) divided 135 adult participants into three groups: a control group, who performed a gambling task, a double-response group, who had to respond twice when seeing the stop-Signal (25 per cent), and an inhibition group, who had to refrain from responding when seeing the Stop-Signal. The training phase consisted of ten blocks of seventy-two trials and only subjects in the stop group made significantly less risky choices than the double-stop group. This suggests that inhibition in one domain can be influenced by inhibition in another. These effects persisted two hours after the training but not after twenty-four hours (Verbruggen et al., 2013).

In one of the very first studies on inhibition training, Houde et al. (2000) attempted to influence logical deductive reasoning by means of ICT. The authors targeted the so-called perceptual matching bias, a systematic reasoning bias caused by the misdirection of attention through the word 'not' in logical statements. They studied eight male adult subjects who had a strong perceptual matching bias. Participants were trained on material, which was different to the test, but which lent itself to being taught how to avoid perceptual matching bias by means of IC. ICT allowed subjects to respond logically in response to deductive reasoning problems (unlike a mere retest of the same problem or a training in logic). Participants showed a marked increase in logical responses following matching-bias ICT and an increased activation of the left prefrontal cortex implicated in EFs.

As we previously discussed for the children, ICT seemed to be able to influence dietary choices. A recent meta-analysis demonstrated that adult participants who had received ICT chose or consumed less unhealthy food or alcohol compared to control groups.[1] Interestingly, the magnitude of the effect was proportional to the number of successful inhibitions, more than the number of trials in which appetitive cues were paired with the need to inhibit. These findings suggest that by training specific behavioural associations between cues and behavioural responses, consumption behaviour can be modulated. The data on stimulus-action associations are very encouraging; both children and adults are similarly responsive to such pairings with transfer to real-life outcomes such as food or alcohol consumption. While this has potentially far-reaching implications for altering real-life behaviour, whether this can be considered far transfer is debatable. So far, studies have not looked at whether this type of IC training also modulates beyond specifically created associations.

It seems as if ICT can indeed lead to improvements in IC as well as transfer effects in both children and adults. Transfer appears to be contingent on several aspects. First, as becomes clear from the studies reviewed at the

start of this subsection, there are a number of factors that can be modified adaptively in inhibition tasks (i.e., response time-window; ISI; SSD). There has been little discussion, however, whether and how these might differentially impact training outcomes. It would appear that adaptively decreasing the response time-window does little to improve IC, whereas shifting the ISI and SSD might lend themselves more to improving IC. This makes sense in light of the fact that decreasing response thresholds presumably leads to an overall speeding of responses and less to improving inhibition. Changing the ISI and SSD, however, would lead to increased proactive inhibition. More work is needed to study the relative contributions of these factors, but, in addition, more attention needs to be paid to the actual training mechanisms.

30.4.3 Attentional Control

In one of the first attempts to train attentional control, Rueda et al. (2005) recruited a total of forty-nine four-year olds and twenty-five six-year olds to participate. Children were divided into an experimental and a control group and were given five days of training. Whereas the experimental group trained on various facets of attentional control by means of different exercises, which got increasingly difficult, the control group watched popular children's videos, which stopped periodically, for which children had to press a button to continue watching. The authors found significant improvements on attentional control as measured by the Eriksen Flanker task, where participants have to respond to the direction of a

---

[1] Control groups entailed both double responses to the stop stimulus (i.e., engaging similar levels of attentional control), responding to the unhealthy images and inhibiting to neutral images, and responding to both healthy and unhealthy images.

centrally presented stimulus in the presence of distractor items, which was stronger for the experimental compared to the control group. Further attentional control also led to improvements on measures of intelligence.

A recent attempt to improve attentional control in eleven-month old infants (Wass et al., 2011) used a battery of gaze-contingent computer tasks targeting attentional control (i.e., butterflies that moved only while infants looked at it, with distractors presented in the periphery of the visual field). Forty-two typically-developing eleven-month old infants took part in five lab visits over a period of fifteen days (average seventy-seven minutes of training). Pre–post tests including assessments of cognitive control, sustained attention, free play and WM were obtained on the first and last day. The control group completed the same number of sessions viewing age-appropriate television clips and animations for an equivalent amount of time. Training difficulty was adaptive in the experimental group. Compared to the control group, infants trained in attentional control were found to have improved cognitive control, sustained attention and changes in looking behaviour during spontaneous free play (i.e., increased number of attentional shifts from object to person). A more recent study using a similar training regime in nine-month olds, showed that training attentional control significantly impacted infants' likelihood to respond to an adult's socio-communicative cues, which persisted six weeks after training (Forssman & Wass, 2018).

30.4.4 Cognitive Flexibility Training

The most common approach to training CF is the task-switching paradigm. Task-switching paradigms require participants to perform two simple tasks, A and B, in single blocks (either A or B) or in mixed-task blocks (switching between both tasks). Mixed-task blocks tap the ability to switch from doing the same task within a mixed block to a different task in a mixed block. In one of the first studies of this in children, Karbach and Kray (2009) allocated fifty-six children aged eight-to-ten years, fifty-six younger adults aged eighteen-to-tewenty-six years and fifty-six older adults aged sixty-two-to-seventy-seven years into one of four training groups: a single-task training group; a mixed-task training group; as well as variants of the mixed-task training, including verbal self-instruction training and training variability. Training occurred over a period of four weeks, with one training session per week lasting between thirty-to-forty minutes (approximately 2.3 hours) and this was not adaptive for any group. Pre–post training comparisons were obtained on measures of inhibition (i.e., Stroop task), verbal and spatial WM as well as fluid intelligence. Task-switching training led to improvements in task-switching, which was greatest for children. Further, task-switching training improved IC as well as WM and fluid intelligence across all age groups.

A similar approach was used in a study with thirty children aged eight-to-twelve years with clinical levels of ADHD symptoms who were split into a group performing a single task and a group performing task-switching (Kray et al., 2012). Task-switching training led to a reduction in switching costs and transfer effects were found for IC as well as WM measures, but not for reasoning.

30.4.5 Metacognition

Whereas most studies have focused on training specific EFs and improving them through the application of adaptive regimes, few have simultaneously targeted metacognitive abilities (for an exception, see Houdé et al., 2000). Also referred to as 'thinking about thinking', metacognition allows reflection on one's own thought processes and performance (Fernandez-Duque et al., 2000). A significant number of studies have suggested that metacognition positively affects EF ability. For instance, the Dimensional Change Card Sort task (DCCS) requires participants to sort bivalent test cards (e.g., red rabbits and blue boats) first according to one dimension (e.g., colour) and then according to the other (e.g., shape). The ability to sort accurately after switching between dimensions improves significantly between the ages of three and five years. It has been argued that metacognition in the form of reflective reprocessing of information allows for the formulation, selection and maintenance in WM of higher order rules (Zelazo & Frye, 1997). Thus, engaging in metacognition via explicit reflection of task rules should allow children challenged by dimensional switches to solve the task more easily. It was found that when children aged three-years were given explicit and corrective feedback following incorrect (i.e., perseverative) sorts on the DCCS as training, they showed greater improvements on the task compared to children in an active control group who received training on relative clauses but without feedback (Espinet et al., 2013; Kloo & Perner, 2003). This suggests that meta-cognitive strategies can yield insight and thus bolster improvements in EFs targeted by training. Interestingly, the authors found significant transfer from metacognition training to the ability to accurately process false-beliefs, a stringent test of theory of mind, which is a core social skill (Kloo & Perner, 2003).

30.5 Discussion

As becomes clear from the overview in Section 30.4, evidence on far-ranging benefits of programmes dedicated to improving specific EF is far from clear-cut. What emerges is that EFs can be trained, and that these training effects can be measured by closely related so-called near transfer tasks, and that this is the case for both TD and AD children as well as adults. However, the benefit of EF training related gains to other cognitive domains seems to depend on the particular study. Overall, intensive and adaptive training studies seem to be more successful in the case of WMT and ICT. However, its success depends on what is being adapted exactly. In some cases, WMT leads to improved ability regarding reading and, in some cases, leads to improved maths performance, while other studies have shown that WMT was not really beneficial at all. When ICT utilizes tasks not only aimed at reducing the response window, it appears to both improve IC and transfer meaningfully to other domains. Interestingly, variants of ICT where cues are associated with specific actions have shown most promise in transferring to real-life behaviour. CF is the least explored in terms of the effects of training (but see Section 30.5.1 for more examples). This is surprising, given that so far it has shown considerable promise in terms of training and transfer effects.

Our review allows us to assess whether it matters at what age EFT might be applied. Recent theoretical advances in developmental cognitive neuroscience have put forward the *Interactive Specialization hypothesis*, which states that increased specialization of cortical circuits arises partly as an emergent property of competition and cooperation between different brain networks (Johnson, 2001, 2011). The central tenet of this theory is that the human cortex early in postnatal development is relatively unspecialized, but becomes increasingly differentiated and dedicated to specific functions over time (Oliver et al., 2000). One hypothesis which follows directly from this is that cognitive training ought to lead to wider transfer effects when applied early in development compared to later

(Wass et al., 2012). This theory of brain development builds on evidence from developmental psychology, showing that cognitive functions are more likely to interact early in development (Karmiloff-Smith, 1992). A meta-analysis published in 2012 argues that age might indeed play a crucial role, in that training younger children leads to wider transfer compared to adults (Wass et al., 2012). As more developmental studies have been conducted, this hypothesis could be tested on recent data. Also, future studies could include age more explicitly into their designs. Whether or not age of training matters is related more generally to whether EFT might work better for some individuals than for others. In Section 30.5.1–30.5.3, we discuss some of the likely factors that may mediate the potential of EFTs, and the topics that future studies in this field will hopefully seek to answer.

30.5.1 Individual Differences

Of considerable interest in the field of cognitive training is the question of who benefits the most from training. Finding answers to this question is critical, as the utility of interventions needs to be measured as much from whether group differences can be found as whether subgroups of individuals might benefit in particular. Studies have suggested that WMT potential might be affected by genetic variation (Soderqvist et al., 2014), temperament (Studer-Luethi et al., 2012, 2016) or brain activation (Nemmi et al., 2016) and WM ability at baseline (Foster et al., 2017; Soderqvist et al., 2012). Some studies have found that WMT worked better for children with low WM skills (Titz & Karbach, 2014), while others report that individuals with higher WM ability benefit more from the training (Foster et al., 2017; Soderqvist et al., 2012). Regarding baseline potential, two accounts dominate the field: the *magnification account*,

which assumes that individuals who already perform well before training would show the largest training-related benefits, because they have the cognitive resources to acquire and implement new strategies; and the *compensation account*, which assumes that high-performing individuals would show less benefit, because they are already performing at optimal levels. This question is particularly pertinent in the context of child development, since performance will be more variable both within and between individuals than during adulthood. It has been argued that whereas magnification effects are found more often after strategy-based memory training (Karbach & Kray, 2016; Lövdén et al., 2012), compensation effects are found after process-based training.

To address this question, Karbach et al. (2017) performed a task-switching training study with 168 participants (42 children, 42 younger and 42 older adults with an age range of eight-to-ten, eighteen-to-twenty-eight and sixty-two-to-seventy-seven years, respectively). Subjects were assigned to one of three groups, identical to the study of Karbach and Kray (2009): namely a single-task training group; a mixed-task training group; as well as a mixed-task training, including verbal self-instruction training. The pre–post measures were identical to Karbach and Kray (2009). Analyses of latent change models showed a training-induced reduction of age differences and individual differences across training and transfer tasks in all three age groups. Further, individuals with lower cognitive abilities at pre-test showed larger training and transfer benefits after training.

One theoretical computational simulation study emphasized the importance of acknowledging individual differences in learning rates as influencing the results we get in WMT studies (Moreau, 2014). Moreau emphasized that difficulties in replicating previously found results of cognitive training might be due to the individual differences in learning rates, or how quickly someone can learn something new, which might be underlying the processes through which WMT is effective. He suggested that WMT studies should have a minimum of forty participants per cell – which would mean many recent WMT studies are severely under-powered – to lower the chances of any presence or absence of WMT effectiveness being due to chance variation in the population (Moreau, 2014). Larger studies, as well as a pre-study assessment in individual difference in learning rates, would help circumvent this problem in future studies.

30.5.2 Motivation and Engagement

EFs represent a set of mental processes that enable individuals to select contextually appropriate behaviour in pursuit of their goals (Ganesan, K., & Steinbeis, N., in press). Recent work has shown that goal values impact EF ability (Botvinick & Braver, 2015). Converging evidence demonstrates that when high-value goals are at stake, adults selectively enhance their goal-directed actions as evidenced by improvements across all EFs (Padmala & Pessoa, 2011). Similar effects have been observed for both children and adolescents (Geier & Luna, 2009, 2012; Padmanabhan et al., 2011; Strang & Pollak, 2014). These motivation–cognition interaction effects have been ascribed to the coordinated integration between striatal and prefrontal cortical areas (Dalley et al., 2011; Haber & Knutson, 2010). Frameworks propose that the striatum relays value-related information to the PFC to select contextually appropriate behaviour and maximize the attainment of high-value outcomes (O'Reilly & Frank, 2006).

This summary is crucial for our understanding of EFs and how these can be modified by means of interventions. It implies that EFs are not just domain-general processes, but that they are harnessed to achieve specific goals. To date, only a few studies have addressed motivational aspects on EF training, except Houdé et al. (2001), showing that access to deductive logic, after inhibition training in young adults, depends on a right ventromedial prefrontal area devoted to motivation (i.e., to emotions and feelings about error-correction and pre–post-test improvement during a logical reasoning task). In a recent study that looked at the effects of motivational components on task-switching training (Dörrenbächer et al., 2014), fifty-six children were assigned to a single- or double-task group in either a low- or high-motivational setting. Motivation was varied as a function of the extent of self-determination experienced by the children. Thus, the high motivation setting included features likely to increase a sense of autonomy, competency and relatedness (Ryan & Deci, 2000). The training comprised four sessions, between thirty-to-forty-five minutes, separated by at least one day and taking place once or twice a week. All children were given a pre–post assessment including a task-switching paradigm, a Stroop task, an AX-CPT task as well as WM tasks. Training was adaptive for each training group, whereby reaction times of a new block within a training session had to be lower or equal to the median RT of the preceding block. It was found that, unsurprisingly, the high motivation setting had a significant effect on children's willingness to train. Further, motivation had an impact on near transfer effects in that children doing the task-switching training in the high motivation setting showed a greater reduction of switch costs post-test compared to their training counterparts in the low motivation setting. In terms of far transfer, effects of motivation were found in the switch group on their overall response latencies on the tasks (i.e., performance speed on the IC tasks were reduced most from pre–post) but not in the interference costs. These findings are intriguing, however, because they would allow arguing that high motivation leads to improvements on far transfer tasks of the same magnitude as the improvements by reducing the response window. Other studies have found similar effects for ICT in adults (Maraver et al., 2016).

30.5.3 Future Directions

The review in Sections 30.4–30.5.2 shows the promise of EFTs when they are done in the right way. We would like to stress that merely shifting a parameter of a task that measures EF ability might not be enough to genuinely improve a cognitive function. We believe that this is evident particularly in the case of ICT, which until recently has been argued to be untrainable. Taking into account that not everyone might benefit from interventions in similar ways (or at all) and that EFs are goal-directed processes, implies that greater care has to be taken with titrating programs to specific populations, as opposed to a wholesale delivery of standardized regimes.

We believe that the field would benefit from more hypothesis-driven approaches as to which transfer effects could be expected given a specific training intervention (Bergman Nutley & Söderqvist, 2017; Moreau & Conway, 2014; Verbruggen & Logan, 2009). Gaining insight into training-related changes in neural activity can help us understand more about the underlying mechanisms at work, and what brain changes (structural and/or functional) we would hypothesize lead to training-related transfer. Strengthened frontal-parietal connections might be one of the underlying neural mechanisms that are sensitive to training-induced plasticity (Buschkuehl et al., 2014; Klingberg, 2010; Langer et al., 2013; Schweizer et al., 2013). Training paradigms that are not challenging enough for the

participants, that do not include a measure of engagement or that lack a proper measure of comparison, such as passive or no-contact controls, will likely be unhelpful in determining the effectiveness of EFTs (Bergman Nutley & Söderqvist, 2017; Bogg & Lasecki, 2015; Moreau & Conway, 2014).

There are further potentially fruitful avenues with regards to EFT. One of these is whether mindsets and individual differences in the belief of behavioural malleability might be an important factor (Haimovitz & Dweck, 2017). Further, it has been shown that the extent to which adults and children engage EF processes is related to computations of effort (Chevalier, 2018; Kool et al., 2010, 2013; Westbrook et al., 2013). The subjective experience of effort may very well be a candidate mechanism that could be affected by interventions aiming to improve EFs. As is evident, the field of EFT has made enormous progress – drawing on a considerable body of research points to exciting vistas and directions the pursuit of which will be helpful in establishing the opportunities and limits of interventions in improving EFs.

References

Alloway, T. P., Bibile, V., & Lau, G. (2013). Computerized working memory training: Can it lead to gains in cognitive skills in students? *Computers in Human Behavior*, *29*, 632–638.

Au, S., Tsai, D., Buschkuehl, M., & Jaeggi, S. M. (2015). Improving fluid intelligence with training on working memory: A meta-analysis. *Psychonomic Bulletin & Review*, *22*, 366–377.

Baddeley, A. D. (1992). Working memory. *Science*, *255*, 556–559.

Baddeley, A. D., & Hitch, G. (1974). Working memory. *The Psychology of Learning and Motivation*, *8*, 47–89.

Beauchamp, K. G., Kahn, L. E., & Berkman, E. T. (2016). Does inhibitory control training transfer?: Behavioral and neural effects on an untrained emotion regulation task. *Social Cognitive and Affective Neuroscience, 11,* 1374–1382.

Beck, S. J., Hanson, C. A., Puffenberger, S. S., Benninger, K. L., & Benninger, W. B. (2010). A controlled trial of working memory training for children and adolescents with ADHD. *Journal of Clinical Child & Adolescent Psychology, 39,* 825–836.

Bergman Nutley, S., & Söderqvist, S. (2017). How is working memory training likely to influence academic performance? Current evidence and methodological considerations. *Frontiers in Psychology, 8,* 69.

Berkman, E. T., Burklund, L., & Lieberman, M. D. (2009). Inhibitory spillover: Intentional motor inhibition produces incidental limbic inhibition via right inferior frontal cortex. *NeuroImage, 47,* 705–712.

Berkman, E. T., Kahn, L. E., & Merchant, J. S. (2014). Training-induced changes in inhibitory control network activity. *Journal of Neuroscience, 34,* 149–157.

Bigorra, A., Garolera, M., Guijarro, S., & Hervás, A. (2016). Long-term far-transfer effects of working memory training in children with ADHD: A randomized controlled trial. *European Child & Adolescent Psychiatry, 25,* 853–867.

Bogg, T., & Lasecki, L. (2015). Reliable gains? Evidence for substantially underpowered designs in studies of working memory training transfer to fluid intelligence. *Frontiers in Psychology, 5,* 1589.

Botvinick, M., & Braver, T. (2015). Motivation and cognitive control: From behavior to neural mechanism. *The Annual Review of Psychology, 66,* 83–113.

Buschkuehl, M., Hernandez-Garcia, L., Jaeggi, S. M., Bernard, J. A., & Jonides, J. (2014). Neural effects of short-term training on working memory. *Cognitive, Affective, & Behavioral Neuroscience, 14,* 147–160.

Chevalier, N. (2018). Willing to think hard? The subjective value of cognitive effort in children. *Child Development, 89,* 1283–1295.

Chevrier, A. D., Noseworthy, M. D., & Schachar, R. (2007). Dissociation of response inhibition and performance monitoring in the stop signal task using event-related fMRI. *Human Brain Mapping, 28,* 1347–1358.

Clark, C. M., Lawlor-Savage, L., & Goghari, V. M. (2017). Working memory training in healthy young adults: Support for the null from a randomized comparison to active and passive control groups. *PLoS ONE, 12,* e0177707.

Cohen, J. R., & Poldrack, R. A. (2008). Automaticity in motor sequence learning does not impair response inhibition. *Psychonomic Bulletin & Review, 15,* 108–115.

Colom, R., Abad, F. J., Quiroga, M. Á., Shih, P. C., & Flores-Mendoza, C. (2008). Working memory and intelligence are highly related constructs, but why? *Intelligence, 36,* 584–606.

Conway, A. R., Kane, M. J., & Engle, R. W. (2003). Working memory capacity and its relation to general intelligence. *Trends in Cognitive Sciences, 7,* 547–552.

Crone, E. A., Wendelken, C., Donohue, S., van Leijenhorst, L., & Bunge, S. A. (2006). Neurocognitive development of the ability to manipulate information in working memory. *Proceedings of the National Academy of Sciences (USA), 103,* 9315–9320.

D'esposito, M., Detre, J. A., Alsop, D. C., Shin, R. K., Atlas, S., & Grossman, M. (1995). The neural basis of the central executive system of working memory. *Nature, 378,* 279.

Dalley, J. W., Everitt, B. J., & Robbins, T. W. (2011). Impulsivity, compulsivity, and top-down cognitive control. *Neuron, 69,* 680–694.

Davidson, M. C., Amso, D., Anderson, L. C., & Diamond, A. (2006). Development of cognitive control and executive functions from 4 to 13 years: Evidence from manipulations of memory, inhibition, and task switching. *Neuropsychologia, 44,* 2037–2078.

Diamond, A. (2013). Executive functions. *The Annual Review of Psychology, 64,* 135–168.

Dörrenbächer, S., Müller, P. M., Tröger, J., & Kray, J. (2014). Dissociable effects of game elements on motivation and cognition in a task-switching training in middle childhood. *Frontiers in Psychology, 5,* 1275.

Dunning, D. L., Holmes, J., & Gathercole, S. E. (2013). Does working memory training lead to generalized improvements in children with low working memory? A randomized controlled trial. *Developmental Science, 16*, 915–925.

Enge, S., Behnke, A., Fleischhauer, M., Kuttler, L., Kliegel, M., & Strobel, A. (2014). No evidence for true training and transfer effects after inhibitory control training in young healthy adults. *Journal of Experimental Psychology-Learning Memory and Cognition, 40*, 987–1001.

Engen, H., & Kanske, P. (2013). How working memory training improves emotion regulation: Neural efficiency, effort, and transfer effects. *Journal of Neuroscience, 33*, 12152–12153.

Ericcson, K. A., Chase, W. G., & Faloon, S. (1980). Acquisition of a memory skill. *Science, 208*, 1181–1182.

Eslinger, P. J., & Grattan, L. M. (1993). Frontal lobe and frontal-striatal substrates for different forms of human cognitive flexibility. *Neuropsychologia, 31*, 17–28.

Espinet, S. D., Anderson, J. E., & Zelazo, P. D. (2013). Reflection training improves executive function in preschool-age children: Behavioral and neural effects. *Developmental Cognitive Neuroscience, 4*, 3–15.

Fernandez-Duque, D., Baird, J. A., & Posner, M. I. (2000). Executive attention and metacognitive regulation. *Consciousness and Cognition, 9*, 288–307.

Forssman, L., & Wass, S. V. (2018). Training basic visual attention leads to changes in responsiveness to social-communicative cues in 9-month-olds. *Child Development, 89*, e199–e213.

Foster, J. L., Harrison, T. L., Hicks, K. L., Draheim, C., Redick, T. S., & Engle, R. W. (2017). Do the effects of working memory training depend on baseline ability level? *Journal of Experimental Psychology: Learning, Memory, and Cognition, 43*, 1677.

Ganesan, K., & Steinbeis, N. (in press). Development and Plasticity of Executive Functions: A Value-Based Account. Current Opinion in Psychology.

Garavan, H., Ross, T., & Stein, E. (1999). Right hemispheric dominance of inhibitory control: An event-related functional MRI study. *Proceedings of the National Academy of Sciences (USA), 96*, 8301–8306.

Geier, C. F., & Luna, B. (2009). The maturation of incentive processing and cognitive control. *Pharmacology Biochemistry and Behavior, 93*, 212–221.

Geier, C. F., & Luna, B. (2012). Developmental effects of incentives on response inhibition. *Child Development, 83*, 1262–1274.

Giedd, J. N., Blumenthal, J., Jeffries, N. O., Castellanos, F. X., Liu, H., Zijdenbos, A., ... Rapoport, J. L. (1999). Brain development during childhood and adolescence: A longitudinal MRI study. *Nature Neuroscience, 2*, 861–863.

Giedd, J. N., & Rapoport, J. L. (2010). Structural MRI of pediatric brain development: What have we learned and where are we going? *Neuron, 67*, 728–734.

Gogtay, N., Giedd, J. N., Lusk, L., Hayashi, K. M., Greenstein, D., Vaituzis, A. C., ... Rapoport, J. L. (2004). Dynamic mapping of human cortical development during childhood through early adulthood. *Proceedings of the National Academy of Sciences (USA), 101*, 8174–8179.

Green, C. T., Long, D. L., Green, D., Iosif, A.-M., Dixon, J. F., Miller, M. R., ... Schweitzer, J. B. (2012). Will working memory training generalize to improve off-task behavior in children with attention-deficit/hyperactivity disorder? *Neurotherapeutics, 9*, 639–648.

Guitart-Masip, M., Nuys, Q. J. M., Fuentemilla, L., Dayan, P., Duzel, E., & Dolan, R. J. (2012). Go and no-go learning in reward and punishment: Interactions between affect and effect. *NeuroImage, 62*, 154–166.

Haber, S. N., & Knutson, B. (2010). The reward circuit: Linking primate anatomy and human imaging. *Neuropsychopharmacology, 35*, 4–26.

Haimovitz, K., & Dweck, C. S. (2017). The origins of children's growth and fixed mindsets: New research and a new proposal. *Child Development, 88*, 1849–1859.

Heckman, J. J. (2006). Skill formation and the economics of investing in disadvantaged children. *Science, 312*, 1900–1902.

Henry, L. A., Messer, D. J., & Nash, G. (2014). Testing for near and far transfer effects with a short, face-to-face adaptive working memory training intervention in typical children. *Infant and Child Development*, *23*, 84–103.

Holmes, J., Gathercole, S. E., & Dunning, D. L. (2009). Adaptive training leads to sustained enhancement of poor working memory in children. *Developmental Science*, *12*, F9–F15.

Houdé, O., Zago, L., Crivello, F., Moutier, S., Pineau, A., Mazoyer, B., & Tzourio-Mazoyer, N. (2001). Access to deductive logic depends on a right ventromedial prefrontal area devoted to emotion and feeling: Evidence from a training paradigm. *NeuroImage*, *14*, 1486–1492.

Houde, O., Zago, L., Mellet, E., Moutier, S., Pineau, A., Mazoyer, B., & Tzourio-Mazoyer, N. (2000). Shifting from the perceptual brain to the logical brain: The neural impact of cognitive inhibition training. *Journal of Cognitive Neuroscience*, *12*, 271–278.

Jaeggi, S. M., Buschkuehl, M., Jonides, J., & Perrig, W. J. (2008). Improving fluid intelligence with training on working memory. *Proceedings of the National Academy of Sciences (USA)*, *105*, 6829–6833.

Jaeggi, S. M., Buschkuehl, M., Jonides, J., & Shah, P. (2011). Short- and long-term benefits of cognitive training. *Proceedings of the National Academy of Sciences (USA)*, *108*, 10081–10086.

Jaffard, M., Longcamp, M., Velay, J.-L., Anton, J.-L., Roth, M., Nazarian, B., & Boulinguez, P. (2008). Proactive inhibitory control of movement assessed by event-related fMRI. *NeuroImage*, *42*, 1196–1206.

Jaušovec, N., & Jaušovec, K. (2012). Working memory training: Improving intelligence–changing brain activity. *Brain and Cognition*, *79*, 96–106.

Johnson, M. H. (2001). Functional brain development in humans. *Nature Reviews Neuroscience*, *2*, 475–483.

Johnson, M. H. (2011). Interactive specialization: A domain-general framework for human functional brain development? *Developmental Cognitive Neuroscience*, *1*, 7–21.

Johnson, M. H. (2012). Executive function and developmental disorders: The flip side of the coin. *Trends in Cognitive Sciences*, *16*, 454–457.

Johnstone, S. J., Roodenrys, S., Phillips, E., Watt, A. J., & Mantz, S. (2010). A pilot study of combined working memory and inhibition training for children with AD/HD. *ADHD Attention Deficit and Hyperactivity Disorders*, *2*, 31–42.

Judd, N., & Klingberg, T., (2021). Training spatial cognition enhances mathematical learning in a randomized study of 17000 children.

Karbach, J., Koenen, T., & Spengler, M. (2017). Who benefits the most? Individual differences in the transfer of executive control training across the lifespan. *Journal of Cognitive Enhancement*, *1*, 394–405.

Karbach, J., & Kray, J. (2009). How useful is executive control training? Age differences in near and far transfer of task-switching training. *Developmental Science*, *12*, 978–990.

Karbach, J., & Kray, J. (2016). Executive functions. In T. Strobach, & J. Karbach (eds.), *Cognitive Training – An Overview of Features and Applications Executive Functions* (pp. 93–103). Cham: Springer International.

Karmiloff-Smith, A. (1992). *Beyond Modularity: A Developmental Perspective on Cognitive Science.* Cambridge, MA: MIT Press.

Kim, C., Johnson, N. F., Cilles, S. E., & Gold, B. T. (2011). Common and distinct mechanisms of cognitive flexibility in prefrontal cortex. *Journal of Neuroscience*, *31*, 4771–4779.

Klingberg, T. (2010). Training and plasticity of working memory. *Trends in Cognitive Sciences*, *14*, 317–324.

Klingberg, T., Fernell, E., Olesen, P. J., Johnson, M., Gustafsson, P., Dahlström, K., . . . Westerberg, H. (2005). Computerized training of working memory in children with ADHD – A randomized, controlled trial. *Journal of the American Academy of Child & Adolescent Psychiatry*, *44*, 177–186.

Kloo, D., & Perner, J. (2003). Training transfer between card sorting and false belief understanding: Helping children apply conflicting descriptions. *Child Development*, *74*, 1823–1839.

Kool, W., McGuire, J. T., Rosen, Z. B., & Botvinick, M. M. (2010). Decision making and the avoidance of cognitive demand. *Journal of Experimental Psychology: General, 139*, 665.

Kool, W., McGuire, J. T., Wang, G. J., & Botvinick, M. M. (2013). Neural and behavioral evidence for an intrinsic cost of self-control. *PLoS ONE, 8*, e72626.

Kray, J., Karbach, J., Haenig, S., & Freitag, C. (2012). Can task-switching training enhance executive control functioning in children with attention deficit/-hyperactivity disorder? *Frontiers in Human Neuroscience, 5*, 180.

Kroesbergen, E. H., Van't Noordende, J. E., & Kolkman, M. E. (2012). Number sense in low-performing kindergarten children: Effects of a working memory and an early math training. In Z. Breznitz, O. Rubinsten, V. J. Molfese, & D. L. Molfese (eds.), *Reading, Writing, Mathematics and the Developing Brain: Listening to Many Voices* (pp. 295–313). Dordrecht: Springer.

Langer, N., von Bastian, C. C., Wirz, H., Oberauer, K., & Jäncke, L. (2013). The effects of working memory training on functional brain network efficiency. *Cortex, 49*, 2424–2438.

Leber, A. B., Turk-Browne, N. B., & Chun, M. M. (2008). Neural predictors of moment-to-moment fluctuations in cognitive flexibility. *Proceedings of the National Academy of Sciences (USA), 105*, 13592–13597.

Lee Swanson, H., Howard, C. B., & Saez, L. (2006). Do different components of working memory underlie different subgroups of reading disabilities? *Journal of Learning Disabilities, 39*, 252–269.

Linzarini, A., Houdé, O., & Borst, G. (2017). Cognitive control outside of conscious awareness. *Consciousness and Cognition, 53*, 185–193.

Liu, Q., Zhu, X., Ziegler, A., & Shi, J. (2015). The effects of inhibitory control training for preschoolers on reasoning ability and neural activity. *Scientific Reports, 5*, 14200.

Logan, G. D., & Burkell, J. (1986). Dependence and independence in responding to double stimulation – A comparison of stop, change, and dual-task paradigms. *Journal of Experimental Psychology–Human Perception and Performance, 12*, 549–563.

Logan, G. D., Schachar, R. J., & Tannock, R. (1997). Impulsivity and inhibitory control. *Psychological Science, 8*, 60–64.

Logue, S. F., & Gould, T. J. (2014). The neural and genetic basis of executive function: Attention, cognitive flexibility, and response inhibition. *Pharmacology Biochemistry and Behavior, 123*, 45–54.

Lövdén, M., Brehmer, Y., Li, S. C., & Lindenberger, U. (2012). Training-induced compensation versus magnification of individual differences in memory performance. *Frontiers in Human Neuroscience, 6*, 141.

Luo, Y., Wang, J., Wu, H., Zhu, D., & Zhang, Y. (2013). Working-memory training improves developmental dyslexia in Chinese children. *Neural Regeneration Research, 8*, 452.

Maraver, M. J., Bajo, M. T., & Gomez-Ariza, C. J. (2016). Training on working memory and inhibitory control in young adults. *Frontiers in Human Neuroscience, 10*, 588.

McKendrick, R., Ayaz, H., Olmstead, R., & Parasuraman, R. (2014). Enhancing dual-task performance with verbal and spatial working memory training: Continuous monitoring of cerebral hemodynamics with NIRS. *NeuroImage, 85*, 1014–1026.

Melby-Lervag, M., & Hulme, C. (2013). Is working memory training effective? A meta-analytic review. *Developmental Psychology, 49*, 270–291.

Melby-Lervåg, M., Redick, T. S., & Hulme, C. (2016). Working memory training does not improve performance on measures of intelligence or other measures of "far transfer" evidence from a meta-analytic review. *Perspectives on Psychological Science, 11*, 512–534.

Metzler-Baddeley, C., Caeyenberghs, K., Foley, S., & Jones, D. K. (2016). Task complexity and location specific changes of cortical thickness in executive and salience networks after working memory training. *NeuroImage, 130*, 48–62.

Mills, K. L., Goddings, A. L., Herting, M. M., Meuwese, R., Blakemore, S. J., Crone, E. A., . . . Tamnes, C. K. (2016). Structural brain development between childhood and adulthood: Convergence across four longitudinal samples. *Neuroimage, 141*, 273–281.

Minear, M., Brasher, F., Guerrero, C. B., Brasher, M., Moore, A., & Sukeena, J. (2016). A simultaneous examination of two forms of working memory training: Evidence for near transfer only. *Memory & Cognition, 44*, 1014–1037.

Miyake, A., Friedman, N. P., Emerson, M. J., Witzki, A. H., Howerter, A., & Wager, T. D. (2000). The unity and diversity of executive functions and their contributions to complex "frontal lobe" tasks: A latent variable analysis. *Cognitive Psychology, 41*, 49–100.

Monchi, O., Petrides, M., Petre, V., Worsley, K., & Dagher, A. (2001). Wisconsin Card Sorting revisited: Distinct neural circuits participating in different stages of the task identified by event-related functional magnetic resonance imaging. *Journal of Neuroscience, 21*, 7733–7741.

Moreau, D. (2014). Making sense of discrepancies in working memory training experiments: A Monte Carlo simulation. *Frontiers in Systems Neuroscience, 8*, 161.

Moreau, D., & Conway, A. R. (2014). The case for an ecological approach to cognitive training. *Trends in Cognitive Sciences, 18*, 334–336.

Nemmi, F., Helander, E., Helenius, O., Almeida, R., Hassler, M., Räsänen, P., & Klingberg, T. (2016). Behavior and neuroimaging at baseline predict individual response to combined mathematical and working memory training in children. *Developmental Cognitive Neuroscience, 20*, 43–51.

O'Reilly, R. C., & Frank, M. J. (2006). Making working memory work: A computational model of learning in the prefrontal cortex and basal ganglia. *Neural Computation, 18*, 283–328.

Olesen, P. J., Macoveanu, J., Tegnér, J., & Klingberg, T. (2006). Brain activity related to working memory and distraction in children and adults. *Cerebral Cortex, 17*, 1047–1054.

Olesen, P. J., Westerberg, H., & Klingberg, T. (2004). Increased prefrontal and parietal activity after training of working memory. *Nature Neuroscience, 7*, 75–79.

Oliver, A., Johnson, M. H., Karmiloff-Smith, A., & Pennington, B. (2000). Deviations in the emergence of representations: A neuroconstructivist framework for analysing developmental disorders. *Developmental Science, 3*, 1–23.

Owen, A. M., McMillan, K. M., Laird, A. R., & Bullmore, E. (2005). N-back working memory paradigm: A meta-analysis of normative functional neuroimaging studies. *Human Brain Mapping, 25*, 46–59.

Padmala, S., & Pessoa, L. (2011). Reward reduces conflict by enhancing attentional control and biasing visual cortical processing. *Journal of Cognitive Neuroscience, 23*, 3419–3432.

Padmanabhan, A., Geier, C. F., Ordaz, S. J., Teslovich, T., & Luna, B. (2011). Developmental changes in brain function underlying the influence of reward processing on inhibitory control. *Developmental Cognitive Neuroscience, 1*, 517–529.

Passolunghi, M. C., & Costa, H. M. (2016). Working memory and early numeracy training in preschool children. *Child Neuropsychology, 22*, 81–98.

Peijnenborgh, J. C., Hurks, P. M., Aldenkamp, A. P., Vles, J. S., & Hendriksen, J. G. (2016). Efficacy of working memory training in children and adolescents with learning disabilities: A review study and meta-analysis. *Neuropsychological Rehabilitation, 26*, 645–672.

Peng, J., Mo, L., Huang, P., & Zhou, Y. (2017). The effects of working memory training on improving fluid intelligence of children during early childhood. *Cognitive Development, 43*, 224–234.

Porter, L., Bailey-Jones, C., Priudokaite, G., Allen, S., Wood, K., Stiles, K., . . . Lawrence, N. S. (2018). From cookies to carrots; the effect of inhibitory control training on children's snack selections. *Appetite, 124*, 111–123.

Redick, T. S. (2015). Working memory training and interpreting interactions in intelligence interventions. *Intelligence, 50*, 14–20.

Redick, T. S., Shipstead, Z., Harrison, T. L., Hicks, K. L., Fried, D. E., Hambrick, D. Z., . . . Engle, R. W. (2013). No evidence of intelligence improvement after working memory training: A randomized, placebo-controlled study. *Journal of Experimental Psychology–General, 142*, 359–379.

Redick, T. S., Shipstead, Z., Wiemers, E. A., Melby-Lervåg, M., & Hulme, C. (2015). What's working in working memory training? An educational perspective. *Educational Psychology Review, 27*, 617–633.

Roberts, G., Quach, J., Spencer-Smith, M., Anderson, P. J., Gathercole, S., Gold, L., ... Wake, M. (2016). Academic outcomes 2 years after working memory training for children with low working memory: A randomized clinical trial. *JAMA Pediatrics, 170*, e154568.

Rubia, K., Russell, T., Overmeyer, S., Brammer, M. J., Bullmore, E. T., Sharma, T., ... Andrew, C. M. (2001). Mapping motor inhibition: Conjunctive brain activations across different versions of go/no-go and stop tasks. *NeuroImage, 13*, 250–261.

Rueda, M. R., Rothbart, M. K., McCandliss, B. D., Saccomanno, L., & Posner, M. I. (2005). Training, maturation, and genetic influences on the development of executive attention. *Proceedings of the National Academy of Sciences (USA), 102*, 14931–14936.

Ryan, R. M., & Deci, E. L. (2000). Self-determination theory and the facilitation of intrinsic motivation, social development, and well-being. *American Psychologist, 55*, 68–78.

Sala, G., & Gobet, F. (2017). Working memory training in typically developing children: A meta-analysis of the available evidence. *Developmental Psychology, 53*, 671.

Schwaighofer, M., Fischer, F., & Bühner, M. (2015). Does working memory training transfer? A meta-analysis including training conditions as moderators. *Educational Psychologist, 50*, 138–166.

Schweizer, S., Grahn, J., Hampshire, A., Mobbs, D., & Dalgleish, T. (2013). Training the emotional brain: Improving affective control through emotional working memory training. *Journal of Neuroscience, 33*, 5301–5311.

Shonkoff, J. P., Garner, A. S., Fa, C. P. A. C., Depe, C. E. C. A., & Pediat, S. D. B. (2012). The lifelong effects of early childhood adversity and toxic stress. *Pediatrics, 129*, E232–E246.

Shonkoff, J. P., & Levitt, P. (2010). Neuroscience and the future of early childhood policy: Moving from why to what and how. *Neuron, 67*, 689–691.

Simmonds, D. J., Pekar, J. J., & Mostofsky, S. H. (2008). Meta-analysis of Go/No-go tasks demonstrating that fMRI activation associated with response inhibition is task-dependent. *Neuropsychologia, 46*, 224–232.

Smid, C.., Karbach, J., & Steinbeis, N. (2020). Towards a science of effective cognitive training. *Current Directions in Psychological Science, 29*, 531–537.

Söderqvist, S., Bergman Nutley, S., Ottersen, J., Grill, K. M., & Klingberg, T. (2012). Computerized training of non-verbal reasoning and working memory in children with intellectual disability. *Frontiers in Human Neuroscience, 6*, 271.

Söderqvist, S., Matsson, H., Peyrard-Janvid, M., Kere, J., & Klingberg, T. (2014). Polymorphisms in the dopamine receptor 2 gene region influence improvements during working memory training in children and adolescents. *Journal of Cognitive Neuroscience, 26*, 54–62.

Soveri, A., Antfolk, J., Karlsson, L., Salo, B., & Laine, M. (2017). Working memory training revisited: A multi-level meta-analysis of n-back training studies. *Psychonomic Bulletin & Review, 24*, 1077–1096.

Strang, N. M., & Pollak, S. D. (2014). Developmental continuity in reward-related enhancement of cognitive control. *Developmental Cognitive Neuroscience, 10*, 34–43.

Studer-Luethi, B., Bauer, C., & Perrig, W. J. (2016). Working memory training in children: Effectiveness depends on temperament. *Memory & Cognition, 44*, 171–186.

Studer-Luethi, B., Jaeggi, S. M., Buschkuehl, M., & Perrig, W. J. (2012). Influence of neuroticism and conscientiousness on working memory training outcome. *Personality and Individual Differences, 53*, 44–49.

Swick, D., Ashley, V., & Turken, U. (2011). Are the neural correlates of stopping and not going identical? Quantitative meta-analysis of two response inhibition tasks. *Neuroimage, 56,* 1655–1665.

Takeuchi, H., Sekiguchi, A., Taki, Y., Yokoyama, S., Yomogida, Y., Komuro, N., . . . Kawashima, R. (2010). Training of working memory impacts structural connectivity. *Journal of Neuroscience, 30,* 3297–3303.

Thompson, T. W., Waskom, M. L., Garel, K.-L. A., Cardenas-Iniguez, C., Reynolds, G. O., Winter, R., . . . Alvarez, G. A. (2013). Failure of working memory training to enhance cognition or intelligence. *PLoS ONE, 8,* e63614.

Thorell, L. B., Lindqvist, S., Bergman Nutley, S., Bohlin, G., & Klingberg, T. (2009). Training and transfer effects of executive functions in preschool children. *Developmental Science, 12,* 106–113.

Titz, C., & Karbach, J. (2014). Working memory and executive functions: Effects of training on academic achievement. *Psychological Research, 78,* 852–868.

Verbruggen, F., Adams, R., & Chambers, C. D. (2012). Proactive motor control reduces monetary risk taking in gambling. *Psychological Science, 23,* 805–815.

Verbruggen, F., Adams, R. C., van't Wout, F., Stevens, T., McLaren, I. P., & Chambers, C. D. (2013). Are the effects of response inhibition on gambling long-lasting? *PLoS ONE, 8,* e70155.

Verbruggen, F., & Logan, G. D. (2008). Response inhibition in the stop-signal paradigm. *Trends in Cognitive Sciences, 12,* 418–424.

Verbruggen, F., & Logan, G. D. (2009). Proactive adjustments of response strategies in the Stop-signal paradigm. *Journal of Experimental Psychology–Human Perception and Performance, 35,* 835–854.

Verbruggen, F., McLaren, I. P., & Chambers, C. D. (2014). Banishing the control homunculi in studies of action control and behavior change. *Perspectives on Psychological Science, 9,* 497–524.

Vogel, E. K., & Machizawa, M. G. (2004). Neural activity predicts individual differences in visual working memory capacity. *Nature, 428,* 748–751.

Wass, S., Porayska-Pomsta, K., & Johnson, M. H. (2011). Training attentional control in infancy. *Current Biology, 21,* 1543–1547.

Wass, S., Scerif, G., & Johnson, M. H. (2012). Training attentional control and working memory – Is younger, better? *Developmental Review, 32,* 360–387.

Westbrook, A., Kester, D., & Braver, T. S. (2013). What is the subjective cost of cognitive effort? Load, trait, and aging effects revealed by economic preference. *PLoS ONE, 8,* e68210.

Wong, A. S., He, M. Y., & Chan, R. W. (2014). Effectiveness of computerized working memory training program in Chinese community settings for children with poor working memory. *Journal of Attention Disorders, 18,* 318–330.

Woud, M. L., Becker, E. S., & Rinck, M. (2011). "Implicit evaluation bias induced by approach and avoidance". Corrigendum. *Cognition & Emotion, 25,* 1309–1310.

Woud, M. L., Maas, J., Becker, E. S., & Rinck, M. (2013). Make the manikin move: Symbolic approach-avoidance responses affect implicit and explicit face evaluations. *Journal of Cognitive Psychology, 25,* 738–744.

Yuan, P., & Raz, N. (2014). Prefrontal cortex and executive functions in healthy adults: A meta-analysis of structural neuroimaging studies. *Neuroscience & Biobehavioral Reviews, 42,* 180–192.

Zelazo, P. D., & Frye, D. (1997). Cognitive complexity and control: A theory of the development of deliberate reasoning and intentional action. In M. Stamenov (ed.), *Language Structure, Discourse and the Access to Consciousness* (pp. 113–153). Amsterdam: John Benjamins.

Zhao, X., Chen, L., & Maes, J. H. (2018). Training and transfer effects of response inhibition training in children and adults. *Developmental Science, 21,* e12511.

31 Curiosity-Driven Learning in Development
Computational Theories and Educational Applications

Pierre-Yves Oudeyer

31.1 Curiosity-Driven Exploration and Learning in Child Development

The timing and ordering of learning experience play a critical role in developmental processes. To make sense and learn skills out of the initial "buzzy blooming confusion," multiple mechanisms interact to canalize the infant through such ordered and progressively more complex learning experiences, harnessing the complexity of the world.

Which activities can be practiced, and what can be learned at a given point in development, is constrained both by the learning opportunities provided by the physical and social environment (caretakers in particular) and by current physical and cognitive abilities. For example, early in life infants cannot locomote due to both insufficient muscular power and lack of adequate sensorimotor coordination. At this stage, they can only observe or physically interact with objects and events in the environment which their parents set for them. Such constrained experience has been hypothesized to constrain and canalize species-typical development (Gottlieb, 1991). West and King (1987) proposed the idea of "ontogenetic niches" to capture the fact that developing organisms face an ordered series of environments that may be exploited by evolutionary processes to ensure adaptive outcomes.

In addition, learning experiences do not passively "happen" to infants. Rather, they play an active role in creating and selecting these experiences. In particular, infants spontaneously explore their body and how it can interact with the environment, physically experimenting with the effects of their arm or vocal tract movements, or the effects of touching, mouthing, grasping, or throwing all kinds of objects, often for the intrinsic pleasure of practicing these activities, without a separate distal goal. Such spontaneous exploration, often called "play" or "curiosity" in colloquial terms, is not random but rather organized, and partly results from brain mechanisms of intrinsic motivation (Gottlieb et al., 2013; Lowenstein, 1994) selecting sensorimotor activities which are "interesting."

Mechanisms of intrinsically motivated exploration and learning and the notion of "interestingness" have long remained studied at an intuitive level in psychology, where concepts like cognitive dissonance (Kagan, 1972), optimal incongruity (Hunt, 1965), intermediate novelty (Berlyne, 1960), or optimal challenge (Csikszenthmihalyi, 1991) were discussed. Furthermore, the relation between intrinsic motivation on one hand, and learning and development on the other hand has been little considered until recently. Yet, important advances and novel theoretical approaches have been achieved in the last decade, with a whole series of operational models in developmental robotics (Baldassarre & Mirolli, 2013; Oudeyer & Smith, 2016; Oudeyer et al., 2007; Twomey & Westermann, 2018), arguments

Large parts of this chapter are adapted from Oudeyer and Smith (2016) and Oudeyer et al. (2016), with permission.

and models of the evolutionary origins of intrinsic motivation systems (Barto, 2013; Singh et al., 2010), and recent findings in neuroscience linking intrinsic motivation with attention (Gottlieb & Oudeyer, 2018), as well as new formal models of infant visual attention (Kidd et al., 2012).

A key idea in these recent approaches is that *learning progress in and for itself* can generate intrinsic rewards driving such spontaneous exploration, leading learners to avoid learning situations that are either too easy or too difficult at a given point of their development. Learning progress refers to the infant's *improvement* of its predictions or control over an activity they practice (Kaplan & Oudeyer, 2007a, 2007b), which can also be described as *reduction* of uncertainty (Friston et al., 2012). Such intrinsically motivating activities have been called "progress niches" (Oudeyer et al., 2007). Thus, learning progress is not simply a consequence of intrinsically motivated exploration, but a primary driver (and accordingly, intrinsic rewards for learning progress/uncertainty reduction may be *primary* rewards). From a machine learning perspective, such a mechanism of information seeking is called "active learning," where the learner probabilistically selects experiments according to their potential for reducing uncertainty.

These advances lead to a definition of curiosity as an epistemic motivational mechanism, which pushes an organism to explore activities for the primary sake of *gaining information* (as opposed to searching for information in service of achieving an external goal, like finding food or shelter). Such a motivational mechanism of curiosity will often be only one of several motivational mechanisms operating in any living being, and, at any given time, curiosity may interact, complement, or conflict with other motivations. From a machine learning perspective, mechanisms of information seeking are called *active learning*, where the learner probabilistically selects experiences

according to their potential for reducing uncertainty (Cohn et al., 1996). They have been used either as an "exploration bonus" mechanism in service of efficient maximization of a task-specific reward, or as primary rewards driving models of curiosity-driven learning (Gottlieb et al., 2013).

As such, active self-exploration bi-directionally interacts with learning, strongly influencing what skills the infant will practice and eventually acquire, and it is bound to have a significant impact on the ordering and organization of development. In fact, through the analysis of robotic experiments in Section 31.3, we argue that such mechanism can be an essential force in the self-organization of developmental structures, and be a pillar of a principled dynamic systems approach to developmental change. Indeed, as we will show, active search for learning progress automatically leads a system to first explore simple activities, and progressively shift to more complex learning experiences, effectively self-generating a learning curriculum adapted to the current constraints, and at the same time itself constraining learning.

The key theoretical idea instantiated in these robotic models is epigenesis (see Chapter 2), in the sense proposed by Gottlieb (1991). Developmental structures in these models are neither learned from "tabula rasa" nor a predetermined result of an innate "program": they self-organize out of the dynamic interaction between constrained cognitive mechanisms (including curiosity, learning, and abstraction), the morphological properties of the body, and the physical and social environment that itself is constrained and ordered by the developmental level of the organism (Oudeyer, 2011; Thelen & Smith, 1996). This self-organization includes the dynamic and automatic formation of behavioral and cognitive stages of progressively increasing complexity, sharing many properties with infant development (Piaget, 1952; Houdé, 2015, for a more recent review).

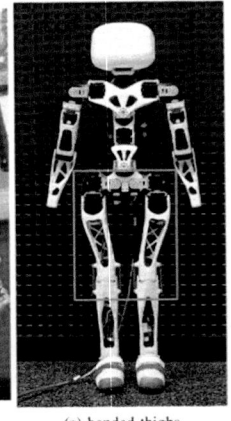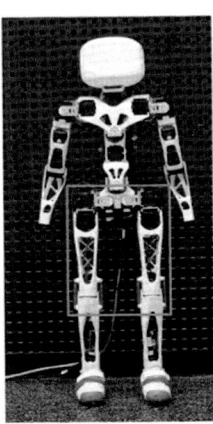

(a) bended thighs   (b) straight thighs

Figure 31.1 Open-source baby robots. Robots can help us model and study the complex interaction between the brain, the body, and the environment during cognitive development. Here we see two open-source robotic platforms used in laboratories. Being open-source allows open science through revealing all details in the experiments as well as replicability. Based on 3D printing, the Poppy platform allows fast and efficient exploration of various body morphologies (Lapeyre et al., 2014), such as leg shape (see alternatives on the right (a) and (b)), and how this can affect development of skills. Left: ICub; www.icub.org, right: Poppy www.poppy-project.org.[1]
A black-and-white version of this figure will appear in some formats. For the color version, please refer to the plate section.

This complex dynamical systems perspective on child development has fueled the use of computational and robotic modeling tools in the field of developmental robotics to design formal mechanistic theories of cognitive development, as well as enable scientists to sharpen their intuitions of these processes and propose new hypotheses (Cangelosi & Schlesinger, 2015, see Figure 31.1). Models of curiosity-driven learning discussed in this category have been designed from this perspective.

31.2 Models of Curiosity-Driven Learning

Diverse theoretical approaches to intrinsic motivation and to the properties that shall make certain activities intrinsically interesting/motivating have been proposed and published by diverse research communities within psychology (e.g., Csikszentmihalyi, 1991; Festinger, 1957; Harlow, 1950; Hull, 1943; Hunt, 1965; Kagan, 1972; Lowenstein, 1994; Montgomery, 1954; Ryan & Deci, 2000; White, 1959) and neuroscience (see Gottlieb & Oudeyer, 2018 for a review), in such a way that still today there is no consensus among these communities on a unified or integrated view of intrinsic motivation and curiosity. Yet, a convincing integrated view was actually proposed in the 1960s by Daniel Berlyne (Berlyne, 1965), and has been used as a fruitful theoretical reference for developing formal mathematical models of curiosity. The central concept of this integrated approach to intrinsic motivation is that of "collative variables," as explained in the following quotations:

---

[1] Both websites last accessed August 23, 2021.

The probability and direction of specific exploratory responses can apparently be influenced by many properties of external stimulation, as well as by many intraorganism variables. They can, no doubt, be influenced by stimulus intensity, color, pitch, and association with biological gratification and punishment, … [but] the paramount determinants of specific exploration are, however, a group of stimulus properties to which we commonly refer by such words as "novelty," "change," "surprisingness," "incongruity," "complexity," "ambiguity," and "indistinctiveness." (Berlyne, 1965, p. 245)

More precisely, Berlyne developed the notion that the most rewarding situations were those with an intermediate level of novelty, between already familiar and completely new situations (Berlyne, 1960). This perspective was echoed by Csikszentmihalyi's flow theory arguing that interesting situations were those of optimal challenge, recently echoed by Kidd et al. (2012), who showed an experiment where infants preferred stimuli of intermediate complexity.

31.2.1 The Learning Progress Hypothesis

Berlyne's concept of intermediate novelty, as well as the related concept of intermediate challenge of Csikszentmihalyi, have the advantage of allowing intuitive explanations of many behavioral manifestations of curiosity and intrinsic motivation. However, recent developments in theory of curiosity, and in particular its computational theory, have questioned its applicability as an operant concept capable of generating an actual mechanism for curiosity. A first reason is that the concept of "intermediate" appears difficult to define precisely, as it implies the use of a relatively arbitrary frame of reference to assess levels of novelty/complexity. A second reason is that while novelty or complexity in themselves may be the basis of useful exploration

heuristics for organisms in some particular contexts, there is in general no guarantee that observing a novel of complex stimulus (be it of intermediate level) provides information that can improve the organism's prediction and control in the world. Indeed, as computational theory of learning and exploration has shown, our environment is full of novel and complex stimuli of all levels, and among them only a few may be associated with actual useful and learnable patterns. As curiosity-driven spontaneous exploration may have evolved as a means to acquire information and skills in rapidly changing environments (Barto, 2013), it appears that heuristics based on maximizing novelty and complexity are suboptimal (Oudeyer et al., 2007; Schmidhuber, 1991).

For these reasons, computational learning theory has explored an alternative mechanism, in which learning progress generates itself intrinsic reward (Oudeyer et al., 2007; Schmidhuber, 1991), and it was hypothesized that this mechanism could be at play in humans and animals (Kaplan & Oudeyer, 2007a; Oudeyer & Smith, 2016). This hypothesis proposes that the brain, seen as a predictive machine constantly trying to anticipate what will happen next, is intrinsically motivated by exploring activities in which predictions are improving (i.e., where uncertainty is decreasing, and learning is actually happening). This means that what is of interest is neither activities which are too easy or too difficult to predict (i.e., where uncertainty is low or where uncertainty is high but not reducible), but activities just beyond the current predictive capacities. So, for example, an infant will be more interested in exploring how its arm motor commands can allow it to predict the movement of its hand in its visual field (initially difficult but learnable) rather than predicting the movement of walls (too easy) or the color of the next car passing through the window (always novel, but not learnable).

As shown by computational studies, this leads in practice systems to the exploration of activities and stimuli of apparently "intermediate complexity." However, this notion of intermediate level is not directly represented in the mechanism: rather, it is a side-effect of selecting actions and stimuli that maximize the derivative of errors in prediction. Furthermore, this concept allows us to bridge several hypotheses related to curiosity and intrinsic motivation, but remains conceptually separated so far.

First, within the learning progress hypothesis, the central concept of prediction errors (and the associated measure of improvement) applies to multiple kinds of predictions. It applies to predicting the properties of external perceptual stimuli (and thus relates to the notion of perceptual curiosity, Berlyne, 1960), as well as the conceptual relations among symbolic items of knowledge (and this relates to the notion of epistemic curiosity, and to the subjective notion of information gap proposed by Lowenstein, 1994). Here the maximization of learning progress leads to behaviors that were previously understood through Berlyne's concept of intermediate novelty/complexity. It also applies to predicting the consequences of one's own actions in particular activities, or to predicting how well one's current skills are capable to solve a given goal/problem: here the maximization of learning progress, measuring a form of progress in competences related to an activity or a goal, allows to reframe Csikszentmihalyi's concept of intermediate challenge in the flow theory as well as related theories of intrinsic motivation based on self-measures of competences (Csikszentmihalyi, 1991; White, 1959).

Second, the learning progress hypothesis allows us to create a new causal link between memory retention and curiosity. As argued, experimental work showed that state curiosity could facilitate memory retention (Kang et al., 2009; Stahl & Feigenson, 2015). These results showed that curiosity and prediction errors had an influence on learning, but curiosity and learning were considered as two separate mechanisms (and indeed, seeing curiosity as search for pure novelty makes it separate from actual learning mechanisms). Furthermore, the experimental protocols were such that novelty/surprise was always imposed by experimenters, with little possibility for subjects to actively seek and explore their environment (and thus limiting the possibility to study the processes by which organisms would encounter such novelty/complexity in a more ecological situation).

The learning progress hypothesis provides a strong complement to this view: it proposes that experiencing learning in a given activity (rather than just intermediate novelty) triggers an intrinsic reward, and thus that learning in itself causally participates to establish state curiosity. Thus, this hypothesis argues that there is a closed self-reinforcing feedback loop between learning and curiosity-driven intrinsic motivation. Here the learner becomes fundamentally active, searching for niches of learning progress, in which in turn memory retention is facilitated. In Section 31.3, we will outline computational experiments that have shown that such an active learning mechanisms can self-organize a progression in learning, with automatically generated developmental phases that have strong similarities with infant developmental trajectories.

31.3 The Playground Experiment: A Developmental Robotics Model of Curiosity-Driven Self-organization of Developmental Trajectories

In this section, we describe a series of robot experiments that illustrate how mechanisms of curiosity-driven exploration, dynamically interacting with learning, physical, and social constraints, can self-organize developmental trajectories and in particular lead a learner to discover successively object affordances and vocal interaction with its peers.

In these Playground Experiments, a quadruped "learning" robot is placed on an infant play mat with a set of nearby objects and is joined by an "adult" robot peer, see Figure 31.2(a) (Kaplan & Oudeyer, 2007b; Oudeyer & Kaplan, 2006; Oudeyer et al., 2007). On the mat and near the learning robot are objects for discovery: an elephant (which can be bitten or "grasped" by the mouth), and

a hanging toy (which can be "bashed" or pushed with the leg). The adult robot peer is preprogramed to imitate the sound made by the learning robot when the learning robot looks to the adult while vocalizing at the same time.

The learning robot is equipped with a repertoire of motor primitives parameterized by several continuous numbers that control movements of its legs, head, and a simulated vocal tract. Each motor primitive is a dynamical system controlling various forms of actions: (a) turning the head in various

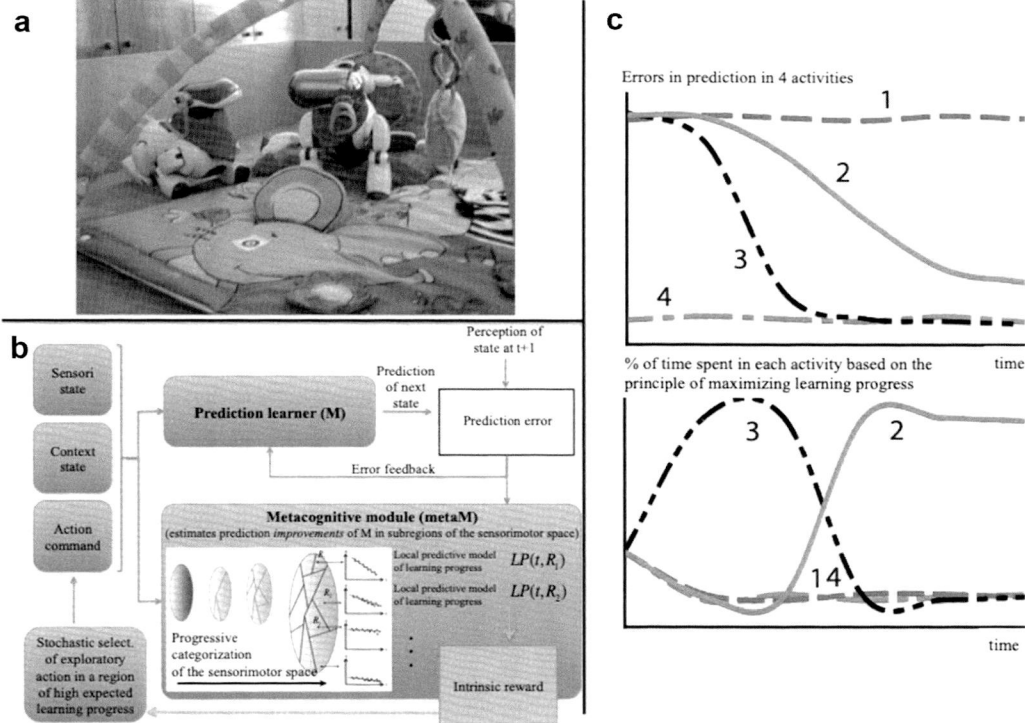

Figure 31.2 The playground experiment (Oudeyer & Kaplan, 2006; Oudeyer et al., 2007). (a) The learning context; (b) The computational architecture for curiosity-driven exploration in which the robot learner probabilistically selects experiences according to their potential for reducing uncertainty, that is, for learning progress; (c) Illustration of a self-organized developmental sequence where the robot automatically identifies, categorizes, and shifts from simple to more complex learning experiences. Figure adapted with permission from Gottlieb et al. (2013)

A black-and-white version of this figure will appear in some formats. For the color version, please refer to the plate section.

directions, (b) opening and closing the mouth while crouching with various strengths and timing, (c) rocking the leg with various angles and speed, and (d) vocalizing with various pitches and lengths. These primitives can be combined to form a large continuous space of possible actions. Similarly, several kinds of sensory primitives allow the robot to detect visual movement, salient visual properties, proprioceptive touch in the mouth, and pitch and length of perceived sounds. For the robot, these motor and sensory primitives are initially black boxes and he has no knowledge about their semantics, effects, or relations.

The robot learns how to use and tune these primitives to produce various effects on its surrounding environment, and exploration is driven by the maximization of learning *progress*, that is, by choosing physical experiences ("experiments") that improve the quality of predictions of the consequences of its actions.

Figure 31.2(b) outlines a computational architecture, called Robust Intelligent Adaptive Curiosity (R-IAC), that makes possible this curiosity-driven exploration and learning process (Moulin-Frier et al., 2014; Oudeyer et al., 2007). It is composed of several modules. A prediction machine (M) learns to predict the consequences of actions taken by the robot in given sensory contexts. For example, this module might learn to predict (with a neural network) which visual movements or proprioceptive perceptions result from using the leg bashing motor primitive with certain parameters. A meta-cognitive module estimates the evolution of errors in prediction of M in various subregions of the sensorimotor space. This module estimates

how much errors decrease in predicting an action, for example, in predicting the consequence of a leg bashing movement when this action is applied toward a particular area of the environment. These estimates of error reduction are used to compute learning progress as an intrinsic reward. This reward is an internal quantity that is proportional to the decrease of prediction errors. The maximization of such reward is the aim of action selection in a computational reinforcement learning architecture (Oudeyer et al., 2007). Importantly, the action selection system chooses most often to explore activities where estimated learning progress is high. However, this choice is probabilistic, which leaves the system open to learning in new areas and open to discovering other activities which might yield learning progress.[2] Since the sensorimotor flow does not come pre-segmented into activities and tasks, a system that seeks to maximize differences in learnability is also used to progressively categorize the sensorimotor space into regions, which models the incremental creation and refining of cognitive categories differentiating activities/tasks.

To illustrate how such an exploration mechanism can automatically generate ordered learning stages, let us first imagine a robot confronted with four categories of activities, as shown in Figure 31.2(c). The practice of each of these four activities, which can be of varying difficulty, leads to different learning rates at different points in time (see the top curves, which show the evolution of prediction errors in each activity if the robot would focus full-time on each). If the robot uses curiosity-driven exploration to decide what and when to practice by focusing on progress niches, it will avoid activities which are already predictable (curve 4) or too difficult to learn to predict (curve 1), in order to focus first on the activity with the fastest learning rate (curve 3) and, eventually, when the latter starts to reach a

---

[2] Technically, the decision on how much time to spend on high learning progress activities and other activities is achieved using Multi-Armed Bandit algorithms for the so-called exploration/exploitation dilemma (Audibert et al., 2009).

"plateau" to switch to the second most promising learning situation (curve 2). Thus, such robots will show a regular developmental course – one that will be "universal" for learners with similar internal processes learning in similar environments. Embodied exploration driven by learning progress creates an organized exploratory strategy: the system systematically achieves these learning experiences in an order and does so because they yield (given the propensities of the learner and the physical world) different patterns of uncertainty reduction.

In the Playground experiment described, multiple experimental runs lead to two general categories of results: self-organization and a mixture of regularities and diversities in the developmental patterns (Oudeyer & Kaplan, 2006; Oudeyer et al., 2007).

31.3.1 Self-organization

In all of the runs, one observes the self-organization of structured developmental trajectories, where the robot explores objects and actions in a progressively more complex stage-like manner while acquiring autonomously diverse affordances and skills that can be reused later on and that change the learning progress in more complicated tasks. The following developmental sequence is typically observed:

1. In a first phase, the robot achieves unorganized body babbling.
2. In a second phase, after learning a first rough model and meta-model, the robot stops combining motor primitives, exploring them one by one, but each primitive is explored itself in a random manner.
3. In a third phase, the robot now begins to experiment with actions toward zones of its environment where the external observer knows there are objects (the robot is not

provided with a representation of the concept of "object"), but in a non-affordant manner (e.g., it vocalizes at the non-responding elephant or tries to bash the adult robot which is too far to be touched).

4. In a fourth phase, the robot now explores affordant experiments: it first focuses on grasping movements with the elephant, then shifts to bashing movements with the hanging toy, and finally shifts to exploring vocalizing toward the imitating adult robot.
5. In the end, the robot has learnt sensorimotor affordances with several objects, as well as social affordances with a peer, and mastered multiple skills, yet none of these specific objectives were preprogramed in the beginning. They self-organize through the dynamic interaction between curiosity-driven exploration, statistical inference, the properties of the body, and the properties of the environment.

These playground experiments do not simply simulate particular skills (such as batting at toys to make them swing or vocalizations) but simulate an ordered and systematic developmental trajectory, with a universality and stage-like structure that may be mistakenly taken to indicate an internally-driven process of maturation. However, the trajectory is created through activity and through the general principle that sensorimotor experiences that reduce uncertainty in prediction are rewarding. In this way, developmental achievements can build on themselves without specific pre-programmed dependencies, but nonetheless – like evolution itself –create structure (see Smith & Breazeal, 2007 and Smith, 2013, for related findings and arguments).

31.3.2 Regularities and Diversity

Because these are self-organizing developmental processes, they generate not only strong regularities but also diversity across individual developmental trajectories. For example, in most runs one observes successively unorganized body babbling, then focused exploration of head movements, then exploration of touching an object, then grasping an object, and finally vocalizing toward a peer robot (preprogrammed to imitate). This can be explained as gradual exploration of new progress niches, and those stages and their ordering can be viewed as a form of attractor in the space of developmental trajectories. Yet, with the same mechanism and same initial parameters, individual trajectories may invert stages, or even generate qualitatively different behaviors. This is due, stochasticity, to even small variability in the physical realities and to the fact that this developmental dynamic system has several attractors with more or less extended and strong domains of attraction (characterized by amplitude of learning progress). We see this diversity as a positive outcome since individual development is not identical but always unique in its own ways. This kind of approach, then, offers a way to understanding individual differences as emergent in the developmental process itself and makes clear how the developmental process might vary across contexts, even with an identical mechanism.

A further result to be highlighted is the early development of vocal interaction. With a single generic mechanism, the robot both explores and learns how to manipulate objects and how to vocalize to trigger specific responses from a more mature partner. While vocal babbling, and more language play and games, have been shown to be key in infant language development, the interest of infants to engage in babbling and such language games has often been associated with an ad hoc language-specific motivation. The Playground Experiment makes it possible to see how the exploration and learning of communicative behavior might be at least partially explained by general curiosity-driven exploration of the body affordances, as also suggested by Oller (2000).

Further models have explored more specifically how social guidance provided by social peers can be leveraged by an intrinsically motivated active learner and dynamically interact with curiosity to structure developmental trajectories (Nguyen & Oudeyer, 2013; Thomaz & Breazeal, 2008). Focusing on vocal development, Moulin-Frier et al. (2014) conducted experiments where a robot explores the control of a realistic model of the vocal tract in interaction with vocal peers, and driven to maximize learning progress. This model relies on a physical model of the vocal tract, its motor control, and of the auditory system. Experiments showed how such a mechanism can explain the adaptive transition from vocal self-exploration with little influence from the speech environment, to a later stage where vocal exploration becomes influenced by vocalizations of peers. Within the initial self-exploration phase, a sequence of vocal production stages self-organizes, and shares properties with infant data: the vocal learner first discovers how to control phonation, then focuses on vocal variations of unarticulated sounds, and finally automatically discovers and focuses on babbling with articulated proto-syllables. As the vocal learner becomes more proficient at producing complex sounds, imitating vocalizations of peers starts to provide high learning progress explaining an automatic shift from self-exploration to vocal imitation.

31.4 Curiosity-Driven Learning in Artificial Intelligence (AI) and Machine Learning

The AI and machine learning literature has also shown how various forms of intrinsically motivated exploration and learning could guide efficiently the autonomous acquisition of repertoires of skills in large and difficult spaces, providing a perspective in which to interpret the evolution of curiosity-driven learning in living organisms.

A first reason is that intrinsically motivated exploration can be used as an active learning algorithm that learns efficient forward and inverse models of the world dynamics through efficient selection of experiences. Indeed, such models can be reused either directly (Baranes & Oudeyer, 2013; Oudeyer et al., 2007), or through model-based planning mechanisms (Lopes et al., 2012; Schmidhuber, 1991; Singh et al., 2004), to solve repertoires of tasks that were not specified during exploration (hence without the need for long re-experiencing of the world for each new task). For example, Baranes and Oudeyer (2013) have shown how intrinsically motivated goal exploration could allow robots to sample sensorimotor spaces by actively controlling the complexity of explored sensorimotor goals and avoiding goals which were either too easy or unreachable. This allowed the robots to learn fast repertoires of high-dimensional continuous action skills to solve distributions of sensorimotor problems such as omnidirectional-legged locomotion or how to manipulate flexible objects. Lopes et al. (2012) showed how intrinsically motivated model-based reinforcement learning, driven by the maximization of empirical learning progress, allows efficient learning of world models when this dynamics is non-stationary, and how this accelerates the learning of a policy that targets to maximize an extrinsic reward (task predefined by experimenters).

A second reason for the efficiency of intrinsic motivation is that by fostering spontaneous exploration of novel skills, and leveraging opportunistically potential synergies among skills, it can create learning pathways toward certain skills that would have remained difficult to reach if they had been the sole target of

the learning system. Indeed, in many contexts, learning a single pre-defined skill can be difficult as it amounts to searching (the parameters of) a solution with very rare feedback until one is very close to the solution, or with deceptive feedback due to the phenomenon of local minima. A strategy to address these issues is to direct exploration with intrinsic rewards, leading the system to explore a diversity of skills and contingencies which often result in the discovery of new sub-spaces/areas in the problem space, or in mutual skill improvement when exploring one goal/skill provides data that can be used to improve other goals/skills, such as in goal babbling (Baranes & Oudeyer, 2013; Benureau & Oudeyer, 2016) or off-policy reinforcement learning (see the Horde architecture, Sutton et al., 2011). For example, Lehman and Stanley (2011) showed that searching for pure novelty in the behavioral space a robot finds a reward in a maze more efficiently than if it had been searching for behavioral parameters that directly optimized the reward. In another model, Forestier and Oudeyer (2016) showed that intrinsically motivated exploration of a hierarchy of sensorimotor models allowed a simulated robot to scaffold the successive acquisition of object reaching, tool grasping, and tool use (note that behaviors aiming at direct search tool use were less efficient).

A third related reason for the efficiency of intrinsically motivated exploration is that it can drive the acquisition of macro-actions, or sensorimotor primitives, which can be combinatorially reused as building blocks to accelerate the search for complex solutions in structured reinforcement learning problems. For example, Singh et al. (2004) showed how intrinsic rewards based on measures of saliency could guide a reinforcement learner to progressively learn "options," which are temporally extended macro-actions, reshaping the structure of the search space and finally learning action policies that solve an extrinsic (abstract) task that is very difficult to solve through standard reinforcement learning exploration. Related uses of intrinsic motivation with a hierarchical reinforcement learning framework were demonstrated in Bakker and Schmidhuber (2004) and Kulkarni et al. (2016).

In a related line of research studying the function and origins of intrinsic motivation, Singh et al. (2010) have shown through computational modeling the potential evolutionary usefulness of intrinsic motivation systems for maximizing extrinsic rewards (e.g., quantity of food collected) in a distribution of changing environments. In such changing environments, it could be more robust for reinforcement learning agents to represent and use an internal reward function that does not directly correspond to this extrinsic reward, but rather includes a component of intrinsic motivation that pushes the system to explore its environment beyond the direct search for the extrinsic reward.

31.5 Applications of Models of Curiosity-Driven Learning in Educational Technologies

Given the strong causal interactions between curiosity-driven exploration and learning that we just reviewed, these topics have attracted the attention of theorists and experimenters on the application domain of education. Long before recent controlled experimental results showing how intrinsic motivation and curiosity could enhance learning, educational experimenters like Montessori (1948) and Froebel (1885) studied how open-ended learning environments could foster individual child development, where learners are active, and where the tutor's role is to scaffold challenges of increasing complexity and provide feedback (rather than instruction). Such experimental

approaches have more recently influenced the development of hands on educational practices, such as the pioneering LOGO experiments of Papert (1980), where children learn advanced concepts of mathematics, computer science, and robotics, and are now disseminating on large scales in several countries (Resnick et al., 2009; Roy et al., 2015).

In parallel, philosophers and psychologists like Dewey, Vygotski, Piaget, and Bruner developed theories of cognitive and social constructivist learning which directly pointed toward the importance of fostering curiosity, free play, and exploration in the classroom. Recently, the large body of research in educational psychology has led others to study systematically how states of intrinsic motivation can be fostered, or on the contrary weakened, in the classroom, for example when the educational context provides strong extrinsic rewards (Deci et al., 2001).

As educational technologies are now thriving, in particular with the wide spreading of Massive Open Online Courses (MOOCs) and educational applications on tablets and smartphones, it has become natural to enquire how fundamental understanding of curiosity, intrinsic motivation, and learning could be leveraged and incorporated in these educational tools to increase their efficiency.

A first line of investigation has been to embed educational training within motivating and playful video games. In a pioneer study, Malone (1980) used and refined theories of intrinsic motivation as proposed by Berlyne, White and psychologists of the 1950–1970s period, to evaluate which properties of video games could make them intrinsically motivating, and to study how such contexts could be used to distill elements of scholarly knowledge to children. In particular, he showed that video games were more intrinsically motivating when including clear goals of progressively increasing complexity, when the system provided clear feedback on the performance of users, and when outcomes were uncertain to entertain curiosity. For example, he showed how arithmetic concepts could be taught in an intrinsically motivating scenarized dart video game. As an outcome of their studies, they could generate a set of guidelines for the design of education-oriented video games.

In a similar study, studying the impact of several of the factors identified by Malone, Cordova and Lepper (1996) presented a study of a population of elementary school children using a game targeting the acquisition of arithmetic order-of-operation rules, scenarized in a "space quest" story. In this specific experimental context, they showed that embedding personalization in the math exercises (based on preferences expressed through a pre-questionnaire) significantly improved intrinsic motivation, task engagement, and learning efficiency, and that this effect was heightened if in addition the software offered personalization of visual displays and a variety of exercise levels children could choose from.

Beyond explicitly including educational elements in video games, it was also shown that "pure" entertainment games such as certain types of action games can enhance attentional control, cognitive flexibility, and learning capabilities by exercising them in an intrinsically motivating playful context (Cardoso-Leite & Bavelier, 2014). Within this perspective, Merrick and Maher (2009) suggested that implementing artificial curiosity in non-player characters in video games could enhance the "interestingness" of video games.

A second line of investigation has considered how formal and computational models of curiosity and intrinsic motivation could be applied to Intelligent Tutoring Systems (ITS) (Nkambou et al., 2010), as well as Massive Open Online Courses (MOOCS) (Liyanagunawardena et al., 2013). ITS, and more recently MOOCs, have targeted the

design of software systems that could help students acquire new knowledge and skills, using artificial intelligence techniques to personalize teaching sequences, or the way teaching material is presented, and in particular proposing exercises that match the particular difficulties or talents of each individual learner. In this context, several approaches were designed and experimented on, so as to promote intrinsic motivation and learning.

Clement et al. (2015) have presented and evaluated an ITS system that directly reused computational models of curiosity-driven learning based on the learning progress hypothesis described in Section 31.3 (Oudeyer et al., 2007). This study considered teaching arithmetic decomposition of integer and decimal numbers, in a scenarized context of money handling, to a population of seven-to-eight years old children (see Figure 31.3). To design the ITS system, a human teacher first provided pedagogical material in the form of exercises grouped along coarsely defined levels and coarsely defined types. Then, an algorithm called ZPDES (Zone of Proximal Development and Empirical Success) was used to automatically personalize the sequence of exercises for each student, and this personalization was made incrementally during the course of interaction with each student. This personalization was achieved by probabilistically proposing to students exercises that maximized learning progress at their current level, that is, the exercises where their errors decrease fastest. In order to dynamically identify these exercises, and shift automatically to new ones when learning progress becomes low, the system used a multi-armed bandit algorithm that balanced exploring new exercises to assess their potential for learning progress, and exploiting exercises that recently lead the student to learning progress. During this process, the coarse structure organizing exercises that was provided by a human teacher is used

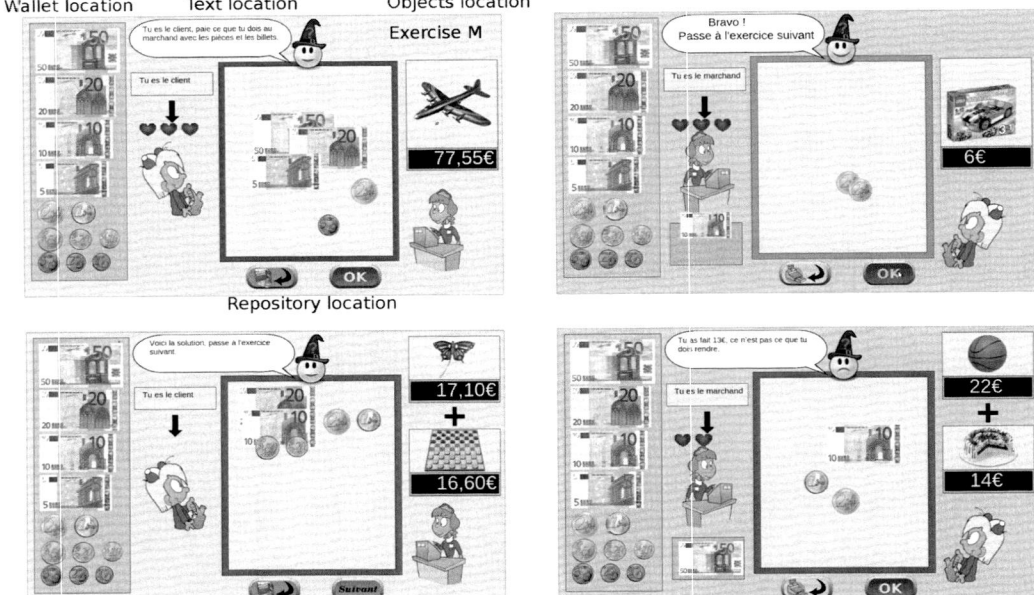

Figure 31.3 Educational game used in Clement et al. (2015): a scenario where elementary school children have to learn to manipulate money is used to teach them the decomposition of integer and decimal numbers. Four principal regions are defined in the graphical interface. The first is the wallet location where users can pick and drag the money items and drop them on the repository location to compose the correct price. The object and the price are present in the object location. Four different types of exercises exist: M (customer/one object), R (merchant/one object), MM (customer/two objects), RM (merchant/two objects). The intelligent tutoring system then dynamically proposes to students the exercises in which they are currently making maximal learning progress, targeting to maximize intrinsic motivation and learning efficiency
A black-and-white version of this figure will appear in some formats. For the color version, please refer to the plate section.

to guide the algorithm toward finding fast which exercises provide maximal learning progress: the system starts with exercise types that are at the bottom of the difficulty hierarchy, and when some of them show a plateau in the learning curve, they are deactivated and new exercises higher in the hierarchy are made available to the student (see Figure 31.4). The use of learning progress as a measure to drive the selection of exercises had two interacting purposes, relying on the bidirectional interaction described above. First, it aimed to propose exercises that could stimulate the intrinsic

motivation of students by dynamically and continuously setting them challenges that were neither too difficult nor too easy. Second, by doing this using learning progress, it aimed at generating exercise sequences that are highly efficient for maximizing the average scores over all types of exercises at the end of the training session. Indeed, Lopes and Oudeyer (2012) showed in a theoretical study that, when faced with the problem of strategically choosing which topic/exercise type to work on, selecting topics/exercises that maximize learning progress is quasi-optimal for important

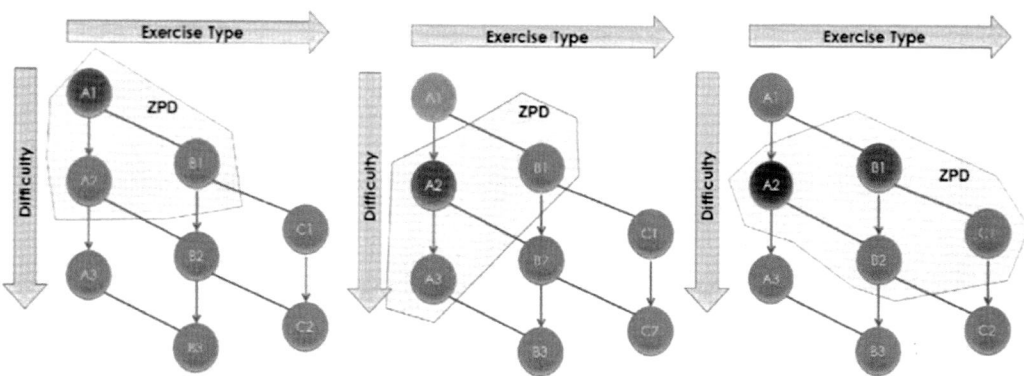

Figure 31.4 Example of the evolution of the zone-of-proximal development (ZPD) based on the empirical results of the student. The ZPD is the set of all activities that can be selected by the algorithm. The expert defines a set of preconditions between some of the activities (A1 → A2 → A3 ...), and activities that are qualitatively equal (A == B). Upon successfully solving A1 the ZPD is increased to include A3. When A2 does not achieve any progress, the ZPD is enlarged to include another exercise type C, not necessarily of higher or lower difficulty, for example, using a different modality, and A3 is temporarily removed from the ZPD. Adapted from Clement et al. (2015)
A black-and-white version of this figure will appear in some formats. For the color version, please refer to the plate section.

classes of learner models. Experiments with 400 children from 11 schools were performed, and the impact of this algorithm selecting exercises that maximize learning progress was compared to the impact of a sequence of exercises hand-defined by an expert teacher (that included sophisticated branching structures based on the errors-repair strategies the teacher could imagine). Results showed that the ZPDES algorithm, maximizing learning progress, allowed students of all levels to reach higher levels of exercises. Also, an analysis of the degree of personalization showed that ZPDES proposed a higher diversity of exercises earlier in the training sessions. Finally, a pre- and post-test comparison showed that students who were trained by ZPDES progressed better than students who used a hand-defined teaching sequence.

Several related ITS systems were developed and tested. For example, Beuls (2013) described a system targeting the acquisition of Spanish verb conjugation, where the ITS

attempts to propose exercises that are just above the current capabilities of the learner. Recently, a variation of this system was designed to foster the learning of musical counterpoint (Beuls & Loeckx, 2015). In another earlier study, Pachet (2004) presented a computer system aiming to help children discover and learn how to play musical instruments, but also capable of supporting creativity in experienced musicians, through fostering the psychological experience of Flow (Csikszenthmihalyi, 1991). This system, called the Continuator (Pachet, 2004), continuously learnt the style of the player (be it a child beginner or expert) and used an automatic improvisation algorithm to respond to the user's musical phrases with musical phrases of the same style and complexity, but different from those actually played by users. Pachet (2004) observed that both children and expert musicians most often experience an "Eureka moment" using this system. Their interest and attention appeared to be strongly attracted by playing with the system, leading children to try and discover different modes of play and to increase the complexity of what they could do. Expert musicians also reported that the system allowed them to discover novel musical ideas and to support creation interactively.

31.6 Conclusion

Computational and robotic models of curiosity-driven exploration and learning have enabled us to formalize various forms of spontaneous exploration mechanisms that had remained elusive in psychology and neuroscience so far. These models have considered curiosity mechanisms from a perspective where the child is viewed as a sense-making organism that explores for the sake of building good predictive models of its world. This perspective has been instrumental in identifying which curiosity mechanisms could guide efficient exploration and learning in large uncontrolled real-world environments. For example, this has allowed us to see the limits of mechanisms pushing organisms to search for high uncertainty or high entropy states (doing this they could be trapped exploring parts of the environments where there is nothing useful to learn). This has also led us to formulate the learning progress (LP) hypothesis, stating that organisms explore situations where they empirically improve various aspects of their world models. Computational and robotic experiments of this LP mechanism have shown that beyond enabling efficient learning of world models in large sensorimotor and cognitive spaces, it also enabled us to self-organize ordered trajectories of development. These self-organized trajectories emerge out of the dynamic interaction between the brain, the body, and the environment, and show similar regularities and diversity to human infant developmental trajectories. Finally, these new theoretical insights provide a new view on

educational perspectives, and have been adapted in educational technology applications, aiming at personalizing the sequences of exercises provided to each learner, in order to maximize both the efficiency of learning and intrinsic motivation.

References

Audibert, J.-Y., Munos, R., & Szepesvari, C. (2009). Exploration–exploitation tradeoff using variance estimates in multi-armed bandits. *Theoretical Computer Science, 410*, 1876–1902.

Bakker, B., & Schmidhuber, J. (2004). Hierarchical reinforcement learning based on subgoal discovery and subpolicy specialization. *Proceedings of the 8th Conference on Intelligent Autonomous Systems* (pp. 438–445). Amsterdam, Netherlands.

Baldassare, G., Mirolli, M. (2013). *Intrinsically Motivated Learning in Natural and Artificial Systems*. Berlin: Springer-Verlag.

Baranes, A., & Oudeyer, P. Y. (2013). Active learning of inverse models with intrinsically motivated goal exploration in robots. *Robotics and Autonomous Systems, 61*, 49–73.

Barto, A. G. (2013). Intrinsic motivation and reinforcement learning. In G. Baldassarre, & M. Mirolli (eds.), *Intrinsically Motivated Learning in Natural and Artificial Systems* (pp. 17–47). Berlin: Springer.

Benureau, F. C. Y., & Oudeyer, P.-Y. (2016). Behavioral diversity generation in autonomous exploration through reuse of past experience. *Frontiers in Robotics and AI, 3*.

Berlyne, D. (1960). *Conflict, Arousal and Curiosity*. New York: McGraw-Hill.

Berlyne, D. (1965). *Structure and Direction in Thinking*. New York: John Wiley and Sons, Inc.

Beuls, K. (2013). Towards an Agent-based Tutoring System for Spanish Verb Conjugation. PhD thesis, Vrije Universiteit, Brussel.

Beuls, K., & Loeckx, J. (2015). Steps towards intelligent MOOCs: A case study for learning counterpoint. In L. Steels (ed.), *Music Learning with Massive Open Online Courses* (pp. 119–144). Amsterdam: IOS Press.

Cangelosi, A., & Schlesinger, M. (2015). *Developmental Robotics: From Babies to Robots.* Cambridge, MA: MIT Press.

Cardoso-Leite, P., & Bavelier, D. (2014). Video game play, attention, and learning: How to shape the development of attention and influence learning? *Current Opinion in Neurology, 27*, 185–191.

Clement, B., Roy, D., Oudeyer, P.-Y., & Lopes, M. (2015). Multi-armed bandits for intelligent tutoring systems. *Journal of Educational Data Mining (JEDM), 7*, 20–48.

Cohn, D. A., Ghahramani, Z., & Jordan, M. I. (1996). Active learning with statistical models. *Journal of Artificial Intelligence Research, 4*, 129–145.

Cordova, D. I., & Lepper, M. R. (1996). Intrinsic motivation and the process of learning: Beneficial effects of contextualization, personalization, and choice. *Journal of Educational Psychology, 88*, 715.

Csikszenthmihalyi, M. (1991). *Flow-the Psychology of Optimal Experience.* New York: Harper Perennial.

Deci, E. L., Koestner, R., & Ryan, R. M. (2001). Extrinsic rewards and intrinsic motivation in education: Reconsidered once again. *Review of Educational Research, 71*, 1–27.

Festinger, L. (1957). *A Theory of Cognitive Dissonance.* Evanston, IL: Row, Peterson.

Forestier, S., & Oudeyer, P.-Y. (2016). Curiosity-driven development of tool use precursors: A computational model. *Proceedings of the 38th Annual Conference of the Cognitive Science Society* (CogSci 2016) (pp. 1859–1864). August 2016, Philadelphia, PA.

Friston, K., Adams, R. A., Perrinet, L., & Breakspear, M. (2012). Perceptions as hypotheses: Saccades as experiments. *Frontiers in Psychology, 3*, 151.

Froebel, F. (1885). *The Education of Man.* New York: A. Lovell & Company.

Gottlieb, G. (1991). Experiential canalization of behavioral development: Theory. *Developmental Psychology, 27*, 4–13.

Gottlieb, J., & Oudeyer, P. Y. (2018). Towards a neuroscience of active sampling and curiosity. *Nature Reviews Neuroscience, 19*, 758–770.

Gottlieb, J., Oudeyer, P.-Y., Lopes, M., & Baranes, A. (2013). Information seeking, curiosity and attention: Computational and neural mechanisms. *Trends in Cognitive Science, 17*, 585–596.

Harlow, H. (1950). Learning and satiation of response in intrinsically motivated complex puzzle performances by monkeys. *Journal of Comparative and Physiological Psychology, 43*, 289–294.

Houdé, O. (2015). Cognitive development during infancy and early childhood across cultures. In J. D. Wright (ed.), *International Encyclopedia of the Social and Behavioral Sciences* (2nd ed., pp. 43–50). Oxford: Elsevier Science.

Hull, C. L. (1943). *Principles of Behavior: An Introduction to Behavior Theory.* New-York: Appleton-Century-Croft.

Hunt, J. M. (1965). Intrinsic motivation and its role in psychological development. *Nebraska Symposium on Motivation, 13*, 189–282.

Kagan, J. (1972). Motives and development. *Journal of Personality and Social Psychology, 22*, 51–66.

Kang, M. J., Hsu, M., Krajbich, I. M., Loewenstein, G., McClure, S. M., Wang, J. T. Y., & Camerer, C. F. (2009). The wick in the candle of learning: Epistemic curiosity activates reward circuitry and enhances memory. *Psychological Science, 20*, 963–973.

Kaplan, F., & Oudeyer, P.-Y. (2007a). The progress-drive hypothesis: An interpretation of early imitation. In K. Dautenhahn, & C. Nehaniv (eds.), *Models and Mechanisms of Imitation and Social Learning: Behavioural, Social and Communication Dimensions* (pp. 361–377). Cambridge: Cambridge University Press.

Kaplan, F., & Oudeyer, P.-Y. (2007b). In search of the neural circuits of intrinsic motivation. *Frontiers in Neuroscience, 1*, 225–236.

Kidd, C., Piantadosi, S. T., & Aslin, R. N. (2012). The goldilocks effect: Human infants allocate attention to visual sequences that are neither too simple nor too complex. *PLoS ONE, 7*, e36399.

Kulkarni, T. D., Narasimhan, K., Saeedi, A., & Tenenbaum, J. (2016). Hierarchical deep reinforcement learning: Integrating temporal abstraction and intrinsic motivation. In M. I. Jordan, Y. LeCun, & S. A. Solla (eds.), *Advances in Neural Information Processing Systems* (pp. 3675–3683). Cambridge, MA: MIT Press.

Lapeyre, M., N'Guyen, S., Le Falher, A., & Oudeyer, P. Y. (2014). Rapid morphological exploration with the Poppy humanoid platform. 2014 IEEE-RAS International Conference on Humanoid Robots (pp. 959–966). IEEE. November 18–20, 2014, Madrid, Spain.

Lehman, J., & Stanley, K. O. (2011). Abandoning objectives: Evolution through the search for novelty alone. *Evolutionary Computation*, *19*, 189–223.

Liyanagunawardena, T. R., Adams, A. A., & Williams, S. A. (2013). MOOCs: A systematic study of the published literature 2008-2012. *The International Review of Research in Open and Distributed Learning*, *14*, 202–227.

Lopes, M., Lang, T., Toussaint, M., & Oudeyer, P.-Y. (2012). Exploration in model-based reinforcement learning by empirically estimating learning progress. *Neural Information Processing Systems (NIPS 2012)*. December 3–8, 2012, Tahoe, USA.

Lopes, M., & Oudeyer, P. Y. (2012). The strategic student approach for life-long exploration and learning. 2012 IEEE International Conference on Development and Learning and Epigenetic Robotics (ICDL) (pp. 1–8). IEEE. November 7–9, 2012, San Diego, CA.

Lowenstein, G. (1994). The psychology of curiosity: A review and reinterpretation. *Psychological Bulletin*, *116*, 75–98.

Malone, T. W. (1980). What makes things fun to learn? A study of intrinsically motivating computer games. *Technical report*. Xerox Palo Alto Research Center, Palo Alto, CA.

Merrick, K. E., & Maher, M. L. (2009). *Motivated Reinforcement Learning: Curious Characters for Multiuser Games*. Berlin: Springer Science & Business Media.

Montessori, M. (1948/2004). *The Discovery of the Child*. New Delhi: Aakar Books.

Montgomery, K. (1954). The role of exploratory drive in learning. *Journal of Comparative and Physiological Psychology*, *47*, 60–64.

Moulin-Frier, C., Nguyen, M., & Oudeyer, P.-Y. (2014). Self organization of early vocal development in infants and machines: The role of intrinsic motivation. *Frontiers in Cognitive Science*, *4*, 1006.

Nguyen, M., & Oudeyer, P.-Y. (2013). Active choice of teachers, learning strategies and goals for a socially guided intrinsic motivation learner. *Paladyn, Journal of Behavioural Robotics*, *3*, 136–146.

Nkambou, R., Mizoguchi, R., & Bourdeay, J. (2010). *Advances in Intelligent Tutoring Systems* (Vol. 308). Berlin: Springer.

Oller, D. K. (2000). *The Emergence of the Speech Capacity*. Mahwah, NJ: Lawrence Erlbaum and Associates, Inc.

Oudeyer, P.-Y. (2011). *Developmental Robotics, Encyclopedia of the Sciences of Learning*, ed. N. M. Seel. Springer Reference Series. Berlin: Springer.

Oudeyer, P.-Y., Gottlieb, J., & Lopes, M. (2016). Intrinsic motivation, curiosity, and learning: Theory and applications in educational technologies. In S. Waxman, D. G. Stein, D. Swaab, & H. Fields (eds.), *Progress in Brain Research* (Vol. 229, pp. 257–284). Amsterdam: Elsevier.

Oudeyer, P.-Y., & Kaplan, F. (2006). Discovering communication. *Connection Science*, *18*, 189–206.

Oudeyer, P.-Y., Kaplan, F., & Hafner, V. (2007). Intrinsic motivation systems for autonomous mental development. *IEEE Transactions on Evolutionary Computation*, *11*, 265–286.

Oudeyer, P.-Y., & Smith, L. (2016). How evolution can work through curiosity-driven developmental process, *Topics in Cognitive Science*, *8*, 492–502.

Pachet, F. (2004). On the design of a musical flow machine. In M. Tokoro, & L. Steels (eds.), *A Learning Zone of One's Own* (pp. 111–134). Amsterdam: IOS Press.

Papert, S. (1980). *Mindstorms: Children, Computers, and Powerful Ideas*. New York: Basic Books, Inc.

Piaget. J. (1952) *The Origins of Intelligence in Children*. New York: International University Press.

Resnick, M., Maloney, J., Monroy-Hernández, A., Rusk, N., Eastmond, E., Brennan, K., & Kafai, Y. (2009). Scratch: Programming for all. *Communications of the ACM, 52*, 60–67.

Roy, D., Gerber, G., Magnenat, S., Riedo, F., Chevalier, M., Oudeyer, P. Y., & Mondada, F. (2015). IniRobot: A pedagogical kit to initiate children to concepts of robotics and computer science. *Proceedings of the RIE 2015.* May 20–22, 2015, Yverdon les bains, Switzerland.

Ryan, R., & Deci, E. (2000). Intrinsic and extrinsic motivations: Classic definitions and new directions. *Contemporary Educational Psychology, 25*, 54–67.

Schmidhuber, J. (1991). Curious model-building control systems. *IEEE International Joint Conference on Neural Networks* (pp. 1458–1463). 18-November 21, 1991, Singapore.

Singh, S., Barto, A. G., & Chentanez, N. (2004). Intrinsically motivated reinforcement learning. *NIPS'04: Proceedings of the 17th International Conference on Neural Information Processing Systems* (pp. 1281–1288). December 2004, Vancouver, BC, Canada.

Singh, S., Lewis, R. L., Barto, A. G., & Sorg, J. (2010). Intrinsically motivated reinforcement learning: An evolutionary perspective. *IEEE Transactions on Autonomous Mental Development, 2*, 70–82.

Smith, L. B. (2013). It's all connected: Pathways in visual object recognition and early noun learning. *American Psychologist, 68*, 618.

Smith, L. B., & Breazeal, C. (2007). The dynamic lift of developmental process. *Developmental Science, 10*, 61–68.

Stahl, A. E., & Feigenson, L. (2015). Observing the unexpected enhances infants' learning and exploration. *Science, 348*, 91–94.

Sutton, R. S., Modayil, J., Delp, M., Degris, T., Pilarski, P. M., White, A., & Precup, D. (2011). Horde: A scalable real-time architecture for learning knowledge from unsupervised sensorimotor interaction. *Proceedings of the 10th International Conference on Autonomous Agents and Multiagent Systems (AAMAS 2011)* (Vol. 2, pp. 761–768). May 2–6, 2011, Taipei, Taiwan.

Thelen, E. S., & Smith, L. B. (1996). *Dynamic Systems Approach to the Development of Cognition and Action.* Cambridge, MA: MIT Press.

Thomaz, A. L., & Breazeal, C. (2008) Experiments in socially guided exploration: Lessons learned in building robots that learn with and without human teachers. *Connection Science, 20*, 91–110.

Twomey, K. E., & Westermann, G. (2018). Curiosity-based learning in infants: A neurocomputational approach. *Developmental Science, 21*, e12629.

West, M. J., & King, A. P. (1987). Settling nature and nurture into an ontogenetic niche. *Developmental Psychobiology, 20*, 549–562.

White, R. (1959). Motivation reconsidered: The concept of competence. *Psychological Review, 66*, 297–333.

32 Neurocomputational Methods

From Models of Brain and Cognition to Artificial Intelligence in Education

Michael S. C. Thomas and Kaska Porayska-Pomsta

In this chapter, we consider computational approaches to understanding learning and teaching. We consider the utility of computational methods in two senses, which we address in separate sections. In Section 32.1, we consider the use of computers to build *models of cognition*, focusing on the one hand on how they allow us to understand the developmental origins of behaviour and the role of experience in shaping behaviour, and on the other hand on how a particular type of model – artificial neural networks – can uncover the way in which the constraints of brain function likely shape the properties of our cognitive systems. In Section 32.2, we consider the use of computers as *tools to aid teaching*, in particular in the use of artificial intelligence in education.

These two approaches naturally cross-fertilize. The origin of computational devices in the early twentieth century lay in an endeavour to build machines that thought as humans did; in order to have a good computer tool to help teachers, the design of the tool needs to be informed by how children learn. One of the goals of Section 32.2 is to provide a basis for informed discussion of whether and how the

developmental cognitive neuroscience and artificial intelligence approaches can guide each other for the benefit of their respective aims and whether artificial intelligence may be able to act as a bridge between developmental cognitive neuroscience research and real-world educational practices.

32.1 Computers as Models of Cognition

Humans are biological entities, whatever the sophistication of our cultures and cultural artefacts. When it comes to education, we are, as it were, primates in the classroom. Understanding the operation of the brain – the biological basis of learning – in terms of computation is one perspective of what biological systems do. It is a valuable perspective that helps us understand and unify various properties of the brain – such as the electrical activity of neurons – and how these properties relate to behaviour. However, there may be limitations to the perspective, for example in the properties of biology or the environment, which are de-emphasized or ignored.[1] More widely, the computational perspective fits into the contemporary cultural context of measurement and optimization familiar in free market societies ('everything has a cost, optimize profits'). Computational modelling is to some extent a method of our time. Those caveats in mind, let us introduce the theoretical framework in which we will consider the use of computational approaches in this section.

---

[1] For example, see the reservations of Rodney Brooks, a leading artificial intelligence and robotics researcher: www.edge.org/response-detail/25336B. Last accessed 23 August 2021. Brooks argues that planetary orbits around the sun can be described and simulated in computational terms, but no one would argue that planets are computers.

The first theoretical framework we will use is *educational neuroscience*. This is an emerging interdisciplinary field that seeks to use new insights into brain mechanisms of learning to inform educational practices (Mareschal et al., 2013; Thomas et al., 2020). It is not reductionist, in the sense that the field comprises a dialogue between neuroscientists, psychologists and educators, with an understanding that education is a much broader phenomenon than the changing of brains. Education is intrinsically a cultural, community-based enterprise based on social interaction. Yet to acquire new knowledge and skills, this must be achieved through changing brains. The interaction between neuroscience and education occurs along two main pathways (Thomas et al., 2019a). The first is an indirect link, where neuroscience findings inform psychological theories, which inform education practices. These might concern specific educational domains, such as literacy or numeracy (see Chapters 26–28) or more general aspects of cognition that impact learning, such as executive function skills, emotion, or motivation (see Chapters 29–31). The second route is a direct one that treats the brain as a biological organ. Insights from neuroscience help to optimize the brain for learning when the child enters the classroom, such as the impact of diet, sleep, exercise or stress.

The second framework we will use is *neuroconstructivism* (Mareschal et al., 2007; Westermann et al., 2007). This is a theory of cognitive development that combines a Piagetian constructivist approach – that more complex knowledge and skills are constructed on the basis of simpler knowledge and skills via the child's interactions with the world – with a contemporary understanding of functional brain development. The development of functional brain systems is viewed as heavily constrained by multiple interacting factors that are both intrinsic and extrinsic to the

developing child. Cognitive development occurs in the context of the constraints operating on the development of the brain that span multiple levels of analysis: from genes and the individual cell to the physical and social environment of the developing child. Neuroconstructivism integrates different views of the brain and cognitive development including probabilistic epigenesis (emphasizing the interactions between experience and gene expression in shaping development), neural constructivism (focusing on the experience-dependent elaboration of small-scale neural structures), the interactive specialization view of brain development (stressing the role of interactions between different brain regions in functional brain development), embodiment (highlighting the role of the physical body in cognitive development), Piagetian constructivism (focusing on the child's pro-active acquisition of knowledge, see also Houdé, 2019, for a current Post-Piagetian approach) and the role of the social environment for the developing child.

32.1.1 Cognition, Computation, Education and the Brain

The view of cognition as computation has been a mainstay of cognitive psychology since the 1980s. It leads to research methods that seek to identify mental representations and processes that manipulate those representations. Cognitive psychology has a long relationship with artificial intelligence research, which constructs machines that can operate in intelligent ways. The collaboration of these fields has led to the identification of possible ways that cognition could work, either in humans or in machines. However, there is only one way that cognition *actually* works in humans and that is constrained by how the brain works. There are things that the brain does that a conventional (digital, symbolic, rule-based, von

Neumann) computer cannot do, and vice versa. From a computational perspective, the goal of neuroconstructivism is to identify how the constraints of being implemented in the brain shape the cognitive processes of the mind. The properties of the brain originate in its biology, and its biology is the outcome of a long evolutionary history. This means the way the brain does things may not necessarily be the best, but it will be optimized (by evolutionary selection) given what was available in ancestor species. For example, a biological constraint is that cognition will be performed by neurons. Neural activity produces metabolic waste products, which must be cleared away, and changes in neural properties and connectivity induced by experience require consolidation to be stabilized as robust memories. Together these factors mean that organisms need to sleep – humans are off-line for a third of their lives. On the face of it, this is not an optimal solution for a cognitive system, and it is a limitation that digital computers do not suffer from.

What, then, are the *implementation constraints* of performing computation in the brain? The basic unit of computation is the neuron, and knowledge is stored in the strength of the connections between neurons. This means knowledge is built into structure. It means that neural processing systems will be content-specific. The brain, then, is built of a set of *content-specific systems* (be they motor or sensory). It then requires a separate, specialist system whose job it is to *modulate* the activity of the various content-specific systems, to make sure that the appropriate parts are activated and inhibited based on the current context and goals (the role of the pre-frontal cortex, see Houdé, 2019). The content-specific systems must be linked by *translators*, for example between sensory and motor information, and their content integrated by *hubs* (such as the hippocampus for episodic memory or

anterior temporal lobe for semantics). The bread and butter of the brain are its sensory and motor systems. These content systems are *hierarchical*, a sequence of layers each picking up increasingly higher order invariances (conceptual structure) in the information to which they are exposed, from immediate low-level motor actions to long-term high-level plans in the motor system and from low-level perceptual features to high-level objects in sensory systems. Activity travels simultaneously up and down these hierarchical systems so that expectations (e.g., of the object you will see) can influence low-level processing. The brain exists to serve the body and there are brain structures dedicated to the evolutionary goals of the organism (eating, sleeping, detecting threats, bonding, mating and fighting). The *emotion* (limbic) system interacts with the modulatory system to influence its goals; it influences regional properties of processing in the cortex through altering *neurotransmitter levels* (e.g., to alter arousal); and it *conditions the body* to be in the appropriate state for the current situation (e.g., fight or flight responses) (see Chapter 1).

With respect to education, there is a *many-to-one* mapping between the content-specific systems of the brain and concepts utilised in psychology. So, for example, 'addition' in mathematics class involves multiple representations of knowledge in different brain systems (visual symbols, representations of quantity), motor sequences (of pencil movements) and strategies (retrieval, execution of procedures) in a complex sequence of activity over time and sometimes involving iterations of physical interaction with the environment (move head and eyes to look at problem, write with pencil, look back to problem). 'Learning' as an educational concept that in the brain involves the on-going interaction between perhaps *eight different neural systems*, including *reward-based* processing systems and a system involved in the *automatization* of movements (Thomas et al., 2019a). Notably, educational psychology tends to focus on the acquisition of abstract knowledge underpinned by cortical mechanisms (e.g., to learn multiplication, the system must link language-encoded times tables to procedural knowledge for linking number symbols, and to the semantic underpinning of quantity). However, from the biological perspective of the social primate sitting in the classroom, this function is probably only the brain's fourth most important priority. Before it come, respectively, movement, emotion and social relations (e.g., leaning on the desk and fiddling with your pencil, feeling anxious about maths, wanting to whisper a question to your friend to find out why Sienna doesn't like you anymore). Learning is optimized when the first three priorities are aligned in the service of the fourth (e.g., motor activities are relevant to the topic, there is excitement and curiosity for learning, and learning is supported by the peer group and the relationship with the teacher).

There are multiple methodological approaches to investigate this complex interactive system within developmental cognitive neuroscience. Computational modelling represents a set of formal methods to specify the representations and processes involved in various components of the cognitive system. Computational methods are widely used in other scientific fields to simulate the behaviour of complex systems, such as in meteorology or astrophysics. Formal models have certain virtues. For example, they enforce precision on sometimes vague implicit or verbal accounts of how systems work; if a theory is implemented as a working system, it can test the viability of the theory to produce the observed behaviour it claims to explain; and models able to unify diverse phenomena provide parsimony. Computational models are particularly important in studying systems with multiple interacting components, where the behaviour of the whole system emerges through complex interactions. Once a model is constructed, it can be applied to new situations and generate novel testable predictions, for example, when its parameters are set to atypical values (e.g., as we'll see in Section 32.1.2, to capture disorders such as dyslexia or Attention Deficit Hyperactivity Disorder for models of reading and decision-making, respectively).

The main disadvantage of models is that, by definition, they require simplification. As Box and Draper (1986) say, 'all models are wrong, some are useful'. This poses the twin challenges of ensuring only irrelevant details are simplified away when building a model and finding a balance between building a model complex enough to capture the target phenomenon but not too complex so that its functioning cannot be understood (Lewandowsky, 1993; McCloskey, 1991). The ultimate goal of modelling is, after all, to progress theoretical understanding.

Computational models of cognition have used different types of computational formalism. Some of them rely on explicit rules for encoding knowledge (*IF x THEN y*) (e.g., Ritter et al., 2018). Some employ formalisms from probability theory, where cognition is viewed as updating a probabilistic understanding of the state of the world in the light of new data (the Bayesian approach; Gopnik & Bonawitz, 2015). Models that focus on the computations that can be performed by neural systems can differ depending on whether they focus on the temporal dynamics of the system (dynamical systems theory; Spencer et al., 2011); or the information encoded in representations (connectionism or artificial neural network models; Spencer et al., 2009; Thomas & McClelland, 2008). In Section 32.1.2, we focus on artificial neural network models, applied to education-relevant cognitive abilities. We do so because these machine-learning systems have the attractive property of learning their knowledge representations by exposure to a structured learning environment; they are therefore ideally suited to studying learning, development and mechanisms of change (Mareschal & Thomas, 2007).

32.1.2 Artificial Neural Network Models of Education-Relevant Cognitive Abilities

Artificial neural network models (henceforth ANNs) have been applied to modelling a range of phenomena in cognitive development, from sensori-motor processing in infancy (e.g., object recognition), routine motor sequences, categorization, aspects of language such as vocabulary, morphology and syntax, to reasoning on Piagetian problems (Botvinick & Plaut, 2004; Elman et al., 1996; Mareschal & Thomas, 2007; Shultz, 2003). Models have addressed development in particular cognitive domains and for restricted behavioural phenomena (e.g., the ability to sort rods of different lengths into serial order; Mareschal & Shultz, 1999). The approach is therefore an analytical one, pulling cognition apart into component parts, and is as a consequence reliant on theories of developmental cognitive neuroscience to identify the relevant components.

The parts of an ANN are as follows. The basic elements are *simple processing units* with activity levels analogous to neurons and electrical neural firing rates. A unit's activity level alters the activity levels of other units to which it is connected, based on the strength of the *connections* between them. The connections are analogous to axons, synapses, neurotransmitters and dendrites. Units have an *activation function* that determines how much they will alter their activation level depending on the level of stimulation (excitation, inhibition) they are receiving from other units. Units are typically organized into *layers*. A layer

represents information through a pattern of activations across its units. In *neural* models, models are tested against their ability to simulate patterns of neural activity. In *cognitive* models, representations correspond to concepts and models are tested against their ability to simulate behaviour.

Layers are usually defined as inputs, outputs and intermediate layers that facilitate the mapping between inputs and outputs. The layers and pathways in a model are referred to as the *architecture* (e.g., the architecture of a model of the reading system is shown in Box 32.1). An untrained ANN has small random connection weights. The ANN is exposed to a *structured learning environment* (or training set), which specifies the sets of input–output mappings it must learn. Input–output pairs are presented to the network and a *learning algorithm* is used to adjust the connection strengths so that the network gradually learns all the input–output pairs through multiple exposures to the mappings. There are a variety of learning algorithms, which generally serve to alter the network connections to optimize some function, be it the accuracy of input–outputs, the conciseness of a set of representations, or how accurately the network can predict the reward gained by a particular action. In *agent-based* models, the system is an agent whose actions alter the subsequent experience of the environment (for more detail, see Elman et al., 1996; McLeod et al., 1998; Thomas & McClelland, 2008). These components are summarised in Table 32.1, left-hand column.

ANNs have been applied to a number of cognitive models relevant to education. Perhaps the most attention has been paid to capturing the development of *reading* (e.g., Harm & Seidenberg, 2004; Plaut et al., 1996; Seidenberg & McClelland, 1989; see Box 32.1 for an example model). These models focus on context-specific pathways, which learn to translate between structured representations

Table 32.1. *Components of two different types of computational model, those used to simulate cognitive mechanisms and those used as theoretically informed artificial intelligence tools to support learning and teaching*

Cognitive model components	*Artificial Intelligence in Education model components*
Stipulation of Theoretical domain of relevance – what is to be modelled (e.g., reading development) and what is to be simplified (e.g., vision and audition)	**Domain model** responsible for representing the knowledge and related operations that are the object of learning (e.g., maths)
Architecture of model specifying inputs, outputs, pathways, internal layers, parameter settings (e.g., pathways linking orthographic, phonological and semantic representations)	**Model of the learner** which represents what the learner knows at any given point as well as their emotions and motivational states
Learning algorithm specifying how structure and parameters of the model will change based on training experiences or development	**Model of pedagogy** taking into account the domain to be mastered and the pedagogical strategies and tactics that are appropriate in that domain
Representational format for inputs and outputs (e.g., code for speech sounds, code for written letters)	**Communication model** offering strategies for how to realize any given pedagogical strategy
Specification of Structured learning environment – frequency and nature of experiences (e.g., associations between written and spoken forms of words); in agent-based modelling, the agent's actions determine the next input from its environment, which may also contain other agents	

of a word's written form (orthography), its spoken form (phonology) and its meaning (semantics). The model is exposed to a learning environment in which it is presented with instances of associations between the written and spoken form of words, encountering them with a frequency based on the occurrence of these words in naturalistic corpuses. The accuracy of the model in reading depends on how often it encounters words, but also on the complexity of the relationship between written and spoken forms, which may be fairly transparent (e.g., Italian) or complex (e.g., English). Box 32.1 provides an example of some of the implementation details of a specific model and how models have been extended and tested by brain imaging data.

Representations of *meaning* in cognitive models are usually depicted in terms of sets of semantic features that define a concept. More recent models have begun to capture semantic representations in terms of a hub, where information from diverse modalities of a concept can be unified (e.g., sound, touch, visual features, smell, movement, verbal descriptions) (e.g., Chen et al., 2017). Meaning has also been represented as sequences of associated concepts over time, structured into events or episodes (Elman & McRae, 2017; Hoffman et al., 2018). Moreover, access to semantics has been proposed to require the operation of executive functions, in the form of external modulatory control processes that activate and inhibit content representations (Hoffman et al., 2018).

Such models acquire generalized representations of meaning, gradually extracting patterns over multiple exposures to individual instances of, say, *dogs* or *cars*. However, the brain also has a structure, called the hippocampus, for snapshot learning of individual *episodic memories*, e.g., where and when you saw a specific dog. Knowledge of individual episodes must somehow be transferred to the cortical representations of general *semantic knowledge*. This process has been studied in models of complementary learning systems, where the hippocampus supports *consolidation* of knowledge in the cortex, partly by replaying memories during sleep (McClelland et al., 1995; O'Reilly et al., 2014).

Models of *numerical cognition* have focused on capturing basic tasks such as number comparison and simple addition, since, developmentally, more complex tasks such as multidigit arithmetic and symbolic mathematical reasoning build on these simpler tasks (Zorzi et al., 2005). In these types of models, the acquisition of number concepts involves the mapping between an analogue code of quantity, representations of number symbols (e.g., Arabic numerals) and verbal numerical expressions (e.g., Campbell, 1994; Dehaene & Cohen, 1995). These models have attempted to account for phenomena such as the distance effect (that is it is easier to select the larger of two numbers when they are far apart than when they are close) and the size effect (that for a given distance, it is easier to compare small numbers than large numbers) (see Dehaene, 2003, for review). Models of simple arithmetic aim to address the fact that competent adults can use a combination of fact retrieval from memory and procedures for transforming the problem if memory search fails, and therefore must combine multiple pathways (Zorzi et al., 2005).

Models have considered *executive functions*, for example, in cognitive control (Botvinick et al., 2001; see Houdé, 2000, 2019, for an inhibitory-control model), in short-term memory (Haarmann & Usher, 2001) and even switching between the bilingual's two languages (Filippi et al., 2014). These models include modulatory mechanisms that influence or retain activation states in the content-specific systems to which they are connected. However, control of behaviour is also sometimes construed within a reinforcement-learning framework, where decisions about behavioural choices depend on a history of the rewards received for different actions. Models of *reward-based decision-making* have been influenced by a growing understanding of the role of the dopamine neurotransmitter system in the striatum, where neural activity has been found to follow the accuracy of the individual's predictions of the rewards they will receive for their actions (Ziegler et al., 2016). These models have been extended to consider the possible origins of impulsivity in Attention Deficit Hyperactivity Disorder, construed in terms of changes to the model's initial computational parameter settings, for example in the weight given to small short-term rewards versus larger longer-term rewards (Ziegler et al., 2016, for a review).

Findings from ANN models of the acquisition of education-relevant abilities point to the importance of the quality of the representations for driving the learning of more complex abilities (e.g., phonology for reading, an analogue code of quantity for numeracy); the importance of sufficient capacity and plasticity in processing systems to acquire target skills; the importance of context-appropriate control of the activation states in content systems; and the importance of representative exposure to the problem domain.

Finally, low-level sensory systems do not tend to be the focus of education-relevant computational models. Nevertheless, they can sometime be relevant because education is seeking to shape brain systems that have

Box 32.1   Example of an ANN Model of Reading development

A great deal of research has focused on developmental models of reading. Initial models addressed how ANNs could learn the mapping between orthography and phonology by repeated exposure to a word's written and spoken forms; how such models could accommodate both regularity in these mappings (*mint, hint, tint*) but also exceptions (*pint*); and how they could extract the general function linking spoken and written forms to enable them to read aloud non-words (e.g., *gint*) (e.g., Seidenberg & McClelland, 1989). Subsequently, models extended to consider the possibility that a written word's meaning could be retrieved either by a direct mapping from orthography to semantics, or by generating its spoken form and using this to access semantics. Similarly, the spoken form could be retrieved either directly from the written form or the written form could be used to retrieve the meaning, which could then be used to retrieve the spoken form (Harm & Seidenberg, 2004; Plaut et al., 1996). In this way, the reading system has multiple pathways and there may indeed be a division of labour between them. For example, it might be more efficient for a system to learn regular mappings via the direct orthography to phonology route, and the exceptions (like *pint*) via the semantic route.

evolved with constraints tailored to other developmental outcomes (so-called *neuronal recycling*; Dehaene, 2005). The computational constraints of these brain systems, at least following a phase of development in infancy and early childhood, may influence behavioural patterns as new culturally determined skills are acquired in school. For example, in some scripts, written letters can be mirror reversals or rotations of each other (e.g., b, d, p, q in English). The early visual system develops to recognize objects irrespective of their orientation, a constraint that must be later overridden to separate these orientation-specific letters (see Ahr et al., 2016a, 2016b, 2017). The result is initial characteristic errors of confusion of these letters (and numbers such as 2 and 5) (see, e.g., Blackburne et al., 2014). Recently, ANN models have been successfully applied to capturing the development of visual object recognition. Advances in so-called deep neural networks have enabled computer scientists to produce much more powerful systems for recognizing complex objects within visual scenes. These models have multiple layers, with each higher layer extracting more complex features from the visual input. Deep networks are very powerful learning systems but very specific to the content on which

they are trained. Two points are notable. First, the types of representations developed in the sequence of layers in the artificial neural networks appear to capture the types of representations found in the hierarchy of processing areas in the ventral (object recognition) visual stream of the human cortex, validating deep learning as a useful perspective on brain function (e.g., Rajalingham et al., 2018). Second, the similarity of the ANN's representations to the brain's representations depends on how many layers the model has. Beyond a certain number of layers, the ANN's performance begins to *exceed* human accuracy on image classification and the layers' representations *cease to be human-like* (Storrs et al., 2017).

Figure 32.1 shows the architecture of one implementation of the multiple pathway architecture (grey elements depict unimplemented input and output systems) (Harm & Seidenberg, 2004). Notably, many of the connections between layers of units are bidirectional, so that activation can flow around the network. In the model, semantics was represented over 1989 units, orthography over 225 units and phonology over 200 units. Intermediate layers helped learn the mappings between these codes. The size of the

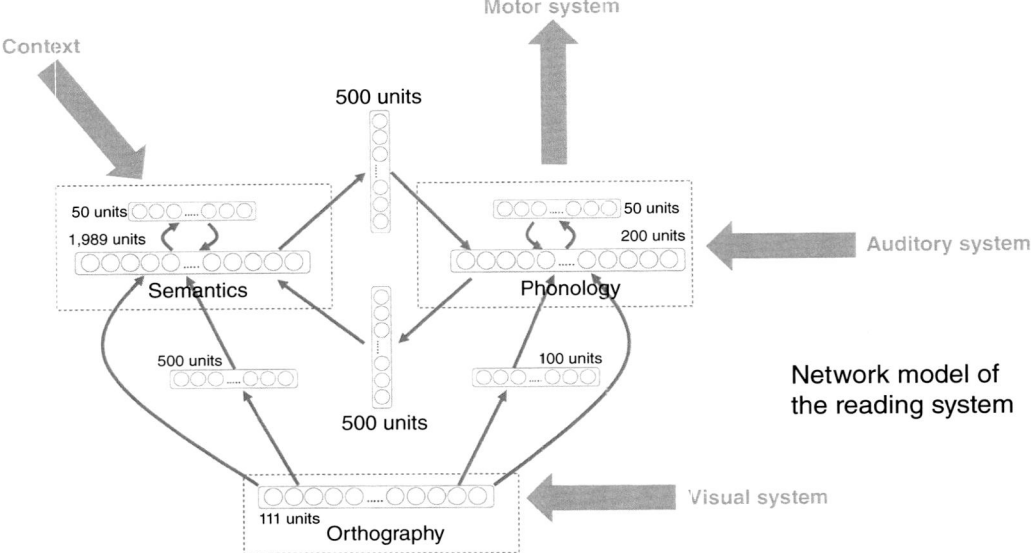

Figure 32.1 Architecture of the Harm and Seidenberg (2004) model of reading, showing the specified representations (semantics, phonology, and orthography), pathways and directions of activation flow between them. Greyed elements (motor, auditory, visual systems, context) were unimplemented, but assumed, components

intermediate layers was determined merely by what worked, or as the authors put it in one case, 'the number 500 was chosen from pilot studies; it is a number large enough to perform the mapping without being too computationally burdensome' (p. 677). The model was trained on 6,103 monosyllabic English words, consisting of all monosyllabic words and their most common inflections. The pathways were trained separately, using an algorithm based on backpropagation through time. This algorithm adjusts connection weights to reduce output errors and accommodates cycling activation. The model was trained for around 700,000 word presentations, first learning an oral language system, then linking written forms to it (see Harm & Seidenberg, 2004, for full details). One notable finding of this model was that, given its multiple pathways, the system initially learned to retrieve meanings from written forms indirectly through accessing phonology,

because this mapping is largely regular, and the pathway from phonology to semantics is already established. However, gradually, the system learned the more complex direct mapping from orthography to semantics, which delivers faster reading.

The dynamics predicted by the computational model were subsequently testable by advances in brain imaging. Dynamical causal modelling techniques applied to functional magnetic resonance imaging (fMRI) data were able to reveal which brain regions dynamically drive which other brain regions during reading (Richardson et al., 2011). Figure 32.2 shows the strength of the dynamic modulation of the activity between connected regions during a reading task, respectively, for low-level vision, visual word processing, phonology and semantics. It reveals that orthography and phonology interact with each other during reading and both drive semantics; but notably, early visual areas

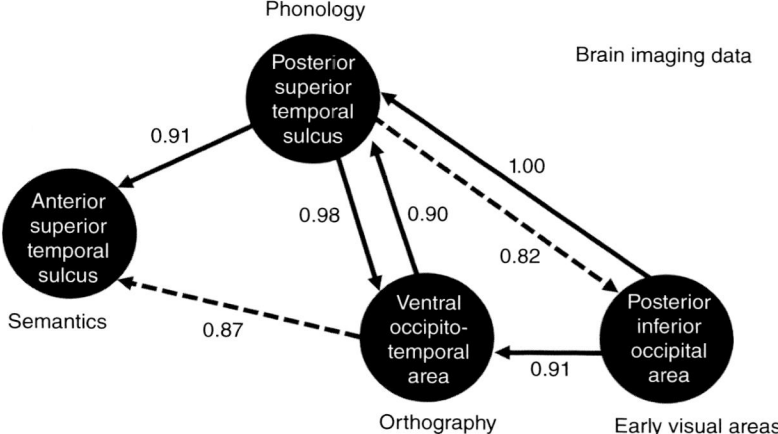

Figure 32.2 Summary of dynamic causal modelling of functional magnetic resonance imaging data, showing which brain regions involved in reading appeared to causally drive other regions (Richardson et al., 2011). Values show probabilities for modulatory connections during the reading task. Solid black arrows indicate connections above threshold. Black dashed arrows indicate strong trends

directly drive activation in both orthographic and phonological areas, with phonology also showing some indication of top down modulation of low-level visual areas. These data confirm the multiple routes, hierarchical nature and interactivity of the reading system.

Subsequent computational models of the reading system have sought to include further constraints from neuroanatomy (e.g., a dorsal route linking auditory perception directly to motor output, for repeating words without retrieving their meaning; Ueno et al., 2011); have considered how alterations in the computational properties of the system, either in the number of units in the mapping pathways or the quality of the phonological representations, could produce developmental trajectories resembling dyslexia (e.g., Harm & Seidenberg, 1999); have investigated how certain kinds of behavioural interventions may ameliorate the developmental deficits (Harm et al., 2003; Thomas et al., 2019b); and have studied how variation in network parameters may produce individual differences in

development and potentially provide a mechanistic link to both genetic levels and environmental variables such as socio-economic status (SES; Thomas, Forrester & Ronald, 2013, 2016). In as much as cognition is viewed as computation, genetic effects on cognition must unpack as modulation of neurocomputational parameters; and correlates of SES include variations in the growth of brain structures and variation in the level of cognitive stimulation.

32.2 Technology As a Tool for Supporting Learning and Teaching

The study of human learning using computational modelling dates back at least to the 1970s and the formal advent of what is now known as Artificial Intelligence in Education (AIEd) – a research field that lies at the intersection of the broader studies in Artificial Intelligence and the Learning Sciences (e.g., Woolf, 2008). Given that computational modelling of learners in context represents a defining characteristic of AIEd technologies (with Intelligent Tutoring Systems providing one example of such technologies), there is a natural overlap between the preceding computational modelling approaches used in educational neuroscience (henceforth EdN) research, and those used in AIEd systems.

However, there are also some fundamental differences between the primary motivation and goals of AIEd and EdN. These differences relate specifically to the emphasis that each field puts on the importance of neurocognitive versus behavioural fidelity of its models, as well as their respective reliance on access to and their immediate application in pedagogical practices at the front-line. In particular, while the primary goal of EdN is to gain fundamental understanding of neural processes related to learning in order to inform a general theory of how the brain works, AIEd is concerned with creating environments, which form an explicit part of educational interventions from their inception to their delivery in real-world educational contexts. In other words, in AIEd systems, neurocognitive fidelity of the models is a highly desirable but not a *necessary* condition for their successful implementation in educational practices.

In the second part of this chapter, we briefly introduce the AIEd perspective as an important area in which computational modelling of learning and teaching behaviours forms a central part. Our goal is to provide a basis for informed discussion of whether and how the AIED and EdN can guide each other for the benefit of their respective aims; and of the extent to which AIEd may be able to act as a bridge between EdN research and real-world educational practices.

32.2.1 Artificial Intelligence in Education (AIEd)

AIEd is a subfield of Artificial Intelligence (AI) and the Learning Sciences (LS), which seeks both to understand the behavioural correlates of learning and teaching processes and to computationally model individual learners as they engage in learning of a particular subject domain in real-time. While utilising AI's techniques and feeding into the Learning Sciences theories and practices, such modelling is essential to enabling educational software environments to provide adaptive, in-the-moment learning and teaching support, for example, pedagogical feedback to learners, or advice to teachers on how to support individual learners in context. AIEd research investigates: (i) how meaningful interactions between teachers and learners develop; (ii) what factors in the physical learning environment contribute to successful learning (be it software environment or a combination of software and a broader context in which learning takes place); and (iii) what kind of pedagogical feedback may be more or less conducive to learning by particular types of learners within a specific learning domain and circumstances (e.g., Porayska-Pomsta & Bernardini, 2013; Woolf, 2008).

There exists a whole plethora of different forms of AIEd technologies, from *Intelligent Tutoring Systems* that focus on supporting mastery learning in one-on-one learning contexts (e.g., Cognitive Tutors – Corbett et al., 1997) to *collaborative learning environments* that support learning interactions amongst groups of learners (e.g., Cukurova et al., 2018). Regardless of their specific application, the key common characteristic to all AIEd environments is that their functionality is underpinned by a mutually informing set of modelling components, including: (i) a *domain model* which is responsible for representing the knowledge and related operations that are the object of learning (e.g., maths); (ii) a *model of the learner* which represents what the learner knows at any given point as well as their emotions and motivational states; (iii) a *model of pedagogy* which takes into account both the domain to be mastered and the pedagogical strategies and tactics that are appropriate in that domain; and (iv) *a communication model*, which offers strategies for how to realize any given pedagogical strategy. The exact way in which these different components will be implemented and utilised in any given system will depend on the context in which they are to be deployed, the specific intervention goals, hardware employed (which may determine what user behaviours can be detected and modelled feasibly in real-time), and data available. However, regardless of their exact implementations, a learner model is generally considered the essential component of any environment that aims to adapt its pedagogy and interaction to individual learners. These components are included in Table 32.1 (right column) and contrasted with those employed in cognitive models of learning and development.

Unlike the computational modelling employed in EdN, which tends to rely on neurocomputational approaches, AIEd environments are *a priori* agnostic with respect to the type of AI that underpins their models. As such, AIEd technologies employ a diverse range of AI techniques from the so-called *good old-fashioned rule-based AI* (GOF AI) to machine learning (ML). GOF AI requires explicit representation of knowledge, which reflects an ontological conceptualization of the world and actions that are possible therein, along with some well-defined measures of success in terms of concrete goals and goal satisfaction constraints. For example, in the context of maths tutoring, the ontological representations will relate to the specific sub-domains of maths – misconceptions in column subtraction and rules that define the possible operations on the given subdomain. The goal satisfaction in this case may be in terms of student's correct or incorrect answers. The rules are typically elicited through questioning of human experts in a given domain, by observing their expertise in real contexts or by hand-annotating data (video recordings, interaction logs, etc.) of humans engaging in specific tasks of interest. By contrast, *machine learning* (ML), such as implemented by artificial neural networks, learns solutions from first principles by applying statistical classification methods to large data sets, as discussed in Section 32.1. Both of these broad approaches have their strengths and weaknesses in terms of the extent to which they lend themselves as a basis for enhancing our theoretical understanding of learning and teaching processes, or for supporting teaching and learning practices.

Specifically, the key advantage of knowledge-based systems is that they require a detailed understanding of the domain, in order for knowledge ontologies to be constructed, thus also potentially leading to a greater understanding of the domains represented, and the fact that the resulting ontologies are transparent, inspectable and often understandable by humans (Davis et al., 1993; Russell & Norvig, 2003). For example, in *Cognitive Tutors* (henceforth CTs; Corbett et al., 1997), which were originally created as a testbed for the ACT-R cognitive theory of rational thought and problem-solving (Anderson et al., 1990), this transparency is key for delivering fine-grained and tailored moment-by-moment feedback to students, and to performing diagnoses (*sic* learner modelling) of learners' developing knowledge and understanding. Here, learner modelling involves keeping track of (i) the learner's progress through a solution and (ii) the growth of learner's knowledge over time. In CTs, the diagnoses are based on the specification of declarative knowledge, for example, ''when both sides of the equation are divided by the same value, the resulting quantities are equal' and procedural knowledge expressed as production rules that apply to a particular stage in a problem-solving episode, for example, 'IF the goal is to solve an equation for variable X and the equation is of the form $aX = b$, THEN divide both sides of the equation by a to isolate X' (Corbett et al., 1997, p. 854). The production rules are annotated for correctness and specificity of the solutions that they offer. During problem-solving a CT keeps track of all the solution steps committed by the learner and identifies the production rules in its database that correspond to learner's solution steps. The annotations associated with each production rule provide the basis for the assessment of the quality of the learner's steps and their problem-solving strategies, which in turn allows the system to choose appropriate feedback. These decisions can be examined in detail and, if necessary or desired, full traces of the diagnoses performed by the CT can be given back to the teachers or learners as an explanation of the system's assessments and of its choices of pedagogical feedback.

CTs provide but one example of how knowledge can be represented in an AI tutoring system and of how learners' knowledge growth can be modelled and supported using a GOF AI approach. Other successful examples of knowledge and learner modelling include constraint-based models, which describe a given subset of a knowledge domain in terms of constraints, and constraint satisfaction conditions, which can be matched to student actions to guide the system's adaptation of its feedback (Ohlsson & Mitrovic, 2007). Topic networks can also be used to represent specific areas of a subject domain taught, allowing the system and the students the flexibility to choose which topics should be covered next (Beal, 2013). On the other hand, models of learners' emotional and motivational states during learning often rely on probabilistic approaches (Conati et al., 2018; Mavrikis, 2008; Porayska-Pomsta & Mellish, 2013), with

the corresponding Bayesian network representations typically being constructed by hand, based on limited, but fine-grained, observational and interaction data, rather than being machine learned. While offering a relatively high degree of inferential transparency, the disadvantage of knowledge-based systems is that they are cumbersome and time-consuming to construct; they are by their very nature limited to small subsets of domains modelled; they may reflect practitioners' theories about their own practices rather than the actual practices; and the data on which they operate may be inaccurate or incomplete, as they rely on directly observable teachers' and learners' behaviours – and these in turn may be difficult to detect and diagnose reliably. Any of these factors individually or in combination may affect the educational efficacy of the GOF AI based systems.

By contrast, ML carries substantial promise both in terms of reducing the effort required to specify knowledge ontologies and in being able to go beyond the knowledge we have ourselves and, in so doing (the questions of bias and correctness of the base models notwithstanding), in driving more accurate decision-making than our own capabilities allow for. Here, one of the most exciting aspects of ML is that it can discover new associations in the world and predict future outcomes based on prior data in complex domains, which may be otherwise hard for us to grasp and analyse efficiently. Recently, given growing availability and access to voluminous educational data (e.g., from MOOCs and commercial educational apps), these advantages of ML have been seized on in the context of learning analytics and educational data mining research (Baker, 2010; Baker & Yacef, 2009; Macfdyen et al., 2014). As well as being very valuable in shedding light onto various relationships between learner behaviours and learning outcomes, these methods are increasingly used to underpin systems that aid *in situ* pedagogical decisions of teachers, for example through dashboards (Martinez Maldonado et al., 2014), that is, reporting tools which offer teachers data and metrics related to learners' activities at an individual student or group levels. Given the disadvantage of ML approaches is their lack of inferential transparency and explainability, there is also a growing tendency to combine ML and GOF AI approaches at different stages of system implementation and levels of functionality to compensate for each of those paradigms' limitations (Li et al., 2011). For example, cognitive tutors described previously, utilise ML to learn any new problem-solving strategies employed by students as they interact with the systems, thus increasing their diagnostic flexibility and reducing both the effort and potential inaccuracies that are involved in constructing such systems.

32.2.2 Cognitive Fidelity versus Computational Efficiency

One critical difference between computational models employed in cognitive neuroscience, including EdN, and those used within AI, including in AIEd, is that the key criterion for the success of the latter is not whether they are able to model the human brain exactly, but rather whether they can autonomously engage in decision-making, and/or semi-autonomously – in a contingently credible interaction with humans. The goal of such systems is not to replace the human and human decision-making (e.g., as driverless cars might do), but to enhance such decision-making either by offering insights that might be otherwise difficult for the human to gain without the help of technology or by triggering some desired thinking and behaviour (e.g., Porayska-Pomsta & Rajendran, 2019). Hernandez-Orallo and Vold (2019) refer to the latter function of AI models as *cognitive enhancers*, which they propose can vary in terms of their autonomy and coupling with the human. For example, dashboards that offer learning analytics to teachers may be considered cognitive enhancers that are loosely coupled with humans, since the decisions that are made on the basis of the information given, and indeed whether such information is considered at all, are left entirely to their users. By contrast, Intelligent Tutoring Systems such as Cognitive Tutors could be considered as relatively tightly coupled enhancers, since their decisions are autonomous and they impact directly on the course of their interactions with the users through accurate learner modelling, while also seeking to optimally compensate or enhance the learners' skills, knowledge and behaviour.

The emphasis on computational efficiency as opposed to cognitive fidelity is a necessary compromise that, arguably, accompanies all AI models, of which AIEd models are a specialized subtype. The tension between cognitive fidelity and computational efficiency was always present in AI developments, leading to two conceptions of AI. The first is a general view of AI where the aim is to replicate human thinking and behaviour exactly, and which is presently still considered unattainable. The second is a narrow view where the aim is for an AI agent to act in a sufficiently human-like manner by emulating to some extent rational thinking and behaviour, given a set of known constraints and constraint satisfaction conditions that define the world within which such an agent operates, that is, in an environment in which thinking/computation can be accomplished (Davis et al., 1993; Russell & Norvig, 1995). The kind of AI systems that are presently developed belong to the narrow AI category, where there is an explicit understanding that the AI models are neither exact replicas of the human brain, nor are they complete. Although from the EdN point of view, this lack of cognitive fidelity or completeness may be considered a limitation, in educational contexts, provided that the models lend themselves to being inspected and modified by the users, these seeming limitations can offer important benefits for learning and teaching. This is because such dependency requires an active effort from the users to engage in completing or correcting those models, which in turn relies on and further develops the users' critical thinking and metacognitive competencies (Bull & Kay, 2016; Conati et al., 2018). The branch of the AIEd research which focuses on this affordance relates to the so-called *Open Learner Models* (OLMs), with research to date demonstrating how OLMs can be used both as a mirror by the learners to help them improve self-monitoring and self-regulation skills (Azevedo & Aleven, 2013; Long & Aleven, 2013; Porayska-Pomsta & Rajendran, 2019) and as a magnifying glass by educational practitioners who want to gain a better understanding of their learners for the purpose of improving their pedagogy (Bull & Kay, 2016; Martinez Maldonado et al., 2014; Porayska-Pomsta, 2016). We consider and exemplify different forms of OLMs further in Section 32.2.3.

32.2.3 Open Learner Models (OLMs)

OLMs are student models, that is, representations of student cognitive and/or affective states that allow users to access their content with varying levels of interactivity and control (Bull, 1995; Bull & Kay, 2016). Originally, OLMs were designed to improve model accuracy by enabling students to adjust the models' diagnoses and predictions, if such were deemed inaccurate by the students. Over time, the use of OLMs revealed substantial educational potential in encouraging learners to self-assess, reflect and ultimately self-regulate,

because engagement with such models requires the students to understand and evaluate their own decisions and behaviours. Different types of OLMs include models that are:

i. *scrutable*, that is, users may view the models' current evaluation of relevant student's states and abilities;
ii. *cooperative* or *negotiable*, where the user and the system work together to arrive at an assessment of student performance; and
iii. *editable*, where users can change directly the models' assessments and even the underlying knowledge representations at will.

In the cognitive tutors' tradition, Long and Aleven (2017) designed a scrutable OLM to help students to self-assess their knowledge in order to share with the system the responsibility for selecting the next problem to work on. Their system employs similar domain knowledge representation and problem selection mechanism to those employed by the Cognitive Tutors, as described in Section 32.2.2. The system evaluates student's problem-solving steps against a set of example solutions and, based on this, using Bayesian Knowledge Tracing, it determines which knowledge components the student needs to learn (Aleven & Koedinger, 2013). The probabilities generated over the knowledge components are visualized for the students in terms of 'skill bars' (Figure 32.3), which they can compare with their own self-assessments. In this approach, student self-reflection constitutes an explicit learning goal, which has been shown to be key in significantly improving learning outcomes for the students who used this OLM.

Mabbott and Bull (2006), who created an OLM that allows the learners to 'persuade' the system to change its assessment of their knowledge, offer an example of a negotiable model. To do so, the learners can register their disagreement with the system's assessment and

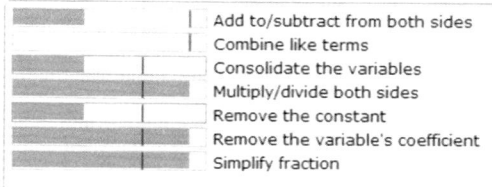

Add to/subtract from both sides
Combine like terms
Consolidate the variables
Multiply/divide both sides
Remove the constant
Remove the variable's coefficient
Simplify fraction

Figure 32.3 Long and Aleven's (2017) skills meter bars indicating the level of student skill mastery A black-and-white version of this figure will appear in some formats. For the colour version, please refer to the plate section.

propose a change. At this point, the system will explain why it 'believes' its current assessment to be correct and will provide evidence to support these beliefs, for example, by showing samples of the learners' previous responses that may indicate a misconception. If the learner still disagrees with the system, they have a chance to 'convince' the system by answering a series of targeted test questions from the system, which keeps a detailed representation of the user on-task interactions and its assessments of the user's understanding given their behavioural patterns and correctness/quality of their solutions.

Basu et al. (2017) designed a fully editable OLM, which allows students to construct models of their knowledge by exploring concepts, properties and relations between them in open-ended exploratory learning environments. This OLM is underpinned with hierarchical representation of tasks and strategies (implemented as a directed acyclic graph) that may be needed to solve a problem. The system allows for the expression of a particular construct or strategy in multiple variations that relate to each other, which in turn gives the system an ability to assess both desired and suboptimal implementations of a strategy by the learner. Based on this, the system can analyse learners' behaviours by comparing their action sequences and the contexts associated therewith against the strategy variants to offer

targeted support when the users seem to flounder. This representation allows for a conceptual support to be given to the user at a fine-grained level of detail, for example, low-level object descriptions in terms of their properties, relations between them and temporal ordering of actions that could be performed on them. In turn, this allows the system to guide the user in editing the model through relatively simple step-by-step interfaces for the different modelling tasks, gradually building users' confidence in their abilities, their buy-in to the system's advice and prompts, ultimately significantly increasing the learning outcomes for the users (Basu et al., 2017).

In the TARDIS system, we implemented a scrutable OLM, in the context of emotional self-regulation in job interview simulations involving AI agents acting as recruiters. TARDIS collects evidence from the simulations, based on low-level signals such as the users gaze patterns, gestures, posture, voice activation, etc., and uses machine learning techniques to predict from this evidence the quality of behaviours known to be important for effective interviews, such as appropriate energy in the voice, fluidity of speech and gaze management (Porayska-Pomsta et al., 2014). Figure 32.4 shows how the data are displayed to the user, with the pie charts referring to four qualities of interest such as energy manifested in the users' interactions (which may indicate engagement), fluidity of the interaction (which may be indicative of user confidence), spatial extent which evaluates expansiveness of gestures (these may need to be controlled during a job interview) and overall activation (i.e., users initiations of interaction and responses to agents' initiations).

The model's assessment over these behaviours is then visualized to the learner as shown by the pie charts in Figure 32.4, as a way to provide the users with a concrete and immediate basis for reflecting on how they may

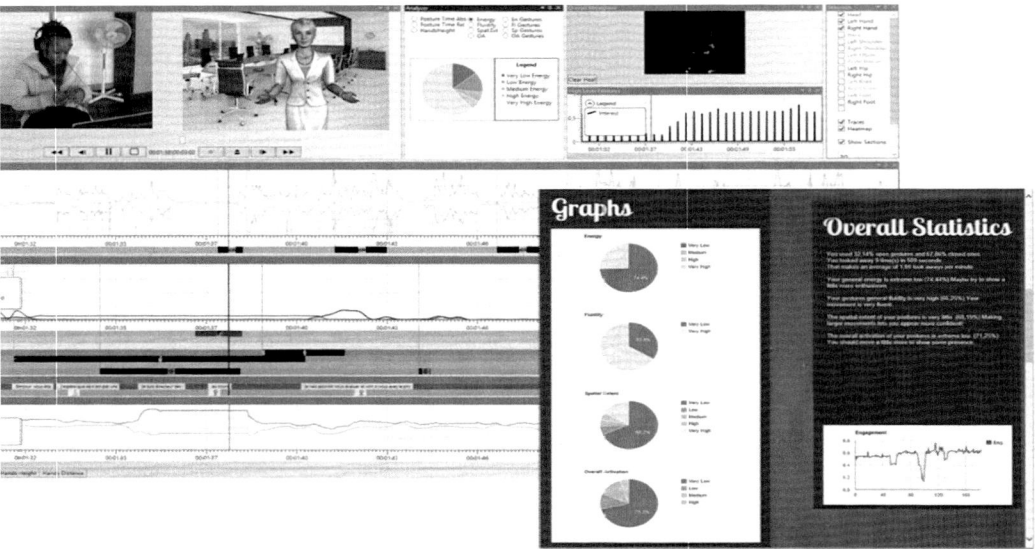

Figure 32.4 TARDIS scrutable OLM showing synchronized recordings of the learners interacting with the AI agents along with the interpretation of the learner's low-level social signals such as gaze patterns, gestures and voice activation in terms of higher-level judgements about the quality of those behaviours, e.g., energy in voice
A black-and-white version of this figure will appear in some formats. For the colour version, please refer to the plate section.

improve their verbal and non-verbal behaviours in subsequent interviews. A time-lined view of learner actions that the system detected and interpretation of those actions is also given. This OLM provides a detailed basis for more nuanced discussion about learners' job interview performance and specific behaviours with human practitioners than would otherwise be possible. The evaluation of this OLM showed significant improvements in key behaviours targeted, including the quality of the responses to interview questions, non-verbal behaviours such as gestures, voice modulation and eye gaze, as well as leading to learners' decreased levels of anxiety and increased levels of self-efficacy and confidence (Porayska-Pomsta & Chryssafidou, 2018). Interestingly, in line with existing OLM research, the accuracy of TARDIS' diagnoses does not seem a pre-requisite of the success of

the intervention. Indeed, some inaccuracies in the model may even be desirable, if the explicit goal of the interaction with an OLM is to provoke the student to self-reflect, self-explain or argue with the system about its diagnosis. Here, the potential of OLMs as mirrors and as props for metacognitive competencies development is clearly apparent, providing a unique opportunity for EdN to study these competencies in systematic and ecologically valid ways, for example by linking the idea of explicitly separating learners' subjective experience from the observation of the behaviour and, thus, through OLM turning such observation into a more objective, almost vicarious experience.

32.2.4 Humanly AI and the Social Brain

Another important question related to cognitive fidelity of the AI models that is of relevance to EdN is that related to the definition of the 'sufficiently humanly behaviour'. In the broader context of AI, this question is central to progressing the state of the art in the field and one which has been asked since the idea of systems that both support and depend on an interaction with humans emerged in the 1960s (e.g., Engelbart, 1962; Licklider, 1960). In this context one of the more intriguing hypotheses is the uncanny valley hypothesis (Mori, 1970, 2005), which states that human-like objects, for example, some forms of robots, elicit emotional responses, for example, empathy, similar to those that are elicited in response to other humans. Although the degree of the emotional responses to such objects tends to be proportionate to the degree of human likeness, beyond a certain degree of similarity and realism, such responses can suddenly become extremely negative (Misselhorn, 2009). Over decades, this hypothesis has led to substantial AI research investigating the questions of AI models' socio-emotional and behavioural credibility in human–computer interaction and of the relationship between human users' empathy toward and social affinity with technological objects that may be attributed some human qualities (e.g., Slater et al., 2006). AI researchers have focused on finding the necessary and sufficient human-like characteristics (their appearance as well as verbal and non-verbal behaviours) of AI agents in a variety of application contexts and with different users, including different educational applications (e.g., Baylor & Kim, 2004; Moreno et al., 2001), social interactions (e.g., Pelachaud & Andre, 2010) and special needs interventions such as for autism (e.g., Porayska-Pomsta et al., 2018).

The questions of credibility relate to both the physical appearance and behaviour of the agents, as well as their seeming trustworthiness as experts in a given learning domain and as educational practitioners. For example, with respect to physical appearance of educational AI agents, Baylor investigated the impact of gender (female, male), ethnicity (e.g., White, Black), role (e.g., expert, motivator, mentor) and realism (e.g., realistic, cartoon) of the agents on learning transfer, self-regulation and self-efficacy. Their results showed that students had greater transfer of learning when the agents were more realistic and when they were represented non-traditionally (as Black versus White) when in the 'expert' role. One explanation for this finding is that the socio-cultural novelty of the 'non-traditional' agents may have been responsible for learners' greater attention. This study also suggests that when agents are perceived by the learners as less intelligent, this can lead to significantly improved self-efficacy, whereas the use of motivational messages, as employed through the motivator and mentor agent roles, can lead to enhanced learner self-regulation and self-efficacy (Baylor & Kim, 2004).

Neuroscience research is also beginning to shed light on the apparent similarities between the neural processes that occur when we engage with other humans versus when we interact with human-like AI. Here the questions tackled also relate to the sufficiently humanly behaviour that is needed to trigger our attributing human intentionality, that is, theory of mind (ToM) to AI (Howard-Jones, 2009). For example, an fMRI study by Krach et al. (2008) suggested that visual appearance is critical in increasing such attributions, showing increased activation in the participants' brain regions that are associated with ToM (Figure 32.6) the more a piece of technology appears to be human. Here the experimental conditions included a computer, a functional robot, an anthropomorphic robot and a human – see Figure 32.5. While the study did not address the questions related to the uncanny valley hypothesis, namely whether and at what point increased realism may lead

Interaction Partner	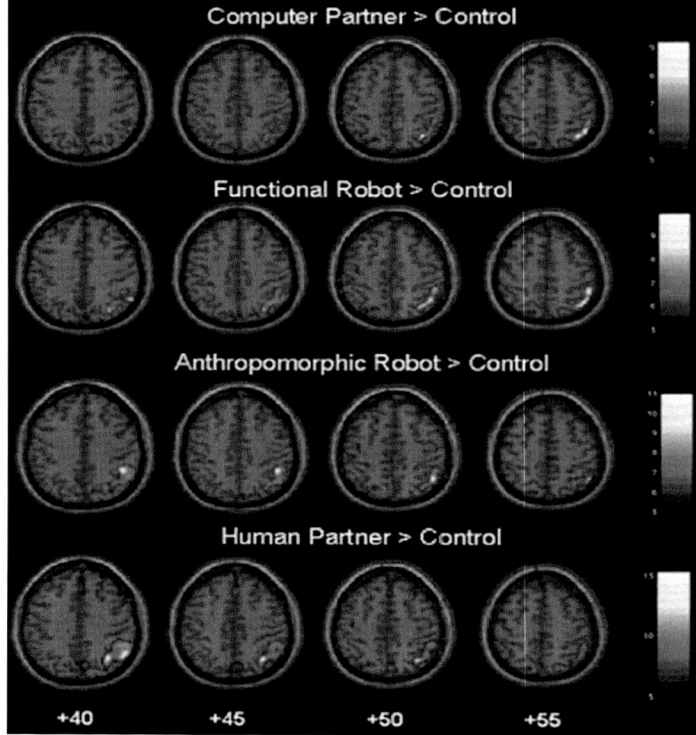			
Condition	Computer Partner (CP)	Functional Robot (FR)	Anthropomorphic Robot (AR)	Human Partner (HP)
Humanlikeness	no human shape; no perceivable button pressing	no human shape; button pressing with artificial hands	humanlike shape; button pressing with humanlike hands	human shape; button pressing with human hands

Figure 32.5 Four conditions examined by Krach et al. (2008)
A black-and-white version of this figure will appear in some formats. For the colour version, please refer to the plate section.

Figure 32.6 Regions associated with 'theory of mind' grow more active as the appearance of a technological opponent becomes more human-like, even when it is clearly not human (Krach et al. 2008)
A black-and-white version of this figure will appear in some formats. For the colour version, please refer to the plate section.

to deactivation of the ToM regions and occurrence of feelings of negativity toward hyper-realistic agents, it does suggest that investment in human-like qualities may be important to learners' mental engagement with AIEd as tools for supporting learning.

However, agents that are more realistic may not be desirable in all learning contexts. For

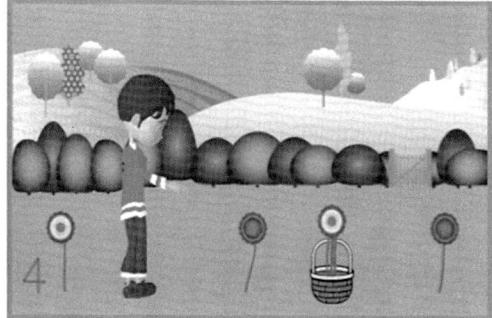

Figure 32.7 A child playing with the ECHOES agent through the multi-touch screen interface (Left). The agent points to a flower that it wants a child to pick and put in the basket in a bid for attention and interaction with the child (Right)
A black-and-white version of this figure will appear in some formats. For the colour version, please refer to the plate section.

example, in the ECHOES project, which developed an interactive system for supporting social interaction skills acquisition by children with autism, a cartoonish agent was employed (Figure 32.7). Here, we placed the emphasis on creating a socially credible, but evidently non-human agent in an attempt to remove some of the social anxiety associated with autism, while at the same time exaggerating some of the features such as the agent's eyes and emotional displays (e.g., surprise, happiness). The ECHOES agent proved to be an effective social partner to children, leading to increases in their initiations of and responses to bids for social interaction during the use of the ECHOES environment (Porayska-Pomsta et al., 2018).

The same types of cartoonish agents as used in ECHOES are presently employed in another project, called unLOCKE, where we investigated the impact of a computerized neuroscience intervention on primary school children's ability to learn counterintuitive facts in maths and science (main intervention) and on their understanding of socially challenging scenarios (active control) (e.g., Wilkinson et al., 2019). In both conditions, children observe agents' actions: in the main

intervention, four agents are placed in TV-like game show settings where they have to answer questions related to counterintuitive science and maths problems. Three agents act as contestants, whereas one agent acts as the show's host. Children first observe how the contestant-agents respond to the challenges posed to them by the host-agent, who also confirms which answer is a correct one. Following this observation phase, children can attempt some problems of their own. In the active control condition, the agents engage in social interaction with one another around key topics such as bullying or social exclusion, before the child is asked to analyse the social scenarios they observe using targeted prompts from the system. In both ECHOES and unLOCKE, the computational modelling relates to agents' behaviours, which must be contingent on the pedagogical goals of any given learning scenario, on the state of the world inhabited by the agents (other agents, objects, etc.) and – in the case of ECHOES – on the actions of the users on the environment. This is achieved through the application of GOF AI planning architecture, which is responsible for managing the agents' immediate reactions and deliberative actions, as well as their emotional displays (Dias & Paiva, 2005).

Both ECHOES and unLOCKE facilitate vicarious engagement with the respective systems, with ECHOES further allowing children to imitate the agent's actions within the environment and to engage in joint attentional activities with the agent. There is emergent evidence from EdN research supporting the value of both human-like technologies, which aligns with AI research to date, and also of employing such technologies to facilitate vicarious learning such as that facilitated in ECHOES and unLOCKE. Specifically, studies have shown that observing others performing actions causes neural activation in the same cortical areas (the mirror neuron system activation) as those that occur when we are carrying out actions ourselves (Rizzolatti & Craighero, 2004). However, the mirror neuron activation seems to be restricted to human movement, suggesting that animation is most conducive to learning when it involves human movement (Howard-Jones, 2009; Tversky & Morrison, 2002). What is not clear from these studies and what might become an interesting area of study at the intersection of AIEd and EdN, is where the boundaries between credibly human and clearly non-human movement and behaviours lie and how the different degrees of humanness can be used to support learning in different learning contexts and with different learner populations. Additionally, there is scope for substantial research involving EdN methods, which focuses on the neural activations of learners engaging in self-inspection and self-regulation with the help of OLMs.

32.3 Conclusion

We have presented two complementary approaches to learning and teaching that both employ computational methods. The first approach, building computational models of cognition, is analytical, in that it relies on developmental cognitive neuroscience theories to identify key components involved in education-relevant abilities. Modelling brings theoretical advances through clarity at the expense of simplification, and provides a platform to consider how the constraints of brain function impact cognition. The multiple components identified in the analytic approach hint at the true complexity of learning in the classroom, while the mechanistic understanding that is the goal nevertheless still requires pedagogic insights to achieve translation into classroom practices.

The second AI approach demands a fuller picture of the learner, the domain to be learned, an appropriate pedagogy for teaching the domain, and ways communication can deliver those aims. As in the first approach, the net result is a push for explicitization and clarification of theory. We saw a range of computational tools available to support teaching and learning, with less need that the computational systems are faithful to constraints of neurocomputation, but a much greater need that systems respect the reality of real-world learning situations. AI in education, in that sense, has the potential to act as a bridge between educational neuroscience research and real-world educational practices.

Computational methods in cognitive science are one tool amongst many, a tool with strengths (rigour) and weaknesses (simplification). We need to ensure that the simplifications intrinsic in computational models do not affect the breadth of questions that are considered within educational neuroscience, in service of its ambition to utilise a mechanistic understanding of mind to achieve wider evidence-informed approaches to educational methods and policy-making.

References

Ahr, E., Borst, G., & Houdé, O. (2016a). The learning brain: Neuronal recycling and inhibition. *Zeitschrift für Psychologie, 224*, 277–285.

Ahr, E., Houdé, O., & Borst, G. (2016b). Inhibition of the mirror-generalization process in reading in school-aged children. *Journal of Experimental Child Psychology, 145*, 157-165.

Ahr, E., Houdé, O., & Borst, G. (2017). Predominance of lateral over vertical mirror errors in reading: A case for neuronal recycling and inhibition. *Brain and Cognition, 116*, 1-8.

Aleven, V., & Koedinger, K. R. (2013). Knowledge component approaches to learner modeling. In R. Sottilare, A. Graesser, X. Hu, & H. Holden (eds.), *Design Recommendations for Adaptive Intelligent Tutoring Systems* (Vol 1 of *Learner Modeling*, pp. 165–182). Orlando, FL: US Army Research Laboratory.

Anderson, J. R., Boyle, C. F., Corbett, A. T., & Lewis, M. W. (1990). Cognitive modelling and intelligent tutoring. *Artificial Intelligence, 42*, 7–49.

Azevedo, R., & Aleven, V. (eds.) (2013). *International Handbook of Metacognition and Learning Technologies*. Berlin: Springer International Handbooks of Education.

Baker, R. (2010). Data mining for education, *International Encyclopedia of Education, 7*, 112–118.

Baker, R., & Yacef, K. (2009). The state of educational data mining in 2009: A review and future visions. *Journal of Educational Data Mining, 1*, 3–17.

Basu, S., Biswas, G., & Kinnebrew, J. S. (2017). Learner modeling for adaptive scaffolding in a computational thinking-based science learning environment. *User Modeling and User-Adapted Interaction, 27*, 5–53.

Baylor, A., & Kim, Y. (2004). Pedagogical agent design: The impact of agent realism, gender, ethnicity, and instructional role. Proceedings of the *7th* International Conference on Intelligent Tutoring Systems (pp. 592–603). 30 August–3

September, Maceió, Alagoas, Brazil. Berlin: Springer.

Beal, C. R. (2013). AnimalWatch: An intelligent tutoring system for algebra readiness. In R. Azevedo, & V. Aleven (eds.), *International Handbook of Metacognition and Learning Technologies* (Springer International Handbooks of Education, p. 26). Berlin: Springer.

Blackburne, L. K., Eddy, M. D., Kalra, P., Yee, D., Sinha, P., & Gabrieli, J. D. (2014). Neural correlates of letter reversal in children and adults. *PLoS ONE, 9*, e98386.

Botvinick, M. M., Braver, T. S., Barch, D. M., Carter, C. S., & Cohen, J. D. (2001). Conflict monitoring and cognitive control. *Psychological Review, 108*, 624–652.

Botvinick, M. M., & Plaut, D. C. (2004). Doing without schema hierarchies: A recurrent connectionist approach to normal and impaired routine sequential action. *Psychological Review, 111*, 395–429.

Box, G. E. P., & Draper, N. R. (1986). *Empirical Model-building and Response Surface*. New York: John Wiley & Sons.

Bull, S. (1995). 'Did I say what I think I said, and do you agree with me?': Inspecting and questioning the student model. *Proceedings of the 7th World Conference on Artificial Intelligence in Education*. 16–19 August 1995, Washington, DC.

Bull, S., & Kay, J. (2016). SMILI: A framework for interfaces to learning data in open learner models, learning analytics and related fields. *International Journal of Artificial Intelligence in Education, 26*, 293–331.

Campbell, J. I. D. (1994). Architectures for numerical cognition. *Cognition, 53*, 1–44.

Chen L., Lambon Ralph, M. A., & Rogers, T. T. (2017). A unified model of human semantic knowledge and its disorders. *Nature Human Behaviour, 1*, 0039.

Conati, C., Porayska-Pomsta, K., & Mavrkis, M. (2018). AI in education needs interpretable machine learning: Lessons from open learner modelling. CML *2018* Workshop on Human Interpretability in Machine Learning (WHI 2018). 14 July 2018, Stockholm, Sweden.

Corbett, A. T., Koedinger, K. R., & Anderson, J. R. (1997). Intelligent tutoring systems. In M. G. Helander, T. K. Landauer, & P. Prabhu (eds.), *Handbook of Human-Computer Interaction* (pp. 849–874). Amsterdam: Elsevier Science.

Cukurova, M., Luckin, R., Millán, E., & Mavrikis, M (2018). The NISPI framework: Analysing collaborative problem-solving from students' physical interactions, *Computers and Education*, *116*, 93–109.

Davis, R., Shrobe, H., & Szolovits, P. (1993). What is knowledge representation? *AI Magazine, 14*, 17–33.

Dehaene, S. (2003). The neural basis of the Weber–Fechner law: A logarithmic mental number line. *Trends in Cognitive Sciences, 7*, 145–147.

Dehaene, S. (2005). Evolution of human cortical circuits for reading and arithmetic: The 'neuronal recycling' hypothesis. In S. Dehaene, J. R. Duhamel, M. Hauser, & G. Rizzolatti (eds.), *From Monkey Brain to Human Brain* (pp. 133–157). Cambridge, MA: MIT Press.

Dehaene, S., & Cohen, L. (1995). Towards an anatomical and functional model of number processing. *Mathematical Cognition, 1*, 83–120.

Dias, J., & Paiva, A. (2005). Feeling and reasoning: A computational model for emotional characters. In C. Bento, A. Cardoso, & G. Dias (eds.), *Portuguese Conference on Artificial Intelligence* (pp. 127–140). Berlin: Springer.

Elman, J. L., Bates, E. A., Johnson, M. H., Karmiloff-Smith, A., Parisi, D., & Plunkett K. (1996). *Rethinking Innateness: A Connectionist Perspective on Development*. Cambridge, MA: MIT Press.

Elman, J. L., & McRae, K. (2017). A model of event knowledge. In G. Gunzelmann, A. Howes, T. Tenbrink, & E. Davelaar (eds.), *Proceedings of the Thirty-Ninth Annual Meeting of the Cognitive Science Society* (pp. 337–342). Austin, TX: Cognitive Science Society.

Engelbart, D. C. (1962). *Augmenting Human Intellect: A Conceptual Framework*. Summary Report AFOSR-3233. Menlo Park, CA: Stanford Research Institute.

Filippi, R., Karaminis, T., & Thomas, M. S. C. (2014). Language switching in bilingual production: Empirical data and computational modelling. *Bilingualism: Language and Cognition, 17*, 294–315.

Gopnik, A., & Bonawitz, E. (2015). Bayesian models of child development. *WIREs Cognitive Science, 6*, 75–86.

Haarmann, H., & Usher, M. (2001). Maintenance of semantic information in capacity-limited item short-term memory. *Psychonomic Bulletin & Review, 8*, 568–578.

Harm, M. W., McCandliss, B. D., & Seidenberg, M. S. (2003). Modeling the successes and failures of interventions for disabled readers. *Scientific Studies of Reading, 7*, 155–182.

Harm, M. W., & Seidenberg, M. S. (1999). Phonology, reading acquisition, and dyslexia: Insights from connectionist models. *Psychological Review, 106*, 491–528.

Harm, M. W., & Seidenberg, M. S. (2004). Computing the meanings of words in reading: Cooperative division of labor between visual and phonological processes. *Psychological Review, 111*, 662–720.

Hernandez-Orallo, J., & Vold, K. (2019). *AI Extenders: The Ethical and Societal Implications of Humans Cognitively Extended by AI*. Palo Alto, CA: Association for the Advancement of Artificial Intelligence.

Hoffman, P., McClelland, J. L., & Lambon Ralph, M. A. (2018). Concepts, control, and context: A connectionist account of normal and disordered semantic cognition. *Psychological Review, 125*, 293–328.

Houdé, O. (2000). Inhibition and cognitive development: Object, number, categorization, and reasoning. *Cognitive Development, 15*, 63–73.

Houdé, O. (2019). *3-System Theory of the Cognitive Brain: A Post-Piagetian Approach*. New York: Routledge.

Howard-Jones, P. (2009). Neuroscience, learning and technology (14–19), *BECTA Report*.

Krach, S., Hegel, F., Wrede, B., Sagerer, G., Binkofski, F., & Kircher, T. (2008). Can machines think? Interaction and perspective taking with robots investigated via FMRI. *PLoS ONE, 3*, e2597.

Lewandowsky, S. (1993). The rewards and hazards of computer simulations. *Psychological Science, 4*, 236–243.

Li, N., Cohen, W. W., Koedinger, K. R., & Matsuda, N. (2011). A machine learning approach for automatic student model discovery. *Proceedings of the 4th International Conference on Educational Data Mining* (pp. 31–40). 6–8 July 2011, Eindhoven, Netherlands.

Licklider, J. C. (1960). Man-computer symbiosis. *IRE Transactions on Human Factors in Electronics, 1*, 4–11.

Long, Y., & Aleven, V. (2013). Supporting students' self-regulated learning with an open learner model in a linear equation tutor. In H. C. Lane, K. Yacef, J. Mostow, & P. Pavlik (eds.), *Proceedings of the 16th International Conference on Artificial Intelligence in Education, AIED 2013* (pp. 219–228). New York: Springer.

Long, Y., & Aleven, V. (2017). Enhancing learning outcomes through self-regulated learning support with an open learner model. *User Modeling and User-Adapted Interaction, 27*, 55–88.

Mabbott, A., & Bull, S. (2006) Student preferences for editing, persuading, and negotiating the open learner model. In M. Ikeda, K. Ashlay, & T.-W. Chan (eds.), *Proceedings of the 8th International Conference on Intelligent Tutoring Systems* (ITS'06, pp. 481–490). Berlin: Springer-Verlag.

Macfdyen LP., Dawson, S., Pardo, A., & Gasevic, D. (2014). Embracing big data in complex educational systems: The learning analytics imperative and the policy challenge. *Research & Practice in Assessment, 9*, 17–28.

Mareschal, D., Butterworth, B., & Tolmie, A. (2013). *Educational Neuroscience*. Oxford: Wiley Blackwell.

Mareschal, D., Johnson, M., Sirios, S., Spratling, M., Thomas, M. S. C., & Westermann, G. (2007). *Neuroconstructivism: How the Brain Constructs Cognition*. Oxford: Oxford University Press.

Mareschal, D., & Shultz, T. R. (1999). Development of children's seriation: A connectionist approach. *Connection Science, 11*, 149–186.

Mareschal, D., & Thomas, M. S. C. (2007). Computational modeling in developmental

psychology. *IEEE Transactions on Evolutionary Computation, 11*, 137–150.

Martinez Maldonado, R., Kay, J., Yacef, K., & Schwendimann, B. (2014). An interactive teachers' dashboard for monitoring groups in a multi-tabletop learning. International Conference on Intelligent Tutoring Systems (pp. 482–492). 5–9 June 2014, Honolulu, Hawaii.

Mavrikis, M. (2008). Data-driven modelling of students' interactions in an ILE. *Proceedings of the 1st International Conference on Educational Data Mining* (pp. 87–96). 20–21 June 2008, Montréal, Canada.

McClelland, J. L., McNaughton, B. L., & O'Reilly, R. C. (1995). Why there are complementary learning systems in the hippocampus and neocortex: Insights from the successes and failures of connectionist models of learning and memory. *Psychological Review, 102*, 419–457.

McCloskey, M. (1991). Networks and theories: The place of connectionism in cognitive science. *Psychological Science, 2*, 387–395.

McLeod, P., Plunkett, K., & Rolls, E. T. (1998). *Introduction to Connectionist Modelling of Cognitive Processes*. New York: Oxford University Press.

Misselhorn, C. (2009) Empathy with inanimate objects and the uncanny valley. *Minds & Machines, 19*, 345–359.

Moreno, R., Mayer, R. E., Spires, H. A., & Lester, J. C. (2001), The case for social agency in computer-based teaching: Do students learn more deeply when they interact with animated pedagogical agents? *Cognition and Instruction, 19*, 177–213.

Mori, M. (1970). Bukimi no tani. *Energy, 7*, 33–35, translated into English by K. F. MacDorman and T. Minato (2005). Proceedings of the Humanoids-2005 workshop: Views of the Uncanny Valley. Tsukuba, Japan.

Mori, M. (2005). On the uncanny valley. Proceedings of the Humanoids-2005 Workshop: Views of the Uncanny Valley. Tsukuba, Japan.

O'Reilly, R. C., Bhattacharyya, R., Howard, M. D., & Ketza, N. (2014). Complementary learning systems. *Cognitive Science, 38*, 1229–1248.

Ohlsson, S., & Mitrovic, A. (2007). Fidelity and efficiency of knowledge representations for intelligent tutoring systems. *Technology, Instruction, Cognition and Learning*, *5*, 101–132.

Pelachaud, C., & Andre, E. (2010). Interacting with embodied conversational agents. In F. Chen, & K. Jokinen (eds.), *Speech Technology* (pp. 123–149). New York: Springer Verlag.

Plaut, D. C., McClelland, J. L., Seidenberg, M., & Patterson, K. E. (1996). Understanding normal and impaired word reading: Computational principles in quasi-regular domains. *Psychological Review*, *103*, 56–115.

Porayska-Pomsta, K. (2016). AI as a methodology for supporting educational praxis and teacher metacognition, *International Journal of Artificial Intelligence in Education*, *26*, 679–700.

Porayska-Pomsta, K., Alcorn, A. M., Avramides, K., Beale, S., Bernardini, S., Foster, M.-E., Frauenberger, C., Pain, H. Good, J., Guldberg, K., Kea-Bright, W., Kossyvaki, L., Lemon, O., Mademtzi, M., Menzies, R., Rajendran, G., Waller, A., Wass, S., & Smith, T. J. (2018). Blending human and artificial intelligence to support autistic children's social communication skills. *ACM Transactions on Human-Computer Interaction (TOCHI)*, *25*, 1–35.

Porayska-Pomsta, K., & Bernardini, S. (2013). Learner modelled environments. In S. Price, C. Jewitt, & B. Brown (eds.), *The SAGE Handbook of Digital Technology Research* (pp. 443–458). Newbury Park, CA: SAGE Publications Ltd.

Porayska-Pomsta, K., & Chryssafidou, E. (2018), Adolescents' self-regulation during job interviews through an AI coaching environment. In C. P. Rosé, R. Martínez-Maldonado, H. U. Hoppe, R. Luckin, M. Mavrikis, K. Porayska-Pomsta, B. McLaren, & B. du Boulay (eds.), *International Conference on Artificial Intelligence in Education* (pp. 281–285). Cham: Springer.

Porayska-Pomsta, K., & Mellish C. (2013). Modelling human tutors' feedback to inform natural language interfaces for learning. *International Journal of Human–Computer Studies*, *71*, 703–724.

Porayska-Pomsta, K., & Rajendran, T. (2019). Accountability in human and artificial intelligence decision-making as the basis for diversity and educational inclusion. In J. Knox, Y. Wang, & M. Gallagher (eds.), *Speculative Futures for Artificial Intelligence and Educational Inclusion* (pp. 39–59). Singapore: Springer Nature.

Porayska-Pomsta, K., Rizzo, P., Damian, I., Baur, T., André, E., Sabouret, N., Jones, H., Anderson, K., & Chryssafidou, E. (2014). Who's afraid of job interviews? Definitely a question for user modelling. In V. Dimitrova, T. Kuflik, D. Chin, F. Ricci, P. Dolog, & G.-J. Houben (eds.), *User Modeling, Adaptation, and Personalization* (pp. 411–422). Cham: Springer International Publishing.

Rajalingham, R., Issa, E. B., Bashivan, P., Kar, K., Schmidt, K., & DiCarlo, J. J. (2018). Large-scale, high-resolution comparison of the core visual object recognition behavior of humans, monkeys, and state-of-the-art deep artificial neural networks. *The Journal of Neuroscience*, *38*, 7255–7269.

Richardson, F. M., Seghier, M. L., Leff, A. P., Thomas, M. S. C., & Price, C. J. (2011). Multiple routes from occipital to temporal cortices during reading. *Journal of Neuroscience*, *31*, 8239–8247.

Ritter, F. E., Tehranchi, F., & Oury, J. D. (2018). ACT-R: A cognitive architecture for modeling cognition. *Wiley Interdisciplinary Reviews: Cognitive Science*, *10*, e1488.

Rizzolatti, G., & Craighero, L. (2004), The mirror neuron system. *Annual Review of Neuroscience*, *27*, 169–192.

Russell, S., & Norvig, P. (1995). A modern, agent-oriented approach to introductory artificial intelligence. *ACM SiGART Bulletin*, *6*, 24–26.

Russell, S. J., & Norvig, P. (2003). *Artificial Intelligence: A Modern Approach* (2nd ed.). Hoboken, NJ: Prentice Hall.

Seidenberg, M. S., & McClelland, J. L. (1989). A distributed, developmental model of word recognition and naming. *Psychological Review*, *96*, 523–568.

Shultz, T. R. (2003). *Computational Developmental Psychology*. Cambridge, MA: MIT Press.

Slater, M., Antley, A., Davison, A., Swapp, D., Guger, C., Barker, C., Pistrang, N., & Sanchez-Vives, M. V. (2006). A virtual reprise of the Stanley Milgram obedience experiments. *PLoS ONE, 1,* e39.

Spencer, J. P., Perone, S., & Buss, A. T. (2011). Twenty years and going strong: A dynamic systems revolution in motor and cognitive development. *Child Developmental Perspectives, 5,* 260–266.

Spencer, J. P., Thomas, M. S. C., & McClelland, J. L. (2009). *Toward a New Unified Theory of Development: Connectionism and Dynamical Systems Theory Re-considered.* Oxford: Oxford University Press.

Storrs, K., Mehrer, J., Walther, A., & Kriegeskorte, N. (2017). Architecture matters: How well neural networks explain IT representation does not depend on depth and performance alone. *Poster Presented at the Cognitive Computational Neuroscience Conference.* 6–8 September 2017, New York. Available from www2.securecms.com/CCNeuro/docs-0/5928796768ed3f664d8a2560.pdf. Last accessed 17 September 2019.

Thomas, M. S. C., Ansari, D., & Knowland, V. C. P. (2019a). Annual research review: Educational neuroscience: Progress and prospects. *Journal of Child Psychology and Psychiatry, 60,* 477–492.

Thomas, M. S. C., Fedor, A., Davis, R., Yang, J., Alireza, H., Charman, T., Masterson, J., & Best, W. (2019b). Computational modeling of interventions for developmental disorders. *Psychological Review, 126,* 693–726.

Thomas, M. S. C., Forrester, N. A., & Ronald, A. (2013). Modeling socio-economic status effects on language development. *Developmental Psychology, 49,* 2325–2343.

Thomas, M. S. C., Forrester, N. A., & Ronald, A. (2016). Multi-scale modeling of gene–behavior associations in an artificial neural network model of cognitive development. *Cognitive Science, 40,* 51–99.

Thomas, M. S. C., Mareschal, D., & Dumontheil, I. (2020). *Educational Neuroscience: Development across the Lifespan.* London: Psychology Press.

Thomas, M. S. C., & McClelland, J. L. (2008). Connectionist models of cognition. In R. Sun (ed.), *Cambridge Handbook of Computational Cognitive Modelling.* Cambridge: Cambridge University Press.

Tversky, B., & Morrison, J.B. (2002) Animation: Can it facilitate? *International Journal of Human–Computer Studies, 57,* 247–262.

Ueno, T., Saito, S., Rogers, T. T., & Lambon, R. (2011). Lichtheim 2: Synthesizing aphasia and the neural basis of language in a neurocomputational model of the dual dorsal-ventral language pathways. *Neuron, 72,* 385–396.

Westermann, G., Mareschal, D., Johnson, M. H., Sirois, S., Spratling, M. W., & Thomas, M. S. C. (2007). Neuroconstructivism. *Developmental Science, 10,* 75–83.

Wilkinson, H. R., Smid, C., Morris, S., Farran, E. K., Dumontheil, I., Mayer, S., Tolmie, A., Bell, D., Porayska-Pomsta, K., Holmes, W., Mareschal, D., Thomas, M., & The UnLocke Team (2019). Domain-specific inhibitory control training to improve children's learning of counterintuitive concepts in mathematics and science. *Journal of Cognitive Enhancement, 4,* 1–19.

Woolf, B. (2008). *Building Intelligent Tutoring Systems.* Burlington, MA: Morgan Kaufman.

Ziegler, S., Pedersen, M. L., Mowinckel, A. M., & Biele, G. (2016). Modelling ADHD: A review of ADHD theories through their predictions for computational models of decision-making and reinforcement learning. *Neuroscience and Biobehavioral Reviews, 71,* 633–656.

Zorzi, M., Stoianov, I., & Umiltà, C. (2005). Computational modeling of numerical cognition. In J. Campbell (ed.), *Handbook of Mathematical Cognition* (pp. 67–84). New York: Psychology Press.

Index